10667227

A Treasury of Jewish Quotations

A Treasury
of Jewish Quotations

EDITED BY JOSEPH L. BARON

ARONSON
B'NAI B'RITH

To Rachel and John
and to
Fannie and Jack

A Treasury of Jewish Quotations has been selected as a volume in the B'nai B'rith Judaica Library. The Library is sponsored by the B'nai B'rith International Commission on Adult Jewish Education in an effort to promote a greater popular understanding of the content of Judaism and the Jewish tradition.

Copyright © 1985 by Bernice S. Baron

© 1956 by Joseph L. Baron
© 1965 by A.S. Barnes and Co., Inc.

All rights reserved. Printed in the United States of America. No part of this book may be used or reproduced in any manner whatsoever without written permission from *Jason Aronson, Inc.* except in the case of brief quotations in reviews for inclusion in a magazine, newspaper, or broadcast.

Library of Congress Cataloging in Publication Data

A Treasury of Jewish quotations.

  Includes indexes.
    1. Quotations, Jewish. I. Baron, Joseph L., 1894-1960. II. Jewish quotations.
PN6095.J4T74 1985   808.88'2   85-3857
ISBN 0-87668-894-6

Manufactured in the United States of America.

Contents

Foreword

It is with a great deal of pleasure and pride that I respond to the invitation to write a Foreword to the new edition of Joseph L. Baron's *Treasury of Jewish Quotations*. When Dr. Baron set out to prepare his book for the press, over thirty years ago, I was happy to offer suggestions and to occasionally help verify a reference. Here in Cincinnati we enjoy the immense resources of the Hebrew Union College and its large library. Dr. Baron and I were classmates at college and it was then, over sixty years ago, that I learned to admire him for his scholarship, his meticulous research, and his imaginative creativity.

His *Treasury of Jewish Quotations* is in many respects a remarkable collection. It is comparable both to John Bartlett's *Familiar Quotations* and H.L. Mencken's *New Dictionary of Quotations*. Like the Mencken book it is arranged according to concept. Mencken goes from "Abbot" to "Zoo"; Baron goes from "Ability" to "Zohar" with numerous references to Zionism. On the way through the alphabet one can stop to browse in the pages of the "ghetto," "loyalty," "politics," "slavery," and "wisdom."

This work represents a tremendous amount of study and research. The entire literature of the world has been scoured to secure apt interesting data on Jews and Judaism. Beginning with the Bible, the author moves through the ages garnering choice bits of wit and learning. Here one finds food for the road, nourishment that will satisfy the thoughtful and the recondite.

What is important for the serious student is that all references are carefully documented; even he who runs may read. In order to expedite the search for an apt citation or a brilliant paragraph the reader can turn to fifty pages of a subject and author index.

This is an invaluable reference work for all writers, men and women, Jews and Gentiles, scholars, journalists, speakers, the intellectually curious. I am indeed pleased that a new edition will now be published as the last edition has long been out of print. This book will grace every reference shelf.

Jacob R. Marcus
American Jewish Archives
Hebrew Union College
Cincinnati, Ohio

Preface

Ever since my college days, for more than forty years now, I have kept an index file of memorable passages which I have come across in my reading. At the suggestion of my friends, Prof. Jacob R. Marcus of Cincinnati and Dr. Solomon Grayzel of Philadelphia, the core of this file is now being published, in the belief that it will prove to be of value to our colleagues and of interest to the general public.

The material comprised in this volume, *A Treasury of Jewish Quotations,* consists of aphorisms, maxims, proverbs, and comments of Jewish authorship, or on Jewish themes, or both. It is the first attempt at an all-inclusive compilation, covering the entire range of Jewish history and thought in all ages, all lands, and all tongues.

The term "Jewish authorship" is employed here in a broad sense, applying also to Spinoza, Marx, and Disraeli, who were born of Jewish parents, and to Onkelos, Elisheba, and Pallière, who chose to identify themselves with the Jewish faith. It does not include Montaigne, Manin, or Metchnikoff, who were only in part of Jewish stock and, culturally, moved outside of the sphere of Jewish creative work; but it does include the authors of the *New Testament,* practically all of whom were Jews, who reflect the idiom of the contemporary Jewish world, and for whose most quotable verses parallels have been traced in recognized Jewish sources.[1]

Jews are a universal people. From the very dawn of history, they have been continuously and everywhere in the forefront of civilization. Individually and collectively, they fashioned their own spiritual faith, and were primary factors in the creation of other religions. They produced exquisite literatures in their own Hebrew and Yiddish media, and gave classic expression to the genius of other languages. They built, and repeatedly rebuilt, their own commonwealth and national life, and merged heart and soul in the socio-political fabric of other nations. And much of their work has become an organic part of world culture, belonging to all mankind.

This collection embraces all these various strains. Thus, to cite illustrations from the American scene, it includes utterances of Louis D. Brandeis, whether or not related to specifically Jewish topics, of Judah P. Benjamin, which belong to the field of strictly American affairs, and of Emma Goldman, which present a highly individualistic attitude, as well as of Solomon Schechter, which deal primarily and authentically with Jewish theological and ecclesiastical subjects.

Books of quotations are not a novel phenomenon in the realm of Jewish letters. There are the Books of *Proverbs* and *Ecclesiastes* in the canon of Holy Scripture, the *Sayings of Ben Sira* and the *Wisdom of Solomon* in the *Apocrypha,* and the *Chapters of the Fathers* in the *Mishna,* the reading of which entered long ago into the sanctifying ritual of the Jewish home and synagogue. And all of these reflect the rich variety of opinion and interest, of mood and temperament, which characterized the intellectual vitality of a dynamic people in its antiquity.

Aphorismic quotations studded, like jewels, the poetry and novella, the homiletical and philosophical writings, and even the scientific and legal works of the

---

[1] See G. Friedlander, *The Jewish Sources of the Sermon on the Mount,* London, 1911; Strack and Billerbeck, *Kommentar zum Neuen Testament aus Talmud und Midrasch,* Munich, 1922; Herford, *Judaism in the New Testament Period,* 1928, p. 187.

centuries that followed. They added pith and charm to Rashi's commentaries, to Judah Halevi's *Cuzari*, to Maimonides' code, and to the cabalistic speculations of the *Zohar*. Collections of these, such as the *Yalḳutim* of the Gaonic period and Ibn Gabirol's *Mibhar HaPeninim* ("Choice of Pearls"), occupied the attention of some of the foremost medieval minds, and these continued to be characterized by the spirit of catholicity and cosmopolitanism. It is noteworthy that Hasdai's *Ben HaMeleḳ VeHaNazir* ("Prince and Dervish") poured into the stream of Jewish culture a current of Persian and Hindu lore, and that Al-Harizi's *Musré HaPilosofim* ("Dicta of the Philosophers") is a Hebrew translation of a Christian, Honain ben Isaac's, Arabic rendition of Greek maxims.

The transmission and popularization of their leaders' bons mots became almost a ritual with the modern Hasidim, who enriched greatly the treasury of Jewish wit and epigrammatic expression. Their work in this field, in the eighteenth and nineteenth centuries, was paralleled by their ideological opponents, the exponents of the Haskala (Enlightenment) movement. Both Nahman of Bratzlav and Solomon Rubin, for example, of the two opposing camps, composed each a volume of moral sayings, entitled *Sefer HaMiddot* (1821 and 1853 respectively). In more recent decades, the stimulus for such collections was renewed by Hayyim Nahman Bialik, the outstanding poet of the present Hebrew renaissance, who personally collaborated with Rabnitzki in the production of the monumental *Sefer HaAgada* and the smaller collection, *Sefer HaMeshalim VeHaPitgamim* ("Book of Proverbs and Apothegms"), and who applied the term *ḳinoos* ("assemblage") to this literary work.

It is hoped that this *Treasury of Jewish Quotations* will take its due place in this historic chain of literary compendia, and will serve not only as a key of reference to thousands of familiar and not-so-familiar quotations, but also as an aid in stimulating the interest of readers of all creeds in the fruit of the world's oldest and longest spiritual tradition. If in some measure as a result of this book, the beauty and fragrance distilled through the ages by the heart and soul of the Jew, the wisdom garnered by his rich and varied experience, will help to illumine the thought, broaden the sympathy, and sustain the faith of men, the editor and publishers of this volume will feel amply rewarded.

Many people have been helpful in the preparation of this work, and I take this opportunity to express my sense of indebtedness to them—to Rabbis David Shapiro of Milwaukee and Bernard Martin of Champaign, Drs. Max Weinreich and Shlomo Noble of New York, Avraham Harman and David I. Marmor of the Israel Office of Information, and Dr. S. Andhil Fineberg of the American Jewish Committee. I recall with sincere thanks a delightful and fruitful day spent in Cambridge with Prof. Harry A. Wolfson, valuable suggestions given by Prof. Jacob R. Marcus of Cincinnati, and the many courtesies extended by the staffs of the Milwaukee Public Library and the Memorial Library at the University of Wisconsin, by John Dulka of the Wisconsin State College Library in Milwaukee, Moses Marx and Dr. Simon Cohen of the Hebrew Union College Library, Rabbi I. Edward Kiev of the Library of the Jewish Institute of Religion, Dr. Judah Rosenthal of the College of Jewish Studies Library in Chicago, and Abraham Berger, Chief of the Jewish Division, and Dr. Alfred Berlstein of the Slavonic Division, of the New York Public Library.

I am very grateful to the publishers and their staff for their warm interest and wise counsel, and to my dear wife for patient and careful aid, through all the stages of publication. Last but not least, a word of tribute to my sister, Anna S. Baron, whose painstaking co-operation and constructive criticism were of enormous help to me in the composition of this volume, and who, alas, has not lived to see its completion and appearance. The memory of her selfless devotion in this, as in her many other labors of love, will abide as a benediction.

J. L. B.

Explanatory Note

The quotations in this volume are arranged topically in alphabetical order and, within each topic, alphabetically according to authors, except for biblical passages which come first and follow the order assigned to them in the Jewish version of Scripture. Both the topics and the items within the topics are numbered.

Where an item is taken out of alphabetical order and placed following another item which it helps to explain, or to which it is otherwise related, the first line is indented to indicate this change.

In cases where a single quotation is attributed to two different authors, each author is listed in a separate citation.

Non-Jewish authors are preceded by an asterisk (*) when cited as original author.

The author's name is followed by a comma, if the volume in the reference is his work, e.g., Spinoza, *Ethics;* and by a period, if the volume in the reference is that of a composite work or a journal, e.g., Ishmael. *Talmud;* Zola. *L'Aurore.*

The books of the Bible and New Testament are abbreviated throughout in their usual form; the key to other abbreviations is found in the List of Abbreviations.

Some books are quoted both from the original and from a translation, and the reference will depend in each case on which source was used. Thus the reference to Berthold Auerbach's novel is given either as *Auf der Höhe,* or *On the Heights.*

Except for biblical and apocryphal sources, the year or century of original composition or publication is given in the reference immediately after the name of the book, and this is followed by the number of the chapter or page. The dates and places of talmudic and midrashic sources, and of some other ancient writers, are listed in the Index of Authors. Where the quotation is taken from a later edition, the year or century of original composition or publication is often put in parentheses.

References to speeches, letters, and newspapers are frequently given with their exact dates. Some critical editions of classics have dual numbers for certain chapters, and where quotations are taken from these editions, the dual numbering is reproduced, as in 5.12, *Seder Eliyahu Rabbah,* ch 15 (14), ed Friedmann, 69.

To facilitate the finding of a specific quotation, two indices are provided:

An Index of Authors, providing biographical information on all the authors quoted, as well as listing all the pages on which they are quoted.

An Index of Select Lines, containing nearly 2,000 of the most familiar quotations, arranged alphabetically according to the first word.

For the benefit of those who are not familiar with the Hebrew and Yiddish words and phrases that appear in this book, there is a Glossary of these terms.

List of Abbreviations

General Abbreviations

* An asterisk denotes a non-Jewish author or proverb.

attr. attributed.

A.V. Authorized Version.

B.C.E. Before the Christian Era.

c. before a number, *circa,* about.

C. Century; *e.g.,* 1C—First Century.

C.E. Common (or Christian) Era.

ch chapter.

ed edition, *or* edited by.

p. page.

Pr proposition, in Spinoza's *Ethics.*

Pt part.

q quoted by (*or* in).

summ. summarized.

tr translated by (*or* in).

Source Abbreviations

ABD I. Abrahams. *Book of Delight. Jewish Publication Society,* 1912.

ABJ J. B. Agus. *Banner of Jerusalem.* Bloch Publishing Co., 1946.

ACWA Amalgamated Clothing Workers of America.

ADL O. R. Agresti. *David Lubin.* Little, Brown & Co., 1922.

AEL Ahad HaAm. *Essays, Letters, Memoirs.* L. Simon, tr. Oxford, East & West Library, 1946.

AGG I. Abrahams. *Glory of God.* Oxford University Press, 1925.

AHE ———. *Hebrew Ethical Wills.* Jewish Publication Society, 1926.

AJ H. Abarbanel. *Judaism.* 1883.

AJA American Jewish Archives.

AJL I. Abrahams. *Jewish Life in the Middle Ages.* Macmillan Co., J.P.S., 1896.

AKS Aaron Cohen. *Keter Shem Tob.* Zolkiew, 1793f; Lwow, 1864.

AMP J. B. Agus. *Modern Philosophies of Judaism.* Behrman House, 1941.

AMR L. Abraham. *Midrash Ribash Tob.* Kecskemet, 1927.

AP Associated Press.

Apoc. *Apocrypha.*

ARN *Abot de Rabbi Nathan.* S. Schechter, ed. London, 1887.

AT Alt Testament.

ATJF N. Ausubel. *A Treasury of Jewish Folklore.* Crown Publishers, 1948.

ATJH ———. *A Treasury of Jewish Humor.* Doubleday & Co., 1951.

AZ *Aboda Zara.*

AZJ *Allgemeine Zeitung des Judentums,* Berlin.

B&P *Blessing and Praise.* Central Conference of American Rabbis, 1923.

Bar. *Baruch.*

BB *Baba Bathra.*

BBR M. Berkowitz. *The Beloved Rabbi.* Macmillan Co., 1932.

BDH C. Bloch. *Hekal LeDibré Hazal.* New York, 1948.

BEJ L. Baeck. *Essence of Judaism.* Kaufmann, Macmillan Co., 1936.

BFZ N. Bentwich. *For Zion's Sake.* Jewish Publication Society, 1954.

BHH P. Birnbaum. *High Holyday Prayer Book.* Hebrew Publishing Co., 1951.

BJS I. Bernstein. *Jüdische Sprichwörter und Redensarten.* Warsaw, 1908.

BK *Baba Kamma.*

BKF S. Bernfeld. *Foundations of Jewish Ethics.* A. H. Koller, tr., (2nd ed.) Macmillan Co., 1929.

BNC B. Borochov. *Nationalism and the Class Struggle.* 1937.

BPA L. Bloy. *Pilgrim of the Absolute.* Pantheon Books, 1947.

BR J. Barzun. *Race: A Study in Modern Superstition.* Harcourt, Brace & Co., 1937.

BRD D. Ben Gurion. *Rebirth and Destiny of Israel.* M. Nurock, tr. Philosophical Library. 1954.

BRN Rohan D'O. Butler. *Roots of National Socialism.* E. P. Dutton & Co., 1942.

BSJ I. Bettan. *Studies in Jewish Preaching.* Hebrew Union College, 1939.

BSL E. R. Bevan and C. Singer (eds.). *Legacy of Israel.* Oxford, 1927.

BSS J. L. Baron. *Stars and Sand.* Jewish Publication Society, 1943.

BTH M. Buber. *Tales of the Hasidim.* Schocken Books, 1947–48.

BWC B. Bokser, *From the World of Cabbalah.* Philosophical Library, 1954.

Cant. *Canticles, Song of Songs.*

Cant. R. *Canticles Rabbah* (Midrash).

CCAR Central Conference of American Rabbis.

CGP C. P. Curtis, Jr. and Ferris Greenlet. *The Practical Cogitator.* Houghton Mifflin Co., 1945.

CHH J. Chotzner, *Hebrew Humor and Other Essays.* London, 1905.

Chron. *Chronicles.*

CHS ———. *Hebrew Satire.* London, Kegan, Paul, Trench, Trubner & Co., 1911.

CJE M. J. Cohen. *Jacob Emden.* Dropsie College, 1937.

CJR *Contemporary Jewish Record.*

CMH C. Clemens. *My Husband Gabrilowitsch.* Harper & Bros., 1938.

Col. *Colossians.*

Cor. *Corinthians.*

CPP I. Cohen. *Parallel Proverbs.* Tel Aviv, Dvir, 1954.

CPQ L. Copeland. *Popular Quotations.* Garden City Books, 1942.

CRK Z. Cahn. *Der Rebbe fun Kotzk* (2nd ed.). New York, 1950.

C-V *Central-Verein Zeitung* (Berlin).

Dan. *Daniel.*

Deut. *Deuteronomy.*

Deut. R. *Deuteronomy Rabbah* (Midrash).

DPB *Daily Prayer Book.* J. H. Hertz, ed.; New York, Bloch Publishing Co., 1948. S. Singer and I. Abrahams, eds.; London, Eyre & Spottiswoode, 1914.

Eccles. *Ecclesiastes.*

Eccles. R. *Ecclesiastes Rabbah* (Midrash).

EOM J. D. Eisenstein. *Otzar Midrashim.* Reznik, Menschel, 1928.

EOV ———. *Otzar Vikuhim.* New York, 1928.

Eph. *Ephesians.*

EPP F. Ewen. *Poetry and Prose of Heinrich Heine.* New York, Citadel Press, 1948.

Esd. *Esdras.*

Est. *Esther.*

Exod. *Exodus.*

Exod. R. *Exodus Rabbah* (Midrash).

Ezek. *Ezekiel.*

FAT C. Fadiman. *The American Treasury.* Harper & Bros., 1955.

FHH H. Fein. *Harvest of Hebrew Verse.* Bruce Humphries, 1934.

FJA E. Fleg. *Jewish Anthology.* Harcourt, Brace & Co., 1925.

FJR M. Friedlander. *Jewish Religion.* London, 1891, 1927.

FNL G. Fraser and T. Natanson. *Leon Blum.* J. B. Lippincott Co., 1938.

FRJ S. Freehof. *Reform Jewish Practice.* Hebrew Union College Press, 1944.

FTH H. Fein. *Titans of Hebrew Verse.* Bruce Humphries, 1936.

Gal. *Galatians.*

Gen. *Genesis.*

Gen. R. *Genesis Rabbah* (Midrash).

Ges. Schr. *Gesammelte Schriften.*

GFR N. M. Glatzer. *Franz Rosenzweig.* Schocken Books, 1953.

GGE M. Güdemann. *Geschichte des Erziehungswesens und der Kultur der Abendländischen Juden* (2 vols.). 1880–88.

GGJ H. Graetz. *Geschichte der Juden* (11 vols.). Leipzig, 1853–70.

GHJ ———. *History of the Jews* (6 vols.). Jewish Publication Society, 1891–98.

GIE H. Greenberg. *The Inner Eye.* New York, 1953.

GIS M. G. Glenn. *Israel Salanter.* Bloch Publishing Co., 1953.

GIT N. M. Glatzer. *In Time and Eternity.* Schocken Books, 1946.

GOJ L. Ginzberg. *On Jewish Law and Lore.* Jewish Publication Society, 1955.

GSS ———. *Students, Scholars and Saints.* Jewish Publication Society, 1928.

Hab. *Habakkuk.*

Hag. *Haggai.*

HBJ J. H. Hertz. *A Book of Jewish Thoughts.* London, 1917.

Heb. *Hebrews.*

HGT Howe and Greenberg. *A Treasury of Yiddish Stories.* Viking Press, 1954.

HHH S. A. Horodetzky. *HaHasidut veHaHasidim* (4 vols.). Dvir, 1922–8.

HJ *Historia Judaica.* New York.

HLH S. A. Horodetzky. *Leaders of Hasidism.* London, 1928.

HMH S. Halkin. *Modern Hebrew Literature.* Schocken Books, 1950.

HMI A. J. Heschel. *Man Is Not Alone.* Jewish Publication Society, 1951.

HMP Honein b. Isaac. *Musré HaPilosofim* (1200?). Al-Harizi, tr. Cracow, 1896.

Hos. *Hosea.*

HPB B. Halper. *Post-Biblical Hebrew Literature,* ii. Jewish Publication Society, 1921.

HSJ G. Horowitz. *Spirit of Jewish Law.* New York, 1953.

HTH J. de Haas. *Theodor Herzl.* Brentano's, 1927.

HUC Hebrew Union College.

IGY Israel Government Year Book.

INJ *Der Israelit des neunzehnten Jahrhunderts.*

Isa. *Isaiah.*

JA *Jewish Affairs* (Johannesburg).

JAI *Journal of Anthropological Institute of Great Britain.*

JAJ O. I. Janowsky. *The American Jew.* Harper & Bros., 1942.

JBH A. Jellinek. *Beth HaMidrasch* (6 vols.). Leipzig, 1853–78.

JCC J. Jacobs. *Jewish Contributions to Civilization.* Jewish Publication Society, 1919.

JE *Jewish Encyclopedia.* I. Singer, ed. Funk & Wagnalls, 1901–5.

Jer. *Jeremiah.*

JF. *The Jewish Frontier* (New York).

JGL *Jahrbuch für jüdische Geschichte und Literatur.* Berlin.

JHSE Jewish Historical Society of England.

JJC M. Joseph. *Judaism as Creed and Life.* London, Geo. Routledge & Sons, 1903, 1910.

JJCW L. Jung. *Judaism in a Changing World.* Oxford University Press, 1939.

Josh. *Joshua.*

JP *The Jewish People, Past and Present.* Jewish Encyclopedic Handbook. CYCO. ii. 1948.

JPS Jewish Publication Society of America.

JQR *Jewish Quarterly Review* (Philadelphia).

JQRo *Jewish Quarterly Review,* Old Series (London).

JRL K. (Mrs. Vaughan) Jennings. *Rahel.* London, 1876.

JS *The Jewish Spectator* (New York).

JSH M. Josephson. *Sidney Hillman.* Doubleday & Co., 1952.

JSS *Jewish Social Studies* (New York).

JTA Jewish Telegraphic Agency.

Jüd. Schr. *Jüdische Schriften.*

Judg. *Judges.*

JWP *Judaism at World's Parliament of Religions.* Union of American Hebrew Congregations, 1894.

JZWL *Jüdische Zeitschrift für Wissenschaft und Leben.* Breslau.

KHD J. Kastein. *History and Destiny of the Jews.* H. Paterson, tr. Viking Press, 1933.

KJG F. Kobler. *Jüdische Geschichte in Briefen.* Vienna, Saturn, 1938.

KJJ G. Karpeles. *Jews and Judaism in the Nineteenth Century.* Jewish Publication Society, 1905.

KJL ———. *Jewish Literature.* Jewish Publication Society, 1895.

KJN J. Klausner. *Jesus of Nazareth.* Macmillan Co., 1926.

KRV E. Key. *Rahel Varnhagen.* A. G. Chater, tr. G. P. Putnam's Sons, 1913.

KTH D. Katz. *Tenuat HaMusar.* Tel Aviv, Betan HaSefer, 5706.

KTJ F. Kobler. *Treasury of Jewish Letters.* London, Ararat, 1952; Jewish Publication Society, 1953.

LAJ L. Lewisohn. *The American Jew.* Farrar, Straus & Young, 1950.

Lam. *Lamentations.*

Lam. R. *Lamentations Rabbah* (Midrash).

LBG A Lief. *Brandeis Guide to Modern World.* Little, Brown & Co., 1941.

LCJ I. Landman. *Christian and Jew.* Horace Liveright, 1929.

LEJ J. L. Lazerov. *Enciklopedie fun Idishe Vitzen.* New York, 1928.

LEJS J. C. Levine. *Echoes of the Jewish Soul.* Bloch Publishing Co., 1931.

Lev. *Leviticus.*

Lev. R. *Leviticus Rabbah* (Midrash).

LEZ S. Liptzin. *Eliakim Zunser.* New York, 1950.

LGF L. Luzzatti. *God in Freedom.* Macmillan Co., 1930.

LGP J. Leftwich. *Golden Peacock.* Sci-Art, 1939.

LGS S. Liptzin. *Germany's Stepchildren.* Jewish Publication Society, 1944.

LJC (London) *Jewish Chronicle.*

LJD B. Lazare. *Job's Dungheap.* Schocken Books, 1948.

LJG M. Lowenthal. *Jews of Germany.* Longmans, Green & Co., 1936.

LP S. Liptzin. *Peretz.* Yivo, 1947.

LR L. Lewisohn. *Rebirth.* Harper & Bros., 1935.

LRB S. Liptzin. *Richard Beer Hofmann.* Bloch Publishing Co., 1936.

LRS K. Lewin. *Resolving Social Conflicts.* Harper & Bros., 1948.

M *Mishna.*

Macc. *Maccabees.*

Mal. *Malachi.*

Matt. *Matthew.*

MBF A. T. Mason. *Brandeis: A Free Man's Life.* Viking Press, 1936.

MCJ C. H. Moehlman. *Christian-Jewish Tragedy.* Leo Hart, 1933.

MEA J. R. Marcus. *Early American Jewry* (2 vols.). Jewish Publication Society, 1951, 1953.

MGU J. Mark. *Gdoilim fun undzer Dor.* New York, 1927.

MGWJ *Monatschrift für Geschichte und Wissenschaft des Judentums.*

Mic. *Micah.*

MJM J. R. Marcus. *The Jew in the Medieval World.* Union of American Hebrew Congregations, 1938.

MKM F. Mehring. *Karl Marx.* Covici, Friede, 1935.

MLL K. Marmor. *Arn Liebermans Briev.* Yivo, 1951.

MND H. L. Mencken. *New Dictionary of Quotations.* Alfred A. Knopf, 1942.

MRH J. S. Minkin. *Romance of Hasidism.* Macmillan Co., 1935.

MRR H. Marcuse. *Reason and Revolution.* Oxford University Press, 1941.

MVAA *Mittheilungen aus dem Verein zur Abwehr des Antisemitismus.* (Berlin).

Nah. *Nahum.*

N & Q *Notes and Queries.* (London).

Neh. *Nehemiah.*

NDI B. Netanyahu. *Don Isaac Abravanel.* Jewish Publication Society, 1953.

NHA L. Newman. *Hasidic Anthology.* C. Scribner's Sons, 1934.

NLG A. Neuman. *Landmarks and Goals.* Dropsie College, 1953.

NMN A. & M. Nordau. *Max Nordau.* New York, 1943.

NOP *Nine One-Act Plays from Yiddish.* B. F. White, tr. Boston, John W. Luce & Co., 1932.

NSR J. Needham. *Science, Religion and Reality.* Macmillan Co., 1925.

NT *New Testament.*

NTA L. I. Newman. *Talmudic Anthology.* Behrman House, 1945.

Num. *Numbers.*

Num. R. *Numbers Rabbah* (Midrash).

Obad. *Obadiah.*

OMB M. Obadiah. *MiPee Bialik.* Tel Aviv, Masada. 5691, 5705.

O.T. *Old Testament.*

PAJHS *Publications,* American Jewish Historical Society.

PCP D. Philipson. *Centenary Papers.* Cincinnati, Ark, 1919.

PDE J. Priestley. *Discourses on Evidence of Revealed Religion,* 1794.

Phil. *Philippians.*

PJC J. Parkes. *Judaism and Christianity.* University of Chicago Press, 1948.

PRE *Pirké de Rabbi Eliezer.* Warsaw, 5612.

PRM D. Philipson. *Reform Movement in Judaism.* Macmillan Co., 1907, 1931.

Prov. *Proverbs.*

Ps. *Psalms.*

PUS A. Pallière. *Unknown Sanctuary.* Bloch Publishing Co., 1928.

PZL *Philo Zitaten Lexikon.* Berlin, Philo, 1936.

RA *Reform Advocate* (Chicago).

RAM P. M. Raskin. *Anthology of Modern Jewish Poetry.* Behrman House, 1927.

RES H. Rogoff. *An East Side Epic.* Vanguard Press, 1930.

Rev. *Revelation.*

RHI D. D. Runes. *Hebrew Impact on Western Civilization.* Philosophical Library, 1951.

Rom. *Romans.*

SA *Shulhan Aruk.*

SAB *Sholom Aleichem Buch.* I. D. Berkowitz, ed. New York, 1926.

Sam. *Samuel.*

SBQ H. Samuel. *A Book of Quotations.* London, Cresset Press, 1947.

Sel. Wr. *Selected Writings.*

Semag Moses of Coucy. *Sefer Mitzvot Ha-Gadol.* 1250.

Semak Isaac of Corbeil. *Sefer Mitzvot Katan.* 1277.

SGZ N. Syrkin. *Geklibene Zionistish-Sociolistishe Shriften.* New York, 1926.

SHB B. Stevenson. *Home Book of Quotations.* Dodd, Mead & Co., 1949.

SHR S. Spiegel. *Hebrew Reborn.* Macmillan Co., 1930.

SHW M. G. Saphir. *Humoristiche Werke* (4 vols.). 1889.

SHZ N. Sokolow. *History of Zionism.* Longmans, Green & Co., 1919.

SMM M. Samuels. *Memoirs of Moses Mendelssohn* (2nd ed.). 1827.

SMMP L. W. Schwartz. *Memoirs of My People.* Jewish Publication Society, 1943.

SMT G. G. Scholem. *Major Trends in Jewish Mysticism.* Schocken Books, 1941, 1946.

SPG M. Samuel. *Prince of the Ghetto.* Alfred A. Knopf, 1948.

SRH N. Slouschz. *Renascence of Hebrew Literature.* Jewish Publication Society, 1909.

SRT S. Shinaver. *Ramatayim Tzofim.* Warsaw, 1881.

SSA S. Schechter. *Seminary Addresses.* Cincinnati, Ark, 1915.

SSJ ———. *Studies in Judaism* (3 vols.). Jewish Publication Society, 1896, 1908, 1924.

SWS M. Samuel. *World of Sholom Aleichem.* Alfred A. Knopf, 1944.

T *Talmud.*

TDS S. Tiktin. *Darstellung des Sachenverhältnisses in seiner hiesigen Rabbinats-Angelegenheit,* 1842.

Thess. *Thessalonians.*

Tim. *Timothy.*

TJ or **Talmud J** *Talmud Jerushalmi.*

TL P. J. Tonger (ed.). *Lebensfreude, Wollen und Wirken.* Cologne.

TMS Thatcher & McNeal. *Source Book for Medieval History.* 1905.

UJE *Universal Jewish Encyclopedia* (10 vols.). I. Landman, ed. New York, 1939–43.

UPB *Union Prayer Book* (newly revised). Central Conference of American Rabbis. i. 1940, ii. 1945.

VA H. Valentin. *Antisemitism.* A. G. Chater, tr. Viking Press, 1936.

WHJ M. Waxman. *History of Jewish Literature* (4 vols.). Bloch Publishing Co., 1930–41.

Wisd. of Sol. *Wisdom of Solomon.*

WUPJ World Union for Progressive Judaism.

WZJT *Wissenschaftliche Zeitschrift für jüdische Theologie.*

Yad Maimonides. *Mishné Torah: Yad Ha-Hazaka,* 1180. Vilna, 1924–28.

YAJ *Yivo Annual of Jewish Social Science.* New York.

YFS *Yivo Filologishe Shriftn.* i. Vilna, 1926.

YHS *Yivo Historishe Shriftn.* ii. Vilna, 1937.

YSS M. M. Yoshor, *Saint and Sage.* Bloch Publishing Co., 1937.

ZCG I. Zangwill. *Children of the Ghetto.* Jewish Publication Society, 1892.

Zech. *Zechariah.*

ZEH L. Zunz. *Zur Geschichte und Literatur,* 1845. Ch. 5: "Die Sittenlehrer—Extracts from Hebrew Moralists." American Jewish Publication Society, 1875.

Zeph. *Zephaniah.*

ZRN H. Zeitlin. *Reb Nahman Braslaver.* New York, Matones, 1952.

ZSA I. Zangwill. *Speeches, Articles and Letters.* Maurice Simon, ed. London, Soncino, 1937.

ZVJ I Zangwill. *Voice of Jerusalem.* Macmillan Co., 1921.

ZWJ *Zeitschrift für die Wissenschaft des Judentums.* Berlin.

ADDENDA

The following item is a valuable addition to the quotations included under topic 24.B, AMERICA: THE JEW AND JUDAISM IN AMERICA, pp. 8–9.

American Jews vigorously repudiate any suggestion that they are in exile. . . . To American Jews, America is home. There, exist their thriving roots; there is the country which they have helped to build; and there they share its fruits and its destiny.
Blaustein, speech in Jerusalem, Aug. 23, 1950.

The full source for the quotation numbered 445.B.60 (under ISRAEL: THE PEOPLE) on p. 209, is as follows:

*Ewer. *The Week-End Book,* 1924, p. 117. Used by L. Browne for title of a book, 1934.

1. ABILITY

1.1 The less their ability, the more their conceit.

Ahad HaAm, letter to Ravnitzki, Feb. 10, 1897, ref. to Hebrew writers at the time.

1.2 The ability of big men is overrated, and that of small men underrated. Give a man opportunity and responsibility, and he will grow.

Brandeis, to A. Lief, April 20, 1935. LBG, 73.

1.3 I pride myself upon recognizing and upholding ability in every party and wherever I meet it.

Disraeli, speech, Feb. 5, 1874.

1.4 Ability will see the Chance and snatch it.
   Who has a Match will find a Place and scratch it.

Guiterman, *A Poet's Proverbs*, 1924, p. 64.

1.5 As long as a man imagines that he cannot do a certain thing, so long . . . is it impossible for him to do it.

Spinoza, *Ethics*, 1677, iii. Definition 28.

2. ABORTION

2.1 It is a capital crime to destroy an embryo in the womb.

Ishmael. *Talmud: Sanhedrin*, 57b.

2.2 A woman convicted of abortion is an infanticide.

Josephus, *Against Apion*, ii. 24.

3. ABRAHAM

3.1 Abraham proclaimed one world before the Holy One.

Eleazar HaKappar. *Tanhuma, Lek Leka, #2*, ed Buber, 30a.

3.2 Like a vial of perfume, Abraham could give fragrance only when moved. So God said, "Get thee out," become a wanderer!

Johanan. *Cant. R.*, 1.3.3, on *Gen.* 12.1. See Abin. *Tanhuma, Lek Leka*, 3. Cf. Berekia. *Gen. R.* to 1.3.

3.3 Abraham was a prototype. His experiences were symbolic of what happened later to Israel.

Levi, Tanhuma. *Tanhuma, Lek Leka, #12*, ed Buber, 35b.

3.4 Abraham discovered the First Cause . . . and demonstrated the importance to all mankind of the principle of Divine Unity.

Maimonides, *Iggeret Teman*, 1172.

3.5 Unlike Noah, who "walked *with* God" [*Gen.* 6.9], Abraham "walked *before* Him" [24.40], because Abraham drew moral force from himself and walked in righteousness by his own effort.

Rashi, *Commentary*, to *Gen.* 6.9. See *Gen. R.*, 30.10.

3.6 When the Holy One contemplated the generations of Enosh and the Flood, He said, How can I build a world with such wicked material? But when he envisioned Abraham, He said, I have found a rock [*petra*] on which to build the world! [*Is.* 51.1].

Yelamdenu, q *Yalkut, #766*, to *Num.* 23.9. See *Matt.* 16.18.

4. ABSENCE

4.1 We recognize the good only in its absence.

Gentili, *Mleket Mahshebet*, 1710, *Va-Yehi*, 9.

4.2 A benefit may be conferred, but not a disability imposed, on a man in his absence.

Judah b. Ilai. *Mishna: Erubin*, 7.11.

5. ABSTINENCE

5.1 Deny yourself not the good which the day brings you, and let not your part in joy overpass you.

Apocrypha: Ben Sira, 14.14.

5.2 Abstainers are physicians of faith and healers of souls.

Bahya, *Hobot HaLebabot*, 1040, 9.2.

5.3 Since he who denies himself wine is a sinner [*Num.* 6.11], how much more so is he who abstains from many things!

Bar Kappara. *Talmud: Taanit*, 11a.

5.4 Who vows not to drink wine or cut his hair is a holy man.

Eleazar b. Pedat. *Talmud: Taanit*, 11a.

5.5 Are there not enough injunctions in the Law that you must impose upon yourself additional prohibitions?

Isaac. *Talmud J: Nedarim*, 9.1.

5.6 The holy law imposes no asceticism. It demands that we . . . grant each mental and physical faculty its due.

Judah Halevi, *Cuzari*, c. 1135, 2.50.

5.7 Abstinence is the beginning of saintliness.

M. H. Luzzatto, *Mesillat Yesharim*, (1740), ch 13, p. 118.

5.8 If you see anyone not taking food or drink when he should, refusing baths and oils, neglecting his clothes, sleeping on the ground, and fancying that he is thus practicing temperance, pity his self-deception and show him the true path of temperance.

Philo, *The Worse Attacks the Better*, 7.

5.9 Man will be called to account in the hereafter for each enjoyment he declined here without sufficient cause.

Rab. *Talmud J: Kiddushin*, 4.12.

5.10 Abstinence is good in its place, i.e., if *forbidden* food, *forbidden* sexual indulgence, *forbidden* money present themselves.

Saadia, *Emunot VeDeot*, 933, 10.4.

5.11 When in doubt, do without.

H. Samuel, *A Book of Quotations*, 1947, p. 191.

5.12 He who denies himself a good life in this world is an ingrate, showing contempt for the King's bounties and grace.

Seder Eliyahu Rabbah, ch 15 (14), ed Friedmann, 69.

6. ACCUSATION

6.1 An accuser may not act as a defender.

Hisda. *Talmud: Rosh Hashana*, 26a.

6.2 Woe to him whose advocate becomes his prosecutor!

Levi. *Talmud J: Sukka*, 3.1. Ref. to use of stolen *Lulab*.

6.3 The Holy One detests him who rushes to accuse a neighbor.

Talmud: Pesahim, 113b.

6.4 I accuse!

*Zola. *L'Aurore*, Jan. 13, 1898. Open Letter to Pres. Faure on Dreyfus case.

7. ACTION

7.1 Through faith man experiences the meaning of the world; through action he is to give to it a meaning.

Baeck, *Essence of Judaism*, (1922) 1936, p. 122.

7.2 Action is what matters. . . . We are present where we act.

Bergson, *Two Sources of Morality & Religion*, 1935, p. 247.

7.3 Action is the proof, the criterion, of the Holy Spirit.

H. Cohen, *Religion der Vernunft*, 1919, ch 7. q FJA, 277.

7.4 The memory of great actions never dies.

Disraeli, *Alroy*, 1833, 10.19.

7.5 Men must beware of looking upon religion as an ideal to be *yearned for*, it should be an ideal to be *applied*.

Dubnow, *Jewish History*, 1903, p. 54f.

7.6 Religion must justify itself through the moral action.

Elbogen. BKF, 1929, p. 52.

7.7 The pestilential marsh is made of stagnant waters; but quickening is life, and quickening is action.

Harrison, *Religion of a Modern Liberal*, 1931, p. 70.

7.8 To refrain from sinful action is itself a religious act.

Huna. *Cant. R.*, 4.4.3.

7.9 Action takes precedence over study.

Judah HaNasi. *Talmud J: Pesahim*, 3.7.

7.10 Wisdom without action is like a tree without fruit.

J. Kimhi, *Shekel HaKodesh*, 12C.

7.11 Everyone can raise himself, but only by his own actions.

Nahman Bratzlav. q HLH, 80f.

7.12 Act while you can: while you have the chance, the means, and the strength.

Simeon b. Eleazar. *Talmud: Sabbath*, 151b.

8. ADAM

8.1 A grain of evil seed was sown in the heart of Adam from the beginning, and how much fruit of ungodliness has it produced!

Apocrypha: II Esd., 4.30.

8.2 The Holy One led Adam through the Garden of Eden, and said: "I created all My beautiful and glorious works for your sake. Take heed not to corrupt and destroy My world!"

Eccles. R., 7.13.

8.3 Adam's dust was collected from all parts of the world.

Meir. *Talmud: Sanhedrin*, 38a.

8.4 So if a man goes west or east, and his time comes to depart from the world, wherever he is, there is where his dust came from, there is where he belongs, and thither he returns.

Pirké de Rabbi Eliezer, ch 11.

8.5 Adam was created single, to teach us that to destroy one person is to destroy a whole world, and to preserve one person is to preserve a whole world; that no man should say to another, "my father was superior to yours!" . . . that though no two men are exactly alike, God stamped us all with the same mould, the seal of Adam; that everyone must say, The world was created for my sake!

Mishna: Sanhedrin, 4.5.

8.6 Adam, the luckiest man,—he had no mother-in-law.

Sholom Aleichem, *SAB*, 1926, p. 350.

8.7 Truth and Peace argued against the creation of Adam, for man is compounded of falsehood and strife, and Love and Righteousness argued for it, because man would dispense kindness and justice. Then God cast down Truth and Peace, and created man.

Simeon b. Pazzi. *Gen. R.*, 8.5.

9. ADAPTABILITY

9.1 Be pliable like a reed, not rigid like a cedar.

Eleazar b. Simeon. *Talmud: Taanit*, 20b.

9.2 Adapt thyself to time and circumstance,
So wilt thou be untroubled every day....
Roar, if upon a lion thou shouldst chance,
But if an ass thou meetest, simply bray.

Falaquera, *HaMebakesh*, (1264) 1779, p. 2b. tr H. W. Ettelson. *JQR*, i. 177.

9.3 The more curved the bow, the deadlier the shot.

Hasdai, *Ben HaMelek VeHaNazir*, c. 1230, ch 30.

9.4 The weather-cock on a church-spire, though made of iron, would soon be broken by the storm-wind if it . . . did not understand the noble art of turning to every wind.

Heine, *English Fragments*, 1828, ch 11.

9.5 He who attempts to resist the wave is swept away, but he who bends before it abides.

Levi. *Gen. R.*, 44.15.

9.6 A rope drawn too taut is apt to break.

Proverb (Yiddish). See BJS, #3729. *JE*, x. 229a.

10. ADORNMENT

10.1 Adorn first yourself, then others.

Simeon b. Lakish. *Talmud: Baba Bathra*, 60b.

11. ADULTERY

11.1 Thou shalt not commit adultery.
Bible: Exod., 20.13. *Deut.*, 5.17.

12. ADVANTAGE

12.1 An advantage over kinsmen is the worst kind of disadvantage.
Apocrypha II Macc., 5.6.

12.2 Life does not give itself to one who tries to keep all its advantages at once.
Blum. q CGP, 97.

12.3 Getting an advantage at the expense of somebody else—that really is what graft is.

Brandeis. *Boston American*, July 22, 1905.

12.4 Next to knowing when to seize an opportunity, the most important thing in life is to know when to forego an advantage.

Disraeli, *Infernal Marriage*, 1828.

12.5 A man cannot see anything to his own disadvantage.

Mar. b. Ashi. *Talmud: Sabbath*, 119a.

13. ADVENTURE

13.1 Failures are made only by those who fail to dare, not by those who dare to fail.

Binstock, *The Power of Faith*, 1952, p. 45.

13.2 The fruit of my tree of knowledge is plucked, and it is this, "Adventures are to the adventurous."

Disraeli, *Coningsby*, 1844, 3.1. *Ixion in Heaven*, 1828, 2.2.

13.3 To realize the impossible is the passion of the adventurer.

I. M. Wise. *Deborah*, Nov. 5, 1896.

14. ADVERSITY

14.1 If you faint in the day of adversity, your strength is small indeed.
Bible: Prov., 24.10.

14.2 In the day of prosperity be joyful, and in the day of adversity consider: God made the one as well as the other.
Bible: Eccles., 7.14.

14.3 Rejoice in adversity even more than in prosperity, for suffering brings forgiveness of sin.

Akiba. *Mekilta*, to *Exod.* 20.20.

14.4 There is no education like adversity.
Disraeli, *Endymion*, 1880.

14.5 I am the hammer, if misery's a stone,
I am the water, if trouble's a spark:
My heart is the stronger with each falling blow,
The moon it resembles, that shines in the dark.

Falaquera, *HaMebakesh*, (1264) 1779.

14.6 A crucible frees silver of dross, wind clears the sky of clouds, and adversity cleanses the heart of evil thoughts.

Jeiteles. *Bikkuré Halttim*, 5591, xi. 189, #41.

14.7 As it is a mark of vulgarity to be over-elated by success, so is it unmanly to be downcast in adversity.

Josephus, *Wars*, 4.1.6.

14.8 In adversity man is quickly persuaded.

Ibid., 6.5.2.

14.9 One's misfortune is always another's benefit.

Levi. *Gen. R.*, 38.10.

15. ADVICE

15.1 We took sweet counsel together.
Bible: Ps. 55.15.

15.2 Beware of unsolicited advice.
Akiba. *Talmud: Sanhedrin*, 76a.

15.3 Advice is not a popular thing to give.
Disraeli, *Lothair*, 1870.

15.4 God said: "Let us make man" [*Gen.* 1.26]. Should anyone say, "Why should I consult my subordinates?" he is told: "Learn from your Creator: He took counsel with the angels."
Jonathan. *Gen. R.*, 8.8.

15.5 Follow the counsel of the old, not of the young, for old people's tearing down is constructive, while youth's building up is destructive.
Simeon b. Eleazar. *Tosefta: Aboda Zara*, 1.19.

15.6 Before the trouble comes, advice obtain;
After it has come, advice is vain.
Zabara. *Sefer Shaashuim*, 13c, ch 2.

16. AFFINITY

16.1 Every bird dwells with its kind.
Apocrypha: Ben Sira, 27.9.

16.2 When the Jews prosper, ye claim kindred with them;
When the Jews suffer, ye are Medes and Persians!
*Longfellow, *Judas Maccabeus*, 1872, 1.2.
See Josephus, *Antiquities*, 9.14.3, 11.8.6, ref. to Samaritans.

16.3 Not for nothing did the starling follow the raven: it is of its kind.
Proverb. q Eliezer. *Talmud: Baba Kamma*, 92b.

16.4 Ishmael the priest favors the priests.
Proverb. q *Talmud: Hullin*, 49a.

16.5 It is seemly to graft grapes of a vine with grapes of a vine, not with berries of a thorn-bush.
Talmud: Pesahim, 49a, ref. to choosing a mate.

17. AGADA

17.1 The precious pearls that lie upon the bed of the talmudic ocean, the agadic passages so rich in beauty and sweetness.
Aboab, *Menorat HaMaor*, c. 1300, Preface.

17.2 Between the rugged boulders of the law which bestrew the path of the Talmud, there grow the blue flowers of romance— parable, tale, gnome, saga; its elements are taken from heaven and earth, but chiefly and most lovingly from the human heart and from Scripture, for every verse and every word in this latter became, as it were, a golden nail upon which it hung its gorgeous tapestries.
E. Deutsch, *The Talmud*, 1867.

17.3 Do you wish to know Him, by whose word the world came into being? Then study Agada.
Sifré #49, to *Deut.* 11.22, ed Friedmann, 85a. Cf Maimonides, *Yad: Melakim*, 12.2.

18. AGE

18.A. The Age

18.A.1 The spirit of the age, as it is revealed to each of us, is too often only the spirit of the group in which the accidents of birth or education or occupation or fellowship have given us a place.
Cardozo, *Nature of the Judicial Process*, 1921, p. 174.

18.A.2 The spirit of the age is the very thing a great man changes.
Disraeli, *Coningsby*, 1844, 9.7.

18.A.3 He who served his age served all ages.
Frishman, *Yahalal*, 1911.

18.A.4 This age of steam, the age of science and sordidness, of divinity mixed with dirt.
Harrison, *Religion of a Modern Liberal*, 1931, p. 129.

18.A.5 The reform which Judaism requires is an education of the age up to the Torah, not a leveling down of the Torah to the age.
S. R. Hirsch. q KHD, p. 400.

18.A.6 The age too is a Bible, through which God speaks to Israel.
G. Salomon. I. Rabbiner Versammlung, *Protokolle*, 1844, 91.

18.B. The Ages of Man

18.B.1 I made man in three stages: when he was young, I overlooked his stumbling;

when he was a man, I considered his purpose; and when he grows old, I watch him till he repent.
Apocalypse of Sedrach, 16.

18.B.2 Youth is a blunder, Manhood a struggle, Old Age a regret.
Disraeli, *Coningsby*, 1844, 3.1.

18.B.3 Your son at five is your master, at ten your slave, at fifteen your double, and after that, your friend or foe, depending on his bringing up.
Hasdai, *Ben HaMelek VeHaNazir*, c. 1230, ch 7.

18.B.4 Solomon wrote first the *Song of Songs*, then *Proverbs*, then *Ecclesiastes*, and this is the way of the world. When young, we compose songs; when older, we make sententious remarks; and when old, we speak of the vanity of things.
Jonathan, *Cant. R.*, 1.1.10.

18.B.5 Adolescence is a kind of emotional seasickness. Both are funny, but only in retrospect.
Koestler, *Arrow in the Blue*, 1952, p .82.

18.B.6 Men's minds, they say, ossify after forty.
Oko. *Menorah Journal*, 1919, v. 135.

18.B.7 At one, like a king, adored by all. At two, like a pig, wallowing in dirt. At ten, he skips like a goat. At twenty, preens and neighs like a horse. Married, he works like an ass. When a father, he snarls like a dog. When old, he dodders like an ape.
Simeon b. Eleazar. See *Abot*, 5.21.

18.C. Age and Youth

18.C.1 We will go with our young and with our old.
Bible: Exod., 10.9.

18.C.2 Your old men shall dream dreams, your young men shall see visions.
Bible: Joel, 3.1.

18.C.3 The glory of young men is their strength, and the beauty of old men is the hoary head.
Bible: Prov., 20.29.

18.C.4 If you gather not in youth, how will you find in old age?
Apocrypha: Ben Sira, 25.3.

18.C.5 An elder in wisdom, tender in years.
Benjamin b. Levi. *Gen. R.*, 99.3.

18.C.6 Youth is a garland of roses; old age a crown of willows.
Dimi. *Talmud: Sabbath*, 152a.

18.C.7 She had lost in youth what she had won in weight.
Heine, *Journey from Munich to Genoa*, 1828, ch 16.

18.C.8 What a man does in youth darkens his face in old age.
Isaac Nappaha. *Talmud: Sabbath*, 152a.

18.C.9 Youth is fair, a graceful stag,
Leaping, playing in a park.
Age is gray, a toothless hag,
Stumbling in the dark.
Peretz, *Sewing the Wedding Gown*, 1906. *NOP*, 127.

18.C.10 A young tree bends, an old tree breaks.
Proverb (Yiddish). BJS, #363.

18.C.11 A reveler in youth, a beggar in old age.
Ibid., #1100.

18.C.12 A glutton in youth, a beggar in old age.
Ibid., #1440.

18.C.13 There is nothing more enviable than to have an old head and a young heart.
Sanders, *Citatenlexikon*, 1899, p. 21.

18.C.14 Tears in youth impair the sight in old age.
Talmud: Sabbath, 151b, on *Eccles.* 12.2.

18.C.15 You are as young as your faith, as old as your doubt; as young as your self-confidence, as old as your fear; as young as your hope, as old as your despair.
S. Ullman, *From the Summit of Four Score Years*, [1920], p. 13.

18.D. Old Age

18.D.1 Rise before the hoary head; honor the face of the old man.
Bible: Lev., 19.32.

18.D.2 They all wax old as a garment, the moth shall eat them up.
Bible: Isa., 50.8f.

18.D.3 Cast me not off in time of old age; when my strength fails, forsake me not.
Bible: Ps. 71.9.

18.D.4 The hoary head is a crown of glory.
Bible: Prov., 16.31.

18.D.5 With the ancient is wisdom and in length of days understanding.
Bible: Job, 12.12. Cf. 32.9.

18.D.6 Old friends and old wine do not lose their flavor.
Algazi, *Zehab Seba*, 1683.

18.D.7 Dishonor not the old: we shall all be numbered among them.
Apocrypha: Ben Sira, 8.6.

18.D.8 Much experience is the crown of the aged.
Ibid., 25.6.

18.D.9 Honorable old age is not marked by length of time . . . but understanding is gray hairs . . . and an unspotted life is ripe old age.
Apocrypha: Wisd. of Sol., 4.8f.

18.D.10 A man is as old as his wife looks.
O. Blumenthal, *Das zweite Gesicht,* 1890.

18.D.11 When a man fell into his anecdotage, it was a sign for him to retire from the world.
See D'Israeli, *Currents of Literature,* Preface, "The world in its anecdotage."

18.D.12 How disgraceful is folly in an old man!
Ibn Gabirol, *Mibhar HaPeninim,* c. 1050, #51.

18.D.13 Old age, mother of forgetfulness.
Ibn Tibbon, *Tzavaah,* 1190.

18.D.14 Old age is a natural disease.
Immanuel, *Mahberot,* (c. 1300) 1491, ch. 4.

18.D.15 Old age is a bad sickness.
Zarfati, *Yad Yosef,* 1617, Introduction.

18.D.16 Respect an old man who has lost his learning through no fault of his. The fragments of the Tables broken by Moses were kept in the Ark of the Covenant alongside of the new.
Judah (b. Ilai). *Talmud: Berakot,* 8b.

18.D.17 Old age, to the unlearned, is winter; to the learned, it is harvest time.
Lazerov, *Enciklopedie fun Idishe Vitzen,* 1928, #499.

18.D.18 Gauge a country's prosperity by its treatment of the aged.
Nahman Bratzlav, *Sefer HaMiddot,* 1821, p. 66.

18.D.19 An old man in a house is a burden; an old woman, a treasure.
Proverb, q Hezekiah b. Hiyya. *T: Arakin,* 19a.

18.D.20 Wine and wisdom improve with age.
S. Rubin, *Sefer HaMiddot,* 1854, 15.12.

18.D.21 The older the unlearned get the more their mind wanders. The older scholars get the more their mind is composed.
Simeon b. Akashia. *Mishna: Kinnim,* 3.6.
See Ishmael b. José. *T: Sabbath,* 152a.

18.D.22 Nobody grows old by merely living a number of years. People grow old only by deserting their ideals.
S. Ullman, *From the Summit of Four Score Years,* [1920], p. 13.

19. AGENT

19.1 As vinegar to the teeth, and as smoke to the eyes, is the sluggard to them that send him.
Bible: Prov., 10.26.

19.2 As the cold of snow on a harvest day is a faithful messenger, . . . refreshing the soul of his master.
Ibid., 25.13.

19.3 Send a wise man and give him no orders; but if you send a fool, rather go yourself.
Apocrypha: Ahikar, 2.41.

19.4 Those on a religious errand are not injured.
Eleazar b. Pedat. *Talmud: Pesahim,* 8a.

19.5 One's agent is like one's self.
Mekilta, to *Exod.* 12.3.

19.6 A dog can't be a butcher, nor a bachelor a matchmaker.
Proverb (Yiddish). BJS, #1138.

19.7 The Almighty has many agents at His disposal.
Talmud: Taanit, 18b. See *Gen. R.,* 10.7.

19.8 No agent for transgression, since we should obey the Master, not the pupil, when the commands conflict.
Talmud: Kiddushin, 42b.

20. ALIENATION

20.1 I shall not be separated from our race!
Apocalypse of Sedrach, 8.

20.2 What have I in common with Jews? I have hardly anything in common with myself.
Kafka, *Diaries,* 1914, p. 11.

20.3 No man can run away from his blood or his true creed.
Remenyi. q *Edouard Remenyi,* 1906, p. 55.

20.4 If a Jew separates himself from his people when they are in trouble, his two angels put their hands over his head and say: "He shall also be excluded from their consolation!"
Talmud: Taanit, 11a.

20.5 Go home to your Jews and tell them that I am not a Jew and I care nothing for Jews and their fate.

Trotsky, to Jewish delegation, 1921. q VA, 262.

21. ALTAR

21.1 Thou shalt not build it of hewn stones; for if thou lift thy sword upon it, thou hast profaned it.
Bible: Exod., 20.22.

21.2 When the Temple was in existence, its altar atoned for Israel. Now a man's table is his altar.

Johanan b. Nappaha. *Talmud: Berakot,* 55a.

22. ALTRUISM

22.1 The world exists only on account of him who disregards his own existence.
Abbahu. *Talmud: Hullin,* 89a.

22.2 The altruism of the Gospels is neither more nor less than inverted egoism.
Ahad HaAm, *Al Parashat Derakim,* (1895) 1921, iv. 45.

22.3 Only a life lived for others is a life worthwhile.
Einstein. *Youth,* June 1932.

22.4 We live largely for the good and happiness of others.
Moscato, *Nefutzot Yehuda,* 1588, p. 135a. q BSJ, 220.

22.5 Both egoism and altruism are necessary to welfare. Both are moral motives. Right living is the right balance between them.
H. Samuel, *Belief and Action,* 1937, p. 130.

22.6 It is true the law teaches that one's own life comes first, but this applies only to things on which life depends. . . . But if it is a question of bread and clothes and wood on one side, and dinners with fish and meat and fruit on the other side, the latter have to be given up as superfluities. . . . This is the real meaning of the law, but it is not worthy of a man to insist upon the law in such cases. He ought not to think of his life.
Shneor Zalman, *Tanya,* (1796) 1896, 52a. q SSJ, ii. 172f.

22.7 Men who are governed by reason . . . desire for themselves nothing which they do not also desire for the rest of mankind.
Spinoza, *Ethics,* 1677, iv. Pr 18, Note.

22.8 My fathers planted for me, and I plant for my children.
Talmud: Taanit, 23a. See *Tanhuma, Kedoshim,* #8, ed Buber, 38b.

22.9 Help us to be among those who are willing to sacrifice that others may not hunger, who dare to be bearers of light in the dark loneliness of stricken lives, who struggle and even bleed for the triumph of righteousness among men.
Union Prayer Book, 1940, i. 45.

23. AMBITION

23.1 Come, let us build . . . a tower, with its top in heaven, and let us make us a name.
Bible: Gen., 11.4.

23.2 You said in your heart, "I will ascend into heaven, above the stars of God will I exalt my throne." You shall be brought down to the nether-world, to the uttermost parts of the pit.
Bible: Isa., 14.13f.

23.3 Seek ye great things for yourself? Seek them not.
Bible: Jer., 45.5. See 49.16; *Obad.,* 1.3.

23.4 Fire ascends and goes out; water descends and is not lost.
Berekia HaNakdan, *Mishlé Shualim,* c. 1260.

23.5 Ambition is bondage.
Ibn Gabirol, *Mibhar HaPeninim,* c. 1050, #173.

23.6 "Go not up . . . that thy nakedness be not uncovered" [*Ex.* 20.23]. Ascend not too high; your faults may show.
Kagan, speech, Aug. 1923. q YSS, 82f.

23.7 Seek not greatness for yourself, covet not honor more than your learning, crave not for royal tables.
Mishna: Abot, 6.4.

23.8 Look for cake and lose your bread.
Proverb (Yiddish). BJS, #1435.

23.9 Who doesn't jump too high doesn't fall too low.
Syrkin. *Neier Veg,* Vilna, Aug. 1906 (SGZ, i. 119).

23.10 Ambition destroys its possessor.
Talmud: Yoma, 86b.

23.11 Man devises new schemes on the grave of a thousand disappointed hopes.
Union Prayer Book, 1922, ii. 325.

24. AMERICA

24.A. Its Meaning and Spirit

24.A.1 America is the youngest of the

nations, and inherits all that went before in history.

Antin, *The Promised Land,* 1912, p. 364.

24.A.2 How young she is! It will be centuries before she will adopt that maturity of custom, the clothing of the grave, that some people believe she is already fitted for.

Baruch, address, May 23, 1944.

24.A.3 We go forth all to seek America. And in the seeking we create her. In the quality of our search shall be the nature of the America that we created.

W. Frank, *Our America,* 1919.

24.A.4 The land of unlimited opportunities.

Goldberger, *Beobachtungen über das Wirtschaftsleben der Vereinigten Staaten,* 1902.

24.A.5 Here at our sea-washed, sunset gates shall stand
A mighty woman with a torch, whose flame
Is the imprisoned lightning, and her name
Mother of Exiles.

E. Lazarus, *New Colossus,* 1883.

24.A.6 We are a nation of immigrants. It is immigrants who brought to this land the skills of their hands and brains to make of it a beacon of opportunity and of hope for all men.

H. H. Lehman, at House Sub-Committee on Immigration and Naturalization, July 2, 1947.

24.A.7 We are a people with a faith in each other, . . . with a faith in reason, . . . with a faith in God . . . and when that is no longer strong within us, we are weak and we are lost, however heavily armed with weapons—even with atomic weapons—we may be.

D. Lilienthal, *This I Do Believe,* 1949, p. 144.

24.A.8 To me Americanism means not only an opportunity to do better . . . but an imperative duty to be nobler than the rest of the world.

London, speech, U.S. Congress, Jan. 18, 1916. RES 73.

24.A.9 The fundamental American tradition is that we came away from the fixed world of Europe to create a dynamic country, with freedom to move, to change, to work; with opportunity to learn; with a

chance to rise in the world; with a duty to keep the free spirit of the country free.

Gilbert Seldes, *The Great Audience,* 1950, p. 269.

24.A.10 God built Him a continent of glory and filled it with treasures untold. . . . Then He called unto a thousand peoples, and summoned the bravest among them. . . . And out of the bounty of earth and the labor of men, out of the longing of hearts and the prayers of souls, out of the memory of ages and the hopes of the world, God fashioned a nation in love, blessed it with a purpose sublime, and called it—America!

Silver, "America," 1917.

24.A.11 In the United States there is more space where nobody is than where anybody is. That is what makes America what it is.

G. Stein, *Geographical History of America,* 1936, p. 17f.

24.A.12 Ours is become a nation too great to offend the least, too mighty to be unjust to the weakest, too lofty and noble to be ungenerous to the poorest and lowliest.

S. S. Wise, address, July 4, 1905.

24.A.13 America is God's Crucible, the great Melting-Pot where all the races of Europe are melting and re-forming.

Zangwill, *The Melting Pot,* 1908, Act 1.

24.B. The Jew and Judaism in America

24.B.1 Not jewels but Jews were the real financial basis of the first expedition of Columbus.

*H. B. Adams, *Columbus and His Discovery of America,* Oct. 10, 1892 (Johns Hopkins Univ. Studies in Historical & Political Science, x. 22).

24.B.2 The twentieth century ideals of America have been the ideals of the Jew for more than twenty centuries.

Brandeis. *Menorah Journal,* Jan. 1915.

24.B.3 Foreigners ourselves, and mostly unable to write English, we had Americanized the system of providing clothes for the American woman of moderate or humble means. . . . Indeed, the Russian Jew had made the average American girl a tailor-made girl.

A. Cahan, *Rise of David Levinsky,* 1917, p. 443.

24.B.4 Gaze at the splendid array of edifices dedicated to every species of noble pnilanthropic work maintained by the Jewish community of this metropolitan city alone [New York], and your heart will beat higher with just pride and exultation at the signal demonstration that the practical Judaism of "good deeds" . . . is so well understood and so conscientiously observed here and now.

Drachman. *The Activities of the Rabbi*, 1892, p. 61.

24.B.5 It is in America that the opportunity of living the Jewish life in freedom has the brightest hopes of realization.

Grayzel, *A History of the Jews*, (1947) 1952, p. 813.

24.B.6 If all Europe were to become a prison, America would still present a loophole of escape. . . . Well then may the Jews take their harps down from the willows, and . . . sit by the Hudson and the Mississippi, to sing their sweet songs of praise and chant the lays of Zion.

Heine. q Peters, *Justice to the Jew*, 1921, p. 237.

24.B.7 We have had a share in the making of this nation. In the mine and in the mill, at the lathe and at the loom, in counting room and council chamber, the Jew has been at work for two centuries and a half for his America. He has sentried his nation's camp; he has been in the mast's lookout on his nation's ship; he has gone out to battle, and he was among them that fell at the firing line. . . . The future will place new solemn obligations upon us for the country's sake and as Judaism's consecration; we shall not shirk our duties.

E. G. Hirsch, *On the 250th Anniversary of the Settlement of the Jews in the U.S.*, Nov. 1905.

24.B.8 We cherish no longer any desire for a return to Palestine, but proudly and gratefully exclaim with the Psalmist [132.14], "Here is my resting place; here shall I reside; for I love this place!"

M. Lilienthal, address. *Israelite*, Sept. 3, 1869.

24.B.9 This synagog is our temple, this city our Jerusalem, this happy land our Palestine.

Poznanaski, sermon, Charleston, S.C., March 19, 1841.

24.B.10 The Jew is neither a newcomer nor an alien in this country or on this continent. . . . He came in the caravels of Columbus, and he knocked at the gates of New Amsterdam only thirty five years after the Pilgrim Fathers stepped ashore on Plymouth Rock.

O. S. Straus, Jan. 18, 1911. *American Spirit*, 293.

24.B.11 It is in America that the last great battle of Judaism will be fought out.

Zangwill, *Children of the Ghetto*, 1892, ii. ch 15.

25. ANARCHY

25.1 Ye shall not do . . . every man whatever is right in his own eyes.

Bible: Deut., 12.8.

25.2 Every man to his tents, O Israel!

Bible: II Sam., 20.1.

25.3 Anarchy stands for the liberation of the human mind from the dominion of religion; the liberation of the human body from the dominion of property; liberation from the shackles and restraints of government.

E. Goldman, *Anarchism*, 1917.

25.4 Anarchism asserts the possibility of organization without discipline, fear or punishment, and without the pressure of poverty.

E. Goldman, *Living My Life*, 1931, i. 402f.

25.5 Anarchy decomposes unity, under the pretext of the most perfect multiplicity; that is, the most unlimited freedom of the members; but under pretense only, for freedom, which has not for its aim the public good, is licentious freedom.

M. Mendelssohn, *National Instruction* (*Jerusalem*, tr Samuels, ii. 183).

26. ANATHEMA

26.1 Woe to you who fulminate anathemas which cannot be reversed!

Apocrypha: Enoch, 95.4.

26.2 The right of proscribing and banishing . . . is contrary to the spirit of religion. Excommunicate . . . a brother who wants . . . to lift his heart to God, along with mine, in salutary participation?!

M. Mendelssohn, *Jerusalem*, 1783, tr Samuels, ii. 66f.

26.3 Reader, . . . see whether you shall not discover more true religion among the multitude of the anathematized than among the incomparably greater multitude of those who anathematized them.

Ibid., ii. 67.

26.4 At this time, Israel has no other force than that of the ban, . . . and there is no greater sin than to violate the ban.
Sefer Hasidim, 13C, #1386, p. 239.

27. ANCESTRY

27.1 "Brother, of what family are you, and out of what tribe?" . . . And he said, "What need have you of a tribe?"
Apocrypha: Tobit, 5.11.

27.2 You are of a good stock, and I bid you welcome.
Ibid., 5.14.

27.3 Man lives not only in the circle of his years but also, by virtue of the subconscious, in the provinces of the generations from which he is descended, and Jewish life, to a very great extent, is based here.
Baeck, *The Jew,* 1950, p. 35.

27.4 All our ancestors are in us. Who can feel himself alone?
Beer-Hoffmann, *Schlaflied für Miriam,* 1898. q LRB, 14.

27.5 There is no pride like the pride of ancestry.
Disraeli, *Young Duke,* 1831.

27.6 Pride of origin is only the smiling sister of prejudice against it.
Goldberg. *Reflex,* July 1927, p. 30.

27.7 A valiant man takes pride in being himself the founder of a race, impotence alone worships the pedigree.
F. Hertz, *Race and Civilization,* 1928, p. 324.

27.8 [Proselytes,] esteem not lightly your pedigree. If we trace ours to Abraham, Isaac and Jacob, you trace yours to the Creator!
Maimonides, letter to Obadiah (*Responsa,* ed Freimann, #42, p. 41).

27.9 Among horses, pedigree plays an important role.
Mendelé, *Di Kliatshé,* 1873.

27.10 If a man has lost the use of his eyes, will the keen sight of his ancestors help him to see?
Philo, *Special Laws,* iv. 36.

27.11 Glorying in ancestors is like seeking fruit among the roots.
J. Steinberg, *Mishlé Yehoshua,* 1885, 40.18, p. 226.

28. ANGELS

28.1 He charges His angels with folly.
Bible: Job, 4.18.

28.2 Michael . . . holds the keys of the kingdom of Heaven.
Apocrypha: III Baruch, 11.2.

28.3 How many angels can dance on the point of a very fine needle without jostling each other?
D'Israeli, *Curiosities: Quodlibets,* 1791, paraphrasing Aquinas.

28.4 One angel does not perform two missions, nor is one mission performed by two angels.
Gen. R., 50.2.

28.5 The Holy One creates a new choir of angels each day: they sing before Him, and depart.
Helbo. *Gen. R.,* 78.1. See PRE, ch 4.

28.6 From each utterance of the Holy One an angel is born.
Jonathan b. Eleazar. *Talmud: Hagiga,* 14a.

28.7 Every one entrusted with a mission is an angel. . . . All forces that reside in the body are angels.
Maimonides, *Guide for the Perplexed,* 1190, 2.6.

28.8 The Angel of Death is all eyes.
Talmud: Aboda Zara, 20b.

29. ANGER

29.1 Anger kills the foolish man.
Bible: Job, 5.2.

29.2 Anger rests in the bosom of fools.
Bible: Eccles., 7.9.

29.3 Anger never went to bed with me.
Adda b. Ahaba. *Talmud: Taanit,* 20b. See *NT: Eph.* 4.26.

29.4 Anger is blindness.
Apocrypha: Patriarchs: Dan., 2.2.

29.5 Never be betrayed into anger, not even on heavenly matters.
Caro, *Maggid Mesharim,* 16C. q SSJ, ii. 216.

29.6 Through anger heroes fall.
Ezobi, *Kaarat Kesef,* 1270.

29.7 Anger begins with madness, and ends with regret.
Hasdai, *Ben HaMelek VeHaNazir,* 1230, ch 30.

29.8 Anger in a house is like a worm in a plant.
Hisda. *Talmud: Sota,* 3b.

29.9 Loss of temper leads to hell.
Jonathan b. Eleazar. *Talmud: Nedarim,* 22a. Cf *NT: Matt.,* 26.11.

29.10 Getting angry is like worshipping idols.
Midrash LeOlam, ch 15.

29.11 Anger and temper are Death's executioners.
Midrash Tehillim, 6.7.

29.12 There are four kinds of temper: easy to provoke and to pacify, the gain cancels the loss; hard to provoke and to pacify, the loss cancels the gain; hard to provoke and easy to pacify, the temper of a hasid; easy to provoke and hard to pacify, the temper of the wicked.
Mishna: Abot, 5.11.

29.13 Loss of temper is disrespect for the Divine Presence.
Rabbah b. Huna. *Talmud: Nedarim*, 22b.

29.14 Attempt not to placate a man at the time of his rage.
Simeon b. Eleazar. *Mishna: Abot*, 4.18. José b. Halafta. *Talmud: Berakot*, 7a.

29.15 Anger deprives a sage of his wisdom, a prophet of his vision.
Simeon b. Lakish. *Talmud: Pesahim*, 66b. See *Sifra, Shemini*, 2.12; *Sifré, Numbers*, #157.

30. ANIMAL

30.1 Thou shalt not muzzle the ox when he treadeth out the corn.
Bible: Deut., 25.4. See *Exod.*, 23.4f, 12.

30.2 A righteous man regards the soul (life) of his beast.
Bible: Prov., 12.10.

30.3 Noxious animals may be killed, but not tortured.
Ahai, *Sheiltot*, c. 760.

30.4 Had the Torah not been given us, we would learn modesty from cats, honest toil from ants, chastity from doves, and gallantry from cocks.
Johanan b. Nappaha. *Talmud: Erubin*, 100b.

30.5 Do not eat before you have fed your beast.
Rab. *Talmud: Berakot*, 40a.

30.6 A good man does not sell his beast to a cruel person.
Sefer Hasidim, 13C, #142, p. 64.

30.7 To relieve an animal of pain or danger is a biblical law, superseding any rabbinic ordinance [on Sabbath observance].
Talmud: Sabbath, 128b.

31. ANSWER

31.1 To answer before hearing is folly and confusion.
Bible: Prov., 18.13. See *Ben Sira*, 11.8; *BB*, 98b.

31.2 Answer not a fool according to his folly, lest you also be like him. Answer a fool according to his folly, lest he be wise in his own eyes.
Bible: Prov., 26.4f.

31.3 Be swift to hear, but with patience make reply.
Apocrypha: Ben Sira, 5.11.

31.4 Who answers speedily errs easily.
Bonsenyor, *Dichos y Sentencias*, 14C, #284.

31.5 The wise is not hasty to answer.
Mishna: Abot, 5.7.

31.6 No answer is also an answer.
Weissmann-Chajes, *Hokma UMusar*, 1875.

32. ANTI-SEMITISM

32.A. Characterization

32.A.1 The last anti-Semite will die only with the last Jew.
V. Adler, at Austrian Social Democratic Party Congress, 1898. *Aufsätze*, viii. 391.

32.A.2 Anti-Semitism is the Socialism of fools.
*Bebel, *Antisemitismus u. Sozialdemokratie*, Oct. 27, 1893. Bahr, *Antisemitismus*, 1894, p. 21, attr. it to Ferdin. Kronawetter.

32.A.3 An anti-Semite may prove "logically" that Jesus never existed and may yet continue to prove "historically" that the Jews had crucified him.
H. Cohen. summ. GIE, 90.

32.A.4 Anti-Semitism is religious fanaticism.
*Coudenhove, *Das Wesen des Antisemitismus*, 1901.

32.A.5 Of all the bigotries that ravage the human temper there is none so stupid as the anti-Semitic. It has no basis in reason, it is not rooted in faith, it aspires to no ideal.
*Lloyd George. Hearst Newspapers, July 22, 1923.

32.A.6 The hatred which breaks out from time to time against the Jews is . . . aimed against Europe. . . . It is the impossible attempt to oust from . . . German culture . . . the very element which enlightens, gives form, is human.

*Mann, address, Free Synagog, April 18, 1937.

32.A.7 Anti-Semitism diverts men from the real tasks confronting them. It diverts them from the true causes of their woes.

*Maritain, *A Christian Looks at the Jewish Question,* 1939.

32.A.8 Who looks to Jesus as his Master, cannot be anti-Semitic.

*Masaryk. q Newman, *Gentile and Jew,* 68.

32.A.9 Anti-Semitism is . . . a movement in which we, as Christians, cannot have any part whatever. . . . Spiritually, we are Semites.

*Pius XI, to Belgian pilgrims, Sept. 1938. See BSS, 328.

32.A.10 Dictators are anti-Semitic because they know or sense that liberty is Semitic in origin and character.

Silver, *World Crisis and Jewish Survival,* 1941, p. 72.

32.A.11 Anti-Semitism . . . is the most dangerous survival of cannibalism.

*Stalin, reply to JTA, Jan. 12, 1931. q. BSS, 316.

32.A.12 Anti-Semitism is a noxious weed that should be cut out. It has no place in free America.

*Taft, address, 1920.

32.A.13 Anti-Semitism is . . . a pathological condition, a peculiar form of sexual perversion. . . . Among all disgraceful phenomena, it is the most disgusting and abominable.

*Tolstoy, conversation with I. Tenoromo (Feinerman), 1889. See *Graf Leo Tolstoi über die Juden,* 1908, p. 44f.

32.A.14 It is the swollen envy of pigmy minds—meanness, injustice.

*Twain. q CMH, 16.

32.A.15 The Jews' quality of a permanent minority renders anti-Semitism permanent.

Valentin, *Antisemitism,* 1936, p. 19.

32.A.16 It is not the Jews who are hated but an imaginary image of them.

Ibid., 305.

32.A.17 One of its fundamental causes is that the Jews exist. . . . We carry the germs of anti-Semitism in our knapsack on our backs.

Weizmann, to Anglo-American Committee, March 8, 1946.

32.A.18 If there were no Jews they would have to be invented, for the use of politicians—they are indispensable, the antithesis of a panacea; guaranteed to *cause* all evils.

Zangwill, *Voice of Jerusalem,* 1921, p. 201.

32.B. Reaction to Anti-Semitism

32.B.1 For the Jews the moral is to answer anti-Semitism with more Semitism, if by Semitism we mean greater devotion to the great ideals which Judaism proclaimed to the world.

Abrahams. LCJ, 1929, p. 180.

32.B.2 A communicable disease . . . can be combated not only by fighting the germs but also by strengthening the resistance of the body under attack. Jews can do very little about fighting anti-Semitism. . . . But they certainly can go on strengthening the morale of their own people.

S. W. Baron. *American Zionist,* Feb. 5, 1953, p. 24.

32.B.3 It is our inescapable duty, as Aryans, to resist, repudiate and eradicate anti-Semitism. . . . This is an indispensable prerequisite for the future progress of European civilization.

*Bonghi, *La Caccia a Giudei. Nuova Antologia,* Ser. 3, vol. 34, Rome, Aug. 16, 1891.

32.B.4 Christianize the Christians.

*Howells. *American Hebrew,* April 4, 1890.

32.B.5 The burden of our history is unmistakable: the enemy of the Jew is the enemy of freedom. Those who organize the pogrom of today will attack tomorrow the general foundation of freedom. That is why the moral stature of the nation is set by its recognition that the claim of the Jew to freedom is the claim of its own people to strike off its chains. When it is silent before the agony of the Jew, it collaborates in the organization of its future servitude.

Laski. *New Statesman and Nation,* Feb. 13, 1943.

32.B.6 Anti-Semitism is not to be overcome by getting people to forget us, but to know us.

M. Levin, *In Search,* 1950.

32.B.7 It is the good behavior of the Jews, their hard work, their efficiency . . . which give momentum to the anti-Semitic drive. Anti-Semitism cannot be stopped by the good behavior of the individual Jew.

Lewin. *JF,* Sept. 1939; LRS, 162.

32.B.8 What if the Jewish revolutionary force leads to anti-Semitism? Anti-Semitism cannot be the guiding negative principle of Jewish life. Only freedom and service can be the guiding principle of the living Jewish people.
Magnes. q BFZ, 114.

32.B.9 Would that I may undo all that anti-Semitism caused me to do in my childhood days!
*Masaryk, "Náš pan Fixl." *Besedy Času,* Feb. 24, 1911.

32.B.10 Jewish institutions of learning are the laboratories where weapons are forged to repel anti-Semitism to the degree that such a course is possible.
Neuman, "The Jewish Defense Complex," 1952. See NLG, 366.

32.B.11 Associate with no man who takes any part in the mendacious race-swindle.
*Nietzsche. q BRN, 163.

32.B.12 If we allow this movement to grow, we will destroy the very pillars on which our civilization rests.
*Richter, 1890. q Simmel, *Anti-Semitism,* 1946, p. 34.

32.B.13 When I used to come home . . . bleeding and crying from the wounds inflicted upon me by the Christian boys, my father . . . made me understand that this is only a passing state in history, as we Jews belong to eternity, when God will comfort His people. Thus the pain was only physical, but my real suffering began later in life, when I emigrated from Rumania to so-called civilized countries and found there what I might call the Higher Anti-Semitism, which burns the soul though it leaves the body unhurt.
Schechter, March 26, 1903. SSA, 36.

33. APATHY

33.1 Thou shalt not stand idly by the blood of thy neighbor.
Bible: Lev., 19.16.

33.2 Hide not yourself from your own flesh.
Bible: Isa., 58.7.

33.3 When you have become indifferent to crimes committed against others, you have dug a pit for yourself.
Asch, *What I Believe,* 1941, p. 190.

33.4 Men do very little from love, a great deal from hate, most of all from indifference.
Brod, *The Master,* 1951, ch 7, p. 326.

33.5 No steam drives wheels with lukewarm water.
Harrison, *Religion of a Modern Liberal,* 1931, p. 94.

33.6 In spiritual matters one can be either cold or hot, not lukewarm.
J. Y. Hurwitz. q GIS, 87. See NT: Rev. 3.16.

33.7 The inertia of indifference is ponderous and hard to move.
H. Samuel, *Belief and Action,* 1937, p. 292.

33.8 Our quarrel is not with Jews who are different, but with Jews who are indifferent.
S. S. Wise, *Rededication,* 1932.

33.9 Indifference is the only infidelity I recognize.
Zangwill, *Children of the Ghetto,* 1892, ii. ch 15, p. 510.

34. APOSTASY

34.1 Who is an apostate? Who publicly desecrates the Sabbath.
Huna. *Talmud: Erubin,* 69a.

34.2 Fallen angels don't write poems. There is lyric poetry, and sacred poetry, and a poetry of love, and a poetry of rebellion; the poets of apostasy do not exist.
Koestler, *The Age of Longing,* 1951, p. 138.

34.3 The Torah does not elucidate in detail theological and metaphysical subjects. . . . If a scholar arrives at a belief in these profound and lofty subjects which does not correspond to the belief of the majority of Jews, he is not therefore an apostate.
S. D. Luzzatto, *Peniné Shadal,* 1883, p. 440f.

34.4 He is a Jew . . . he left his old religion for an estate, and has not had time to get a new one. But stands like a dead wall between Church and Synagog, or like the blank leaves between the Old and New Testament.
*Sheridan, *The Duenna,* 1775, Act 1. See Jason in Longfellow, *Judas Maccabeus,* 1872, 4.3.

34.5 An apostate who transgresses the law in public is like a heathen in all respects.
Talmud J: Erubin, 6.2.

34.6 Apostasy is automatically excluded for anyone with self-respect.
J. Wassermann, *My Life as German and Jew,* 1933, p. 233.

13

35. APPEARANCE

35.1 Man looks on the outward appearance, but the Lord looks on the heart.
Bible: 1 Sam., 16.7.

35.2 Let your garments be always white and your head lack no oil.
Bible: Eccles., 9.8.

35.3 Praise none for his beauty; abhor none for his appearance.
Apocrypha: Ben Sira, 11.2.

35.4 A man is known by his appearance.
Ibid., 19.29.

35.5 Most women are not so young as they are painted.
Beerbohm.

35.6 If men be judged by their beard and their girth,
Then goats are the wisest of creatures on earth.
J. S. Delmedigo, or Moses Metz, 17C. q *JE*, ii. 613b.

35.7 Man must seek not only to be guiltless before his God and fellow-men, but also to *appear* guiltless.
M. Lazarus, *Ethics*, 1900, i. 125. See *NT: 1 Cor.*, 5.22.

35.8 Pinch your cheeks and keep their color rosy.
Proverb (Yiddish). BJS, #3381. Suhl, *With One Foot in America*, 1947.

35.9 Sometimes in vessels seemingly empty, grains of gold can be discovered.
Zohar, Exodus, 95a.

36. ARABS

36.1 There will be not only peace between us and the Arabs, . . . but close friendship and co-operation.
Ben Gurion, to Anglo-American Com. of Inquiry, March 19, 1946.

36.2 Laboring orphan, peace unto you. . . . Whether you be akin to me in blood or no, responsibility for you rests upon me. It is for me to brighten your eyes. . . . Not for any aim and not from any motive save the motive of a brother, friend, companion.
Brenner, on seeing an overworked Arab boy. *Kuntres* (Tel Aviv) 1921, p. 77. q SHR, 389.

36.3 Was it not Arabs and Jews, in the earlier Dark Ages, . . . who held the torch high on the northern littoral of Africa and illumined the darkness of the plateau of Spain? Let us once more kindle a torch, you and we. The world is darker now than then!
Golding, *The Jewish Problem*, 1938, p. 198.

36.4 In the midst of wanton aggression, we yet call upon the Arab inhabitants of the State of Israel, to return to the ways of peace and play their part in the development of the State, with full and equal citizenship and due representation in all its bodies and institutions, provisional or permanent.
Israel, *Declaration of Independence*, May 14, 1948.

36.5 These Arabs are not heathens. Idolatry was eliminated from their speech and hearts long ago, and they affirm properly the unity of God. . . . Those who worship in mosques today have their hearts directed only toward heaven.
Maimonides, *Responsa*, ed Freimann, #369, p. 335f.

36.6 (In) the brilliant revival of learning that spread from Baghdad in the ninth and tenth centuries, . . . the leading part was played . . . by Syrians, Persians, Jews and others who were neither of Arab race nor domiciled in Arabia.
C. & D. Singer, *The Jewish Factor*, 1927 (BSL, 180f).

36.7 Conversations and negotiations with Arabs are not unlike chasing a mirage in the desert: full of promise and good to look at, but likely to lead you to death by thirst.
Weizmann, *Trial and Error*, 1949, p. 216.

37. ARGUMENT

37.1 A legal decision depends not on the teacher's age, but on the force of his argument.
Abbahu. *Talmud: Baba Bathra*, 142b.

37.2 Do not argue with the obstinate.
Ibn Gabirol, *Mibhar HaPeninim*, c. 1050, #232.

37.3 Do not attempt to confute a lion after he is dead.
Joshua b. Hanania. *Talmud: Gittin*, 83b.

37.4 Prepare your proof before you argue.
Samuel HaNagid, *Ben Mishlé*, 11C, #61.

37.5 If you are proved right, you accomplish little; but if you are proved wrong, you gain much: you learn the truth.
Sefer Hasidim, 13C.

38. ARK

38.1 It was not the priests that bore the Ark, but the Ark that bore its bearers.
Berekia. *Exod. R.,* 36.4.

39. ARMS

39.1 You come to me with a sword and a spear and a javelin, but I come to you in the name of the Lord of hosts!
Bible: I Sam. 17.45.

39.2 His quiver is an open sepulchre.
Bible: Jer., 5.16.

39.3 They shall make fires of their weapons and use them as fuel.
Bible: Ezek., 39.9.

39.4 Every one with one hand wrought in the work, and with the other held his weapons.
Bible: Neh., 4.11.

39.5 The terror created by weapons has never stopped men from employing them.
Baruch, at UN Atomic Energy Commission, June 14, 1946.

39.6 Cannon-balls and musket-balls are often the scouring-balls to cleanse the fouled world.
Boerne, *Fragmente & Aphorismen,* 1840, #122.

39.7 An end to these bloated armaments!
Disraeli, speech, 1862.

39.8 On earth, that is always right which has more and better arms.
Franzos, *Deutsche Dichtung,* 9.5.

39.9 Powder makes men equal: a citizen's musket fires as well as a nobleman's.
Heine, *English Fragments,* 1831, ch 13.

39.10 A man who invents a terrible explosive does more for peace than a thousand mild apostles.
Herzl, note to Baroness von Suttner, 1895.

39.11 Collect iron, crown a king, and learn to laugh.
Jabotinsky, *Samson,* ch 30.

39.12 There is no instance of our forefathers having triumphed by arms, or failed without them, when they committed their cause to God.
Josephus, *Wars,* 5.9.4.

39.13 One must not walk out on the Sabbath with a sword, bow, shield, lance or spear. . . . R. Eliezer objects: But these are ornaments. Said the Rabbis: These are a disgrace, not ornaments!
Mishna: Sabbath, 6.4. See Johanan b. Zakkai. *Mekilta,* to *Exod.,* 20.22.

39.14 Do not enter a house of learning with weapons.
Talmud: Sanhedrin, 82a.

39.15 He who goes about in this hard world without armor on his breast will be wounded.
Varnhagen. q KRV, 107.

40. ART

40.1 Make holy garments . . . for splendor and for beauty.
Bible: Exod., 28.2.

40.2 Art is not based on actuality, but on the wishes, dreams and aspirations of a people.
Berenson, Dec. 23, 1941, *Rumor & Reflections,* 1952, p. 54.

40.3 The artist must penetrate into the world, feel the fate of human beings, of peoples, with real love. There is no art for art's sake. One must be interested in the entire realm of life.
Chagall. q *JS, Sept.* 1951, p. 21.

40.4 He who has art in his life can never be entirely lost.
Gabrilowitsch. q CMH, 46.

40.5 The true artist sees the harmony, the wholeness, the tendencies toward perfection in things everywhere.
Guggenheimer, *Creative Vision,* 1950, p. 105f.

40.6 In matters of art I am a supernaturalist. I believe that the artist cannot find all his types in nature, but that the most remarkable types are revealed to him in his soul.
Heine, *The Salon,* 1831.

40.7 The beautiful artistic form is only for the eyes, and does not correspond to reality.
q M. Ibn Ezra, *Shirat Yisrael,* (12C) 1924, p. 100.

40.8 The interior of a poor house is richer in color than the room of a prominent merchant, and the effect of light, through a dilapidated window-pane, on colored objects casts a spell . . . which one cannot see through large panes of plate glass.
Israels, letter to Boer. KJG, 270.

40.9 For an artist there are no limitations . . . he must not be told, "Paint no evil." The only demand which may be made of him is that he employ the right means which art affords.
Ibid., (KJG, 271).

40.10 Art is the truest League of Nations, speaking a language and preaching a message understood by all peoples.
O. H. Kahn, *Of Many Things,* 1926, p. 27.

40.11 Those who love art and are truly susceptible to its spell, do die young in the sense that they remain young to their dying day.
Ibid., p. 28.

40.12 True art is eternal, but it is not stationary.
Ibid., p. 67.

40.13 The essence of photography lies not in its fixation of the visible and actual but, if it is to be considered an art, in . . . the external projection . . . of an inner vision of the artist.
Lerski. *Israel Miscellany,* i. 76.

40.14 The artist is one to whom all experience is revelation.
Lewisohn, *Creative Life,* 1924, p. 66.

40.15 Wherever deep experience attains intense expression, there is art.
Ibid., 95.

40.16 An artist who fails, by representations of reality, to express the invisible, that which lies behind the phenomenon, whatever we call it—soul, spirit, life—is no artist.
Liebermann, *Ueber Kunst. Ges. Schr.,* 1922, p. 19.

40.17 I have portrayed you more like yourself than you are.
Liebermann, to a complainant who found no likeness in his portrait. q Baeck, *Judaism & Philosophy,* 16.

40.18 Art is always and everywhere the secret confession and, at the same time, the immortal movement, of its time.
Marx, *A Critique of Political Economy,* 1859.

40.19 Art is a reaching out into the ugliness of the world for vagrant beauty and the imprisonment of it in a tangible form.
G. J. Nathan, *Critic and the Drama,* 1922, p. 3.

40.20 Art is a gross exaggeration of natural beauty: there never was a woman so beautiful as the Venus di Milo, . . . or human speech so beautiful as Shakespeare's, or the song of a nightingale so beautiful as Ludwig van Beethoven's.
Ibid., p. 6.

40.21 The artist creates the work of art . . . to free his nervous system from a tension. . . . The artist writes, paints, sings or dances the burden of some idea or feeling off his mind.
Nordau, *Degeneration,* (1893) 3.3, p. 324.

40.22 When a Jewish artist expresses himself sincerely, he will reflect something specially Jewish in his work: he will create Jewish art.
Pann. *Menorah Journal,* 1920, vi. 220.

40.23 Art is a form of catharsis.
Parker, *Sunset Gun,* 1928, p. 75.

40.24 It is the height of folly to take the arts as the standard of measurement for mankind.
Philo, *Eternity of the World,* 27.

40.25 The three criteria of a work of art: harmony, intensity, continuity.
Schnitzler, *Buch der Sprüche & Bedenken,* 1927, p. 173.

40.26 The artist is content with aspiration, whereas the mediocre must have beauty. And yet the artist attains beauty without willing it, for he is only striving after truthfulness.
Schoenberg. Armitage, *Schoenberg,* p. 257.

40.27 The pyramidal effect is essential to all the arts—the effect of starting from the level, rising to the supreme height, and sinking back to the original level again. This in truth is the meaning of key in music; in art, as in life, the secret of happiness is first of all to get as far away from home as you can, and then get back to your home: every work of art is a sort of Prodigal Son, that learns to appreciate the fixed point in space as in ethics, by straying from it.
Sokolow. q *Avukah Annual,* 1932, p. 410.

40.28 Criticism clearly recognizes in every work of art an organism governed by its own law.
Spingarn, *New Criticism,* March 9, 1910.

40.29 To let one's self go—that is what art is always aiming at.
Spingarn, *Creative Criticism,* 1917.

40.30 Almost all art cycles are short in their development though often long in their degeneration.
L. Stein, *Journey into the Self,* 1950, p. 168.

40.31 My ideal of a picture is that every part of it should oblige the looker-on who has any real sense for a whole to see the rest.

Ibid., p. 179.

40.32 It is only through the self-portraiture of great artists that the genius of mankind becomes comprehensible to earthbound mortals.

S. Zweig, *Adepts in Self-Portraiture,* 1928.

41. ASPIRATION

41.1 Lead me to a rock that is too high for me.

Bible: Ps., 61.3.

41.2 He who lives aspires! He who is dead, renounces!

Beer-Hoffmann, *Der Graf von Scharolais,* 1904.

41.3 To see the true, to love the beautiful, to desire the good, and to do the best.

M. Mendelssohn, motto.

41.4 I want to soar the boundless blue
Where winds and tempests have their birth,
And let the clouds conceal for me
Not heaven, but the earth.

Peretz, *"I Am a Rainworm,"* 1900, tr Jacob Robbins. LGP, 83.

41.5 We cannot and shall not change our aspirations in accordance with the mode of the day or the mood of the moment.

Riesser, 1842. q Baron. *Liberal Judaism,* Apr. 1945, p. 10.

41.6 Upward to God, upward to God, Sons of earth, together!

Union Prayer Book, 1922, ii. 95.

41.7 Aspiration is achievement.

Zangwill, *Voice of Jerusalem,* 1921, p. 364.

42. ASS

42.1 He shall be a wild ass of a man.

Bible: Gen., 16.12.

42.2 The Lord opened the mouth of the ass.

Bible: Num., 22.28.

42.3 When you see an ass mount a ladder, you will find sense in fools.

Huppat Eliyahu Rabbah, (EOM, 171a).

42.4 If one says you have the ears of an ass, pay no attention; but if two tell you that, get yourself a halter.

Proverb. q *Gen. R.,* 45.7. *Cf Raba. T: BK,* 92b.

42.5 The pace of an ass depends on his barley.

Talmud: Sabbath, 51b.

43. ASSIMILATION

43.1 I want now to be of today. It is painful to be conscious of two worlds. The Wandering Jew in me seeks forgetfulness.

Antin, *The Promised Land,* 1912, p. xiv.

43.2 Death and suicide are the most radical reliefs from disease. Similarly, assimilation is the most radical solution of the Jewish problem.

Borochov, "National Self-Help," Aug. 6, 1915 (BNC, 85).

43.3 Be a Jew in your tent, and a man outside.

J. L. Gordon, *"Hakitza Ammi,"* 1863.

43.4 I would deplore the spiritual and moral fate of any country that imposed among the duties of citizenship an obligation of amnesia, of becoming oblivious of oneself, of erasing one's memories, one's past, one's intimate group relationships.

H. Greenberg, address, 1951 (GIE, 76. See 181).

43.5 We have honestly endeavored everywhere to merge ourselves in the social life of surrounding communities and to preserve the faith of our fathers. We are not permitted to do so.

Herzl, *The Jewish State,* 1896, ch 1.

43.6 Assimilation offers the only chance to life, liberty, and the pursuit of happiness to this able but unbeloved stock.

*Hooton, *Twilight of Man,* 1939, p. 231.

43.7 The ruling nation seeks to transform other peoples into its own image.

Ibn Verga, *Shebet Yehuda,* 1550. q LAJ, 43.

43.8 Joining a new community or nation or class or set is . . . above all a question of reception. Jewish assimilation in East-Central Europe has obviously failed in this respect; by bringing Jew and Gentile nearer to each other, . . . it merely extended the area of possible friction.

Jabotinsky, *The War and the Jew,* 1942, p. 115.

43.9 Ezekiel complained: "Ye did not" and "Ye did follow the ordinances of the nations round about you" [5.7, 11.12]. He meant: Ye did not follow the good, but the corrupt, among them.

Joshua b. Levi. *Talmud: Sanhedrin,* 39b.

43.10 Had the youthful Moses . . . accepted [assimilation] . . . he would never have brought the chosen people out of their house of bondage . . . spoken with the Eternal . . . [or] come down with the light of inspiration shining in his countenance and bearing in his arms the tables of the law, graven in the language of the outlaw.

*Joyce, *Ulysses*, (1918) 1934, p. 140f.

43.11 Now we will suffer loss of memory;
> We will forget the tongue our mothers knew;
> We will munch ham, and guzzle milk thereto,
> And this on hallowed fast-days, purposely. . . .
> To Gentile parties we will proudly go;
> And Christians, anecdoting us, will say:
> "Mr. and Mrs. Klein—the Jews, you know. . . ."

Klein, *Poems: Hath Not a Jew*, 1940, p. 70f.

43.12 To those thousands upon thousands of wretched Jews who sigh in the ghettoes of Russia, Rumania, Persia and Morocco, . . . we say: Assimilation will burden you with new chains and bonds; you will find salvation only when you dwell upon a soil which belongs to you. Assimilation will give you only a makeshift freedom; the law will confer this freedom upon you, passions and prejudices will constantly repeal it.

Lazare, *Nationalism & Jewish Emancipation*, 1889 (LJD 99).

43.13 There is no greater sin than to cause one's nation to disappear from the world.

Levinsohn, *Zerubabel*, 1853, i. 84.

43.14 It would be an easy solution of the minority problem if it could be done away with through individual assimilation. Actually, however, such a solution is impossible for any underprivileged group.

Lewin. *JF*, Sept. 1939. LRS, 164.

43.15 In the diaspora the Jewish soul is capable only of submission. . . . True and wholesome assimilation can only take place where the Jewish soul is free, and the Jewish soul can be free only in its own soil.

Margolis. *Maccabean*, Feb. 1907

43.16 The Chinese Jews
> Have longer queues

Than ordinary Chinamen.
Menorah Journal, 1931, xvii. 198.

43.17 I admonish you not to alter, God forbid, your Jewish names, language and manner of dress. Let your watchword be, "Jacob came *whole* to the city of Shechem" [*Gen.* 33.18].

Sofer, *Tzavaah*, Nov. 24, 1836.

43.18 The more assimilation the more and mightier anti-Semitism.

*Sombart, *The Future of the Jews*, 1911.

43.19 When the emperor proposed, "Let us all be one people," Tanhuma replied: "Very well, but since we, who are circumcised, cannot possibly become like you, you become like us."

Tanhuma b. Abba. *T: Sanhedrin*, 39a.

43.20 It appears to be only when the gifted Jew escapes from the cultural environment created and fed by the particular genius of his own people, . . . that he comes into his own as a creative leader in the world's intellectual enterprise.

*Veblen. *Political Science Quarterly*, March 1919.

43.21 Assimilation is evaporation, the Mendelssohnian solution is *dis*solution

Zangwill. *JQRo*, 1905, xvii. 410.

44. ASSOCIATION

44.1 Woe to the wicked and woe to his neighbor! Hail the righteous and hail his neighbor!

Ishmael b. Johanan. ARN A ch. 9, p. 39.

44.2 If you touch pitch, it will cleave to your hand.

Apocrypha: Ben Sira, 13.1.

44.3 How can jar and kettle associate, when, whichever smite, the one is always smashed?

Ibid., 13.2.

44.4 In a long journey and a small inn, one knows one's company.

Disraeli, *Count Alarcos*, 1839.

44.5 If you come near to the shadow of a king, you come near a lion. Others will fear you, but your fear too will be great.

Hai Gaon, *Musar Haskel*, c. 1000.

44.6 If a prince wear a Bohemian glass stone on his finger, it will be taken for a diamond; should a beggar wear a genuine diamond ring, everyone will feel convinced it is only glass.

Heine, *The Salon*, 1834.

44.7 Sometimes a man's fitness for a post of trust is determined by his associations.

Hook. *N.Y. Times Magazine*, July 9, 1950.

44.8 I'd rather be the partner of a wise man in Gehenna than the companion of a fool in Eden.

N. Z. Horowitz. q *HaDoar*, 1945, p. 673.

44.9 One must not pass all the time in study; one must also seek intercourse with people.

Katz, *Toldot Jacob Joseph*, 1780. q HLH, 33.

44.10 It's not what you do. . . . It's who you know. . . . It's contacts.

Miller, *Death of a Salesman*, 1949, Act 2.

44.11 The scroll's sheath is saved with the scroll.

Mishna: Sabbath, 16.1.

44.12 What is attached to the defiled will be defiled, and what is attached to the pure will be pure.

Mishna: Kelim, 12.2.

44.13 A king's servant is like a king.

Proverb. q Ishmael School. *Talmud: Shebuot*, 47b.

44.14 Together with the thorn the cabbage is smitten.

Proverb. q Raba. *Talmud: Baba Kamma*, 92a.

44.15 You can't act the part of a broom without getting soiled.

Proverb. q Schechter, June 5, 1904. SSA 75.

44.16 Attach yourself to the captain, and they'll bow to you.

Proverb. q *Sifré, #6*, to *Deut.* 1.7, ed Friedmann, 66b.

44.17 Because beside a thorn it grows,
The rose is not less fair;
Tho wine from gnarled branches flows,
'Tis sweet beyond compare.

Santob de Carrion, *Proverbios Morales*, 1350.

44.18 Who's close to the anointed smells of ointment (Who's close to fat grows fat).

Simeon b. Tarfon. *Talmud: Shebuot*, 47b.

44.19 We're perfumed: we shook hands with an aristocrat!

A taunt. q Rami b. Hama. *Talmud: Zebahim*, 96b.

45. ASTROLOGY

45.1 Be not dismayed at the signs of heaven.

Bible: Jer., 10.2. See *Isa.*, 47.13f.

45.2 The planets cannot affect earthly affairs for good or ill unless empowered to do so by the Lord of all.

Baraita of Samuel, 776, ch 9.

45.3 The Holy One forbade astrology in Israel.

Gen. R., 44.12.

45.4 Israel has no *mazal* [tutelary planet; lucky star].

Johanan, Rab, Samuel. *Talmud: Sabbath*, 156a. Cf Hanina b. Hama. *Ibid.*

45.5 God lifted Abraham above the vault of heaven, and said to him: You are a prophet, not an astrologer!

Johanan. *Gen. R.*, 44.12.

45.6 God said to Abraham: He who is below the stars, fears them. You are above them. Ignore them.

Levi. *Ibid.*

45.7 Astrology is a disease, not a science. . . . it is a tree under the shadow of which all sorts of superstitions thrive. . . . Only fools and charlatans lend value to it.

Maimonides, letter to Marseilles, 1195. *Responsa*, ii. 25b.

46. ASYLUM

46.1 Appoint cities of refuge . . . that the manslayer . . . through error may flee thither.

Bible: Num., 35.11.

46.2 A closed country is a dying country.

Ferber, radio broadcast, 1947.

46.3 Give me your tired, your poor,
Your huddled masses yearning to breathe free,
The wretched refuse of your teeming shore,
Send these, the homeless, tempest-tossed, to me.

E. Lazarus, "The New Colossus," 1883.

46.4 Whenever I meet one of those melancholy processions of Russo-Jewish refugees . . . I ask myself whether one of those pitiable Jewesses . . . is not perchance carrying beneath her heart some future Messiah of art or science? Spinoza's mother may well have disembarked as such a fugitive on the low shores of the Netherlands.

*Leroy-Beaulieu, *Israel Among the Nations*, 1895, p. 262.

46.5 I would welcome the exiled Russian Jew to South Africa, not merely with pity, but with a feeling of pride that any member of that great people . . . should find a refuge and a home among us; and with the certainty that, however broken, crushed and dwarfed he might appear to be by the long ages of suffering and wrong which have passed over him, he would recuperate and rise.

*Schreiner, *A Letter on the Jews,* July 1, 1906.

46.6 Homicides had more cities of refuge in ancient Palestine than the Rumanian Jews have in the whole world.

Zangwill, "Send-Off to Dr. Schechter," April 1902.

47. ATHEISM

47.1 The fool has said in his heart: There is no God.

Bible: Ps., 14.1, 53.1. See 42.4.

47.2 Even atheism can be uplifted through charity. If someone seeks your aid, act as if there were no God, as if you alone can help.

Moshe Leib of Sasov. See BTH, ii. 89.

47.3 Atheism is the source of all iniquities.

Philo, *Decalog,* 18.

47.4 He who denies his Creator is most despicable, for he who denies the Commander will not hesitate to deny His commands.

Reuben b. Strobilus. *Tosefta: Shebuot,* 3.6.

47.5 The space of the whole universe is
emptied . . .
And frightening when there is no
God.

Shneor, "On the Banks of the Seine," 1908. q *Judaism,* ii. 29.

47.6 Yes, it has come to this! Men who . . . can form no idea of God . . . unblushingly accuse philosophers of Atheism.

Spinoza, *Theologico-Political Treatise,* 1670, ch 2.

47.7 Fervid atheism is usually a screen for repressed religion.

Stekel, *Autobiography,* 1950, p. 74.

47.8 Of two men who have no experience of God, he who denies Him is perhaps nearer to Him than the other.

S. Weil, *Gravity and Grace,* tr 1952, p. 167.

47.9 The soul of man does not thrive on godlessness.

Wolfson. *Menorah Journal,* 1921, vii. 79.

48. ATOM

48.1 Behind the black portent of the new atomic age lies a hope which, seized upon with faith, can work our salvation. If we fail, then we have damned every man to be the slave of Fear.

Baruch, at U.N. Atomic Energy Commission, June 14, 1946.

48.2 Science has brought forth this danger, but the real problem is in the minds and hearts of men.

Einstein. *N.Y. Times Magazine,* June 23, 1946, p. 44.

48.3 The vast dilemma of the human
race
Is pulsing, restless, in the atom's
space.
What magnitudes, that sleep in
shrunken size,
At man's command, are ready to
arise!

L. Ginsberg, "Atomic Bomb." *P.M.,* 1945.

48.4 Atomic energy bears that same duality . . . expressed in the Book of Books thousands of years ago: "See, I have set before thee this day life and good, and death and evil . . . therefore choose life" [*Deut.* 30, 15, 19].

D. E. Lilienthal, *This I Do Believe,* 1949.

48.5 The Atom is not the natural enemy of the Adam. Indeed, it can serve as his greatest helpmate.

Sarnoff, *Youth in a Changing World,* June 12, 1954.

49. ATONEMENT

49.1 On this day shall atonement be made for you, to cleanse you; from all your sins shall ye be clean before the Lord.

Bible: Lev., 16.30.

49.2 "For you to cleanse you"—only through your own cleansing, through self-purging, can you appear "clean before the Lord."

Mendel of Kotzk, *Emet VeEmuna,* (1940), p. 62.

49.3 The priest shall atone for the soul that . . . sins through error.

Bible: Num., 15.28.

49.4 By mercy and truth iniquity is expiated.

Bible: Prov., 16.6.

49.5 The Day of Atonement atones for sins against God, not for sins against man, unless the injured man has been appeased.
Eleazar b. Azariah. *Mishna: Yoma*, 8.9.

49.6 To atone is to be *at one* with God, to sink self into the not-self, to achieve a mystic unity with the source of being, wiping out all error and finding peace in self-submergence.
Goldberg, *The Wonder of Words*, 1938, p. 5.

49.7 On the eve of each New Moon, repent and make restitution by word and deed. Enter the new month as pure as a new-born babe.
Horowitz, *Shné Luhot HaBerit*, 1649.

49.8 The Day of Atonement will achieve nothing for him who says, I'll sin and the Day of Atonement will atone.
Mishna: Yoma, 8.9.

49.9 We do not ask that our past sins be forgiven in the sense that their effects may be cancelled. . . . .All we can and do ask for is better insight, purer faith, fuller strength.
Montefiore, *Liberal Judaism*, 1903, p. 164.

50. AUTHOR

50.1 The writer of art has in mind the psychology of his characters; the writer of trash, the psychology of his readers.
Bickel, *Detaln un Sach-Hakeln*, 1943, p. 256.

50.2 I have a very high regard for the writer's calling. If he is not truth's ordained priest, then he is fit only for the scrap-heap.
Brandes, letter to Clemenceau, March 1915.

50.3 An author may influence the fortunes of the world to as great an extent as a statesman or a warrior.
Disraeli, *Life & Writings of D'Israeli*, 1848.

50.4 The author who speaks about his own books is almost as bad as a mother who talks about her own children.
Disraeli, speech, Nov. 19, 1870.

50.5 We find great men often greater than the books they write.
D'Israeli, *Literary Character*, 1795, ch 15.

50.6 Licentious writers may be very chaste men, for the imagination may be a volcano while the heart is an Alp of ice.
Ibid.

50.7 I ask myself constantly your question, "For whom do I toil?" Yet . . . I always return to my work. . . . We cannot, dear friends, do otherwise; we must write and publish.
Finn, letter to J. L. Gordon, April 17, 1871.

50.8 By the time a writer discovers he has no talent for literature, he is too successful to give it up.
G. S. Kaufman. q Leon Gutterman. JTA 1952.

50.9 If you were to ask me what a writer's ambition should be, I would answer with a formula: to trade a hundred contemporary readers for ten readers in ten years and for one reader in a hundred years.
Koestler. q Breit. *N.Y. Times*, Apr. 1, 1951. See *Arrow in the Blue*, 1952, p. 27.

50.10 There is no such thing as a dirty theme. There are only dirty writers.
G. J. Nathan, *Testament of a Critic*, 1931, p. 179.

50.11 Not every human being can be an author, but every author could be a human being.
Saphir, *Badenmantel-Gedanken*. SHW, i. 376.

51. AUTHORITY

51.1 What is founded on tradition or prophetic inspiration can not be overthrown by any science in the world.
Adret, *Responsa*, 13C. q KTJ, 249.

51.2 If you wish to hang, select a large tree.
Akiba. *Talmud: Pesahim*, 112a.

51.3 We fully acknowledge the old authorities' greatness and our own insignificance; but, like pygmies riding on giants' shoulders, we see farther than the giants, when we use their knowledge and experience.
q Z. Anav, *Shibbolé HaLeket*, 13C, Preface.

51.4 We must not be guided in our decisions by admiration for great men.
Asher b. Yehiel, c. 1300. q Weiss, *Dor*, v. 63.

51.5 What if the Tosafists and other authorities disagree with my opinion? The spirit of God made me as it made them!
Bacharach, *Havot Yair*, 1699, #155.

51.6 The great majority of people have a strong need for authority which they can

admire, to which they can submit, and which . . . sometimes even ill-treats them. . . . It is the longing for the father that lives in each of us from his childhood days.
Freud, *Moses and Monotheism*, p. 172.

51.7 To deny the authority of a religious work, great or small, is to earn the title of *epiḳoros*.
Hagiz, *Leḳet HaKemah*, (1697) 1897, p. 103a.

51.8 Every religious authority is, as a matter of course, superior to the succeeding generations.
Y. T. Heller, *Tosefot*, 1614, to *Eduyot*, 5.1. q HSJ, 67.

51.9 Counsel searching for authority for lack of argument.
Jessel. q Goodhart, *Five Jewish Lawyers*, 22.

51.10 I consider the subordination of reason to the authority of any person to be idolatry.
Maier. *Rabbinische Gutachten*, 1842, ii. 64.

51.11 We must not reject a proven doctrine because it is opposed to some isolated opinion of this or that great authority. . . . No man must surrender his private judgment. The eyes are directed forwards, not backwards.
Maimonides, Letter to Marseilles, 1195. *Responsa*, ii. 26a.

51.12 Notwithstanding my desire and delight to follow the earlier authorities, I do not consider myself "a donkey carrying books." I will explain their methods and I appreciate their value, but . . . I will plead, in all modesty, my right to judge by the light of my eyes. . . . The Lord gives wisdom in all times and ages.
Nahmanides, *Hasagot*, 13C, Preface. q SSJ, i. 111.

51.13 It is not by a perpetual Amen to every utterance of a great authority that truth or literature gains anything.
Schechter, *Studies in Judaism*, 1896, i. 164.

51.14 Authority, not majority.
Stahl, at Erfurt Parliament, April 15, 1850. See *Die gegenwärtigen Parteien in Staat & Kirche*, 1868, p. 22.

51.15 Every nation, every epoch, every thoughtful human being, has again and again to establish the landmarks between freedom and authority: for, in the absence of authority, liberty degenerates into license, and chaos ensues; and authority becomes tyranny unless it is tempered by freedom.
S. Zweig, *The Right to Heresy*, 1936, p. 7.

52. AWE

52.1 How full of awe is this place!
Bible: Gen., 28.17.

52.2 We are encompassed by questions to which only awe can respond.
Baeck, *Judaism and Science*, 1949, p. 6.

52.3 Enter into your Creator's presence with the deepest awe.
Eliezer b. Isaac, *Orhot Hayyim*, 11C.

52.4 Walk not irreverently even four cubits, for "the whole earth is full of His glory" [*Isa.* 6.3].
Joshua b. Levi. *Talmud: Kiddushin*, 31a.

52.5 Lord our God, impose Thine awe upon all Thy works . . . that they may all form one band to do Thy will with a perfect heart.
Rosh Hashana Prayer. See *DPB*, ed Singer, 239.

52.6 Of all the ways of awakening inner reverence in man, the best is the contemplation of the works of God. Their transcendent greatness must inspire awe.
Vidas. *Reshit Hoḳma*, 1578, 1.2.

53. BABY

53.1 Out of the mouth of babes and sucklings hast Thou founded strength.
Bible: Ps., 8.3.

53.2 Too many midwives kill the baby.
Twerski. Cf *Gen. R.*, 60.3.

54. BABYLON

54.1 By the rivers of Babylon, there sat we down, yea, we wept.
Bible: Ps., 137.1.

54.2 When the Torah was forgotten in Israel, sages came from Babylon and restored it—Ezra, Hillel, and Hiyya and his sons.
Simeon b. Lakish. *Talmud: Sukḳa*, 20a.

55. BARE

55.1 Thou shalt not go up by steps to Mine altar, that your nakedness be not uncovered thereon.
Bible: Exod., 20.23.

55.2 Who walks barefoot has callous soles.
Herzl, *Das neue Ghetto*, 1896.

55.3 Cover your head, that the fear of Heaven be upon you.

Nahman b. Isaac's mother. *Talmud: Sabbath*, 156b.

55.4 The barefoot recalls the comfort in his father's home.

Proverb (Palestine). *Lam. R.*, 1.34.

55.5 All shoemakers go barefoot.

Proverb (Yiddish). q Weissman-Chajes, *Hokma UMusar*, p. 19.

55.6 Who plants thorns should not walk barefoot.

Twerski, *Rashi*, 1946.

56. BASTARD

56.1 A bastard shall not enter the assembly of the Lord.

Bible: Deut., 23.3.

56.2 Bastards are innocent sufferers. God will comfort them.

Daniel the Tailor. *Lev. R.*, 32.8.

56.3 None is as bold as a bastard.

Midrash HaNe'elam, Genesis (VaYera), 118.

56.4 A learned bastard is ahead of an ignorant High Priest.

Mishna: Horayot, 3.8.

56.5 Most bastards are bright.

Abba Saul. *Talmud J: Kiddushin*, 4.11.

57. BEARD

57.1 The glory of a face is its beard.

Joshua b. Karha. *Talmud: Sabbath*, 152a.

57.2 Better a Jew without a beard than a beard without a Jew.

Mendelé, *Dos Kleine Mentshelé*, (1864) 1879.

57.3 Learn to barber on someone else's beard.

Proverb (Yiddish). BJS, #337.

58. BEAUTY

58.1 Beauty is a fading flower.

Bible: Isa., 28.1.

58.2 Grace is deceitful, and beauty is vain.

Bible: Prov., 31.30.

58.3 Truth is the vital breath of Beauty; Beauty the outward form of Truth.

Aguilar, *Amete and Yafeh*, 1850.

58.4 Of what profit are beauties if they die in the earth?

Apocalypse of Sedrach, 7. Cf Eleazar. *Talmud: Berakot*, 5a.

58.5 As the lamp shining on the holy candlestick, so is the beauty of a face on a stately figure. As the golden pillars upon the silver base, so are beautiful feet upon firm heels.

Apocrypha: Ben Sira, 27.17f.

58.6 If the vision of a beautiful woman, or of any lovely thing, comes suddenly to a man's eyes, let him ask himself: whence this beauty if not from the divine force which permeates the world? and why be attracted by the part? better be drawn after the All! . . . Such perception of beauty is an experience of the Eternal.

Baal Shem, *Tzavaat Ribash*, 1797, 18 (See AHE, 297f).

58.7 Beauty can inspire miracles.

Disraeli, *The Young Duke*, 1831.

58.8 Read only beautifully written . . . and handsomely bound books, in a tastefully furnished room. Let your eye rest on graceful objects. . . . Beauty must be everywhere.

Efodi. See *Maasé Efod*, (1403) 1865, p. 20; AJL, 355.

58.9 Keep away from the hideous and from what looks hideous.

Eliezar b. Hyrcanus. *Tosefta: Hullin*, 2.24.

58.10 A comely form, my darling son, is thine;
Corrupt it not, for 'tis a gift divine.

Ezobi, *Kaarat Kesef*, 1270. *JQRo*, viii. 539.

58.11 What is all beauty but the trace
Of my heart shining in my face?

Fleg, *Wall of Weeping*, 1919, tr H. Wolfe, 1929, p. 27.

58.12 Only to Beauty
Time belongs;
Men may perish
But not their songs.

L. Ginsberg, "Only to Beauty." N.Y. *Herald Tribune*, 1936.

58.13 "I will be beautiful before Him" —I will prepare beautiful ritual objects before Him.

Ishmael b. Elisha. *Mekilta*, to *Exod.* 15.2.

58.14 Only that is beautiful which is worthy.

Linetzki. q I. Goldberg. *Menorah Journal*, 1919, v. 42.

58.15 The mind needs to relax by contemplating pictures and other beautiful objects.

Maimonides, *Eight Chapters*, 1168, #5.

58.16 Each conception of spiritual beauty is a glimpse at God.
M. Mendelssohn.

58.17 Ugliness is the greatest of all sins.
Peretz. q M. Samuel, *Prince of the Ghetto*, 146.

58.18 Is not beauty an ephemeral thing, wasting away almost before it comes to its prime?
Philo, *Joseph*, 23. Cf *Posterity of Cain*, 33.

58.19 Beauty of body lies in symmetry of parts, in a good complexion and vigor of flesh, and short is its period of prime. But beauty of mind lies in harmony of doctrine, in concert of virtues, which time does not fade or impair . . . they are adorned with the complexion of truth, and the accord of words with deeds, and of thoughts and intentions with both.
Philo, *Moses*, iii. 15.

58.20 Rather little with beauty than much without it.
Proverb. q M. Ibn Ezra, *Shirat Yisrael*, (12C) 1924, p. 69.

58.21 Beauty aims at neither morals nor truth.
Spingarn, *Creative Criticism*, 1917.

58.22 Three give satisfaction: a beautiful home, a beautiful wife, and beautiful clothes.
Talmud: Berakot, 57b.

58.23 Tinnius Rufus asked, "Which is more beautiful, God's work or man's?" Akiba replied: "Unquestionably, man's work; for nature supplies only the raw material, while human skill makes of it works of art and of good taste."
Tanhuma, Tazria, 7.

58.24 When you see handsome people or fine trees, pronounce the benediction: Praised be He who created beautiful things.
Tosefta: Berakot, 7.4.

59. BEE

59.1 Of no account among flying things is the bee, but her fruit is supreme among products.
Apocrypha: Ben Sira, 11.3.

59.2 While Honey lies in Every Flower,
    no doubt,
  It takes a Bee to get the Honey out.
Guiterman, *A Poet's Proverbs*, 1924, p. 13.

59.3 Men say to the bee: Neither of your honey nor of your sting!
Proverb. q *Num. R.*, 20.10.

60. BEGGING

60.1 Rather die than beg.
Apocrypha: Ben Sira, 40.28.

60.2 I've tasted all, and found nothing as bitter as asking.
Ibn Gabirol, *Mibhar HaPeninim*, c. 1050, #569.

60.3 Hire yourself out for the meanest labor rather than beg.
Talmud J: Berakot, 9.2.

61. BEGINNING

61.1 The beginning bears witness to the end, and the end will at long last bear witness to the beginning.
Baeck, *Essence of Judaism*, 1936, p. 286.

61.2 To be old is a glorious thing when one has not unlearned what it means to begin.
Buber, *Report on Two Talks*, 1932 (*Eclipse of God*, 15).

61.3 A daring beginning is half way to winning.
Heine, "To the Young," *Romancero*, 1851.

61.4 All beginnings are hard.
Mekilta, to *Exod.* 19.5.

61.5 The beginning is half of the whole.
Proverb. q Philo, *Husbandry*, 38.

61.6 A beginning is more than half of the whole.
Arama, *Akedat Yitzhak, Bereshith*, 15C.

61.7 We do not begin with a tale of woe.
Talmud: Baba Bathra, 14b.

62. BEHAVIOR

62.1 Circumstances are beyond the control of man; but his conduct is in his own power.
Disraeli, *Contarini Fleming*, 1832, 7.2.

62.2 There is no truer index to intelligence than good behavior.
Ibn Gabirol, *Mibhar HaPeninim*, c. 1050, #2.

62.3 It is not family ties alone which constitute relationship, but agreement in the principles of conduct.
Josephus, *Against Apion*, ii. 28.

62.4 Make your God's name beloved of all, by righteous conduct toward Gentiles and Jews.
Seder Eliyahu Rabbah, ch 28.

63. BELIEF

63.1 He believed in the Lord, and He counted it to him for righteousness.
Bible: Gen., 15.6.

63.2 Because ye believed not in Me, . . . ye shall not bring this assembly into the land which I have given them.
Bible: Num., 20.12.

63.3 A fire was kindled . . . because they believed not in God.
Bible: Ps., 78.21f.

63.4 Believe in the Lord . . . , so shall ye be established; believe His prophets, so shall ye prosper.
Bible: II Chron., 20.20.

63.5 The Torah does not oblige us to believe absurdities.
Albo, *Ikkarim,* 1428, 1.2.3.

63.6 Belief in the impossible does not produce happiness.
Ibid., 1.22.1.

63.7 Believing in God, they were saved from the flame.
Apocrypha: I Macc., 2.59.

63.8 A disbelieving soul has a memorial there: a pillar of salt.
Apocrypha: Wisd. of Sol., 10.7.

63.9 I make it a rule to believe only what I understand.
Disraeli, *Infernal Marriage,* 1828, 1.4.

63.10 Man is a being born to believe, and if no church comes forward with all the title deeds of truth, . . . he will find altars and idols in his own heart and his own imagination.
Disraeli, speech, Oxford, Nov. 25, 1864.

63.11 Believe nothing that is not proved by reason or by God.
Falaquera, *Iggeret HaVikuah,* (13C), 1875.

63.12 That's also a Jewish characteristic, very, very Jewish: to believe with absolute faith, with glowing faith, with all their hearts and souls, and all the same just very slightly not to believe, the tiniest little bit, and that tiny little bit is the decisive thing.
Hazaz, "The Sermon," (*Abanim Rothot,* 1946), tr Lask. *JS,* May 1952, p. 16.

63.13 The Jew was not commanded to believe, but to search after the knowledge of God.
Hess, *Rome and Jerusalem,* (1862) p. 98.

63.14 Who believes in what is contrary to reason shows contempt for God's greatest gift—excepting the miracles of revelation.

M. Ibn Ezra, *Shirat Yisrael,* (12C) 1924, p. 99.

63.15 Belief cannot be commanded.
S. D. Luzzatto, *Igrot,* 252.

63.16 There is not . . . in the Mosaic law a single command, "Thou shalt believe" or "not believe." . . . Faith is not commanded. . . . Where the question is of eternal truth, there is nothing said of believing, but *understanding* and *knowing.*
M. Mendelssohn, *Jerusalem,* 1783, tr Samuels, ii. 106.

63.17 The Jew believes only what he has seen with his eyes.
L. Philippson, *Israelitische Religionslehre,* 1861, i. 35. Cf *NT: John,* 20.29; Maimonides, *Yad: Yesodé,* 8.1.

63.18 Who sincerely believes in God thereby disbelieves in all else, . . . beginning with those forces within himself which exalt themselves so highly, reason and sense-perception.
Philo, *Rewards,* 5.

63.19 See that you are not taken at your own word!
Proverb. q Levi. *Deut. R.,* 2.1.

63.20 If you hear your neighbor died, believe it; if you hear he became rich, believe it not.
Proverb, q Papa. *Talmud: Gittin,* 30b.

63.21 Jews are believers, sons of believers.
Simeon b. Lakish. *Talmud: Sabbath,* 97a.

63.22 The whole Torah depends altogether on belief.
Vidas, *Reshit Hokma,* 1578, p. 84b.

63.23 The Jews worship a God that you cannot see. . . . In fact, they only believe in things that you cannot see.
*Wilde, *Salome,* 1898.

63.24 I am a fool of the Lord: I believe.
Yehudi, *Tiferet HaYehudi,* 1908, p. 22.

64. BENEDICTION

64.A. Benedictions

64.A.1 Blessed be the glory of the Lord from His place.
Bible: Ezek., 3.12.

64.A.2 . . . the name of the Lord from this time forth and for ever.
Bible: Ps., 113.2. Cf 41.14; *Dan.,* 2.20.

64.A.3 . . . Thy glorious name, that is exalted above all . . . praise.
Bible: Neh., 9.5.

64.A.4 . . . Thou, Lord of righteousness, who rulest over the world.

Apocrypha: Enoch, 22.14.

64.A.5 . . . the Lord to whom all praise is due for ever and ever.

Hanania, Nephew of Joshua. *Mekilta,* to *Exod.,* 13.3.

64.A.6 . . . His name whose glorious kingdom is for ever and ever.

Idem. Mishna: Yoma, 3.8.

64.A.7 Praise ye the Lord to whom all praise is due.

Ishmael b. Elisha. *Mishna: Berakot,* 7.3.

64.B   About Benedictions

64.B.1 Pronounce a benediction before tasting anything.

Akiba. *Sifra,* to *Lev.* 19.24.

64.B.2 Praise God daily that He did not make you a heathen, or a boor.

Judah b. Ilai. *Tosefta: Berakot,* 7.18.

64.B.3 Preparing for a pleasure doubles the enjoyment. This advantage has he who recites a benediction with devotion.

Judah Halevi, *Cuzari,* c. 1135, 3.17.

64.B.4 Recite a hundred benedictions daily.

Meir. *Talmud: Menahot,* 43b.

64.B.5 We take a drink only for the sake of the benediction.

Peretz. q SPG, 179.

64.B.6 He who recites unnecessary benedictions is guilty of taking God's name in vain.

Simeon b. Lakish, Johanan. *Talmud: Berakot,* 33a.

65.   BIBLE
65.A.   Evaluation

65.A.1 The Bible . . . is the classical book of noble ethical sentiment. In it the mortal fear, the overflowing hope, the quivering longings of the human soul . . . have found their first, their freshest, their fittest utterance.

F. Adler, *Creed and Deed,* 1877, p. 200.

65.A.2 This small book is the charter of peace, the charter of freedom, the charter of the future life of mankind.

Berggrav. q N.Y. Times Magazine, June 9, 1946.

65.A.3 The Jews were the only ones whose sacred Scriptures were held in ever greater veneration as they became better known.

Bossuet, Discours sur l'Histoire Universelle, 1681, ii. ch 13 (1722, p. 315).

65.A.4 When read intelligently the Bible reveals itself as the immortal epic of a people's confused, faltering, but indomitable struggle after a nobler life in a happier world.

Browne, *The Graphic Bible,* (1928) 1939, p. 16.

65.A.5 One day when the net result of our European way of life comes to be summed up, this whole as yet so boundless concern of French Philosophism will dwindle into the thinnest of fractions, or vanish into nonentity! Alas, while the rude History and Thoughts of those same *"Juifs misérables,"* the barbaric War-song of a Deborah and Barak, the rapt prophetic Utterance of an unkempt Isaiah, last now, with deepest significance, say only these three thousand years,—what has the thrice-resplendent *Encyclopédie* shrivelled into within these threescore! This is a fact which, explain it, express it, in what way he will, your Encyclopedist should actually consider. *Those* were tones caught from the sacred Melody of the All, and have harmony and meaning forever; *these* of his are but outer discords, and their jangling dies away without result.

Carlyle, Diderot, 1833, at end.

65.A.6 Humanity can never deny the Bible in its heart, without the sacrifice of the best that it contains, faith in unity and hope for justice, and without a relapse into the mythology and the "might makes right" of thirty centuries ago.

Darmsteter, *Selected Essays,* 276.

65.A.7 The three first verses in *Genesis* in the King James version are the most superb sentences in the English language.

C. W. Eliot. Menorah Journal, 1919, v. 151.

65.A.8 The Bible is like an old Cremona; it has been played upon by the devotion of thousands of years until every word and particle is public and tunable.

Emerson, Quotation and Originality, 1859.

65.A.9 We call upon the German people once again: "Guard what you have!" Let no man rob you of your priceless . . . sacred books!

Faulhaber, Judaism, Christianity & Germany, 1933.

65.A.10 The Bible is the epic of the world. It unrolls a vast panorama in which the ages move before us in a long train of solemn imagery from the creation of the world onward. . . . All life's fever is there, its hopes and joys, its suffering and sin and sorrow.

*Frazer, 1895. q HBJ, 132. See *Folk-Lore in the O.T.*, 1919, i. p. xi.

65.A.11 Israel's Sacred Books stand so happily combined together, that, even out of the most diverse elements, the feeling of a whole still rises before us. They are complete enough to satisfy, fragmentary enough to excite, barbarous enough to rouse, tender enough to appease; and for how many other contradicting merits might not these books, might not this one book, be praised!

*Goethe, *Wilhelm Meister's Travels*, 1821, ch 11.

65.A.12 What a book! great and wide as the world, rooted in the abysmal depths of creation and rising aloft into the blue mysteries of heaven. . . . Sunrise and sunset, promise and fulfilment, birth and death, the whole human drama, everything is in this book. . . . It is the book of books, *Biblia*.

Heine, *Ludwig Boerne*, 1840, 2.

65.A.13 The Bible, that great medicine chest of humanity.

Heine, *Ludwig Marcus*, 1844 (EPP, 668).

65.A.14 I owe my enlightenment entirely to an old, simple book, as plain and modest as nature itself . . . a book as weekday like and unpretending as the sun which warms us or the bread which nourishes us; a book which greets us with all the intimate confidence, blessed affection and kind glance of an old grandmother . . . . This is called with cause the Holy Scripture. He who lost his God may find Him again in this book, and he who has never known Him will inhale here the breath of God's word. The Jews who are connoisseurs of valuables, knew very well what they were about when, in the conflagration of the Second Temple, they left the gold and silver vessels of sacrifice, the candelabra and lamps, even the High Priest's breastplate with its large jewels, and rescued only the Bible. This was the real treasure of the Temple.

Heine, *Germany*, Preface to 2d ed, 1852.

65.A.15 The Jews . . . trudged around with it all through the Middle Ages as with a portable fatherland.

Heine, *Confessions*, 1854. EPP, 663.

65.A.16 The Prophets and Hagiography will be abolished in the future, but not the Pentateuch.

Johanan b. Nappaha. *Talmud J: Megilla*, 1.5.

65.A.17 Throughout the world rejected,
From every corner hunted,
Thy book shall be thy banner,
Thy country and thy watchword.

D. Levi, "The Bible," 1846, tr Mary A. Craig. *JQRo*, ix. 381.

65.A.18 The Bible is a chronicle of crises in the life of men and nations.

Magnes, 1944. *Gleanings*, 1948, p. 63.

65.A.19 In the Old Testament of the Jews, the book of Divine righteousness, there are men, events and words so great that there is nothing in Greek or Indian literature to compare with it.

*Nietzsche, *Beyond Good and Evil*, 1885.

65.A.20 To have bound this New Testament, so completely rococo in taste, with the Old Testament into one book, as the Bible, is perhaps the greatest piece of audacity and "sin against the Holy Spirit" which literary Europe has on its conscience.

Ibid., #52. See *Genealogy of Morals*, 3.22.

65.A.21 The Bible in its various transformations is the great book of consolation for humanity.

*Renan, *History of Israel*, 1888, i. p. xi.

65.A.22 The Bible is our patent of nobility.

Schechter, March 26, 1903. SSA, 38.

65.A.23 We search the world for truth. . . .
And, weary seekers of the best,
We come back laden from our quest,
To find that all the sages said
Is in the Book our mothers read.

*Whittier, "Miriam," 1870.

65.A.24 The Bible is for the government of the people, by the people, and for the people.

*Wycliffe, Preface to first English tr of the Bible, 1384.

65.A.25 It is precisely in the Old Testament that is reached the highest ethical note ever yet sounded . . . by man.

Zangwill, *Chosen Peoples. Menorah Journal*, 1918, iv. 259.

65.A.26 The Bible is an anti-Semitic book. "Israel is the villain, not the hero, of his own story." Alone among epics, it is out for truth, not high heroics.

Ibid., (273).

65.B. Influence

65.B.1 The tales of this Old Testament breathed Protestantism before there were Protestants, and the spirit of Lutheranism when Doctor Martin was yet unborn.

*Arndt, *Versuch in vergleichender Völkergeschichte*, 1843, p. 21.

65.B.2 What built St. Paul's Cathedral? Look at the heart of the matter, it was that divine Hebrew Book,—the word partly of the man Moses, an outlaw tending his Midianitish herds, four thousand years ago, in the wilderness of Sinai!

*Carlyle, *The Hero as Man of Letters*, 1840.

65.B.3 Our Jewish Bible has implanted itself in the table-talk and household life of every man and woman in the European and American nations.

*Emerson, *Representative Men: Plato*, 1845.

65.B.4 If we are to repudiate the Old Testament and banish it from our schools and national libraries, then we must disown our German classics. We must cancel many phrases from the German language . . . . We must disown the intellectual history of our nation.

*Faulhaber, *Judaism, Christianity & Germany*, 1933, p. 16f.

65.B.5 They had no state, holding them together, no country, no soil, no king, no form of life in common. If, in spite of this, they were one, more one than all the other peoples of the world, it was the Book that sweated them into unity.

Feuchtwanger, *Power*, 1925, p. 165.

65.B.6 Great consequences have flowed from the fact that the first truly popular literature in England—the first which stirred the hearts of all classes of people and filled their minds with ideal pictures and their every-day speech with apt and telling phrases—was the literature comprised within the Bible.

*Fiske, *The Beginnings of New England*, 1889.

65.B.7 We must not forget that the Sun of Homer, to use Schiller's well-known phrase, smiles only upon the fortunate few who enjoy life's eternal graces, whereas the Sun of the Bible penetrates into the proudest palaces and the humblest shanties; that the Sun of Homer smiles, spreading a bewitchingly beautiful glimmer over the surface of life, whereas the Sun of the Bible radiates warmth and strength, and has called into being a system of morality, which has become the corner-stone of human civilization.

I. Friedlander, *Past and Present*, 1919, p. 89.

65.B.8 It is from Daniel that the modern world has learned the idea of a world history.

*Gunkel, *What Remains of the O.T.*, (1914) 1948, p. 43.

65.B.9 The Hebrew Scriptures have acted like salt to keep the Christian teaching from corruption, and the witness of Judaism has been a constant reminder that that salt has not lost its savor.

*Herford. *Menorah Journal*, 1919, v. 145.

65.B.10 The Bible has been the Magna Charta of the poor and the oppressed.

*T. H. Huxley, *Controverted Questions*, 1892.

65.B.11 Throughout the history of the western world, the Scriptures . . . have been the greatest instigators of revolt against the worst forms of clerical and political despotism.

Ibid.

65.B.12 If it be true, as it obviously is, that the Bible is a creation of the Jews, it is also true, though not so obvious, that the Jews are a creation of the Bible.

Jacobs, *Jewish Contributions to Civilization*, 1919, p. 63.

65.B.13 From that Eastern fountain countless multitudes of men have for centuries gone on drawing ennobling consolation in misery, judicious doctrines of practical wisdom, and warm enthusiasm for all that is exalted.

*Lotze, *Microcosmus*, 1856, 8.3, tr 1885, ii. 402.

65.B.14 A people's entry into universal history is marked by the moment at which it makes the Bible its own in a translation.

F. Rosenzweig, *Kleine Schriften*, 1937, q KHD, 368.

65.B.15 We are at home with the nonconformist Amos and the protesting Job because it is they who taught us the nature of non-conformity and protest. They talk to us in our own language, and that

because we have made their language ours.
L. Roth, *Jewish Thought as a Factor in Civilization*, 1954, p. 39.

65.B.16 The early Hebrews had created the Bible out of their lives; their descendants created their lives out of the Bible.
Sachar, *A History of the Jews*, 1940, p. 88.

65.B.17 Where is there a chapel or a shrine
Wherein you do not catch the echo
Of the son of Amram's voice or Psalms of David's praises?
Where is there the canvas, marble, or the bronze
Which does not speak the language of the ancients . . .
And the dreams and visions of their light . . . ?
Shneor, "Tahat Tzilelé HaMandolina," 1912. q WHJ, iv. 296.

65.B.18 Not only the spiritual substance but the very styles of the literature of Israel have impressed themselves on some of the greatest of modern literatures. The vivid simplicity of Hebrew narrative and the majestic eloquence of the prophets did much to mould the youth of our own and of the German language and the styles of our earliest writers.
*G. A. Smith, *The Hebrew Genius*, 1927 (BSL, 12).

65.B.19 Written in the East, these characters live for ever in the West; written in one province, they pervade the world; penned in rude times, they are prized more and more as civilization advances; product of antiquity, they come home to the business and bosoms of men, women and children in modern times.
*Stevenson, q HBJ, 132.

65.B.20 Puritanism was a Protestant renaissance of the Old Testament and a reversion to biblical precedents for the regulation of the minutest details of daily life.
Straus, *Origin of Republican Form of Government*, 1885, p. 143.

65.B.21 Hence have sprung much of the English language and half of the English manners. To this day the country is biblical.
*Taine, *History of English Literature*, (1864) 1873, ii. 168.

65.B.22 From century to century, even unto this day, through the fairest regions of civilization, the Bible dominates exist-

ence. Its vision of life moulds states and societies. Its Psalms are more popular in every country than the poems of the nation's own poets. Besides this one book with its infinite editions, . . . all other literatures seem "trifles light as air."
Zangwill. *North American Review*, April 1895.

65.C. Interpretation

65.C.1 From Creation [*Gen*.1.1] to Revelation [*Exod*. 20.2] all is parable.
Abba Mari, *Minhat Kenaot*, c. 1300, p. 153.

65.C.2 When two biblical passages contradict each other, a third is introduced to decide between them.
Akiba. *Mekilta*, to *Exod*. 12.5.
Ishmael School. *Sifra*, #1.

65.C.3 The Bible spoke in the language of men.
Akiba. *Talmud: Berakot*, 31b. Cf *NT: Rom*., 6.19.
Ishmael b. Elisha. *Sifré to Num*., #112.

65.C.4 Look at the end of the verse [judge not half a passage].
Beruria. *Talmud: Berakot*, 10a.

65.C.5 Scripture can be understood only by aid of philology.
Ibn Janah, *HaRikma*, c. 1030.

65.C.6 The Bible follows no chronological order.
Ishmael b. Elisha. *Talmud: Pesahim*, 6b.

65.C.7 A biblical verse may yield many lessons.
Ishmael School. *Talmud: Sanhedrin*, 34a, on *Jer*. 23.29.

65.C.8 I can always reconcile two contradictory passages.
Jacob Tam, *Sefer HaYashar*, (12C) ed Vienna, 78b.

65.C.9 Verses like . . . "Timma was concubine" [*Gen*. 36.12] and "I am the Lord thy God" [*Exod*. . . . 20.2] . . . are equally of divine origin.
Maimonides, *Commentary to Mishna: Sanhedrin*, 1168, 10.1.

65.C.10 We do not reject the eternity of the universe because certain passages in Scripture confirm the creation, for . . . it is not difficult to find for them a suitable interpretation.
Maimonides, *Guide for the Perplexed*, 1190, 2.25.

65.C.11 The literal meaning of the [biblical] words may lead us to conceive cor-

rupt ideas and to form false opinions about God.
Ibid., 2.29.

65.C.12 When a biblical verse is contradicted by proof, we do not accept the Bible.
Maimonides, *Responsa*, iii. Note to Judah Alfakhar's letter to Kimhi, q Ahad Ha-Am, *Supremacy of Reason.*

65.C.13 A biblical verse cannot be deprived of its literal meaning.
Mar b. Huna. *Talmud: Sabbath*, 63a.

65.C.14 Scripture, though apparently speaking of matters here below, is always pointing to things above.
Nahmanides, *Commentary*. q SSJ, i. 127.

65.C.15 Exegesis has no such certain demonstration as mathematics.
Nahmanides, *Milhamot Adonai.* q *JQRo*, v. 89.

65.C.16 There are innumerable ways of explaining the Torah.
Nahmanides. q *JQRo*, i. 299.

65.C.17 As I have been rewarded for what I interpreted, so have I been rewarded for what I left uninterpreted.
Nahum of Gimzo. *Talmud: Pesahim*, 22b.

65.C.18 Let us follow the rules of that wise architect, Allegory.
Philo, *Dreams*, 2.2. See 1.16, *Joseph*, 6.

65.C.19 A passage should be explained . . . according to the context.
Rashi. q Liber, *Rashi*, 111.
Maimonides, *Iggeret Teman*, 1172, see tr B. Cohen, p. ix.

65.C.20 The Bible is a parable of man's advance to the family, to the tribe, to a nation with a national ideal, to a nation with a universal ideal.
F. Rosenzweig, *Diary*, Feb. 9, 1906. q GFR, 6f.

65.C.21 The Bible must be construed in its literal sense, except for the statements in it which cannot be so construed.
Saadia, *Emunot VeDeot*, 933, 7.2. See 2.3.

65.C.22 Higher Criticism, higher anti-Semitism.
Schechter, March 26, 1903. SSA, 35.

65.C.23 Scripture is often to be understood figuratively.
Simeon b. Gamaliel II. *Sifré*, to *Deut.*, #25.

65.C.24 "And it came to pass" always introduces a tale of woe.
Talmud: Megilla, 10b.

65.C.25 The more critically and humanly we consider the Bible, the greater the merit of the people that produced it.
Zhitlovsky. *The Day* (N.Y.), Nov. 26, 1922.

65.C.26 The Torah contains sublime and recondite truths. Treasures innumerable are concealed therein. Hence, David said, "Open mine eyes that I may behold wondrous things out of Thy Law" [*Ps.* 119.18].
Zohar, Gen., 132a. See *Exod.*, 12a.

65.C.27 The biblical tales are only the Torah's outer garments, and woe to him who regards these as being the Torah itself!
Zohar, Num., 152a.

65.D. Reading

65.D.1 They read in the book, in the Law of God, distinctly; and they gave the sense, and caused them to understand the reading.
Bible: Neh., 8.8.

65.D.2 Read each week the regular portion of the Pentateuch, twice the Hebrew text and once the translation.
Ammi b. Nathan. *Talmud: Berakot*, 8a.

65.D.3 Those who are satisfied to read the biblical text without understanding it . . . are like a donkey laden with books.
Bahya, *Hobot HaLebabot*, 1040, 3.4.

65.D.4 I string together, like pearls, the words of the Pentateuch, the Prophets, and the Hagiographa, and they are as thrilling as on the day when they were revealed in flame on Sinai.
Ben Azzai. *Lev. R.*, 16.4.

65.D.5 May the history of your nation be written with equal honesty, and may you then be able to have it read in your churches for general edification, as we do ours!
Bernays. q Carmen Sylva, *From Memory's Shrine*, 70.

65.D.6 The Bible is always . . . with me. Indeed, I am not apt to dip pen in ink without first looking into the Book of Books.
Bialik. q OMB, 37.

65.D.7 Who reads a verse in its proper season promotes the good of the world.
Joshua b. Haninia. *Talmud: Kalla Rabbati*, ch 1.

65.D.8 Reading the Bible will in itself not satisfy the needs of our faith; there must go with it the proper interpretation and necessary understanding.

Krochmal, *Moré Nebuké HaZman*, (1851) 1924, ch 17, p. 314.

65.D.9 Because the children of Israel were without Torah for three days, they became rebellious. Hence the elders and prophets instituted Torah reading on Mondays, Thursdays, and the Sabbath.

Mekilta, to *Exod.* 15.22.

65.D.10 That Bible, which his mother had given him as a companion in his exile, had been a source of dreams to him. Although he did not read it in any religious spirit, the moral, . . . vital energy of that Hebraic Iliad had been to him a spring in which, in the evenings, he washed his naked soul of the smoke and mud of Paris.

*Rolland, *Jean-Christophe in Paris: Market-Place*, 3.

66. BIGOTRY

66.1 Sometimes I think that what we need in Israel is more belief for the "believers" and more freedom for the "freethinkers," and above all, love, a bit more love.

Z. J. Kook. q *Commentary*, 1954, p. 258.

66.2 He who is afraid of bigots, and debases himself before them, bears a mean soul that was born to slavery.

Krochmal, letter (*Kerem Hemed*, 1833, p. 91f; *Kitbé Ranak*, 418). q SSJ, i. 53.

66.3 Nothing is so sure of itself as fanaticism.

Lewisohn, *Creative Life*, 1924. p. 197.

66.4 A bigot converts the main issue in piety into a side issue, and a side issue into the main issue.

Mendel of Kotzk. q BTH, ii. 281.

67. BIRD

67.1 If a bird's nest chance to be before you . . . you shall not take the dam with the young.

Bible: Deut, 22.6.

67.2 In vain the net is spread in the sight of any bird.

Bible: Prov., 1.17.

67.3 Pigeons on the grass alas.

G. Stein. *Four Saints in Three Acts,* 1934.

68. BIRTH

68.1 The children are come to birth, and there is no strength to bring forth.

Bible: II Kings, 19.3.

68.2 When I was born, I drew in the common air, fell upon the earth, which is of like nature, and the first voice which I uttered was crying, as all others do.

Apocrypha: Wisd. of Sol., 7.3.

68.3 Wherever a child is born, and the old miracle of motherhood with all its heroism and love is enacted afresh, there the angels' choir chant anew the sweet tidings of glory and peace and good will.

Enelow, *Selected Works,* 1935, i. 170.

68.4 The Shekina rests only on families of pure birth in Israel.

Hama b. Hanina. *Talmud: Kiddushin,* 70b.

68.5 When a woman is in labor, the child may be delivered, if need be, member by member, for her life comes before that of the unborn child; but if the greater part of the child has proceeded forth, it may not be touched injuriously, for one life may not be set aside for another.

Mishna: Oholot, 7.6.

68.6 Be it born to the glory of God!

Saying (Yiddish). q *JQRo,* ii. 4.

68.7 Conceived in heathendom, born in holiness.

Talmud: Baba Bathra, 149a.

69. BIRTH AND DEATH

69.1 The day of death [rather] than the day of birth.

Bible: Eccles., 7.1.

69.2 Man enters and departs this life crying and weeping. He comes and he leaves in love and ignorance.

Eccles. R., 5.14.

69.3 As you came sinless so may you depart sinless!

Johanan. *Talmud: Baba Metzia,* 107a. Cf Berekia. *Eccles. R.,* 3.2.1.

69.4 Birth and death are like two ships in a harbor. There is no reason to rejoice at the ship setting out on a journey [birth], not knowing what she may encounter on the high seas, but we should rejoice at the ship returning to port [death] safely.

Levi. *Exod. R.,* 48.1.

69.5 A baby enters the world with hands clenched, as if to say, "The world is mine; I shall grab it." A man leaves with hands open, as if to say, "I can take nothing with me."

Meir. *Eccles. R.,* 5.14.

69.6 Among Jews, a birthday is no holiday; but the anniversary of a death, that a Jew remembers.

Mendelé, *Dos Kleine Mentshelé*, 1864.

69.7 If there is to be birth, there must be death.

H. Samuel, *Belief and Action*, 1937, p. 94.

69.8 On the day of your birth you wept, and those about you were glad. On the day of your death you will laugh, while those about you will sigh.

Satanov, *Mishlé Asaf*, 1789, 1792, 15.5. q SRH, 43.

70. BIRTHRIGHT

70.1 He sold his birthright to Jacob, and Jacob gave Esau bread and pottage of lentils.

Bible: Gen., 25.33f.

71. BITTER

71.1 Their grapes are grapes of gall, their clusters are bitter.

Bible: Deut., 32.32.

71.2 Embittered in mind, as a bear robbed of her whelps.

Bible: II Sam., 17.8.

71.3 Call me Marah, for the Almighty dealt very bitterly with me.

Bible: Ruth, 1.20.

71.4 There is a kind of cheese which is full of bacteria, and gourmets pay a high price for it and consume it with relish. Just so is Jewish life: its bitterness is its wondrous savor.

Mendelé, *Shlomo Reb Hayyims*, 1899.

71.5 Sugar in the mouth won't help if you're bitter at heart.

Proverb (Yiddish). BJS, #1081.

72. BLESSING
72.A. Blessings

72.A.1 Be a blessing . . . and in you shall all the families of the earth be blessed.

Bible: Gen., 12.2f.

72.A.2 God give you of the dew of heaven and of the fat places of the earth, and plenty of corn and wine!

Ibid., 27.28.

72.A.3 God make you as Ephraim and as Manasseh!

Ibid., 48.20.

72.A.4 The Lord bless you and keep you. The Lord make His face to shine upon you, and be gracious unto you. The Lord lift up His countenance upon you, and give you peace.

Bible: Num., 6.24ff.

72.A.5 Blessed be when you come in, and . . . when you go out.

Bible: Deut., 28.6.

72.A.6 Blessed be he who comes in the name of the Lord.

Bible: Ps., 118.26.

72.A.7 The blessing of the Lord be upon you; we bless you in the name of the Lord.

Ibid., 129.8.

72.A.8 They shall be for a blessing, not for a curse; they shall be the head, not the tail.

Apocrypha: Jubilees, 1.16.

72.A.9 God make you as Sarah, Rebekah, Rachel and Leah!

Daily Prayer Book, ed Singer, 122. Cf *Ruth*, 4.11.

72.B. About Blessing

72.B.1 The blessing of the Lord, it makes rich.

Bible: Prov., 10.22.

72.B.2 A father's blessing establishes his seed.

Apocrypha: Ben Sira, 3.9.

72.B.3 A weary wayfarer through a desert came at last upon a tiny oasis, where a mighty tree grew near a spring. He sat down in the shade of its luxuriant branches, ate of its luscious fruit, drank of the clear water, and rested and refreshed himself. When he was ready to depart, he said to the tree: Wherewith can I bless you, seeing that you are already blessed with beauty and shade, with magnificent branches and delicious fruit, with a precious location and a spring for your roots. Let me then wish you that all your offshoots be like you!

Isaac, to his host Nahman. *T: Taanit*, 5b. Johanan b. Nappaha. *Num. R.*, 2.12.

72.B.4 Do not underestimate a common man's blessing.

Ishmael b. Elisha. *Talmud: Berakot*, 7a.

72.B.5 Rather the curse of Ahijah the prophet than the blessing of Balaam the wicked.

Johanan b. Nappaha. *Talmud: Taanit*, 20a.

72.B.6 Blessings from above descend

only where there is some substance, not just emptiness, below.
Zohar, Gen., 88a.

73. BLIND

73.1 Put no stumbling block before the blind.
Bible: Lev., 19.14. See *Deut.,* 27.18.

73.2 Better blind of eye than blind of heart.
Apocrypha: Ahikar, 2.48.

73.3 Not the eye but the heart is blind.
Ibn Gabirol, *Mibhar HaPeninim,* c. 1050, #414.

73.4 Love blinds us to faults, hatred to virtues.
M. Ibn Ezra, *Shirat Yisrael,* (12C) 1924, p. 138.

74. BLOOD

74.1 The voice of your brother's blood cries to Me from the ground.
Bible: Gen., 4.10.

74.2 It is the blood that makes atonement.
Bible: Lev., 17.11.

74.3 The blood is the life.
Bible: Deut., 12.23.

74.4 In your blood, live!
Bible: Ezek., 16.6.

74.5 Woe to him that builds a town with blood!
Bible: Hab., 2.12.

74.6 Precious will be their blood in his sight.
Bible: Ps., 72.14.

74.7 In the blood is the source of all sickness.
Talmud: Baba Bathra, 58b.

74.8 From the blood of battlefields spring daisies and buttercups.
Zangwill, *Melting Pot,* 1908, Act 4.

75. BLUE

75.1 Blue is not merely a color; it is a mystery.
M. Najara. q MND, 112.

76. BOAST

76.1 Is not Ephraim's gleaning better than Abiezer's vintage?
Bible: Judg., 8.2.

76.2 Let not him that girds on his armor boast as he that puts it off.
Bible: I Kings, 20.11.

76.3 Should the axe boast against him that hews therewith?
Bible: Isa., 10.15.

76.4 I am holier than thou.
Ibid., 65.5.

76.5 There are men who . . . do little and say much, who . . . sound loud bells that the report of their goodness be heard afar. To such, the heavens have no voice.
Arama, *Akedat Yitzhak,* 15C, i. 13b, adapted *B&P,* 19.

76.6 The boastful is Gehenna's prey.
Hoshaia Rabbah. *Talmud: Aboda Zara,* 18b.

76.7 God created Paradise and said: The boastful may not enter!
q M. Ibn Ezra, *Shirat Yisrael,* (12C) 1924, p. 134.

76.8 Why was not the Book of *Ezra* named for its author, Nehemiah? Because he claimed credit for himself [*Neh.* 5.19].
Jeremiah b. Abba. *Talmud: Sanhedrin,* 93b.

76.9 Man often boasts and does not fulfil.
Nahman. *Talmud: Shebuot,* 46a.

76.10 Wisdom departs from a boastful sage, and prophecy from a boastful prophet.
Rab. *Talmud: Pesahim,* 66b.

76.11 Wretch, why do you boast in a world which is not yours?
Simeon the Just. *Talmud: Nedarim,* 9b.

77. BODY

77.1 No man is reconciled to bodily defects.
Abayé. *Talmud: Ketubot,* 75b.

77.2 God, who loves the soul, cannot despise the body, so essential to the preservation of the individual and the species.
Anatoli, *Malmad HaTalmidim,* (1149), p. 79b.

77.3 The body is formed out of a troubled fountain and a corrupt spring; it is built of a fetid drop.
Bahya, *To the Soul,* c.1040. Cf Akabia. *Mishna: Abot,* 3.1.

77.4 The body often seems to have more insight than the soul, and man thinks frequently far better with his back and belly than with his head.
Heine, *Romantic School,* 1833, ii. ch 2.

77.5 O God, Thou hast formed the body of man with infinite goodness. Thou hast united in him innumerable forces incessantly at work like so many instruments, so as to preserve in its entirety this beautiful house containing his immortal soul, and these forces act with all the order, concord and harmony imaginable. If weakness or violent passion disturb this harmony, these forces act against one another. . . . Then Thou sendest Thy messengers, the diseases which announce the approach of danger, and bid man prepare to overcome them.

M. Herz, "Physicians' Prayer," attributed to Maimonides. *Deutsches Museum,* 1783.

77.6 What a marvelous machine it is, the human body. A chemical laboratory, a power-house. Every movement, voluntary or involuntary, full of secrets and marvels!

Herzl, *Diary,* Jan. 24, 1902.

77.7 Respect your own body as the receptacle, messenger and instrument of the spirit.

S. R. Hirsch, *Nineteen Letters* (1836), #11, p. 112.

77.8 Man owes it to keep his body clean, as a worthy dwelling for the soul, God's portion from on high.

Lipkin, on Yom Kippur, 1849. See GIS, 28.

77.9 A good, sound body, which does not disturb the equilibrium in man, is a divine gift . . . but it is not impossible to conquer a bad constitution by training.

Maimonides, *Guide for the Perplexed,* 1190, 3.8.

77.10 "There was a little city" [*Eccles.* 9.14],—i.e., the human body.

Midrash HaNe'elam, ed 5625, ch 1, p. 8b.

77.11 The human body has three kings: brain, heart, and liver.

Ibid., 12b.

77.12 If you marvel at the waters of the sea, that the sweet and the salty do not mingle, think of the tiny human head, where the fluids of its many fountains do not mingle.

Num. R., 18.22.

77.13 Is not the body the soul's house? Then why should we not take care of the house that it fall not into ruins?

Philo, *The Worse Attacks the Better,* 10.

77.14 The body is from the "other side"; and to promote the side of holiness, we need to load the body heavily with Torah.

Ragoler, *Maalot HaTorah,* (1828) 1946, p. 85.

77.15 The human body as such . . . is altogether pure, for defilement is not a matter subject to sense perception or logic.

Saadia, *Emunot VeDeot,* 933, 6.4 (6.17). Cf *NT: Phil.,* 3.21.

77.16 The noble man has his soul rule his body; the wicked has his body rule his soul.

Satanov, *Mishlé Asaf,* 1789. q WHJ, iii. 125.

77.17 If a gourd has a hole as tiny as a needle's eye, all its air escapes; yet man, with so many cavities and orifices, retains his breath. Verily, "Thou doest wonders"! [*Ps.* 86.10].

Tanhum b. Hiyya. *Gen. R.,* 1.3.

78. BONE

78.1 Bone of my bones.
Bible: Gen., 2.23.

78.2 Our bones are dried up, and our hope is lost.
Bible: Ezek., 37.11.

78.3 It shall be health to your navel and marrow to your bones.
Bible: Prov., 3.8.

79. BOOK

79.1 Oh that my words were now written! Oh that they were inscribed in a book!
Bible: Job, 19.23.

79.2 Oh would that mine adversary had written a book!
Ibid., 31.35.

79.3 Of making many books there is no end.
Bible: Eccles., 12.12.

79.4 Preserve the books which I shall deliver to you. Set them in order, anoint them with cedar oil.
Apocrypha: Assumption of Moses, 1.17.

79.5 A book skilfully composed is a delight to the taste.
Apocrypha: II Macc., 15.39.

79.6 We have preserved the Book, and the Book has preserved us.
Ben Gurion. *Israel Government Year Book,* 5712, Introd.

79.7 A book may be as great a thing as a battle.
Disraeli, *Memoir of Isaac D'Israeli,* 1848.

79.8 The Sword and the Book came from Heaven wrapped together, and the Holy One said: "Keep what is written in this Book, or be delivered to the sword." Eleazar. *Lev. R.,* 35.6.

79.9 Books are holy—aye, and the cases are full of them. . . . Happy art thou, Israel. When others embalmed the bodies of their heroes and mighty ones, thou didst embalm the souls of thy poor and afflicted. Wherefore the bodies have hardened to stone, but thy souls, Israel, live and move like shadows in broken chests and yellowing leaves.

Feierberg, *Shadows*, 1893. q Steinberg, *The Making of the Modern Jew*, 1933, p. 216f.

79.10 A book, like a child, needs time to be born. Books written quickly—within a few weeks—make me suspicious of the author. A respectable woman does not bring a child into the world before the ninth month.

Heine, *Thoughts and Fancies*, 1869. EPP, 653.

79.11 The Jew's books, like the Jew, should be spread abroad, so that in them all the nations of the earth shall be blessed.

Heine. q Zangwill, *Dreamers of the Ghetto*, 1898, p. 352.

79.12 A book is the most delightful companion. . . . An inanimate thing, yet it talks. . . . It stimulates your latent talents. There is in the world no friend more faithful and attentive, no teacher more proficient. . . . It will join you in solitude, accompany you in exile, serve as a candle in the dark, and entertain you in your loneliness. It will do you good, and ask no favor in return. It gives, and does not take.

M. Ibn Ezra, *Shirat Yisrael*, (12C) 1924, p. 93.

79.13 Books are word-embroidered sheaths of the sciences.

Ibid., 117.

79.14 Make your books your companions; let your cases and shelves be your pleasure-grounds and orchards. Bask in their paradise, gather their fruit, pluck their roses, take their spices. If your soul be satiate and weary, change from garden to garden, from furrow to furrow, from prospect to prospect. Then will your desire be renewed, and your soul be filled with delight.

Ibn Tibbon, *Tzavaah*, 1190. AHE, 63.

79.15 Take particular care of your books. Cover your shelves with a fine covering, guard against damp and mice. Write a complete catalog of your books, and examine them. . . . When you lend a book, make a memorandum, and when it is returned, cancel it. Each Passover and Tabernacles call in all your books that are out on loan.

Ibid., q AJL, 353.

79.16 Spend your money on good books, and you'll find its equivalent in gold of intelligence.

Immanuel, *Mahberot*, c. 1300 (1491), ch 14.

79.17 Books were created for the people, not the people for books.

Kaminer, "Shir HaAm." *HaAsif*, 5645.

79.18 Do not consider it a proof just because it is written in books, for a liar who will deceive with his tongue will not hesitate to do the same with his pen.

Maimonides, *Iggeret Teman*, 1172 (*Responsa*, ii. 5d).

79.19 People of the Book (*Ahl' ul kitab*).

*Mohammed, *Koran*, 625, "Table," 5.22; "Spider," 29.45.

79.20 Israel's glory sinks to the earth only when he lets his Book fall to the ground.

Moscato, *Nefutzot Yehuda*, 1588, p. 86, q BSJ, 211.

79.21 The Bible is the worst printed book in the world.

*Moulton, *Literary Study of the Bible*, 1899, p. 45.

79.22 A basket full of books! (A man full of learning but without method, or with little independence of thought).

Nahman b. Jacob. *Talmud: Megilla*, 28b.

79.23 Books lead us into the society of those great men with whom we could not otherwise come into personal contact. They bring us near to the geniuses of the remotest lands and times. A good library is a place, a palace, where the lofty spirits of all nations and generations meet.

Niger, *Geklibene Shriftn*, 1928, i. 32.

79.24 Lo, truth is a flame—will ye quench it with fire?

"On Burning of Maimonides' Works," at Montpellier, 1232. q *Bookmen's Holiday*, p. 285, Note 49.

79.25 If a drop of ink fell at the same time on your book and on your coat, clean first the book and then the garment.

Sefer Hasidim, 13C, #653, p. 175.

79.26 If you drop gold and books, pick up first the books and then the gold.

Ibid., #655, p. 175.

79.27 Books are made for use, not to be hidden away.
Ibid, #673, p. 178; #1740, p. 417.

79.28 Books must be treated with respect.
Ibid., #1741, p. 417.

79.29 Books which teach and speak of whatever is highest and best are equally sacred, whatever be the tongue in which they are written, or the nation to which they belong.
Spinoza, *Theologico-Political Treatise,* 1670, ch 10.

79.30 Let's bring a book and see!
Talmud: Kiddushin, 30a.

80. BOOR

80.1 A boor is not sensitive to sin.
Hillel. *Mishna: Abot,* 2.5.

80.2 Who is a boor? He who does not raise his sons for Torah.
Jonathan. *Talmud: Berakot,* 47b.

81. BOOTHS

81.1 Ye shall dwell in booths seven days.
Bible: Lev., 23.42.

81.2 The booth is designed to teach us not to put our trust in the size or strength or improvements of a house, nor in the help of any man, even the lord of the land, but in the Creator, for He alone is mighty, His promises alone are sure.
Aboab, *Menorat HaMaor,* c.1300, 3.4.6.1.

82. BOREDOM

82.1 He who harps on a matter estranges a familiar friend.
Bible: Prov., 17.9.

82.2 There are those who need more time to tell than it took the event to happen. They are the farmer-generals of boredom.
Boerne, *Aus Meinem Tagebuche,* May 25, 1830.

82.3 Boredom is an emptiness filled with insistence.
L. Stein, *Journey into the Self,* 1950, p. 261.

82.4 The life of the working family is too monotonous, and it is this monotony that wears out the nervous system. Hence the desire for alcohol—a small flask containing a whole world of images. Hence the need for the Church and her ritual.
Trotsky, *Problems of Life,* 1923, p. 62.

83. BORROWING and LENDING

83.1 If you lend money to any of My people, . . . you shall not be to him as a creditor; neither shall ye lay upon him interest.
Bible: Exod., 22.24.

83.2 I have not lent, neither have men lent to me; yet every one of them curses me.
Bible: Jer., 15.10.

83.3 A good man shows favor and lends.
Bible: Ps., 112.5.

83.4 The borrower is a servant to the lender.
Bible: Prov., 22.7.

83.5 Scholars shall not take even a mote of interest from non-Jews.
Amram Gaon, *Shaaré Tzedek,* (9C) 1792, 40a.

83.6 Become not a beggar by banqueting on borrowing.
Apocrypha: Ben Sira, 18.33.

83.7 Who builds his house with other people's money is as one who gathers stones for his own sepulchre.
Ibid., 21.8.

83.8 To lend on interest is to transgress every prohibition in the Torah. Lending without interest is like fulfilling all the commandments of the Torah.
Exod. R., 31.13.

83.9 Do not lock the door in the face of borrowers.
Hanina. *Talmud: Yebamot,* 122b.

83.10 Hire your daughter out as a servant rather than borrow. By serving, she may win freedom, but debt grows ever larger.
Huna. *Talmud: Arakin,* 30b.

83.11 Money lending is the price of our existence.
Isaac of Vienna, c.1250. q LJG, 58.

83.12 Lend money, and acquire an enemy.
Proverb (Yiddish). BJS, #330.

83.13 Borrow, and you'll sorrow.
Ibid., #332.

83.14 Who wants to borrow, should come tomorrow.
Ibid., #335.

83.15 To lend is more meritorious than to give alms.
Simeon b. Lakish. *Talmud: Sabbath,* 63a.

83.16 A borrower may not lend the thing he borrowed.
Simeon b. Lakish. *Talmud: Gittin,* 29a.

84. BRAND
84.1 Is not this man a brand plucked out of the fire?
Bible: Zech., 3.2.

85. BREAD
85.1 I have broken the staff of your bread.
Bible: Lev., 26.26.

85.2 Man does not live by bread only.
Bible: Deut., 8.3.

85.3 Feed him with the bread of affliction.
Bible: 1 Kings, 22.27.

85.4 Bread is not to the wise.
Bible: Eccles., 9.11.

85.5 Cast your bread upon the waters, for you shall find it after many days.
Ibid., 11.1.

85.6 No flour, no Torah; no Torah, no flour.
Eleazar b. Azariah. *Mishna: Abot,* 3.17.

85.7 Anything is good with bread.
Mendelé, *Dos Kleine Mentshelé,* 1864.

85.8 He who has bread wants cake.
Mendelé, *Fishke der Krumer,* 1869.

85.9 You talk of Reform, Haskala; what the people want is bread.
Mendelé. q Peretz, *Mendelé,* 1910. *Alle Verk,* x. 127.

85.10 Praised be Thou, Lord our God, King of the universe, who bringest forth bread from the earth.
Nehemiah. *Gen. R.,* 15.7.

85.11 Bread is baked better in a full oven.
Simeon b. Eleazar. *Talmud: Betza,* 17a.

85.12 Give, O Lord, each one his bread, each body what it needs.
Talmud: Berakot, 29b.

85.13 You can't compare him who has bread with him who has not.
Talmud: Yoma, 18b, 67a.

85.14 Bread is the staple of a meal.
Wesseley, *Ruah Hen,* 1780, ch 16.

86. BREVITY
86.1 It is stupid to make a long introduction to a short story.
Apocrypha: II Macc., 2.32.

86.2 Where brevity suffices, length is a mistake.
M. Ibn Ezra, *Shirat Yisrael,* (12C) 1924, p. 36.

86.3 Length is folly's style.
Ibid.

86.4 Brevity aids memory.
Ibid., 37.

86.5 Like a high hat crowning a low brow is a long preface to a short treatise.
Somerhausen, *Hitze Shenunim,* 1840.

86.6 It is much easier to write a long book than a short one.
I. M. Wise, "World of My Books." *Deborah,* Jan. 7, 1897.

87. BRIBE
87.1 While accepting bribes to do injustice is an act of utter depravity, to accept them to do justice shows a half depravity.
Philo, *Special Laws,* iv. 11.

87.2 If you grease the wheels, you can ride.
Sholom Aleichem, *Gymnazie,* 1902. NOP, 229.

87.3 When bribery increased, the span of life decreased.
Talmud: Sota, 47b.

88. BROTHERHOOD
88.1 Am I my brother's keeper?
Bible: Gen., 4.9.

88.2 I seek my brethren.
Ibid., 37.16.

88.3 Have we not all one father? Has not one God created us?
Bible: Mal., 2.10.

88.4 Behold, how good and how pleasant it is for brethren to dwell together in unity!
Bible: Ps., 133.1.

88.5 A brother offended is harder to be won than a strong city.
Bible: Prov., 18.19.

88.6 Better a neighbor who is near than a brother far off.
Ibid., 27.10. *Ahikar,* 2.49.

88.7 In years of prosperity men become brothers.
Gen. R., 89.4.

88.8 All Jews, including proselytes, are like brothers.
Maimonides, *Yad: Matnot Aniyim,* 1180, 10.2.

88.9 Nature has mother-like borne and reared all men alike, and created them genuine brothers.

Philo, *Every Good Man Is Free*, 12.

88.10 Implicit in Hebraism lay a belief in human brotherhood which cannot be reconciled with racial or sectarian enmities. Indeed it may be said that the world as a whole has not yet risen to the height of this great Hebraic argument.

*Selbie, *Influence of O. T. on Puritanism*, 1927. BSL 415f.

88.11 In the Titanic tragedy, all creeds were at last united in the brotherhood of Death. If one could only hope for a brotherhood of Life!

N. Straus. q Analyticus, *Jews Are Like That*, 225.

89. BUILDING

89.1 When you build a new house . . . make a parapet for the roof.

Bible: Deut., 22.8.

89.2 Israel has forgotten his Maker, and builded palaces.

Bible: Hos., 8.14.

89.3 Except the Lord build the house, they labor in vain that build it.

Bible: Ps., 127.1.

89.4 Often, in regarding these old churches, I know not which most to admire, the beauty of their vicinity, their great size, or the equally great and rock-like firm souls of their builders. They well knew that only their far-off descendants could complete the work; yet they . . . calmly placed one stone upon another until death called them from the work.

Heine, *Journey from Munich to Genoa*, 1828, ch 32.

89.5 When I lately stood with a friend before [the cathedral of] Amiens. . . he asked me how it happens that we can no longer build such piles? I replied: Dear Alphonse, men in those days had convictions, we moderns have opinions, and it requires something more than an opinion to build a Gothic cathedral.

Heine, *Confidential Letters to August Lewald*, 1837, #9.

89.6 It is not wreckers that we need, but builders.

Ussishkin, letter to Ahad HaAm, 1899.

89.7 Woe to him who makes a door before he gets a house, who builds a gate and has no yard!

Yannai Rabba. *Talmud: Sabbath*, 31b.

90. BURDEN

90.1 Cast your burden upon the Lord, and He will sustain you.

Bible: Ps., 55.23.

90.2 Blessed be the Lord: day by day He bears our burden.

Ibid., 68.20.

90.3 What is too heavy for you, lift not.

Apocrypha: Ben Sira, 13.2.

90.4 Rather death than becoming a burden.

Eliezer b. Isaac, *Orhot Hayyim*, c.1050.

90.5 Bear the public burden, but impose it not heavily on others.

J. M. Epstein, *Kitzur Shné Luhot Ha-Berit*, 1683, p. 8a.

90.6 Unhappy Atlas that I am! I'm doomed
   To bear a world, a very world of sorrows!

Heine, *Pictures of Travel: Return Home*, 1826, #26.

90.7 Man himself assumes the burden under which he falls.

A. Ibn Ezra, *Commentary*, to *Zech.* 12.13, c.1160.

90.8 Lay no burden on the public which the majority cannot bear.

Ishmael b. Elisha. *Talmud: Baba Bathra*, 60b. See *T: Taanit* 14b.

90.9 The beam's owner shall bear its weight.

Proverb. q Abin Halevi. *Talmud: Berakot*, 64a.

90.10 The load according to the camel.

Proverb. q Ishmael School. *Talmud: Sota*, 13b.

90.11 I'll carry the load if you'll help me to lift it.

Proverb. q Raba. *Talmud: Baba Kamma*, 92b.

91. BURIAL

91.1 He shall be buried with the burial of an ass.

Bible: Jer., 22.19.

91.2 Let my coffin be set open to the earth.

Judah HaNasi. *Talmud J: Ketubot*, 12.3.

91.3 Bury me among the poor, that my grave may shine on theirs and their graves on mine.

Sholom Aleichem, last will, 1916. q HGT, 39.

92. BUSH

92.1 The bush burned with fire, and the bush was not consumed.
Bible: Exod., 3.2.

92.2 O bush, O bush! Precisely because you are the lowest of trees did the Holy One reveal Himself in you.
Aha b. Raba. *Talmud: Sabbath*, 67a.

93. BUSINESS

93.1 Busy here and there.
Bible: I Kings, 20.40.

93.2 In the field of modern business, so rich in opportunity for the exercise of man's finest and most varied mental faculties and moral qualities, mere money-making cannot be regarded as the legitimate end . . . since with the conduct of business human happiness or misery is inextricably interwoven.
Brandeis, address, Brown University, 1912.

93.3 Better to lease one garden and cultivate it than to lease many and neglect them. As the proverb goes: Who leases a garden eats birds; who leases gardens is eaten by birds.
Eccles. R., 4.6.

93.4 When a wise man busies himself with many affairs, his wisdom becomes confused.
Exod. R., 6.2.

93.5 Not everyone who does much business becomes wise.
Hillel. *Mishna: Abot*, 2.5.

93.6 In business, all depends on aid from Heaven.
Isaac. *Talmud: Megilla*, 6b.

93.7 To be a successful businessman you need extraordinary talents; and if you have such talents, why waste them on business?
Lipkin. q KTH, i. 272.

93.8 Shop and nothing but shop soon converts a man into a boot, an overall, a barrel of sugar, a banknote, or a mortgage squeezer. . . . How unlike the "image of God" such men are, allied by instinct and capacity to the brute!
Lubin, 1885. q ADL, 98.

93.9 Some people think of business when they are at the synagog. Is it too much to ask them to think of God when they are at business?
Nahman Kasovir. q Katz, *Toldot Jacob Joseph*, (1780) 1903, p. 39f.

93.10 The bigger the merchant the smaller the Jew.
Peretz, *"Fir Dores Fir Tzavoes,"* 1901. *Alle Verk*, iv. 237.

94. CABALA

94.1 Cabala is the core, the essence, the spirituality of Judaism.
Horodetzky, *HaHasidut VeHaHasidim*, 1927, i. p. xi.

94.2 Study Cabala, for without it the fear of God is impossible.
S. Horowitz, *Tzavaah*, 1690. AHE, 256.

94.3 Cabala is the cloak of fools.
Leon of Modena, *Ari Nohem*, (17C) 1840, ch 2.

94.4 In the Cabala I find what I find in Paul; in the Cabala I hear the voice of Plato.
Mirandola, 15C. q HUC Jubilee Volume, 1925, p. 325f.

94.5 You cannot penetrate into the mysteries of Cabala by independent thought and reflection.
Nahmanides, *Commentary to Pentateuch*, 13C. q JE, ix. 88b.

94.6 Salt adds flavor to food, though it is not itself a food. The same is true of the Cabala. In itself hardly comprehensible, and tasteless, it adds flavor to the Torah.
Shneor Zalman, *Tanya, Leviticus* (1796) 1928, p. 6f.

94.7 The men with ascetic eyes and sensual lips
Dandle eternity on their fingertips.
Stampfer, "Kabbalist." *Jerusalem Has Many Faces*, 1950, 16.

95. CALENDAR

95.1 Events are sometimes the best calendar.
Disraeli, *Venetia*, 1837.

95.2 The catechism of the Jew is his calendar.
S. R. Hirsch, *Betrachtungen zum jüd. Kalendarjahr*, (*Ges. Schr.*, i. 1).

95.3 The Jewish calendar is the most brilliant achievement of its kind.
*Scaliger, *De Emendatione Temporum*, 1583, 101.

96. CANDOR

96.1 There is no wisdom like frankness.
Disraeli, *Sybil*, 1845, 4.9.

96.2 Even brute force is not devoid of dignity when it acts openly and aboveboard.
Lassalle, *Science and Workingmen*, 1863.

96.3 In the narrative books of the Bible, the good and the bad appear without disguise. All is set forth with a frankness that made the heart of the Hebrew tent-dweller the heart of the world thereafter.

*Stedman, *Nature & Elements of Poetry,* 1892.

97. CANTOR

97.1 Asked why he was not pleased with a certain precentor, a king replied, "Because he prays to impress me, not God."
Bahya, *Hobot HaLebabot,* 1040, 5.5.

97.2 He should lead in prayer who has a large family and no means of support, . . . a man meek, loved by the people, skilled as a singer, and thoroughly learned in all branches of Jewish lore.
Judah b. Ilai. *Talmud: Taanit,* 16a. Cf *M: Taanit,* 2.2.

97.3 "The song of fools" [*Eccles.* 7.5] refers to precentors, delegated to interpret the prayers, but who, by singing, disturb the ritual, and give the worshipers a chance to chatter and gossip.
Katz, *Ben Porat Yosef, Tzav,* 1781.

97.4 He who would lead a congregation in prayer must remove hatred from his heart, and pray also for his enemy.
M. Katzenellenbogen, *She-elot UTeshubot,* 1553, #64.

97.5 I protest against cantors who . . . cannot concentrate on the meaning of the prayers because they are preoccupied with the impression they are striving to make and the plaudits they are eager to win. Needless to say that prayers chanted by choristers are altogether senseless and savorless to the Lord.
Lenczicz, *Amudé Shesh,* 1617. See BSJ, 302.

97.6 A precentor may grow hoarse if he prays before the lectern, not if he prays before the living God.
Levi Yitzhok. q M. Zitrin, *Shibhé Tzaddikim* (5643), 225.

97.7 A cantor is a fool: standing on a platform, he believes he is on a pedestal.
Zabara, *Sefer Shaashuim,* 13C, ch 5.

97.8 All cantors are fools, but not all fools are cantors.
Proverb (Yiddish). BJS, #1549.

98. CAPITAL PUNISHMENT

98.1 Whoso sheds man's blood, by man shall his blood be shed.
Bible: Gen., 9.6. See *Lev.,* 24.17.

98.2 Give life for life.
Bible: Exod., 21.23. See *Mekilta, ad loc.*

98.3 The condemning judge must fast on the day of execution.
Akiba. *Sifra,* to *Lev.* 19.26, ed Weiss, 90a.

98.4 The death penalty will seem to the next generation, as it seems to many even now, an anachronism too discordant to be suffered, mocking with grim reproach all our clamorous professions of the sanctity of life.
Cardozo, *Law and Literature,* 1931, p. 93f.

98.5 A criminal may not be condemned to death unless he had been warned against the crime by two witnesses.
José b. Halafta. *Mishna: Makkot,* 1.9.

98.6 Capital cases cannot be tried by a court of less than twenty-three members.
Maimonides, *Yad: Sanhedrin,* 5.2, 1180, tr Hershman, 17.

98.7 A Sanhedrin that effects one execution in seven years is branded a murderous court. Eleazar b. Azariah: one in seventy years. Tarfon and Akiba: Were we members of a Sanhedrin, no one would ever be put to death. Simeon b. Gamaliel: They would multiply murderers in Israel!
Mishna: Makkot, 1.10.

98.8 Choose an easy death for him who must be executed.
Rabbah b. Abbuha. *Talmud: Sanhedrin,* 52a.

99. CASUISTRY

99.1 The Babylonian Amoraim created the dialectic, close-reasoning, Jewish spirit, which in the darkest days preserved the dispersed nation from stagnation and stupidity. It was . . . the eternal spring which kept the mind ever bright and active.
Graetz, *History of the Jews,* 1893, ii. 635.

99.2 The essence of rabbinical study is casuistry.
Israel Bruna, *Responsa,* (15C) 1798, #100.

99.3 Spend not much time or thought in needless casuistry.
Jacob b. Asher, *Tokaha,* 14C. AHE, 204.

99.4 Are you not from Pumbedita, where they draw an elephant through a needle's eye?
Sheshet. *Talmud: Baba Metzia,* 38b.

100. CAT

100.1 Said the cat: If I should have eyes

of silver and ears of gold, I would not leave off thieving.
Apocrypha: Ahikar, 8.26.

100.2 If cats wore gloves, they'd catch no mice.
Proverb. See ATJF, p. 638.

100.3 On a fat victim, the cat and the weasel feasted together.
Proverb. q Papa. *Talmud: Sanhedrin,* 105a.

100.4 However you throw the cat, it will always land on its feet.
Weissmann-Chajes, *Hokma UMusar,* 1875.

101. CAUSE

101.1 What is found in the effect was already in the cause.
Bergson, *Creative Evolution,* 1908, ch 1.

101.2 A spoiled broth may lead to divorce.
Lipkin. q KTH, i. 272.

101.3 No one effect is ever the effect of a single cause, but only of a combination of causes; and the essence of causation is in the combination.
H. Samuel, *Belief and Action,* 1937, p. 268.

101.4 God is the free cause of all things.
Spinoza, *Ethics,* 1677, i. Appendix.

102. CAUTION

102.1 He who observes the wind shall not sow, and he who regards the clouds shall not reap.
Bible: Eccles., 11.4.

102.2 Be not like a bird that sees the seeds but not the trap.
Ibn Tibbon, *Tzavaah,* c.1190.

102.3 It is the part of caution not to be over-cautious.
Proverb. q Bahya, *Hobot HaLebabot,* 1040, Introduction.

103. CEMETERY

103.1 What has a Cohen to do in a cemetery?
Levi b. Abba. *Exod. R.,* 5.14, ref. to *Lev.* 21.1.

103.2 Walk reverently in a cemetery, lest the deceased say: Tomorrow they will join us, and today they mock us!
Hiyya Rabbah. *Talmud: Berakot,* 18a.

103.3 It is forbidden to use the cemetery for any other purpose, to eat, drink, work, read Scripture or study Mishna there.
Maimonides, *Yad: Ebel,* 1180, 14.13.

103.4 Cemeteries must not be treated disrespectfully. Cattle may not be fed there, nor a watercourse turned nor grass plucked.
Talmud: Megilla, 29a.

104. CENSORSHIP

104.1 How can you look on when the sanctuary is being consumed by rotten books?
Abba Mari, letter to Adret, 1304. KTJ, 251.

104.2 Only the suppressed word is dangerous.
Boerne, *Ankündigung der Wage,* 1818.

104.3 It is most unworthy to suppress books or silence teachers.
Judah Löw, *Beer HaGola,* 1598, ch 7.

104.4 It was needless for the Government to ban the book [Heine's *Reisebilder,* vol. 2]—people would have read it without that.
Moser. q Heine, *Journey from Munich to Genoa,* 1829, ch 7.

105. CEREMONY

105.1 Men cling to sanctified phrases not only because of the insights they contain but even more because, through ritual and repetition, they have become redolent with the wine of human experience. . . . The ritual may be diluted by English and by modernisms, but the Hebraic God is still a potent symbol of the continuous life of which we individuals are waves.
M. R. Cohen, *A Dreamer's Journey,* 1949, p. 218.

105.2 Judaism without ceremonial is an absurdity, a ragged garb which protects not, adorns not.
I. Deutsch, letter to A. Muhr, April 24, 1838.

105.3 Human actions are vehicles to spiritual heights. Having reached these, I care not for religious ceremonies.
Elisha b. Abuya. q Judah Halevi, *Cuzari,* 3.65.

105.4 Judaism looks upon religious ceremonies as a means for strengthening our religio-ethical sentiments. . . . When ceremonies no longer . . . fulfill this purpose, . . . they become entirely worthless . . .

and the reign of superstition has been inaugurated.

A. Geiger, *"Der Formglaube," WZJT*, 1839. q PCP, 134.

105.5 A ceremony is not adequately discharged unless it is performed with beauty and dignity.

M. H. Luzzatto, *Mesillat Yesharim*, 1740, ch 19.

105.6 Ceremonies are no aid to blessedness.

Spinoza, *A Theologico-Political Treatise*, 1670, ch 5.

105.7 Our ceremonialism is a training in self-conquest, while it links the generations . . . and unifies our atoms dispersed to the four corners of the earth as nothing else could.

Zangwill, *Children of the Ghetto*, 1892, ii. ch 2.

106. CERTAINTY

106.1 Certainty even with regard to the essential dogmas appears to be impossible.

F. Adler, *Creed and Deed*, 1877, p. 1.

106.2 Better a small certainty than a large peradventure.

Berekia HaNakdan, *Mishlé Shualim*, c.1260.

106.3 We must distinguish between the sound certainty and the sham, between what is gold and what is tinsel; and then, when certainty is attained, we must remember that it is not the only good, that we can buy it at too high a price.

Cardozo, *Growth of the Law*, 1924, p. 16. See *Nature of the Judicial Process*, 166.

106.4 Never take anything for granted.

Disraeli, speech, Oct. 5. 1864.

106.5 Between "sure" and "perhaps," the "sure" has it.

Huna, Judah. *Talmud: Ketubot*, 12b.

106.6 There is no certainty without some doubt.

Levita, *Tishbi*, 1541, *v. Vadai.*

106.7 We can say nothing with certainty about anything, because the picture presented to us is not constant.

Philo, *Drunkenness*, 41.

106.8 Better an ounce from the ground than a pound from the roof.

Rab. *Talmud: Pesahim*, 113a.

106.9 Doubt cannot override a certainty.

Rabbah. *Talmud: Yebamot*, 38b.

106.10 Our life is wrought of dreams and waking, fused
Of truth and lies. There lives no certitude.

Schnitzler, *Paracelsus*, 1899.

107. CHANCE

107.1 Time and chance happens to them all.

Bible: Eccles., 9.11.

107.2 Deification of accidents serves of course as rationalization for every people that is not master of its own destiny.

Arendt, *Origins of Totalitarianism*, 1951, p. 246.

107.3 He who ascribes things to mere accident is like a bird that sees a net and deems it of no special purpose.

Bahya b. Asher, *Kad HaKemah*, 14C.

107.4 Great things spring from casualties.

Disraeli, *Sybil*, 1845.

107.5 A consistent man believes in destiny, a capricious man in chance.

Disraeli, *Vivian Grey*, 1827, 6.7.

107.6 It is Accident that has become decisive for the structure of Jewish history. And Accident . . . in the language of religion is called Providence.

A. S. Steinberg, *Dubnow Festschrift*, 1930, p. 34. q Arendt, *Origins of Totalitarianism*, p. 246, Note 64.

107.7 If you win, you win a charcoal; if you lose, you lose a pearl.

Yannai. *Talmud J: Berakot*, 4.4.

108. CHANGE

108.1 Can an Ethiopian change his skin, or a leopard his spots?

Bible: Jer., 13.23.

108.2 I am the Lord, I change not.

Bible: Mal., 3.6.

108.3 Everything subject to time is liable to change.

Albo, *Ikkarim*, 1428, 2.7, tr ii. 42.

108.4 Nought endures but change.

Boerne, *Memorial Address on Jean Paul*, Dec. 2, 1825.

108.5 Other seasons, other song-birds,
Other song-birds, other songs.
They perchance could give me pleasure
Had I only other ears!

Heine, *Atta Troll*, 1841, ch 27. See *JQRo*, xiv. 557.

108.6 Whoever would change men must change the conditions of their lives.

Herzl, *Diary*. q LR, 31.

108.7 A woman can dye her hair but not change her character.

Immanuel, *Mahberot*, c.1300 (1491), ch 17.

108.8 A change of name or place may sometimes save a person.

Johanan. *Talmud J: Sabbath*, 6.9.

108.9 You Westerners always crave excitement; you are always eager to change everything. You cannot leave things as they are; so you destroy the most beautiful gift granted to man on earth: the joy of finding everything again as one had known it.

Nordau, *Menschliches u. Unmenschliches von Heute*, 1915.

108.10 Never say, "Times have changed." We have an old Father, bless His name! who has never changed and will never change.

Sofer, *Tzavaat Moshé*, Nov. 24, 1836.

108.11 What is freedom if not the possibility of change?

Twerski. *Hegyonot. HaPoel HaTzair*, 1951. xliv. #38.

108.12 Like a language, a religion was dead when it ceased to change.

Zangwill, *Dreamers of the Ghetto*, 1898, p. 521.

109. CHAOS

109.1 The earth was without form and void.

Bible: Gen., 1.2.

109.2 Woe to them that call evil good, and good evil.

Bible: Isa., 5.20.

109.3 Broken down is the city of confusion.

Ibid., 24.10. See 34.11.

110. CHARACTER

110.1 A man's character is known by his walk, dress and greeting.

Abot de R. Nathan, B ch 31, ed Schechter, p. 68.

110.2 A character is tested through business, wine, and conversation.

Ibid.

110.3 A man is known through his portion, potion, and passion.

Ilai. *Talmud: Erubin*, 65b. tr Zangwill.

110.4 Three types . . . offend me greatly: a poor man who is haughty, a rich man who lies, and an old man an adulterer.

Apocrypha: Ben Sira, 25.2.

110.5 Four are intolerable: an arrogant poor man, a deceitful rich man, a lecherous old man, and a president who lords it over the community.

Talmud: Pesahim, 113b.

110.6 The reason for so much bad science is not that talent is rare—not at all. What is rare is character.

Freud. q J. Wortis. *Journal of Orthopsychiatry*, Oct. 1940.

110.7 The most beautiful as well as the most ugly inclinations of man are not part of a fixed and biologically given human nature, but result from the social process which creates man.

Fromm, *Escape from Freedom*, 1941, p. 12.

110.8 Man is always trying to make something for himself rather than something of himself.

Heifetz. q Leon Gutterman. JTA 1952.

110.9 Ask me not what I have, my loved one,
Ask me rather what I am.

Heine, *Early Poems*, #13.

110.10 Before his death, none is to be praised as a character.

Heine, *Gedanken und Einfälle*, 1869.

110.11 Every man must strive first for the improvement of his own character, and then of the character of others.

M. Ibn Ezra, *Shirat Yisrael*, (12C) 1924, p. 198.

110.12 The meek is known in anger, a hero in war, and a friend in time of need.

Ibn Gabirol, *Mibhar HaPeninim*, c. 1050, #490.

110.13 The time-honored ideal of an ethical character is a pure heart, clear convictions, coupled with a firm, constant will, unwaveringly directed towards the good.

M. Lazarus, *Ethics of Judaism*, 1901, ii. 44, #202.

110.14 It is possible to be a sage in some things and a child in others, to be at once ferocious and retarded, shrewd and foolish, serene and irritable.

Lippmann, *A Preface to Morals*, 1929, p. 183f.

110.15 Man is not born endowed with either virtue or vice, just as he is not born skilled in any particular art.

Maimonides, *Eight Chapters*, 1168, #8, ed Gorfinkle, 85. Cf Aristotle, *Nichomachaean Ethics*, 2.1.

110.16 Not trade but traits lead to riches or poverty.

Meir. *Mishna: Kiddushin,* 4.14.

110.17 Whoever has a generous eye, a humble mind, and a modest spirit is a disciple of Abraham our father; whoever has an evil eye, a haughty mind, and an over-ambitious spirit is a disciple of Balaam the wicked.

Mishna: Abot, 5.19.

110.18 Character is shaped by deeds, and character is partly habit.

Montefiore, *Liberal Judaism,* 1903, p. 119.

110.19 Because man is half angel, half brute, his inner life witnesses such unlike natures. . . . Not until the very hour of death can it be certain which of the two won.

Moses of Coucy, *Semag,* 1245.

110.20 Character, like a delectable dish, must be achieved with a proper recipe: of some traits, like modesty, man should take a large dose, and of others, like pride, fierceness, cruelty, he should take but little. Man should weigh carefully the measure of each ingredient, and he will attain the goal of the good.

Orhot Tzaddikim, 15C, Introduction.

110.21 Man is like a precious stone: cut and polished by morals, adorned by wisdom.

Satanov, *Mishlé Asaf,* 1789.

110.22 He who sins not among the wicked is a better man than he who sins not among the righteous.

Sefer Hasidim, 13C, #1947, p. 471.

110.23 Our destiny is really nothing more than our character; our character but . . . the sum total of all our capacities and gifts.

Varnhagen, letter to Count Astolf Custine, Dec. 17, 1816.

110.24 Of genius there is no dearth; but character is a rare article.

Willstätter, 1934. q RHI, 272.

111. CHARIOT

111.1 Woe to them that . . . trust in chariots!

Bible: Isa., 31.1.

111.2 When man . . . perfects himself according to the commandments, he becomes a very chariot and throne of glory, in the likeness of the heavenly Chariot and Throne.

I. Horowitz, *Shné Luhot HaBerit,* 1649, 38b.

111.3 The hand that does charity becomes a limb in the Chariot of the Holy One.

Shneor Zalman, *Tanya,* (1796) 1896, 23.

112. CHARITY
112.A. Characterization

112.A.1 Withhold not good from [its *baal*] him to whom it is due.

Bible: Prov., 3.27. See *Ben Sira,* 4.3.

112.A.2 Here the needy appears as the *baal* of the good deed, as having a God-given, legal claim to it, as being by natural right its proprietor. Truly an unfathomable depth of philanthropy . . . is expressed in this single and apparently innocent word.

Cornill, Israel and Humanity, Jan. 8, 1895.

112.A.3 He who refuses a suppliant the aid which he has the power to give, is accountable to justice.

Josephus, *Against Apion,* ii. 27.

112.A.4 He who is gracious to the poor lends to the Lord.

Bible: Prov., 19.17.

112.A.5 Charity suffers long, . . . rejoices in the truth, bears all things, believes all things, hopes all things, endures all things. Charity never fails.

New Testament: I Cor., 13.4–8.

112.A.6 Now abides faith, hope, charity, these three; but the greatest of these is charity.

Ibid., 13.13.

112.A.7 Wealth is fleeting, honor winged, but charity abides.

Steinberg, *Mishlé Yehoshua,* 1885, 11.2, p. 64.

112.B. Duty

112.B.1 You shall not harden your heart, nor shut your hand from your needy brother, but . . . lend him sufficient for his need.

Bible: Deut., 15.7f.

112.B.2 We should be grateful for the rogues among the poor; were it not for them, we would sin each time we ignore an appeal.

Eleazar b. Pedat. *Talmud: Ketubot,* 68a.

112.B.3 What you save from frivolity, add to your charity.

Elijah b. Raphael, *Tzavaah,* 18C.

112.B.4 Shutting one's eye from charity is like worshipping idols.

Joshua b. Karha. *Talmud J: Peah,* 4.20.

112.B.5 To him who has the means and refuses the needy, the Holy One says: Bear in mind, fortune is a wheel!

Nahman. *Tanhuma, Mishpatim,* #8, ed Buber, 43a.

112.B.6 A community which has no synagog and no shelter for the poor, must first provide for the poor.

Sefer Hasidim, 13C, #1529, p. 374f.

112.B.7 Every Jew must either give or take charity for Passover.

Sholom Aleichem, *A Pesachdike Expropriacie,* 1908.

112.B.8 Care of the poor is incumbent on society as a whole.

Spinoza, *Ethics,* 1677, iv. Appendix 17.

112.B.9 Even a poor man, a subject of charity, should give charity.

Zutra. *Talmud: Gittin,* 7b.

112.C. Value

112.C.1 Happy is he who considers the poor; the Lord will deliver him in the day of evil.

Bible: Ps., 41.2.

112.C.2 He has scattered abroad, he has given to the needy, . . . his horn shall be exalted in honor.

Ibid., 112.9. See *Talmud: Baba Bathra,* 10b.

112.C.3 Charity [*tzedaka,* righteousness] delivers from death.

Bible: Prov., 10.2.

112.C.4 Charity delivers from death and purges away all sin.

Apocrypha: Tobit, 12.8.

112.C.5 Who gives to the poor shall not lack.

Bible: Prov., 28.27.

112.C.6 By benevolence man rises to a height where he meets God. Therefore do a good deed before you begin your prayers.

Ahai Gaon, *Sheiltot,* c.760.

112.C.7 Turn not away your face from any poor man, and the face of God will not turn away from you.

Apocrypha: Tobit, 4.7. See *Matt.,* 5.42.

112.C.8 If you have much, give much; if you have little, be not afraid to give according to that little; for you lay up a good treasure for yourself against the day of need.

Apocrypha: Tobit, 4.8–10. See *II Enoch,* 51.1.

112.C.9 Charity equals all the other commandments.

Assi. *Talmud: Baba Bathra,* 9a.

112.C.10 A penny for the poor will obtain a view of the Shekina.

Dosetai b. Yannai. *Talmud: Baba Bathra,* 10a, on *Ps.* 17.15.

112.C.11 Who withholds charity from the needy withdraws himself from the luster of the Shekina and the light of the Law.

Jacob b. Asher, *Tur Yoré Deah,* c. 1300, #247.

112.C.12 Charity is a magnet with more power to attract the divine influence than any other precept.

Shneor Zalman, *Torah Or, BeShalah,* (1837). q MRH, 217.

112.C.13 As lightning springs out of its concealment in dark clouds to flash through the world, so the divine light, imbedded in matter, emerges through charitable deeds. . . . Thus through charity, a sort of divine revelation occurs in the soul.

Shneor Zalman, *Seder Tefillot,* 1816.

112.C.14 Charity and loving-kindness intercede greatly and promote peace between Israel and their Father in Heaven.

Eleazar b. José. *Tosefta: Peah,* 4.21.

112.C.15 Who shears his property for alms is saved from Gehenna. The shorn sheep cross the stream, the unshorn are swept down.

Ishmael School. *Talmud: Gittin,* 7a.

112.C.16 Charity is as potent for atonement as the altar.

Johanan b. Zakkai. *Abot de R. Nathan,* ch 4.

112.C.17 Charity equals in importance the whole Temple cult.

Eurydemos b. José. *Sifra,* to *Lev.* 23.22, ed Weiss, 101b. See *Talmud: Sukka,* 49b.

112.C.18 A table spread for the poor is an altar for the rich.

Targum Jerushalmi, to *Exod.,* 40.6.

112.C.19 Whom the Holy One loves, He sends a golden opportunity for charity, by which he may draw the cord of grace.

Zohar, Gen., 104a. See *Talmud: Baba Bathra,* 10a.

112.C.20 The more charity, the more peace.

Hillel. *Mishna: Abot,* 2.7.

112.C.21 If you really want to do charity. God provides the means.

Isaac Nappaha. *Talmud: Baba Bathra* 9b.

112.C.22 Nobody is ever impoverished through the giving of charity.

Maimonides, *Yad: Matnot Aniyim,* 1180, 10.2.

112.C.23 The charitable will have children healthy and wise.

Joshua b. Levi. *Talmud: Baba Bathra,* 9b.

112.C.24 Great is charity, for it brings near the redemption.

Judah b. Ilai. *Talmud: Baba Bathra,* 10a.

112.C.25 Knowledge puffs up, but charity edifies.

New Testament: 1 Cor., 8.1. See 13.1–3.

112.C.26 The door which does not open to the poor will open to the physician.

Levi. *Pesiḳta Rabbati,* ch. 11. ed Friedmann 42b.

112.C.27 What you do not give in charity voluntarily, the heathen will take from you forcibly.

Eleazar b. Pedat. *Talmud: Baba Bathra,* 9a.

112.C.28 Charity removes the stain of sin.

Shneor Zalman, *Likkuté Torah: Re-eh,* 1848.

112.C.29 Charity is one of the remedies against alien thoughts.

Shneor Zalman. q Teitelbaum, *HaRab MeLadi,* ii. 225.

112.C.30 What you give to charity in health is gold; in sickness, is silver, and after death, is copper.

Tosafot of the Pentateuch, 13C.

112.C.31 Who helps the poor is their creator. It is said of Abraham and his servants, "the souls that they had made" [*Gen.* 12.5].

Zohar, Exod., 198a.

112.D. Limitations

112.D.1 The character of a people may be ruined by charity.

Herzl, to Baron de Hirsch, *Diary,* June 2, 1895.

112.D.2 Either from the character of those who take, or from the method of those who give, Jewish charity does not tend to the demoralization of individual recipients.

*Potter. C. Booth, *Life & Labor of People in London,* 1902, iii. ch 4, p. 166.

112.D.3 Charity will not end poverty, disease, idleness, ignorance.

Mendelé, *Di Kliatshé,* 1873.

112.D.4 Spend not on charity more than a fifth of your wealth.

Usha Synod, c.140. q Ilai. *Talmud: Ketubot,* 50a.

112.E. Manner and Form

112.E.1 Draw out your soul to the hungry.

Bible: Isa., 58.10.

112.E.2 I was a father to the needy, and the cause of him that I knew not, I searched out.

Bible: Job, 29.16.

112.E.3 To delay alms over night on a fast is like shedding blood.

Eleazar b. Pedat. *Talmud: Sanhedrin,* 35a.

112.E.4 Watch not the poor while he eats in your home.

Eliezer b. Isaac, *Orhot Hayyim,* c.1050.

112.E.5 Do not humiliate a beggar: God is at his right hand.

S. Horowitz, *Tzavaah,* 17C.

112.E.6 Who gives the poor money is blessed six-fold; who gives him morale is blessed seven-fold.

Isaac Nappaha. *Talmud: Baba Bathra,* 9b. Ref. to *Isa.* 58.8ff.

112.E.7 Charity demands the utmost care and diligence, for it may save a life.

Jacob b. Asher, *Tur Yoré Deah,* c.1300, #247.

112.E.8 Charity delivers from death only when giver and recipient do not know the one who the other is.

Johanan b. Nappaha. *Talmud: Sanhedrin,* 10b, on *Prov.* 11.4.

112.E.9 "Happy is he who *considers* the poor." We must be considerate of the sensibilities of the poor.

Jonah. *Lev. R.,* 34.1, on *Ps.* 41.2.

112.E.10 He gives twice who gives quickly.

Leon of Modena, *Tzemah Tzaddik,* 1600.

112.E.11 Give graciously, cheerfully, and sympathetically.

Maimonides, *Yad: Matnot Aniyim,* 1180, 10.4.

112.E.12 There are eight rungs in charity. The highest is when you help a man to help himself.

Ibid., 10.7.

46

112.E.13 What nation on earth has customs as strange as ours? Our poor *demand* alms, as if they were collecting a debt, and our benefactors . . . invite paupers to their table.

Mendelé, *Shem VeYefet BaAgala*, 1890.

112.E.14 Who gives charity with a smile is truly a right-minded man.

Nahman Bratzlav. q BHH, 487.

112.E.15 To boast of the help you gave a brother in need is to cancel the good of your deed.

Samuel HaNagid, *Ben Mishlé*, 11C, #8.

112.E.16 Charity must be given in secret.

Talmud: Sabbath, 104a. See *Baba Bathra*, 9b. *Matt.* 6.1.

112.E.17 It is better not to give alms than to give it in public, with embarrassment for the recipient.

Yannai Rabba. *Talmud: Hagiga*, 5a.

112.F. Scope

112.F.1 As tiny scales join to form a strong coat of mail, so little donations combine to form a large total of good.

Eleazar b. Pedat. *Talmud: Baba Bathra*, 9b, on *Isa.* 59.17.

112.F.2 Let us supply the man in need also with that about which he is silent.

Philo, *Prosperity and Exile of Cain*, 44.

112.G. Application

112.G.1 In relieving human suffering I never ask whether the cry of need comes from one of my own faith or not; but what is more natural than that I should find my highest purpose in bringing to the followers of Judaism, oppressed for a thousand years and starving in misery, the possibility of physical and moral regeneration . . . and thus furnish humanity with much new and valuable material?

M. Hirsch, 1891. See O. S. Straus. *Forum*, July, 1896.

112.G.2 As between relatives and poor strangers, relatives come first.

Joseph. *Talmud: Baba Metzia*, 71a.

112.G.3 Divided as we may be by religion, we are united by charity.

Rashi, to a monk he had cured gratis. q Liber, *Rashi*, 44.

112.G.4 To promote peace, we support the poor of the heathen, visit their sick and bury their dead, along with the poor, the sick, and the dead of Israel.

Talmud: Gittin, 61a

112.G.5 If an orphan boy and an orphan girl need support, or apply for a marriage grant, the girl is cared for first.

Tosefta: Ketubot, 6.8. See Caro, *Yoré Deah,* 1564, #251.

112.H. Administration

112.H.1 It is permissible to assign charity to the poor on the Sabbath.

Eleazar b. Pedat. *T: Sukka* 5a.

112.H.2 A charity pledge may be taken even on Sabbath eve.

Rabbah b. Abbuha. *Talmud: Baba Bathra,* 8b.

112.H.3 Applicants for clothes are investigated, not applicants for food.

Judah b. Ezekiel. *Talmud: Baba Bathra,* 9a.

112.H.4 A public fund is collected by no less than two, disbursed by no less than three.

Mishna: Peah, 8.7.

112.H.5 We do not transfer from one charity fund to another.

Proverb, based on *Talmud: Arakin,* 6ab.

112.H.6 "I will punish all that oppress" [*Jer.* 30.20], —even collectors for charity, who sometimes exact contributions beyond the givers' means.

Rab. *T: Baba Bathra,* 8b.

112.I. Acceptance

112.I.1 An old, sick or distressed person, who stubbornly declines charity, is guilty of suicide; yet one who frets and defers . . . troubling the community, . . . shall live to provide for others.

Caro, *Yoré Deah,* 1564, #255. See Hanina. *Talmud J: Peah,* 8.8.

112.I.2 The great sages were porters, smiths, hewers of wood and drawers of water, . . . accepting nothing from the community.

Maimonides, *Yad: Matnot Aniyim,* 1180, 10.18.

112.I.3 Who has for two meals may accept nothing from a charity kitchen; and for fourteen meals, nothing from a public fund.

Mishna: Peah, 8.7.

112.I.4 He who is not in need and takes charity will end up being in need; he who is in need and does not accept charity will yet come to support others.

Ibid., 8.9.

113. CHARM

113.1 Charm and lightness of form . . . is a condition of art.
Benda, *Belphégor*, (1919) 1929, p. 130.

113.2 Three possess charm: a place to its residents, a woman to her husband, and a bargain to the customer.
Johanan b. Nappaha. *Talmud: Sota*, 47a.

113.3 Charm is character exercising its influence.
Magnin, *How to Live*, 1951, p. 89.

113.4 Charm is more than beauty.
Proverb (Yiddish). BJS, #1587.

114. CHEER

114.1 A merry heart makes a cheerful countenance.
Bible: Prov., 15.13.

114.2 He who has a merry heart has a continual feast.
Ibid., 15.15.

114.3 A merry heart is a good medicine.
Ibid., 17.22.

114.4 Cheer prolongs man's days.
Apocrypha: Ben Sira, 30.22.

114.5 The sleep of a cheerful heart is like dainties.
Ibid., 30.25.

114.6 No wealth like health, no pleasure like cheer.
Ibn Gabirol, *Mibhar HaPeninim*, c. 1050, #457.

114.7 When you do a good deed, do it with a cheerful heart.
Isaac. *Lev. R.*, 34.8.

114.8 Receive everybody cheerfully.
Ishmael b. Elisha. *Mishna: Abot*, 3.12.

115. CHILDREN

115.A. Propagation

115.A.1 Be fruitful and multiply, and replenish the earth.
Bible: Gen., 1.28.

115.A.2 To refrain from begetting is to impair the divine image.
Eleazar b. Azariah. *Gen. R.*. 34.14.

115.A.3 Who brings no children into the world is like a murderer.
Eliezer b. Hyrcanus. *Talmud: Yebamot*, 63b.

115.A.4 Let not the fear of bad offspring deter you. . . . You do your duty and the Holy One will do what pleases Him.
Hamnuna. *Talmud: Berakot*, 10a.

115.A.5 A childless person is like dead.
Joshua b. Levi. *Talmud: Nedarim*, 64b.

115.A.6 After ten fruitless years, a man takes another wife.
Mishna: Yebamot, 6.6.

115.A.7 Was not the world created only for propagation?
Shammai School. *Talmud: Hagiga*, 2b. on *Isa.* 45.18.

115.A.8 No marital relations in years of famine.
Simeon b. Lakish. *Talmud: Taanit*, 11a. See *Zohar, Gen.*, 204a.

115.B. A Blessing

115.B.1 Lo, children are a heritage of the Lord. . . . Happy the man that has his quiver full of them.
Bible: Ps.. 127.3, 5.

115.B.2 In my children, I speak clearly with the Eternal.
Herzl, *Das Palais Bourbon*, 1895.

115.B.3 Children . . . constitute man's eternity.
Peretz, *Der Dichter*, 1910. LP, 321.

115.B.4 See how precious children are: the Shekina did not go with the Sanhedrin and priestly watches into exile, but it did go with the children.
Judah b. Ilai. *Lam. R.*, 1.6.33.

115.B.5 Your children are the best surety, better than patriarchs and prophets; for their sake I give you the Torah.
Meir. *Cant. R.*, 1.4.

115.B.6 Each child carries his own blessing into the world.
Proverb (Yiddish). BJS, #3278.

115.B.7 To his father and mother, no child is superfluous.
Ibid., #3292.

115.B.8 A child: a staff for the hand and a hoe for the grave!
Talmud: Yebamot, 65b.

115.B.9 No children, no bliss, here or hereafter.
Zohar, Gen., 66a. See 187a, 188a.

115.C. Childhood

115.C.1 Childhood and youth are vanity.
Bible: Eccles., 11.10.

115.C.2 Sinful breath cannot be compared with innocent breath.
Abayé. *Talmud: Sabbath*, 119b.

115.C.3 Blessed lot of childhood, whose troubles the silent night of slumber lulls into oblivion!

Auerbach, *Ivo der Hajrle,* 1843.

115.C.4 A garden of God is our child-hood, each day
A festival radiant with laughter and play.

M. J. Lebensohn, *"HaYaldut."* *Kinor Bat Tziyon,* 1870, p. 50. q WHJ, ii. 234.

115.C.5 Children without childhood are a frightful sight.

Mendelé, *BeSeter Raam,* 1913, p. 4.

115.D. Training

115.D.1 Train a child in the way he should go, and when he is old he will not depart from it.

Bible: Prov., 22.6.

115.D.2 You are responsible for your son till he is thirteen; then say, "Blessed be He who has rid me of responsibility for this."

Eleazar b. Simeon. *Gen. R.,* 63.10.

115.D.3 Be faithful shepherds of your flocks, . . . and be in your conduct a light to their paths.

Elijah b. Raphael, *Tzavaah,* 18C. AHE, 305.

115.D.4 Mothers should introduce their children to the Torah.

Exod. R., 28.2.

115.D.5 As soon as a child learns to talk, his father must teach him the verse, "Moses commanded us a law" [*Deut.* 33.4].

Hamnuna. *Talmud: Sukka,* 42a. See *Tosejta: Hagiga,* 1.2.

115.D.6 Train children in their youth, and they won't train you in your old age.

Lazerov, *Enciklopedie Jun Idishé Vitzen,* 1928, #504.

115.D.7 The principal cause of misdeeds is familiarity with falsehood . . . right from the cradle, the work of nurses and mothers.

Philo, *Special Laws,* iv. 10.

115.D.8 Who rears his son to be right-eous is like an immortal.

Rashi, *Commentary,* to *Gen.* 18.19.

115.D.9 Little children do not lie till they are taught to do so.

Saadia, letter, 928. KTJ, 89.

115.D.10 Who rears a family is dis-turbed in mind and in heart.

Seder Eliyahu Zuta, ch 8, ed Friedmann, 185.

115.D.11 Bless our children, ( ) God, and help us so to fashion their souls by precept and example that they may ever love the good, flee from sin, revere Thy word, and honor Thy name.

Union Prayer Book, 1940, i. 131.

115.E. Treatment

115.E.1 Who spares the rod hates his son.

Bible: Prov., 13.24.

115.E.2 Gold must be hammered, and a child must be beaten.

Alphabet of Ben Sira, 4.

115.E.3 The best security for old age: respect your children.

Asch. q Leon Gutterman, JTA, 1952.

115.E.4 We must bow reverently before all children: they are our masters, we work for them.

Boerne.

115.E.5 Love, cherish and esteem the children of other people.

D'Israeli, letter to Thomas Holcroft, 1784. N & Q, 1949, 193.

115.E.6 Play no favoritism: because Jo-seph got a multi-colored coat, the brothers "hated him" [*Gen.* 37.4].

Eleazar b. Azariah. *Gen. R.,* 84.8.

115.E.7 Love equally all your children. Sometimes the favored disappoint, and the neglected make you happy.

Berekia HaNakdan, *Mishlé Shualim,* c. 1260.

115.E.8 When you lead your sons and daughters in the good way, let your words be tender and caressing, in terms of disci-plines that win the heart's assent.

Elijah Gaon, *Alim LiTerufa,* 1836. AIIE 319.

115.E.9 Honor children of the ignorant: Torah may issue from them.

Judah b. Bathyra. *Talmud: Sanhedrin,* 96a.

115.E.10 Reprimand not a child im-mediately on the offence. Wait till the irri-tation has been replaced by serenity.

Moses Hasid, *Iggeret HaMusar,* 1717. AHE, 291.

115.E.11 Parents must not so exasperate a child that he cannot constrain himself from rebelling against them.

Sefer Hasidim, 13C, #954, p. 234f.

115.E.12 If you wish to give a child food, first tell his mother.

Simeon b. Gamaliel II. *Talmud: Sabbath,* 10b.

115.F. Miscellaneous

115.F.1 And a little child shall lead them.
Bible: Isa., 11.6.

115.F.2 No kids, no wethers; no wethers, no sheep. . . . No children, no adults; no adults, no sages.
Eleazar b. Pedat. *Gen. R.,* 42.3.

115.F.3 It is easier to grow a legion of olive trees in Galilee than to rear one child in the Land of Israel.
Eleazar b. Simeon. *Gen. R.,* 20.6.

115.F.4 What a child says on the street, the parents said at home.
Proverb. q Abayé. *Talmud: Sukka,* 56b.

115.F.5 One father willingly maintains ten children, but ten children are unwilling to maintain one father.
Proverb. q Epstein, *Kitzur Shné Luhot HaBerit,* 12b.

115.F.6 A small child is a pig, a big child is a wolf.
Proverb (Yiddish). BJS, #3289.

115.F.7 Small children disturb your sleep, big children your life.
Ibid., #3318.

115.F.8 Small children, small joys; big children, big annoys.
Ibid., #3321. *JE,* x. 228b.

115.F.9 Why children, if one is unable to provide for them? . . . Why rear them, unless they grow in knowledge and wisdom?
Saadia, *Emunot VeDeot,* 933, 10.9.

115.F.10 One may have twelve sons, and still die barren.
Sackler, *Tzaddik's Journey. Reflex,* Nov. 1927, p. 75.

116. CHOICE

116.1 Ye have chosen the Lord, to serve Him.
Bible: Josh., 24.22.

116.2 Morality may consist solely in the courage of making a choice.
Blum. q CGP, 97.

116.3 The power of choice must involve the possibility of error—that is the essence of choosing.
H. Samuel, *Belief and Action,* 1937, p. 94.

116.4 In choosing a wife, a teacher, or a surgeon, do not be influenced by affection or friendship.
Sefer Hasidim, 13C, #787, p. 198.

117. CHRISTIANITY

117.1 All the values which unfolded in Christianity, love, pity, patience, insight, restraint, the essentials of our civilization, are Jewish values.
Asch, *What I Believe,* 1941, p. 121.

117.2 The blood shed on the Cross for the redemption of mankind, as well as that which is shed invisibly every day in the Chalice of the Sacrament of the Altar, is naturally and supernaturally Jewish blood.
*Bloy, *Le Salut par les Juifs,* 1892. Pilgrim, 245.

117.3 Everything, to the last item, that elevates the Christian faith above the other religions is of Jewish origin.
*Breysig, *Kulturgeschichte der Neuzeit,* 1901, ii. 678.

117.4 What you call Christianity, I call Prophetic Judaism.
H. Cohen, to F. A. Lange. q AMP, 58.

117.5 His Christianity was muscular.
Disraeli, *Endymion,* 1880, ch 14.

117.6 Christianity is Judaism for the multitude.
Disraeli. q SHZ, i. 141.

117.7 He [Christ], though a born Dauphin of Heaven, is democratically minded . . . he is not a God of shaven and shorn bookish pedants and laced men-at-arms . . . he is a modest God of the People, a citizen God, *un bon dieu citoyen.*
Heine, *City of Lucca,* 1831, ch 7.

117.8 If, as many think, we still live in the youth of mankind, then Christianity belongs to the most extravagant of its college ideas, which do far more credit to its heart than to its head.
Heine, *Germany from Luther to Kant,* 1834.

117.9 These religions [Christianity and Islam] are the preparation and preface to the Messiah we expect.
Judah Halevi, *Cuzari,* c. 1135, 4.23.

117.10 To a Jew, the interesting part of Christianity is the part that he rejects. The morals are the morals of Judaism . . . . But the other part—the Hellenistic and pagan and sacramental—that is new and interesting and strange . . . and for the life of us, literally, we and our fathers have not been able to believe it, and we reject it with both hands.
Magnes. q BFZ, 290. See Darmsteter, *Selected Essays,* 1895, p. 256.

117.11 The yearning pity for the sinner and the outcast, the humility of the true saver of souls, who, while never ceasing to accentuate the horror of sin, bridges over and even annuls the moral chasm between the basest criminal and himself, have been delightful characteristics of both the two great branches of Christianity in their highest and purest forms.

Montefiore. *JQRo*, Jan. 1896, viii. 215.

117.12 It is a denial of this world, a severance from reality, an abdication, a means of redemption *from*, not *for*, life.

Peretz, *Vegn vos Firn op fun Yidishkeit,* 1911. LP, 372.

117.13 The first founder of Christianity was Isaiah. By introducing into the Jewish world the concept of ethical religion, of justice, and of the relative unimportance of sacrifices, he antedated Jesus by more than seven centuries.

*Renan, *Le Judaisme comme race et comme réligion,* 1883.

117.14 It is through Christianity that Judaism has really conquered the world. Christianity is the masterpiece of Judaism, its glory and the fulness of its evolution.

*Renan, *History of Israel,* 1895, v. 355.

117.15 These doctrines which certain churches put forward concerning Christ, I neither affirm nor deny, for I freely confess that I do not understand them.

Spinoza, *Theologico-Political Treatise,* 1670, ch 1.

117.16 *Micah* 6.6–8 and *Psalm* 73.23–28 give us the complete Gospel.

*Wellhausen, *Isr. & jüd. Geschichte,* ed 1901, 389f, note 1.

117.17 To speak of Jews as rejecting Christ when it was a Jew who spread his gospel is a strange popular blunder.

Zangwill. *North American Review,* April 1895.

118. CHRISTIANS

118.1 The Christians . . . have many admirable traits and righteous principles. . . . Happy are they and happy are we when they treat us according to their faith!

Emden, Preface to *Seder Olam,* 1757. JJCW, 128.

118.2 I do not regard a Christian as a stranger, because he believes in divine creation and Providence.

Ibn Verga, *Shebet Yehuda,* (1550) 1855, p. 10.

118.3 Christians are not heathens. They believe in God and do not tolerate bloodshed. . . . We must pray for their welfare.

Lampronti, *Pahad Yitzhak,* 1750.

118.4 That which makes me a Christian in your eyes
Makes you a Jew in mine.

*Lessing, *Nathan the Wise,* 1779, 4.7.

118.5 Some preach Christ of envy and strife, and some also of good will.

New Testament: Phil., 1.15.

118.6 They are all so-called Christian nations, but . . . this superimposed religion . . . does not penetrate into the core of their souls. It has no relation to their daily experience. . . . It is a key to open a heaven after death and not a key with which to force open the portals of this life.

Peretz, *Vegn vos Firn op fun Yidishkeit,* 1911. LP, 372.

118.7 As the Jew, so the Christian (*Wie es sich jüdelt, so christelt sich*).

Proverb. q Zoozmann, *Zitatenschatz.*

118.8 As the Christian, so the Jew.

Proverb. q Jacobs, *Jewish Ideals,* 237.

118.9 Not long ago I was reading the Sermon on the Mount with a rabbi. At nearly each verse he showed me very similar passages in the Hebrew Bible and Talmud. When we reached the words, "Resist not evil," he did not say, "This too is in the Talmud," but asked, with a smile, "Do the Christians obey this command?" I had nothing to say in reply, especially as at that particular time, Christians, far from turning the other cheek, were smiting the Jews on both cheeks.

*Tolstoy, *My Religion,* 1884, ch 2.

118.10 But for these nations, who believe in our essential doctrines,—creation, the virtues of the patriarchs, revelation, retribution, resurrection—we might have slipped from the faith.

Yaabetz, *Maamar HaAhdut,* 1554, ch 3, 1794, p. 4b.

119. CHURCH AND STATE

119.1 No religion can long continue to maintain its purity when the church becomes the subservient vassal of the state.

F. Adler, *Creed and Deed,* 1877, p. 227.

119.2 Religion may be the concern of a people, but it must never become a concern of the state.

Baeck, *Essence of Judaism,* 1936, p. 48.

119.3 Religion should be not the root ... that bears only certain fruits, but the fructifying dew which quickens all plants.

Boerne, *Das Gespenst der Zeit*, 1821.

119.4 Religion cannot sink lower than when somehow it is raised to a state religion ... it becomes then an avowed mistress.

Heine, *Letters from Berlin*, March 16, 1822.

119.5 We shall never ask any support for our ... institutions by the state; and if offered, we should ... reject it with scorn and indignation.

M. Lilienthal, *Platform of Judaism*, June 5, 1868.

119.6 When church and state are in the field against each other, mankind is the victim of their discord; and when they agree, the brightest jewel of human happiness is gone, for they seldom agree but for the purpose of banishing from their realms a third moral entity, liberty of conscience.

M. Mendelssohn, *Jerusalem*, 1783. tr Samuels, ii. 4.

120. CIRCUMCISION

120.1 This is My covenant: ... every male among you shall be circumcised.

Bible: Gen., 17.10.

120.2 It is possible to worship God without being circumcised.

Ananias. q Josephus, *Antiquities*, 20.2.4.

120.3 Circumcision is a sign of the covenant between man and his Creator, not to pollute himself with unchastity.

A. Ibn Ezra, *Yesod Mora*, 1158, ch 7, 1840, p. 31. See Nahmanides, letter to his son Solomon, c. 1267 (AHE, 232).

120.4   With a wound
—What better sign exists?—the child is made
A Jew forever! quickly taught the life
That he must lead, an heir to lasting pain.

Schwartz, *Shenandoah*, 1941, p. 27.

120.5 The sign of circumcision is ... so important, that ... it alone would preserve the nation forever.

Spinoza *Thelogico-Political Treatise*, 1670, ch 3.

120.6 Praised be Thou ... who hast sanctified us by commandments and bidden us enter the Covenant of Abraham our father.

Tosefta: Berakot, 7.12.

120.7 To maintain the purity of the Covenant is to observe the whole Torah.

Zohar, Gen., 197a.

120.8 Circumcision ... is an institution, not a mere ceremony. ... The son who, on principle, remained uncircumcised will hardly, on principle, remain in Judaism.

Zunz, *Die Beschneidung*, 1844. *Ges. Schr.*, ii. 199.

121. CIRCUMSTANCE

121.1 Man is not the creature of circumstances, circumstances are the creatures of men.

Disraeli, *Vivian Grey*, 1826, 6.7.

121.2 There is no sense in my attempting ever to flee from circumstances and conditions which cannot be avoided but which I might bravely meet and frequently mend and often turn to good account.

Glueck. E. R. Murrow, *This I Believe*, 1952, p. 59.

121.3 He who doesn't lose his head under certain circumstances has no head to lose.

Shatzky, to J. L. Baron, 1953.

121.4 To defy external forces, to rise above circumstances, is to proclaim the sovereignty of the human spirit.

Weizmann. *N.Y. Herald Tribune* Annual Forum, Oct. 21, 1947.

122. CITIZENSHIP

122.1 The most important office, ... that of private citizen.

Brandeis. *Boston Record*, April 14, 1903.

122.2 Whatever is a privilege rather than a right, may be made dependent upon citizenship.

Cardozo, *People vs. Crane*, 1915.

122.3 According to Aristotle, the "stateless" must be a God or a beast; nowadays he is usually a Jew.

Namier, *Conflicts*, 1943.

122.4 Bad officials are elected by good citizens who do not vote.

G. J. Nathan.

123. CITY

123.1 A city and mother in Israel.

Bible: II Sam. 20.19.

123.2 From out of the populous city men groan, and the soul of the wounded cries out.

Bible: Job, 24.12.

123.3 There haven't been civilizations without cities. But what about cities without civilizations?

Bellow, *Adventures of Augie March,* 1949.

123.4 Lo! I was Sodom! I was Nineveh!
Look, and remember, Cities of Today! . . .
Each of us sought to pluck the stars from heaven.
Men have forgotten us, but God has not forgiven.

Fleg, *Wall of Weeping,* 1919, tr Wolfe, 1929, pp. 33, 37.

123.5 There is hardly one in three of us who live in the cities who is not sick with unused self.

Hecht, *A Child of the Century,* 1954, p. 626.

123.6 From Kiev I learned . . . that cities have souls.

S. Levin, *Youth in Revolt,* 1930, p. 187.

123.7 When I . . . changed the town of Speyer into a city, I thought that I would add to its honor by bringing in Jews.

*Rudiger, Bishop of Spires, 1084. *Orient,* 1842, p. 391.

123.8 I have seen a city chiseled out of moonlight,
Its buildings beautiful as silver foothills,
While universes shimmered in its corners.

Stampfer, *Jerusalem Has Many Faces,* 1950, p. 57.

123.9 I cannot stand the life of the big cities, with their host of conventions and artificialities, where there are no true friends . . . where the friends of today will fall upon one another tomorrow . . . if an unclaimed piece of bread, or a little lump of gold, is thrown among them.

Trumpeldor, letter, Nov. 21, 1911. q Lipovetzky, *Joseph Trumpeldor,* 42.

124. CIVILIZATION

124.1 Increased means and leisure are the two civilizers of man.

Disraeli, speech, April 3, 1872.

124.2 A civilization is judged by its quality, not its speed.

Edman. *N.Y. Times Book Review,* Jan. 18, 1953, p. 3.

124.3 All these funnels of countless factories are altars on which there smoke burnt offerings to the Golden Calf.

Mendelé, *Di Kliatshé,* 1873.

124.4 Civilization is built on a number of ultimate principles: . . . respect for human life, the punishment of crimes against property and persons, the equality of all good citizens before the law—or, in a word, justice.

Nordau, address, VIII Zionist Congress, 1907.

124.5 "Civilized?" The word does ill befit
Those that internecine wars permit.

Sanders, *366 Sprüche,* 1892, #210.

124.6 Civilization should have but one aim—to liberate man from all that is mystic, from the vague impulsiveness of instinctive action, and to cultivate the purely rational side of his being.

Zollschan, *Das Rassenproblem,* 1910, p. 298.

125. CLARITY

125.1 Write the vision and make it plain upon tables, that he may run that reads it.
Bible: Hab., 2.2.

125.2 Open your mouth, and let your words be clear.

Judah b. Bathyra. *Talmud: Berakot,* 22a.

125.3 A thinker who cannot set forth weighty thoughts in simple and clear language should be suspected, primarily, of lacking talent for thought.

Klatzkin, *In Praise of Wisdom,* 1943, p. 307.

125.4 One of the most essential things for a scholar is to write, . . . even an ordinary letter, in clear language.

S. Luria. q Isserles, *Responsa,* #6.

125.5 Truth and clarity, logically arranged, is classic style in all languages.

q I. M. Wise, "World of My Books." *Deborah,* Oct. 29, 1896.

125.6 What is clarity? To speak without erring, and to be brief without repeating.

Zabara, *Sefer Shaashuim,* 13C, 7.5, ed Davidson, 66.

126. CLASS

126.1 In Germany people are arranged like books in a library. The big and weighty stand below, the light and little above. You must stoop to get to a folio, climb to reach a duodecimo.

Boerne, *Der Narr im weissen Schwan,* ch 2.

126.2 As property has its duties as well as its rights, rank has its bores as well as its pleasures.
Disraeli, *Sybil*, 1845.

126.3 Religion, philosophy and politics leave me cold if they do not help to . . . put an end to all caste spirit and all class rule.
Hess. *Ben Chananja*, 1862. q *HJ*, Apr. 1951, p. 21.

126.4 The Jews have been a people without classes.
Oppenheim, *A Psycho-Analysis of the Jews*, 1926.

126.5 There was one point by which it [Israel] was distinguished from the other nations of antiquity, namely, its comparative absence of caste, its equality of religious relations.
*Stanley, *History of the Jewish Church*, (1862) 1896, i. 141.

126.6 My [peasant] neighbor and I are both God's creatures. My work is in town, his in the country. As he does not presume to do my work, I do not presume to do his. And we have learned: It is all the same . . . provided one directs one's heart to Heaven.
Talmud: Berakot, 17a.

127. CLEANNESS

127.1 With the pure Thou dost show Thyself pure.
Bible: II Sam., 22.27.

127.2 Wash yourself, make yourself clean, put away the evil of your doings.
Bible: Isa., 1.16.

127.3 Be clean, ye that bear the vessels of the Lord.
Ibid., 52.11.

127.4 Who shall ascend the mountain of the Lord? . . . He that has clean hands and a pure heart.
Bible: Ps., 24.3f.

127.5 Happy Israel, before whom do you purify yourselves, and who cleanses you? Your Father in Heaven [*Ezek.* 36.25].
Akiba. *Mishna: Yoma*, 8.9.

127.6 The whole philosophy of monotheism is contained in this rallying cry of Rabbi Akiba.
H. Cohen. q Newman, *Living With Ourselves*, 1950, p. 20.

127.7 God is the bath wherein Israel is cleansed!
Finkelstein. *Avukah Annual*, 1932, p. 94.

127.8 Eating bread without first washing the hands is like prostituting oneself.
Ammi, Assi. *Talmud: Sota*, 4b. See *DPB*, ed Singer, 4.

127.9 As the sun is not defiled by shining on dung and mire, so the pure in mind, though encompassed by the defilements of earth, cleanse and are not themselves defiled.
Apocrypha: Patriarchs, Benjamin, 8.3.

127.10 Self mortification robs you of the strength you need for devotions and Torah; a bath invigorates you.
Baal Shem. See BTH, i. 52.

127.11 Washing your hands before a meal . . . is in itself a trivial act . . . but when you wash your hands by the command of God, . . . the souls of all the generations that lived and died to sanctify His name come into some kind of touch with you!
Berdichevsky, *Din uDebarim*, 1900, p. 63. q SHR, 372.

127.12 Just as it is forbidden to declare the unclean clean, so is it forbidden to declare the clean unclean.
Eleazar. *Talmud J: Terumot*, 5.3.

127.13 Pass not your unwashed hands over your eyes.
Eliezer b. Isaac. *Orhot Hayyim*, c. 1050.

127.14 Sickness and poverty are found in foul dwellings.
Eliezer Halevi, *Tzavaah*, c. 1350.

127.15 He who is physically unclean has no soul.
J. M. Epstein, *Kitzur Shné Luhot Ha-Berit*, 1683, p. 61b.

127.16 As custodians must keep clean the statues of the king, so must we keep clean our body, the icon of the Holy One.
Hillel. *Tosefta: Sota*, 4.13.

127.17 Laborers are paid for engaging in dirty work; Jews are promised reward for keeping clean.
Hiyya b. Abba. *Cant R.*, 5.16.4.

127.18 Death does not defile, nor does ritual water purify. To wash after contact with the dead is a command we must not question.
Johanan b. Zakkai. *Pesikta Kahana*, ed Buber, 36a. Ref. to *Num.* 19.

127.19 The chief solicitude of the Jew for twenty-five or thirty centuries has been to be clean.
*Leroy-Beaulieu, *Israel Among the Nations*, 1895, p. 125.

127.20 The Jews, both men and women, bathe in all lands, at all seasons of the year, without any prejudice to their health.
*Locke, *Some Thoughts Concerning Education,* 1692, #7.

127.21 A house that was invaded by thieves, or tax and customs collectors, is unclean.
Maimonides, *Responsa,* ed Freimann, #149, p. 143.

127.22 Physical cleanliness leads to the sanctification of the soul from reprehensible opinions.
Maimonides, *Yad: Tumat Oklin,* 1180, 15.12.

127.23 Impurity does not sing, for it knows no joy. It is the source of melancholy.
Nahman Bratzlav, *Likuté Moharan,* (1874), 54a.

127.24 Clothing, bed, table, especially dishes, indeed everything that we ever take in our hands, must be clean, sweet, pure; and above and beyond all, the body, made in the image of God.
Orhot Tzaddikim, 15C, ch 1.

127.25 It is a purification of the spirit to keep the body clean.
Pseudo-Phocylides, *Nuthetikon,* c. 100 B. C. E.

127.26 Have no spot on your clothes and shoes when you go to synagog.
Sefer Hasidim, 13C, #1064, p. 270.

127.27 To him who wishes to defile himself, the doors are open; to him who wishes to purify himself, aid will be given.
Simeon b. Lakish. *Talmud: Sabbath,* 104a.

127.28 Wash your face, hands and feet daily in honor of your Maker.
Talmud: Sabbath, 50b.

127.29 Cleanliness is the genius of plenty; filth, of poverty.
Talmud: Pesahim, 11b.

127.30 No dirt comes from Heaven.
Talmud: Sanhedrin, 59b.

127.31 Hold on to a defiling object, and no amount of ablution, even in holy water, will purify you. Drop the reptile and the slightest immersion will cleanse you.
Tosefta: Taanit, 1.8.

127.32 A soldier must admire the singular attention that was paid (in Israel) to the rules of cleanliness.
*Washington, *Instructions for Soldiers,* 1777.

127.33 Dirty hands are unfit for the recital of Grace.
Zuhamai. *Talmud: Berakot,* 53b.

128. CLERGY

128.1 Not so much what a man says in the pulpit, but what he does out of the pulpit, gives power to his ministry.
Berkowitz, sermon, June 15, 1901. BBR, 255.

128.2 A Catholic priest walks as if heaven belonged to him; a Protestant clergyman . . . as if he had taken a lease of it.
Heine, *City of Lucca,* 1831, ch 4.

128.3 He who is not well versed in the laws of marriage and divorce should not officiate at these ceremonies.
Samuel. *Talmud: Kiddushin,* 6a.

128.4 Clericalism, as history shows, has ever been one of the chief hindrances to social progress.
H. Samuel, *Belief and Action,* 1937, p. 47.

128.5 Among all professions, that of the clergy stands in need of knowledge the fullest, of sympathy the deepest, of unselfishness the most perfect, of character the most spotless.
S. Singer, "Where the Clergy Fail," Jan. 17, 1904. *Lectures and Addresses,* 1908, p. 24.

128.6 Popular religion may be summed up as respect for ecclesiastics.
Spinoza, *Theologico-Political Treatise.* 1670, Preface.

129. CLEVERNESS

129.1 He takes the wise in their own craftiness.
Bible: Job, 5.13.

129.2 When wisdom enters, subtlety comes along.
Abbahu. *Talmud: Sota,* 21b.

129.3 Shrewdness is often annoying, like a lamp in a bedroom.
Boerne, *Fragmente & Aphorismen,* 1840, #276.

129.4 There is no cleverness like the cleverness of a Jew.
Ibn Verga, *Shebet Yehuda,* (1550) 1855, #12, p. 35.

129.5 His very subtlety has led him into error.
Raba. *Talmud: Baba Metzia,* 96b.

129.6 To want to be the cleverest of all is the biggest folly.
Sholom Aleichem, *SAB,* 1926, p. 350.

129.7 The devil brought curses on the world through cleverness.
Zohar, Gen., 35b.

130. CLOCK

130.1 Even the costliest clock owns no more than sixty minutes an hour.
Sam Liptzin, *A Vort far a Vort*, 1955, p. 13.

130.2 A clock that stands entirely still is "right" by coincidence twice a day.
A. Myerson, *Speaking of Man*, 1950, p. 60. See Hershfield, *Now I'll Tell One, 1938*, p. 71.

130.3 A watch is the symbol of man. His heart, too, beats incessantly. . . . The slightest breeze may change his course; and his moods, swinging between hope and despair, may be brought to a sudden halt by the least jar.
Zunser, *Der Zeiger*, 1861. See Liptzin, *Eliakum Zunser*, 77.

131. COAL TO NEWCASTLE

131.1 Would you bring straw to Afrayim, . . . fleece to Damascus, or witchcraft to Egypt?
Proverb. q Aha. *Gen. R.*, 86.5.

132. COMFORT

132.1 Comfort ye, comfort ye My people.
Bible: Isa, 40.1. See 52.9.

132.2 As one whom his mother comforts, so will I comfort you.
Ibid., 66.13. See *Zech.*, 1.17.

132.3 Thy rod and Thy staff, they comfort me.
Bible: Ps., 23.4.

132.4 When my cares are many, . . . Thy comforts delight my soul.
Ibid., 94.19.

132.5 Sorry comforters are ye all.
Bible: Job, 16.2.

132.6 She has none to comfort her among all her lovers.
Bible: Lam., 1.2.

132.7 Heaven gives us comfort; from people we expect assistance.
Boerne, *Vermischte Aufsätze*, #22, July 1829.

132.8 Be comforted, master, that you returned pure and whole the jewel entrusted to you!
Eleazar b. Arak, to Johanan b. Zakkai, who had lost a son. *ARN*, ch 14.

132.9 Man finds some consolation in trouble befalling others.
Josippon, c. 940, ch 22.

132.10 Do not attempt to console your neighbor while his dead still lies before him.
Simeon b. Eleazar. *Mishna: Abot*, 4.18.

132.11 What trade have we with comfort well-bestowed,
Who are the world's uncomfortable goad!
L. Untermeyer, "Lost Jerusalem," *Roast Leviathan*, 1923.

133. COMMANDMENTS

133.A. Classification and Number

133.A.1 The main purpose of precepts performed with our bodies and limbs is to arouse our attention to those performed with the heart and mind, which are the pillars of the service of God.
Bahya, *Hobot HaLebabot*, 1040, 8.3.21.

133.A.2 The commandments are divided first into those which effect the welfare of the body and those which effect the welfare of the soul, and secondly into the practical and the speculative.
Caspi, *Yoré Deah*, 14C, ch 2. AHE, 133.

133.A.3 613 commandments were given to Moses, 365 negative, corresponding to the days of the year, and 248 positive, corresponding to the number of joints in the human body.
Simlai. *Talmud: Makkot*, 23b.

133.A.4 Moses was given 613 precepts. David summed these up in eleven [*Ps.* 15], Isaiah in six [33.16f], Micah in three [6.8], Isaiah again in two [56.1], and finally Habakkuk based them all on one principle, Faith [2.4].
Ibid., 23b–24a.

133.B. Character

133.B.1 The commandment . . . is not too hard for you, nor far off. It is not in heaven . . . nor beyond the sea. . . . But the word is very nigh to you, in your mouth and heart, that you may do it.
Bible: Deut., 30.11–14.

133.B.2 The precepts of the Lord are right, rejoicing the heart; the commandment of the Lord is pure, enlightening the eyes. . . . The ordinances of the Lord are true, they are righteous altogether, more desirable than gold, . . . sweeter than honey.
Bible: Ps., 19.9–11.

133.B.3 Thy statutes have been my songs in the house of my pilgrimage.
Ibid., 119.54.

133.B.4 The commandment is a lamp, and the teaching is a light.
Bible Prov., 6.23.

133.B.5 A commandment is to the Torah what a lamp is to the sun.
Johanan b. Nappaha. *Midrash Tehillim*, 17.7.

133.B.6 Each commandment . . . has a unique musical quality . . . which evokes reverent joy and song within us.
Kook, *Eder HaYekor*, 1906, p. 44. q ABJ, 199.

133.B.7 The Holy One does not come to Israel with burdensome laws.
Rab. *Pesikta Rabbati*, ch 16, ed Friedmann, 84b.

133.B.8 The lightest and weightiest of the precepts are alike. The command for fringes is in the ritual next to the *Shema*.
Seder Eliyahu Rabbah, ch 24 (26), ed Friedmann, 132.

133.C. Purpose

133.C.1 Ye shall keep My statutes . . . which if a man do, he shall live by them.
Bible: Lev., 18.5. See *Deut.*, 6.24.

133.C.2 *"Live* by them"—not die under them.
Ishmael. *Talmud: Sanhedrin*, 74a.

133.C.3 The sacred commandments were given for the sake of righteousness, to arouse pious thoughts and to form character.
Apocrypha: Aristeas, 144.

133.C.4 The Holy One desired to make Israel worthy, so He gave them many laws and commandments.
Hanania b. Akashia. *Mishna: Makkot*, 3.16.

133.C.5 A truth, to produce results, must be impressed upon the mind and heart repeatedly and emphatically. This is the essential concept of the *Edoth* (symbolic observances).
S. R. Hirsch, *Nineteen Letters*, (1836) #13, p. 118.

133.C.6 The essence of all precepts is to make the heart upright.
A. Ibn Ezra, *Commentary*, to *Deut.* 5.18. *Yesod Mora*, (1158) 1840, ch 7, p. 30.

133.C.7 With each new command, God adds holiness to Israel.
Issi b. Akabia. *Mekilta*, to *Exod.* 22.30.

133.C.8 The commandments were not given for physical enjoyment.
Judah b. Ilai. *Talmud: Erubin*, 31a.

133.C.9 The Torah is the mighty stream of spirituality. . . . It would have caused no useful fruits to grow . . . had not the *mitzva* been there to lead its divine floods into the houses, the hearts and minds of the individual members of the people.
M. Jung, 1917. q HBJ, 200.

133.C.10 The commandments are the canals through which flow constantly the Torah's abundant faith and love.
Kook. q Tzoref, *Hayye HaRav Kook*, 1947, p. 189.

133.C.11 The purpose of the laws of the Torah is . . . to promote compassion, loving-kindness and peace in the world.
Maimonides, *Yad: Sabbath*, 1180, 2.3.

133.C.12 If you will enter into life, keep the commandments.
New Testament: Matt., 19.17.

133.C.13 Their purpose is to unify the nation and refine man's nature.
Pines, *Yaldé Ruhi*, 1872.

133.C.14 The precepts were given expressly to purify mankind.
Rab. *Gen. R.*, 44.1. See *Tanhuma, Shemini*, ed Buber, #12, 15b.

133.C.15 Israel is shielded by its precepts as a dove by its wings.
Talmud: Sabbath, 130a.

133.C.16 How well suited is this people to the commandments, which are as a bridle in their mouths and as a yoke on their necks!
Targum, to *Cant.* Cf Gollancz, *Targum*, 24.

133.D. Observance

133.D.1 Hear, O Israel, the statutes . . . that ye may learn them, and observe to do them.
Bible: Deut., 5.1.

133.D.2 The important thing is not how many separate injunctions are obeyed, but how and in what spirit we obey them.
Baal Shem. q SSJ, i. 29.

133.D.3 Rush toward a light precept, and flee from sin, for one precept leads to another, and one sin entails another.
Ben Azzai. *Mishna: Abot*, 4.2.

133.D.4 All the commandments follow three ways: faith, word, and deed. As one is basic in mathematics, so the essence of every commandment, whether it depends on speech or action, is faith of heart. If it has not that, all else is meaningless.

A. Ibn Ezra, *Yesod Mora*, 1158, ch 7, 1840, p. 27.

133.D.5 As one should not be slow when baking *matza*, lest it leaven, so one should not be slow when performing a *mitzva*.

Joshua b. Karha. *Talmud: Nazir*, 23b. Josiah. *Mekilta*, to *Exod*. 12.17.

133.D.6 Be as scrupulous about a light precept as about a weighty one, for you know not the reward which good deeds yield.

Judah HaNasi. *Mishna: Abot*, 2.1.

133.D.7 Think what you like, but carry out the commandments.

q Loewe, *Rabbinic Anthology*, p. xcvi, jibe at Breslau school.

133.D.8 He who undertakes to fulfill faithfully one precept is worthy of the Holy Spirit.

Nehemiah. *Mekilta*, to *Exod*. 14.31.

133.D.9 If you perform a precept with impatience, irritation and weariness, you blow out its reward [*Mal*. 1.13].

Saadia, letter to a Jewish community, 928. See KTJ, 87.

133.D.10 Do especially the precepts that are generally neglected.

Sefer Hasidim, 13C, #1, p. 2; #586, p. 160.

133.D.11 Forego not an occasion to observe a religious precept.

Simeon b. Lakish. *Talmud: Yoma*, 33a.

133.D.12 It is forbidden to observe a precept through a transgression.

Simeon b. Yohai. *Talmud: Sukka*, 30a.

133.D.13 If a man nails up a mezuza, did I not give him the house? If he attaches holy fringes, did I not give him the garment?

Yalkut Shimoni, to *Job* 41.3.

134. COMMERCE

134.1 Tyre, the crowning city, whose merchants are princes, whose traffickers are the honorable of the earth.

Bible: Isa., 23.8.

134.2 It is naught, it is naught, says the buyer; but when he is gone his way, then he boasts.

Bible: Prov., 20.14.

134.3 If the goods are near at hand, the owner consumes them; if they are at a distance, they consume him.

Alphabet of Ben Sira, 19.

134.4 A merchant shall hardly keep himself from wrong doing, and a huckster will not be acquitted of sin.

Apocrypha: Ben Sira, 26.29.

134.5 A peg will stay between the joinings of stones, and sin will intrude between buyer and seller.

Ibid., 27.2.

134.6 When prices drop, buy.

Bar Kappara. *Talmud: Berakot*, 63a.

134.7 Who buys what he does not want sells what he wants.

Bonsenyor, *Dichos y Sentencias*, 14C, #524.

134.8 The old idea of a good bargain was a transaction in which one man got the better of another. The new idea of a good contract is a transaction which is good for both parties to it.

Brandeis, address, Brown University, 1912.

134.9 Transact no business with your kith and kin.

Hai Gaon, *Musar Haskel*, c. 1000. HPB, 75.

134.10 Merchants throughout the world have the same religion.

Heine. *Letters from Berlin*, #2, March 16, 1822.

134.11 Give me a wide and noble field
 Where I may perish decently!
O let me in this narrow world
 Of shops be not condemned to
 die!

Heine, *New Poems: Anno 1829*, 1853.

134.12 The Creator, . . . to make commerce in the earth, gave not to every place all things, but parted his benefits amongst them.

Manasseh b. Israel, *Vindication of the Jews*, 1656, vi.

134.13 If the wheat is of the quality represented in the sale, neither seller nor buyer may cancel the transaction.

Mishna: Baba Bathra, 5.6.

134.14 Merchants show first their inferior wares.

Num. R., 16.12.

134.15 Merchants, for the sake of gain, cross the seas and compass the wide world, letting nothing stand in their way, summer heat or winter cold, violent gales or contrary winds, old age or physical ailment, the society of friends or the pleasure beyond words which we take in wife, child/en and all else that is our own, . . . all the gracious amenities of civic life.

Philo, *Migration of Abraham*, 39.

134.16 Sell your merchandise while the dust of your buying trip is still on your boots.

Rab. *Talmud: Pesahim*, 113a.

134.17 There are only two or three times in a man's life when there are absolutely no clouds on the horizon, when everything insures that securities will go up. When that time comes, sell short.

N. Rothschild.

135. COMMUNISM

135.1 Cast in your lot among us; let us all have one purse.

Bible: Prov., 1.14.

135.2 Communism has its origins in the socialism of Proudhon, of Louis Blanc, of Saint-Simon, of Babeuf, who, if they were Jews, concealed that fact well.

Fleg, *Why I Am a Jew*, 1929, p. 77.

135.3 Communism, though it be at present but little discussed, and now yearns away its life in forgotten garrets on wretched straw-pallets, is still the gloomy hero to whom a great if transitory part is assigned in the modern tragedy, and which only waits its cue to enter on the stage. We should never lose sight of this.

Heine, *Lutetia*, June 20, 1842.

135.4 It is with dread and horror that I think of the time when these gloomy iconoclasts will attain power; when their heavy hands will break without pity all the marble statues of beauty which are so dear to my heart. They will . . . fell my groves of laurel and plant potatoes in their place, . . . and ah! my book of songs will be used by the grocers to make paper cornets in which to put coffee or snuff for the cold women of the future.

Ibid., Preface to French ed, 1855.

135.5 The theory of Communism may be summed up in one sentence: Abolish all private property.

Marx, *Communist Manifesto*, 1848.

135.6 Let the ruling classes tremble at a Communist revolution. The proletarians have nothing to lose but their chains. They have a world to win. Workers of all countries, unite!

Ibid.

136. COMMUNITY

136.1 In the merely religious congrega-tion . . . there is not the mutual criticism which organizes men into a moral society.

S. Alexander, *Space, Time and Deity*, (1920) 1927, ii. 412.

136.2 It is now more than ever necessary to preserve the Jewish community in a vital form.

Einstein, *Cosmic Religion*, 1929, p. 76.

136.3 Many of the precepts apply only to certain individuals, places and circumstances. It is only when all Jews are together as a community that the whole Torah can be fulfilled.

J. M. Epstein, *Kitzur Shné Luhot Ha-Berit*, 1683, p. 6b.

136.4 Conquer the communal organizations!

Herzl, address, II Zionist Congress, 1898.

136.5 Separate not yourself from the community.

Hillel. *Mishna: Abot*, 2.4.

136.6 Join a community, by which alone your work can be made universal and eternal in its results.

S. R. Hirsch, *Nineteen Letters*, (1836) #12, p. 116.

136.7 The wolf grabs the sheep that strays from the flock.

q M. Ibn Ezra, *Shirat Yisrael*, (12C) 1924, p. 147.

136.8 A community is too heavy for anyone to carry alone.

Isaac. *Deut. R.*, 1.10.

136.9 Communal activity is as meritorious as studying Torah.

Jeremiah. *Talmud J: Berakot*, 5.1.

136.10 Prayers for the community take precedence over those for ourselves . . . and he who sets its claims above his private interests is especially acceptable to God.

Josephus, *Against Apion*, 2.23.

136.11 Why is the Confession couched in the plural? . . . Because all Israel is one body, and every Jew is a member of that body. Hence follows mutual responsibility among all the members.

I. Luria. q Hertz, *DPB*, 906.

136.12 By virtue of his nature, man seeks to form communities.

Maimonides, *Guide for the Perplexed*, 1190, 3.49.

136.13 The wicked son is he who excludes himself from the community.

Mekilta, to *Exod.* 13.8.

136.14 A community's fiscal authority may not be of less than two.
Mishna: Shekalim, 5.2.

136.15 The community is to the civilized man what the atmosphere is to the body. If it is pure and wholesome, he is healthy. If it is close and stifling, he stifles. If it is cut off, he dies.
H. Samuel, *Belief and Action,* 1937, p. 178.

136.16 Who shares in the community's trouble will also share in its consolation.
Seder Eliyahu Zuta, ch 1, ed Friedmann, 167. *T: Taanit* 11a.

136.17 The community is Israel's rampart.
Simeon b. Lakish. *Talmud: Baba Bathra,* 8a.

136.18 I believe in a world where there is a great deal of power at the local level, at the bottom, at the community, like a pyramid. What we've done is reverse it: the power is on the top, the weakness at the bottom. Russia is the best example of that. We must go back to communities.
Tannenbaum. q H. Breit. *N.Y. Times,* March 11, 1951.

136.19 When a man puts on the phylactery of the hand, he should stretch out his left arm as though to draw to him the Community of Israel and to embrace her with the right arm [*Cant.* 2.6].
Zohar, Lev., 55a.

137. COMPENSATION

137.1 First I charge a retainer, then I charge a reminder, next I charge a refresher, and then I charge a finisher.
J. P. Benjamin.

137.2 What people give you, you must repay with what you have, or, more expensively, with what you are.
Boerne, *Ueber den Umgang mit Menschen,* 1824.

137.3 Each country has some cheerful compensation for a sad privation: the heartless North has its iron strength, the sickly South its golden sun, . . . the famished French are refreshed by a bountiful wit, and England's fog is transfigured by liberty.
Boerne, *Denkrede auf Jean Paul,* 1825.

137.4 The soil produces no flowers unless it had first been watered by the rain.
q M. Ibn Ezra, *Shirat Yisrael,* (12C) 1924, p. 82.

137.5 Birds come down only where there are seeds to be picked.
Ibid.

137.6 To the tune of my fee, dance for me.
Midrash Tehillim, 16.13, ed Buber, 62b.

137.7 I could see virtue in every client— and the greater the fee the greater the virtue.
W. B. Rubin, on his 81st birthday. *Milwaukee Sentinel,* Sept. 2, 1954.

137.8 Exact no fee for teaching Torah. God gave it gratis.
Talmud: Derek Eretz, ch 3.

138. COMPETITION

138.1 If you have run with footmen and they have wearied you, then how can you contend with horses?
Bible: Jer., 12.5.

138.2 Compete not with evil-doers.
Bible. Ps., 37.1.

138.3 I considered all labor and all excelling in work, that it is a man's rivalry with his neighbor.
Bible: Eccles., 4.4.

138.4 Just: who gave no cut-throat competition to his neighbor.
Aha b. Hanina. *Talmud: Sanhedrin,* 81a. See Simlai. *Makkot,* 24a.

138.5 To vie is not to rival.
Disraeli, *The Young Duke,* 1831.

138.6 The competitive urge is a fine, wholesome direction of energy. But . . . the desire to win must be wedded to an ideal, an ethical way of life. It must never become so strong that it dwarfs every other aspect of the game of life.
Holman. E. R. Murrow, *This I Believe,* 1952, p. 74.

138.7 Everybody dislikes his fellow-craftsman.
Levi. *Gen. R.,* 19.4.

138.8 Promote yourself, but do not demote another.
Lipkin. q KTH, i. 271.

138.9 The emancipation of the masses can become a reality only with the abolition of the competitive system of society.
London, speech, U.S. Congress, 1916. RES, 87.

138.10 It is by competition only, by unlimited liberty, and equality of the laws of buying and selling, that the general welfare can be obtained.

M. Mendelssohn, Pref. to *Vindiciae Judaeorum*, 1782.

138.11 The powerful force of competition . . . will not disappear in a Socialist society, but . . . will be sublimated. . . . The liberated passions will be channelized into techniques.

Trotsky, *Literature and Revolution*. 1925, p. 230.

139. COMPOSITION

139.1 We have not found . . . abridging to be a light business. On the contrary, we have sweated and sat up late over it.

Apocrypha: II Macc., 2.26.

139.2 The great legislator of the Hebrews orders us to pull off the fruit for the first three years, and not to taste them. He was not ignorant how it weakens a young tree to bring to maturity its first fruits. Thus, on literary compositions, our green essays ought to be picked away. The word *zamar*, by a beautiful metaphor from *pruning trees*, means in Hebrew to *compose verses*.

D'Israeli. *Curiosities: Literary Composition*, 1793.

139.3 Composing is like organizing a meal. The different dishes must be so arranged as to rouse the appetite and renew the pleasure with each course.

q M. Ibn Ezra, *Shirat Yisrael*, (12C) 1924, p. 35.

139.4 The best composition is the little which holds much, that instructs and does not weary.

q *Ibid.*, 120.

139.5 If a composer doesn't write from the heart, he simply can't compose good music.

Schoenberg. Armitage, *Schoenberg*, 249.

140. COMPROMISE

140.1 It is forbidden to arbitrate . . . but let the law take its course, let justice cut through the mountain.

Eliezer b. José. *Talmud: Sanhedrin*, 6b.

140.2 It is meritorious to compromise.

Joshua b. Karha. *Tosefta: Sanhedrin*, 1.3.

140.3 Abraham said to the Holy One: There can be no absolute justice and an abiding world. If Thou wouldst hold the cord by both ends, Thou must forego a little.

Levi. *Gen. R.*, 39.6.

140.4 A temporary compromise is a diplomatic act, but a permanent compromise is the abandonment of a goal.

L. Stein, *Journey into the Self*, 1950. p. 145.

141. CONCEIT

141.1 The haughtiness of men shall be bowed down: The Lord alone shall be exalted in that day.

Bible: Isa., 2.11. See 2.17.

141.2 Woe unto them that are wise in their own eyes.

Ibid., 5.21. See *Prov.*, 3.7, 26.12; *Rom.*, 12.16.

141.3 Because . . . you said: I am a god, . . . and your heart is lifted up because of your riches, . . . I will bring strangers upon you.

Bible: Ezek., 28.2, 5, 7.

141.4 Pride has beguiled you . . . that say in your heart: "Who shall bring me down to earth?"

Bible. Obad., 1.3.

141.5 The haughty of eye and proud of heart I will not suffer.

Bible: Ps., 101.5.

141.6 Everyone proud in heart is an abomination to the Lord.

Bible: Prov., 16.5.

141.7 Pride goes before destruction, and a haughty spirit before a fall.

Ibid., 16.18. See *Ben Sira*, 1.30.

141.8 He who esteems himself highly because of his knowledge is like a corpse at the wayside: the passer-by turns his head away in disgust and walks quickly by.

Akiba. *Abot de R. Nathan*, ch 11.

141.9 A man afflicted with haughtiness will be disturbed by the slightest breeze.

Alexandri. *Talmud: Sota*, 5a.

141.10 God overthrows the throne of the proud, and sets the humble in their place.

Apocrypha: Ben Sira, 10.14. See 10.16.

141.11 Pride in religious activity affects people more readily than all other injurious influences.

Bahya, *Hobot HaLebabot*, 1040, introd. to 6. See 4.6, 8.5.

141.12 How can a creature that twice passed through a cloaca of urine and blood be proud and arrogant?

Ibid., 6.5.

141.13 No counsel can be given on how to break pride. We must struggle with it all the days of our life.
Ber. q BTH, i. 100.

141.14 I can tolerate a fool better than him who is wise in his own eyes.
Berekia HaNakden, *Mishlé Shualim*, c. 1260, ch 58.

141.15 Nothing is more dangerous for a poor man than pride.
Brenner, *HaYerushalmi*, ch 1. Cf *Talmud: Pesahim*, 113b.

141.16 Pride blinds.
S. Cohen, *Mishlé Agur*, 1803, 28.

141.17 A man of haughty spirit, . . . the Shekina laments over him.
Eleazar b. Pedat. *Talmud: Sota*, 5a.

141.18 Pride and envy, . . . with which even the pious among us seem infected, form the greatest menace to our spiritual integrity.
Eybeshitz, *Keshet Yehonathan*, (1784) 1873, p. 6a.

141.19 I am glad I am guilty of some sins, else I might be guilty of one of the greatest sins of all—conceit.
M. Hurwitz, *Imré Noam*, (1877) 1907, p. 4b.

141.20 O habitants of homes of clay,
 Why lift ye such a swelling eye,
 Ye are but as the beasts that die,
 What do ye boast of more than they?
Ibn Gabirol, *Selected Religious Poems*, 61.

141.21 Pride and greed are the ferment which prevents the Redemption, and these are unhappily exemplified in the conduct of scholars, judges, leaders and servants of the people.
Margolioth, *Hibburé Likkutim*, 1715, Introd.

141.22 Haughtiness toward men is rebellion to God.
Nahmanides, letter to his son Nahman, c. 1268. HPB, 174.

141.23 Arrogance is the gate to many evils.
.*Orhot Tzaddikim*, 15C, ch 1.

141.24 Arrogance, companion of indigence.
Parhon, *Mahberet HeAruk*, 1160.

141.25 Leaven is forbidden because of the rising it produces, and none who ap-proaches the altar should be puffed up.
Philo, *Special Laws*, i. 53.

141.26 Arrogance is equivalent to all the other sins.
Rab. *Talmud: Sukka*, 29b.

141.27 Because you are sinless, exalt not yourself above other men.
Seder Eliyahu Rabbah, ch 18, ed Friedmann, p. 104.

141.28 A haughty man is like an idolator.
Simeon b. Yohai. *Talmud: Sota*, 4b.

141.29 Walking with a haughty air is like pushing the Shekina.
Talmud: Berakot, 43b. Cf Joshua b. Levi. .*Kiddushin*, 31a.

141.30 When haughtiness multiplies, discord increases.
Talmud: Sota, 47b.

141.31 If ever man becomes proud, let him remember that a mosquito preceded him in the divine order of creation!
Tosefta: Sanhedrin, 8.8.

141.32 God said: There's no room in the world for both the arrogant and Me.
Ukba. *Talmud: Sota*, 5a.

141.33 Pride is the root of all evils.
Vital, *Shaaré HaKedusha*, (c. 1600) 1876, p. 15a.

141.34 Who gives himself airs here is humbled hereafter.
Yalkut, to *Ezek*. 21.31.

142. CONCENTRATION

142.1 The whole art of practical success consists in concentrating all efforts at all times upon one point.
Lassalle, *Open Letter to the Central Committee*, 1863.

142.2 None ever got ahead of me except the man of one task.
Rossi, *Meor Enayim*, 1573.

142.3 Stick to your brewery, and you will be the great brewer of London. Be brewer and banker and merchant and manufacturer, and you will soon be in the *Gazette*.
N. M. Rothschild, to Sir Thomas Buxton. q Emerson, *Conduct of Life: Power*, 1860.

142.4 The eternal secret of all great art, yes of every mortal achievement . . . : Concentration.
S. Zweig, *World of Yesterday*, 1943, p. 149.

143. CONFESSION

143.1 Who confesses and forsakes [his sins] shall obtain mercy.
Bible: Prov., 28.13.

143.2 He cleanses a soul from sin, when it makes confession.
Apocrypha: Psalms of Solomon, 9.12.

143.3 To confess one's sins is to honor the Holy One.
Joshua b. Levi. *Talmud: Sanhedrin,* 43b.

143.4 He is brazen who recounts his sins openly.
Kahana. *Talmud: Berakot,* 34b.

143.5 If anything discreditable be in you, be the first to tell it.
Proverb, q Raba. *Talmud: Baba Kamma,* 92b.

143.6 A litigant's admission is worth a hundred witnesses.
Talmud: Gittin, 64a. *Kiddushin,* 65b.

144. CONFORMITY

144.1 The spirit of Judaism is conformity in deed and freedom in dogma.
M. Mendelssohn, letter to Wolf, July 11, 1782.

144.2 Be not conformed to this world.
New Testament: Rom., 12.2.

144.3 Fair fame is won as a rule by all who cheerfully take things as they find them and interfere with no established custom.
Philo, *Migration of Abraham,* 16.

144.4 Rejoice not among weepers, weep not among rejoicers.
Talmud: Derek Eretz, ch 7. *Kalla,* 10. See *Matt.* 11.17; *Rom.,* 12.15.

145. CONQUEST

145.1 The blood of Canaan's conquerors,
It will not cease to flow.
Their mighty song still calls to me,
The song of blood and fire:
"Ascend the hill, descend the vale,
Possess what you desire!"
Chernihovsky, "A Melody," 1916, tr FTH, 66.

145.2 Great conquerors are the powerful mixers of cultures and races, they loosen the bonds binding the spirit to the supernatural, and prepare the way for liberty and individuality.
F. Hertz, *Race and Civilization,* 1928, p. 307.

145.3 Conquerors here are the conquered in the hereafter.
Sefer Hasidim, 13C, #14, p. 15.

145.4 This abominable nation [Jews] has succeeded in spreading its customs throughout all lands; the conquered have given their laws to the conquerors.
Seneca, De Superstitione, fragm. 36. q Augustine, *City of God,* 6.11.

145.5 Minds are not conquered by force, but by love and high-mindedness.
Spinoza, *Ethics,* 1677, iv. Appendix 11.

146. CONSCIENCE

146.1 I know my transgression, and my sin is ever before me.
Bible: Ps., 51.5.

146.2 I'd rather be called a fool all my life than lose my conscience for one moment.
Akabia b. Mahalalel. *Mishna: Eduyot,* 5.6.

146.3 A good digestion depends upon a good conscience.
Disraeli, *Young Duke,* 1831, ch 12.

146.4 Real human progress depends not so much on inventive ingenuity as on conscience.
Einstein. *Avukah Annual,* 1932, p. 3.

146.5 You can eat better on ten percent—but you sleep better on five.
Hershfield, *Now I'll Tell One,* 1938, p. 25.

146.6 One pang of conscience is worth more than many lashes.
José b. Halafta. *Talmud: Berakot,* 7a.

146.7 The armies most successful in war are those in which every combatant has a clear conscience.
Josephus, *Wars,* 2.20.7.

146.8 Be master of your will and slave to your conscience.
Lazerov, *Enciklopedie fun Idishe Vitzen,* 1928, #445.

146.9 Conscience is, like charity, a Semitic importation. Israel introduced it into the world.
Leroy-Beaulieu, Israel Among the Nations, 1895, p. 194f.

146.10 Be not wicked in your own esteem.
Simeon b. Nathaniel. *Mishna: Abot,* 2.13.

147. CONSEQUENCE

147.1 Can a man take fire in his bosom, and his clothes not burn?
Bible: Prov., 6.27.

147.2 If you chop wood, chips will fall.
Proverb (Yiddish). BJS, 1075.

147.3 A hen can't be slaughtered without blood being shed.

Proverb (Yiddish). BJS, #1169.

147.4 Let his head be cut off, and let him not die!

Simeon b. Yohai. *Talmud: Ketubot*, 6a.

147.5 Some paradox of our natures leads us when once we have made our fellow men the objects of our enlightened interest, to go on to make them the objects of our pity, then of our wisdom, ultimately of our coercion.

Trilling, *The Liberal Imagination*, 1950.

148. CONSERVATISM

148.1 A conservative Government is an organized hypocrisy.

Disraeli, speech, House of Commons, March 17, 1845.

148.2 There is, in all the world, perhaps nothing more stubbornly conservative than the talmudic Jew.

*Leroy-Beaulieu, *Israel Among the Nations*, 1895, p. 63.

148.3 The very survival of Judaism is due to the strictest conservatism known to history.

Rathenau, *Staat und Judentum*, 1911.

148.4 Jews derive their notions of liberty and social justice from the Torah of Moses; and in view of the honorable antiquity of that source, should not those notions be properly described as conservative?

*Solovyov, "Talmud": *Ruskaya Mysl*, 1886.

148.5 All radicalism and all conservatism has its value and its danger. It is through the dialogue between them that the march of progress is maintained.

Valentin, *Antisemitism*, 1936, p. 254.

148.6 No man can be a conservative unless he has something to lose.

J. P. Warburg.

149. CONSISTENCY

149.1 The wise man does not expect consistency or harmony . . . for he sees that man is a mosaic of characteristics and qualities that only rarely achieve an internal and intrinsic harmony.

A. Myerson, *Speaking of Man*, 1950, p. 9.

149.2 It is also said of me that I now and then contradict myself. Yes, I improve wonderfully as time goes on.

G. J. Nathan, *The Theatre in the Fifties*, 1953, p. 298.

149.3 The Jewish God is no philosopher and his path is tangled with logical contradictions.

L. Roth, *Jewish Thought as a Factor in Civilization*, 1954, p. 22.

149.4 Whatever the faults of the Rabbis were, consistency was not one of them.

Schechter, *Some Aspects of Rabbinic Theology*, 1910, p. 46.

149.5 He begins with a pitcher and ends with a barrel.

Talmud: Baba Kamma, 27a.

150. CONTEMPLATION

150.1 While I was musing, the fire was kindled.

Bible: Ps., 39.4.

150.2 A great work always leaves us in a state of musing.

D'Israeli, *Literary Character*, 1795, ch 8.

150.3 The act of contemplation creates the thing contemplated.

Ibid., ch 11.

150.4 Contemplation imbues the righteous with a sense of true reverence and humility, and makes him heedless of anyone who may scoff at him and his devotions.

Isserles, gloss to *Orah Hayyim*, 1.1., on *Ps.* 16.8.

150.5 He who meditates over words of Torah, finds ever new meanings in them.

Rashi, *Commentary*, to *Cant.* 5.15.

150.6 Contemplation, weighty contemplation, must be the foundation of any creative work.

Shofman, *Kol Kitbé*, iv. 138.

151. CONTENTMENT

151.1 The slave is a freeman if content with his lot, the freeman's a slave if he seeks more than that.

Al-Harizi, *Tahkemoni*, 13C, ch 42.

151.2 He who enjoys his labor and is content . . . avoids intestinal trouble and heart-ache. . . . True riches is contentment.

Anav, *Sefer Maalot HaMiddot*, (13C), ch 23, q JJC, 293.

151.3 With little or with much, be content.

Apocrypha: Ben Sira, 29.23.

151.4 Discontent is the source of trouble, but also of progress.

B. Auerbach, *On the Heights*, 1865.

151.5 Who is rich? He who rejoices in his lot.

Ben Zoma. *Mishna: Abot*, 4.1.

151.6 Most people are dissatisfied, because too few know that the distance between one and nothing is greater than that between one and a thousand.

Boerne, *Der Narr im weissen Schwan,* ch 2.

151.7 I look on contentment as the very epitome of depravity.

Brod, *The Master,* 1951, ch 6, p. 273.

151.8 The Jews have always been malcontents.

Lazare, *Antisemitism,* (1892), 1903, p. 276.

151.9 The cautious seeks happiness through union with God, and is content here with little.

Maimon b. Joseph, *Letter of Consolation,* 1160.

151.10 Be satisfied with life always but never with one's self.

G. J. Nathan, *Testament of a Critic,* 1931, p. 15.

151.11 Fortune cannot make you happy, if you lack contentment.

Sanders, *Citatenlexikon,* 709.

151.12 The eye is never satisfied with seeing; endless are the desires of the heart. . . . Discontent abides in the palace and in the hut, rankling alike in the breast of prince and pauper.

Union Prayer Book, 1945, ii. 310.

151.13 Ever insurgent let me be,
Make me more daring than devout;
From sleek contentment keep me free
And fill me with a buoyant doubt.

L. Untermeyer, *Prayer. Challenge,* 1915, p. 7.

151.14 The noblest within us is brought forth not in contentment but in discontent, not in truce but in fight!

Vladeck. ACWA, *Documentary History,* 1918, p. 19.

152. CONTRAST

152.1 The Holy One created light out of darkness.

Berekia. *Lev. R.,* 31.8.

152.2 Judaism knew how to reconcile two seemingly contradictory exigencies: in God, justice and mercy; in man, fear and love.

*Bonsirven, *Sur les Ruines du Temple,* 1928, ch 1.

152.3 Everything is known and better understood by its contrary.

Guglielmo, *Trattato dell' Arte del Ballare,* 15C (1873), q *Menorah Journal,* 1954, xlii. 93.

152.4 I belong to a world full of contrast and change.

Hasdai, *Sefer HaTapuah,* c. 1230, tr Gollancz, 94.

152.5 Since every event is engendered by its opposite, it is also necessary that being shall come from non-being.

Ibn Gabirol, *Mekor Hayyim,* 11C. q BWC, 175.

152.6 Without contrast, there can be no progress.

Marx, *Poverty of Philosophy,* 1847. q MKM, 149.

152.7 It is the dark part of the eye that sees.

Philo, *Allegorical Interpretations,* 2.17.

152.8 I sense how meaningless is light
without darkness,
How lauded righteousness exists
because of wickedness. . . .
What is the image of a God without a Satan at His back?

Shneor, "Song of the Prophet," 1903. tr FTH, 163.

152.9 The life and movement of a nation take their course through the contradictions embodied in classes, parties and groups.

Trotsky, *Literature and Revolution,* 1925, p. 96.

152.10 The worst demoralization arises from nations, individuals, congregations habituating themselves to the contradiction between their theoretical convictions and practical mode of life.

M. Wassermann. *Verhandlungen der II israelitischen Synode,* 1871, p. 160.

152.11 There is no true good except it proceed from evil.

Zohar, Exod., 184a.

152.12 If there were no folly there would be no wisdom. . . . White is known and valued only by contrast with black. . . . A man does not know what sweet is until he tastes bitter.

Zohar, Lev., 47b.

153. CONTROVERSY

153.1 For three years there was a dispute between the Schools of Shammai and of Hillel. Then a heavenly voice proclaimed:

Both are the words of the living God!
Gamaliel II. *Talmud J: Berakot*, 1.4.

153.2 Satires which censors can understand deserve to be suppressed.
Kraus, "Controversy." *Poems*, 1930, p. 113.

153.3 A controversy waged in the name of Heaven, such as between Hillel and Shammai, will yield permanent value.
Mishna: Abot, 5.17.

153.4 He who is unyielding in a dispute is a transgressor.
Rab. *Talmud: Sanhedrin*, 110a.

153.5 A struggle that revolves about the Book ends in love.
Rashi, *Commentary, Kiddushin* 30b, to Hiyya b. Abba's homily on *Num.* 21.14.

153.6 A nation without controversy is politically dead.
H. Samuel, *Grooves of Change*, 1946, p. 316.

154. CONVERSATION

154.1 We never converse willingly when talking is our profession.
Heine, *Baths of Lucca*, 1829, ch 5.

154.2 Do not converse with a fool.
Ibn Gabirol, *Mibhar HaPeninim*, c. 1050, #232.

154.3 Let us converse a little, and we shall be relieved.
Lipkin, *Iggeret HaMusar*, 1858.

154.4 Even scholars' ordinary talk deserves to be studied.
Rab. *Talmud: Sukka*, 21b. See SSJ, i. 144f.

154.5 Even the conversation of Jews is Torah.
Zera. *Midrash Tehillim*, 5.5, ed Buber, 26b.

155. CONVERSION

155.A. From Judaism

155.A.1 All that forsake Thee shall be ashamed.
Bible: Jer., 17.13.

155.A.2 Every Jew is an "organ of the Shekina." As long as the organ is joined to the body, however tenuously, there is hope; once it is cut off, all hope is lost.
Baal Shem, 1759. *Shibhé HaBesht*, (1903, p. 27).

155.A.3 Every case of apostasy from Judaism is . . . detrimental to the development of religion.
*Berner. q Karples, *Jews and Judaism*, 81.

155.A.4 The renegades who deserted to the New Covenant need only smell a *tsholnt* to feel a certain nostalgia for the synagog.
Boerne. q Heine, *Ludwig Boerne*, 1840.

155.A.5 Certainly I accepted baptism out of conviction . . . the conviction that it is better to be a professor in the Imperial Academy at St. Petersburg than a teacher in a *heder* in Vilna.
Chwolson. q Morgenstern, *Testament of the Lost Son*, 139.

155.A.6 What person will not despise the vile being who . . . forsakes the religion of his youth, abandons his kindred and people, and desecrates another faith by externally observing its rites while internally being unconvinced of its divine institution?
*Dohm, *Civil Improvement of Jews*, 1781, p. 94.

155.A.7 A Jew may be religious . . . or non-religious. But when he . . . formally adopts Christianity, he steps out altogether from the Jewish nationality.
Dubnow, *Pisma o Starom i Novom Yevreistvie*, 1907, p. 17.

155.A.8 The baptismal certificate is the admission ticket into European civilization.
Heine, *Thoughts and Fancies*, 1869.

155.A.9 The converted Jew remains a Jew no matter how much he objects to it.
Hess, *Rome and Jerusalem*, (1862), p. 98.

155.A.10 No Christian shall compel . . . Jews to accept baptism.
*Innocent III, *Epistle*, 1199. TMS, 212.

155.A.11 It is as easy to convert Jews as to convert the devil himself.
*Luther. q *JE*, iv. 250.

155.A.12 If . . . the corner-stones of my house fail, . . . shall I shift my effects to the upper story? . . . Christianity is built on Judaism, and if this falls, that becomes one heap of ruins with it.
M. Mendelssohn, *Jerusalem*, 1783. See tr Samuels, ii. 85.

155.A.13 When you baptize a Jew, hold him under water for five minutes.
*Proverb (Bulgarian). q MND, 613.

155.A.14 It is proper to mourn at the

demise of a body, and all the more so at the loss of a body and soul.

Sefer Hasidim, 13C, #192, p. 74.

155.A.15 In converting Jews . . . we raise the price of pork.

Shakespeare, Merchant of Venice, 1597, Act 3.

155.A.16 I am a Jew and will remain a Jew. I would not become a Christian even if I could become an emperor. Changing one's religion is a matter for consideration by a free man; it is an evil thing for a prisoner.

Süss Oppenheimer, before his execution, to Pastor Rieger. q Stern, *The Court Jew*, 262.

155.B. To Judaism

155.B.1 Many peoples shall . . . say: Come, let us go up . . . to the house of the God of Jacob; He will teach us of His ways, and we will walk in His paths.

Bible: Isa., 2.3. See 14.1.

155.B.2 Many nations shall join themselves to the Lord that day, and shall be My people.

Bible: Zech., 2.15. See 8.23.

155.B.3 The Holy One waits for the nations . . . to come under His wings.

Abbahu, or Hama b. Hanina. *Num. R.*, 10.1.

155.B.4 Every Jew should endeavor to bring men under the wings of the Shekina even as Abraham did.

Abot de R. Nathan, ch 12, ed Schechter, 27a.

155.B.5 A would-be proselyte is neither persuaded nor dissuaded.

Eleazar b. Pedat. *Talmud: Yebamot*, 47b.

155.B.6 If one wishes to adopt Judaism, in the name of God and for the sake of Heaven, welcome and befriend him, do not repel him.

Eleazar of Modin. *Mekilta*, to *Exod.* 18.6.

155.B.7 Proselytes are hard on Israel, like a sore on the skin.

Helbo. *Talmud: Yebamot*, 47b, 109b.

155.B.8 He who attracts a gentile to God is as though he created him.

José b. Zimra. *Gen. R.*, 39.14. See *Sifré*, #32, to *Deut.* 6.5.

155.B.9 To all who desire to come and live under the same laws with us, our lawgiver gives a gracious welcome.

Josephus, *Against Apion*, ii. 28.

155.B.10 How precious are proselytes to the Omnipresent!

Judah b. Simon. *Ruth R.*, 3.5.

155.B.11 A proselyte refers to Abraham as "my father."

Judah HaNasi. *Talmud: Bikkurim*, 1.4, ref. to *Gen.* 17.4.

155.B.12 All who adopt Judaism and profess the unity of God's Name are Abraham's disciples. . . . Abraham is the father . . . also of his disciples and proselytes. . . . There is absolutely no difference between you and us.

Maimonides, letter to Obadiah the Proselyte. *Responsa*, ed Freimann, # 42, p. 41.

155.B.13 Whoever wishes to adopt Judaism . . . is constrained to accept, not the Torah and commandments, but the precepts which were promulgated for the sons of Noah.

Maimonides, *Responsa*, ed Freimann, #124, p. 117.

155.B.14 The proselyte is like a born Jew with respect to all the commandments.

Mekilta, to *Exod.* 12.49.

155.B.15 Since . . . according to the Rabbis, the just and virtuous of every nation shall enjoy eternal felicity hereafter, the reason for proselyting falls to the ground.

M. Mendelssohn, *Letter to Lavater*, 1770.

155.B.16 Ye [Pharisees] compass sea and land to make one proselyte.

New Testament: Matt., 23.15.

155.B.17 Proselytes are like stags that left their habitat to join the sheepfold, and are treated with special consideration.

Num. R., 8.2.

155.B.18 A poor man, in search of a lost bag of pennies, passed through a city where he found fame and fortune. Do you suppose he would resume his search for the missing pennies?

Potocki, 1749, before his execution, reply to friends who pleaded that he return to Christianity. See J. Hurwitz, *Amudé Bet Yehuda*, 1766, p. 46.

155.B.19 A would-be convert who accepts all the laws of the Torah except one, is not admitted into the fold.

Sifra, to *Lev.* 19.34, 91a.

155.B.20 A proselyte is like a new-born infant.

Simeon b. Lakish. *Talmud: Yebamot*, 62a.

155.B.21 Proselytes are dearer to God than Jewish saints.
Simeon b. Yohai. *Mishnat R. Eliezer*, ed Enelow, 302.

155.B.22 A proselyte is dearer to God than was Israel at Sinai, for he accepts Heaven's yoke without having witnessed the thunders . . . and trumpet blasts which attended the Revelation.
Simeon b. Lakish. *Tanhuma, Lek Leka*, 6, ed Buber, 32.

155.B.23 He who embraces Judaism to marry a Jewess, or through love or fear of Jews, is not a genuine proselyte.
Talmud: Gerim, 1.3.

155.B.24 If any person . . . betake himself to their nefarious sect . . . he shall sustain with them the deserved punishments [be burned].
Theodosian Code, 16.8.1, Aug. 13, 339.

155.B.25 It is more grievous than death and more cruel than murder if anyone of Christian faith be polluted by Jewish disbelief.
Ibid., 16.8.19, April 1, 409.

155.B.26 If you . . . require no other advocate [than your righteousness] before your Father, then come to us and be of the divine covenant.
I. M. Wise, letter, 1860. *Selected Writings*, 403.

156. CONVICTION

156.1 He who holds convictions, respects convictions.
Baeck, *Essence of Judaism*, 1936, p. 286.

156.2 Let everyone act according to his convictions, and rest perfectly assured that this will not displease his Creator.
M. Mendelssohn, letter to Paul, B-s-t April 24, 1773.

156.3 He who once silences his convictions is unclean.
Varnhagen, *Briefe*, (1877).

157. CORRECTION

157.1 Lord, correct me, but in measure.
Bible: Jer., 10.24.

157.2 Whom the Lord loves He corrects.
Bible: Prov., 3.12.

157.3 Happy is the man whom God corrects.
Bible: Job, 5.17.

157.4 That which is crooked cannot be made straight.
Bible: Eccles., 1.15.

157.5 Corrections of misstatements rarely correct a situation.
Brandeis, letter to Julian W. Mack, Oct. 4, 1933.

157.6 Everything needs improvement: mustard and lupine need sweetening, wheat needs grinding, and man needs correction.
Hoshaia Rabba. *Talmud: Aboda Zara*, 44b.

157.7 There is a form of meekness which leads to Gehenna, as when a man, in order to be agreeable, fails to correct his child or pupil, or keeps silence when justice is miscarried.
Sefer Hasidim, 13C, #1924f., p. 466.

158. CORRUPTION

158.1 Your silver has become dross, your wine mixed with water.
Bible: Isa., 1.22.

158.2 A worm can enter a fruit only after it has begun to rot.
Ansky, *Dybbuk*, 1918, Act 3.

158.3 A little corruption in government is too much corruption.
D. L. Cohn. *N.Y. Times Magazine*, Oct. 18, 1951, p. 10.

158.4 Smelling like a municipal budget.
Hoffenstein, "Entr' Acte," vi, *Year In, You're Out*, 1930 (*Complete Poetry*, 1954, p. 244).

159. COSMOPOLITANISM

159.1 Above all nations is humanity; above all creeds is God.
Blumenthal (LCJ, 1929, p. 274).

159.2 My home, the earth, all men, my friends,
And life, a lover's song.
J. Cahan, "A Great Hour," 1901. RAM, 106.

159.3 All nations, without exception, must go up with the Jews towards Jerusalem.
H. Cohen, *Religiöse Postulate*, 1907, p. 14.

159.4 I trust that . . . the State of Israel will lend still greater scope, force and content to our "cosmopolitanism."
H. Greenberg, "An Open Letter," Feb. 1951. GIE, 329.

159.5 Every civilized people that is the bearer of an idea is in the service of *all* mankind.
J. Guttmann, *Idee der Versöhnung*, 1909, p. 14. q BKF, 165.

159.6 Cosmopolitanism has sprung almost completely from Judea's soil.

Heine, *Shakespeare's Maidens: Jessica*, 1839.

159.7 A world-temple must be built unto God, for His name shall be praised from the rising of the sun to the setting thereof.

S. Hirsch, *Die Reform in Judentum*, 1844.

159.8 Cosmopolitanism is likely to be an alibi for not doing one's duty to one's own people.

Kaplan, *Future of the American Jew*, 1948, p. 90.

159.9 It is significant that in antiquity only the two nationally conscious peoples [Israel and Hellas] developed a conscious cosmopolitanism and universalism.

H. Kohn, *Idea of Nationalism*, 1944, p. 36.

159.10 It is only a parliament of nations, with law and power, the power and majesty of the people, that . . . will bring on earth the rule which is in heaven, the rule of Equity.

Lubin, letter. *Israelite*, Oct. 31, 1912.

159.11 We Jews are the true cosmopolitans, the world citizens by the grace of God, or, if you will, by God's disfavor.

*Raabe, *Der Hungerpastor*, 1864.

159.12 God keeps not only Israel but all men.

Sifré, #40, to *Deut.* 11.12, ed Friedmann, 78b.

159.13 If I were asked where I belonged, I should answer that a Jewish mother had borne me, Germany had nourished me, Europe formed me, my home was the earth, and the world my fatherland.

Toller, *I was a German*, 1934, p. 286.

159.14 If the Jew has been able to enter into all incarnations of humanity and to be at home in every environment, it is because he is a common measure of humanity. . . . One touch of Jewry makes the whole world kin.

Zangwill, *Problem of the Jewish Race*, 17.

160. COURAGE

160.1 Be strong and of good courage.
Bible: Josh., 1.9.

160.2 You have no fire so exceeding hot as to make me a coward.
Apocrypha: IV Macc., 10.14.

160.3 Bravery is fear sneering at itself.
Bodenheim, *Blackguard*, 1923.

160.4 Courage is fire, and bullying is smoke.
Disraeli, *Count Alarcos*, 1839.

160.5 We have trained our courage, not to wage war for self-aggrandizement, but to preserve our laws.
Josephus, *Against Apion*, ii. 37.

160.6 Courage is never to let your actions be influenced by your fears.
Koestler, *Arrow in the Blue*, 1952, p. 131.

160.7 Money lost, nothing lost. Courage lost, all is lost.
Lazerov, *Enciklopedie fun Idishe Vitzen*, 1928, #423.

160.8 Who train themselves in wisdom cultivate true courage.
Philo, *Virtues*, 1.

161. COURTESY

161.1 The more eminent, the more courteous to inferiors.
Boerne, *Schilderungen aus Paris: Französische Sprache*, 1822.

161.2 It's not an act of courtesy to carry the cane for the cripple.
Schnitzler, *Buch der Sprüche & Bedenken*, 1927, p. 224.

162. COURTSHIP

162.1 The Lord has created a new thing in the earth: a woman shall court a man.
Bible: Jer., 31.22.

162.2 It is natural for a man to woo a woman, not for a woman to woo a man: the loser seeks what he lost [the rib].
Dosetai b. Yannai. *Talmud: Nidda*, 31b.

162.3 Let your daughter die unmarried rather than beseech a man.
Hai Gaon, *Musar Haskel*, c. 1000.

162.4 The Law commands us, in taking a wife, not to be influenced by dowry, not to carry her off by force, nor yet to win her by guile and deceit.
Josephus, *Against Apion*, ii. 24.

162.5 Be quick in buying land, but deliberate in acquiring a wife.
Papa. *Talmud: Yebamot*, 63a.

163. COVENANT

163.1 I set My bow in the cloud . . . a token of a covenant . . . [that] the waters shall no more become a flood to destroy all flesh.
Bible: Gen., 9.13, 15.

163.2 That day the Lord made a covenant with Abram, saying: "Unto thy seed have I given this land."
Ibid., 15.18.

163.3 The Lord God made a covenant with us in Horeb . . . not with our fathers, but with us . . . who are here alive this day.
Bible: Deut., 5.2f. See 29.13f.

163.4 The Covenant . . . formed the gateway to their history, a symbolic act of the highest pregnancy, revived three thousand years later as the root of modern nationalism and democracy. For the Covenant was concluded . . . between God and the whole people, every member in complete equality.
H. Kohn, *Idea of Nationalism*, 1944, p. 37.

163.5 The covenant at Sinai, the Magna Charta of Judaism.
*Moore, *Judaism*, 1927, i. 262.

163.6 The souls of all future generations also took part when the Covenant was concluded between God and Israel.
Samuel b. Nahman. *Tanhuma, Nitzabim*, 8, ed Buber, 25b.

163.7 At Sinai, our fathers united and concluded a mutual covenant to do lovingkindness . . . and not to forsake their father's tongue.
Seder Eliyahu Rabbah, ch 21 (23), ed Friedmann, 123.

163.8 Torah, God, and circumcision are all called *Covenant*. All three are inseparably linked together.
Zohar, Lev., 73b.

164. CREATION
164.A. The World

164.A.1 In the beginning God created the heaven and the earth.
Bible: Gen., 1.1.

164.A.2 God went on creating worlds and destroying them till He created this world and said "it was very good" [*Gen.* 1.31].
Abbahu. *Gen. R.*, 3.7.

164.A.3 Earth on nothing He founded,
And on emptiness stretched out the sky.
Meshullam b. Kalonymus, tr Zangwill.

164.A.4 With ten utterances was the world created.
Mishna: Abot, 5.1.

164.A.5 Seven things He created before the world: Torah, penitence, Eden, Gehenna, Throne of Glory, Temple, and Messiah's name.
Talmud: Pesahim, 54a.

164.B. Purpose

164.B.1 The Lord has made everything for His own purpose.
Bible: Prov., 16.4.

164.B.2 He has created the world on behalf of His people.
Apocrypha: Assumption of Moses, 1.12. See *IV Ezra*, 6.55.

164.B.3 Man was not made for the world, but the world for man.
Apocrypha: II Baruch, 14.18. See *IV Ezra*, 8.44.

164.B.4 Man was created for the world, not the world for man.
Gentili, *Mleket Mahshebet, VaYera*, 8. 1710.

164.B.5 This world came into being on account of the righteous.
Apocrypha: II Baruch, 15.7. See *Talmud: Berakot*, 6b.

164.B.6 I added that the Lord had made cattle because beef-soup strengthened man; that jackasses were created for the purpose of serving as comparisons, and that man existed that he might eat beef-soup, and realize that he was no jackass.
Heine, *Harz Journey*, 1824.

164.B.7 The goal of creation is the messianic era.
Johanan b. Nappaha. *Talmud: Sanhedrin*, 98b.

164.B.8 God created heaven and earth only "that men should fear."
Judah b. Ezekiel. *Talmud: Sabbath* 31b, on *Eccles.* 3.14.

164.B.9 As to the purpose of creation . . . it was the will of God.
Maimonides, *Guide for the Perplexed*, 1190, 3.13.

164.B.10 The Holy One created everything only for His glory.
Mishna: Abot, 6.11.

165. CREATIVITY

165.1 The lash may force men to physical labor; it cannot force them to spiritual creativity.
Asch, *What I Believe*, 1941, p. 173.

165.2 Man is made to create, from the poet to the potter.
Disraeli, *Contarini Fleming,* 1832.

165.3 Not capital is the chief thing . . . the happiness of life is not in it, nor the savor of life. The chief thing is creation.
A.D. Gordon. q SHR, 416.

165.4 The poet and the artist create by nature, not because of what they acquired by learning.
M. Ibn Ezra, *Shirat Yisrael,* (12C) 1924.

165.5 We are what we create.
Oppenheim, *War and Laughter,* 1916.

165.6 To live means to create.
M. Steinberg, *A Partisan Guide,* 1945.

165.7 There is continuous creation, out of the new ideas discovered in the Torah.
Zohar, Gen., Introduction, 52.

165.8 This implies that man can become a co-creator with God.
Ber, *Or HaEmet,* (1899), p. 13.

166. CREDULITY

166.1 The thoughtless believes every word.
Bible: Prov., 14.15.

166.2 Believe not every tale.
Apocrypha: Ben Sira, 19.15.

166.3 There are three fields in which all human beings are credulous: money, matrimony and medicine.
Fishbein. Noah D. Fabricont, *Amusing Quotations for Doctors and Patients* (Greene & Stratton, 381 4th Ave., N.Y., 1950), p. 89.

166.4 Let Apella the Jew believe it.
Horace, Satires, 1.5, line 100.

166.5 It is curious . . . that the same race which had been critical over a Moses should have been credulous over a Sabbathai Zevi.
Magnus, *Jewish Portraits,* 1901, p. 166.

166.6 The folly of an accusation, unhappily, is no sufficient reason that it should not meet with credit.
Nordau, speech, II Zionist Congress, Aug. 8, 1898.

166.7 Religion beats me. I'm amazed at folk
Drinking the gospels in and never scratching
Their heads for questions.
Sassoon, *The Old Huntsman,* 1917.

167. CREED

167.1 It is improper to lay down basic creeds, since we must believe everything in the holy Torah.
Abravanel, *Rosh Amana,* (1505) 1861.

167.2 We do not deny dogma, but prefer to remit it to the sphere of individual conviction.
F. Adler, *Creed and Deed,* 1877, p. 1.

167.3 Man's creed is that he believes in God, and therefore in mankind, but not that he believes in a creed.
Baeck, *Essence of Judaism,* 1936, p. 261.

167.4 Judaism is not a creed; the Jewish God is simply a negation of superstition, an imaginary result of its elimination.
Einstein, *The World As I See It,* 1934.

167.5 Any stigma . . . will serve to beat a dogma.
Guedalla, *Masters and Men,* 1923, p. 36.

167.6 We have no articles of belief in the commonly accepted interpretation of the term, viz., that we should or must believe what cannot be known or comprehended.
S. Hirsch. I Rabbiner Versammlung, *Protokolle,* 1844, p. 54.

167.7 Ancient Judaism has no symbolical books, no articles of faith . . . and, according to the spirit of true Judaism, must hold them inadmissible.
M. Mendelssohn, *Jerusalem,* 1783, tr Samuels, ii. 107.

167.8 Let us thank God that Judaism has no dogmas.
M. A. Stern, *Offene Briefe.* INJ, 1844, p. 296. q PRM, 128.

167.9 The man who had eaten pudding or rabbit would have been stoned; while he who denied the immortality of the soul might be a high priest.
Voltaire, Philosophical Dictionary, 1764, v. Jews, #1.

167.10 Judaism has its dogmas; hence there may be built up a theology of Judaism.
I. M. Wise, 1893, *Judaism at World's Parliament of Religions,* 3.

168. CRITICISM

168.1 The test of democracy is freedom of criticism.
Ben Gurion. q McDonald, *My Mission in Israel,* 247.

168.2 It is much easier to be critical than to be correct.

Disraeli, speech, House of Commons, Jan. 24, 1860.

168.3 He wreathed the rod of criticism with roses.

D'Israeli, *Miscellanies,* 1796 (ref. to P. Bayle).

168.4 We do not hesitate to criticize Judaism . . . for we believe in the invincibility of its higher ideals.

Dubnow, *Pisma o Starom i Novom Yevreistvie,* 1907, p. 125.

168.5 Love your critics and hate your flatterers.

Gerondi, *Shaaré Teshuba,* (13C) 1505, ch 3.

168.6 Criticism is much more sharp and incisive among Jews.

Graetz. *JQRo,* 1888, i. 6.

168.7 Write not asses criticism?

Heine, *Atta Troll,* 1841, ch 5.

168.8 To silence criticism is to silence freedom.

Hook *N.Y. Times Magazine,* Sept. 30, 1951, p. 46.

168.9 Wise is the singer who . . . considers the judgment of men.

M. Ibn Ezra, *Selected Poems,* 92.

168.10 A man's mind is hidden in his writings; criticism brings it to light.

Ibn Gabirol, *Mibhar HaPeninim,* c. 1050, #215.

168.11 Love without criticism is not love.

José b. Hanina. *Gen. R.,* 54.3.

168.12 I shall have the courage to point out the ulcers of my people and to cure them.

Lazare, *Job's Dunghill,* (1948) p. 44.

168.13 A sound critique is the only means whereby to purify Judaism of the many accretions which distort and degrade it.

S. D. Luzzatto, letter to Reggio, Nov. 26, 1838.

168.14 Present-day Jews lack prophetic self-criticism. . . . For fear of the majority, Jews do not dare to look into their own conscience. . . . That is today their great fault.

*Masaryk, *Grundlagen des Marxismus,* 1899, Sect. 120.

168.15 Whoever makes verses plays nine pins; and whoever plays nine pins, be he king or peasant, must allow a fellow to tell him the pins he has thrown.

M. Mendelssohn, to Frederick the Great, 1760.

168.16 No chronically happy man is a trustworthy critic.

G. J. Nathan, *The Theatre in the Fifties,* 1953, p. 296.

168.17 The fool runs away from criticism.

Samuel HaNagid, *Ben Mishlé,* 11C, #37.

168.18 The self-critical spirit of the Jews is one of the strangest phenomena in history. . . . We cannot find an instance of another people which, having been driven from its soil by peoples at least as bad as (actually much more than) itself, should wander about the world saying: "It served us right. We lost our homeland because of our sins."

M. Samuel, *Prince of the Ghetto,* 1948, p. 121.

168.19 Many journalists and critics are like cockatoos: they pull in their claws when fed, and shut an eye when given a drink.

Saphir, *Humoristische Abende,* 1830.

168.20 Jewish literature unflinchingly exposes the flaws even of a Moses and a David.

Zangwill, *Chosen Peoples. Menorah Journal,* 1918, iv. 273.

169. CROWN

169.1 In all the world, three precious
crowns there be . . .
Of strength, of Torah, and of
beauty are the three.

Chernihovsky, *Shlosha Ketarim,* 1923. q WHJ, iv. 265.

169.2 There are three crowns: of priesthood, royalty, and Torah. Aaron took the first, David the second. As to the third, it is available to anyone in the world worthy of it.

Sifré, Numbers, #119.

Johanan b. Nappaha. *T: Yoma,* 72b.

169.3 Can two kings wear one crown?

Simeon b. Pazzi, *Talmud: Hullin,* 60b.

169.4 There are three crowns: of Torah, of priesthood, and of royalty; but the crown of a good name excels them all.

Simeon b. Yohai. *Mishna: Abot,* 4.13.

170. CRUCIFIXION

170.1 Perhaps the saddest thing to admit is that those who rejected the Cross have to carry it, while those who welcomed it are so often engaged in crucifying others.

*Berdyaev, *Christianity & Antisemitism,* (1938) 1952, p. 12.

170.2 If it hadn't been for such damned cusses as you, our Lord Jesus Christ would be alive and well to this day.

*Dumont, to a Jewish sutler, 1861.

170.3 In every land is our Gethsemane, A thousand times have we been crucified.

F. K. Frank, *A Jew to Jesus,* 1915, p. 3.

170.4 How strange! The very people who had given the world a God, and whose whole life was inspired by devotion to God, were stigmatized as deicides!

Heine, *Confessions,* 1854. EPP, 664. See LJD, 77f.

170.5 If the Jews did commit an inexplicable crime nearly two thousand years ago, we have had no authority given to us —even if we could determine who were the descendants of the persons guilty of that crime—to visit the sins of the fathers upon the children . . . unto the three hundredth or four hundredth generation. That awful power is not ours.

*Peel, speech, House of Commons, Feb. 11, 1848.

170.6 You confess that Jesus publicly called our Pharisees and priests "races of vipers, whited sepulchres." If one of us should run incessantly through the streets of Rome calling the Pope and Cardinals vipers and sepulchres, would he not be punished?

*Voltaire, "Sermon du Rabbi Akib." *Nouveaux Mélanges,* 1765.

170.7 The process of education must end the Christ-killing lie about the Jew and affirm anew the Christ-bearing truth of the Jew in the world.

S. S. Wise. LCJ, 1929, p. 167.

171. CRUELTY

171.1 He that is cruel troubles his own flesh.

Bible: Prov., 11.17.

172. CULTURE

172.1 Neither the pleasure derived from gold, nor any other of the possessions which are prized by shallow minds, confers the same benefit as the pursuit of culture.

Apocrypha: Aristeas, 8.

172.2 Our arid, desiccating culture . . . while giving us wheels by which to propel ourselves with greater ease across this patient earth, seems to have taken away from us our wings.

Blau. *The Wonder of Life,* 1925, p. 105.

172.3 Exaggerated respect for athletics, an excess of coarse impressions brought about by the technical discoveries of recent years, the increased severity of the struggle for existence due to the economic crisis, the brutalization of political life: all these factors are hostile to the ripening of the character and the desire for real culture, and stamp our age as barbarous, materialistic, and superficial.

Einstein, *World As I See It,* 1934, p. 258f.

172.4 It is the principal task of culture, its real *raison d'être,* to defend us against nature.

Freud, *Future of an Illusion,* 1949, p. 26.

172.5 What we desire in Palestine is to . . . do with our own hands all the necessary labor, from the highest and most complicated and easiest to the coarsest and hardest and meanest. . . . Only then will we have a culture, for only then will we have a life of our own.

A. D. Gordon, *Work and Culture,* 1911.

172.6 Culture destroys in the artist that fresh accentuation, that vivid coloring, that impulsiveness of thought, that directness of feeling, so often to be admired in circumscribed and uncultured natures.

Heine, *Rossini and Meyerbeer,* 1837.

172.7 Culture is always a product of mixing.

F. Hertz, *Race and Civilization,* 1928, p. 308.

172.8 All culture is commissioned to convert, as far as lies within its power, pain into enjoyment, necessity into freedom.

Klatzkin, *In Praise of Wisdom,* 1943, p. 23.

172.9 By culture we understand the harmonious development of all the powers and capacities of man.

Perles. *Menorah Journal,* 1922, viii. 317.

172.10 This divine ordinance imparts both light and sweetness to the soul which has the eyes to see.

Philo. q Walsh, *Curiosities of Literature,* p. 1043.

172.11 A Jewish culture in America can

exist only in symbiosis with an American culture.

M. Samuel. *Jewish Frontier,* Nov. 1951, p. 14.

172.12 Man is covered with a very thin veneer of culture. Scratch a little—and the beast will appear.

Stekel, *Autobiography,* 1950, p. 74.

172.13 Nine-tenths of what the world celebrated as Viennese culture in the nineteenth century was promoted, nourished, and created by Viennese Jewry.

S. Zweig, *World of Yesterday,* 1943, p. 22.

173. CURIOSITY

173.1 Be not curious in unnecessary matters: for more things are shown to you than men understand.

Apocrypha: Ben Sira, 3.23.

173.2 The Semitic peoples lack almost entirely a sense of curiosity and the faculty of laughter.

*Rénan, *Histoire génerale des langues sémitiques,* 1855, i. 9, 11.

173.3 Natural curiosity, the mother of science.

C. Singer. NSR, 1925, p. 118.

174. CURSE

174.1 Revile not God, nor curse a ruler of your people.

Bible: Exod., 22.27. See 21.17; *Eccles.,* 10.20.

174.2 You shall not curse the deaf.

Bible: Lev., 19.14.

174.3 So perish all Thine enemies, O Lord!

Bible: Judg., 5.31.

174.4 Let them be blotted out of the book of the living!

Bible: Ps., 69.29. See *Deut.,* 29.19.

174.5 As the wandering sparrow, as the flying swallow, so the curse that is causeless shall come home.

Bible: Prov., 26.2.

174.6 Blaspheme God, and die.

Bible: Job, 2.9.

174.7 Perish the day wherein I was born!

Ibid., 3.3.

174.8 A mother's curse roots up the young plant.

Apocrypha: Ben Sira, 3.9.

174.9 Do not take lightly the curse of a common man.

Isaac Nappaha. *Talmud: Megilla,* 28a. See *Berakot,* 56a.

174.10 Let yourself be cursed, rather than curse.

Proverb. q Rab. *Talmud: Sanhedrin,* 49a.

175. CUSTOM

175.1 See how the people act, and that is the law.

Abayé. *Talmud: Berakot,* 45a.

175.2 Customs out of time and place cannot maintain themselves.

Z. H. Chajes, *Darké HaTorah,* 1842, p. 7b.

175.3 Customs may not be as wise as laws, but they are always more popular.

Disraeli, speech, House of Commons, March 11, 1870.

175.4 Customs create exegesis, not exegesis customs.

Finkelstein, *The Pharisees,* 1940, p. 131.

175.5 Custom is second nature.

Gentili. *Mleket Mahshebet, Tazria,* #2, 1710.

175.6 Men will sooner surrender their rights than their customs.

Güdemann, *Gesch. des Erziehungswesens,* 1888, iii. ch 1.

175.7 Custom cancels a law.

Hoshaia. *Talmud J: Yebamot,* 12.1.

175.8 The custom of our fathers is the law.

Isserles, *Darké Moshé,* on *Tur Yoré Deah,* 116, 376.4.

175.9 *Minhag* ("custom"), when inverted, spells Gehenna.

Jacob Tam. q Mintz, *Responsa,* 1617, #43, 66. *JE,* iv. 397a.

175.10 Do not deviate from the custom of the land.

José. *Tosefta: Ketubot* 6.6.

175.11 Change not the custom of your fathers.

José b. Zabda. *Talmud J: Erubin,* 3.9.

175.12 If the court is in doubt, follow the popular custom.

Joshua b. Levi. *Talmud J: Peah,* 7.5.

175.13 We observe lovingly Israel's customs.

Kook, *Eder HaYekor,* 1906, p. 44. q ABJ, 199.

175.14 "Turn not to the *obot*" [*Lev.* 19.3],—use your own judgment, and depend not entirely on the customs of your fathers.

Kremer, c. 1650. q JJCW, 161.

175.15 Everything according to local custom.

Mishna: Sukka, 3.11; *Ketubot*, 6.4.

175.16 Customs and ceremonies must change with the varying needs of different generations.

Philipson, *Reform Movement in Judaism*, (1907) 1930, p. 3.

175.17 Customs are unwritten laws, not engraved on pillars or inscribed on paper, which may be eaten by moths, but impressed on the souls of those living under the same constitution.

Philo, *Justice*, (*Special Laws*, iv. 28), on *Deut.* 19.14.

175.18 We ought not, in our words or actions, follow only popular and beaten tracks.

Philo, *Every Good Man Is Free*, 1.

175.19 When you come to a town, follow its customs.

Proverb. q Meir. *Gen. R.*, 48.14.

175.20 Customs of later generations are Torah.

Rashi, *Pardes*, (c. 1220) 1870, #1, #174.

175.21 Custom in its decay degenerates into a kind of religious fashion, the worst disease to which religion is liable, and the most difficult to cure.

Schechter, *Studies in Judaism*, 1896, i. 144.

175.22 In most places, Jews follow the same customs as Gentiles.

Sefer Hasidim, 13C, #1301, p. 321.

175.23 Never deviate from custom. When Moses ascended on high he ate no bread [*Ex.* 34.28], and when the angels came down below, they ate bread [*Gen.* 19.3].

Tanhum b. Hanilai. *Talmud: Baba Metzia*, 86b.

175.24 Each Jewish custom has something in it which may be interpreted poetically and thus acquire a genuinely modern form, with perhaps a wholly new and important spiritual content.

Zhitlovsky, *Gezamelte Shriften*, iv. 271.

176. CYNIC

176.1 Cynicism is, after all, simply idealism gone sour.

Herberg, *Judaism and Modern Man*, 1951, p. 177.

176.2 It takes a clever man to turn cynic, and a wise man not to.

Hurst.

176.3 The so-called sophisticated who prides himself on cynicism, is only seeking to escape his own inadequacies.

Magnin, *How to Live*, 1951, p. 11.

176.4 The cynicism that is born of defeat is pitiable and worthless. It is only the cynicism that is born of success that is penetrating and valid.

G. J. Nathan, *Monks Are Monks*, 1929, p. 56.

177. DANCE

177.1 Without dancing you can never attain a perfectly graceful carriage, which is of the highest importance in life.

Disraeli, *Vivian Grey*, 1827.

177.2 Yes, the dance throughout all ages
Was a pious act of faith.

Heine, *Atta Troll*, 1841, ch 6.

177.3 No dancing before eating.

Mendelé, *Di Kliatshé*, 1873.

177.4 My heart lifted my feet, and I danced.

Nathan of Nemirov, *Letters*. q ZRN, 217.

177.5 At sixty as at six, the sound of a timbrel makes her nimble.

Proverb. q Hisda. *Talmud: Moed Katan*, 9b.

178. DANGER

178.1 Who loves danger shall perish therein.

Apocrypha: Ben Sira (Greek version), 3.26.

178.2 There is a city . . . full of all good things, but its approach is narrow, along a steep path, flanked by fire on one side and deep water on the other. . . . Now, if this city be given to a man for an inheritance, how shall he receive it unless he pass through the danger set before him?

Apocrypha: II Esd., 7.6–9.

178.3 The danger of failure is greatest at the beginning of an enterprise and not far from its consummation. Shipwrecks occur near shore.

Boerne, *Fragmente & Aphorismen*, 1840, #156.

178.4 Men love to risk their lives, conquering pinnacles. They love the spice of danger in it. And that's what life is.

Harrison, *Religion of a Modern Liberal*, 1931, p. 125.

178.5 When a man is in danger, Satan presses charges against him.

Hiyya b. Abba. *Talmud J: Sabbath*, 2.6.

178.6 Three need to be guarded: a patient, a groom and a bride.

Judah b. Ezekiel. *Talmud: Berakot,* 54b.

178.7 Seek not to evade taxes, and stand not before an ox when it goes up from pasture.

Judah HaNasi. *Talmud: Pesahim,* 112b.

178.8 Play with life, O mortal. Seek danger, and if thou findest it not, create it.

Klatzkin, *In Praise of Wisdom,* 1943, p. 312.

178.9 Only in danger's hour do we men learn
    All that a man may be.

Lassalle, *Franz von Sickingen,* 1859.

178.10 It is improper to consider personal danger when the public welfare is at stake.

Maimonides, *Iggeret Teman,* 1172.

178.11 When Israel came to the Red Sea, with Pharaoh's army in hot pursuit, they were like the dove which, to escape a hawk, flew into a rock's cleft, only to find there a lurking serpent.

Mekilta, to *Exod.* 14.13. *Cant. R.,* 2.14.2.

178.12 The finer the cloth, the more dangerous the moth.

Moscato, *Nefutzot Yehuda,* 1588, 65b.

178.13 Breed not a savage dog, nor keep a loose stairway.

Nathan. *Talmud: Ketubot,* 41b.

178.14 Danger is my old friend, and though I do not long for Death, I don't think that even he can say that I fear him.

Trumpeldor. q Lipovetzky, *Joseph Trumpeldor,* 51.

178.15 Never expose yourself to danger. A miracle may not occur; and if it does, it is deducted from your credit.

Yannai. *Talmud: Sabbath,* 32a.

179. DARKNESS

179.1 Darkness which may be felt.
Bible: Exod., 10.21.

179.2 Woe to the house whose windows open in the dark!
Exod. R., 14.2.

180. DAUGHTER

180.1 Many daughters have done valiantly, but you excel them all.
Bible: Prov., 31.29.

180.2 Have you daughters? Give heed to their bodies, and show them not a pleasant countenance.

Apocrypha: Ben Sira, 7.24.

180.3 A daughter is to her father a treasure of sleeplessness.
Ibid., 42.9.

180.4 It is a good omen when the first baby is a daughter.
Hisda. *Talmud: Baba Bathra,* 141a.

180.5 "The Lord blessed Abraham with all"—with not having a daughter.
Meir. Kiddushin, 5.17, on *Gen.* 24.1.

180.6 The world cannot be without sons and daughters; yet happy he who has sons, and woe to him who has daughters!
Judah HaNasi. *Talmud: Pesahim,* 65a.

180.7 The sheep will follow one another:
    A daughter acts as acts her mother.
Proverb. q *Talmud: Ketubot,* 63a; I Myers, *Gems from the Talmud,* 31.

180.8 You reprove your daughter, and mean your daughter-in-law.
Proverb (Yiddish). BJS, #1653; ATJF, P. 638.

180.9 A mother is always attached to her daughter, but not so a daughter to her mother.
Talmud: Baba Bathra, 80a.

181. DAVID

181.1 Saul has slain his thousands, and David his ten thousands!
Bible: I Sam., 18.7, 21.11, 29.5.

181.2 David . . . the sweet singer of Israel.
Bible: II Sam., 23.1.

181.3 David, king of Israel, is alive and vigorous!
Judah HaNasi. *Talmud: Rosh Hashana,* 25a.

181.4 David's dynasty will endure for ever.
Maimonides, *Yad: Melakim,* 1180, 1.9.

181.5 A harp hung over David's bed. At midnight, a North wind blew on it, and it played of itself. Then the king arose and studied Torah till the break of day.
Simeon HeHasid. *Talmud: Berakot,* 3b. Cf Levi. *Lam. R.,* 2.22.

182. DAWN

182.1 I will awake the dawn.
Bible: Ps., 108.3.

182.2 The day laughs in forecast while the dawning is still young because the sunrise is coming. For beam heralds beam, and the dimmer light leads the way for the clearer.
Philo, *Change of Names,* 30.

182.3 A thief and a rogue are afraid of the dawn.
Talmud: Hullin, 91b.

183. DAY

183.1 Day unto day utters speech.
Bible: Ps., 19.3.

183.2 Days are scrolls: write on them what you want to be remembered.
Bahya, *Hobot HaLebabot*, 1040, 8.3.11.

183.3 Peevish carpers say:
"Two nights enclose each day."
But cheerful men indite:
"Two days enclose each night."
O. Blumenthal. q TL, p. 30.

183.4 Days have an odor, not merely a color and a tone.
Shenberg, *Under the Fig Tree*, 96.

183.5 The days hover like shadows about man. Each day, in which no good was done, returns to its Creator in disgrace. Each day, in which good was done, weaves a garment for the human soul, which it dons when it departs from the body.
Zeitlin. *HaTekufa*, 1920, vi 315.

183.6 No day without night, and no night without day.
Zohar, Gen., 46a, 162a.

184. DAY OF GOD

184.1 Behold, the day of the Lord comes, cruel, and full of wrath and fierce anger.
Bible: Isa., 13.9.

184.2 Their silver and their gold shall not be able to deliver them in the day of the Lord's wrath.
Bible: Ezek., 7.19.

184.3 The day of the Lord is near in the valley of decision.
Bible: Joel, 4.14. See 2.1, 11.

184.4 Behold, the day comes, it burns as a furnace; all the proud, all that work wickedness, shall be stubble, and the day that comes shall set them ablaze. . . .
But to you that fear My name shall the sun of righteousness arise with healing in its wings.
Bible: Mal., 3.19f.

184.5 The day of the Lord comes as a thief in the night.
New Testament: I Thess., 5.2.

184.6 O come, day of God,
And fill our spirits
With peace and with gladness
from heaven.
Union Prayer Book, 1922, ii. 95.

185. DEATH
185.A. Description

185.A.1 He was gathered to his people.
Bible: Gen., 25.8.

185.A.2 I am going the way of all the earth.
Bible: Josh., 23.14.

185.A.3 Thus will they quench my coal.
Bible: II Sam., 14.7. Cf 21.17.

185.A.4 Before the silver cord is snapped asunder, and the golden bowl is shattered.
Bible: Eccles., 12.6.

185.A.5 The dust returns to the earth whence it was, and the spirit returns unto God who gave it.
Ibid., 12.7.

185.A.6 I am going out at one door, and I shall go in at another.
Baal Shem. q BTH, i. 84.

185.A.7 The day of death is when two worlds meet with a kiss: this world going out, the future world coming in.
José b. Abin. *Talmud J: Yebamot*, 15.2.

185.A.8 Death is an illusion; its ritual uncleanness is the symbol of its falsehood. What people call death is the intensification and reinvigoration of life.
Kook, *Orot HaKodesh*, 1938, p. 392. q ABJ, 190.

185.A.9 Behold a pale horse, and his name that sat on it was Death.
New Testament: Rev., 6.8.

185.A.10 Death is the means of transition to future life, which is the ultimate goal of mortal existence.
Saadia, *Emunot VeDeot*, 933, 3.7. tr Rosenblatt, 160.

185.A.11 Death is frozen time. Time is molten death.
Werfel, *Between Heaven and Earth*, 1944, p. 223.

185.A.12 Death, the terror of the rich, the desire of the poor.
Zabara, *Sefer Shaashuim*, 12C, 7.25.

185.B. Imminence

185.B.1 There is but a step between me and death.
Bible: I Sam., 20.3.

185.B.2 Death is always imminent.
Berenson, May 22, 1944. *Rumor and Reflection*, 309.

185.B.3 None can say to the Angel of Death, "Wait till I make up my accounts."
Eccles. R., 8.8.

185.B.4 Every creature who thinks he pursues is pursued. Disease, old age and death . . . pursue each of us.
Philo, *Cherubim*, 23.

185.B.5 Death does not knock on the door.
Proverb (Yiddish). YFS, i. 418.

185.B.6 The aim so far, the grave so near.
Rodenberg, "Autumnal Airs," 1864. *Poems, tr Vocke*, 1869, p. 42.

185.C. Inevitability

185.C.1 No man can by any means redeem his brother.
Bible: Ps., 49.8.

185.C.2 Their inward thought is that their houses shall continue for ever, . . . they call their lands after their own names. But man abides not in honor; he is like the beasts that perish.
Ibid., 49.12f. See *Eccles.*, 3.19.

185.C.3 What living man shall not see death?
Ibid., 89.49.

185.C.4 One event happens to them all.
Bible: Eccles., 2.14.

185.C.5 How can my flesh be delighted, when I am informed that I shall live long, since there is no escape from the destruction of death? . . . Shall ants that languish and perish, shall creeping things that melt away like water, exalt themselves?
Bedersi, *Behinat HaOlam*, c.1310, ch 9.

185.C.6 Where is the Torah and where the commandment that will shield us from death and judgment!
Hamnuna Zuti. *Talmud: Berakot*, 31a.

185.C.7 Death, the fusty pedant, spares the rose as little as the thistle; he forgets not a lonely blade of grass in the remotest wilderness; he thoroughly and incessantly destroys.
Heine, *Journey from Munich to Genoa*, 1828, ch 34.

185.C.8 Death in the inmost chambers waits.
Of what avail if I bar the gates?
Immanuel, tr Enelow, *Selected Works*, i. 121.

185.C.9 I Shadar ben Aar reigned over a million provinces, rode on a million steeds, slew a million heroes, and when the Angel of Death came to me, I could not prevail against him.
Mendelé, *Di Kliatshé*, 1873, ch 21.

185.C.10 One man [Moses] saved sixty myriads at the time of the Golden Calf, yet sixty myriads could not save him [from death]!
Samuel b. Nahman. *Deut. R.*, 7.10.

185.D. Finality

185.D.1 I shall go to him, but he will not return to me.
Bible: II Sam., 12.23.

185.D.2 We must needs die, and are as water spilt on the ground, which cannot be gathered up again.
Ibid., 14.14.

185.D.3 He that goes down to the grave shall come up no more.
Bible: Job, 7.9. See *Job*, 10.21.

185.D.4 So man lies down and rises not; till the heavens be no more, they shall not awake, nor be roused out of their sleep.
Ibid., 14.12.

185.D.5 There is no remedy when a man comes to his end, and none was ever known that returned from Hades.
Apocrypha: Wisd. of Sol., 2.1.

185.D.6 Nought abides but death.
Boerne, *Memorial Address on Jean Paul*, Dec. 2, 1825.

185.D.7 We are not like a tree but like leaves, plucked by the wind and left to decay.
Shimonovitz, *"Lo Etz Anahnu,"* 1921. *Shirim*, i. 335f.

185.D.8 Death finally terminates the combat, and grief and joy, success and failure, all are ended.
Union Prayer Book, 1922, ii. 325.

185.E. Causes

185.E.1 No death without antecedent sin.
Ammi. b. Nathan, *Talmud: Sabbath*, 55a (refuted 55b).

185.E.2 God created man for incorruption . . . but by the envy of the devil, death entered the world.
Apocrypha: Wis. of Sol., 2.23f.

185.E.3 For three sins women die in childbirth: carelessness with menstruation, the dough-offering, and the Sabbath lights.
Mishna: Sabbath, 2.6.

185.E.4 The Angel of Death always finds an excuse.
Proverb (Yiddish). BJS, #2273. *JE*, x. 229a.

185.E.5 For one who dies of natural causes, ninety-nine die of an evil eye.

Rab. *Talmud: Baba Metzia,* 107b.

185.E.6 Delayed elimination kills more than does starvation.

Raba. *Talmud: Sabbath,* 33a.

185.E.7 An Arab who lost a brother was asked, "What was the cause of his death?" He replied, "Life."

Zabara, *Sefer Shaashuim,* 13c, 7.27.

185.F. Death of Righteous

185.F.1 Let me die the death of the righteous!

Bible: Num., 23.10.

185.F.2 The righteous is taken away from the evil to come.

Bible: Isa., 57.1.

185.F.3 Precious in the sight of the Lord is the death of His saints.

Bible: Ps., 117.15.

185.F.4 The death of the righteous is like the burning of the Temple.

Akiba. *Talmud: Rosh Hashana,* 18b. Cf *Lam. R.,* 1.37.

185.F.5 The death of the righteous is an atonement.

Ammi. Eleazar. *Talmud: Moed Katan,* 28a.

185.F.6 The righteous are mightier in death than in life.

Hama b. Hanina. *Talmud: Hullin,* 7b. See *Megilla,* 15a.

185.F.7 The righteous die that they may rest from their struggles.

Johanan b. Nappaha. *Gen. R.,* 9.5.

185.F.8 Death was decreed for all, so that men may not be righteous just for the sake of life.

Jonathan b. Eleazar. *Gen. R.,* 9.5.

185.F.9 The Destroyer does not discriminate: he may even begin with the righteous.

Joseph. *Talmud: Baba Kamma,* 60a.

185.F.10 When the perfect man is . . . near death, his knowledge increases mightily, . . . and his love for the object of his knowledge becomes more intense, and it is in this great delight that his soul separates from his body.

Maimonides, *Guide for the Perplexed,* 1190, 3.51.

185.F.11 The Creator knows that the righteous may waver, so He takes him away in his righteousness.

Samuel HaKatan. *Eccles. R.,* to 7.15.

185.F.12 The angels asked why Moses should die, and the Holy One answered, "That he may be equal to all men."

Sifré #339, to *Deut.* 32.50, ed Friedmann, p. 141a.

185.F.13 When the righteous departs, evil enters.

Talmud: Sanhedrin, 113b.

185.F.14 The good die young that they may not degenerate; the wicked live on that they may have a chance to repent, or to produce a virtuous progeny.

Zohar, Gen., 56b.

185.G. Place and Time

185.G.1 You shall come to your grave in ripe age, like as a shock of corn comes in its season.

Bible: Job, 5.26.

185.G.2 Though a plague last seven years, none dies before his time!

Ashi. *Talmud: Sanhedrin,* 29a.

185.G.3 Many a young foal's skin served as saddle on its mother's back.

Proverb. q Nehemiah. *Gen. R.,* 67.8.

185.G.4 The day of death is concealed, that man may build and plant.

Tanhuma, Kedoshim, 8, ed Buber, 38b.

185.H. Bitterness

185.H.1 How bitter is the thought of death to him who lives at peace!

Apocrypha: Ben Sira, 41.1.

185.H.2 Look upon death with indifference, for its bitterness is commensurate with its fear.

q Ibn Gabirol, *Mibhar HaPeninim,* c.1050, #515.

185.H.3 There's no bad mother, and no good death.

Proverb (Yiddish). *JE,* x. 228b.

185.I. Defiance

185.I.1 He will swallow up death for ever.

Bible: Isa., 25.8.

185.I.2 I shall not die but live, and declare the works of the Lord.

Bible: Ps., 118.17.

185.I.3 God implanted in Jewish breasts souls that scorn death.

Josephus, *Wars,* 3.8.4.

185.I.4 In the messianic future there will be no death.

Joshua b. Levi. *Gen. R.,* 26.2, on *Isa.* 25.8.

185.I.5 O death, where is thy sting? O grave, where is thy victory?
New Testament: I Cor., 15.55.

185.J. Acceptance

185.J.1 The righteous has hope in his death.
Bible: Prov., 14.32.

185.J.2 The Lord gave, and the Lord hath taken away; blessed be the name of the Lord.
Bible: Job, 1.21.

185.J.3 Hail, Death! How welcome is your decree to the unhappy!
Apocrypha: Ben Sira, 41.2.

185.J.4 Fear not death, it is your destiny.
Ibid., 41.3.

185.J.5 Death is the absence of life. . . . There is no evil in it.
M. R. Cohen, *A Dreamer's Journey,* 1949, p. 262.

185.J.6 Is there not a certain satisfaction in the fact that natural limits are set to the life of the individual, so that at its conclusion it may appear as a work of art?
Einstein. *La Pensée,* 1947 (*Out of My Later Years,* 231).

185.J.7 Life, not death, is man's misfortune. It is death which gives liberty to the soul and permits it to depart to its own pure abode, there to be free from all calamity.
Eleazar b. Yair. q Josephus, *Wars,* 7.8.7.

185.J.8 Why should we fear death who welcome the repose of sleep?
Ibid.

185.J.9 Death . . . comes as a friend and comforter to man.
Franzos, *Picture of Christ,* 1868. *Jews of Barnow,* 292.

185.J.10 The man of wisdom . . . rejoices at the prospect of death, when the soul is disenthralled from the body.
Hasdai, *Sefer HaTapuah,* c.1230, tr Gollancz, 103.

185.J.11 It is impossible to escape death, and what is inescapable you may as well anticipate readily.
M. Ibn Ezra, *Shirat Yisrael,* (12C) 1924, p. 89.

185.J.12 Why do we dread death so much? . . . Death is our redeemer. . . . We should thankfully enjoy its blessed wine.
Ibn Gabirol, *Ahi Tebel.* q JP, 1952, iii 93.

185.J.13 It is equally cowardly not to wish to die when one ought to do so, and to wish to die when one ought not.
Josephus, *Wars,* 3.8.5.

185.J.14 I often feel that death is not the enemy of life, but its friend, for it is the knowledge that our years are limited which makes them so precious.
Liebman, *Peace of Mind,* 1946, p. 135.

185.J.15 For each one of us the moment comes when the great nurse, death, takes man, the child, by the hand and quietly says, "It is time to go home. Night is coming. It is your bedtime, child of earth. Come; you're tired. Lie down at last in the quiet nursery of nature and sleep. Sleep well. The day is gone. Stars shine in the canopy of eternity."
Ibid., 136.

185.J.16 Genesis can only take place through destruction, and without the destruction of the individuals, the species themselves would not exist permanently.
Maimonides, *Guide for the Perplexed,* 1190, 3.12.

185.J.17 "*Tob Meod,* very good"—read it: "*Tob mot,* death is good."
Meir. *Gen. R.,* 9.5, on *Gen.* 1.31.

185.J.18 Fear not death. It is just a matter of going from one room to another, ultimately to the most beautiful room.
Mendel of Kotzk, *Emet VeEmuna,* (1940), p. 30.

185.J.19 The dead must be amused when people bewail him, as if to say: It were better if you lived longer and suffered more!
Nahman Bratzlav. q HHH, iii. 72.

185.J.20 As no reasonable man chafes at having to repay a debt or deposit, . . . so he must not fret when nature reclaims its own.
Philo, *Abraham,* 44. See *Yalkut, Proverbs,* #964.

185.J.21 Better a noble death than a wretched life.
Proverb (Yiddish). BJS, #1700. *JE,* x. 228b.

185.J.22 After man's span of life, comes the Great Joy. The day Adam died became a holiday.
Seder Eliyahu Rabbah, ch 16, ed Friedmann, 81.

185.J.23 Death in a good cause is no

punishment, but an honor, and death for freedom is glory.

Spinoza, *Theologico-Political Treatise,* 1670, ch 20.

185.K. Contemplation

185.K.1 It is better to go to the house of mourning than to go to the house of feasting; for that is the end of all men, and the living will lay it to his heart.
Bible: Eccles., 7.2.

185.K.2 Remember thy end, and you shall never do amiss.
Apocrypha: Ben Sira, 7.36.

185.K.3 Remember his doom, for it is also yours—his yesterday, yours today!
Ibid., 38.22.

185.K.4 Who thinks of death improves himself.
Bahya, *Hobot HaLebabot,* 1040, 8.3.16.

185.K.5 One should never think of death, one should think of life. That is real piety.
Disraeli, (Waldershare in) *Endymion,* 1880.

185.K.6 He who reflects on death is already half dead!
Heine, *Lutetia,* Feb. 13, 1841.

185.K.7 Is there a reasonable person who at any significant moment does not deep in his soul think of anything but death?
Schnitzler, *Der einsame Weg,* 1903.

185.K.8 There is a veiled reference to death, resurrection and the hereafter in the Grace, so that man may not be haughty and smug after a meal. Let him contemplate that all snow begins pure white and turns into slush, that he with all his beauty will change into a small heap of corrupted matter.
Sefer Hasidim, 13C, #305, p. 95f.

185.K.9 A free man thinks of death least of all things; and his wisdom is a meditation not of death but of life.
Spinoza, *Ethics,* 1670, iv. Prop. 67.

185.L. Preparation

185.L.1 Set your house in order.
Bible: II Kings, 20.1.

185.L.2 O my soul, prepare provisions abundantly and not sparsely, while you are still among the living, and still able!
Bahya, *Hobot HaLebabot,* 1040, 7.7. tr Hyamson, iv. 46.

185.L.3 If you would endure life, be prepared for death.
Freud, *Reflections on War and Death,* tr 1918.

185.L.4 Of wood and of iron you seek
   to make sure,
   Of silk and of velvet and wares
   not a few.
   Nor should I neglect, O my
   friend, were I you,
   A piece of white linen ere long
   to secure.
Frug, "Hot and Cold," tr H. Frank. *JQRo,* xiv. 562.

185.L.5 One must not hold life too precious. One must always be prepared to let it go.
M. Steinberg. q *Jewish Frontier,* Oct. 1951, p. 54.

185.L.6 The provision is scant, and the road is long.
Ukba. *Talmud: Ketubot,* 67b.

186. DEBT

186.1 Debt is a prolific mother of folly and of crime.
Disraeli, *Henrietta Temple,* 1837, 2.1.

186.2 The beautiful shopkeeper's virtue, which sacrifices everything to meet a note on the day it is due!
Heine, *English Fragments,* 1831, ch 5.

186.3 Retire without supper, and rise without debt.
q Ibn Tibbon, *Tzavaah,* c.1190.

186.4 Pay your debts before you dispense alms.
Sefer Hasidim, 13C, #1247, p. 308.

186.5 We presume a debt is not paid before it is due.
Talmud: Baba Bathra, 5b.

187. DECALOG

187.1 The writing was the writing of God, graven upon the tables.
Bible: Exod., 32.16.

187.2 The broken tables were put with the new in the Ark.
Joseph. *Talmud: Menahot,* 99a.

187.3 The Ten Commandments are addressed in the singular, for at Sinai all Israel were of one heart.
Judah HaNasi. *Mekilta,* to *Exod.* 20.2.

187.4 "Remember" and "Observe" were spoken in one utterance.
Mekilta, to *Exod.* 20.8 (*Deut.* 5.12). *Talmud: Rosh Hashana,* 27a.

187.5 All the 613 commandments are included in the decalog.
Rashi, *Commentary*, to *Exod.* 24.12.

187.6 Behold, in this decalog is contained the whole law.
Abraham Saba, *Zeror HaMor, Jethro*, 15C, 78b.

187.7 When Moses descended from Sinai and saw Israel's offense, he noticed that the inscription had fled from the Tables. Dumbfounded, he broke the Tables, and then and there it was decreed that Israel be taught through trouble and subjection, through exile and anguish, through oppression and indigence.
Seder Eliyahu Rabbah, ch 19 (21), ed Friedmann, 117.

187.8 The letters carried Moses and the Tables as he came down from Sinai; but when they saw the dance about the Golden Calf, they flew up. Letterless, the Tables of stone became unbearably heavy, dropped from Moses' hands, and were shattered.
Pirké de R. Eliezer, ch 45. See *Talmud: Pesahim*, 87b; M. Steinberg, *A Partisan Guide*, 1945, p. 199.

187.9 Hard, stiff, abrupt as the cliffs from which they were taken, they remain as the firm, unyielding basis on which all true spiritual religion has been built up and sustained. . . . They represent to us . . . the granite foundation . . . without which all theories of religion are but as shifting and fleeting clouds; they give us the two fundamental laws, which all subsequent Revelation has but confirmed and sanctified—the Law of our duty towards God, and the Law of our duty towards our neighbor.
*Stanley, *History of the Jewish Church*, (1862) 1896, i. 159.

188. DECEIT

188.1 He that works deceit shall not dwell within My house.
Bible: Ps., 101.7.

188.2 None deceives unless he first be faithless to God.
Hanania b. Hakinai. *Tosefta: Shebuot*, 3.6.

188.3 Creating a false impression is deception.
Meir. *Talmud: Hullin*, 94a. *Tosefta: Baba Kamma*, 7.8.

188.4 It is forbidden to deceive anyone, Jew or heathen.
Samuel. *Talmud: Hullin*, 94a.

188.5 Verbal fraud is worse than monetary fraud.
Simeon b. Yohai. *Talmud: Baba Metzia*, 58b.

189. DEED

189.1 Not by the Creed but by the Deed.
F. Adler, motto of Ethical Culture Society, 1876.

189.2 Your deeds will bring you near or drive you far.
Akabia b. Mahalalel. *Mishna: Eduyot*, 5.7.

189.3 All depends on deeds.
Akiba. *Mishna: Abot*, 3.15.

189.4 Your works are to this city as a firm pillar.
Apocrypha: II Baruch, 2.2.

189.5 It is in the deed that God reveals Himself in life.
Baeck, *Essence of Judaism*, 1936, p. 50.

189.6 Our answer must be given in deeds, not words.
Bahya, *Hobot HaLebabot*, 1040, 7.10.

189.7 Great deeds are great legacies, and work with wondrous usury.
Disraeli, *Alroy*, 1833, 10.19.

189.8 Whose works exceed his wisdom is like a tree with few branches and many roots: all the raging winds will not move him.
Eleazar b. Azariah. *Mishna: Abot*, 3.17.

189.9 He who performs a good deed gains an advocate.
Eliezer b. Jacob. *Mishna: Abot*, 4.11.

189.10 Who has much learning but no good deeds is like an unbridled horse, that throws off the rider as soon as he mounts.
Elisha b. Abuya. *Abot de R. Nathan*, ch 24.

189.11 Practice makes the artist.
Hanau, *Tzohar HaTeba*, 1733, Introduction.

189.12 The divine sings in noble deeds.
Heschel, *The Earth is the Lord's* 1950, p. 64.

189.13 It were better if he, who does not practice the Torah he learns, had never been born.
Hiyya (Cf Johanan). *Lev. R.*, 35.7.

189.14 My deeds shall both my witnesses and judges be.

M. Ibn Ezra, "Hekitzoti." *Poems,* ed Brody, 1945, p. 7.

189.15 Out of divine precepts and deeds shall we build our ramparts.

Johanan b. Nappaha. *Cant. R.,* to 8.8.

189.16 Be always like a helmsman, on the lookout for good deeds.

Johanan b. Nappaha. *Lev. R.,* 21.5.

189.17 When a man departs this life, neither silver nor gold nor jewels accompany him, only Torah and good deeds.

José b. Kisma. *Mishna: Abot,* 6.9.

189.18 Man can approach God only by doing His commands.

Judah Halevi, *Cuzari,* c.1135, 2.46.

189.19 There is a haphazard sort of doing good, which is nothing but temperamental pleasure-seeking.

Lewald, *Gefühltes und Gedachtes,* (1900), p. 186.

189.20 True wisdom can be attained only through practice.

Maimonides. q CPP, #1718.

189.21 No reward except for deeds.

Mathia b. Heresh. *Mekilta,* to *Exod.* 12.6.

189.22 Scripture does not say of the people of Nineveh that God saw their sackcloth and fasting, but "God saw their works"!

Mishna: Taanit, 2.1, on *Jonah* 3.10.

189.23 Giving must culminate in service and action in character. But in order to *be,* enough doing must precede.

Montefiore, *Liberal Judaism,* 1903, p. 118f.

189.24 Be rich in good works.

New Testament: I Tim., 6.18.

189.25 Be doers of the word, not hearers only.

New Testament: James, 1.22.

189.26 By works was faith made perfect.

Ibid., 2.22.

189.27 Their works do follow them.

New Testament: Rev., 14.13.

189.28 Everyman has three friends: Family, Property, and Good Deeds. When his time comes to depart, he pleads with them to save him. Family replies, "No man can . . . redeem his brother" [*Ps.* 49.8]. Property replies, "Riches profit not in the day of wrath" [*Pr.* 11.4]. But Good Deeds respond: "Go in peace. We shall not desert you. We shall accompany, yea, precede you on the way, as Isaiah [58.8] says, 'Thy righteousness shall go before thee.'"

Pirké de R. Eliezer, ch 34.

189.29 Say little and do much.

Shammai. *Mishna: Abot,* 1.15.

189.30 Not theory but practice is the essential thing.

Simeon b. Gamaliel I. *Mishna: Abot,* 1.17.

189.31 We can judge a man faithful or unfaithful only by his works.

Spinoza, *Theologico-Political Treatise,* 1670, ch 14.

189.32 The best faith is not necessarily possessed by him who displays the best reasons, but by him who displays the best fruits of justice and charity.

Ibid.

189.33 Man's deeds are the measure of his days.

J. Steinberg, *Mishlé Yehoshua,* 1885, 23.11, p. 127.

189.34 The question was raised in Lydda: Which is greater, study or practice? Tarfon said, Practice. Akiba said, Study, for it leads to practice. And they all agreed with Akiba.

Talmud: Kiddushin, 40b.

189.35 Long, long are the shadows cast by our deeds.

A. Zweig, *The Crowning of a King,* 1938.

190. DEFENSE

190.1 If one comes to kill you, get ahead and kill him.

Shila. *Talmud: Berakot,* 58a. See 62b.

190.2 It is a duty to save a woman from rape, and anyone from idolatry, even at the cost of the assailant's life.

Simeon b. Yohai. *Talmud: Sanhedrin,* 74a.

191. DEFINITION

191.1 God has no definition.

Albo, *Ikkarim,* 1428, ii. ch 6.

191.2 Genius, the divine, are undefinable.

Baeck, *Essence of Judaism,* 1936, p. 25.

191.3 I hate definitions.

Disraeli, *Vivian Grey,* 1827, 2.6.

192. DELIBERATION

192.1 He is not wise who deliberates after stumbling.
Ibn Gabirol, *Mibhar HaPeninim*, c.1050, #208.

192.2 Be deliberate in judgment.
Mishna: Abot, 1.1.

193. DEMOCRACY

193.1 The chief claim of the Hebrew world to our regard lies in the fact that the ideals of democracy . . . first developed within this area . . . and all later democratic legislation is largely an unfolding of what is there set forth in principle.
*Bailey & Kent, *Hebrew Commonwealth*, 1922, p. 13f.

193.2 Democracy is evangelical in essence and its motive power is love.
Bergson, *Two Sources of Morality & Religion*, 1935, p. 271.

193.3 Industrial democracy should ultimately attend political democracy.
Brandeis, *The Employer and Trades Union*, April 21, 1904.

193.4 Their affliction, as well as their religion, has prepared the Jews for democracy.
Brandeis, *The Jewish Problem*, June 1915.

193.5 Democracy . . . substitutes self-restraint for external restraint. It is more difficult to maintain than to achieve.
Brandeis, letter to R. W. Bruere, Feb. 25, 1922.

193.6 The fatal drollery called a representative government.
Disraeli, *Tancred*, 1847, 2.13.

193.7 Nature herself vindicates democracy. For nature plants gifts and graces where least expected, and under circumstances that defy all the little artifices of man.
F. Frankfurter, address, Aaronsburg, Pa., Oct. 23, 1949.

193.8 Democracy is always a beckoning goal, not a safe harbor. For freedom is an unremitting endeavor, never a final achievement.
Ibid.

193.9 Democracy is a system that creates the . . . conditions for the full development of the individual.
Fromm, *Escape from Freedom*, 1941, p. 274.

193.10 I remember reading in Josephus that there were in Jerusalem republicans who opposed the royally-inclined Herodians, fought them fiercely, called no man "master," and hated Roman absolutism most bitterly. Freedom and equality was their religion. What madness!
Heine, *Shakespeare's Maidens: Jessica*, 1839.

193.11 Democracy is predicated not on faith in man but on the conviction . . . that no man is good enough or wise enough to be entrusted with irresponsible power over his fellow-men.
Herberg, *Judaism and Modern Man*, 1951, p. 181.

193.12 In contrast to totalitarianism, democracy can face and live with the truth about itself.
Hook. *N.Y. Times Magazine*, Sept. 30, 1951, p. 44.

193.13 Only that government is legitimate in which the king's seal of authority is voluntarily acknowledged by his subjects.
Jaffe, *Lebush Ir Shushan*, 1590, #369. q *JE*, vii. 60b.

193.14 Democracy which began by liberating man politically has developed a dangerous tendency to enslave him through the tyranny of majorities and the deadly power of their opinion.
Lewisohn, *The Modern Drama*, 1915.

193.15 It is citizen participation that nourishes the strength of a democracy.
D. E. Lilienthal, *This I Do Believe*, 1949, p. 91.

193.16 Democracy does not mean perfection. It means a chance to fight for improvement.
M. London. q RES, 154.

193.17 The best of constitutions, democracy.
Philo, *Unchangeableness of God*, 36.

193.18 The basic axioms of democracy —human dignity, equality and freedom— are all as Jewish as the Hebrew language.
Rifkind, American Jewish Tercentenary address, Nov. 14, 1954.

193.19 The Jewish belief in democracy is based simply on the faith that God created man in His image, that all men are His equal children, and that each possesses within him a spark of the divine which may not be violated.
Ibid.

193.20 I believe democracy to be of all forms of government the most natural, and the most consonant with individual liberty. In it no one transfers his natural right so absolutely that he has no further voice in affairs, he only hands it over to the majority of a society, whereof he is a unit. Thus all men remain, as they were in the state of nature, equals.

Spinoza, *Theologico-Political Treatise*, 1670, ch 16.

193.21 People who want to understand democracy should spend less time in the library with Aristotle and more time on the buses and in the subway.

Strunsky, *No Mean City*, 1944, ch 2, p. 22.

193.22 Democracy is moral before it is political.

Wirth, *Judaism and Democracy*, 7.

194. DEMONS

194.1 It is forbidden to traffic with demons.

Caro, *Yoré Deah*, 1564, 179.16.

194.2 Man, if you knew how many demons thirst for your blood, you would abandon yourself entirely . . . to the Almighty.

Kaidanover, *Kab HaYashar*, 1705, ch 5. q MRH, 52.

194.3 Demons bother only those who bother them.

Sefer Hasidim, 13C, #379, p. 115.
Talmud: Pesahim, 110b.

194.4 Do not go out alone on Wednesday or Saturday nights, for Igrath bath Mahalath is abroad then with her eighteen myriad dangerous demons.

Talmud: Pesahim, 112b.

195. DESERT

195.1 The desert shall rejoice, and blossom as the rose.

Bible: Isa., 35.1.

195.2 Clear ye in the wilderness the way of the Lord, make plain in the desert a highway for our God.

Ibid., 40.3.

195.3 I envy you your deserts—not just because they are deserts, but because you can afford to keep them deserts.

Ben Gurion, in Southern California, 1951.

195.4 The desert causes our otherwise so-important everyday to evaporate, nothing remains of our small differences and conventionalisms. The atmosphere is charged with something of the eternal mystery of the universe; burning sun, lambent air, and glowing sand, sand, sand.

Ehrenpreis, *The Soul of the East*, 1928, p. 74f.

195.5 In the wilderness Israel received the Torah, and thus in the wilderness, without land or soil, Israel became a nation.

S. R. Hirsch, *Nineteen Letters*, (1836), #8, p. 75.

195.6 The green pastures of Israel have sprung from a twofold desert: the waterless land and the arid past of the nation.

Koestler, *Promise and Fulfilment*, 1949, p. 199.

196. DESIRE

196.1 Desire fulfilled is a tree of life.
Bible: Prov., 13.12.

196.2 Put a knife to your throat if you be . . . given to appetite.
Ibid., 23.2.

196.3 All the labor of man is for his mouth, and yet the appetite is not filled.
Bible: Eccles., 6.7.

196.4 None departs from the world with even half of his desires gratified. If he has a hundred, he wants two hundred, and if he has two hundred, he wants them doubled again.
Aibu. *Eccles. R.*, 1.13, 3.10.

196.5 We desire much which, if granted, we would not like.
B. Auerbach, *Brosi und Moni*, 1852.

196.6 Desires becloud, weapons beshroud, pearls are thorns, roses are nettles, conceits are flames, and ducats are flies.
Bedersi, *Behinat HaOlam*, c.1310, ch 4.

196.7 Desires must be purified and idealized, not exterminated.
Elijah Gaon, *Commentary*, on *Prov.* 11.17.

196.8 There is more appetite than meat on earth.
Herzl, *Das Palais Bourbon*, 1895.

196.9 Life is the oil, man the wick, and appetite the fire.
I Hurwitz, *Mishlé Yisachar*, 1887, 9.7.

196.10 Desire blinds the wise.
A. Ibn Ezra, *Commentary*, to *Eccles.* 7.26.

196.11 The fruit of desire is poverty.
q M. Ibn Ezra, *Shirat Yisrael*, (12C) 1924, p. 86.

196.12 If you can't have what you want, want what you can have.
Ibn Gabirol, *Ethics*, 1045.

196.13 Who clings faithfully to God desires nothing for himself.
Itzikl of Radvil, *Or Yitzhak*, to *Abot* 6.1.

196.14 The will is never satisfied by desire for gain. . . . It is as if one should try to slake one's thirst with salt water.
Leo Hebraeus, *Philosophy of Love*, (1502) 1937, p. 13.

196.15 A poor man can be as sensuous about his dry morsel of bread as a rich man about his sumptuous meal.
Lipkin. q KTH, i. 272.

196.16 Those who desire to be men in truth, not brutes in the appearance of men, must constantly endeavor to reduce the wants of the body.
Maimonides, *Guide for the Perplexed*, 1190, 3.8.

196.17 He wins much who wants little.
Mosenthal, *Gesammelte Gedichte*, 1866; *Sprüchen*, 17.

196.18 Worldly desires are like columns of sunshine radiating through a dusty window, nothing tangible, nothing there.
Nahman Bratzlav. q Dubnow, *Toldot HaHasidut*, 303.

196.19 Appetite is never satisfied, but remains in want and athirst.
Philo, *Allegorical Interpretation*, 3.51.

196.20 Nothing ever escapes desire, but, like a forest fire, it proceeds onward, consuming and destroying everything.
Philo, *Decalogue*, 32.

196.21 What you can't acquire, don't desire.
Proverb (Yiddish). BJS, #1015.

196.22 Desire has no eyes.
Refiman, *Toldot Rabbenu Zerahia*, 1853, p. 46.

196.23 Desire is the essence of a man.
Spinoza, *Ethics*, 1677, iv. Pr 18, Proof.

196.24 No man can be wise against his own wishful thinking.
Werfel, *Between Heaven and Earth*, 1944, p. 215.

196.25 We often mistake a desire of the body for a yearning of the soul.
Wolfson. "Escaping Judaism." *Menorah*, 1921, vii. 158.

197. DESPAIR

197.1 My God, my God, why hast Thou forsaken me?
Bible: Ps., 22.2.

197.2 The day you transfix with melancholy and benumbing despair is lost, broken off the chain of your life.
B. Auerbach, *Lucifer*, 1847.

197.3 Despair is the conclusion of fools.
Disraeli, *Alroy*, 1833, 10.17.

197.4 The worst poison: to despair of one's own power!
Heine, *Book of Songs*, 1827.

197.5 To be disheartened by vicissitudes of heaven is natural, but to be despondent at the attack of a human foe is unmanly.
Herod. q Josephus, *Wars*, 1.19.4.

197.6 Even when the sharp sword is already on his neck, man must not despair nor cease to pray.
Johanan b. Nappaha. *Talmud: Berakot*, 10a.

197.7 Despair not. It is darkest before dawn. . . . Before light was created, all was darkness upon the face of the deep.
Kagan, *Hafetz Hayyim*, 1873. See YSS, 168.

197.8 No sickness like despair.
Lipkin. q KTH, i. 272.

197.9 Never despair because of your sins. Counterbalance them now with many good deeds.
Midrash LeOlam, vi. (JBH, iii. 112f).

197.10 Despair not because of persecution!
Mishna: Abot, 1.7.

197.11 No matter how you turn the mud of despair, it remains mud.
Nahman Bratzlav. q ZRN, 217.

197.12 Who despairs is not a man.
Philo, *The Worse Attacks the Better*, 38.

198. DESTINY

198.1 All things come alike to all: there is one event to the righteous and to the wicked.
Bible: Eccles., 9.2.

198.2 All men are appointed by God to share the greatest evil as well as the greatest good.
Apocrypha: Aristeas, 197.

198.3 There is no Fate. . . . Man is the creator of his destiny.
E. Auerbach, *Die Prophetie*, 1920, p. 67.

198.4 We ourselves are our Deity and destiny.

M. Beer, *Die Bräute von Aragonien,* 1823, Act 4, Sc. 7.

198.5 The road is predestined, but the way we walk it, the attitude with which we bear our fate, can be of great influence over events.

Beer-Hoffmann, 1945. q *New Palestine,* Nov. 1950.

198.6 No man but has his hour, no thing but has its place.

Ben Azzai. *Mishna: Abot,* 4.3.

198.7 No man touches what is destined for his neighbor; no government infringes even by a hair's breadth on the time of another.

Ben Azzai. *Talmud: Yoma,* 38a. See *Ruth R.,* 1.3, 11.18.

198.8 Our destiny repeats itself, because we create it.

Brod, *The Master,* 1951, p. 30.

198.9 We make our fortunes, and we call them fate.

Disraeli, *Alroy,* 1833, 5.4.

198.10 Man's feet are his fate: they lead him to where he is wanted.

Johanan b. Nappaha. *T: Sukka,* 53a.

198.11 I verily believe that if it would rain dollars from heaven, the coins would only knock holes in my head.

Heine, *Harz Journey,* 1824, p. 80.

198.12 Yes, withered and stripped and trampled down
By destiny's footsteps appalling—
My friends, this is ever the fate upon earth
Of all that is sweet and enthralling!

Heine, *Germany: A Winter Tale,* 1844, ch 23.

198.13 An evil fate pursues me
With unrelenting spite;
If I sold lamps and candles,
The sun would shine all night.
I cannot, cannot prosper
No matter what I try—
Were selling shrouds my business,
No man would ever die!

A Ibn Ezra, "When Love Passed By," tr S. Solis Cohen.

198.14 Guard thee against Fate; like venom
With a little honey mingled,
Are his gifts. Yet should he bring thee
Good at morn, accept, enjoy it,
Knowing surely that ere nightfall
Into evil will he turn it.

M. Ibn Ezra, *Selected Poems,* 1934, p. 41.

198.15 The religion of Israel freed mankind from that worship of Luck and Fate which is at the basis of all savagery.

Jacobs, *Jewish Contributions to Civilization,* 1919, p. 73.

198.16 There is no escape from Fate, for works of art and places any more than for living beings.

Josephus, *Wars,* 6.4.8.

198.17 If a man is destined to drown, he will drown even in a spoonful of water.

Proverb (Yiddish). BJS, #1014; ATJF, p. 642.

199. DESTRUCTION

199.1 When you besiege a city . . . destroy not its trees.

Bible: Deut., 20.19.

199.2 To destroy any object is a violation of this.

Abayé. *Talmud: Sabbath,* 129a.

199.3 To make a lamp burn fast is a violation of this.

Zutra. *Talmud: Sabbath,* 67b.

199.4 They shall not hurt nor destroy in all My holy mountain.

Bible: Isa., 11.9, 65.25.

199.5 To destroy is still the strongest instinct of our nature.

Beerbohm, *Yet Again,* 1923, p. 6.

199.6 Destructiveness is the outcome of unlived lives.

Fromm, *Escape from Freedom,* 1941, p. 184.

199.7 'Tis easier to abolish than to establish.

M. Ibn Ezra, *Shirat Yisrael,* (12C) 1924, p. 92.

199.8 We must not kill in vain even a snake or a spider.

Kaidanover, *Kab HaYashar,* 1705, ii. ch 3.

199.9 A people cannot be destroyed except from within.

Lewisohn, *Israel,* 1925, p. 224.

199.10 An imbecile destroys all he gets. Papa. *Talmud: Hagiga,* 4a.

199.11 One should be trained not to be wasteful.
Talmud: Semahot, 9.

200. DETAIL

200.1 There is no such thing as an unimportant detail. A sixteenth note is just as significant as a whole note.
Gabrilowitsch. q CMH, 7.

200.2 It is just the minutiae of life that make up the essence of life.
Klatzkin, *In Praise of Wisdom,* 1943, p. 19.

200.3 The good Lord dwells in the detail.
A. M. Warburg. q Baeck, *Judaism and Science,* 5.

201. DEVOTION

201.1 Better a little with devotion than much without it.
Jacob b. Asher, *Tur Orah Hayyim,* i., c.1300.

201.2 "For the commandment is a lamp" [*Prov.* 6.23]. And the spark which kindles the commandment is devotion.
Peretz, *Torah. Alle Verk,* vi. 74.

202. DIASPORA

202.1 The Lord shall scatter you among the peoples. . . . But from thence ye will seek the Lord your God, and you shall find Him.
Bible: Deut., 4.27, 29.

202.2 Seek the peace of the city whither I have caused you to be carried away captive, and pray unto the Lord for it; for in the peace thereof shall ye have peace.
Bible: Jer., 29.5, 7.

202.3 I will sift the house of Israel among all the nations, as corn is sifted in a sieve.
Bible: Amos, 9.9.

202.4 I have spread you abroad as the four winds of heaven.
Bible: Zech., 2.10.

202.5 Do not move to a foreign land, lest you adopt idolatry.
Akiba. *ARN,* ch 26. See *Tosefta: Aboda Zara,* 4.6.

202.6 I will scatter this people among the Gentiles that they may do good to the Gentiles.
Apocrypha: II Baruch, 1.4. See *Zohar, Gen.,* 244a.

202.7 Each land shall be full of you and each sea; and every one shall be incensed at your customs.
Apocrypha: Sibyls, iii. 271f.

202.8 The thousandfold lie which constitutes *Galuth.*
Buber, *Kampf um Israel,* 1933. q LAJ, 45.

202.9 The Jewish nation in the diaspora . . . is in a state of permanent danger.
Dubnow, *Pisma,* 1907, p. 322.

202.10 In this "land of two streams" the peculiar traits of the diaspora Jew were developed—his ability to feel at home in foreign lands and yet to remain a foreigner in his own home, his power of merging with his environment while adhering to tradition, his longing for the land of his fathers and his capacity for growing up with the land of his children.
Elbogen, *History of the Jews,* (1920) 1926, p. 20.

202.11 God scattered Israel among the nations for the sole purpose that proselytes should be numerous among them.
Eleazar b. Pedat. *Talmud: Pesahim,* 87b.

202.12 Blow out the light of the *Galuth* —a new candle must be lit!
Feierberg, *LeOn?* 1898. q HMH, 86.

202.13 In every country, even unto the giving of your life, be men of your country; and at the same time be Jews.
Fleg, *Why I Am a Jew,* 1929, p. 91.

202.14 In the diaspora we can have no living culture . . . because in the diaspora we have no life of our own.
A. D. Gordon, *Work and Culture,* 1911. LR, 75.

202.15 Israel's entire *Galuth* history is one vast altar, upon which it sacrificed all that men desire and love for the sake of acknowledging God and His Law.
S. R. Hirsch, *Nineteen Letters,* (1836), #9, p. 84.

202.16 The Holy One did a great favor to Israel in dispersing them among the nations.
Hoshaia Rabba. *Talmud: Pesahim,* 87b.

202.17 What brought about the Jews' dispersion? Their desire to be close to Gentiles.
Johanan b. Nappaha. *Talmud: Pesahim,* 118b.

202.18 Ye shall suffice for the world, to

furnish every land with inhabitants sprung from your race.

Josephus, *Antiquities,* 4.6.4.

202.19 The Jewish people in the diaspora is a body without a head or heart. . . . Indeed, it is not even a body, but scattered bones.

Judah Halevi, *Cuzari,* c.1135.

202.20 The diaspora is a perversion of the divine order, which assigns to each nation its own suitable place.

Judah Löw.

202.21 In the very circumstance of dispersion may lie fulfilment.

D. Kaufmann, *George Eliot & Judaism,* 1877, p. 87.

202.22 We are a nation in whose heart the love for home, for Zion, struggles with a lust for dispersion, for *Galuth.*

Liebenstein. *Jewish Frontier,* Sept. 1950, p. 26.

202.23 The Jewish people . . . has need of an intense center and a periphery. The complete salvation and working power of Judaism is dependent upon neither alone, but upon both together.

Magnes, "Land of Israel & Diaspora," 1923. q BFZ, 132.

202.24 Before all be fulfilled, the People of God must be first dispersed into all places and countries of the world.

Manasseh b. Israel, *A Declaration to the Commonwealth of England,* 1655 (ed L. Wolf, 1901, p. 79.).

202.25 Devote yourselves to the constitution of the land in which you have settled, but remain steadfast in the religion of your fathers. Bear both burdens as well as you can.

M. Mendelssohn, *Jerusalem,* 1783.

202.26 Canaan is too small for God's children. The Land of Israel will spread through all lands!

Peretz, *Der Dichter,* 1910. *Alle Verk,* x. 24.

202.27 With the dispersion of the Jews all over the world, the universal mission of Judaism began.

Philipson, *Reform Movement in Judaism,* 1907, p. 5.

202.28 So populous are the Jews that no one country can hold them. . . . While they hold the Holy City . . . to be their mother city, yet those . . . are in each case

accounted by them to be their fatherland in which they were born and reared.

Philo, *Flaccus,* 7.

202.29   We have sat by every river,
Not only of Babylon, . . .
So that now we love
Every inch of earth.
In each far-flung region
There is a Jewish hearth.

A. Raisen, "Jewish Song." LGP, 16f.

202.30 We have been dispersed to all the ends of the earth in order that we may learn from the nations their best, while we may teach them the fundamentals of our pure, illuminating, ancient faith.

Rapoport, letter to S. D. Luzzatto, Apr. 28, 1841.

202.31 Blessed are Israel in all their settlements: even though they wander wearily in all directions . . . they are always in the center!

Seder Eliyahu Rabbah, ch 5, ed Friedmann, 25.

202.32 Were Jews to find rest in the diaspora, they would lose their desire to return to the land of their fathers.

Simeon b. Lakish. *Lam. R.,* 1.3.

202.33 The debris of this devoted Syriac people which took up the Hellenic challenge so gallantly and was shattered so remorselessly by the impact of Rome is drifting about in the world down to this day. . . . This pulverized social ash is familiar to us as the Jewish "Diaspora."

*Toynbee, *Study of History,* 1934, ii. 286.

202.34 If a ruler rises up against you in Europe to inflict death upon you, a kingdom in Asia permits you to live therein; and if they expel you and burn you in Spain, the Lord wills it that you are received and allowed to live freely in Italy. . . . This is a mysterious and sublime favor which heretofore you have deemed the reverse.

Usque, *Consolação às Tribulaçoes de Yisrael,* 1553. q NLG, 128.

202.35 Israel is fated to be enslaved by all the Gentiles of the world in order that it may uplift those sparks which have also fallen among them. . . . Therefore it was necessary that Israel should be scattered to the four winds.

Vital, *Sefer HaLikkutim,* 16C, p. 89b. q SMT, 284.

202.36 As the world cannot be without the four cardinal points, so the nations cannot be without Israel.
Zohar, Exod., 5b, on *Zech.* 2.10.

202.37 Wherever Jews dwell, God is found among them.
Zohar, Num., 126a.

203. DIFFERENCE

203.1 What has the straw to do with the wheat?
Bible: Jer., 23.28.

203.2 Diversity in the Creed, Unanimity in the Deed.
F. Adler, *Creed and Deed,* 1877, p. 172.

203.3 The difference is no less real because it is of degree.
Cardozo, *Heidemann vs. American District Tel. Co.,* 1921.

203.4 Praised be Thou . . . who endowest the mind with intelligence to distinguish between day and night.
Daily Prayer Book, ed Singer, 5.

203.5 A true democracy rests on the differences between its citizens, as individuals or as groups.
H. Greenberg, *The Inner Eye,* 1953, p. 183.

203.6 The refrain "it was good" is omitted in the account of the second day of creation, because on that day distinctions were introduced,—"divide waters from waters" [*Gen.* 1.6].
Hanina b. Hama. *Gen. R.,* 4.6.

203.7 It is impossible that all men should agree, since their characters, temperaments and fates differ.
M. Ibn Ezra, *Shirat Yisrael,* (12C) 1924, p. 96.

203.8 Differences are likely to lead to . . . the world's advancement, and add to the charms of social intercourse. Nothing leads to boredom more than uniformity of manners and thoughts.
Jacobs, *Jewish Contributions to Civilization,* 1919, p. 53.

203.9 The very first petition in the *Amida* is for discrimination.
Loewe, *Rabbinic Anthology,* 1938, p. lix.

203.10 Our likeness to other creatures is the greatest system of facts of our life; our differences are relatively minor.
Myerson, *Speaking of Man,* 1950, p. 117.

203.11 As a shepherd divides the sheep from the goats.
New Testament: Matt., 25.32.

203.12 Woe to him who knows not the difference between good and bad.
Proverb. q Papa. *Talmud: Sanhedrin,* 103a.

203.13 No one frog jumps twice alike.
L. Stein, *Journey Into the Self,* 1950, p. 154.

203.14 Praised be Thou . . . who distinguishest between holy and profane.
Zutra I. *Talmud: Berakot,* 29a.

204. DIGNITY

204.1 Grant them esteem, O Lord.
Bible: Ps., 9.21.

204.2 Is not this the chief function of our religion, to engender in us a sense of human worth?
Eybeshitz, *Yaarot Debash,* 1779, i. 99a. See BSJ, 357.

204.3 I have been wont to bear my head right high.
Heine, *Book of Songs: To My Mother,* 1827, #1.

204.4 To be invested with dignity means to represent something more than oneself.
Heschel, *The Earth Is the Lord's* 1950, p. 109.

204.5 If one does not love Judaism even in a dusty dress, one will not love it in a fancy dress either . . . [but] everyone who loves it should wish it to be dignified at all times.
S. R. Hirsch, letter to Simon May, Dec. 15, 1839. q *HJ,* April 1951, p. 41.

204.6 The dignity of a neighbor, who was created in the divine image, is equivalent to God's dignity.
Judah Löw. q Bokser, *From World of Cabbalah,* 79.

204.7 Dignity demands determination of will in good forms; good forms by themselves do not make for dignity.
Pappenheim. *Bertha Pappenheim zum Gedächtnis,* 1936, 29.

204.8 In deference to human dignity a negative command of the Torah may be disregarded.
Rabina b. Huna. *Talmud: Menahot,* 37b.

204.9 Love forgets dignity.
Simeon b. Eleazar. *Talmud: Sanhedrin,* 105b.

204.10 Man's dignity is not greater than God's. If the Holy One makes winds to blow, clouds to rise, rain to descend, the earth to produce, and tables to be set, certainly Rabban Gamaliel can wait on scholars!

Zadok. *Talmud: Kiddushin*, 32b.

205. DILIGENCE

205.1 The hand of the diligent makes rich.

Bible: Prov., 10.4. See 13.4.

205.2 A man diligent in his business shall stand before kings.

Ibid., 22.29.

205.3 Only the industrious are inwardly cheerful and peaceful.

B. Auerbach, *Der Lauterbacher*, 1843.

205.4 Diligence is the right hand of success.

S. Rubin, *Sefer HaMiddot*, 1854.

205.5 The ant, though small and poor, bores the eternal hills.

J. Steinberg. *Luah Ahiasaf*, 5660, p. 283.

205.6 Some who are diligent lose, and some who are indolent win.

Talmud: Pesahim, 50b.

206. DIPLOMACY

206.1 If you will be a servant to this people this day, . . . they will be your servants for ever.

Bible: I Kings, 12.7.

206.2 Israel's salvation will be achieved by prophets, not by diplomats.

Ahad HaAm, "First Zionist Congress," 1897. *Ten Essays*, 31.

206.3 I have ceased to wonder at many things; but that two diplomats can look at each other without laughing, that still amazes me daily.

Boerne, *Der Narr im weissen Schwan*, ch 2.

206.4 A pupil of diplomacy has to learn three things: to speak French, to speak nothing, and to speak falsehood.

Boerne, *Fragmente & Aphorismen*, 1840, #46.

206.5 I never refuse. I never contradict. I sometimes forget.

Disraeli, on his success with Queen Victoria, 1877.

206.6 Diplomacy is to do and say
The nastiest things in the nicest way.

Goldberg. *Reflex*, Oct. 1927, p. 77.

207. DIRECTION

207.1 Only direction is reality, the goal

is always fiction, even the attained goal.

Schnitzler, *Buch der Sprüche & Bedenken*, 1927, p. 232.

207.2 In the direction a man follows in this world will he be led in the world of eternity.

Zohar, Gen., 100a.

208. DISCIPLINE

208.1 Every artist and every athlete knows how stern a regimen is imposed by an ideal.

Edman, *Adam*, 1929, p. 173.

208.2 Only in fetters is liberty:
Without its banks could a river be?

L. Ginsberg, "Fetters." *Commonweal*, 1935.

208.3 Blessed were our ancestors, whose discipline was such that they were punished even for succumbing to sleep.

Johanan b. Nappaha. *Talmud: Tamid*, 28a.

208.4 Man is free in his imagination, but bound by his reason.

Lipkin, *Iggeret HaMusar*, 1858. GIS, 128.

208.5 Whoever preaches absence of discipline is an enemy of progress.

Nordau, *Degeneration*, (1893), 5.2, p. 560.

209. DISGUISE

209.1 Mankind is pure and simple only at a masque ball, where the waxen mask covers the usual mask of flesh.

Heine, *Letter from Berlin*, 1822.

209.2 We clothe the wolf our action in the sheep's clothing of our beautiful phrases.

London. q Rogoff, *An East Side Epic*, 210.

209.3 God has not stamped on every man a peculiar countenance for nothing; why then should we, in the most solemn concerns of life, render ourselves unknown to one another by disguise?

M. Mendelssohn, *Jerusalem*, 1783, tr Samuels, ii. 170.

209.4 There are many who owe their happiest hours to a coat of mourning; many who carry an aching heart under a comedian's cloak.

Saphir. q Peters, *The Jew as a Patriot*, 210.

210. DISGUST

210.1 Devour not voraciously lest you become offensive.
Apocrypha: Ben Sira, 31.17.

210.2 He will be judged who disgusts a neighbor.
Talmud: Hagiga, 5a.

211. DISPLAY

211.1 Display not your wisdom before the king.
Apocrypha: Ben Sira, 7.5.

211.2 It is forbidden . . . to display unusual ability in the presence of the handicapped.
Finkelstein. *Religions of Democracy,* 1941, p. 3.

211.3 A man who shows me his wealth is like the beggar who shows me his poverty; they are both looking for alms, the rich man for the alms of my envy, the poor man for the alms of my guilt.
Hecht, *A Child of the Century,* 1954, p. 33.

211.4 Who quibbles to display his learning, is a false speaker.
Mekilta, to *Exodus* 23.7.

212. DISPOSITION

212.1 No good above a good disposition.
Apocrypha: Ben Sira, 30.16.

212.2 A man's disposition is his destiny.
Lassalle, *Die Philosophie Herakleitos,* 1858, ii. 452.

213. DIVINATION

213.1 Ye shall practice neither divination nor soothsaying.
Bible: Lev., 19.26.

213.2 Divinations, soothsayings and dreams are vain.
Apocrypha: Ben Sira, 34.5.

214. DIVORCE

214.1 A man may divorce his wife if he finds another woman more beautiful.
Akiba. *Mishna: Gittin,* 9.10.

214.2 If a man divorces his first wife, the very altar weeps.
Eleazar b. Pedat. *Talmud: Gittin,* 90b.

214.3 A woman may not be divorced except by her own consent.
Gershom b. Judah, summary of decree, c. 1000. See Asher b. Yehiel, *Responsa,* 43.1.

214.4 A man may divorce his wife for merely spoiling his food.
Hillel School. *Mishna: Gittin,* 9.10.

214.5 No man may divorce his wife unless he found her guilty of an immoral act.
Shammai School, *ibid.* Cf *Matt.,* 5.32, 19.6.

214.6 He who sends away his wife is a hateful person.
Johanan. *Talmud: Gittin,* 90b.

214.7 If a woman says, "My husband is distasteful to me, I cannot live with him," the court compels the husband to divorce her, because a wife is not a captive.
Maimonides, *Yad: Ishut,* 1180, 14.8.

214.8 When a divorced man marries a divorced woman, there are four minds in the bed.
Talmud: Pesahim, 112a.

215. DOG

215.1 Against any of the children of Israel shall not a dog whet his tongue.
Bible: Exod., 11.7.

215.2 A dog knows its master, a cat does not.
Eleazar b. Zadok. *Talmud: Horayot,* 13a.

215.3 When one dog barks, all others bark with him.
Exod. R., 31.9.

215.4 The worst dog gets the best bone.
Peretz, *Mesiras Nefesh,* c. 1910. *Alle Verk,* vii. 155.

215.5 Show a dog a finger, and he wants the whole hand.
Proverb (Yiddish). BJS, #1140.

215.6 If you lie with dogs, you rise with fleas.
Ibid., #1142.

215.7 None smarter than a beaten dog.
Sholom Aleichem, *Menahem Mendel,* 1895.

215.8 Barking dogs don't bite, but they themselves don't know it.
Sholom Aleichem. *Sholom Aleichem Buch,* 1926, p. 350. Ref. to anti-Semites.

215.9 Who breeds a wild dog in his house keeps kindness away.
Simeon b. Lakish. *Talmud: Sabbath,* 63a.

215.10 When dogs howl, the Angel of Death is in town; when dogs frolic, the prophet Elijah is in town.
Talmud: Baba Kamma, 60b.

215.11 Two dogs in a kennel snarl at each other; but when a wolf comes along, they become allies.
Talmud: Sanhedrin, 105a.

215.12 Who was bitten by a dog will tremble at its bark.
Zohar, Exod., 45a.

216. DOUBT

216.1 Do not rely on If and Perhaps.
Bahya, *Hobot HaLebabot*, 1040, 8.3.13.

216.2 I'll give you a definite maybe.
Goldwyn, attributed to.

216.3 The worst of worms: the dagger thoughts of doubt.
Heine, *Sonnets: To August Wilhelm von Schlegel*, 1821.

216.4 No greater joy than to resolve a doubt.
J. Hurwitz, *Tzel HaMaalot*, 1764, p. 31. See Isserles, *Responsa*, #5.

216.5 Who grieves over the doubtful will rejoice over the sure.
M. Ibn Ezra, *Shirat Yisrael*, (12C) 1924, p. 123.

216.6 I may be wrong, and sometimes am, but I never have any doubts.
Jessel. q Goodhart, *Five Jewish Lawyers*, 19.

216.7 Doubt is the father of laziness.
S. D. Luzzatto, *Igrot Shadal*, #46.

216.8 May the Lord deliver us from doubt!
Maimonides, *Iggeret Teman*, 1172.

216.9 Faith and doubt are twin offspring of mystery.
Mattuck, sermon, Jan. 2, 1927. q SBQ, 49.

216.10 The path to sound credence is through the thick forest of skepticism.
G. J. Nathan, *Materia Critica*, 1924, p. 5.

216.11 He who doubts is damned.
New Testament: Rom., 14.23.

216.12 The safest course is to suspend judgment.
Philo, *Drunkenness*, 49.

216.13 Skepticism often makes big calls on our faith.
M. Samuel, *Prince of the Ghetto*, 1948, p. 178.

216.14 Some people are never in doubt; either they know nothing or they are sure; but often their ignorance is really their best guarantee.
L. Stein, *Journey into the Self*, 1950, p. 256.

216.15 From the womb of doubt is born truth.
J. Steinberg, *Mishlé Yehoshua*, 1885, 20.1, p. 114.

216.16 No people are more superstitious than skeptics.
Trotsky, *Literature and Revolution*, 1925, p. 27.

216.17 Doubts make men wise.
Uceda, *Midrash Samuel*, to *Abot*, 1.11, 1579.

216.18 Without helpful doubts . . . the human family cannot advance.
I. M. Wise, "Wandering Jew," 1877. *Selected Writings*, 182.

217. DOWRY

217.1 The money a man takes with his wife is not honest money.
Abraham b. David. q *Tur Eben HaEzer*, 66. q HSJ, 268.

217.2 Sell the Holy Scrolls in the synagog to give a poor girl a dowry.
Proverb. ATJF, p. 640.

217.3 A father must provide for his daughter a trousseau and dowry.
Talmud: Ketubot, 52b.

218. DRAMA

218.1 Moral actions, not moral views, are material for the drama.
Boerne, *Dramaturgische Blätter*, #42.

218.2 Drama—what literature does at night.
G. J. Nathan, *Testament of a Critic*, 1931, p. 179.

219. DREAM

219.1 Behold, this dreamer comes!
Bible: Gen., 37.19.

219.2 Dreams lift up fools.
Apocrypha: Ben Sira, 34.1.

219.3 He who can reflect on his dreams, no longer dreams.
Boerne, *Für die Juden*, 1819.

219.4 Dreams do not die
If they bloomed once in the soul.
Fichman, *Kol Shiré*, ii. 23. q WHJ, iv. 307.

219.5 Dreams are like a microscope through which we look at the hidden occurrences in our soul.
Fromm, *The Forgotten Language*, 1951, p. 167.

219.6 Dream is the incomplete form of prophecy.
Hanina b. Isaac. *Gen. R.*, 17.5.

219.7 Sir, do not mock our dreamers. . . . Their words become the seeds of freedom.

Heine, *English Fragments*, 1828, ch 1.

219.8 Every creed of man was once a dream.

Herzl. q S. S. Wise, *Sermons & Addresses*, 1905, p. 8.

219.9 A dream not interpreted is like a letter not read.

Hisda. *Talmud: Berakot*, 55a.

219.10 Dreams are real.

Isaac. *Eccles. R.*, 1.1.1.

219.11 A dream only reflects the dreamer's thoughts.

Jonathan b. Eleazar. *Talmud: Berakot*, 55b.

219.12 A dream brought me into the sanctuaries of God.

Judah Halevi, *Selected Religious Poetry*, 9.

219.13 Dreams are of no consequence.

Meir. *Talmud: Gittin*, 52a. *Horayot*, 13b.

219.14 The meaning of a dream depends on the interpreter.

Nahum Gimzo, (Eleazar b. Pedat). *Talmud: Berakot*, 55b.

219.15 A dream never shows the impossible, e.g., a golden palm, or an elephant going through a needle's eye.

Raba. *Talmud: Berakot*, 55b.

219.16 A man's dreams are an index to his greatness.

Z. Rabinowitz, *Pri Tzaddik*, 1906, i. to *Gen.* 28.12.

219.17 I will not change one golden dream for all your dreams of gold.

P. M. Raskin.

219.18 Depend not on dreams.

Sefer Hasidim, 13C, #221, p. 76.

219.19 Dreams are a secretion of our thoughts, and through them our thought is purified.

P. Shapiro. q BTH, i. 134.

219.20 Fritters in a dream are not fritters, but a dream.

Sholom Aleichem, *Menahem Mendel: London*, 1892, #8.

219.21 No wheat without chaff: no dream without nonsense.

Simeon b. Yohai. *Talmud: Berakot*, 55a.

220. DRESS

220.1 They sewed fig-leaves together and made themselves aprons.

Bible: Gen., 3.7.

220.2 A woman shall not wear what pertains to a man, neither shall a man put on a woman's garment.

Bible: Deut., 22.5.

220.3 Dress mirrors a nation's pain and sorrow, its pleasures and joys.

A Brüll, *Trachten der Juden*, 1873. q AJL, 273.

220.4 On no account adopt foreign fashions in dress.

Eliezer Halevi, *Tzavaah*, c. 1350. AHE, 212.

220.5 Clothes are man's glory.

Exod. R., 18.5.

220.6 Folly rests its honor in its dress.

Ezobi, *Kaarat Kesef*, 1270. JQRo, viii. 538.

220.7 A man may walk about in simple dress.
And yet within a priceless soul possess.

Ibid., (539).

220.8 The fool carries all his greatness on his clothes.

Foundations of Religious Fear, 12C, tr H. Gollancz.

220.9 Let not his humble vesture make thee blind
To one whose greatness is a learned mind.

Hasdai, *Ben HaMelek VeHaNazir*, 1230, ch 26. q CHH, 124.

220.10 My garments are my honorers.

Johanan. *Talmud: Baba Kamma*, 91b.

220.11 Who does not respect clothes will not benefit from them.

Jose b. Hanina. *Talmud: Berakot*, 62b.

220.12 "Clean hands and a pure heart" does not refer to clean gloves and a white shirt.

Kranz, on *Ps.* 24.4. See AJL, 292, Note 1.

220.13 My glory, honor, all depend
Upon my shirt and cloak and hat:
Alas! An age that honors clothes
Though worn by horse or ass!

Lonzano, *Tokahat Musar*, 1572, Canto 3, lines 127f. q Rhine. *JQR*, 1910, i. 367.

220.14 Gorgeous headgear and embroidered apparel give rise to pride and border upon lust.

M. H. Luzzatto, *Mesillat Yesharim*, 1740, ch 13, p. 124.

220.15 A wise man should wear neither princely apparel . . . to attract attention,

nor paupers' clothes which bring disrespect.
Maimonides, *Yad: Deot,* 1180, 5.9.

220.16 Avoid excessive finery which sets people gaping at you.
Orhot Tzaddikim, 15C, ch 1.

220.17 If need be, spare from your stomach and spend on your back.
Proverb. q Abayé. *Talmud: Baba Metzia,* 52a.

220.18 My name in my town; elsewhere, my gown.
Proverb. q *Talmud: Sabbath,* 145b.

220.19 Judge not a man by his dress; not garments but character stress.
G. Rosenzweig, *Hamisha Ve-Elef,* 1903, #508.

220.20 Beautiful clothes will not hide a hump.
Twerski. q CPP, #404.

221. DRINK

221.1 Woe to them that rise early in the morning to follow strong drink, that tarry late into the night till wine inflame them!
Bible: Isa., 5.11.

221.2 The drinking was according to the law: none did compel.
Bible: Esther, 1.8.

221.3 I hate a scholar who frequents taverns.
Apocrypha: Ben Sira, 21.23.

221.4 Food without drink is like a wound without a plaster.
q Brüll, *Jahrbücher,* vii.

221.5 Who drinks, first chinks.
Disraeli, *Count Alarcos,* 1839.

221.6 "Man comes from dust and ends in dust" [Holy Day Musaf prayer]—and in between, let's have a drink.
Proverb (Yiddish). BJS, #24.

221.7 What, then, will become of the world
When no one will drink any more?
E. Salomon, *Fiducit,* 1834.

222. DROWNING

222.1 A drowning man will catch at any rope.
Maimonides, *Iggeret Teman,* 1172.

223. DRUNKENNESS

223.1 A workman given to drunkenness will never become rich.
Apocrypha: Ben Sira, 19.1.

223.2 Drink not wine to drunkenness.
Apocrypha: Tobit, 4.15.

223.3 On Simhat Torah all drunkards are sober.
Proverb (Yiddish). q *Kibitzer,* Oct. 8, 1909.

223.4 The intoxicated is legally responsible, but exempt from prayer.
Talmud: Erubin, 65a.

224. DUST

224.1 Dust you are, and unto dust shall you return.
Bible: Gen., 3.19. See *Eccles.* 3.20.

224.2 His enemies shall lick the dust.
Bible: Ps., 72.9.

224.3 I am dust under the soles of your feet!
Lev. R., 2.12.

224.4 When ye depart from there, shake off the dust under your feet for a testimony against them.
New Testament: Mark, 6.11.

225. DUTY

225.1 We want . . . not religion as a duty, but duty as a religion.
F. Adler, *Creed and Deed,* 1877, p. 97.

225.2 Who does no more than his duty is not doing his duty.
Bahya, *Hobot HaLebabot,* 1040, 5.5, tr Hyamson, iii. 66.

225.3 Obedience to duty means resistance to self.
Bergson, *Two Sources of Morality & Religion,* 1935, p. 12.

225.4 Duty must be accepted as the dominant conception in life.
Brandeis, at Menorah Conference, Nov. 8, 1914.

225.5 Duty scorns prudence.
Disraeli, *Life of Lord George Bentinck,* 1852.

225.6 Think ever that you are born to perform great duties.
Disraeli, *Venetia,* 1837.

225.7 Judaism enjoins 613 duties, but knows no dogmas.
S. R. Hirsch, *Nineteen Letters,* (1836), #15, p. 146.

225.8 Only the obligations of the strong assure the rights of the weak.
Hoffenstein, *Pencil in the Air,* 1923, p. 147.

225.9 While occupied with one religious duty, a man is exempt from the performance of other religious duties.

José HaGelili. *Talmud: Sukka*, 26a. Shammai School. *Talmud: Berakot*, 11a.

225.10 A moral obligation is no less compelling because it may end in failure.

Laski, *The State in Theory & Practice*, 1935.

225.11 To earn redemption, you need religious duties.

Mathia b. Heresh. *Mekilta*, to *Exod.* 12.6.

225.12 A man will do unawares what is not imposed on him.

Raba. *Talmud: Shebuot*, 34b.

225.13 It is not incumbent on you to finish the work, neither are you free to exempt yourself from it.

Tarfon. *Mishna: Abot*, 2.16.

226. EAGLE

226.1 His fellow creatures . . . believe that the eagle cannot sing, and know not that he only lifts his voice in music when far from their realm, that in his pride he will only be heard by the sun. And he is right, for it might occur to some of the feathered mob down below there to criticize his song.

Heine, *Journey from Munich to Genoa*, 1828, ch 6.

226.2 Wherever the carcass is, there will the eagles gather.

New Testament: Matt., 24.28.

226.3 'Tis a disgrace for an eagle to perish in its gilded cage!

Shneor, "Song of the Prophet," 1903, tr FTH, 168.

227. EAR

227.1 The ear tries words, as the palate tastes food.

Bible: Job, 34.3.

227.2 The mouth and the ear are a bow and a fiddle; and when the ear is shut, the mouth is mute.

Bialik, *Debarim SheBe'al Peh*, i. 233.

227.3 The ears are the gates to the mind.

M. Ibn Ezra, *Shirat Yisrael*, (12C) 1924, p. 114.

227.4 Why is the ear-lap soft? That it might be bent into the ear when an unworthy thing is said.

Ishmael School. *Talmud: Ketubot*, 5b.

227.5 Why was his ear singled out for punishment when a bondman refuses liberation [*Exod.* 5.6]? Because the ear heard at Sinai, "They are My servants" [*Lev.* 25.55], yet this man submitted voluntarily to the yoke of a human master!

Johanan b. Zakkai. *Tosejta: Baba Kamma*, 7.5.

227.6 Let your ear hear what your mouth speaks.

Jose b. Halafta. *Talmud J: Berakot*, 2.4.

227.7 Woe to the ears that hear this!

Judah b. Ilai. *Midrash Tehillim*, 17.4.

227.8 The road has ears, aye, the wall has ears!

Levi. *Leviticus Rabbah*, 32.2.

227.9 The human ear is so formed that it can sleep through the sound and wake at the echo.

Schnitzler, *Buch der Sprüche & Bedenken*, 1927, p. 227.

227.10 Is there an ear so fine that it can hear the sigh of the withering rose?

Ibid.

228. EARTH

228.1 All the earth is Mine.

Bible: Exod., 19.5. *Lev.*, 25.23. Cf *Job*, 41.3.

228.2 He created it not a waste. He formed it to be inhabited.

Bible: Isa., 45.18.

228.3 The earth is the Lord's, and the fulness thereof.

Bible: Ps., 24.1. See *I Sam.*, 2.8.

228.4 The heavens are the heavens of the Lord; but the earth has He given to the children of men.

Bible: Ps., 115.16.

228.5 Speak to the earth, and it shall teach you.

Bible: Job, 12.8.

228.6 One generation goes, another generation comes, but the earth abides forever.

Bible: Eccles., 1.4.

228.7 The Lord of heaven made the earth to be possessed by all men in common.

Apocrypha: Sibyl, 3.47.

228.8 O Earth, today I am on you, tomorrow you will be on me.

Benjacob. *Pirhé Tzajon*, 1841, p. 15.

228.9 "The place whereon you stand is holy ground" [*Exod.* 3.5]. Wherever man stands is holy ground. Whatever spot on earth you occupy can be sanctified to God.

Elimelek, *Noam Elimelek*, (1787) 1942, p. 62.

228.10 All talk turns on the subject of the earth.

Gen. R., 13.2.

228.11 Our object is, that here on earth
We may mount to the realms of
heaven.

Heine, *Germany: A Winter Tale,* 1844, ch 1.

228.12 Have you ever watched children swinging? in order to lift themselves higher . . . they have to dig their toes into the earth.

Opatoshu, *In Polish Woods,* (1921) 1928, p. 112.

228.13 The pagans do not know God, and love only the earth. The Jews know the true God, and love only the earth. The Christians know the true God, and do not love the earth.

*Pascal, *Pensées,* 1670, xv.

228.14 To be of the eternal, you must be of the earth.

Peretz, *Der Dichter,* 1910. *Alle Verk,* x. 19.

228.15 I got a religion that wants to take heaven out of the clouds and plant it right here on the earth where most of us can get a slice of it.

Shaw, *Bury the Dead,* 1936, p. 82.

229. EATING

229.1 Let us eat and drink, for tomorrow we die.

Bible: Isa., 22.13.

229.2 Every man has the right to eat.
Heine. q EPP, 50.

229.3 The glutton's gullet consumes his gold and washes down his silver.

Hiyya b. Nehemiah. *Lev. R.,* 18.1, on *Eccles.* 12.6.

229.4 Do not talk while eating, lest the windpipe act before the gullet, and life be endangered.

Johanan b. Nappaha. *Talmud: Taanit,* 5b.

229.5 Guard against heavy meals: more heinous than homicide is suicide.

Judah b. Asher, *Tzavaah,* 14C. AHE, 172.

229.6 Work before eating, rest after eating. Eat not ravenously, filling the mouth gulp after gulp without breathing space.

Maimonides, *Shaaré HaMusar.* AHE, 113f.

229.7 Chew well with your teeth and you'll feel it in your toes.

Meir. *Talmud: Sabbath,* 152a.

229.8 There is a universal law . . . which none can amend or repeal, and against which no protest or preachment can avail, a law . . . most persistent and inexorable, the law of—eating.

Mendelé, *Di Kliatshé,* 1873, ch 17.

229.9 Eat a third, drink a third, and leave a third of your stomach empty, so that if you get angry, you'll have your fill.

Nathan. *Talmud: Gittin,* 70a.

229.10 Jews begin a meal with Torah and a benediction; the heathen, with frivolous talk.

Rab. *Talmud: Megilla,* 12b.

229.11 You eat to live, you do not live to eat.

Saadia, letter to an Egyptian community, 928. KTJ, i. 89.

229.12 A change of diet is the beginning of bowel trouble.

Samuel. *Talmud: Ketubot,* 110b.

229.13 Who eats in the street acts like a dog.

Talmud: Kiddushin, 40b.

229.14 Sixty runners will not overtake him who breakfasts early.

Talmud: Baba Kamma, 92b.

229.15 Sometimes one meal prevents many meals.

Zabara, *Sefer Shaashuim,* 13C, ch 8.

229.16 The less you eat, the less you ail.

Ibid., ed Davidson, 88; ed Hadas, 116.

230. ECCLESIASTES

230.1 Unfortunately . . . Ecclesiastes is in the Bible. Otherwise it would certainly be an extremely popular book. It is so modern, it is so sceptical, it is so blasé, it is so fashionably free from enthusiasm, from all fervor or deep conviction.

Harrison, *Religion of a Modern Liberal,* 1931, p. 1.

230.2 Nowhere else can we see so plainly the singularity, the variety, the unexpectedness of Jewish genius. . . . The Song of Songs and Koheleth seem like a love-song and a pamphlet of Voltaire found astray among the folios of a theological library. This is what gives them their value.

*Renan, *History of Israel,* 1895, v. 137, 148f.

230.3 I know nothing grander than Ecclesiastes in its impassioned survey of mortal pain and pleasure, its estimate of failure and success; none of more noble sadness; no poem working more indomitably for spiritual illumination.
*Stedman, *Nature & Elements of Poetry*, 1892, p. 211f.

231. ECONOMICS

231.1 It is economic slavery, the savage struggle for a crumb, that has converted mankind into wolves and sheep. . . . My prison-house . . . is but an intensified replica of the world beyond, the larger prison locked with the levers of Greed, guarded by the spawn of Hunger.
Berkman, *Prison Memoirs of an Anarchist*, 1912, p. 225.

231.2 Economic facts are the ever recurring decisive forces, the chief points in the process of history.
E. Bernstein, *Evolutionary Socialism*, 1899, i.

231.3 Our whole evolutionary thinking leads us to the conclusion that economic independence lies at the very foundation of social and moral well-being.
F. Frankfurter, *Law and Politics*, 1936.

231.4 If it were not for economic repression, . . . all these social evils would disappear.
Mendelé, *Di Kliatshé*, 1873, ch 17.

231.5 Every new industry and every new commercial connection is equivalent to battalions. All politics are economic politics.
Rathenau. q BRN, 231.

232. EDUCATION
232.A. Definition

232.A.1 Education is that which remains, when one has forgotten everything he learned in school.
Einstein, 1936. *Out of My Later Years*, 36.

232.A.2 Education is, Making Men.
Guiterman, *The Light Guitar*, 1923, p. 20.

232.A.3 Learning is the raising of character by the broadening of vision and the deepening of feeling.
M. Sulzberger. *Menorah Journal*, 1916, ii. 58.

232.B. Duty

232.B.1 Thou shalt teach them diligently unto thy children.
Bible: Deut., 6.7.

232.B.2 The father to the children shall make known Thy truth.
Bible: Isa., 38.19. See Deut., 4.9.

232.B.3 What is the grossest form of neglect? If a man does not . . . devote every effort toward the education of his children.
Apocrypha: Aristeas, 248.

232.B.4 Moses ordained that Jews be addressed each holiday on the subject of that holiday, and he said to Israel: If you do this, it will be as if you established God's sovereignty.
Midrash Abkir. Yalkut Shimoni, #408, to Exod. 35.1.

232.B.5 We must endeavor to teach even the unintelligent.
Rashi, *Commentary*, to *Exod.* 13.14.

232.B.6 Lead your young flocks in the steps of the wise. . . . Thus ye may be confident your learning will abide.
Trabotti, *Farewell Address*, 1653. AHE, 282.

232.B.7 The Jewish religion, because it was a literature-sustained religion, led to the first efforts to provide elementary education for all the children in the community.
*Wells, *Outline of History*, 1920, 19.4, p. 235.

232.C. Aims

232.C.1 A Jew, however poor, if he had ten sons would put them all to letters, not for gain as the Christians do, but for the understanding of God's law, and not only his sons, but his daughters.
*Abelard School, *Commentary to Ephesians*, ch 6, c. 1141. A. Landgraf, *Commentarius Cantabrigiensis in Epistolae Pauli*, Notre Dame, 1939, ii. 434.

232.C.2 Teach your children letters, that they may have understanding all their life, reading unceasingly the law of God.
Apocrypha: Patriarchs, Levi, 13.2.

232.C.3 The highest task of education is training for duty.
B. Auerbach, *Ivo der Hajrle*, 1843.

232.C.4 The aim of education must be the training of independently acting and thinking individuals, who, however, see in the service of the community their highest life problem.

Einstein, 1936. *Out of My Later Years,* 32.

232.C.5 Education . . . should concern itself primarily . . . with the liberation, organization, and direction of power and intelligence, with the development of taste, with *culture.*

Flexner, *Universities,* 1930, p. 53.

232.C.6 No one has yet fully realized the wealth of sympathy, kindness and generosity hidden in the soul of the child. The effort of every true educator should be to unlock that treasure—to stimulate the child's impulses and call forth the best and noblest tendencies.

E. Goldman, *Living My Life,* 1931, i. 409.

232.C.7 The aim [of Jewish education] is to develop a sincere faith in the holiness of life and a sense of responsibilty for enabling the Jewish people to make its contribution to the achievement of the good life.

Kaplan, *Future of the American Jew,* 1948, p. 44.

232.C.8 Busy yourself as much as possible with the study of divine things, not to know them merely, but to do them; and when you close the book, look round you, look within you, to see if your hand can translate into deed something you have learned.

Moses of Evreux, 1240.

232.C.9 As the nation of the future, they [Jews] are the world-historical nation *par excellence,* the nation among nations, whose education—whenever the Jew has not changed and corrupted his nature through modern culture—is still always patriarchal, hierarchal, and mnemonic (dwelling on the memory of its past history).

*Rosenkranz, *Philosophy of Education,* (1848) 1886, p. 249.

232.C.10 No man can better display the power of his skill and disposition than in so training men that they come at last to live under the dominion of their own reason.

Spinoza, *Ethics,* 1677, iv. Appendix 9.

232.D. Methods

232.D.1 It is precept by precept, precept by precept, line by line, line by line; here a little, there a little.

Bible: Isa., 28.10.

232.D.2 When you teach your son, use a carefully edited text.

Akiba. *Talmud: Pesahim,* 112a.

232.D.3 Arrange the ordinances in order, like a set table.

Akiba. *Mekilta,* to *Exod.* 21.1.

232.D.4 All education starts with forbidding.

Baeck, *Essence of Judaism,* 1936, p. 217.

232.D.5 Getting education is like getting measles; you have to go where measles is.

Flexner, to Albert Jay Nock. q FAT, 287.

232.D.6 The prevailing philosophy of education tends to discredit hard work.

Flexner, *Universities,* 1930, p. 47.

232.D.7 He who learns by Finding Out
  has sevenfold
  The Skill of him who learned by
  Being Told.

Guiterman, *A Poet's Proverbs,* 1924, p. 73.

232.D.8 Reviewing a lesson a hundred times cannot be compared with reviewing it a hundred and one times.

Hillel. *Talmud: Hagiga,* 9a. See *Sanhedrin,* 99a.

232.D.9 A soul that is sick, humble and subservient . . . is not capable of absorbing wisdom, particularly when subjected to arrogant and cruel masters.

Huke HaTorah, 12C or 13C. S Asaf, *Mekorot LeToldot HaHinuk,* 1925, i. 11.

232.D.10 If a student crams, his learning diminishes; and if he "gathers little by little, it shall increase" [*Prov.* 13.11].

Huna. *Talmud: Erubin,* 54b.

232.D.11 A boy must be urged on, with rewards appropriate to his intelligence and age, until he realizes that he must study because it is the will of God.

Isaac b. Eliakim, *Leb Tob,* 1620, ch 9. q GSS, 31.

232.D.12 Only the lesson which is enjoyed can be learned well.

Judah HaNasi. *Talmud: Aboda Zara,* 19a.

232.D.13 A teacher should give his pupil opportunity for independent practice without suggestions from himself, and thus set upon him the stamp of indelible memory in its purest form.

Philo, *Change of Names,* 48.

232.D.14 Training through love breeds love.

Stekel, *Autobiography,* 1950, p. 44.

232.E. Value

232.E.1 All your children shall be taught of the Lord, and great shall be the peace of your children.
Bible: Isa., 54.13.

232.E.2 Nations . . . borrow billions for war; no nation has ever borrowed largely for education. Probably no nation is rich enough to pay for both war and civilization. We must make our choice; we cannot have both.
Flexner, *Universities,* 1930, p. 302.

232.E.3 As the day adds to the vision of the seeing and the blindness of the bat, so does instruction help to enlighten the wise and to bewilder the fool.
Ibn Gabirol, *Mibhar HaPeninim,* c. 1050, #228.

232.E.4 Where Jewish education is neglected, the whole content of Judaism is reduced to merely an awareness of anti-Semitism. Judaism ceases then to be a civilization, and becomes a complex.
Kaplan, *Future of the American Jew,* 1948, p. 44.

232.E.5 It is a woeful mistake to suppose that the educated are kinder or more tolerant: education creates vested interests, and renders the beneficiaries acutely jealous and very vocal.
Namier, *Conflicts,* 1943, p. 141.

232.E.6 A mixture of misery and education is highly explosive.
H. Samuel.

232.E.7 Who trains his son in good deeds from childhood on, trains him to be a good pilot, who knows how to steer his ship to port.
Sefer Hasidim, 13C, #12, p. 10.

232.E.8 When there is a chance to act against Jews, the highly educated joins in the chorus of the low, illiterate mob.
Taubels, letter to her sister, 1848.

232.E.9 On the bitter day of expulsion from Spain, most of those who were proud of their intellectual attainment changed their glory, while the women and uncultivated masses surrendered themselves and their property for the sanctification of the Name. . . . Verily, "the Lord preserveth the simple" [*Ps.* 116.6].
Yaabetz, *Or Hayyim,* 1555, ch 5.

233. EFFORT

233.1 If a man strives . . . to do what is in his power, God will aid him to accomplish what is beyond his power.
Bahya, *Hobot HaLebabot,* 1940, 8.3.21.

233.2 If you're told, "I toiled and didn't get," believe not; "I didn't toil and got," believe not; "I toiled and got," believe.
Isaac Nappaha. *Talmud: Megilla,* 6b.

233.3 Only live fish swim up-stream.
Lazerov, *Enciklopedie fun Idishe Vitzen,* 1928, #444.

233.4 The more valuable the thing, the more effort it demands.
Saadia, *Emunot VeDeot,* 933, ch 2, Introduction.

233.5 The good attained by effort is twice as precious.
Ibid., 3.1.

233.6 Move heaven and earth.
Saying, based on *Bible: Hag.,* 2.6.

233.7 We must strive and have faith. We shall triumph in the end.
Schapira, last words, May 8, 1898. q *Eretz Israel,* 1932, 29.

233.8 Mountains of charcoal are burnt in the thickness of the earth
To bequeathe to the world the precious diamond;
Countless winds are blowing and are vainly spent
For the sake of one breath in man.
Shneor, "Song of the Prophet," 1903, tr FTH, 165.

233.9 For each little effort toward holiness, Heaven endows man richly.
Talmud: Yoma, 39a.

233.10 The prophetic spirit rests on a man only after he has bestirred himself to receive it.
Zohar, Gen., 77b.

234. EGYPT

234.1 Abhor not an Egyptian, for you were a stranger in his land.
Bible: Deut., 23.8.

234.2 You rely on . . . this bruised reed, on Egypt.
Bible: II Kings, 18.21.

234.3 I will spur Egypt against Egypt.
Bible: Isa., 19.2.

234.4 Blessed be Egypt My people, and Assyria My handiwork, and Israel Mine inheritance.
Ibid., 19.25.

234.5 Egypt is a very fair heifer, but the gadfly out of the North is come.

Bible: Jer., 46.20.

234.6 When Israel crossed the Red Sea, the angels were about to break forth in song, but the Holy One rebuked them: My children [Egyptians] are drowning, and ye would sing?!

Johanan b. Nappaha: *T: Megilla,* 10b. Johanan b. Eleazar. *T: Sanhedrin,* 39b.

234.7 The Egyptian disposition is by nature most jealous.

Philo, *Flaccus,* 5.

234.8 There is no nation so despised of the Holy One as Egypt.

Zohar, Exod., 17a.

235. ELIJAH

235.1 Elijah cast his mantle upon him [Elisha].

Bible: I Kings, 19.19.

235.2 Elijah went up by a whirlwind into heaven.

Bible: II Kings, 2.11. See *I Macc.,* 2.58.

235.3 Elijah the prophet . . . shall turn the heart of the fathers to the children and the heart of the children to the fathers.

Bible: Mal., 3.23f.

235.4 A prophet like fire, whose word was like a burning furnace.

Apocrypha: Ben Sira, 48.1.

235.5 Blessed is he who sees you [Elijah], and dies.

Ibid., 48.11.

235.6 Elijah is in charge of seating the righteous in Eden.

Sefer Hasidim, 13C, #1044, p. 261, based on *Ketubot* 77b.

235.7 Israel was assured long ago that Elijah would not come on a Sabbath or festival eve because of their preoccupation then.

Talmud: Erubin, 43b.

236. EMANCIPATION

236.1 There is only one object . . . for which we have at present the strength . . . and that is the *moral* object—the emancipation of ourselves from the inner slavery and spiritual degradation which assimilation has produced in us.

Ahad HaAm, "I Zionist Congress," 1897. *Ten Essays,* 25f.

236.2 The cause of Jewish regeneration is closely bound up with that of Italian re-

generation, because there is only one justice and it is the same for all.

*Azeglio, *Dell' emancipazione civile degl' Israeliti,* 1848. q *JSS,* 1953, xv. 122.

236.3 At last the day has come when we see the curtain torn, which separated us from our compatriots and brothers! At last we have regained the rights of which we were deprived for more than eighteen hundred years! . . . Thanks to the Supreme Being and the sovereign nation, we are recognized not only as humans, not only as citizens, but also as Frenchmen! Almighty God, what a happy turn Thou hast wrought for us!

Berr, *Lettre d'un Citoyen,* 1791.

236.4 Civic equality should not be granted to Jews as a reward; it should be conferred on them as an inalienable right.

Boerne, *Briefe aus Paris,* #60, Dec. 4, 1831.

236.5 To the Jews as a nation, we must deny everything; to Jews as individuals, we must grant everything.

*Clermont-Tonnère, Dec. 23, 1789 (summ. in *Le Moniteur*).

236.6 Fifty thousand Frenchmen arose this morning as slaves; it depends on you whether they shall go to bed as free men.

*Grégoire, motion for Jewish emancipation, National Assembly, Oct. 1, 1789.

236.7 There will come a time when people in Europe will no longer ask who is a Jew or a Christian, for the Jew, too, will live according to European laws and contribute to the welfare of the State. Only a barbarian situation can hinder it.

*Herder, *Ideen zur Philosophie der Geschichte,* 1791, 4.16.5.

236.8 If it be true that the emancipation of the Jews in exile is incompatible with Jewish nationality, then Jews ought to forego emancipation.

Hess, *Rome and Jerusalem,* 1862.

236.9 I bless emancipation if Israel regards it as . . . only a new condition of its mission, and as a new trial, much severer than the trial of oppression; but I would grieve if Israel understood itself so little . . . that it would welcome emancipation as the end of the *Galuth* and the highest goal of its historic mission.

S. R. Hirsch, *Nineteen Letters,* (1836), #16, p. 167.

236.10 As I am at one and the same time both a Jew and a German, the Jew in me

cannot be emancipated without the German nor the German without the Jew.
J. Jacoby, letter to A. Küntzel, May 12, 1837.

236.11 Our emancipation will not be complete until we are free of the fear of being Jews.
Kaplan, *Future of the American Jew*, 1948, p. 81.

236.12 The more thoroughly the emancipation of Jewry is carried out, the more certainly does it mean the dissolution of Jewry.
*Kautsky, *Rasse & Judentum*, 1914, p. 92.

236.13 A new emancipation must be initiated—an emancipation from the sordid fallacies of scientific materialism, from the ominous identification of the state with society, . . . from that inner servility which consents to our being merely the object, never the codeterminants of the historic process in which we are involved.
Lewisohn, *The American Jew*, 1950.

236.14 Not outer emancipation is the blessing for which we supernaturalists long, but inner emancipation, deliverance from the influence of the exotic.
S. D. Luzzatto, letter to Reggio, Nov. 26, 1838.

236.15 Let us do justice to them. . . . Let us open to them every career in which ability and energy can be displayed. Till we have done this, let us not presume to say that there is no genius among the countrymen of Isaiah, no heroism among the descendants of the Maccabees.
*Macaulay, address, House of Commons, Apr. 17, 1833.

236.16 The emancipation of the Jews in its last significance is the emancipation of mankind from Judaism.
Marx, *On the Jewish Question*, 1844. *Selected Essays*, 89.

236.17 The emancipation of the Jews will bring about the emancipation of mankind. The victory of Judaism will be the victory of the entire world, and precisely the victory of spiritual Judaism, of the Judaism of the Prophets.
Ivensky, *Marx the Jew*. q *HaDoar*, July 30, 1954, p. 661.

236.18 In the nineteenth century exceptional laws for the Jews can be nothing more than a blunder and an absurdity.
*Mazzini, letter to his mother, Nov. 9, 1835. q *JSS*, xv. 120.

236.19 If you wish the Jews to become better men and useful citizens, then banish every humiliating restriction, open to them every avenue of gaining a livelihood.
*Mirabeau, *On Mendelssohn & Political Reform of Jews*, 1787. q GHJ, v. 433.

236.20 I humbly conceive it to be the duty of the Civil Magistrate to break down that superstitious wall of separation (as to civil things) between us Gentiles and the Jews, and freely (without their asking) to make way for their free and peaceable habitation amongst us.
*R. Williams, *The Fourth Paper*, London, 1652.

236.21 It is high time that the Jews . . . be accorded, not rights and liberties, but right and liberty, not miserable, humiliating privileges, but complete, elevating citizenship!
Zunz, *Die gottesdienstliche Vorträge der Juden*, 1832, Preface, p. iii.

237. END

237.1 Your beginning was small, yet your end should greatly increase.
Bible: Job, 8.7.

237.2 Better is the end of a thing than its beginning.
Bible: Eccles., 7.8.

237.3 Always think of the end, and you will never do amiss.
Apocrypha: Ben Sira, 7.36.

237.4 It all depends on how it ends.
Gabishon, *Omer HaShikha*, c. 1600 (1748).

237.5 Each beginning needs an end.
Hasdai, *Ben HaMelek VeHaNazir*, c. 1230.

237.6 All is well that ends well.
Proverb. q *Pesikta Zutarti*, (1097), to *Gen.* 47.28, 113b.

237.7 The end often begins much sooner than we believe.
Schnitzler, *Anatol: Dissolution*, 1893, tr Colbron.

237.8 Learn to end well.
Talmud: Derek Eretz, 1.24.

237.9 Who begins with trouble ends with ease.
Tanhuma, Ekeb, #5, ed Buber, 9b.

238. ENDURANCE

238.1 For the sake of the Lord, endure every wound.
Apocrypha: II Enoch, 50.3.

238.2 Endurance is a mighty charm.
Apocrypha: Patriarchs, Joseph, 2.7.

238.3 A people that patiently lets itself be trampled, deserves to be trampled and crushed.
Boerne, *Briefe aus Paris,* #33, Feb. 11, 1831.

238.4 You will not attain what you love if you do not endure much that you hate, and you will not be freed from what you hate if you will not endure much from what you love.
M. Ibn Ezra, *Shirat Yisrael,* (12C) 1924, p. 113.

238.5 Jewish ecstasy does not lie in action. It is rather a capacity for enduring.
Kastein. q RHI, 509.

238.6 Our sages instructed us to bear in silence the prevarications and preposterousness of Ishmael.
Maimonides, *Iggeret Teman,* 1172, tr Cohen, p. xviii.

238.7 A man can bear more than ten oxen can pull.
Proverb (Yiddish). See *JE,* x. 228b.

238.8 "These are the names of the sons of Ishmael: Mishma, Dumah, and Massa" —Listen, Be Silent, Endure.
Targum Pseudo-Jonathan, to Gen. 25.14.

239. ENEMY

239.1 A man's enemies are the men of his own house.
Bible: Mic., 7.6.

239.2 Rejoice not when your enemy falls.
Bible: Prov., 24.17.

239.3 If your enemy be hungry, give him bread to eat.
Ibid., 25.21.

239.4 Who is a hero? He who turns an enemy into a friend.
Abot de R. Nathan, ch 23.

239.5 I am very careful in the choice of enemies.
Ahad HaAm, letter to J. Klausner, Sept. 18, 1904. AEL, 306.

239.6 If you can't cut off your enemy's hand, kiss it and appease him.
Amram, *Noam HaMiddot,* 1854, #12.

239.7 Envy not an enemy's prosperity; rejoice not at his adversity.
Apocrypha: Ahikar, 2.17.

239.8 If your enemy meet you with evil, meet him with wisdom.
Ibid., 2.20.

239.9 An enemy is not hidden in adversity.
Apocrypha: Ben Sira, 12.8.

239.10 Pray for an enemy as for yourself.
Baal Shem. See HLH, 10.

239.11 Every man's enemy is within himself.
Bahya, *Hobot HaLebabot,* 1040, Introduction.

239.12 Let not a single enemy seem trifling in your eyes.
Ibn Gabirol, *Mibhar HaPeninim,* c. 1050, #253.

239.13 A single enemy is one too many.
Asher b. Yehiel, *Hanhaga,* c. 1320.

239.14 We must show consideration even to avowed enemies.
Josephus, *Against Apion,* ii. 29.

239.15 The man who never made an enemy never made anything.
Muni.

239.16 Love your enemies.
New Testament: Matt., 5.44. Cf 12.30.

239.17 Pray for your enemy that he serve God.
Orhot Tzaddikim, 15C.

239.18 Who are your bitterest enemies? The unknown who suspect how much you would despise them if you knew them.
Schnitzler, *Buch der Sprüche & Bedenken,* 1927, p. 229.

239.19 Aid an enemy before you aid a friend, to subdue hatred.
Tosefta: Baba Metzia, 2.26.

240. ENGLAND

240.1 Here, as in no other country, the teachings of Holy Writ are venerated. . . . Here, as in no other empire in the world, there breathes a passionate love of freedom, a burning hatred of tyrant wrong.
H. Adler, at unveiling of Memorial to Jewish soldiers who fell in the South African War, 1905.

240.2 A cemetery with ornamental tombstones—that is all that English Judaism is.
Ahad HaAm, letter to J. Klausner, Feb. 28, 1908. AEL, 311.

240.3 Nowhere in the modern world have the Jews found so tranquil and peaceful a home as here in this England of ours.
*Bryce, speech, JHSE, Feb. 5, 1906.

240.4 We are indeed a nation of shopkeepers.
Disraeli, *Young Duke,* 1831, 1.11.

240.5 Loyalty to the flag for which the sun once stood still, can only deepen our devotion to the flag on which the sun never sets.

Goldsmid, 1902.

240.6 An Englishman is a man who lives on an island in the North Sea governed by Scotsmen.

Guedalla, *Supers and Supermen*, 1920, p. 55.

240.7 The most repulsive race which God in His wrath ever created.

Heine, *Shakespeare's Maidens*, 1839, Introduction.

240.8 Their superiority consists in that they have no imagination.

Heine, *Lutetia*, July 29, 1840.

240.9 Silence—a conversation with an Englishman.

Heine.

240.10 England the great, England the free, England with her eyes scanning the seven seas, will understand us.

Herzl, address, IV Zionist Congress, London, 1900.

240.11 The Englishman accepts a fit of delirium if it appears with footnotes, and is conquered by an absurdity if it is accompanied by diagrams.

Nordau, *Degeneration*, (1893), 2.2, p. 78.

240.12 The only letter which Englishmen write in capitals is I. This is the most pointed comment on their national character.

A. Rubinstein, attrib. to. SHB, 561.

240.13 The Hebrews have determined our literature more than all other influences combined; the English heart and mind are now partly made of Hebrew thought and ideals.

*Tucker, *Foreign Debt of English Literature*, 1907, 253.

240.14 The unchristian oppressions, incivilities and inhumanities of this nation against the Jews have cried to Heaven against this nation and the kings and princes of it.

*R. Williams, *The Fourth Paper*, London, 1652.

240.15 The Romans merely took Palestine. The English have taken the whole of its history and literature. But they have taken it because—despite all the aberrations and iniquities of Imperialism—it represents their own ideal of justice for all races.

Zangwill, *War for the World*, (1915) 1921, p. 131.

241. ENTHUSIASM

241.1 Every production of genius must be the production of enthusiasm.

D'Israeli, *Curiosities: Solitude*, 1793.

241.2 Enthusiasm begets heroism.

Dubnow, *Jewish History*, 1903, p. 80.

241.3 I delight in your enthusiasm of today, but I have no faith in fireworks enthusiasm. I do not believe in those holy rockets which so brilliantly soar up to heaven, but get extinguished before they reach it. No, "an eternal fire shall burn upon the holy altar; it shall never be extinguished" [*Lev.* 6.6]. What a shame it would be to build a gorgeous temple and then, when finished, to leave it empty and desolate!

M. Lilienthal, *Platform of Judaism*, June 5, 1868.

241.4 There are those who fulfil all the commandments, but lack the joy and fervor that should accompany them. When they come to the other world and enter Paradise, they grumble, "What's all the fuss about this?" until they are driven out from there.

Solomon of Karlin. q YHS, ii. 178.

241.5 Years wrinkle the skin, but to give up enthusiasm wrinkles the soul.

S. Ullman, *From the Summit of Years, Four Score*, (1920?). p. 13.

242. ENVY

242.1 Envy is the rottenness of the bones.
Bible: Prov., 14.30.

242.2 Envy slays the silly.
Bible: Job, 5.2. See *Wisd. of Sol.*, 6.23.

242.3 Envy and anger shorten life.
Apocrypha: Ben Sira, 30.24. See *Abot*, 2.11.

242.4 Envy is hatred without a cure.
Bahya b. Asher, *Kad HaKemah*, 14C.

242.5 Envy spoils our complexions.
Disraeli, *Young Duke*, 1831.

242.6 Envy a man nothing save his virtues.
Eleazar b. Judah, *Rokeah*, 13C.

242.7 Envy, appetite and ambition lead to ruin.
Eleazar HaKappar. *Mishna: Abot*, 4.21.

242.8 The taste of another's luck is always tart.

Hoffenstein, *Pencil in the Air*, 1923, p. 148.

242.9 Envy has a thousand eyes, but none with correct vision.

I. Hurwitz, *Mishlé Yisachar*, 1887, p. 71.

242.10 Woe to the man who is envied, and alas, if none envy him!

Ibid.

242.11 Who sows envy reaps regret.

Immanuel, *Mahberot*, c. 1300, ch 9.

242.12 It is impossible in prosperity to escape envy.

Josephus, *Wars*, 1.10.6.

242.13 Envious wives will ruin their husbands.

Lev. R., 25.6.

242.14 Without envy, the world could not abide, for none would marry or build a house.

Midrash Tehillim, 37.1, ed Buber, 126b.

242.15 The hungry has sixty toothaches when another smacks his lips.

Proverb. q Raba. *Talmud: Baba Kamma*, 92b.

242.16 I no longer envy anybody anything but such things as no one has.

Varnhagen. q KRV, 32.

243. EPIGRAM

243.1 The feathered arrow of an epigram has sometimes been wet with the heart's blood of its victim.

D'Israeli, *Curiosities: Censured Authors*, 1793.

243.2 The epigram is a beautiful meaning in few and clear words. . . . It slings at the mark without delay.

M. Ibn Ezra, *Shirat Yisrael*, (12C) 1924, p. 117.

243.3 The aphorism should be a light vessel holding a heavy load.

Klatzkin, *In Praise of Wisdom*, 1943, p. 303.

243.4 Shake an aphorism, and a life falls out while a banality remains.

Schnitzler, *Buch der Sprüche & Bedenken*, 1927, p. 234.

244. EQUALITY

244.1 He made the small and the great, and cares for all alike.

Apocrypha: Wisd. of Sol., 6.7.

244.2 All men have one entrance into life, and the like exit.

Ibid., 7.6.

244.3 Equality . . . is the result of human organization. . . . We are not born equal.

Arendt, *Origins of Totalitarianism*, 1951, p. 297.

244.4 Where only compeers meet, boredom will soon preside, and stupidity will serve as secretary.

Boerne.

244.5 I am no leveller; I look upon an artificial equality as equally pernicious with a factitious aristocracy; both depressing the energies and checking the enterprise of a nation.

Disraeli, *Coningsby*, 1844.

244.6 Before God there is . . . no respect of persons.

Eleazar HaKappar. *Mishna: Abot*, 4.22. See *Rom.*, 2.11.

244.7 Freedom and equality! They are not to be found on earth below or in heaven above. The stars on high are not alike, . . . and all obey an iron-like law.

Heine, *English Fragments*, 1828, ch 1.

244.8 Jerusalem was destroyed because the small and the great were made equal.

Isaac Nappaha. *Talmud: Sabbath*, 119b.

244.9 Neither all men, nor all places, nor all seasons are alike.

Judah b. Baba. *Mishna: Yebamot*, 16.3.

244.10 The twelve tribes are not listed in the same order everywhere in Scripture, to teach us that the offspring of Jacob's wives take no precedence over those of his hand-maidens.

Levi. *Exod. R.*, 1.6.

244.11 The best way of making good citizens of the Jews . . . is to make brothers of them, equal to everybody else under the law.

*Mazzini. *Jeune Suisse*, Nov. 4, 1835. q *JSS*, xv. 120.

244.12 Moses treated Joshua, his subordinate, as an equal.

Mekilta, to *Exod.* 17.9.

244.13 Jews seek superiority only because they are denied equality.

Nordau, speech, I Zionist Congress, Aug. 29, 1897.

244.14 What is permitted one Jew is permitted another.

Papa. *Talmud: Betza*, 25a.

244.15 Even where Jews enjoy complete equality with the rest of the population, they do so by the good will of that population. And that is not complete equality.
*Parkes, *An Enemy of the People: Anti-semitism*, (1943) 1946, p. 133.

244.16 What right have I . . . to be puffed up and insolent . . . since we can all claim to be children of one common mother nature?
Philo, *Decalogue*, 10.

244.17 Equality is the mother of Justice, queen of all virtues.
Philo, *Noah's Work as a Planter*, 28. See Wolfson, *Philo*, i. 107, ii. 391.

244.18 At the baths, all are equal.
Proverb (Yiddish). BJS, #321. ATJF, p. 641.

244.19 All were alike . . . when they fled for their lives.
Solomon b. Judah, Letter on Earthquake, Dec. 1033.

244.20 God has granted to all men the same intellect [*Ps.* 33.15].
Spinoza, *Theologico-Political Treatise*, 1670, ch 3.

244.21 Not all fingers are alike.
Talmud: Pesahim, 112b.

244.22 All men, women and children met at the foot of Mount Sinai. This in itself is a proclamation of equality.
I. M. Wise, *Outlines of Judaism*, 1869. *Selected Writings*, 216.

245. ERROR

245.1 Who can discern errors?
Bible: Ps., 19.13.

245.2 A false notion involving a principle of faith . . . prevents the soul from attaining perfection.
Abravanel, *Rosh Amana*, (1505) 1861, p. 14a.

245.3 He who upholds the law of Moses and believes in its principles . . . is classed with the sages and pious, though he holds erroneous theories.
Albo, *Ikkarim*, 1428, 1.2.

245.4 It is not dishonorable to commit an error.
Al-Rabi, *Matté Aharon*, c. 1410.

245.5 Where error has once crept in, it stays.
Dimi of Nehardea. *Talmud: Baba Bathra*, 21a.

245.6 If err we must, let us err on the side of tolerance.
F. Frankfurter, 1952. q *N.Y. Times Magazine*, Nov. 23, 1952.

245.7 Let people err innocently rather than presumptuously.
Ishmael b. Elisha. *Talmud: Baba Bathra*, 60b.
Simeon b. Gamaliel. *Tosefta: Sota*, 15.10.

245.8 The errors of sages are regarded as willful sins; the sins of the ignorant are accounted as unwitting errors.
Judah b. Ilai. *Talmud: Baba Metzia*, 33b.

245.9 It is impossible to be human and not to err.
Maimonides, *Introduction to Zeraim*, 1168.

245.10 Great men . . . have been characterized by the greatness of their mistakes as well as by the greatness of their achievements.
A. Myerson, *Speaking of Man*, 1950, p. 32.

245.11 Error due to lack of study is a sin.
Rabbinic maxim. q GSS, 250.

245.12 An expert is a person who avoids the small errors as he sweeps on to the grand fallacy.
Stolberg.

246. ETERNITY

246.1 The prophet and the martyr do not see the hooting throng. Their eyes are fixed on the eternities.
Cardozo, *Law and Literature*, 1931, p. 36.

246.2 You have nothing eternal if not on the side of the good.
Fano, *Hikkur Din*, c. 1600 (1698), 5.1.

246.3 Every instant is to me an eternity . . . and I need no priest to promise me a second life, for I can live enough in this life when I live backwards in the life of those who have gone before me, and win myself an eternity in the realm of the past.
Heine, *Ideas*, 1826, ch 3.

246.4 The eternity of the spirit does not begin after death, but is, like God, always present.
Hess, *Rome and Jerusalem*, (1862), p. 215.

246.5 Men are children of this world,
Yet hath God set eternity in their hearts.
M. Ibn Ezra, *Selected Poems*, 46.

246.6 Some win eternity after years of toil, others in a moment.

Judah HaNasi. *Talmud: Aboda Zara,* 10b, 17a.

246.7 It was not the picturesqueness of the Jews that fascinated him, but the element of the eternal that was their birthright.

*Malraux, *Voices of Silence,* 1953, ref. to Rembrandt.

246.8 The noble exploits of our time are our passport to eternity.

P. Nathan, letter from Italy, 1887.

246.9 The race remains forever, though particular specimens perish.

Philo, *Eternity of the World,* 13.

246.10 If we had been made so as to live forever, we could never have lived at all.

H. Samuel, *Belief and Action,* 1937, p. 96.

246.11 There is something higher than modernity, and that is eternity.

Schechter. q *Menorah Journal,* 1924, x. 473.

246.12 Eternity is a thrust upon
A bit of earth, a senseless stone.
A grain of dust, a casual clod
Receives the greatest gift of God.

L. Untermeyer, *Irony. Challenge,* 1914, p. 92.

246.13 Most Jews have a dimension of eternity. . . . Our myths are the temporal myths of Caesar and Pericles, of Charlemagne, Washington, Hitler, but the myths of the Jews are timeless—the patriarchs and prophets who never die, the Messiah who never comes.

*E. Wilson. *New Yorker,* May 15, 1954, p. 141.

246.14 God will one day reestablish the world and strengthen the spirit of men so that they may prolong their days for ever.

Zohar, Gen., 38b.

247. EULOGY

247.1 I decree that no praises be spoken of me.

Aaron of Karlin, *Tzavaah.* q *YAJ,* 139.

247.2 What will a paean help me in my tomb? . . . Give me bread and clothes now!

Imber, *Barkai,* 1899.

247.3 Orators and Amen-sayers will be punished for false eulogies.

Talmud: Berakot, 62a.

247.4 A eulogy should not be extravagant. To ascribe to one merits which are not his is really to reproach him.

Zohar, Gen., 232b.

248. EUROPE

248.1 United, France and Germany can accomplish and prevent anything. . . . On their union depends, therefore, not only their own welfare but also the destiny of all of Europe.

Boerne, *Introduction à la Balance,* 1836.

248.2 Europe has fallen into the hands of clowns.

Brandes, *Hellas,* 1926, p. 219.

248.3 Jewish life in Europe was not a failure. Europe had failed.

Grayzel, *A History of the Jews,* 1952, p. 812.

248.4 All Europe raises itself to the level of the Jews.

Heine, *Shakespeare's Maidens: Jessica,* 1839.

248.5 In a cultural sense the Jews were the first Europeans.

C. & D. Singer, *The Jewish Factor,* 1927. BSL, 180.

248.6 The question is sometimes raised whether Jews are Europeans. They are more, for they have helped to make Europe.

Zangwill. q LGP, p. xxiv.

249. EUTHANASIA

249.1 Only He who gave the soul may take it back!

Hanina b. Teradion. *Talmud: Aboda Zara,* 18a.

249.2 If a patient in agony begs to die, another may not touch him.

Sefer Hasidim, 13C, #315, p. 100.

250. EVIL

250.1 You meant evil against me, but God meant it for good.

Bible: Gen., 50.20.

250.2 Bring the precious out of the vile.

Bible: Jer., 15.19.

250.3 These words might well stand as a motto for the bent of the Hebrew ethical genius.

*G. A. Smith, *The Hebrew Genius,* 1927. BSL, 8.

250.4 Shall we receive good at God's hand, and not evil?

Bible: Job, 2.10. See *Lam.,* 3.38.

250.5 Evil, like parental punishment, is not intended for itself.
Albo, *Ikkarim*, 1428, 2.13.

250.6 Evil is not wholly evil; it is misplaced good.
S. Alexander, *Space, Time and Deity*, 1920.

250.7 Evil is only a throne for good.
Baal Shem. q HLH, 40.

250.8 First learn evil, to shun it; then learn good, to do it.
Bahya, *Hobot HaLebabot*, 1040, 5.5.

250.9 That which to mortals seems most calamitous is not infrequently converted into a blessing.
J. P. Benjamin, 1861.

250.10 A power of evil exists only in myth.
H. Cohen, *Ethnik des reinen Willens*, 1907, 452. q SMT, 36.

250.11 There is no more demoralizing theory than that which imputes all human evils to capitalism or any other single agency.
Gompers, *Seventy Years of Life & Labor*, 1925, ii. 402.

250.12 Most evils that befall man are due to lust and anger.
Ibn Shem Tob, *Commentary* on Maimonides' *Moré*, to 3.8.

250.13 Not a moment without evil bestowment.
Judah Halevi.

250.14 God uses evil to educate His children for a place in His kingdom.
Kohler, *Jewish Theology*, 1918, p. 178.

250.15 All evils are negations.
Maimonides, *Guide for the Perplexed*, 1190, 3.10.

250.16 The treasuries of evil are in ourselves; with God are those of good things only.
Philo, *Flight & Finding*, 15. See *Change of Names*, 4; *Seder Eliyahu Rabbah*, ch 8, ed Friedmann, p. 40.

250.17 The exit of evil works the entrance of virtue.
Philo, *Sacrifices of Abel and Cain*, 39.

250.18 Do not court evil, and evil won't come to you.
q. *Tanhuma, Hukkat*, 1, ed Buber, 50a.

250.19 Let us not paralyze our capacity for good, by brooding on man's capacity for evil.
Sarnoff, *Youth in a Changing World*, June 12, 1954.

250.20 Whatever hinders man's perfecting of his reason and capability to enjoy the rational life, is alone called evil.
Spinoza, *Ethics*, 1677, iv. Appendix 5.

250.21 Evil is more contagious than good.
A. Stern, letter to Luzzatti, Apr. 1923. LGF, 500.

250.22 Sufficient unto the hour is the evil thereof.
Talmud: Berakot, 9b. Cf *NT: Matt.*, 6.34.

250.23 Regard as enormous the little wrong you did to others, and as trifling the great wrong done to you.
Talmud: Derek Eretz, 1.29.

250.24 The fact that evil confronts good gives man the possibility of victory.
Yehiel Michael of Zlotshov. q BTH, i. 145.

251. EVIL INCLINATION

251.1 The greater the man the greater his evil inclination.
Abayé. *Talmud: Sukka*, 52a.

251.2 A pious man said to victorious veterans returning from battle, "Now equip yourselves for the *Great* War!" "And what is that?" they asked. He replied, "The War on the Evil Urge!"
Bahya, *Hobot HaLebabot*, 1040, 5.5.

251.3 Guard against the inner thief, the evil instinct!
M. Cohen, *Sefer Hasidim Zuta*, (1473) 1866, p. 2.

251.4 Israel complained: "If a potter leaves a pebble in the clay, and the jar leaks, is not the potter responsible? Thou has left in us the Evil Urge. Remove it, and we shall do Thy will!" God replied, "This I will do in time to come."
Exod. R., 46.4.

251.5 Man makes a harness for his beast; all the more should he make one for the beast within himself, his Evil Will.
Hama b. Hanina. *Talmud J: Sanhedrin*, 10.1.

251.6 The Evil Urge attacks man daily with renewed vigor.
Isaac Nappaha. *Talmud: Sukka*, 52a.

251.7 The Evil Urge begins like a guest and proceeds like the host.
Isaac Nappaha. *Gen. R.*, 22.6,

251.8 The Evil Will lures man in this world, then testifies against him in the world to come.

Jonathan b. Eleazar. *Talmud: Sukka,* 52a.

251.9 In the messianic future, the Holy One will execute the Evil Will. The righteous, to whom it will then seem as an enormous mountain, will weep and say, How did we conquer such a height? The wicked, to whom it will look like a hair, will weep and say, Why did we not overcome it?

Judah b. Ilai. *Talmud: Sukka,* 52a.

251.10 The Evil Will is more powerful when wrapped in the prayer-shawl of piety.

S. Levin.

251.11 In every evil thought there is a spark of divinity, which has sunk to a very low degree, and begs to be elevated.

Opatoshu, *In Polish Woods,* (1921) 1938, p. 113.

251.12 The Evil Will dominates only over what the eyes see.

q Raba. *Talmud: Sota,* 8a.

251.13 Without the Evil Inclination, no man would build a house, take a wife, beget a family, and engage in work.

Samuel b. Nahman. *Gen. R.,* 9.7. Cf *Eccles. R.,* 3.11.3.

251.14 The Evil Inclination is a good thing, for if it did not involve man in a struggle for the Holy One, what reward could man expect for doing good?

Sefer Hasidim, 13C, #2, p. 4.

251.15 The very fire of the Evil Inclination must be employed in the service of God.

Shneor Zalman, *Likkuté Torah, Deut.* (1848) 1928, p. 160.

251.16 Torah can temper the Evil Urge, as fire bends iron.

Simeon b. Eleazar. *Abot de Rabbi Nathan,* ch 16.

251.17 As leaven can be removed only by burning, so can the Evil Urge be combatted only by the fire of Torah.

Azulai, *Simhat HaRegel,* (1782) 1909, p. 3a.

251.18 God created the Evil Will, but He also created its antidote, the Torah.

Talmud: Kiddushin. 30b.

251.19 Torah, prayer, and the contemplation of death will help you in your struggle with the Evil Inclination.

Simeon b. Lakish. *Talmud: Berakot,* 5a.

251.20 Always incite the Good Will to combat the Evil Will.

Ibid. See *Sukka,* 52b.

251.21 Thou hast given us the Evil Will that we may be rewarded for resisting him; but we want neither him nor the reward!

Talmud: Yoma, 69b.

251.22 The Evil Will hankers only for that which is forbidden.

Talmud J: Sabbath, 14.3. *Yoma,* 6.4.

251.23 May it be Thy will . . . to break the yoke of the Evil Will in our hearts!

Tanhum b. Hanilai. *Talmud J: Berakot,* 4.2.

251.24 He who obeys his inclination is like an idolator. "There shall no strange god be in thee" [*Ps.* 81.10] means, Make not the stranger in you your ruler!

Yannai. *Talmud J: Nedarim,* 9.1.

252. EVOLUTION

252.1 The concept of development . . . is indispensable for the understanding of the origin and growth of the Jewish religion.

Baeck, *Essence of Judaism,* 1936, p. 14.

252.2 Life does not proceed by the association and addition of elements, but by dissociation and division.

Bergson, *Creative Evolution,* (1908) 1911, ch 1.

252.3 Life is tendency, and the essence of a tendency is to develop in the form of a sheaf, creating, by its very growth, divergent directions among which its impetus is divided.

Ibid., ch 2.

252.4 There are no shortcuts in evolution.

Brandeis, at Boston Typothetae, April 22, 1904.

252.5 The question is this: is man an ape or an angel? I am on the side of the angels. I repudiate with indignation and abhorrence these new-fangled theories.

Disraeli, speech, Nov. 25, 1864.

252.6 When I consider how we fret
About a woman or a debt,
And strive and strain and cark and cuss,
And work and want and sweat and fuss,
And then observe the monkey swing
A casual tail at everything,
I am inclined to think that he

Evolved from apes like you and me.

Hoffenstein, *Year In, You're Out*, 1930. (*Complete Poetry*, 1954, p. 148f.)

252.7 The doctrine of evolution . . . agrees with the cosmic secrets of Cabala more than any other philosophic doctrine.

Kook, *Orot HaKodesh*, 1938, p. 555. q ABJ, 184.

253. EXAGGERATION

253.1 The Torah and the sages sometimes spoke in hyperbole.

Ammi. *Talmud: Hullin*, 90b.

253.2 Each vine shall yield a thousand branches, each branch a thousand clusters, each cluster a thousand grapes, and each grape a barrel of wine.

Apocrypha: II Baruch, 29.5.

253.3 Were all my organs mouths, and the hair of my head voices, even then I could not give Thee the meed of praise.

Ibid., 54.8.

253.4 If all the skies were sheets, all the trees quills, and all the seas ink, these would not suffice to record what I learned from my teachers, and I did not absorb from them more than this fly, dipping in the Great Sea, takes from its waters.

Johanan b. Zakkai. *Talmud: Soferim*, 16.8.

253.5 There were 365 thoroughfares in the great city of Rome, and each had 365 palaces; each palace had 365 stories, and each story had enough food for the whole world.

Jose b. Halafta. *Talmud: Pesahim*, 118b.

253.6 Could we with ink the ocean fill,
Were every blade of grass a quill,
Were the world of parchment made,
And every man a scribe by trade,
To write the love
Of God above
Would drain the ocean dry;
Nor would the scroll
Contain the whole,
Though stretched from sky to sky.

Meir b. Isaac Nehorai, "Akdamut," c. 1060. See Singer, *DPB*, 125.

253.7 If the seas were ink, the reeds pens, the skies parchment, and all men scribes, they would not suffice to describe the complexity of government.

Rab. *Talmud: Sabbath*, 11a. See *Yoma*, 76a.

254. EXCELLENCE

254.1 It is a wretched taste to be gratified with mediocrity when the excellent lies before us.

D'Israeli, *Curiosities: Quotation*, 1793.

254.2 Thoroughness is a part of excellence.

Schechter, March 20, 1904. *Seminary Addresses*, 60.

254.3 All things excellent are as difficult as they are rare.

Spinoza, *Ethics*, 1677, v. Pr 42, Note.

255. EXCESS

255.1 Be not righteous overmuch, neither make yourself overwise.

Bible: Eccles., 7.16.

255.2 In overeating nests sickness, and excess leads to loathing.

Apocrypha: Ben Sira, 37.30.

255.3 Even virtue in extreme becomes a vice.

Ezobi, *Kaarat Kesef*, 1270.

255.4 When the body gets full, the mind gets dull.

Gabishon, *Omer HaShikha*, c. 1600.

255.5 A Jest, unduly pushed, becomes no Jest;
Remember always, too far East is West.

Guiterman, *A Poet's Proverbs*, 1924, p. 37.

255.6 There are three things of which you may easily have too much, while a little is good: yeast, salt, and hesitation.

Joshua of the South. *Talmud J: Berakot*, 5.3.

255.7 To renounce delicacies habitually is a better rule against excess than fasting occasionally.

Kol Bo, c. 1300, #67.

255.8 The particle "too" is a dangerous foil,
It even the meaning of "honest" may spoil.

Kuh, *Hinterlassene Gedichte*, 1792.

255.9 Be not too sweet lest you be consumed, nor too bitter lest you be spewed out.

Lazerov, *Enciklopedie fun Idishe Vitzen*, 1928, #421.

255.10 A wise man will carefully avoid excess, lest he give the impression of haughtiness.

Maimonides, *Yad: Deot*, 1180, 5.7.

255.11 There are three whose life is no life: the over-compassionate, the hot-tempered, and the hyper-fastidious.
Talmud: Pesahim, 113b.

255.12 If you grasp too much, you do not grasp; if you grasp a little, you grasp.
Talmud: Rosh Hashana, 4b.

255.13 Too much oil quenches the wick.
Yalkut, Psalms, #979.
Bahya, *Hobot HaLebabot,* 1040, 10.7.

256. EXCLUSION

256.1 Include me out.
Goldwyn, attributed to.

257. EXILE

257.1 I will send a faintness into their heart in the lands of their enemies; the sound of a driven leaf shall chase them; they shall flee . . . and fall when none pursues.
Bible: Lev., 26.36. See *Deut.,* 28.65ff.

257.2 My people are gone into captivity for want of knowledge.
Bible: Isa., 5.13.

257.3 The house of Israel went into captivity . . . because they broke faith with Me.
Bible: Ezek., 39.23.

257.4 How shall we sing the Lord's song in a foreign land?
Bible: Ps., 137.4.

257.5 The three great causes of exile: lack of courage, of honor, and of government.
Abravanel, *Maayené Yeshua,* 1551, p. 76.

257.6 Why is this great community driven like cattle? Surely because they refuse to deny the faith of their fathers.
Ben Avigdor, *The Spanish Exile,* q LEJS, 55.

257.7 Our soul demands great things, but our body has no ground on which to stand.
Berdichevsky, *BaHomer UbaRuah,* 1908, p. 29f.

257.8 The *Galuth* condition of the Jewish nation is not only tragic, but also hopeless. Our *Galuth* tragedy is not temporary, but permanent. We do not fight for a Jewish cause; we suffer for foreign interests.
Borochov, "National Self-Help," Aug. 6, 1915. BNC, 85.

257.9 Tribes of the wandering foot and weary breast,

How shall ye flee away and be at rest?
The wild dove hath her nest, the fox his cave,
Mankind their country—Israel, but the grave.
*Byron, *Hebrew Melodies,* 1815.

257.10 Exile is not only a punishment but also a sin.
J. Cahan, "Bat HaGalut," 1904. q WHJ, iv. 301.

257.11 The Orient dwells an exile in the Occident, and its tears of longing for home are the fountain-head of Jewish poetry.
*Delitzsch, *Jüdische Poesie,* 1836, p. vii. q KJL, 24.

257.12 Long as the Jewish Exile.
Figure of speech (Yiddish). BJS #806. ATJF, 641.

257.13 What, in fine, are you, O Israel, but a poor *bahur* among the peoples, eating one day with one of them, and another day with the other! . . . You kindled a perpetual lamp for the whole world, and about you alone the world is dark, O People, slave of slaves, desperate and despised!
J. L. Gordon, "Two Joseph ben Simons." *Kol Shiré,* iv. 102. q SRH, 198.

257.14 Wherever Jews live as a minority . . . is *Galuth.*
H. Greenberg, address, 1951. GIE, 71.

257.15 He who does not know exile will not understand how luridly it colors our sorrows, how it pours the darkness of night and poison into all our thoughts. . . . Only he who has lived in exile knows what love of fatherland is—patriotism with all its sweet terrors and its nostalgic trials.
Heine, *Ludwig Börne,* 1840. EPP, 652.

257.16 Exile deepened the moral strain in the people. . . . Ethical monotheism, the emphasis on sanctity of mind, purification through suffering, charity towards the poor and miserable, love of God and neighbor, all these were the fruits of that hard school.
F. Hertz, *Race and Civilization,* 1928, p. 194.

257.17 In exile, the Jewish people cannot be regenerated.
Hess, *Rome and Jerusalem,* (1862), p 166.

257.18 Israel can accomplish its task be-

ter in exile than in the full possession of good fortune.
S. R. Hirsch, *Nineteen Letters*, (1836), #9, p. 82.

257.19 Exile is a form of imprisonment. . . . The refugee is like a plant without soil or water.
M. Ibn Ezra, *Shirat Yisrael*, (12C) 1924, p. 34.

257.20 Exile atones for everything.
Johanan. *Talmud: Sanhedrin*, 37b.

257.21 Woe to the children, for whose sins I destroyed My house, burnt My temple, and exiled My people among the nations! Woe to the father who had to banish his children, and woe to the children who had to be banished from their father's table!
Jose b. Halafta. *Talmud: Berakot*, 3a.

257.22 My heart is in the East,
And I am in the ends of the West.
How then can I taste what I eat,
And how can food to me be sweet?
Judah Halevi, *Poems,* ed. Harkavy, ii. 7.

257.23 Where is the Hebrew's fatherland? . . .
His cup is gall, his meat is tears,
His passion lasts a thousand years.
E. Lazarus, "Crowing of the Red Cock," 1881. *Poems,* ii. 3.

257.24 As winnowed grain is flung into the air,
So, 'midst all peoples God shall scatter thee,
And thou shalt bear, as well as thine own griefs,
The griefs and burdens of all other races.
D. Levi, *IL Profeta: Orient,* 1884. q *JQRo,* ix. 395.

257.25 Here in exile, God Himself is in exile.
Levi Yitzhok. q HLH, 45.

257.26 It is easier to take a Jew out of the exile than to take the exile out of the Jew.
S. Levin. q A. Zeitlin. See *HaDoar,* June 18, 1954, p. 600.

257.27 A sick man may find some relief in complaining about his pain. But how bitter is the lot of him who falls sick in a strange, unfriendly house, where he fears even to heave a sigh lest he be driven out altogether. We, four million Jewish souls, are in such a circumstance in our land.

. . . Our wound is as deep as the sea, and we are forbidden to open our mouth!
Lipshitz, letter to A. Asher, Oct. 27, 1881.

257.28 The captive is like the drowning.
Maimon b. Joseph, *Letter of Consolation,* 1160.

257.29 Exile is caused by idolatry, immorality, bloodshed, and failure to release the land.
Mishna: Abot 5.9.

257.30 We become more united in exile than in Palestine.
Peretz, *Verk,* ed Kletzkin, xi. 277.

257.31 With Israel in exile, the kingdom of Heaven is not at peace.
Samuel b. Nahman. *Midrash Tehillim,* to *Ps.* 9.1.

257.32 Exile is as hard as all other punishments combined.
Sifré, #43, to *Deut.* 11.17, ed Friedmann, 82a.

257.33 As long as the Community of Israel is in exile, the Divine Name remains incomplete.
Zohar, VaYetzé, 154b-155a (Soncino ii. 97).

257.34 The exile under Ishmael is the hardest of all.
Zohar, Exod., 17a.

257.35 Banishment is often the only means of saving the nobler possessions of the world.
A. Zweig, *The Crowning of a King,* 1938.

258. EXODUS

258.1 Remember this day, in which ye came out from Egypt.
Bible: Exod., 13.3.

258.2 Israel was redeemed because they had not changed their names, abandoned their language, borne tales, or practiced immorality.
Eleazar HaKappar. *Mekilta,* to *Exod.* 12.6.

258.3 Strangest of recorded births! From out the strongest and most splendid despotism of antiquity comes the freest republic. From between the paws of the rock-hewn Sphinx rises the genius of human liberty, and the trumpets of the Exodus throb with the defiant proclamation of the rights of man.
*George, *Moses,* 1878.

258.4 Not in vain does the story of the Exodus stand at the center of Jewish history and thought. The abandonment of old homes and the breaking up of old gods is symbolic of the will to liberty in the Jewish people.

Gutkind. *Freeland*, Jan. 1953, vii. 7.

258.5 Israel's exodus from Egypt will remain forever the springtime of the entire world.

Kook. q Tzoref, *Hayye HaRav Kook*, 1947, p. 191.

258.6 In each generation every man must regard himself as though he personally had gone forth from Egypt.

Mishna: Pesahim, 10.5.

258.7 Sound the loud timbrel o'er
          Egypt's dark sea!
       Jehovah has triumphed—His people are free!

*T. Moore, "Sound the Loud Timbrel," *Sacred Songs*, 1816–1820.

259. EXPECTATION

259.1 What we anticipate seldom occurs; what we least expect generally happens.

Disraeli, *Henrietta Temple*, 1837, 2.4.

259.2 Be sure to get your bear before you skin him.

I. J. Singer, *The Sinner*, tr Samuel (1933), p. 74.

260. EXPEDIENCE

260.1 Expediency may tip the scales when arguments are nicely balanced.

Cardozo, *Woolford Realty Co. vs. Rose*. *U.S. Reports*, v. 286, p. 330.

260.2 In the end, Vespasian's friends overcame his scruples by telling him that against Jews there could be no question of impiety, and that he ought to prefer expediency to decency when the two were incompatible.

Josephus, *Wars*, 3.10.10.

261. EXPERIENCE

261.1 Experience is more forceful than logic.

I. Abravanel, *Commentary*, to *Deut.* 17. 15.

261.2 None so wise as the experienced.

Arama, *Akedat Yitzhak*, 15C, ch 14. See *Ben Sira*, 34.10.

261.3 The experience of facts, . . . only that converts.

B. Auerbach, *Auf der Höhe*, 1865.

261.4 You may dispute principles, not experiences.

Boerne, announcement of *Zeitschwingen*, 1819.

261.5 Experience is like a pitiless beauty.

Years pass before you win her, and by the time she finally surrenders, you have both grown old and no longer need one another.

Boerne, *Der Narr im weissen Schwan*, ch 2.

261.6 Not years but experiences age us; hence man would be the unhappiest of creatures were he a diligent pupil of experience. That each new generation and each new era starts out from the cradle is what keeps mankind eternally young.

Boerne, *Fragmente & Aphorismen*, 1840, #240.

261.7 Often a liberal antidote of experience supplies a sovereign cure for a paralyzing abstraction built upon a theory.

Cardozo, *Paradoxes of Legal Science*, 1928, p. 125.

261.8 Wisdom is not to be obtained from text-books, but must be coined out of human experience in the flame of life.

M. R. Cohen, *A Dreamer's Journey*, 1949, p. 118.

261.9 Experience is a good school, but the fees are high.

Heine.

261.10 Experience makes a person better or bitter.

S. Levenson. q Leon Gutterman, JTA, 1952.

261.11 Who has eaten of the dish knows its taste.

Levi. *Deut. R.*, 2.26f.

261.12 One may eat potatoes for forty years, yet that won't make one a botanist!

S. Levin, at Zionist Congress, 1929. q *HaDoar*, 6.3.55, p. 545.

261.13 What happens *to* a man is less significant than what happens *within* him.

Mann, *In Quest of the Bluebird*, 1938, p. 60.

262. EXPERIMENT

262.1 No amount of experimentation can ever prove me right; a single experiment may at any time prove me wrong.

Einstein, of his Theory of Relativity.

263. EXPLANATION

263.1 The only correct actions are such as require no explanation.

Auerbach, *Auf der Höhe*, 1865.

263.2 It is unwise to wish everything explained.

Disraeli, *Coningsby*, 1844.

263.3 If you cannot explain, you do not understand.
Lipkin. q KTH, i. 277.

264. EXPRESSION

264.1 All religion is an attempt to express . . . what is essentially inexpressible. Every new religion has to create its own language.
Baeck, *Essence of Judaism,* 1936, p. 148.

264.2 It's not the gag, it's how you deliver it.
Berle.

264.3 The expressed is never fruitless.
Boerne, *Ankündigung der Wage,* 1818.

264.4 'Tis not thy words, but *how* thou
    speakest them
    That leads thee to the pleasant
       things of life.
Frishman, "A Dream and Its Meaning." q CHS, 90.

264.5 The intrinsic, the most essential, is never expressed.
Heschel, *Man Is Not Alone,* 1951, p. 4.

264.6 My God, . . . grant me the gifts of articulation,
Expression, the mind's translation!
Kook. *Zikaron,* 1945, p. 17. q ABJ, 131.

264.7 When I carried the thought in my heart, it uplifted me; and when I expressed it, it lost its influence.
Lipkin. q KTH, 275.

264.8 A letter depends on how you read it, a melody on how you sing it.
Peretz, *A Gilgul fun a Nign,* 1901. *Alle Verk,* vi. 33.

264.9 The early Hebraic expression of its mysteries will never be surpassed.
*Stedman, *Nature & Elements of Poetry,* 1892, p. 244.

265. EYE

265.1 The eyes of a fool are in the ends of the earth.
Bible: Prov., 17.24.

265.2 Man was created with two eyes, so that with one he may see God's greatness, and with the other his own lowliness.
Agnon, *Haknasat Kalla,* 1922.

265.3 Man's eye is like a fountain of water, and it is not satisfied with riches till filled with dust.
Apocrypha: Ahikar, 2.66.

265.4 God created nothing more evil than the eye; it must therefore weep over everything.
Apocrypha: Ben Sira, 31.15.

265.5 Man is the eye of the universe.
Berdichevsky, *BaDerek,* 1922, i. 17. q HMH, 92.

265.6 As dear as a Jew's eye.
*Harvey, *Works,* 1593, ii. 146.

265.7 A bride with beautiful eyes need not worry about her figure.
Hoshaia Zeera. *Talmud: Taanit,* 42a.

265.8 The eye tells what the heart means.
Lazerov, *Enciklopedie fun Idishe Vitzen,* 1928, #446.

265.9 A man's eyes are in front, not behind.
Maimonides, Letter to Marseilles, 1195. *Responsa,* ii. 26b.

265.10 The light of the body is the eye.
New Testament: Matt., 6.22.

265.11 The soul is imprisoned in the body, and the Lord . . . built two windows in the wall of the prison. . . . Unfortunately, the windows have curtains—eyelids; and a man whose soul is impure, feeling himself scrutinized, lets down the curtains and conceals the soul.
Peretz, *Mesiras Nefesh.* q SPG, 22.

265.12 Believe one eye more than two ears.
The eye is little, yet it sees the world.
The eyes are larger than the mouth.
The eyes are bigger than the stomach.
    Proverbs (Yiddish). BJS, Nos. 47, 51, 54f.

265.13 The eye is small and devours all.
Proverb (Yiddish). YFS, i. 411.

265.14 No organ as precious as the eye.
Simeon b. Eleazar. *Sifré,* to *Num.,* #84.

265.15 Stumbling is only with the eyes.
Talmud: Derek Eretz, 1.4

265.16 When one says, Take the mote out of your eye, the other replies, Take the beam out of yours!
Tarfon. *Talmud: Arakin,* 16b. Cf *Baba Bathra,* 15b. *Matt.* 7.3.

266. FACE

266.1 A pretty face is half a dowry.
Sholom Aleichem, *Heintike Kinder,* 1899.

266.2 The mould of the heart is shown in the face.
Zohar, Gen., 96b.

267. FACT

267.1 Create facts and more facts—that

is the cornerstone of political strategy. Facts are more convincing than phrases.

Borochov. *Yidisher Kempfer*, May 4, 1917. BNC, 91.

267.2 Face facts, and proceed.

Fleischer, motto. q *Commentary*, June 1954, p. 564.

267.3 If the romance does not become a fact, at least the fact can become a romance.

Herzl, *Diary*, 1895.

267.4 A *fait accompli* is not open to discussion.

Johanan b. Zakkai. *Talmud: Rosh Hashana*, 29b.

267.5 Fools must be refuted, not by arguments, but by facts.

Josephus, *Against Apion*, ii. 8.

267.6 It [Judaism] bowed before truth, but it had never made a covenant with facts only because they were facts.

Schechter, *Studies in Judaism*, 1896, i. p. xxi.

268. FAILURE

268.1 You are weighed in the balances, and are found wanting.

Bible: Dan., 5.27.

268.2 Failure, when sublime, is not without its purpose.

Disraeli, *Alroy*, 1833, 10.19.

268.3 Our failures . . . for the most part spring from our successes.

Sarnoff, *Youth in a Changing World*, June 12, 1954.

269. FAITH

269.1 If ye will not have faith, surely ye shall not be established.

Bible: Isa., 7.9.

269.2 The righteous shall live by his faith.

Bible: Hab., 2.4.

269.3 All Thy commandments are faith.

Bible: Ps., 119.86.

269.4 The way of the faithless is harsh.

Bible: Prov., 13.15.

269.5 When Israel gained faith, *then* . . . could they sing.

Abbahu, on *Exod.* 15.11, *Exod. R.*, 23.2.

269.6 Their faith merits that I divide the sea for them.

Abtalion. *Mekilta*, to *Exod.* 14.15.

269.7 Faith is to do His will.

Apocrypha: Ben Sira, 15.15.

269.8 Slow of faith is all the race of men.

Apocrypha: Sibyl, 4.40.

269.9 Faith must be conquered and acquired.

Asch, *What I Believe*, 1941, p. 49.

269.10 In the struggle with evil, only faith matters.

Baal Shem. See BTH, i. 60.

269.11 When God wants to punish a man, He deprives him of faith.

Baal Shem. q A. Cohen, *Keter Shem Tob*, (1864), p. 93.

269.12 In Judaism faith is . . . the capacity of the soul to perceive the abiding . . . in the transitory, the invisible in the visible.

Baeck, *Essence of Judaism*, 1936, p. 118.

269.13 Men reach the sublime pinnacle of faith when they learn to transform tragedy into soul energy.

J. L. Baron, "Spirit of Faith," 1930. (Burstein, *Books of Moses*, p. 217.)

269.14 The dynamite of doubt is useful in wrecking old structures; but to build new buildings, we must have the dynamics of faith.

J. L. Baron, *In Quest of Integrity*, 1936, p. 13.

269.15 A brilliant mind without faith is like a beautiful face without eyes.

S. Cohen, *Mishlé Agur*, 1803, 11.

269.16 He who has a piece of bread in his basket and asks, What will I eat tomorrow? belongs to those who are of little faith.

Eleazar of Modin. *Mekilta*, to *Exod.* 16.4. Eliezer b. Hyrcanus. *Talmud: Sota*, 48b. Cf *Matt.*, 6.30ff.

269.17 Faith not based on understanding is worse than atheism.

J. L. Gordon, letter to Smolenskin, 1871. *Igrot*, i. 172. q Rhine, *Leon Gordon*, 54.

269.18 To rely on our faith would be idol-worship. We have only the right to rely on God.

Heschel, *Man Is Not Alone*, 1951, p. 174.

269.19 Poverty, sickness and terror are easier to bear with faith.

Ibn Gabirol, *Mibhar HaPeninim*, c.1050, #122.

269.20 Faith is the summit of the Torah.

Ibid., #123.

269.21 I believe in the sun even when it is not shining. I believe in love even when not feeling it. I believe in God even when He is silent.

Inscription in a Cologne cellar, where Jews hid from the Nazis. q Kolitz, *The Tiger Beneath the Skin*, 81.

269.22 Faith is devotion to God.

Katz, *Toldot Jacob Joseph*, 1780. q HLH, 31.

269.23 Faith is the song of life. . . . Woe to him who wishes to denude life of the splendor of its poetry.

Kook, *HaMahshaba HaYisraelit*, 1920, p. 23. q ABJ, 143.

269.24 The happiness of the Jewish people depends not upon its political emancipation, but upon its faith and morality.

S. D. Luzzatto, letter to Jost, 1840. See SRH, 89.

269.25 The exiles will be gathered only as a reward for faith.

Mekilta, to *Exod.*, 14.31.

269.26 Faith is a Jewish commodity. With faith our father Jacob crossed the Jordan, supported only by a staff; with faith Jews open big stores. Everything you see here is built only on faith.

Mendelé, *Travels of Benjamin III*, 1878.

269.27 Where reason ends, faith begins.

Nahman Bratzlav, *Likkuté Etzot*, (1816) 1875, 3.

269.28 Your faith has made you whole.

New Testament: Mark, 5.34.

269.29 Faith is the substance of things hoped for, the evidence of things not seen.

New Testament: Heb., 11.1.

269.30 Faith, if it has not works, is dead.

New Testament: James, 2.17.

269.31 We know of some very religious people who came to doubt God when a great misfortune befell them, even though they themselves were to blame for it; but we have never yet seen anyone who lost his faith because an undeserved fortune fell to his lot.

Schnitzler, *Buch der Sprüche & Bedenken*, 1927, p. 40.

269.32 The foundation of service is faith.

Zerahia, *Sefer HaYashar*, 13C or 14C (1526).

269.33 God banished Israel only when they no longer had faith.

Zohar, Gen., 291b.

270. FALL

270.1 How are the mighty fallen!
Bible: II Sam., 1.19.

270.2 Within itself the fall
Bears the ascension.

Anski, *Dybbuk*, 1918, Act 1.

270.3 From a roof so high to a pit so deep!

Judah HaNasi. *Talmud: Hagiga*, 5b.

270.4 The fall is not the worst; but overthrow
With strength unconquered, power unimpaired,
This is the worst that heroes can endure.

Lassalle, *Franz von Sickingen*, 1859.

270.5 Buttered bread always falls on its face.

Proverb (Yiddish). BJS, #579.

271. FALSEHOOD

271.1 Thou shalt not bear false witness against thy neighbor.
Bible: Exod., 20.13.

271.2 Thou shalt not utter a false report.
Ibid., 23.1.

271.3 I said in my haste: All men are liars.
Bible: Ps., 116.11.

271.4 A lying tongue is but for a moment.
Bible: Prov., 12.19.

271.5 Lying lips are an abomination to the Lord.
Ibid., 12.22.

271.6 A lie has no legs.
Alphabet of Rabbi Akiba. Jellinek, *Bet HaMidrasch*, 1855, iii. 51.

271.7 A lie is a foul blot on a man.
Apocrypha: Ben Sira, 4.28.

271.8 When Falsehood saw he had no legs, he made himself wings.

Ben Zion. *Luah Ahiasaf*, 1897, p. 76.

271.9 The gravest sins are forbidden in Scripture once, but falsehood is forbidden many times.

M. Cohen, *Sefer Hasidim Zuta*, 1573.

271.10 The art of survival is the art of lying to yourself heroically, continuously, creatively. The senses lie to the mind; the mind lies to the senses. The truth-seeker is a liar; he is hunting for happiness, not truth.

De Casseres, *Fantasia Impromptu*, 1933.

271.11 The prevaricator is like an idolater.

Eleazar b. Pedat. *Talmud: Sanhedrin*, 92a.

116

271.12 You may modify a statement in the interests of peace.

Eleazar b. Simeon. *Talmud: Yebamot,* 65b.

271.13 Occasionally even a liar tells the truth.

M. Ibn Ezra, *Shirat Yisrael,* (12C) 1924, p. 79.

271.14 People tend to lie because of impotence.

Ibid., 122.

271.15 Lying is a European power.

Lassalle. q J. R. Macdonald, *Socialist Movement,* 164.

271.16 Falsehood begets falsehood.

Levi. *Midrash Tehillim,* 7.11, ed Buber 35a.

271.17 Who doesn't lie can't be a marriage broker.

Mendelé, *Eltern und Kinder,* 1868.

271.18 Confess each time you lie, and get used to the truth.

Mordecai of Czernobil, *Likkuté Torah,* (1867), 6b.

271.19 Falsehood derives from fear.

Nahman Bratzlav, *Sefer HaMiddot,* 1821.

271.20 Lying kills the divinity in man.

Nahman Bratzlav. q HLH, 97.

271.21 False witnesses are despised even by their own employers.

Nathan b. Mar Zutra. *Talmud: Sanhedrin,* 29a.

271.22 Messiah will come only when the world will realize that to speak an untruth is adultery.

P. Shapiro, *Midrash Pinhas,* (1876), 26b. See SSJ, ii. 164.

271.23 A liar's punishment is that he is not believed even when he tells the truth.

Simeon b. Yohai. *Talmud: Sanhedrin,* 89b.

271.24 Falsehood is frequent, truth is rare.

Talmud: Sabbath, 104a.

271.25 If you wish to establish a lie, mix a little truth with it.

Zohar, Num., 161a.

272. FAME

272.1 Warn your offspring not to be dazzled by fame or wealth.

Apocrypha: Aristeas, 196.

272.2 What is fame? A many-colored cloak, without warmth, without protection.

B. Auerbach, *Christian Gellert's Last Christmas,* 1869.

272.3 If you wish to live long, don't become famous.

Baal Shem. q *Reshumot,* 1925, i. 406.

272.4 Fame always brings loneliness.

V. Baum, *Grand Hotel,* (1929) 1931, p. 134.

272.5 Fame is the beauty-parlor of the dead.

De Casseres, *Fantasia Impromptu,* 1933.

272.6 Study two chapters for knowledge, rather than the whole Mishna for fame. Earn a modest living from your own small capital, rather than borrow to be known as a man of affairs. Give a little of your own, rather than much of what is not yours, just to be known as a philanthropist.

Isaac Nappaha. *Lev. R.,* 3.1.

272.7 Our ancients issued works anonymously, disclaiming any ambition for fame.

Sefer Hasidim, 13C, #1528, p. 374.

272.8 Fame has also this great drawback, that if we pursue it, we must direct our lives so as to please the fancy of men.

Spinoza, *De Intellectus Emendatione,* 1677.

273. FAMILIARITY

273.1 May one behave familiarly with Heaven?

Abayé. *Talmud: Berakot,* 34a.

273.2 As true as God be true to me, I sat by Solomon Rothschild, and he treated me just like an equal, quite *familionaire.*

Heine, (Hyacinth in) *Baths of Lucca,* 1828, ch 8.

273.3 Growing familiarity has the deadly effect of enabling one to predict the other person's responses; and when that happens, the stimulating quality and creative tension of a relationship are finished.

Koestler, *Arrow in the Blue,* 1952, p. 244.

273.4 When we continually see an object, however sublime it may be, our regard for it will be lessened, and the impression we have received of it will be weakened.

Maimonides, *Guide for the Perplexed,* 1190, 3.47.

274. FAMILY

274.1 Whatever is great and good in the institutions and usages of mankind is an application of sentiments that have drawn their first nourishment from the soil of the family. The family is the school of duties . . . founded on love.

F. Adler, *Creed and Deed*, 1877, p. 204.

274.2 I have carried iron and removed stones, and they were not heavier than for a man to settle in his father-in-law's house.

Apocrypha: Ahiḳar, 2.46.

274.3 Lighter than bran is a son-in-law who lives in the house of his father-in-law.

Talmud: Baba Bathra, 98b.

274.4 Honor your father-in-law and mother-in-law, because henceforth they are your parents.

Apocrypha: Tobit, 10.12.

274.5 Children may not be parted from their parents, nor a wife from her husband, even if they be captive.

Philo. q Eusebius, *Preparation of the Gospel*, 8.7.

274.6 None may interfere between two who sleep on the same pillow.

Proverb (Yiddish). BJS, #3827.

274.7 No man can examine the leprosy of his own relations.

Sifré, Num., #105.

274.8 If one in a family is a tax-collector or a robber, they are all tax-collectors or robbers, for they will shield the sinner.

Simeon. *Talmud: Shebuot*, 39a.

274.9 "Your tent is in peace" refers to him who loves his wife as himself and honors her more than himself, who leads his children in the right path, and arranges for their early marriage.

Talmud: Yebamot, 62b, on *Job* 5.24.

274.10 A little hurt from a kin is worse than a big hurt from a stranger.

Zohar, Gen., 151b.

275. FARMING

275.1 The seventh year you shall let it [your land] rest and lie fallow, that the poor of your people may eat.

Bible: Exod., 23.11. Cf *Lev.* 25.3–7.

275.2 You shall not wholly reap the corner of your field, nor gather the gleaning of your harvest . . . leave them to the poor and the stranger.

Bible: Lev., 19.9f.

275.3 Because of the thorns uproot not a garden.

Al-Harizi, *Taḥkemoni*, 13C, ch 1.

275.4 How can he become wise who holds the plough, glories in the goad, drives cattle and talks about bullocks?

Apocrypha: Ben Sira, 38.25.

275.5 A time will come when all craftsmen will take up farming.

Eleazar b. Pedat. *Talmud: Yebamot*, 63a.

275.6 Even if the field were ploughed breadthwise and lengthwise, business would still be more profitable.

Ibid.

275.7 Not the Atlantic sweeps a flood
Potent as the ploughman's blood.
He, his horse, his ploughshare,
These are the only verities.

Golding, "Ploughman at the Plough."

275.8 On the day the plough is again in the strengthened hands of the Jewish farmer, the Jewish question will be solved.

Herzl, address, I Zionist Congress, Aug. 31, 1897.

275.9 Only in the tilling of the soil is the redemption of the Jew.

Mendelé, *BiYeshiva Shel Maala*, 1895.

275.10 A century of *Kultur* is not equal to a decade of agriculture on a soil of your own.

Zangwill, at Zionist Congress, Aug. 23, 1903.

275.11 In the plow lies our bliss.

Zunser, "In the Plow." q Liptzin, *Eliakim Zunser*, 43f.

276. FASHION

276.1 There are people who dress also inwardly as the fashion ordains.

B. Auerbach, *Drei einzige Töchter*, 1875.

276.2 The concepts of morality too are subject to fashion; and he who cannot incline to the ideas in vogue in his century, is misunderstood and decried by his contemporaries.

M. Mendelssohn, to Hennings.

276.3 There are fashions in immortality as there are trivial fashions. Books and pictures read differently to different generations.

Rothenstein, *Men and Memories*, 1931, i. 66.

277. FASTING

277.1 Is not this the fast that I have chosen? To loose the fetters of wickedness, to undo the bands of the yoke, and to let the oppressed go free? Is it not to deal your bread to the hungry, and that you bring

the outcast poor to your house? When you see the naked, that you cover him, and that you hide not yourself from your own flesh?
Bible: Isa., 56.7.

277.2 The fasts . . . shall be to the house of Judah joy and gladness and cheerful seasons.
Bible: Zech., 8.19.

277.3 Fasting is more effective than charity, for the latter is done with money, the former with one's person.
Eleazar b. Pedat. *Talmud: Berakot,* 32b.

277.4 He who fasts is called a holy man.
Eleazar (b. Pedat). *Talmud: Taanit,* 11a.

277.5 No excessive fasting, lest you become a public charge.
Jose b. Halafta. *Tosefta: Taanit,* 2.12.

277.6 Prolonged fasting is no act of piety.
Judah Halevi, *Cuzari,* c.1135, 2.50.

277.7 Fasting and penance sadden, while devotion is only through joy.
Katz, *Toldot Jacob Joseph,* 1780.

277.8 Who indulges in fasting is called a sinner.
Samuel. *Talmud: Taanit,* 11a.

277.9 If hunger makes you irritable, better eat and be pleasant.
Sefer Hasidim, 13C, #66, p. 49.

277.10 A scholar may not fast, if it interferes with his study.
Simeon b. Lakish. *Talmud: Taanit,* 11b.
See *TJ: Demai,* 7.3.

277.11 People in a besieged or flooded city, passengers on a storm-tossed boat, and those persecuted by heathens or robbers, may not weaken themselves by fasting.
Tosefta: Taanit, 2.12.

277.12 The merit of a fast day is in the charity dispensed then.
Zutra. *Talmud: Berakot,* 6b.

278. FAT

278.1 Jeshurun waxed fat, and kicked.
Bible: Deut., 32.15.

279. FATHER

279.1 If your father's understanding fail, be considerate.
Apocrypha: Ben Sira, 3.13.

279.2 It is an honor for children and father to be with one another.
Exod. R., 34.3.

279.3 He who brings up, not he who begets, is the father.
Ibid., 46.5.

279.4 A father loves best his worst son.
Gentili, *Mleket Mahshebet, Noah,* 1710, #46.

279.5 Joseph resisted the enticements of his master's wife, because at the moment of temptation he saw his father's image.
Judah Halevi b. Shalom. *Tanhuma, Va-Yesheb.*

279.6 When I was a boy I used to do what my father wanted. Now I have to do what my boy wants. My problem is: When am I going to do what I want?
Levenson.

279.7 Formerly I was my father's son, now I am my son's father.
A. Mendelssohn, son of Moses and father of Felix.

279.8 A father's love is for his children; the children's love is for their children.
Proverb. q Huna. *Talmud: Sota,* 49a.

279.9 Let not a father ask his married daughter to attend to him, without first obtaining her husband's permission.
Sefer Hasidim, 13C, #930, p. 229.

280. FAULT

280.1 Clear Thou me from hidden faults.
Bible: Ps., 19.13.

280.2 No one sees his own fault.
Al-Harizi, *Tahkemoni,* 13C, ch 18.

280.3 The defects of great men are the consolation of dunces.
D'Israeli, *Literary Character,* 1795.

280.4 We have a bat's eyes for our own faults, and an eagle's for the faults of others.
J. L. Gordon, *Mishlé Yehuda,* 1860, #9, p. 21.

280.5 If you seek a faultless brother, let a flawless time be your guide.
Hasdai, *Ben HaMelek VeHaNazir,* c.1230, ch 13.

280.6 Each work has faults which only its maker knows; each treasure has flaws which only its owner sees.
Herzl, *Buch der Narrheit,* 1888.

280.7 All hands to work! Old faults must be corrected!
Herzl, letter to IV Convention, Federation of American Zionists. *Maccabean,* Oct. 1901, Supplement, p. iv.

280.8 It is easier to acknowledge one's sin than one's fault.
Jeiteles. *Bikkuré Halttim,* 5589, ix. #24, p. 224.

280.9 With all her faults, I love her still.
M. H. Rosenfeld, title and refrain of a song, 1883.

281. FEAR

281.1 Fear not, for I am with thee.
Bible: Gen., 26.24. See *Isa.,* 43.1.

281.2 Yea, though I walk through the valley of the shadow of death, I will fear no evil, for Thou art with me.
Bible: Ps., 23.4.

281.3 You shall not be afraid of the terror by night, nor of the arrow that flies by day.
Ibid., 91.5.

281.4 Be not afraid of sudden terror.
Bible: Prov., 3.25.

281.5 The Lord is with me, I shall not fear.
Adon Olam. DPB, ed Singer, p. 3.

281.6 Fear is a surrender of the succors which reason offers.
Apocrypha: Wisd. of Sol., 17.12.

281.7 Fear builds walls to bar the light.
Baal Shem. See BTH, i. 42.

281.8 I'd be ashamed were God to see me fear anyone besides Him.
Bahya, *Hobot HaLebabot,* 1040, 10.6.

281.9 There is nothing to fear but fear.
Boerne, *Kritiken,* 1823, #21.

281.10 The most dangerous person is the fearful; he is most to be feared.
Boerne, *Der Narr im weissen Schwan,* ch 2.

281.11 Whoever wishes to accomplish a great task must be free of the fear of men, utterly free.
Brod, *The Master,* 1951, p. 321.

281.12 'Tis fools who never fear.
Heine, *Romancero: Enfant Perdu,* 1850.

281.13 In the democratic countries, the fear of arson, massacre and expulsion has been eliminated from Jewish life. But Jews have developed a new fear, the fear of living and acting openly and collectively as Jews.
Kaplan, *Future of the American Jew,* 1948, p. 75.

281.14 Fear him who fears you.
Lazerov, *Enciklopedie fun Idishe Vitzen,* 1928, #466.

281.15 Death is experienced only once, but he who fears it dies each minute.
Rubin, *Sefer HaMiddot,* 1854, 24.4.

281.16 We cannot banish dangers, but we can banish fears. We must not demean life by standing in awe of death.
Sarnoff, *Youth in a Changing World,* June 12, 1954.

281.17 All the roads are barricaded off with dread.
Schwarzman, "The Night Has Covered Me," LGP, 212.

281.18 Dumb animals fear a live infant but not a dead giant.
Simeon b. Eleazar. *Talmud: Sabbath,* 151b.

281.19 There is no hope unmingled with fear, and no fear unmingled with hope.
Spinoza, *Ethics,* 1677, iii. Def 13, Explanation.

281.20 Is there any worse slavery than the fear of man, however you may gild and polish your chains?
Varnhagen, to Brinckmann. q JRL, 250.

281.21 Jacob must be distressed because of fear of Esau.
Yehiel Michael. See BTH, i. 148f, on *Gen.* 32.8.

282. FEAR OF GOD

282.1 Fear the Lord thy God.
Bible: Deut., 6.13.

282.2 Serve the Lord with fear, and rejoice with trembling.
Bible: Ps., 2.11.

282.3 The fear of the Lord is clean, enduring for ever.
Bible: Ps., 19.10.

282.4 The fear of the Lord is the beginning of wisdom.
Ibid., 111.10. *Prov.,* 1.7, 9.10.

282.5 The fear of the Lord is to hate evil.
Bible: Prov., 8.13. Cf 16.6.

282.6 The end of the matter, all having been heard: fear God, and keep His commandment; for this is the whole man.
Bible: Eccles., 12.13.

282.7 Man should be ever subtle in the ways of fearing God.
Abayé. *Talmud: Berakot,* 17a.

282.8 Let the fear of Heaven be upon you.
Antigonus. *Mishna: Abot,* 1.3.

282.9 None is greater than he who fears God.
Apocrypha: Ben Sira, 10.24. See 19.24, 40.27.

282.10 Who fears the Lord is afraid of nothing.
Ibid., 34.14.

282.11 Fear not, my child, because we have become poor; you have much wealth if you fear God.
Apocrypha: Tobit, 4.21.

282.12 There is no freedom without . . . fear of God.
Baeck, *Essence of Judaism,* 1936, p. 252.

282.13 The Holy One desires only that men fear Him.
Eleazar b. Pedat. *Talmud: Sabbath,* 31b.

282.14 Learning without fear is as a tower without foundation.
Foundations of Religious Fear, 12C, tr H. Gollancz.

282.15 Everything is in the hands of Heaven except the fear of Heaven.
Hanina. *Talmud: Berakot,* 33b.

282.16 Your noblest quality before God is your fear of Him.
q M. Ibn Ezra, *Shirat Yisrael,* (12C) 1924, p. 145.

282.17 The righteous fear only God.
Ibn Gabirol, *Mibhar HaPeninim,* c. 1050, #5.

282.18 Fear of God, which Wisdom makes a crown for the head, humility makes a sole for the shoe.
Isaac b. Eleazar. *Talmud J: Sabbath,* 1.3.

282.19 May your fear of Heaven be as strong as your fear of man!
Johanan b. Zakkai. *Talmud: Berakot,* 28b.

282.20 The true service of God is through love *and* fear.
Judah Löw, *Netibot Olam,* 1595. q BWC, 78.

282.21 Love of God and fear of God should be yoke-fellows.
Moses Hasid, *Iggeret HaMusar,* 1717. See AHE, 291.

282.22 Fear only two: God, and him who fears not God.
Lazerov, *Enciklopedie fun Idishe Vitzen,* 1928, #451.

282.23 Dwellers above and dwellers below, they shake and they quake in the fear of Thy name. Dwellers in chasms, dwellers in graves, they quiver and shiver for fear of Thy name.
Levi Yitzhok. q BTH, i. 209.

282.24 Always envision the fear of Me.
Meir. *Talmud: Berakot,* 17a.

282.25 Fear of God is the thread on which the virtues are strung together like pearls. Loosen the knot of fear, and all the precious virtues will fall apart.
Orhot Tzaddikim, 15C, Introduction.

282.26 He who has learning but not fear of Heaven has the inside, but not the outside, keys to the treasury. He cannot enter.
Rabbah b. Huna. *Talmud: Sabbath,* 31ab.

282.27 There is a difference between fear of God and being afraid of Him.
M. Samuel, *World of Sholom Aleichem,* 1943, p. 28.

282.28 The divine assurance, "Fear not," comes only to one who is truly God-fearing.
Seder Eliyahu Rabbah, ch 23 (25), ed Friedmann, 128.

282.29 The only truly precious thing which the Holy One has in His treasury is the fear of Heaven.
Simeon b. Yohai, on *Isaiah* 33.6. *Talmud: Berakot,* 33b.

282.30 There is a palace that opens only to him who fears God.
Tikkuné Zohar, 13C, ch 11, p. 26b.

282.31 Fear of God is the gateway of faith.
Zohar, Prolog, 11b.

282.32 Who fears punishment is not yet endowed with that fear of God which leads to life. He fears the lash, not the Lord.
Ibid.

282.33 Fear involves humility, and humility involves grace!
Zohar, Num., 145a.

283. FEAST

283.1 For men, no feast without wine; for women, none without fancy dress.
Judah b. Bathyra. *Talmud: Pesahim,* 109a.

283.2 It is as difficult to feast with the right motive on the eve of Yom Kippur as it is to fast with the right motive on the day of Yom Kippur.
Lipkin. q KTH, i. 272.

283.3 Through much feasting a scholar destroys his home.
Talmud: Pesahim, 49a.

283.4 No festival without a feast.
Talmud: Moed Katan, 9a.

284. FEELING
284.A. Sentiment

284.A.1 We shall not overcome our opponents with reason, but with sentiment.
Ben Yehuda, letter to Smolenskin, Dec. 2, 1880.

284.A.2 Creation signifies, above all, emotion. . . . It is the emotion which drives the intelligence forward in spite of obstacles.
Bergson, *Two Sources of Morality & Religion*, 1935, p. 37.

284.A.3 Emotional ambivalence . . . lies at the root of many important cultural institutions.
Freud, *Totem and Taboo*, (1913) 1950, p. 157.

284.A.4 Not merely the skyscraper's height but its mass and proportions are the result of an emotion as well as of calculation.
Gershwin. O. M. Sayler, *Revolt in the Arts*, 1930, p. 265.

284.A.5 Only feeling understands feeling.
Heine, *Lutetia*, Feb. 13, 1841.

284.A.6 Among Jews a great civilization of the heart has persisted through two thousand years as an uninterrupted tradition. They have been able to play so great a part in European culture because they have had so little to learn by way of feeling, and needed only to acquire knowledge.
Heine, letter to Joseph Lehman, Oct. 5, 1854.

284.A.7 From true emotion spring phrases of beauty.
S. Levin, *Youth in Revolt*, 1930.

184.A.8 Thou shalt not be afraid of thy hidden impulses.
Liebman, *Peace of Mind*, 1946, p. 202.

284.A.9 The most delightful of companions is he who combines the mind of a gentleman with the emotions of a bum.
G. J. Nathan, *Autobiography of an Attitude*, 1925, p. 50.

284.A.10 Men are ruled by their feelings and offer furious resistance . . . when reason seeks to impose its discipline on them.
Nordau, *Conventional Lies*, Pref. to 59th ed., 1909.

284.A.11 Emotions . . . become more violent when expression is stifled.
Philo, *Joseph*, 2.

284.A.12 Always remember that right feeling is the vital spark of strong writing.
Pulitzer, to editors of N. Y. *World*, Dec. 29, 1895.

284.A.13 When you cannot love or hate any more, then where is the charm of life?
Schnitzler, *Professor Bernhardi*, 1912.

284.A.14 Sentimentality is feeling acquired below cost.
Schnitzler. q W. Mahrholtz, *Deutsche Literatur*, 1931, 78.

284.A.15 When a man is a prey to his emotions, he is not his master.
Spinoza, *Ethics*, 1677, iv. Preface.

284.A.16 My feelings at that moment could only be expressed in camera.
Sutro, *Mollentrave on Women*, 1905, Act 1.

284.A.17 A thing only belongs to us when it is felt . . . as beautiful, necessary, and vivid.
S. Zweig, *Emile Verhaeren*, 1910, tr Bitherll, 218.

284.B. Sensitivity

284.B.1 Exaggerated sensitiveness is an expression of the feeling of inferiority.
A. Adler, *Social Interest*, 1939.

284.B.2 Hurt not the feelings of the afflicted.
Apocrypha: Ben Sira, 4.3.

284.B.3 A warmth as of life is on the Hebrew, a chill as of marble is on the Greek. In Jewish history the most tenderly religious character is the most sensitive to earth.
*Bagehot, *Macaulay*, 1852. *Literary Studies*, ii. 19.

284.B.4 The sources of beauty and satisfaction may be found close at hand within the range of one's own sensibilities.
Glueck. E. R. Murrow, *This I Believe*, 1952, p. 59.

284.B.5 Since the destruction of the Temple all gates of prayer have been closed, except to the cry of hurt feelings.
Hisda. *Talmud: Baba Metzia*, 59a.

284.B.6 A scholar without sensibility is less than an ant.
Lev. R., 1.15.

284.B.7 Abash not him who has a physical blemish or family stain.
Orhot Tzaddikim, 15C, ch 21.

284.B.8 I will inure my mind to the feelings of a human being . . . because a man should not forget what he is.
Philo, *Decalogue*, 10.

284.B.9 If there was a hanging in his family, don't tell him, "Hang this up for me."

Proverb. q *Talmud: Baba Metzia,* 59b.

284.B.10 Bring not your small children to visit one who was bereaved of his small children.

Sefer Hasidim, 13C, #103, p. 56.

284.B.11 "Where the burnt-offering is sacrificed shall the sin-offering be sacrificed"—so as not to expose sinners.

Simeon b. Yohai, on *Lev.* 6.18. *Talmud: Sota,* 32b.

284.B.12 Taunt not a penitent or a proselyte about his past.

Talmud: Baba Metzia, 58b.

285. FELLOWSHIP

285.1 I am a companion of all them that fear Thee.

Bible: Ps., 119.63.

285.2 Be kind to your companions, but be firm.

Disraeli, *Venetia,* 1837.

285.3 Honor your colleague as you honor your teacher.

Eleazar b. Shammua. *Mishna: Abot,* 4.12.

285.4 Give me comradeship, or give me death!

Honi HaMe'agel. q Raba. *Talmud: Taanit,* 23a.

285.5 A man without comrades is like the left without the right.

Ibn Gabirol, *Mibhar HaPeninim,* c. 1050, #255.

285.6 When one dies, all his company fear.

Johanan. *Talmud: Sabbath,* 106a.

285.7 We are born for fellowship.

Josephus, *Against Apion,* 2.23.

285.8 To follow the straight path, choose a good colleague; to avoid the evil path, avoid a wicked colleague.

Joshua b. Hanania. *Mishna: Abot,* 2.9.

285.9 Acquire a companion.

Joshua b. Perahia. *Mishna: Abot,* 1.6.

285.10 The ability to unite is the ability to sense the great factor which makes for our fellowship.

Katznelson, *Ketabim,* ix. 301.

285.11 There are three kinds of companions: some are like food, indispensable; some like medicine, good occasionally; and some like poison, unnecessary at any time.

Samuel HaNagid, *Ben Mishlé,* 11C, #101.

285.12 When the way is long, company is pleasant.

Talmud: Sukka, 52a.

285.13 What others see with us doubles its value.

Varnhagen, letter to Brinckmann, Nov. 30, 1819. JRL 201.

286. FENCE

286.1 There are no fences on high.

Elijah b. Raphael, *Tzavaah,* 18c.

286.2 Set a fence round your words.

Hillel. *Talmud: Nidda,* 3b.

287. FIGHT

287.1 Strive not with a man in his day; stand not up against a river in its flood.

Apocrypha: Ahikar, 2.65.

287.2 Strive for the right till death, and the Lord will fight for you.

Apocrypha: Ben Sira, 4.28.

287.3 They fought with gladness the battle of Israel.

Apocrypha: I Macc., 3.2.

287.4 If a man advises you how to keep unholy thoughts from disturbing you in your prayers and studies, know that he is of no account. For this is the service of men in the world to the very hour of death: to struggle time after time with the extraneous, and time after time to uplift and fit it into the nature of the Divine Name.

Baal Shem. q BTH, i. 66.

287.5 Only those are crowned who have nobly striven.

Didascalia, ii. ch 14.

287.6 Man is a pugnacious animal; and the task of finding an outlet for that fruitful source of destruction is omnipresent.

Laski, *A Grammar of Politics,* 1925, p. 25.

287.7 No devil cares a jot for all your tears;
You have two fists, what need for idle fears?

Mosen, "Zuruf." *Gedichte,* 1836.

287.8 Men of peace become men of war, when they oppose and attack those who seek to overturn the firmness of the soul.

Philo, *Confusion of Tongues,* 11.

287.9 The thrill, believe me, is as much in the battle as in the victory.

Sarnoff, *Youth in a Changing World,* June 12, 1954.

288. FINANCE

288.1 There is no such thing as an innocent purchaser of stocks.

Brandeis, before Senate Committee on Interstate Commerce, Dec. 14, 1911. q LBG, 303.

288.2 In finances, be strict with yourself, generous with others.

Maimonides, *Yad: Deot*, 1180, 5.13.

288.3 A financier is a pawn-broker with imagination.

Pinero, *Second Mrs. Tanqueray*, 1893, Act 2.

289. FINGER

289.1 A finger does not know it has a separate life until it hurts.

H. Greenberg, "Notes on Marxism," 1935. GIE, 247.

290. FINISH

290.1 Who does not finish what he began is deposed.

Eleazar b. Pedat. *Talmud: Sota*, 13b.

290.2 You started, you finish.

Gen. R., 60.2. See Rab. *Talmud: Berakot*, 14b.

290.3 Scripture credits with performance not him who begins a task, but him who completes it.

Hama b. Hanina. *Talmud: Sota*, 13b.

290.4 He who began a precept is told: Finish it!

José. *Talmud J: Rosh Hashana*, 1.8.

290.5 Indeed, well begun
Is already half-won;
But the final and choicest awards, my good friend,
Bear in mind, on successful conclusions depend.

Sanders, *366 Sprüche*, 1892, #366.

290.6 He sins who does not finish the good deed he started.

Seder Eliyahu Zuta, ch 8, ed Friedmann, 188.

290.7 Who takes the trouble to start a thing should have the pleasure of finishing it.

Tanhuma, Ekeb, 5.

291. FIRE

291.1 According to its fuel, so will the fire be.

Apocrypha: Ben Sira, 28.10.

291.2 Fire is the symbol of civilization. . . . Jewish legend declares fire to be a heavenly gift to man. . . . God endowed Adam with the intuition to take two stones —named Darkness and Shadow of Death— rub them against each other, and so discover fire.

Hertz, *Daily Prayer Book*, 1948, p. 748. See *Gen. R.* 11.2; *Talmud: Pesahim*, 54a.

291.3 Who answers with fire is God.

J. Ibn Ghayat, *Elijah's Prayer*, 12C.

291.4 If fire grabbed the wet, what chance have the dry?

Seder Eliyahu Rabbah, ch 14, ed Friedmann, 65.
Meshullam b. Kalonymus, *Enosh Ma Yizkor*, 10C.

291.5 Blessed is the match that is consumed in kindling flame. Blessed is the flame that burns in the secret-fastness of the heart.

Senesh, *Blessed Is the Match*. q M. Syrkin, same title, 70.

291.6 Can fire be near tow and not singe it?

Talmud: Sanhedrin, 37a. See *Tanhuma, Metzora*, #13, ed Buber, 26b.

291.7 He has a pot for every fire.

Twerski. q CPP, #399.

291.8 If you need a flame, fan it.

Uceda, *Midrash Samuel*, 1579, ch 9.

292. FISH

292.1 Where there are no fish, even a crab is called a fish.

Bialik, *Arieh Baal Goof*, ch 6.

292.2 There is no fishing for trout in dry beaches.

Disraeli, *Count Alarcos*, 1839.

292.3 What does a fish know about the water in which he swims all his life?

Einstein. G. Schreiber, *Portraits & Self-Portraits*, 1936.

292.4 Try the Brook that none esteem;
Do not fish the Famous Stream.

Guiterman, *A Poet's Proverbs*, 1924, p. 28.

292.5 Sell not the fish which you haven't yet caught.

I. Hurwitz, *Mishlé Isachar*, 1887.

292.6 Like fish, like men: the greater swallow the smaller.

Talmud: Aboda Zara, 4a.

293. FLAG

293.1 With a flag you can lead people wherever you want.

Herzl, *Diary*, June 3, 1895.

293.2 I would suggest a white flag with seven gold stars: the white field symbolizing our pure life; the stars, the seven golden hours of our working day.
Herzl, *The Jewish State*, 1896, ch 5.

293.3 No stain adheres to our flag. Blood aplenty—but our own! On this flag is inscribed: "The Eternal is my banner!"
L. Holländer, speech, April 1914.

293.4 Let but an Ezra rise anew
To lift the banner of the Jew!
E. Lazarus, "The Banner of the Jew," c. 1882. *Poems*, 1889, ii. 11.

293.5 That flag of stars and stripes is yours:
It is the emblem of the promised land.
E. Lieberman, "I Am an American," ii.

293.6 We have a flag, and it is blue and white: the talith with which we wrap ourselves when we pray—that is our symbol.
D. Wolffsohn. *Moledeth*, reminiscence.

294. FLATTERY

294.1 A flattering mouth works ruin.
Bible: Prov., 26.28.

294.2 Let the wise strike you with many blows, and let not the fool salve you with sweet salve.
Apocrypha: Ahiḳar, 2.73.

294.3 Flattery is the destruction of all good fellowship: it is like a qualmish liqueur in the midst of a bottle of wine.
Disraeli, (Hunsdrick in) *Vivian Grey*, 1827.

294.4 Flatterers are destined for Gehenna. They will ultimately fall into the hands of those they flatter.
Eleazar b. Pedat. *Talmud: Sota*, 41b.

294.5 A community where flattery prevails will end in exile.
Ibid., 42a.

294.6 One whose praise was sung with much exaggeration said: I am below what they say and above what they think.
M. Ibn Ezra, *Shirat Yisrael*, (12C) 1924, p. 142.

294.7 Flattery is friendship diseased.
Philo, *Allegorical Interpretation*, 3.64.

294.8 Everybody flatters the king.
Proverb. q Ishmael. *Num. R.*, 10.4.

294.9 To flatter is to steal.
Proverb (Yiddish). YFS, i. 418.

294.10 None are more taken in by flat-

tery than the proud, who wish to be the first and are not.
Spinoza, *Ethics*, 1677, iv. Appendix 21.

295. FLESH

295.1 Flesh of my flesh.
Bible: Gen., 2.23.

295.2 All flesh is grass.
Bible: Isa., 40.6.

295.3 Jewish thought never identified "the flesh" with the evil impulse, nor regarded flesh and spirit as hostile to one another.
*Herford, *Judaism in the NT Period*, 1928, p. 95.

295.4 The more flesh the more worms.
Hillel. *Mishna: Abot*, 2.7.

295.5 The spirit indeed is willing, but the flesh is weak.
New Testament: Matt., 26.41.

295.6 It is the spirit that quickens, the flesh profits nothing.
New Testament: John, 6.63.

296. FLIGHT

296.1 A fugitive and a wanderer shall you be in the earth.
Bible: Gen., 4.12.

296.2 Thou shalt not deliver unto his master a bondman that escaped . . . unto thee.
Bible: Deut., 23.16.

296.3 Hide the outcast; betray not the fugitive.
Bible: Isa., 16.3.

296.4 O that I had wings like a dove! for then I would fly away and be at rest.
Bible: Ps., 55.7.

296.5 If we go through history, Madame, we find that all great men were obliged to run away once in their lives: Lot, Tarquin, Moses, Jupiter, Madame de Stael, . . . Mahomet, the whole Prussian army . . . to which I could add very many other names, as, for instance, those whose names stand on the blackboard of the Exchange.
Heine, *Ideas*, 1826, ch 13.

296.6 The shorter the flight, the easier the return.
Hiyya Rabbah. *Eccles. R.*, to *Eccles.*, 11.9.

297. FLOWERS

297.1 In many a flower one can tell,
Nests a glittering parable.
In hedges, where the sunlight pours,

The bushes burst with metaphors.
Ginsberg, "Spring Landscape." *Christian Century.*

297.2   In every calix I . . . seek a heart.
Heine, *New Spring: Lyrics,* 1844, #4.

297.3   Knowest thou the hidden language
By these lovely flowerets spoken?
Truth by day-time, love at night-
time—
'Tis of this that they're the
token!
Ibid., #33.

297.4   The flowers of the field, they are kith and kin to me.
A. M. Klein, *Hath Not a Jew,* 1940, p. 35.

298.   FOLLY

298.1   A little folly outweighs wisdom and honor.
Bible: Eccles., 10.1.

298.2   There is a remedy for every illness but folly.
Al-Rabi. See *JE,* ii. 59b.

298.3   Folly . . . is a vigorous plant, which sheds abundant seed.
D'Israeli, *Curiosities: Ridiculous Titles.*

298.4   Every folly . . . imparts to us an accelerated velocity downwards.
S. Levin, *Youth in Revolt,* 1930, p. 209.

299.   FOOD
299.A.   Kashrut

299.A.1   Thou shalt not seethe a kid in its mother's milk.
Bible: Exod., 23.19, 34.26, *Deut.,* 14.21.

299.A.2   Eat neither fat nor blood.
Bible: Lev., 3.17, 7.23. See *Gen.,* 9.4.

299.A.3   Whatever parts the hoof, is wholly cloven-footed, and chews the cud, among the beasts, that ye may eat.
Bible: Lev., 11.3.

299.A.4   Whatever has fins and scales in waters, . . . ye may eat.
Ibid., 11.9.

299.A.5   What dies of itself or is torn of beasts, ye shall not eat.
Ibid., 22.8. Cf *Exod.,* 22.30.

299.A.6   As if one could not eat tripe and yet be a good Jew!
Lassalle, *Diary,* Feb. 2, 1840.

299.A.7   If our slaughter-houses were placed under the supervision of the Jewish *shohet,* . . . disease would be less prevalent and the average duration of life would be increased.
*Leroy-Beaulieu, *Israel Among the Nations,* 1895, p. 159. See Ripley, *Races of Europe,* 1899, p. 384.

299.A.8   The dietary laws train us to master our appetites . . . and not to consider . . . eating and drinking the end of man's existence.
Maimonides, *Guide for the Perplexed,* 1190, 3.35.

299.A.9   Some say that all the animals that are unclean in this world will be declared clean by the Holy One in time to come.
Midrash Tehillim, 146.4, ed Buber, 268a.

299.A.10   A physician restricts the diet of only those patients whom he expects to recover. So God prescribed dietary laws for those who have hope of a future life. Others may eat anything.
Tanhum b. Hanilai. *Lev. R.,* 13.2.

299.A.11   It is better to eat oysters openly than to open oysters secretly.
Zangwill, *Send-Off to Dr. Schechter,* April 1902.

299.B.   General

299.B.1   Who eats disagreeable food violates three prohibitions: he hurts his health, wastes food, and offers a benediction in vain.
Akiba. *Abot de R. Nathan,* ch 26, ed Schechter, 83.

299.B.2   *Kugel,* this holy national dish, has done more for the preservation of Judaism than all three issues of the magazine [*ZWJ*].
Heine, letter to Moser, Dec. 14, 1825.

299.B.3   It is *tsholnt* alone that unites them still in their old covenant.
Heine, *On Boerne,* 1840.

299.B.4   Food can never make one noble.
Heine, *Atta Troll,* 1841, ch 5.

299.B.5   "Schalet, ray of light immortal!
Schalet, daughter of Elysium!"
So had Schiller's song re-
sounded,
Had he ever tasted Schalet,
For this Schalet is the very
Food of heaven, which, on Sinai,
God Himself instructed Moses
In the secret of preparing.
Heine, *Princess Sabbath,* 1850. Parody on Schiller's *Hymn to Joy.*

299.B.6 No scholar should live in a town where vegetables are unobtainable.

Huna. *Talmud: Erubin,* 55b. See *Berakot,* 57b.

299.B.7 Eat nothing that will prevent you from eating.

Ibn Tibbon, *Tzavaah,* c. 1190.

299.B.8 Domestic strife is due only to food.

Judah b. Ezekiel. *Talmud: Baba Metzia,* 59a.

299.B.9 God performs many miracles ... but He doesn't grow corn in the houses of the pious.

Maaseh Book, (1602) 1934, #10, p. 17.

299.B.10 Dainty dishes ... create distempers of soul and body.

Philo, *Special Laws,* i. 35.

299.B.11 When the barley is gone from the jar, strife comes knocking at the door.

Proverb. q Papa. *Talmud: Baba Metzia,* 59a.

299.B.12 Many hymns and few noodles!

Proverb (Yiddish). BJS, #1479.

299.B.13 Food must not be treated disrespectfully.

Talmud: Sefer Torah, 3.11.

299.B.14 The meal is according to the road and the inn.

Tanhuma, Naso, #23, ed Buber, 19a.

300. FOOL

300.1 Fools hate knowledge.

Bible: Prov., 1.22.

300.2 The confidence of fools shall destroy them.

Ibid., 1.32.

300.3 A bridle for the ass, and a rod for the back of fools.

Ibid., 26.3.

300.4 As a dog returns to his vomit, a fool repeats his folly.

Ibid., 26.11.

300.5 Bray a fool in a mortar, . . . yet will not his foolishness depart from him.

Bible: Prov., 27.22.

300.6 The world has been handed over to fools!

Aha b. Jacob. *Talmud: Sanhedrin,* 46b.

300.7 A nod to the wise is sufficient; the fool requires a blow.

Alphabet of Ben Sira, 12.

300.8 When water will stand up without earth, the sparrow fly without wings, the raven turn white as snow, and bitter be sweet as honey, then may the fool become wise.

Apocrypha: Ahikar, 2.62.

300.9 Teaching a fool is like gluing together a potsherd.

Apocrypha: Ben Sira, 22.7.

300.10 Mourn for the dead seven days, but for a fool all his life.

Ibid., 22.12.

300.11 Sand and salt and a weight of iron are easier to bear than a senseless man.

Ibid., 22.15. See Heine, *Ideas,* 1826, ch 15.

300.12 The fool thinks that all are fools.

Eccles. R., to *Eccles.* 10.3.

300.13 Fools are prisoners of death.

Ibn Gabirol, *Mibhar HaPeninim,* c. 1050, #14.

300.14 A hint to the wise, a fist to the fool.

Midrash Mishlé, to *Prov.* 22.6.

300.15 What one fool spoils a thousand wise men cannot mend.

Proverb. q Emden, *Torat HaKenaot,* 1752, ch 9.

300.16 A fool will return to his folly.

Proverb. q Joshua b. Levi. *Lev. R.,* 16.9.

300.17 A fool is a misfortune.

Proverb (Yiddish). BJS, #2450.

300.18 A fool must not be shown half the work.

Proverb, *ibid.* #2473.

300.19 You can tell when a fool speaks: he grinds much and produces little.

Sholom Aleichem, *Menahem Mendel,* 1895.

300.20 If you pound a fool in the groats, you can't make a soup of it.

Ibid.

300.21 If all the fools were drowned in Noah's flood, the seed was saved.

L. Stein, *Journey into the Self,* 1950, p. 154.

300.22 Fools make feasts, and wise men eat them.

J. Steinberg, *Mishlé Yehoshua,* 1885, 7.6, p. 48.

300.23 A fool is not aware of his folly.

Talmud: Sabbath, 13b.

300.24 When a fool is whipped, he forgets the first lash even before the rod comes down with the next.

Tanhuma, Noah, 24, ed Buber, 26b.

300.25 Every fool delights in his cap.
I. M. Wise, "World of My Books." *Deborah,* Sept. 17, 1896.

300.26 A fool always laughs.
Zabara, *Sefer Shaashuim,* 13C, ch 9.

301. FORCE

301.1 Who tries to force good fortune will be forced by misfortune.
Abin Halevi. *Talmud: Berakot,* 64a.

301.2 No compulsion can make a single Jew a sincere Christian.
*Coutinho, 1497. See *JE,* iv. 318a.

301.3 Coercion in religion is useless.
Ibn Verga, *Shebet Yehuda,* (1550) 1855, #3, p. 3.

301.4 What we grievously lament is the implicit trust placed on physical force, as a safeguard for upholding national rights.
L. Levi, *International Law,* 1888, p. 5.

301.5 No empire which exists by force can be said to have its public law founded on a solid basis.
Ibid., 5.

301.6 Who forces time is forced back by time; who yields to time finds time on his side.
Talmud: Erubin, 13b.

301.7 "Must" is neither sweet nor soft.
Twerski. q CPP, #1572.

301.8 The All Merciful absolves anyone who acts under coercion.
Zera. *Talmud: Aboda Zara,* 54a.

302. FORESIGHT

302.1 It were well, my friends, it were well, while the vessel is still in port, to foresee the coming storm, and not to put out into the midst of the hurricane to meet your doom. For the victims of unforeseen disaster there is left at least the meed of pity; but he who rushes to manifest destruction incurs opprobrium to boot.
Agrippa II. q Josephus, *Wars,* 2.16.4.

302.2 A good quality which men should cherish is foresight.
Simeon b. Nathaniel. *Mishna: Abot,* 2.9.

303. FOREST

303.1 The forest has ears.
Midrash Agada, VaYetzé.

303.2 Who is afraid of leaves should not go into the forest.
Morawczyk, *Minha Hadasha,* 1576.

303.3 No bears and no forest!
Proverb. q *Talmud: Sota,* 47a.

303.4 Dark, secret forests that awaken buried springs in man. Forests that quiver with stillness. Forests where men pray. Forests where men dance.
Toller, *Machine Wreckers,* 1922, 2.2.

304. FORGETTING

304.1 O Israel, you should not forget Me.
Bible: Isa., 44.21.

304.2 The end of all learning is forgetting.
Agnon, *Shebuat Emunim,* 1943.

304.3 A day's happiness makes misfortune to be forgotten, and a day's misfortune makes happiness to be forgotten.
Apocrypha: Ben Sira, 11.25.

304.4 Our name shall be forgotten in time, and no man shall have our works in remembrance.
Apocrypha: Wisd. of Sol., 2.4.

304.5 Were it not for the ability to forget, a man would never be free from melancholy.
Bahya, *Hobot HaLebabot,* 1040, 2.5, tr. Hyamson, ii. 19.

304.6 It is the lot of man to suffer, it is also his fortune to forget.
Disraeli, *Vivian Grey,* 1827.

304.7 Who is busy with communal affairs forgets his learning.
Exod. R., 6.2.

304.8 To study and forget is like bearing children and burying them.
Joshua b. Karha. *Talmud: Sanhedrin,* 99a.

304.9 Forgetfulness is universal. He who wields the whip remembers not that only the day before, he himself was scourged.
Mendelé, *Shlomé Reb Hayyims,* 1899.

304.10 Women and elephants never forget.
Parker, *Death and Taxes,* 1931, p. 46.

304.11 Beware of what leads to forgetting the commandments: too much eating and drinking, too much acquisition of money and property, too much ambition and worry and fear.
Ragoler, *Maalot HaTorah,* (1828) 1946, p. 33, on *Deut.* 8.11.

305. FORGIVING

305.1 Pardon, I pray Thee, the iniquity of this people!
Bible: Num., 14.19.

305.2 I, even I, . . . blot out thy transgression for Mine own sake, and thy sins will I not remember.

Bible: Isa., 43.25.

305.3 Let the Lord avenge the wrong; you show forgiveness.

Apocrypha: Asenath, ii. See Apoc.: Patriarchs, Gad, 6.7.

305.4 Add not sin to sin, counting on forgiveness.

Apocrypha: Ben Sira, 5.5.

305.5 Forgive your neighbor . . . and then, when you pray, your sins will be forgiven you.

Ibid., 28.2. See 28.3.

305.6 Each night, before retiring, forgive whomever offended you.

Asher b. Yehiel, *Hanhaga,* c. 1320.

305.7 The most beautiful thing man can do is to forgive.

Eleazar b. Judah, *Rokeah,* 13C.

305.8 If your neighbor wronged you, forgive him at once, for "thou shalt love thy neighbor as thyself." Would you vengefully punish your one hand for having hurt the other?

J. M. Epstein, *Kitzur Shné Luhot Ha-Berit,* 1683, p. 9b.

305.9 When I have forgiven a fellow everything, I am through with him.

Freud. q Koestler, *Arrow in the Blue,* 26.

305.10 The sweetest revenge is to forgive.

I. Friedmann, *Imré Bina,* 1912, p. 71 q CPP, #1676.

305.11 As soon as one repents, one is forgiven.

Hanina b. Papa. *Talmud: Hagiga,* 5a.

305.12 Since I myself stand in need of God's pity, I have granted an amnesty to all my enemies.

Heine, *Memoirs,* ed Karpeles, tr Cannan, ii. 227.

305.13 God will pardon: that's His business.

Heine, on his death-bed, 1856.

305.14 Who avenges subdues one, who forgives rules over two.

I. Hurwitz, *Mishlé Yisachar,* 1887, 28.

305.15 The highest and most difficult of all moral lessons, to forgive those we have injured.

J. Jacobs, at Royal Academy, Madrid. *Jewish Ideals,* 1895.

305.16 God forgives sins committed against Him, but offenses against man must first be forgiven by the injured person.

Jose HaCohen. *Talmud: Rosh Hashana,* 17b.

305.17 Father, forgive them, for they know not what they do.

New Testament: Luke, 23.34.

305.18 He who forgives . . . will himself be forgiven.

Raba. *Talmud: Yoma,* 23a.

305.19 In grief unspeakable, I give you my hand. You, of all women the most pitiable, say to your son that in the name and spirit of him he has murdered, I forgive, even as God may forgive, if before an earthly judge he make a full confession of his guilt, and before a Heavenly One he repent.

M. Rathenau, mother of Walter, to his assassin's mother, 1922.

305.20 To be able to forget and forgive is the prerogative of noble souls.

Stekel, *Autobiography,* 1950, p. 44.

306. FORM

306.1 All form has its value only in what it suggests.

F. Adler, *Creed and Deed,* 1877, p. 96.

306.2 It is the ancient cask with its ancient form that is holy, and sanctifies all that is in it.

Ahad HaAm, *Sacred and Profane,* 1891. *Selected Essays,* 44.

306.3 We give to things a form which corresponds to the measure of form which we carry within us.

Asch, *What I Believe,* 1941, p. 8.

306.4 A religion, however lofty, can influence mankind only by external forms that give it a mould capable of resistance, by the necessary mummery without which mankind does not take ideas seriously.

J. Darmsteter, *Selected Essays,* 1895, p. 59.

306.5 When we change the form, we snap the bond of continuity and the celebration is no more the loved one of old, but something new and cold and contains little of the glow which warms the soul.

A. Geiger, *Prayer Book,* 1860, Pref. q WHJ, iii. 365.

306.6 Forms are necessary as vehicles and expressions of the spirit, as well as a means of fortifying it.

A. Geiger. q Enelow, *CCAR,* 1924, p. 244.

306.7 New forms! Are not the ancient forms flexible . . . enough to lend expression to every sentiment and thought? . . . Those who have talent know how to create something even within the limits of old forms.

Nordau, *Degeneration,* (1893), 5.1, p. 544f.

306.8 Formlessness is more complex than form.

Pasternak, *Safe Conduct,* ii. ch 4, tr Scott 1945, p. 52.

306.9 In the strange world in which we live—it may be safely asserted—that a square is not a circle.

Ponte, *Don Juan,* 1787, 1.5.

306.10 As the breath of the craftsman, so the shape of the vessel.

Proverb. q *Zohar, Exodus,* 86a.

306.11 All these traditional solemnities without traditional roots are false, like the rabbi's gown, and, in a certain sense, his entire contemporary position.

F. Rosenzweig, letter to his parents, Jan. 6, 1917. GFR, 45.

307. FORTUNE

307.1 Who foregoes fortune will postpone misfortune.

Abin Halevi. *Talmud: Berakot,* 64a.

307.2 When God is with you, your neighbors are not against you.

Agnon, *Sippur Pashut,* 1935.

307.3 Today a king, tomorrow he shall fall.

Apocrypha: Ben Sira, 10.10.

307.4 Many downtrodden have sat on a throne.

Ibid., 11.5.

307.5 Are you fortunate when you've made your fortune? There's a difference.

Boerne, *Der Narr im weissen Schwan,* ch 2.

307.6 Misfortune is the ballast which maintains our equilibrium on the sea of life, when we no longer have fortunes to carry.

Boerne, *Fragmente & Aphorismen,* 1840, #199.

307.7 Inner superiority to worldly fortune is the essence of genuine nobility, spirituality, or . . . the truly philosophic life.

M. R. Cohen, *A Dreamer's Journey,* 1949, p. 57.

307.8 Time, like a scale, raises the light and lowers the heavy.

Elijah Gaon, *Alim LiTerufa,* 1836. See AHE, 313.

307.9 The world is like a fountain-wheel: the buckets ascend full and descend empty. Who's rich today may not be so tomorrow.

Exod. R., 31.14.

307.10 The world is like a pump-wheel, through which the full is emptied and the empty filled.

Nahman. *Lev. R.,* 34.9.

307.11 Things goes pretty smooth for us lately, Mawruss, . . . I guess we are due for a *schlag* somewheres, ain't we?

Glass, (Abe in) *Potash and Perlmutter,* 1909, p. 83.

307.12 Good fortune . . . depends on the stars.

Hanina b. Hama. *Talmud: Sabbath,* 156b.

307.13 Good Fortune is a giddy maid,
    Fickle and restless as a faun;
    She smooths your hair, and then
      the jade
    Kisses you quickly and is gone.
Misfortune to her heart, however,
To clasp thee tightly, ne'er omits;
She says she's in a hurry never,
Sits down beside thy bed and
    knits.

Heine, *Romancero,* 1851, Bk 2, Motto.

307.14 Fortune is never permanently either adverse or favorable; one sees her veering from one mood to the other.

Herod. q Josephus, *Wars,* 1.19.4.

307.15 When your fortune ascends all become your friends.

J. Hurwitz, *Tzel HaMaalot,* 1764, p. 70.

307.16 Show not your power in time of might, you know how fortune is given to flight.

Ibn Gabirol, *Mibhar HaPeninim,* c. 1050, #445.

307.17 Good fortune—remember it's fickle; misfortune—remember it'll pass.

Ibid., #502.

307.18 The world is like a ladder: one goes up, another goes down.

Immanuel, *Mahberot,* c. 1300, ch 19. See *Lev. R.,* 8.1.

307.19 When God is with you, each tree will bear you fruit.

Isaac b. Samuel of Acre, *Meirat Enayim,* 14C.

307.20 There's a wheel of fortune revolving in the world.

Ishmael School. *Talmud: Sabbath,* 151b.

307.21 If you run after fortune, you may be running away from contentment.

Lazerov, *Enciklopedie fun Idishe Vitzen,* 1928, #490.

307.22 Men are very prone to despise him who has ill fortune, and to make much of those whom fortune favors.

Manasseh b. Israel, *Declaration to the Commonwealth of England,* 1655. q GHJ, v. 42.

307.23 There is nothing more inconstant than fortune, which tosses human affairs up and down like dice.

Philo, *Moses,* i. 6.

307.24 Clockwise moves the revolution of the divine plan which the masses call Fortune. In its constant flow among cities, nations and countries, it overturns existing arrangements, giving one now what another had before, so that the whole world may become, as it were, one city, and enjoy . . . democracy.

Philo, *Unchangeableness of God,* 36.

307.25 I profit not by my master's fortune, but suffer from his misfortune.

Proverb. *Lam. R.,* Proem, 24.

307.26 Weep for him who knows not his fortune; laugh for him who knows not his fortune.

Proverb. q Papa. *Talmud: Sanhedrin,* 103a.

307.27 From fortune to misfortune is just a span, but from misfortune to fortune is quite a distance.

Proverb (Yiddish). BJS, #814. ATJF, p. 641.

307.28 Fortune is shallow, misfortune deep. Fortune dulls, misfortune whets.

J. Rosenfeld. q *Davke,* 1952, xiii. 379.

307.29 In this world a dog may become a lion and a lion a dog. Not so in the world to come.

Ruth R., 3.2.

307.30 Misfortune does not come single.

Weissmann-Chajes, *Hokma uMusar,* 1875, 7.

308. FOWL

308.1 I know his geese and hens [all his affairs].

Figure of speech. q Lipperheide, *Spruchwörterbuch,* 444.

308.2 Yesterday a chicken, today an egg! [retrogression].

Gen. R., 37.4.

308.3 There are people who believe they know the fowl thoroughly, because they saw the egg from which it emerged.

Heine, *Gedanken und Einfälle,* 1869.

308.4 The duck stoops as it waddles, but its eyes peer afar.

Proverb. q Raba. *Talmud: Megilla,* 14b.

309. FOX

309.1 A fox in its hour—bow to it.

Eleazar b. Pedat. *Talmud: Megilla,* 16b.

309.2 Each fox lauds its tail.

I. B. Levinsohn, *Yehoshafat.*

309.3 A fox does not die from the dust of his den.

Proverb. q Adda b. Ahaba. *Talmud: Ketubot,* 71b.

309.4 Chase two foxes at once, and you won't catch either.

Steinberg, *Mishlé Yehoshua,* 1885, 71.8, p. 328.

309.5 The fox feels safe only as long as the leopard can catch other prey.

Zabara, *Sefer Shaashuim,* 13C, ch 2.

310. FRANCE

310.1 God chose the French nation to restore our rights and to make possible our rebirth.

Berr, *Lettre d'un Citoyen,* 1791.

310.2 France is the dial of Europe.

Boerne.

310.3 France! What a fine example it set to civilization and progress since the immortal era of 1789! As we watch daily the growing realization of this noble concept of civic and political equality among civilized peoples, and its extension to our Jewish brethren, . . . we can say to ourselves with justifiable pride: "This is the sun of our France, whose rays will brighten and illumine the entire world!"

Crémieux, to Alliance Israélite Universelle, 1876.

310.4 Honor to the French! they have taken good care of the two greatest human needs—good eating and civic equality.

Heine, *Journey from Munich to Genoa,* 1828, ch 29.

310.5 France is sacred territory,
Blessed fatherland of freedom.

Heine, *Atta Troll,* 1841, ch 11.

310.6 A little French, that's wonderful!
D. Kalisch, *Der gebildete Hausknecht,* 1858.

310.7 We French are a conservative nation and we like even our disorders to have a cachet of organized continuity.
Koestler, *Age of Longing,* 1951, p. 132.

310.8 While you stay in France to oppose the Vichy traitors directly, I the Jew will know how to organize a French diaspora and to sweep out any aspiring Hitler from our beloved country.
G. Mandel, to E. Herriot, May 18, 1940.

310.9 I cannot go without my luggage, and that is much too big for your plane. My luggage is—France.
G. Mandel, to a Briton who offered to take him on one of the last planes to leave France, in 1940.

310.10 They talk of the "sick man," and say we are in the evening of our greatness. But really it is dawn, and we are just beginning to wake.
Mendès-France. q *N.Y. Times,* Dec. 11, 1955, p. 78.

310.11 Note that the leading French philosopher (Bergson), the foremost French novelist (Proust), the chief French controversialist (Benda), and the favorite French essayist (Maurois) are Jews or half-Jews.
*Michaud, *Modern Thought & Literature in France,* 1934, p. 226.

310.12 The French Jews remain a distinct element among the French people, and here lies the special value of their contribution to our civilization.
*Siegfried. *American Hebrew,* Nov. 22, 1929.

310.13 I think of that mobility and restlessness of Israel. . . . A Montaigne, a Proust, a Bergson have managed to root firmly in our rich and complex literature what may be called the Franco-Semitic element.
*Thibaudet. See André Spire. *Menorah Journal,* 1924, x. 257; Maurois, *Proust: Portrait of a Genius,* 1950, 5; Thibaudet, *Histoire de la Littérature Française,* 1936, ii. 295.

311. FREEDOM

311.1 Proclaim liberty throughout the land unto all the inhabitants thereof.
Bible: Lev., 25.10.

311.2 The spirit of freedom is the newly-born Messiah.
S. Adler, Passover sermon, New York, 1857.

311.3 What is national freedom if not a people's inner freedom to cultivate its abilities along the beaten path of its history?
Ahad HaAm. *HaShiloah,* 1902, vi. 377.

311.4 Our fathers sustained many a mighty struggle for independence . . . determined to refuse obedience to a conqueror's behests.
Anan b. Anan. q Josephus, *Wars,* 4.3.10.

311.5 We are still in the spirit and power of our liberty.
Apocrypha: Il Baruch, 85.7.

311.6 Only he is free who cultivates his own thoughts . . . and strives without fear of man to do justice to them.
B. Auerbach, *Schatzkästlein des Gevattersmanns,* 1875.

311.7 Man's freedom is his inner worth;
His guilt alone can rob him of it.
M. Beer, *Clytemnestra,* 1823, i. 3.

311.8 The cause of Freedom and the cause of Peace are bound together.
Blum, *Les Problèmes de la Paix,* 1931.

311.9 To want to be free is to be free.
Boerne, *Der ewige Jude,* 1821.

311.10 The difference between liberty and liberties is as great as between God and gods.
Boerne, *Fragmente und Aphorismen,* 1840, #54.

311.11 Governments which suppress freedom of speech . . . act like children who shut their eyes in order not to be seen.
Boerne, *Die Freiheit der Presse in Baiern,* 1818.

311.12 There is no man who does not love liberty; but the just demands it for all, the unjust only for himself.
Boerne, *Der Narr im weissen Schwan,* ch 2.

311.13 Because I was born a slave, I love liberty more than you.
Boerne, *Briefe aus Paris,* #74, Feb. 7, 1832.

311.14 Experience teaches us to be most on our guard to protect liberty when the government's purposes are beneficent.
Brandeis, dissent, *Olmstead vs. U.S.,* 1928.

311.15 Free trade is not a principle, it is an expedient.
Disraeli, speech, April 25, 1843.

311.16 God forbid that such a thing should happen in Israel, as to condemn honest inquiries on account of their differing opinions.
Duran, *Magen Abot*, 15C. q SSJ, i. 171.

311.17 Long since we determined to serve neither Romans nor any other, save God.
Eleazar b. Yair. q Josephus, *Wars,* 7.8.6.

311.18 Those who fell in battle may fitly be felicitated, for they died defending . . . liberty.
Ibid., 7.8.7.

311.19 Positive freedom consists in the spontaneous activity of the total, integrated personality.
Fromm, *Escape from Freedom*, 1941, p. 258.

311.20 The Jewish faith is in no way endangered by Germany's liberation movement. . . . If a religion can exist only under serfdom, let it perish, for it is not of divine origin.
Fürst, 1848. *AZJ*, xii. 756.

311.21 I hold a jail more roomy . . . than would be the whole world if I were to submit to repression.
Gompers, *Seventy Years of Life & Labor*, 1925, ii. 203.

311.22 Freedom of speech and of the press have not been granted to the people . . . but to say the things which displease.
Ibid., 213.

311.23 Man must have the right to speak his mind before he can be asked to mind his speech.
J. Gordon, "Growing Up Jewishly," CCAR, 1952.

311.24 Judaism, which is throughout rationalistic, is the sole stronghold of free hought in the religious sphere.
Graetz. *JQRo,* 1888, i. 12.

311.25 I really do not know whether I deserve that a laurel wreath be laid on my coffin. . . . But ye may lay a sword on my coffin, for I was a brave soldier in the war of freedom for mankind.
Heine, *Journey from Munich to Genoa*, 1828, ch. 31.

311.26 Liberty is a new religion, the religion of our age.
Heine, *English Fragments*, 1828, ch 13.

311.27 Since the Exodus, Freedom has always spoken with a Hebrew accent.
Heine, *Germany to Luther,* 1834. q Zangwill, *Dreamers,* 360.

311.28 That being is free . . . whose will coincides with the divine law.
Hess, *Rome and Jerusalem,* (1862), p. 133.

311.29 To be free is to be bound—bound in the fetters of obligation. . . . To live in a free country . . . and be the sport of ignoble ideas, the plaything of vicious desires, is to be a slave.
M. Joseph, *Judaism as Creed and Life,* 1903, p. 176.

311.30 There is a freedom greater even than the freedom conferred by citizenship and the possession of full human rights. It is the freedom of the soul—of the soul that "walks at liberty because it has sought God's precepts," that visualizes the best and strenuously aspires after it. That greatest of boons has still to be attained.
M. Joseph, "Song of Songs." *Jewish Guardian*, Apr. 15, 1927, p. 9.

311.31 Everyone should worship God in accordance with the dictates of his own conscience, and not under constraint.
Josephus, *Life,* 23.

311.32 To deprive opponents of religion of freedom of speech and opinion is to undermine religion and weaken it.
Judah Löw, *Beer HaGola,* (1598), p. 151.

311.33 The deadliest foe of democracy is not autocracy but liberty frenzied.
O. H. Kahn, speech, Univ. of Wis., Jan. 14, 1918.

311.34 In the Berlin congregation there must be room for every tendency in Judaism, but never for zealotry and heresy-hunting.
Karpeles, "Unsere Orthodoxie." *AZJ,* 1898.

311.35 Life without free faith and free science would resemble an extinguished planet, destitute of light and heat!
Luzzatti, *Themistius,* 1885. LGF, 99.

311.36. Liberty and serenity in the search for truth, liberty and sincerity in the practice of faith!
Luzzatti, address, Jan. 3, 1921. LGF, 255.

311.37 The destiny of Israel, more than that of any other people, depends on the establishment of universal freedom.
Magnes, 1941, *Gleanings,* 1948, p. 62.

311.38 Convert not into law any immutable truth, without which civil happiness may very well subsist. . . . Leave thinking and speaking to us, just as it was given us, as an unalienable heirloom . . . as an unalterable right, by our universal Father.
M. Mendelssohn, *Jerusalem*, 1783, tr Samuels, ii. 171.

311.39 Reward and punish no doctrine; hold out no allurement or bribe for the adoption of theological opinions. . . . Suffer no one to be a searcher of hearts and a judge of opinions, . . . to assume the right which the Omniscient has reserved to Himself.
Ibid., ii .172.

311.40 Every virtuous man is free.
Philo, *Every Good Man Is Free*, 1.

311.41 That man alone is free who has God for his leader.
Ibid., 3.

311.42 To speak freely what is dictated by a clear conscience befits the nobly born.
Ibid., 15.

311.43 If to die for a garland of olive or parsley is glory in the arena, a far greater glory is it to die for freedom!
Ibid., 17.

311.44 Let us never endure the loss of that greatest of all human blessings, liberty, the beginning and fountain of all happiness!
Ibid., 20.

311.45 When is a man free? Not when he is driftwood on the stream of life, . . . free of all cares or worries or ambitions. . . . He is not free at all—only drugged, like the lotus eaters in the Odyssey. . . . To be free in action, in struggle, in undiverted and purposeful achievement, to move forward towards a worthy objective across a fierce terrain of resistance, to be vital and aglow in the exercise of a great enterprise —that is to be free, and to know the joy and exhilaration of true freedom. A man is free only when he has an errand on earth.
Silver.

311.46 Not only is freedom of thought and speech compatible with piety and the peace of the State, but it cannot be withheld without destroying at the same time both the peace of the State and piety itself.
Spinoza, *Theologico-Political Treatise*, Sub Title, 1670.

311.47 He alone is free who lives with free consent under the entire guidance of reason.
Ibid., ch 16.

311.48 Freedom is absolutely necessary for progress in science and the liberal arts.
Ibid., ch 20.

311.49 "They are My servants" [*Lev.* 25.55]—not servants' servants.
Talmud: Baba Metzia, 10a.

311.50 The first step toward liberty is to miss liberty; the second, to seek it; the third, to find it.
Zunz, address, Feb. 1849. *Ges. Schr.* 1875, i. 305.

312. FREE WILL

312.1 I have set before you life and death, the blessing and the curse; therefore choose life.
Bible: Deut., 30.19.

312.2 I know that man's way is not his own; it is not in man to direct his steps as he walks.
Bible: Jer., 10.23.

312.3 There is no man that has power over the wind, . . . nor over the day of death, and there is no discharge in war.
Bible: Eccles., 8.8.

312.4 That which is determined shall be done.
Bible: Dan., 11.36.

312.5 All is foreseen, yet man is endowed with free will.
Akiba. *Mishna: Abot*, 3.15. See Ben Azzai. *Mekilta*, to *Exod.* 15.26.

312.6 Right and wrong is the work of our hands.
Apocrypha: Ps. of Sol., 9.4.

312.7 Everybody acts not only under external compulsion but also in accordance with inner necessity.
Einstein, *The World As I See It*, 1934, p. 238.

312.8 You were born, you live, and you will die under compulsion. Likewise, without your consent, you are destined to render an account before the King of kings.
Eleazar HaKappar. *Mishna: Abot*, 4.22.

312.9 A man is led the way he wishes to follow.
Huna. *Talmud: Makkot*, 10b.

312.10 The world is an exedra: you may go out [astray] if you wish.
Judah b. Ilai. *Talmud: Menahot*, 29b.

312.11 My ship has no rudder and is driven by the wind that blows in the undermost regions of death.
Kafka, *The Hunter Graccus. Parables*, 103.

312.12 Every man ought to act as if his will were omnipotent, without drawing less upon the virtue of resignation, as if he were impotent.
Luzzatti, *Fioretti*, 1912, Preface. LGF, 321.

312.13 Every person is fit to be as righteous as Moses or as wicked as Jeroboam, wise or foolish, kind or cruel, . . . and may tend, of his own free will, to whichever side he pleases.
Maimonides, *Yad: Teshuba*, 1180, 5.2. See *Guide*, 3.17.

312.14 On the second day, God created the angels, with their natural propensity to good. Later He made beasts with their animal desires. But God was pleased with neither. So He fashioned man, a combination of angel and beast, free to follow good or evil.
Midrash. q *Semak*, 1277, # 53. See *JQRo*, ii. 3.

312.15 Sin . . . was not determined by the King.
Nahmanides, tr Lucas, *The Jewish Year*, 1898, p. 135.

312.16 Without our faith in free will the earth would be the scene not only of the most horrible nonsense but also of the most intolerable boredom.
Schnitzler, *Buch der Sprüche & Bedenken*, 1927, p. 56.

312.17 Man can by no means be called free because he is able not to exist or not to use his reason, but only in so far as he preserves the power of existing and operating according to the laws of human nature.
Spinoza, *Political Treatise*, 1677, 2.7. See *Ethics*, i. Ap.

312.18 God does not predetermine whether a man shall be righteous or wicked; that He leaves to man himself.
Tanhuma, Pikkudé, 3.

313. FRIENDSHIP

313.1 Lovely and pleasant in their lives, even in their death they were not divided.
Bible: II Sam., 1.23.

313.2 I was wounded in the house of my friends.
Bible: Zech., 13.6. See *Ps.*, 41.10, 55.13f.

313.3 There are friends that one has to his own hurt; but there is a friend that sticks closer than a brother.
Bible: Prov., 18.24.

313.4 Faithful are the wounds of a friend, but the kisses of an enemy are importunate.
Ibid., 27.6.

313.5 Bring all men into friendship with you.
Apocrypha: Aristeas, 228.

313.6 Be on guard against your friends.
Apocrypha: Ben Sira, 6.13.

313.7 Who finds a faithful friend finds a treasure.
Ibid., 6.14. See 6.15f, 7.18.

313.8 A new friend is as new wine.
Ibid., 9.10.

313.9 A friend is not known in prosperity.
Ibid., 12.8.

313.10 There is a friend who is one only in name.
Ibid., 37.1.

313.11 Never weary of making friends.
Asher b. Yehiel, *Hanhaga*, c. 1320.

313.12 When a friend changes, regard him as an enemy.
Caspi, *Commentary*, to *Prov.* 24.21.

313.13 My friends and gnats together
Have gone with the sunny weather.
Heine, *Romancero: Mrs. Care*, 1851.

313.14 Friendship is man's greatest gift.
M. Ibn Ezra, *Shirat Yisrael*, (12C) 1924, p. 136.

313.15 A friend will prove himself in time of trouble.
Ibid.

313.16 Let not a thousand friends seem too many in your eyes.
Ibn Gabirol, *Mibhar HaPeninim*, c. 1050, #253.

313.17 Some friends are like a sun-dial: useless when the sun sets.
Jeiteles. *Bikkuré Halttim*, 5589, ix. 225.

313.18 Some friends are like the shadow
They follow us when our sun shines.
Kuh, *Epigramme. Hintergelassene Gedichte*, 1792.
Mandelkern, *Shiré Sfat Eber*, iii. 1901, #132, p. 72.

313.19 Who looks for a faultless friend will have none.
Lazerov, *Enciklopedie fun Idishe Vitzen*, 1928, #465.

313.20 Beware of friends, not enemies.
Ibid., #467.

313.21 False friends, like birds, migrate in cold weather.
Ibid., #478.

313.22 A friend in the market is better than gold in the chest.
Levi b. Gershon, *Commentary to Prov.*

313.23 One who asks for friendship as a favor can never be a friend.
Lewisohn, *Israel*, 1925.

313.24 Friendship is like a treasury: you cannot take from it more than you put into it.
Mandelstamm, *Mishlé Binyamin*, 1884, 7.3.

313.25 None remembers an old friendship, . . . none takes such delight in it, as a poor man.
Mendelé, *BiYeshiva shel Maalah*, 1895.

313.26 It may be easier to be true to a friendship for a person long dead than one who is alive.
Morgenstern, *Testament of the Lost Son*, 1950, p. 248.

313.27 Your enemies you have to take, wherever and however you find them; but fortunately, I can choose my friends.
Schnitzler, *Professor Bernhardi*, 1912, Act 4.

313.28 Rather the bite of a friend than the kiss of an enemy.
Sholom Aleichem, *Menahem Mendel*, 1895.

313.29 Friendship—one heart in two bodies.
Zabara, *Sefer Shaashuim*, 13C, ch 7.

314. FRINGES

314.1 Let them make . . . fringes in the corners of their garments, and put with the fringe . . . a thread of blue, . . . that ye may look upon it and remember the commandments of the Lord.
Bible: Num., 15.38f.

314.2 The fringes are implements for the observance of a commandment, and have no sanctity in themselves.
Maimonides, *Responsa*, ed Freimann, #5, p. 5.

314.3 Why is blue specified for the holy fringes? Because it is the color of sea and sky, suggestive of the sapphire of the Throne of Glory.
Meir. *Talmud: Menahot*, 43b. See *Sifré, Num.*, #115.

314.4 An all-blue cloak cannot exempt itself of that which four threads of blue can exempt it!
Num. R., 18.3. Cf *Talmud J: Sanhedrin*, 10.1.

314.5 Who scrupulously observes this precept is worthy to receive the Divine Presence.
Simeon b. Yohai. *Talmud: Menahot*, 43b.

314.6 This precept is equal to all the precepts put together.
Talmud: Menahot, 43b.

315. FRUIT

315.1 We cannot eat the fruit while the tree is in blossom.
Disraeli, *Alroy*, 1833, ch 4.

315.2 Our fruits testify for us!
Levi. *Gen. R.*, 16.3. Cf *Matt.*, 7.16.

316. FUNERAL

316.1 Deal graciously with the departed that you may be dealt with graciously: mourn, inter, and accompany him to the grave.
Akiba. *Talmud J: Ketubot*, 7.5.
Meir. *Talmud: Ketubot*, 72a.

316.2 We usually meet all of our relatives only at funerals where somebody always observes: "Too bad we can't get together more often."
Levenson.

316.3 In deference to the poor, all decedents are carried on a plain bier.
Talmud: Moed Katan, 27b.

316.4 Funerals became so expensive that the bereaved would abandon the dead. Then Gamaliel ordered that he be buried in simple linen, and the people followed his example.
Ibid.

317. FUTILITY

317.1 For what vanity hast Thou created all the children of men!
Bible: Ps., 89.48.

317.2 Vanity of vanities, all is vanity.
Bible: Eccles., 1.2.

317.3 The ocean spills upon the sands
Water with a thousand hands,
And when the water all is spilled,
The sands are dry, the ocean filled.
Hoffenstein, *Year In, You're Out*, 1930.
(*Complete Poetry*, 1954, p. 182).

317.4 What remains to mortals for all their travail upon earth?
M. Ibn Ezra, *Selected Poems*, 51.

317.5 The recognition of universal futility is our greatest sorrow—but also our greatest consolation.
Klatzkin, *In Praise of Wisdom*, 1943, p. 311.

318. FUTURE

318.1 To know the future and to act accordingly is most desired by man.
Abravanel, *Commentary*, on *Deut.* 18.14, (1579) 1862, 38a.

318.2 Perhaps a human being does not die until he no longer sees anything but the past and the present moment.
Baeck, *The Pharisees*, 1947, p. vii.

318.3 We will live not as pall-bearers of a dead past, but as the creators of a more glorious future.
M. R. Cohen. *International Journal of Ethics*, 1915, p. 469.

318.4 The past is for wisdom, the present for action, but for joy the future.
Disraeli, *Alroy*, 1833, 7.12.

318.5 I never think of the future. It comes soon enough.
Einstein. Interview on Belgenland, Dec. 1930.

318.6 The future belongs to the Church which is the first to become fitted to the Future.
Zangwill, speech, Oct. 24, 1898.

319. GAMBLING

319.1 A gambler transgresses all the Ten Commandments.
Leon of Modena, *On Games of Chance*, 1596.

319.2 A gambler always loses. He loses money, dignity, and time. And if he win, he weaves a spider's web round himself.
Maimonides, *Shaaré HaMusar*.

319.3 Gambling is a form of robbery.
Maimonides, *Yad: Eduyot*, 1180, 10.4.

319.4 A gambler is disqualified as witness or judge.
Mishna: Sanhedrin, 3.3.

319.5 The first winner is the last loser.
Proverb (Yiddish). BJS, #880.

319.6 Gamblers do not contribute to the common welfare.
Sheshet. *Talmud: Sanhedrin*, 24b.

320. GENERALIZATION

320.1 When Haman saw that Mordecai bowed not down . . . he sought to destroy all the Jews.
Bible: Esther, 3.5f.

320.2 Curse not a whole Christian nation because some wrong you.
Ashkenazi, *Maasé HaShem*, 1583.

320.3 We are like mice: one eats the cheese and all are blamed.
Ibn Verga, *Shebet Yehuda*, (1550) 1855, #8, p. 27.

320.4 We cannot learn from general principles: there may be exceptions.
Johanan. *Talmud: Kiddushin*, 34a.

320.5 As smoke to the eye and vinegar to the teeth are glittering generalities with no specific facts behind them.
Lubin. q ADL, 57.

320.6 Guilt and worthlessness are personal.
Proskauer, *A Segment of My Times*, 1950, p. 180.

320.7 Only what is in the particular is in the general.
Talmud: Sota, 46b.

321. GENERATIONS

321.1 Consider the present generation as good as the past, and the sages of our time as good as those who were before.
Adda b. Hunya. *Eccles. R.*, to *Eccles.* 1.4.

321.2 The fathers' finger-nails rather than the sons' bodies.
Aha. *Gen. R.*, 45.7.
Johanan b. Nappaha. *Talmud: Yoma*, 9b. See *Erubin*, 53a.

321.3 The casual conversation of the patriarchs' slaves is more important than the religious laws of their descendants.
Aha. *Gen. R.*, 60.8.

321.4 Nothing the wisdom of old surpasses;
Our fathers were wise, and their children are asses.
Eternal their laws, beyond question or doubt;
Our business is only to carry them out.
J. Cahan, "The Frogs," 1902. tr FJA, 367.

321.5 Our fathers removed the ceiling of the Temple, but we have smashed its walls!
Eliezer b. Hyrcanus. *Talmud J: Yoma*, 1.1.

321.6 According to the generation is the music thereof.

Peretz, *A Gilgul fun a Nign,* 1901. *Alle Verk,* vi. 73.

321.7 We are greater than our ancestors, for we study Torah in spite of persecution.

Simeon b. Lakish. *Talmud: Yoma,* 9b.

321.8 The Holy One showed Adam each generation with its expositors, each generation with its sages, and each generation with its leaders.

Simeon b Lakish, *Aboda Zara,* 5a.

321.9 Jephtha in his generation was like Samuel in his.

Talmud: Rosh Hashana, 25b.

321.10 If our ancestors were angels, we are human; and if they were humans, we are asses.

Abba b Zabina. *T: Sabbath,* 112b.

322. GENIALITY

322.1 Try always to be on the best terms with your relatives and all men, including the heathen on the street, that you may be beloved above and well-liked below.

Abayé. *Talmud: Berakot,* 17a.

322.2 All the good gifts in the world, given with a dour face, Scripture regards as nothing; but a genial reception, even though unaccompanied by any gift, is regarded as everything.

Abot de Rabbi Nathan, ch 13.

322.3 Goodwill, friendly speech, is like the gentle sunshine in early spring. It invigorates and awakens all the buds.

B. Auerbach, *Brosi und Moni,* 1852.

322.4 An agreeable person is a person who agrees with me.

Disraeli, (Hugo Bohun in) *Lothair,* 1870, ch 35.

322.5 Treat all men with courtesy, amiability, and respect.

Elijah Gaon, *Alim Li Terufa,* 1836.

322.6 Good will is the best charity.

Proverb (Yiddish). BJS, #1341.

322.7 Receive everybody in a friendly manner.

Shammai. *Mishna: Abot,* 1.15.

322.8 One should always maintain a sweet disposition toward people.

Talmud: Ketubot, 17a.

323. GENIUS

323.1 It is only the thrust of genius that

has ever forced the inertia of Humanity to yield.

Bergson, *Les Deux Sources de la Morale,* 1932, p. 181.

323.2 Fortune has rarely condescended to be the companion of genius.

D'Israeli, *Curiosities: Poverty of the Learned,* 1791.

323.3 Talent may be acquired by laborious application; genius is a . . . gift of grace . . . which can never be acquired if it be not in man. Talent cannot overcome impediments . . . of overwhelming force; . . . genius conquers the severest reverses.

Geiger, *Judaism and Its History,* 1865, tr Mayer, 54f.

323.4 A great genius forms itself on another great genius less by assimilation than by friction. One diamond grinds another.

Heine, *Germany from Luther to Kant,* 1834.

323.5 Is genius, like a pearl in the oyster, only a splendid disease?

Heine. q Zangwill, *Dreamers of the Ghetto,* 362.

323.6 Genius really means to be able to see and feel what will come to pass ten years hence.

Jabotinsky, 1931. q *The War and the Jews,* 1942, p. 18.

323.7 A Genius: a stupid kid with very happy grandparents.

Levenson. q FAT, 1010.

323.8 Good sense travels on the well-worn paths; genius, never. And that is why the crowd, not altogether without reason, is so ready to treat great men as lunatics.

Lombroso, *The Man of Genius,* 1889, Preface.

323.9 Great geniuses reach their goal with one step, whereas common minds must be led to it through a long row of objectives.

M. Mendelssohn, letter to Lessing's friends, 1786.

323.10 Genius creates by a single conception.

D'Israeli, *Literary Character,* 1795, ch 8.

323.11 Genius is like a flint of many edges, but it is the edges that give the sparkle.

Saphir, *Warum giebt es kein Narrenhaus.* SHW, i. 367.

323.12 Genius learns only from itself; talent chiefly from others. Genius learns from nature, from its own nature; talent learns from art.

Schoenberg, *Problems of Teaching Art*, 1911. q E. Wellesz, *Arnold Schoenberg*, 10.

324. GENOCIDE

324.1 O Lord, God of Israel, why is this come to pass in Israel, that there should be today one tribe lacking in Israel?

Bible: Judg., 21.3.

324.2 Let not a tribe be blotted out from Israel.

Ibid., 21.17.

324.3 We must . . . prohibit genocide.

Lemkin, *Axis Rule in Occupied Europe*, 1944, p. 79.

324.4 No ruler has a right to destroy a whole race or nation.

Sofer, *Hatham Sofer, Orah Hayyim*, 1855, #208.

324.5 Moses refused to obey the command, "you shall utterly destroy" the Canaanite cities [*Deut.* 20.17], saying, Shall I slay the innocent with the guilty?

Tanhuma, Tzav, 5, ed Buber, 8b.

325. GENTILES

325.1 In thy seed shall all the nations of the earth be blessed.

Bible: Gen., 22.18.

325.2 Thou shalt not abhor an Edomite, for he is thy brother.

Bible: Deut., 23.8.

325.3 That we also may be like all the nations.

Bible: I Sam., 8.20.

325.4 Learn not the way of the nations.

Bible: Jer., 10.2.

325.5 Why are the nations in an uproar?

Bible: Ps., 2.1.

325.6 Declare His glory among the nations.

Bible: I Chron., 16.24.

325.7 God of all, . . . as Thou hast sanctified Thyself in us before them, so glorify Thyself in them before us.

Apocrypha: Ben Sira, 36.1, 4.

325.8 Seventy bullocks were sacrificed in the Temple on Succoth, to atone for all the seventy nations.

Eleazar b. Pedat. *Talmud: Sukka*, 55b.

325.9 A gentile who observes the Torah is as good as a High Priest.

Jeremiah. *Sifra*, #143, to *Lev.* 18.5, ed Weiss, 86a.

Meir. *Baba Kamma*, 38a; *AZ*, 3a.

325.10 If you accustom your tongue to talk against your brother gentile, you will come to slander also your fellow Jew.

Johanan b. Nappaha. *Deut. R.*, 6.9.

325.11 God says: Both gentile and Jew are My handiwork. I cannot destroy the former for afflicting the latter!

Johanan b. Nappaha. *Talmud: Sanhedrin*, 98b.

325.12 Gentiles outside of Palestine are not to be condemned as idolaters, for they only follow their fathers' practices.

Johanan b. Nappaha. *Talmud: Hullin*, 13b.

325.13 Righteous gentiles have a share in the world to come.

Joshua b. Hanania. *Tosefta: Sanhedrin*, 13.2.

325.14 Antonine asked: Is it not written [*Obad.* 1.18], "There will be no remnant to the house of Esau"? Rabbi replied: That refers only to those who act like Esau.

Talmud: Aboda Zara, 10b.

325.15 Any decent gentile has a share in the world to come.

I. Lipschütz, *Tiferet Israel*, 1845, to *Sanhedrin* 10.1.

325.16 Gentiles who follow a moral code and worship God, though they differ from us in dogmas, . . . are like Jews in all respects of law.

Meiri, c.1300. q Ashkenazi, *Shitta Mekubetzet*, to *BK* 113b.

325.17 To promote peace, poor gentiles may not be denied gleanings, forgotten sheaves, and the corners of the field.

Mishna: Gittin, 5.8.

325.18 In a town inhabited by gentiles and Jews, we appoint gentile and Jewish administrators, collect from both, support the poor, visit the sick, bury the dead, condole with the bereaved, and provide laundry facilities, for both.

Talmud J: Gittin, 5.9.

325.19 Gentiles of the present age are not heathens.

Rashi. q JJCW, 115.

Caro, *Bet Yosef*, to *Tur Hoshen Mishpat*, 1559, #266.

325.20 If a Jew attempt to kill a non-Jew, help the non-Jew.

Sefer Hasidim, 13C, #1849, p. 445.

325.21 If you know that a Jew robbed a gentile, it is your duty to testify to it in court.

Sherira Gaon, 10C. See *JE*, v. 624a.

325.22 Gentiles should have the option to seek judgment either in a Jewish or a non-Jewish court.

Simeon b. Gamaliel. *Sifré, Deut.*, #16, ed Friedmann, 68b.

325.23 A gentile usually makes himself heard.

Talmud: Hullin, 133b.

325.24 To rob a non-Jew is more heinous than to rob a Jew, for it involves also the desecration of the Name.

Tosefta: Baba Kamma, 10.15.

325.25 Who robs a gentile will rob also a Jew.

Seder Eliyahu Rabbah, ch 26 (28), ed Friedmann, p. 140.

325.26 Those who lie to, or steal from, non-Jews are also blasphemous, for it is due to them that some say: Jews have no law.

Moses of Coucy, *Semag,* 1250.

325.27 It is just as wrong to rob Esau as to rob Israel.

Nahmanides, *Commentary,* to *Deut.,* 2.10.

326. GENTLENESS

326.1 The only rank which elevates a woman is that which a gentle spirit bestows upon her.

Pinero, *Sweet Lavender,* 1893.

326.2 Cultivate gentleness.

Rabina. *Talmud: Taanit,* 4a.

326.3 Bear in mind that true wisdom is always joined with mildness, that malice never converts.

Riesser. AJZ, 1838, p. 113.

326.4 Be gentle like Hillel, not impatient like Shammai.

Talmud: Sabbath, 30b.

327. GERMANY

327.A. General

327.A.1 What language is as rich and powerful, as spirited and graceful, as beautiful and tender as ours?

Boerne, (Ruhdorf in) *Der Narr im weissen Schwann,* ch 5.

327.A.2 Out of German soil issued forth all those great ideas which the more able, more enterprising or more fortunate peoples put into practice and utilized. Germany is the source of all European revolutions, the mother of those discoveries which transformed the shape of the world. Gunpowder, printing, religious reform came out of its womb—ungrateful and execrated

daughters that married princes and jeered at their plebian mother.

Boerne, *Menzel der Franzosenfresser,* 1836.

327.A.3 Is not Germany Europe's Ghetto? Do not all Germans wear a yellow patch on their hat? . . . And the insult which all of them, young and old, once hurled lightly and superciliously, day and night, at each Jew: *Mach' Mores Judl* must they not now hear it themselves?

Ibid.

327.A.4 Deutschland ueber Allah.

Guedalla, ref. to Germany's influence in Turkish court.

327.A.5 Germans need neither freedom nor equality. They are a speculative race, . . . dreamers who live only in the past and future, and have no present.

Heine, *English Fragments,* 1828, ch 1.

327.A.6 Of my fair fatherland, I once was proud. . . . It was a dream.

Heine, *New Poems: Abroad,* 1844, #3.

327.A.7 Christianity . . . has somewhat softened the brutal Germanic lust for battle, but could not destroy it; and when the cross, that restraining talisman, 'falls to pieces, then will break forth again the ferocity of the old fighters, the insane Berserker rage whereof northern poets have sung . . . and at last Thor with his giant hammer will leap aloft and shatter the gothic cathedrals.

Heine, *Religion and Philosophy in Germany,* 1834.

327.A.8 The German is like a slave who obeys the mere nod or word of his master, and needs neither whips nor chains. Servility is inherent in him—it is in his soul.

Heine, *Thoughts and Fancies,* 1869. EPP, 765.

327.A.9 All wisdom derives from the German, and he himself remains a fool.

Proverb (Yiddish). YFS, i. 415.

327.A.10 What's truly German must for ever stand.

Rodenberg, *Das Heidelberger Schloss,* 1864.

327.B. The Jew in Germany

327.B.1 The Federal Government, and with it the vast majority of the German people, is conscious of the immeasurable suffering that was brought upon the Jews in Germany and in the occupied territories during the period of National Socialism. . . . Unspeakable crimes were perpetrated in the name of the German people, which impose upon them the obligation to make moral and material amends.

* Adenauer, speech, Bundestag, Sept. 27, 1951.

327.B.2 You [Germans] are so fond of classes and exult in cowering a hundred degrees beneath your superiors as long as you can stand one notch above your inferiors. Because you are slaves yourselves, you cannot do without enslaving [Jews].

Boerne, *Der ewige Jude,* 1821.

327.B.3 I know how to treasure the undeserved fortune of being at one and the same time a German and a Jew, of being able to strive toward all the virtues of the Germans and yet not to share in any of their faults.

Boerne, *Briefe aus Paris, #74,* Feb. 7, 1832.

327.B.4 Poor Germans! Living on the lowest floor, oppressed by the seven stories of the higher estates, they feel relieved to speak of people who live even lower than they, in the cellar. That they are not Jews is a comfort to them who are never aulic councilors.

Ibid.

327.B.5 It is wonderful that a deep elective affinity prevails between both races, Jews and Germans . . . the two being so much alike that primeval Palestine may be regarded as an oriental Germany, just as Germany today may be regarded as the home of the Holy Word.

Heine, *Shakespeare's Maidens: Jessica,* 1839.

327.B.6 Germany—and in this respect Austria was one with her long before the *Anschluss*—has ever been the paramount workshop of modern anti-Semitism.

Jabotinsky, *The War and the Jew,* 1942, p. 57.

327.B.7 Ungrateful fatherland, thou shalt not have my bones!

Koreff. q LGS, 62.

327.B.8 The German people are the least anti-Semitic of all.

Neumann, *Behemoth,* 1942, p. 121.

327.B.9 A day will come when Zionism will be needed by you, proud Germans, as much as by those wretched Ostjuden. . . . A day will come when you will beg for asylum in the land you now scorn.

Nordau, speech, Berlin, Jan. 23, 1899.

327.B.10 Germany, after devoting herself entirely to military life, would have had no talent left if it were not for the Jews, to whom she has been so ungrateful.

*Renan, *Recollections of Infancy and Youth,* 1883.

327.B.11 No nation has contributed more to the cruelty of the Jewish fate in our time, and, nevertheless, no nation shows more similarities in character and destiny with Judaism than the Germans.

*Tillich, address, Feb. 16, 1942. *Congress Weekly,* Feb. 27, 1942.

328. GHETTO

328.1 Ghetto life made the Jew a sloven, it never made him a brute.

Abrahams, *Jewish Life in the Middle Ages,* 1896, p. 153.

328.2 The outlook of the ghetto divided the universe into two: this world for the gentiles—the hereafter for the Jews.

Ben Gurion, speech, Apr. 18, 1940. BRD, 106.

328.3 On Sundays they were prohibited from leaving the ghetto lane, to spare them from being beaten up by drunkards. . . . On public holidays, they had to re-enter the ghetto gate by sharp six in the evening lest over-exposure to the sun ruin their complexions. . . . Then, too, a great many of the streets—because their bumpy pavement was bad for the feet—were altogether closed to them.

Boerne, *Juden in der freien Stadt Frankfurt,* c. 1817. *Fragmente & Aphorismen,* 1840, #96. q LJG, 211.

328.4 In those gloomy, tumbledown Jewish houses, intellectual endeavor was at white heat. The torch of faith blazed clear in them. . . . In the abject, dishonored son of the Ghetto was hidden an intellectual giant.

Dubnow, *Jewish History,* 1903, p. 126 f.

328.5 It is only in the ghetto, where there is human nature, that I have ideas for sketches.

J. Epstein. q *Jewish Frontier,* March 1951.

328.6 Most American Jews remain in the Ghetto even when they move to the fashionable suburbs and join country clubs. . . . It is not always, perhaps it is seldom, their fault.

Fischer, *Men and Politics,* 1941, p. 242.

328.7 The Jew obtained a territory on the day he was imprisoned in these Jewries, and the Israelites lived since then exactly like a people that had a fatherland of its own.

Lazare, *Antisemitism,* (1892) 1903, p. 259.

328.8 Israel is the Diogenes of the nations . . . he lives in a barrel and his dwelling-place is narrow and restricted; yet under the dust and ashes of the ghetto, there burns the flame of the Torah, which radiates light and warmth for the entire people.

Mendelé, *BaYamim HaHem,* 1912, 17.

328.9 The ghetto . . . was for the Jew of the past not a prison, but a refuge.

Nordau, speech, I Zionist Congress, Aug. 29, 1897.

328.10 The ghetto:
> kaleidoscope of shifting misery
> and shifting chance.
> Refuge of sorrows,
> dream and pawnshop:
> the stubborn penny profit,
> the moonbeam's radiance.
> Heine sings
> in the enchanted garden
> the song he stole from the
>   nightingale;
> Shylock counts the gold
> coin by coin;
> Spinoza ponders
> his eternal Treatise of eternal
>   glory.

*Ortiz-Vargas, "El Ghetto." *Las Torres de Manhattan,* 1939, p. 145f.

328.11 How should I have come to
>   beauty?
> Whence, oh whence, my little
>   one?
> On the roads where dogs kept
>   duty?
> Or where aliens barred the sun?

A. Raisen. q *Jewish Affairs,* May 1952, p. 20.

328.12 Were I of Jew blood, I do not think I could ever forgive the Christians; the ghettos would get in my nostrils like mustard or lit gunpowder.

*Stevenson, 1891. q BSS, p. 43.

328.13 The modern invisible ghetto wall is no less real than the old.

Wirth, *The Ghetto,* 1928, p. 280.

328.14 The history of the ghetto is from more than one aspect the story of the longest and bravest experiment that has ever been made in practical Christianity.

Zangwill, *Voice of Jerusalem,* 1921, p. 27.

329. GIANT

329.1 There were the giants . . . great of stature and expert in war. . . . They perished because they had no wisdom, they perished through their own foolishness.

Apocrypha: I Baruch, 3.26 ff.

329.2 When men could no longer sustain them, the giants turned against them and devoured mankind.

Apocrypha: Enoch, 7.4.

329.3 My colleague regarded windmills as giants; I, however, in the braggart giants of the day see only noisy windmills.

Heine, *City of Lucca,* 1828, ch 17.

330. GIFT

330.1 Take no gift, for a gift blinds them that have sight.

Bible: Exod., 23.8.

330.2 He that hates gifts shall live.

Bible: Prov., 15.27.

330.3 The king by justice establishes the land, but he who exacts gifts overthrows it.

Ibid., 29.4.

330.4 A gift destroys the understanding.

Bible: Eccles., 7.7.

330.5 The receiver of a gift is not the chooser.

Abravanel. q Waxman, *Mishlé Yisrael,* #3965.

330.6 A gift is good from an owner, not from a robber.

Proverb. q *Cant. R.,* 7.7.

330.7 Get one by trade, rather than a thousand as gifts.

Samuel HaNagid, *Ben Mishlé,* 11C.

330.8 Take nothing from anyone, and you won't need to return.

Simeon b. Lakish. *Gen. R.,* 78.12.

330.9 The free man, who lives among the ignorant, strives, as far as he can, to avoid receiving favors from them.

Spinoza, *Ethics,* 1677, iv. Pr 70.

331. GIRL

331.1 The man who wants a girl that is good, clever and beautiful doesn't want one; he wants three.

G. Berg. q L. Gutterman, JTA, 1952.

331.2 A girl in good shape is often the reason why a man is in bad shape.

Cantor. q *ibid.*

331.3 How like a lovely flower,
> So fair, so pure thou art;
> I watch thee and a prayer
> Comes stealing through my heart;

I lay my hands upon thee
And ask God to adjure
That thou shalt be forever
So sweet, so fair, so pure.
Heine, *Return Home,* 1827, #49.

331.4 It is a common phenomenon that just the prettiest girls find it so difficult to get a man. That was already the case in antiquity . . . all the three Graces have remained single.
Heine, *Gedanken und Einfälle,* 1869.

331.5 Men seldom make passes
    At girls with glasses.
Parker, "News Item." *Enough Rope,* 1926, p. 85.

331.6 A homely girl hates mirrors.
Proverb. ATJF, p. 643.

332. GIVING

332.1 The horseleech has two daughters: Give, Give.
Bible: Prov., 30.15.

332.2 More than the calf wants to suck, the cow wants to suckle.
Akiba. *Talmud: Pesahim,* 112a.

332.3 All God's creations borrow from each other: day from night and night from day, the moon from the stars and the stars from the moon, . . . the sky from the earth and the earth from the sky.
Exod. R., 31.15.

332.4 A blanket warms a person, but not a stone.
I. Friedman. q P. Shapiro, *Bet Pinhas,* 60.

325.5 Love that is hoarded moulds at last
    Until we know some day
    The only thing we ever have
    Is what we gave away.
L. Ginsberg, "Song." *The Liberator,* 1930.

332.6 By the hand alone, a hand is washed;
    Wouldst thou take, then thou must give.
Heine. q Herzl, address, London Maccabeans, 1901. See 375.6.

332.7 Water, having penetrated the earth, is collected in cloud and sea; light, having pierced the earthly crust and brought forth plants . . . is concentrated again into sun, moon and stars . . . the earth must receive that it give—thus one glorious chain of love, of giving and receiving, unites all creatures; none is by or for itself, but all things exist in continual reciprocal activity—one for all, and All for the One.
S. R. Hirsch, *Nineteen Letters,* (1836), #3, p. 29 f.

332.8 What we get out of life is in direct proportion to what we put into it.
Lehman. E. R. Murrow, *This I Believe,* 1952, p. 99.

332.9 Give and it shall be given to you.
New Testament: Luke, 6.38.

332.10 It is more blessed to give than to receive.
New Testament: Acts, 20.35.

332.11 God loves the cheerful giver.
New Testament: II Cor., 9.7.

332.12 Yet this the need of woman, this is her curse:
    To range her little fingers, and give, and give,
    Because the throb of giving's sweet to bear.
Parker, *Enough Rope,* 1926, p. 40.

332.13 They who give, hoping to receive a requital, such as praise or honor, . . . are in reality making a bargain.
Philo, *Cain,* 34.

332.14 If you don't give Jacob, you give Esau.
Proverb (Yiddish). BJS, #849.

332.15 The sick you ask, the well you give.
Proverb. q Sholom Aleichem, *Dos Groise Gevins,* 1903.

332.16 Not a handful of rain descends from above without the earth sending up two handfuls of moisture to meet it.
Simeon b. Eleazar. *Gen. R.,* 13.13.

332.17 I always give much away, and so gather happiness instead of pleasure.
Varnhagen, letter to Ludwig Robert, Aug. 13, 1827. JRL, 209.

333. GLOOM

333.1 Why art thou cast down, my soul, why moanest thou within me?
Bible: Ps., 42.6, 12; 43.5.

333.2 Sadness dulls the heart more than the grossest sin.
Aaron of Karlin. q YAJ, 1950, p. 138.

333.3 Sadness obstructs communion with God.
Baal Shem, *Tzavaat HaBesht,* 1797.

333.4 If all the World looks drear, perhaps the meaning
Is that your Windows need a little cleaning.
Guiterman, *A Poet's Proverbs,* 1924, p. 12.

333.5 Gloom obstructs our comprehension of the divine mysteries.
Moses Hasid, *Iggeret HaMusar,* 1717.

333.6 Melancholy is a symptom of oncoming sickness.
Nahman Bratzlav, *Sefer HaMiddot: Atzvut,* 1821.

334. GLORY

334.1 The glory is departed from Israel.
Bible: I Sam., 4.21.

334.2 Let not the wise man glory in his wisdom, nor the mighty man in his might, let not the rich man glory in his riches; but let him that glories glory in that he understands and knows Me.
Bible: Jer., 9.22 f.

334.3 What is the highest form of glory? To honor God. And this is done not with gifts and sacrifices, but with purity of soul and holy conviction.
Apocrypha: Aristeas, 234.

334.4 All men are fond of glory, and even those philosophers who write against that noble passion prefix their names to their works.
D'Israeli, *Curiosities: Fame Contemned,* 1791.

334.5 God created three glories: Childhood, Youth, and Woman.
Jabotinsky.

334.6 Warlike valor is not a Jewish characteristic. . . . In the historic consciousness of our people glory is reserved to quite another heroism: it belongs to the deeds of our saints and sages.
Klatzkin, *Krisis und Entscheidung,* 1921. LR, 170f.

334.7 Some, elated by boldness and aided by bodily strength, array themselves in full armor for war and slay innumerable hosts, . . . being accounted by the multitude exceedingly glorious, though in fact they have been savage and brutal both in nature and practice, having thirsted for human blood.
Philo, *Courage,* 1.

334.8 Who seeks no glory here is fit for glory there.
Phineas. *Pesikta Rabbati,* ed Friedmann, 2a.

335. GOD

335.A. Existence

335.A.1 We need no ladders to the sky, we need only . . . observe the structure and functions of man's bodily organs . . . to know that the Creator exists. Job said, "from my flesh shall I see God."
Abba Mari, *Minhat Kenaot,* (1303). *Job* 19.26, *Ps.* 35.10. See Shneor Zalman, *Likkuté Torah, Deut.* (1848), p. 4; J. L. Gordon, *Diglé Yehuda,* 90.

335.A.2 As a house implies a builder, a dress a weaver, a door a carpenter, so the world proclaims God, its Creator.
Akiba. *Midrash Temura,* ch 3.

335.A.3 Evidence of God I have found in the existence of Israel.
Fleg, *Why I Am a Jew,* 1929, p. 93.

335.A.4 The foundation and pillar of all wisdom is to recognize that there is an original Being . . . and that all . . . exist only through the reality of His being.
Maimonides, *Yad: Yesodé HaTorah,* 1180, 1.1.

335.A.5 We comprehend only that He exists, not His essence.
Maimonides, *Guide for the Perplexed,* 1190, 1.58.

335.A.6 The existence and essence of God are one and the same.
Spinoza, *Ethics,* 1677, i. Pr 20.

335.A.7 Hard as the world is to explain *with* God, it is harder yet without Him.
Montefiore, *Liberal Judaism,* 1903, p. 190.

335.A.8 Who can look upon statues or paintings without thinking at once of a sculptor or painter? . . . And when one enters a well-ordered city . . . what else will he suppose but that this city is directed by good rulers? So he who comes to the truly Great City, this world, and beholds hills and plains teeming with animals and plants, . . . the yearly seasons passing into each other, . . . and the whole firmament revolving in rhythmic order, must he not . . . gain the conception of the Maker and Father and Ruler also?
Philo, *Special Laws,* i. 6.

335.A.9 God necessarily exists.
Spinoza, *Ethics,* 1677, i. Pr 11, Proof.

335.A.10 Surely there must be a king who rules over the orbs of heaven and orders them!
Zohar, Gen., 86a.

335.B. Meaning

335.B.1 It is in God that morality has its foundation and guarantee.

Baeck, *Essence of Judaism,* 1936, p. 150.

335.B.2 In nature I have always sought God, God only, and in art the divine; and where I did not find God, I saw nothing but miserable botch-work. History, men, and books I have judged in like manner.

Boerne. q Brandes, *Main Currents,* tr 1924, vi. 64.

335.B.3 A man who writes of himself without speaking of God is like one who identifies himself without giving his address.

Hecht, *A Child of the Century,* 1954, p. 7.

335.B.4 The beginning and end of all things is in God.

Heine, *Romantic School,* Pref., Apr. 2, 1833. Cf. *Isa.* 44.6.

335.B.5 The most vital question of humanity, the existence of God.

Heine, *Memoirs,* ed Karpeles, i. 288.

335.B.6 God is of no importance unless He is of supreme importance.

Heschel, *Man Is Not Alone,* 1951, p. 92.

335.B.7 The Holy One is the heart of Israel.

Hiyya b. Abba. *Pesikta Kahana,* ch 5, p. 41b.

335.B.8 God is the reconciliation of the many in the One.

H. Kohn, *Die politische Idee des Judentums,* 1924. LR 123.

335.B.9 The whole human story, with all its tragedy and its triumph, is like a page torn from the middle of a book, without beginning or end—an undecipherable page, when cut out of its context. . . . The context of man is the Power greater than man. The human adventure is part of a universal sonnet—one line in a deathless poem.

Liebman, *How Can I Believe in God Now,* 1943.

335.B.10 The idea of God in the Jewish Church, which can be traced to nothing short of Mount Sinai, was the very reverse of a negation or an abstraction. It was the absorbing thought of the national mind. It was not merely the Lord of the Universe, but "the Lord who had brought thee out of the land of Egypt, out of the house of bondage."

*Stanley, *History of the Jewish Church,* (1862) 1896, i. 136.

335.C. Name

Tetragrammaton

335.C.1 I appeared to Abraham, to Isaac, and to Jacob as God Almighty, but by My name YHVH I made Me not known to them.

Bible: Exod., 6.3.

335.C.2 Moses conceived the Deity as a Being who has always existed, does exist, and always will exist, and he therefore called Him Jehovah, which in Hebrew signifies these three phases.

Spinoza, *Theologico-Political Treatise,* 1670, ch 2.

335.C.3 An English word expressing at once "he was, he is, and he will be," would be an equivalent for Jehovah, but it would have to convey the meaning . . . also of causation. There is no such term in any language except the Hebrew, so far as I know.

I. M. Wise, *Outlines of Judaism,* 1869. *Selected Writings,* 213 f.

Other Names

335.C.4 God said: My name is according to My work: when I judge, it is *Elohim* [God]; when I war on the wicked, it is *Zebaot* [Hosts]; when I suspend judgment, it is *Shaddai* [Almighty], and when I show compassion, it is *Adonai* [Lord].

Abba b. Memel. *Exod. R.,* 3.6. See *Tanhuma, Shemot,* #20, ed Buber, 88b.

335.C.5 They worship the same God . . . though He is called by different names, such as Zeus or Dis.

Apocrypha: Aristeas, 15.

335.C.6 *Ehyé asher Ehyé* may, of course, be soundly interpreted as "I am that I am." But *Ehyé* is an imperfect tense . . . "I will be." God revealed Himself as the . . . yet to be perfected "I".

Bergmann, *Jawne und Jerusalem,* 1919. LR, 140.

335.C.7 God is called the Heart of Israel.

Hiyya b. Abba. *Cant. R.,* 5.2.1. (*Ps.* 73.26).

335.C.8 God is called *Makom* [Place], because He contains and is not contained, He is a place for all to flee to, and He is Himself the space which holds Him.

Philo, *Dreams,* i. 11; *Alleg. Interpretations,* 3.17.

Jose b. Halafta. *Gen. R.,* 68.9.

Mystery

335.C.9 Thou shalt not take the name of the Lord thy God in vain.

Bible: Exod., 20.7. *Deut.,* 511. *Ps.* 24.3f.

335.C.10 The name of the Lord is a strong tower.
Bible: Prov., 18.10.

335.C.11 Do not get into the habit of exclaiming, God! but speak always of "the Creator, blessed be He."
Eliezer Halevi, Tzavaah, c. 1350. AHE, 213.

335.C.12 God's full name appeared first when the world was complete.
Gen. R., 13.3, ref. to "Lord God," Gen. 2.4.

335.C.13 Yea, all Thy deeds of small or greatest fame
Are letters of Thy name.
M. J. Lebensohn, "HaTefilla," #8. Kinor Bat Tziyon, 3, tr FHH, 24.

335.C.14 Human lips are now forbidden to utter His name, for being the only God, He needs no name.
Peretz, Der Dichter, 1910. Alle Verk, x. 23.

335.C.15 The Jews alone know the true name of God.
*Reuchlin. q Darmsteter, Selected Essays, 268.

335.C.16 In each generation didst Thou make plain part of the mystery of Thy name.
Saadia, "Shield and Quickener." q AGG, 49.

335.C.17 God's name, graven on Israel's escutcheon at Sinai, was obliterated when Israel sinned.
Simeon b. Yohai. Lam. R., Proem, 24.

Sanctification

335.C.18 Miracles were performed for our ancestors, because they sacrificed their lives for the sanctification of the Name.
Abayé. Talmud: Berakot, 20a.

335.C.19 What is the Sanctification of the Name? Conduct which leads people to love the name of Heaven.
Abayé. Talmud: Yoma, 86a.

335.C.20 To avoid a transgression or to perform a precept, not from fear or ambition but purely out of love of God, is to sanctify His name in public.
Maimonides, Iggeret HaShemad, 1160. Yad: Yesodé HaTorah, 1180, 5.10.

335.C.21 When Jews do the will of God, the Name is glorified; when they do not, the Name is desecrated.
Simeon b. Eleazar. Mekilta, to Exod. 15.2.

335.C.22 To act so as to manifest a sublime faith, to do more than what the formal law requires, to practice goodness not out of fear nor for one's own glory, but for the glory of God, that is what it means to Sanctify the Name.
*Solovyov, "Talmud." Ruskaya Mysl, 1886.

Desecration

335.C.23 Ye shall not profane My holy name.
Bible: Lev., 22.32.

335.C.24 God may overlook idolatry, but not a profanation of the Name.
Hanina b. Hama. Lev. R., 22.6.

335.C.25 If you must, sin privately, but profane not the Name publicly.
Hanina b. Hama. Talmud: Kiddushin, 40a.

335.C.26 If you feel the Evil Urge overwhelming you, go to a place where you are unknown, dress in black, do the sordid thing, and profane not the Name openly.
Ilai. Talmud: Moed Katan, 17a.

335.C.27 What is a profanation of the Name? For example, not to pay the butcher at once where it is customary to pay in cash.
Rab. Talmud: Yoma, 86a.

335.C.28 If the positive principle of Kiddush HaShem is an ideal of conduct which only holy men can attain, the corresponding negative principle of Hillul HaShem imposes an unconditional obligation on every Jew. If any act, though permitted by law, may provoke the defamation of Israel and of God, then, in spite of its abstract legality, it becomes a great sin and crime.
*Solovyov, "Talmud." Ruskaya Mysl, 1886.

335.D. Attributes

335.D.1 All the attributes of God, with which the mind endows Him, were to Jewish philosophy so many negations, intended to contrast the Divine and the mortal natures.
Baeck, Essence of Judaism, 1936, p. 90f.

335.D.2 We must . . . not take God's attributes literally. . . . They are metaphorical.
Bahya, Hobot HaLebabot, 1040, 1.10. tr Hyamson, i. 53.

335.D.3 In many shapes do men Thine image frame;

Through all their visions Thou
art yet the same.
Hymn of Glory, c. 1200.

335.D.4 There is no distinction between
Thy divinity, Thy unity, Thy eternity, and
Thy existence; for it is all one mystery.
Ibn Gabirol, *Royal Crown*, 11C.

335.D.5 They attribute to Him mercy,
although this is surely nothing but a weakness of the soul, . . . which cannot be applied to God. . . . He has no sympathy with
one nor anger with another.
Judah Halevi, *Cuzari*, c. 1135, 2.2.

335.D.6 God is identical with His attributes, so that it may be said that He is
the knowledge, the knower, and the
known.
Maimonides, *Eight Chapters*, 1168, #8,
ed Gorfinkle, 100. *Yad: Yesodé HaTorah*,
2.10.

335.D.7 All attributes ascribed to God
are attributes of His acts, and do not imply
that God has any qualities.
Maimonides, *Guide for the Perplexed*,
1190, 1.54.

335.D.8 Thought is an attribute of God,
or God is a thinking being.
Spinoza, *Ethics*, 1677, i. Pr 1.

335.D.9 Power, Love, Wisdom—there
you have a real trinity which makes up the
Jewish God.
Zangwill, *Children of the Ghetto*, 1892,
ii. ch 2, p. 342.

335.E.   Personal

335.E.1 It is from the god's personality
that religion draws its greatest efficacy.
Bergson, *Two Sources of Morality & Religion*, 1935, p. 164.

335.E.2 The center and soul of all religion, the belief in a personal God, is the
pillar of the religion of Israel. And it
fathomed this truth with incomparable and
triumphant energy, and expressed it with
incomparable poetic power.
*Cornill, *Culture of Ancient Israel*, 1914,
p. 144.

335.E.3 Is it more unphilosophical to believe in a personal God, omnipotent and
omniscient, than in natural forces unconscious and irresistible? Is it unphilosophical
to combine power with intelligence?
Disraeli, (Paraclete in) *Lothair*, 1870.

335.E.4 The God of the Hebraic religion
is either a living, active, "feeling" God or
he is nothing.
Herberg, *Judaism and Modern Man*,
1951, p. 61.

335.E.5 In the one living, true God there
are two supreme and primary powers:
goodness and authority . . . and between
these two there is a third, which brings
them together, Reason.
Philo, *Cherubim*, 9.

335.E.6 The impersonal God is the most
wretched reflection of technologized and
thought-weary brains, the modern old folks'
home of senile pantheism.
Werfel, *Between Heaven and Earth*,
1944, p. 171.

335.F.   Incorporeal

335.F.1 Man shall not see Me and live.
Bible: Exod., 33.20.

335.F.2 Ye heard the voice of words, but
ye saw no form.
Bible: Deut., 4.12.

335.F.3 The Lord was not in the wind,
. . . not in the earthquake, . . . not in the
fire. And after the fire a still small voice.
Bible: I Kings, 19.11f.

335.F.4 Any representation of God form-
ing itself in our minds applies to something
other than God.
Bahya, *Hobot HaLebabot*, 1040, 1.10.

335.F.5 Thou art living, but not through
a soul and breath, for Thou art the soul of
the soul.
Ibn Gabirol, *Royal Crown*, 11C.

335.F.6 The soul fills, carries and sur-
vives the body, and the Holy One fills,
carries and outlives the universe. The soul
is one, and the Holy One is one. The soul
is pure, does not eat, sees and is unseen, and
never sleeps, and the Holy One is pure, does
not eat, sees and is unseen, and neither
slumbers nor sleeps.
Lev. R., 4.8.

335.F.7 I believe with perfect faith that
the Creator . . . is not a body, is free from
all properties of matter, and has no form
whatever.
Maimonides, *Commentary to Mishna:
Sanhedrin*, 1168, 10.1. *Thirteen Principles*, #3.

335.F.8 Though we speak of the "Creator," we must not construe the term in a
corporeal sense. A physical agent must
himself move, . . . needs materials, time,

space and tools. All this is far removed from God.

Saadia, *Emunot VeDeot*, 933, 2.11.

335.F.9 God is totally distinct from both the upper and lower worlds and can in no way be compared to the soul of man.

Shneor Zalman, *Iggeret HaKodesh*, iii. 1805.

335.F.10 Jews worship with the mind alone. They believe in one God, supreme and . . . immortal, and deem it impious, out of perishable matter, to fashion effigies of God after the likeness of men.

*Tacitus, *History*, 5.5.

335.G. Eternal

335.G.1 The Lord shall reign for ever and ever.

Bible: Exod., 15.18. See *Dan.* 3.33, 4.31.

335.G.2 When this our world shall be
   no more,
  In majesty He still shall reign,
  Who was, who is, who will for
   aye
  In endless glory still remain.

Adon Olam, tr F. de Sola Mendes.

335.G.3 Eternity is Thine!

Ibn Gabirol, *Royal Crown*, 11C.

335.G.4 Eternity is the very essence of God.

Spinoza, *Ethics*, 1677, v. Pr 30, Proof. See i. Pr 19.

335.H. One

335.H.1 The Lord, He is God; there is none else beside Him.

Bible: Deut., 4.35. See 32.39; *II Sam.*, 7.28.

335.H.2 Hear, O Israel, the Lord our God, the Lord is one.

Bible: Deut., 6.4.

335.H.3 In that day the Lord shall be one, and His name one.

Bible: Zech., 14.9.

335.H.4 I have no father, I have no brother, I have no son.

Abbahu. *Exod. R.*, 29.5, on *Isa.* 44.6.

335.H.5 People should get to know what the unity of God really means. To attain a part of this indivisible unity is to attain the whole. The Torah and all its ordinances are from God. If I therefore fulfill but one commandment in and through the love of God, it is as though I have fulfilled them all.

Baal Shem. q SSJ, i. 29f.

335.H.6 One and unique is His oneness, inconceivable and infinite is His unity.

Daniel b. Judah, "Yigdal," 14C.

335.H.7 Only one God is not made of plaster.

Hoffenstein, *Pencil in the Air*, 1923, p. 149.

335.H.8 I believe with a perfect faith that the Creator . . . is a Unity, that there is no unity . . . like His, and that He alone is our God.

Maimonides, *Commentary to Mishna: Sanhedrin*, 1168, 10.1. *Thirteen Principles*, #2.

335.H.9 When the heathen will forsake their idols, God will be One.

Rashi, *Commentary*, to *Zech.* 14.9.

335.H.10 God is one, that is, only one substance can be granted in the universe, and that substance is absolutely infinite.

Spinoza, *Ethics*, 1677, i. Pr 14, corollary 1.

335.I. Omnipresent

335.I.1 He is God in heaven above, and on earth beneath.

Bible: Josh., 2.11.

335.I.2 The whole earth is full of His glory.

Bible: Isa., 6.3.

335.I.3 The Lord is great beyond the border of Israel.

Bible: Mal., 1.5.

335.I.4 Whither shall I go from Thy spirit, or . . . flee from Thy presence? If I ascend into heaven, Thou art there; if I make my bed in the nether-world, behold, Thou art there. If I take the wings of the morning and dwell in the uttermost parts of the sea, even there would Thy hand lead me, and Thy right hand would hold me.

Bible: Ps., 139.7–10.

335.I.5 Within me is the Lord.

M. Ibn Ezra, *Selected Poems*, 6.

335.I.6 The infinite heights are too small to contain Thee, yet perchance Thou canst niche in the clefts of me.

Ibn Gabirol, *Selected Religious Poems*, 16.

335.I.7 O Lord, where shall I find
   Thee?
  All hidden and exalted is Thy
   place;
  And where shall I not find
   Thee?

Full of Thy glory is the infinite
space.
Judah Halevi, tr Davis. *JQRo*, x. 117.
(*Selected Poems*, 168).

335.I.8 Wherever you find man's footprints, there God is before you.
Mekilta, to *Exod*. 17.6.

335.I.9 God, surrounding all things, is Himself not surrounded.
Philo, *Fugitives*, 14. *Allegories*, 1.14, 3.17.

335.I.10 God is the world's Place, not the world God's Place.
Jose b. Halafta, *et alia. Gen. R.*, 69.9.

335.I.11 There is no place devoid of Him.
Saadia, *Sefer HaYerushot*, Introd., ed J. Müller. *Oeuvres Complètes*, ix.

335.I.12 Whatsoever is, is in God.
Spinoza, *Ethics*, 1677, i. Pr 15.

335.I.13 God is the indwelling, not the transient cause, of all things.
Ibid., Pr 18.

335.I.14 Wherever a Jew goes, his God goes with him.
Tanhuma. *Deut. R.*, 2.16.

335.I.15 "Holy, holy, holy"—in heaven, on earth, and to all eternity.
Targum Jonathan, to *Isa.*, 6.3.

335.J. Omnipotent

335.J.1 Who is like unto Thee, O Lord, among the mighty?
Bible: Exod., 15.11.

335.J.2 There is no restraint to the Lord to save by many or by few.
Bible: I Sam., 14.6.

335.J.3 The Lord on high is mighty.
Bible: Ps., 93.4.

335.J.4 Thy power is not in multitude, nor Thy might in strong men.
Apocrypha: Judith, 9.11.

335.J.5 God's power is identical with His essence.
Spinoza, *Ethics*, 1677, i. Pr 34.

335.K. Omniscient

335.K.1 The Lord is a God of knowledge.
Bible: I Sam., 2.3.

335.K.2 Thou knowest the hearts of all the children of men.
Bible: I Kings, 8.39. See *II Kings*, 19.27.

335.K.3 Thou understandest my thought afar off.
Bible: Ps., 139.2.

335.K.4 Thou art wise, but not that Thou didst learn from another.
Ibn Gabirol, *Royal Crown*, 11C.

335.K.5 I believe with perfect faith that the Creator . . . knows every deed of the children of men, and all their thoughts.
Maimonides, *Commentary to Mishna: Sanhedrin*, 1168, 10.1. *Thirteen Principles*, #10.

335.L. Just

335.L.1 All His ways are justice.
Bible: Deut., 32.4.

335.L.2 The Lord of hosts is exalted through justice.
Bible: Isa., 5.16.

335.L.3 The Lord is a God of justice.
Ibid., 30.18.

335.L.4 Thy righteousness is like the mighty mountains. Thy judgments are like the great deep.
Bible: Ps., 36.7. See 119.142.

335.L.5 God's justice must comprise all His children.
Crescas, *Or Adonai*, c.1400 (1556).

335.L.6 The Holy One said: Mercy or Justice alone will not do. I shall create the world with the two combined!
Gen. R., 12.15.

335.L.7 All believe that He . . . is a Leveler, who renders equal small and great.
Johanan HaCohen, *HaOhez BeYad*, Rosh Hashana hymn, 9C.

335.M. Merciful

335.M.1 Lord, Lord, God merciful and gracious, long-suffering, and abundant in loving-kindness and truth.
Bible: Exod., 34.6.

335.M.2 Let us fall into the Lord's hand, for His mercies are great.
Bible: II Sam., 24.14. See *Hos.*, 14.4.

335.M.3 He retains not His anger forever, He delights in mercy.
Bible: Mic., 7.18.

335.M.4 All the paths of the Lord are mercy and truth.
Bible: Ps., 25.10.

335.M.5 The earth, O Lord, is full of Thy mercy.
Ibid., 119.64.

335.M.6 The Lord is good to all. His tender mercies are over all His works.
Ibid., 145.9. See 110.5.

335.M.7 Surely His compassions fail not. They are new every morning.
Bible: Lam., 3.23f.

335.M.8 He does not afflict willingly nor grieve the children of men.
Ibid., 3.33.

335.M.9 Even in anger, the Holy One is compassionate.
Eleazar b. Pedat. *Talmud: Pesaḥim,* 87b.

335.M.10 The All-Merciful turns the scale of judgment toward mercy.
Hillel. *Tosefta: Sanhedrin,* 13.3.

335.M.11 God shows mercy also to cattle and birds.
Judah b. Pazzi. *Deut. R.,* 6.1.

335.M.12 God prays: May My mercy overcome My anger!
Rab. *Talmud: Beraḳot,* 7a.

335.M.13 Lord of all worlds, not in reliance upon our own merit do we lay our supplications before Thee, but trusting in Thine infinite mercy alone.
Union Prayer Book, 1940, i. 101. *DPB,* ed Singer, 7. See *Apocrypha: Testament of Moses,* 12.7f. *Talmud: Yoma,* 87b.

335.N. Benevolent

335.N.1 The mountains may depart, the hills be removed, but My kindness shall not depart from you.
Bible: Isa., 54.10.

335.N.2 His anger is but for a moment, His favor for a lifetime.
Bible: Ps., 30 6.

335.N.3 Thy loving-kindness, O Lord, is in the heavens. Thy faithfulness reaches unto the skies.
Ibid., 36.6. See 57.11.

335.N.4 God draws all men to Himself by His benignity.
Apocrypha: Aristeas, 207.

335.N.5 When all within is dark, and
    former friends misprize,
From them I turn to Thee, and
    find love in Thine eyes.
When all within is dark, and I
    my soul despise,
From me I turn to Thee, and
    find love in Thine eyes.
When all Thy face is dark, and
    Thy just angers rise,
From Thee I turn to Thee, and
    find love in Thine eyes.
Ibn Gabirol, *Royal Crown,* 11C, tr Abrahams.

335.N.6 When the Holy One cursed the serpent, or Canaan, He yet provided for their food.
Jose b. Halafta. *Talmud: Yoma,* 75a.

335.N.7 God is perfect goodness, and all that comes from Him is absolutely good.
Maimonides, *Guide for the Perplexed,* 1190, 3.12.

335.N.8 God is love.
New Testament: I John, 4.8.

335.N.9 Beneficence is the peculiar prerogative of a god.
Philo, *Change of Names,* 22.

335.N.10 God chastises with one hand and blesses with the other.
Proverb (Yiddish). BJS, #710.

335.N.11 The whole world is sustained by God's charity.
Talmud: Beraḳot, 17b.

335.N.12 Infinite as is Thy power, even so is Thy love.
Union Prayer Book, 1940, i. 12.

335.N.13 God gives us a thousand joys for each affliction, a thousand smiles for each pang.
I. M. Wise. *American Israelite,* Aug. 31, 1866.

335.O. Creator

335.O.1 Who meted out heaven with the span, . . . and weighed the mountains in scales?
Bible: Isa., 40.12.

335.O.2 I form the light and create darkness; I make peace and create evil.
Ibid., 45.7.

335.O.3 We are the clay, and Thou art our potter.
Ibid., 64.7. Cf *Jer.* 18.6.

335.O.4 His wisdom and power in creating an ant or bee is no less than in the making of the sun and its sphere.
Judah Halevi, *Cuzari,* c.1135, 3.17.

335.O.5 I believe with perfect faith that the Creator, blessed be His Name, is the author and guide of everything created.
Maimonides, *Commentary to Mishna: Sanhedrin,* 1168, 10.1.

335.O.6 God never leaves off making; as it is the property of fire to burn and of snow to chill, so it is of God to make.
Philo, *Allegorical Interpretation,* i. 3.

335.O.7 God left unfinished the north corner of the world and said: Whoever

claims to be a god, let him complete this corner!
Pirké de Rabbi Eliezer, ch 3.

335.O.8 In His goodness He reneweth each day the work of creation.
Prayer, pre-Maccabean. *DPB*, ed Singer, 37.

335.P. Providence

335.P.1 God will provide.
Bible: Gen., 22.8.

335.P.2 It is He that gives you power to get wealth.
Bible: Deut., 8.18.

335.P.3 The Lord kills and quickens . . . He lowers and also lifts.
Bible: 1 Sam., 2.6f.

335.P.4 The Lord is my shepherd, I shall not want.
Bible: Ps., 23.1.

335.P.5 Man and beast Thou preservest, O Lord.
Ibid., 36.7.

335.P.6 It is of the Lord that a man's doings are established.
Ibid., 37.23.

335.P.7 Unto God the Lord belong the issues of death.
Ibid., 68.21.

335.P.8 A man's heart devises his way, but the Lord directs his steps.
Bible: Prov., 16.9. See 19.21.

335.P.9 Who provides for the raven his prey?
Bible: Job, 38.41.

335.P.10 A snake never bites, a lion never rends, a government never interferes unless so ordered from above.
Abba b. Kahana. *Eccles. R.*, 10.11.1.

335.P.11 The Holy One takes wealth from one and gives it to another.
Abba of Serungaya. *Num. R.*, 22.8. Cf BJS, #648.

335.P.12 In our finest achievements it is not we who attain success, but God who brings all things to fulfillment.
Apocrypha: Aristeas, 195.

335.P.13 Good and evil, life and death, poverty and wealth come from God.
Apocrypha: Ben Sira, 11.14.

335.P.14 He who created the day has also provided for it.
Eliezer b. Hyrcanus. *Mekilta*, to *Exod.* 16.4.

335.P.15 A finger is not pricked here below unless decreed on high.
Hanina b. Hama. *Talmud: Hullin*, 7b.

335.P.16 Jerusalem said to Babylon: Had they not fought me on high, would you have prevailed? . . . Only a slain lion did you slay, ground meal did you grind, a burnt city did you burn!
Joshua. *Lam. R.*, 1.13.

335.P.17 A lady asked what God has been doing since creation. José b. Halafta replied: He has been building ladders, for some to ascend, for others to descend.
Lev. R., 8.1. *Tanhuma, Matot*, 9, ed Buber, 161.

335.P.18 Divine Providence does not extend to the individual members of the species, except in the case of mankind.
Maimonides, *Guide for the Perplexed*, 1190, 3.17.

335.P.19 You are not master of your words, nor have you power over your hand; everything is of the Lord, who forms your heart.
Nahmanides, letter to his son, c.1268.

335.P.20 If God does not approve, a fly won't make a move.
Proverb (Yiddish). BJS, #614.

335.P.21 What God has sent, no man can prevent.
Ibid., #700.

335.P.22 Man proposes, and God laughs.
Ibid., #2346.

335.P.23 Whom God would regale, man cannot quail.
Proverb (Yiddish). *JE*, x. 228b.

335.P.24 All appointments are from Heaven, even that of a janitor.
Rab. *Talmud: Baba Bathra*, 91b. See *NT: John*, 3.27.

335.P.25 He provides all for all.
Saadia, *Sefer HaYerushot*, Introd., ed J. Müller. *Oeuvres Complètes*, ix.

335.P.26 When man completes a product, his relation to it ends; but God's power continues to permeate His creatures.
Shneor Zalman, *Tanya*, 1796, *Yihud*, ch 2.

335.P.27 Other nations of antiquity, when they were defeated, acknowledged that their gods had been defeated. The Jews always saw in their defeat the *triumph* of their God.
Silver, *World Crisis & Jewish Survival*, 1941, p. 51.

335.P.28 There is not a single blade of grass below but has a director up above, who taps it and says, "Grow!"
Simeon. *Gen. R.*, 10.6.

335.P.29 A bird does not fall into a trap without the will of God.
Simeon b. Yohai. *Talmud J: Shebiit*, 9.1. See *Matt.*, 10.29.

335.P.30 He who made this one rich can make him poor, and He who made that one poor can make him rich.
Talmud: Temura, 16a.

335.Q. Healer

335.Q.1 I am the Lord that healeth thee.
Bible: Exod., 15.26.

335.Q.2 Heal me, O Lord, and I shall be healed.
Bible: Jer., 17.14.

335.Q.3 He has torn, and He will heal us.
Bible: Hos., 6.1. See *Job*, 5.18.

335.Q.4 With Thee is the fountain of life.
Bible: Ps., 36.10.

335.Q.5 He heals the broken in heart, and binds up their wounds.
Ibid., 147.3.

335.Q.6 My cure comes from God, the Maker of physicians.
Apocrypha: Testament of Job, ed Kohler.

335.Q.7 The Holy One heals with the very wound He inflicts.
Levi. *Lev. R.*, 18.5. *Mekilta*, to *Exod.* 14.24.

335.Q.8 He first prepares the plaster, then inflicts the wound.
Simeon b. Lakish. *Talmud: Megilla*, 13a. Simeon b. Yohai. *Cant. R.*, 4.5.1.

335.R. Protector

335.R.1 The Lord your God who goes before you shall fight for you.
Bible: Deut., 1.30.

335.R.2 Underneath are the everlasting arms.
Ibid., 33.27.

335.R.3 Neither is there any Rock like our God.
Bible: I Sam., 2.22.

335.R.4 He drew me out of many waters.
Bible: II Sam., 22.17.

335.R.5 God is with us!
Bible: Isa., 8.10.

335.R.6 Thou hast been a stronghold . . . to the needy in his distress.
Ibid., 25.4.

335.R.7 Thou, O Lord, art a shield about me.
Bible: Ps., 3.4.

335.R.8 The Lord also will be a high tower for the oppressed.
Ibid., 9.10.

335.R.9 The Lord preserveth the faithful.
Ibid., 31.24.

335.R.10 The Lord shall guard thy going out and thy coming in.
Bible: Ps., 121.8.

335.R.11 How little does he need to worry whom the Lord supports! Saul sinned once and met with disaster; David sinned twice and escaped evil.
Huna. *Talmud: Yoma*, 22b.

335.R.12 God is called Protector of Israel though He protects all men.
Judah HaNasi. *Sifré to Deut.*, #38, ref. to *Ps.* 121.4.

335.R.13 Gog and Magog will say: The ancients were fools in plotting against Israel. We will first take issue with their Protector in Heaven, and then with them.
Levi. *Lev. R.*, 27.11.

335.R.14 If God be for us, who can be against us?
New Testament: Rom., 8.31.

335.S. Redeemer

335.S.1 The Lord is my strength and song. He is become my salvation.
Bible: Exod., 15.2.

335.S.2 I am the Lord thy God who brought thee out of the land of Egypt, out of the house of bondage.
Ibid., 20.2. *Deut.*, 5.6.

335.S.3 The Holy One of Israel is thy Redeemer.
Bible: Isa., 54.5.

335.S.4 The Lord is my light and my salvation; whom shall I fear?
Bible: Ps., 27.1.

335.S.5 The Lord redeems the soul of His servants.
Ibid., 34.23. See 31.6.

335.S.6 God is unto us a God of deliverances.
Ibid., 68.21.

335.S.7 He will redeem their soul from oppression and violence.
Ibid., 72.14.

335.S.8 He will redeem Israel from all his iniquities.
Ibid., 130.8.

335.S.9 Thou art a God of the afflicted . . . a savior of those without hope.
Apocrypha: Judith, 9.11.

335.S.10 Fear thou not, for I behold thee,
    I will strengthen and enfold thee,
    Yea, My right hand shall uphold thee!
    I am thy salvation!
A. Ibn Ezra, tr Lucas. *Jewish Year*, 1898, p. 33.

335.T. King

335.T.1 The Lord is king.
Bible: Isa., 33.22.

335.T.2 With a mighty hand . . . will I be king over you.
Bible: Ezek., 20.33.

335.T.3 The Lord reigneth, let the earth rejoice!
Bible: Ps., 97.1.

335.T.4 Thine is the kingdom, O Lord! . . . Thou rulest over all.
Bible: I Chron., 29.11f.

335.T.5 A Jew submits first to the sovereignty of God, then to that of the Law.
Joshua b. Karha. *Mishna: Berakot*, 2.2.

335.T.6 The Lord is king, the Lord was king, the Lord shall be king for ever and ever.
Kalir, "The Lord Is King." ZVJ, 158.

335.U. Father

335.U.1 The Lord your God bore you as a man bears his son.
Bible: Deut., 1.31.

335.U.2 Ye are the children of the Lord your God.
Ibid., 14.1.

335.U.3 O Lord, Thou art our Father.
Bible: Isa., 64.7. See *Ps.*, 68.6, 103.13.

335.U.4 When are you His children? When you obey Him.
Abba b. Kahana. *Tanhuma, Ekeb.*

335.U.5 You are His children even when you do not act as such.
Meir. *Sifré* 32.5, to *Deut.* 14.1. Cf *Talmud: Kiddushin*, 36a.

335.U.6 They shall all be called children of the living God.
Apocrypha: Jubilees, 1.25.

335.U.7 When Jeremiah preached repentance, Israel said: "How can we approach the Almighty? Have we not angered Him, do not the very hills on which we served idols testify against us?" Said God to the prophet: "Tell them, when ye come to Me, do ye not come to your Father in Heaven?" [*Jer.* 31.1].
Isaac. *Pesikta de R. Kahana*, ch 25, ed Buber, 148a.

335.V. Anthropomorphism

335.V.1 It repented the Lord that He had made man on the earth.
Bible: Gen., 6.6.

335.V.2 The Lord smelled the sweet savor.
Ibid., 8.21.

335.V.3 I the Lord am a jealous God.
Bible: Exod., 20.5. *Deut.*, 5.9. See *Nah.*, 1.2.

335.V.4 God is not a man that he should lie, neither the son of man that He should repent.
Bible: Num., 23.19.

335.V.5 I am God, not man, . . . I will not come in fury.
Bible: Hos., 11.8f.

335.V.6 The Holy One wrapped Himself in a prayer-shawl.
Aha, or Simon. *Tanhuma, VaYera*, #9, ed Buber, 46a.

335.V.7 The prophets had to speak in a language understood by the masses, . . . so they said that He is a jealous and avenging God.
Albo, *Ikkarim*, 1428, 2.4.

335.V.8 God is not as man that He should be threatened, neither as the son of man that He should be turned by entreaty.
Apocrypha: Judith, 8.16.

335.V.9 A God lacking in wrath would be like a man lacking in conscience. . . . Those that are so stirred up over the wrathful God of the Jews do not know, or forget, that the divine wrath is . . . also a Christian doctrine.
*Cornill, *Culture of Ancient Israel*, 1914, p. 147ff.

335.V.10 If the infinite God had not appeared to the prophets as a King on a throne, they would not know to whom they were praying.
Eleazar b. Judah, *Sodé Raza*, 13C, ed Kamelhar, 32.

335.V.11 He who sees his God suffer bears more easily his own afflictions. The merry gods of old . . . were holiday gods. . . . Therefore, they were never loved from the very soul and with all the heart. To be *so* loved, one must be a sufferer.

Heine, *City of Lucca*, 1828, ch 6.

335.V.12 A curtain would open in the Temple on festivals, disclosing the intertwined Cherubim, and the pilgrims would be told: Behold, the divine love for you is as the love of man and woman!

Kattina. *Talmud: Yoma*, 54a.

335.V.13 We describe God in creature figures, to make it acceptable to the ear.

Mekilta, to *Exod.* 19.18.

335.V.14 The anthropomorphism and the rejection of anthropomorphism are both needed in our conception of God.

Montefiore, 1927. BSL, 519.

335.V.15 God was the perfect Rabbi: He too loved and studied the Law.

Montefiore, *A Rabbinic Anthology*, 1938, p. xxvi.

335.V.16 It is wrong to compare God to any creature. . . . The Torah, the Prophets, and the agadists spoke only metaphorically.

Nissim. q Habib, *En Yaakob, Berakot,* 59a.

335.V.17 The Holy One sits on an exalted throne, high in the air. His glory appears as the color of electrum, a wreath on His head, the crown of the Tetragrammaton on His brow. His eyes run to and fro in all the earth. He is half fire, half ice. On His right is life, on His left death. A fiery rod is in His hand. A curtain is spread before Him, and within what is called the Paragode, seven angels minister before Him. His footstool is like fire and hail. Beneath the throne of His glory is like sapphire, and around it flashing fire.

Pirké de Rabbi Eliezer, ch 4.

335.V.18 As long as Jews are in trouble while others are at peace, you may say, "Awake, why sleepest Thou, O Lord" [*Ps.* 44.23].

Rehaba. *Talmud: Sota,* 48a.

335.V.19 The Holy One sits on His throne of glory, one third of the day studying, one third of the day judging, and one third of the day dispensing loving-kindness.

Seder Eliyahu Rabbah, ch 17, ed Friedmann, p. 84.

335.V.20 In each generation, the Holy One strikes His hands against His heart, then against His arms, and cries secretly over (His transgressing children). Why secretly? Because it is unbecoming for a lion to cry before a fox, for a king before his subjects, for a teacher before his pupils, for a master before his servants.

Ibid., p. 87.

335.V.21 God is without passions, neither is He affected by any emotion of pleasure or pain.

Spinoza, *Ethics,* 1677, v. Pr 17.

335.V.22 God is described as a lawgiver or prince, and styled just, merciful, etc., merely in concession to popular understanding.

Spinoza, *Theologico-Political Treatise,* 1670, ch 4.

335.V.23 Judaic anthropomorphism was of the most transcendent type that ever hath entered into the heart of man.

*Stedman, *Nature & Elements of Poetry,* 1892, p. 83.

335.V.24 I the Eternal am the same before a man sins and after he repents.

Talmud: Rosh Hashana, 17b.

335.V.25 The change is not in God, but in man.

Albo, *Ikkarim,* 1428, 2.8, tr Husik, ii. 49.

335.W. Near

335.W.1 The Lord is nigh to them that are of a broken heart.

Bible: Ps., 34.19.

335.W.2 The nearness of God is my good.

Ibid., 73.28.

335.W.3 The Lord is nigh to all that call upon Him.

Ibid., 145.18.

335.W.4 The Lord is far from the wicked.

Bible: Prov., 15.29.

335.W.5 The Lord is with you while you are with Him.

Bible: I Chron., 15.2.

335.W.6 The nearness and farness are on man's side.

Albo, *Ikkarim,* 1428, 2.8.

335.W.7 When men learn righteousness, they are on the way to God.

Arama, *Akedat Yitzhak,* 15C, 11a, on *Isa.* 40.3.

335.W.8 Thou art nearer to men than the breath of their nostrils and the counsels of their reins.

Bahya, *Hobot HaLebabot, Bakasha*, 1040.

335.W.9 Thou art far, farther than the heaven of heavens, and near, nearer than my body is to me.

q Bahya b. Asher, *Kad HaKemah*, 14C, *v. Emuna* and *Hashgaha*.

335.W.10 God is closer to all than the body is to the soul.

Eleazar b. Judah, *Shaaré HaSod*, 13C (*Kokebé Yitzhak*, 1862, xxvii. 9).

335.W.11 No iron wall can separate Israel from their Father in Heaven.

Joshua b. Levi. *Talmud: Pesahim*, 85b.

335.W.12 How exalted above His world is the Most High! yet, let a man enter a synagog and pray silently, and the Holy One listens, even as a friend in whose ear one whispers a secret.

Judah b. Simeon. *Talmud J: Berakot*, 9.1.

335.W.13 Remove lust from the midst of thee;
Thou wilt find thy God within thy bosom
Moving gently.

Judah Halevi, *Selected Poems*, 115.

335.W.14 Man came into the world only to achieve nearness to God.

M. H. Luzzatto, *Mesillat Yesharim*, (1740) 1936, p. 18.

335.W.15 Lift me not high . . . unless Thou goest with me!

Philo, *Migration of Abraham*, 31.

335.W.16 When the need is highest, God is nighest.

q M. Samuel, *World of Sholom Aleichem*, 44.

335.W.17 O Lord, . . . Thou art as close to us as breathing and yet art farther than the farthermost star.

Union Prayer Book, 1940, i. 39.

335.X. God and Man

335.X.1 The glory of God is, to a large extent, placed not merely within human reach, but under human control.

Abrahams, *Glory of God*, 1925, p. 72.

335.X.2 "The Lord is thy shade"—as man acts, God reacts.

Baal Shem, on *Ps.* 121.5. q AMR, ii. 102.

335.X.3 The Holy One mirrors your laughter and weeping, your scowl and smile. As you are with Him, so is He with you.

Hayyim b. Isaac, *Nefesh HaHayyim*, 1824, i. ch 7.

335.X.4 You depend on Him, not He on you.

Bahya, *Hobot HaLebabot*, 1040, 3.6.

335.X.5 The fate of God is dependent on that of the world.

Bergmann, *Jawne und Jerusalem*, 1919. LR, 137.

335.X.6 The mystics unanimously bear witness that God needs us.

Bergson, *Two Sources of Morality & Religion*, 1935, p. 243.

335.X.7 Judaism has a central, unique and tremendous idea that is utterly original—the idea that God and man are partners in the world and that, for the realization of His plan and the complete articulation of this glory upon earth, God needs a committed, dedicated group of men and women.

T. Gaster, at American Council for Judaism, Apr. 30, 1954.

335.X.8 God redeemed Himself, as it were, when He redeemed Israel.

Hanania, Nephew of Joshua. *Talmud J: Sukka*, 4.3.

335.X.9 His glory is on me and mine on Him.

Hymn of Glory, c. 1200. q ZVJ, 160.

335.X.10 When Jews do the will of God, they "strengthen God" [*Ps.* 60.14], when they do not, they weaken the Rock [*Deut.* 32.18].

Levi b. Perata. *Lam. R.*, 1.6, #33. See *Mekilta* to *Exod.* 15.6.

335.X.11 The Almighty shares in the affliction of the community and of the individual.

Mekilta, to *Exod.* 12.41.

335.X.12 If God pursues you, it is He alone with whom you can take refuge.

Midrash, on *Exod.* 14.27. See Goitein, *Jews & Arabs*, p. 166.

335.X.13 "Ye are My witnesses . . . I am God." When ye are My witnesses, I am God; when ye are not My witnesses, I am, as it were, not God.

Midrash Tehillim, 123.2, ed Buber, 255a, on *Isa.* 43.12.

Simeon b. Yohai. *Pesikta de R. Kahana*, on *Isa.* 43.10.

335.X.14 Reason has long since decided that God needs nothing, but that all things need Him.

Saadia, *Emunot VeDeot*, 933, 3.10.

335.X.15 God is King when His children decorate themselves with good deeds and Torah.

Seder Eliyahu Rabbah, ch 2, ed Friedmann, p. 13.

335.X.16 God Himself records His need
      for man.
In braided filigree of bloom
    and leaf,
In dawns and starshine, cadenced lake and wood,
In glaciered mountains and in coral reef,
He strains to make His hunger understood.
For whom this vast unfoldment of His might,
This drama of creation without end?
For whom this cosmic theme of growth and light,
If not for man whom He yearns to befriend?

Steinbach. *N. Y. Times*, May 2, 1954.

335.X.17 The power above is set in motion by the impulse from below, even as vapor ascends to form the cloud. If the community of Israel did not first give the impulse, the One above would not move to meet her, for yearning below makes completion above.

Zohar, Gen., 35a.

335.Y. Communion

335.Y.1 Ye that did cleave unto the Lord your God are alive every one of you this day.

Bible: Deut., 4.4.

335.Y.2 As the girdle cleaves to the loins of a man, so have I caused to cleave unto Me the whole house of Israel.

Bible: Jer., 13.11.

335.Y.3 I have set the Lord always before me.

Bible: Ps., 16.8.

335.Y.4 Religion ... regards God, above all, as a Being who can hold communication with us: now this is just what the God of Aristotle ... is incapable of doing.

Bergson, *Two Sources of Morality and Religion*, 1935, p. 230.

335.Y.5 The perfection of the creatures consists in their union with Him, the primary Source.

Cordovero, *Pardes Rimonim*, 1591, 55a.

335.Y.6 All benedictions begin with "Praised be Thou"—as though man were addressing an intimate friend.

Eleazar b. Judah, *Sefer Raziel HaGadol*, (13C) 1701, 8b.

335.Y.7 He who enters the mystery of adhesion to God, *debekut*, attains equanimity, and he who has equanimity attains solitude, and from there he comes to the holy spirit and to prophecy.

Issac b. Samuel of Acre, *Meirat Enayim*, 14C. See SMT, 96.

335.Y.8 God: Make an opening for Me no wider than a needle's eye, and I will open for you a gate through which armies can pass.

Jose. *Pesikta de R. Kahana*, ch 35, p. 146b.

335.Y.9 A man should have no other purpose in whatever he does, be it great or small, than to be drawn to God as iron to a magnet.

M. H. Luzzatto, *Mesillat Yesharim*, (1740) 1936, p. 17.

335.Y.10 Let not God be a stranger to you.

Mendel of Kotzk, on *Ps.* 81.10. See BTH, ii. 278.

335.Y.11 Faith, love and sorrow are three elements that mysteriously blend in human experience, each having its own tale to tell of the relation which we bear to the Supreme Being.

O. J. Simon, *Faith and Experience*, 1895, p. 204.

335.Y.12 We belong to the Lord, and our eyes are turned to the Lord!

Temple refrain, at Water Drawing ceremony on Succoth. q Judah HaNasi. *Mishna: Sukka*, 5.4.

335.Y.13 In the mystery of the Trinity ... lies the chief infraction against the faith of Israel, which rests on the certainty of a free and direct communion between Creator and Creation.

Werfel, *Between Heaven and Earth*, 1944, p. 144.

335.Y.14 Let your God be your companion.

Zera. *Midrash Tehillim*, 104.3, ed Buber, 220b.

335.Z. Argument with God

335.Z.1 You have striven with God and with men, and have prevailed.
Bible: Gen., 32.29.

335.Z.2 If the Lord be with us, why then is all this befallen us? where are all His wondrous works which our fathers told us of?
Bible: Judg., 6.13.

335.Z.3 How long, O Lord, shall I cry, and Thou wilt not hear? . . . The bitter and impetuous nation marches through the breadth of the earth to take possession of homes that are not his. . . . Thou who art of eyes too pure to behold evil, . . . why lookest Thou at traitors and keepest silent when the wicked swalloweth the more righteous?
Bible: Hab., 1.2, 6, 13.

335.Z.4 Why, O God, hast Thou cast us off forever? Why doth Thine anger smoke against the flock of Thy pasture?
Bible: Ps., 74.1.

335.Z.5 He is not a man . . . that I should answer Him, that we should come together in judgment. There is no arbiter betwixt us that might lay his hand upon us both. Let Him take His rod away . . . then would I speak and not fear Him.
Bible: Job, 9.32–35. See 14.2f.

335.Z.6 There is no possible argument with the Creator, for each word of His is true, each decision just.
Akiba. *Mekilta, to Exod. 14.29.*

335.Z.7 I desire to speak face to face with God . . . Yea, verily, the son has a suit with the Father.
Apocalypse of Sedrach, 3.

335.Z.8 Why didst Thou weary Thy undefiled hands and create man, when Thou didst not intend to have mercy on him?
Ibid., 4.

335.Z.9 If Thou didst love man, why didst Thou not slay the devil? . . . He fights Thee, and what can wretched man then do to him?
Ibid., 5.

335.Z.10 Why should they bear in pain, only to bury in grief?
Apocrypha: II Baruch, 10.15.

335.Z.11 I see that the world, which was made on account of us, abides, but we, on whose account it was made, depart!
Ibid., 14.19.

335.Z.12 Are their deeds any better that inhabit Babylon? Has He for this rejected Zion?
Apocrypha: II Esdras, 3.28.

335.Z.13 If the world has been created for our sakes, why do we not enter into possession of our world? How long shall this endure?
Ibid., 6.58f.

335.Z.14 O dire calamity, that a man, righteous and alms-giving, should have become blind!
Apocrypha: Tobit, 7.7.

335.Z.15 I have not yet cleared all my accounts with my fathers' God.
Barash, *The Jew that Stayed Behind in Toledo.* q HMH, 169.

335.Z.16 Why do they pray to Me? Tell them to thunder against Me. Let them raise their fists against Me and claim recompense for their shame!
Bialik, "In the City of Slaughter," 1904.

335.Z.17 Murmur not because the world goes well with the powerful and wicked. God's ways are admirable, even though our poor eyes may not be able to see the good He does for Israel.
Eleazar b. Judah, *Rokeah*, 13C. ZEH, 18.

335.Z.18 Moses, Hannah and Elijah chided Heaven [*Num.*, 11.2.; *I Sam.*, 1.10; *I Kings*, 18.37].
Eleazar b. Pedat. *Talmud: Berakot*, 31b–32a.

335.Z.19 Never reproach Providence.
Eleazar b. Pedat. *Talmud: Sukka*, 53a.

335.Z.20 Who is like unto Thee, mighty and hard, hearing the blasphemous insults of that wicked [Titus] and keeping silent?
Hanan. *Talmud: Gittin*, 56b., on *Ps.* 89.9.

335.Z.21 "Who is like Thee, O Lord, among the *elim*" [*Exod.* 15.11]?—among the mute?
Ishmael School. *Ibid.*

335.Z.22 Wherefore bends the just one, bleeding
'Neath the cross's weight laborious,
While upon his steed the wicked
Rides all-proudly and victorious? . . .
Thus are we for ever asking,
Till at length our mouths securely
With a clod of earth are fastened,—

That is not an answer, surely?

Heine, *Latest Poems: Appendix to "Lazarus,"* 1853.

335.Z.23 Why didst Thou for a thousand years forget them,
While enemies from all around beset them?

A. Ibn Ezra. q WHJ, i. 236.

335.Z.24 How long, O Lord, will Israel's heart be riven?
How long will ye cry to a dotard God
To let us keep the breath that He has given?
How long will you sit on your throne, and nod?

Klein, "Job Reviles." *Hath Not a Jew,* 1940, p. 46.

335.Z.25 You, dear Lord, told us that we are Your "own treasure." . . . If so, why do You torment us? Why do You not help us?

Levi Yitzhok. q Cahn, *Der Rebbe fun Kotzk,* 7.

335.Z.26 Lord of the universe! I saw an ordinary Jew pick up his Tefillin from the floor, and kiss them; and You have let Your Tefillin, the Jewish people, lie on the ground for more than two thousand years, trampled by their enemies,—why do You not pick them up? Why do You not act as a plain Jew acts? Why?

Levi Yitzhok. q S. L. Hurwitz, *Otzar HaTorah,* 188.

335.Z.27 When Moses, on his visit in Heaven, foresaw Akiba's learning and martyrdom, he cried out: "Is this the Torah, and this its reward?" The Holy One replied: "Be silent, for such is My decree!"

Rab. *Talmud: Menahot,* 29b.

335.Z.28 When the Temple was destroyed, Mother Rachel complained: "If I, a creature of flesh and blood, dust and ashes, was not envious of my rival and did not expose her to shame, why shouldst Thou, eternal and merciful King, be jealous of vain idols, and have my children . . . dealt with wantonly by their enemies?" Whereupon the mercy of the Holy One was roused, and He said: "For your sake, Rachel, I will restore Israel!"

Samuel b. Nahman. *Lam. R.,* Proem 24.

335.Z.29 It is more revolutionary to believe in God and take Him to task sensibly than not to believe in Him and denounce Him in unmeasured language.

M. Samuel, *World of Sholom Aleichem,* 1943, p. 15.

335.Z.30 Father in Heaven, remember how many poverty-stricken Jews, tortured by the nations, engage constantly, each day, in Torah, how many blind Jews, who are without food, yet provide for their children's instruction in Torah. . . . Father in Heaven, we do not quarrel with Thee, but let our deeds speak for us!

Seder Eliyahu Rabbah, ch (19), ed Friedmann, 110.

335.Z.31 Indulge not in complaints when you see the righteous suffer and the wicked prosper.

Seder Eliyahu Zuta, ch 10, ed Friedmann, 189.

335.Z.32 Moses said: "Lord, is it right to give them and then kill them? Is a donkey told, Here is a heap of barley and we'll cut off your head? or a man, Have a talent of gold and go to hell?"

Simeon b. Yohai. *Sifré, Num.,* #95.

335.Z.33 Why is God especially severe toward us . . . who serve Him as no others do? . . . I would be no Jew and no human being if the question did not torture me daily, and only in death will it be silenced on my lips.

S. Zweig, *Der begrabene Leuchter,* 1937, p. 45.

336. GOLD

336.1 Mine is the silver, and Mine the gold.

Bible: Hag., 2.8.

336.2 Gold has made many reckless.

Apocrypha: Ben Sira, 8.2.

336.3 Who loves gold shall not go unpunished.

Ibid., 31.5.

336.4 Make not gold your hope: it is the first step to idolatry.

Asher b. Yehiel, *Hanhaga,* c. 1320.

336.5 The fetters which bind the people are forged from the people's own gold.

Brandeis. *Harper's Weekly,* Nov. 22, 1913.

336.6 A key of gold will open many a lock.

I. Friedmann, *Imré Bina,* 1912, p. 90.

336.7 Gold comes from dust.

Hasdai, *Ben HaMelek VeHaNazir,* c. 1230, ch 48.

336.8 Ah, that yellow load of sin!

Heine, *Romancero: Vitzliputzli,* 1851, #1.

336.9 In Cabul there are people chained to silver and gold.

Huna. *Talmud: Sabbath,* 54a.

336.10 It is good at home, and a fortunate thing to have on a trip.

Isaac. *Gen. R.,* 16.2.

336.11 With golden bullets you always hit the target.

Lazerov, *Enciklopedie fun Idishe Vitzen,* 1928, #431.

336.12 With a golden hammer you can break open iron gates.

Ibid.

336.13 Gold is society's blood. Too little or too much is unhealthy.

Ibid., #473. q NHA, 15.

336.14 A golden pen is no guarantee for glorious writing.

Sam Liptzin, *A Vort far a Vort,* 1955, p. 16.

336.15 Slaves of gold . . . the more they own, the more anxious they are.

Nahman Bratzlav. q BHH, 487.

336.16 Gold's father is dirt, yet it regards itself as noble.

Proverb (Yiddish). BJS, #726.

336.17 Here is Satan's dominion. . . .
Darkness is packed in his gold,
And gold in his darkness.

Shneor, "Song of the Gold Miner," c 1910. *Shirim,* 1952, ii. 221. tr FTH, 139.

336.18 Gold was created for the sake of the Temple.

Simeon b. Lakish. *Gen. R.,* 16.2.

336,19 Gold is a boon . . . as a medium of exchange.

Abbahu. *Gen. R.,* 16.2.

337. GOLDEN CALF

337.1 Not a generation but is somehow afflicted for the sin of the Golden Calf.

Assi. *Exod. R.,* 43.2.
Jose. *Talmud J: Taanit,* 4.5.

337.2 There is no catastrophe which does not contain some particle of the Golden Calf.

Isaac Nappaha. *Talmud: Sanhedrin,* 102a.

337.3 When the Holy One complained about the Calf, Moses said: Didst Thou not put us under taskmasters who worshipped calves?

Johanan b. Nappaha. *Exod. R.,* 43.7.

337.4 The High Priest would not enter the Holy of Holies attired in gold, lest it recall the Golden Calf.

Joshua b. Levi. *Pesikta Kahana,* ch 27, ed Buber, 159a.

338. GOLDEN RULE

338.1 Thou shalt love thy neighbor as thyself.

Bible: Lev., 19.18.

338.2 Be considerate of your companion as of yourself.

Apocrypha: Ben Sira, 31.15.

338.3 Love the Lord through life, and one another with a true heart.

Apocrypha: Patriarchs, Dan, 5.3.

338.4 What you yourself hate, do to no man.

Apocrypha: Tobit, 4.14.

338.5 Seek for your neighbor what you would seek for yourself.

Hasdai, *Sefer HaTapuah,* c. 1230, tr Gollancz, 92f.

338.6 What is hateful to you, do not to another: this is the whole Torah, the rest is commentary. Now go and study it.

Hillel. *Talmud: Sabbath,* 31a. Cf *ARN,* ch 26.

338.7 Whatever ye would that men should do to you, do ye even so to them: for this is the law and the prophets.

New Testament: Matt., 7.12.
Maimonides, *Yad: Ebel,* 14.1.

339. GOOD

339.A. Goodness

339.A.1 Seek good, not evil, that ye may live.

Bible: Amos, 5.14.

339.A.2 There is none that does good, no, not one.

Bible: Ps., 14.3.

339.A.3 The Manichaean divides the universe between good and evil. . . . There is no such clear-cut continuity in values. . . . Elements emerge from the chaos of evil and are built up into good.

S. Alexander, *Space, Time and Deity,* (1920) 1927, ii. 411.

339.A.4 Who's good to all is bad to all.

Al-Harizi, *Tahkemoni,* c. 1220, Introduction.

339.A.5 The good will always claim victory over the beautiful.

Heine, *Briefe aus Berlin,* Jan. 26, 1822.

339.A.6 There are three sorts of good: the profitable, the pleasurable, and the virtuous.

Leo Hebraeus, *Philosophy of Love,* (1501) 1937, p. 4.

339.A.7 It is not good, if it entails evil for others.

Lipkin. q KTH, i. 273.

339.A.8 Unfortunately, goodness and honor are rather the exception than the rule among exceptional men, not to speak of geniuses.

Lombroso. *Die Welt,* Nordau issue, 1909.

339.A.9 Faith in human goodness is a link that unites us.

Luzzatti, letter to D. Askowith. *God in Freedom,* xxii.

339.A.10 Seek the good in everyone, and reveal it, bring it forth.

Nahman Bratslav, *Likkuté Moharan,* (1806) 1936, p. 279.

339.A.11 There is some good in everything.

Nahum of Czernobiel. See HLH, 40.

339.A.12 Can anything good come out of Nazareth?

New Testament: John, 1.26.

339.A.13 Better good than pious.

Proverb (Yiddish). YFS, i. 414.

339.A.14 Goodness is not theory or pious aspiration. It is action, and action prescribed.

L. Roth, *Jewish Thought,* 1954, p. 32.

339.A.15 Regard as trifling the great good you did to others, and as enormous the little good others did to you.

Talmud: Derek Eretz, 1.29.

339.A.16 To work on oneself, to make clear that which confuses and depresses us, even if it entail the greatest pain—that is what is meant by being good.

Varnhagen, *Briefe,* 1877.

339.B. The Highest Good

339.B.1 On the way to the highest goal I must take my fellow-beings with me.

F. Adler, *Life and Destiny,* 1903, p. 82.

339.B.2 What is the highest good? To know that God is the Lord.

Apocrypha: Aristeas, 195.

339.B.3 To be true to the best—that is our vocation on earth.

M. Joseph, *Judaism as Creed and Life,* 1903, p. 75.

339.B.4 The highest good is not something visible, but that which is felt within the heart.

S. D. Luzzatto, letter to Jost, 1840.

339.B.5 The true good can find its home . . . only in the sovereign part of the soul, . . . the reasoning faculty.

Philo, *Virtues,* 35.

339.C. Good for Evil

339.C.1 We are God-fearing men, and it does not befit us to requite evil for evil, or to smite a fallen enemy. Let us heal his wounds.

Apocrypha: Asenath, ii.

339.C.2 What people has repaid love for hate, blessings for curses, . . . as much as did the Jews?

B. Heller, *Epistle to an Apostate,* 1951, p. 58.

339.C.3 In imitation of God, it is our duty not only to confer an act of kindness upon those who harm us, but to do it at the very moment we are wronged.

Lipkin. See GSS, 192.

339.C.4 You may prevent your foe from hurting you, but you must not injure him beyond the point of making him powerless to harm you.

I. Lipschütz, *Tzavaah,* 1861. q *JQRo,* iii. 474.

339.C.5 Requite good for evil, as God requites good for evil.

Meir. *Exod. R.,* 26.2. See *Matt.* 5.44, *Rom.* 12.21.

339.C.6 Him who pelts you with stones, you pelt with bread.

Proverb (Yiddish). BJS, #1276.

339.C.7 Blessed are they who pay good for good to the Lord, and good for evil to men.

Saadia, letter to an Egyptian community, 928. KTJ, 90. See Spinoza, *Ethics,* 1677, iv. Pr. 46.

340. GOSSIP

340.1 Go not up and down as a talebearer among thy people.

Bible: Lev., 19.16.

340.2 Where no wood is, the fire will go out; and where there is no whisperer, contention ceases.

Bible: Prov., 26.20. See 17.9.

340.3 If you hear an evil matter, bury it seven fathoms underground.

Apocrypha: Ahikar, 2.54.

340.4 Have you heard something? Let it die with you. Be of good courage: it will not burst you.

Apocrypha: Ben Sira, 19.10.

340.5 Be not like a fly, seeking sore spots; cover up your neighbor's flaws, and reveal them not to the world.

Eliezer b. Isaac, *Orhot Hayyim*, c. 1050.

340.6 God loves not talebearers even when they are right. . . . The talebearer is a cannibal.

q M. Ibn Ezra, *Shirat Yisrael*, (12C) 1924, p. 40.

340.7 Gossip is more hideous than capital crime.

Ishmael School. *Talmud: Arakin*, 15b.

340.8 A gossiper is like an infidel.

Jose b. Zimra. *Ibid.*

340.9 Gossip kills three: the speaker, the spoken of, and the listener.

Samuel b. Nahman. *Num. R.*, 19.2.

340.10 Of ten measures of gossip that came down to the world, women took nine.

Talmud: Kiddushin, 49b.

340.11 The gossiper stands in Syria and kills in Rome.

Talmud J: Peah, 1.1.

340.12 Gossip from pedlars and vermin from rags!

Yalta. *Talmud: Berakot*, 51b.

341. GOVERNMENT

341.1 It is not impracticable to have many leaders, . . . concurring in one counsel. . . . Why should not their administration be for a year or three? . . . Again, why should not their power be limited and regulated by laws?

I. Abravanel, *Commentary*, on *Deut.* 17.15. HPB, 221f.

341.2 What is the greatest achievement in ruling an empire? That the subjects should live continually in a state of peace, and justice be administered speedily in cases of dispute.

Apocrypha: Aristeas, 291.

341.3 The Government does nothing for nothing.

Bar Kappara. *Eccles. R.*, 11.1.1.

341.4 We must remember that the people do not belong to the government but that governments belong to the peoples.

Baruch, at U.N. Atomic Energy Commission, June 14, 1946.

341.5 Government is the art of the momentarily feasible, of . . . the least bad attainable, and not of the rationally most desirable.

Berenson, Feb. 17, 1944. *Rumor & Reflection*, 248.

341.6 Government . . . is the common enemy. All weapons are justifiable in the noble struggle . . . against this terrible curse.

Berkman, *Prison Memories of an Anarchist*, 1912, p. 71.

341.7 A government can be too strong, just as it can be too weak, and . . . people rush from one extreme to the other.

Blum, *For All Mankind*, (1941) 1946, p. 55.

341.8 To strengthen a weak government, we must reduce its power.

Boerne, *Fragmente & Aphorismen*, 1840, #42.

341.9 Governments are sails, the people is the wind, the state is the boat, and time is the sea.

Ibid., #194.

341.10 Governments perpetrate wrong more often out of cowardice than out of wantonness.

Ibid., #281.

341.11 Accountancy—that is government.

Brandeis, before House Committee on Interstate and Foreign Commerce, Jan. 30, 1914.

341.12 Government is not an exact science.

Brandeis, *Truax vs. Corrigan*, 1921.

341.13 I have not much faith in "good government." What we need is the development of the individual.

Brandeis, to A. Lief, April 16, 1934. LBG, 34.

341.14 The greatest of all evils is a weak government.

Disraeli, *Coningsby*, 1844.

341.15 A government of statesmen or of clerks? Of Humbug or of Humdrum?

Ibid., 2.4.

341.16 Government . . . is neither business, nor technology, nor applied science. It is the art of making men live together in peace and with reasonable happiness.

F. Frankfurter, *The Public and Its Government*, 1930, p. 160. *New Republic*, Oct. 31, 1928.

341.17 More and more government is conceived as the biggest organized social effort for dealing with social problems.

Frankfurter, *Law and Politics*, 1939, p. 4.

341.18 Pray for the welfare of the government, since but for the fear of it, men would swallow one another alive.

Hanania Sgan Kohanim. *Mishna: Abot*, 3.2.

341.19 Our lawgiver ... gave to his constitution the form of what . . . may be termed a "theocracy," placing all sovereignty and authority in the hands of God.

Josephus, *Against Apion*, ii. 16.

341.20 The "Theocracy" of Moses was not a government by priests, as opposed to kings; it was a government by God Himself, as opposed to the government by priests or kings.

*Stanley, *History of the Jewish Church*, (1862) 1896, i. 141.

341.21 Many writers fall into the error of defining this theocracy as a government by priests. . . . The very fact that . . . with the single exception of Eli, no priest was ever elected to the magistracy during the entire period of the Commonwealth, decidedly negatives any such interpretation.

Straus, *Origin of Republican Form*, (1885) 1926, p. 108f.

341.22 Nothing could have a greater future or a more beneficent role than the monarchy, if it could only make up its mind to become a social monarchy.

Lassalle, letter, Feb. 1864. q BRN, 134.

341.23 You can't run a government solely on a business basis.

H. H. Lehman.

341.24 Bureaucracy is the biggest eater and the biggest loafer that ever oppressed the sons of man.

Lubin. q ADL, 228.

341.25 Of cities, there are two kinds: the better enjoys a democratic government, which honors equality, and has law and justice for its rulers,—such a constitution is a hymn to God; the worse . . . is ochlocracy, mob-rule.

Philo, *Confusion of Tongues*, 23.

341.26 Every government other than the autocratic is powerless and incompetent. Autocracy and democracy are not antitheses which exclude each other; on the contrary, they can only become operative through union. It is only upon a democratic basis that autocratic rule can and

should rest; democracy is only justified where it has an autocratic superstructure.

Rathenau. q BRN, 230.

341.27 The ultimate aim of government is ... to free every man from fear, that he may live in all possible security. . . . In fact, the true aim of government is liberty.

Spinoza, *Theologico-Political Treatise*, 1670, ch 20.

341.28 Hell cries aloud: Bring me the two daughters whose motto is "Give, Give!" [*Prov.* 30.15], namely, Sectarianism and Government!

Ukba. *Talmud: Aboda Zara*, 17a.

341.29 Always respect the Government.

Yannai. *Talmud: Zebahim*, 102a.

342. GRACE

342.1 The Lord gives grace and glory.

Bible: Ps., 84.12.

342.2 To the humble He gives grace.

Bible: Prov., 3.34.

342.3 I bend the knee ... to every form of grace.

Chernihovsky, "Before Statue of Apollo," 1911, tr Snowman.

342.4 As in life, in song the highest
Good of all is simply grace.

Heine, *Jehuda Ben Halevi*, 1851, tr. M. Armour.

342.5 Grace without beauty is a magnet which draws mysteriously but firmly, a luster which does not dazzle but is salutary, a charm which does not startle but blesses.

Saphir, *Nachtschatten der Zeit und des Lebens*.

343. GRACE OF GOD

343.1 The Pharisaic position tried to hold the balance between man's duty to *strive* to earn pardon and his *inability* to attain it without God's gracious gift of it.

Abrahams, *Studies in Pharisaism & the Gospels*, 1917, i. 147.

343.2 Compassionate them that have no wealth of good works!

Apocrypha: II Esdras, 8.36.

343.3 If an account were kept of what we owe the Creator, no man would ever receive reward in the world to come. He will receive it only by divine grace.

Bahya, *Hobot HaLebabot*, 1040.

343.4 God said to Israel: If you see the merit of your fathers failing, or that of your mothers, come and cling to My grace.

Berekia. *Talmud J: Sanhedrin*, 10.1.

343.5 When we are worthy and have good deeds to our credit, God gives us our reward; and when we have nothing of our own, God blesses us for the sake of His love, for He is good.

Judah Halevi b. Shalom. *Midrash Tehillim* to *Ps.* 72.

343.6 Thou hast created me not from necessity but from grace.

Ibn Gabirol, *Royal Crown,* 11C.

343.7 Man has no claim upon God. Even Moses came before God only with an appeal for grace.

Johanan. *Deut. R.,* 2.1, on *Deut.* 3.23.

343.8 Even before God gave Israel the commandments, He had advanced them their rewards, as a double portion of manna on Fridays.

Jose b. Halafta. *Mekilta,* to *Exod.* 19.2.

343.9 There is for all mankind but one source of felicity—a gracious God.

Josephus, *Antiquities,* 4.8.2.

343.10 Thine is the love, O God, and
　　　Thine the grace,
　　That folds the sinner in its mild
　　　embrace:
　　Thine the forgiveness bridging
　　　o'er the space
　　'Twixt man's works and the
　　　task set by the King.

Nahmanides, tr Lucas, *Jewish Year,* 1898, p. 136.

343.11 God's creation was purely an act of grace.

Saadia, *Emunot VeDeot,* 3, Exordium. 933.

344. GRAMMAR

344.1 My grammar, 'tis of thee,
　　Sweet incongruity,
　　Of thee I sing.
　　I love each mood and tense,
　　Each freak of accidence,
　　Protect me from common sense,
　　Grammar, my king!

Goldberg, *The Wonder of Words,* 1938, p. 466f.

344.2 Grammar is to speech what salt is to food.

M. Ibn Ezra, *Shirat Yisrael,* (12C) 1924, p. 110.

345. GRATITUDE

345.1 There was a little city . . . and there came a great king against it. . . . Now there was found in it a poor man and wise, and he by his wisdom delivered the city; yet no man remembered that same poor man.

Bible: Eccles., 9.14f.

345.2 Is it not most shameful that, in requiting favors, man should be left behind by a dog?

Philo, *Decalogue,* 23.

345.3 The wine belongs to the owner and thanks are given the butler.

Proverb. q Raba. *Talmud: Baba Kamma,* 92b.

345.4 Give someone of your nuts, and you'll have the shells thrown at you.

Proverb (Yemenite). Moses Levi Nahum.

345.5 Ingratitude to man is ingratitude to God.

Samuel HaNagid, *Ben Mishlé,* 11C. #8.

346. GRAVE

346.1 Graves, they say, are warmed by
　　　glory;
　　Foolish words and empty story!

Heine, *Latest Poems: Epilogue,* 1853.

346.2 Little houses in a row,
　　Down a quiet lane;
　　Neither doors nor windows know,
　　Peace and darkness reign.
　　Though you cannot pay the rent,
　　You will dwell there with the best.
　　Where the weary, broken, spent,
　　Find eternal rest!

Peretz, *Sewing the Wedding Gown,* 1906. NOP, 126.

346.3 Each passing day brings you closer to the grave.

Proverb (Yiddish). BSJ, #964.

346.4 Man joins house to house, and at the end four ells suffice.

Saadia.

346.5 It is pleasant to find rest among one's ancestors.

Talmud J: Moed Katan, 2.4.

346.6 The grave levels all distinctions and makes the whole world kin.

Union Prayer Book, 1922, ii. 325.

347. GREATNESS

347.1 It is not the great that are wise.

Bible: Job, 32.9.

347.2 Greatness with the mob is inferiority with those who seek true rank.

Abulafia. *Shaare Tzedek,* 1295. q SMMP, 29; SMT, 152.

347.3 True greatness needs no setting. . . . True greatness must have the setting which befits it.

Anski, *Dybbuk,* 1918, Act 1.

347.4 There is no greatness that does not rest on true morality.

B. Auerbach, *Auf der Höhe*, 1865.

347.5 Greatness is the Creator's robe, and he who comes into His presence in this robe is thrown out.

Bahya, *Hobot HaLebabot*, 1040, 6.8.

347.6 Great men are but life-sized.

Beerbohm, *A Point To Be Remembered*, 1918. *And Even Now*, 149.

347.7 Greatness lies . . . in a strong will and a good heart.

Franzos, *Two Saviors*, 1870. *Jews of Barnow*, 126.

347.8 Greatness is so often a courteous synonym for great success.

Guedalla.

347.9 I know the great are small, as small as myself.

Herzl, *Diary*, June 11, 1900.

347.10 With the great who do not bear the burdens of the small, "the Lord will enter into judgment" [*Isa.* 3.14].

Isaac Nappaha. *Ruth R.*, Proem 6. Cf. *Deut. R.*, 1.10.

347.11 When the great sustain the small, "there is no breach and no outcry in our streets" [*Ps.* 144.14].

Johanan b. Nappaha. *Talmud J: Rosh Hashana*, 2.8.

347.12 A man becomes great not only because of his virtues but also because of his faults.

Klausner, *From Jesus to Paul*, 1944, p. 587.

347.13 There is exalted greatness in everything small.

Kook, *Orot HaKodesh*, 1938, p. 106. q ABJ, 154.

347.14 By your friends I gauge your wealth; by your enemies, your greatness.

Lazerov, *Enciklopedie fun Idishe Vitzen*, 1928, #442.

347.15 Bigness can become an expression of the heroic size of man himself as he comes to a new-found greatness.

D. Lilienthal, *Big Business: A New Era*, 1952, p. 204.

347.16 The serpent's downfall was according to his greatness.

Meir. *Gen. R.*, 19.1.

347.17 Before a man attains greatness he must descend to lowliness.

Nahman Bratzlav. q *Commentary*, Oct. 1951, p. 349.

347.18 Greatness flees from him who seeks it, and follows him who flees from it.

Samuel. *Talmud: Erubin*, 13b.

347.19 Many a man might have become great in later years if he had not in his younger years believed himself to be that already.

Sanders, *Citatenlexikon*, 1899, p. 297.

347.20 Happy the generation in which the greater defer to the lesser, and all the more so the lesser to the greater!

Talmud: Rosh Hashana, 25b.

347.21 Do not dissipate your powers in petty activities: you were fashioned for great things.

Ussishkin. q Schwartz, *Ussishkin Belgratov*, 5710, p. 102.

347.22 All greatness loves to be surprising.

Werfel, *Poems: Night Rain*, tr E. A. Snow.

347.23 Great men are instructive and attractive text-books, whose paragraphs are deeds.

I. M. Wise, "Moses," 1889. *Selected Writings*, 153.

348. GREECE

348.1 It has been found in writing, concerning the Spartans and the Jews, that they are brethren, of the stock of Abraham.

Apocrypha: I Macc., 12.21.

348.2 Hellas, why do you put your trust in mortal governors . . . ? Why do you proffer vain gifts to the dead and sacrifice to idols? Who put error in your heart?

Apocrypha: Sibyl, 3.545ff.

348.3 The Greeks' haughty kings, pioneers of evils to mankind.

Ibid., 3.552f.

348.4 Greece, not Palestine, is the Holy Land, and until humanity . . . discards its indifference to truth and its hatred for reason, . . . we shall witness . . . a continuous and progressive decay of our civilization.

Brandes, *Hellas*, 1926, p. 193.

348.5 Let the beauty of Greek dwell in the schools of Jews!

Hiyya b. Abba, Johanan, Simeon b. Gamaliel. *Talmud: Megilla*, 9b, play on word *Japheth* and *Genesis* 9.27. Cf. Bar Kappara. *Talmud J: Megilla*, 1.9.

348.6 Girls may be taught Greek: it is an ornament.

Johanan b. Nappaha. *Talmud J: Peah*, 1.1.

348.7 Let not the wisdom of the Greeks
   beguile thee,
   Which hath no fruit but only
   flowers.
Judah Halevi, *Selected Poems*, 16.

348.8 The Jews seek signs, the Greeks
seek wisdom.
New Testament: I Cor., 1.22.

349. GREED

349.1 Thou shalt not covet.
Bible: Exod., 20.14.

349.2 Woe to them that join house to
house, that lay field to field, till there be
no room, and ye dwell alone in the land.
Bible: Isa., 5.8.

349.3 Greed is the root of all sin.
Aboab, *Menorat HaMaor*, c. 1300, Introd.
to 1.

349.4 Lovers of money and fame dispatch on expeditions to the ends of the
earth and beyond the sea. . . . All these are
war-makers.
Philo, *Prosperity and Exile of Cain*, 34.

349.5 When the camel demanded horns,
they cut off his ears.
   Proverb. q Rab. *Talmud: Sanhedrin*,
106a.

349.6 A fly is greedy for a sore.
   Simeon b. Halafta. *Pesikta Kahana*, ch
3, p. 23b.

349.7 Avarice, ambition, lust, etc. are
species of madness.
Spinoza, *Ethics*, 1677, iv. Pr. 44, Note.

349.8 Who sets his eyes on what is not
his, loses also what is his.
Talmud: Sota, 9a.

349.9 What you have is not yours, why
want what you have not?
Talmud: Derek Eretz, 1.24.

349.10 To covet is to violate all the Ten
Commandments.
   Yakim. *Pesikta Rabbati*, ch 21, ed Fried-
mann, 107a.

350. GREETING

350.1 Be the first to greet everyone,
whatever his faith.
Asher b. Yehiel, *Hanhaga*, c. 1320.

350.2 On the Sabbath, the outgoing
Temple watch would greet the incoming
watch: May He who put His name on this
house, put among you love, brotherhood,
peace and friendship!
   Helbo. *Talmud: Berakot*, 12a.

350.3 He who does not return a greeting
is called a robber.
   Huna. *Talmud: Berakot*, 6b.

350.4 May He who suspends the earth
over nil, inscribe you for life on this day
of good will.
Maharil. q Agnon, *Days of Awe*, 26.

350.5 Meet everybody with a friendly
greeting.
   Mathia b. Heresh. *Mishna: Abot*, 4.15.

350.6 To welcome a fellow man is to
welcome the Shekina.
Mekilta, to *Exod*. 18.12.

350.7 If you greet one only because you
owe him money, you violate the law against
"usury of any word" [*Deut*. 23.20].
   Simeon b. Yohai. *Talmud: Baba Metzia*,
75b.

351. GRIEF

351.1 Would I had died for you, O Absalom, my son, my son!
Bible: II Sam., 19.1.

351.2 Grief is the agony of an instant;
the indulgence of grief the blunder of a
life.
Disraeli, *Vivian Grey*, 1827, 6.7.

351.3 It is only kindred griefs that draw
forth our tears, and each weeps really for
himself.
Heine, *Italy*, 1828.

351.4 From grief too great to banish
   Come songs, my lyric minions.
Heine, tr L. Untermeyer.

351.5 Everything that grows begins little
and becomes big, except grief: it starts
big and becomes little, till it disappears.
Ibn Gabirol, *Ethics*, 1045.

351.6 Joy has its friends, but grief its
loneliness.
R. Nathan, *A Cedar Box*, 1929, Sonnet 7.

351.7 One man's grief is another man's
joy.
   J. Steinberg, *Mishlé Yehoshua*, 1885.

351.8 To brood over our sorrow is to
embitter our grief.
Union Prayer Book, 1940, i. 74.

351.9 Not unavailing will be our grief,
if it send us back to serve and bless the living.
Ibid.

351.10 No grief in the presence of God.
Zohar, Gen., 163a.

352. GROTESQUE

352.1 Too many of today's artists have persuaded themselves that the grotesque is more expressive than the higher grace. It is always easier to caricature than to reveal, to shout than to sing, to pretend than to be true.

Guggenheimer, *Creative Vision*, 1950, p. 9.

353. GROWTH

353.1 The smallest shall become a thousand, and the least a mighty nation.

Bible: Isa., 60.21.

353.2 My stream became a river, and my river became a sea.

Apocrypha: Ben Sira, 24.31.

353.3 It is essential to abiding worthy results that the process be that of a gradual slow unfolding.

Brandeis, letter to J .W. Mack, June 3, 1925, ref. to Hebrew University. q LBG, 74.

353.4 There is danger in perpetual quiescence as well as in perpetual motion . . . a compromise must be found in a principle of growth.

Cardozo, *The Growth of the Law*, 1924, p. 17.

353.5 Who does not increase, decreases.

Hillel. *Mishna: Abot*, 1.13.

353.6 "Neither shalt thou set thee up a pillar, which the Lord thy God hateth" [*Deut*. 16.22]. Do not make, through custom and habit, even of a commandment a stationary, pillar-like fixture. In regard to the form and meaning of the precepts, man should not stand still, but proceed from strength to strength and from stage to stage.

Isaac of Vorki, as recorded by his son, Jacob David of Omshinov. *Niflaot Yitzhak*, ed Moses M. Walden, 1914, p. 20f.

353.7 Growth is coherence capable of moving itself.

Philo, *Allegorical Interpretation*, 2.7.

354. GRUMBLING

354.1 Refrain from grumbling; it may lead to other sins.

Eleazar HaKappar. *Talmud: Derek Eretz*, 1.15, 7.13.

354.2 This instinct for grumbling of the rough and stiff-necked but honorable John Bull is perhaps the bulwark of British greatness abroad and of British freedom at home.

Heine, *English Fragments,* 1828, ch 4.

355. HABIT

355.1 A silk thread begins as the flimsiest of things, a worm's mucus, yet how strong it is when doubled many times! . . . So it is with transgressions. They grow strong with persistence.

Bahya, *Hobot HaLebabot*, 1040, 7.7.

355.2 Habit is a hard mistress.

Boerne, *Der ewige Jude*, 1821.

355.3 Who stoops too often will remain bent.

Harrison, *Religion of a Modern Liberal*, 1931, p. 76.

355.4 A sin repeated seems permitted.

Huna. *Talmud: Yoma*, 86b.
Raba. *ibid.*, 87a.

355.5 Habit is master of all things.

Ibn Gabirol. q Ibn Tibbon, *Tzavaah*. AHE, 62.

355.6 Bad habits are easier to abandon today than tomorrow.

Lazerov, *Enciklopedie fun Idishe Vitzen*, 1928, #492.

355.7 We naturally like what we have been accustomed to. . . . This is one of the causes which prevent men from finding truth.

Maimonides, *Guide for the Perplexed*, 1190, 1.31.

355.8 Habit and character are closely interwoven, habit becoming, as it were, second nature.

Maimonides, *Shaaré HaMusar*. AHE, 105.

355.9 Who lives near a waterfall is scarcely disturbed by its roar.

Moscato, *Nefutzot Yehuda*, 1588, 1b. q BSJ, 205.

355.10 Only those accustomed to the sun can endure its glare.

Ibid., 87b.

355.11 Lot's wife . . . we may properly call Habit, a nature at variance with Truth. When one tries to lead it, it lags behind, looks round upon its ancient and customary ways, and remains among them like a lifeless pillar.

Philo, *On Drunkenness*, 40.

355.12 When a peasant becomes king, he does not take the basket off his shoulder.

Proverb. q Abayé. *Talmud: Megilla*, 7b.

355.13 He who is inured to pain bears it patiently.
Zohar, Exod., 2b.

356. HAIR

356.1 Absalom gloried in his hair, so he was hanged by his hair.
Mishna: Sota, 1.8.

356.2 The first gray hair is a summons from the Angel of Death.
Proverb (Yiddish). YFS, i. 416.

356.3 The Holy One plaited Eve's hair, then brought her to Adam.
Simeon b. Menasya. *Talmud: Erubin,* 18a. *Nidda,* 45b.

356.4 A woman who exposes her hair for self-adornment brings poverty to her house, renders her children of no account, and maintains an evil spirit in her home.
Zohar, Num., 125b–126a.

357. HALF

357.1 The half was not told me.
Bible: I Kings, 10.7.

357.2 As the twilight is more eerie than complete darkness, so a half education is more dangerous than absolute ignorance.
Franzos, *Shylock of Barnow,* 1873. *Jews of Barnow,* 63.

357.3 They do not grant half favors in Heaven.
Talmud: Yoma, 69b.

358. HAND

358.1 His hand shall be against every man, and every man's hand against him.
Bible: Gen., 16.12.

358.2 The hands are the hands of Esau.
Ibid., 27.22.

358.3 O hands, mild, fair-fingered, worn with toil!
Apocalypse of Sedrach, 11.

358.4 Let not your hand be stretched out to take, and closed at the time of giving back.
Apocrypha: Ben Sira, 4.31.

358.5 The world is full of wonderful sights and great mysteries, but one small hand before our eyes obstructs their view.
Baal Shem. q Nahman Bratzlav, *Likkuté Moharan,* 1936, 235.

358.6 A beautiful hand is an excellent thing in woman; it is a charm that never palls. . . . The expression of the hand is inexhaustible; and when the eyes we may have worshiped no longer flash or sparkle,

. . . the immortal hand, defying alike time and care, still vanquishes . . . and small, soft, and fair, by an airy attitude, a gentle pressure, or a new ring, renews with untiring grace the spell that bound our enamored and adoring youth!
Disraeli, *Henrietta Temple,* 1837.

358.7 It was a lovely hand, not that of a young girl, who, half lamb and half rose, has only thoughtless, vegetable-animal hands—this hand, on the contrary, had something spiritual in it, . . . like the hands of handsome human beings who are highly refined and accomplished, or who have greatly suffered.
Heine, *Journey from Munich to Genoa,* 1828, ch 15.

358.8 A beautiful hand adorns the whole person.
Heine, *Der Rabbi von Bacharach,* 1840, ch 2.

358.9 One hand washes the other . . . or both stay dirty.
Martin, *The Landsmen,* 1952, p. 65.

358.10 Our hands are tied and we are reproached for not using them.
M. Mendelssohn, Pref. to *Vindiciae Judaeorum,* 1782.

358.11 Let not your left hand know what your right hand does.
New Testament: Matt., 6.3.

358.12 Who lifts a hand against another, even if he does not strike him, is called a wicked man.
Simeon b. Lakish. *Talmud: Sanhedrin,* 58b.

359. HAPPINESS

359.1 Pronounce no man happy before his death, for by his latter end shall a man be known.
Apocrypha: Ben Sira, 11.28.

359.2 This, too, is a virtue: to be happy.
Boerne, *Fragmente & Aphorismen,* 1840, #277.

359.3 Man is born for happiness.
J. Frank, 18C. See HMH, 30.

359.4 We're born to be happy, all of us.
Alfred Sutro, *The Perfect Lover,* Act 2.

359.5 The happiness we owe to a lie is not true happiness.
Heine, *Norderney,* 1826.

359.6 I desire not happiness if it be an island in a sea of misery.
Herzl, *Solon in Lydia,* 1900.

359.7 Happiness is a perfume which you cannot pour on others without getting a few drops on yourself.
Mann, *In Quest of the Bluebird*, 1938, p. 96.

359.8 The best way to attain happiness is not to seek it.
Montefiore, *Liberal Judaism*, 1903, p. 41.

359.9 The foolish man seeks happiness in the distance.
Oppenheim, "The Wise." (*War and Laughter*, 1916, p. 77).

359.10 It is impossible for man, who is bound up in a mortal body, to be entirely and altogether happy.
Philo, *Change of Names*, 4.

359.11 To be able to live in strict accord with nature is what the men of old have defined as the end of happiness.
Philo, *Noah's Planting*, 12.

359.12 Knowledge of Him is the consummation of happiness.
Philo, *Special Laws*, i. 63.

359.13 Happiness and life are two different things; and it's no wonder that men came to ascribe bliss to the dead alone.
F. Rosenzweig, letter to his mother, Apr. 5, 1918. GFR 67.

359.14 Bliss *is* virtue, not its reward.
Spinoza, *Ethics*, 1677, v. Pr 42.

359.15 What is happiness other than the grace of being permitted to unfold to their fullest bloom all the spiritual powers planted within us.
Werfel, *Between Heaven and Earth*, 1944, p. 27.

360. HARMONY

360.1 Judaism from its inception always . . . demanded harmony between thought, feeling and deed.
Augsburg Synod, Declaration, July 17, 1871.

360.2 The aim and value of the duties of the heart consist in securing the equal cooperation of body and soul in the service of God, that heart, tongue and other bodily organs testify alike, support and confirm, not contradict and differ from, each other. This harmony is called in Scripture wholeheartedness.
Bahya, *Hobot HaLebabot*, 1040, Introduction.

360.3 It is man's duty to forge a oneness out of the manifoldness of his soul.
H. Kohn, *Die politische Idee des Judentums*, 1924. LR 123.

361. HARVEST

361.1 Thou crownest the year with Thy goodness.
Bible: Ps., 65.12.

361.2 The hills are girded with joy.
Ibid., 65.13.

361.3 They that sow in tears shall reap in joy.
Ibid., 126.5.

361.4 Not all that grows up high
And blossoms fair is homeward brought to store.
Fichman, "Harvest," 1941 (*Pe-at Sadeh*, 1944, p. 8), tr D. Vardi. *Israel Miscellany*, i. 66.

361.5 In empty barns when the harvests fail
You may find some forgotten grain.
S. J. Imber, *When Harvests Fail*. LGP, 251.

362. HASID

362.1 He who hears himself cursed and remains silent is a hasid.
Alexandri. *Midrash Tehillim*, 16.11.

362.2 Hasidim . . . willingly offered themselves for the Law.
Apocrypha: I Macc., 2.42.

362.3 The love of service burns in the hasid's heart, and he is glad to fulfil the will of his Creator.
Eleazar b. Judah, *Rokeah, Hasidut*, 13C. See SMT, 95.

362.4 It may be proper to call me a kosher Jew, but as to being a hasid, a saint —I haven't reached that stage yet.
Elijah Gaon. q Glenn, *Israel Salanter*, 31.

362.5 The true hasid is he who devotes himself in love entirely to the service of the Higher Power, who . . . does not withdraw from the world, but lives in it, with it, and for it.
S. R. Hirsch, *Nineteen Letters*, (1836), #15, p. 149.

362.6 He who is very strict with himself, and bends slightly from the middle course, is called hasid.
Maimonides, *Yad: Deot*, 1180, 1.5.

362.7 Already in the *Psalms* the word, *hasidim*, is used—side by side with the much more common *tzaddikim*, "righteous"—as a party name for those who feel themselves to be the true Church of God, the poor and oppressed.

*Meyer, *Ursprung u. Anfänge d. Christentums,* 1921, ii. 41f. q Toynbee, *Stady of History,* v. 543.

362.8 Whenever Jews envisaged the Holy One, they were hasidim.
Midrash Tehillim, 149.1.

362.9 Not all Hasidim are hasidim.
Peretz, *Torah,* 1906. *Alle Verk,* vi. 75.

362.10 A hasid is one who all his life devotes himself to one particular religious commandment.
Saadia, *Emunot VeDeot,* 933. q SMT, 97.

363. HASTE

363.1 The race is not to the swift.
Bible: Eccles., 9.11.

363.2 Be not in a hurry, like the almond, first to blossom and last to ripen. Be rather like the mulberry, last to blossom and first to ripen.
Apocrypha: Ahikar, 2.7.

363.3 There is one that toils and labors and runs, and is so much more behind.
Apocrypha: Ben Sira, 11.11.

363.4 Notwithstanding Solomon, in a race speed must win.
Disraeli, (Sidonia in) *Coningsby,* 1844.

363.5 Only a genius or a fool will rush into writing.
q M. Ibn Ezra, *Shirat Yisrael,* (12C) 1924, p. 77.

363.6 Patience gives peace, haste regret.
Ibn Gabirol, *Mibhar HaPeninim,* c. 1050, #114.

363.7 Who rushes love rushes hate.
Ibn Verga, *Shebet Yehuda,* 1550.

363.8 Levi Yitzhok asked a man, who seemed to be in a great hurry, why he rushed so. "I am in pursuit of my livelihood," replied the man. "And how do you know," asked the rabbi, "that your livelihood runs ahead of you? May be it is behind you, and what you need is to pause till it overtakes you."
Kahana, *Sefer HaHasidut,* 1922, p. 237.

363.9 Who acts in haste, falls into debt.
Nahman Bratzlav, *Sefer HaMiddot, Mammon,* 1821.

363.10 What is rapid is not always superior.
Philo, *Noah's Work as a Planter,* 39.

363.11 Quickly got, quickly lost.
Proverb (Yiddish). BJS, #542.

363.12 Any plan formulated in a hurry is foolish.
Rashi, *Commentary,* to *Job* 5.13.

363.13 Who rushes is often late.
Zabara, *Sefer Shaashuim,* 13C, ch 8, ed Davidson, 81.

363.14 Follow the wise tailor, who studies his measures carefully before cutting his cloth, for there is no good in haste.
Ibid., p. 86.

364. HATRED

364.1 Thou shalt not hate thy brother in thy heart.
Bible: Lev., 19.17.

364.2 Hatred stirs up strifes.
Bible: Prov., 10.12.

364.3 Who bears hatred is irritable and prematurely old.
B. Auerbach, *On the Heights,* 1865.

364.4 If you must hate, if hatred is the leaven of your life, which alone can give flavor, then hate what should be hated: falsehood, violence, selfishness.
Boerne, *Der ewige Jude,* 1821.

364.5 An hour spent in hate is an eternity withdrawn from love.
Boerne *Fragmente & Aphorismen,* #191.

364.6 May no hatred of us rise in any heart, and no hatred of any man in our heart.
Eleazar. *Talmud J: Berakot,* 4.2.

364.7 Hate ruins the very savor of food, the peace of sleep, and all reverence in the soul.
Eleazar b. Judah, *Rokeah,* 13C.

364.8 A hater is like a murderer.
Eliezer. *Talmud: Tosefta Derek Eretz,* 6.13.

364.9 Hatred and envy caused the fall of angels.
Heine, *Romantic School,* 1833, ii. ch 3.

364.10 Who sows hatred reaps remorse.
Ibn Gabirol, *Mibhar HaPeninim,* c. 1050, #616.

364.11 Hate is a greater tie than love. The person we hate occupies our mind far more than the person we love.
Klatzkin, *In Praise of Wisdom,* 1943, p. 305.

364.12 Hatred increases in proportion to the amount of shared convictions and interests.
Koestler, *Arrow in the Blue,* 1952, p. 257.

364.13 You cannot conquer the world for the God of love by a jihad of hate.
Lazaron, *Common Ground*, 1938, p. 317.

364.14 To hate a man is to hate his Creator.
Pesikta Zutarti, to Num. 10.35, ed Buber, 100a.

364.15 Hatred upsets the social order.
Simeon b. Eleazar. *Talmud: Sanhedrin*, 105b.
Simeon b. Yohai. *Gen. R.*, 55.8.

364.16 Hatred can never be good.
Spinoza, *Ethics*, 1677, iv. Pr 45.

364.17 The simple cunning of the wasp, the bee,
Is how to sting, and sting, and still be free.
The poisons human beings generate
Fix them forever to the things they hate.
Stampfer, *Jerusalem Has Many Faces*, 1950, p. 88.

364.18 Unprovoked hatred is worse than the three cardinal sins.
Talmud: Yoma, 9b.

364.19 The terrible thing about hatred is that he who is seized with it as a rule does not wish to be rid of it.
Valentin, *Antisemitism*, 1936, p. 306.

365. HEAD

365.1 They shall be the head and not the tail.
Apocrypha: Jubilees, 1.16.

365.2 In my head I carry my jewelry all.
Heine, *Germany: A Winter Tale*, 1844, ch 2.

365.3 The body follows the head.
Proverb, q Johanan b. Nuri. *T: Erubin*, 41a.

365.4 If the head is gone, what good is the body?
Simlai. *Pesikta de R. Kahana*, .ch 16, p. 112b.

366. HEALING

366.1 God created medicines out of the earth, and let not a discerning man reject them.
Apocrypha: Ben Sira, 38.4.

366.2 Proclaim the healing of the earth!
Apocrypha: Enoch, 10.7.

366.3 The cure is hard if the sickness is old.
Morawczyk, *Minha Hadasha*, 1576, ch 4.

366.4 The pleasure of recovery has in it a touch of the joy of resurrection.
Twerski, *Hegyonot. HaPoel HaTzair*, 1951, #38, p. 19.

367. HEALTH

367.1 There is no wealth like health.
Apocrypha: Ben Sira, 30.16.

367.2 There are thousands of diseases, but only one health.
Boerne, *Dramaturgische Blätter: Aphorismen*, 2.

367.3 Trust not your health: many lay down never to rise again.
Eliezer b. Isaac, *Orhot Hayyim*, c. 1050.

367.4 Three, if drawn out, prolong life: praying, eating, easing.
Judah b. Ezekiel. *Talmud: Berakot*, 54b.

367.5 The well-being of the soul can be obtained only after that of the body has been secured.
Maimonides, *Guide for the Perplexed*, 1190, 3.27.

367.6 Cold water for the eyes in the morning and hot water for the limbs at night are better than all the salves in the world.
Samuel. *Talmud: Sabbath*, 108b.

367.7 Up to forty, food; after forty, drink.
Ibid., 152a.

367.8 Drink plenty of water with your meals.
Talmud: Berakot, 40a.

367.9 Too much sitting aggravates hemorrhoids; too much standing injures the heart; too much walking hurts the eyes. Hence, divide your time between the three.
Talmud: Ketubot, 111b.

367.10 Three things sap one's strength: worry, travel, and sin.
Talmud: Gittin, 70a.

368. HEARING

368.1 An intelligent man will not only never say something stupid, he will also never listen to something stupid.
Boerne, *Fragmente & Aphorismen*, 1840, #200.

368.2 Who hears badly answers badly.
Bonsenyor, *Dichos y Sentencias*, 14C, #294.

368.3 Why are fingers fashioned like

pegs? So that if a man hears an unworthy thing, he may plug his ears.

Eleazar b. Pedat. *Talmud: Ketubot*, 5b.

368.4 The wise reports what he saw, the fool what he heard.

Hasdai, *Ben HaMelek VeHaNazir*, c. 1230, ch 7.

368.5 Take care to hear more than to speak.

M. Ibn Ezra, *Shirat Yisrael*, (12C) 1924, p. 132. See *NT: James*, 1.19.

368.6 Hearing is not like seeing.

Mekilta, to *Exod.*, 19.9.

369. HEART

369.A. Apothegms

369.A.1 My son, give me your heart.

Bible: Prov., 23.26.

369.A.2 Let us lift our heart with our hands to God in heaven.

Bible: Lam., 3.41.

369.A.3 The people's heart is the foundation on which the land will be built.

Ahad HaAm, "Lo Zu HaDerek." *HaMelitz*, March 15, 1889. *Al Parashat Derakim*, 1921, i. 7.

369.A.4 Any wound, only not a heart wound.

Apocrypha: Ben Sira, 25.13.

369.A.5 The heaviness of the heart breaks strength.

Ibid., 38.18.

369.A.6 You must sow hearts, if you wish to reap hearts.

Boerne, *Ueber den Umgang mit Menschen*, 1824.

369.A.7 Their hearts are in the right place.

Disraeli, *Infernal Marriage*, 1828, 1.1.

369.A.8 The highest good is a good heart, the greatest evil an evil heart.

Eleazar b. Arak. *Mishna: Abot*, 2.9.

369.A.9 Even the poorest heart has some jewel on which it hangs.

Franzos, *Die Juden von Barnow*, 1877.

369.A.10 My heart is like the ocean,
With tempest, ebb and flow,
And many pearls full precious
Lie in its depths below.

Heine, *Return Home*, 1823, #8.

369.A.11 A good heart includes all other virtues.

Johanan b. Zakkai. *Mishna: Abot*, 2.9.

369.A.12 The Holy One (Rashi: The Merciful) wants the heart.

Judah b. Ezekiel. *Talmud: Sanhedrin*, 106b.

369.A.13 For Thy songs, O God, my heart is a harp.

Judah Halevi. q Magnus, *Jewish Portraits*, 14.

369.A.14 It is the same whether a man offers much or little, provided his heart is directed to Heaven.

Mishna: Menahot, 13.11.

369.A.15 Each thing has a heart, and the world as a whole has a heart.

Nahman Bratzlav, *Tale of the Seven Beggars*. See Ansky, *Dybbuk*, Act 3.

369.A.16 The life of our heart alone is true and real.

Varnhagen. q KRV, 80.

369.B. The Great Heart

369.B.1 God gave Solomon wisdom . . . and largeness of heart.

Bible: 1 Kings, 5.9.

369.B.2 Happy the man . . . in whose heart are the highways.

Bible: Ps., 84.6.

369.B.3 Keep your heart, for out of it are the issues of life.

Bible: Prov., 4.23.

369.B.4 He has set the world in their heart.

Bible: Eccles., 3.11.

369.B.5 I build my hospital in the human heart.

*Cumberland, (Sheva in) *The Jew*, 1793.

369.B.6 When the heart is narrow, the tongue is wide.

Ibn Gabirol, *Mibhar HaPeninim*, c. 1050, #329.

369.C. The Knowing Heart

369.C.1 These words . . . shall be upon thy heart.

Bible: Deut., 6.6.

369.C.2 Give thy servant an understanding heart.

Bible: 1 Kings, 3.9.

369.C.3 I will give them a heart to know Me.

Bible: Jer., 24.7. See 31.33.

369.C.4 The heart knows its own bitterness, and with its joy no stranger can intermeddle.

Bible: Prov., 14.10.

171

369.C.5 May He give you an open heart for His law.
Apocrypha: II Macc., 1.4.

369.C.6 The heart is the tabernacle of the human intellect.
Maimonides, *Shaaré HaMusar. Responsa*, ii. 39c.

369.C.7 One heart is mirror to another.
Proverb (Yiddish). BJS, #1084.

369.C.8 The heart is like a clock.
Ibid., #1086.

369.C.9 The heart sees better than the eye.
Proverb (Yiddish). YFS, i. 416.

369.C.10 I trust your wisdom only when it comes from the heart, your goodness when it comes from the mind.
Schnitzler, *Buch der Sprüche & Bedenken*, 1927, p. 230.

369.C.11 The heart knows whether it is baling or baleful.
Seder Eliyahu Rabbah, ch 21 (23), ed Friedmann, 121.
Simeon b. Lakish. *Talmud: Sanhedrin*, 26a.

369.D. The Feeling Heart

369.D.1 I will take away the stony heart . . . and I will give you a heart of flesh.
Bible: Ezek., 36.26. Cf *Zech.*, 7.12.

369.D.2 Thou hast given us a heart that we may fear Thee and call upon Thy name.
Apocrypha: Baruch, 3.7.

369.D.3 Oh, ye hard-hearted, ye shall find no peace.
Apocrypha: Enoch, 5.4.

369.D.4 Of steel and iron, cold and hard and dumb,
Forge for yourself a heart, O man, and come!
Bialik, "In the Slaughter Town," 1904. LGP, 30.

369.D.5 Words which come from the heart enter the heart.
q M. Ibn Ezra, *Shirat Yisrael*, (12C) 1924, p. 156.

369.D.6 Out of the abundance of the heart the mouth speaks.
New Testament: Matt., 12.34.

369.D.7 Hearts starve as well as bodies:
give us
Bread, but give us roses!
J. Oppenheim, "Bread and Roses" (*Poems of Justice*, ed. T. C. Clark, 1929, p. 125).

369.D.8 Each heart has its own smart.
Proverb (Yiddish). BJS, #1083.

369.D.9 Not each laughing heart is joyful.
Ibid., #1088.

369.D.10 When the heart is full, the eyes overflow.
Sholom Aleichem, *Dos Groise Gevins*, 1895.

369.D.11 The heart, especially the Jewish heart, is a fiddle: you pull the strings, and out come songs, mostly plaintive.
Sholom Aleichem, *Stempenyu*, 1888.

369.D.12 The heart is the great clock, showing weal and woe.
Varnhagen, *Briefe*, 1877.

369.E. The Wicked Heart

369.E.1 The heart is deceitful above all things, and very weak.
Bible: Jer., 17.9.

369.E.2 Associate not with the double-hearted.
Apocrypha: Enoch, 91.4.

369.E.3 Out of the heart proceed evil thoughts, murders, adulteries.
New Testament: Matt., 15.19.

369.F. The Guiding Heart

369.F.1 A man's heart changes his countenance, for good or ill.
Apocrypha: Ben Sira, 13.25. See *Gen. R.*, 73.12.

369.F.2 It is not the mind, it is the heart that makes free.
Boerne, *Der ewige Jude*, 1821.

369.F.3 All is governed by the heart's desire.
Emden, *Sheelat Yaabetz*, 1739–59, ii. 8a.

369.F.4 To the place my heart loves, my feet carry me.
Hillel. *Tosefta: Sukka*, 4.3.

369.F.5 The evil of the eye depends on the evil of the heart.
A. Ibn Ezra, *Yesod Mora*, 1158, ch 7, ed 1840, p. 31.

369.F.6 The heart is king. . . . Wherever it leads, the organs follow.
M. H. Luzzatto, *Mesillat Yesharim*, 1740, ch 16.

369.F.7 The heart determines all action.
Sefer Hasidim, 13C, #643, p. 173.

369.F.8 The eyes follow the heart, not the heart the eyes, for there are blind people who commit all the abominations in the world.

Sifré, Numbers, #115.

369.G. Searching of Heart

369.G.1 There were great searchings of heart.

Bible: Judg., 5.16.

369.G.2 Create in me a clean heart, O God!

Bible: Ps., 51.12.

369.G.3 A broken and a contrite heart, O God, Thou wilt not despise.

Ibid., 51.19. See *Jer.,* 17.10.

369.G.4 There was an earthquake in my heart.

U. Z. Greenberg, *Maasé BiYerushalmi Kadmon.*

369.G.5 It is absurd that a man should be forbidden to enter the Temple save after washing his body . . . and yet attempt to sacrifice and pray with a heart still polluted and disordered.

Philo, *Unchangeableness of God,* 2.

369.G.6 Purify our hearts that we may serve Thee in truth.

Sabbath prayer. *DPB,* ed Singer, 139; *UPB,* 1940, i. 58.

369.G.7 In me the cave-man clasps the seer,
And garlanded Apollo goes
Chanting to Abraham's deaf ear.
In me the tiger sniffs the rose.
Look in my heart, kind friends, and tremble,
Since there your elements assemble.

Sassoon, *The Heart's Journey,* 1928, #8, p. 14.

369.G.8 The sea at times gives up its pearls
When tempests rock its deep abyss;
The heart, when stirred, likewise unfurls
Its youthful dreams, its secret bliss.

J. Steinberg, "The Heart." FTH, 115.

369.H. The Whole Heart

369.H.1 Be whole-hearted.

Bible: Gen., 17.1.

369.H.2 I was single-hearted toward Him.

Bible: II Sam., 22.24.

369.H.3 I will give them one heart.

Bible: Ezek., 11.19.

369.H.4 Make one my heart to fear Thy name.

Bible: Ps., 86.11.

369.H.5 Let not your heart be divided regarding God.

Sifré, #32, to *Deut.* 6.5, ed Friedmann, 73a.

369.H.6 There is nothing so whole as a broken heart.

q Stampfer. *Reconstructionist,* June 13, 1952, p. 29.

369.H.7 Unite our hearts to love and revere Thee!

Union Prayer Book, 1940, i. 118. *DPB,* ed Singer, 40.

370. HEATHEN

370.1 They have no heart.

Apocrypha: Jubilees, 22.18.

370.2 The heathen spirit is wingless. It cannot lift itself to heights from which the totality of being is visible, and it therefore loses itself in details. It lacks fantasy for that which it cannot apprehend with the senses; it must hold the thing in its hand.

Asch, *What I Believe,* 1941, p. 157.

370.3 Who caters to a heathen causes exile for his children.

Hezekiah b. Hiyya. *Talmud: Sanhedrin,* 104a.

370.4 The country and glassware of heathens are impure.

Jose b. Joezer, Jose b. Johanan. *Talmud: Sabbath,* 15a.

370.5 Praised be Thou . . . who hast not made me a heathen.

Judah b. Ilai. *Tosefta: Berakot,* 7.18. *Talmud: Menahot,* 43b. *DPB,* ed Singer, 5.

371. HEAVEN

371.1 The heavens declare the glory of God.

Bible: Ps., 19.2.

371.2 We build a heaven, knowing very well
The bricks were baked in hell.

Auslander, "And Jacob Wrestled" (*Harper's Magazine,* Jan. 1935). *No Traveller Returns,* 113.

371.3 The heavens are always present.

Bahya, *Hobot HaLebabot,* 1040, 2.5.

371.4 Back, my soul, into thy nest;
Earth is not for thee;

Still in heaven find thy rest,
There thou canst be free.

Judah Halevi, tr M. Simon. *JQRo*, xvi. 206.

371.5 Why should I want Heaven, if there's slavery there! All of you . . . are mechanical bodies, unable to act of your own accord.

Mendelé (Ashmedai in) *Di Kliatshé*, 1873, ch 20.

371.6 Ye skies, how fair the paths about your spaces!
There freedom shines forever like a star!

Morpurgo, "Song," 1867, tr Salaman, *Songs of Many Days*, 47.

371.7 God bent the eyes of all other creatures downwards, . . . but the eyes of man He set high, that he may behold heaven.

Philo, *Noah's Planting*, 4. See Plato, *Timaeus*, 90.

371.8 All things on earth are copies of what is in heaven.

Zohar, Exod., 15b.

372. HEBRAISM and HELLENISM

372.1 Hebraism and Hellenism,—between these two points of influence moves our world. . . . The final aim of both . . . is no doubt the same: Man's perfection and salvation.

Arnold, Culture and Anarchy, 1869, p. 110.

372.2 The uppermost idea with Hellenism is to see things as they really are; the uppermost idea with Hebraism is conduct and obedience.

Ibid., 111f.

372.3 Whereas the prophets and scribes . . . made the belief in one universal God and the observance of the law of righteousness part of the life of the Jewish people, the Hellenic philosophers and poets did not affect the ideas of the main body of their fellows.

Bentwich, *Hellenism*, 1919, p. 59f.

372.4 The Hellenes paid homage first and foremost to external beauty and physical strength; the Judeans to inner beauty and spiritual heroism.

Dubnow, *Jewish History*, 1903, p. 77.

372.5 Hellenism and Judaism represent different streams of life, and they need not therefore be antagonistic to each other. Are

they not, perhaps, the two arms of humanity aspiring to eternity, stretched toward the height, each in its own direction?

Ehrenpreis, *The Soul of the East*, 1928, p. 37.

372.6 There are two races in every country, the Judeo-Christians and the Graeco-Romans. . . . There are some people for whom success, power and riches carry their own justification. . . . Then there are others . . . who hunger and thirst after righteousness, for whom . . . action is subordinate to morals.

Ferrero, Peace and War, 1933, p. 200ff.

372.7 Creation, liberty: two ideas foreign to Greek thought which are the substance of Jewish thought. God, creator and free, creates man in His image; and man . . . in his turn freely creates.

Fleg, *Why I Am a Jew*, 1929, p. 59.

372.8 All the wonders of the Greek civilization heaped together are less wonderful than the single Book of Psalms. . . . Greece had . . . all that this world could give her; but the flowers of Paradise . . . blossomed in Palestine alone.

Gladstone, Place of Ancient Greece, 1865.

372.9 All men are either Jews or Greeks: either they are driven by ascetic, image-hating, spiritualizing impulses, or they are cheerful, taking pride in self-government, realistic.

Heine, *Reisebilder: Norderney*, 1826.

372.10 Greco-Oriental spirituality is self-centered and individualistic. . . . Hebraism, on the other hand, holds salvation, like life itself, to be communal, and sees man's self-transcending service to fellow-man as the true service of God. Yet such is the ultimate paradox of life, that the self-absorption of the Buddhist or Yogi culminates in self-annihilation, while the sacrificial service enjoined by prophet and rabbi turns out to be the way toward personal fulfilment.

Herberg, *Judaism and Modern Man*, 1951, p. 55.

372.11 The Greeks stressed the holiness of beauty; the Jews emphasized the beauty of holiness.

E. G. Hirsch, sermon. q GSS, 7.

372.12 The spirit of science is still Greek in its origin, and the passion for justice is still Hebrew, and these sum up civilization. . . . The two together make a progressive humanity possible.

Husik, *Philosophical Essays*, 1952, p. 19.

372.13 While the Greek developed the plastic sense to perfection, the Jew did not see so much as he heard; he lived in time. His senses did not encircle the contours; rather were they intent on the inner flow. His organ was the ear.

H. Kohn, *Idea of Nationalism*, 1944, p. 31.

372.14 For the Greek only the defined and finite were beautiful and perfect . . . thus the most perfect figure was the circle. . . . In Greek philosophy the Jew Philo was the first to place a higher value on the infinite than on the proportionate finite.

Ibid., 32.

372.15 The wisdom of the Greeks, when compared to that of the Jews, is absolutely bestial; for apart from God there can be no wisdom, not any understanding and insight.

*Luther. q Chamberlain, *Foundations*, ii. 278.

372.16 Alien and antagonistic to Judaism and Christianity alike is the spirit of Athens, which breathes a selfish and swaggering morality, and in general practices the cult of the beautiful, the big, the showy in place of the good, the true, the real.

S. D. Luzzatto, letter to S. Rosenthal, Aug. 13, 1839.

372.17 Man is endowed with heart and mind . . . Judaism lay primary stress on the heart, Atticism on the mind.

S. D. Luzzatto, letter to E. Lolli, Jan. 21, 1864.

372.18 When Socrates and Plato began to speak of truth and justice, they were no longer Greeks, but Jews.

*Nietzsche. q Baeck, *Judaism and Ethics*, 22.

372.19 If the delicacy of modern thought is a Greek contribution, its seriousness is a heritage from Judaea.

Oko. *Menorah Journal*, 1919, v. 126f.

372.20 The quest for righteousness is oriental, the quest for knowledge occidental. . . . Modern civilization is the outcome of these two great movements of the mind of man, who today is ruled in heart and head by Israel and by Greece.

*Osler, address, London, April 27, 1914.

372.21 The Greek grasped the present moment, and was the artist; the Jew wor-

shipped the timeless spirit, and was the prophet.

I. M. Wise, "The Wandering Jew," 1877. *Selected Writings*, 185.

373. HEBREW

373.1 Hebrew is our very flesh and blood, and each encounter with it is a fixture of our soul.

Bialik. q OMB, 46f.

373.2 The Hebrew language has about thirty words to express justice and humanity, but not a single one for slave.

J. S. Bloch, 1882. *My Reminiscences*, 35.

373.3 Thirty years had passed above my head
Ere the language of my folk I learned.
Then at last I was redeemed from deafness.

Brod. q LR, 191.

373.4 The tongue of God, the tongue of angels, the tongue of the prophets.

*Buxtorf. q White, *Warfare of Science*, 1898, ii. 185.

373.5 Our Hebrew language is called the Holy Tongue because the Holy One brought it into being. . . . Its words are not accidental, but the result of wondrous design and sublime wisdom, based on profound mysteries and meanings.

J. S. Delmedigo, *Koah HaShem*, 1631.

373.6 The language in which God, angels and men spoke together, not through the ambiguous murmur of a Castilian spring, Typhonian cave or Dorian wood, but as friends talk face to face.

*Reuchlin, *De Merifico Verbo*, 1494. q LJG, 145.

373.7 Hebrew is God's language, in which He gave us the Torah.

Sofer, *Elé Dibré HaBerit*, 1819.

373.8 The recollection that it was the Hebrew language in which the Revelation was given, in which the Prophets expressed their high ideals, in which generations of our fathers breathed forth their suffering and joys, makes this language a holy one for us.

L. Ginzberg, *Students, Scholars and Saints*, 1928, p. 204.

373.9 Hebrew is the original tongue of mankind.

Dunash Ibn Tamim, *Commentary* to *Sefer Yetzira*, 956. See Gesner, *Mithridates*, 16C; White, *Warfare of Science with Theology*, 1898, ii. 181.

373.10 The whole of antiquity affirms that Hebrew . . . was the beginning of all human speech.

*Jerome. q White, *Warfare of Science with Theology*, ii. 175.

373.11 One cannot understand Israel without understanding Hebrew.

Fleg, *Why I Am a Jew*, 1929, p. 48.

373.12 Hebrew is the historical chain which links all the dispersed parts of our people into one national body. If we drive it out of Jewish communal life in Germany . . . we destroy our national unity, and become strangers to all other Jews.

Z. Frankel, letter to A. Geiger, 1845.

373.13 The language of our fathers is "the middle bar" [*Exod.* 26.28] which embraces all the scattered children of Israel. . . . It is also the force which knits together the successive generations.

S. D. Luzzatto, letter to Moses Porto, April 2, 1855.

373.14 The Hebrew language . . . is the only glue which holds together our scattered bones. It also holds together the rings in the chain of time. . . . It binds us to those who built pyramids, to those who shed their blood on the ramparts of Jerusalem, and to those who, at the burning stakes, cried *Shema Yisrael!*

Peretz, *Bildung*, 1890. *Alle Verk*, xii. 14.

373.15 The Hebrew Tongue's eternal slave am I.

J. L. Gordon, *Ahabat David uMichal*, 1857, Introduction.

373.16 The tongue of Jerusalem on our lips, and the ideas of Europe in our minds.

J. L. Gordon, letter to M. M. Dolitzki, Nov. 10, 1881.

373.17 Hebrew, key to the casket which holds the precious treasure.

Heine, *Confessions*, 1854.

373.18 It is worth studying the Hebrew language for ten years in order to read *Psalm* 104 in the original.

*Herder. q Hertz, *DPB*, 582.

373.19 Our sages always regarded our language as a shield against assimilation in all its forms.

Herzog. q *HaDoar*, March 18, 1953, p. 348.

373.20 Our forefathers are to be rebuked for neglecting Hebrew.

M. Ibn Ezra, *Shirat Yisrael*, (12C) 1924, p. 59.

373.21 As the man in Seneca, that through sickness lost his memory and forgot his own name, so the Jews, for their sins, . . . speak the language of all the world and not their own.

*Lightfoot, *Erubhin*, 1629. q White, *Warfare of Science with Theology*, 1898, ii. 184.

373.22 The Hebrew language of the Old Testament, with its small number of words for abstract ideas, and its great simplicty of construction, is favorable neither to scientific investigation nor to intellectual conversation; but it is in an equal degree more fitted for the most faithful deliniation of the ever-recurring fundamental characteristics of human life, and for the majestic expression of divine sublimity.

*Lotze, *Microcosmus*, 1856, 8.3, tr 1885, ii. 402. See A. Darmsteter, *Life of Words*, 1886, p. 92.

373.23 The words of the Hebrew tongue have a peculiar energy. It is impossible to convey so much so briefly in any other language.

*Luther, *Table Talk*, 1569, 34.

373.24 Hebrew idioms run into the English tongue with a particular grace and beauty. . . . They give a force and energy to our expressions, warm and animate our language, and convey our thoughts in more ardent and intense phrases than any that are to be met with in our own tongue.

*J. Addison. *Spectator*, #405, June 14, 1712.

373.25 It's all Hebrew to me; I can't understand a word.

*Molière, *L'Étourdi*, 1653. iii.

373.26 The knowledge of Hebrew is the golden hinge upon which our national and religious existence turns. Flowing down from the hills of eternity, the Hebrew language has been set apart by God as the receptacle of truths destined to sway mankind and humanize the world.

Morais.

373.27 Many have known the indescribable charm that the language of the Bible holds, . . . have sensed the mystic perfume these venerable texts exhale. . . . Through the Hebrew syllables with their sonorous cadence, something of the soul of Israel reached me. . . . When I opened the psalter the words had . . . an emotional and religious value that I could never again find in French or in Latin.

Pallière, *Unknown Sanctuary*, 1928, p. 54.

373.28 A quiver full of steel arrows, a cable with strong coils, a trumpet of brass, crashing through the air with two or three sharp notes, such is Hebrew. A language of this kind is not adapted to the expression of philosophic thought, or scientific result, or doubt, or the sentiment of the Infinite. The letters of its books are not to be many; but they are letters of fire. This language is not destined to say much, but what it does is beaten out upon an anvil. It is to pour out floods of anger, and utter cries of rage against the abuses of the world, calling the four winds of heaven to the assault of the citadels of evil. Like the jubilee horn of the sanctuary, it will be put to no profane use; it will never express the innate joy of the conscience or the serenity of nature; it will sound the note of the holy war against injustice and the call to the great assemblies; it will have accents of rejoicing and accents of terror; it will become the clarion of the neomenia and trumpet of judgment.

*Renan, *History of Israel,* 1888, i. 86.

373.29 In this language there survive historic Jewish concepts, . . . peculiar and unique ancient Hebraic relics, for which there are no parallels in any other language. There are in it words, phrases, idioms and expressions, rooted so deep in remotest time, that no other tongue can reach. In it each figure of speech has the flavor of distant ages, the relish of old wines, which stir longings and yearnings that transcend the limits of speech. Thus he who speaks or writes in this language enters the mysterious realm of the sublime.

M. Ribalow, *Im HaKad el HaMabua,* 1950, p. 317.

373.30 O Ezra the Scribe, our spiritual hero! Who will lift the dust from your eyes that you may see, after 2500 years, the language which you fashioned and cultivated with all your might blossom forth anew? Yes, indeed, it lives, and in a land which is not its native home!

S. Rubin, letter, Sept. 26, 1858.

373.31 Of all these ritual languages . . . Hebrew is . . . the only one which has ever showed signs of renewing its old vitality—like the roses of Jericho which appear to be dead and shrivelled but which, when placed in water, recover their vitality and bloom.

H. Samuel, Foreword to Zangwill, *Chosen Peoples,* 1918.

373.32 Hellenistic Judaism is the only one . . . which dared to . . . dispense with the Sacred Language. The result was death. It withered away and terminated in total . . . apostasy.

Schechter, Aug. 28, 1904. *Seminary Addresses,* 88f.

373.33 As the Torah was given in the Holy Tongue, so was the world created in the Holy Tongue.

Simeon b. Pazzi. *Gen. R.,* 18.4.

373.34 Hebrew may be called primarily a language of the senses. . . . There is a prevalence . . . of the harder, heavier consonants. . . . Much use is made of the explosive letters. . . . Thus though the liquids and softer gutturals also abound in the vocabulary, it is urgency more than beauty, emphasis more than melody, which strike the ear as characteristic of Hebrew. So far the language was suited to a people who first heard the voice of their God in thunder and tempest. . . . One remembers the summons to the prophet to "call with the throat" [*Isa.* 58.1].

*G. A. Smith, *The Hebrew Genius.* BSL, 10f.

373.35 We who have no national monuments, no solid ground, and no outer authority, have one treasure, salvaged from the ruins of our sanctuary, and that is our holy tongue. . . . Who rejects this tongue rejects the entire people!

Smolenskin, 1870. q KJG, 402. See letter 13, to D. Kaufmann. q KJG, 407.

373.36 There is no such thing as creedless Hebrew. He who conjures up Hebrew at the same time involuntarily opens sluices for the obstructed springs of an ancient religious civilization.

Spiegel, *Hebrew Reborn,* 1930, p. 405.

373.37 It has been said of the Hebrew language that its every word is a poem.

*Stedman, *Nature & Elements of Poetry,* 1892, p. 87.

373.38 Hebrew should properly become the international language of mankind. . . . If the aim and function of culture is to make the world not lighter but weightier, to augment its mystery, to kindle in it the lights of symbols, to refine life in holiness, to create the . . . new Adam, who stands with his feet on the secular ground of technique and, with his spirit, builds the divine world of soul, . . . then Hebrew should be its primary tool.

Syrkin. *Dos Neie Leben*, 1923. SGZ, ii. 193f.

373.39 There is a vast storehouse filled with treasures. The key, the Hebrew language, is in our guardianship. Have we a right to throw the key into the ocean of oblivion? . . . I fear that, in the case of such dereliction of duty, the twentieth century will have in store for us, not a ghetto, but a grave.

H. Szold, 1896.

373.40 I found the Holy Tongue beyond all belief cultivated, graceful, and dignified. . . . No other language expresses so much with so few words and such powerful phrases; no language is so rich in many-sided and meaningful forms of expression and modes of imagery. No language so delights and quickens the human heart.

*Zwingli. q Raisin, *Gentile Reactions to Jewish Ideals*, 587.

374. HELL

374.1 Ye shall be burned with torches the livelong day throughout the age, being ashamed of your lying futile idols.

Apocrypha: Sibyl, Fragments iii. 44f.

374.2 Heaven has a thousand gates, Hell but one, and men succeed more rarely than we think, with more difficulty than we believe, in letting themselves be damned.

Boerne, *Der Gott in Hoefflingen*, 1823.

374.3 Yannai and Simeon b. Lakish: There is no Gehenna, but the sun will burn up the wicked. Our Rabbis: There will be a Gehenna. Judah b. Ilai: There will be neither a consuming sun nor a Gehenna, but a fire issuing from the wicked will burn them up.

Gen. R., 6.6. *Talmud: Nedarim*, 8b.

374.4 In hell, a kingdom of ill reputation,
  A crowd of gay damsels will sit at
    my side;
  But in heaven there's boredom and
    mental starvation,
  To hoary old men and old crones
    I'll be tied.

Immanuel, *Mahberot*, (c. 1300) 1491, ch 16. CHH, 94.

374.5 How anyone can believe in eternal punishment, . . . or in any soul which God has made being "lost," and also believe in the love, nay, even in the justice, of God, is a mystery indeed.

Montefiore, *Liberal Judaism*, 1903, p. 58.

374.6 Hell, the fire that shall never be quenched.

New Testament: Mark, 9.43.

374.7 One path leads to paradise, but a thousand to hell.

Proverb (Yiddish). JE, x. 228b.

374.8 Three face no future Gehenna: the very poor, the sick with bowel-trouble, and the prisoner. Some add: and he who is afflicted with a shrew for a wife.

Talmud: Erubin, 41b.

374.9 Gehenna is without limit.

Talmud: Taanit, 10a.

374.10 Let the belly burst rather than go down into the pit.

Tarfon. *Talmud: Nidda*, 13b. Cf. *Matt.* 5.29f, 18.8f.

374.11 Gehenna's doors close forever behind heretics, apostates, informers, deniers of the Torah and resurrection, deviators from the customs, promoters of sin, tyrants, and those who lay hands on the Temple.

Tosefta: Sanhedrin, 13.5.

374.12 Sinners are punished in Gehenna for twelve months, half of the time in fire and half in snow. When they enter the fire, they say, "This is really Gehenna!" When they go into the snow, they say, "This is the real winter of the Almighty!"

Zohar, Gen., 238b.

375. HELP

375.1 Vain is the help of man.

Bible: Ps., 60.13.

375.2 To help one another is our wisdom, our renown, and our sweet consolation.

F. Adler, *Creed and Deed*, 1877, p. 132.

375.3 Give aid to all, expect it from none.

B. Auerbach, *Briefwechsel mit Jakob*, ii. 95.

375.4 If you want to help pull a friend out of the mire, don't hesitate to get a little dirty.

Baal Shem. See BTH, i. 7.

375.5 Help yourself, then Heaven will help you.

Boerne, *Briefe aus Paris*, #106, Feb. 9, 1833.

375.6 As one hand washes the other, so must one man help another.

Leon of Modena, *Tzemah Tzaddik*, 1600.
S. Cohen, *Mishlé Agur*, 1803. See 332.6.

375.7 Help not evil, and evil won't befall you.

Proverb. q *Gen. R.*, 22.8.

375.8 The Lord will help,—only help me, Lord, until the Lord will help.
Proverb (Yiddish). BJS, #667.

376. HEREAFTER

376.1 The netherworld cannot praise Thee . . . they that go down into the pit cannot hope for Thy truth.
Bible: Isa., 38.18.

376.2 There the wicked cease from troubling . . . the weary are at rest. . . . The small and the great are there alike, and the servant is free from his master.
Bible: Job, 3.17, 19.

376.3 No work, no advice, no knowledge, no wisdom in the grave.
Bible: Eccles., 9.10.

376.4 A foundation of religion cannot be something which is not discernible to experience. . . . The Torah has therefore avoided mentioning the hereafter.
Judah Löw, *Derek HaHayyim,* (1589), 12b–14a. q BWC, 161.

376.5 I am content with the conviction that God's eyes are ever upon me, that His providence and justice will follow me into the future life . . . that my true happiness consists in the development of the powers of my soul. It is such felicity that awaits me in the life to come. More I do not desire to know.
M. Mendelssohn, *Phaedon,* 1767, toward the end.

376.6 As to what happens to us after death, we have no conception, and we form no theory.
Montefiore, *Liberal Judaism,* 1903, p. 58.

376.7 The dead do not feel the scalpel.
Talmud: Sabbath, 13b.

376.8 If you fulfilled My commands joyfully, My divine attendants will come out to meet you, and I Myself will bid you welcome!
Talmud: Derek Eretz, 3.7.

377. HEREDITY

377.1 Out of the wicked comes forth wickedness.
Bible: I Sam., 24.14.

377.2 Brothers and sisters are not alike in bodily form; the chemical composition of their blood may be quite different.
Boas, *Mind of Primitive Man,* (1911) 1938, p. 38f.

377.3 A scion is proved by its stock.
Proverb. q *Cant. R.,* 1.1.6.

377.4 The offspring of an idolater or slave and a Jewess, whether married or not, is legitimate and a Jew.
Raba. *Talmud: Yebamot,* 45b.

377.5 Most children resemble their mother's brothers.
Abba Saul. *Talmud J: Kiddushin,* 4.11.

377.6 Scholars' children usually are not scholars.
Talmud: Nedarim, 81a.

377.7 What environment can do, heredity cannot do.
Tanhuma, VaYetzé, 13.

378. HERESY

378.1 The heretics of fifty years ago are the saints of today.
Schreiber, *Reformed Judaism,* 1892, p. 81.

378.2 He who denies the heavenly source of one verse or point in the Torah has "despised the word of the Lord" [*Num.* 15.31].
Talmud: Sanhedrin, 99a.

379. HERITAGE

379.1 Yea, I have a goodly heritage.
Bible: Ps., 16.6.

379.2 Our riches are not in money, nor in estates or land, but in scriptures . . . which have become absorbed into our blood.
Asch, *Sabbatai Zevi,* (1908) 1930, 1.1.

379.3 We receive with our life the mind of centuries; and he who in truth becomes a human being is the whole humanity in himself.
Auerbach, *On the Heights,* 1865.

379.4 Have we any heritage save the sanctuaries of God?
Judah Halevi, *Selected Poems,* 15.

379.5 From the Jewish heritage, I have derived my world outlook, a God-centered interpretation of reality in the light of which man the individual is clothed with dignity, and the career of humanity with cosmic meaning and hope; a humane morality, elevated in its aspirations yet sensibly realistic; a system of rituals which interpenetrates my daily routines and invests them with poetry and intimations of the divine.
M. Steinberg, *To Be or Not to Be a Jew. Common Ground,* 1943.

379.6 Mine literally is a double past— the American and the Jewish. . . . I am twice anchored in traditions, hence twice

secured against the peril of being "unpossessed."
Ibid.

380. HERO

380.1 What would history be without heroes, who give us a far view into the realm of the spirit?
Auerbach, *Tausend Gedanken des Kollaborators,* 1876.

380.2 The heroic hours of life do not announce their presence by drum and trumpet.
Cardozo, *Law and Literature,* 1931, p. 170.

380.3 To believe in the heroic makes heroes.
Disraeli, *Coningsby,* 1844, 3.1.

380.4 The Jewish heroes were not men of battle, but men of faith.
M. Gaster, *Maaseh Book,* 1934, p. xviii.

380.5 Heaven preserve thee, worthy race,
. . . From heroes and heroes' deeds.
Heine, *Germany: A Winter Tale,* 1844, ch 10.

380.6 Judaism knows its own heroism well, a quiet heroism: death for faith and truth, death for the sanctification of the Name.
Klatzkin, *Krisis und Entscheidung,* 1921. LR, 172.

380.7 Certainly the heroism of the defenders of every other creed fades into insignificance before this martyr people, who for thirteen centuries confronted all the evils that the fiercest fanaticism could devise, enduring obloquy and spoliation and the violation of the dearest ties, and the infliction of the most hideous sufferings, rather than abandon their faith.
*Lecky, *Spirit of Rationalism,* 1868, ii. 270.

380.8 Soldiers fight and kings are heroes!
Proverb. q MND, 1125.

380.9 No man is a hero to his valet or his relatives.
Zangwill, *Dreamers of the Ghetto,* 1898, p. 369.

381. HERZL

381.1 He touched beggars and they became kings.
q Learsi, *Fulfillment,* 80.

381.2 Our people had a Herzl, but Herzl never had a people.
Nordau, at VII Zionist Congress, July 27, 1905.

381.3 The hour of redemption has struck, and the man who will bring it is here!
Wolffsohn, letter to Isaac Ruelf, Nov. 1895.

381.4 Herzl is the first statesman the Jews have had since the destruction of Jerusalem.
Zangwill. *Daily News,* 1901. ZVJ, 67.

381.5 One of those creators of ideas who disclose themselves triumphantly in a single country, to a single people, at vast intervals.
S. Zweig, *World of Yesterday,* 1943, p. 109.

382. HILLS

382.1 I lift mine eyes unto the mountains: whence shall come my help?
Bible: Ps., 121.1.

382.2 God, give me hills to climb,
And strength for climbing!
Guiterman, "Hills." *Death & General Putnam,* 1935, p. 20.

382.3 Mountains hanging by a hair.
Mishna: Hagiga, 1.8.

383. HISTORY
383.A. General

383.A.1 Bring the history of the past not as a gloomy memento mori, but as a friendly forget-me-not, whose lessons we may recall with love.
Boerne, *Fragmente & Aphorismen,* 1840, #161.

383.A.2 The concept of history is the product of Prophetism.
H. Cohen, *Die Religion der Vernunft,* 1919, p. 307.

383.A.3 History is the study of other people's mistakes.
Guedalla, *Supers and Supermen,* 1920, p. 54.

383.A.4 History is a logical whole which unfolds step by step under the guidance of inexorable laws.
Lassalle, *Science and the Workingmen,* 1863.

383.A.5 A people's memory is history; and as a man without a memory, so a people without a history cannot grow wiser, better.
Peretz, *Vegn Geshichte,* 1890. *Alle Verk,* xii. 35.

383.A.6 The Jewish thinkers were the first who sought for a general theory of the progress of our species . . . The Jew, thanks to a kind of prophetic sense which renders the Semite at times marvelously apt to see the great lines of the future, has made history enter into religion.

*Renan, *Life of Jesus*, 1863, p. 101. See Berdyaev, *Meaning of History*, 1934, p. 28; Hyatt, *Prophetic Religion*, 1947, p. 76.

383.A.7 History is not merely the record of a string of occurrences. It is an attempt to seize occurrences in their pattern.

L. Roth, *Jewish Thought*, 1954, p. 37.

383.A.8 Ages employed in making history have no time for studying it.

Schechter, *Studies in Judaism*, 1896, i., p. xvi.

383.A.9 Men related in chronicles and histories their own opinions rather than actual events.

Spinoza, *Theologico-Political Treatise*, 1670, ch 6.

383.A.10 The chief value of history, if it is critically studied, is to break down the illusion that peoples are very different.

L. Stein, *Journey into the Self*, 1950, p. 254.

383.A.11 The history of the world is the judge of the world.

H. Ullmann. *Geist der Zeit* (Berlin), 1938.

383.A.12 History has no time to be just. . . . She keeps her eyes fixed on the victorious, and leaves the vanquished in the shadows.

S. Zweig, *The Right to Heresy*, 1936, p. 15.

383.B.   Jewish

383.B.1 The history of the Jews obstructs the history of mankind as a dam obstructs a river, in order to raise its level.

*Bloy, *Le Salut par les Juifs*, 1892. Pilgrim, 1947, p. 248.

383.B.2 In nothing is Scriptural history more strongly contrasted with the histories of highest note in the present age, than in its freedom from the hollowness of abstractions.

*Coleridge, *The Statesman's Manual*, 1816.

383.B.3 The historian's special interest in the Jewish nation is due to its being the only one that is met with at every turn of history.

Darmsteter, *Selected Essays*, 241.

383.B.4 The history of the Jewish people is like an axis crossing the history of mankind from one of its poles to the other.

Dubnow, *Jewish History*, 1903, p. 11.

383.B.5 A nation . . . which has witnessed the rise and decay of the most ancient empires, and which still continues to hold its place in the present day, deserves . . . the closest attention.

Graetz, *History of the Jews*, 1895, v. 705.

383.B.6 Owing to this really astounding objectivity the work of the Hebrew historian far surpasses anything produced elsewhere in the ancient East.

*Gunkel, *What Remains of the OT*, 1914, tr 1928, p. 30.

383.B.7 The history of the Jewish religion was the profoundest and richest that any nation had, and indeed was . . . the religious history of the human race.

*Harnack, *Wesen des Christentums*, (4th ed, 1901) p. 89.

383.B.8 The greatest poem of all time— the history of the Jews.

*Herder. q Magnus, *Jewish Portraits*, 146. See KJL, 296.

383.B.9 "Blood and fire and pillars of smoke" [*Joel* 3.3], this is the whole history of the Jews, the rest is commentary; study it.

Kaminer, *Baraitot de R. Yitzhak. HaKol*, 1885.

383.B.10 The strength of Judaism consists in this, that as soon as one period of history comes to an end, another begins. A new idea replaces the old, fresh forces come into play, and the result is continuous progress.

Krochmal, *Moré Nebuké HaZeman*, 1851.

383.B.11 [Jewish] history encloses the length of all our histories.

*Pascal, *Pensées*, 1670, #620.

383.B.12 The history of the Jewish people is one of the most beautiful in existence. I do not regret having dedicated my life to it.

*Renan, *Le Judaisme comme race et réligion*, 1883. *History of Israel*, 1888, i. p. xv.

383.B.13 To see in history a moral purpose and a task for a people on earth is a great discovery, far more important than the accounts of battles and intrigues that have plagued humanity from time immemorial.

J. Singer, sermon, 1926. *Buffalo Jewish Review*, Sept. 9, 1926, p. 58.

383.B.14 Jewish history, beyond all histories, is composed of tragedies.
*Whitehead. *Atlantic Monthly*, March 1939, p. 320.

384. HOLIDAY

384.1 This day is holy . . . mourn not, nor weep.
Bible: *Neh.*, 8.9.

384.2 For want of a national soil, Jews in the diaspora could not build national structures. So they built out of the substance of time. They took a specific day of the year, and kneaded and molded it until they fashioned it into an edifice. Thus each Jewish holiday is a whole construction.
Bialik. q Karu. *HaBoker*, May 21, 1950.

384.3 Devote your festival half to yourself and half to God.
Joshua b. Hanania. *Talmud: Pesahim*, 68b.

384.4 The Sabbath and holidays are the primary reason for Jewish endurance and glory.
Judah Halevi, *Cuzari*, c. 1135, 3.10.

384.5 Festivals promote the good feeling that men should have to each other in their social and political relations.
Maimonides, *Guide for the Perplexed*, 1190, 3.43.

384.6 The sabbaths are for rest and the festivals for joy, not for fasting and weeping and crying.
Maimonides, *Responsa*, ed Freimann, #41, p. 40.

384.7 To eat and drink on a festival in the company of your family without providing for the poor and distressed, is not "the joy of the commandment" but the joy of your stomach. It is a disgrace.
Maimonides, *Yad: Yom Tob*, 1180, 6.18.

384.8 Honor a festival with food, drink, and clean clothes.
Mekilta, to *Exod*. 12.16.

384.9 The festivals are ten in number. . . . The first is that which anyone will perhaps be astonished to hear called a festival. This festival is every day.
Philo, *The Festivals*.

384.10 The river of life . . . flows from birth toward death. Day follows day with wearisome monotony. Only the holidays twine themselves together to form the circle of the year. Only through the holidays does life experience the eternity of the river that returns to its source. Then life becomes eternal.
F. Rosenzweig, *Das Büchlein vom gesunden und kranken Menschenverstand*, 1921. GFR, 211.

384.11 The holidays are occasions for social intercourse.
Saadia, *Emunot VeDeot*, 933, 3.2.

384.12 Israel had no greater days of joy than Ab Fifteenth and the Day of Atonement, when Jerusalem's maidens danced in the vineyards, in borrowed white dresses, so as not to embarrass those who had none of their own.
Simeon b. Gamaliel II. *Mishna: Taanit*, 4.8.

385. HOLINESS

385.1 Ye shall be holy men unto Me.
Bible: *Exod.*, 22.30. See *Lev.* 11.44, 19.1; *Josh.* 7.13.

385.2 God, the Holy One, is sanctified through righteousness.
Bible: *Isa.*, 5.16.

385.3 Holy, holy, holy is the Lord of hosts.
Ibid., 6.3.

385.4 O God, Thy way is in holiness.
Bible: *Ps.*, 77.14.

385.5 Who follows the rabbis' rulings is called a holy man.
Abayé. *Talmud: Yebamot*, 20a.

385.6 Everything created by God contains a spark of holiness.
Baal Shem. See Anski, *Dybbuk*, 1918, Act 1.

385.7 The hallowing of man is man's proper work.
Dinemann, *Judentum und Christentum*, (2d ed, 1919), 34.

385.8 Saintliness, too, can be egoistic, . . . sinful.
H. Greenberg, "Gandhi," Feb. 1, 1948. GIE, 158.

385.9 Holiness is the essence of all moral perfection.
Kohler, *Jewish Theology*, 1918, p. 101.

385.10 There is nothing in the universe absolutely secular.
Kook, *Orot HaKodesh*, 1938, p. 143. q ABJ, 154.

385.11 The sanctification of God . . . through man, may be called absolutely the most audacious, the most exalted, ecstatic and blissful of thoughts. The expression "I am sanctified" . . . is the noblest word framed by human tongue!

M. Lazarus, *Ethics,* (1899) 1901, ii. 15, #184.

385.12 The Hebrew form of thought rebels against the very idea of a distinction between the secular and religious aspects of life.

*Macmurray, *Clue to History,* 1939, p. 29.

385.13 When the Bible says, "be holy," it means exactly the same as if it said, "do My commandments."

Maimonides, *Sefer HaMitzvot,* iv.

385.14 None can be called saint before death, for none can be trusted to win against the Evil Urge till the end of life.

Midrash Tehillim, 16.2.

385.15 Sainthood comes after death.

Proverb based on *Aharé Mot, Kedoshim, Emor,* the names of consecutive sections in *Leviticus.* See Immanuel, *Mahberot,* ch 9, 21, ed Lemberg, 1870, pp. 72, 168.

385.16 Holiness toward God and justice toward men usually go together.

Philo, *Abraham,* 37.

385.17 The holiness of God, Sabbath and Israel is all the same.

Seder Eliyahu Rabbah, ch 24 (26), ed Friedmann, 133.

385.18 If ye sanctify yourselves, it is as though ye sanctified Me.

Sifra, Kedoshim, 1, ed Weiss, 86b.

385.19 Not what a man does, but how he does it, is profane or sacred.

Steinthal, *Ueber Juden und Judentum,* (1906) 1925.

385.20 If you sanctify yourself a little, you are sanctified much.

Talmud: Yoma, 39a.

385.21 We may add to the sacred from the profane.

Ibid., 81b.

385.22 The Holy Land was not holy while it belonged to the Perizites and Jebusites, and any land in which Israel should find his soul again would be also a Holy Land.

Zangwill, *The False Romantic.* ZSA, 124.

385.23 Only the holy may use holy things.

Zohar, Gen., 167b.

386. HOLLAND

386.1 The whole of Holland is proof of what man can create on the most thankless soil.

Herzl, *Diary,* Sept. 30, 1898.

386.2 In the struggle against sea and Inquisition, the people of the Netherlands grew more vigorous than the furious elements.

Luzzatti, *Evolution in Science & Morality,* 1876. LGF, 195.

386.3 What makes people so crowd together on a barren soil . . . and by industry and art metamorphose lone fens into a garden of God? . . . What else but liberty, mild government, equitable laws, and the hospitable manner in which men of all complexions . . . and creeds are admitted, protected, and quietly allowed to follow their business?

M. Mendelsshon, Pref. to *Vindiciae Judaeorum,* 1782.

386.4 Amsterdam, that city of the saints, the home of the true faith, of the brotherhood of man and the fatherhood of God.

Zangwill, *Dreamers of the Ghetto,* 1898, p. 84.

387. HOME

387.1 All the children of Israel had light in their dwellings.

Bible: Exod., 10.23.

387.2 How goodly are thy tents, O Jacob, thy dwellings, O Israel.

Bible: Num., 24.5.

387.3 I will walk within my house in the integrity of my heart.

Bible: Ps., 101.2.

387.4 The purity of the Jewish home life was a constant antidote to the poisonous suggestions of life in slums.

Abrahams, *Jewish Life in the Middle Ages,* 1896, p. 68.

387.5 The hearth was their rallying-point and the center of their union. There the scattered atoms gained consistency sufficient to withstand the pressure of the world. Thither they could come to recreate their torn and lacerated spirits. There was the well-spring of their power.

F. Adler, *Creed and Deed,* 1877, p. 206.

387.6 The dwelling provides an instrument for measuring the degree of civilization a people has attained.

Alsberg, *Die gesunde Wohnung,* 1866.

387.7 Be not like a lion in your home, tyrannous and terrible toward your servants.
Apocrypha: Ben Sira, 4.30. See Adda b. Ahaba. *Taanit* 20b.

387.8 May the Lord establish the man who follows peace at home.
Apocrypha: Psalms of Solomon, 12.6.

387.9 Make not those who live under your roof dread your presence.
Eliezer b. Isaac, *Orhot Hayyim,* c. 1050.

387.10 Dine on onions, but have a home. Subtract from your diet and add to your dwelling.
Judah b. Ilai. *Talmud: Pesahim,* 114a.

387.11 The alchemy of home life went far to turn the dross of the Ghetto into gold.
Magnus, *Jewish Portraits,* 1905, p. 27.

387.12 He who uses his private house as a sort of stronghold of defiance, and allows there no freedom of speech, . . . is a tyrant with smaller resources.
Philo, *Special Laws,* iii. 25.

387.13 When a house falls, woe to the windows!
Proverb. q Josiah. *Mekilta,* to *Exod.* 17.3.

387.14 Homelessness is harder on a man than on a woman.
Rab. *Talmud: Ketubot,* 28a.

387.15 In his home, even a weaver is a ruler.
Raba. *Talmud: Megilla,* 12b.

387.16 Everyone is king in his home.
Abot de R. Nathan, ch 28.

387.17 A cottage is all that I ask,
　　The face of a friend at the door,
　　As I pass from the wind and the rain
　　To shelter me—that and no more.
A. Raisen, "On Life's Journey," tr E. Lieberman.

387.18 He who maintains peace at home helps to maintain it in Israel. . . . Everyone is king in his home.
Simeon b. Gamaliel II. *Abot de R. Nathan,* ch 28.

387.19 It is a joy to live in one's own house.
Talmud J: Moed Katan, 2.4.

387.20 And though these shattering walls are thin,
　　May they be strong to keep hate out
　　And hold love in.
L. Untermeyer, "Prayer for This House." *This Singing World,* 1923, p. 67.

387.21 You will always be treated as a guest if you, too, can play the host. The only man who is invited to dinner is the man who can have dinner at home if he likes.
Weizmann, *Trial and Error,* 1949, p. 274.

388. HOMELAND

388.1 The national center will not be a "secure home of refuge" for our people, but it will be *a home of healing for its spirit.*
Ahad HaAm, *Summa Summarum,* 1912. *Ten Essays,* 160.

388.2 It is good to live and die in one's own country.
Apocrypha: Aristeas, 249.

388.3 He who abandons his fatherland, stands in mid-air, with no ground to sustain him.
B. Auerbach, *Waldfried,* 1874.

388.4 I often envy the lot of the most miserable people who live on their own land.
Axelrod, 1917. q Rifkind, *Zionism and Socialism,* 16f.

388.5 A homeland cannot be bought with money or conquered by the sword. It has to be created with one's own toil and sweat.
Ben Gurion. *N.Y. Times,* March 28, 1954.

388.6 Because I was born to no fatherland, I yearn for one more fervently than you; and because my birthplace was no larger than the *Judengasse* and beyond its locked gates a foreign country began for me, even the city does not suffice now as my fatherland, nor a county, nor a province, only the entire greater fatherland, as far as its speech extends.
Boerne, *Briefe aus Paris,* #74, Feb. 7, 1832.

388.7 When the fatherland faded from my eyes I found it again in my heart.
Heine, *English Fragments,* 1828, ch 1.

388.8 A sensitive person longs more for his homeland than for his food.
q M. Ibn Ezra, *Shirat Yisrael,* (12C) 1924, p. 34.

388.9 Jews have no country or place of their own in all Christendom where they can live and move and have their being, except by the purely voluntary permission and good will of the lord under whom they wish to dwell.
*John of France, Charter, 1361. q PJC, 125.

388.10 History is no longer enough for the Jews—history, the heroic fatherland of time. They are yearning for a small, simple home on earth. More young Jews are returning to Palestine. This is a return to self, to one's own roots, to growth.
Kafka. q Janouch, *Conversations.* q *JF*, March 1953, p. 33.

388.11 A Jewish life must have a Jewish land.
S. Levin, *The Arena*, 1932, p. 241. See OMB, 98.

388.12 It is better to sink roots into the soil like a tree . . . than to flutter like a bird, skipping from branch to branch.
Nordau, *From the Kremlin to the Alhambra*, 1879.

388.13 The Jews have no fatherland of their own, though they have many motherlands. . . . They are everywhere guests, nowhere at home.
Pinsker, *Auto-Emancipation*, 1882.

388.14 Gypsies and Jews are men without a country.
*Ripley, *Races of Europe*, 1899, p. 368.

388.15 Man is free to choose his fatherland. He is not bound to the soil like a serf, or rooted in the ground like a tree.
Weill, *Le Lévitique*, 1891, p. 51.

388.16 A fatherland focuses a people.
Zangwill, *Children of the Ghetto*, 1892, ii. ch 15.

389. HONESTY

389.1 If you sell . . . or buy . . . ye shall not wrong one another.
Bible: Lev., 25.14.

389.2 Happy are they that are upright in the way.
Bible: Ps., 119.1.

389.3 Honesty is the precondition for genuine scientific and scholarly work.
Baeck, *Judaism and Science*, 1949, p. 5.

389.4 The first question at the Last Judgment will be: Did you deal honestly with your fellow man?
Kohler. *JE*, vii. 361a, based on Raba. *Talmud: Sabbath*, 31a.

389.5 Honest with a penny, trusted with a dollar.
Lazerov, *Enciklopedie fun Idishe Vitzen*, 1928, #429.

389.6 As the rabbi must inspect periodically the slaughtering-knives of the *shohatim* in his town, to see that they have no defect, so must he go from store to store to inspect the weights and measures of the store-keepers.
Lipkin. q Glenn, *Israel Salanter*, 24.

389.7 To be honest in business is to fulfill the whole Torah.
Mekilta, to *Exod.* 15.26.

389.8 Point out to your customer, regardless of his creed, the defects in your merchandise.
Moses b. Jacob, *Semag*, 1250, #1245.

389.9 A tailor who does not appropriate some of his customer's cloth, a cobbler who patches with good leather, a storekeeper who gives the correct weight and a full measure, will have a greater portion in the world to come than many a rabbi.
Moses Isaac. q MGU, 254.

389.10 To have no occasion for lying does not yet mean to be honest.
Schnitzler, *Buch der Sprüche & Bedenken*, 1927, p. 226.

389.11 Be absolutely honest with gentile as with Jew.
Sefer Hasidim, 13C, #1216, p. 303.

389.12 What? Pass a law against counterfeit money? You must be a scoundrel indeed if you need such a law to keep you honest!
Solomon HaCohen, *Responsa*, 1594, iii. 108.

390. HONEY

390.1 Where there's honey there are flies.
Proverb (Yiddish). YFS, i. 416.

391. HONOR

391.1 Before honor goes humility.
Bible: Prov., 15.33.

391.2 Leave not a stain on your honor.
Apocrypha: Ben Sira, 33.22.

391.3 Honor has its deepest source in self-preservation, but this very source appears purified in it.
Auerbach, *Lucifer*, 1847.

391.4 Who is honored? He who honors.
Ben Zoma. *Mishna: Abot*, 4.1.

391.5 The Jew who is not weak enough to disavow his faith must be strong enough to forego honors.
I. Deutsch, Dec. 7, 1840.

391.6 Where there is no honor, there is no disgrace.
Duran, *Tiferet Yisrael*, 1591.

391.7 Cherish your colleague's honor as your own.
Eliezer b. Hyrcanus. *Mishna: Abot*, 2.10.

391.8 Let your skill exalt you, not another's shame.
Israeli, *Manhig HaRofeim,* c. 930. See *Legacy of Islam,* 326.

391.9 The world delights more to honor those who delight it than those who instruct it.
Jacobs, 1885. *JAI,* 1886, xv. 368.

391.10 The man honors the place, not the place the man.
Jose b. Halafta. *Mekilta,* to *Exod.* 19.13.

391.11 He who promotes his own honor at the expense of his neighbor's has no portion in the world to come.
Judah b. Hanina. *Gen. R.,* 1.5.

391.12 Which is the right course a man should choose? That which honors him in his own eyes and in the eyes of his fellow men.
Judah HaNasi. *Mishna: Abot,* 2.1.

391.13 States, like men, never protest their honor loudly unless they have a bad case to argue.
Laski, *A Grammar of Politics,* 1925, p. 167.

391.14 None is as dependent as he who seeks honor.
Lipkin. q KTH, i. 271.

391.15 There can be no such thing as offending national honor. One may offend national pride or injure national interest.
London, speech, U.S. Congress, March 6, 1916. q RES, 77.

391.16 Accept no dignity of which you are not worthy.
q Schechter, June 5, 1910. *Seminary Addresses,* 195.

391.17 An elder must not burden the community with demands for honors.
Simeon b. Eleazar. *Sifra,* 91a, to *Lev.* 19.32.

391.18 Those who cry out the loudest against the misuse of honor and the vanity of the world, are those who most greedily covet it.
Spinoza, *Ethics,* 1677, v. Pr 10, Note.

391.19 Who runs after honor comes behind him who flees from it.
Talmud J: Aboda Zara, 3.1.

391.20 Honor flees from him who runs after it, and follows him who flees from it.
q Elijah HaCohen, *Shebet Musar,* 1712, ch 17.

391.21 He who runs after honor, gets the honor; and he who flees from it, is allowed to flee.
Sholom Aleichem, *Yidishé Folks Tzeitung,* 1902.

392. HOPE

392.1 The hope of Israel, the Lord.
Bible: Jer., 17.13. See *Ps.,* 130.7.

392.2 Return to the stronghold, ye prisoners of hope.
Bible: Zech., 9.12.

392.3 Hope deferred makes the heart sick.
Bible: Prov., 13.12.

392.4 The righteous, even when brought to death, has hope.
Ibid., 14.32.

392.5 Even as ye hope, so sees your heart.
Apocrypha: Ben Sira, 34.5.

392.6 In God we hope.
Apocrypha: II Macc., 2.18.

392.7 In the absence of Hope and of an ideal of progress, we strike upon one great difference between the classical Greeks and the Hebrews. . . . In the darkest hour of adversity the Prophets did not despair of Israel.
*Butcher, *Some Aspects of the Greek Genius,* 1893, 163f.

392.8 I am a Jew because in every age when the cry of despair is heard, the Jew hopes.
Fleg, *Why I Am a Jew,* 1929, p. 94.

392.9 Many the hopes that have vanished, after the ball.
C. K. Harris, "After the Ball," 1892.

392.10 Hopes are fallacious which depend not on one's own strength, but on the misadventures of another.
Herod I. q Josephus, *Wars,* 1.19.4.

392.11 I hope always, I desire much, I expect little.
Jabotinsky, 1937. q *Jewish Affairs,* July 1950, p. 17.

392.12 As long as there is life, there is hope.
Johanan. *Talmud J: Berakot,* 9.1.

392.13 Hope and faith, however dim they be,
Can turn the grave beneath to paradise.
M. J. Lebensohn, *Koheleth.* q *JS,* July 1952, p. 28.

392.14 God desires not . . . sacrifices, but hope.
Midrash Tehillim, 40.2, ed Buber, 129a.

392.15 The beginning of all participation in good things is hope.
Philo, *Abraham,* 2.

392.16 Hope is the source of all happiness. . . . None is to be considered a man who does not hope in God.
Philo, *Rewards,* 2.

392.17 The morning air was like life's elixir, and hope went singing skyward with the lark.
Sassoon, *Sherton's Progress,* 1936.

392.18 The more poverty, the more hope.
Sholom Aleichem, *A Boidem,* 1899.

392.19 Hope deceives.
q Zunz, *Nachlese zur Spruchkunde,* 1869. *Ges. Schr.* iii. 265.

393. HORN

393.1 Blow the horn in Zion.
Bible: Joel, 2.1.

393.2 Blow the horn at the new moon.
Bible: Ps., 81.4.

393.3 We blow a ram's horn to recall the Binding of Isaac.
Abbahu. *Talmud: Rosh Hashana,* 16a.

393.4 Every note has importance, as every atom . . . is a mystery.
Benamozegh. q Palliére, *Unknown Sanctuary,* 169.

393.5 As we blow, first we stand, then we sit, to confuse Satan.
Isaac b. Phineas. *Talmud: Rosh Hashana,* 16a.

393.6 A toot binds and a toot releases.
Samuel. *Talmud: Moed Katan,* 16a, (ref. to ban).

393.7 The Shofar blast neither makes nor unmakes a Jew.
Sokolow, *Baruch Spinoza,* tr *Avukah Annual,* 1932, p. 730.

394. HORSE

394.1 Woe to them that . . . rely on horses.
Bible: Isa., 31.1. See *Ps.,* 33.17.

394.2 The glory of his snorting is terrible. He paws in the valley, and rejoices in his strength. . . . He swallows the ground with storm and rage. . . . He smells the battle afar off.
Bible: Job, 39.20f, 24f.

394.3 A canter is the cure for every evil.
Disraeli, *Young Duke,* 1831, 2.11.

394.4 Formerly mules pulled cars, now cars pull mules.
Nehemiah. *Mekilta,* to *Exod.* 14.25.

394.5 Drive your horse with oats, not with a whip.
Proverb (Yiddish). BJS, #2965. ATJF, p. 640.

395. HOSPITALITY

395.1 Let a stranger live with you, and he'll estrange your way of life.
Apocrypha: Ben Sira, 11.34.

395.2 Let a stranger in . . . and he'll turn you out.
Ibid., 11.36. See Aha. *Lev. R.,* 17.7.

395.3 Mankind is divisible into two great classes: hosts and guests.
Beerbohm, *Hosts and Guests,* 1919. *And Even Now,* 128.

395.4 A grateful guest says: "Bless that host! How many wines, portions, cakes he brought out for me!" An ingrate says: "What did I have? A piece of bread, a bite of meat, a bit of wine. And he served for the sake of his wife and children!"
Ben Zoma. *Tosefta: Berakot,* 7.2.

395.5 Let all who are hungry come and eat.
Huna. *Talmud: Taanit,* 20b.

395.6 Whatever your host tells you, do.
Huna b. Nathan. *Talmud: Pesahim,* 86b.

395.7 A woman watches a guest more grudgingly than a man.
Isaac. *Talmud: Baba Metzia,* 87a.

395.8 A little refreshment goes a long way. Its denial alienated two tribes, Ammon and Moab, from Israel [*Deut.* 23.4f].
Jose b. Kisma. *Talmud: Sanhedrin,* 103b.

395.9 The poor does for the host more than the host for the poor.
Joshua b. Hanania. *Lev. R.,* 34.8.

395.10 Nowhere does the Torah say, Invite your guest to pray; but it does tell us to offer him food, drink and a bed.
Kagan. q YSS, 197.

395.11 It is improper for a guest to give of his portion to a child of the host.
Meir. *Talmud: Derek Eretz,* 7.9.

395.12 On the day a guest arrives, a calf is slaughtered in his honor; the next day, a sheep; the third day, a fowl, and on the fourth day he is served just beans.
Midrash Tellihim, 23.3, ed Buber, 99b. Cf *Num. R.,* 21.25; *Pesikta Kahana,* ch 30, ed Buber, 175b.

395.13 Forget not to entertain strangers: for thereby some entertained angels unawares.
New Testament: Heb., 13.2.

395.14 In the house of a wise man none is ever slow to perform the duties of hospitality.
Philo, *Abraham,* 22.

395.15 Having served your guest food and drink, escort him.
Proverb. q *Gen. R.,* 48.20.

395.16 One guest does not bring along another.
Proverb, based on *Talmud: Baba Bathra,* 89b.

395.17 Fill your house with guests, and you'll settle your daughter.
Proverb. q *JQRo,* i. 432.

395.18 House-guests and fish spoil on the third day.
Proverb. ATJF, p. 639.

395.19 Hospitality to wayfarers is greater than welcoming the Shekina.
Rab. *Talmud: Sabbath,* 127a.

395.20 A dish tastes best
When shared with a guest.
Sanders, *Citatenlexikon,* 1899, p. 253.

395.21 The host breaks bread and the guest says Grace.
Simeon b. Yohai. *Talmud: Berakot,* 46a.

396. HOUSE OF GOD

396.1 The house of God . . . the gate of heaven!
Bible: Gen., 28.17.

396.2 Let them make Me a sanctuary that I may dwell among them.
Bible: Exod., 25.8.

396.3 Behold, heaven and the heaven of heavens cannot contain Thee, how much less this house that I have builded!
Bible: I Kings, 8.27.

396.4 My house shall be called a house of prayer for all peoples.
Bible: Isa., 56.7.

396.5 The heaven is My throne and the earth My footstool; where is the house that ye may build unto Me?
Ibid., 66.1.

396.6 I have been to them a little sanctuary in the countries where they are come.
Bible: Ezek., 11.16.

396.7 In that day there shall be no more a trafficker in the house of the Lord of hosts.
Bible: Zech., 14.21.

396.8 Lift up your heads, O ye gates, and be ye lifted up, ye everlasting doors; that the King of glory may come in.
Bible: Ps., 24.7, 9.

396.9 Lord, I love the habitation of Thy house.
Ibid., 26.8.

396.10 My soul yearns, yea, pines for the courts of the Lord.
Ibid., 84.3.

396.11 Happy are they that dwell in Thy house.
Ibid., 84.5.

396.12 A day in Thy courts is better than a thousand [elsewhere].
Ibid., 84.11.

396.13 Strength and beauty are in His sanctuary.
Ibid., 96.6.

396.14 This is the gate of the Lord; the righteous shall enter it.
Ibid., 118.20.

396.15 The soul requires a sanctuary.
Disraeli, *Lothair,* 1870.

396.16 When Israel forgot his Maker, he would build temples.
H. Gollancz, "Pentecost and Palestine," 1912. *Sermons,* 46.

396.17 Where is God? . . . In each human heart.
Hasdai, *Ben HaMelek VeHaNazir,* c. 1230, ch 22.

396.18 God says: If you come to My house, I will come to yours.
Hillel. *Tosefta: Sukka,* 4.3. *Talmud: Sukka,* 53a.

396.19 Every house a temple, every heart an altar, every human being a priest.
M. Lazarus, *Ethics of Judaism,* 1900, i. 35.

396.20 God dwells wherever man lets Him in.
Mendel of Kotzk. q BTH, ii. 277.

396.21 In my Father's house are many mansions.
New Testament: John, 14.2.

396.22 Ye are the temple of God.
New Testament: I Cor., 3.16.

396.23 Nought but a pious soul is His fit abode.
Philo, *Cherubim,* 29. See 30; *Dreams* 1 23; *Sobriety* 13.

396.24 The mind of the wise is the palace of God.
Philo, *Rewards,* 20.

396.25 Why do men make crypts of stone
To snare a living God?
J. S. Untermeyer, *On Temples. Dreams Out of Darkness*, 1921, p. 19.

396.26 We are, unless we build some shrine or ark,
A dying rabble in a wilderness.
Zangwill, *Bezalel*.

397. HUMANISM

397.1 Neither faith in the dignity of the human soul, which is the essence of humanism, nor its opposite, contempt for the human species and all its ideals, is susceptible of logical proof and disproof. Belief in man, as in God, is . . . an act of will, which has a way of proving itself through the kind of deeds and policies that it inspires.
J. B. Agus, *Banner of Jerusalem*, 1946, p. 187.

397.2 In their struggle for the ethical good, teachers of religion must have the stature to give up the doctrine of a personal God, . . . that source of fear and hope which in the past placed such vast power in the hands of priests. In their labors they will have to avail themselves of those forces which are capable of cultivating the Good, the True, and the Beautiful in humanity itself.
Einstein, 1941. *Out of My Later Years*, 28f.

397.3 The prevailing mood [in humanistic religion] is that of joy, while the prevailing mood in authoritarian religion is that of sorrow and of guilt.
Fromm, *Psychoanalysis and Religion*, 1950, p. 37.

397.4 Man is the cornerstone; and from the true conception of man have the Jewish thinkers risen to the noblest conception of the Deity.
E. G. Hirsch. *Reform Advocate*, 1893, v. 244.

397.5 My brother, mankind! My fatherland, the world! My religion, virtue!
M. J. Lebensohn, letter to Senior Sachs, July 15, 1850.

397.6 The best religion is humanity, the best divine service, love thy neighbor as thyself. The motto which we inscribe on our banner is the fatherhood of God and the brotherhood of man.
M. Lilienthal, address, 1876.

398. HUMILITY

398.1 I am the least in my father's house.
Bible: Judg., 6.15.

398.2 I dwell . . . with him that is of a contrite and humble spirit.
Bible: Isa., 57.15.

398.3 The humble shall inherit the land.
Bible: Ps., 37.11. See *NT: Matt.*, 5.5.

398.4 The Lord upholds the humble.
Bible: Ps., 147.6.

398.5 Take your seat a little below your rank, for it is better to be asked to come up than to be told to go down.
Akiba. *Lev. R.*, 1.5.

398.6 Humble yourself in all greatness.
Apocrypha: Ben Sira, 3.18.

398.7 Glorify your soul in humility.
Ibid., 10.28.

398.8 Blessed is he who speaks with humble tongue and heart to all.
Apocrypha: II Enoch, 52.13.

398.9 Humility destroys envy.
Apocrypha: Patriarchs, Gad, 5.3.

398.10 To find truth, bend down humbly [*Ps.* 85.12].
Baal Shem. q Simeon Zeeb, *Derash Tob*, 1928, p. 10.

398.11 The test of the real service of God is that it leaves behind it the feeling of humility.
Baal Shem. q SSJ, i. 30.

398.12 Repentance begins with humility.
Bahya, *Hobot HaLebabot*, 1040, 6.8.

398.13 If humility is Christianity, you, Jews, are the true Christians!
*Blake, *Selections from Jerusalem*, 1804–1820, f 27.

398.14 Everything heroic in man is insignificant and perishable . . . unless it be the fruit of humility.
H. Cohen. q Hertz, *DPB*, 705.

398.15 God revealed Himself in a bush, to teach us that the loftiest may be found in the lowliest.
Eleazar b. Arak. *Mekilta de Simeon b. Yohai*.

398.16 Learn from the Creator: He revealed Himself on Sinai, not on high mountains, in a bush, not in majestic trees.
Joseph b. Hiyya. *Talmud: Sota*, 5a.

398.17 No crown carries such royalty as that of humility.
Eleazar b. Judah, *Rokeah*, 13C.

398.18 Only the humble will rise at the Resurrection.

Eleazar b. Pedat. *Talmud: Sota,* 5a, ref. to *Isa.* 26.19.

398.19 Be obscure, that you may endure.

Eleazar b. Pedat. *Talmud: Sanhedrin,* 14a.

398.20 Humility comes . . . only with maturity.

Finkelstein, *The Pharisees,* 1940, p. xxix.

398.21 As water flows to the lowest level, so Torah finds its way to the lowly of spirit.

Hanina b. Iddi. *Talmud: Taanit,* 7a, ref. to *Isa.* 55.1.

398.22 Scripture likens Torah to water, wine and milk, for, like these, it can be preserved only in humble containers.

Hoshaia. *Talmud: Taanit,* 7a.

398.23 The tempest spares the hyssop on the wall,
But 'neath its wrath the proudest cedars fall.

Hasdai, *Ben HaMelek VeHaNazir,* c. 1230, ch 30. q CHH, 125.

398.24 My lowliness is my loftiness, my loftiness my lowliness.

Hillel. *Lev. R.,* 1.5. Cf *Matt.* 23.12, *Luke* 14.11.

398.25 Of all Moses' virtues, the Bible singles out for mention only his humility [*Num.* 12.3]; and his humbleness is cited in reference to men [not to God], and that is true humility.

E. Hurwitz, *Noam Megadim,* (1807) 1859, p. 53b.

398.26 The green shoots of lowliness are love.

Ibn Gabirol, *Mibhar HaPeninim,* c.1050, #170.

398.27 The summit of intelligence is lowliness.

Ibid., #652.

398.28 Wherever in Scripture you find reference to God's greatness (power), you find reference also to His humility (grace).

Johanan b. Nappaha. *Talmud: Megilla,* 31a. *DPB,* ed Singer, 214f.

398.29 Where there is greatness, there is humility.

Wesseley, *Yen Lebanon,* Preface, 1775.

398.30 The humble is regarded as though he brought all the offerings.

Joshua b. Levi. *Talmud: Sanhedrin,* 43b, ref. to *Ps.* 51.19.

398.31 Humility before Him is true honor.

Judah Halevi, *Cuzari,* c. 1135, 5.25.

398.32 Humility is the seed of contentment.

Kagan. See YSS, 116.

398.33 One who is well aware that he is humble is no longer humble.

Klatzkin, *In Praise of Wisdom,* 1943, p. 303.

398.34 People become smaller when they want to be bigger.

Lazerov, *Enciklopedie fun Idishe Vitzen,* 1928, #498.

398.35 Be very, very humble, for man's hope is worms.

Levitas. *Mishna: Abot,* 4.4.

398.36 The greatest minds are those which, even in the act of creation, remain humble.

Luzzatti, *Fioretti,* 1912, Preface. LGF, 314f.

398.37 Be humble before all men.

Meir. *Mishna: Abot,* 4.10.

398.38 Who does not exalt himself will be exalted by others.

Meir. *Talmud: Moed Katan,* 28b.

398.39 On the way to humility, beware of self-exaltation.

Moses of Evreux, 1240.

398.40 Humility for the sake of approval is the worst arrogance.

Nahman Bratzlav, *Likkuté Moharan,* 1811.

398.41 Humility is the first virtue, for if you are aware of God's greatness and man's lowliness, you will fear God and avoid sin.

Nahmanides, letter to his son Nahman, c. 1268.

398.42 The test of humility is in your attitude to subordinates.

Orhot Tzaddikim, 15C, ch 2.

398.43 A leper is cleansed with cedarwood and hyssop [*Lev.* 14.4], to remind him that he was stricken for exalting himself like the tallest tree, and that he may be healed by humbling himself like the lowest plant.

Pesikta Kahana, ch 4, ed Buber, 31a.

398.44 Who, when he lays to heart that ashes and water are the beginning of his existence, can be puffed up by conceit? That is why the lawgiver required those about to sacrifice to besprinkle themselves.

Philo, *Dreams,* i. 36.

398.45 If you remember your own nothingness, you remember also God's transcendence.

Philo, *Sacrifice of Abel and Cain*, 14.

398.46 God exalts the self-humbling and humbles the self-exalting.

Samuel. *Talmud: Erubin*, 13b.

398.47 Good deeds without humility are like a dish without salt.

Sefer Hasidim, 13C, #1045, p. 262.

398.48 As the fruit multiplies, the tree bends; as wisdom grows, humility increases.

J. Steinberg, *Mishlé Yehoshua*, 1885, 39.11, p. 220.

398.49 Be humble, that you may not be humbled.

Talmud: Derek Eretz, 1.27.

398.50 Love humility, and prolong your life.

Ibid., 7.15.

398.51 Even if you be otherwise perfect, you fail without humility.

Talmud: Kalla Rabbati, 3.

398.52 Because of his humility, Moses was worthy to receive the Torah.

Tanhuma, Bereshit, #1, 6b.

398.53 We lower when we want to lift. . . . The upward movement in us is vain . . . if it does not come from a downward movement.

S. Weil, *Gravity and Grace*, 1952, p. 145f.

398.54 Don't make yourself so little, you're not so big!

S. S. Wise. q J. P. Rudin, *Concerning a King*, March 12, 1954.

399. HUMOR

399.1 Humor is a gift not of the mind, but of the heart.

Boerne, *Memorial Address on Jean Paul*, Dec. 2, 1825.

399.2 Only relatively civilized people have a sense of humor.

Brill, *Basic Writings of Sigmund Freud*, 1938, p. 21.

399.3 In all ages those who have had something to say and have been unable to say it without danger . . . have gladly donned the cap and bell. He for whom the forbidden saying was intended was more likely to tolerate it if he was able to laugh at it, and to flatter himself . . . that what he disliked was obviously absurd.

Freud, *Interpretation of Dreams*, 1900. *Basic Writings*, 422.

399.4 This determination of self-criticism may make clear why it is that a number of the most excellent jokes . . . should have sprung into existence from the soil of Jewish national life. . . . I do not know whether one often finds a people that makes so merry unreservedly over its own shortcomings.

Freud, *Wit and Its Relation to the Unconscious*, tr 1917, iii., 705.

399.5 Comic operas do not lie.

Goldberg, *Major Noah*, 1936, iv.

399.6 Humor,—the truth in an intoxicated condition.

G. J. Nathan, *The Theatre*, etc., 1921, p. 132.

399.7 Humor is the red thread in the gray linen.

J. Rosenfeld. q Twerski. *Davké*, 1952, xiii., 379.

399.8 Pleasantry in pain, that makes humor.

Saphir, *Fliegende Album*, 1846.

400. HUNGER

400.1 The sheep should have his belly full who quarrels with his mate.

Disraeli, *Count Alarcos*, 1839.

400.2 An empty stomach is not a good political adviser.

Einstein, *Cosmic Religion*, 1931, p. 107.

400.3 Hunger is a good seasoning for any dish.

Gentili, *Mleket Mahshebet, Noah*, 1710.

400.4 Hunger is the best cook.

Ginzberger, *Der Zuchts Spiegel*, 1610.

400.5 Hunger, a kind of suffering like burning slowly and incessantly on a still fire.

Mendelé, *Di Antdekung fun Volin*.

400.6 A hungry dog will swallow its own dung.

Proverb. q Raba. *Talmud: Baba Kamma*, 92b.

400.7 A hungry Jew sings, a hungry squire whistles, a hungry peasant beats his wife.

Proverb (Yiddish). See BJS, #1773.

401. HUNT

401.1 Like Nimrod, a mighty hunter before the Lord.

Bible: Gen., 10.9.

401.2 The hunting dog will become the portion of wolves.

Apocrypha: Ahikar, 8.20.

401.3 I cannot comprehend, when I see such a noble animal [deer] how educated and refined people can take pleasure in its chase or death.

Heine, *Harzreise*, 1824.

401.4 My ancestors did not belong to the hunters so much as to the hunted, and the idea of attacking the descendants of those who were our comrades in misery goes against my grain.

Heine, *Norderney*, 1826.

401.5 I cannot comprehend how a Jew could even dream of killing animals merely for the pleasure of hunting. . . . When the act of killing is prompted by sport, it is downright cruelty.

Landau, *Noda BiYehuda*, (1776) 1811, p. 48. q HSJ, 115.

401.6 Who hunts game with dogs will not partake of Leviathan.

Meir of Rothenburg, *Responsa*, (13C) 1891, #27, p. 7.

401.7 When a Jew says he's going hunting to amuse himself, he lies.

Rathenau. q Einstein, *World As I See It*, 146.

401.8 "The way of sinners" [*Ps. 1.1*],— animal contests and hunting.

Simeon b. Pazzi. *Talmud: Aboda Zara*, 18b.

402. HUSBAND

402.1 Every man should bear rule in his own house.

Bible: Esther, 1.22.

402.2 A husband's patience atones for all crimes.

Heine, *Latest Poems: Ascension*, 1853.

402.3 A faithless husband makes a faithless wife. As the proverb goes: he among the large pumpkins, she among the little.

Johanan. *Talmud: Sota*, 10a.

402.4 Though her husband be a carder, she calls him to her side.

Papa. *Talmud: Yebamot*, 118b.

402.5 A husband is sufficient ornament for his wife!

Philo's wife, when asked, at a banquet, why she wore no jewels. q Antonius, Sermon 123 (Yonge, iv. 275).

402.6 Even with an ant for a husband, a woman may be placed among the great.

Proverb. q Abayé. *Talmud: Yebamot*, 118b.

402.7 Husband and wife are one flesh, but different purses.

Proverb. q Lipperheide, *Spruchwörterbuch*, 587.

402.8 A henpecked husband gets no relief in court.

Talmud: Baba Metzia, 75b.

403. HYPOCRISY

403.1 This people draw near, and with their mouth and lips do honor Me, but have removed their heart far from Me, and their fear of Me is a commandment of men learned by rote.

Bible: Isa., 29.13.

403.2 Behold, in the day of your fast ye pursue your business, and exact all your labors!

Ibid., 58.3.

403.3 There is no sincerity in their mouth; their inward part is a yawning gulf, their throat is an open sepulchre; they make smooth their tongue.

Bible: Ps., 5.10.

403.4 Smoother than cream were the speeches of his mouth, but his heart was war; his words were softer than oil, yet were they keen-edged swords.

Ibid., 55.22.

403.5 Fear not the Pharisees or the non-Pharisees, but the hypocrites who ape the Pharisees, who act like Zimri and scheme for the reward of Phineas [*Num. 25.11–14*].

Alexander Jannaeus, to Queen Salome. *Talmud: Sota*, 22b.

403.6 Young swallows fell out of their nest. A cat caught them and said, "If it were not for me, great evil would have befallen you." Said they, "Is this why you put us in your mouth?"

Apocrypha: Ahikar, 8.25.

403.7 The idolater worships one object, but there is no limit to the number of men the hypocrite worships.

Bahya, *Hobot HaLebabot*, 1040, 5.4.

403.8 Catch the fleeting colors of that she-chameleon Cant, and show what excessive trouble we are ever taking to make ourselves miserable and silly.

Disraeli, *Young Duke*, 1831.

403.9 The cold and glistening serpent-skin of hypocrisy.

Heine, *Baltic: Purification*, 1825.

403.10 I know the tune, and I know the text.

I know the people who wrote it;
I know that in secret they drink but wine,
And in public a wickedness vote it.

Heine, *Germany: A Winter Tale,* 1844, ch 1.

403.11 Many men fear not God, yet wrap themselves in the *talith.*

A. Ibn Ezra, *Yesod Mora,* (1158) 1840, ch 5, p. 23.

403.12 Well may he sit with downcast look,

His eyes glued to his Hebrew book. . . .
But yet in truth, his heart within
Is hard as stone, and black with sin!

Kalonymus b. Kalonymus, *Eben Bohan,* c. 1322. q CHH, 109.

403.13 Fear not the seven-headed hydra, but the double-tongued man.

Lazerov, *Enciklopedie fun Idishe Vitzen,* 1928, #415.

403.14 We have a Sunday code and a weekday code. . . . We preach good and practice evil. We clothe the wolf of our action in the sheep's clothing of our beautiful phrases.

London, speech, U.S. Congress, 1915. q RES, 210.

403.15 The Supreme Judge will call to account those who wrap themselves hypocritically in the mantle of true Pharisees.

Nahman b. Isaac. *Talmud: Sota,* 22b.

403.16 Woe to you, scribes and Pharisees, hypocrites! . . . Ye blind guides, who strain at a gnat and swallow a camel.

New Testament: Matt., 23.23f.

403.17 Woe to you, scribes and Pharisees, hypocrites! for ye are like whited sepulchres, which indeed appear beautiful outward, but within are full of dead men's bones and of all uncleanness.

Ibid., 23.27.

403.18 Be not soft with your mouth and hard in your heart.

Seder Eliyahu Rabbah, ch 18, ed Friedmann, 106.

403.19 The Holy One detests him who speaks one thing with his mouth and another in his heart.

Talmud: Pesahim, 113b.

403.20 Expose hypocrites, to prevent the profanation of the Name.

Talmud: Yoma, 86b.

403.21 I hated this weak pomp of charity,

This pauper feast to aid the stricken poor,
I watched these too-thin ladies seek their door
In sweetly pious insincerity;
Holding themselves so righteously alone,
Turning their Christian backs on Mrs. Cohn.

J. S. Untermeyer, "Church Sociable." *Growing Pains,* 1918, p. 35.

404. IDEA

404.1 A person's behavior springs from his ideas.

A. Adler, *Social Interest,* 1939.

404.2 An idea not capable of realization is an empty soap-bubble.

B. Auerbach, *Sträflinge,* 1846.

404.3 In the struggle of ideas, we must be most cautious when our opponents come close to us and agree with us.

Boerne, *Fragmente und Aphorismen,* 1840, #115.

404.4 One should conquer the world, not to enthrone a man, but an idea, for ideas exist for ever.

Disraeli, *Tancred,* 1847.

404.5 We [Jews] preserved our unity through ideas, and because of them we have survived to this day.

Freud, letter to Jacob Meitlis, Nov. 30, 1938.

404.6 You talk of our having an idea; we do not have an idea. The idea has us, and martyrs us, and scourges us, and drives us into the arena to fight and die for it, whether we like or no.

Heine. q de Haas, *Theodor Herzl,* i. 69f.

404.7 You cannot confine an idea behind prison bars. . . . Ideas cannot be shut in nor shut out.

M. London. q Rogoff, *An East Side Epic,* 205f.

404.8 Ideas are duty free.

q Zunz, *Nachlese zur Spruchkunde,* 1869, #51, p. 89.

405. IDEAL

405.1 An ideal is a port toward which we resolve to steer.

F. Adler, *Life and Destiny,* 1903.

405.2 The Real is the sole foundation of the Ideal.

Aguilar, *Amete and Yafeh*, c. 1850.

405.3 He who can work in the realm of the real and live in that of the ideal, has attained the highest.

Boerne. q TL, p. 169.

405.4 The road to perdition has ever been accompanied by lip service to an ideal.

Einstein, 1936, *Out of My Later Years*, 32.

405.5 Ideals enacted are ideals corrupted . . . visions realized are visions disrupted.

Kallen. *Menorah Journal*, Autumn 1951, p. 113.

405.6 A great people cannot live without an ideal.

Nordau, address, Madrid, 1915.

405.7 There are many fine ideals which are not realizable, and yet we do not refrain from teaching them.

Smolenskin, *Maamarim*, (1925) i. 144. q SHR, 240.

405.8 False ideals cannot be shattered by criticism. Right ideals must take up the battle against them.

Werfel, *Between Heaven and Earth*, 1944.

405.9 We restless idealists are none other than the court jesters of Providence, who even pay for their own fools' caps.

I. M. Wise. *Deborah*, Jan. 7, 1897, p. 5.

405.10 The Heaven of today is the earth of tomorrow.

Yehiel Mikhal of Zloców. q BTH, i. 157.

405.11 Every dogma has its day, but ideals are eternal.

Zangwill, speech, Nov. 13, 1892.

406. IDLENESS

406.1 Idleness teaches much mischief.

Apocrypha: Ben Sira, 33.27.

406.2 Idleness is the mother of famine.

Apocrypha: Tobit, 4.13.

406.3 None of those who are dedicated to God ought to be idle.

Didascalia, ii. ch 62. q *JE*, iv. 590b.

406.4 Who does not work on week-days will end up working also on the Sabbath.

Dosetai b. Yannai. *Abot de R. Nathan*, ch 11.

406.5 Idleness leads to lewdness.

Eliezer b. Jacob. *Mishna: Ketubot*, 5.5.

406.6 Idleness leads first to boredom, then to sin.

Eliezer Halevi, *Tzavaah*, c. 1350.

406.7 Idleness is fatal.

Jose. *Abot de R. Nathan*, ch 11.

406.8 Idleness leads to idiocy.

Simeon b. Gamaliel II. *Mishna: Ketubot*, 5.5.

407. IDOLATRY

407.1 Thou shalt have no other gods before Me.

Bible: Exod., 20.3. *Deut.*, 5.7.

407.2 Thou shalt not make unto thee a graven image.

Bible: Exod., 20.4. *Deut.*, 5.8.

407.3 Gods of silver or of gold ye shall not make unto you.

Bible: Exod., 20.20. See *Isa.* 2.8.

407.4 These men have set up their idols in their mind.

Bible: Ezek., 14.3.

407.5 They that sacrifice men kiss calves.

Bible: Hos., 13.2.

407.6 Be it known to you, O king, that we will not serve your gods, nor worship the golden image which you have set up.

Bible: Dan., 3.18.

407.7 It was not in insolence . . . that I did . . . not bow before proud Haman . . . but that I might not set a man's glory above God's!

Apocrypha: Additions to Esther, C 5–7.

407.8 If the gods steal, by whom shall they make them to swear?

Apocrypha: Ahikar, 8.22.

407.9 These gods cannot save themselves from rust and moths.

Apocrypha: Jeremy, 12.

407.10 They can show no mercy to the widow, . . . these gods.

Ibid., 38f.

407.11 The worship of those unnameable idols is the beginning and cause and end of every evil.

Apocrypha: Wisdom of Solomon, 14.27.

407.12 People made their bellies their gods, their fine clothes their law, and their home maintenance their ethics.

Bahya, *Hobot HaLebabot*, 1040, 9.2.

407.13 We cannot extract a nail from a board without damage to the wood, or eradicate phallic idols without loss of souls.

Eleazar b. Shammua. *Sifré*, #131, to *Num.* 25.3.

407.14 A Jew may not enter a building

dedicated to idol-worship even to protect himself from inclement weather.

Finkelstein, *Religions of Democracy,* 1941, p. 7.

407.15 Words can become idols, and machines. . . . Science and the opinions of one's neighbors can become idols, and God has become an idol for many.

Fromm, *Psychoanalysis and Religion,* 1950, p. 118.

407.16 If Zeus is a god, licentiousness is no sin. If Aphrodite is a goddess, chastity cannot be a virtue.

Graetz. *JQRo,* 1889, i. 9.

407.17 Man was made mortal, because the Holy One foresaw that some . . . would proclaim themselves gods.

Hama b. Hanina. *Gen. R.,* 9.5.

407.18 Ultimately all idolatry is worship of the self projected and objectified: all idolization is self-idolization.

Herberg, *Judaism and Modern Man,* 1951, p. 96.

407.19 The representatives of inchoate force, the lords of fire and water, have not forgiven and will never forgive our victory of idea over matter. . . . Fire, ever since Abraham rebelled against it, has pursued us. Water, ever since Moses subdued it, seeks to overcome us.

Kurzweil. *Israel Argosy,* Autumn 1952, p. 117.

407.20 Every idol demands sacrifices.

S. Levin, *The Arena,* 1932, p. 50.

407.21 The law against idolatry outweighs all other commandments.

Mekilta, to *Exod.* 12.6.

407.22 When asked why God did not exterminate all idols, Gamaliel replied: You worship the sun, moon, stars and planets, . . . and even man. Shall He then destroy His world because of fools?

Ibid., 20.5. *Mishna: Aboda Zara,* 4.7.

407.23 The Torah warns us not to make idols of God's commandments.

Mendel of Kotzk, on *Deut.* 4.23. See BTH, ii. 279.

407.24 No man can serve two masters . . . God and Mammon.

New Testament: Matt., 6.24.

407.25 Let none who has a soul worship a soulless thing.

Philo, *Decalogue,* 16.

407.26 Whoever professes idolatry rejects the Ten Commandments . . . and whoever rejects idolatry professes the entire Torah.

Sifré, #111, *Num.* 15.22, ed Horovitz, 116.

407.27 When God is dethroned, His throne does not remain empty for long. Some false god, some Wotan, Moloch, Mammon or Mars soon occupies it.

Silver, *World Crisis,* 1941, p. 80.

408. IGNORANCE

408.1 No safety in ignorance if proper inquiry would avail.

Cardozo, *People vs. Sheffield Farms,* 1918.

408.2 Where the population is large, ignorance too is large.

Costa, *Tratado de Cortesia y Politica,* 1726.

408.3 Ignorance never settles a question.

Disraeli, speech, House of Commons, May 14, 1866.

408.4 We have become increasingly and painfully aware of our abysmal ignorance.

A. Flexner, *Universities,* 1930, p. 17.

408.5 God has chosen me because I am an *am ha-aretz.*

J. Frank. q M. Buber, *Hasidism,* 22.

408.6 Canonization of ignorance has never been the rule in Israel.

Geiger, *Judaism and Its History,* 1865, p. 285.

408.7 The ignorant is not pious.

Hillel. *Mishna: Abot,* 2.5.

408.8 No greater indigence than ignorance.

M. Ibn Ezra, *Shirat Yisrael,* (12C) 1924, p. 123.

408.9 An ignorant Jew may be torn like a fish.

Johanan b. Nappaha. *Talmud: Pesahim,* 49b.

408.10 Who is ignorant? He who does not educate his children.

Jonathan b. Joseph. *Talmud: Sota,* 22a.

408.11 Disaster comes only because of ignorance.

Judah HaNasi. *Talmud: Baba Bathra,* 8a.

408.12 Nothing is so sure of itself as ignorance.

Lewisohn, *Creative Life,* 1924, p. 197.

408.13 Who pleads ignorance admits negligence, and must pay.

Nahman. *Talmud: Baba Metzia,* 35a.

408.14 Do not live near an ignorant man who is pious.

Simeon b. Lakish. *Talmud: Sabbath*, 63a.

409. ILLUSION

409.1 Illusions commend themselves to us because they save us pain and allow us to enjoy pleasure instead. We must therefore accept it without complaint when they sometimes collide with a bit of reality against which they are dashed to pieces.

Freud. q CGP, 40.

409.2 Our grandeur lies in our illusions.

Hoffenstein, "Grandeur."

409.3 Who rides on delusions rides to destruction.

q M. Ibn Ezra, *Shirat Yisrael*, (12C) 1924, p. 85.

409.4 It is better to ask for a moon that does not exist than to consent to a moonless world.

Lewisohn, *Creative Life*, 1924, p. 104.

409.5 Society's preservation and man's happiness depend on illusion. Nature itself, which certainly represents the will of God, deludes us in many respects, as when it leads us by the cords of love to reproduce the race. If a youth would consider the trouble of rearing a family, not one in a thousand would marry, but nature closes our eyes to the future (and indeed, wherever popular knowledge rises, the birth rate declines). The same is true of other passions, which nature utilizes to deceive men and goad them toward the attainment of ends which, when attained, turn out to be but vanity.

S. D. Luzzatto, *Igrot Shadal*, 1882, v. 661.

409.6 Blessed be the illusion which makes life worth living.

Nordau, *Morals and the Evolution of Man*, 1920.

409.7 It's the first duty of friendship to preserve a friend's illusions.

Schnitzler, *Anatol: Questioning Fate*, 1893.

409.8 It is only delusion, not knowledge, that bestows happiness.

S. Zweig, *World of Yesterlay*, 1943, p. 228.

410. IMAGE OF GOD

410.1 God created man in His own image.

Bible: Gen., 1.27.

410.2 This one sentence is enough to prove the divine origin of Israel's Holy Writ.

*Cornill, *Das Alte Testament und die Humanität*, 1895, 9.

410.3 In the likeness of God made He him.

Bible: Gen., 5.1.

410.4 This principle is even greater than "love your neighbor as yourself" [*Lev.* 19.18], for it teaches us not to retaliate when a neighbor puts us to shame.

Ben Azzai. *Sifra, Kedoshim*, 4.12. Cf *Gen. R.*, 24.7.

410.5 Beloved is man who was created in the divine image.

Akiba. *Mishna: Abot*, 3.14.

410.6 No creature in heaven or on earth can conceive any image of God.

Donnolo, *Hakemoni*, 982.

410.7 Man is preceded on the road by a company of angels who proclaim: Make room for the Image of the Holy One!

Joshua b. Levi. *Midrash Tehillim*, 55.19, to *Ps.* 17.7.

410.8 Because of the divine image . . . man is superior even to angels.

Judah Löw, *Derek HaHayyim*, 1589.

410.9 It is in respect of the mind, the sovereign element of the soul, that the word "Image" is used.

Philo, *Creation*, 23. See *Special Laws*, iii. 36.

411. IMAGINATION

411.1 The imagination of man's heart is evil from his youth.

Bible: Gen., 8.21.

411.2 Lack of imagination causes cruelty.

Brandeis. q *Louisville Herald*, July 1, 1911.

411.3 Imagined woes pain none the less.

Heine, *City of Lucca*, 1829, ch 17.

411.4 A sinful imagination is worse than sin.

Talmud: Yoma, 29a.

411.5 The poet is in command of his fantasy, while it is exactly the mark of the neurotic that he is possessed by his fantasy.

Trilling, "Freud and Literature," 1940. *The Liberal Imagination*, 1950, p. 45.

412. IMITATION

412.1 The Jews have not merely a tendency to imitation, but a genius for it.

Whatever they imitate, they imitate well.

Ahad HaAm, *Imitation & Assimilation*, 1893. *Selected Essays*, 117.

412.2 Man may be well defined as a mimetic animal.

D'Israeli, *Curiosities: Paradoxes*, 1817.

412.3 Everything in the world can be imitated, except truth, for truth that is imitated is no longer truth.

Mendel of Kotzk. q BTH, ii. 284.

412.4 When a jackass brays, no one pays any attention to him, not even other jackasses. But when a lion brays like a jackass, even the lions in the neighborhood may be pardoned for exhibiting a little surprise.

G. J. Nathan, *Testament of a Critic*, 1931.

413. IMITATION OF GOD

413.1 Be holy, for I am holy.

Bible: Lev., 11.44. See *Sifra, Shemini*, 12.

413.2 Jews imitate God by philanthropy.

*Aristides Mareianus, *Apology*, 2C. q JE, ii. 94b.

413.3 As He clothes the naked, visits the sick, comforts mourners, and buries the dead [*Gen.* 3.21, 18.1, 25.11, *Deut.* 34.6], so you do likewise.

Hama b. Hanina, on *Deut.* 13.5. *Talmud: Sota*, 14a.

413.4 Look on the glory of God, and awaken the glory in thee.

Judah Halevi, *Selected Poems*, 1924.

413.5 Man never acts in a manner more resembling God than when he bestows benefits.

Philo, *Special Laws*, iv. See tr Yonge, iii. 372.

413.6 "This is my God, *veanvehu*"—read it, *ve-ani-ve-hu*, "I shall be like Him"! As He is gracious and merciful, so will I be.

Abba Saul. *Mekilta*, to *Exod.* 15.2 *Talmud: Sabbath*, 133b.

414. IMMIGRATION

414.1 Not the absorption capacity of the land, but the creative ability of a people, is the true yardstick with which we can measure the immigration potentialities of the land.

Ben Gurion, speech, Palestine Labor Party, 1931.

414.2 A regrettable product of our Diaspora, emigration, is frequently the only means of mitigating Jewish suffering, not merely of a personal, but of a national character. Under the conditions of our history, this fatal necessity of emigration takes on the character of a powerful instrument of national survival.

Dubnow, *Pisma*, 1907. q JP, 1948, ii. 317.

414.3 Can we not rely on Him who provides for all the thousands in Algiers to provide for forty-five souls more?

Isaac b. Sheshet, *Responsa*, 14C, on refugees. q J. L. Baron, *The Immigrant*, 1923, p. 12.

414.4 An unprejudiced study of immigration justifies me in saying that the evils are temporary and local, while the benefits are permanent and national.

O. S. Straus, address, May 22, 1907. *American Spirit*, 222.

414.5 America was largely populated by misrepresentation, and on the whole it has been a good thing for the newcomers. The average man is industrious but inert. . . . A rainbow was needed—a land where the roads were paved with gold, where every man was as good as everybody else, where every man's native-born son had a fine chance to be elected President. No colonization without misrepresentation.

Strunsky, *No Mean City*, 1944, p. 14.

415. IMMORTALITY

415.1 Without my flesh I shall see God.

Bible: Job, 19.26.

415.2 Like footsteps in a gallery, our lightest movements are heard along the ages.

S. Alexander, *Moral Order and Progress*, (1889) 1899, 413.

415.3 If there were this life only, nothing could be more bitter.

Apocrypha: II Baruch, 21.13.

415.4 All souls are prepared to eternity.

Apocrypha: II Enoch, 23.5 .

415.5 The righteous live forever.

Apocrypha: Wisdom of Solomon, 5.15. See 2.23, 3.1–4, 4.1.

415.6 I have no particular taste for postmortem immortality. I am immortal now, while I am gloriously alive.

Blau, "My Uncertain God." *Menorah Journal*, 1924, x. 476.

415.7 Egyptian immortality was to be attained through power. . . . Only when the doctrine was presented as one of salvation for the righteous, . . . did the masses of Jerusalem become converted to it.

Finkelstein, *The Pharisees*, 1940, p. 147f.

415.8 We . . . are in reality as unable to conceive the separate existence of our soul as . . . to comprehend the resurrection of our body.

M. Friedlander, *Jewish Religion*, (1891) 1927, p. 165.

415.9 It must require an inordinate share of vanity and presumption, too, after enjoying so much that is good and beautiful on earth, to ask the Lord for immortality in addition to it all.

Heine, *City of Lucca*, 1829, ch 9.

415.10 Deprived of the hope for immortality, man . . . is the most wretched being on earth.

M. Mendelssohn, *Phaedon*, 1767.

415.11 The survival of personality is neither conceivable nor desirable.

Nordau. *What Happens After Death?* 1916. q NMN, 95.

415.12 We feel and know that we are eternal.

Spinoza, *Ethics*, 1677, v. Pr 23, Note.

415.13 The Jewish religion is characterized in an eminent degree by the dimness of its conception of a future life. From time to time there are glimpses of the hope of immortality. But, for the most part, it is in the present life that the faith of the Israelite finds its full accomplishment. . . . Not from want of religion, but (if one might use the expression) from excess of religion, was this void left in the Jewish mind. The Future Life was not denied or contradicted,—but it was overlooked, set aside, overshadowed by the consciousness of the living, actual presence of God Himself.

*Stanley, *History of the Jewish Church*, (1862) 1896, i. 139f.

415.14 Death is not the end; the earthly body vanishes, the immortal spirit lives on with God.

Union Prayer Book, 1940, i. 275.

416. IMPOSSIBLE

416.1 Number me the days that are not yet come, gather me the raindrops that are scattered, make me the withered flowers to bloom again.

Apocrypha: II Esdras, 5.36.

416.2 Most of the things worth doing in the world had been declared impossible before they were done.

Brandeis. Arbitration Proceedings, N.Y. Cloak Industry, Oct. 13, 1913. q LBG, 282.

416.3 In two words: im-possible.

Goldwyn. q Alva Johnston, *The Great Goldwyn*.

416.4 Turrets flying in the air.

Isaac. *Talmud: Sanhedrin*, 106b.

416.5 To will the impossible is usually a sin of indolence.

Lewald, *Gefühltes und Gedachtes*, 1900, p. 30.

416.6 People say: If you cannot pass, you must return. We say: If you cannot pass, you must pass.

Lipkin. q KTH, i. 277.

416.7 We do not ascribe to God the power of doing what is impossible . . . and this assumption does not imply weakness in God.

Maimonides, *Guide for the Perplexed*, 1190, 3.15.

416.8 You can never fill a sack full of holes.

Proverb. ATJF, p. 639.

416.9 There is no such thing as impossible. . . . Had anyone said a hundred years ago that the small Greek nation . . . would again set up their kingdom, all the people would have laughed at him.

Smolenskin, *Maamarim*, 1925, i. 144. q SHR, 240.

416.10 The actually probable is often the apparently impossible.

L. Stein, *Journey into the Self*, 1950, p. 261.

417. IMPUDENCE

417.1 Audacity leads to sin.

Hamnuna. *Talmud: Taanit*, 7b.

417.2 Deliver me . . . from the impudent and from impudence!

Judah HaNasi. *Talmud: Berakot*, 16b. *DPB*, ed Singer, 7.

417.3 Audacity avails even with God.

Nahman b. Jacob. *Talmud: Sanhedrin*, 105a.

417.4 Impudence is sovereignty without a crown.

Proverb. q Sheshet. *Talmud: Sanhedrin*, 105a.

417.5 The impudent may be called wicked.

Rabbah b. Huna. *Talmud: Taanit*, 7b.

417.6 The impudent is a bastard.

Talmud: Kallah.

418. INDEPENDENCE

418.1 You have no peace of mind if you

depend on others, even on parents or children.

Ahai b. Josiah. *Abot de R. Nathan*, ch 30.

418.2 Make your Sabbath a week-day, and depend not on others.

Akiba. *Talmud: Sabbath*, 118a.

418.3 It is not life if a man looks to a stranger's table.

Apocrypha: Ben Sira, 40.29. See *Talmud: Berakot* 6b, *Betza* 32b.

418.4 Depend on another's board, and you'll go without meals.

Gabishon, *Omer HaShikha*, c. 1600 (1748), p. 63.

418.5 Rely not on the broken reed of human support.

Asher b. Yehiel, *Hanhaga*, c. 1320. AHE, 120.

418.6 Without moral and intellectual independence, there is no anchor for national independence.

Ben Gurion, speech, Aug. 13, 1948. BRD, 279.

418.7 Noah's dove prayed: Lord of the world, rather a bitter olive leaf given by Thee than sweets and honey provided by man!

Eleazar. *Talmud: Sanhedrin*, 108b.
Jeremiah b. Eleazar. *Talmud: Erubin*, 18b.

418.8 I have none but myself to depend on.

Eleazar b. Dordia. *Talmud: Aboda Zara*, 17a.

418.9 May not the children of Israel find it necessary to derive their livelihood from one another!

Judah b. Ezekiel. *Talmud: Yoma*, 53b.

418.10 Live on the coarsest food, and depend not on others.

Orhot Tzaddikim, 15C.

418.11 Better a spoonful from God than a bushel from man.

Proverb (Yiddish). See *JE*, x. 228b.

418.12 Hire yourself out for alien service, rather than depend on your fellow-man.

Samuel b. Nahman. *Talmud: Baba Bathra*, 110a.

418.13 A scholar who depends on his own labor . . . may be called happy.

Seder Eliyahu Rabbah, ch 18, ed Friedmann, 91.

418.14 Who depends on his wife's earnings will not be successful.

Talmud: Pesahim, 50b.

418.15 Independence is never given to a people, it has to be earned; and having been earned, it has to be defended.

Weizmann. q G. Hoffman, *Land & People of Israel*, 46.

419. INDIVIDUAL

419.1 Every one shall die for his own iniquity.

Bible: Jer., 31.30.

419.2 Son of man, stand upon thy feet, and I will speak to thee.

Bible: Ezek., 2.1. See Herford, *Judaism in NT Period*, 1928, p. 32f.

419.3 If there is any miracle in the world, any mystery, it is individuality.

Baeck, *Judaism and Ethics*, 1949, p. 21.

419.4 God needs me as I am, and He needs you otherwise! Only because you are Edom may I be Jacob.

Beer-Hoffman, *Jacob's Dream*, 1916. q LRB, 62.

419.5 In the study of the individual one can never overestimate the fact that the individual was meant for society.

Bergson, *Two Sources of Morality & Religion*, 1935, p. 95.

419.6 Democracy . . . insists that the full development of each individual is not only a right, but a duty to society.

Brandeis, *The Jewish Problem*, 1915, p. 5.

419.7 Individualism understands only a part of man; collectivism understands man only as a part. Neither advances to the wholeness of man, to man as a whole.

Buber, *Between Man and Man*, 1947, p. 200.

419.8 All that is valuable in human society depends upon the opportunity for development accorded to the individual.

Einstein, Sept. 15, 1933.

419.9 It is only to the individual that a soul is given. And the high destiny of the individual is to serve rather than to rule.

Einstein, 1939. *Out of My Later Years*, 23.

419.10 The ideal which holds us together beyond any other is our belief in the work of the individual, whatever his race or religion.

Frankfurter, at Aaronsburg, Oct. 23, 1949.

419.11 Every man, no matter how great or small, must be viewed not as a means to an end, but as an end in himself.

H. Greenberg, "To a Communist Friend," 1936. GIE, 254.

419.12 Every single man is a world which is born and which dies with him; beneath every gravestone lies a world's history.

Heine, *Journey from Munich to Genoa,* 1828, ch 30.

419.13 The tree is the supreme wonder . . . the forest is only a mirage.

S. Levin, *The Arena,* 1932, p. 54.

419.14 The problem of civilization today is how to secure the largest possible measure of individual liberty consistent with the welfare of society.

London, speech, Congress, Aug. 24, 1921. q RES, 234.

419.15 Perhaps no code of national law and custom has observed the balance between group life and individual life more successfully than that of Israel.

*J. R. Macdonald, *Socialist Movement,* 1911, p. 20.

419.16 The Creator made all men different in features, intelligence and voice, in order to promote honesty and chastity.

Meir. *Tosefta: Sanhedrin,* 8.6.

419.17 Confusion—the process of fusing together—is the annihilation of individual properties, . . . and is indeed a most proper name for vice.

Philo, *Confusion of Tongues,* 38.

419.18 The Ten Commandments are addressed in the singular, for each single person, when he obeys God and the Law, equals in worth a whole nation, even the world.

Philo, *Decalogue,* 10. See *Yalkut* to *Exod.* 20.2.

419.19 No king . . . may despise an insignificant private person.

Philo, *Decalogue,* 10.

419.20 This new world must be based on the recognition that the individual human being is the cornerstone of our culture and our civilization.

Proskauer, *Declaration of Human Rights,* 1945. *A Segment of My Times,* 217.

419.21 "In the sight of *all* the people": one Jew being absent would have withheld the Revelation.

Simeon b. Yohai. *Mekilta,* to *Exodus* 19.11.

419.22 Brains differ as completely as palates.

Spinoza, *Ethics,* 1677, i. Appendix.

419.23 The welfare, right and honor of every individual, even the lowest, is the community's concern.

Stahl, *Philosophie des Rechts,* (1837) 1854, ii. 312. q MRR, 370.

419.24 One ear of corn is not exactly like another.

Talmud J: Sanhedrin, 4.9.

419.25 All of you are pledges one for the other: all of you, aye the world, exist through the merit of a single righteous man among you, and if but one man sin, the whole generation suffers.

Tanhuma: Nitzabim, ed Buber, 25a.

419.26 Every single man is a new thing in the world, and is called upon to fulfill his particularity in this world.

Yehiel Michael of Zlotchov. q Buber, *Way of Man,* 17.

419.27 In the coming world, they will not ask me: "Why were you not Moses?" They will ask me: "Why were you not Zusya?"

Zusya. q BTH, i. 251.

420. INEVITABLE

420.1 What is unavoidable is not reprehensible.

Proverb. Rabnitzki & Bialik, *Sefer Ha-Meshalim,* 165.

421. INFERIORITY

421.1 The feeling of inferiority rules the mental life.

A. Adler, *Social Interest,* 1939, p. 102.

422. INFLUENCE

422.1 They that turn the many to righteousness shine as the stars for ever and ever.

Bible: Dan., 12.3.

422.2 The king's giving the ring to Haman was more effective than all the forty-eight prophets' and seven prophetesses' preachment to Israel.

Abba b. Kahana. *Talmud: Megilla,* 14a, ref. to *Esther* 3.10.

422.3 The promoter of a good deed is credited as its doer.

Abbahu. *Talmud: Sanhedrin,* 99b.
Elisha b. Abuya. *Sifré* to *Deut.* 4.9.

422.4 We live truly in our radiations. We grow and develop in proportion as we help others to grow and develop.

F. Adler, *Life and Destiny,* 1903, p. 84.

422.5 As the sun which glows on summer days still lives as concentrated warmth in wine, and somewhere on some winter night warms up a human heart, so is the sunshine in that man's life whose vocation it is to impart to others the conceptions of his own mind. Nay, there is here far more; for the refreshing draft here offered is not diminished, though thousands drink thereof.

B. Auerbach, *Christian Gellert's Last Christmas*, 1869.

422.6 He who is charitable and just fills the world with kindness.

Eleazar. *Talmud: Sukka*, 49b.

422.7 Who stimulates others to do good is greater than the doer.

Eleazar. *Talmud: Baba Bathra*, 9a.
Caro, *SA: Yoré Deah*, 1574, 249.5.

422.8 A smoldering spark . . . when blown up and made to blaze, lights a great pile, so the least particle of virtue, when warmed into life by great hopes.

Philo, *Migration of Abraham*, 21.

422.9 A saloon won't spoil the good and a school won't mend the bad.

Proverb (Yiddish). BJS, #773.

422.10 To put debased money into circulation is an offense, but to put degenerate men and women into circulation is an offense far graver.

H. Samuel, *Belief and Action*, 1937, p. 146.

422.11 To cause a man to sin is worse than to murder him.

Simeon b. Yohai. *Sifré, #252, to Deut. 23.8.*

422.12 The ultimate influence of a nation, or an individual, is measured more by the amount of character revealed than by the stir produced in human events.

Weizmann. *N.Y. Herald Tribune* Annual Forum, Oct. 21, 1947.

423. INGENUITY

423.1 Ingenuity will shine in a man even if he is carrying a log of wood.

S. Jacobs, letter, Nov. 30, 1761. q MEA, i. 210.

423.2 Inspiration soon dies and is with difficulty reborn, but ingenuity only sleeps and is easily awakened.

L. Stein, *Journey into the Self*, 1950, p. 261.

424. INHERITANCE

424.1 Who comes for the inheritance is often made to pay for the funeral.

Proverb (Yiddish). BJS, #1877.

424.2 Dowries and inheritances bring no luck.

Ibid., 1878.

425. INITIATIVE

425.1 The margin between that which men naturally do, and that which they can do, is so great that a system which urges men on to action and develops individual enterprise and initiative is preferable, in spite of the wastes that necessarily attend their process.

Brandeis, *Efficiency & Trusts*, 1912. *American Legal News*, 1913.

425.2 When the work of initiation is at an end, the initiator dies or—becomes a renegade.

Heine, *Germany from Kant to Hegel*, 1834.

425.3 We want initiative, competition, efficiency.

Trotsky, *Problems of Life*, 1923, p. 114.

426. INNER AND OUTER

426.1 Speedy external gains have always entailed internal loss.

Baeck, *Essence of Judaism*, 1936, p. 11.

426.2 I have seen you, O world, gather shells and discard kernels, attract the empty and repel the full.

Bedersi, *Behinat Olam*, c. 1310, ch 12.

426.3 The bitter and the sweet come from the outside, the hard from within, from one's own efforts.

Einstein. G. Schreiber, *Portraits & Self Portraits*, 1936.

426.4 'Twas the outward gleam, not his inner grace.

Ezobi, tr I. Gollancz. *LJC*, July 19, 1901.

426.5 None may enter the academy who is not inwardly as outwardly.

Gamaliel II. *Talmud: Berakot*, 28b.

426.6 The idea in Judaism is mightier than the vessel which first contained it . . . Break the vessel and save its precious contents.

Geiger, *Judaism and Its History*, 1865, tr Mayer, 45.

426.7 The harder the shell, the sweeter the almond.

Heine, *Germany from Luther to Kant*, 1834.

426.8 Jewish ethics, with its emphasis on the motives of the heart and its concern for the actions of men, has shown itself able to preserve the tension between the inner and the outer.

Herberg, *Judaism & Modern Man*, 1951, p. 102.

426.9 It is only the attainment of the higher level of inner religious life which justifies an abandonment of our religious forms, that on a lower level are both a duty and a necessity.

Holdheim, address, April 2, 1846. *JQRo*, i. 212.

426.10 A cup is judged by what is drunk from it.

M. Ibn Ezra, *Shirat Yisrael*, (12C) 1924, p. 93.

426.11 "Pure gold, within and without" [*Exod.* 25.11]. A scholar who is not inside as he is outside is no scholar.

Raba. *Talmud: Yoma*, 72b.

426.12 Meir found a pomegranate: he ate the fruit and threw away the rind (ref. to his association with Elisha b. Abuya).

Rabbah b. Shela. *Talmud: Hagiga*, 15b.

426.13 The "forms" of religion are not dissociable from their "matter". . . . "Outward" and "inward" are corporeal metaphors which represent the spiritual only faultily. A holy life is defined in actions and dispositions to action which . . . make up the concrete fullness of living.

L. Roth, *Jewish Thought*, 1954, p. 32.

426.14 The roads to freedom do not run through the lands out yonder, but rather through our inner selves.

Schnitzler, *Der Weg ins Freie*, 1908. q LGS, 134.

426.15 When a Roman princess saw Joshua b. Hanania and remarked, "O glorious wisdom in such a homely vessel!" he replied, "Wine is not kept in vessels of gold."

Talmud: Taanit, 7a.

426.16 Without inwardness there can be no external world, and without imagination there can be no reality.

Werfel, *Realism and Inwardness*, 1930. *Between Heaven and Earth*, 1944, p. 58.

427. INNOCENCE

427.1 I will wash my hands in innocence.
Bible: Ps., 26.6.

427.2 God will not cast away an innocent man.
Bible: Job, 8.20.

427.3 The innocent man is a laughing-stock.
Ibid., 12.4.

427.4 Let us all die in our innocence.
Apocrypha: I Macc., 2.37.

428. INQUISITION

428.1 The bloodhounds of bigotry.
M. M. Noah.

428.2 The fires of the Inquisition, lighted exclusively for the Jews, were destined eventually to consume their oppressors.

*Prescott, *Reign of Ferdinand & Isabella*, (1837) i. 264.

428.3 They introduced from Rome a ferocious monster, . . . that at its name alone all Europe trembled. . . . Its breath kills more speedily than the basilisk, . . . and it feeds only on human bodies. . . . Every green thing it treads on, . . . it blights and withers . . . and leaves everything within its range desolate.

Usque, *Consolação às Tribulaçoes de Yisrael*, 1553, ch 25.

428.4 Would you believe that while the flames were consuming these innocent victims, the inquisitors and the other savages were chanting *our* prayers? These pitiless monsters were invoking the God of mercy . . . while committing the most atrocious crime.

*Voltaire, "Sermon du Rabbin Akib." *Nouveaux Mélanges*, iii. 1765. BSS, 203.

429. INSPIRATION

429.1 We can never rely on inspiration. When we most want it, it does not come.
Gershwin.

429.2 When the minstrel sees two beautiful eyes,
　　Then songs from his inmost bosom arise.

Heine, *Book of Songs: Quite True*, 1827.

429.3 Words of the pious kindle sparks in the souls of people naturally open to religion . . . while those who are not so gifted must have recourse to theological dialectics.

Judah Halevi, *Cuzari*, c. 1135, 5.16.

430. INSTABILITY

430.1 Unstable as water, you shall not excel.
Bible: Gen., 49.4.

430.2 Your goodness is as a morning cloud . . . that early passes away.
Bible: Hos., 6.4.

430.3 Like the chaff which the wind drives away.
Bible: Ps., 1.4.

431. INSTINCT

431.1 We must always remember that the sphere of life is essentially that of instinct.

Bergson, *Two Sources of Morality & Religion*, 1935, 119.

431.2 Build fences, so as not to forget the peril of instinct.

Braude, see Glenn, *Israel Salanter*, 73.

432. INSTITUTION

432.1 Judaism lives not in an abstract creed, but in its institutions.

J. Auerbach. III Versam. deut. Rabbiner, 1846. *Protokolle*, 130.

432.2 Man is as the Lord made him. But we can change our institutions.

Brandeis, to A. Lief, Dec. 7, 1940. q LBG, 93.

432.3 The number of new political ideas is very small. . . . But the institutions are found in constant change and must be seized in their own peculiar historical forms.

G. Jellinek, *Declaration of the Rights of Man*, 1895, ch 6. tr M. Farrand, 1901, p. 57f.

432.4 No important institution is ever merely what the law makes it. It accumulates about itself traditions, conventions, ways of behavior, which . . . are not less formidable in their influence.

Laski, *The American Presidency*, 1940.

433. INSULT

433.A. About Insults

433.A.1 He who offends, though only with words, must appease.

Isaac Nappaha. *Talmud: Yoma*, 87a.

433.A.2 Insults borne for Thy sake are an honor!

Judah Halevi, *Pride of a Jew*. q Jacobs, *Jewish Ideals*, 119.

433.A.3 Taunt not your neighbor with your own blemish!

Nathan. *Talmud: Baba Metzia*, 59b.

433.A.4 Adorning oneself by besmirching a neighbor . . . is like pouring good wine in a cracked cask.

Orhot Tzaddikim, 15C, Introduction.

433.A.5 One stigmatizes others with one's own blemishes.

Samuel. *Talmud: Kiddushin*, 70b.

433.A.6 To avoid an insult, you may tell a white lie.

Sefer Hasidim, 13C, #106, p. 57.

433A.7 God grant that you neither shame nor be shamed.

Simeon b. Halafta. *Talmud: Moed Katan*, 9b.

433.A.8 Throw yourself into a blazing furnace rather than shame a neighbor in public.

Simeon b. Yohai. *Talmud: Berakot*, 43b. Cf *NT: Matt.* 5.22.

433.A.9 Shaming another in public is like shedding blood.

Talmud: Baba Metzia, 58b.

433.B. Insults

433.B.1 I never forget a face, but in your case I'll make an exception.

Groucho Marx.

433.B.2 Sawdust Caesar.

George Seldes, title of book on Mussolini, 1932.

433.B.3 Judge Gary never saw a blast furnace until after his death.

Stolberg, *The Story of the C. I. O.*, 1938, p. 67.

434. INTEGRITY

434.1 Let integrity and uprightness preserve me.

Bible: Ps., 25.21.

434.2 Mark the man of integrity, and behold the upright!

Ibid., 37.37.

434.3 Who walks in a way of integrity . . . shall minister to Me.

Ibid., 101.6.

434.4 It is integrity that invests man with immortality, and bestows upon him the privilege of direct communion with God.

Bahya b. Asher, *Kad HaKemah*, 14C, p. 71. See BSJ, 116.

434.5 The quality of insight is determined by the degree of our ultimate integrity. Sound vision is the reward of maturity, and maturity is intellectual, emotional, spiritual integrity.

Guggenheimer, *Creative Vision*, 1950, p. 4.

434.6 What health can there be for him who is not whole with his Master?

Maimon b. Joseph, *Letter of Consolation*, 1160.

434.7 Man can be whole only when he comprises both love and fear.

Z. Rabinowitz, *Pri Tzaddik*, 1906.

435. INTELLIGENCE

435.1 A man shall be commended according to his intelligence.
Bible: Prov., 12.8.

435.2 Intelligence . . . is the faculty of manufacturing artificial objects, especially tools to make tools.
Bergson, *Creative Evolution,* (1908) 1911, ch 2.

435.3 It is the very essence of intelligence to coordinate means with a view to a remote end, and to undertake what it does not feel absolutely sure of carrying out.
Bergson, *Two Sources of Morality & Religion,* 1935, p. 128.

435.4 We regard intelligence as man's main characteristic, and we know that there is no superiority which intelligence cannot confer on us, no inferiority for which it cannot compensate.
Ibid., p. 171.

435.5 Intelligence is a shrewd calculator before it is an appreciative philosopher.
Guggenheimer, *Creative Vision,* 1950, p. 72.

435.6 In everything, the more the cheaper, except in intelligence, the more the dearer.
Hasdai, *Ben HaMelek VeHaNazir,* c. 1230, ch 25.

435.7 The beginning of intelligence is discrimination between the probable and improbable, and acceptance of the inevitable.
Ibn Gabirol, *Mibhar HaPeninim,* c. 1050. #209.

435.8 The intelligent will know his time, guard his tongue, and attend to his business.
Ibid., #212.

435.9 When intelligence expires, charity departs.
Jeiteles. *Bikkuré Halttim,* 5587.

435.10 To be intelligent is to be open-minded, active-memoried, and persistently experimental.
L. Stein, *Journey into the Self,* 1950, p. 109.

435.11 Intelligent means one who can see implications and draw conclusions.
Talmud: Hagiga, 14a.

435.12 Men are not narrow in their intellectual interests by nature; it takes special and vigorous training to accomplish that end.
Viner, *Scholarship in Graduate Training,* 1953.

435.13 An intelligent man will seek knowledge in details before venturing to discourse on great subjects.
Zunz, *Azariah de Rossi. Kerem Hemed,* v. 130.

436. INTENTION

436.1 Scripture credits him who intended to do a good deed and was forcibly prevented, as though he had done it.
Ammi b. Nathan. *Talmud: Sabbath,* 63a.

436.2 If the intention is not pure, the deed is not acceptable.
Bahya, *Hobot HaLebabot,* 1040, Introduction.

436.3 Rather a little [prayer] with intention than much without it.
Caro, *Shulhan Aruk: Orah Hayyim,* 1564, 1.1.

436.4 The intention is the foundation of the deed.
M. Ibn Ezra, *Shirat Yisrael,* (12C) 1924, p. 141.

436.5 Precepts do not require intention.
José. *Talmud: Pesahim,* 114b.

436.6 Precepts do require intention.
Simeon b. Lakish. *Ibid.*

436.7 The heart's intention is the measure of all things.
Maimonides, letter to Hasdai Halevi. *KTJ,* i .197. See *Guide for the Perplexed,* 3.51.

436.8 The validity of the words depends on the heart's intention.
Meir. *Talmud: Berakot,* 15a.

436.9 Better sin with good intent than conformity with evil intent.
Nahman b. Isaac. *Talmud: Nazir,* 23b.

436.10 If a man eats lamb, thinking it is pork, he requires atonement and forgiveness.
Sifré, Num., #153.

436.11 It is the heart, the disposition, the intent that give value to the deed.
Steinthal, *Ueber Juden und Judentum,* 1906, p. 30.

436.12 In retribution, the Holy One adds good intentions to good deeds, but not evil intentions to evil deeds.
Tosefta: Peah, 1.4. *Talmud: Kiddushin,* 39b.

437. INTERPRETATION

437.1 Do not interpretations belong to God?
Bible: Gen., 40.8.

437.2 Who multiplies commentaries, multiplies nonsense.
Caspi, *Commentary,* to *Jer.,* end.

437.3 The rabbinic methods of interpretation . . . are all of Sinaitic origin.
Z. H. Chajes, *Mebo HaTalmud,* 1845, ch 3, tr 1952, p. 23.

437.4 The dead letter needs to be made living by interpretation.
L. Ginzberg, *Commentary on Jer. Talmud,* 1941, Intr. GOJ, 3.

437.5 Whenever a person's words can be interpreted so as to agree with fully established facts, it is the duty of every educated and honest man so to interpret them.
Maimonides, *Guide for the Perplexed,* 1190, 3.14.

437.6 Nothing can be said so rightly that it cannot be twisted into wrong.
q Spinoza, *Theologico-Political Treatise,* 1670, ch 12.

437.7 The Torah can be interpreted in forty-nine different ways, and God told Moses, Decide according to the majority.
Yannai. *Talmud J: Sanhedrin,* 4.2.

438. INTUITION

438.1 A man's heart tells him his opportunities better than seven watchmen on a tower.
Apocrypha: Ben Sira, 37.14.

438.2 Intuition precedes all creation.
Bialik. q OMB, 51.

438.3 The supreme task of the physicist is to arrive at those universal elementary laws from which the cosmos can be built up by pure deduction. There is no logical path to these laws; only intuition, resting on sympathetic understanding of experience, can reach them.
Einstein, address, 1918. *Ideas and Opinions,* 226.

438.4 A man who acts intuitively is dearer in the sight of God than a sinner whom calculating caution returned to good.
q M. Ibn Ezra, *Shirat Yisrael,* (12C) 1924, p. 96.

438.5 Intuition is an integral part of the processes of the human mind. . . . But . . . although reason may err . . . , it does carry within itself the means of remedy, and intuition does not.
H. Samuel, *Belief and Action,* 1937, p. 72f.

438.6 Beauty is the result of intuition; when the one ceases to be, the other ceases also.
Schoenberg. Armitage, *Schoenberg,* p. 257.

438.7 A religion based upon mystical intuition, unchecked by reason, is capable of all sorts of grossness and stupidities.
M. Steinberg. *Reconstructionist,* Nov. 1, 1935.

439. INVENTION

439.1 God made man upright, but they sought out many inventions.
Bible: Eccles., 7.29.

439.2 Mechanical inventions . . . diminish distance vainly; they contribute nothing to the rapprochement of minds.
Bergson, letter to L. Brunschwicq. q *Reflex,* 1927, 119.

439.3 When were there seen such great inventions as in our generation? And as a result, have there been less war, murder, theft, poverty, disease, envy, hatred and untimely death?
S. D. Luzzatto *Yesodé HaTorah,* 1880, p. 11f.

439.4 All our inventions have endowed material forces with intellectual life, and degraded human life into a material force.
Marx, speech, London, April 14, 1856.

439.5 Now life can be taken easily, quickly, with good guns and clever devices, which a merciful generation invented for the benefit of men!
Mendelé, *Di Kliatshé,* 1873.

440. INVENTORY

440.1 Keep careful accounts, and strike an annual balance. Apply the same rule to your moral conduct.
Elijah b. Raphael, *Tzavaah,* 18C. AHE, 308.

440.2 Who inspects his property daily will save a dollar.
Samuel. *Talmud: Hullin,* 105a.

441. INVITATION

441.1 Say not to your neighbor, Dine at my house for I dined at yours. It sounds like usury.
Talmud: Pirké Ben Azzai, 6.2.

441.2 When you are invited, decline; when you are invited again, hesitate; and when you are asked a third time, [accept].
Talmud J: Berakot, 5.3, ref. to leading in prayer.

442. IRELAND

442.1 "Ireland has the honor of being the only country which never persecuted the Jews." . . . "Because she never let them in."
*Joyce, *Ulysses,* (1914) 1934, p. 37.

443. IRON

443.1 The iron entered his soul.
Bible: Ps., 105.18, Vulgate mistranslation.

443.2 Iron sharpens iron; so a man sharpens the countenance of his friend.
Bible: Prov., 27.17.

443.3 Iron axes that break iron.
Raba. *Talmud: Sanhedrin,* 96b. (Scholars who contradict scholars).

444. IRONY

444.1 The antiquity of their race, their sense of its long-suffering and isolation, . . . leads the stronger or more reflective spirits to revenge themselves by a kind of scorn upon the upstart Western peoples among whom their lot is cast. The mockery one finds in Heinrich Heine could not have come from a Teuton.
*Bryce, *Studies in Contemporary Biography,* (1903) 1927, 19f.

444.2 If their irony has at times a touch of the Satanic, this comes from the hell of the Ghetto and the long damnation of the Judengasse. . . . Irony, sarcasm, have ever been the weapons of the weak when persecuted or degraded. . . . Moreover, the irony of the Jews spares no one; they ridiculed themselves as well as others.
*Leroy-Beaulieu, *Israel Among the Nations,* 1895, p. 258.

444.3 Satire and irony are the weapons of clever slaves. I wince whenever a new Jewish book or play is acclaimed by other Jews as merciless, mordant, hard, witty.
Lewisohn. q M. Syrkin. JAJ, 94.

445. ISRAEL

445.A. The Name

445.A.1 Your name shall be called . . . Israel, for you have striven with God and with men, and have prevailed.
Bible: Gen., 32.29.

445.A.2 Israel means "seeing God."
Philo, *Dreams,* ii. 26.

445.A.3 Read *Ish raah el,* "a man who saw God."
Seder Eliyahu Rabbah, ch 25 (27), ed Friedmann, 138f.

445.A.4 *Yisra-el:* God attached His name to Israel's, like a king who clasps a precious key to his chain, that it be not lost.
Yannai. *Talmud J: Taanit,* 2.6.

445.B. The People

Character

445.B.1 I will make of you a great nation.
Bible: Gen., 12.2.

445.B.2 It is a people that shall dwell alone, and shall not be reckoned among the nations.
Bible: Num., 23.9.

445.B.3 You are a holy people unto the Lord your God.
Bible: Deut., 7.6.

445.B.4 Who is like Thy people, . . . a nation one in the earth.
Bible: II Sam., 7.23. Cf *I Chron.* 17.21. Eleazar b. Azariah. *Talmud: Berakot,* 6a.

445.B.5 Israel is the core of the human race and the rest of humanity is like the peeling.
Abravanel, *Commentary* on *Exod.,* Introd. q NDI, 302.

445.B.6 Those that do not regard these books as . . . Divine revelation must admit that Israel is the super-people of the world!
*Faulhaber, *Judaism, Christianity & Germany,* 1933.

445.B.7 We are the heartbeat of a world that wills
To find its noblest self and to fulfill
The law of Justice which it seeks to know;
We are God's people, for we will it so,
The stars our quest and truth our watchword still!

Fleg, *Why I Am a Jew,* 1929, p. xv.

445.B.8 Israel is the people of Revelation. . . . It must have had a native endowment that it could produce . . . such heroes of the spirit.
Geiger, *Judaism and Its History,* 1865, p. 61f.

445.B.9 As an olive tree does not lose its foliage in summer or winter, so Israel will never be lost, here or hereafter.

Joshua b. Levi. *Talmud: Menahot,* 53b, on *Jer.* 11.16.

445.B.10 Israel among the nations is like the heart amidst the organs of the body: it is the sickest and healthiest of them.

Judah Halevi, *Cuzari,* c. 1135, 2.36.

445.B.11 Israel did not derive its high position from Moses, but Moses attained his for Israel's sake.

Ibid., 2.56.

445.B.12 Israel, the holy people, is higher than all the world.

Levi Yitzhok. q HLH, 43.

445.B.13 Israel, the only democracy of antiquity.

*Michelet. q *JQRo,* ix. 394.

445.B.14 "Do homage to the wheat" [*Ps.* 2.12]. The stalk and the chaff had an argument, each claiming that the field had been tilled for its sake. At threshing time, the chaff was scattered to the wind and the stem was given to the flames, while the wheat was carefully gathered on the floor. So among the nations, each claiming that the world was created for its sake. But wait for the Day of Judgment!

Midrash Tehillim, 2.14, ed Buber, 16a, on *Cant.* 7.3.

Pesikta Rabbati, ch 10, ed Friedmann, 36a.

455.B.15 A golden harp is Israel—its strings
Are heaven's own rays,
That trembling, pour a melody that sings
Of holiness when poet plays.
Alas, the melody is sad and low,
For God has tuned the harp strings so.

C. Shapiro, *Collected Poems,* 75. q WHJ, iv. 211.

445.B.16 The Jews, like the Greeks, were a unique fact in the development of man. . . . There were other pastoral peoples in the Levant. . . . Other groups were ground between the upper and nether millstones of war, invasion, and captivity. . . . But it was this particular race, . . . that became the vehicle of the new ideas. These ideas have the originality and unpredictability of genius.

*Ward, *Faith and Freedom,* 1954, p. 49.

445.B.17 Moses was the greatest of all artists . . . and he left to posterity that imperishable statue of truth . . . : its pedestal is the earth, its head reaches heaven's dome; the name of that inimitable colossus is Israel, the immortal, a nation graced by the choice of God.

I. M. Wise, "Moses," 1889. *Selected Writings,* 168.

445.B.18 There is no God but God, and Israel is His prophet; not Moses, not Christ, not Mohammed, but Israel, the race in whom God was revealed.

Zangwill. *North American Review,* April 1895.

Beloved of God

445.B.19 Israel is My son, My first-born.
Bible: Exod., 4.22. See *Deut.,* 14.1.

445.B.20 Is Ephraim My darling son? . . . for as often as I speak of him, . . . My heart yearns for him.
Bible: Jer., 31.20.

445.B.21 Beloved is Israel, called "Children of God" [*Deut.* 14.1], and presented with a priceless, world-creative treasure.

Akiba, on *Prov.* 4.2. *Mishna: Abot,* 3.14.

445.B.22 Only when they do My will are they My children.
Exod. R., 46.4.

445.B.23 Even if they be foolish, transgressors, full of flaws, they are still "Sons of God."

Meir. *Sifré,* #308, to *Deut.* 32.5, ed Friedmann, 133a.

445.B.24 What great nation . . . has God so nigh to them?
Bible: Deut., 4.7. See *Ps.,* 148.14.

445.B.25 God is like a brother when Israel is in trouble.

Hanania b. Hakinai. *Mekilta,* to *Exod.* 14.15.

445.B.26 A man is proud to call a distinguished philosopher his kin, but the Holy One calls all Israel His close relatives.

Simeon b. Lakish, on *Ps.* 148.14. *Talmud J: Berakot,* 9.1.

445.B.27 The portion of the Lord is His people.
Bible: Deut., 32.9. See 4.20; *Jer.,* 2.3.

445.B.28 The Lord will not forsake His people.
Bible: I Sam., 12.22.

445.B.29 Can a woman forget her sucking child . . . ? Yea, these may forget, yet will I not forget you.

Bible: Isa., 49.14f. See Talmud: Berakot, 32b.

445.B.30 Your Maker is your husband.

Bible: Isa., 54.4. See Jer., 51.5.

445.B.31 I will betroth you unto Me for ever.

Bible: Hos., 2.21. See 11.4.

445.B.32 Sanctification is the term for the marriage ceremony; and when we say in our prayers, "God who sanctified us," we may indeed connote by it, "God who wedded us."

Abudraham, Hibbur Perush HaBerakot VeHaTefilot, 1340.

445.B.33 Israel is a young woman of good family, the Holy One is a princely wooer, and Moses is His envoy.

Johanan. Cant. R., 1.2.3.

445.B.34 Thou hast loved us, taken pleasure in us, and exalted us above all tongues. Thou hast sanctified us by Thy commandments, brought us near to Thy service, and called us by Thy great and holy name.

Prayer for Festivals. DPB, ed Singer, 227.

445.B.35 I have loved you with an everlasting love.

Bible: Jer., 31.3. See DPB, ed Singer, 96; UPB i. 118.

445.B.36 The Lord will be a refuge to His people.

Bible: Joel, 4.16.

445.B.37 Israel is like a crown, whose artisan is told, Set in it as many jewels, pearls and emeralds as you can, for it will adorn the head of the king.

Judah b. Simon. Lev. R., 2.5, on Isa. 49.3.

445.B.38 To hate Israel is to hate God. . . . To rise against Israel is to rise against God. . . . To help Israel is to help God.

Sifré, Num., #84.

445.B.39 Beloved are Israelites, for the Holy One encompassed them with precepts: tefillin on head and arm, fringes on clothes, mezuzot on door-posts.

Talmud: Menahot, 43b.

445.B.40 Israelites are dearer to the Holy One than angels.

Talmud: Hullin, 91b.

445.B.41 The Holy One and the community of Israel are called one when they are together, not when they are parted.

Zohar, Lev., 93b.

Chosen People

445.B.42 I will take you to me for a people and I will be to you a God.

Bible: Exod., 6.7. See II Sam. 7.24; Jer., 24.7.

445.B.43 I have set you apart from the peoples that ye should be Mine.

Bible: Lev., 20.26.

445.B.44 You only have I known of all the families of the earth; therefore will I visit upon you all your iniquities.

Bible: Amos, 3.2.

445.B.45 Are ye not as the children of the Ethiopians unto Me, O children of Israel? saith the Lord.

Ibid., 9.7.

445.B.46 Israel's great advantage . . . is their belief in God's unity and their acceptance of the Torah. But . . . all are fit to believe and confess the same.

Abraham b. Hiyya HaNasi, Hegyon HaNefesh, (12C) 1860, 8a.

445.B.47 Whoever adopts these principles belongs to Israel, regardless of his national or racial origin.

Yahuda, Eber VeArab, 1946, p. 45, Note 10.

445.B.48 For the elect there shall be light and joy and peace, and they shall inherit the earth.

Apocrypha: Enoch, 5.7. See 58.2.

445.B.49 Praised be Thou . . . who hast chosen Thy people Israel in love.

Benediction, pre-Maccabean. DPB, ed Singer, 40. See Hamnuna. Talmud: Berakot, 11b.

445.B.50 With keen and passionate pleasure I would blot out from the prayer book of the Jew of our day the "Thou hast chosen us" in every shape and form.

Brenner, MiKan uMiKan, 1911. q SHR, 386.

445.B.51 The belief in Israel's election . . . creates a useful self-consciousness over against the ruling Church.

Einhorn. II Rabbiner Versammlung, 1845.

445.B.52 In charging itself with the burden of His law, Israel feels itself chosen, not as a master but as a servant. . . . It separates itself from others only for the purpose of uniting them.

Fleg, Why I Am a Jew, 1929, p. 65.

445.B.53 History, not Jehovah, chose the Jew; but it chose him for tragedy.
Goldberg. *Reflex*, July 1927, p. 30.

445.B.54 Every people regards itself as chosen, and it exhibits the higher self-consciousness if it does not put forward its defects as merits.
Güdemann, *Das Judentum*, 1902, p. 44. q JJC, 118.

445.B.55 The character of Israel as the chosen people does not involve the inferiority of other nations. . . . It was the *noblesse oblige* of the God-appointed worker for the entire human race.
Güdemann, *Das Judentum*, 1902, p. 44. q *JE*, iv. 46a.

445.B.56 It is in no arrogant temper that we claim to be the chosen people. We thereby affirm, not that we are better than others, but that we ought to be better.
M. Joseph, *Judaism as Creed and Life*, 1903, p. 117f.

445.B.57 We . . . advocate the elimination from our own liturgy of all references to the doctrine of Israel as the Chosen People.
Kaplan, *Future of the American Jew*, 1948, p. 79.

445.B.58 God selected a people for His special education, and precisely the rudest and unruliest, in order to begin with it from the very beginning. . . . He was bringing up in them the future teachers of the human race.
*Lessing, *Education of the Human Race*, 1778, Nos. 8, 18.

445.B.59 "Thou hast chosen us from among all nations"—what, O Lord, did You have against us?
Proverb (Yiddish). BJS, #309.

445.B.60 How odd of God to choose the Jews.
Saying, used by L. Browne for title of book, 1934.

445.B.61 It's not so odd. The Jews chose God.
Saying. q L. Roth, *Jewish Thought*, 1954, p. 39.

445.B.62 The Chosen People . . . felt in humility and reverence . . . that its destiny was to think, to suffer. . . . And its admission of proselytes . . . proved that it did not interpret its mission to be

. . . racial integrity, but rather the binding tie for all peoples.
S. Schulman. *Menorah Journal*, 1924, x. 317.

445.B.63 The most notorious historical example of the idolization of an ephemeral self is the error of the Jews. . . . They persuaded themselves that Israel's discovery of the One True God had revealed Israel itself to be God's Chosen People.
*Toynbee, *A Study of History*, 1939, iv. 262.

445.B.64 It is clear to me that no people can continue being *chosen*, nor unceasingly designate itself as such, without upsetting in the eyes of other peoples the normal order of things. The whole idea is plainly absurd and immoral.
J. Wassermann. LCJ, 1929, p. 120.

445.B.65 A chosen people is really a choosing people. Not idly does Talmudical legend assert that the Law was offered first to all other nations and only Israel accepted the yoke.
Zangwill, *Chosen Peoples. Menorah Journal*, 1918, iv. 261. See *War for the World*, 1915, 1921, p. 133.

445.C. Mission

445.C.1 Ye shall be Mine own treasure from among all peoples, . . . a kingdom of priests and a holy nation.
Bible: Exod., 19.5f.

445.C.2 I have set you for a light of the nations: to open the blind eyes, to bring out prisoners from the dungeon.
Bible: Isa., 42.6f. See 49.6.

445.C.3 Ye are My witnesses, says the Lord.
Ibid., 43.10. See 43.21.

445.C.4 The remnant of Jacob shall be amidst many peoples, as dew from the Lord, as showers upon the grass.
Bible: Mic., 5.6.

445.C.5 What will the Gentiles do if ye be darkened through sin?
Apocrypha: Patriarchs, Levi, 14.4.

445.C.6 God shall be glorified among the Gentiles through you.
Ibid., Naphtali, 8.4.

445.C.7 The Jews were for all mortal men the guides to life.
Apocrypha: Sibyls, 3.195.

445.C.8 It is justly said of the Jewish people . . . that they were "entrusted with the oracles of God."
*Arnold, *Culture and Anarchy*, 1869.

445.C.9 The destiny of God rests on the shoulders of Israel.
H. Cohen.

445.C.10 The idea, I confess, is a noble one; but it is merely an idea, lacking real substance, and resting on air. . . . There is no special Jewish work to do, which others of non-Jewish descent could not do just as well.
Felsenthal. *Maccabean*, March 1903, pp. 131, 133.

445.C.11 It is the most perseverant nation in the world: it is, it was, and will be, to glorify the name of Jehovah through all ages.
*Goethe, *Wilhelm Meister's Travels*, 1829, ch 11.

445.C.12 We are God's stake in human history. We are the dawn and the dusk, the challenge and the test. . . . We carry the gold of God in our souls to forge the gate of the kingdom.
Heschel, *The Earth Is the Lord's*, 1950, p. 109.

445.C.13 The Jew assumes for himself the historic post of a sentinel and soldier of righteousness. . . . He protests by his very existence against the doctrine that might makes right, that numbers decide truth, and that possession condones every offense.
E. G. Hirsch. *Reform Advocate*, 1891, i. 425.

445.C.14 Because men had eliminated God from life, nay, even from nature, and found the basis of life in possessions and its aim in enjoyment, . . . it became necessary that a people be introduced into the ranks of the nations which, through its history and life, should declare God the only creative cause of existence, fulfillment of His will the only aim of life, and which should bear the revelation of His will . . . unto all parts of the world as the motive and incentive of its coherence.
S. R. Hirsch, *Nineteen Letters*, (1836) 1899, #7, p. 66f.

445.C.15 Israel has not sent out any missionaries to carry its faith to mankind. But what need had it of missionaries when it itself went to the nations as the messenger of the Lord of Hosts, and engraved its belief on the stony hearts of men with the stylus dipped in its own heart's blood.
Holdheim. q Philipson, *Centenary Papers*, 93.

445.C.16 The world depends on Israel's piety.
Isaac the Blind, *Bahir*, c. 1200.

445.C.17 Israel may be considered as contributing the element of form to the world's otherwise chaotic and undisciplined character. And if Israel should, God forbid, perish, the whole world would fail.
Judah Löw. q BWC, 170.

445.C.18 God warned Israel to proclaim Him as God to the world.
Lev. R., 6.5.

445.C.19 Israel's mission is . . . to realize its ideals on its own soil and in its own State.
Livneh, *BeShaar HaTekufa*. *JS*, Dec. 1952, p. 12.

445.C.20 It may take fifty years more . . . or ten thousand years more for Israel's task to be accomplished; accomplished it will be some day . . . when there will be collective righteousness, the righteousness of the State, the righteousness of the Nation, and righteousness among the Nations as well as righteousness practiced by the individual. This is the mission of Israel.
Lubin, letter to Enelow, June 1912. q ADL, 76f. See 331.

445.C.21 The Israelites are and have to remain a distinct nation, having essentially the prerogative of sanctifying life.
Manasseh b. Israel, *Nishmat Hayyim*, 1652.

445.C.22 The great majority of Jews is like the great majority of voters. It fears war. It fears troubled times. . . . They know the cost of bearing God and His agents, the prophets. . . . Secretly they would prefer . . . to make no noise in the world . . . to purchase peace with prudent silence. . . . Israel wishes to be forgotten. . . . But the whole of Israel's mysticism demands that Israel should pursue its resounding and painful mission. . . . A people of merchants, the same people one of prophets.
*Péguy. *Notre Jeunesse*, 1910, xi. 12. *Basic Verities*, 131–7.

445.C.23 Almighty and merciful God, Thou hast called Israel to Thy service and found him worthy to bear witness unto Thy truth among the peoples of the earth. Give us grace to fulfill this mission with zeal tempered by wisdom and guided by regard for other men's faith.
Union Prayer Book, 1940. i. 34.

445.C.24 Israel has a mission still: Truth-seeking in the world of thought, and right-doing in the world of action!

S. S. Wise, *Sermons and Addresses*, 1905, p. 122.

445.C.25 We are proud and happy in that the dread Unknown God of the infinite Universe has chosen our race as the medium by which to reveal His will to the world. . . . Our miraculous survival through the cataclysms of ancient and modern dynasties is a proof that our mission is not yet over.

Zangwill, *Children of the Ghetto*, 1892, ii. ch 2, p. 342.

445.C.26 What our preachers really preach is that the mission of Israel is *sub*mission, for never do they set up our own ideal—our supposed mission of Peace and Brotherhood upon earth.

Zangwill, speech, 1903. q ZVJ, 89.

445.C.27 Assume whatever attitude you wish toward this national dream of ours regarding a world mission of the Jewish people in its own land, but there is no question that this national dream, this national faith, wove a halo of heroic, tragic beauty about the historic fate of the Jewish people in exile.

Zhitlovsky. *Serp*, 1908, ii. 310. *Gez. Shr.*, vii. 234f.

445.D.   The Land

445.D.1 The Lord appeared unto Abram and said: "Unto thy seed will I give this land."

Bible: Gen., 12.7. See 13.14f.

445.D.2 God of Israel, . . . remember Thy covenant . . . that their seed should never fail from the land which Thou hast given them.

Apocrypha: Assumption of Moses, 3.9.

445.D.3 A land flowing with milk and honey.

Bible: Exod., 3.8.

445.D.4 From Dan to Beer-Sheba.

Bible: Judg., 20.1.

445.D.5 To consummate the purchase of a house in Israel, the deed may be written even on the Sabbath.

Adda, or Aha, or Hanina, b. Papa. *Talmud: Baba Kamma*, 80b.

445.D.6 Burial in Israel is like burial under the altar.

Anan. *Talmud: Ketubot*, 11a. See Eleazar b. Pedat. *Ibid.; Gen. R.*, 96.5.

445.D.7 Japheth's land is cold, Ham's is hot, Shem's is . . . moderate.

Apocrypha: Jubilees, 8.30.

445.D.8 This country made us a people; our people made this country.

Ben Gurion, at Anglo-American Comm. of Inquiry, March 19, 1946.

445.D.9 What need for nature to be fair in a scene like this, where not a spot is visible that is not heroic or sacred.

Disraeli, *Tancred*, 1847.

445.D.10 As a deer's skin shrinks when life has expired, so Israel expands when inhabited, and contracts when uninhabited.

Hanina b. Hama. *Talmud: Gittin*, 57a.

445.D.11 Stones in the Land of Israel are heavier than in other lands.

J. Israel, *Yalkut Hadash*, 1648.

445.D.12 Nothing can be perfect, except in Israel.

Judah Halevi, *Cuzari*, c. 1135, 5.23.

445.D.13 The Torah cannot assume perfection except in Israel.

Nahmanides. See Heller, *Zionist Idea*, 117.

445.D.14 All the weaning of the centuries, all the enlightenment of modern times, have been unable to banish a longing for that land from their hearts.

Kaufmann, *George Eliot and Judaism*, 1877.

445.D.15 Palestine has the size of a county and the problems of a continent.

q Koestler, *Promise and Fulfillment*, 196.

445.D.16 Only in the Holy Land can the spirit of our people develop and become a light for the world.

Kook. *Azkara*, 1937, i. q ABJ, 63.

445.D.17 Land of the muses, perfection of beauty, wherein every stone is a book, every rock a graven tablet.

M. J. Lebensohn, "Judah Halevi." *Shiré Bat Tziyon*, 1852. q SRH, 133.

445.D.18 Anyone who spreads an evil report about the Land of Israel—even if it be true—is a spy.

J. L. Maimon. *JS*, Oct. 1951, quoting a rabbi of Volozhin.

445.D.19 Living in Israel is itself an atonement for one's sins.

Meir. *Sifré*, #333, to *Deut.* 32.44. See *TJ: Shekalim*, 3.3.

445.D.20 Residence in Israel is equivalent to the observance of all the biblical precepts.

Eleazar b. Shammua. *Sifré,* #80, to *Deut.* 13.29.

445.D.21 Who walks four cubits in Israel is assured of a place in the world to come.

Johanan. *Talmud: Ketubot,* 111a.

445.D.22 Even a Canaanite bondwoman, if she lives in Eretz Israel, is assured of belonging to the world to come.

Abbahu. *Ibid.*

445.D.23 Sinning in Eretz Israel is worse than elsewhere. . . . It is like rebellion right within the king's own palace.

Meir of Rothenburg, *Responsa,* (13C) 1891, #14, p. 5.

445.D.24 A man or woman may compel the members of his or her family to move to Israel, but none may be compelled to leave it.

Mishna: Ketubot, 13.11.

445.D.25 The very name Palestine stirs within us the most elevated sentiments. . . . All find consolation in that land, some by its memories, others by its hopes.

S. Munk, 1863. q HBJ, 119.

445.D.26 No matter where I go, it is always to Israel.

Nahman Bratzlav, 1807. q ZRN, 200.

445.D.27 The Land of Israel is the holiest of lands.

Num. R., 7.8.

445.D.28 The Land of Israel extends to the Euphrates River.

Samuel. *Gen. R.,* 16.3.

445.D.29 From each Jewish heart an invisible path leads to the Land of Israel.

Shimonovitz, *BaDerek,* 1923. *Shirim,* ii. 110.

445.D.30 Love for Israel must be a fire burning in the Jew's heart.

Shneor Zalman, *Tanya,* 1796. q HLH, 148.

445.D.31 That little land of revelation which, like some precious, jeweled clasp, draws three continents together on the shore of the Western Sea.

Silver, *Vision and Victory,* 1949.

445.D.32 A sage who leaves Israel diminishes in worth.

Simeon b. Eleazar. *Abot de R. Nathan,* ch 28.

445.D.33 Each land has some unique property, but the Land of Israel is endowed with all of these, lacking none.

Simeon b. Yohai. *Sifré,* #37, to *Deut.* 11.10.

445.D.34 As long as food is available, even though prices are exorbitant, it is forbidden to move from Israel to a foreign land.

Simeon b. Yohai. *Talmud: Baba Bathra,* 91a.

445.D.35 If, God forbid, there be no Jew in Israel, it would spell the end of the nation, though there be Jews elsewhere.

Sofer, *Hatam Sofer, Yoré Deah,* 1841, 234.

445.D.36 Palestine is the center of the world, Jerusalem the center of Palestine, and the Temple the center of Jerusalem. . . . In the Holy of Holies there was a stone, the foundation of the world.

Tanhuma, Kedoshim, 10, ed Buber, p. 78.

445.D.37 Reside in Israel, even among a majority of idolators, rather than outside of Israel, even among a majority of Jews.

Tosefta: Aboda Zara, 4.3.

445.D.38 Those who live outside of Israel may be considered heathen.

Ibid., 4.5.

445.D.39 It was the Jewish genius that bestowed its radiance upon Palestine.

*Whitehead. *Atlantic Monthly,* March 1939, p. 318.

445.D.40 The air of the Land of Israel makes one wise.

Zera. *Talmud: Baba Bathra,* 158b.

445.D.41 The life of souls is the air of thy land.

Judah Halevi, *Selected Poems,* 5.

445.D.42 Residents of Israel are in a holy atmosphere.

Alshek, *Commentary,* to *Kedoshim,* 1593.

445.D.43 Abraham did not enter into a covenant with God till after he had entered the Holy Land.

Zohar, Gen., 79b.

445.D.44 The air of Israel makes . . . people happy and gay.

J. Zucker. q *New Palestine Magazine,* Jan. 1951, p. 2.

445.E. Fall

445.E.1 The virgin of Israel is fallen, she shall rise no more.

Bible: Amos, 5.2.

445.E.2 She that was great among the nations, princess among the provinces, how she is become tributary!
Bible: Lam., 1.1.

445.E.3 The destruction of Israel's independence is . . . the fulfillment of the divine purpose in sending Israel forth into the world upon its priestly mission.
Einhorn. *Jewish Times* (N.Y.), June 1, 1869.

445.E.4 Come, let us bow down before the people of Israel that has known for eighteen centuries how to keep alive its anguish as if the disaster occurred only yesterday.
*Mickiewicz, Aug. 11, 1845.

445.E.5 The holier the place, the greater the desolation.
Nahmanides, letter to his son Nahman, 1267.

445.F. Restoration

445.F.1 He will . . . assemble the dispersed of Israel.
Bible: Isa., 11.12. Cf 49.22.

445.F.2 There shall be a highway for the remnant of His people.
Ibid., 11.16.

445.F.3 The Lord will set them in their own land.
Ibid., 14.1.

445.F.4 The Lord binds up the bruise of His people.
Ibid., 30.26.

445.F.5 The ransomed of the Lord shall return . . . with singing to Zion.
Ibid., 35.10. See 51.11; *Jer.*, 31.11.

445.F.6 The nations . . . shall bring your sons in their bosom, and your daughters shall be carried upon their shoulders.
Bible: Isa., 49.22.

445.F.7 For a small moment have I forsaken you, but with great compassion will I gather you.
Ibid., 54.7.

445.F.8 They shall build the old waste places . . . and you shall be called the repairer of the breach, the restorer of paths.
Ibid., 58.12.

445.F.9 Again will I build you . . . virgin of Israel.
Bible: Jer., 31.3.

445.F.10 He that scattered Israel will gather and guard him as a shepherd his flock.
Ibid., 31.9.

445.F.11 There is hope for your future . . . children will return to their own border.
Ibid., 31.16.

445.F.12 I shall be as dew to Israel; he shall blossom as the lily.
Bible: Hosea, 14.6.

445.F.13 In that day will I raise up David's fallen tabernacle.
Bible: Amos, 9.11.

445.F.14 I will plant them upon their land, and they shall no more be plucked up.
Ibid., 9.15.

445.F.15 All nations shall call you happy, for ye shall be a delightsome land.
Bible: Mal., 3.12.

445.F.16 Jews must settle where their roots are, where the Shekina hovers over them as nowhere else.
Alshek, *Commentary*, to *Kedoshim*, 1593.

445.F.17 We have conquered the swamps of Nahalal and of Nouris, and now we are draining the fields of Gedara. In the swamps of Kabara, too, we must stand in the front ranks and win. . . . Ours is the privilege of dying for Kabara, because we claim for ourselves the privilege of living upon it.
Ben Barak. *HaPoel HaTzair*, Nov. 13, 1924. q SHR, 409.

445.F.18 We have gathered up human particles . . . and combined them into the fruitful and creative nucleus of a nation revived . . . ; in the desolate spaces of a ruined and abandoned Homeland, we have . . . built villages and towns, planted gardens and established factories; . . . we have breathed new life into our muted and abandoned ancient language. . . . Such a marvel is unique in the history of human culture.
Ben Gurion, *Farewell Address*, Dec. 7, 1953.

445.F.19 Tel Hai has gone up in flames, but the heart of Israel is alive!
Brenner, March 1920. q Lipovetzky, *Jos. Trumpeldor*, 98.

445.F.20 You ask me what I wish: my answer is, a national existence. . . . You ask me what I wish: my answer is . . . all we have forfeited, . . . our beauteous country, our holy creed, our simple manners, and our ancient customs.
Disraeli, *Alroy*, 1833, 8.6.

445.F.21 A race that persist in celebrating their vintage, although they have no fruits to gather, will regain their vineyards.

Disraeli, *Tancred,* 1846.

445.F.22 Israel is not lost. "*Barkai!* It dawns in the East!"—as the young priests exclaimed in the old Jerusalem temple, when they noticed the first rays of the rising sun.

Felsenthal. *Maccabean,* March 1903, p. 138.

445.F.23 You will live the life of Israel, and the life will be as a living fountain.

A. D. Gordon, "A Dream." q LEJS, 25.

445.F.24 Ah, well it is that we have forsaken Europe and all its splendors, and have become comrades to all the barefoot who burn in fever and whisper love to the sands and stones in Canaan.

U. Z. Greenberg, *Jerusalem,* tr C. A. Cowen, 1939.

445.F.25 Ye shall be reborn, ye fearsome cities!
A breath of security will always hover
O'er your banks where our colors have fluttered!

Léon Halévy. q Hess, *Rome & Jerusalem,* (1862), p. 146.

445.F.26 Where ruin was, a ransomed folk
Upbuilds its homes anew!

Ibn Gabirol, *The Heavens Shall Yield Their Dew.*

445.F.27 Let your spirits' desires
For the land of our sires
Eternally burn,
From the foe to deliver
Our own holy river
To Jordan return.

Imber, *Watch on the Jordan,* 1886, tr ZCG, ch 15, p. 189.

445.F.28 The Land of Israel was the birthplace of the Jewish people. Here their spiritual, religious and national identity was formed. Here they achieved independence and created a culture of national and universal significance. . . . Impelled by this historic association, Jews strove throughout the centuries to go back to the land of their fathers and regain their Statehood.

Israeli Declaration of Independence, May 14, 1948.

445.F.29 Every Jew has the right to immigrate to Israel.

Israeli Kneset, Law of the Return, adopted July 5, 1950.

445.F.30 Mass immigration to Israel by forceful means is forbidden.

Jose b. Hanina, Judah, Zera. *Talmud: Ketubot,* 111a.

445.F.31 Those who will find here a hold for their souls, an anvil for their hands, and vitality for their hearts, will build both their lives and the land.

Katznelson, "From the Inside." *HaPoel HaTzair,* 1912. *Ktabim,* i. 15.

445.F.32 O God, defend Masadah!

Lamdan, "Masada." *HaPoel HaTzair,* 1927.

445.F.33 The Spirit is not dead, proclaim the word, . . .
I ope your graves, my people, saith the Lord,
And I shall place you in your promised land.

E. Lazarus, "New Ezekiel," c. 1883. *Poems,* ii. 15.

445.F.34 In that day, wonder of centuries,
All who behold thee shall exclaim, "Behold
The people who for ages were hewn down
Upon a thousand altars, . . .
Arising from the wrecks of shattered fanes
Unhurt and pure!"

D. Levi, *Il Profeta,* 1884. q *JQRo,* ix, 395.

445.F.35 The ruin and desolation of the land was and is to us its glory and its opportunity. Here the creative effort of the Jew must build first the very soil he is to dig, bring the very water that is to make it tillable, fight the diseases of man and beast and plant which to the natives had been mere objects of superstitious fear.

Lewisohn, *Israel,* 1925, p. 167. Cf. 643.3.

445.F.36 There is singing again on Mount Scopus. And there is rejoicing in the Holy City of Jerusalem.

Lipsky, *Inauguration of Hebrew University,* March 1925.

445.F.37 If Palestine is to be restored . . . it must be by settling Jews on its soil. The condition to which the land has been reduced . . . is such that restoration is only possible by a race that is prepared for sentimental reasons to make and endure sacrifices for that purpose.

*Lloyd George. Hearst Newspapers, July 1923.

445.F.38 God will raise up the tabernacle of David from the dust. . . . Then He will also send His spirit into our sacred language, to revive it, to put it back upon the pedestal on which it once stood.

M. Mendelssohn. q Kayserling, *Moses Mendelssohn*, 1862, p. 568, app. 57; q HMH, 77.

445.F.39 The Holy One will turn the Ninth of Ab into joy . . . and will Himself build Jerusalem and gather therein the exiles of Israel.

Midrash Zuta, Eka, #28, ed Buber, 1894, p. 74. See *Ps.* 147.2; *Yalkut, Eka*, nos. 7, 104; Abin. *Pesikta Kahana*, ch 13, ed Buber, 104a.

445.F.40 I have seen these Jewish agricultural settlements. They are one of the most wonderful moral demonstrations of the human race. . . . Here are colonies in which people are working on a voluntary cooperative basis with no element of dictatorship or compulsion behind them, actually reclaiming soil hitherto . . . untillable and making it productive. . . . I came back with a humble feeling that I should like to give up this game of House of Commons and politics and join them in the clean, healthy life they are living.

*Morrison, speech, House of Commons, 1936.

445.F.41 Bring us in peace from the four corners of the earth, and make us go upright to our land!

Prayer, pre-Maccabean. *DPB*, ed Singer, 40.

445.F.42 I have pitched my tent on these ancient hills and my desire is to tie together the ends of the thread that history broke.

R. Rubin. q *Jewish Affairs*, July 1951, p. 29.

445.F.43 This people is for peace and for health in a land full of fevers.

Sampter, *The Book of the Nations*, 1917.

445.F.44 Lead me to toil at dawn.
My land wraps itself in light as in the prayer shawl.
New homes stand forth as do phylacteries.
And like phylactery-bands, the highways . . . glide.

Thus a town beautiful recites the morning prayer to its Creator.

Shlonsky. q HMH, 205f.

445.F.45 They may even, if occasion offers, . . . raise up their empire afresh, and God may a second time elect them.

Spinoza, *Theologico-Political Treatise*, 1670, ch 3.

445.F.46 We must work and struggle to redeem our land, and fight with the courage of those for whom there is no possible retreat.

Vitkin, *Manifesto*, 1906. q HMH, 97.

445.F.47 Palestine should be as distinctly Jewish as England is English.

Weizmann, 1919.

445.F.48 The Jews demand no privilege. . . . They solicit no favors. They ask no more than an assured opportunity of peacefully building up their national home by their own exertions and of succeeding on their merits.

Zionist Organization, Memorandum to League of Nations. q Lloyd George, 1923.

445.F.49 No people ever reverts to its ancient position.

Zunz. q *Menorah Journal*, 1919, v. 127.

445.G. The State

445.G.1 After two thousand years of untold . . . suffering, the Jewish people cannot possibly be content with attaining at last to the position of a small and insignificant nation, with a State tossed about like a ball between its powerful neighbors.

Ahad HaAm, *I Zionist Congress*, 1897. *Ten Essays*, 26.

445.G.2 The State of Israel will prove itself not by material wealth, not by military might or technical achievement, but by its moral character and human values.

Ben Gurion, Statement, March 1949.

445.G.3 The State of Israel represents and speaks only on behalf of its own citizens, and in no way presumes to represent or speak in the name of the Jews who are citizens of any other country.

Ben Gurion, address, Jerusalem, Aug. 23, 1950.

445.G.4 The Jewish Renaissance has come—the nation is reborn, and the Jewish State in its beginning is already here.

Brandeis, address, April 1915.

445.G.5 In Basle I founded the Jewish State. If I said it today, it would be greeted with laughter; but in five years, perhaps, certainly in fifty years, everyone will see it. A State is founded essentially on the will of the people for the State.

Herzl, *Diaries*, Sept. 30, 1897.

445.G.6 This mission of Israel is by no means incompatible with a re-nationalization of a Jewish political life. The Jewish State, if truly Jewish, would be founded on the precepts of the Prophets.

E. G. Hirsch.

445.G.7 We, the members of the National Council, representing the Jewish people in Palestine and the Zionist movement of the world, . . . Hereby proclaim the establishment of the Jewish State in Palestine, to be called Israel.

Israeli Declaration of Independence, May 14, 1948.

445.G.8 If Palestine is to be Jewish it cannot be a State, and if it is to be a State it cannot be Jewish.

Lazaron, *Common Ground*, 1938, p. 113.

445.G.9 The Land of Israel will be small . . . but the people of Israel will make it great. . . . Not in opulence but in eminence will their destiny be fulfilled, and the elixir of their pride will be distilled not out of dominion or far-flung borders, but out of the faithful and skillful building of the good society.

Silver, *Vision and Victory*, 1949.

445.G.10 The General Assembly, acting in discharge of its functions . . . 1. Decides that Israel is a peace-loving State which accepts the obligations contained in the Charter and is able and willing to carry out these obligations; 2. Decides to admit Israel to membership in the United Nations.

U.N. General Assembly, Australian Resolution, adopted May 11, 1949.

445.G.11 In this hour a message of hope and good cheer issues from this place, from this sacred city, to all oppressed people and to all who are struggling for freedom and equality.

Weizmann, opening the Kneset, Feb. 14, 1949.

446. JABNEH

446.1 Give me Jabneh and its sages!
Johanan b. Zakkai. *Talmud: Gittin*, 56b.

447. JEALOUSY

447.1 Jealousy is cruel as the grave.
Bible: Cant., 8.6.

447.2 Be not jealous of the wife of your bosom.
Apocrypha: Ben Sira, 9.1.

447.3 Jealousy is . . . a tiger that tears not only its prey but also its own raging heart.
Beer, *Schwert und Hand*, 1831, 3.4.

447.4 Jealousy makes a man silly . . . and a woman more subtle.
Boerne, *Fastenpredigt über die Eifersucht*.

447.5 The jealousy of scribes increases wisdom.
Proverb. q Dimi of Nehardea. *Talmud: Baba Bathra*, 21a.

447.6 Jealousy is disguised self-love, and the salt in the ocean of love.
Saphir, *Papilloten*. SHW., iv. 58.

447.7 Love without jealousy is not true love.
Zohar, Gen., 245a.

448. JERUSALEM

448.1 How is the faithful city become a harlot!
Bible: Isa., 1.21.

448.2 Jerusalem: She shall be built!
Ibid., 44.28.

448.3 I send My four judgments against Jerusalem: the sword, the famine, the evil beasts, and the pestilence.
Bible: Ezek., 14.21.

448.4 Jerusalem, . . . your father was Amorite, your mother Hittite.
Ibid., 16.3.

448.5 Jerusalem shall be called City of Truth.
Bible: Zech., 8.3.

448.6 Fair in situation, the joy of the whole earth!
Bible: Ps., 48.3. See *Jer.*, 39.9.

448.7 Pray for the peace of Jerusalem.
Ibid., 122.6.

448.8 If I forget thee, O Jerusalem, let my right hand forget her cunning. Let my tongue cleave to the roof of my mouth, if I remember thee not, if I set not Jerusalem above my chiefest joy.
Ibid., 137.5f.

448.9 Jerusalem shall be built again as His house unto all the ages . . . the gates with sapphire and emerald, and all the walls with precious stone. The towers shall be built with gold, . . . the streets shall be paved with carbuncles, . . . and all her houses shall say Hallelujah.
Apocrypha: Tobit, 13.15–18.

448.10 Jerusalem . . . has been and will remain for ever the capital of the Jewish people.

Ben Gurion, Dec. 3, 1947. *Ben Gurion Selections*, 77.

448.11 All possible winds blow in Jerusalem. It is said that every wind before going where it listeth comes to Jerusalem to prostrate itself before the Lord.

Bertinoro, letter to his father, 1488. KTJ, 309.

448.12 Jerusalem at midday in midsummer is a city of stone in a land of iron with a sky of brass.

Disraeli, *Tancred*, 1847.

448.13 Jerusalem is destined to become a lantern to the nations.

Hoshaia. *Pesikta, Kumi.* 144b.

448.14 Jerusalem will become the metropolis of the world.

Johanan. *Exod. R.*, 23.10. See *Talmud: Baba Bathra*, 75b.

448.15 Jerusalem will expand, its gates reaching Damascus.

Johanan b. Nappaha. *Cant. R.*, 7.5.

448.16 The Holy One said: I will not enter the heavenly Jerusalem until I can enter the earthly Jerusalem!

Johanan b. Nappaha. *Talmud: Taanit*, 5a. *Zohar, VaYchi*, 231a.

448.17 Jerusalem is in the very center, for which reason it has sometimes been called the "navel" of the country.

Josephus, *Wars*, 3.3.5. See *Ezek.*, 5.5, 38.12; *Jubilees*, 8.19; *Sanhedrin*, 37a.

448.18 As the heart in the midst of the body, so is Jerusalem situated in the midst of the inhabited earth.

*Caesarius of Heisterbach, 13C. q White, *Warfare of Science with Theology*, i. 99.

448.19 Oh, city of the world, most
    chastely fair,
In the far west, behold, I sigh
    for thee. . . .
Oh, had I eagles' wings I'd fly to
    thee,
And with my falling tears make
    moist thine earth. . . .
Oh, that I might embrace thy
    dust, the sod
Were sweet as honey to my fond
    desire.

Judah Halevi, *City of the World*, tr Amy Levy.

448.20 All members of a household may be compelled to move to Jerusalem, but not to leave it.

Mishna: Ketubot, 13.11.

448.21 O Jerusalem, Jerusalem, that kills the prophets and stones them that are sent to you, how often would I have gathered your children, even as a hen gathers her chickens under her wings, and ye would not.

New Testament: Matt., 23.27.

448.22 That which the Hebrews call the City of God is Jerusalem, literally, "Vision of Peace."

Philo, *Dreams*, ii. 39.

448.23 Jerusalem is situated on seven hills.

Pirké de Rabbi Eliezer, ch 10.

448.24 Ten measures of beauty came down to earth: nine were taken by Jerusalem, and one by the rest of the world.

Talmud: Kiddushin, 49b.

448.25 In the din and tumult of the age, . . . the still small voice of Jerusalem remains our only music.

Zangwill, *Voice of Jerusalem*, 1921, p. 9.

448.26 Jerusalem, like Heaven, is more a state of mind than a place.

Ibid., 91.

449. JESUS

449.1 He never taught any law or practice contrary to the Written Law. Only after his death . . . many of his disciples introduced practices and doctrines altogether foreign to him, removing thereby the cornerstone of the Law while winning the multitudes.

Afendopolo, *Asara Maamarot*, 15C.

449.2 Jesus was so much filled with the last and deepest thoughts of his people that he appears to us as the incarnation of the genius of Judaism.

*Breysig, *Kulturgeschichte der Neuzeit*, 1901, ii. 678.

449.3 The Nazarene wrought a double kindness to the world: he supported the Torah of Moses with full strength, . . . and sought to perfect Gentiles with ethical qualities.

Emden, Preface to *Seder Olam*, 1757. JJCW, 132 f.

449.4 He has become the most fascinating figure in history. In him is combined what is best and most mysterious and most enchanting in Israel—the eternal people whose child he was.

Enelow, *A Jewish View of Jesus*, 1920, p. 181.

449.5 The Jew believes in the religion *of* Jesus; he cannot bring himself to accept the religion *about* Jesus.

*Fagnani. Landman, *Christian and Jew*, 1929, p. 292.

449.6 It is an historic fact that he instituted no rite, no sacrament, no Church. Born a Jew, he wished to live and to die a Jew, and from the swaddling clothes of circumcision to the embalmed shroud of sepulchre, followed only the rites of his religion.

*Hyacinthe. q Pallière, *Unknown Sanctuary*, 230 f.

449.7 Jesus is, for the Jewish nation, *a great teacher of morality and an artist in parable.* . . . If ever the day should come and his ethical code be stripped of its wrappings of miracles and mysticism, the Book of the Ethics of Jesus will be one of the choicest treasures in the literature of Israel for all time.

Klausner, *Jesus of Nazareth*, 1926, p. 414.

449.8 If one cannot say that it was he who made divinity human, I am ready to rank him among the foremost of those who have made humanity divine.

Krauskopf, *A Rabbi's Impressions*, 1901, p. 43.

449.9 All these matters relating to Jesus . . . and the Ishmaelite . . . only served to clear the way for King Messiah, to prepare the whole world to worship God with one accord.

Maimonides, *Yad: Melakim*, 11.4. *Code*, xiv. tr Hershman, p. xiii.

449.10 You, noble martyr, who will head the procession,
A new Sanhedrin will welcome you. . . .
And you will be cleansed from the taint
Of the dead they have slaughtered,
And the Scrolls of the Law they have burned in the market place.

Shneor, "Last Words of Don Henriquez," 1922. *Shirim*, 1952, i. 394; LGP, 109.

449.11 If it were permitted to reason consistently in religious matters, it is clear that we all ought to become Jews, because Jesus was born a Jew, lived a Jew, died a Jew, and he said expressly that he was fulfilling the Jewish religion.

*Voltaire, *Philosophical Dictionary*, v. *Toleration*, 1764.

449.12 Jesus was not a Christian, he was a Jew. He did not proclaim a new faith, but taught men to do the will of God. According to Jesus, as to the Jews generally, this will of God is to be found in the Law and the other canonical Scriptures.

*Wellhausen, *Einleitung in die drei ersten Evangelien*, 1905, p. 113. q KJN, 95. See PDE, 1794, i. 130.

449.13 Jesus was not a being come down from heaven, but one who attained to heavenly heights. He was not a God who walked on earth like a man but a man who walked with God on earth. He was not a God who lived humanly, but a man who lived divinely. . . . To us he belongs—not his Church, but he—the man, the Jew, the prophet.

S. S. Wise. q LCJ, 292.

449.14 The Jewish reclamation of Jesus . . . will come about as a result of a wider . . . conception of the scope of Jewish learning . . . and of a general restoration of our lost literary treasures. . . . Then in a cloistered synagog in a re-Judaized Galilee a sage . . . will con over a new tome which will be an old tome revised . . . and he will comment in the spirit of an ancient rabbi. . . . "Come and see, how great is the power of Israel. Once there was a child in Galilee. He was taken captive . . . to the great city of Rome. There they made a God of him. . . . But the mind of the child was not at rest until he returned to Galilee and saw his name inscribed in an ancient tome among the names of his castigated Pharisees. . . ."

Wolfson, Introd. to Jacobs, *Jesus as Others Saw Him*, 1925.

450.   JEWS
450.A.   Name

450.A.1 We shall not abandon the name of Jew, which, though much reviled, has been linked with the purest knowledge of God, the noblest freedom of the spirit and refinement of morals.

A. Geiger, letter to L. R. Bischoffsheim, Oct. 8, 1872.

450.A.2 When people talk about a wealthy man of my creed, they call him an Israelite; but if he is poor, they call him a Jew.

Heine, Manuscript Papers.

450.A.3 We accept this word, supposedly a term of abuse, and we shall convert it into a title of honor.

Herzl. *Die Welt*, first issue, June 3, 1897.

450.A.4 A Jew is called *Yud*, for as the letter *Yod* is the only one in our alphabet which cannot be magnified (if written longer vertically it becomes a *Vav*, and horizontally a *Daled*), so the Jew who magnifies himself ceases to be a Jew.

Simha Bunam. q *Imré Tzaddikim*, (5669) 5704, p. 7, #30.

450.B. Definition

450.B.1 We are Jews through history and through birth.

B. Auerbach. q WHJ, iv. 579.

450.B.2 We are a race by religion, not a race by blood.

H. Bloch, *Hekal LeDibré Hazal*, 1948, p. 49.

450.B.3 Jews are a distinct nationality.

Brandeis, address, June 28, 1915.

450.B.4 The Jews are a race apart. They have made laws according to their own fashion, and keep them.

*Celsus, *A True Discourse*, c.178.

450.B.5 We consider ourselves no longer a nation, but a religious community.

CCAR, *Pittsburg Platform*, 1885.

450.B.6 My people, a fragile remnant, nevertheless a people.

Disraeli, *Alroy*, 1833, 7.1.

450.B.7 It is not birth that makes the Jew, but conviction, the profession of faith.

Geiger, *Das Judentum u. s. Geschichte*, 1865, i. 42.

450.B.8 We are a people, one people (*ein Volk, e i n Volk*).

Herzl, *Jewish State*, 1896, ch 1.

450.B.9 The Jews are a nation, destined to be resurrected.

Hess, *Rome and Jerusalem*, 1862. q LJG, 258.

450.B.10 Anyone who repudiates idolatry is a Jew.

Johanan b. Nappaha. *Talmud: Megilla*, 13a.

450.B.11 A Jew's a Jew.

*Lessing, (Templar in) *Nathan der Weise*, 1779, 1.6.

450.B.12 The common fate of all Jews makes them a group in reality.

Lewin. *JF*, Sept. 1939. *Resolving Social Conflicts*, 166.

450.B.13 A group is best defined as a dynamic whole based on inter-dependence rather than on similarity.

Lewin. *Menorah Journal*, 1940. *Resolving*, 184.

450.B.14 To be a Jew is to be a friend of mankind, to be a proclaimer of liberty and peace.

Lewisohn, *Israel*, 1925, p. 280.

450.B.15 All the forces of democracy are Israel.

Lubin, letter, March 1918. q ADL, 352. See ADL, 69f.

450.B.16 *I* determine who is a Jew.

*Lueger, *Goering. q Namier, *Conflicts*, 121.

450.B.17 Jews are a distinct people even though they abandon their own vernacular.

*Masaryk, *Grundlagen des Marxismus*, 1899, Sect. 120.

450.B.18 Israel is a religious people. . . . A secular, non-religious Israel is a monstrosity.

Montefiore, *Rabbinic Anthology*, 1938, p. 116.

450.B.19 A Jewish half-breed descended from two full-blooded Jewish grandparents is considered a Jew.

*Nazi decree, March 15, 1938. *Reichsgesetzblatt*, 1938, i. #24, p. 245. q Lemkin, *Axis Rule*, 286.

450.B.20 He is not a Jew who is one outwardly.

New Testament: Rom., 2.28.

450.B.21 They are not all Israel who are of Israel.

Ibid., 9.6.

450.B.22 I know the blasphemy of them that say they are Jews and are not, but are the synagog of Satan.

New Testament: Rev., 2.9.

450.B.23 We are more than a people. . . . We are of a pure blood.

Peretz, *Verk*, ed Kletzkin, xi. 277.

450.B.24 The Jews are not a race but only a people, after all.

*Ripley, *Races of Europe*, 1899, p. 400.

450.B.25 Our nation is a nation only by virtue of its Torah.

Saadia, *Emunot VeDeot*, 933, 3.7.

450.B.26 There is no Jewish nation, but only Germans, Frenchmen, Englishmen, who profess the Jewish religion.
Sanhedrin, reply to Napoleon, 1806.

450.B.27 The Jews are a fact . . . and they need no definition. . . . It is the definitions of the others that are troubling you. . . . For them, you are one, indivisible, inside and outside, a Jew.
M. Sulzberger. *Menorah Journal*, 1916, ii. 58.

450.B.28 We are what we will to be.
Max Wiener, *Religion in dieser Zeit*, 1933.

450.C. Alienation

450.C.1 A Jew who sinned is still a Jew.
Abba b. Zabdai. *Talmud: Sanhedrin*, 44a.

450.C.2 A Jew has it not in his power to change his essence.
Arama, *Akedat Yitzhak, Ki Tetzé*, 82a, 15C. q FRJ, 143.

450.C.3 Every Jew is obligated by his birth; Judaism is inalienable.
Holdheim, I Rabbiner Versammlung, *Protokolle*, 1844, 56.

450.C.4 Once a Jew, always a Jew, whatever be his creed.
*Hollingsworth, *Remarks*, 1852, p. 21. q SHZ, i. 36f.

450.D. Description

450.D.1 Is it not that Thou goest with us that we are distinguished?
Bible: Exod., 33.16.

450.D.2 A people of saviors, anointed for thorns and chosen for pain.
Beer-Hofmann, *Der Tod Georgs*, 1900, p. 216. q LGS, 242.

450.D.3 The great despoiled ones of history.
Blum, *Nouvelles Conversations. Révues Blanches*, 1901, 360.

450.D.4 They are distinguished from the rest of mankind in practically every detail of life, especially by not honoring any of the usual gods and by extreme reverence for one particular divinity.
*Dio Cassius, *Roman History*, 230, iii. 47.17.2.

450.D.5 Jewry at all times . . . was preeminently a spiritual nation.
Dubnow, *Jewish History*, 1903, p. 177.

450.D.6 They are the only people today that consist of men of all peoples, . . . they are a Society of Nations.
Fleg, *Why I Am a Jew*, 1929, p. 9.

450.D.7 Not a people, not a community, are we but a flock—the holy flock of the Lord, and the whole earth is an altar for us.
J. L. Gordon, "The Flock of the Lord," 1882. See SRH, 202.

450.D.8 "Brotherhood" is a designation for Israel.
Hanania b. Hakinai. *Mekilta*, to *Exod.* 14.15.

450.D.9 The Jews, the Swiss Guard of deism.
Heine, *Germany from Luther to Kant*, 1834.

450.D.10 We are not even a body, only scattered limbs.
Judah Halevi, *Cuzari*, c. 1135, 2.30.

450.D.11 The chimerical nationality of the Jew is the nationality of the merchant, of the monied man generally.
Marx, *On the Jewish Question*, 1844. *Selected Essays*, 93.

450.D.12 One might call the Jew the Old Man of Europe.
Oppenheim, *A Psycho-Analysis of the Jews*, 1926.

450.D.13 Since the days of antiquity we have been a people of the spirit, whose Torah was for us as a land, government and laws.
Smolenskin, *Maamarim*, 1935, ii. 145.

450.D.14 The Jews and Parsees are manifestly fossils of the Syriac Society . . . under the Achaemenian Empire.
*Toynbee, *A Study of History*, 1934, i. 90f.

450.D.15 The great misunderstood of history.
Zangwill. *North American Review*, April 1895.

450.D.16 He [the Jew] is the common measure of humanity.
Zangwill, *Problem of the Jewish Race*, 17.

450.D.17 The community of Israel is that which keeps "the covenant and the kindness" [*Deut.* 7.9].
Zohar, Gen., 47b.

450.E. Character

Courage

450.E.1 You must teach these scoundrels that no disaster, whether inflicted by God or man, will ever reduce the valor of the Jews.
Herod. q Josephus, *Wars*, 1.19.4. See 6.1.5.

450.E.2 Coward? Not he, who faces death,
Who singly against the world has fought,
For what? A name he may not breathe,
For liberty of prayer and thought.
E. Lazarus, "Each Crime That Wakes," 1882.

450.E.3 In time of distress, Jews least of all . . . try to escape by recourse to drink or suicide.
*Nietzsche, *Dawn of Day*, 1886, #205.

450.E.4 The Jewish nation is ready for agreement and friendship . . . yet is not of the contemptuous kind which surrenders through cowardice to wrongful aggression.
Philo, *Special Laws*, iv. 41.

450.E.5 Their valor under the Maccabees, their exploits in the campaign which ended with Titus' destruction of Jerusalem, their desperate rebellion under Bar Kochba, and later on, their defense of Naples against Balisarius, or of the passes in the Pyrenees against the Franks, place the Jews on a par with the greatest heroes known to history.
*Schleiden, *Importance of Jews in . . . Learning*, 1876.

450.E.6 If the statistics are right, the Jews constitute but one per cent of the human race. It suggests a nebulous dim puff of star dust lost in the blaze of the Milky Way. Properly the Jew ought hardly to be heard of; but he is heard of, has always been heard of. . . . He has made a marvelous fight in this world, in all the ages; and he has done it with his hands tied behind him.
*Twain, "Concerning the Jews." (*Harper's Magazine*, 1898).

Humaneness

450.E.7 The Jewish nation to a higher degree than any other possesses . . . all domestic virtue, loving care for the needy, profound reverence for parents.
*Bail, *Les Juifs au XIXme Siècle*, 38. q GHJ, v. 522.

450.E.8 Israel gave the world the sense of true humanity.
*Cornill, *Israel and Humanity*, Jan. 8, 1895.

450.E.9 If the Jew is so generous, if beneficence is his main virtue, it is because

he has not forgotten the time of persecution.
*Du Camp, *Paris Bienfaisant*, 1888, p. 440.

450.E.10 The Jewish race are people of gentle instincts.
*Gerard, *My Four Years in Germany*, 1917, p. 188.

450.E.11 From the first moment we come upon the Hebrews, they have within them . . . a tenderness and compassion from man to man . . . which are essentially at one with Hosea and Isaiah.
*Hamilton, *Spokesmen for God*, 1936, 1949, p. 106.

450.E.12 Jews are characterized by modesty, mercy, and benevolence.
Hiyya b. Abba. *Deut. R.*, 3.4 Cf. *Talmud: Yebamot*, 79a.

450.E.13 Whoever is merciful is certainly of the children of Abraham.
Shabetai b. Marinus. *Talmud: Betza*, 32b.

450.E.14 Jews are first to feel universal disaster or joy.
Simeon b. Lakish. *Lam. R.*, 2.3.

450.E.15 Jews excel not only in prayers but also in charity.
*R. Simon, tr of Leon of Modena, *Historia dei Riti Hebraici* (1674) 1684. q Pallière, *Unknown Sanctuary*, 32.

Impetuosity

450.E.16 Israel promised "we shall do" before "we shall hear" [*Exod.* 24.7].
Ahaba b. Zera. *Cant. R.*, to 2.3.
Hama b. Hanina. *Talmud: Sabbath*, 88a.

450.E.17 The Torah was given to Israel because they are impetuous [and need discipline].
Meir. *Talmud: Betza*, 25b.

450.E.18 Rash people, you still persist in your rashness!
Talmud: Sabbath, 88a. Cf *Ketubot*, 112a.

450.E.19 The Jews are historically over-impetuous, they are effervescent, they rush along precipitously.
Werfel, *Between Heaven and Earth*, 1944, p. 202.

Intelligence

450.E.20 Surely this is . . . a wise and understanding people.
Bible: Deut., 4.6.

450.E.21 Here we start with a pure race of unusual intellectual vigor and power, the Jews, long thrown by circumstances into an environment which has brought out many of their faculties in a very high degree. They are the oldest civilized race now remaining on earth; they are artistic, musical, literary, exceptionally philosophic, and hereditarily cultivated.

*Allen, "Idiosyncracy." *Mind,* 1883, viii. 504.

450.E.22 For ages the Jews have shown a marked excellence in what may be called the "commerce of imperceptibles." They . . . excel on every Bourse in Europe. . . . The works of Spinoza . . . have shown the power of the race in dealing with other kinds of abstraction.

*Bagehot, *Economic Studies,* 1879: *Ricardo. Works & Life,* vii. 228f.

450.E.23 A Jew may be foolish once; he is seldom that twice.

Boerne, *Menzel der Franzosenfresser,* 1836.

450.E.24 Often when I found in China an artist of unusual talent, or a mind more vivid than others among my students, the chances were good that he had Jewish blood in him. It is a creative strain.

*Buck, *My Several Worlds,* 1954, p. 297.

450.E.25 The Jews are a people of artists, of intrinsic dreamers. That's what makes them achieve the impossible, and that is why they have survived.

*D'Annunzio. q Hunterberg, *Tragedy of the Ages,* 50.

450.E.26 Jewish origin is a patent of wisdom.

*Deotyma, quoting her mother. q *YAJ,* v. 53.

450.E.27 Thinking became just as characteristic a feature of the Jews as suffering.

Graetz, *Geschichte der Juden,* iv. Pref., 1853.

450.E.28 Superior intelligence is preeminently the possession of the Jewish people. . . . It has enabled them to produce genius with such a frequency that it becomes monotonous and irksome to less gifted peoples.

*Hooton, *Anthropological Appraisal,* May 15, 1938. *Twilight of Man,* 1939, p. 244.

450.E.29 The development of the neo-Hebraic idiom from the ancient Hebrew confirms, by linguistic evidence, the plasticity, the logical acumen, the comprehensive and at the same time versatile intellectuality of the Jewish race.

Jellinek, *Der jüdische Stamm,* 1869, p. 195. q KJL, 32.

450.E.30 The Jewish mind is an instrument of precision; it has the exactness of a pair of scales.

*Leroy-Beaulieu, *Israel Among the Nations,* 1895, p. 179.

Intensity

450.E.31 The same passionate intensity which makes the grandeur of the ancient Hebrew literature still lives among them.

*Bryce, *Studies in Contemporary Biography,* 1903, pp. 20, 23.

450.E.32 The Jews when good are better, and when bad are worse, than the Christians.

Heine, *Gedanken und Einfälle,* 1869, ii.

450.E.33 These people have been compared to sand and stars: when they fall, they fall as low as the sand, and when they rise, they rise as high as the sky.

Judah b. Ilai. *Talmud: Megilla,* 16a.

450.E.34 Jews are the intensive form of any nationality whose language and customs they adopt.

E. Lazarus, *Epistle to the Hebrews,* 1882.

450.E.35 The Jews have a radical quality which goes to the root of things, whether in capitalism or socialism.

Magnes. q Bentwich, *For Zion's Sake,* 114.

450.E.36 The Jews are like other people, only more so.

Proverb. q Koestler, *Promise and Fulfilment,* 287.

Mercantilism

450.E.37 Unjust and stupid, we despise
The Jew that buys, and sells, and buys,
As if we acted otherwise!
Nay, we do worse; for not content,
Like other thieves, with a home rent,
We rob on every Continent.

*Alfieri, *A Satire: The Love of Money,* tr Leigh Hunt.

450.E.38 Jews cannot flourish among Yankees, who are said to out-Jew them in trading.

*Dow, *Dealings of God, Man and the Devil,* (4th ed, 1833).

450.E.39 It takes nine Jews to equal one Genoese.
*Proverb (Italian). q MND, 450.

450.E.40 It takes ten Jews to make a Greek, and ten Greeks to make an Armenian.
*Proverb (Turkish). q Golding, *Jewish Problem*, 39.

450.E.41 Ours is not a maritime country; neither commerce nor the intercourse which it promotes with the outside world has any attraction for us.
Josephus, *Against Apion*, 1.12.

450.E.42 It was not the publican nor the financier whom the sons of Israel honored and aspired to emulate; it was the rabbi, the interpreter of the law, the scribe, the scholar, the *hakham*.
*Leroy-Beaulieu, *Israel Among the Nations*, 1895, p. 182.

450.E.43 Our zeal and earnestness is displayed not in the cause of gain, but in that of religion.
Philo, *Ambassadors*, 32.

450.E.44 The words which have to do with banking and finance are largely of Italian origin. . . . In many European countries the pawn-shop is called Lombard, and its coat of arms consists . . . of three balls, the *palle* of the Florentine Medici. On the other hand, the words which the Jews have made internationally familiar have nothing to do with business.
M. Samuel, *World of Sholom Aleichem*, 1944, p. 53.

450.E.45 The Jews generally give value. They make you pay, but they deliver the goods. In my experience, the men who want something for nothing are invariably Christians.
*G. B. Shaw, *Saint Joan*, 1923, Scene 4. See LJG, 212.

450.E.46 The Jew could not comprehend the Gothic inwardness, the castle, the Cathedral; nor the Christian the Jew's superior, almost cynical, intelligence and his finished expertness in money-making.
*Spengler, *Decline of the West*, 1928, ii. 317.

Polarity

450.E.47 It is hard to fathom this people's character: they give for the Golden Calf, and they give for the Holy Tabernacle.
Abba b. Aha. *Talmud J: Shekalim*, 1.1.

450.E.48 A curious people these Jews, with glaring faults and shining virtues.
Brod, *The Master*, 1951, ch 5, p. 244.

450.E.49 Jews are of the stuff of which gods are made; today trampled under foot, tomorrow worshipped on the knees. While some of them crawl in the filthy mire of commerce, others rise to the loftiest peaks of humanity. . . . You will find among them every possible caricature of vulgarity, and also the ideas of purest humanity.
Heine, *Ludwig Boerne*, 1840.

450.E.50 A Jew is a great paradox, a living bundle of contrasts: wise and foolish, calculating like a merchant and fanciful like a child, burning like fire and freezing like ice, believer and heretic, scholar and ignoramus, meek and conceited, bashful and arrogant, mighty and innocent, disobedient and prompt performer, soft and hard, brave like a lion and craven like a hare, kind and cruel, spendthrift and miser, dandy and beggar.
Mendelé, *In a Sturm Tzeit*, 1913.

450.E.51 What a strange people, verily— made to set before us every contrast! It gave God to the world, and barely believes in Him. . . . It has founded the hope of man in a kingdom of Heaven, and all its wise men tell us . . . that we must occupy ourselves only about earthly things!
*Renan, *History of Israel*, 1895, v. 157.

Sobriety

450.E.52 They cannot be charged with any of those debauches which are grown into reputation with whole nations of Christians, to the scandal and contradiction of their name and profession.
*L. Addison, *Present State of [Barbary] Jews*, 1675.

450.E.53 Israel is yet ready to show to the nations a phenomenon the like of which has never been seen: a peasantry not given to drink, . . . laborers not given to brawls.
J. L. Gordon, letter to J. Syrkin, July 14, 1892. *Igrot*, ii. 405.

450.E.54 The Jews are a chaste, temperate, I might say an abstract race, and in purity of morals they are most nearly allied to the Germanic races.
Heine, *Shakespeare's Maidens: Jessica*, 1838.

450.E.55 Among the theocratically governed nations of the East, the Hebrews seem to us as sober men among drunkards;

but to antiquity they seemed like dreamers among waking folk.

*Lotze, *Microcosmus,* (1856) tr 1885, 7.5, ii. 267.

Social Idealism

450.E.56 There is one characteristic in the Jews which we ought to emulate with profit. . . . It is their great idealism, and their no less great practicality.

*Bonghi, "La Caccia a Giudei," *Nuova Antologia,* Aug. 16, 1891.

450.E.57 Every inheritance of the Jewish people, every teaching of their secular history and religious experience, draws them powerfully to the side of charity, liberty and progress.

*Coolidge, *Spiritual Unification of America,* 1925.

450.E.58 You find the . . . Hebrew invariably arrayed in the same ranks as the leveller and the latitudinarian, prepared to support the policy which may even endanger his life and property, rather than tamely continue under a system which seeks to degrade him.

Disraeli, *Coningsby,* 1844, 4.15.

450.E.59 Those who rage today against the ideals of reason and of individual freedom, and seek to impose an insensate state of slavery by means of brutal force, rightly see in the Jews irreconcilable opponents.

Einstein, *The World As I See It,* 1934, p. 143.

450.E.60 No citizen has proved himself more zealous for liberty than the Jew, . . . none has displayed more sense of order and justice, none shown more benevolence towards the poor or more readiness in voluntarily contributing towards the expenses of the district.

*Gerville, speech, Paris City Hall, Jan. 29, 1790. q GHJ, v. 444.

450.E.61 The Aryan gentleman asks concerning an action: Is it honorable according to a code? Is it correct? Is it gentlemanly? Is it "quite cricket?" The Jewish gentleman asks: Is it righteous? What is its relation to an eternal justice, an eternal mercy? It is perfectly true that, according to the standards of chivalric Europe . . . , the Jew is no gentleman.

Lewisohn, *Israel,* 1925, p. 260.

450.E.62 A mighty longing for freedom is what characterizes the Jew.

Magnes, 1911. *Gleanings,* 1948, p. 58.

450.E.63 Sheer egotism compels us to the purest love of mankind as a whole. . . . Our hearts are like a sponge, receptive to all the newest humanitarian ideas; and our sympathy goes out to all the unfortunate, all the oppressed.

Peretz. q *JA,* June 1952, p. 28. See *Alle Verk,* xii. 318.

450.E.64 The quality most distinguishing them has been a large idealism; the power of grasping great impersonal conceptions, of tenaciously clinging to them, and living for their practical realization. It is these qualities which have made the Jews in all ages the ethical leaders of the race, and which today find their expression in the fields of social and political reform.

*Schreiner, *A Letter on the Jew,* July 1, 1906.

450.E.65 A people who can't sleep themselves and let nobody else sleep.

I. B. Singer, (Asa Heshel in) *Family Moskat,* 1950.

450.E.66 Deep down in the sorely tried soul of the Jewish masses, there reposes a fund of idealism, an ardent faith in a better future unshaken by time or disappointments. Defraud them of the millenial ideal which sustains their courage, . . . and you push them into the arms of a demoralization that lies in wait.

Slouschz, *Renascence of Hebrew Literature,* 1909, p. 287.

Spirituality

450.E.67 Every noble and amiable quality becomes a nation whose task is the sanctification of life.

Aaron Halevi, *Sefer HaHinuk,* c. 1300. q LEJ, ii. 17, Note 2.

450.E.68 The spiritual discipline of the school came to mean for the Jew what military discipline is for other nations.

Dubnow, *Jewish History,* 1903, p. 19.

450.E.69 This is Israel's excellence: When Moses told them, "Arise and journey," they did not ask, How can we go into the desert without provisions? But they believed and followed him.

Eliezer b. Hyrcanus. *Mekilta,* to *Exod.* 12.39, 15.22.

450.E.70 Monotheism had not taken root in Egypt. . . . And it is proof of a special psychical fitness in the mass which had become the Jewish people that it could bring forth so many persons . . . to take upon themselves the burden of the Mosaic religion.

Freud, *Moses and Monotheism,* 1939, p. 174f.

450.E.71 The preference which through two thousand years the Jews have given to spiritual endeavor has had its effect; it has helped to build a dike against brutality and the inclination to violence which are usually found where athletic development becomes the ideal of the people.

Ibid., 181.

450.E.72 Golgotha is not the only mountain on which a Jewish god bled for the salvation of the world. Jews are the people of the spirit, and whenever they return to the spirit, they are great and splendid and put to shame and overcome their knavish oppressors. Rosenkranz profoundly compared them to the giant Antaeus, except that the giant was strengthened whenever he touched earth, while the Jews gain new strength whenever they touch heaven.

Heine, *Ludwig Boerne,* 1840.

450.E.73 If they are not prophets, they are the sons of prophets.

Hillel. *Talmud: Pesahim,* 66b.

450.E.74 The least learned Jew is as packed with religious merits and good deeds as a pomegranate is with seeds.

Huna. *Cant. R.,* 4.4.3.

450.E.75 There is not a Jew who does not observe a hundred precepts a day, who is not encompassed by precepts of piety.

Meir. *Tosefta: Berakot,* 7.24.

450.E.76 Jewish life is dark without, and beautiful within.

Mendelé, *BaYamim HaHem,* 1912.

450.E.77 Among other nations, the vital problems are: a good crop, extension of the boundaries, strong armies, colonies; among us, if we wish to be true to ourselves, the vital questions are: conscience, freedom, culture, ethics.

Peretz, *Verk,* ed Kletzkin, xi. 277f.

450.E.78 One nation alone among all the select nations of the earth that desire wisdom and among whom religious continence is honored.

Philo, *Questions in Genesis,* ii .58.

Strength

450.E.79 We belong to a race which can do everything but fail.

Disraeli. q Herzl, HTH, i. 353.

450.E.80 I see now that the Greeks were only beautiful youths, but that the Jews have ever been men, strong, invincible men, not only in old days, but even to this day, in spite of eighteen centuries of persecution and misery.

Heine, *Memoirs,* 1884, ed Karpeles, tr Cannan, ii. 252.

450.E.81 Israel's body is soft as a reed, its spirit is hard as iron.

Kaminer, *Shir HaAm. HaAsif,* 5645.

450.E.82 Only world empires conquered Israel.

Mekilta, to *Exod.* 14.5.

450.E.83 The Jews are beyond all doubt the strongest, toughest, and purest race at present living in Europe.

*Nietzsche, *Beyond Good and Evil,* 1885, #251.

450.E.84 Jews are strong. Despite heathen blandishment and oppression, they adhere to their laws and customs like lions and lionesses.

Zohar, Gen., 237b.

Miscellaneous

450.E.85 Behold, it is a stiff-necked people.

Bible: Exod., 32.9. See *Deut.* 10.16; Abin. *Exod. R.,* 42.9.

450.E.86 "Stiff-necked" is not said disparagingly. It is a compliment. It means: If you are a Jew, be ready to be crucified.

Ammi b. Nathan. *Exod. R.,* 42.9.

450.E.87 Israel is stubborn like a stubborn heifer.

Bible: Hos., 4.16.

450.E.88 Jews exhibit purity, intelligence, and love of study.

*Ambrose, *Enarratio in Psalmos,* 4C, 1.41, xiv. 943.

450.E.89 Nor war nor wisdom yields our Jews delight,
They will not study and they dare not fight.

*Crabbe, *The Borough,* 1810.

450.E.90 Specifically Jewish collective qualities . . . belong nowhere but to the realm of mythology. One may find amongst us exactly the same characters as in the Gentile world.

P. Bernstein, *Jew-Hate,* (1926) 1951, p. 59.

450.E.91 The best Christians in Europe today are to be found among the Jews.

*Coudenhove-Kalergi, *Adel,* 1921.

450.E.92 Men find the bad among us easily enough. They take the worst of us as samples of the best; they take the lowest of us as presentations of the highest; and they say, "All Jews are alike."
*Dickens, (Riah in) *Our Mutual Friend,* 1865.

450.E.93 All the tendencies of the Jewish race are conservative. Their bias is to religion, property, and natural aristocracy.
Disraeli, *Lord George Bentinck,* 1852. See *Coningsby,* 4.15.

450.E.94 The pursuit of knowledge for its own sake, an almost fanatical love of justice, and the desire for personal independence—these are the features of Jewish tradition which make me thank my stars that I belong to it.
Einstein, *The World As I See It,* 1934, p. 143.

450.E.95 Each country has the kind of Jews it deserves.
Franzos, "Tote Seelen" in *Neue Freie Presse,* Mar. 31, 1875, paraphr. J. de Maistre's *toute nation a le gouvernment qu'elle mérite.*

450.E.96 A race which, in the face of uninterrupted and unparalleled persecution . . . has managed to preserve its mental and moral vigor, and has remained a powerful factor in the life of civilized humanity, can well afford to own to its share of human frailty. The Jewish historian need not apologize for them. All he may do is to account for it, by pointing to the historical factors which have produced it.
Friedlaender, *Jews of Russia and Poland,* 1915, p. x.

450.E.97 I don't like 'Ebrews. They work harder; they're more sober; they're honest; and they're everywhere.
*Galsworthy, *Loyalties,* 1922, 3.1.

450.E.98 The Israelitish people never was good for much, as its own leaders . . . have a thousand times reproachfully declared: it possesses few virtues, and most of the faults of other nations; but in cohesion, steadfastness, valor, and . . . obstinate toughness, it has no match. It is the most perseverant nation.
*Goethe, *Wilhelm Meister's Travels,* 1829, ch 11.

450.E.99 Shaftesbury observes that Jews are by nature somber and melancholy. That is natural for a people always engulfed in terror. Hence the jarring and sinister look,

the constrained and timid air that dominates their faces and determines their attitudes. . . . Gentiles, confess with contrition that it is the fruit of your work! The Jews have produced the effects, you have established the causes. Who is more to blame?
*Grégoire, *La Régéneration . . . des Juifs,* 1789, ch 6.

450.E.100 I love it not, this folk, and yet I know
That what disfigures it, is our own work;
We lame them, and are angry when they limp,
And yet, withal, this wandering shepherd race
Has something great about it, Garceran.
We are today's, we others; but their line
Runs from Creation's cradle.
*Grillparzer, *Jewess of Toledo,* tr Danton. *German Classics,* ed Francke & Howard, 1913, vi. 355.

450.E.101 If Israel is the stubborn nonconformist among the nations, he is also the unconquerable optimist.
*Herford. *Menorah Journal,* 1919, v. 206.

450.E.102 The great moment has found a small people.
Herzl. q ZVJ, 292. See *Diaries,* May 1, 1900.

450.E.103 The Jews are with us as a perpetual lesson to teach us modesty and civility.
*O. W. Holmes. *American Hebrew,* Apr. 4, 1890. *Over the Teacups,* 1892, p. 197.

450.E.104 Made homeless in space, they had to expand into new dimensions. . . . It made them cunning and grew them claws to cling on with as they were swept by the wind . . . reduced to drift-sand, they had to glitter if they wanted to avoid being trodden on . . . to get an equal chance they had to start with a plus.
Koestler, *Twilight in the Night,* 1946, p. 356.

450.E.105 Jews have always lacked a sense of color.
Koestler, *Promise and Fulfilment,* 1949, p. 197.

450.E.106 The Jew is the most nervous and, in so far, the most modern of men. . . . The Jew is born old.
*Leroy-Beaulieu, *Israel Among the Nations,* 1895, p. 169, 173.

450.E.107 The supreme faculty of the Jew is his suppleness, his gift of adaptation. . . . In the matter of nobility of character, dignity of life, and generosity of feeling, the Jew puts the Christians to shame.
Ibid., 217, 221.

450.E.108 The failings of the Jews have rather the character of cowardice and meanness than of cruelty and atrocity.
Luzzatto, *Discorso*, 1638. q GHJ, v. 85.

450.E.109 The Jew is what we made him.
*Macaulay. q Peters, *Jew as a Patriot*, 221.

450.E.110 The Jews' vices are those which we have produced in them; their virtues are their own.
*Michelet, *Bible of Humanity*, 1864, p. 254f. Cf Liebknecht, *Souvenirs*, 1901, p. 185.

450.E.111 People wanted to make them contemptible by treating them scornfully for twenty centuries . . . and by pushing them all the deeper down into the mean trades—and, indeed, they have not become cleaner under this process. But contemptible? They have never ceased believing themselves qualified for the highest functions; neither have the virtues of all suffering people ever failed to adorn them.
*Nietzsche, *Dawn of Day*, 1886, #205, tr Volz, p. 204.

450.E.112 By nature we are like all human beings, yet our people is unlike others, because our life is different, our history is different, our teacher is the Exile.
Peretz, *Idishe Bibliotek*, i. Pref., 1890. *Alle Verk*, xii. 7.

450.E.113 What invested the Jew of all times with an economic, and in part also spiritual, superiority over other people has been, first, his thrift and temperance, cultivated by his religious law and moral code; second, his actually boundless attachment to and care of his wife and children; and third, his capacity and desire for learning, which stands out even more significantly and irresistibly among the poor than among the rich.
Rülf, *Das Erbrecht*, 1893, p. 114.

450.E.114 Talk what you will of the Jews,—that they are cursed: they thrive wherever they come; they are able to oblige the prince of their country by lending him money; none of them beg; they keep to-gether; and as for their being hated, why Christians hate one another as much.
*Selden, *Table-Talk*, 1689.

450.E.115 I am a Jew: Hath not a Jew eyes? Hath not a Jew hands, organs, dimensions, senses, affections, passions? fed with the same food, hurt with the same weapons, subject to the same diseases, healed by the same means, warmed and cooled by the same winter and summer, as a Christian is? If you prick us, do we not bleed? If you tickle us, do we not laugh? If you poison us, do we not die? and if you wrong us, shall we not revenge?
*Shakespeare, *Merchant of Venice*, 1597, 3.1.

450.E.116 We have recognized three chief qualities in the Jewish character: firm faith in the living God, an intense feeling of their human and national personality, and an irresistible striving to realize and materialize their faith and their feeling, to clothe them in flesh and blood as soon as possible.
*Solovyov, *The Jews*, 1882. *Solovyov Anthology*, 1950, 116.

450.E.117 The Jews are what their history has made them.
Wirth, *The Ghetto*, 1928, p. 288.

450.E.118 Israel's vices are on the surface, his virtues lie deep.
Zangwill. *North American Review*, April 1895.

450.E.119 The Jews, such as they are today, are our work, the work of our eighteen hundred years of idiotic persecution.
*Zola, *Nouvelle Campagne*, 1896.

450.F. Types

450.F.1 The real miracle of Palestine is the Jew who masters the labor of orchard and garden, field and vineyard, quarry and harbor, water and power, factory and craft, highway and byway. That sort of Jew the Diaspora never made.
Ben Gurion, March 2, 1932. *Rebirth and Destiny*, 49.

450.F.2 Here in Israel they are killing the myth that there is a physical type of Jew. The thing that's so startling here is that Jews from India are so Indian and Jews from Persia so Persian.
Jo Davidson. q D. A. Schmidt. *N.Y. Times*, Dec. 19, 1951.

450.F.3 A *sabra,* that's the Hebrew word for the flower of the cactus, prickly outside and sweet inside. They use it to mean a native son. The *sabra* is the symbol of tomorrow.
Ibid.

450.F.4 Perhaps . . . these free-born
          children of the Revival
     Are . . . lowlier in soul than
          the . . . children of the Dias-
          pora.
     They lack the depth achieved
          by children of affliction . . .
     The longings for redemp-
          tion. . . .
     Which have nurtured count-
          less generations in the hero-
          ism of martyrdom—
     In the aspiration for sanctity
          and purity, and for some-
          thing lowly in living.
Shimonowitz, "Dewdrops at Night." q HMH, 176.

450.F.5 Every one who has travelled in the East of Europe, where the genuine Sephardim still as far as possible avoid all intercourse with German Jews, . . . begins to comprehend the significance of Judaism in the history of the world. This is nobility in the fullest sense of the word, genuine nobility of race! Beautiful figures, noble heads, dignity in speech and bearing.
Chamberlain, Foundations, (1899) 1911, i. 273.

450.F.6 I observed some few of those Jews [in Venice] especially some of the Levantines to be such goodly and proper men, that I said to myself our English proverb: To look like a Jew (whereby is meant sometimes a weather-beaten wasp-faced fellow, sometimes a phrenetic and lunatic person, sometimes one discon-tented) is not true. For indeed I noted some of them to be most elegant and sweet-featured persons, which gave me occasion the more to lament their religion.
Coryat, Crudities, 1611.

450.F.7 Were I a Jew and living in northern Europe, I would pilgrimage to Saloniki annually. I would visit my kins-men, . . . and, joyous in the beauty of the chosen people—as it had been permitted to maintain itself and develop—I would breathe deeply and throw my head back.
Kielland. q Ehrenpreis, Soul of the East, 41.

450.F.8 The Jews of the Holy City still retain a noble beauty . . . The forehead is loftier, the eye larger and more frank in its expression, the nose more delicate in its prominence, and the face a purer oval. I have remarked the same distinction in the countenances of those Jewish families of Europe, whose members have devoted themselves to Art or Literature.
Taylor, The Lands of the Saracen, 1855, p. 81.

450.F.9 It is not the body which marks the Jew; it is his soul. . . . The ghetto face is purely psychic, just like the actor's, the soldier's, the minister's face.
Fishberg, *The Jews,* 1911, p. 166.

450.F.10 The Jewish physiognomy ex-ists, only it is not molded in the mother's womb but in the cradle. . . . It is not the face that makes Jacob, it is Jacob's life that molds his face.
Goldenweiser. *Reflex,* Oct. 1927, p. 11f.

450.F.11 Jews have their own peculiar honorable expression, not because they spring from Abraham, Isaac and Jacob, but because they are business men, and the Frankfort Christian shopman looks as much like a Frankfort Jewish shopman as one rotten egg looks like another.
Heine, *City of Lucca,* 1828, ch 4.

450.F.12 The Jewish type was moulded and stamped by the Ghetto. . . . Those fetid and doleful prisons were the crucibles in which . . . medieval Europe fused the various elements of Judaism into that as-tonishingly hard and ductile metal—the modern Jew.
Leroy-Beaulieu, Israel Among the Na-tions, 1895, p. 121f. See Ripley, *Races of Europe,* 1899, p. 377.

450.F.13 Jews differ from one another in mind as in face.
Hamnuna. *Talmud: Berakot,* 58a.

450.F.14 All Jewish beauty is of a pe-culiarly moving kind; for the conscious-ness of the deep misery, the bitter scorn, and the evil chances amid which her kin-dred and friends dwelt, gave to her lovely features a depth of sorrow and an ever-watchful apprehension of love, such as most deeply touches our hearts.
Heine, *Rabbi of Bacharach,* 1840, ch 1.

450.F.15 In China the Jews are hardly to be distinguished from the Chinese, in Africa they resemble the Negroes, in Germanic North Europe they look like the Nordic type, in Russia the Russian.

F. Hertz, *Race and Civilization*, 1928.

450.F.16 Dark Syroid Jews are often taken for Spaniards or Italians, Armenoids for South Slavs or other Alpines, and blond, blue-eyed Jews for Northwest Europeans.

Boas, *Aryans and Non-Aryans*, 1934.

450.F.17 The Jewish type has conserved its purity through the centuries.

Hess, *Rome & Jerusalem*, (1862) #4, p. 59.

450.F.18 There is not even a standardized German-Jewish type. The Swabian Jew is different from the Jew of Hamburg or Luebeck—not because Jews are peculiarly adaptable, but because the influence of environment has always proven more effective than imported traditions.

*Ossietzky. *Weltbühne*, July 1932; *Menorah Journal*, 1938.

450.F.19 There is no Jewish type, although there are Jewish types. . . . This came about through isolation in the ghetto, and the prohibition of mixed marriage.

*Renan, *Le Judaisme comme Race et Réligion*, 1883.

450.F.20 Jewesses are beautiful, only poverty disfigures them.

Ishmael. *Mishna: Nedarim*, 9.10.

450.F.21 Among the Jews whom Nebuchadnezzar drove into exile there were youths who shamed the sun by their beauty.

Johanan. *Talmud: Sanhedrin*, 92b.

450.F.22 Russian and Polish Jewesses may fairly be numbered amongst the handsomest of women.

M. Lilienthal, *My Travels in Russia*, 279.

450.F.23 Two lovely sisters still and sweet
As flowers, stand side by side:
Their soul-subduing looks might cheat
The Christian of his pride.

*Wordsworth, "A Jewish Family," 1828.

450.F.24 Heavenly splendor lights up her face,
And she, like the enchanted princess of folk tales,
Enraptures all being with the poetry of her plight.

*Zablocki, "Jewess." q W. Belza, *Zydzi w Poezyi Polskiej*, 1883, p. 60; 1906, p. 44.

450.F.25 As the ethrog has taste and fragrance, the palm taste but no fragrance, the myrtle fragrance but no taste, and the willow neither taste nor fragrance, so some Jews have learning and good deeds, some learning but no deeds, some deeds but no learning, and some neither learning nor deeds. Said the Holy One: Let them all be tied together, and they will atone one for the other.

Lev. R., 30.12. Cf. *Pesikta Kahana*, 185a.

450.F.26 The communal demands did not weigh heavily upon them, and they only remembered the way to the synagog on the Day of Atonement. Nevertheless they deluded themselves into the belief that they were good Jews, because they loved Heine, believed in *Daniel Deronda*, and left nothing to be desired in their praise of *kugel* and *sholnt*. They protested that they were *auch Juden* [also Jews]. I say they are mere *Bauch Juden* [belly Jews].

Nordau, speech, II Zionist Congress, Aug. 28, 1898.

450.F.27 There is a tragedy in the face of that old Jewess seated upon her bale, with her arm around the colored box that contains her worldly possessions; a racial memory that is full of sad happenings and dark incidents. It is not a European face nor yet completely Oriental; there is the legend written on it of the hunted animal with a soul.

*O'Connor, *Vision of Morocco*, 1924, p. 6.

450.F.28 The Jewish boys are magnificent, and I felt something I rarely feel, pride in my race, in so much freshness and vivacity.

F. Rosenzweig, letter from Warsaw, May 23, 1918. GFR, 74.

450.F.29 Where shall we look in our search for genuine Jews today?

A. Zweig, *Caliban*, 1927. q LR, 156.

450.G. Nobility

450.G.1 Our very existence in dispersion is possible only because we feel ourselves to be "the aristocrats of history."

Ahad HaAm, letter to Rabnitzki, Apr. 17, 1910. AEL, 268.

450.G.2 All Jews are of royal descent.

Akiba, Ishmael, Simeon b. Gamaliel. *Talmud: Sabbath*, 128a.

Simeon b. Yohai. *Mishna: Sabbath*, 14.4.

450.G.3 Even the poor among Jews are noblemen, reduced in circumstances, for they are children of Abraham, Isaac and Jacob.

Akiba. *Mishna: Baba Kamma*, 8.6. See *Talmud: Sukka*, 31a. *DPB*, ed Singer, p. 8.

450.G.4 The Godlike, heavenly race of the blessed Jews!

Apocrypha: Sibyls, 5.249.

450.G.5 Jewish history admonishes the Jews: *Noblesse oblige!*

Dubnow, *Jewish History*, 1903, p. 180.

450.G.6 Every Jew is destined to have progeny as numerous as the generation that left Egypt, and all of them will be of a princely character, not in the sense of conquerors but of a holy nation.

Eliezer b. Jose. *Mekilta*, to *Exod*, 19.4.

450.G.7 The sufferance, which is the badge of the Jew, has made him, in these days, the ruler of the rulers of the earth.

*Emerson, *Conduct of Life: Fate*, 1860.

450.G.8 Viewed as a nation, Israel is the most ancient and perhaps the most gifted of all those which the Germans call *Kultur-Völker*. The breadth and antiquity of her culture have won for her a sort of aristocracy of birth among the nations.

*Leroy-Beaulieu, *Israel Among the Nations*, 1895, p. 191.

450.G.9 Though we boast of rank, we must admit that we are but of pagan stock while the Jews are of the blood of Christ. ... The Glory came from them, not from us.

*Luther, *Das Jesus ein geborener Jude war*, 1523.

450.G.10 The Jewish people is, aside from accidental modifications, a perpetual aristocracy under the appearance of a theocracy.

S. Maimon, *Autobiography*, (1793) 1947, p. 108.

450.G.11 There is not in the sublimest of Gentiles a majesty comparable to that of the Jew elect. He may well think his race favored of heaven, though heaven chastise them still. The noble Jew is grave in age, but in his youth he is the arrow to the bow of his fiery eastern blood, and in his manhood he is . . . a figure of easy and superb preponderance, whose fire has mounted to inspirit and be tempered by the intellect.

*Meredith, *Tragic Comedians*, 1892. *Works*, 1910, xv. 20f.

450.G.12 Israelites, whose is the sonship, the glory, the covenants, the giving of the Law, the service, and the promises; whose are the fathers, and of whom is Christ according to the flesh.

New Testament: Rom., 9.4f.

450.G.13 Our people was subjected to a frightful selection over a period of two thousand years; those who were weak and faint-hearted and without honor, fell off; but we may assert with pride that we had only noblemen as ancestors, only men and women who remained loyal in each trouble.

F. Oppenheimer, *Alte und neue Makkabäer*, 1906.

450.G.14 Who would not be proud of so illustrious a descent and so glorious a destination as they alone can boast of?

*Priestley, *Discourse on the Evidence of Revealed Religion*, 1794.

450.G.15 We are perhaps the sons of dealers in old clothes, but we are the grandsons of prophets.

Weizmann, speech, March 18, 1923.

450.H. Challenge and Role

450.H.1 The Jewish genius is not of the kind that plants its seed, and leaves it for the silent centuries to assimilate it and mature its fruits. It needs living hearts for its soil, and the whole world is only wide enough to provide them.

Abrahams, *Jewish Life in the Middle Ages*, 1896, p. xix.

450.H.2 They are so disseminated through all the trading parts of the world, that they are become the instruments by which the most distant nations converse with one another, and by which mankind are knit together in a general correspondence. They are like the pegs and nails in a great building, which, though they are but little valued in themselves, are absolutely necessary to keep the whole frame together.

*Addison. *Spectator*, #495, Sept. 27, 1712.

450.H.3 The Greeks had chosen wisdom as their pursuit; the Romans, power; and the Jews, religion.

Anatoli, *Malmad HaTalmidim*, 1149, p. 103b.

450.H.4 We Jews are, as it were, the sons of the revolution, the daughters of the revolution. We should be aware of it. We can always be, what Dr. Toynbee calls a "creative minority."

Baeck, *Judaism*, 1949, p. 27.

450.H.5 To be a Jew is a destiny.

Baum, *And Life Goes On*, 1931, p. 193.

450.H.6 His own distress, as well as his conscious or half conscious messianic heritage, makes the Jew a ferment in the society in which he lives. His own misery makes him more sensitive to general injustice and social inequality.

Bentwich. q Heller, *Zionist Idea*, 38.

450.H.7 To be a Jew . . . is to be strong with a strength that has outlived persecutions. It is to be wise against ignorance, honest against piracy, harmless against evil, industrious against idleness, kind against cruelty!

*Bottome, *The Mortal Storm*, 1938, p. 72.

450.H.8 The Jewish people in the Diaspora is . . . the herald of international reconciliation and amity. As a people of peoples, it is the symbol of the "metahistorical" aim of mankind.

I. Breuer, *Der neue Kusari*, 1934.

450.H.9 By right of deeper insight into the moral needs of man, it has been their [the OT Jews'] prerogative to be for all succeeding ages the consolers and interpreters of suffering humanity.

*Butcher, *Some Aspects of Greek Genius*, (1891), p. 77.

450.H.10 Judaism was a normal school to train up teachers for the whole world.

*Channing, *The Universal Father*, 1872. *Works*, 1888, p. 949a.

450.H.11 The descendants of the teachers of religion and martyrs of the faith dare not be insignificant, not to say wicked.

Dubnow, *Jewish History*, 1903, p. 180.

450.H.12 Today every Jew feels that to be a Jew means to bear a serious responsibility not only to his own community, but also toward humanity.

Einstein, address, April 17, 1938.

450.H.13 Jews, belonging as they do to a minority group, can best fulfill the function of the constructive critic: they are less conditioned . . . than other men to accept things as they are.

Goodhart, *Five Jewish Lawyers*, 1949, p. 63.

450.H.14 Can it be doubted that it has been and is a substantial benefit to the human race that there should be, amongst its members, and especially its Christian members, this nonconformist nation, to represent liberty of thought, freedom of conscience, independence of judgment, the right of the human mind to settle for itself its relation with God?

*Herford. *Menorah Journal*, 1919, v. 145f.

450.H.15 As the East needed a Chinese wall in order not to be disturbed in its *immobile* existence, in like manner the Jews are the yeast of western humanity, destined from the beginning to impress upon it the distinguishing mark of *mobility*.

Hess, *Die europäische Triarchie*, 1841, p. 111. q *HJ*, April 1951, p. 8f.

450.H.16 They are the living witnesses of the true faith.

*Innocent III, Bull, 1199.

450.H.17 The Jews are as indispensable to the world as the winds.

Joshua b. Levi. *Talmud: Taanit*, 3b, on *Zech.* 2.10.

Ketia b. Shalom. *Talmud: Aboda Zara*, 10b.

450.H.18 To make Israel the central figure of the world's history, the leaven of peoples, the awakener of nations, is absurd; nevertheless this is what the friends and the enemies of the Jews are guilty of.

Lazare, *Antisemitism*, (1892) 1903, p. 358.

450.H.19 Jews . . . form a secretly corrective element against our passions. . . . When anti-Semitism breaks out in Europe, it betokens that the people there feel ill at ease under the Jewish mind, hampered in their evil designs. . . . Then the Jews have to suffer. But they *will* suffer—and survive. And we may all be certain that their strong sense of this world, their inborn socialism, will play an important part in the upbuilding of a new humanity, struggling slowly out of its crises.

*Mann, address, Free Synagog, April 18, 1937.

450.H.20 Israel, which is not of the world, is to be found at the very heart of the world's structure, stimulating it, exasperating it, moving it. Like an alien body, like an activating ferment injected into the mass, it gives the world no peace, it bars slumber, it teaches the world to be discontented and restless as long as the world has not God.

*Maritain, *A Christian Looks at the Jewish Problem*, 1939, p. 29.

450.H.21 The Jews in all times have taught the world how, without armies and

231

legions, to resist foreign domination, the Jews who form the most spiritual people on earth.

*Mickiewicz. q M. Bersano Begey, *Vita e Pensiero di A. Tomianski,* 1918; LGF, 504, Note 2.

450.H.22 In the ancient world also Judaism was an effective leaven of cosmopolitanism and of national decomposition, and to that extent a specially privileged member of the Caesarian state, the polity of which was really nothing but a citizenship of the world.

*Mommsen, *History of Rome,* 1866, 5.11; tr 1891, iv. 643.

450.H.23 It is not an Ibn Gabirol or a Maimonides, still less a Spinoza, who fulfilled the Jewish mission most truly or rendered the greatest service to the Jewish cause. No. It was the many little obscure Jewish communities through the ages, persecuted and despised, who kept alive the flame of purest monotheism and the supremacy and divineness of the Moral Law. Montefiore, 1927. BSL, 515f.

450.H.24 The Jews' vocation is to serve God!

*Paracelsus. q S. L. Steinheim, *Glaubenslehre der Synagoge,* 1856, p. 352.

450.H.25 Israel itself is a prophet, is itself the prophetic race.

*Péguy. *Notre Jeunesse,* 1910. *Basic Verities,* 1943, 131f.

450.H.26 In the hands of the Jew, the reddest of all flags has been placed forcibly, and he has been told: "Go, go on and on, with all liberators, with all fighters for a better tomorrow, with all destroyers of Sodoms. But never may you rest with them. . . . Pay everywhere the bloodiest costs of liberation, but be unnamed in all emancipation proclamations, or be rarely and scarcely mentioned." . . . The people cursed and blessed to be the last of the redeemed, to be eternally bleeding, the highest soaring expression of the divine in life.

Peretz. *The Day,* 1906. *Alle Verk,* xii. 319. LP, 18.

450.H.27 If sand is not put into lime, the lime will not last. So, if it were not for Israel, the Gentiles could not abide.

Pesikta Rabbati, ch 11, ed Friedmann, 45b.

450.H.28 The Jewish nation is to the whole inhabited world what the priest is to the State.

Philo, *Special Laws,* ii. 29.

450.H.29 It pleased God to make one nation the medium of all His communications with mankind. . . . This the nation of the Jews has done to a considerable degree in all ages. . . . As civilization extended, they by one means or another became most wonderfully dispersed through all countries; and at this day they are almost literally everywhere, the most conspicuous, and in the eye of reason and religion, the most respectable, nation on the face of the earth.

*Priestley, *Evidence of Revealed Religion,* 1794, i. 152f.

450.H.30 Do you know why we Jews were born into this world? In order to call every human being to Sinai. You don't want to go there? Well, if I don't call you, Marx will. If Marx doesn't, then Spinoza. If not Spinoza, Christ will summon you.

Rathenau, to Hans Breisig, 1919. q *Reconstructionist,* Oct. 31, 1952, p. 20.

450.H.31 The Jew was designed to serve as leaven in the progress of every country, rather than to form a separate nation on the globe.

*Renan, *History of Israel,* 1895, v. 189.

450.H.32 You must be the conscience of the world, the forgotten sense of shame to the nations.

Shneor, *The Middle Ages Are Approaching,* 1913. q HMH, 160.

450.H.33 Israel passes over Europe like the sun: wherever it appears new life shoots up, but when it is withdrawn, all that once flourished withers away.

*Sombart. q VA, 279f.

450.H.34 Israel has been, in the words of Athanasius, "a school of the knowledge of God to all nations."

*C. C. J. Webb. NSR, 1925, p. 339.

450.H.35 The people of Christ has been the Christ of peoples, both in its apostolate and in its martyrdom.

Zangwill, *Children of the Ghetto,* 1892, ii. 358.

450.I. Contributions to Civilization

450.I.1 There were no Jews round the table of King James I's compilers of the Authorized Version, but David Kimhi was present in spirit. The influence of his Commentary on the Bible is evident on every page of that noble translation.

Abrahams, *Jewish Life in the Middle Ages*, 1896, p. xix.

450.I.2 The Hebrews have done more to civilize men than any other nation. . . . The doctrine of a supreme, intelligent . . . sovereign of the universe, . . . I believe to be the great essential principle of all morality, and consequently of all civilization.

*J. Adams, letter to F. A. Vanderkemp, Feb. 16, 1809.

450.I.3 We drink from the pure source of Hebrew truth.

*Bede, *De Temporum Ratione*, 8C, ch 67.

450.I.4 The Jews gave to the world its three greatest religions, reverence for law, and the highest conceptions of morality.

Brandeis, *The Jewish Problem*, 1915.

450.I.5 On every sacred day you read to the people the exploits of Jewish heroes, the proofs of Jewish devotion, the brilliant annals of past Jewish significance. . . . Every Sunday . . . if you wish to express . . . thanksgiving to the Most High, or if you wish . . . solace in grief, you find both in the works of Jewish poets.

Disraeli. q Monypenny, *Life of B. Disraeli*, iii. 68.

450.I.6 The highest conception of God, man and nature are all Jewish.

*C. W. Eliot, address, Nov. 1905.

450.I.7 All the greatness of the white races comes from that sublime Judeo-Christian idea whose light was shed over the world from Palestine through the agency of the Bible and the great teachers of the Pharisees. Through its influence the State lost its divine character and put itself at the service of mankind; the spirit of criticism and the desire of better things were given the freedom of the world; the thirst for truth and justice increased with every effort made to quench it.

*Ferrero, *Paganism & Christianity*, 1931. *Peace & War*, 190.

450.I.8 Intellectual life in the occident is immensely indebted to the Jews. One cannot think about early scholasticism . . . without at the same time thinking about the influence of Jewish theology and philosophy.

*Hashagen, *Europa im Mittelalter*, 1951, p. 196.

450.I.9 'Tis a little people but it has done great things. . . . It had but a precarious hold on a few crags and highlands between the desert and the deep sea, yet its thinkers and sages with eagle vision took into their thought the destinies of all humanity, and rang out in clarion voice a message of hope to the downtrodden of all races.

J. Jacobs, *Jewish Contributions*, 1919, p. 10.

450.I.10 Had there been no Jews, there would have been no Torah.

Judah Halevi, *Cuzari*, c. 1135, 2.56.

450.I.11 Judaism gave to the world not only the fundamental ideas of the great monotheistic religions but the institutional forms in which they have perpetuated and propagated themselves.

*G. F. Moore, *Judaism*, 1927, i. 285.

450.I.12 Assyria gave to the world through its kings and armies the principle of world-conquest, world-empire, and world-exploitation. In direct answer and refutation, Israel gave to the world, through the mouth of its inspired prophets, the principle of world-justice, world-peace, world-brotherhood.

J. Morgenstern. *Menorah Journal*, 1919, v. 87.

450.I.13 Israel first gave form to the cry of the people, to the plaint of the poor, to the obstinate demand of those who "hunger and thirst after righteousness."

*Renan, *History of Israel*, 1895, v. 361.

450.I.14 We are largely indebted to the Jews for our first knowledge of philosophy, botany, medicine, astronomy, cosmography, not less than for the elements of grammar, the sacred languages, and almost all branches of biblical study.

*Santos, *Memorias de Litterature Portuguesa*.

450.I.15 We did not invent the art of printing; we did not discover America . . . we did not inaugurate the French Revolution . . . we were not the first to utilize the power of steam or electricity. . . . Our great claim to the gratitude of mankind is that we gave to the world the word of God, the Bible. We stormed heaven to snatch down this heavenly gift, as the Puritanic expression is; we threw ourselves into the breach and covered it with our bodies against every attack; we allowed ourselves to be slain by hundreds and thousands rather than become unfaithful to it; and bore witness to its truth and watched over its purity in the face of a hostile world.

Schechter, March 16, 1903. *Seminary Addresses*, 37.

450.I.16 Without Hebrew no Reformation, and without Jews no Hebrew, for they were the only teachers of that language.

*Schleiden, *Importance of Jews in . . . Learning,* 1876.

450.I.17 The western mind had sunk into ineptitude during the centuries that preceded the scholastic revival. Systematic thought had ceased to be; philosophy had wholly vanished; science had perished; even the love of nature was submerged. But still beyond the sunrise trickled the ancient spring of Hellenic wisdom. From these healing waters man could still renew his youth, and it was the Wandering Jew who bore westward the magic draught.

Singer, *Jewish Factor in Medieval Thought,* 1927. BSL, 182f.

450.I.18 Hebraic mortar cemented the foundations of our American democracy, and through the windows of the Puritan churches, the New West looked back to the Old East.

O. S. Straus, address, Nov. 29, 1905. *PAJHS,* xiv. 74.

450.I.19 Monotheism, the supreme importance of perfectibility in this sad, sublunar world, the refusal to be bullied by superior force, the right to persist as a minority—these are the leading elements in the Jewish contribution to human progress.

Weizmann. *N.Y. Herald Tribune* Annual Forum, Oct. 21, 1947.

450.I.20 The laws of Moses as well as the laws of Rome contributed suggestion and impulse to the men and institutions which were to prepare the modern world; and if we could have but eyes to see the subtle elements of thought which constitute the gross substance of our present habit, both as regards the sphere of private life, and as regards the action of the state, we should readily discover how very much besides religion we owe to the Jew.

*Wilson, *The State,* 1890, p. 143f.

450.J.   Attitude to Jews

Barometer

450.J.1 Jews have always been the barometer as well as lightning rod of all public storms.

Antokolski, letter to Turgeniev, June 4, 1881.

450.J.2 The Jew in the Diaspora, always in the minority, serves as a measure of the culture of the nations among whom he dwells.

Auerbach, *Lebensgeschichte Spinozas,* 1871, p. xvii. q *JQR,* 1910, i. 151.

450.J.2a A nation's attitude toward the Jews is the measure of its cultural maturity.

*Masaryk.

450.J.3 The social position of the Jews is the barometer indicating the moral condition of the nations.

*Kalmykowa, 1881. q BSS, 228.

450.J.4 The treatment of the Jews in every country is the thermometer of that country's civilization.

*Napoleon. See Straus, *Under Four Administrations,* 418.

450.J.5 Throughout history and in all countries of the world, the Jews have been the touchstone of the nations.

H. Samuel, *A Book of Quotations,* 1947, p. 97.

450.J.6 The nations which have received and in any way dealt fairly and mercifully with the Jew have prospered, and the nations that have tortured and oppressed him have written out their own curse.

*Schreiner, *A Letter on the Jew,* July 1, 1906.

450.J.7 When democracy yields to dict..torship, the Jew is the first to feel the mailed fist of arbitrary power. . . . Wherever democracy reigns supreme, the Jew is accorded equal treatment.

*Bankhead, address, B'nai Brith, May 9, 1938.

Appreciation

450.J.8 Whoever defends Israel is exalted by the Holy One.

Aha. *Pesikta Kahana,* ch 31, ed Buber, 176a.

450.J.9 If we part at the threshold of the gospels, it shall be, not with anger, but with love, and a grateful remembrance of our long and pleasant journey from Genesis to Malachi.

*Bonney, *JWP,* p. xxi. Aug. 27, 1893.

450.J.10 As I read [Josephine Lazarus' *The Spirit of Judaism*], I found myself reading as a Jew, and wellnigh the words of scornful reprobation and rejection burst from my lips: no, no, and no a thousand times. By all the disabilities of my people in the past, by all the insults and the injuries they have suffered and are suffering still, by their persecutions and expatriations, by the Ghetto's sordid Hell, this people shall be my people, and their God my God!

*Chadwick, "Christian Unity." q S. S. Wise, *Sermons and Addresses,* 121.

450.J.11 Oh, let us respect them; let us wait for that glorious day which will make them the head of the nations. Oh, the time is at hand when every one shall think himself happy that can but lay hold of the skirt of a Jew. Our salvation came from them. . . . Let us not, for God's sake, be unmerciful to them! No! let it be enough if we have all their spiritual riches.

*Collier, 1656. Tovey, *Anglia Judaica,* 279.

450.J.12 You cannot bring me too good a word, too dazzling a hope, too penetrating an insight from the Jews. I hail every one with delight, as showing the riches of my brother, my fellow soul, who could thus think and thus greatly feel. Zealots eagerly fasten their eyes on the differences between their creed and yours, but the charm of study is in finding the agreements, the identities, in all the religions of men.

*Emerson, speech, May 28, 1869.

450.J.13   The Prophets caught the Spirit's flame,
      From thee the Son of Mary came,
      With thee the Father deigned to dwell,—
      Peace be upon thee, Israel!

*O. W. Holmes, "At the Pantomime," 1874.

450.J.14 O Jews, you seem to live in the inner chamber of the heart!

*Ifra Hormiz. c.350. q *Talmud: Nidda,* 20b.

450.J.15 In the infancy of civilization, when our island was as savage as New Guinea, when letters and arts were still unknown to Athens, when scarcely a thatched roofed hut stood on what was afterwards the site of Rome, this contemned people had their fenced cities and cedar palaces, their splendid Temple, their fleets of merchant ships, their schools of sacred learning, their great statesmen and soldiers, their natural philosophers, their historians and their poets.

*Macaulay, address, House of Commons, April 17, 1833.

450.J.16 Let us extend a brotherly hand to this illustrious people, and requite it, as far as possible, for all that fate had meted out to it in the course of dark and terrible ages.

*Nebesky, response to S. Kapper's Czech poems, 1843.

450.J.17 To meet a Jew is a blessing, especially if one lives among Germans.

*Nietzsche. q VA, 65.

Apathy and Tolerance

450.J.18 Have mercy upon all Jews, Turks, Infidels, and Heretics.

Book of Common Prayer: Good Friday, 1662.

450.J.19 Just as no freedom may be granted to Jews in their communities to exceed the limits legally set for them, so they should in no way suffer through a violation of their rights.

*Gregory I, *Sicut Judaeis,* vii. 25, c.600.

450.J.20 The Jews are a treasure to the king, a good treasure.

Ibn Verga, (Archbishop Gil of Toledo in) *Shebet Yehuda,* (1550) 1855, #10, p. 32.

450.J.21 How hot the nineteenth century waxed about one Jew [Dreyfus] and how wearily the twentieth has taken the case of millions!

*Vansittart.

Ingratitude

450.J.22 You have seized upon Moses and Aaron and the Ten Commandments, which were our natural property, and placed them over the communion tables; yet make the pretense of Christian communion a reason for excluding us from the advantages of the commonwealth.

*Arnall, *Complaints of the Children of Israel,* 1736.

450.J.23 The treatment of the Jews is the greatest ingratitude on the part of Christianity.

*Balfour, address, Parliament, 1905.

450.J.24 Jews who enrich general culture and civilization are like laborers who toil in a factory which they do not own. The profit never accrues to them but always to the owner.

Bialik, at Kovno, 1930. *Debarim She-Be'al Peh,* 1.

450.J.25 The Jew is the Prometheus of history. . . . He received the fire of monotheism from heaven and gave it to man. For his care and solicitude he has been chained to the rock of the ages while the vultures of hatred, persecution, riot and massacre have preyed upon his heart.

*Chandler, *The Jews of Rumania,* Oct. 10, 1913.

450.J.26 The Jews were looked upon in the middle ages as an accursed race. . . . No one in those days paused to reflect that Christianity was founded by the Jews . . . that the infallible throne of Rome itself was established by a Jew.

Disraeli, *Coningsby,* Pref. to 5th ed, 1849.

450.J.27 Judaism suffered the tragic fate of King Lear.

Dubnow, *Jewish History,* 1903, p. 120.

450.J.28 We have taken your Bible over and made it ours, and said never a word of appreciation of the genius for God which produced it. . . . We have called peace a Christian attitude, forgetting that it was a Jew who first used those words, which now belong to humanity, about beating swords into plowshares and spears into pruning hooks.

*Edmonds. *Federal Council Bulletin,* June 1931.

450.J.29 Jews are not fit for Heaven, but on earth are most useful.

*G. Eliot, *Spanish Gypsy,* 1868, i.

450.J.30 Single, gifted Jews are lionized. . . . But these are somehow . . . extracted from their race, regarded as separate and not as reflecting the nature of that people—an unjust attitude not exercised toward any other. And what a train of great names in art and science this people summons from its past!

*Gale. Landman, *Christian and Jew,* 1929, p. 133.

450.J.31 Such an injustice as that inflicted by the Gentile Church on Judaism is almost unprecedented in the annals of history. The Gentile church stripped it of everything; she took away its sacred book; herself but a transformation of Judaism, she cut off all connection with the parent religion. The daughter first robbed her mother, and then repudiated her.

*Harnack, *Expansion of Christianity,* 1902, i. 5, tr J. Moffat, 1904, i. 81.

450.J.32 The help of the Jew has been sought and used and then cast away with no word of thanks.

*Herford. *Menorah Journal,* 1919, v. 212. See *Judaism in the NT Period,* 1928, p. 237f.

450.J.33 Their sacred writings . . . have been adopted by all civilized communities, while they themselves have been fugitives everywhere, without security anywhere.

*Hone, *The Every-Day Book,* (1826) 1838, i. 300.

450.J.34 Every nation keeps its own ledger; ours alone is kept by strangers, who place the achievement of individual Jews to their own credit, and leave us only with the debit side.

Namier, *Conflicts,* 1943, p. 131.

Hostility

450.J.35 Christian civilization has been guilty of a strange syllogism in regard to Jews. Christianity orders me to love all men without distinction. The Jews are men. Therefore, I hate them, I persecute and torment them.

*d'Azeglio, *Dell' emancipazione civile degli Israeliti,* 1848, p. 6. q *JSS,* 1953, xv. 121.

450.J.36 You have always persecuted the Jews, but . . . now you seek, what you did not seek before, to justify your persecution. You do not hate the Jews because they deserve it; you hate them and seek, as best you can, to show that they earn your hostility; you hate them because they—earn . . .

Boerne, *Der ewige Jude,* 1821.

450.J.37 While . . . Jews were in a peaceful state, the religious ceremonies and observances of that people were much at variance with the splendor of this empire, the dignity of our name, and the institutions of our ancestors. And they are the more odious to us now, because that nation has shown by arms what were its feelings toward our supremacy.

*Cicero, *Flaccus,* 59 B.C.E., 28.

450.J.38 In every work of fiction, . . . wherever Jews are introduced, I find they are invariably represented as beings of a mean, avaricious, unprincipled, treacherous character.

*Edgeworth, *Harrington,* 1816.

450.J.39 If it be the mark of a good Christian to hate Jews, what excellent Christians we all are!

*Erasmus, letter to Hoogstraten, 1519. See GHJ, iv. 463.

450.J.40 Hatred for Judaism is at bottom hatred for Christianity.
Freud, *Moses and Monotheism*, 1939, p. 145.

450.J.41 We tolerate no Jew among us. How can we concede him participation in the highest culture when he denies its origin?
*Goethe. q SHR, 67f. See Conversation with von Müller, Sept. 23, 1823; L. Geiger, *Die deutsche Literatur und die Juden*, 1910, p. 101ff.

450.J.42 The Jew must be gold to pass for silver; he is deemed guilty until he is proved innocent; he alone is not judged by his best, but by his worst. He is attacked not only by the ignorant through lack of knowledge, but by the scholar through lack of sympathy.
Harrison, *Religion of a Modern Liberal*, 1931, p. 24.

450.J.43 Only utter hypocrites continue to give their hatred a religious hue . . . the great multitude confesses that material interests are what are really at stake. . . . Here in Frankfort, for example, only twenty-four believers in the law of Moses can be married annually, lest their population increases and too much competition with Christian business people be created.
Heine, *Shakespeare's Maidens: Jessica*, 1839.

450.J.44 It is for his virtues, not his vices, that the Jew is hated.
Herzl. q Zangwill, *Zionism*, Oct. 1899.

450.J.45 The Jew is an irritant that brings forever to the conscience of the people their shortcomings. This is the cause of hatred against the Jew.
E. G. Hirsch. *Reform Advocate*, 1891, i. 425.

450.J.46 By attacking Israel, the heathen hope to undermine the foundations of the Holy One.
Hiyya b. Abba. *Exod. R.,* 51.5.

450.J.47 The people hate Jews because of envy, and . . . for hatred due to envy there is no cure.
Ibn Verga, *Shebet Yehuda*, (1550) 1855, p. 11.

450.J.48 A good Law, but an execrable people!
*Innocent XII, to a Jewish delegation that presented him with a Scroll at his inauguration as Pope, 1692.

450.J.49 To be detested by the whole race of man one must carry within him something truly great.
Lazare, *Notes on a Conversion.* LR, 49.

450.J.50 It is the vocation of Israel which the world execrates. To be hated by the world is their glory.
*Maritain, *A Christian Looks*, 1939, p. 30.

450.J.51 Who hateth me but for my happiness? . . .
Rather had I, a Jew, be hated thus
Than pitied in a Christian poverty.
*Marlowe, *Jew of Malta*, 1590, 1.1.

450.J.52 O ye believers, choose not Jews and Christians as allies. . . . He who befriends them is one of them.
*Mohammed, *Koran: Table*, 5.56.

450.J.53 Who could believe it that in the year of grace 1812, anyone would still harbor an antipathy to the Jews!
*Napoleon, letter to Kubloscher of Danzig, 1812.

450.J.54 The Jew as devil, the Jew whose badge was a scorpion, the symbol of falsity, owes his origin to religion, not to economics.
*Parkes, *Judaism and Christianity*, 1948, p. 126.

450.J.55 Judeophobia is a psychosis. As a psychosis it is hereditary and . . . incurable.
Pinsker, *Auto-Emancipation*, 1882.

450.J.56 The Jews are the chosen people of the world's hatred.
Ibid.

450.J.57 One may kill as many as seven Jews with impunity.
*Proverb (Moroccan). q Zangwill, *Problem of Jewish Race*, 7.

450.J.58 It lifts forty sins from the soul to kill a Jew.
*Proverb (Ukrainian). q MND, 613.

450.J.59 In the early days of every German Jew there comes a painful moment, which he remembers for the rest of his life, when he first becomes fully aware of the fact that he came into the world as a second class citizen, and that no proficiency and no merit can release him from that status.
Rathenau, *Staat und Judentum*, 1911.

450.J.60 The enemies of Jewry are for the most part the enemies of the modern spirit.

*Renan. q Ellis, *Questions of Our Day,* 38.

450.J.61 Our genius is an offense,
Our brains a subject for penitence.

M. Rosenfeld, "Exile Song." LGP, 43.

450.J.62 Hatred of Jews starts where common sense stops.

Saphir, *Lebende Bilder.* SHW, ii. 162.

450.J.63 Who called into being the liberal movement in Austria? . . . the Jews! By whom were the Jews betrayed and deserted? By the Liberals. Who created the Pan-German movement in Austria? The Jews! By whom were the Jews left in the lurch . . . nay more, spat on like dogs? . . . By the Germans! And the same thing will happen to them at the hands of the Socialists and Communists.

Schnitzler, *Weg ins Freie,* 1907. q LGS, 134f.

450.J.64 This hatred of the world against us can spring only from one thing: If the death of a man shall be revenged, shall not the death of gods be revenged seventy times and seven? And will you ever forgive us for having slain all your gods, gods of east and west and south and north, Zeus and Odin and Astaroth?

Shneor. q M. Samuel. *Reflex,* Aug. 1927, p. 115.

450.J.65 The eternal hatred for an eternal people!

Smolenskin, *Am Olam,* 1873.

450.J.66 The world is divided into two groups of nations—those that want to expel the Jews and those that do not want to receive them.

Weizmann, attributed to.

450.K. Persecution

450.K.1 They set over them taskmasters to afflict them with their burdens. . . . But the more they afflicted them, the more they multiplied and the more they spread abroad.

Bible: Exod., 1.11f.

450.K.2 My people has been lost sheep. . . . All that found them have devoured them, and their adversaries said: "We are not guilty," because they have sinned against the Lord.

Bible: Jer., 50.6f.

450.K.3 Innocent or not, let the Jew be fried!

*Arbues, c. 1480. q MND, 610.

450.K.4 It matters not, the Jew must still be burned!

*Lessing, (Patriarch in) *Nathan der Weise,* 1779, 4.2.

450.K.5 We are ashamed to write down all that the Cossacks and Tatars did unto the Jews, lest we disgrace the species man who is created in the image of God.

q from an old Chronicle. Asch, *Kiddush HaShem,* tr Rufus Learsi, 1926, motto.

450.K.6 In the decay and dregs of centuries men have adopted a spirit of cruelty and barbarism towards the Jews. They were accused of being the cause of all the disasters which happened, and . . . of crimes of which they never even dreamed. . . . People and kings . . . agreed in the purpose of destroying this nation, and have not succeeded. The bush of Moses, surrounded by flames, has ever burned without being consumed.

*Basnage, Prospectus to *L'Histoire et la Réligion des Juifs,* 1706. q GHJ, v. 196.

450.K.7 Since the Merchants Guild is composed of honest, upright people, therefore no Jew, blasphemer, murderer, thief, adulterer, perjurer, or anyone otherwise spotted and stained with heinous vices and sins, shall be suffered in our Guild.

*Berlin Merchants Guild, *By-Laws,* 1716.

450.K.8 In Frankfurt the law forbids all Jews to marry, except for fifteen couples annually. . . . At this we rejoice, for it shows humanity's great progress: even the art of execution has been refined. . . . Less than four thousand years ago this political whim, to reduce the Jewish population, occurred also to an Egyptian Pharaoh; but Christendom has milder means: it prohibits Jews to marry.

Boerne, *Der Narr im weissen Schwan,* ch 3.

450.K.9 By the torture, prolonged from age to age,
By the infamy, Israel's heritage,
By the Ghetto's plague, by the garb's disgrace,
By the badge of shame, by the felon's place,
By the branding tool, the bloody whip,
And the summons to Christian fellowship—

We boast our proof that at least the Jew
Would wrest Christ's name from the Devil's crew.
*Browning, "Holy Cross Day," 1855.

450.K.10 Except the Jews (*kromye zhydov*).
*Catherine II, Manifesto inviting foreigners to settle in Russia, 1762. The phrase became a refrain in czarist legislation.

450.K.11 Everybody rails at us, everybody points us out for their maygame and their mockery. If you playwriters want a butt, or a buffoon, or a knave to make sport of, out comes a Jew to be baited and buffeted through five long acts, for the amusement of all good Christians. Cruel sport! merciless amusement!
*Cumberland, (Sheva in) *The Jew*, 1793, 1.1.

450.K.12 We have damned you for the very attitudes which we ourselves made inevitable. . . . We have driven you together like sheep in a storm and now call you clannish. . . . Your prosperity has been an evidence of a mercenary mind, ours of the favor of God.
*Edmonds, *Federal Council Bulletin*, June 1951.

450.K.13 Since the destruction of the Temple, the Jewish world has been so afflicted . . . that I could justify their exemption from divine judgment.
Eleazar b. Azariah. *Talmud: Erubin*, 65a.

450.K.14 My throat is parched from crying Violence!
Gershon b. Judah, c. 1000. q WHJ, i. 247.

450.K.15 Whenever an act of cruelty was to be perpetrated on the Jews, fables . . . were forged, and the brutal passions of the mob set loose upon the life and wealth of fugitive Israelites.
*Hone, *The Every-Day Book*, (1826) 1838, i. 385.

450.K.16 Though the acts of violence against the Jews proceeded much from bigotry, they were still more derived from avidity and rapine. So far from desiring in that age to convert them, it was enacted by law in France that if any Jew embraced Christianity, he forfeited all his goods . . . to the king. . . . These plunderers were careful lest the profits accruing from . . . that unhappy race should be diminished by their conversion.
*Hume, *History of England*, 1754, ch 12 (1879, i. 633).

450.K.17 Jews, like the fratricide Cain, are doomed to wander about the earth as fugitives and vagabonds, and their faces must be covered with shame. They are . . . to be condemned to serfdom.
*Innocent III, letter to Count Nevers, 1208. q GHJ, iii. 500.

450.K.18 What a shame it is they should be more miserable under Christian princes than their ancestors were under Pharaoh!
*Innocent IV, letter, 1247.

450.K.19 "Give, Give!" do the wicked shout:
"Supply us with money!" is their battle-cry.
Isaac Halevi, 11C. q Zunz, *Synagogale Poesie*, 10.

450.K.20 The Jew-baiter never tires.
Johanan b. Nappaha. *Talmud: Sanhedrin*, 104b.

450.K.21 The nations ruined and enslaved you on account of your intelligence and purity.
Judah Halevi, *Cuzari*, c. 1135, 3.10.

450.K.22 His cup is gall, his meat is tears,
His passion lasts a thousand years.
E. Lazarus, "Crowing of the Red Cock," 1881. *Poems*, 1888, ii. 3.

450.K.23 If the apostles . . . had behaved towards us Gentiles as we Gentiles behave towards the Jews, not one Gentile would have become a Christian.
*Luther, *Das Jesus ein geborener Jude war*, 1523.

450.K.24 The Jews are the last serfs still existing in Europe.
Luzzatti. *Corriere della Sera*, March 3, 1913.

450.K.25 I sometimes go out in the evening with my wife and children. "Papa," inquires one of them in innocent simplicity, "what is it those lads call out after us? Why do they throw stones at us? . . ." "Yes, dear papa," says another, "they always run after us . . . and shout, 'Jew-boy!' Is it a disgrace . . . to be a Jew? . . ." I cast down my eyes and sigh to myself, Poor humanity! To what a point have these things come!
M. Mendelssohn, letter to Winkopp. q Hensel, *Mendelssohn Family*, i. 25.

450.K.26 Edom's princes covet money, and therefore flay Israel alive.

Midrash Agadat Bereshith, ch 57, ed Buber, 1925, 48b.

450.K.27 If you beat my Jew, I'll beat yours!

*Niebergall, *Der Datterich,* 1841, adapted from J. P. Hebel, *Die zwei Postillions,* 1811.

450.K.28 To rob a Jew they consider not a crime but an act of justice.

Num. R., 10.2.

450.K.29 If there be a class of our fellow-beings to whom reparation is due from every Christian State in Europe . . . the Jews are that class. I defy you to read the early history of this country, narrated, not by indignant Jews, but by the popular historians of your own faith, without shuddering at the atrocities committed by Christian sovereigns and a Christian people.

*Peel, speech, House of Commons, Feb. 11, 1848.

450.K.30 Strange inconsistency! to persecute in the name of religion those who had given the religion. . . . Catholic Spain, Protestant Germany, Greek Russia massacred and murdered Jews while singing the psalmody Jewish patriarchs and prophets had written. Oh! Christianity, what crimes have been committed in thy name!

*Peters, *Justice to the Jew,* (1899) 1921, p. 229.

450.K.31 I am sorry for the pogroms, but they help maintain the discipline of the army.

*Petliura. q *Reflex,* July 1927, p. 91.

450.K.32 The whole Jewish race is in the position of an orphan compared with all the nations on every side.

Philo, *Special Laws,* iv. 34.

450.K.33 If the Jew is right, he is beaten all the more.

Proverb (Yiddish). *JE,* x. 229a.

450.K.34 He who has never been persecuted is not a Jew.

Rab. *Talmud: Hagiga,* 5a.

450.K.35 To be a Jew means to be in exile.

F. Rosenzweig, letter to R. Hallo. *Briefe,* 1935.

450.K.36 A people . . . wise-hearted with the sorrows of every land.

Sampter, *Book of the Nations,* 1917.

450.K.37 Every age has its own idolatry, and the eternal wandering Jew will always be the chosen victim of the Moloch in fashion.

Schechter, *Studies in Judaism,* 1896, i. 331.

450.K.38 You call me misbeliever, cut-throat dog,
And spit upon my Jewish gaberdine.

*Shakespeare, *Merchant of Venice,* 1597, 1.3.

450.K.39 He hath . . . laughed at my losses, mocked at my gains, scorned my nation, thwarted my bargains, cooled my friends, heated mine enemies; and what's his reason? I am a Jew.

Ibid., 3.1.

450.K.40 No Jew . . . shall enter upon any honors or dignities; to none of them shall the administration of a civil duty be available.

Theodosian Code, Novellae, 3.2, Jan. 31, 438.

450.K.41 A Jew-baiter becomes a chief.

*Titus. q *Talmud: Gittin,* 56b.

450.L. Reaction

450.L.1 Pour out Thy wrath upon the nations that know Thee not . . . for they have devoured Jacob . . . and laid waste his habitation.

Bible: Jer., 10.25.

450.L.2 When I hear mockery, I boldly answer: My Redeemer liveth!

Abitur, hymn based on *Ps.* 121, 10C.

450.L.3 The best defense against hostile attitudes directed toward Jews is a firm identification with Judaism, coupled with full participation in the broad community life of America.

American Jewish Committee, *Tentative Statement,* 1951.

450.L.4 Woe to the nations that rise up against my race!

Apocrypha: Judith, 16.17.

450.L.5 Hold firm! Do not let your misfortune and the wickedness of others rob you of your love for mankind! Be too proud to deem yourselves unhappy! Despite all shocks to your spirit, despite all temptation to despair, cry out with me: God exists for a' that, and the spirit of humanity will conquer for a' that!

Auerbach, *Genesis des Nathans,* 1881, p. 24. q LGS, 98.

450.L.6 The attention and pity of Christians should be aroused for men whom God has preserved for so long in spite of a burden of suffering under which any other people would have been completely entombed.

*Basnage, *L'Histoire et la Réligion des Juifs*, 1706, vi. 1:4. q Parkes, *Judaism & Christianity*, 155.

450.L.7 Their situation forces them [Jews] to be careful of consciously giving offense. This fact does not in the least mitigate the hatred . . . but serves rather to rob that antecedent hatred of normal and excusable outlets, and all hatred is intensified when its selected object will not supply it with any decent or tolerable motivation.

P. Bernstein, *Jew-Hate*, 1926. LR, 177.

450.L.8 That I was born a Jew has never embittered me against the Germans, has never deluded me. Indeed, I would not deserve enjoying the light of day if I were to respond to the divine grace, which permitted me to be at once both German and Jew, with base murmuring against a mockery which I have always scorned, against pain which I have long since gotten over.

Boerne, *Briefe aus Paris*, #74, Feb. 7, 1832.

450.L.9 In every century of history, with their hands tied behind them and their hearts burdened to the breaking point with a bitter load of hatred and persecution, Jews have yet managed . . . to plant in the garden of life, in the soil of the soul, the most beautiful and fragrant flowers that bloom and blossom there.

*Chandler, *Jews of Rumania*, in Congress, Oct. 10, 1913.

450.L.10 Our forefathers bore their destiny with heroism, with inner dignity in devout trust. Let us learn from them!

Elbogen, "Haltung." *C-V Zeitung*, April 8, 1933.

450.L.11 Despite all this, we praise God . . . and diligently pray for the welfare of all men, especially of the nations among whom we dwell, . . . for when they enjoy peace, we have peace.

Emden, Pref. to *Seder Olam*, 1757. See JJC, 134.

450.L.12 I bow before the strength of the martyred soul of the great Jewish people, which for centuries has been so awfully wronged, that power which, when once relieved, has always felt warm and keen for liberty.

*Gorky. q *Maccabean*, April 1902, ii. 213.

450.L.13 It is not the business of the Jews to petition for justice, but it is the duty of Christians to be just.

*Hone, *The Every-Day Book*, (1826) 1838, i. 298.

450.L.14 If I can't bite, my wrath will bite into my own bowels. That's why our whole race is ulcerated in the bloodiest literal sense. Fifteen hundred years of impotent anger has gnawed our intestines, sharpened our features and twisted down the corners of our lips.

Koestler, *Thieves in the Night*, 1946, p. 229.

450.L.15 We are unable to safeguard our fellow Jews or our growing children today against those handicaps which are the result of their being Jewish. However, we can try to build up a Jewish education . . . to counteract the *feeling of inferiority* and the *feeling of fear* which are the most important sources of the negative balance.

Lewin, "Self-Hatred." *CJR*, 1941. *Resolving*, 198.

450.L.16 Brethren, be strong and of good courage. If persecution come, let it not discomfort you. . . . These events are but the test and proof of your faith and love.

Maimonides, *Iggeret Teman*, 1172, tr Cohen, p. iii.

450.L.17 It is by virtue that I wish to shame the opprobrious opinion commonly entertained of a Jew, not by controversial writings.

M. Mendelssohn, *Letter to Lavater*, Dec. 12, 1769.

450.L.18 All logical methods of combatting the hostility against us are futile. . . . Prejudice and bad faith will yield to no proof.

Pinsker, *Auto-Emancipation*, 1882.

450.L.19 When the toll of bricks is doubled, then comes Moses!

q Stanley, *History of the Jewish Church*, (1862) 1892, i. 104.

450.L.20 I have never conversed with a well-informed Jew without experiencing shame and humiliation.

*Pückler-Muskau, *Tutti-Frutti*, 1834, p. 94.

450.L.21 The adversaries of our people and faith say: Your frightful fate . . . proves that you have been rejected. Shame on such logic! Who is the rejected, the perpetrator or the victim of injustice? Israel is that Servant of God, whom the prophet Isaiah . . . portrayed so strikingly in his Chapter 53: "despised and forsaken of men . . . but he was . . . crushed because of our iniquities, and with his stripes we were healed!"

Rülf, address, in Kovno synagog, 1869. q *JGL*, 1912, p. 201f.

450.L.22 Still have I borne it with patient shrug,
For sufferance is the badge of all our tribe.

*Shakespeare, *Merchant of Venice*, 1597, 1.3.

450.L.23 What good will our denunciation do? . . . Sir, when the student of history shall turn the pages of the past . . . will he not ask, . . . "Had the great free nation of the West no word for an hour like that? . . . Was America heartless or afraid to speak?" Sir, it is not the Jews of Moscow and Odessa, it is we and our children who have most at stake in the answer to that question.

*Stafford, speech, Jan. 21, 1906.

450.L.24 May this demonic scene be a lesson to our non-Jewish Jews. Let them see what they have gained by sacrificing their religious ceremonies and customs, their patriarchal way of life, their *esprit de corps* . . . in order to amalgamate with Amalek.

Taubels, letter on anti-Jewish riot in Prague, 1848.

450.L.25 Vain to present the right cheek after the left has been struck . . . they strike the right cheek too. Vain to interject words of reason into their crazy shrieking. They say: Gag him. . . . Vain to seek obscurity. They say: The coward! . . . Vain to live for them and die for them. They say: He is a Jew.

J. Wassermann, *My Life as German and Jew*, 1933, p. 226f.

450.L.26 The Jew's revenge . . . was characteristic of him. He destroyed the gods of his persecutors. He dissipated the illusions, exposed the superstitions, battled against ignorance, protested against slavery, demanded freedom of belief, thought and speech, and raised his voice against prejudice and oppression. He carried skep-

ticism and learning from land to land, gave the impulses to the world's progress and stood at the cradle of every idea of light and freedom. That was the Jew's revenge.

I. M. Wise, "Wandering Jew," 1877. *Selected Writings*, 195.

450.M. Preservation

450.M.1 I will not . . . destroy them utterly . . . for I am . . . their God.
Bible: Lev., 26.44.

450.M.2 If these ordinances [sun and moon] depart, . . . then the seed of Israel also shall cease from being a nation before Me forever.
Bible: Jer., 31.35f.

450.M.3 Be of good courage, my people. . . . Ye were sold to the nations, but not for destruction.
Apocrypha: 1 Baruch, 4.5f.

450.M.4 You denied air to the Jews, but that guarded them against putrefaction. You poured the salt of hatred into their heart, but that kept their heart fresh. You incarcerated them the whole winter long in a cellar and stopped up its entrance with dung; but you, freely exposed to the frost, are half-frozen. When spring comes, we shall see who blossoms first!
Boerne, *Briefe aus Paris*, #74, Feb. 7, 1832.

450.M.5 There seems to be but one way to kill Jews, and that is with kindness. Let them be, and they cease to be.
Browne, *Wisdom of Israel*, 1945, p. xvi.

450.M.6 The Persians, the Greeks, the Romans are swept from the earth; and a petty tribe, whose origin preceded that of those great nations, still exists unmixed among the ruins of its native land. If anything among the nations wears the character of a miracle, that, in my opinion is here legibly impressed.
*Chateaubriand, *Travels in Greece*, 1806f, tr 1814, p. 391.

450.M.7 A people still, whose common ties are gone;
Who, mixed with every race, are lost in none.
*Crabbe, *The Borough*, 1810, Letter 4.

450.M.8 Empires and dynasties flourish and pass away; the proud metropolis becomes a solitude, the conquering kingdom even a desert: but Israel still remains.
Disraeli, *Alroy*, 1833, 4.2. See his speech, May 25, 1854.

450.M.9 Jewry, being a spiritual entity, cannot suffer annihilation: the body, the mould, may be destroyed, the spirit is immortal.

Dubnow, *Jewish History*, 1903, p. 177.

450.M.10 The river of Jewish life is still flowing on; and it may be that, when London and Petersburg have in their turns fallen to ruins, the waters of Siloa, which flow so softly, shall still refresh the world.

*Farrar, *The Jews. Social & Present Day Question*, 1891, p. 359. See *The Bible*, 22.

450.M.11 Judaism has been preserved throughout the long years of Israel's dispersion by two factors: its separative ritualism, which prevented close and intimate contact with non-Jews, and the iron laws of the Christian theocracies of Europe, which encouraged and enforced isolation.

Fishberg, *The Jews*, 1911, p. 555.

450.M.12 We should survive. First, because . . . there is a great deal of fine literature and art and music for us to create. . . . Secondly, . . . for the same reason that I want the Red Indian and the Basque to survive. . . . From day to day the world tends to become more and more monotone and monochrome. . . . We must hang on to what separates us, our traditions, . . . lest we bore each other and ourselves to extinction.

Golding, *The Jewish Problem*, 1938, p. 209f.

450.M.13 In its journey through the wilderness of life, . . . the Jewish people has carried along the Ark of the Covenant, which breathed into its heart ideal aspirations, and even illumined the badge of disgrace affixed to its garment with a shining glory. . . . Such a people, which disdains its present and has the eye fixed steadily on its future, which lives as it were on hope, is on that very account eternal, like hope.

Graetz, *Geschichte der Juden*, 1853, iv. Preface.

450.M.14 Kingdoms come and go, but Israel abides for ever.

Isaac Nappaha. *Eccles. R.*, to *Eccles.* 1.4.

450.M.15 Jerusalem was indeed once a great city, and the Temple magnificent; but the Jews themselves were greater than either. . . . Exiled and dispersed, reviled and persecuted, . . . the Jews were divinely preserved for a purpose worthy of a God.

*Jerome. q N. Maclean, *His Terrible Swift Sword*, p. 60.

450.M.16 There is within us the infinite and universal Idea which saves us from the common fate of the ephemeral.

Krochmal, *Moré Nebuḳé HaZman*, 1851. q FJA, 274.

450.M.17 They are a piece of stubborn antiquity, compared with which Stonehenge is in its nonage. They date beyond the Pyramids.

*Lamb, *Imperfect Sympathies*, 1821.

450.M.18 From age to age all the prizes of the world, which only a fool would underestimate, have been set upon betrayal, withdrawal, apostasy, disappearance, merging with the nations. Yet . . . we are here. That is the marvel.

Lewisohn, *Adam*, 1929.

450.M.19 Pride and humiliation hand in
    hand
      Walked with them through
      the world where'er they
      went;
      Trampled and beaten were
      they as the sand,
      And yet unshaken as the
      continent.

*Longfellow, "Jewish Cemetery at Newport," 1852.

450.M.20 We are in possession of the divine assurance that Israel is indestructible and imperishable, and will always continue to be a pre-eminent community.

Maimonides, *Iggeret Teman*, 1172, tr Cohen, p. v.

450.M.21 Israel is wasted, his seed is not.

*Merneptah, inscription on monument at Thebes (Luxor), c. 1210 B.C.E.

450.M.22 There must be no surrender whatever by either Jew or Christian of the fullness of his inheritance. God still needs the Jews as Jews.

*Parkes, *Jews, Christians and God*, 1942, p. 14.

450.M.23 This people is . . . singular by their duration. . . . For whereas the nations of Greece and Italy, . . . and others who came long after, have long since perished, these ever remain, and in spite of the endeavors of many powerful kings who have a hundred times tried to destroy them.

*Pascal, *Pensées*, 1670, #620.

450.M.24 When they have become a
    legend,
    and Rome a fable,
    that old men will tell of in the
    city's gate,

the tellers will be Jews and
their speech Hebrew.
Reznikoff, "In Memoriam: 1933."

450.M.25 I believe that the Jewish people . . . will live eternally.
Smolenskin, letter to David Frishman, #1.

450.M.26 They have been preserved in great measure by Gentile hatred.
Spinoza, *Theologico-Political Treatise*, 1670, ch 3.

450.M.27 The Jew is the emblem of eternity. He whom neither slaughter nor torture of thousands of years could destroy, . . . he who was the first to produce the oracles of God, he who has been for so long the guardian of prophecy, and who transmitted it to the rest of the world—such a nation cannot be destroyed. The Jew is everlasting as is eternity itself.
*Tolstoy. q Baron, *Stars and Sand*, 46.

450.M.28 All things are mortal but the Jew; all other forces pass, but he remains. What is the secret of his immortality?
*Twain, "Concerning the Jews." *Harper's Magazine*, 1898.

450.M.29 A people that has learned to live without a country is unconquerable.
Zangwill, *Future of the Jewish People*, 1903.

450.M.30 Israel is like the silkworm, that precious creature which produces from itself a fine thread out of which is woven the costliest kingly raiment, and leaves behind, before it dies, a seed out of which it comes to life as before.
Zohar, Gen., 178a.

450.N. The Jewish Problem

450.N.1 Fundamentally, the Jewish question is a battle between the honorable and the honorless.
Inscription on a monument to Theodor Fritsch, in Zellendorf. See Baron, *In Quest of Integrity*, 36.

450.N.2 The Jewish question—that's the wide canal which drains all the impurities, all the dirt and mud and sewage of man's soul.
Mendelé, *BeYeshiba shel Maala*, 1895.

450.N.3 As long as a Jewish question exists, as long as justice is denied us, civilization is written down a lie.
Nordau, speech, VIII Zionist Congress, Aug. 14, 1907.

450.N.4 *Moah* vs. *Koah* [mind vs. might]—that is the Jewish problem in a nutshell.
*Sombart, *Jews & Modern Capitalism*, 1913, p. 260.

450.O. Identification

450.O.1 I am a Hebrew, and I fear the Lord.
Bible: Jon., 1.9.

450.O.2 Think not . . . that you will escape in the king's house more than all the Jews.
Bible: Esther, 4.13.

450.O.3 I consider it an honor to be a Jew. I am proud of it, and I want all to know that I am one.
Antokolski. q Anski, *Gezamelté Shriften*, x. 36.

450.O.4 Far be it from me that I should spare my own life in any time of affliction; for I am not better than my brethren.
Apocrypha: I Macc., 13.5.

450.O.5 I and my children are happy that we belong . . . not to those who slaughter and not to those who look on indifferently.
Ben Gurion, to Anglo-American Committee, March 19, 1946.

450.O.6 It is true that I am a Jew, and when my ancestors were receiving their Ten Commandments from the immediate hand of Deity, amidst the thunderings and lightnings of Mt. Sinai, the ancestors of the distinguished gentleman who is opposed to me were herding swine in the forests of Scandinavia.
Benjamin, reply in Senate to taunt, "that Jew from Louisiana," c. 1857.
(Another version: The gentleman will please remember that when his half-civilized ancestors were hunting the wild boar in Silesia, mine were princes of the earth.)

450.O.7 Rather than be a beast among beasts, I choose to perish with the lambs.
Bialik. q SHR, 431.

450.O.8 Some reproach me for being a Jew, some pardon me for it, and some even praise me for it, but all think of it.
Boerne, *Briefe aus Paris*, #74, Feb. 7, 1832.

450.O.9 As nuts are betrayed for customs duty by their rattle, so Jews cannot deny their identity.
Cant. R., 6.11.1.

450.O.10 Yes, I am a Jew, and when the ancestors of the right honorable gentleman were brutal savages in an unknown island, mine were priests in the Temple of Solomon.

Disraeli, reply to a taunt by Daniel O'Connell.

450.O.11 I am a Jew, and it always seemed to me not only shameful but downright senseless to deny it.

Freud. q Puner, *Freud*, 171. See his Pref. to Hebrew tr of *Totem & Taboo*, Dec. 1930 (tr Strachey, 1950, p. xi).

450.O.12 A Jew doloris causa, a Pole honoris causa.

Golomb, ref. to Julian Tuwim. *Yidishe Kultur*, May 1945, 33.

450.O.13 Moses pleaded: "Joseph's remains are taken into the Land, and I am not to enter?" God replied: Joseph asserted he was a Hebrew [*Gen.* 39.14, 40.15], whereas you kept silence when referred to as an Egyptian [*Exod.* 2.19].

Levi. *Deut. R.*, 2.8.

450.O.14 To counteract fear and make the individual strong to face whatever the future holds, there is nothing so important as a clear and fully accepted belonging to a group whose fate has a positive meaning.

Lewin. *CJR*, 1941. *Resolving Social Conflicts*, 198.

450.O.15 I am a Jew, and I consider nothing Jewish alien to me.

S. D. Luzzatto, *Igrot Shadal*, vi. 780.

450.O.16 For me the factors that decide whether one belongs to a people or a nation are those of heart, mind, character and soul. . . . If I examine myself closely I find that I am hurt more if a Bavarian declaims against Prussians than if he does so against the Jews.

Rathenau, *Briefe*, 1930, i. 220. q LGS, 144f.

450.O.17 There are Jews whom I really hate, hate as Jews. These are the ones who pretend before others, and sometimes also before themselves, that they are not Jews.

Schnitzler, *Der Weg ins Freie*, 1908.

450.O.18 Never should it cross our minds for an instant to shrink from proclaiming that we are Jews.

Sefer Hasidim, 13C. q ZEH, 18.

450.O.19 We, the Jewish people, can defend our honor by a moral act. We remember all those who . . . have been stigmatized as Jews. The world reminds us

that we are of them, that we are Jews. And we answer: Yes, it is our pride and glory that we are!

Weltsch. *Jüdische Rundschau*, April 4, 1933. LR, 341.

450.O.20 We must solve our problems by cold logic, but we must assert . . . that it was not cold, calculating logic which led us back to our people, nor was it a sense of pity for the humiliated and persecuted masses, but a great and profound respect for a great people that deserves our love, the feeling of pride that we belong to it, and that it depends on our resources, small as these may be, that its voice shall once again be heard in the concert of nations, in the History of Humanity.

Zhitlovsky. *Folks Stimme*, #1, 1906. *Gez. Shr.*, v. 27f.

450.P. Consciousness

450.P.1 Never did the fact of Jewish birth play such a decisive role . . . as among the assimilated Jews. . . . They were obsessed by it as one may be by a physical defect, . . . addicted to it as . . . to a vice.

Arendt, *Origins of Totalitarianism*, 1951, p. 84.

450.P.2 When it is rational to say, "I know not my father or my mother, let my children be aliens to me, that no prayer of mine may touch them," then it will be rational for the Jew to say, "I will seek to know no difference between me and the Gentile, I will not cherish the prophetic consciousness of our nationality—let the Hebrew cease to be, and let all his memorials be antiquarian trifles, dead as the wall-paintings of a conjectured race."

*Eliot, *Daniel Deronda*, 1876, ch 42.

450.P.3 If you do not let your son grow up as a Jew, you deprive him of those sources of energy which cannot be replaced by anything else. He will have to struggle as a Jew and you ought to develop in him all the energy he will need for the struggle. Do not deprive him of that advantage.

Freud, to Max Graf. q *Psychoanalytical Quarterly*, 1942.

450.P.4 Without a certain self-consciousness, neither individuals nor peoples can survive. It is their backbone.

Güdemann, *Das Judentum*, 1902, p. 44. q JCC, 118.

450.P.5 If all pride of ancestry were not a foolish contradiction in a champion of the Revolution and its democratic principles, the present writer might take pride in the fact that his ancestors belonged to the House of Israel, and that he is a descendant of those martyrs who gave the world a God and morality, and who fought and suffered on all the battlefields of thought.

Heine, *Confessions*, 1854.

450.P.6 [Fascism] discovers that the source of all this pressure towards progress, equality, freedom and common humanity is the Jew. . . . For Hitler the Jewish consciousness is a poison. I have learned from the greatest genius of the Jewish race to recognize it as the Water of Life.

*Macmurray, *Clue to History*, 1937, p. 225ff. See Frishman, *Al HaYahadut. Kol Kitbé*, 1939, viii. 16f.

450.Q. Unity

450.Q.1 I will give them one heart and one way.

Bible: Jer., 32.39.

450.Q.2 I will make them one nation in the land.

Bible: Ezek., 37.22.

450.Q.3 Children of Israel, be one band, and thus prepare yourselves for the redemption!

Alkali. *Habatzelet*, vii. Oct. 22, 1876.

450.Q.4 We are one . . . people, who received one law from the One.

Apocrypha: II Baruch, 48.24.

450.Q.5 We have been held together and upheld by common remembering.

Buber. *Kampf um Israel*, 1933. LAJ, 133.

450.Q.6 As with nuts, if you take one from a heap, all the rest topple over, so with Jews, if one is smitten, all feel it.

Cant. R., 6.11.1.

450.Q.7 All Jews are comrades.

Joshua b. Levi. *Talmud J: Hagiga*, 3.6.

450.Q.8 This was Israel's excellence: at Sinai they were of one accord in accepting joyfully the kingdom of God. Moreover, they pledged themselves for one another.

Judah HaNasi. *Mekilta*, to *Exod.* 20.2.

450.Q.9 All Jews constitute one soul and one body.

Kagan, *Shmirat HaLashon*, 1879, on *Gen.* 46.27.

450.Q.10 Israel continues to resemble quick-silver, that strange, liquid metal, whose restless globules run in all directions without mingling with anything they touch, but reunite in larger masses as soon as they meet again.

*Leroy-Beaulieu, *Israel Among the Nations*, 1895, p. 359.

450.Q.11 When is God exalted in heaven? When His people are one band on earth.

Lev. R., 30.12, on *Amos* 9.61.

450.Q.12 Jewish solidarity is never one that seeks power or exerts force; it is historically and actually a solidarity the fruits of which are charity and peace.

Lewisohn, *Israel*, 1925, p. 251.

450.Q.13 The only bond that unites Jews is religion.

P. Nathan. q Ahad HaAm. AEL, 265.

450.Q.14 One God, one Law, one people, and one land.

Peretz, *Der Dichter*, 1910. *Alle Verk,* x. 21.

450.Q.15 Only when Jews are united on earth is there a firm foundation for God's chambers on high.

Simeon b. Yohai. *Sifré, #346*, to *Deut.* 33.5.

450.Q.16 Israel can be reconciled to God only when all Jews are one brotherhood.

Talmud: Menahot, 27a.

450.Q.17 Jews will not be redeemed until they form a single union.

Yalkut Shimoni, to *Amos* 9.

450.Q.18 As God is One, though His name has seventy ramifications, so is Israel one, though dispersed among the seventy nations.

Zohar, Exod., 16b. See also 57a, 121b.

451. JOB

451.1 The devout archives commission of the Temple . . . accepted this book into the holy canon . . . because they knew . . . that doubt is deeply fixed in man's nature—and justified.

Heine, *Ludwig Marcus*, 1844. EPP, 668.

451.2 The introduction to the Book of Job is certainly fiction.

Maimonides, *Guide for the Perplexed*, 1190, 3.22.

451.3 Job never existed.

Simeon b. Lakish. *Talmud J: Sota*, 5.6.

451.4 The story of Job is a parable.

Talmud: Baba Bathra, 15a.

451.5 [In Job,] Hebrew poetry, scattering on its flight its richest treasures of re-

flection and music, soars to its highest glory.
*G. A. Smith, *The Hebrew Genius*, 1927. BSL, 27.

451.6 The sublimest poem of antiquity is impersonal, yet written in the Hebrew tongue. The Book of Job . . . towers with no peak near it. . . . Who composed it? Who carved the Sphinx, or set the angles of the Pyramids? The shadow of his name was taken, lest he should fall by pride, like Eblis.
*Stedman, *Nature & Elements of Poetry*, 1892, p. 86.

452. JOY

452.1 Ye shall rejoice before the Lord your God.
Bible: Deut., 12.12. See *II Sam.*, 6.21.

452.2 Weeping may tarry for the night, but joy comes in the morning.
Bible: Ps., 30.6.

452.3 Serve the Lord with gladness.
Ibid., 100.2. See 118.24.

452.4 The end of mirth is heaviness.
Bible: Prov., 14.13.

452.5 Nothing better than that a man should rejoice in his works.
Bible: Eccles., 3.22.

452.6 Eat your bread with joy, drink your wine with a merry heart.
Ibid., 9.7.

452.7 The joy of the Lord is your strength.
Bible: Neh., 8.10.

452.8 Who lives in joy does his Creator's will.
Baal Shem.

452.9 Rejoicing on a festival is a religious duty.
Joshua b. Hanania. *Talmud: Pesahim*, 68b.

452.10 Contrition on a fast day does not bring you closer to God than a devout heart's joy on a Sabbath or festival.
Judah Halevi, *Cuzari*, c. 1135, 2.50.

452.11 When Jews become saintly, they sing and rejoice.
Midrash Tehillim, 149.1.

452.12 Common sense is strengthened by joy.
Nahman Bratzlav. See HLH, 96.

452.13 When you feel most like crying, then rejoice.
Nathan of Nemirov. q ZRN, 217.

452.14 Joy has its friends, but grief its loneliness.
R. Nathan, *A Cedar Box*, 1929.

452.15 In this world, there is no perfect joy, unmixed with anxiety, no perfect pleasure, unmixed with envy; but in the future, the Holy One will make our joy and pleasure perfect.
Pesikta Kahana, ch 29, ed Buber, 170a.

452.16 Joy . . . is found only in the good things of the soul.
Philo, *The Worse Attacks the Better*, 37.

452.17 Where there is rejoicing, there should be also trembling.
Rab. *Talmud: Berakot*, 30b, on *Ps.* 2.11.

452.18 Joy waits for no man.
Tanhuma, Shemini, 3, ed Buber p. 22.

452.19 Joylessness is indeed a grievous sin. [*Deut.* 28.47].
Yerahmiel b. HaYehudi, *Tiferet Banim*, 1908, p. 8.

452.20 How many joys have turned into sighs!
Zabara, *Sefer Shaashuim*, 13C, ch 2, ed Davidson, 21.

452.21 Joy breaks down all partitions, then you see that all is nought, that there is only God.
H. Zeitlin, "Orot," *HaTekufa*, 1919, iv. 525.

453. JUBILEE

453.1 Hallow the fiftieth year. . . . It shall be a jubilee to you, and ye shall return every man to his possession and family.
Bible: Lev., 25.10.

453.2 Moses, in . . . ordering a general and incompensated cancelation of all mortgages every fiftieth year, had opposed a barrier to the invasions of force.
*Proudhon, *System of Economical Contradictions*, 1846, ch 7, #1, tr Tucker, 1888, i. 326.

454. JUDAH

454.1 Judah is a lion's whelp.
Bible: Gen., 49.9.

454.2 The sceptre shall not depart from Judah.
Ibid., 49.10.

454.3 *Judaea capta. Judaea devicta* (Judea captured, vanquished).
Inscriptions on Roman coins, 70.

455. JUDAISM[1]

[1] First mention of the word "Judaism," in *II Maccabees*, 2.21.

455.A. Description

455.A.1 The other religions . . . worshipped force because of fear; this one religion [Judaism] worshipped righteousness because of conscience.

*Abbott, *Life & Literature of Ancient Hebrews*, 1901, p. 381.

455.A.2 Judaism is the national creative power, which in the past expressed itself in a primarily religious culture.

Ahad HaAm, letter to I. Abrahams, Mar. 30, 1913. AEL, 27.

455.A.3 Judaism is based upon the principle of Divine Unity, which signifies the unity and equality of all men.

Astruc, speech, Leipzig Synod, 1869.

455.A.4 Judaism rightly understood is far in advance of Christianity; but I cannot do with a watch that gains time any better than with one that loses.

Auerbach, *Dichter & Kaufmann*, 1839. q *Menorah Journal*, 1921, vii. 158.

455.A.5 The essence of Jewish thought lies in its gift for the ideal reconstruction of the world.

Blum. q *Opinion*, July 1955, p. 15.

455.A.6 Judaism is a religion of ideals; Christianity, of an ideal person.

*Burkitt. q Loewe, *Rabbinic Anthology*, 1938, p. xcix.

455.A.7 The religion of reason.

H. Cohen, title of his last work, 1919.

455.A.8 The religion of the Jews is, indeed, a light; but it is as the light of the glow-worm, which gives no heat, and illumines nothing but itself.

*Coleridge, *Table-Talk*, April 13, 1830.

455.A.9 The Jewish faith is predominantly the faith of liberty.

*Coolidge, *Spiritual Foundation of America*, 1925.

455.A.10 If it be the last and highest task of religion to make us better human beings, . . . then Israel's religion has certainly no cause to shrink from such a test. When all the rest of mankind was still covered by the darkest night of . . . inhumanity, the religion of Israel breathed a spirit of true humanity, which must fill even the outsider with reverence and admiration.

*Cornill, *Das Alt Testament u.d. Humanität*, 1895, p. 23. q BKF, 40f.

455.A.11 The great distinctive feature of the Hebrew religion . . . is its utilitarianism. . . . It asserts . . . a God who in His inexorable law is here and now; a God of the living as well as of the dead; a God of the market place as well as of the temple.

*George, *Moses*, 1878.

455.A.12 Doctor, the mischief take the old Jewish religion! I don't wish it to my worst enemy. It brings nothing but abuse and disgrace. I tell you it aint a religion, but a misfortune.

Heine, *City of Lucca*, 1829, ch 9.

455.A.13 And where, indeed—if not in Judaism, broadened by Hellenism—shall one find the religion of the future?

Heine. q Zangwill, *Dreamers of the Ghetto*, 358.

455.A.14 A strong and deep flowing current of faith and religious power, of unquenchable hope and unconquerable perseverance, pursuing its way across the centuries like the Nile. . . , undeterred by the cataracts of persecution, unwasted by the barren deserts of neglect and scorn.

*Herford. *Menorah Journal*, 1919, v. 148.

455.A.15 Judaism is a *religion of time* aiming at the *sanctification of time*. . . . The Sabbaths are our great cathedrals.

Heschel, *The Sabbath*, 1951, p. 251.

455.A.16 Judaism is a historical religion, . . . in contradistinction to Paganism, which is a natural cult.

Hess, *Rome and Jerusalem*, (1862), p. 182.

455.A.17 Judaism is one of the incurable diseases.

Ibn Verga, *Shebet Yehuda*, (1550) 1855, #64, p. 96. See Heine, *The New Jewish Hospital at Hamburg*, 1842.

455.A.18 Countless are the figures under which Judaism appears in the Bible and the writings of the sages. Now it is compared to water, because it cleanses men from what is animal and low, and dulls and cools the passions; and now to wine, because time cannot injure it, nay, it increases in power with advancing age; to oil, because it mixes not with foreign elements, preserving ever its distinctiveness; to honey, because it is sweet and lovely, free from religious hatred; to a wall, because it protects its professors from the violence of the wicked; to manna, because it proclaims human equality before God, and asserts His justice; and lastly it is compared to a crown, because it invests every son of earth with sovereignty, and raises him higher than all nature.

A. Jellinek. q AJ, 1883, p. 43.

455.A.19 Our religion has three elements: fear, love, and joy, by each of which one can draw near to God.

Judah Halevi, *Cuzari*, c. 1135, 2.50.

455.A.20 Judaism is the funded cultural activity which the Jewish people has transmitted from generation to generation.

Kaplan. *Menorah Journal*, 1927, xiii. 121.

455.A.21 The fundamental principle of Judaism is Love.

Karpeles, *Jewish Literature*, 1895, p. 228, based on *M: Abot*, 2.9.

455.A.22 Here are the three doctrines which shall be taught here as the essence of Judaism: First, there is a God, one, indivisible, eternal, spiritual, most holy and most perfect. Second, there is an immortal life and man is a son of eternity. Thirdly, love thy fellow men without distinction of creed or race as thyself.

M. Lilienthal, *Modern Judaism*, 1865.

455.A.23 The whole superfluity of mystic natural philosophy, which so uselessly burdened the other religions of antiquity, was cast aside by the Hebrews, that they might devote themselves to the great problem of the spiritual world—the problem of sin and of righteousness before God.

*Lotze, *Microcosmus*, (1856) 7.2, tr 1885, ii. 268.

455.A.24 The principal dogma of Judaism is the belief in the divine origin of the Torah and the acceptance of the yoke of the commandments.

S. D. Luzzatto, *Peniné Shadal*, 1833, p. 440.

455.A.25 Old Testament religion is clearly about this world, and about nothing else.

*Macmurray, *Clue to History*, 1939, p. 31.

455.A.26 The monotheism of the Jew is in reality the polytheism of many needs.

Marx, *On the Jewish Question*, 1844. *Selected Essays*, 92.

455.A.27 Buddhism negates life. Judaism affirms it.

Melamed, *Spinoza and Buddha*, 1933, p. 9.

455.A.28 Judaism is not revealed religion, but revealed legislation.

M. Mendelssohn, Preface to *Vindiciae Judaeorum*, 1782.

455.A.29 Judaism is the belief that all life should be sanctified and transfigured by religion. . . . Man is to humanize himself by . . . conscious adherence to . . . the moral law.

Montefiore, *Liberal Judaism*, 1903, p. 113.

455.A.30 The jeer was justified that Judaism had become a religious community composed of atheists.

Nordau, *The Tragedy of Assimilation*.

455.A.31 Judaism is a tendency rather than a doctrine. It is the attitude of . . . viewing life and death, man and the world, from the point of view of eternity.

Oko. *Menorah Journal*, 1919, v. 124.

455.A.32 Judaism is not so much a church-going institution as a view of life: its teachings are concerned with the whole tangled web of existence.

Philipson, *Reform Movement in Judaism*, (1907) 1930, p. 40.

455.A.33 Judaism which served us so well in the past, will serve us equally well in the future. It will promote the cause of truth, the cause of progress, and of the modern spirit.

*Renan. q Karpeles, *Jews and Judaism*, 80.

455.A.34 The great insights of Judaism . . . derive from a unique religious humanism which . . . rejected all that was extreme and excessive . . . all that deified man or degraded him. Judaism was a movement of purification and equilibrium, achieving for the religious life of man what Greece achieved for his artistic and intellectual life, a sobriety of measure and order which we are wont to call classicism.

Silver, address, H. U. C., June 7, 1952.

455.A.35 The union of the qualities so often disjoined in man, so little heeded in many forms of ancient religion, "justice and mercy," "truth and love," became . . . the substance of the Creed of the Jewish Church.

*Stanley, *History of the Jewish Church*, (1862) 1896, i. 137.

455.A.36 Judaism is more related to time and history than to space and nature. Therefore it could exist when it lost its space. . . . Being tied up with time is being tied up with the future, with the prophetic message of the coming period of justice and peace.

*Tillich, address, Feb. 16, 1942. *Congress Weekly*, Feb. 27, 1942.

455.B. National and Universal

455.B.1 Judaism cannot conceive of mankind without itself, nor of itself without mankind.

Baeck, *Essence of Judaism*, 1936, p. 255.

455.B.2 To Judaism the existence of the Jewish people is essential and indispensable, not only for its realization in life, but for its very idea.

S. W. Baron, *Social & Religious History*, 1952, i. 3.

455.B.3 Mankind cannot rise to the essential principles on which society must rest unless it meet with Israel. And Israel cannot fathom the deeps of its own national and religious tradition unless it meet with mankind.

Benamozegh. q Pallière, *Unknown Sanctuary*, 243.

455.B.4 All nations, without exception, must go up with the Jews towards Jerusalem . . . for they too will become priests and Levites.

H. Cohen, *Religiöse Postulate*, 1907, p. 14.

455.B.5 Faith in the progress of man, creating through this progress the kingdom of God, this is the faith of Israel. . . . To fulfill this promise, he desires . . . to make of himself, according to the word of the Talmud, "cement" between the nations.

Fleg, *Why I Am a Jew*, 1929, p. 67.

455.B.6 Israel never forgot to hold all mankind in his embrace, and . . . was ever guided by the truth that his religion came into existence for the whole world.

Geiger, *Judaism and Its History*, 1865, tr Mayer, 70.

455.B.7 Like the Gulf Stream, . . . Judaism, passing through all the nations of the old world, part of them and yet distinct from them, ever recognized by its depth and intensity, has at last reached this new world without having lost its individuality. And here it is still able, by the loftiness of its ethical truth and by the purity of its principles, to give intellectual and moral stamina to a never-ending future humanity.

M. H. Harris, 1887. Cf Z. B. Vance, *Scattered Nation*, 1882.

455.B.8 Israel's most cherished ideal is the universal brotherhood of mankind.

S. R. Hirsch, *Nineteen Letters*, (1836), #15, p. 142.

455.B.9 All laws and institutions of Judaism which . . . imply exclusiveness and particularism . . . have lost all religious significance and obligation.

Holdheim, *Letter to the Jews in Arad*, 1848.

455.B.10 It was in Israel that ethics broke down national barriers for the first time.

Max Joseph, *Zur Sittenlehre des Judentums*, 1902, p. 18. q BKF, 168.

455.B.11 While Judaism in its entirety is for the Jew, its creed and its ethics are for mankind.

Morris Joseph, *Judaism as Creed and Life*, 1910, p. 382.

455.B.12 Judaism is a nation and a religion at one and the same time.

Klausner, *From Jesus to Paul*, 1944, p. 593.

455.B.13 As the idea of a common humanity forms its beginning, so Judaism will attain its final goal only in a divine covenant comprising all humanity.

Kohler, *Jewish Theology*, 1918, p. 48.

455.B.14 In the face of the brutalizing nationalism of our times, we must cry out the universal message of Israel: Not the blood cult, state cult, hate cult, war cult of nationalism, but one humanity on earth as there is one God in heaven.

Lazaron, *Common Ground*, 1938, p. 129.

455.B.15 Israel had to be particularistic in order to formulate and hold up the universal ideal.

Lazarus, *Ethics of Judaism*, 1901, i. 217, #159.

455.B.16 Judaism looks upon all human beings as children of one Father; thinks of them all as created in the image of God, and insists that a man be judged not by his religion, but his action.

S. D. Luzzatto, *Yesodé HaTorah*, (1880), p. 44.

455.B.17 The Jews were the only people in their world who conceived the idea of a universal religion, and labored to realize it by a propaganda often more zealous than discreet.

*G. F. Moore, *Judaism*, 1927, i. 22f.

455.B.18 On the Feast of Booths, Israel would offer seventy bullocks, corresponding to the seventy nations of the world, and prayed that they might live in tranquility.

Phineas b. Hama. *Pesikta Kahana,* ch 30, ed Buber, 175b. See *Midrash Tehillim,* ch 109, ed Buber, 243a.

455.B.19 An apostolic mission, and intercourse between churches, became possible only later, in the days of the Roman Empire; but the idea of a universal religion was already fully in existence in Israel of old.

*Renan, *Le Judaisme comme Race et Réligion,* 1883. See *Conférences d' Angleterre,* 1880, p. 103.

455.B.20 The prophet says, "Open the gates," not that Priests, Levites, Israelites may enter, but "the righteous nation that keeps faithfulness may enter" [*Isa.* 26.2].

Sifra, to *Lev.,* 18.5, ed Weiss, 86a.

455.B.21 Judaism is a missionary religion, or it is nothing.

O. J. Simon, *Faith and Experience,* 1895, p. 137.

455.B.22 This is the time when Judaism can arise from lethargy and establish its claim as the universal religion.

I. M. Wise, *Apologetics of Judaism,* 1887. *Selected Writings,* 226.

455.B.23 Now, for the first time in history, is the hour of Judaism. . . . The formula for the religion of the future will be a Jewish formula—Character, not Creed. The provincial period of Judaism is over. . . . It is the world the Jewish preacher should address, not a Kensington congregation. Perhaps, when the Kensington congregation sees the world is listening, it will listen too.

Zangwill, *Children of the Ghetto,* 1892, ii. ch 15, p. 513f.

455.B.24 The very first line of Genesis is universal. . . . The genealogy of all races and colors from Adam strikes the same broad note, while Abraham, the founder of Judaism, actually asks God, in what I have always considered the epoch-making sentence in the whole Bible, "Shall not the Judge of all the earth do right?" [*Gen.* 18.25]. A righteous God is not a tribal God.

Zangwill, *War for the World,* (1915) 1921, p. 133.

455.C.   Judaism and Other Religions

455.C.1 Here in America, more than in any other land, we may witness the realization of a miracle in the merging of the two streams, the Christian and the Jewish.

Asch, *Tales of My People,* 1948, Foreword, ix.

455.C.2 I must forbear impugning a religion that has its good sides.

M. Mendelssohn, *Letter to Lavater,* 1770.

455.C.3 We are richer for possessing both the ethical teaching of the Rabbis and the lofty enthusiasm and paradoxes of the Sermon on the Mount.

Montefiore, *A Rabbinic Anthology,* 1938, p. xliv.

455.C.4 He who desires to be a good and worthy disciple of Christ must first become a Jew, must first acquire an intimate knowledge of the language and culture of the Jews. He must become a disciple of Moses before he joins the Apostles.

*Surenhuys, *Mishna,* i., introd., 1698. q GGJ, x. 313.

455.D.   Orthodoxy

455.D.1 Orthodoxy in Judaism is something like snakes in Ireland.

G. Deutsch. q Enelow. *CCAR Year Book,* 1924, p. 238.

455.D.2 Only he can be considered a conforming Jew who believes that the Torah, including all the interpretations found in the Talmud, was given by God Himself to Moses on Mount Sinai to be delivered to the Jews and to be observed by them forever.

S. Eger, in TDS, 1842, Appendix 1.

455.D.3 All the commandments of the Holy Torah are equally divine. . . . "Love thy neighbor" and "A garment of diverse kinds . . . shall not come upon thee," stand side by side in the same paragraph.

M. Friedlander, *Jewish Religion,* (1891) 1927, p. 239.

455.D.4 Differences in ritual as well as in religious customs have always existed side by side in rabbinical Judaism.

A. Kohn. *Rabbinische Gutachten,* 1842, i. 115.

455.D.5 Judaism is inherently liberal, and the word "orthodox" has, strictly speaking, no place in it.

F. A. Levy, *Crossroads in Judaism,* 1954, p. 14.

455.D.6 Judaism has no future without adherence to the commandments and without belief in miracles and prophecy.

S. D. Luzzatto, *Igrot Shadal,* 1882, ii. 633.

455.D.7 The Torah is meant to be an everlasting commandment, without change, deduction, or addition.

Maimonides. q Enelow. *CCAR Year Book,* 1924, p. 236.

455.D.8 Indifference and hypocrisy between them keep orthodoxy alive.

Zangwill, *Children of the Ghetto,* 1892, ii. ch 15.

455.E.   Reform

455.E.1 Judaism experiences a continuous renaissance.

Baeck, *The Essence of Judaism,* 1936, p. 13.

455.E.2 Only he who despairs of his future disposes of his possessions. . . . Vessels require fixing from time to time. They need polishing and cleansing, but one does not break them.

Bialik, address, Kovno, 1930. *JS,* Dec. 1951, p. 10f.

455.E.3 We recognize in Judaism a progressive religion, ever striving to be in accord with the postulates of reason.

CCAR, *Pittsburgh Platform,* 1885.

455.E.4 Judaism, as a part of Jewish national culture, represents . . . an evolving, not a traditional, principle.

Dubnow, *Pisma o Starom i Novom Yevreistvie,* 1907, p. 27.

455.E.5 In all its stages, Judaism shows its capacity for continuous development.

Einhorn, letter. *AZJ,* 1844, p. 87.

455.E.6 Judaism is movement, not stagnation. "I will *walk* among you," as the ancient promise has it.

Enelow. *CCAR Year Book,* 1924, p. 240.

455.E.7 Judaism has never been content to be a faith divorced from life or a practice at variance with belief.

A. Geiger. *WZJT,* 1836, ii. 220. See PRM, 42.

455.E.8 Judaism is not a finished tale. There is much in its present form that must be changed or abolished. It can assume a higher position in the world only if it will rejuvenate itself.

A. Geiger, Inaugural Sermon, Breslau, Jan. 4, 1840.

455.E.9 Merely to seek greater ease and comfort . . . through the destruction of the eternal code set up for all ages by the God of Eternity, is not and never can be Reform. Judaism seeks to lift us to its height, how

dare we attempt to drag it down to our level?

S. R. Hirsch, *Nineteen Letters,* (1836), #17, p. 171.

455.E.10 Only by the absolute separation of the political and religious elements in Judaism is a thoroughgoing reform possible.

Holdheim, *Autonomie der Rabbinen,* 1843, Preface, vii.

455.E.11 The Talmud voices the convictions of its times, and from that standpoint it is right. I voice the convictions of my time, and from this standpoint I am right.

Holdheim, *Das Ceremonialgesetz in Messiasreich,* 1845, p. 50. q PRM, 441.

455.E.12 To discard . . . all that is not of an exclusively religious character in Judaism, all that recalls its national origin, . . . to abolish circumcision and the dietary laws, to introduce Sunday as the Sabbath, to substitute the vernacular for the Hebrew in the singing of the Psalms, is not only . . . to slacken the ties that bind the Jew to his brethren as well as to his fathers, but also to destroy, little by little, all that is peculiarly characteristic of Judaism, and to reduce it, by imperceptible degrees, to a mere name, a mere shadow.

*Leroy-Beaulieu, *Israel Among the Nations,* 1895, p. 140.

455.E.13 Though liberal Judaism has ceased to be a strictly legal religion, it does not abandon the great Jewish conception that religion is a discipline as well as a faith.

Montefiore, *Liberal Judaism,* 1903, p. 121.

455.E.14 The all-important truth that Judaism spells development and not stagnation . . . is the intent and content of the reform movement.

Philipson, *Reform Movement in Judaism,* (1907) 1930, p. 3.

455.E.15 Liberal Judaism is the Judaism of the future; it is the only type of Judaism that is valiantly grappling with the intellectual religious problem; it is the most active, the most energetic spiritual force in Judaism today.

Wolfson, *Escaping Judaism. Menorah Journal,* 1921, vii. 81.

455.E.16 It is because I am with you in admiring the Rabbis that I would undo much of their work. . . . The Rabbis constructed a casket, if you will, which kept the jewel safe. . . . But the hour has come now to wear the jewel on our breasts before all the world. The Rabbis worked for their time—we must work for ours.

Zangwill, *Children of the Ghetto*, 1892, ii. ch 15, p. 511.

455.E.17 We must reform ourselves and not our religion. We should attack only evil practices that crept in our religious life whether from within or from without, but not the holy heritage.

Zunz, letter to Geiger, May 4, 1845. q WHJ, iii. 377.

455.E.18 Suicide is not a reform.

Zunz. q SSJ, iii. 80.

455.F. Conservative

455.F.1 Positive-Historical Judaism . . . [is] my Judaism.

Z. Frankel, speech, Frankfurt, July 18, 1845.

455.F.2 The maintenance of the twin principles of authority and development in Jewish law . . . together with the emphasis upon the worldwide peoplehood of Israel—these are the basic postulates of Conservative Judaism.

Gordis, *CCAR Year Book*, 1951, p. 272.

455.F.3 Judaism functions only so long as it is co-extensive with the whole of the Jew's life.

Kaplan, *Judaism as a Civilization*, 1934.

455.F.4 Judaism is, in the first instance, a divine religion, *not* a mere complex of racial peculiarities and tribal customs.

Schechter. *JQRo*, 1888, i. 126; SSJ, 1896, i. 180.

455.F.5 Conservative Judaism . . . consists largely in attempting to strike a "happy medium" between the two extremes, in the effort to hold on to as much of the tradition as is tenable and to make such adjustments in Jewish life and thought as circumstances forcibly compel.

M. Steinberg, *Making of the Modern Jew*, 1933, p. 286.

455.F.6 Reconstructionism declares Judaism to be the evolving religious civilization of the Jewish people.

M. Steinberg. *Reconstructionist*, 1950, xvi. #1.

456. JUDGMENT
456.A. Divine

456.A.1 The Lord will judge His people.

Bible: Deut., 32.36. See *Hos.*, 4.1.

456.A.2 The Lord will judge the ends of the earth.

Bible: I Sam., 2.10.

456.A.3 Enter not into judgment with Thy servant, for in Thy sight shall no man living be justified.

Bible: Ps., 143.2.

456.A.4 I will investigate the records of all nations: if they have any merits, I will redeem them; if not, I will destroy them.

Alexandri. *Talmud: Aboda Zara*, 4a.

456.A.5 They shall be cast into the judgment of fire, and shall perish in wrath and in grievous judgment for ever.

Apocrypha: Enoch, 91.9. Ref. to heathens.

456.A.6 All these things will be laid bare in the scales and in the books on the day of the Great Judgment.

Apocrypha: II Enoch, 52.15. See *Jubilees* 5.13.

456.A.7 If there is no judgment [below], there is judgment [above].

Eleazar b. Pedat. *Gen. R.*, 26.6.

456.A.8 Prayer, righteousness and penitence annul the evil decree.

Ibid., 44.12. *Talmud J: Taanit*, 2.1.

456.A.9 The world is judged by the majority of its people, and an individual by the majority of his deeds. Happy he who performs a good deed: that may tip the scale for him and the world.

Eleazar b. Simeon. *Talmud: Kiddushin*, 40b.

Simeon b. Eleazar. *Tosefta: Kiddushin*, 1.14.

456.A.10 Like the blind man who lifted a lame man to steal from the king's orchard could not escape complicity and punishment, so the soul and body will be reunited for judgment and retribution.

Ishmael b. Elisha. *Lev. R.*, 4.5.

456.A.11 Three ledgers are opened in Heaven on Rosh Hashana: one of the thoroughly righteous, who are forthwith inscribed in the Book of Life; another of the thoroughly wicked, who are put into the Book of Death; and a third of the intermediate, whose fate is suspended till Yom Kippur. If they gain merits in the penitential period, they are entered for Life; otherwise, for Death.

Johanan b. Nappaha. *Talmud: Rosh Hashana*, 16a.

456.A.12 Man is judged each day.
Jose b. Halafta. *Tosefta: Rosh Hashana,*
1.13.

456.A.13 The world is like the sea, and
man a fragile little boat, floating toward
Eternity. . . . There God sits on His
throne . . . and judges every newcomer.
Son of man, it will depend entirely on
your cargo of good deeds, whether you
will be sent to the regions glowing with
perpetual light or to those where everlasting darkness reigns.
Kalonymus b. Kalonymus, *Eben Bohan,*
c. 1322. q CHH, 109f.

456.A.14 The great trumpet is sounded;
the still small voice is heard; the angels are
dismayed, fear and trembling seizes them
as they proclaim: Behold the Day of Judgment! . . . As a shepherd seeks out his
flock, and has them pass beneath his crook,
so dost Thou cause to pass . . . every living soul, appointing the measure of every
creature's life, and decreeing their destiny.
Kalonymus b. Meshullam, *"Untané To-
kef,"* c. 1000.

456.A.15 All are judged on Rosh Ha-
shana, and their verdict is sealed on the
Day of Atonement.
Meir. *Talmud: Rosh Hashana,* 16a.

456.A.16 When Jews appear for Divine
Judgment, the angels say to them: "Fear
not, the Judge . . . is your Father!"
Midrash Tehillim, 118.10, ed Buber,
242b. Cf *Berakot,* 28b.

456.A.17 Man is judged each moment.
Nathan. *Talmud: Rosh Hashana,* 16a.

456.A.18 When a man is led to the Last
Judgment, he is asked: Did you deal honestly, did you fix times for study, did you
do your duty in procreation, did you hope
for salvation, . . . and if "the fear of the
Lord is his treasure" [*Isa.* 33.6] it is well
with him.
Raba. *Talmud: Sabbath,* 31a.

456.A.19 Man's advocates are repentance and good deeds.
Talmud: Sabbath, 32a.

456.A.20 Even if nine hundred and
ninety-nine argue against a man, and only
one argues in his favor, he is saved.
Ibid.

456.B. Human

456.B.1 Neither shall you favor a poor
man in his cause.
Bible: Exod., 23.3. See *Lev.* 19.15.

456.B.2 In righteousness judge your
neighbor.
Bible: Lev., 19.15.

456.B.3 Ye shall hear the small and the
great alike; ye shall not be afraid of the
face of any man; for the judgment is
God's.
Bible: Deut., 1.17.

456.B.4 Execute the judgment of truth
and peace in your gates.
Bible: Zech., 8.16.

456.B.5 No sentimentality in judgment.
Akiba. *Mishna: Ketubot,* 9.2f.

456.B.6 Know before whom you stand:
not before Akiba ben Joseph, but before the
Creator of the universe.
Akiba, charge to litigants. *Talmud J:
Sanhedrin,* 1.1.

456.B.7 If a wicked man and a pious
man are before you in court, do not say:
I will turn judgment against the wicked.
Eliezer b. Hyrcanus. *Mekilta to Exod.*
23.6.

456.B.8 A court may not listen privately
to one of the litigants before the other has
an opportunity to appear.
Hanina b. Hama. *Talmud: Sanhedrin,*
7b.

456.B.9 Judge not your neighbor till
you've been in his place.
Hillel. *Mishna: Abot,* 2.4.

456.B.10 A court may not permit one
litigant to sit and compel the other to stand,
one to speak all he desires and the other
to be brief.
Judah b. Ilai. *Talmud: Shebuot,* 30a.

456.B.11 When the litigants stand before you, regard them as guilty. When they
have acquiesced in the verdict and left, regard them as innocent.
Judah b. Tabbai. *Mishna: Abot,* 1.8.

456.B.12 Judge everyone according to
his merits.
Mishna: Abot, 1. 6.

456.B.13 Scrutinize the facts rather than
the litigants . . . so that neither affection
nor hatred becloud your decision.
Philo, *Special Laws,* iv. 12.

456.B.14 Judge a case involving one
penny as meticulously as that involving a
hundred.
Simeon b. Lakish. *Talmud: Sanhedrin,*
8a.

456.B.15 Examine witnesses thoroughly, and be careful with your words, lest you suggest to them falsehood.

Simeon b. Shetah. *Mishna: Abot*, 1.9.

456.B.16 A suspect of one violation is not necessarily suspect in regard to the whole Torah.

Talmud: Erubin, 69a.

456.B.17 Let him whose coat a court has taken, sing his song and go his way.

Talmud: Sanhedrin, 7a.

456.B.18 None may be condemned save in his presence.

Ibid., 79b.

456.B.19 One litigant may not come to court in fine attire if the other is in rags. Both should be told to dress alike.

Talmud: Shebuot, 31a.

456.C. Judge

456.C.1 Seek not to be a judge.

Apocrypha: Ben Sira, 7.6. See *NT: Matt.*, 7.1.

456.C.2 In the world to come I may have to account for declining to serve as a judge when I was able to do so.

Assi. *Tanhuma, Mishpatim*, #2.

456.C.3 Each court of three judges serving in Israel is on a level with the court of Moses.

Dosa b. Harkinas. *Mishna: Rosh Hashana*, 2.9.

456.C.4 A judge must not trample over the people.

Eleazar b. Pedat, on *Exod.* 20.23. *Talmud: Sanhedrin*, 7b.

456.C.5 Disaster comes because of the kind of judges we have.

Eleazar b. Simeon. *Talmud: Sabbath*, 139a.

456.C.6 Woe to the generation that judges its judges!

Johanan b. Nappaha. *Talmud: Baba Bathra*, 15b.

456.C.7 Only those are appointed to the Sanhedrin who have stature, wisdom, good appearance, maturity, a knowledge of [the tricks of] sorcery, and familiarity with all the seventy languages of mankind.

Johanan. *Talmud: Sanhedrin*, 17a.

456.C.8 A judge must have these seven qualifications: wisdom, humility, fear of God, disdain of gain, love of truth, love of his fellow men, and a good reputation.

Maimonides, *Yad: Sanhedrin*, 2.7.

456.C.9 Only he is seated in the Sanhedrin who is able to prove the cleanness of a reptile from biblical texts.

Rab. *Talmud: Sanhedrin*, 17a.

456.C.10 If you are a judge, be not an advocate.

Judah b. Tabbai. *Mishna: Abot*, 1.8.

456.C.11 A witness may not act as a judge.

Akiba. *Talmud: Baba Kamma*, 90b. *Rosh Hashana*, 26a.

456.C.12 He who renders true judgment is a co-worker with God.

Mekilta, to *Exod.* 18.13.

456.C.13 A judge who accepts a bribe, who perverts justice, will lose his vision [*Exod.* 23.8].

Mishna: Peah, 8.9.

456.C.14 A judge who accepts bribes brings terror into the world.

Isaac Nappaha. *Talmud: Baba Bathra*, 9b.

456.C.15 An honest judge attracts the Shekina, a dishonest one drives it away.

Jonathan b. Eleazar. *Talmud: Sanhedrin*, 7a.

456.C.16 When corrupt judges multiplied . . . people threw off the yoke of Heaven and imposed upon themselves the yoke of men.

Talmud: Sota, 47b.

456.C.17 These are ineligible to serve as judges or witnesses: a gambler, a usurer, and a dealer in forbidden produce.

Mishna: Sanhedrin, 3.3.

456.C.18 A very old man, a eunuch, or a childless person is not appointed to a Sanhedrin, since these are apt to lack tenderness.

Maimonides, *Yad: Sanhedrin*, 2.3.

456.C.19 A judge is disqualified for a case involving one he loves or hates.

Papa. *Talmud: Ketubot*, 105b.

456.C.20 A habitual borrower is unfit to be a judge.

Rabbah b. Shela. *Talmud: Ketubot*, 105b.

456.C.21 He who was sued and convicted is disqualified as judge.

Talmud: Baba Bathra, 58b.

456.C.22 A judge must bear in mind that when he tries a case he is himself on trial.

Philo, *Special Laws*, iv. 9.

456.C.23 A judge should always visualize a sword suspended over him, and Gehenna gaping under him.
Jonathan b. Eleazar. *Talmud: Yebamot*, 109b.

456.C.24 Appointing an unworthy judge is like introducing idolatry.
Simeon b. Lakish. *Talmud: Sanhedrin*, 7b.

456.C.25 A judge is a "talebearer" if, after a case is concluded, he says, "I was for acquittal but my colleagues were for conviction."
Talmud: Sanhedrin, 31a.

456.C.26 A judge sins if he looks not for merits in the accused.
Zohar, Exod., 257a.

457. JUSTICE

457.A. Divine

457.A.1 Wilt Thou indeed sweep away the righteous with the wicked? . . . Shall not the Judge of all the earth do justly?
Bible: Gen., 18.23, 25.

457.A.2 Why does the way of the wicked prosper?
Bible: Jer., 12.1.

457.A.3 Where is the God of justice?
Bible: Mal., 2.17.

457.A.4 There are righteous men, to whom it happens according to the work of the wicked.
Bible: Eccles., 8.14.

457.A.5 Fear not, ye righteous, when ye see sinners growing strong and prosperous . . . ye shall become companions of the hosts of heaven.
Apocrypha: Enoch, 104.6.

457.A.6 The prosperity of the wicked here is an index to the reward of the righteous hereafter.
Eleazar b. Pedat. *Midrash Tehillim*, 37.3.

457.A.7 Who leads mankind to virtue here cannot be damned hereafter.
M. Mendelssohn, *Letter to Lavater*, 1769.

457.A.8 Happy the righteous who fare here as the wicked hereafter! Woe to the wicked who fare here as the righteous do hereafter!
Nahman b. Hisda. *Talmud: Horayot*, 10b.

457.A.9 In this world we see the godless prosper and the faithful suffer. There must, therefore, be another world in which all will be recompensed in justice and righteousness.
Saadia, *Emunot VeDeot*, 933, 9.1.

457.A.10 If you see a wicked person prosper, know that he is being rewarded here for some merit of his or his parents, or that he is being elevated temporarily to make his ultimate degradation all the harder.
Sefer Hasidim, 13C, #226, p. 79.

457.A.11 Cain said to Abel: There is no Judgment, no Judge, and no other world; there is neither reward for the righteous nor punishment for the wicked; neither was the world created nor is it governed with kindness; else why was your offering accepted and mine rejected?
Targum Jerushalmi, to Gen. 4.8. *Mikraot Gdolot*, i. 262a.

457.A.12 To explain the relative peace of the wicked and suffering of the righteous is beyond us.
Yannai. *Mishna: Abot*, 4.15.

457.B. Human

457.B.1 Just balances, just weights . . . shall ye have.
Bible: Lev., 19.36.

457.B.2 Justice, justice shall you pursue.
Bible: Deut., 16.20.

457.B.3 Seek justice, relieve the oppressed.
Bible: Isa., 1.17.

457.B.4 Zion shall be redeemed with justice.
Ibid., 1.27.

457.B.5 Woe to him who builds his house by . . . injustice, who uses his neighbor's services without wages.
Bible: Jer., 22.13.

457.B.6 Let justice well up as waters, and righteousness as a mighty stream.
Bible: Amos, 5.24.

457.B.7 Happy are they that keep justice . . . at all times.
Bible: Ps., 106.3.

457.B.8 Justice is not a prize tendered to the good-natured, nor is it to be withheld from the ill-bred.
Aarons, *Hach vs. Lewinsky et al.*, p. 9. April 19, 1945. *Wisconsin* 189–251.

457.B.9 If there is no justice, there is no peace.
Bahya b. Asher, *Kad HaKemah*, 14C.

457.B.10 Justice is not to be taken by storm. She is to be wooed by slow advances.
Cardozo, *Growth of the Law*, 1924, p. 133.

457.B.11 True justice is tempered with mercy.
Crescas, *Or Adonai*, c.1400 (1556). q RHI, p. 796.

457.B.12 Justice is truth in action.
Disraeli, speech, House of Commons, Feb. 11, 1851, ref. to Joubert, *Pensées*, 1838: "Grace is beauty in action."

457.B.13 The passion to shape the forms of justice has been one of the dominant forces in the life of the Jewish people from the time of the mighty tablets to the days in which we now live.
Goodhart, *Five Jewish Lawyers*, 1949, p. 66.

457.B.14 I ask not for pity, I ask but for justice!
Gottlober, *Netzah Yisrael*. q SRH, 153.

457.B.15 Justice has but one form, evil has many.
M. Ibn Ezra, *Shirat Yisrael*, (12C) 1924, p. 121.

457.B.16 A king's justice is better than a season's harvest.
Ibn Gabirol, *Mibhar HaPeninim*, c. 1050, #369.

457.B.17 Nothing can be permanently useful which is unjust.
Levi, *International Law*, 1888, p. 6.

457.B.18 If only truth and justice were the rule, there would be no need for mercy.
Mendelé, *Di Kliatshé*, 1873.

457.B.19 The enemy comes only because of the violation of just balances and just weights.
Pesikta Kahana, ch 3, ed Buber, 22b.

457.B.20 The whole Bible is a hymn to Justice,—that is, in the Hebrew style, to charity, to kindness to the weak on the part of the strong, to voluntary renunciation of the privilege of power.
*Proudhon, *System of Economical Contradictions*, 1846, ch 7, #1, tr Tucker, 1888, i. 326.

457.B.21 Rather suffer an injustice than commit one.
Proverb (Yiddish). BJS, #498.

457.B.22 The Hebrew prophet never appeals to rewards and punishments beyond the grave. He hungers for justice and for speedy justice. . . . An unjust world is, in his eyes, a monstrosity.
*Renan, *History of Israel*, 1889, ii. 423.

457.B.23 Justice toward others, courage for ourselves.
Varnhagen. q KRV, p. 230.

458. KADDISH

458.1 The Kaddish is not a prayer for the dead, but a mandate to the living. . . . It bids man rise above his sorrow . . . and fixes his view upon the welfare of mankind. It lifts his hope and vision to a day . . . when mankind shall at last inhabit the earth as children of the one God and Father, and justice reign supreme in peace.
R. Hertz, *Positive Judaism*, 1955, p. 41.

458.2 If there is any bond strong enough to chain heaven to earth, it is this prayer.
Kompert. q HBJ, 186.

459. KARAITE

459.1 It is proper to show respect to Karaites, to draw near them with right action, and to conduct ourselves toward them in modesty, truth and peace.
Maimonides, *Responsa*, ed Freimann, #371, p. 339f.

460. KID

460.1 One kid, one kid, that father bought for two zuzim.
Passover Hagada.

461. KIDDUSH

461.1 What a work of genius is that simple, homely and beautiful creation of the Jewish spirit—the Kiddush! It is the very essence of poetry wrought into an institution of family life. It has cultivated and nourished the idealism of generations. It has proven a factor of incalculable worth in linking loving hearts to home, to kindred, to Israel and to God.
Berkowitz, *Sabbath Sentiment*, (1898) 1921, p. 13.

461.2 Recite Kiddush on Sabbath eve, and your days will be lengthened here and hereafter.
Pirké de Rabbi Eliezer, 18.

462. KINDNESS

462.1 Let not kindness and truth forsake you.
Bible: Prov., 3.3.

462.2 It is a duty to cultivate kindness.
Aaron Halevi, *Sefer HaHinuk*, c.1300, #601.

462.3 Blessed is the man whose heart bears no malice.

Apocrypha: II Baruch, 44.4.

462.4 Man is honored for his wisdom, loved for his kindness.

S. Cohen, *Mishlé Agur,* 1803, 57.

462.5 The meed of charity is in its measure of kindness.

Eleazar b. Pedat. *Talmud: Sukka,* 49b.

462.6 If you do one a favor, remind him not of it.

Elijah b. Raphael, *Tzavaah,* 18C.

462.7 You are rich, though you do not know it. You have wells of kindness within your heart. At times man will bless you more for a smile, a kindly glance, a gesture of forgiveness, than for treasures of gold.

Kabak, *BaMishol HaTzar.* See *Reconstructionist,* Nov. 26, 1954, p. 18.

462.8 God commanded the ravens, symbols of cruelty, to feed Elijah [*I Kings* 17.4] to show that cruelty may be turned to kindness.

Nahman Bratzlav, *Likkuté Moharan,* (1936) ii. 10f.

462.9 "Loving kindness is a sin offering for nations" [*Prov.* 14.34].

Nehunia b. HaKana. *Talmud: Baba Bathra,* 10b.

462.10 Though I be invested with sovereignty of earth and sea, I will make myself affable and accessible to the poorest.

Philo, *Decalogue,* 10.

462.11 The one thing most alien to men —humanity.

Pinsker, *Auto-Emancipation,* 1881.

462.12 The highest wisdom is kindness.

Proverb. ATJF, p. 640.

462.13 The Torah begins and ends with kindness: God clothing Adam and Eve, and burying Moses [*Gen.* 3.21, *Deut.* 34.6].

Simlai. *Talmud: Sota,* 14a.

462.14 The highest form of kindness is that shown to the dead, for it involves no thought of recompense from the recipient.

Tanhuma, VaYehi, ed Buber, 107a.

462.15 Charity is limited to the living, the poor, and money; kindness applies also to the dead, the rich, and personal service.

Tosefta: Peah, 4.19.

463. KING

463.1 He shall not multiply horses . . . wives . . . silver and gold . . . that his heart may not be lifted up above his brethren.

Bible: Deut., 17.16f, 20.

463.2 This will be the manner of the king: he will take your sons . . . to plough his ground . . . and to make his instruments of war . . . He will take your daughters to be perfumers and cooks and bakers. He will take your fields . . . even the best of them . . . And ye shall cry out . . . and the Lord will not answer you in that day.

Bible: I Sam., 8.11–14, 18.

463.3 Long live the king!

Ibid., 10.24.

463.4 He made you king to do justice and righteousness.

Bible: I Kings, 10.9.

463.5 Behold, your king comes to you, triumphant and victorious, lowly, and riding upon an ass.

Bible: Zech., 9.9.

463.6 Happy are you, O land, when your king is a free man!

Bible: Eccles., 10.17.

463.7 Only he whose thoughts are pure, who shuns sin and is modest in his manners deserves to be king.

Abravanel, *Commentary,* to *Deut.* 17.14, (1495) 1862, p. 36d. q NDI, 177.

463.8 A monarch is unnecessary, harmful, and very dangerous.

Ibid., to *Deut.* 17.15.

463.9 Kings were first set up not by popular vote, but by force: the strongest prevailed.

Ibid.

463.10 God save the king!

Apocrypha: Aristeas, 178.

463.11 What is the essence of kingship? To rule oneself well, and not to be led astray by wealth or fame.

Ibid., 211.

463.12 No one is king by his own power.

Ibid., 224.

463.13 You are a great king . . . because you excel in mercy.

Ibid., 290.

463.14 They [Jews] stand alone among nations in their stiff-necked resistance to kings.

Apocrypha: III Macc., 3.19.

463.15 He set the kingdom beneath the priesthood.

Apocrypha: Patriarchs, Judah, 21.2.

463.16 Kings perish, and their glory vanishes like a shadow.

Apocrypha: Testament of Job, ed Kohler, ch 7.

463.17 Kings! Why, what's a king? . . . Is their blood purer than our own? We are all the seed of Abraham!

Disraeli, *Alroy*, 1833, 9.1.

463.18 He remains a king also in underwear.

Fulda, *Der Talisman*, 1892.

463.19 Only he is fit to be king who knows how to work.

Gentili, *Meḵet Mahshebet, Pinhas, #2*, 1710.

463.20 Every inch a king was he.

Heine, *Romancero: The Poet Firdusi, #2*, 1851.

463.21 Judah's royal throne had six steps leading to the seat, which were to remind the king, as he ascended, of the six commandments for rulers: not to multiply horses, wives and gold [*Deut.* 17.16f.], and not to wrest judgment, respect persons or accept bribes [*ibid.* 16.19]. Above the throne was a sign: Know before Whom you sit!

Huna, *Esther Rabbah*, 1.12.

Johanan. *Pesiḵta Kahana*, ch 1, ed Buber, 6b.

463.22 A king is like fire, necessary when far, scorching when near.

Ibn Gabirol, *Mibhar HaPeninim*, c. 1050, #366.

463.23 Royal association is like a high mountain: abounding in goodly fruits, but also in wild beasts.

Ibid., #370.

463.24 The king, in essence, is the people.

Ibn Verga, *Shebet Yehuda*, (1550) 1855, #7, p. 21.

463.25 It is the misfortune of kings that they will not listen to the truth.

J. Jacoby, to Frederick Wilhelm IV, Nov. 2, 1848.

463.26 A king who confiscates an offender's property is a robber.

Maimonides, *Yad: Melakim*, 3.8.

463.27 If a king repeals a religious command, he is not obeyed.

Ibid., 3.9.

463.28 Woe to the land whose king is a slave!

Pirḵe de Rabbi Eliezer, ch 24.

463.29 If a king says, I will uproot mountains, he will uproot them, and not go back on his word.

Samuel. *Talmud: Baba Bathra*, 3b.

463.30 It is unseemly for a king to be false.

Talmud: Tamid, 32a.

463.31 The authority of the king of Israel was limited by law and tradition . . . and in this sense the ancient Hebrew polity was the mother of constitutional government in the modern age.

Weizmann, opening Constituent Assembly, Feb. 14, 1949.

463.32 No king loves his superior.

Zabara, *Sefer Shaashuim*, 13C, ch 7.

464. KINGDOM OF GOD

464.1 The kingdom shall be the Lord's.

Bible: Obad., 1.21.

464.2 His kingdom is an everlasting kingdom.

Bible: Dan., 3.33, 4.31.

464.3 The kingdom of God . . . embraces all the moral motives effective in the modern conception of society.

H. Cohen, *Das Gottesreich*, 1913. *Jüd. Schr.*, iii. 171.

464.4 May He establish His kingdom . . . speedily and soon.

Kaddish. Pre-Maccabean prayer.

464.5 The kingdom of heaven is at hand.

New Testament: Matt., 3.2.

464.6 The kingdom of God is within you.

New Testament: Luke, 17.21.

464.7 May we be co-workers with Thee in the building of Thy kingdom which has been our vision and goal through the ages.

Union Prayer Book, 1940, i. 45.

464.8 May Thy kingdom come speedily, that worship of Thy name and obedience to Thy law may unite all men in brotherhood and peace.

Union Prayer Book, 1945, ii. 22.

464.9 All the roadways, small and great,
Lead unto Thy kingdom's gate.

Yehoash, "House of God," tr Goldstick. LGP, 137.

465. KISS

465.1 Oh, they loved dearly; their souls kissed, they kissed with their eyes, they were both but one single kiss!

Heine, *Ideas*, 1826, ch 5.

465.2 O what falsehood lies in kisses!

Heine, *Return Home*, 1827, #73.

465.3 Tell me who first did kisses suggest?

It was a mouth all glowing and blest!

Heine, *New Spring: Lyrics*, 1844, #25.

465.4 Short their words and long their kisses,
And their hearts are overflowing.

Heine, *Lyrical Interlude: Donna Clara*, 1823.

465.5 Kissing is not customary among Jews. How does one, out of a clear sky, kiss, especially a child his father?

Mendelé, *Dos Vintshfingerl*, 1865.

465.6 When a knave kisses you, count your teeth.

Proverb. q MND, 636.

465.7 Rather an honest slap than a false kiss.

Proverb (Yiddish). BJS, #500.

465.8 The universe hangs on a kiss, exists in the hold of a kiss.

Shneor, "The Kiss," 1906. tr FJA, 333.

466. KNOWLEDGE
466.A. In General

466.A.1 He that increases knowledge increases sorrow.

Bible: Eccles., 1.18.

466.A.2 Knowledge shall be increased.

Bible: Dan., 12.4.

466.A.3 None is poor but he who lacks knowledge.

Abayé. *Talmud: Nedarim*, 41a.

466.A.4 Man knows much more than he understands.

A. Adler, *Social Interest*, 1939.

466.A.5 The prayer for knowledge is first among the Benedictions.

Ammi b. Nathan. *Talmud: Berakot*, 33a.

466.A.6 No mercy for him who is without knowledge.

Ibid.

466.A.7 Kindle the light of knowledge in Jacob.

Apocrypha: Patriarchs, Levi, 4.3.

466.A.8 There is no new knowledge without a new problem.

Baeck, *Judaism and Science*, 1949, p. 6.

466.A.9 The avenues . . . to the knowledge of Torah are three: reason, Scripture, and tradition.

Bahya, *Hobot HaLebabot*, 1040, Introduction.

466.A.10 Men can know with the heart and not only with the mind.

Bokser, *From World of Cabbalah*, 1954, p. 189.

466.A.11 The tree of knowledge is the tree of death.

Disraeli, (Egremont in) *Sybil*, 1845.

466.A.12 Knowledge of mankind is knowledge of their passions.

Disraeli, *Young Duke*, 1831, ch 2.

466.A.13 People get to know one another not at banquets but in toil and grief.

Ehrenburg. *Christian Register*, Dec. 1944.

466.A.14 With true knowledge it is as though the Temple were built.

Eleazer b. Pedat. *Talmud: Sanhedrin*, 92a.

466.A.15 Knowledge leads to wealth.

Ibid.

466.A.16 There is no other source of knowledge but the intellectual manipulation of carefully verified observations.

Freud. q Puner, *Freud*, 267.

466.A.17 Defense demands knowledge, and knowledge brings us self-assurance, pride and loyalty.

E. Fuchs, *Ges. Reden und Aufsätze*, 1919, p. 285.

466.A.18 The broadest range of knowledge condemns us to the narrowest inaction.

Heine, *Lutetia*, Dec. 4, 1842.

466.A.19 The blossom of knowledge is Life.

S. R. Hirsch, *Horeb*, 1838.

466.A.20 Many are ordained, but few know.

Isserlein, *Pesakim*, 1519, #255.

466.A.21 Without knowledge, how can there be discernment?

Judah HaNasi. *Talmud J: Berakot*, 5.2.

466.A.22 He is great who is not ashamed to admit he does not know.

Judah HaNasi, *Talmud J: Hagiga*, 1.8.

466.A.23 Knowledge and action are twins, each glorifying the other.

J. Kimhi, *Shekel HaKodesh*, 12C.

466.A.24 The unknown must be deduced from the known.

Ibid. q JE, vii. 496b.

466.A.25 We can add to our knowledge, but we cannot at will subtract from it.

Koestler, *Arrow in the Blue*, 1952, p. 278.

466.A.26 Love and fear of God can be guided only by knowledge.

Lipman-Mühlhausen, *Nitzahon*, c. 1400, #124.

466.A.27 One loves God only by dint of knowledge, and the degree of love corresponds to the degree of knowledge.

Maimonides, *Yad: Teshuba*, 1180, 10.6.

466.A.28 Secular knowledge bears the same relation to the Torah as zero bears to one. Knowledge without Torah is 0; Torah without knowledge is 1; the two together are 10.

M. Perles. q GSS, 222.

466.A.29 If you lack knowledge, what do you have? If you have knowledge, what do you lack?

Proverb (Palestine). q Levi. *Eccles. R.* to 7.23.

466.A.30 Who wants to know everything ages early.

Proverb (Yiddish). BJS, #1360.

466.A.31 To know a man you must ride in the same coach with him.

Proverb (Yiddish). *JE*, x. 228b.

466.A.32 Knowledge is not enough, unless it leads you to understanding, and, in turn, to wisdom.

Sarnoff, *Youth in a Changing World*, June 12, 1954.

466.A.33 Men make mistakes not because they think they know when they do not know, but because they think others do not know.

Sholom Aleichem, *Yidishe Folks Tzeitung*, 1902.

466.A.34 When you do not know, be not ashamed to admit it.

Talmud: Derek Eretz, 1.22.

466.A.35 Let your tongue acquire the habit of saying, "I do not know," lest you be led to lie.

Ibid., 2.1. q Zera. *Talmud: Berakot*, 4a.

466.A.36 Only through the disclosed can one reach the undisclosed.

Zohar, Gen., 154a.

466.A.37 True knowledge is the mother of deed.

Zunz. q SSJ, iii. 117.

466.B. Of Self

466.B.1 Preoccupation with watching other people's blemishes would prevent me from investigating my own, a task more urgent.

Bahya, *Hobot HaLebabot*, 1040, 5.5.

466.B.2 You must learn to know others, in order to know yourself.

Boerne, *Kritiken*, #4: *Cooper's Novels.*

466.B.3 We cannot achieve self-respect if we are afraid of self-knowledge.

M. R. Cohen, *A Dreamer's Journey*, 1949, p. 230.

466.B.4 To be conscious that you are ignorant is a great step to knowledge.

Disraeli, *Sybil,* 1845, 1.5.

466.B.5 Learn to know thyself, cast dreams away.

Judah Halevi, tr Lucas, *Jewish Year,* 23.

466.B.6 An individual is a person, when and because he knows himself as such; a group is a people, when and because it knows itself as such.

Kaplan, *Future of the American Jew,* 1948, p. 63.

466.B.7 In our very being there is rooted a mighty desire to know ourselves and our Creator, to understand the primary basis of all real beings.

Krochmal, *Moré Nebuké HaZman,* 1851, ch 17, ed 1924, p. 314.

466.B.8 Man lives with himself for seventy years, and doesn't know himself.

Lipkin. q KTH, i. 270.

466.B.9 "Know thyself" means: devote time each day to studying yourself, . . . ferreting out your weakness, working at self-improvement, purifying your immortal soul.

Lipkin. q J. Meisl, *Haskalah,* 1919, p. 175; LEZ, 68.

466.B.10 It is one of the great tragedies of modern Judaism that it knows itself so little.

Schechter, *Studies in Judaism,* 1908, ii. 156.

466.C. Of God

466.C.1 The ox knows his owner, and the ass his master's crib; but Israel does not know, My people does not consider.

Bible: Isa., 1.3.

466.C.2 My people are gone into captivity for want of knowledge.

Ibid., 5.13. See *Hos.* 4.6.

466.C.3 The earth shall be full of the knowledge of the Lord as the waters cover the sea.

Bible: Isa., 11.9, 65.25.

466.C.4 He judged the cause of the poor . . . Is not this to know Me?

Bible: Jer., 22.16. See 31.34.

466.C.5 Let us know, eagerly strive to know the Lord.

Bible: Hos., 6.3.

466.C.6 I desire . . . the knowledge of God rather than burnt-offerings.

Ibid., 6.6.

466.C.7 I know that my Redeemer liveth!
Bible: Job, 19.25.

466.C.8 The people that know their God shall show strength.
Bible: Dan., 11.32.

466.C.9 To know Thee is perfect righteousness; yea, to know Thy power is the root of immortality.
Apocrypha: Wisdom of Solomon, 15.3.

466.C.10 To avoid wrong and to seek good means to know God.
Baeck, *Essence of Judaism,* 1936, p. 248.

466.C.11 The ultimate result of your knowledge of God should be the conviction that of His real essence you are completely ignorant.
Bahya, *Hobot HaLebabot,* 1040, 1.10, tr Hyamson, i. 50.

466.C.12 Know before whom you labor and by whom you are employed!
Eleazar b. Arak. *Mishna: Abot,* 2.14.

466.C.13 Only in working out some end can you know God.
S. R. Hirsch, *Nineteen Letters,* (1836), #4, p. 32.

466.C.14 He is made known to us by His power, though the nature of His real being passes knowledge.
Josephus, *Against Apion,* ii. 16.

466.C.15 The conception of the believer that everything is naught and void except what is related to the Creator, that is the Knowledge of God.
Krochmal, *Moré Nebuķé HaZman,* 1851, ch 6, ed 1924, p. 30.

466.C.16 God knows what God is.
S. Maimon. q *Menorah Journal,* 1924, x. 13.

466.C.17 Every time you establish by proof the negation of a thing in reference to God, you become more perfect; while with every additional positive assertion you follow your imagination and recede from the true knowledge of God.
Maimonides, *Guide for the Perplexed,* 1190, 1.59.

466.C.18 Knowledge of Him is the consummation of happiness.
Philo, *Special Laws,* i. 63.

466.C.19 The mind's highest good is the knowledge of God, and the mind's highest virtue is to know God.
Spinoza, *Ethics,* 1677, iv. Pr 28.

466.C.20 The Jewish doctrine of God has never been thought out, perhaps because the genius of Judaism shies at schematics, and prefers the "healthy contradictions" of life.
Zangwill, *Voice of Jerusalem,* 1921, p. 44.

466.D. Beyond Knowledge

466.D.1 His discernment is past searching out.
Bible: Isa., 40.28.

466.D.2 Such knowledge is too wonderful for me, too high.
Bible: Ps., 139.6.

466.D.3 God is great, beyond our knowledge.
Bible: Job, 36.26.

466.D.4 Reason must always leave God as unknowable.
Abrahams. q V. Fisher. *American Zionist,* Nov. 5, 1953, 15.

466.D.5 The height of heaven, the breadth of the earth, and the deep,—who can trace them out?
Apocrypha: Ben Sira, 1.3.

466.D.6 Seek not to understand what is too wonderful for you.
Ibid., 3.21.

466.D.7 The sky for height, the earth for depth, and an intelligent mind for breadth are unsearchable.
Bedersi, *Behinat HaOlam,* c. 1300, ch 1.

466.D.8 The fact is, truth is veiled, but, like the Shekina over the tabernacle, the veil is of dazzling light!
Disraeli, *Venetia,* 1837.

466.D.9 We are all fools, poor fools, with an eternal bandage covering our eyes, and an eternal thirst for knowledge filling our spirits.
Franzos, *Nameless Graves,* 1873. *Jews of Barnow,* 301.

466.D.10 Woe to them that see and know not what they see, that stand and know not whereon they stand!
Jose b. Halafta. *Talmud: Hagiga,* 12a.

466.D.11 Who can affirm of the Cause of All either that he is or that he is not a body, that he has or has not such and such qualities?
Philo, *Allegories,* 3.73.

466.D.12 He is above and beyond any form or likeness or evaluation or conception or association, as it was said, "To whom then will ye liken God?" [*Isa.* 40.18].

Saadia, *Sefer HaYerushot*, Introduction, ed J. Müller, *Oeuvres Complètes*, ix.

466.D.13 In science, as well as in religion, one has to operate with basic terms which cannot be defined and with basic propositions which cannot be proved, and in science, too, with every new insight comes a new obscurity.

Silver, address, H.U.C., June 7, 1952.

466.D.14 Seven things are concealed: the day of death, the day of comfort, the depth of judgment, what's in another's heart, what may prove to be profitable, when David's dynasty will be restored, and when tyranny will end.

Talmud: Pesahim, 54b. Cf. *Gen. R.,* 65.12.

467. LABOR

467.A. Work

467.A.1 In toil shall you eat . . . all the days of your life.
Bible: Gen., 3.17. See 3.19.

467.A.2 Six days shall you labor, and do all your work.
Bible: Exod., 20.9, 23.12. *Deut.,* 5.13.

467.A.3 Be strong, . . . and work.
Bible: Hag., 2.4.

467.A.4 When you eat the labor of your hands, happy shall you be.
Bible: Ps., 128.2.

467.A.5 Man is born to labor.
Bible: Job, 5.7.

467.A.6 All things toil to weariness.
Bible: Eccles., 1.8.

467.A.7 Only through labor is one at home in the world.
B. Auerbach, *Das Landhaus am Rhein,* 1869.

467.A.8 The true right to a country— as to anything else—springs not from political or court authority, but from work.
Ben Gurion, *Earning a Homeland,* 1915. BRD, 5.

467.A.9 We don't consider manual work as a curse, or a bitter necessity, not even as a means of making a living. We consider it as a high human function, as the basis of human life, the most dignified thing in the life of the human being, and which ought to be free, creative. Men ought to be proud of it.
Ben Gurion, to Anglo-American Committee of Inquiry, March 19, 1946.

467.A.10 Hebrew has but one word— *Avoda*—for work and worship.
Bergmann, *Jawneh und Jerusalem,* 1919. LR, 133.

467.A.11 Comes the Hebrew individual of our generation with but one simple slogan: Work!
Brenner. *HaPoel HaTzair,* 1911, #22. *Kol Kitbé,* vi. 106. q ABJ, 51.

467.A.12 The superb . . . man is not he who is able to derive esthetic pleasures from delicate food and charming furniture, from beautiful music or keen discussion, but he who produces goods and increases the wealth of life through labor.
Brenner, *Ahdut HaAboda,* 1919. q SHR, 385.

467.A.13 No rain, no fruit; no toil, no good.
S. Cohen, *Mishlé Agur,* 1803, ch 15.

467.A.14 As others toil for me, I must toil for others.
Eccles. R., 2.20.

467.A.15 Every craftsman and artist takes pride in his work.
Eleazar b. Azariah. *Abot de R. Nathan,* B, ch 21.

467.A.16 In his work the individual is at least securely attached to a part of reality, the human community.
Freud, *Civilization and Its Discontents,* 1930, p. 34, Note.

467.A.17 The drive for relentless work was one of the fundamental productive forces, no less important for the development of our industrial system than steam and electricity.
Fromm, *Escape from Freedom,* 1941, p. 94.

467.A.18 Labor alone will heal us!
A. D. Gordon, *On Labor. Avukah Annual,* 1925–30, p. 130.

467.A.19 Weeds spring up of themselves and thrive; but to produce wheat, how much toil and trouble must be endured!
Hanina b. Pazzi. *Gen. R.,* 45.4.

467.A.20 Under the sign of labor we go into the Promised Land.
Herzl, *Diaries. Excerpts,* 14.

467.A.21 The sanctity of labor must be declared, for man has been placed on earth to work, to employ and develop his powers.
S. Hirsch, *Die Reform in Judentum,* 1844.

467.A.22 There is work which is abandonment of work.

q M. Ibn Ezra, *Shirat Yisrael*, (12C) 1924, p. 132.

467.A.23 Only manual work can make you blessed [*Deut.* 2.7].

Jacob. *Midrash Tehillim*, 23.3. Cf. Meir. *Tosefta: Berakot* 7.8.

467.A.24 Labor is more precious than ancestral merit.

Jeremiah. *Gen. R.*, 74.12.

467.A.25 Man dies when he stops working.

José. *Abot de R. Nathan*, ch 11.

467.A.26 Work is the great anodyne. It brings us forgetfulness of sorrow, courage to face it.

Joseph, *Judaism as Creed and Life*, (2d ed) 1910, p. 283.

467.A.27 If you have no regular work, find something to do—perhaps in a neglected yard or field.

Judah b. Bathyra. *Abot de R. Nathan*, ch 11.

467.A.28 Great is labor: it confers honor on the laborer.

Judah b. Ilai. *Talmud: Nedarim*, 49b.

467.A.29 Hard work is the cure for most ills.

Laski, 1924. q K. Martin, *Harold Laski*, 1953, p. 64.

467.A.30 Labor is the source of all wealth and all culture.

Lassalle, Preamble to Gotha Program. q M. Kaufmann, *Socialism & Modern Thought*, 1895, p. 103.

467.A.31 Let us discard the soiled clothes, the garments of merchants and speculators, and turn joyously to the tilling of our soil and the enjoyment of its fruit.

J. L. Levontin, letter to S. D. Levontin, Jan. 24, 1882.

467.A.32 Work, that you may have the right to live. Work, that you may perfect your body and soul. Work, that you may share in the common perfection.

A. Lieberman, letter to his brother Abraham, 1875. MLL, 41.

467.A.33 A coin earned by manual labor is worth more than all the revenue the Prince of the Captivity derives from gifts.

Maimonides, letter to Joseph Aknin. q AJL, 229.

467.A.34 See how the Torah values labor: who steals and kills a sheep pays fourfold; but for an ox, a work animal, fivefold.

Meir. *Tosefta: Baba Kamma*, 7.10.

467.A.35 From common labor you won't earn much.

Mendelé, *Dos Kleine Mentshelé*, 1864.

467.A.36 Toil, that's for common horses. They plow the fields, haul burdens, do everything. But noble horses, they live happily in the stable, near the hay and oats, take a ride once in a while with the gentlemen, gallop briskly, and take pride in their fine figures.

Mendelé, *Di Kliatshé*, 1873.

467.A.37 Behold, the fowls of the air, they sow not, nor reap, nor gather into barns, yet your heavenly Father feeds them.

New Testament: Matt., 6.26.

467.A.38 Work alone lends value to life.

Nordau, to Yehuda, 1922.

467.A.39 As the eye needs light to see, so the soul needs labor to comprehend.

Philo, *Sacrifices of Abel and Cain*, 6.

467.A.40 What food is to life, labor is to virtue.

Ibid., 9.

467.A.41 Where muscles strain and sweat beads the brow, product and producer blend in a fabric of sinew and nerves which is indestructible.

Pines, Preamble to "Land & Labor" Association By-Laws, 1892. q BRD, 51f.

467.A.42 If need be, hire yourself out to flay carcasses in the market place, and say not: "I am a priest, a great man, and this thing is detestable to me."

Rab. *Talmud: Pesahim*, 113a.

467.A.43 Where the peasant plows the hard ground, . . . where the laborer breaks the stones and constructs the roads, there Thy eternal light shines in order and harmony.

A. S. Rabinovich, *Souls of Israel*. LEJS, 67f.

467.A.44 From the Carmel and the Tabor
We proclaim the law of labor,
Love and song and toil.

Raskin, *Song of the Halutzim*. RAM, 48.

467.A.45 Love work.

Shemaiah. *Mishna: Abot*, 1.10.

467.A.46 Work is a splendid means of warming oneself up.

Sheshet. *Talmud: Gittin*, 67b.

467.A.47 The wood you chop makes you warm without your burning it.
B. Auerbach, *Little Barefoot*, 1856, ch 1.

467.A.48 Labor ennobles.
Simeon b. Yohai. *Talmud: Nedarim*, 49b.

467.A.49 Only he who labored before the Sabbath can eat on the Sabbath.
Talmud: Aboda Zara, 3a.

467.A.50 The Shekina is with Israel only after they did some work.
Tarfon. *Abot de R. Nathan*, ch 11.

467.A.51 Who works for a living is greater than he who fears God.
Ulla. *Talmud: Berakot*, 8a.
Hiyya b. Abba. *Midrash Tehillim*, on 128.1, #1, 257a.

467.A.52 The genius of the Hebrew language coined the term *malak* for angel, which is identical with *melaka* for work or labor, so that angel and working factor are identical.
I. M. Wise, 1893, *JWP*, 102f.

467.A.53 It is more difficult not to work than to work.
Wolffsohn, letter to Jacobus Kahn, 1908.

467.A.54 The best form of prayer is work.
Zangwill, *The East Africa Offer*, 1905.

467.B. Workers

467.B.1 I wonder why an employee should have to be subservient to his employer, and should have to please and praise him.
Bahya, *Hobot HaLebabot*, 1040, 4.4.

467.B.2 It is hard to be a worker; it is a hundred times harder to be a Jewish worker; it is a thousand times harder to be a Jewish worker in Eretz Israel.
Ben Gurion, address, March 1932.

467.B.3 Don't assume that the interests of employer and employee are necessarily hostile. . . . The opposite is more apt to be the case.
Brandeis, *Economic Exhortation to Organized Labor*, Feb. 5, 1905.

467.B.4 America . . . cannot develop citizens unless the workingmen possess industrial liberty; and industrial liberty is impossible if the right to organize be denied.
Brandeis. *Collier's Weekly*, Sept. 14, 1912.

467.B.5 There are thousands upon thousands of Jewish proletarians, . . . the worst exploited and most impoverished of all workers.
*Engels. q LJG, 256.

467.B.6 Let us make of this new union a structure that is a temple within and a fortress without!
Goldfarb. q Josephson, *Sidney Hillman*, 138.

467.B.7 The labor of a human being is not a commodity . . . of commerce.
Gompers, *Seventy Years of Life & Labor*, ii. 296. Incorporated in Clayton Anti-Trust Law, 1914.

467.B.8 The wealth of a country is its working people.
Herzl, *Altneuland*, 1902.

467.B.9 The strike is the weapon of the industrial jungle.
Hillman. q Josephson, *Sidney Hillman*, 142.

467.B.10 What labor is demanding all over the world today is not a few material things like more dollars and fewer hours of work, but the right to a voice in the conduct of industry.
Hillman, speech, 1918. q Josephson, *loc. cit.*, 190.

467.B.11 Sweatshops are an expedient of hell. . . . God in heaven and Judaism protest that he that works shall . . . not be robbed of his manhood.
E. G. Hirsch. *Reform Advocate*, 1894, viii. 205.

467.B.12 It may be arranged for a waiter to eat after he serves; but delicacies he may have at any time, to avoid tantalizing him.
Isaac b. Hanina. *Talmud: Ketubot*, 61a.

467.B.13 Workingmen we all are, so far as we have the desire to make ourselves useful to human society in any way whatever.
Lassalle, *The Workingmen's Programme*, 1862.

467.B.14 Blessed is the land that has a labor question.
Lubin, letter, 1888. q ADL, 59.

467.B.15 A laborer may withdraw from his job even in the middle of the day.
Rab. *Talmud: Baba Kamma*, 116b.

467.B.16 The friends of humanity cannot but wish that in all countries the laboring classes should have a taste for comforts and enjoyments, and that they should be stimulated by all legal means in their exertions to procure them. There cannot be a better security against a superabundant population.

Ricardo, *Principles of Political Economy*, 1817, 5.

467.B.17 The laborer has the advantage.
Talmud: Baba Metzia, 77b.

467.B.18 The trade union movement was an unconscious rebellion against the isolation forced on man by the industrial revolution. . . . The union recreated a society . . . to which a man could feel he really belonged. It filled a need.

F. Tannenbaum. q H. Breit. *N.Y. Times*, March 11, 1951.

467.B.19 Workers need poetry more than bread. They need that their life should be a poem. They need some light from eternity. Religion alone can be the source of such poetry.

S. Weil, *Gravity and Grace*, 1952, p. 235.

468. LAMB

468.1 I was like a lamb that is led to the slaughter.
Bible: Jer., 11.19.

468.2 Though lions to their enemies, they were lambs to their friends.
Disraeli, *Infernal Marriage*, 1828, 2.4.

468.3 Between the shepherd and the wolf, the lamb is torn.
Judah Halevi b. Shalom. *Exod. R.*, 5.21.

469. LAMENT

469.1 Alas for those who are gone and are no more!
Eleazar b. Jose. *Talmud: Sanhedrin*, 111a.

469.2 Alas for the world that has lost its leader, alas for the ship that has lost its pilot!
Rab. *Talmud: Baba Bathra*, 91ab.

470. LAND

470.1 Land shall not be sold in perpetuity, for the land is Mine.
Bible: Lev., 25.23.

470.2 I often envy the lot of the most miserable people who live on their own land.
Axelrod, 1917. q Rifkind, *Zionism and Socialism*, 16f.

470.3 The soil is the source of life, creativity, culture, and real independence.
Ben Gurion, *Hazon VeDerek*, 1951, ii. 160.

470.4 Each people has as much heaven over its head as it has land under its feet.
Bialik. q GIE, 225.

470.5 The term *Luftmensch* was Max Nordau's contribution to our literature, and it expresses all too well the severance of Jewish labor from the soil.
Borochov. *Der Yidisher Kempfer*, 1916. BNC, 63.

470.6 The landlessness of the Jewish people is the source of its malady and tragedy.
Borochov, *Nationalism & Class Struggle*, (1907) 1937, p. 72.

470.7 A man who owns no land is not a man.
Eleazar b. Pedat. *Talmud: Yebamot*, 63a. See Hanin. *Talmud: Menahot* 103b.

470.8 Man's alienation from the earth . . . was the beginning of all trouble and misery that have plagued him ever since.
Hofshi, *Man & Agriculture*. tr *Freeland*, Sept. 1952, p. 8.

470.9 Like garden, like gardener.
Proverb. q Kahana. *Talmud J: Sanhedrin*, 2.6.

471. LANGUAGE

471.1 The whole earth was of one language and of one speech.
Bible: Gen., 11.1.

471.2 Hebrew is the father, Yiddish the mother, of the Jewish soul.
Berdichevsky, summ. Z. Reisen, *Lexikon*, s.v. Berdichevsky.

471.3 Anyone who is thoroughly familiar with the language and literature of a people cannot be wholly its enemy.
Bergson, *Two Sources of Morality & Religion*, 1935, p. 275.

471.4 Anything can be exchanged, except the national tongue.
Bialik, letter, May 15, 1923. *Dbir*, 1923, i. p. viii.

471.5 Language is but spirit crystalized and substantialized.
Ibid., p. ix.

471.6 Language, the key to a nation's heart.
Ibid., p. xiii.

471.7 The conjugation of the Semitic languages, so rich in voices and so poor in moods and tenses, supposes a psychological state very different from that which has produced the Aryan conjugation, with its wealth of moods and tenses, and its poverty of voices. We are in the presence of two moulds utterly different.

A. Darmsteter, *Life of Words*, London 1886, p. 14.

471.8 Every time a dead language is exhumed, a new nationality may be created.

Flexner, *Universities*, 1930, p. 21.

471.9 The Romans would never have found time to conquer the world if they had been obliged first to learn Latin.

Heine, *Ideas*, 1826, ch 7. Source in *Epistolae Obscurorum Virorum*.

471.10 Is it not an anomaly in national development that a nation like the Jews has, on the one hand, kept itself racially purer than all other civilized peoples, but on the other hand, . . . has adopted the language of every country in which it has settled, and so, by giving up its own Semitic idiom, has inevitably lost with its language its soul and the noblest sides of its character?

*Hommel, *Die semitische Völker u. Sprachen*, 1883, p. 67.

471.11 A language is an organism. To digest it one must be, paradoxically, swallowed up by it.

S. Levin, *Youth in Revolt*, 1930, p. 76.

471.12 The Jewish people represents the only instance of a people that has created two languages of its own.

S. Levin, *The Arena*, 1932, p. 88.

471.13 What is lofty may be said in any language, and what is mean should be said in no language.

Maimonides, *Commentary to Mishna: Abot*, 1168, 1.17.

471.14 Wretched are you, O man, because of your speech! This fine endowment of yours has been your curse. All dogs bark alike . . . All frogs in all swamps and marshes croak alike. But men are divided in languages according to their nationalities and one does not understand the other, thus destroying their bond of brotherhood, and having them regard one another like strangers.

Mendelé, *Di Kliatshé*, 1873, ch 11.

471.15 The Holy Tongue means: Guard your tongue and sanctify it with holy words. When a Jew pours out his heart before God in plain Yiddish, that is a perfectly Holy Tongue.

Nahman Bratzlav, *Likkuté Moharan.* q ZRN, 292.

471.16 The Judeans who were exact in language retained their learning; the Galileans who were careless in language did not retain their learning.

Rab. *Talmud: Erubin*, 53a.

471.17 I speak ten languages—all of them in Yiddish.

C. Rappaport, *Reminiscences. YAJ*, vi. 236.

471.18 Abstraction is unknown in Semitic languages, metaphysics impossible.

*Renan, *Histoire des langues sémitiques*, 1855, p. 18.

471.19 What was wanting in the Semite far more even than a taste for the plastic arts was mythology, which, quite as much as painting and sculpture, is the mother of polytheism. The principle of mythology is the investing of words with life; whereas the Semitic languages do not readily lend themselves to personifications of this kind.

*Renan, *History of Israel*, 1888, i. 39. See *Journal asiatique*, April–May, 1859.

471.20 There is no future in this country for a Judaism that resists either the English or the Hebrew languages.

Schechter, address, Aug. 28, 1904. *Seminary Addresses*, 89.

471.21 The power of a language can scarcely be gauged. Language is more than language. Within language lie concealed magic forces of nature and of blood, . . . a heritage of emotions, habits of thought, traditions of taste, inheritances of will— the imperative of the past. It is impossible to measure the power and influence of all this upon the soul, upon its consciousness and upon its subterranean strata.

Spiegel, *Hebrew Reborn*, 1930, p. 21.

471.22 Jews are linguistic amphibia.

Steinschneider.

471.23 Languages are spiritual organisms, vital works of art, each of them having its measure of creative power, splendor, depth, logic to explore and to construct the world of nature in life.

Syrkin. *The Day*, March 1923. SGZ, ii. 212.

471.24 As no man is dead so long as the mirror put to his lips reveals a breath, so no race is extinct so long as there comes from its lips the breath of speech.

Zangwill, *Voice of Jerusalem*, 1921, p. 255.

471.25 One writer of genius is enough to consecrate and immortalize a language.
Zangwill. q *JS*, May 1952, p. 19.

472. LAUGHTER

472.1 He that sits in heaven laughs.
Bible: Ps., 2.4.

472.2 Even in laughter the heart aches.
Bible: Prov., 14.13.

472.3 I said of Laughter, "It is to be praised!" (A.V.: "it is mad.")
Bible: Eccles., 2.2.

472.4 As the crackling of thorns under a pot, so is the laughter of the fool.
Ibid., 7.6.

472.5 A fool lifts his voice in laughter, but a wise man smiles in silence.
Apocrypha: Ben Sira, 21.20.

472.6 Laughter is a universal bond that draws all men closer.
Ausubel, *Treasury of Jewish Folklore*, 1948, p. 266.

472.7 Strange, when you come to think of it, that of all the countless folk who have lived . . . on this planet, not one is known in history or in legend as having died of laughter.
Beerbohm, "Laughter," 1920. *And Even Now*, 1921, p. 315.

472.8 Laughter is man's friend, for it lightens all his burdens.
O. Blumenthal, *Das zweite Gesicht*, 2d ed 1898, Preface p. 4.

472.9 Who cannot laugh stoutly cannot weep stoutly.
Ibid., p. 5.

472.10 A home without laughter is a home without love.
J. Gordon, *Your Sense of Humor*, 1950, p. 37.

472.11 Seriousness shows itself more majestic when laughter leads the way.
Heine, *English Fragments*, 1828, ch 13.

472.12 The enduring love is the love that laughs.
G. J. Nathan, *The World in Falseface*, 1923, p. 246.

472.13 God is the creator of laughter that is good.
Philo, *The Worse Attacks the Better*, 33.

472.14 Weep before God—laugh before people.
Proverb (Yiddish). ATJF, p. 639.

472.15 The laugh of the Jew! It is never a right one,

For laughing and groaning with him are the same.
M. Rosenfeld, *Songs of Labor*, 67.

472.16 Wails and words can be stifled, but in laughter . . . even the gagged can indulge.
Saphir, *Literatur-Briefe*. SHW, iv. 81.

472.17 Do not laugh heartily in this world.
Simeon b. Yohai, on *Ps.* 126.2. *Talmud: Berakot* 31a.

472.18 Laughter, as also jocularity, is merely pleasure; therefore, so long as it be not excessive, it is in itself good.
Spinoza, *Ethics*, 1677, iv. Pr 45, Note.

473. LAW

473.1 The law of the Medes and Persians, which alters not.
Bible: Dan., 6.9, 13.

473.2 Many of the evils in life arise out of the fact that men have invented laws directly contrary to those of nature.
Acosta. q SMM, 93.

473.3 The example of the Hebrew nation laid down the parallel lines on which all freedom has been won—the doctrine of national tradition and the doctrine of the higher law; the principle that a constitution grows from a root, by process of development, and not of essential change; and the principle that all political authorities must be tested and reformed according to a code which was not made by man.
*Acton, "Freedom in Antiquity," Feb. 26, 1877. *History of Freedom*, 1907, p. 4f.

473.4 The fundamental principle of the Hebraic commonwealth was that there are great moral laws . . . not dependent upon the will of monarch, oligarchy, aristocracy, or public assembly.
*Abbot, *Life & Literature of Ancient Hebrews*, 1901, p. 111.

473.5 The Jews were in the beginning the most unstable of nations; they submitted to their law and came out the most stable of nations. . . . The Jews who adhered to their law became . . . a nation of a firm set if ever there was one.
*Bagehot, *Physics & Politics*, 1872, iii. *Works & Life*, viii. 19.

473.6 The Law! It is the arch-crime of the centuries. The path of Man is soaked with the blood it has shed. Can this great criminal determine Right? Is a revolutionist to respect such a travesty? It would mean the perpetuation of human slavery.

Berkman, *Prison Memoirs*, 1912, p. 71.

473.7 If nature had as many laws as the State, God Himself could not reign over it.

Boerne, *Der Narr im weissen Schwan*, ch 2.

473.8 If we desire respect for the law, we must first make the law respectable.

Brandeis. q *Cleveland Plain Dealer*, Oct. 15, 1912.

473.9 The law ... must have a principle of growth.

Cardozo, *Growth of the Law*, 1924, p. 20.

473.10 When men are pure, laws are useless; when men are corrupt, laws are broken.

Disraeli, *Contarini Fleming*, 1832.

473.11 Let the law pierce through the mountain! (Jastrow: justice under all circumstances).

Eliezer b. Jose HaGelili. *Talmud: Yebamot*, 92a.

473.12 If facts are changing, law cannot be static.

F. Frankfurter, address, 1912. *Law and Politics*, 1939, p. 6.

473.13 The Jew who fails to understand the importance of law misses the very essence of his people's contribution to humanity.

S. Goldman. *Reflex*, Dec. 1927, p. 19.

473.14 King and law are two brothers, mutually indispensable.

Ibn Gabirol, *Mibhar HaPeninim*, c. 1050, #364.

473.15 A man is allowed by law to be a fool, if he likes.

Jessel. q Goodhart, *Five Jewish Lawyers*, 22.

473.16 Be content to have the laws for your masters, ... for God suffices as your ruler!

Josephus, *Antiquities*, 4.8.17.

473.17 Even as there are laws of poetry, so there is poetry in law.

Kook. q H. Weiner. *Commentary*, 1954, p. 255.

473.18 The roots of valid law ... are, and can only be, within the individual conscience.

Laski, *The State in Theory and Practice*, 1935.

473.19 Old laws always survive old fortresses.

S. Levin, *Youth in Revolt*, 1930, p. 69.

473.20 The real law in the modern state is the multitude of little decisions made daily by millions of men.

Lippmann, *A Preface to Morals*, 1929, p. 275.

473.21 The law is an inexhaustible reservoir of good stories because it deals with humanity between the hammer and the anvil.

E. Lipsky. q *N.Y. Times Book Review*, Jan. 2, 1955, p. 5.

473.22 Laws will not alter persuasions.

M. Mendelssohn, *Jerusalem*, 1783, tr Samuels, ii. 19.

473.23 How noble man can be if he conform with law!

Montefiore, *Liberal Judaism*, 1903, p. 117. See BSL, 521.

473.24 May it be Thy will ... that no wrong occur through me, that I err not in a matter of law ... and call not the unclean clean or the clean unclean!

Nehunya b. HaKana. *Mishna: Berakot*, 4.2.

473.25 Those who live in accordance with law are free; and right reason is unerring law.

Philo, *Every Good Man Is Free*, 7.

473.26 A rabbinic decree must not assume the character of a jest.

Raba. *Talmud: Erubin*, 68b.

473.27 The law of the state is the law.

Samuel. *Talmud: Gittin*, 10b.

473.28 A court issues only such decrees which the public can endure.

Simeon b. Gamaliel. *Tosefta: Sota*, 15.10.

473.29 A law is something which must have a moral basis, so that there is an inner compelling force for every citizen to obey.

Weizmann, *Trial and Error*, 1949, p. 403.

474. LAWYER

474.1 Whene'er a bitter foe attack thee,
Sheathe thy sword, thy wrath restrain:
Or else will magistrates and lawyers
Divide thy wealth, thy purse retain.

Archevolti, *Arugat HaBosem*, 1602, p. 119a. q Rhine. *JQR*, 1910, i. 369.

474.2 What the lawyer needs to redeem himself is not more ability ... but the moral courage in the face of financial loss and personal ill-will to stand for right and justice.

Brandeis, address, June 22, 1907.

474.3 A lawyer who has not studied economics and sociology is very apt to become a public enemy.

Brandeis, address, Jan. 3, 1916.

474.4 The lawyer has spoiled the statesman.

Disraeli, *Young Duke*, 1831, 5.6, ref. to Lord Brougham.

474.5 The Bar is never a bed of roses. It is either all bed and no roses, or all roses and no bed.

R. Isaacs. q Goodhart, *Five Jewish Lawyers*, 42.

474.6 Woe unto you, lawyers! for ye lade men with burdens grievous to bear, and ye yourselves touch not the burdens with one of your fingers.

New Testament: Luke, 11.46.

474.7 Lawyers are just like physicians: what one says, the other contradicts.

Sholom Aleichem, *Finf un Zibtzig Toisnt*, 1902.

474.8 Administrators of the law should aspire to become the medium of universal divine justice.

Zunz, *Gottesdienstliche Vorträge der Juden*, 1832, Preface.

475. LAZINESS

475.1 Cursed be he who does the Lord's work with a slack hand.

Bible: Jer., 48.10.

475.2 Go to the ant, you sluggard, consider her ways, and be wise.

Bible: Prov., 6.6.

475.3 The sluggard will not plow when winter sets in, therefore he shall beg in harvest.

Ibid., 20.4.

475.4 The sluggard says, "There is a lion outside."

Ibid., 22.13. Cf. 26.13.

475.5 The door is turning on its hinges, and the sluggard is still in bed.

Ibid., 26.14.

475.6 By slothfulness the rafters sink in, and through idleness of the hands the house leaks.

Bible: Eccles., 10.18.

475.7 A lazy man is like a filthy stone, everyone flees from its stench.

Apocrypha: Ben Sira, 22.1.

475.8 Consult not the sluggard concerning much work.

Ibid., 37.11.

475.9 Brains to the sluggard are like wings to the ant, or a torch to the blind, an added load of no use or aid.

Bedersi, *Behinat HaOlam*, c. 1310, ch 38.

475.10 A sleeping cat doesn't catch the rat.

A. Ibn Ezra, *Shirim*, ed Kahana, i. 25.

475.11 Poverty due to laziness is incurable.

Immanuel, *Mahberot*, c. 1300 (1491), ch 19.

475.12 Laziness is the beginning of all vices.

A. Kohn, "The Fourth Commandment." *Jeschurun.*

475.13 Fear is not the cause of indolence, but indolence is the cause of fear.

M. H. Luzzatto, *Mesillat Yesharim*, (1740), ch 9, p. 66.

475.14 As a rule, there is no laziness as such, but laziness in regard to some specific activity.

Twerski, "Hegyonot." *HaPoel HaTzair*, 1951, xliv. #38.

476. LEADERSHIP

476.1 Those only can attract the mob and bend it to their will who can descend to its level and pander to its tastes.

Ahad HaAm, "Pinsker," 1902. *Ten Essays*, 86.

476.2 Poor is the generation whose leader is a woman!

Berekia. *Midrash Tehillim*, 22.20, to *Ps.* 22.6.

476.3 We live in an age of prudence. The leaders of the people now generally follow.

Disraeli, *Coningsby*, 1844, 1.3.

476.4 A gentle leader here will lead also in the hereafter.

Eleazar b. Pedat. *Talmud: Sanhedrin*, 92a.

476.5 He who is kind to a Jewish spiritual leader is rewarded as though he were kind to the entire people of Israel.

Eliezer b. Jose. *Cant. R.*, 2.5.

476.6 God said to Moses and Aaron: "My children are obstinate, ill-tempered, troublesome. In assuming leadership over them, expect to be cursed and even stoned by them."

Exod. R., 7.3.

476.7 People are more easily led than driven.

Fink, *Release from Nervous Tension*, 1943.

476.8 A leader may not be appointed without consulting the community.
Isaac. *Talmud: Berakot*, 55a .

476.9 One leader, not two, for a generation.
Johanan b. Nappaha. *Talmud: Sanhedrin*, 8a.

476.10 As the generation, so the leader.
José b. Maon. *Talmud J: Sanhedrin*, 2.6. See *Talmud: Arakin*, 17a.

476.11 Take God for your supreme commander and elect as His lieutenant the one who is preeminent for valor; for divided control, besides being a hindrance to those for whom prompt action is imperative, is withal apt to injure those who practice it.
Josephus, *Antiquities*, 4.8.41.

476.12 Woe to the generation whose leader you are, seeing that you know nothing of the scholars' troubles and struggles!
Joshua b. Hanania, to Gamaliel. *Talmud: Berakot*, 28a.

476.13 The serpent was dragged into a ditch, into fire, and amidst thorns, when its head followed its tail!
Joshua b. Levi. *Deut. R.*, 1.10.

476.14 Leadership shortens life.
Judah b. Ezekiel. *Talmud: Berakot*, 55a.

476.15 No fanatic can be a leader in Israel.
Mendel of Kotzk, *Emet VeEmuna*, (1940) p. 136.

476.16 A leader must not think that God chose him because he is a great man. Does a peg in the wall, on which the king hangs his crown, boast that its beauty attracted the king's attention?
Moses of Kobryn. See BTH, ii. 167.

476.17 A leader must always show respect for the community.
Nahman b. Jacob, on *I Chron.* 28.2. *Talmud: Sota*, 40a.

476.18 The pilot of a ship is worth as much as all the crew.
Philo, *Virtues*, 34.

476.19 A gifted leader is one who is capable of touching your heart.
Potofsky. q Josephson, *Sidney Hillman*, 80.

476.20 A leader who inspires fear, and not for the sake of Heaven, will not see his son become a scholar.
Rab. *Talmud: Rosh Hashana*, 17a.

476.21 Woe to the city where all are leaders.
Roquemartine, *Zekut Adam*, 13C, p. 7.

476.22 A community head may not do common labor in public.
Samuel. *Talmud: Kiddushin*, 70a.

476.23 When people do not appreciate a good leader, they get a wicked leader.
Sefer Hasidim, 13C, #225, p. 79.

476.24 One of unblemished ancestry should not be put at the head of a congregation, for if a leader becomes too proud, it is good to be able to say to him, "Look back and see whence you came!"
Simeon b. Yehozadok. *Talmud: Yoma*, 22b.

476.25 Once a person is put in charge of a community, be he the most worthless, he is regarded as the mightiest of the mighty.
Talmud: Rosh Hashana, 25b.

476.26 God weeps over a community leader who is domineering.
Talmud: Hagiga, 5b.

476.27 We have leaders, but we have not yet learned how to follow.
S. S. Wise, *Sermons and Addresses*, 1905, p. 11.

476.28 The commander cannot shoot side by side with his soldiers: he must retain perspective.
Wolffsohn, to Herzl.

476.29 To save a people, leaders must be lost.
Zangwill, *Theodor Herzl*.

477. LEARNING

477.A. Evaluation

477.A.1 Learning—learning—learning: that is the secret of Jewish survival.
Ahad HaAm, letter to J. L. Magnes, Sept. 18, 1910. AEL 269.

477.A.2 A natural love of learning, . . . man's highest possession.
Apocrypha: Aristeas, 1.

477.A.3 Without learning, no Judaism.
Z. Frankel.

477.A.4 He who does not learn forfeits his life.
Hillel. *Mishna: Abot*, 1.13.

477.A.5 He who possesses both learning and piety is like an artist with his tools ready to hand.
Johanan b. Zakkai. *Abot de R. Nathan*, 22.

477.A.6 Happy he who comes in the hereafter possessed of learning!
Joseph b. Joshua. *Talmud: Pesahim*, 50a.

477.A.7 Who does not learn, cannot truly love God.

Lipman-Mühlhausen, *Nitzahon,* c. 1400, #124.

477.A.8 The advancement of learning is the highest commandment.

Maimonides, letter to Joseph Ibn Gabir, 1191. KTJ, 199.

477.A.9 One may be learned, and yet be a big fool.

Mendelé, *Dos Kleine Mentshelé,* 1864.

477.A.10 It is this intellectual element in Judaism which enabled the Jews to go through unheard-of degradations and persecutions, and yet never . . . to suffer degradation in the soul.

Montefiore, *A Rabbinic Anthology,* 1938, p. xl.

477.A.11 Paul, you are beside yourself: much learning makes you mad.

New Testament: Acts, 26.24.

477.B. Process

477.B.1 Let the lesson you study be like a song!

Abayé. *Talmud: Sabbath,* 106b.

477.B.2 Review your lesson twice the next day, for each time you will discover something you did not know before.

Alnaqua, *Menorat HaMaor,* (14C) 1932, iii. 317.

477.B.3 He who, for the sake of learning, lowers himself by exposing his ignorance, will ultimately be elevated.

Ben Azzai. *Gen. R.,* 81.2. *Talmud: Berakot,* 63b.

477.B.4 Torah abides only with him who regards himself as nothing.

Johanan. *Talmud: Sota,* 21b.

477.B.5 Learning in youth is like writing on new paper; learning in old age is like writing on crumpled paper.

Elisha b. Abuya. *Mishna: Abot,* 4.20. Cf. *ARN,* ch 24.

477.B.6 The lessons of youth are not easily forgotten.

Abayé. *Talmud: Sabbath,* 21b.

477.B.7 Learning in old age is like writing on sand; learning in youth is like engraving on stone.

Ibn Gabirol, *Mibhar HaPeninim,* c. 1050, #53.

477.B.8 Who studies Torah in old age is like an old man married to a young woman.

Simeon b. Gamaliel II. *Abot de R. Nathan,* ch 23.

477.B.9 We cannot learn men from books.

Disraeli, *Vivian Grey,* 1827, 5.1.

477.B.10 A shy person is not apt to learn.

Hillel. *Mishna: Abot,* 2.5.

477.B.11 If a man is passionately devoted to his studies, heedless of cost or consequence, his learning will endure.

Huna. *Talmud: Erubin,* 54a.

477.B.12 Be not ashamed to learn truth from any source.

Ibn Gabirol, *Mibhar HaPeninim,* c. 1050, #64.

477.B.13 A foolish student will say, "Who can possibly learn the whole Torah?" A wise student will say, "I'll learn two laws each day, till I master the whole Torah."

Johanan. *Cant. R.,* 5.11.2.

477.B.14 To learn from the young is like eating unripe grapes and drinking new wine.

Jose b. Judah of Kfar Babli. *Mishna: Abot,* 4.20.

477.B.15 I learned much from my teachers, more from my colleagues, and most from my pupils.

Judah HaNasi. *Talmud: Taanit,* 7a.

477.B.16 I learned much from my teachers, more from my books, and most from my troubles.

Kaminer, *Baraitot de Rabbi Yitzhak* 1885.

477.B.17 We learn consciously from those we like, but unconsciously from those we dislike.

Klausner, *From Jesus to Paul,* 1944, p. 464.

477.B.18 Learning must be sought; it will not come of itself.

Simeon b. Lakish. *Midrash Mishlé,* 2.4.

477.B.19 If a student finds his lessons as hard as iron, it is because he has failed to systematize his studies.

Simeon b. Lakish. *Talmud: Taanit,* 8a.

477.B.20 The perfect method of learning is analogous to infection. It enters and spreads.

L. Stein, *Journey into the Self,* 1950, p. 231.

477.B.21 Who understands his lesson will not forget it readily.

Tanhum. *Talmud J: Berakot,* 5.1.

477.B.22 Be sure to ask your teacher his reasons and sources.

Rashi, *Commentary, Baba Metzia,* 33b.

477.C. Miscellaneous

477.C.1 We may prevent people from learning, but we cannot make them unlearn.

Boerne, *Fragmente & Aphorismen*, 1840, #103.

477.C.2 Child of Nature, learn to unlearn.

Disraeli, *Contarini Fleming*, 1832, 1.1.

477.C.3 Learn from modern inventions. From a train: to be late one minute may mean to be late altogether. From a telegraph: each word counts. From a telephone: what you say here is heard there.

A. J. Friedman. q *Reshumot*, i. 406.

477.C.4 You may learn three things from a railroad: if you are late one minute, you miss it; the slightest deflection from the rails leads to catastrophe; a passenger without a ticket may expect punishment.

Lipkin. q KTH, i. 278.

477.C.5 Torah, like a fine woolen garment, is hard to acquire and easy to lose; while silly and trivial subjects are, like cheap burlap, easy to get and hard to forget.

Gamaliel II. *Abot de R. Nathan*, ch 28. Cf B, ch 31.

477.C.6 The trouble with most men of learning is that their learning goes to their heads.

Goldberg. *Reflex*, Dec. 1927, p. 41.

477.C.7 Where others gather [learn], you scatter [teach]; and where others scatter, you gather.

Hillel. *Tosefta: Berakot*, 7.24.

477.C.8 The road to learning is endless.

Jacob b. Asher, *Tokeha*, 14C.

477.C.9 He comes to teach and stays to learn. This is intended to illumine, and is itself illumined.

Judah HaNasi. *Talmud: Pesahim*, 25b.

477.C.10 Love of learning is by nature curious and inquisitive, . . . prying into everything, reluctant to leave anything, material or immaterial, unexplored.

Philo, *Migration of Abraham*, 39.

477.C.11 We do not find sacred learning and [secular] greatness combined in one person.

Talmud: Sanhedrin, 36a.

477.C.12 In precious lore well-read, but hungry for a slice of bread.

Talmud J: Bikkurim, 3.3.

477.C.13 People are wont to copy the mistakes [of great men], but not their corrections.

Talmud J: Moed Katan, 2.2.

478. LEAVEN

478.1 We stress the thorough search for, and elimination of, leaven on the eve of Passover because leaven symbolizes the Evil Urge, which we must search out in all the recesses of our mind, and of which even a tiny bit may become disastrous.

David b. Zamiro, *Responsa*, (16C) 1781, #576.

478.2 A little leaven infects the whole lump.

Didascalia. See *I Cor.* 5.6; *Gal.*, 5.9.

478.3 "No leaven be seen in thee, neither . . . in all thy borders" [*Exod.* 13.7]. Let nothing stale or sour be seen in you, and you will not see it in others.

Katz, *Tzofnat Paaneah*, (1782) 1833, p. 228.

478.4 Leaven can be removed only by burning.

Raba. *Talmud: Pesahim*, 5b.

478.5 Jews are not only the "salt of the earth," they are also an extremely valuable ferment. They produce extraordinary ideas. They provide initiative, energy; they start things. But this compliment is of a doubtful sort. There is a very fine difference between a ferment and a parasite. If the ferment is increased by ever so little beyond a certain point, it becomes a parasite. So those who wish to be polite call us "ferments"; others, who are not so scientific, call us "parasites."

Weizmann, address, March 23, 1923.

479. LEGEND

479.1 To him who knows how to read the legend, it conveys more truth than the chronicle.

M. Buber, *Hasidism*, 1948, p. 4 .

480. LEISURE

480.1 The wisdom of a learned man comes through leisure, and he who has little business shall become wise.

Apocrypha: Ben Sira, 38.24.

480.2 We need leisure, among other reasons, because with us every man is of the ruling class.

Brandeis, *Hours of Labor*, Jan. 11, 1906.

480.3 The best test of the quality of a civilization is the quality of its leisure. Not what the citizens . . . do when they are obliged to do . . . but what they do when they can do anything by choice, is the criterion of a people's life.

Edman, *Adam*, 1929, p. 3.

480.4 Aristotle justifies slavery with the argument that the masters require leisure. . . . Sacred Scripture, on the other hand, ordains leisure . . . that the day of rest . . . may be enjoyed by all who work during the week.

M. Lazarus, *Ethics of Judaism*, 1901, ii. 19, Note 1.

481. LENIN

481.1 All Jews should set up a statue to Lenin for not being a Jew.

Zangwill, *Voice of Jerusalem*, 1921, p. 224.

482. LETTER

482.1 If you leave a letter unopened long enough, it answers itself.

Hershfield, *Now I'll Tell One*, 1938, p. 33.

482.2 Letters enlighten.

I. Horowitz, *Tzavaah*, 17C.

482.3 Letters are like bodies, and their meanings like souls.

A. Ibn Ezra, *Yesod Mora*, 1158, ed 1840, ch 1, p. 4.

482.4 Let the reader of the letter be its messenger.

Talmud: Baba Metzia, 83b.

483. LETTER OF THE LAW

483.1 It is a principle of Jewish tradition . . . not simply to cling to the dry letter of the law, but to be guided by its spirit.

Chorin. *Rabbinische Gutachten*, 1842, i. 23. See Aub. ii. 10.

483.2 God said: I have not dealt with you according to the strict letter of the law.

Haggai. *Deut. R.*, 4.3.

483.3 Jerusalem was destroyed because judgments . . . did not go beyond the requirements of the law.

Johanan. *Talmud: Baba Metzia*, 30b.

483.4 Rather let a letter be uprooted than the Torah be forgotten.

Johanan. *Talmud: Temura*, 14b.

483.5 What is the whole Talmud . . . except an adaptation of the letter to the needs of life?

Klausner, *From Jesus to Paul*, 1944, p. 603.

483.6 "Lest . . . ye make a graven image . . . of anything which the Lord . . . commanded" [*Deut.* 4.23]. . . . The commandments themselves, the letters of the Law, may become graven images.

Mendel of Kotzk, *Emet VeEmuna*, (1930, p. 10f).

483.7 The letter kills, but the spirit gives life.

New Testament: II Cor., 3.6. See *Rom.*, 7.6.

483.8 Ignore a letter of the Torah rather than profane the Name.

Simeon b. Yehozadak. *Talmud: Yebamot*, 79a.

483.9 To act according to the strict letter of the law is not the way of the hasidim.

Talmud J: Terumot, 8.4.

483.10 The sages of all times overlooked the letter of the law whenever the times demanded it.

Weiss, *Dor*, (1876) 1911, ii. 50. See Moore, *Judaism*, i. 259.

484. LEVITE

484.1 The Levites are dedicated to the Lord, not to the priests.

Sifré, #116, to *Num.* 18.6, ed Horovitz, 133.

485. LEVITY

485.1 Levity leads to lewdness.

Akiba. *Mishna: Abot*, 3.13.

485.2 Levity is a life-belt for the stream of life.

Boerne, *Fragmente & Aphorismen*, 1840, #121.

485.3 Where there is revelry, there is no wisdom.

Ibn Gabirol, *Mibhar HaPeninim*, c. 1050, #9.

486. LIBERALISM

486.1 Like science, liberalism insists on a critical examination of the content of all our beliefs, principles, or initial hypotheses . . . so that they will be progressively better founded in experience and reason.

M. R. Cohen. *Nation*, Aug. 5, 1931, p. 128.

486.2 Liberalism is too often merely a way of speaking.

Janowsky, *People at Bay*, 1938, iii.

486.3 Liberalism is nothing but secularized Judaism.

*Lagarde. q VA, 62.

486.4 It is in the ancient liberal faith . . . that our course be governed not by the dead hand of yesterday's facts and prejudices but by the living realities of today and our aspiration for tomorrow. It is this genius for making change serve the eternal unchanging values we cherish that is the very essence of American liberalism.

D. Lilienthal, *Big Business*, 1952, p. xi-xii.

487. LIBERALITY

487.1 The liberal devises liberal things.
Bible: Isa., 32.8.

487.2 There is he that scatters and yet increases.
Bible: Prov., 11.24.

487.3 I want to be fair, but a man should be hanged
Who's any less liberal than I.
Adams, "Broadmindedness." *Book of Quotations*, 649.

487.4 Give to God as He has given to you, with goodness of eye, and as your hand has attained.
Apocrypha: Ben Sira, 35.10.

487.5 Let not your eye be grudging when you give alms.
Apocrypha: Tobit, 4.16.

487.6 As there are soft, medium and hard nuts, so there are Jews who give unsolicited, others who give when solicited, and still others who do not give even when solicited.
Cant. R. 6.11.1.

487.7 As a lamp is not diminished by kindling even a million candles, so will he not lose who gives to a good cause.
Exod. R., 36.3.

487.8 Jews spend at Easter, Moors at marriage, Christians in suits.
*Herbert, *Outlandish Proverbs*, 1640. *Jacula Prudentum* #244.

487.9 The superior man is liberal with his wisdom, as clouds with their rains.
M. Ibn Ezra, *Shirat Yisrael*, (12C) 1924, p. 116.

487.10 It is better to listen to one who is lenient and permits, for anybody can be strict and forbid.
Rashi, Commentary, Betza, 2b.

487.11 The liberal in charity increases his wealth.
Yalkut, Mishlé, #947.

488. LIFE

488.A. Affirmation

488.A.1 All that a man has will he give for his life.
Bible: Job, 2.4.

488.A.2 A living dog is better than a dead lion.
Bible: Eccles., 9.4.

488.A.3 Saving a life supersedes the Sabbath.
Eleazar b. Azariah. *Mekilta*, to *Exod.* 31.13.

488.A.4 Life is the highest good, and death the worst evil.
Heine, *Ideas*, 1826, ch 3.

488.A.5 Firmly rooted in all is nature's law—the will to live.
Josephus, *Wars*, 3.8.5.

488.A.6 All of Schopenhauer's hate for Judaism and the Jews . . . arose largely from the fact that he could not forgive Judaism for its affirmation of life.
Klausner, *From Jesus to Paul*, 1944, p. 525.

488.A.7 God bade Abraham offer his son, and an angel stopped him [*Gen.* 22.2, 11]. Thus the Bible teaches: None but God can command us to destroy a life, but a mere angel suffices to have us save one, even if it contravenes a divine command.
Mendel of Kosov. See BTH, ii. 96.

488.A.8 Who closes a patient's eye before he expires is a murderer.
Mishna: Sabbath, 23.5.

488.A.9 Nothing but idolatry, incest and bloodshed must stand in the way of saving a life.
Talmud: Yoma, 82a.

488.B. Negation

488.B.1 Wherefore is light given to him that is in misery, and life unto the bitter in soul—who long for death, but it comes not!
Bible: Job, 3.20f.

488.B.2 What profit has man of all his labor . . . under the sun?
Bible: Eccles., 1.3, 2.22.

488.B.3 From the day man comes forth from his mother's womb till the day he returns to the mother of all living: preoccupation and anxiety. . . . From him who sits on an exalted throne to him who is clothed with dust and ashes, . . . naught

but anger and jealousy, strife and contention!

Apocrypha: Ben Sira, 40.1–3, 5.

488.B.4 This mundane life is like a drink
of salt water, which seems to quench, but
actually inflames. . . . Life is a series of
vexations and pains, and sleepless nights
are the common lot.

Elijah Gaon, *Alim LiTerufa*, 1836. AHE,
313f.

488.B.5 Life is a terrible disease, cured
only by death.

Hai Gaon, *Musar Haskel*, c. 1000.

488.B.6 Life is a disease, the whole world
a hospital, and Death is our physician.

Heine, *City of Lucca*, 1829, ch 5.

488.B.7 It were better if man had not
been created; but inasmuch as he has been
created, let him examine his works.

Hillel School. *Talmud: Erubin*, 13b.

488.B.8 To be unborn were better worth
Than . . . struggling in this snare
of earth!

Ibn Gabirol, "Dwellers in Clay." *Selected
Poems*, 62.

488.B.9 Man is born for tears and sorrow.

M. J. Lebensohn, *Kol Shiré Mikal*, iii. 9.

488.B.10 Life is a blister on top of a
tumor, and a boil on top of that.

Sholom Aleichem. q SWS, 50.

488.B.11 Life is a wreath of curling
smoke, and men spit out their bitter last
days as one spits out the butt of a cigar.

J. Steinberg. q FTH, 108.

488.C. Brevity

488.C.1 Lord, . . . let me know how
short lived I am.

Bible: Ps., 39.5. Cf 89.48.

488.C.2 We end our years like a sigh [*or*
like a tale that is told]. . . . for it is speedily
gone, and we fly away.

Ibid., 90.9f.

488.C.3 My days are swifter than a
weaver's shuttle.

Bible: Job, 7.6.

488.C.4 "His days are as a passing
shadow" [*Ps.* 144.4]. Not as the shadow of
a wall or a tree, but as that of a flitting
bird.

Aha. *Eccles. R.*, 1.2.

488.C.5 Short and sorrowful is our life.
. . . It passes away as the trace of a cloud,

it is scattered as a mist when chased by the
sun's rays and overcome by its heat.

Apocrypha: Wisdom of Solomon, 2.1, 4.

488.C.6 As a ship passing through bil-
lowy waters . . . leaves no trace behind,
. . . or as when a bird flies through the air,
no token of her passage is found, . . . so
we, at our very birth, cease to be.

Ibid., 5.10f, 13.

488.C.7 Man worries over the loss of his
treasure, but not over his days' diminish-
ing measure.

Bedersi, *Behinat HaOlam*, c. 1310.

488.C.8 I, a thing of clay, the creature
of a day.

Ibn Gabirol, *Royal Crown*, tr Lucas,
Jewish Year, 1898, 146.

488.C.9 Life is short, labor long.

Israeli, *Sefer HaYesodot*, 9C.
Judah Halevi, *Cuzari*, c. 1135, 5.2.

488.C.10 Here today, and tomorrow in
the grave.

Johanan b. Zakkai. *Talmud: Berakot*,
28b.

488.C.11 The goal is far, and short the
day.

Judah Halevi. Cf *Selected Poems*, 120.

488.C.12 Though a man live a thousand
years, yet at his demise it seems to him as
though he had lived but an hour.

Zohar, Gen., 223b.

488.D. Meaning

488.D.1 To love the Lord . . . that is
your life and length of days.

Bible: Deut., 30.20.

488.D.2 The days of our years are threescore years and ten, or even by reason of
strength four-score years; yet is their pride
but travail and vanity.

Bible: Ps., 90.10.

488.D.3 My days are like a lengthening
shadow.

Ibid., 102.12. Cf 144.4; *I Chron.*, 29.15;
Eccles. R., 1.2.

488.D.4 As for man, his days are as
grass. . . . The wind passes over him and he
is gone, and his place knows him no more.

Ibid., 103.15f. See *Isa.* 40.24, 64.6; *Job*,
7.10, 14.2.

488.D.5 Everything is given on trust,
and the net is spread. The store is open,
the shopkeeper gives on credit, but the
ledger too is open, and the hand makes
the entry. Whoever wishes may come and

borrow, but the collectors make their daily round.

Akiba. *Mishna: Abot*, 3.16.

488.D.6 I have only one life, and it is short enough. Why waste it on things I don't want most?

Brandeis. q *Current Literature*, March 1911.

488.D.7 The man who regards life . . . as meaningless is not merely unfortunate but almost disqualified for life.

Einstein, *The World As I See It*, 237.

488.D.8 To the last moment we play a comedy with ourselves.

Heine, *Ideas*, 1826, ch 20.

488.D.9 The meaning of man's life lies in his perfecting the universe. He has to distinguish, father and redeem the sparks of holiness scattered throughout the darkness of the world. This service is the motive of all precepts and good deeds.

Heschel, *The Earth Is the Lord's*, 1950, p. 72.

488.D.10 We are a part of the eternities and have a part to play in their orchestrated symphonic movements.

E. G. Hirsch. *Reform Advocate*, 1916, lii. 231.

488.D.11 To work out ends of righteousness and love are you called; not merely to enjoy or suffer.

S. R. Hirsch, *Nineteen Letters*, (1836), #4, p. 32.

488.D.12 Man was not brought into this world to enjoy himself.

A. Ibn Ezra, *Commentary*, to *Ps.* 73.17.

488.D.13 Man was created to learn wisdom.

Ibid., to *Job* 5.21.

488.D.14 Man eats to live, he does not live to eat. . . . He was created to serve God and to cleave to Him, not to accumulate wealth and erect buildings which he must leave behind.

A. Ibn Ezra, *Yesod Mora*, 1158, ch 7 (1840, pp. 27, 32).

488.D.15 Man's years are dreams; death alone can tell their meaning.

M. Ibn Ezra, *Selected Poems*, 126.

488.D.16 Man was created so that he might perfect his soul.

Jacob of Radzimin. q BTH, ii. 276.

488.D.17 We are all of us artists in life, and very poor daubs most of us make of it.

J. Jacobs. q ZVJ, 362.

488.D.18 Some men stand like question marks in the Book of Life, and we know not why and wherefore they are here on earth.

Mandelstamm, *Mishlé Binyamin*, 1884.

488.D.19 Life is too short to be little.

Maurois.

488.D.20 Man was created so that he might lift up the heavens.

Mendel of Kotzk. q BTH, ii. 276.

488.D.21 A long life, a short life,— what's the difference? A life of beauty!

Nordau, *Tales for Maxa*, 1905. Cf LEJS, 19.

488.D.22 Life is that incurable disease from which all have thus far died, and only those survive who are never born.

Saphir, *Leben, Liebe, Langweile*. SHW, i. 189.

488.D.23 The meaning of our life is the road, not the goal. For each answer is delusive, each fulfillment melts away between our fingers, and the goal is no longer a goal once it is attained.

Schnitzler, *Buch der Sprüche & Bedenken*, 1927, p. 32.

488.D.24 There is evil in the world, but it can be overcome through repentance and aspiration, and therein lies the true meaning and adventure of life.

Silver, address, H. U. C., June 7, 1952.

488.D.25 The day is short, the labor long, the workers are idle, the reward is great, and the Master is urgent.

Tarfon. *Mishna: Abot*, 2.15.

488.D.26 Do you know why the tree grows, and puts out leaves that wither in the autumn? You ask for sense and purpose? I am, thou art, we are. That is the end of wisdom. Sense is given to life by men.

Toller, *Machine Wreckers*, 1926, 3.2.

488.D.27 Our life would be altogether vanity, were it not for the soul which, fashioned in Thine image, gives us assurance of our higher destiny and imparts to our fleeting days an abiding value.

Union Prayer Book, 1940, i. 101.

488.D.28 Life is not a matter of extent but of content.

S. S. Wise, *Sermons and Addresses*, 1905, p. 55.

488.D.29 Eternal God, our life is but
A sea in which our tears are shed.

We know not from what
depth we come,
Nor whither we are led. . . .
Yehoash, *A Prayer,* tr Goldstick. LGP,
135.

488.D.30 Health alone does not suffice.
To be happy, to become creative, man must
always be strengthened by faith in the
meaning of his own existence.
S. Zweig, *Mental Healers,* 1932, p. 357.

488.E. Life and Death

488.E.1 Creatures of the world, their
very life depends on death, for some are
the food of others.
Al-Harizi, *Tahkemoni,* 1218. q WHJ, i.
240.

488.E.2 All creatures pass over a frail
bridge, connecting life and death: life is its
entrance, death its exit.
Bahya, *Hobot HaLebabot,* 1040, *Tokeha.*

488.E.3 Our clock of life, wound up in
the womb, begins to run down at the very
moment of birth. Every day we die a little.
Binstock, *The Power of Faith,* 1952, p.
19.

488.E.4 Life is but a constant dying.
Gentili, *Mleket Mahshebet, Hayye Sarah,*
i, 1710.

488.E.5 Death is nothing but cooling
night,
And life is nought bu: sultry
day.
Heine, *Return Home,* 1826, #87.

488.E.6 A warm true-hearted death is
better than a cold false life.
Heine, *Journey from Munich to Genoa,*
1828, ch 12.

488.E.7 The dead have peace, but the
living weep. . . .
Oh, why do the living weep for
the dead?
And why not weep for them-
selves instead?
Hoffenstein, *Year In, You're Out,* 1930.
Complete Poetry, 1954, p. 265f.

488.E.8 Plan for this world as if you
were to live forever; plan for the hereafter
as if you were to die tomorrow.
Ibn Gabirol, *Mibhar HaPeninim,* c. 1050,
#512.

488.E.9 Die that you may not die; live
not that you may live. Die here where you
must die, not hereafter where you need
not die.
Judah HaNasi. *Abot de R. Nathan,* B, ch
32.

488.E.10 Grass suckles on earth's
strength;
Then sheep devour the verdant
wave
Of green; then man at length
devours the sheep,
And him devours the grave.
A. D. Lebensohn, "HaTemura." *Shiré
Sfat Kodesh,* 1842; *Kol Shiré,* 1895, i.
223. q WHJ, iii. 222.

488.E.11 Why look for the living among
the dead?
Levi. *Exod. R.,* 5.14. Cf *Luke,* 24.5.

488.E.12 Some who live are dead, and
some who are dead still live.
Philo, *Fugitives,* 10. Cf *Matt.,* 10.39.

488.E.13 The righteous are called
alive in death; the wicked are called dead
even when alive.
Hiyya Rabba. *Talmud: Berakot,* 18ab.

488.E.14 When far from Thee, I die
while yet in life;
But if I cling to Thee, I live,
though I should die.
Judah Halevi, *Selected Poems,* 87.

488.E.15 Life begins where Death ap-
pears to be,
And where things mould and
rot, your eyes may see
The poppies below most red.
Shneor, "Manginot HaZugot," 1908. q
WHJ, iv. 291.

488.E.16 Alexander asked the Elders of
the South what a man should do to live.
They replied, Let him kill himself [doing
good]. He asked what a man should do
to kill himself. They replied, Let him live
[in self-indulgence]!
Talmud: Tamid, 32a.

489. LIGHT

489.1 Let there be light!
Bible: Gen., 1.3.

489.2 Cause a lamp to burn continually.
Bible: Exod., 27.20.

489.3 Let us walk in the light of the
Lord.
Bible: Isa., 2.5.

489.4 In Thy light do we see light.
Bible: Ps., 36.10.

489.5 Light is sown for the righteous.
Ibid., 97.11.

489.6 Light is sweet.
Bible: Eccles., 11.7.

489.7 Younger men have seen the light.
Apocrypha: I Baruch, 3.20.

489.8 The light of a candle is serviceable only when it precedes man on his way, useless when it trails behind.
Bahya b. Asher, *Kad HaKemah*, 14C, 37. q BSJ, 115.

489.9 I shall kneel down to light.
Chernihovsky, "Before Statue of Apollo," 1911.

489.10 A little light will dispel much darkness.
Eilenburg, *Tzeda LaDerek*, 1623.

489.11 Israel gives light to Him who gives light to the world.
Exod. R., 36.2.

489.12 Lord, may it be Thy will to place us . . . on the side of light.
Hamnuna. *Talmud: Berakot*, 17a.

489.13 Light is perceived only out of darkness.
Hasdai, *Ben HaMelek VeHaNazir*, c. 1230, ch 18.

489.14 What you see depends on where the light falls.
Lerski. q *Israel Miscellany*, i. 77.

489.15 Ye are the light of the world.
New Testament: Matt., 5.14.

489.16 A lantern at night is as good as a companion, and moonlight is as good as two.
Rab. *Talmud: Berakot*, 43b.

489.17 I light the path for wanderers
But pathless stray myself.
Shneor, "Song of the Prophet," 1903, tr FTH, 161.

489.18 God to Israel: You and I together will give light to Zion.
Simeon b. Lakish, on *Isa.* 60.1. *Pesikta Kahana*, ch 21, ed Buber, 129b.

489.19 Of what use is a lamp in broad daylight?
Simeon b. Pazzi. *Talmud: Hullin*, 60b.

489.20 A light for one is a light for a hundred.
Talmud: Sabbath, 122a.

489.21 There is a palace of light that opens only to him who occupies himself with the light of Torah.
Tikkuné Zohar, 13C, ch 11, p. 26b.

489.22 Light is the symbol of the divine.
Union Prayer Book, 1940, i. 7.

489.23 How can a little candle shine at midday?
Zohar, Gen., 20a.

490. LIGHTNING

490.1 The thunder and the lightning are inseparable.
Apocrypha: Enoch, 60.14.

490.2 No mortal eye has ever fully seen a flash of lightning . . . for no matter how firmly we look, our eyes are sure to be dazzled.
B. Auerbach, *Little Barefoot*, 1856, ch 15.

490.3 Lightning never strikes twice in the same place—it doesn't have to.
Hershfield, *Now I'll Tell One*, 1938, p. 36.

490.4 Lightning strikes the tallest trees.
Steinman. *Davar*, 5711. q CPP, #1127.

491. LILY

491.1 As a lily among thorns, so is my love among the daughters.
Bible: Cant., 2.2.

491.2 The slender water-lily
Peeps dreamily out of the lake;
The moon, oppressed with love's sorrow,
Looks tenderly down for her sake.
Heine, *New Spring*, 1844, #15.

491.3 Consider the lilies of the field . . . they toil not, neither do they spin: and yet . . . even Solomon in all his glory was not arrayed like one of these.
New Testament: Matt., 6.28f.

492. LIMITATION

492.1 Restrictions by others chain the mind; by oneself, paralyze it.
Boerne, *Kritiken*, #16.

492.2 Many men are all wool, but none is more than a yard wide.
Brandeis, Interview, June 1935. q MBF, 620.

492.3 We all of us live in a limited circle.
Disraeli, *Endymion*, 1880.

492.4 We all of us live too much in a circle.
Disraeli, *Sybil*, 1845, 3.7.

492.5 That which protects, may exclude. Sometimes to save the common, may be to imperil the uncommon.
Harrison, *Religion of a Modern Liberal*, 1931, p. 90.

492.6 There is an end to speech and a limit to the listener's endurance.
M. Ibn Ezra, *Shirat Yisrael*, (12C) 1924, p. 36.

492.7 One feels free within one's own limitations, but not within the limitations imposed by others.
L. Stein, *Journey into the Self*, 1950, p. 256.

493. LION

493.1 The young lions roar after their prey.
Bible: Ps., 104.21.

493.2 In heart a lion, in mien a fox.
Ezobi, *Kaarat Kesef*, 1270. *JQRo*, viii. 535.

493.3 The lion you spoke of turns out to be a fox.
Johanan b. Nappaha. *Talmud: Baba Kamma*, 117a.

493.4 A handful does not satisfy a lion.
Simeon HeHasid. *Talmud: Berakot*, 3b.

493.5 Can two whelps kill a lion?
Talmud: Sanhedrin, 95a.

493.6 If you saw not the lion, you saw his den.
Targum Sheni, to *Esther* 1.2.

493.7 A lion gets excited over a heap of flesh, not of straw.
Yannai School. *Talmud: Berakot*, 32a.

494. LIP

494.1 Our lips are with us: who is lord over us?
Bible: Ps., 12.5.

494.2 The lips of truth shall be established for ever.
Bible: Prov., 12.19.

494.3 Sweetness of the lips increases learning.
Ibid., 16.21.

494.4 Your lips are a thread of scarlet.
Bible: Cant., 4.3.

494.5 Your lips, O my bride, drop honey.
Ibid., 4.11.

494.6 Let your lips be closed like a pair of millstones that cleave together.
Vital, *Shaare Kedusha*, (c. 1600) 1740.

495. LISTENING

495.1 It is unseemly to listen at the door.
Apocrypha: Ben Sira, 21.24.

495.2 As ye speak no slander, so listen to none, for if it had no hearers, it would have no bearers.
Eliezer HaLevi, *Tzavaah*, 14C.

495.3 Man was endowed with two ears and one tongue, that he may listen more than speak.
Hasdai, *Ben HaMelek VeHaNazir*, c. 1230, ch 26 (Honein, *Musré HaPilosofim*, II, ch 2 #17, where it is ascribed to Plato). Falaquera, *HaMebakesh*. CHH, 68.

495.4 Listen and you will learn.
Ibn Gabirol, *Mibhar HaPeninim*, c. 1050, #19.

495.5 He who closes his ears to the views of others shows little confidence in the integrity of his own views.
Lehman. E. R. Murrow, *This I Believe*, 1952, p. 110.

495.6 It is as bad to listen to bad language as to use it.
Maimonides, *Guide for the Perplexed*, 1190, 3.43.

495.7 The girl with the patient eardrum is the girl who first nabs a husband.
G. J. Nathan, *The Theatre*, 1921, p. 233.

495.8 When two students listen patiently to one another in legal discussion, the Holy One listens to them too; and if they do not, they cause the Shekina to depart from Israel.
Simeon b. Lakish. *Talmud: Sabbath*, 63a.

496. LITERATURE

496.1 Jewish literature is literature written in our own language; it does not include books written by Jews in other languages.
Ahad HaAm, "Spiritual Revival," 1902. AEL, 91.

496.2 If we compare . . . sacred and profane literatures, the depth of human affection is deepest in the sacred. A warmth as of life is on the Hebrew, a chill as of marble is on the Greek.
*Bagehot, Macaulay, 1858. See Shelley, 1856.

496.3 Our Hebrew literature is a sacred literature: its readers are few, select individuals, and it is therefore not conducive to cheap, ragged stuff.
Brenner, 1909. q *HaDoar*, Aug. 25, 1950, p. 968.

496.4 Is this the time to stroll in the gardens and pick roses while the tents of Jacob are covered with thistles?
J. L. Gordon, letter to Kaplan, May 2, 1881. *Igrot*, i. 314.

496.5 The whole world is Israel's sepulchrel And his books? The epitaph of his funeral monument.

J. L. Gordon, "At the Death of Smolenskin," 1885. Kol Shiré, v. 135. q ZVJ, 258.

496.6 In the present chilly period in history, it is necessary to give our people something warm. . . . With wine—imagination, poetry—and with hope it is possible to maintain the strength of a fainting heart. Beware of cold dishes—icy criticism of old Jewish customs, chilly ridicule of Jewish matters. . . . This is not the time for these.

Kaminer. q *JP*, 1952, iii. 184f.

496.7 In the true novel, as opposed to reportage and chronicle, the main action takes place inside the characters' skull and ribs.

Koestler, *Yogi and Commissar*, 1944.

496.8 Wars and victories . . . are but vain noise and tumult; but letters and learning look to eternity.

S. Luzzatto, *Discorso*, 1638. *Commentary*, June 1952, 590.

496.9 Literature is all that enhances, by means of the word, both your knowledge and your ability to employ that knowledge. Literature embraces all spheres and forms of life and creativity, that which pertains to facts and ideas as well as that which depends on fantasy and feeling.

Niger, *Geklibene Shriften*, 1928, i. 64f.

496.10 The poets and historians of old . . . did not confine themselves to soothing and tickling the ears with rhythmic sounds. . . . But the cooks and confectioners of our time . . . are always building up the outward senses with some new color, shape, scent or flavor, so as to utterly destroy the most important part of us, the Mind.

Philo, *Noah's Planting*, 38.

496.11 No critic of authority now tests literature by the standards of ethics.

Spingarn, *New Criticism*, March 9, 1910.

496.12 There is no literature at once so grand and so familiar to us [as the Hebrew]. Its inherent racial genius was emotional and therefore lyrical, . . . and of so fiery and prophetic a cast that its personal outbursts have a loftiness beyond those of any other literature.

*Stedman, *Nature & Elements of Poetry*, 1892, p. 82f.

497. LITHUANIA

497.1 A Lithuanian repents before he sins.

Proverb (Yiddish). YFS, i. 419.

497.2 We are in . . . perhaps the only Jewish country in the world.

Slouschz, *Masa BeLita*, 1899. *Renascence of Hebrew Literature*, 1909, p. 93.

498. LIVELIHOOD

498.1 He slays his neighbor who takes away his living.

Apocrypha: Ben Sira, 34.22.

498.2 Assume not that a livelihood depends on one means only.

Bahya, *Hobot HaLebabot*, 1040, 4.3.

498.3 To earn a livelihood is as hard as parting the Red Sea.

Eleazar b. Azariah. *Talmud: Pesahim*, 118a. Cf Issi. *Gen. R.*, 20.9.

498.4 He who provides life provides also a living.

Peretz, *Yohanan Melamed's Maaselech. Alle Verk*, vi. 181.

498.5 Salvation may be earned through an angel [*Gen.* 48.16], but a livelihood requires the intervention of God [*Ps.* 145.16].

Samuel b. Nahman. *Gen. R.*, 20.9.

498.6 Did you ever see a beast or bird with a craft? Yet they sustain themselves without trouble, and they were created to serve me. Surely I, who was created to serve my Creator, should support myself without trouble, were it not that I became corrupt and ruined my ready livelihood.

Simeon b. Eleazar. *Mishna: Kiddushin*, 4.14. Cf *Talmud: Kiddushin* 82b. Meir. *TJ: Kiddushin*, 4.11.

499. LOGIC

499.1 Wisdom is like gold ore in the ground, mixed with rock and sand; logic is the mercury used to extract the gold dust.

M. Ibn Ezra, *Shirat Yisrael*, (12C) 1924, p. 119.

500. LONDON

500.1 London is roost for every bird.

Disraeli, *Lothair*, 1870, ch 11.

500.2 London—a nation, not a city.

Ibid., ch 27.

500.3 This downright earnestness of all things, this colossal uniformity, this machine-like movement, this troubled spirit in pleasure itself, this exaggerated London, smothers the imagination and rends the heart. . . . Send no poet to London.

Heine, *English Fragments*, 1828, ch 2.

501. LONGEVITY

501.1 Who would live long must cultivate a tough heart.

Gabishon, *Omer HaShikha,* c. 1600 (1748), 60.

501.2 Longevity is the result of freedom from grief and worry.

Maimonides, *Commentary to Mishna: Sanhedrin,* 10.1, Introd.

501.3 I have never sought honor at the expense of a colleague, or carried hatred to my couch at night. . . . I have never accepted a gift, insisted on my rights, or requited evil for evil.

Nehunya b. HaKana, explaining his long life. *Talmud: Megilla,* 28a. See Hanina b. Hama. *Talmud: Hullin,* 24b.

501.4 A cause conducive to longevity is the sobriety of the Jew.

Ripley, Races of Europe, 1899, p. 384.

502. LONGING

502.1 Never yearn for things beyond your reach.

Apocrypha: Aristeas, 223.

502.2 The longing makes the Messiah.

Herzl, *Altneuland,* 1902.

502.3 How glad I am! How longing drives me on!

Mosenthal, *Die lustige Weiber von Windsor,* 1849.

502.4 Longing counts not the hours.

Schnitzler, *The Lady with the Dagger,* 1904.

503. LONGING FOR GOD

503.1 As the hart pants after the water brooks, so pants my soul after Thee, O God.

Bible: Ps., 42.1.

503.2 My soul thirsts for God, for the living God.

Ibid., 42.2. Cf 63.2.

503.3 Whom have I in heaven but Thee? and beside Thee I desire none upon earth.

Ibid., 73.25.

503.4 Lord, light up all Thy light for me one moment—
And mothlike I will plunge into it, and be utterly consumed.

J. Cahan, "The Face of God," 1902. q HMH, 188.

503.5 Would that I might behold His face within my heart!
Mine eyes would never ask to look beyond.

Judah Halevi, *Selected Poems,* 115.

503.6 All my being is athirst for Thee.

Judah HeHasid, *Hymn of Glory,* c. 1200. ZVJ, 161.

503.7 The yearning for the dominion of God's will is our supreme desire; it pulsates mightily in our most inward life, and those who wish to perceive their Jewish soul will sense it in this mighty longing within their inner essence.

Kook, *Ikbé HaTzon,* 25. q ABJ, 205.

503.8 As the palm-tree shoots straight up, so Jews direct their hearts to their Father in Heaven. As the palm-tree longs, so do the righteous long—for God.

Num. R., 3.1.

503.9 Brute force is shattered, and with night all round about, Thy affianced spouse, loving, yearning, Calls on Thy faithfulness; she pleads with her eyes, and asks, is she still Thine.
Is hers Thy love for aye?

Rashi, "Seliha." q Liber, *Rashi,* 178.

504. LOOK

504.1 His wife looked back . . . and she became a pillar of salt.

Bible: Gen., 19.26.

504.2 A look may last for ever.

Heine, *New Poems: Emma,* 1853, #2.

504.3 The look explains the word.

q M. Ibn Ezra, *Shirat Yisrael,* (12C) 1924, p. 140.

504.4 A severe glance may frighten more than a hundred slaps.

Mendelé, *Eltern und Kinder,* 1868.

505. LORDSHIP

505.1 Why did Joseph die before his brothers? Because he assumed airs of authority.

Hama b. Hanina. *Talmud: Berakot,* 55a.

505.2 Alas for lordship, which buries its possessors: there was not one prophet who did not outlive four kings.

Johanan b. Nappaha. *Talmud: Pesahim,* 87b.

505.3 Hate lordship.

Shemaiah. *Mishna: Abot,* 1.10.

506. LOSS

506.1 Sometimes loss comes through honor, and honor through loss.

Apocrypha: Ben Sira, 20.11.

506.2 I sought your penny, and lost my pound.

Bialik. q SHR, 304.

506.3 Men occasionally find a new truth, but never an old button.
Fulda, "The Fur Coat."

506.4 Lose with truth and right rather than gain with falsehood and wrong.
Maimonides, *Tzavaah. Responsa*, ii. 38c.

506.5 God, . . . give me the heart to fight—and lose.
L. Untermeyer, "Prayer." *Challenge.* 1914, p. 7.

507. LOVE

507.A. General

507.A.1 Love covers all transgression.
Bible: Prov., 10.12.

507.A.2 Better a dinner of herbs where love is, than a stalled ox and hatred therewith.
Ibid., 15.17.

507.A.3 Love is the voice of God. Love is the rule of heaven!
Aguilar, *Vale of Cedars*, 1850, ch 34, p. 219.

507.A.4 Men do not sacrifice their lives for reasonable things. They move mountains only under the imperative of love.
Baron, *In Quest of Integrity*, 1936, p. 13.

507.A.5 Love is a load: blessed is he who bears heavy ones.
Beer-Hofmann, *Der junge David*, 1933.

507.A.6 We are even more anxious to hide our love than our hatred.
Boerne, *Denkrede auf Jean Paul*, Dec. 2, 1825.

507.A.7 To live is to love.
Boerne, *Der ewige Jude*, 1821.

507.A.8 You are not loved when you are lovely, but when you are loved you are found to be lovely.
Boerne, *Umgang mit Menschen*, 1824.

507.A.9 Love is a form of flattery which pleases all, . . . even God.
Ibid.

507.A.10 He who loves brings God and the World together.
Buber, *At the Turning*, 1952, p. 44.

507.A.11 Death is where love is not.
Chernihovsky, "Agadot HaAviv," c.1900. *Kitbé*, i. 112.

507.A.12 We are all born for love.
Disraeli, *Sybil*, 1845.

507.A.13 Where we do not respect, we soon cease to love.
Disraeli, *Young Duke*, 1831.

507.A.14 To love and be loved,—this On earth is the highest bliss.
Heine, *Italien*, xvi. 1828.

507.A.15 Love blinds to faults, hatred to virtues.
M. Ibn Ezra, *Shirat Yisrael*, (12C) 1924, p. 138.

507.A.16 A needle's eye is not too narrow for two lovers, but the whole world is not wide enough for two enemies.
Ibn Gabirol, *Mibhar HaPeninim*, c.1050, #281.

507.A.17 If not love, why live?
Immanuel, *Mahberot*, c.1300 (1491), ch 3.

507.A.18 Love is the pivot of the Torah.
Ibid. q KJL, 223.

507.A.19 People associate love with sentimental feeling alone. But love includes much more. The act of love should bring all levels of the human being into play, his intuitions, his emotions, and his logic and mind as well.
Z. J. Kook. q H. Weiner. *Commentary*, 1954, p. 258.

507.A.20 There are three kinds of love: of pleasure, of profit, and of virtue.
Leo Hebraeus, *Philosophy of Love*, (1502) 1937, p. 4.

507.A.21 A heart without affection is like a purse without money.
Mandelstamm, *Mishlé Binyamin*, 1884.

507.A.22 Love: a fire nourished by physical things. It burns, crackles, till the material turns to ashes, and the blaze ends in smoke.
Mendelé, *Shlomé Reb Hayyims*, 1899.

507.A.23 Love which is physical, like that of Amnon and Tamar, vanishes with the object; love which is not physical, like that of David and Jonathan, is imperishable.
Mishna: Abot, 5.16.

507.A.24 Work done for love's sake seems short and seems sweet.
Montefiore, *Bible for Home Reading*, 1896, i. 33.

507.A.25 Love is the fulfilling of the law.
New Testament: Rom., 13.10.

507.A.26 He who loves not abides in fear.
New Testament: I John, 3.14. See 4.18.

507.A.27 Hell's afloat in lovers' tears.

Parker, "Wisdom," *Sunset Gun*, 1928.

507.A.28 Love is that celestial virgin that serves as an intermediator between God who gives and the soul which receives. The entire written law is nothing but a symbol of love.

Philo. q F. Hertz, *Race & Civilization*, 202. See Friedländer, *Das Judentum in der vorchristlichen griechischen Welt*, 1897, p. 30f.

507.A.29 Those who love deeply cannot age.

Pinero, *Princess and Butterfly*, 1897.

507.A.30 Love brings to life whatever is dead around us.

F. Rosenzweig, letter to Edith Hahn, Jan. 16, 1920. GFR 90.

507.A.31 Love disregards propriety (upsets the natural order).

Simeon b. Eleazar. *Talmud: Sanhedrin*, 105b.

Simeon b. Yohai. *Gen. R.*, 55.8.

507.A.32 No love, save intellectual love, is eternal.

Spinoza, *Ethics*, 1677, v. Pr 34, Corollary.

507.A.33 We love the things we love, in spite of what they are.

L. Untermeyer, "Love." *New Adam*, 1920, p. 28.

507.A.34 Everyone loves alone, as everyone prays alone.

Varnhagen, *Briefe*, 1877.

507.A.35 Happy is the man that saith: Above

All earthly might and fame I crave for love.

Yehoash, "*Psalms*," tr I. Goldstick. LGP, 135.

507.A.36 Let Loving-kindness and Mercy pass through you,

And Truth be the Law of your mouth.

For so ye are channels of the divine sea,

Which may not flood the earth, but only steal in

Through rifts in your souls.

Zangwill, "The Circle of Love." *Dreamers*, 524.

507.A.37 In love is found the secret of divine unity.

Zohar, *Exod.*, 216a.

507.A.38 Love alone dominates fear.

Ibid.

507.B. Love for God

507.B.1 Thou shalt love the Lord thy God with all thy heart, and with all thy soul, and with all thy might.

Bible: Deut., 6.5.

507.B.2 I came into the world to show another way, to cultivate love of God, of Israel, and of the Torah, and there is no need for fasting and mortification.

Baal Shem. q Baruch of Mezbizh, *Butzina de Nehora*, 1880.

507.B.3 In Judaism, love towards God is never a mere feeling; it belongs to the sphere of ethical activity.

Baeck, *Essence of Judaism*, 1936, p. 129.

507.B.4 O God, ... if Thou wert to burn me, I'd love Thee all the more.

Bahya, *Hobot HaLebabot*, 1040, 10.1.

507.B.5 God is love, and the object of love: herein lies the whole contribution of mysticism.

Bergson, *Two Sources of Morality and Religion*, 1935, 240.

507.B.6 The [ideal] Jew's thoughts are as a mass of heated coal, which love for God has fused and set aglow.

Eleazar b. Judah, *Rokeah*, 13C. q JJC, 256.

507.B.7 The Congregation of Israel said, Even in my distress and bitterness, my Beloved shall lodge between my breasts!

Joshua b. Levi, on *Cant.* 1.13. *Talmud: Sabbath*, 88b.

507.B.8 Man's love of God is identical with his knowledge of Him.

Maimonides, *Guide for the Perplexed*, 1190, 3.51.

507.B.9 "Love the Lord ... with all thy heart"—with both your good and evil inclinations; "with all thy soul"—even when He takes your life; "with all thy might"—with all your possessions.

Mishna: Berakot, 9.5.

507.B.10 As the love of God is man's highest happiness and blessedness, and the ultimate end and aim of all human actions, it follows that he alone lives by the Divine law who loves God not from fear of punishment, or from love of any other object, ... but solely because he has knowledge of God.

Spinoza, *Theologico-Political Treatise*, 1670, ch 4.

507.C. Love of Mankind

507.C.1 Teach not the love of scholars only, but the love of all.
Abot de Rabbi Nathan, ch 16.

507.C.2 Blessed is he who implants peace and love.
Apocrypha: II Enoch, 52.11.

507.C.3 Love one another from the heart.
Apocrypha: Patriarchs, Gad, 6.3.

507.C.4 The most touching chapter about love of the enemy is contained in the history of . . . Israel. . . . No wrong, no physical violence, have availed to stifle the human love in their hearts.
Baeck, *Essence of Judaism,* 1936, p. 221.

507.C.5 I know no better test of a man than his possession of the affection of those most intimate with him.
J. P. Benjamin, letter to his daughter Minette.

507.C.6 I love Jews and Christians, not because they are Jews or Christians, I love them because they are human, born to freedom.
Boerne, *Der ewige Jude,* 1821.

507.C.7 How can he love God who loves not His works?
Boerne, *Der Narr im weissen Schwan,* ch 5.

507.C.8 Everyone has in his life a beautiful day when, like the first human beings in Eden, he finds love without care and trouble. But when this day is past, you earn love, as you earn bread, by the sweat of the brow.
Boerne, *Umgang mit Menschen,* 1824.

507.C.9 Let the time be dark with hatred,
I believe in years beyond—
Love at last shall bind the peoples
In an everlasting bond.
Chernihovsky, "Credo," 1892. FJA, 354f.

507.C.10 Love is based on equality and freedom.
Fromm, *Escape from Freedom,* 1941, p. 161.

507.C.11 The love of people is at the same time a love for God. For when we love one, we necessarily love one's handiwork.
Judah Löw. q BWC, 79.

507.C.12 Whether a man really loves God can be determined by the love he bears toward his fellow men.
Levi Yitzhok. q BTH, i. 227.

507.C.13 Love, that ye may be loved.
M. Mendelssohn, Pref. to *Vindiciae Judaeorum,* 1782.

507.C.14 True love of man is to know his pain and bear his sorrow.
Moshe Leib. q Berger, *Esser Tzahtzohot,* 1910, p. 52.

507.C.15 If a man say, I love God, and hates his brother, he is a liar. He who loves God loves his brother too.
New Testament: I John, 4.20f.

507.C.16 We need love and creative imagination to do constructive work.
Ollendorf. *Das Jahr des jüdisches Frauenbundes,* 1928f.

507.C.17 To be pious towards God is to be affectionate towards men.
Philo, *Abraham,* 37.

507.C.18 As a rule, men love one another from a distance.
Sholom Aleichem, *Di erste Communé,* 1904.

507.C.19 Love all, Jews and Gentiles, and envy none.
Vital, *Shaaré HaKedusha,* (c. 1600) 1876.

507.C.20 Would that my eyes would shine and send forth light,
To be a beacon in another's night.
Yehoash, *Psalms,* tr I. Goldstick. LGP, 135.

507.D. Romantic Love

507.D.1 Your love is better than wine.
Bible: Cant., 1.2.

507.D.2 Awake not, nor stir up love, until it please.
Ibid., 2.7, 3.5, 8.4.

507.D.3 My beloved is mine, and I am his.
Ibid., 2.16.

507.D.4 The king is held captive in the tresses.
Ibid., 7.6.

507.D.5 Set me as a seal upon your heart.
Ibid., 8.6.

507.D.6 Love is strong as death.
Ibid.

507.D.7 Many waters cannot quench love, neither can floods drown it.
Ibid., 8.7.

507.D.8 If a man would give all the substance of his house for love, he would be utterly contemned.
Ibid.

507.D.9 Wine and song rejoice the heart, but better than both is the affection of lovers.
Apocrypha: Ben Sira, 40.20.

507.D.10 The magic of first love is the ignorance that it can ever end.
Disraeli, *Henrietta Temple*, 1837.

507.D.11 Amid the gloom and travail of existence suddenly to behold a beautiful thing, and as instantaneously to feel an overwhelming conviction that with that fair form for ever our destiny must be entwined; that there is no more joy but in her joy, nor sorrow but when she grieves; that in her sigh of love, in her smile of fondness, hereafter is all bliss; to feel our flaunty ambition fade away like a shrivelled gourd before her vision; to feel fame a juggle and posterity a lie; and to be prepared at once, for this great object, to forfeit and fling away all former hopes, ties, schemes, views; to violate in her favor every duty of society; this is a lover, and this is love!
Ibid.

507.D.12 True love is . . . a divine gift, without which it is a sin against God and man to enter into any marriage.
Franzos, *Hané*, 1873. *Jews of Barnow*, 119.

507.D.13 He to whom to die 'tis given
On the battlefield, is blest;
But a foretaste 'tis of heaven,
Dying on a woman's breast.
Heine, *Germany 1815*, st 21.

507.D.14 Scratch a lover and find a foe!
Parker, *Enough Rope*, 1926, p. 60.

507.D.15 Love tastes sweet, but only with bread.
Proverb (Yiddish). q *JE*, x. 228b.

507.D.16 When love was strong, we could have made our bed on a sword's blade; now, when it has become weak, a bed of sixty cubits is not large enough for us.
Talmud: Sanhedrin, 7a.

507.D.17 Each goose is a swan in the eyes of its lover.
Twerski, *Rashi*, 1946.

508. LOYALTY

508.1 Entreat me not to leave thee, and to return from following after thee; for whither thou goest, I will go; and where thou lodgest, I will lodge; thy people shall be my people, and thy God my God; where thou diest, will I die, and there will I be buried; the Lord do so to me, and more also, if aught but death part thee and me.
Bible: Ruth, 1.16f.

508.2 Stone the dog that left its master and followed you.
Apocrypha: Aḥikar, 2.35.

508.3 Fidelity sleeps on the hardest stone
More sweetly than Betrayal on the softest pillow.
Beer, *Struensee*, (1827) 1829, Act 3, Sc. 13.

508.4 Multiple loyalties are objectionable only if they are inconsistent.
Brandeis, *The Jewish Problem*, 1915.

508.5 It is such a beautiful sentiment! And such a purely German sentiment. . . . Did I not know that fidelity is as old as the world, I would believe that a German had invented it.
Heine, *Harz Journey*, 1824.

508.6 People don't mind if you betray humanity, but if you betray your club, you are considered a renegade.
Koestler, *Age of Longing*, 1951, p. 133.

508.7 A healthy loyalty is not passive and complacent, but active and critical.
Laski, *Dangers of Obedience*, 1930, p. 30.

508.8 Praised be He who inspires people with a love for their town!
Simeon b. Lakish. *Gen. R.*, 34.15.

509. LOYALTY TO JUDAISM

509.1 Who is on the Lord's side, let him come to me!
Bible: Exod., 32.26.

509.2 We are of them that are peaceable and faithful in Israel.
Bible: II Sam., 20.19.

509.3 There exists no other race of men that has proved its fidelity to religious conviction for an equal period, under equal difficulties, and amid equal temptations.
F. Adler, *Creed and Deed*, 1877, p. 203.

509.4 The honor of the emperor is not identical with dishonor to the ancient laws.
Agrippa I, letter to Caligula, 40. KTJ, i. 54.

509.5 Woe unto you who despise the humble dwelling and inheritance of your fathers!

Apocrypha: Enoch, 99.14.

509.6 If all the nations that are within the king's dominions obey him by forsaking . . . the worship of their fathers, yet will I and my sons and my brethren walk in the covenant of our fathers.

Apocrypha: I Macc., 2.19f.

509.7 There shone out in that intense moment the sterner and sublimer qualities which later Hellenism, and, above all, the Hellenism of Syria, knew nothing of—uncommon fidelity to an ideal, endurance raised to the pitch of utter self-devotion, a passionate clinging to purity. They were qualities for the lack of which all the riches of Hellenic culture could not compensate. It was an epoch in history.

*Bevan, *House of Seleucus,* 1902, ii. 174.

509.8 Everything for our Judaism!

Brodnitz. *C-V Zeitung,* Sept. 14, 1933.

509.9 Truly it is beyond wonder how that contemptible and degenerate issue of Jacob, once so devoted to ethnic superstition and so easily seduced to the idolatry of their neighbors, should now in such an obstinate and peremptory belief adhere unto their own doctrine, expect impossibilities, and, in the face and eye of the Church, persist without the least hope of conversion. This is a vice in them, that were a virtue in us; for obstinacy in a bad cause is but constancy in a good.

*Browne, *Religio Medici,* 1643, #25.

509.10 The Jews owe it to themselves and to humanity to hold their own against the all-devouring dogmatism of Christianity. They have done a great work in the past, and they can do a great work in the future.

*T. Davidson. q S. S. Wise, *Sermons,* 1905, p. 122.

509.11 Almighty God! . . . I only want a grave
Where I may rest at peace. . . .
That I may know, when I have closed my eyes,
Beneath that tree that grows upon my tomb,
My great-grandchild, one summer's day will come,
And read the words upon my gravestone,

And that to him the words, the language of my fathers,
Be understood and known.

Einhorn, "Prayer," 1910. *Gez. Lider,* 1952, p. 20. LGP, 516.

509.12 Why the people of Israel adhered to their God all the more devotedly the worse they were treated by Him, that is a question we must leave open.

Freud, *Moses and Monotheism,* 1939.

509.13 Do not conceal, but magnify and be proud of your race, your names and your religion. . . . Train your children in Hebrew, and tell in your homes the magnificent traditions of your race.

*Hall, speech at corner-stone of Shaaré Torah synagog, Worcester, Mass., April 29, 1906.

509.14 Neither the slander of their neighbors and of foreign visitors, to which as a nation they are exposed, nor the frequent outrages of Persian kings and satraps, can shake their determination; for these laws, naked and defenseless, they face tortures and death in its most terrible form, rather than repudiate the faith of their forefathers.

*Hecataeus of Abdera, 4–3C B.C.E. q Josephus, *Against Apion,* i. 22.

509.15 Queer people this! Downtrodden for thousands of years, weeping always, suffering always, abandoned always by its God, yet clinging to Him tenaciously, loyally, as no other under the sun. Oh, if martyrdom, patience and faith in despite of trial, can confer a patent of nobility, then this people is noble beyond many another.

Heine. q A. Meissner, *Heinrich Heine,* 138. KJL, 362f.

509.16 Your conscientiousness in your faith is the best pledge to me for your conscientiousness as a physician.

*Henry IV of Navarre, to Filotheo Eliahu Montalto, who agreed to come to Paris as Queen Maria de Medici's physician if he could practice Judaism openly.

509.17 A return to the Jewish people presupposes a return to Judaism.

Herzl.

509.18 The greatest honor I can give my children is love for our people, loyalty to self.

Herzl, *Kishinef and the Sardines. Die Welt,* May 8, 1903.

509.19 Unconditional agreement with the culture of the present day—harmony between Judaism and science—but also unconditional steadfastness in the faith and traditions of Judaism.

Hildesheimer, address, 1861.

509.20 Be a Jew; be it really and truly . . . then will you be respected, not in spite of it but because of it.

S. R. Hirsch, *Nineteen Letters,* (1836), #15, p. 156.

509.21 Never may I live to become so abject a captive as to abjure my race or forget the traditions of my forefathers!

Josephus, *Wars,* 6.2.1.

509.22 They bear their degradation partly from necessity, partly from their own free will. For whoever wishes to do so, can become the friend and equal of his oppressor by uttering one word, and without any difficulty.

Judah Halevi, *Cuzari,* c. 1135, 1.115, 4.23.

509.23 Perhaps no other religion has had so many martyrs as the Jewish, whose followers have sacrificed all their interests, without even the comfort that their martyrdom would be rewarded by outward acknowledgment of their courage. On the contrary, they have, in addition to the loss of their property and lives, had to bear taunts and scorn, and yet they have proved faithful to their creed.

Lasker, speech, Prussian Chamber of Deputies, March 27, 1865. q AJ, 1883, p. 82.

509.24 The vicissitudes endured by the Jewish race . . . may well be a subject of pride to the Hebrew and of shame to the Christian. The annals of mankind afford no more brilliant instance of steadfastness under adversity, of unconquerable strength through centuries of hopeless oppression, of inexhaustible elasticity in recuperating from apparent destruction, and of conscientious adherence to a faith whose only portion in this life was contempt and suffering.

*Lea, *History of the Inquisition of Spain,* 1906, i. 35.

509.25 Where can we find a race more faithful to its traditions, to its Law, to its God, in short, to its ideal? What a history it has had! Its poets have called it "the passion of a people." How enduring and mighty has been that passion, from Nebu-

chadnezzar to Antiochus, from Hadrian to Torquemada!

*Leroy-Beaulieu, *Israel Among the Nations,* 1895, p. 283.

509.26 Non-Jews are less sensitive to an overemphasis of one's Jewishness than to the tendency of aping things non-Jewish. . . . Loyalty to the Jewish group furthers rather than hinders friendly relations with non-Jews.

Lewin. *JF,* Sept. 1939. *Resolving Social Conflicts,* 166f.

509.27 Don't assume, Jewish intellectuals, that you are doing your duty by working . . . for so-called Humanity. . . . You are lighting a fire beneath the open sky, while your own family in your own house is freezing.

Peretz, *Bildung,* 1890. *Alle Verk,* xii. 20ff. LP 334–8.

509.28 Like all rivers, as long as they follow their course on land are fresh and sweet, but when they enter the ocean become bitter and useless, so Israel, as long as they maintain their trust in their Creator are blessed and sweet, and when they turn away and put their trust in vanity, become cursed and evil and useless to the world.

Pirké de R. Eliezer, ch 9.

509.29 There were found but very few, when the day of departure [from Spain] arrived, who were not prepared to abandon their country rather than their religion. This extraordinary act of self-devotion by a whole people for conscience' sake may be thought, in the nineteenth century, to merit other epithets than those of "perfidy, incredulity, and stiff-necked obstinacy," with which the worthy Curate of Los Palacios, in the charitable feeling of that day, has seen fit to stigmatize it.

*Prescott, *Ferdinand and Isabella,* (1837) 1868, ii. 143.

509.30 Nominal Christians are numerous, but merely nominal Jews, though there are some, are comparatively very few.

*Priestley, *Evidence of Revealed Religion,* 1794, i. 94.

509.31 We have no reason to repudiate the religion of our fathers; we have every reason to love it. We can see in it . . . the highest ideals which humanity in our days can comprehend.

Riesser. q Baron. *Liberal Judaism,* April 1945, p. 7.

509.32 We shall willingly sacrifice all for our fatherland, all except creed and faith, truth and honor, for Germany's heroes and Germany's sages have never taught us that one becomes a German through such sacrifice.

Riesser. q *ibid.,* 8.

509.33 Distress is no excuse for disloyalty.

Saadia, *Emunot VeDeot,* 933, 5.8. tr Rosenblatt, 233.

509.34 I'd rather be maid to this people than mistress to any other!

Talmud: Sanhedrin, 99b.

509.35 Our bodies are in your hands, but not our souls! You cannot uproot our Torah except by force.

Yehiel b. Joseph, to Queen Blanche, 1240. q Official, *Disputation,* (EOV, 82a).

509.36 Let individuals traffic with the Eternal for the sake of temporal goods; we shall cling all the more steadfastly to Judaism! Not even a single law should be sacrificed for political equality. That is not man's ultimate goal.

Zunz, *Gutachten über die Beschneidung,* April 2, 1844. *Ges. Schr.,* ii. 203.

510. LUCK

510.1 Throw a lucky man into the sea, and he will come up with a fish in his mouth.

Lazerov, *Enciklopedie fun Idishe Vitzen,* 1928, #422.

510.2 Even in misfortune, one must have luck.

Proverb. q S. Levin, *In Milhomé Tzeiten,* 68, Oct. 10, 1914.

510.3 If you have luck, even your ox will calve.

Proverb (Yiddish). BJS, #2221.

510.4 Intelligence is not needed for luck, but luck is needed for intelligence.

Proverb (Yiddish). q *JE,* x. 229a.

510.5 He with whom luck plays the game hits the mark without his aim.

Ibid.

510.6 Better an ounce of luck than a pound of gold.

Proverb (Yiddish). YFS, i. 414.

510.7 Long life, progeny and livelihood depend on luck.

Raba. *T: Moed Katan,* 28a.

510.8 Everything depends on luck, even a scroll in the Temple.

Zohar, Numbers, 134a.

511. LULAB

511.1 A dried up lulab is disqualified.

Mishna: Sukka, 3.1.

511.2 For it says: "The dead praise not the Lord" [*Ps.* 115.17].

Judah b. Pazzi. *Talmud J: Sukka,* 3.1.

512. LUST

512.1 The lips of a strange woman drop honey, and her mouth is smoother than oil; but her end is bitter as wormwood, sharp as a two-edged sword.

Bible: Prov., 5.3f.

512.2 Who indulges in lustful thoughts will not be admitted into the compartment of the Holy One.

Ammi b. Nathan. *Talmud: Nidda,* 13b.

512.3 With a female singer have no converse, lest you be taken in her snare. On a maiden fix not your gaze, lest you be entrapped in penalties with her.

Apocrypha: Ben Sira, 9.4f.

512.4 Gaze not upon beauty which is not yours. By the comeliness of a woman many have been ruined, and this way passion flames like fire.

Ibid., 9.8.

512.5 Wine and woman make the heart lustful.

Ibid., 19.2. See 23.1, 6.

512.6 Who gazes lustfully will lose his virility.

Eleazar b. Pedat. *Talmud: Sanhedrin,* 92a.

512.7 When the serpent came to Eve, he infected her with lasciviousness. When Israel came to Sinai, they were rid of it.

Johanan b. Nappaha. *Talmud: Sabbath,* 145b.

512.8 "Lusted lust" [*Num.* 11.4]. When dulled by surfeit, people crave desire for pleasure even more than pleasure itself.

Katz, *Toldot Jacob Joseph,* 1780, p. 261.

512.9 A man should not walk behind a woman on the road.

Nahman b. Isaac. *Talmud: Berakot,* 61a.

512.10 To be carnally minded is death.

New Testament: Rom., 8.6. See *Matt.,* 5.28.

512.11 No task of civilization has been so painfully laborious as the subjugation of lasciviousness. The pornographist would take from us the fruit of this, the hardest struggle of humanity.

Nordau, *Degeneration,* (1893), 5.2, p. 557.

512.12 The licentious age early.
Raba. *Talmud: Sabbath,* 152a.

512.13 He who sins only with his eyes is also an adulterer.
Simeon b. Lakish. *Lev. R.,* 23.12. See *Matt.* 2.28. Ishmael School. *Talmud: Sabbath,* 64a. *Berakot,* 61a.

512.14 Entertain no wanton thoughts by day, and you'll avoid pollution at night.
Talmud: Aboda Zara, 20a.

513. LUXURY

513.1 Delight not in excessive luxury, for double is its poverty.
Apocrypha: Ben Sira, 18.32.

513.2 Luxury in dress is a mark of pride and a cause of envy.
Hanok, *Reshit Bikkurim,* 1708.

513.3 Luxury feeds more poor people than philanthropy.
Lazerov, *Enciklopedie fun Idishe Vitzen,* 1928, #414.

513.4 If the spirit rule and the body be humbled, man will seek nothing beyond the necessary. He will be satisfied with little and will disdain superfluity.
Maimonides, *Shaaré HaMusar. Responsa,* ii. 38d.

513.5 The more we desire the superfluous, the more we meet with difficulties. . . . The more necessary a thing is for living beings, the more easily it is found and the cheaper it is.
Maimonides, *Guide for the Perplexed,* 1190, 3.12.

514. MACCABEES

514.1 As part of the eternal world-wide struggle for democracy, the struggle of the Maccabees is of eternal world-wide interest.
Brandeis, message, Dec. 1915. *Brandeis on Zionism,* 82.

514.2 The little Maccabean band was like a rock in the midst of a surging sea. Standing almost alone in their day, the heroes beat back the forces that threatened to involve all mankind in a common demoralization.
M. Joseph, *Judaism as Creed and Life,* 1903, p. 216f.

514.3 But for the heroism of the Maccabees the heathen must, finally, have swallowed up the Jews.
Klausner, *Jesus of Nazareth,* 1926, p. 14f.

515. MACHINE

515.1 Machines . . . have imparted to our organism an extension so vast, have endowed it with a power so mighty, . . . that surely none of all this was foreseen in the structural plan of our species. . . . The body, now larger, calls for a bigger soul.
Bergson.

515.2 The mystery of mysteries is to view machinery making machinery.
Disraeli, *Coningsby,* 1844, 4.2.

515.3 Machines and their development provide the greatest opportunity in the whole history of mankind to improve the lot of the individual human being.
D. Lilienthal, *Big Business,* 1952, p. 203.

515.4 Machinery, gifted with the wonderful power of shortening and fructifying human labor, we behold starving and overworking it.
Marx, *Revolution of 1848,* April 14, 1856.

515.5 The increase of net incomes, estimated in commodities, which is always the consequence of improved machinery, will lead to new savings and accumulations . . . and the demand for labor will be as great as before.
Ricardo, *Political Economy,* 1817, p. 31.

515.6 I know not, I care not, I am a machine!
M. Rosenfeld, "In the Factory," *Songs of Labor,* tr Stokes & Frank, 1914.

515.7 A vampire stretching out its bloody claws to clutch your souls. A god, a devil chaining you to drudgery. A monster made to lame your bodies, blunt your minds, and foul your honorable trade.
Toller, *Machine Wreckers,* (1922) 1926, 2.2

516. MADNESS

516.1 Do I lack madmen?
Bible: I Sam., 21.16.

516.2 None is so crazy but that he may find a crazier comrade who will understand him.
Heine, *Harz Journey,* 1824.

516.3 Socrates is supposed to have said: "You must do a crazy thing once in a while to keep from going nuts."
Hershfield, *Now I'll Tell One,* 1938, p. 114.

516.4 Were it not for madmen, the world would remain waste.
Maimonides, *Commentary to Mishna: Zeraim,* 1168, Preface.

516.5 You may find even madness providentially beneficial.
Midrash Tehillim, 34.1, ed Buber, 123a.

517. MAGIC

517.1 No enchantment with Jacob, no divination with Israel.
Bible: Num., 23.23. See *Deut.,* 18.10–12.

517.2 Who abstains from magic is closer to God than angels.
Ahaba b. Zera. *Talmud: Nedarim,* 32a.

517.3 Who whispers a charm over a wound has no portion in the world to come.
Akiba. *Mishna: Sanhedrin,* 10.1.

517.4 Who practices magic will be harassed by magic.
Levi. *Talmud: Nedarim,* 32a.

517.5 Beware of the error of amulet-writers. What you hear from them or read in their works . . . is utter nonsense.
Maimonides, *Guide for the Perplexed,* 1190, 1.6.

517.6 Who puts a Bible or tefillin in a cradle to induce a baby to sleep, denies the Torah, for he turns sacred objects, intended to quicken the soul, into media of physical therapy.
Maimonides, *Yad: Akum,* 11.12, 1180.

517.7 The magician mumbles, and knows not what he mumbles.
q Nahman b. Isaac. *Talmud: Sota,* 22a.

517.8 Among the Jews alone, of all the nations of the world, were the detestable arts of necromancy strictly forbidden.
*Priestley, *Evidence of Revealed Religion,* 1794, i. 51.

517.9 Who indulges in conjuring angels or demons, or in magic, will come to no good end. . . . Man has only one good recourse, prayer to God.
Sefer Hasidim, 13C, #221, p. 76.

518. MAIMONIDES

518.1 Every Jew who has . . . traversed the hard and bitter road from blind faith to free reason must have met with Maimonides . . . and found in him a source of strength and support for his first steps, which are the hardest and the most dangerous.
Ahad HaAm, "Supremacy of Reason," 1904. *Ten Essays,* 210.

518.2 Go to the left, my heart, or to the right, but believe all our great master Moses ben Maimon believed, last of the Gaonim in time, but first in rank.
Bedersi, *Behinat HaOlam,* c.1310, ch 41.

518.3 From Moses to Moses, there was none like Moses.
Popular tribute. q Graetz, *Dibré Yemé Israel,* iv. 406.

519. MAJORITY

519.1 A majority is always the best repartee.
Disraeli, *Tancred,* 1847, 2.14.

519.2 A majority is like the whole.
Huna b. Hoshaiah. *Talmud: Horayot* 3b.

519.3 A heavenly voice proves nothing. The law of Sinai commands us to "decide according to the majority" [*Exod.* 23.2]
Joshua b. Hanania. *Talmud: Baba Metzia,* 59b.

519.4 The majority rules.
Talmud: Yebamot, 40a.

520. MAN

520.1 Am I in the place of God?
Bible: Gen., 50.19.

520.2 Quit yourselves like men.
Bible: I Sam., 4.9.

520.3 A man after his own heart.
Ibid., 13.14.

520.4 Thou art the man!
Bible: II Sam., 12.7.

520.5 Cease ye from man . . . for how little is he to be accounted.
Bible: Isa., 2.22.

520.6 What is man that Thou art mindful of him. . . ? Yet Thou hast made him but little lower than the angels.
Bible: Ps., 8.5f.

520.7 Surely every man at his best estate is altogether vanity.
Ibid., 39.6. See 62.10.

520.8 I am fearfully and wonderfully made.
Ibid., 139.14.

520.9 Man is like unto a breath.
Ibid., 144.4.

520.10 Shall mortal man be just before God?
Bible: Job, 4.17.

520.11 They that dwell in houses of clay,

whose foundation is in the dust, who are crushed before the moth!
Ibid., 4.19.

520.12 Man, born of woman, is of few days and full of trouble.
Bible: Job, 14.1.

520.13 Behold, even the moon has no brightness, and the stars are not pure in His sight; how much less man, that is a worm, and the son of man, that is a maggot!
Ibid., 25.5f.

520.14 Man has no preeminence above the beast, for all is vanity.
Bible: Eccles., 3.20.

520.15 If a man say, "I am God," he lies. If he say, "I am the Son of Man," he should repent. And if he say, "I shall ascend to heaven," he will not do it. He will not make good his promise.
Abbahu. *Talmud J: Taanit,* 2.1.

520.16 Not even face to face with the sun's rays are men able to stand, being mortals, mere veins and flesh wedded to bones.
Apocrypha: Sibyl, Fragment 1, 12–14.

520.17 Under all the false, overloaded and glittering masquerade, there is in every man a noble nature beneath.
B. Auerbach, *On the Heights,* 1865.

520.18 The ideal of man is to be a revelation himself, clearly to recognize himself as a manifestation of God.
Baal Shem. q *JE,* ii. 385a.

520.19 Man is the only creature on earth that has come to have knowledge of his grandparents and his grandchildren.
Baeck, *Judaism and Ethics,* 1949, p. 18.

520.20 Man alone is conscious of his individuality.
Ibid., 21.

520.21 Man, a miniature world, in whom there is the completion of the cosmic order, and its beauty, glory and perfection.
Bahya, *Hobot HaLebabot,* 1040, 2.4.

520.22 Man is like a musical box. An imperceptible jolt, and he plays a different tune.
Boerne, *Fragmente & Aphorismen,* 1840, #189.

520.23 Humanity is the immortality of men.
Boerne, *Kritiken,* 1825, #5.

520.24 Oh, these human beings. They are as wise as Gods, and as blundering as babes. They make of their lives an intricate network, in which they soon find themselves entangled.
Daixel, *After Midnight. Tzen Einakters,* 1925; *NOP,* 102f.

520.25 If man lives in slime—and there is slime always at the core of the soul—it is nevertheless this briefly animated dust that beholds stars, writes symphonies, and imagines God.
Edman, *Adam,* 1929, p. 168.

520.26 Man eats and drinks, procreates, performs natural functions and dies like an animal; he stands erect, speaks, thinks and has vision like an angel.
Eleazar b. Pedat. *Gen. R.,* 14.3. Cf 8.11.

520.27 Let man ever bear in mind that the Holy One dwells in him.
Eleazar b. Pedat. *Talmud: Taanit,* 11b.

520.28 Queer, how helpless a man becomes
In autumn at the window, at night when it rains.
Esselin, "Harbst Dermont." *Unter der Last,* 1936, p. 107.

520.29 I am a Jew because for Israel man is not yet created; men are creating him.
Fleg, *Why I Am a Jew,* 1929, p. 95. See Fromm, *Escape from Freedom,* 13.

520.30 Who displeases man displeases God.
Hanina b. Dosa. *Mishna: Abot,* 3.10.

520.31 Man, the aristocrat among animals.
Heine. *City of Lucca,* 1829, ch 9. Cf *Atta Troll,* ch 5.

520.32 Men, who form the other kind of livestock.
Heine, *Atta Troll,* 1841, ch 6.

520.33 Humanity is a living organism, of which races and peoples are the members.
Hess, *Rome and Jerusalem,* (1862), p. 123.

520.34 Where there are no men, you try to be a man.
Hillel. *Mishna: Abot,* 2.5.

520.35 My son I have lost, but not my heir; humanity is my heir.
M. Hirsch, reply to a message on loss of his son, 1887.

520.36 Inhabitants of earthen huts! . . . We acknowledge that we are worms, that our bodies are fragments of clay. How, then, can presumption make its nest in our hearts? Yea, and of what profit to man, when his end is in the grave?
Ibn Gabirol, *Shiré* (ed 5688, iii. 87). q Asch, *Sabbatai Zevi*, 3.5, tr White & Boyes, 106f.

520.37 Whatever God created in the world, He created its parallel in man.
José HaGelili. *Abot de R. Nathan*, ch 31, ed Schechter 46a.

520.38 On every creature's form there is of God a seal and a token.
Judah Halevi, *Selected Poems*, 146.

520.39 All men are God's creatures, and manifest the glory of His work. All are sacred to His Holy Name.
Judah Löw, *Beer HaGola,* (1598) p. 150. See BWC, 89.

520.40 Man—thirst in his throat, fear in his heart, sin in his lap, hate in his growth.
E. Kalir, *Maasé Elohenu,* c.750.

520.41 The aim of man is to be the Temple of God.
Katz, *Toldot Jacob Joseph*, 1780. q HLH, 31.

520.42 Man embodies within himself all sorts of creatures . . . the cat playing with a mouse, the weasel stealing into a coop and turning the heads of the fowl, monkeys aping others, dogs wagging their tails to anyone who throws them a bone, a spider luring a fly, entangling it in its web, and sucking out its vitals, gnats following somebody, buzzing his ears, etc.
Mendelé, *Di Kliatshé*, 1873.

520.43 It is because man is half angel, half brute, that his inner life witnesses such a bitter warfare.
Moses of Coucy. q Hertz, *DPB*, 25.

520.44 One human being is worth as much as the whole creation.
Nehemiah. *Abot de Rabbi Nathan*, ch 31.

520.45 Man at birth is the weakest of all creatures.
Orhot Tzaddikim, 15C, Introduction.

520.46 Of all the treasures which the universe has in its store, there is none more sacred and godlike than man, the glorious cast of a glorious image.
Philo, *Special Laws*, iii. 15.

520.47 Man is a little world and the world a large man.
Philo, *Who Is the Heir of Divine Things,* 31.

520.48 Man is the purpose of creation.
Saadia, *Emunot VeDeot*, 933, iv. Introduction.
Abravanel, *Mifalot Elohim*, 1592, p. 54d.

520.49 Man is the axle of the world and its foundation.
Saadia, *Emunot VeDeot*, 933, 4.1, tr Rosenblatt, 182.

520.50 Diogenes carried not only a lantern, with which he was in search of a man, but, in case he should find one, he carried also a—cudgel.
Saphir, *Badenmantel-Gedanken.* SHW, i. 376.

520.51 Men are divided into two categories: scabs and scabs. If you have no money, you're plainly a scab; and if you have money, you're surely a scab, otherwise you wouldn't have money.
Sholom Aleichem, *Roite Yidelech*, 1900.

520.52 A Jew should always carry with him two purses, so that he may reach into the one or the other according to his needs: one with "I am but dust and ashes," and another with "For my sake was the world created."
Simha Bunam; Mendel of Kotzk. See BTH, ii. 249f.

520.53 To man there is nothing more useful than man.
Spinoza, *Ethics*, 1677, iv. Pr 18, Note.

520.54 Man is to man a God.
Ibid., iv. Pr 35, Note.

520.55 The real man is within, the flesh is only a vestment.
Zohar, Gen., 20b.

520.56 Every man is a composite of the heavenly and the earthly.
Ibid., 130b.

521. MANNERS

521.1 When you . . . eat with a ruler, consider well who is before you.
Bible: Prov., 23.1.

521.2 Enter not a house suddenly.
Akiba. *Talmud: Pesahim*, 112a. See *Ben Sira*, 21.22.

521.3 Good manners is thoughtfulness of God and of men.
Anav, *Sefer Maalot HaMiddot,* (13C) ch 23.

521.4 In the midst of a discourse, speak not.

Apocrypha: Ben Sira, 11.8.

521.5 A fool peeps through the door; the cautious acts humbly.

Ibid., 2.23.

521.6 Eat like a man what is put before you, but be not ravenous.

Ibid., 31.16.

521.7 The world is governed not by morality, but by a hardened form of it, manners.

B. Auerbach, Little Barefoot, 1856.

521.8 Both in writing and in speaking, say "he and I," not "I and he."

M. Cohen, Sefer Hasidim Zuta, c.1473.

521.9 Nowadays, manners are easy and life is hard.

Disraeli, Sybil, 1845.

521.10 Without manners no Torah, without Torah no manners.

Eleazar b. Azariah. Mishna: Abot, 3.17.

521.11 Good manners may in Seven Words be found:
Forget Yourself and think of Those Around.

Guiterman, A Poet's Proverbs, 1924, p. 3.

521.12 Fine manners are the oil that lubricates social contacts. . . . Ability is adorned by nothing as much as by affability.

Harrison, "What Is a True Gentleman?" Israelite, Jan. 14, 1926.

521.13 The test of good manners: to bear patiently with bad ones.

Ibn Gabirol. See ATJH, p. 212.

521.14 The Torah teaches incidentally good manners.

Ishmael b. Elisha. Sifré, #42, to Deut. 11.14.

521.15 Manners provide the lubrication without which frictions would develop.

Magnin, How to Live, 1951, p. 87.

521.16 Do not interrupt while another speaks.

Simeon b. Yohai. Sifré, #103, to Num., 12.6.

521.17 If you empty a cup of wine in one draught, you're a sot.

Talmud: Betza, 25b.

521.18 Be ever decorous when you enter and when you leave.

Talmud: Pirké Ben Azzai, 2.1.

522. MARRIAGE

522.A. Matrimony

522.A.1 It is not good that the man should be alone; I will make him a helpmate against him.

Bible: Gen., 2.18.

522.A.2 If he is worthy, she is a helpmate; if he is unworthy, she is against him.

Eleazar b. Pedat. Talmud: Yebamot, 63a.

522.A.3 Therefore shall a man leave his father and his mother, and shall cleave unto his wife, and they shall be one flesh.

Bible: Gen., 2.24.

522.A.4 Among the ancient Hebrews, youths and young girls were wont to meet on the Day of Atonement . . . to cement their affections and plight their troth. For marriage itself was esteemed an act of purification. . . . Marriage is the foundation of all morality.

F. Adler, Creed and Deed, 1877, p. 86.

522.A.5 He who remains unmarried impairs the divine image.

Akiba. Talmud: Yebamot, 63b.

522.A.6 If husband and wife are worthy, the Shekina abides with them; if not, fire consumes them.

Akiba: Talmud: Sota, 17a.

522.A.7 The Holy One took the two letters of esh, "fire," added the two letters of His name Yh, the yad to form ish, "man," "husband," and the heh to form ishah, "woman," "wife," and He said: If together they follow My ways, My name abides between them and delivers them from trouble; if not, My name is removed from between them, and they become a consuming fire (of passion).

Pirké de R. Eliezer, ch 12. See Talmud: Kalla Rabbati, ch 1.

522.A.8 Without a hedge the vineyard is laid waste, and without a wife, a man is a homeless wanderer. Who trusts an armed band of vagabonds?

Apocrypha: Ben Sira, 36.25.

522.A.9 When one is married, it is all over with willfulness.

Auerbach, Landolin von Reutershofen, 1879, ch 6.

522.A.10 Happiness in marriage is not a gift, but an opportunity. It is an obligation, not an experiment. . . . The chief purpose of marriage is . . . the making of a home, the rearing of children, and the working together for economic security. Brickner, "Five Rules." *National Jewish Post*, Sept. 5, 1947.

522.A.11 I have always thought that every woman should marry, and no man. Disraeli, *Lothair*, 1870, ch 30.

522.A.12 Here's to matrimony, the high sea for which no compass has yet been invented! Heine.

522.A.13 He who marries is like the Doge who wedded the Adriatic Sea; he doesn't know what's in it: treasures, pearls, monsters, unknown storms. Heine, *Gedanken und Einfälle*, 1869, #5.

522.A.14 Without a wife, a man is incomplete. Hiyya b. Gamada. *Gen. R.*, 17.2.

522.A.15 Man is not even called Man till united with woman. *Zohar, Gen.*, 55b, on *Gen.* 5.2.

522.A.16 An unmarried man is deficient, "blemished," and nothing blemished may approach the altar. *Zohar. Lev.*, 5b. See *Zohar, Num.*, 145b.

522.A.17 In the consciousness of belonging together, in the sense of constancy, resides the sanctity, the beauty of matrimony, which helps us to endure pain more easily, to enjoy happiness doubly, and to give rise to the fullest and finest development of our nature. Lewald. q TL, p. 385.

522.A.18 It is better to marry than to burn. *New Testament: 1 Cor.*, 7.9.

522.A.19 Many embark on matrimony: most succeed, some come to grief. *Num. R.*, 9.4.

522.A.20 Marriage is something special. I guess you have to deserve it. Odets, *Golden Boy*, 1937, 2:3, p. 138.

522.A.21 We approach our virgin brides as pure as themselves, proposing as the end of marriage not pleasure but legitimate offspring. Philo, *Joseph*, 9.

522.A.22 There are four motives in marriage: physical pleasure, material advantage, social prestige, and rearing a family. Only those prompted by the last, the heavenly motive, will find satisfaction: they

will have children who will redeem Israel. *Seder Eliyahu Zuta*, ch 3, ed Friedmann, 177.

522.A.23 I ask you, my friend, who started all this business of marriage and of wives? Sholom Aleichem, *Gymnazie*, 1902. NOP, 235.

522.A.24 Marriage is certainly in harmony with reason, if the desire for physical union is not engendered solely by bodily beauty, but also by the desire to beget children and bring them up wisely. Spinoza, *Ethics*, 1677, iv. Appendix 20.

522.A.25 More than man desires to marry, woman desires to be married. *Talmud: Yebamot*, 113a.

522.B. Monogamy

522.B.1 Of all the rabbis named in the Talmud there is not one who is mentioned as having lived in polygamy. Greenstone, "Polygamy." *JE*, x. 121a.

522.B.2 One wife is enough for any man. A. Ibn Ezra. q AJL, 119.

522.B.3 "A virgin of his own people shall he take to wife"—*wife*, not wives. Samuel, on *Lev.* 21.14. *Talmud: Yebamot*, 59a.

522.C. Time

522.C.1 One two three four five six
     seven eight.
     Marry your girl before it's too
     late.
     Do not reflect, do not delay,
     Or someone else will snatch her
     away.
Bialik, "One Two Three." LGP, 46.

522.C.2 "You shall make them known to your . . . children's children"—we must marry early, that we may teach children's children. Ishmael b. Elisha, on *Deut.* 4.9. *Talmud: Kiddushin*, 61a.

522.C.3 When a bachelor attains the age of twenty and is still unmarried, the Holy One says, "Let him rot!" Ishmael School. *Talmud: Kiddushin*, 29b.

522.C.4 First study, then marry; but if you cannot live without a wife, reverse the order. Said Johanan: "With a millstone round his neck, he should engage in study?" *Talmud: Kiddushin*, 29b.

522.D. Mate

522.D.1 Who marries a woman he does not love violates five commandments of the Torah.

Akiba. *Abot de Rabbi Nathan*, ch 26. Meir. *Tosefta: Sota*, 5.11.

522.D.2 Marry your daughter and sorrow will depart from your house, but bestow her upon a man of understanding.

Apocrypha: Ben Sira, 7.25.

522.D.3 Success in marriage does not come merely through finding the right mate, but through being the right mate.

Brickner, "Five Rules." *National Jewish Post*, Sept. 5, 1947.

522.D.4 Since creation, God has engaged in making matches, a task as difficult as dividing the Red Sea.

Jose b. Halafta. *Gen. R.*, 68.4.

522.D.5 A man's mate is from the Holy One.

Abbahu. *Gen. R.*, 68.3.

522.D.6 Forty days before the creation of a child, a Voice proclaims in heaven: So-and-so's daughter for so-and-so's son!"

Rab. *Talmud: Sota*, 2a.

Samuel. *Talmud: Moed Katan*, 18b.

522.D.7 Man has free will in the choice of a proper wife.

Sefer Hasidim, 13C, #19, p. 24.

522.D.8 Marriages made in heaven are not exported.

Hoffenstein, *Pencil in the Air*, 1923, p. 147.

522.D.9 Nowhere do human beings act as irresponsibly as in this matter of choosing a mate.

S. Levin, *The Arena*, 1932, p. 52.

522.D.10 Marrying a daughter to a boor is like throwing her to a lion.

Meir. *Talmud: Pesahim*, 49b.

522.D.11 Step down in life to take a wife; one step ascend to choose a friend.

Papa. *Talmud: Yebamot*, 63a; Myers, *Gems from the Talmud*, 43.

522.D.12 Betroth not a woman you have not seen.

Rab. *Talmud: Kiddushin*, 41a.

522.D.13 Wait till your daughter reaches her majority and can express her consent, before you give her in betrothal.

Ibid.

522.D.14 Who marries for money will have unworthy children.

Ibid., 70a.

522.D.15 A youth need not obey his parents if they urge him to marry not the girl he loves but another with money.

Sefer Hasidim, #953, p. 234. See #1096, p. 279.

522.D.16 Two who quarrel constantly should not marry one another.

Rab. *Talmud: Kiddushin*, 71b.

522.D.17 "The Lord will not . . . pardon him" who marries his daughter to an old man, or takes a wife for his infant son.

Rab, Abayé, Raba. *Talmud: Sanhedrin*, 76a. Ref. to *Deut.* 29.19.

522.D.18 Before taking a wife, investigate her brothers, for most children resemble their mother's brothers.

Raba. *Talmud: Baba Bathra*, 110a.

522.D.19 In the vineyard dances, the Jerusalem maidens would call: "Young man, lift your eyes and see what you choose. Set not your eyes on beauty, but on family."

Simeon b. Gamaliel. *Mishna: Taanit*, 4.8.

522.D.20 Marry into a good family, to insure good offspring.

Eleazar b. Pedat. *Talmud: Baba Bathra*, 109b.

522.D.21 A girl of good stock, though poor and an orphan, is worthy to marry a king.

See Feldman, *Jewish Child*, 21, based on *Num. R.*, 1.5.

522.D.22 Marry into a family of pure, kind and honorable proselytes rather than into a family of Jews who lack these qualities.

Sefer Hasidim, #1097, p. 279.

522.D.23 If need be, sell all you have and marry the daughter of a scholar, and your daughter to a scholar.

Talmud: Pesahim, 49a.

522.D.24 Who marries a worthy woman is kissed by Elijah and loved by the Holy One; who marries an unworthy woman is despised by the Holy One and lashed by Elijah.

Talmud: Tosefta Derek Eretz, 3.12. Cf *T: Kiddushin*, 70a.

522.D.25 Woe to him who disqualifies his descendants and tarnishes his family's reputation by marrying an unworthy woman!

Ibid., 3.12.

522.D.26 Marry not a woman for her money or beauty, for these vanish and the damage remains.

Zabara, *Sefer Shaashuim*, 13C, ch 12, ed Davidson, 137.

522.E. Intermarriage

522.E.1 The courting of young men, the choice of a partner by young women, will solve the last of the Jewish problems.
O. Bauer. q *JF*, Oct. 1951, p. 14.

522.E.2 A complete assimilation of the Jewish stock by intermarriage presents not the slightest biological difficulty. . . . Such an assimilation would distribute the superiorities of the Jewish mind through a much larger proportion of mankind.
*Hooton, *Anthropological Appraisal*, May 15, 1938. *Twilight*, 249f.

522.E.3 The Jew has no preference for or any aversion to one race or another, provided he can marry a woman of his religion.
Neubauer. *JAI*, 1886, xv. 19.

522.E.4 Because the Book of Esther tells of an intermarriage, there is no mention in it of the name of God.
Sefer Hasidim, 13C, #703, p. 183.

522.E.5 No Jew shall receive a Christian woman in marriage, nor shall a Christian man contract a marriage with a Jewish woman. . . . This misdeed shall be considered as the equivalent of adultery.
Theodosian Code, 3.7.2, March 14, 388.

522.E.6 The marriage of a Jew with a Christian . . . is not forbidden, if the laws of the State permit the parents to rear the children of such a union also in the Jewish faith.
Versammlung deutscher Rabbiner, *Protokolle*, 1844, p. 73. q PRM, 150.

522.E.7 Sects that do not intend to marry should not intersect.
Zangwill. q *JS*, Sept. 1954, p. 13.

522.F. Wedding

522.F.1 A man is forbidden to dwell with his wife one hour without the *ketuba* (marriage contract).
Caro, *Eben HaEzer: Ketubot*, 1565, 66.3.

522.F.2 A wedding may not be held in a festival week, because we must not mix one joy with another.
Hanina, Hoshaia, Samuel. *Talmud: Moed Katan*, 8b.

522.F.3 A groom may not enter the bridal chamber till the bride gives him permission.
Hanina. *Pesikta de R. Kahana*, 1a.
Nehunia. *Pesikta Rabbati*, ch 5, ed Friedmann, 17b.

522.F.4 Honeymoon for a month, trouble for life.
Hasdai, *Ben HaMelek VeHaNazir*, c. 1230, ch 30.

522.F.5 Every bride is beautiful and graceful.
Hillel School. *Talmud: Ketubot*, 17a.

522.F.6 Blue sky,
Young flowers—
Grander still is a comely bride!
Opatoshu, *Last Revolt*, 1952, ch 43, p. 275.

522.F.7 No powder, no rouge, no hairdo, yet a graceful gazelle!
Palestine bridal song. q Dimi. *Talmud: Ketubot*, 17a.

522.F.8 No wedding agreement without disagreement.
Simeon b. Gamaliel. *Talmud: Sabbath*, 130a.

522.F.9 A great man should not disdain to serve as best man to one of minor position. The Holy One was best man at Adam's wedding.
Talmud: Erubin, 18b. See Hama b. Hanina. *Talmud: Baba Bathra*, 75a. *Pirké de R. Eliezer*, ch 12.

523. MARTYRDOM

523.1 He was despised and forsaken of men, a man of sorrows and acquainted with grief.
Bible: Isa., 53.3. See 53.7.

523.2 For Thy sake are we killed all the day.
Bible: Ps., 44.23.

523.3 You have only the choice between Islam and death!
*Abdul Mumen, after conquest of Morocco, 1146.

523.4 All my life I wondered when I could love God "with all thy soul" [*Deut.* 6.5], even if He take my life. Now the opportunity has come. I will fulfil it with joy!
Akiba. *Talmud: Berakot*, 61b.

523.5 My dear children, if ye be called upon to suffer martyrdom, go to your death with whole-hearted joy!
Alexander Süsskind b. Moses, *Tzavaah*, 1794. AHE, 330.

523.6 A Jew would either live as a Jew or die on the cross.
Ammi b. Nathan. *Exod. R.*, 42.9.

523.7 If our time is come, let us die manfully for our brethren's sake and not leave a cause of reproach against our glory!
Apocrypha: I Macc., 9.10.

523.8 Fear not this butcher, but show yourself worthy of your brothers, and accept your death!
Apocrypha: II Macc., 7.29.

523.9 Twist hard your racks, blow your furnace hotter. I do not so pity my old age as to break the Law of my fathers!
Apocrypha: IV Macc., 5.32f.

523.10 Sons of Abraham, die nobly for righteousness' sake!
Ibid., 6.23.

523.11 Through all the torments I will show you that in behalf of virtue, the sons of the Hebrews alone are unconquerable.
Ibid., 9.18.

523.12 How sweet is every form of death for the sake of our fathers' righteousness!
Ibid., 9.29. See 17.9f.

523.13 Damned and accursed be you, Balchira, and all your powers. You cannot take aught from me save the skin of my body!
Apocrypha: Martyrdom of Isaiah, 5.9f.

523.14 Let us die rather than transgress the commands of the Lord of hosts, the God of our fathers.
Apocrypha: Testament of Moses, 9.6.

523.15 It is the pride of Judaism that the idea and the demand of martyrdom were created by it.
Baeck, *Essence of Judaism,* 1936, p. 177.

523.16 Whoever chooses to die in the service of God . . . is worthy of Divine grace in the bliss of the life hereafter.
Bahya, *Hobot HaLebabot,* 1040, 4.4, tr Hyamson, iii. 40.

523.17 The figure of the martyr . . . dates from the persecution of Antiochus; all subsequent martyrologies derive from the Jewish books.
*Bevan, *House of Seleucus,* 1902, ii. 175.

523.18 The blood shed on the Cross for the Redemption of mankind, as well as that which is shed invisibly every day in the Chalice of the Sacrament of the Altar, is naturally and supernaturally Jewish blood.
*Bloy, *Le Salut par les Juifs,* 1892 (*Pilgrim,* 245).

523.19 When persecuted, let us not be perplexed; let us love neither this world nor the praise of men nor the glory of rulers; but let him who is worthy of martyrdom rejoice in the Lord, obtaining thereby a great crown, and ending life with a confession.
Didascalia, 5.6. q *JE,* iv. 592b.

523.20 The Lord, as it were, dips His purple in the blood of every righteous martyr. On the Day of Judgment, if the nations of the world deny their guilt, the Holy One will don that royal purple, display the marks of all the victims, and give His verdict.
Eleazar b. Pedat. *Midrash Tehillim,* 9.13.

523.21 If you be told: Give your life for the sanctification of the Name, answer: I give it! Only let him cut off my head at once, not like in the (Roman) persecution, when they put glowing iron balls under the martyr's armpits and drove splinters of reed under his nails.
Hiyya b. Abba. *Pesikta Kahana,* ch 10, ed Buber, 78a.

523.22 In time of persecution, submit to martyrdom even for a slight precept.
Johanan b. Nappaha. *Talmud: Sanhedrin,* 74a.

523.23 None can take the place in heaven reserved for martyrs.
Joseph b. Joshua. *Talmud: Pesahim,* 50a.

523.24 Fear not death, for if ye die in the battle of the Lord, ye will receive your reward.
Josippon, iv. ch 20. q HPB, 55.

523.25 O Jewish people, what part of the earth has not been moistened with your blood? To our misfortune, Christ was born of you and you became the Christ of the peoples, the outraged Christ, the thorn-crowned Christ, the Christ of the pierced side and the cross, the Christ forever insulted and stricken, to whom none even gives the sponge of vinegar. O martyr people, you are beautiful with the beauty of your sorrows!
Lazare, *Notes on a Conversion.* LR, 49.

523.26 The martyrs . . . are less celebrated than the heroes who die for their country. But truly they seem to us greater. To die for one's country—what joy, what secure prize of glory! But to die for a despised and mocked creed, for a scorned idea, what obscure desolation without prize and without terrestrial joys!
Luzzatti, *Themistius,* 1885. LGF, 94.

523.27 He who sacrifices himself as a martyr, rather than acknowledge Mahomet as the messenger of God, certainly performs a most meritorious action. But if a person asks whether he is bound to give up his life in such a case, then we must answer conscientiously according to the precepts of Judaism, No. We advise him to leave a country where such religious coercion prevails.

Maimonides, *Iggeret HaShemad,* 1160.

523.28 Better slain by the sword than bereft of the Torah!

Official, *Disputation of Yehiel of Paris,* 1240. EOV, 82a.

523.29 Our twenty centuries in Europe
have the shape of a cross.
On which we have hung in disaster and glory.

Oppenheim, "Hebrews." *The Sea,* 1924, p. 526.

523.30 A glorious death in defense . . . of our laws is a kind of life.

Philo, *Ambassadors,* 29.

523.31 God forbid that we ostracize, revile or shame the Maranos.

Rashi, *Pardes,* (1220), 23d.

523.32 Better death of body than of soul! My portion is the living God!

Rimos, *Lamentation,* on day before martyrdom, 1430. AHE 247.

523.33 Martyrdom has always been a proof of the intensity, never of the correctness, of a belief.

Schnitzler, *Buch der Sprüche & Bedenken,* 1927, p. 32.

523.34 After her seven sons had been martyred by Hadrian, Miriam bat Tanhum said: "My sons, go and tell father Abraham, Be not so proud of building an altar for the offering of your son. I built seven altars and brought seven sons as burnt-offerings!"

Seder Eliyahu Rabbah, ch 28 (30), ed Friedmann, 153.
Judah b. Ezekiel. *Talmud: Gittin,* 57b.

523.35 Enough of playing the martyr! Learn to be heroes instead!

Shneor, "Medieval Days Draw Near," 1913, tr M. Samuel.

523.36 Each practice, for which Jews gave their lives, such as circumcision, is still firmly followed by them.

Simeon b. Eleazar. *Sifré,* #76, to *Deut.* 12.23.

523.37 Maranos! What a splendid record of noble deeds, . . . of triumphant suffering, is called to memory at the mere mention of the word! What powerful endurance is described in the history of these Jewish martyrs! What an inspiration to attempt even the impossible in the cause of liberty of conscience!

Sokolow, *History of Zionism,* 1919, i. 32.

523.38 When Hanina b. Teradion, wrapped in a Scroll, was being burned, he said to his daughter: "If I were burned alone, it would indeed be hard to bear; but to be burned with a Scroll—be assured that He who has regard for the Torah will have regard for me!"

Talmud: Aboda Zara, 18a.

523.39 There is not a thoroughfare in all of Rome where someone is not slain by the sword, and this wicked nation will continue to shed innocent Jewish blood. My last counsel to you is: Have a care one for the other; love peace and justice; perhaps there is yet some hope!

Yeshebab the Scribe, last words before martyrdom. *Midrash Elé Ezkera* (tr Gollancz, *The Targum,* 142).

523.40 God, whose decisions are inscrutable, desires that we die for our holy religion. Death is at hand, unless you prefer, for a short span of life, to be unfaithful to your religion. We prefer a glorious death to a shameful life. . . . Many pious men and congregations have given us this example.

Yom Tob of Joigny, charge to the Jews of York, 1190.

524. MARX

524.1 As a German and a Jew, Marx is authoritarian from head to heels.

*Bakunin. q MKM, 429.

524.2 Marx was above all a revolutionary, and his great aim in life was . . . the emancipation of the modern proletariat.

*Engels, *Farewell to Marx,* March 17, 1883. MKM, 555.

524.3 The historical materialism essential to Marxism is the total negation of the historical spirituality essential to Judaism.

Fleg, *Why I Am a Jew,* 1929, p. 77.

524.4 Marx was a Talmudist devoted to sociology and applying his native power of exegesis to the criticism of economic theory. He was inspired by that ancient Hebraic materialism which . . . never ceased to dream of Paradise realized on earth. But Marx was . . . also a rebel, . . . and he derived his gift for sarcasm and invective, as Heine did, from his Jewish ancestry.

Lazare, *Antisemitism*, (1892) 1903, p. 315f.

524.5 I, I am not a Marxist.

Marx. q *Reflex*, Nov. 1917, p. 43.

524.6 Marxian messianism suffered from the very fault which it ascribed to Jews: Marxism is too practical, too materialistic.

*Masaryk, *Grundlagen des Marxismus*, 1899, Sect. 120.

524.7 If Socialism has become scientific, we owe this to Karl Marx.

*Plehanoff. *Iskra*, March 1, 1903.

524.8 Marxism is contrary to the Torah, which protects private property.

I. J. Rabinowitz. q MGU, 131.

524.9 For all his secularization, Marx himself is a great Jewish apocalyptic prophet. Certainly Communism owes its immense vitality more to its biblical vision of the mighty put down and the poor raised up than to its theories of value or its interpretation of history.

*Ward, *Faith and Freedom*, 1954, p. 56. See p. 189.

525. MATERIAL

525.1 Ye shall no more give the people straw to make bricks.

Bible: Exod., 5.7.

525.2 Not from every pine can you a mast design.

Judah Halevi, letter to Aaron Alamani (*Diwan*).

525.3 With the same bricks one may erect . . . a palace or a prison. . . . The same letters are used in Holy Writ and heretical works.

Peretz, *A Gilgul fun a Nign*, 1901. *Alle Verk*, vi. 33.

525.4 A heap of bricks is not yet a house.

Ibid. Alle Verk, 35; LP, 239.

526. MATERIALISM

526.1 The materialist is a Calvinist without a God.

E. Bernstein, *Evolutionary Socialism*, 1899.

526.2 The educated descendants of a people which in its infancy cast aside the Golden Calf and put its faith in the invisible God cannot worthily in its maturity worship worldly distinction and things material.

Brandeis. *Menorah Journal*, Jan. 1915.

526.3 Men's ideas are the direct emanations of their material state.

Marx, *The German Ideology*, 1846.

526.4 The liver, which is bigger than, and works for, the heart, says to it: Before thinking of Torah, think of food and drink.

Midrash HaNe'elam. q *Zohar, Genesis*, 138b.

526.5 Whose God is their belly.

New Testament: Phil., 3.19.

526.6 The soul intent on corporal pleasures or external things is hammered like on an anvil.

Philo, *Posterity of Cain*, 34.

526.7 The religious materialism of the Jews springs not from disbelief but from a superabundance of faith eager for its fulfillment, not from the weakness but from the strength and energy of the human spirit which, unafraid of being defiled by matter, purifies it and uses it for its own ends.

*Solovyov, *The Jews*, 1882. *Solovyov Anthology*, 115.

526.8 Just as bad music is nothing else than organized emptiness of time, so materialistic thinking is nothing else than organized emptiness of the spirit.

Werfel, *Between Heaven and Earth*, 1944, p. 243.

527 MATHEMATICS

527.1 Arithmetic is the first of the sciences and the mother of safety.

Brandeis, letter to N. Hapgood, Sept. 25, 1911.

527.2 As far as the propositions of mathematics refer to reality, they are not certain; and as far as they are certain, they do not refer to reality.

Einstein, "Geometry and Experience," lecture before Prussian Academy of Sciences, Jan. 27, 1921. *Ideas and Opinions*, 1954, p. 233.

527.3 A Russian peasant once propounded this mathematical theory: "Four and four make eight, with this I can agree; some say that five and three also make eight—but that's a Jewish trick."

Jabotinsky, *The War and the Jew*, 1942, p. 159.

527.4 Geometry gives us the sense of equality produced by proportion. It also heals by means of fine music all that is harsh and inharmonious or discordant in the soul, under the influence of rhythm, meter and melody.

Philo, *Cherubim*, 30.

527.5 Mathematics . . . is not a continent or an ocean whose arc can be mapped out and its content defined: it is limitless as that space which it finds too narrow for its aspirations; its possibilities are as infinite as the worlds which are forever crowding in and multiplying upon the astronomer's gaze; it is as incapable of being restricted within assigned boundaries or being reduced to definitions of permanent validity, as the consciousness, the life, which seems to slumber . . . in every atom of matter, in each leaf and bud and cell, and is forever ready to burst forth into new forms of vegetable and animal existence.

Sylvester, address, Feb. 22, 1877. *Collected Math. Papers,* ed Baker, 1909, iii. 77f.

528. MATTER

528.1 Matter never becomes evil except when it is forced to conspire in secret against the usurpations of the spirit.

Heine, *Germany from Luther to Kant,* 1834.

528.2 The desirable works of this world are desirable before God, even though they are physical in character.

Judah Löw. q BWC, 77.

528.3 All material things pass away, are lost and turn into nothing, because they are not true reality.

Krochmal, *Moré Nebuké HaZman,* (1851) 1924, ch 6, p. 29.

528.4 Man's shortcomings and sins are all due to the substance of the body and not to its form, while all his merits are exclusively due to his form.

Maimonides, *Guide for the Perplexed,* 1190, 3.8.

528.5 There exists no object in the world that can completely annihilate another. Even fire . . . merely effects a separation of the parts of a thing and a reunion between each part and its original element.

Saadia, *Emunot VeDeot,* 933, 7.7. tr Rosenblatt, 278.

529. MATURITY

529.1 People look with sympathetic eyes only at the blossom and the fruit, and disregard the long period of transition during

which the one is ripening into the other.

B. Auerbach, *Little Barefoot,* 1856, ch 4.

529.2 Maturity implies otherness. . . . The art of living is the art of living with.

J. Gordon, "Growing Up Jewishly," CCAR, 1952.

529.3 "When Moses was grown up, he went out unto his brethren, and looked on their burdens" [*Exod.* 2.11]. How do we know that Moses was grown up? Because he went out unto his brethren, and was ready to bear the burdens and share the plight of his people. Maturity is sensitivity to human suffering.

Ibid.

529.4 Sound within silence, struggle within serenity, war within peace—these are the confusions that dissolve as the mind matures.

Guggenheimer, *Creative Vision,* 1950, p. 153.

529.5 One is not called *Man* before reaching the age of twenty-five.

Midrash Abkir. q *Yalkut, Exod.,* #167.

530. MEANS

530.A. Medium

530.A.1 Perfection of means and confusion of goals seem to characterize our age.

Einstein, *Out of My Later Years,* 1950, p. 113.

530.A.2 Methods and means cannot be separated from the ultimate aim.

E. Goldman, *My Further Disillusionment,* 1924, p. 174.

530.A.3 Darkness is not the road to light, dictatorship and paternalism are not the paths to freedom and independence, terror is no express train to the golden age.

H. Greenberg, "To a Communist Friend," 1936. GIE, 256.

530.A.4 God can never be saved by the devil.

Heine, *Romantic School,* ii. ch 3, 1833.

530.A.5 The character of the end depends on the character and functions of the means employed.

M. H. Luzzatto, *Mesillat Yesharim,* (1740), ch 1, p. 17.

530.A.6 A divine precept is detestable if performed by means of a transgression, as is written, "I . . . hate robbery even when committed for the sake of a burnt-offering" [*Isa.* 61.8].

Simeon b. Yohai. *Talmud: Sukka,* 30a.

530.B. Resources

530.B.1 Eat and drink below your means, clothe yourself according to your means, and honor your wife and children beyond your means.

Assi. *Talmud: Hullin*, 84b.

530.B.2 On food, spend as much as you can afford; on clothes, less than you can afford; on your home, more than you can afford.

Levi. *Gen. R.*, 20.12.

530.B.3 Be satisfied with little, and manage your household according to your means.

Nahman Bratzlav. See HLH, 98.

531. MEASURE

531.1 They shall eat bread by weight, and with anxiety, and drink water by measure, and in appalment.

Bible: Ezek., 4.16.

531.2 Everything needs measure.

Leon of Modena, *Tzemah Tzaddik*, c.1600. q CPP, #1466.

531.3 Anything can give pleasure, if you know the right measure.

Mandelstamm, *Mishlé Binyamin*, 1885, 4.1, adapted.

531.4 With what measure ye measure, it shall be measured to you.

Meir. *Talmud: Sanhedrin*, 100a. *Mishna: Sota*, 1.7. *Matt.* 7.2.

531.5 No prescribed measure for these: the corner of the field for the poor and stranger [*Lev.* 19.9], the first fruits for priests [*Exod.* 23.19], the offering on festivals [*Exod.* 23.17, *Deut.* 16.16], lovingkindness, and study of Torah.

Mishna: Peah, 1.1.

531.6 All depends on the measure.

Mishna: Baba Metzia, 3.7.

531.7 Rather measure ten times and cut once than do the reverse.

Proverb (Yiddish). BJS, #533.

532. MEDDLING

532.1 Every fool will be meddling.

Bible: Prov., 20.3.

533. MEDIATOR

533.1 If there be for him an angel, an intercessor, one among a thousand, to vouch for man's uprightness, then He is gracious.

Bible: Job, 33.23f.

533.2 A rabbi once told me, among other *heinous stuff*, that he did not expect the felicity of the next world on account of any merits but his own; whoever kept the law would arrive at the bliss, by *coming upon his own legs*.

*L. Addison, *Present State of the Jews*, 1675.

533.3 I am the angel who intercedes for the nation of Israel.

Apocrypha: Patriarchs, Levi, 5.6.

533.4 Judaism demands no mediation . . . every one shall be his own priest, his own mediator between himself and God.

A. Geiger, *Judaism and Its History*, 1865, p. 98f.

533.5 A man in trouble does not cry to an archangel, to Michael or Gabriel, but directly to God, who answers him.

Isaac. *Talmud J: Berakot*, 9.1.

533.6 Let us invoke no mediator, but direct our thoughts to God.

Maimonides, *Commentary to Mishna: Sanhedrin*, 10.1, 1168, Introd.

533.7 When we are told that the Jewish God is distant, we smile with astonishment at the strange accusation. So near is He, that He needs no Son to bring Him nearer to us, no intercessor to reconcile Him with us or us with Him.

Montefiore, *Liberal Judaism*, 1903, p. 56. See p. 203.

533.8 Since the Temple was destroyed . . . nobody prays on behalf of Israel. Upon whom then do we depend? Upon our Father in Heaven!

Phineas b. Yair. *Mishna: Sota*, 9.15.

533.9 Three keys have been entrusted to no messenger: of childbirth, resurrection, and rain.

Zohar, Gen., 102b.

534. MEEKNESS

534.1 Be not like the lintel, which no hand can reach, but like the threshold, trodden by all. When the building falls, the threshold remains.

Eleazar HaKappar. *Abot de R. Nathan*, 26.

534.2 Where the mighty swarm, God is hidden.

Hoffenstein, *Pencil in the Air*, 1923, p. 148.

534.3 Meekness is the greatest of virtues.

Joshua b. Levi. *Talmud: Aboda Zara*, 20b.

534.4 Meekness of spirit is the halo of the wise.

J. Kimhi. q Hertz, *DPB*, 915.

534.5 We shall bless them that cursed us, and we shall lift up them that pulled us down.

Lubin, letter, June 28, 1900. q ADL, 155f.

534.6 May my soul be silent to them that curse me, and be like dust to all.

Mar b. Abina. *Talmud: Berakot,* 17a. DPB, ed Singer, 54.

534.7 The meek attract the Shekina, the proud . . . drive it away.

Mekilta, to *Exod.* 20.18.

534.8 The meek do prematurely inherit the earth—six or more feet of it.

A. Myerson, *Speaking of Man,* 1950, p. 99.

534.9 The offended who do not offend, the reviled who do not revile, they who act out of love and rejoice in their trials, are "as the sun . . . in its might" [*Judg.* 5.31].

Talmud: Sabbath, 88b.

534.10 Happy is he who hears himself abused and ignores it, for a hundred evils will pass him by.

Talmud: Sanhedrin, 7a.

534.11 If ever there was a race which was forgiving to the point of flabbiness, it is the race which styles itself "the merciful, sons of the merciful," and of which I have written . . . "The only Christians in Europe, turning the other cheek."

Zangwill, *Legend of the Conquering Jew.* ZVJ, 197.

535. MEETING

535.1 Mountains do not meet, but men do.

Proverb. Source in responsa. See BDH, Note.

536. MEMORY

536.1 Remember and do all My commandments.

Bible: Num., 15.40.

536.2 Thou shalt remember the Lord thy God.

Bible: Deut., 8.18.

536.3 Remember the days of old.

Ibid., 32.7. Cf *Isa.,* 46.9.

536.4 Remember not the former things, consider not the things of old.

Bible: Isa., 43.18.

536.5 Remember unto me, O my God, for good all that I have done for this people.

Bible: Neh., 5.19.

536.6 Blessed be he that remembers what is forgotten!

Agnon, "Hemdat." *Israel Argosy,* Autumn 1952, p. 95.

536.7 Remember famine in time of fullness, and poverty and want in the days of wealth.

Apocrypha: Ben Sira, 18.25.

536.8 There are memories . . . stored below the scene illuminated by consciousness. Yes, I believe that all our past life is there, preserved even to the most infinitesimal details, and that we forget nothing.

Bergson, *Dreams,* 1914, p. 33.

536.9 The remembrance of forbidden fruit is the earliest thing in the memory of each of us, as it is in that of mankind.

Bergson, *Two Sources of Morality and Religion,* 1935, p. 1.

536.10 A scattered nation which remembers its past and connects it with the present, will undoubtedly have a future as a people and probably even a more glorious life than the one in the past.

Levanda. q WHJ, iv. 612.

536.11 Memories are all we really own.

E. Lieberman, "Violin Concerto." *N.Y. Times,* Oct. 4, 1953.

536.12 To remember much is not necessarily to be wise.

S. D. Luzzatto, *Letters,* #73.

536.13 Fatness, arrogance and money rob one of memory.

Mendelé, *Shlomé Reb Hayyims,* 1899.

536.14 Remember the virtues you lack and the faults you have; forget the good you did and the wrong you received.

Orhot Tzaddikim, 15C, ch 2.

536.15 It is well in wealth to remember your poverty, in distinction your insignificance, . . . in peace the dangers of war, on land the storms of the sea, in cities the life of loneliness.

Philo, *Special Laws,* ii. 33.

536.16 Remembrance is a gentle goddess,
Recalling joys of long ago;
Mollifying bygone sorrows
In the sunset after-glow.

Sanders, *366 Sprüche,* 1892, #233.

536.17 Man's memory is long on injustice endured, and short on injustice done.

Sanders, *Citatenlexikon,* 1899, p. 232.

536.18 It is easy to write memoirs, when one has a poor memory.

Schnitzler, *Buch der Sprüche & Bedenken*, 1927, p. 232.

536.19 Like a cloud sailing in the blue of the sky above, Judaism winds its way through history, refreshed by the memories of its hoary and holy past as by a soft breeze. To this very day the pious Jew blesses his children with the words, "The Lord make thee as Ephraim and Manasseh."

*Sombart, *Jews and Modern Capitalism*, 1913, p. 241.

537. MEMORY OF THE DEPARTED

537.1 The memory of the righteous shall be for a blessing.

Bible: Prov., 10.7.

537.2 There is no remembrance of them of former times, neither shall there be any remembrance of them of latter times.

Bible: Eccles., 1.11.

537.3 When the dead is at rest, let his memory rest.

Apocrypha: Ben Sira, 38.23.

537.4 When mentioning a righteous man, add a blessing for him.

Isaac. *Gen. R.*, 49.1. See *Talmud: Kiddushin*, 31b. *Sefer Hasidim*, #352.

538. MERCY

538.1 A throne is established through mercy.

Bible: Isa., 16.5. See *I Macc.*, 2.57.

538.2 I desire mercy, and not sacrifice.

Bible: Hos., 6.6.

538.3 Show mercy and compassion every man to his brother.

Bible: Zech., 7.9.

538.4 Mercy and truth are met together.

Bible: Ps., 85.11. See 89.15.

538.5 The merciful man does good to his own soul.

Bible: Prov., 11.17.

538.6 By clemency . . . you will lead to repentance. See Pr. 16.6.

Apocrypha: Aristeas, 188.

538.7 A man will show no mercy . . . and then plead to God for mercy!

Apocrypha: Ben Sira, 28.4.

538.8 Have compassion for all, not only men, but also beasts.

Apocrypha: Patriarchs, Zebulun, 5.1.

538.9 The glory of God is not visible except to those who are profoundly moved by compassion for their fellow-men.

M. R. Cohen. *New Republic*, Aug. 31, 1918, p. 143. *Faith of a Liberal*, 76.

538.10 If you are merciful, the Merciful will be merciful to you.

Gamaliel II. *Tosefta: Baba Kamma*, 9.30. See Judah HaNasi. *Talmud: Baba Metzia*, 85a; *Gen. R.*, 33.3. *II Sam.* 22.26.

538.11 How can he be merciful to others who is merciless to himself?

Hasdai, *Ben HaMelek VeHaNazir*, c. 1230, ch 12.

538.12 None shall add bonds or heap suffering on the troubled.

Philo. q Eusebius, *Preparation of the Gospel*, 8.7.

538.13 Who is merciful to the merciless will be merciless to the merciful.

Simeon b. Lakish. *Eccles. R.*, 7.16.

538.14. He who asks mercy for another while he himself is in the same need, will be answered first.

Talmud: Baba Kamma, 92a.

539. MERIT

539.1 The old Jewish doctrine of the "merit of the fathers" has a counterpart— the idea that the righteousness of the living child favorably affects the fate of the dead father. . . . Thus is a bridge built over the chasm of the tomb. Thus do the hearts of fathers and children beat in eternal unison.

Abrahams, 1919.

539.2 Angels came bearing baskets full of flowers. . . . And the angel said to me: These flowers are the merits of the righteous.

Apocrypha: III Baruch, 12.1, 5.

539.3 You have a treasure of works laid up with the Most High, but it shall not be shown to you until the last times.

Apocrypha: IV Ezra, 7.77.

539.4 There is no sphere in heaven where the soul remains a shorter time than in the sphere of merit; there is none where it abides longer than in the sphere of grace (love).

Baal Shem. q SSJ, i. 31.

539.5 A man's merits and demerits, earned in this world, precede him on the Day of Judgment in the world to come.

Jonathan b. Eleazar. *Talmud: Sota*, 3b. Joshua b. Levi. *Talmud: Aboda Zara*, 2a.

539.6 Who provides on land has on the sea. Who lays up merits here has treasures hereafter.

Jonathan b. Eleazar. *Pesikta Rabbati*, ed Friedmann, 198b.

539.7 He who does not himself do good, cannot depend on his father's works and merits.

Midrash Tehillim, 146.2, on *Ps.* 128.2.

539.8 Who did not earn merits in life will not benefit by what's done for him after death.

Sefer Hasidim, 13C, #35, p. 37.

539.9 Even a Jew devoid of Torah is as packed with merits [precepts] as a pomegranate is with seeds.

Simeon b. Lakish. *Talmud: Berakot*, 57a.

540. MESSIAH

540.A. Messianic Faith

540.A.1 It is the comforting and uplifting faith in Messiah which has sustained the Jews through the fateful times of oppression.

I. Deutsch, address, July 2, 1839.

540.A.2 Jews have no Messiah to expect, for they already had him at the time of Hezekiah.

Hillel b. Gamaliel III. *Talmud: Sanhedrin*, 99a.

540.A.3 The Messianic idea is the most glistening jewel in the glorious crown of Judaism!

Klausner, *Messianic Idea in Israel*, 1955, p. 25.

540.A.4 The Jewish Messianic faith is the seed of progress which has been planted by Judaism throughout the whole world.

Ibid., p. 531.

540.A.5 I believe with perfect faith in the coming of the Messiah; and, though he tarry, I will wait daily for his coming.

Maimonides, *Commentary to Mishna: Sanhedrin*, 1168, 10.1. *Thirteen Principles*, #12.

540.A.6 From this belief in the Messiah who is to come, from the certainty which they have of conquering with him, from the power of esteeming all present things of small importance in view of such a future, springs the indestructible nature of the Jews.

*Rosenkranz, *Philosophy of Education*, (1848) 1886, p. 249.

540.A.7 The existence of Judaism depends upon clinging to the Messianic hope.

Skreinka, *Entwickelungsgeschichte der jüdischen Dogmen*, 1861, p. 75.

540.A.8 Whenever anyone—prophet or deceiver—throughout the two thousand years of exile plucked this string, the entire soul of the people was brought into vibration.

S. Zweig, *The World of Yesterday*, 1943, p. 104.

540.B. Person

540.B.1 There shall come forth a shoot out of the stock of Jesse . . . He shall judge with righteousness the poor, . . . and with the breath of his lips shall he slay the wicked.

Bible: Isa., 11.1, 4.

540.B.2 The Holy One gave His robes—glory and majesty—to Messiah.

Abin. *Num. R.,* 14.3.

540.B.3 On the day the Temple was destroyed, Messiah was born.

Abin. *Talmud J: Berakot*, 2.4. See *Lam. R.,* 1.16.51.

540.B.4 Israel's last redeemer was born before its first enslaver.

Gen. R., 85.1. Ref. to Messiah and Pharaoh.

540.B.5 Messiah's name was one of seven things created before the creation of the world.

Talmud: Pesahim, 54a.

540.B.6 Messiah, who will some day punish Edom [Rome], lives there.

Exod. R., 1.26.

540.B.7 Messiah has been living in the most beautiful palace in heaven . . . but his hands are fettered with golden chains!

Manasseh b. Naphtali. q Heine, *Ludwig Boerne*, 1840.

540.C Advent

540.C.1 Each time he hears Jews groan, he tries to break his chains. . . . But God has vowed not to release him till the Jews . . . tear the chains from his hands.

Asch, *Sabbatai Zevi*, (1908), 1930, Epilogue, p. 130f.

540.C.2 The Son of David will come when all the souls destined for earthly bodies will have been born.

Assi. *Talmud: Yebamot*, 62a.

540.C.3 If you fulfill the law of kindness to birds, you will fulfill also the law of freeing the Hebrew slaves, . . . and you will thereby hasten the advent of King Messiah.
Deut. R., 6.7.

540.C.4 When you see the Powers fighting, look for King Messiah.
Eleazar b. Abina. *Gen. R.,* 42.2.

540.C.5 Messiah will come in a generation fit for extinction.
Eleazar b. Pedat. *Pesikta Rabbati,* ch 1, ed Friedmann, 4b.

540.C.6 Just before Messiah's advent, insolence will increase and honor dwindle . . . the government will turn to heresy . . . academies will become bawdy houses . . . scholarship will degenerate, piety will be scorned, truth will cease, youths will be impudent. . . and a man's enemies will be the members of his own household.
Eliezer b. Hyrcanus. *Mishna: Sota,* 9.15. Cf *Cant. R.,* 2.13.4. *Talmud: Sanhedrin,* 97a.

540.C.7 Messiah is coming now, as he has been coming in all past ages; as one of the Talmudists distinctly taught, "Messiah's days are from Adam until now."
Gottheil, 1893. *JWP,* 32.

540.C.8 The Son of David will come at a time of such want that even a fish will be unprocurable for an invalid.
Hanina. *Talmud: Sanhedrin,* 98a.

540.C.9 Messiah will come in a generation all good or all bad.
Johanan b. Nappaha. *Talmud: Sanhedrin,* 98a.

540.C.10 Grass will grow in your cheeks long before he will come!
Johanan b. Torta, to Akiba, who proclaimed Bar Kochba as Messiah. *Lam. R.,* 2.2.4.

540.C.11 The Messiah will come only when he is no longer necessary; he will come only on the day after his arrival.
Kafka, *Parables,* tr Greenberg, 65.

540.C.12 All these matters concerning Messiah's advent will not be known to anyone until they happen.
Maimonides, *Yad: Melakim,* 1180, 12.2.

540.C.13 Messiah cannot yet have come, since we see the nations actually warring and fighting as violently as possible.
Saadia, *Emunot VeDeot,* 933, 8.8.

540.C.14 No one knows about the advent of Messiah.
Sefer Hasidim, 13C, #212, p. 77.

540.C.15 When will Messiah come? "Today, if ye hearken to His voice."
Simeon b. Yohai. *Talmud: Sanhedrin,* 98a (*Ps.* 95.7).

540.C.16 The redeemer will come when men despair of the redemption.
Talmud: Sanhedrin, 97a.

540.C.17 When good and evil are finally separated, Messiah will come.
Vital. q SMT, 305.

540.C.18 Three come unawares: Messiah, a find, and a scorpion.
q Zera. *Talmud: Sanhedrin,* 97a.

540.D. The End

540.D.1 The vision belongs to the time of the end.
Bible: Dan. 8.17. See 10.4.

540.D.2 Jacob wished to reveal the end, and it was hidden from him.
Gen. R., 96.1, 98.2.

540.D.3 God adjured Israel not to seek to hasten the end.
Helbo. *Cant. R.,* 2.7.

540.D.4 Blasted be the bones of those who calculate the end, for when the calculated time comes and Messiah does not appear, people despair of his ever coming.
Jonathan. *Talmud: Sanhedrin,* 97b.

540.D.5 What delays the end? The Attribute of Justice.
Ibid.

540.D.6 Who calculates Redemption's time will have no share in it.
José. *Talmud: Tosefta Derek Eretz,* 6.13.

540.D.7 "I will hasten it in its time" [*Isa.* 60.22]. If you be worthy, "I will hasten it"; if not, "in its time."
Joshua b. Levi. *Cant. R.,* 8.14. *Talmud: Sanhedrin,* 98a.

540.D.8 All the calculated ends have already passed, and it now depends entirely on repentance and good deeds.
Rab. *Talmud: Sanhedrin,* 97b.

540.D.9 Should anyone try to tell you when the end will be, tell him, "The day of vengeance is in My heart" [*Isa.* 63.3]!
Simeon b. Yohai. *Eccles. R.,* 12.9.

540.D.10 The world was to exist six thousand years: two thousand of chaos, two thousand of Torah, and two thousand

of Messiah; but through our many sins, all these years have been lost.
Tanna debe Eliyahu. q *Talmud: Sanhedrin,* 97ab.

540.E.   In Messiah's Days

Eschatological

540.E.1   He shall open the gates of Paradise, and remove the threatening sword against Adam. He shall give to the saints to eat from the Tree of Life, the spirit of holiness shall be upon them, and all saints shall clothe themselves with joy.
Apocrypha: Patriarchs, Levi, 18.

540.E.2   Then the actual wedding will take place between God and Israel.
Exod. R., 15.31.

540.E.3   Women will bear daily. . . . Trees will yield fruit daily. . . Eretz Israel will bring forth ready cakes and woolen robes.
Gamaliel II. *Talmud: Sabbath,* 30b.

540.E.4   The Holy One will repair the damage [of Adam's sin]. He will heal the wound of the world.
Hama of Sepphoris. *Gen. R.,* 10.4. See 20.5.

540.E.5   The Tempter will lose his sway in the Messianic future.
Hiyya. *Gen. R.,* 48.11.

540.E.6   The future redeemer will, like the former [Moses], come riding on an ass, and cause manna to fall and a well to rise.
Isaac. *Eccles. R.,* 1.9. See *Exod.* 4.20, *Zech.* 9.9.

540.E.7   Messiah will throw Satan . . . into Gehenna.
Pesikta Rabbati, ch 36, ed Friedmann, 161b.

540.E.8   Said Messiah: "Lord of the universe, I accept cheerfully all trials, if only all souls be saved, not only those living in my days, but also . . . those who have passed away from the days of Adam to the present time!"
Ibid.

540.E.9   In Messiah's days I will rejoice greatly at the fall of wicked Rome, . . . the deliverance from Gehenna, the elimination of the Evil Urge, the forgiveness of sin, the abolition of the Angel of Death, and the everlasting World to Come.
Pesikta Rabbati, ch 37, ed Friedmann, 163ab, on *Isa.* 61.2.

540.E.10   In the hour of Messiah's appearance, the Holy One will don the robe of Justice.
Ibid., 163b.

540.E.11   In the Messianic age, night will become day [*Isa.* 30.26], and the primordial light will be restored.
Samuel. *Exod. R.,* 18.11. Cf *Gen. R.,* 3.6.

National

540.E.12   In the future, Israel will be subject to the yoke of no man.
Eleazar b. Jacob. *Cant. R.,* 1.5.

540.E.13   The Messianic time is the time when Israel shall will the planting of the national ensign.
*Eliot, *Daniel Deronda,* 1876, ch 42.

540.E.14   Messiah will chastise the empire [Rome].
Gen. R., 97. NV, Soncino ed, 906.

540.E.15   Messiah will restore the kingdom of David.
Maimonides, *Yad: Melakim,* 11.1, tr Hershman, xiv. 238.

540.E.16   Three days before Messiah's advent, Elijah will appear on the mountains of Israel and bewail them: "O Mountains of Israel, how long will you remain waste and desolate?!" Then will he proclaim world peace . . . and the Holy One will . . . redeem Israel.
Pesikta Rabbati, ch 35, ed Friedmann, 161a.

540.E.17   The only difference between the present and the Messianic age is our present subjection to foreign Powers.
Samuel. *Talmud: Berakot,* 34b.

Moral and Spiritual

540.E.18   In the end of days, you will return to the Lord your God.
Bible: Deut., 4.30.

540.E.19   The mountain of the Lord's house shall be established as the top of the mountains, and . . . all nations shall flow unto it.
Bible: Isa. 2.2. See *Apocrypha: Patriarchs, Levi,* 18.

540.E.20   He shall judge between nations . . . and they shall beat their swords into plowshares, and their spears into pruning-hooks; nation shall not lift sword against nation, neither shall they learn war any more.
Ibid., 2.4. *Mic.,* 4.3.

540.E.21 The wolf shall dwell with the lamb, the leopard shall lie down with the kid, the calf and the young lion and the fatling together, and a little child shall lead them.

Ibid., 11.6.

540.E.22 In the Messianic era all the peoples of the world will of their own accord take shelter under the wings of the Shekina.

José b. Halafta. *Talmud: Aboda Zara*, 3b.

540.E.23 Messiah's first message will be Peace!

José HaGelili. *Talmud: Tosefta Derek Eretz*, 2.13.

540.E.24 The essential function of the Messiah will consist in uniting and perfecting all, so that this will be truly one world.

Judah Löw. q BWC, 176.

540.E.25 When Messiah comes, war will end, God's blessing will be on all men, and none will risk his life for money.

Maimonides, *Commentary to Mishna: Sanhedrin*, 1168, 10.1.

540.E.26 In Messiah's days there will be no hunger or war, no jealousy or strife; prosperity will be universal, and the world's chief occupation will be to know the Lord.

Maimonides, *Yad: Melakim*, 1180, 12.5.

540.27 True Jews and true Christians have always expected a Messiah who should make them love God, and by that love triumph over their enemies.

Pascal, Pensées, 1670, #607.

540.F. Messianic Conceptions

540.F.1 So paradoxical is the Messianic idea that it glows as the brightest of stars on the horizon, when seen in perspective from the distance, and it turns into dust and ashes, like a glowing ember, if it is brought too close and grasped too tightly. As in the case of the God-idea itself, we must beware to resist the popular temptation to fashion earthly images of the Messiah who is the symbol of the Goal of life.

J. B. Agus. *Jewish Frontier*, July 1952, p. 6.

540.F.2 The thought underlying the Messianic conception is that the soul must not allow itself to be subjugated to anyone but God.

Baeck, *Essence of Judaism*, 1936, p. 252.

540.F.3 Israel's Messianic goal is . . . the union of all peoples in the knowledge of the One Supreme God, the unification of all mankind, and their elevation to purity and holiness.

Einhorn. N.Y. *Jewish Tribune*, June 1, 1869.

540.F.4 Those who believe in a superhuman nature of Messiah are guilty of idolatry.

M. Friedlander, *Jewish Religion*, (1891) 1927, p. 160.

540.F.5 Judaism does not hold that the Messiah redeems mankind from sin, but declares that when mankind shall have set itself free from the sway of sin through *its own powers of amendment*, and shall have matured to true moral perfection, *then*, for it, *the Messiah will have come.*

J. Guttmann, *Idee der Versöhnung*, 1909, p. 15, q BKF, 166.

540.F.6 An architect of hidden worlds, every pious Jew is, partly, the Messiah.

Heschel, *The Earth Is the Lord's*, 1950, p. 71.

540.F.7 Every Jew has within him the potentiality of a Messiah, and every Jewess that of a Mater Dolorosa.

Hess, *Rome and Jerusalem*, (1862) 1918, p. 45.

540.F.8 Israel required no Messiah in the generally accepted sense of the word because it itself suffered and agonized for its faith, . . . died for its faith and was resurrected time and again.

Holdheim. q Philipson, *Centenary Papers*, 94.

540.F.9 To the Jew, the world of the future is not a beyond, but . . . the time of oneness, . . . of the union of all men in brotherly at-oneness and of the oneness of all nature in peace.

H. Kohn, *Politische Idee des Judentums*, 1924. LR, 126f.

540.F.10 Messiah's advent has no absolution power.

Maimonides, *Iggeret HaShemad*, 1160.

540.F.11 Do not imagine that King Messiah will perform signs and wonders, . . . revive the dead, or do similar things. It is not so.

Maimonides, *Yad: Melakim*, 11.3, 1180. tr Hershman, xiv. 239.

540.F.12 If there arise a king from the House of David who . . . observes the precepts . . . prevails upon Israel to walk in the way of the Torah . . . and fights the battles of the Lord, it may be assumed that he is the Messiah. If he does these things and succeeds, rebuilds the sanctuary on its site, and gathers the dispersed of Israel, he is beyond all doubt the Messiah. He will prepare the whole world to serve the Lord with one accord.

Ibid., 11.4, tr Hershman, xiv. 240. See p. xxiii.

540.F.13 The sages and Prophets did not long for the days of the Messiah that Israel might exercise dominion over the world. . . . Their aspiration was that Israel be free to devote itself to the Law and its wisdom, with no one to oppress or disturb it, and thus be worthy of life in the world to come.

Ibid., 12.4, tr Hershman, xiv. 242.

540.F.14 The ancient Greeks and Romans tell of a golden age in the past. . . . Our Messiah alone belongs to the future. He still has to make his appearance, and not solely for the benefit of his own people. The whole world must be judged and redeemed.

Peretz, *Der Dichter*, 1910. *Alle Verk*, x. 11; LP, 310.

540.F.15 A Jew waits for Messiah to come and redeem the world from fear and pain, from the cataclysmic conflicts between rich and poor. All shall enjoy the earth. This means, in popular imagination, that bread and clothes shall grow, ready-made, on trees. Do you have more winged ideals?

Peretz, *Advice to the Estranged*. LP, 348.

540.F.16 There is no difference between the present and Messianic future with respect to poverty. "The poor shall never cease."

Samuel. *Talmud: Sabbath*, 63a, quoting *Deut.* 15.11.

540.F.17 Israel must always await the Messiah. It must never acknowledge any person or event as the complete fruition of its hopes. Indeed, the essence of Jewish Messianism is the hope in an infinite ideal.

S. Schulman. *Menorah Journal*, 1924, x. 318.

540.F.18 I make a sharp distinction between the present realities and the Messianic hope, . . . a hope which the nation cannot forget without ceasing to be a nation. A time will come when there shall be neither enemies nor frontiers, when war shall be no more, and men will be secure in the dignity of man.

Weizmann, speech, Zionist Congress, 1937.

541. MEZUZA

541.1 Consecration of the Jewish home as a temple of God . . . is the aim of mezuza, the sacred inscription on the door post [*Deut.* 6.9].

S. R. Hirsch, *Nineteen Letters*, (1836) 1899, #13, p. 120.

541.2 Some put a mezuza on the post, and "sin couches at the door."

Kalonymus b. Kalonymus, *Eben Bohan*, c. 1322, #46, ed 1865, p. 41. (*Gen.* 4.7).

541.3 Fools pervert for temporal benefit the religious duty of mezuza, of proclaiming the unity of God and the love and service due Him, as though this were an amulet.

Maimonides, *Yad: Tefillin*, 1180, 5.4.

542. MIDDLE

542.1 Keep to the middle of the road.

Bahya, *Hobot HaLebabot*, 1040, 8.3.25, tr Hyamson, iv. 97.

542.2 The way of life is like a path between two forbidding roads, one of fire and one of ice. The slightest bend in either direction is fatal. What shall one do? Let him walk in the middle.

Judah b. Ilai. *Tosefta: Hagiga*, 2.6.

542.3 Follow the middle course again and again, until it involves little effort, and by repetition becomes a fixed habit.

Maimonides, *Yad: Deot*, 1180, 1.7.

542.4 The six branches of the candelabrum in the Temple were bent toward the stem, teaching us that the mean is most honored.

Nathan. *Sifré*, #59, to *Num.* 8.2.

542.5 The middle road is really the royal road. . . . Hence virtues are means.

Philo, *Migration of Abraham*, 26.

542.6 What is now called the "golden mean" is the road that leads to golden means.

Saphir, *Badenmantel-Gedanken*. SHW, i. 376.

542.7 Men with vision walk in the middle.

Tosefta: Baba Kamma, 2.12.

543. MIDDLE AGES

543.1 In the long night of the Middle Age, religion was the polar light.

Boerne, *Der Narr im weissen Schwan, ch* 2.

543.2 Who wants to write the history of the Jews in the fourteenth century must portray a cemetery.
Güdemann, *Geschichte des Erziehungswesens*, 1888, iii. ch 1.

543.3 From the eleventh to the end of the sixteenth century, abominable years fell out, and the Jews suffered from it not a whit more than did those among whom they lived.
Lazare, *Antisemitism*, (1892) 1903, p. 122.

543.4 Above all this [medieval persecution] the genius of that wonderful people rose supreme. While those around them were grovelling in the darkness of besotted ignorance, . . . the Jews were still pursuing the path of knowledge, amassing learning, and stimulating progress with the same unflinching constancy that they manifested in their faith.
*Lecky, *Spirit of Rationalism in Europe*, 1868, ii. 271.

543.5 The whole of Europe had its Middle Age, a period of brutality and decadence in the worst imaginable sense. The Jews alone constituted a distinct exception. In spite of dispersion and oppression, which deprived them often of the simplest human rights . . . they continued, throughout that period, to cultivate their spiritual life. . . . Trouble and misery only tended to ennoble their character and to spur them to increased mental and moral effort.
*Schleiden, *Jews in the Revival of Learning*, 1876.

544. MIDNIGHT

544.1 And it came to pass at midnight.
Bible: Exod., 12.29.

544.2 At midnight I will rise to give thanks unto Thee.
Bible: Ps., 119.62.

544.3 Midnight is when the Holy One goes into the Garden of Eden to have joyous converse with the righteous there.
Zohar, Num. 193a.

545. MILITARY

545.1 A king is not saved by the multitude of a host.
Bible: Ps., 33.16. See 20.8.

545.2 Terrible as an army with banners.
Bible: Cant., 6.4,10.

545.3 The introduction of compulsory services is . . . the prime cause of the moral collapse of the white race.
Einstein, *The World As I See It*, 208.

545.4 Our soldiers have won more esteem for us than our great thinkers have won. It is a bitter reflection, but it is true.
R. Kohut, *More Yesterdays*, 1950, p. 29.

545.5 They talk about conscription as being a democratic institution. Yes; so is a cemetery.
M. London, speech, U. S. Congress, April 25, 1917.

545.6 Militarism is defeatism in the moral sphere.
H. Samuel.

546. MIND

546.1 God set the mind . . . to be man's sacred guide in all things.
Apocrypha: IV Macc., 2.23.

546.2 Who has his mind right sees all things rightly.
Apocrypha: Patriarchs, Benjamin, 3.2.

546.3 If the mind be not quite pure, actions can't be acceptable.
Bahya, *Hobot HaLebabot*, 1040, Introduction.

546.4 There is no state of mind, however simple, which does not change every moment.
Bergson, *Introduction to Metaphysics*, 1903, tr Hulme, 44.

546.5 The functions of the mind are common to the whole of humanity.
Boas, *Mind of Primitive Man*, (1911) 1938, p. 143.

546.6 A closed mind is a dying mind.
Ferber, radio broadcast, 1947.

546.7 The faith of Israel demands no abdication of the mind.
Fleg, *Why I Am a Jew*, 1929, p. 94.

546.8 To occupy the mind with Torah is to clear it of fear and folly.
Hanania Sgan Kohanim. *Abot de R. Nathan*, ch 20.

546.9 The glory of the world is commensurate with the glory of the mind which views it.
Heine, *Thoughts and Fancies*, 1869. EPP, 653.

546.10 A man's faith is not perfected till his mind is perfected.
Ibn Gabirol, *Mibhar HaPeninim*, c.1050, #211.

546.11 Your mind is rich enough in subtlety: you must enrich it also in wisdom.
Leo Hebraeus, *Philosophy of Love*, (1502) 1937, p. 13.

546.12 The mind is the Holy of Holies, and to admit evil thoughts is like setting up an idol in the Temple.
Levi Yitzhok. q BTH, i. 230.

546.13 Never, never, never will the intellect possess a monopoly over the heart.
Luzzatti, *Evolution*, Aug. 15, 1876. LGF, 210.

546.14 The intellect . . . is the link that joins us to God.
Maimonides, *Guide for the Perplexed*, 1190, 3.51.

546.15 This superiority of yours has been your degradation! You, O man, have been endowed with the advantage of an intellect . . . and thereby lost your naturalness. . . . The more searching of the heart the more errors, the more revealing of mysteries the more agonies, the more inventions the more catastrophes.
Mendelé, *Di Kliatshé*, 1873, ch 11.

546.16 Man's mind is his essence; he is where his thoughts are.
Nahman Bratzlav. See BHH, 487.

546.17 Often, when asked for a definition of "mind," I replied: If you have a mind, you know, and need not be told; and if you have no mind, no amount of explanation will help you.
Neumark, *Essays*, 24.

546.18 When mind, the charioteer or pilot of the soul, is master . . . life proceeds rightly; but when irrational sense obtains supremacy, a terrible confusion overtakes the man.
Philo, *Allegories*, 3.79. Cf *Husbandry*, 11.

546.19 The mind is the sight of the soul.
Philo, *Unchangeableness of God*, 10.

546.20 Where brains are what you need, force will not succeed.
Proverb (Yiddish). BJS, #2232.

546.21 Let the mind always rule over the heart.
Shneor Zalman, *Tanya*, 1796.

546.22 Nothing is in itself absolutely sacred, or profane, or unclean, apart from the mind, but only relatively thereto.
Spinoza, *Theologico-Political Treatise*, 1670, ch 12.

546.23 The erudite is superior to the keen dialectician.
Talmud: Horayot, 14a. See *Talmud J: Horayot*, 3.5.

546.24 Intellect obscures more than it illumines.
Zangwill, *Children of the Ghetto*, 1892, ii. ch 15.

547. MINORITY

547.1 Jews have always constituted a minority, and a minority is constantly compelled to think; that is the blessing of their fate.
Baeck, *Essence of Judaism*, 1936, p. 3.

547.2 Because it has been a minority, Judaism has become a measuring test for the height to which morality has risen upon earth. . . . For all justice is justice for the few.
Ibid., 281.

547.3 When, in 1873, I first joined the University, . . . I was made familiar with the fate of being . . . under the ban of the "compact majority." The foundations were thus laid for a certain degree of independence of judgment.
Freud, *Autobiographical Study. Problem of Lay-Analysis*, 1927.

547.4 No minority is as weak as one whose members are scattered.
Graetz. *JQRo*, 1888, i. 5.

547.5 When the ledgers of a people show red, the outlook for minority peoples is black.
Lowenthal. q Sachar, *Sufferance Is the Badge*, 9.

547.6 All revolutions are the work of a minority.
Nordau.

548. MIRACLE

548.1 Blessed be the Lord . . . who only doeth wondrous things.
Bible: Ps., 72.18.

548.2 Wonderful are Thy works, and that my soul knoweth.
Ibid., 139.14.

548.3 Elijah's great work was not that he performed miracles, but that, when fire fell from heaven, the people did not speak of miracles, but all cried, "The Lord is God!"
Baruch of Mezbizh. q BTH, i. 93.

548.4 Miracles and rites constitute no essential part of Judaism.
Darmsteter, *Selected Essays*, 1895, p. 273.

548.5 Miracles are for those who have little faith.
I. Friedman. q BTH, ii. 62.

548.6 At the very creation, the Holy One stipulated with the sea to divide and the heavens to be silent before Moses, with the sun and moon to stand still for Joshua, with the ravens to feed Elijah, with the fire not to harm Hananiah, Mishael and Azariah, with the lions not to injure Daniel, with the sky to open for Ezekiel, and with the fish to vomit forth Jonah.

Jeremiah b. Eleazar. *Gen. R.*, 5.5. See Maimonides, *Guide for the Perplexed*, 2.29.

548.7 On these matters [miracles], everyone is welcome to his own opinion.

Josephus, *Antiquities*, 2.16.5.

548.8 The Torah is not in heaven: we pay no heed to a heavenly Voice.

Joshua b. Hanania. *Talmud: Baba Metzia*, 59b.

548.9 If the people at Carmel had not proclaimed, "The Lord is God," Elijah could not have effected a miracle.

Joshua b. Levi. *Talmud J: Taanit*, 3.4.

548.10 A miracle cannot prove what is impossible; it is useful only to confirm what is possible.

Maimonides, *Guide for the Perplexed*, 1190, 3.24.

548.11 We pay no heed to one who, by miracles and wonders, seeks to refute Moses, whose prophecy was established not by signs but by revelation, which we witnessed with our own eyes and ears.

Maimonides, *Yad: Yesodé HaTorah*, 1180, 8.3. See 8.1.

548.12 If a thousand believing hasidim were to gather around a block of wood, it too would work miracles.

Mendel of Rymanov. q BTH, ii. 9.

548.13 We do not acknowledge the infallibility of miracles.

Mendelssohn, *Supplementary Remarks*, 1770. q SMM, 95.

548.14 Miracles occur, but food is rarely provided by them.

Nahman b. Jacob. *Talmud: Sabbath*, 53b.

548.15 No man can share in the Torah of Moses unless he believes that all our affairs and events, concerning the masses or the individual, are miracles, attributing nothing to the natural order of the world.

Nahmanides, *Commentary*, Introduction. q SSJ, i. 120.

548.16 God worked miracles only for the Prophets.

Samuel b. Hofni. *Shaalot uTeshubot HaGaonim*, ed 1864, #99.

548.17 God performs wonders for the righteous, as He did for the Prophets.

Hai Gaon. *Ibid*. See *Hananel* and *HaKoteb* in *En Yaakob*, to *Hagiga*, 14b.

548.18 Miracles only appear as something new because of man's ignorance.

Spinoza, *Theologico-Political Treatise*, 1670, ch 6.

548.19 Miracles cannot be cited (as proofs).

Talmud: Yebamot, 121b.

548.20 In danger, one must not rely on a miracle.

Talmud: Kiddushin, 39b.

548.21 Never depend on a miracle.

Yannai Rabbah. *Talmud: Sabbath*, 32a.

548.22 Miracles do not happen each day.

Zera. *Talmud: Megilla*, 7b. See *Pesahim*, 50b.

548.23 Miracles are not performed in halves, letting half be delivered and half be destroyed.

Zohar, Gen., 113ab.

549. MISER

549.1 To the small of heart wealth is unfitting.

Apocrypha: Ben Sira, 14.3.

549.2 Who withholds from himself gathers for another.

Ibid., 14.4.

549.3 A miser once dreamed he had
  given away
  Some bread to a beggar he'd met
    in the day;
  He woke with a start, and solemn-
    ly swore,
  That as long as he lived he would
    slumber no more.

Ben-Zeb. CHS, 159.

549.4 The niggard, like a nut, can be enjoyed only when cracked.

Dari, *Divan*. q Pinsker, *Likkuté Kadmoniyot*, #151.

549.5 Miserliness and want amount to the same.

Erter, *HaTzofé LeBet Israel*, 1858, p. 4.

549.6 The biggest miser with his money is the biggest spendthrift with his desires.

q M. Ibn Ezra, *Shirat Yisrael*, (12C) 1924, p. 82.

549.7 Soliciting a miser is like fishing in the desert.
Ibn Gabirol, *Mibhar HaPeninim,* c.1050, #583.

549.8 The miser does not own his wealth; his wealth owns him.
J. Jeiteles. *Bikkuré Halttim,* 5571.

549.9 Parsimony enriches not, and benevolence impoverishes not.
Proverb (Yiddish). See *JE,* x. 229a.

549.10 A miserly man and a fat cow are useful only after death.
Sholom Aleichem. *Sholom Aleichem Buch,* 1926, p. 350.

550. MISERY

550.1 Better death than a wretched life.
Apocrypha: Ben Sira, 30.17.

550.2 There are three whose life is no life: he who depends on another's table, who has to pass through another's apartment to reach his own, and who is henpecked.
Ben Azzai. *Abot de R. Nathan,* ch 25. Cf *Talmud: Betza,* 32b.

550.3 Great misery may lodge in a little bosom.
Heine, *Buch Le Grand,* 1826, ch 19.

550.4 One's little miseries make one realize the more the greater miseries of others.
L. Stein, *Journey into the Self,* 1950, p. 228.

550.5 Rebels are bred in misery.
Toller, *Machine Wreckers,* (1922) 1926, 3.2.

550.6 It is misery, not pleasure, which contains the secret of the divine wisdom.
S. Weil, *Gravity and Grace,* 1952, p. 145.

551. MODERATION

551.1 There should be moderation in all things.
Apocrypha: Aristeas, 223.

551.2 Temperance is most beneficial to health.
Ibid., 237.

551.3 Moderation prolongs life.
Apocrypha: Ben Sira, 37.31.

551.4 If a man abound overmuch, he sins. Sufficient are moderate means with righteousness.
Apocrypha: Wisdom of Solomon, 5.19f.

551.5 There is moderation even in excess.
Disraeli, *Vivian Grey,* 1826, 6.1.

551.6 God spare me from the imprudence of wealth and the degradation of poverty.
q M. Ibn Ezra, *Shirat Yisrael,* (12C) 1924, p. 143.

551.7 Abandon both extremes and set about the right mean.
Ibn Gabirol, *Ethics,* 1045.

551.8 Good deeds are such as are equibalanced . . . between the *too much* and the *too little.*
Maimonides, *Eight Chapters,* ch 4, ed Gorfinkle, 54. See Aristotle, *Nichomachaean Ethics,* 2.6.

551.9 Sumptuous nourishment excites to wanton debauchery.
Pseudo-Phocylides, *Nuthetikon,* 55, c. 100 B.C.E.

552. MODESTY

552.1 The noblest of all ornaments is modesty.
Eleazar b. Judah, *Rokeah,* 13C.

552.2 Man's finest virtue is that of which he is unaware.
M. Ibn Ezra, *Shirat Yisrael,* (12C) 1924, p. 96.

552.3 Diffidence is an index to nobility.
Ibn Gabirol, *Mibhar HaPeninim,* c. 1050, #176. See #335.

552.4 Diffidence and faith are intertwined.
Ibid., #178.

552.5 Modesty is meekness and wisdom combined.
Ibid., #330.

552.6 Let him who cannot be an Elijah be content to be an Elisha.
Immanuel, *Tophet VeEden,* c. 1300, 11, tr Gollancz, 34.

552.7 The brazen-faced go to Gehenna, the shame-faced to Eden.
Judah b. Tema. *Mishna: Abot,* 5.20.

552.8 A small act done modestly is a thousand-fold more acceptable to God than a big act done in pride.
Orhot Tzaddikim, 15C, ch 2.

552.9 Nothing is more precious to the Holy One than modesty.
Pesikta Rabbati, ch 45, ed Friedmann, 185b.

552.10 Beware of the modest: you have no idea with what affected pride they cherish their weaknesses.
Schnitzler, *Buch der Sprüche & Bedenken,* 1927, p. 226.

553. MOMENT

553.1 What the long process of time has slowly created, a single moment may suffice to destroy.
F. Adler, *Creed and Deed*, 1877, p. 24.

553.2 There are moments that conceal eternities in their breast.
Ehrenpreis, *Soul of the East*, 1928, p. 192.

553.3 Moments are sparks of eternity.
Hofstein, "Stepping It Out." LGP, 192.

553.4 Get up and out, my man, the day is bursting with moments.
O. Williams, "The Answer." *That's All That Matters*, 1945, p. 54.

553.5 Great moments are always outside of time.
S. Zweig, *World of Yesterday*, 1943, p. 148.

554. MONEY

554.1 Money answers all things.
Bible: Eccles., 10.19.

554.2 Money covers the shame.
Aaron Berekia, *Maabar Yabbok*, (1626) ch 14.

554.3 Money cleaves to those who handle it.
Agnon, *Haknasat Kalla*, (1922) 1931, i. 176.

554.4 If the hands are empty, the "spirit" cannot soar aloft.
Ahad HaAm, to E. Lewin-Epstein, May 16, 1909. AEL, 312.

554.5 The love of money leads to idolatry.
Apocrypha: Patriarchs, Judah, 19.1. See *NT: I Tim.* 6.10.

554.6 Cash is the best broker.
Ashi. *Talmud: Baba Metzia*, 63b.

554.7 To acquire money requires valor; to keep money requires prudence, and to spend money well is an art.
Auerbach, *Landhaus am Rhein*, 1869, i. ch 7.

554.8 Try to save something while your salary is small; it's impossible to save after you begin to earn more.
Benny. q Leon Gutterman, JTA, 1952.

554.9 Money is a wonderful thing, but it is possible to pay too high a price for it.
A. Bloch. E. R. Murrow, *This I Believe*, 1952, p. 10.

554.10 If we have no money, no one respects us.
Esther Rabbah, 2.4.

554.11 The greatest temptation is money. Men who will endure suffering, persecution and degradation for their religion seem unable to curb the passion for material gain.
Eybeshitz, *Yaarot Debash*, 1779, i. 53d. q BSJ, 335.

554.12 Money is a liberal's faithful servant and a miser's hard master.
I. Friedmann, *Imré Bina*, 1912, p. 90.

554.13 The dollar permits, the dollar forbids, the dollar elects the very ill-bred as community head.
Hagiz, *Leket HaKemah*, (1697) 1897, p. 103.

554.14 The fundamental evil of the world arose from the fact that the good Lord had not created money enough.
Heine, *English Fragments*, 1828, ch 8.

554.15 Put not all your money in one basket.
Hiyya Rabbah. *Gen. R.*, 76.3.

554.16 Some people think they are worth a lot of money just because they have it.
Hurst. q Leon Gutterman, JTA, 1952.

554.17 Money will take wing.
A. Ibn Ezra, *Commentary*, to *Exod.* 20.2.

554.18 Always keep your money in three parts: a third in land, a third in merchandise, and a third in cash.
Isaac Nappaha. *Talmud: Baba Metzia*, 42a.

554.19 All the organs depend on the heart, and the heart depends on the purse.
Johanan b. Nappaha. *Talmud J: Terumot*, 8.4.

554.20 Money legitimates a bastard.
Joshua b. Levi. *Talmud: Kiddushin*, 71a.

554.21 I must atone for my money.
O. Kahn.

554.22 It is proper to command money, not to serve it.
Leon of Modena, *Tzemah Tzaddik*, 1600. q CPP, #1522.

554.23 A small coin before the eyes will hide all from sight.
Lipkin. q KTH, i. 272.

554.24 Money degrades all the gods of man and converts them into commodities.
Marx, *Jewish Question*, 1844. *Selected Essays*, 92.

554.25 Money is man's work and being, alienated from himself, and this alien being rules him, and he prays to it.
Ibid.

554.26 Money is the best advocate.
Mendelé, *Di Alté Maasé,* 1895.

554.27 When a man marries for money, a month comes and a month goes, and the dowry is no more.
Nahman b. Isaac. *Talmud: Kiddushin,* 70a.

554.28 A small coin before the eye will hide the biggest mountain.
Nahman Bratzlav, *Likkuté Moharan,* (1806) 1936, p. 235.

554.29 Abolish the lust for money, and Messiah will come.
Ibid.

554.30 Where your treasure is, there will your heart be also.
New Testament: Matt., 6.21.

554.31 Not greedy of filthy lucre.
New Testament: 1 Tim., 3.3.

554.32 Money, it has been said, is the cause of good things to a good man, of evil things to a bad man.
Philo, *Noah's Work as a Planter,* 41.

554.33 There's no money for provision, but there is for waste.
Proverb. q Raba. *Talmud: Hagiga,* 5a.

554.34 Money won, virtue gone.
Proverb (Yiddish). BJS, #900.

554.35 Money attracts money.
Proverb (Yiddish). BJS, #912.

554.36 Money answers all questions.
Ibid., #915.

554.37 He who'll pay has the say.
Ibid., #2236.

554.38 The best friend is the dollar.
Ibid., #3001.

554.39 He who saves is worth more than he who earns.
Proverb (Yiddish). *JE,* x. 229a.

554.40 Money is an elevator-shoe to make small people appear as tall as others.
Saphir.

554.41 Money and credit are curious articles. Money is needed most when you don't have it, and credit you have most when you don't need it!
Saphir, *Badenmantel-Gedanken.* SHW, i. 377.

554.42 If you have money, you're wise and handsome, and you can sing.
Sholom Aleichem, *Olam Haba,* 1904.

554.43 As a cousin of mine once said about money, money is always there but the pockets change; it is not in the same pockets after a change, and that is all there is to say about money.
G. Stein. q CGP, 313.

554.44 Money is a hard master, but also an excellent servant.
J. Steinberg, *Mishlé Yehoshua,* 1885, 29.31, p. 159.

554.45 The Torah is considerate of Israel's money.
Talmud: Yoma, 39a.

554.46 None is in control of himself when his money is at stake.
Ibid., 85b.

554.47 No one throws money away.
Talmud: Ketubot, 36b.

554.48 All money is Mine.
Talmud: Derek Eretz, 3.3.

554.49 Your law of Nature is the law of money!
Money lends mastery to the man who gives
Another work. Not mind, not rank, but money!
. . . Money bids you crush
The Indian peoples, children of the Spring.
And money bids you spread destruction wide
Through Eastern wonderlands, with devil's brews
Of opium and brandy. Money bids you burn
The garnered store of riper lands for gain.
Toller, (Jimmy in) *Machine Wreckers,* (1922) 1926, 4.1.

554.50 Money sometimes makes fools of important persons, but it may also make important persons of fools.
Winchell. q Leon Gutterman, JTA 1952.

554.51 Money is the monomania of the century.
I. M. Wise, 1893. *JWP,* 402.

554.52 Hands that hold money must not be nervous.
Wolffsohn, to Herzl, 1900. q Cohn, *David Wolffsohn,* 98.

555. MONKEY

555.1 "O what ugly creatures there are in the world!" sighed the monkey.
J. Cahan, *Kitbé* (Tel Aviv, 5710), iii. 320.

555.2 Are not apes all good comedians?
Heine, *Atta Troll,* 1841, ch 5.

315

555.3 No notice need be taken of the nonsensical idea that monkeys were created for our pastime.

Maimonides, *Guide for the Perplexed,* 1190, 3.25.

556. MONOTHEISM

556.1 The idea of the supremacy of monotheism was no abstract idea which merely proclaimed the thought of a single God for all; it was also bound up with the dream of a future international realm of justice, liberty and peace.

Bendixon. q VA, 239.

556.2 The monotheism of Judaism is the immovable bulwark of moral culture for all future ages.

H. Cohen.

556.3 Absolute monotheism . . . is rationalism; it is the negation of all the absurdities by which the religious views . . . of the ancient nations were dominated.

Graetz. *JQRo,* 1888, i. 11.

556.4 Monotheism means not only the positive search for unity but also, negatively, the refusal to set man in the throne of God.

Roth, *Jewish Thought,* 1927. BSL, 469.

556.5 The Holy One, the Torah, and Israel are one.

Zohar, Lev., 73b, based on.

557. MONUMENT

557.1 While Nahshon lived, he badly
    wanted bread;
    Now he is gone, he gets a stone
      instead.

Benjacob, *Epitaph. Mitkamim,* 19, q CHH, 69.

557.2 Replace dead monuments with living memories.

J. Gordon, *Your Sense of Humor,* 1950, p. 210.

557.3 Let Monuments be raised to those
    alone
    Who need no Monuments of
      Bronze or Stone.

Guiterman, *A Poet's Proverbs,* 1924, p. 100.

557.4 The pious rites which it [Torah] provides for the dead do not consist of costly obsequies or conspicuous monuments.

Josephus, *Against Apion,* ii. 26.

557.5 It is unnecessary to erect monu-

ments to the pious; their teachings [words, deeds] are their memorials.

Simeon b. Gamaliel II. *Gen. R.,* 82.11. *TJ: Shekalim,* 2.7.

558. MOON

558.1 The moon was created so that the sun be not regarded a god.

Hanina. *Gen. R.,* 6.1.

558.2 The moon was created only to facilitate study.

Simeon b. Lakish. *Talmud: Erubin,* 65a.

558.3 When God created the two great lights [*Gen.* 1.16], the moon asked, "Can two kings wear one crown?" Said God, "Go, then, and make yourself the lesser, to rule the night."

Simeon b. Pazzi. *Talmud: Hullin,* 60b.

559. MORALITY

559.1 The fundamental principle of the Hebraic commonwealth was that there are great moral laws . . . not dependent upon the will of monarch, oligarchy, aristocracy, or public assembly.

*Abbott, *Life & Literature of Ancient Hebrews,* 1901, p. 111.

559.2 The bloom of human life is morality; whatever else we may possess, health and wealth, power, grace, knowledge, have a value only as they lead up to this, have a meaning only as they make this possible.

F. Adler, *Creed and Deed,* 1877, p. 24.

559.3 Judaism is not merely ethical, but ethics constitutes its . . . essence.

Baeck, *Essence of Judaism,* 1936, p. 52.

559.4 In the ethical field every man is to be a creative artist.

Ibid., 156.

559.5 Morality is the grammar of religion; it is easier to act correctly than to act beautifully.

Boerne, *Fragmente & Aphorismen,* 1840, #184.

559.6 Ethics is the vital principle of Judaism. Its religion aims to be, and is, moral doctrine. Love of God is knowledge of God, and that is knowledge of the ultimate moral purpose of mankind.

H. Cohen, *Innere Beziehungen der Kantischen Philosophie zum Judentum,* 1910. *Jüd. Schr.,* i. 303.

559.7 Moral conduct is a prerequisite to worship.

David of Talna, *Magen David,* 1852, p. 61.

559.8 As all morality that sprang from Judaism is social ethics, so all morality grown out of the soil of India is individual ethics. The one is ruled by the tendency to reform the world, the other sees the chief task of the individual in making himself free from the world.

F. Hertz, *Race and Civilization*, 1928, p. 212.

559.9 Immorality in a house is like a worm in a plant.

Hisda. *Talmud: Sota*, 3b.

559.10 Rational law demands justice and the recognition of God's bounty. What has he, who fails in this, to do with offerings, Sabbath, circumcision, which reason neither demands nor forbids.

Judah Halevi, *Cuzari*, c. 1135, 2.48.

559.11 Morality is its own reason and aim.

M. Lazarus, *Ethics of Judaism*, 1900, i. 154. #116.

559.12 If the public law of Europe is ever to deserve the title of model and exemplar for all civilized nations, it must . . . seek to reverse the old maxim of "Nothing which is useful can be unjust" for the better one of "Nothing can be permanently useful which is unjust."

L. Levi, *International Law*, 1888, p. 5f.

559.13 Science does not make us happy; the highest morality alone is capable of conferring true happiness upon us.

S. D. Luzzatto, letter to Jost, 1840. See SRH, 89.

559.14 Intellect is a broken reed to lean on; our only hope is to enjoy the practice of goodness and kindness and love.

S. D. Luzzatto, *Yesodé HaTorah*, 1880, p. 9.

559.15 It is possible to settle wine on the lees or put a moratorium on money for a while, but not to freeze ethics. . . . The attempt to arrest man's moral sensibilities leads to their obliteration. Man's moral forces must function in order to remain alert and alive; otherwise, the heart congeals and petrifies.

Magnes, 1948, *Gleanings*, 63.

559.16 Morality and beauty are in their innermost essence identical.

Nordau, *Degeneration*, (1893) 3.3, p. 328.

559.17 Morality will conquer war even as it has conquered human sacrifice, slavery, feuds, head-hunting and cannibalism.

Nordau, *Morals and the Evolution of Man*, 1920.

559.18 Man is unique, knowing of himself good and evil.

Onkelos, *Targum, Gen.*, 3.22.

559.19 The whole Torah depends on moral qualities.

Orhot Tzaddikim, 15C, Introduction.

559.20 A straight line is the shortest in morals as in geometry.

Rachel.

559.21 Moral action is the meeting-place between the human and divine.

Roth, *Jewish Thought . . . in Civilization*, 1954, p. 30.

559.22 Morality is more important than learning.

Abba Saul. *Talmud: Semahot*, 11.

559.23 Morality was made for man, not man for morality.

Zangwill, *Children of the Ghetto*, 1892, ii. ch 6.

560. MOSES

560.1 When Moses held up his hand, Israel prevailed; and when he let down his hand, Amalek prevailed.

Bible: Exod., 17.11.

560.2 The man Moses was very meek.

Bible: Num., 12.3.

560.3 There has not arisen a prophet since in Israel like Moses.

Bible: Deut., 34.10.

560.4 Moses was . . . the father of civil liberty for all humanity.

*Abbott, *Life and Literature of Ancient Hebrews*, 1901, p. 48.

560.5 [Moses], all the world is your sepulchre.

Apocrypha: Testament of Moses, 11.8.

560.6 God spoke to Moses . . . only for the sake of Israel.

Eleazar b. Ahaba. *Sifra*, to *Lev.* 1.1.

560.7 "When Moses . . . went out to his brethren" [*Exod.* 2.11], then the Holy One determined to speak to him.

Eliezer b. José. *Exod. R.*, 1.27.

560.8 Moses carried on his shoulder a stray kid back to the herd, and God said: "You who lead so tenderly a mortal's flock, will surely tend with compassion My flock!"

Exod. R., 2.2.

560.9 It was one man, the man Moses, who created the Jews.

Freud, *Moses and Monotheism*, 1939, p. 168.

560.10 That the greatest prophet left his work unfinished contains a profound truth: he must not be regarded as the Atlas who bears the whole world upon his shoulders, who completes a work without the cooperation of others. . . . It is not known where he is buried [*Deut.* 34.6], and our ancient teachers remark: "His grave should not serve for a place of pilgrimage whither men go to do honor to *one,* and thus raise him above the level of man."

Geiger, *Judaism and Its History*, 1865, p. 62.

560.11 It is in these . . . Mosaic institutions [Sabbath and land regulations] that, as in the fragments of a Colossus, we may read the greatness of the mind whose impress they bear . . . of one of those star souls that dwindle not with distance, but, glowing with the radiance of essential truth hold their light while institutions and languages and creeds change and pass.

*George, *Moses*, 1878.

560.12 Leader and servant of men! Lawgiver and benefactor; toiler toward the promised land seen only by the eye of faith! Type of the high souls who in every age have given to earth its heroes and its martyrs, whose deeds are the precious possession of the race, whose memories are its sacred heritage! With whom among the founders of empire shall we compare him?

Ibid.

560.13 He was the liberator of his people, but he spurned crowns and scepters, and did not, as many others after him did, put a new yoke on the neck from which he had taken the old one.

Gottheil, 1893, *Judaism at World's Parliament of Religions*, 160.

560.14 How small Sinai appears when Moses stands upon it! . . . There was a time when I felt little affection for Moses, probably because the Hellenic spirit predominated in me, and I could not forgive the lawgiver of the Jews his intolerance of images and of all plastic representation. I failed to see that despite his hostility to art, Moses was himself a great artist; only his artistic temperament, like that of his Egyptian fellow countrymen, was directed solely towards the colossal and indestructible. But unlike the Egyptians, he did not shape his works of art out of brick and granite. He built pyramids of men and carved obelisks out of human material. He took a poor shepherd tribe and transformed it into a people to defy the centuries—a great, eternal, holy people, God's people, an exemplar to all other peoples, the prototype of mankind: he created Israel!

Heine, *Confessions*, 1854.

560.15 Moses bore himself as a simple commoner, who desired in nothing to appear different from the crowd, save only in being seen to have their interests at heart.

Josephus, *Antiquities*, 3.8.8.

560.16 All other prophets saw through blurred lenses, but Moses saw through a polished lens.

Lev. R., 1.14. *Talmud: Yebamot*, 49b.

560.17 Moses, father of wisdom, father of the Prophets.

Ibid., 1.15. *Alphabet of Rabbi Akiba, Kuf.*

560.18 Moses with his law is most terrible; there never was any equal to him in perplexing, affrighting, tyrannizing, threatening, preaching, and thundering.

*Luther, *Table-Talk*, 276.

560.19 I believe with perfect faith that the prophecy of Moses . . . was true, and that he was the chief of the prophets.

Maimonides, *Commentary to Mishna: Sanhedrin*, 1168, 10.1. *Thirteen Principles, #7.*

560.20 Having faith in Israel's shepherd [Moses] is the same as having faith in the Creator.

Mekilta, to *Exod.* 14.31. See Judah b. Simeon. *Num. R.*, 7.2.

560.21 Moses was equal to all Israel, and all Israel to Moses.

Ibid., 18.1.

560.22 Everything that is essential to the life of the people is derived from Moses, and all laws are given in his name.

*Pedersen, *Israel*, (1920) 1926, p. 18.

560.23 Moses is the most exalted personality in ancient history.

*Ranke, *Weltgeschichte*, 1888, i. 42.

560.24 A colossus among the great mythical figures of humanity.

*Renan, *History of the People of Israel*, 1888, i. 135.

560.25 Moses refused to be at ease while his people was in trouble.
Seder Eliyahu Zuta, ch 1, ed Friedmann, 167, on *Exod.* 17.12.
Talmud: Taanit, 11a.

560.26 'Tis Moses up to heaven come,
　　To heaven come, to heaven come,
　　Through all the circles seven come,
　　To fetch the Torah down!
Simhat Torah hymn, unknown poet of Gaonic period. ZVJ 165.

560.27 Moses was the author of the great principle that the governments and religions of nations must be built upon the same basis of truth as is individual character.
I. M. Wise, "Moses," 1889. *Selected Writings,* 175.

560.28 Moses was wedded to the Shekina.
Zohar, Gen., 21b–22a. See SMT, 226f.

561. MOTHER

561.1 Eve, . . . the mother of all living.
Bible: Gen., 3.20.

561.2 You arose a mother in Israel.
Bible: Judg., 5.7.

561.3 As the mother, so her daughter.
Bible: Ezek., 16.44.

561.4 Despise not your mother when she is old.
Bible: Prov., 23.22.

561.5 Honor your mother at heart, in speech, and by action.
Elijah b. Raphael, *Tzavaah,* 18C. AHE, 305.

561.6 Show the utmost honor to your aged mother-in-law.
Elijah Gaon, *Alim LiTerufa,* 1836. AHE, 322.

561.7 When kid and leopard dwell together, daughter-in-law and mother-in-law will dwell together.
Huppat Eliyahu Rabbah. EOM, 171a.

561.8 Let me rise before the approaching Glory of God!
Joseph b. Hiyya, on hearing his mother's footsteps. *Talmud: Kiddushin,* 31b.

561.9 God could not be everywhere, so He created mothers.
Kompert. q KJL, 123; Hess, *Rome & Jerusalem,* 87.

561.10 There is no bad mother and no good death.
Proverb (Yiddish). BJS, #2153.

561.11 There is as yet no chair in Paradise for a good stepmother.
Ibid., #3706.

561.12 A daughter-in-law and a mother-in-law do not ride in the same coach.
Proverb (Yiddish). JE, x. 229a.

561.13 He who dwells with his mother-in-law for thirty days deserves a flogging.
Rab. *Talmud: Kiddushin,* 12b.

561.14 I saw a Jewish lady only yesterday with a child at her knee, and from whose face towards the child there shone a sweetness so angelical that it seemed to form a sort of glory round both. I protest I could have knelt before her, too, and adored in her the divine beneficence in endowing us with the maternal storge which began with our race and sanctifies the history of mankind.
Thackeray, Pendennis, 1849.

561.15 Imagine a young, loving mother, . . . the dearest friend, the most intimate confidante of her children, their companion in games, music, society, dress, life and thoughts. Almighty God, what a . . . sure support this is! *Such a mother is God's deputy on earth.*
Varnhagen. q KRV, 173.

562. MOTIVE

562.1 God did not reveal the reward of each separate precept, so that they may all be performed without questioning.
Abba b. Kahana. *Deut. R.,* 6.2. See *Pesikta Rabbati,* ch 23, ed Friedmann, 121b. Cf *Tanhuma, Ekeb,* 3, ed Buber, 9a.

562.2 That is not virtue which looks for a reward.
F. Adler, *Creed and Deed,* 1877, p. 19.

562.3 For commandments done not out of love and fear of God, man will receive no reward in the world to come.
Alphabet of R. Akiba (JBH, i. 23). q BKF, 73.

562.4 Be not like slaves who serve their master for a reward . . . and let the fear of Heaven be upon you.
Antigonus. *Mishna: Abot,* 1.3.

562.5 I don't want Your this world, I don't want Your world to come; I want only You.
Baal Shem. q ZRN, 137. See JE, ii. 386b; Z. E. Shapiro, *Igra de Pirka,* 5618, #2. q Berger, *Eser Orot,* 25.

562.6 I desire not Thy Paradise, heavenly or earthly; I desire only Thee, to be absorbed in Thee [*Ps.* 73.25].

Shneor Zalman, *Liḳuté Torah, Deut.* (1851) 1928, p. 25a. See Heilman, *Bet Rabbi,* 1892, i. 16a.

562.7 There is an old saying: If you wish to find out whether your motive is pure, test yourself in two ways: whether you expect recompense from God or anyone else, and whether you would perform the act in the same way if you were alone, unbeknown to others.

Bahya, *Hobot HaLebabot,* 1040, 5.5.

562.8 Say not, "I do not want forbidden food, forbidden clothes, or forbidden sexual relations"; rather say, "I do indeed want these but will not have them, because my Father in Heaven forbade them."

Eleazar b. Azariah. *Sifra,* to *Lev.* 20.26.

562.9 "Happy is the man that ... delights in His commandments" [*Ps.* 112.1]: "in His commandments," not in their reward.

Eleazar b. Pedat, or b. Shammua. *Talmud: Aboda Zara,* 19a.

562.10 Only a law fulfilled for itself is a "Torah of lovingkindness."

Eleazar b. Pedat, on *Prov.* 31.26. *Talmud: Suḳka,* 49b.

562.11 Elijah can serve God also without a world to come.

Elijah Gaon. q Brainin. *MiMizrah Umi-Maarab,* 1899.

562.12 When you erect a building, buy a vessel, or make a new garment, say, "I do it in honor of the Shekina's union with God."

Epstein, *Kitzur Shné Luhot HaBerit,* 1683 (1698), 8a.

562.13 Let all who serve the community do so for the sake of Heaven.

Gamaliel III. *Mishna: Abot,* 2.2.

562.14 Let all your actions be in the name of Heaven.

Jose HaCohen. *Mishna: Abot,* 2.12.

562.15 The conception of *simha shel mitzva,* "joy in the pious act," precludes the motivation of reward.

Güdemann, *Das Judentum in seinen Grundzügen,* 1902, p. 86.

562.16 There is no difference between those who repent out of love, and those who repent out of fear.

Hama b. Hanina. *Talmud: Yoma,* 86a.

562.17 Prompted by love is greater than prompted by fear.

Simeon b. Eleazar. *Talmud: Sota,* 31a.

562.18 An assembly dedicated to Heaven will endure, and one not so dedicated will not endure.

Johanan HaSandlar. *Mishna: Abot,* 4.11.

562.19 As the bee gathers for its owner, so Israelites accumulate merits and good deeds for the glory of their Father in Heaven.

Levi. *Deut. R.,* 1.6.

562.20 Who thinks of reward serves himself, not God.

Lipkin, *Etz Pri,* 1880, p. 26.

562.21 If doing good were recompensed with Gehenna, and doing wrong with Paradise, it would still be proper to do good.

Lipkin. q KTH, i. 271.

562.22 To serve God out of love is to fulfill the Torah. . . . But this is a high level of piety, and not every sage attains it.

Maimonides, *Yad: Teshuba,* 1180, 10.2. See *Yad: Deot,* 3.2f.

562.23 Love virtue for its own sake alone.

Philo, *Sobriety,* 3.

562.24 Who seeks reward for a deed "is an evil man" [*Prov.* 11.21].

Phineas. *Lev. R.,* 36.3.

562.25 Not the sermon is he after but the fee that comes thereafter.

Proverb (Yiddish). BJS, #1025.

562.26 I don't mean the Hagada, but the dumplings.

Ibid., #1090.

562.27 Not to *haroses* do they incline but to the four cups of wine.

Ibid., #1603.

562.28 Engage in Torah and charity even with an ulterior motive, for the habit of right doing will lead also to right motivation.

Rab. *Talmud: Pesahim,* 50b.

562.29 It were better that he, who practices virtue not for its own sake, had never been born.

Raba. *Talmud: Beraḳot,* 17a.

562.30 Not out of love for Mordecai, but out of hatred for Haman.

Raba. *Talmud: Megilla,* 16a.

562.31 Make a vest, or verse—
If 'tis done for hire,
It is done the worse.

M. Rosenfeld, "For Hire," tr Stokes & Frank.

562.32 If one serves God out of love, not for reward, even Satan becomes his advocate.
Sefer Hasidim, 13C, #15, p. 17.

562.33 Fear of punishment is a much stronger motive than desire for reward.
Ibid., #411, p. 123.

562.34 Say not, I will study Torah to become rich, or to be called Rabbi, or to obtain reward.
Sifré, #41, to *Deut.* 11.13.
Talmud: Nedarim, 62a.

562.35 Fear must not motivate a decision.
Simeon b. Gamaliel II. *Talmud: Sabbath*, 13a.

562.36 To seek justice for the sake of personal gain is adultery.
Tanhum b. Hiyya. *Pesikta Rabbati*, ch 22.

562.37 Men erect synagogs and colleges, and place there richly adorned Scrolls, not for the glory of God, but to make themselves a name. Hence, the powers of evil prevail over Israel.
Zohar, Gen., 25b.

562.38 God takes account of a good motive.
Ibid., 28b.

562.39 Worship inspired by fear is worship, but it does not rise to the highest part of the supernal sphere. That is reserved for worship inspired by love.
Zohar, Exod., 216a.

563. MOURNING

563.1 Reason would not have us grieve for the dead, who are set free from evil, but all men do grieve over them, because they think of themselves and of their own advantage.
Apocrypha: Aristeas, 268.

563.2 Let your weeping be bitter and your wailing passionate; make mourning such as befits him: a day or two on account of gossip—and be consoled on account of your sorrow.
Apocrypha: Ben Sira, 38.17.

563.3 Woe to the losers, not to the lost:
     He is at rest, we're the distressed.
Bar Abin. *Talmud: Moed Katan*, 25b.

563.4 It seems to me as if the entire people of Israel has been sitting for two thousand years and weeping over graves.
Feierberg, *LeOn?* 1898.

563.5 Who does not patiently subdue his mourning prolongs his grief.
Ibn Gabirol, *Mibhar HaPeninim*, c. 1050, #144.

563.6 All go to the house of mourning and each weeps over his own sorrow.
Ibn Shuaib, *Olat Shabbat*, 1469, #53.

563.7 Everyone who mourns Jerusalem will see its joy, and everyone who mourns it not will not see its joy.
Johanan, on *Isa.* 66.10. *Midrash Zuta, Eka*, #28, ed Buber, 1894, p. 74.

563.8 Blessed are they that mourn, for they shall be comforted.
New Testament: Matt., 5.4.

563.9 On the day of a funeral, a mourner is forbidden to eat of his own bread.
Rab. *Talmud: Moed Katan*, 27b.

563.10 No mourning rites on the Sabbath.
Samuel. *Talmud: Moed Katan*, 24a.

563.11 He who witnesses the parting of a soul, or the burning of a Scroll, must rend his garments in mourning.
Simeon b. Eleazar. *Talmud: Sabbath*, 105b.

563.12 They used to carry food to the house of mourning, the rich in silver and gold baskets, the poor in wicker baskets. Then, in deference to the poor, all had to carry in wicker baskets.
Talmud: Moed Katan, 27a.

563.13 What is the measure of mourning? Three days for weeping, seven for lamenting, and thirty for abstaining from a haircut and pressed clothes. Thereafter, the Holy One says: Ye are not more compassionate toward the departed than I am.
Ibid., 27b.

564. MOUTH

564.1 Set a guard, O Lord, to my mouth.
Bible: Ps., 141.3.

564.2 A fool's mouth is his ruin.
Bible: Prov., 18.7.

564.3 Your own mouth condemns you.
Bible: Job, 15.6.

564.4 The heart of fools is in their mouth, but the mouth of the wise is in their heart.
Apocrypha: Ben Sira, 21.26.

564.5 As you enclose your vineyard with thorns, so make doors and bolts to your mouth.
Ibid., 28.24.

564.6 Blessed is he whose mouth is mercy and gentleness.

Apocrypha: II Enoch, 42.13.

564.7 The mouth is a door, and should be kept closed.

Bahya b. Asher, Kad HaKemah, 14C, p. 3.

564.8 Nature has given us two ears, but only one mouth.

Disraeli, Henrietta Temple, 1837, 6.24.

564.9 We have a table, knife and meat; all we need is a mouth to eat!

Johanan. T: Kiddushin, 46a.

564.10 Does not God a heart demand, and not a shouting mouth?

Lonzano, Tokahat Musar, 1572, Canto 3, line 229. Ref. to cantors.

564.11 From a man's mouth we can tell who he is.

Proverb. q Zohar, Numbers, 187a.

564.12 Give your ear to all, your hand to a friend, but your mouth only to your wife.

Proverb (Yiddish). BJS, #84.

564.13 His power is only with his mouth.
Rashi, Commentary, Isaiah, 41.14.

564.14 Were I at Sinai, I would have asked God for two mouths, one for its ordinary functions, and one for Torah. On second thought, however, I feel, since the world is being ruined by man's one mouth, how frightfully worse it would be if he had two mouths!

Simeon b. Yohai. TJ: Berakot, 1.2.

564.15 Prayer is the mighty weapon of the mouth. Why is Israel called "worm" [Isa. 41.14]? The worm's only weapon is its mouth, but with it, it fells mighty cedars.

Tanhuma, Beshallah, #9, 111a.

564.16 The mouth that forbids is the mouth that permits.

Tosefta: Eduyot, 3.6. Tohorot, 8.5.

564.17 Israel's only power to prevail is in its mouth.

Zohar, Genesis, 178a.

565. MUCK

565.1 Whichever way you rake the muck, it remains muck.

Yitzhak Meir of Ger. See Buber, Way of Man, 36.

566. MUD

566.1 Long live the world of mud!
J. Cahan, "The Frogs," 1902, tr M. Samuel. FJA, 367.

566.2 When we in mud descended,
    Soon we understood each other.
Heine, Return Home, 1823, #91.

566.3 The year is lush when Tebeth has slush.

Hisda. Talmud: Taanit, 6b.

567. MULTITUDE

567.1 Thou shalt not follow a multitude to do evil.

Bible: Exod., 23.2.

567.2 Multitudes, multitudes in the valley of decision!

Bible: Joel, 4.14.

567.3 To lose one's self in the multitude, body and soul, is one of the elemental human passions.

Wolfson, "Escaping Judaism." Menorah Journal, 1921, vii. 159.

568. MURDER

568.1 Thou shalt not murder.
Bible: Exod., 20.13.

568.2 Who sheds blood destroys the divine image.

Akiba. Tosefta: Yebamot, 8.4.

568.3 He who kills an innocent person is responsible for the blood of all the victim's potential descendants to the end of time.

Mishna: Sanhedrin, 4.5, comment on Gen. 4.10.

568.4 Be killed, and kill not. Is your blood redder than his?

Raba, to one ordered, on pain of death, to kill another. Talmud: Pesahim, 25b.

568.5 Shelter not a fleeing murderer, be he Jew or Gentile.

Sefer Hasidim, 13C, #181, p. 72. Cf Tarfon. Nidda, 61a.

569. MUSIC

569.A. Evaluation

569.A.1 Where there's music, pour not out talk.

Apocrypha: Ben Sira, 32.4.

569.A.2 As a seal of carnelian on a necklace of gold is a concert of music at a banquet of wine.

Ibid., 32.5f. See Opatoshu, Last Revolt, ch 43, p. 274.

569.A.3 Music is a universal language, and needs not be translated. With it soul speaks to soul.

B. Auerbach, Auf der Höhe, 1865.

569.A.4 Music washes away from the soul the dust of everyday life.
B. Auerbach.

569.A.5 Music is prayer. Whether uttered by a child in its stammering, or by a crude person in crude speech, or by the cultivated in ardent, witty words, Heaven hearkens to them with equal love and returns to each as a text the echo of his feelings.
Boerne.

569.A.6 O Music! miraculous art! . . . A blast of thy trumpet, and millions rush forward to die; a peal of thy organ, and uncounted nations sink down to pray.
Disraeli, *Contarini Fleming*, 1832.

569.A.7 The essence of music is a revelation. . . . It is spirit, yet in need of time, rhythm; it is matter, yet independent of space.
Heine, *Letters on the French Stage*, 1837, #9.

569.A.8 Hidden in a brief adagio
There is a sermon on the transient hour;
And lured from inner depths by sweep of bow
May be a vision of the perfect flower,
Immortal blossom of divine intent
Whose humblest seed explains the firmament.
Lieberman, "Violin Concerto." *N.Y. Times*, Oct. 4, 1953.

569.A.9 Each science, religion, philosophy, even atheism, has its particular song. The loftier the religion or science, the more exalted is its music.
Nahman Bratzlav, *Likkuté Moharan*, (1806) 1874, 18a.

569.A.10 Music evokes the spirit of prophecy.
Ibid., 62b (1936, p. 145).

569.A.11 There are palaces that open only to music.
Tikkune Zohar, 13C, ch 11, p. 266.

569.A.12 In the high spheres there are temples which may be opened only with music.
Shneor Zalman, q Teitelbaum, *HaRab MeLadi*, i. 20.

569.A.13 There are places that open only to music.
Zeitlin, *Orot. HaTekufa*, 1919, iv. 525.

569.A.14 Stronger is music than death.
Werfel, *Poems*, tr E. A. Snow, *The Beyond*, 1945.

569.B.   In Nature

569.B.1 Sing, O heaven, be joyful, O earth, and break forth into singing, O mountains!
Bible: Isa., 49.13.

569.B.2 The morning stars sang together.
Bible: Job, 38.7.

569.B.3 The righteous should sanctify himself so that the Shekina sings from his throat.
Elimelek, *Noam Elimelek*, (1787) 1942, p. 220.

569.B.4 Nature is saturated with melody; heaven and earth are full of song.
Nahman Bratzlav. q HLH, 97.

569.B.5 The whole world is nothing more than a singing and a dancing before the Holy One, blessed be He. Every Jew is a singer before Him, and every letter in the Torah is a musical note.
Nathan b. Naphtali Herz. q Peretz. SPG, 180.

569.B.6 Grasshoppers are said to live on air because, I suppose, their singing makes their lack of food a light matter.
Philo, *Contemplative Life*, 4.

569.C.   Song

569.C.1 This song shall testify before them as a witness.
Bible: Deut., 31.21.

569.C.2 My song is my strength, the strength of rocks.
Ezobi, *Kaarat Kesef*, 1270. *JQRo*, viii. 535.

569.C.3 Song is a faithful messenger.
M. Ibn Ezra, *Selected Poems*, p. 15.

569.C.4 The inner history of a people is contained in its songs.
Jellinek. *Der Orient*, 1844, p. 669.

569.C.5 Who sings in this world will sing also in the next.
Joshua b. Levi. *Talmud: Sanhedrin*, 91b.

569.C.6 Through true song one may rise to the power of prophecy.
Opatoshu, *In Polish Woods*, 1921, p. 162.

569.C.7 Song charms away the passions.
Philo, *Special Laws*, i. 62.

569.C.8 The ears that listen to song should be torn away.
Rab. *Talmud: Sota*, 48a.

569.C.9 Where there's song in a house, there's ruin on its threshold.
Raba. *Ibid.*

569.C.10 With the daily rejuvenation of the world new songs are created.
Yitzhak Meir. q *HaOlam,* 1908; Idelsohn, *Jewish Music,* 415.

569.C.11 Beware of singers, they are mostly thieves; trust no word of theirs, for they are liars; they dally with women, and long after other people's money.
Zabara, *Sefer Shaashuim.* q Abrahams, *Book of Delight,* 41.

569.D. Melody

569.D.1 Whatever the tune, the fool won't hear it.
Berekia. *Lam. R.,* Proem 12.

569.D.2 Who reads Scripture without chanting and studies the sages without melody is "not good" [*Ezek.* 20.25].
Johanan b. Nappaha. *Talmud: Megilla,* 32a.

569.D.3 All melodies come from the source of sanctity.
Nahman Bratzlav, *Likkuté Moharan,* (1806) 1874, 54a.

569.D.4 There are melodies that must have words . . . and melodies that sing themselves without words. The latter are of a higher grade. But these, too, depend on a voice and lips, . . . hence are not yet altogether pure, not yet genuine spirit. Genuine melody sings itself without a voice. It sings inside, within the heart, in man's very entrails!
Peretz, *Mekubolim,* 1906. *Alle Verk,* vi. 53. See LP, 227.

569.E. Religious Music

569.E.1 Sing unto the Lord, for He has done gloriously.
Bible: Isa., 12.5.

569.E.2 O sing unto the Lord a new song.
Bible: Ps., 98.1. See 100.2.

569.E.3 I will sing unto the Lord as long as I live.
Ibid., 104.33.

569.E.4 The individual may pray in prose or even in wordless silence; a congregation must sing or disband.
Abrahams, *Poetry and Religion,* 1920, p. 22.

569.E.5 "I will open my riddle with the harp" [*Ps.* 49.5]—by means of songs and hymns I open the larger world of mystery.
Elimelek, *Noam Elimelek,* (1787) 1942.

569.E.6 Cultivate song and music in our synagogs.
Leon of Modena, letter, 1623. KTJ, 418.

569.E.7 Song is obligatory in the ritual of the sanctuary.
Samuel. *Talmud: Arakin,* 11a.

569.E.8 Do these bought singers reach
    His favor?
And is His ear arrested by these
    paid praises?
Or are they not as hired
    mourners
Whose wailings measure the
    purse not the pulse of the be-
    reaved?
J. S. Untermeyer, "On Temples." *Dreams Out of Darkness,* 1912, p. 19f.

569.E.9 Fear and faith and song go together.
Zeitlin, *Orot. HaTekufa,* 1919, iv. 526, on *Exod.* 14.31–15.1.

569.F. Jewish Music

569.F.1 Sweet are the songs of Israel (The sweet singer of Israel).
Bible: II Sam., 23.1.

569.F.2 Every people has its own melody. . . . But Israel sings all of them, in order to bring them all to God.
Abraham Yaakov. q BTH, ii. 71.

569.F.3 The Jewish *scherzo* in fact is little more than an *adagio.*
H. Adler. q Sterling, *Jew and Civilization,* 181.

569.F.4 In my work termed "Jewish" . . . I have but listened to an inner voice, deep, secret, insistent, ardent, . . . a voice which surged up in me on reading certain passages in the Bible. . . . This entire Jewish heritage moved me deeply, it was reborn in my music.
Bloch. q Mary Tibaldi-Chiesa. *Musica Hebraica,* 1938.

569.F.5 There exists no music that is distinctly Jewish.
Ewen. *Reflex,* Sept. 1927, p. 45.

569.F.6 Wherever a Jewish group maintained Jewish spiritual culture, there Jewish song was cultivated.
Idelsohn, *Jewish Music,* 1929, p. 492.

569.F.7 Of that medieval music of ours, the poet's words are true: "It rejoices so pathetically, it laments so joyously."
Karpeles, *Jewish Literature,* 1895, p. 375.

569.F.8 When does a Jew sing? When he's hungry.

Mendelé, *Travels of Benjamin III*, 1878.

569.F.9 The cruel suffering of the Jews is piteously told in their music, and I am carried back to my mother's knees when I hear it.

Remenyi. q Kowalsky. *Edouard Remenyi*, 1906, p. 55.

569.F.10 Jewish music must satisfy the musical demands while remaining Jewish; and it should not be necessary to sacrifice the Jewish characteristics to artistic forms.

Sulzer, *Shir Zion*, i. 1838, Preface. q Idelsohn, *Jewish Music*, 249.

570. MYRTLE

570.1 A myrtle among reeds is still a myrtle.

Proverb. q Abba b. Zabda. *Talmud: Sanhedrin*, 44a.

571. MYSTERY

571.1 The secret things belong to the Lord our God.

Bible: Deut., 29.28.

571.2 There are three things which are too wonderful for me, yea, four which I know not: the way of an eagle in the air, the way of a serpent upon a rock, the way of a ship in the midst of the sea, and the way of a man with a young woman.

Bible: Prov., 30.18f.

571.3 Seek to know only what has followed Creation, not what preceded it.

Bar Kappara. *Gen. R.*, 1.10. Cf 8.2.

571.4 All is mystery; but he is a slave who will not struggle to penetrate the dark veil.

Disraeli, *Contarini Fleming*, 1832.

571.5 The fairest thing we can experience is the mysterious. It is the fundamental emotion which stands at the cradle of true art and true science. He who knows it not and can no longer wonder, no longer feel amazement, is as good as dead. . . . It was the experience of mystery . . . that engendered religion.

Einstein, *The World As I See It*, 1934, p. 5.

571.6 The revealed aspect of Torah is holy, and its mystery aspect is the Holy of Holies.

I. Horowitz, *Shné Luhot HaBerit*, (1649), 8ṫa.

571.7 How doth my soul within me yearn . . .
Thy secret mysteries to learn!

Judah HeHasid, *Hymn of Glory*, c. 1200, tr Lucas.

571.8 Why does the Bible begin with the letter *beth* [ב]? Because just as *beth* is closed on all sides but one, so you may not investigate what is above or below or behind Creation, but only what has been since Creation.

Levi. *Talmud J: Hagiga*, 2.1.

571.9 We are deceived by localisms and the accidental. . . . Because we live through most of the day, we fasten our wonderment on night. Because most of the great poets have been men, it is women that have been thought to be the mystery. But Adam is not less a riddle than Eve.

S. Levin, *Youth in Revolt*, 1930, p. 273.

571.10 How God rules the universe . . . is a complete mystery.

Maimonides, *Guide for the Perplexed*, 1190, i. 72.

571.11 It were better if he, who speculates on what is above, beneath, before or after, had never come into the world.

Mishna: Hagiga, 2.1.

571.12 Moses banished from the sacred legislation the lore of occult rites and mysteries and all such imposture and buffoonery.

Philo, *Special Laws*, i. 59.

571.13 What a dark world—who knows?—
Ours to inhabit is!
One touch and what a strange
Glory burst on us,
What a hid universe!

Zangwill, *Blind Children*, 1903.

572. MYSTICISM

572.1 Judaism is unquestionably and supremely a religion of reason. But, paradoxically enough, it only made its appeal to the Jew and held him tightly in its grip because he was—and is—by nature and inclination a mystic. . . . The Jew believed and lived not by logic but by love, not by ratiocination but by intuition. It was by these standards that he was led
To one changeless Life in all the Lives,
And in the Separate, One Inseparable.

Abelson, *Zohar*, ed Soncino, 1949, Introd., p. xxvi.

572.2 Mysticism is nothing but an over-whelming concentration of religious feeling.

Agus, *Banner of Jerusalem*, 1946, p. 228.

572.3 Jewish mysticism is never release from will or . . . from self; on the contrary it is a doctrine of the most intense moral activity. . . . Jewish mysticism is not pantheistic. . . . God and the world are never identified. . . . What distinguishes Jewish mysticism is rather that it enlarges man . . . so that the effect of his action reaches the infinite, so that his ethical act also becomes a cosmic act.

Baeck, *The Pharisees*, 1947, p. 98f.

572.4 The culmination of mysticism is an entry into contact . . . with the creative effort manifested by Life. . . . Plotinus . . . said, "Action is a weakening of contemplation." He remained faithful to Hellenic intellectualism. . . . In short, mysticism, in the absolute sense . . . was never attained by Greek thought.

Bergson, *Two Sources of Morality and Religion*, 1935, 209f.

572.5 No current of thought or feeling has contributed so much as the thought and feeling of Jewish prophets to arouse the mysticism which we call complete. . . . The reason is that, if other currents carried certain souls towards a contemplative mysticism . . . pure contemplation they remained, and nothing more. To cover the interval between thought and action an impetus was needed. . . . We find this impetus in the prophets.

Ibid., 229.

572.6 Religion is to mysticism what popularization is to science.

Ibid., 227.

572.7 When the mystical Jew dies, the Jew is dead.

W. Frank, *Our America*, 1919.

572.8 I myself am just at present a Mystic, following the advice of my physician to avoid stimulants to thought.

Heine, *Harz Journey*, 1824.

572.9 Man is by nature a mystic.

Kook, *HaMahshaba HaYisraelit*, 1920, p. 26.

572.10 Expanses, expanses,
Expanses divine, my soul doth crave.
Enclose me not in cages
Of matter or mind.

Through heavenly vastness my soul doth soar
Unfenced by walls of heart
Or walls of deed—
Of ethics, logic, or mores—
Above all these it soars and flies,
Above the expressible and nameable,
Above delight and beauty.

Kook. *Zikaron*, 1945, p. 17. q ABJ, 130.

572.11 Mystics . . . are enemies to society of the direst kind.

Nordau, *Degeneration*, (1893) 5.2, p. 557.

572.12 Tell me, ye mystics, if these things are good and profitable, why do you shut yourselves up in profound darkness and reserve their benefits for three or four alone, when by producing them in the market-place you might extend them to every man and thus enable all to share . . . a better and happier life?

Philo, *Special Laws*, i. 59.

572.13 I saw the mystic dance of flesh and flame.

Stampfer, *Jerusalem Has Many Faces*, 1950, p. 37.

573. MYTHOLOGY

573.1 Judaism . . . is fundamentally opposed to mythology.

Baeck, *Essence of Judaism*, 1936, p. 84.

573.2 The history of the development of the religion of Israel is the memory of its holy wars against mythology.

Neumark, *Toldot HaPilosofia*, 1921, i. 3. q AMP 387.

573.3 Not only wealth and glory and the like are idols and unsubstantial shadows, but also those personages which the myth-makers invented. . . . To promote the seductiveness they have fitted the falsehood into melody, meter and rhythm. Further, they have brought in sculpture and painting to cooperate in the deception.

Philo, *Special Laws*, i. 5. See *Giants*, 13.

574. NAME

574.1 As is his name, so is he.

Bible: 1 Sam., 25.25.

574.2 A name better than sons and daughters.

Bible: Isa., 56.5.

574.3 A good name is rather to be chosen than great riches.

Bible: Prov., 22.1.

574.4 A good name is better than precious ointment.
Bible: Eccles., 7.1.

574.5 What is a good pedigree? A good name.
Al-Harizi, *Tahkemoni,* c. 1220, ch 34.

574.6 A name endures while beauty wanes.
Apocrypha: Ahikar, 2.49.

574.7 There are some who have left a name behind them.
Apocrypha: Ben Sira, 44.8.

574.8 Whenever my opponents see themselves in danger of foundering on the rock of Boerne, . . . they throw out as their sheet-anchor the name of Baruch.
Boerne, *Menzel der Franzosenfresser,* 1836.

574.9 Every man has three names: one his father and mother gave him, one others call him, and one he acquires himself.
Eccles. R., 7.1.3.

574.10 No monument gives such glory as an unsullied name.
Eleazar b. Judah, *Rokeah,* 13C. ZEH, 13.

574.11 One's name has an influence on one's life.
Eleazar b. Pedat. *Talmud: Berakot,* 7b.

574.12 Who aggrandizes his name loses his name.
Hillel. *Mishna: Abot,* 1.13.

574.13 As long as time endures, there will always be royally enthroned the names of Abraham, Moses, Isaiah.
Joel Jacoby, "Klagen eines Juden," 1837, p. 28. q LGS, 53.

574.14 Happy is he who grew up with a good name, and departed this world with a good name.
Johanan. *Talmud: Berakot,* 17a.

574.15 The earned name is worth much more than the given name.
Phineas b. Hama. *Eccles. R., 7.4.*

574.16 If unjust hatred clings to our name, should we not, instead of denying it, use all our strength to secure honor for it?
Riesser. q Baron. *Liberal Judaism,* April 1945, p. 9.

574.17 A Jew should not accept the name of a heathen idol or saint.
Sefer Hasidim, 13C, #195, p. 74.

574.18 Your name Mark does not fit you at all. Forsooth, your name is Mordecai; and what nobility and heroism are in that name!
*Stasov, to Antokolski, 1897, reported by Joel Engel to Jacob Weinberg. q *HaDoar,* Sept. 7, 1951, p. 735.

574.19 When a man supplicates God, he should identify himself with certainty; hence he mentions his mother's name, not his father's.
Zohar, Gen., 84a.

574.20 A change of name acts as an atonement for sin.
Ibid., 133b.

575. NATION

575.A. Definition

575.A.1 A nation is a totality of men united through community of fate into a community of character.
O. Bauer, *Die Nationalitätsfrage,* 1907, p. 135.

575.A.2 A nation is best defined as a people possessing a developed national consciousness.
F. Hertz, *Nationality in History and Politics,* 1944, p. 23.

575.A.3 A nation is a historical group of men of recognizable cohesion, held together by a common enemy.
Herzl, *The Jewish State,* 1896.

575.B. Character

575.B.1 The nations are as a drop of a bucket, and are counted as the small dust of the balance.
Bible: Isa., 40.15.

575.B.2 What is national existence if not the existence of a national spirit? What is a nation's importance if not the importance of the spiritual treasures it has added to human culture?
Ahad HaAm. *HaShiloah,* 1902, vi. 377.

575.B.3 Individuals may form communities, but it is institutions alone that can create a nation.
Disraeli, speech, Manchester, 1866.

575.B.4 A nation is a work of art and a work of time.
Disraeli, *The Spirit of Whiggism,* 1836.

575.B.5 Pleasure, pride, dominion and superstition, these are the four afflictions which corrupt the spirit of a nation. . . . The essence of nationality is the essence of a people's spirituality.
Krochmal, *Moré Nebuké HaZman,* (1851) 1924, ch 7, p. 36.

575.B.6 A nation is just as sacred as an individual.

Syrkin, "International." *Idisher Kempfer,* 1916. SGZ, ii. 223.

576. NATIONALISM

576.A. General

576.A.1 The new nationalism adopted by America proclaims that each race or people, like each individual, has the right and duty to develop, and that only through such differentiated development will high civilization be attained.

Brandeis, *True Americanism,* July 4, 1915.

576.A.2 Internationalism of the ordinary variety, which ignores entirely the facts and potentialities of nationhood, is a structure built on thin air. Like a harp with many strings, mankind has many national characteristics, out of the scale of whose tonalities great music is made, not by dissolving these characteristics into nothingness.

Brod. *Jewish Frontier,* July 1940, p. 27.

576.A.3 Nationalism is an infantile disease. It is the measles of mankind.

Einstein, to George Sylvester Viereck, 1921.

576.A.4 National memories lie deeper in man's heart than we generally imagine.

Heine, *Norderney,* 1826.

576.A.5 It is impossible to reach the level of moral perfection without the wholehearted love of one's nation.

Kook. *Azkara,* 1937, i. 90.

576.A.6 Since mankind is not a hodgepodge, not even *tutti-frutti,* but a garden, we shall have to put up with the fact that not all trees have the same bark.

Landauer, 1913. *Sein Lebensgang,* 1929, i. 450. q LGS, 234f.

576.A.7 Nationalism means two things which liberalism must deny: the complete subjugation of the individual to the group and the predominance of the interest of the group over the claims of humanity.

Mattuck. WUPJ *Bulletin,* #20, Sept. 1948, p. 6.

576.A.8 All nationalism is bad which turns out to be an ultimate value in and by itself; nationalism can . . . be good while serving a higher value and aim than itself.

E. Simon. *Jewish Social Studies,* Oct. 1952, p. 371.

576.A.9 Those who favor love of one's nation set a ladder on the ground, whose top reaches the heavens, and they go up rung by rung until they reach the top, while those who advocate love of all humanity wish to leap up to heaven in one bound.

Smolenskin, *Maamarim,* 1925, i. 17. q SHR, 238.

576.A.10 The time will come when national pride will be looked upon as selflove or other vanity is now, and war as brawling.

Varnhagen. q KRV, 196.

576.B. Jewish

576.B.1 The Prophets of Israel saw the Return from the Captivity . . . as part of the universal ideal of world peace. . . . Religion and nationality are fused in Judaism, and Jewish nationalism is historically an aspect of . . . Judaism.

Bentwich. London *Jewish Chronicle,* 1937.

576.B.2 Jewish nationalism generates in the people . . . a mighty affirmation of life, and with it a sense of unshakable rootedness.

Blumenfeld. *Jüdische Rundschau,* Sept. 9, 1915.

576.B.3 The nationality of the Jews came to a beautiful and enviable end: it turned into universalism.

Boerne, letter, Feb. 2, 1833.

576.B.4 The Jewish nation *lives* and *will* live! Other nations may love us or hate us, but they will never succeed in wiping us out, either by persecution or by assimilation.

Borochov, *National Self-Help,* Aug. 6, 1915. BNC, 86.

576.B.5 Let us recognize that we Jews are a distinct nationality of which every Jew, whatever his country, station, or shade of belief, is necessarily a member. Let us insist that the struggle for liberty shall not cease until equality of opportunity is accorded to nationalities as to individuals.

Brandeis, address, April 25, 1915.

576.B.6 We were to be dispersed among the peoples and to experience . . . all the evils of nationalism, so that when the time was ripe, we could found and live a new kind of nationalism in the Holy Land.

Brod, *Im Kampf um das Judentum,* 1920, p. 41. q LGS, 271.

576.B.7 Whoever ascribes to the nation or to the community the attributes of the absolute and of self-sufficiency betrays the religion of Israel.
Buber, *At the Turning*, 1952, p. 36.

576.B.8 Our nationalism does not tend to erect barriers. We wish only to throw a bridge across the abyss created by an abnormal life.
Chinese Jewish Community, letter to Tagore. q LGF, 498.

576.B.9 We accept European culture and at the same time we wish to preserve the best in our national culture.
Dubnow, *Pisma o Starom i Novom Yevreistvie*, 1907, p. 225.

576.B.10 The basis of our national idea consists in the fact that all the scattered parts of the Jewish Diaspora constitute one indivisible people, united by common interests.
Ibid. q *JP*, 1948, ii. 317.

576.B.11 We Jews should once more become conscious of our existence as a nationality and regain the self-respect that is necessary to a healthy existence.
Einstein, *World As I See It*, 1934, p. 156.

576.B.12 Is not Jewish nationalism an empty phrase if we do not connect with it Jewish religion and Jewish ethics, Jewish culture and the Jewish mode of life which gave it its individuality?
L. Ginzberg, *Students, Saints and Scholars*, 1928, p. 124.

576.B.13 Three essential traits of nationalism originated with the ancient Jews: the idea of the chosen people, the consciousness of national history, and national Messianism.
Kohn, *Idea of Nationalism*, 1944, p. 36.

576.B.14 The idea of a Jewish "nationality" runs counter to the interests of the Jewish proletariat because directly or indirectly it arouses within it a mood hostile to assimilation, a ghetto mood.
*Lenin, 1903. q *JF*, Aug. 1950, p. 6.

576.B.15 In the first half millenium of the Christian era, amid darkness, confusion, the conflict of creeds and the downfall of classical civilization, the Jews learned the lesson of being a nation by force of the spirit alone.
Lewisohn, *Israel*, 1925, p. 32.

576.B.16 An Israel that talks straight nationalism and is not linked with the world redemptive character of Judaism, is

a retreat, not an advance, a subtraction from the world's liberating forces.
M. Samuel, *The Gentleman and the Jew*, 1950.

576.B.17 The Jewish national idea was not narrow, but embodied a universalistic charge, "in thee shall all the families of the earth be blessed" [*Gen.* 12.3].
*Solovyov, *Talmud. Ruskaya Mysl*, 1886.

576.B.18 What sort of a nation . . . is a Jewish nation that consists of Georgian, Daghestanian, Russian, American and other Jews, the members of which do not understand each other, . . . will never see each other, will never act together, whether in time of peace or of war? . . . No, it is not for such paper "nations" that the Social Democratic Party draws up its national program.
*Stalin, 1913, *Marxism and the National Question*, 11f.

576.B.19 Faith in Israel means faith in the spiritual strength of the world.
Syrkin, 1924. See SGZ, ii. 53ff.

576.B.20 The content of Judaism, the substance of the Jewish national idea, the meaning of Jewish culture reside in the social-revolutionary critique and hope, of which Jews are the historic announcers, in the tidings of redemption, which the Jewish people brings to mankind. This is the highest, the first and last, justification of Jewish nationalism, of the separate existence of the Jewish people.
Syrkin, *Jewish Nationalism*. SGZ, i. 208.

577. NATURE

577.1 While the earth remains, seedtime and harvest, cold and heat, summer and winter, and day and night shall not cease.
Bible: Gen., 8.22.

577.2 Deep calls unto deep at the voice of Thy cataracts.
Bible: Ps., 42.8.

577.3 Sun, moon and stars . . . are obedient.
Apocrypha: Jeremy, 60. See *Enoch*, 2.1.

577.4 In all its partitions and iron walls, under all its cloaks and covers, Nature is of the very essence of the Deity.
Baal Shem. q Horodetzki. *HaShiloah*, 1907, xvii. 354.

577.5 History teaches us virtue, but nature preaches incessantly vice.
Boerne, *Fragmente & Aphorismen*, 1840, #198.

577.6 Nature leads us to wisdom by way of the confectioner: it surfeits us with the pleasures we should avoid.
Ibid., #247.

577.7 Like a great poet, Nature knows how to produce the greatest effects with the most limited means.
Heine, *Harz Journey*, 1824.

577.8 Knowledge and action release man from the fetters of nature.
Ibn Gabirol, *Fons Vitae*, 11C.

577.9 A wolf changes his hair, but not his nature.
Immanuel, *Mahberot*, (c. 1300) 1491.

577.10 What is contrary to nature is contrary to God.
Kompert, *Christian and Leah*, 1895, 65.

577.11 Our daily activity implies unruffled, perfect confidence in the invariability of natural laws.
Lévy-Bruhl, *La mentalité primitive*, 1922, p. 17.

577.12 To be able to live in strict conformity with nature is what the men of old defined as the end of happiness.
Philo, *Noah's Planting*, 12.

577.13 Only through intimacy with nature could human beings learn the meaninglessness of luxury and thus set themselves free.
Schatz, *Memoir*. SMMP, 429.

577.14 The letters of the Hebrew words *Elohim* ("God") and *HaTeba* ("Nature") have the same numerical value.
Shneor Zalman, *Likkuté Amarim*, (1796), p. 159.

577.15 There does not exist a vacuum in nature.
Spinoza, *Ethics*, 1677, i. Pr 15, Note.

577.16 The power of nature is the power of God.
Spinoza, *Theologico-Political Treatise*, 1670, ch 16.

577.17 Let man who needs a scripture
      for his eyes
      Peruse the star-built altars in the
      skies!
Steinbach. *New York Times*, May 2, 1954.

577.18 For the Jew, nature and men are nothing of themselves; they are for the service of God.
*Taine, *History of English Literature*, (1864) 1873. ii. 5.

577.19 Stolen seed should properly not grow, but Nature follows its course, and fools who do wrong will have to render an account.
Tosefta: Aboda Zara, 6.7.

578. NECESSITY

578.1 It Ain't Necessarily So.
I. Gershwin, *Porgy and Bess*, 1935.

578.2 To be distressed at a necessary condition of life is absurd.
Ibn Pulgar, *Ezer HaDat*, 14C, 53a.

578.3 Nothing in war so rouses the martial spirit as necessity.
Josephus, *Wars*, 3.7.4.

578.4 One of the great tasks of culture is to convert necessity into freedom.
Klatzkin, *In Praise of Wisdom*, 1943, p. 22.

578.5 Every necessity creates its own consoling philosophy, and turns itself into a virtue.
S. Levin, *Youth in Revolt*, 1930, p. 77.

578.6 Necessity is blind until it becomes conscious. Freedom is the consciousness of necessity.
Marx. q Engels, *Anti-Dühring*, 1877.

578.7 Necessity breaks iron.
Proverb (Yiddish). BJS, #2533.

578.8 Nothing in the universe is contingent, but all things are conditioned to exist and operate in a particular manner by the necessity of the divine nature.
Spinoza, *Ethics*, 1677, i. Pr 29.

578.9 The eternal and infinite Being, which we call God or Nature, acts by the same necessity as that whereby it exists.
Ibid., iv. Preface.

578.10 We are drawn toward a thing because we believe it is good. We end by being chained to it because it has become a necessity.
S. Weil, *Gravity and Grace*, 1952, p. 99.

579. NECK

579.1 Thy neck is as a tower of ivory.
Bible: Song, 7.5.

579.2 If the neck is beautiful, it needs no string of pearls.
Immanuel, *Mahberot*, (c.1300) 1491, ch 14.

579.3 Neck is a simile for the Temple: as the neck gives symmetry and beauty to the body, so does the Temple to the whole world.
Zohar, Gen., 209b.

580. NEED

580.1 One often needs most the unnecessary.

Auerbach. q TL, p. 284.

580.2 From each according to his abilities, to each according to his needs.

Marx, *Critique of the Gotha Program*, 1875.

580.3 Thy people's needs are many and their talent is small!

Ne'ila Prayer. *Talmud: Berakot*, 29b.

580.4 When the need is highest, God is nighest.

Proverb (Yiddish). q SWS, 44.

580.5 A voice proclaims daily from Mt. Horeb: The whole world is sustained for the sake of My son Hanina, and all he needs for his weekly subsistence is but a measure of carobs!

Rab. *Talmud: Berakot*, 17b.

580.6 Need alone is negative, and the greatest productions of man spring from an affirmation.

Weizmann, *Trial and Error*, 1949, p. 176.

581. NEGATION

581.1 We can unite in firm negation of idolatry and find perhaps more of a common faith in this negation than in any affirmative statement about God. Certainly we shall find more of humility and of brotherly love.

Fromm, *Psychoanalysis and Religion*, 1950, p. 119.

581.2 From a negative statement you may not infer the positive.

Meir. *Talmud: Nedarim*, 11a.

581.3 From a positive statement you may infer the negative.

Proverb, based on preceding.

581.4 From negation arises party, not movement.

Rathenau, *Von kommenden Dingen*, 1917.

581.5 The Jew is the spirit of negation, a protest against the dogmas of creeds.

I. M. Wise, "Wandering Jew," 1877 (*Selected Writings*, 182).

582. NEGRO

582.1 Negroes are victims of harsh discrimination and flagrant injustices, which cry aloud to God and to man for remedy and redress. . . . If our prayers and repentance . . . truly touch us, . . . we shall proceed, in cooperation with all men of good will, to remove barriers and eliminate injustices.

CCAR, Statement, February 1942.

582.2 The influence of the Negro upon the psychology of the American has been tremendous. . . . We taught him things; he taught us feelings. We gave him knowledge; he has helped to give us passion, which is not the meaner of the gifts.

Goldberg, *Tin-Pan Alley*, 1930.

582.3 We owe to the Negro our love because of the martyrdom to which we have subjected him.

London, speech, U.S. Congress, 1922. q RES, 250.

582.4 Jews, by reason of the mandate of their ethical teaching, . . . by reason of their own insecure position in large sections of the world . . . must be as ardent for the defense of Negro rights as they are of their own.

National Jewish Monthly, editorial, April, 1942.

583. NEIGHBOR

583.1 In everyone there is something of his fellow-man. . . . Hence, "love your neighbor"—for he is really you yourself.

Cordovero, *Tomer Deborah*, (1588) 1928, p. 5.

583.2 Love your Neighbor, yet respect
him too;
Don't pull down the Fence, 'twixt
him and you.

Guiterman, *A Poet's Proverbs*, 1924, p. 7.

583.3 Cling to a good neighbor . . . shun an evil neighbor.

José HaCohen. *Mishna: Abot*, 2.9. See *Abot* 1.7.

584. NEWS

584.1 As cold waters to a faint soul, so is good news from a far country.

Bible: Prov., 25.25.

584.2 Mortals and angels wrestled for the Holy Tables of the Law. The angels have won and captured the Tables.

Bar Kappara, breaking the news of Judah HaNasi's death. *Talmud: Ketubot*, 104a.

584.3 NEWS is that which comes from the North, East, West and South, and if it comes from only one point of the compass, then it is a class publication and not news.

Disraeli, speech, House of Commons, March 26, 1855.

584.4 No news, good news.
Ludovic Halevy, *La Belle Hélène*, 1864.

584.5 A people without reliable news is, sooner or later, a people without the basis of freedom.
Laski, *A Grammar of Politics*, 1925, p. 147f.

584.6 Your friend has a friend, and his friend has a friend [and so news travels].
Talmud: Baba Bathra, 29a.

585. NEW YORK

585.1 The Deepest City in the world.
Oppenheim, "New York from a Skyscraper."

585.2 City of prose and fantasy, of capitalist automatism, its streets a triumph of cubism, its moral philosophy that of the dollar. New York impressed me tremendously because, more than any other city, it is the fullest expression of our modern age.
Trotsky, *My Life*, 1930.

585.3 New York is the great stone desert.
Zangwill, *The Melting Pot*, 1909, Act 2.

586. NIGHT

586.1 Watchman, what of the night?
Bible: Isa., 21.11.

586.2 "Night unto night revealeth knowledge" [*Ps.* 19.3]. The revelations of nature cannot be easily heard during the day, when men move noisily about in their daily work. But in the evening, when men sit in silence, the voice of the heavens may be heard.
Arama, *Akedat Yitzhak*, 15C, i. 13b; adapted CCAR, *B&P*, 19.

586.3 By night . . . all flowers are gray, —the sinfullest rose quite as much as the most virtuous parsley.
Heine, *Journey from Munich to Genoa*, 1828, ch 20.

586.4 The darkness moves before the
    pale gray light,
    Trembles and doubts and never
    understands
    That day should lay unconsecrated
    hands
    Upon the holy kingdom of the
    night.
Salaman, "Two Dawns." *Songs of Many Days*, 1923, p. 13.

586.5 The milkman alone is enough to redeem the night from its undeserved evil reputation.
Strunsky, *Belshazar Court*, 1914, p. 102.

586.6 Come, drink the mystic wine of
    Night,
    Brimming with silence and the
    stars;
    While earth, bathed in this holy
    light,
    Is seen without its scars.
L. Untermeyer, "The Wine of Night." *Challenge*, 1915, p. 34.

587. NIGHTINGALE

587.1 My heart loves to hear the nightingale's song, though the songster is above me and afar.
M. Ibn Ezra. q AJL, 164.

588. NOBILITY

588.1 There is no price too high which the man without self-respect would not pay for the fiction of nobility and the right to treat others as being lower than himself.
H. Greenberg, "From Bakhmut to Vienna," 1938. GIE, 371.

588.2 Pedigree is of no avail to him who is not himself noble.
Hasdai, *Ben HaMelek VeHaNazir*, c.1230, Introduction.

588.3 He is noble who both nobly feels and acts.
Heine, *Atta Troll*, 1841, ch 5.

588.4 All men, born equal, are a noble race.
Heine, *Harz Journey*, 1824, #2.

588.5 What is the noblest pedigree? Lovingkindness to men.
Ibn Gabirol, *Mibhar HaPeninim*, c.1050, #395.

588.6 No pedigree as noble as virtue, no heritage equal to honor.
Maimonides, *Shaaré HaMusar*. q AHE, 110.

588.7 At the Throne of Glory it is not the nobly-born that are beloved, but the nobly-risen.
Peretz, *Drei Matones*, c.1910. *Alle Verk*, vii. 18.

588.8 We ought to call noble only those who are temperate and just, even though they belong to the class of domestic slaves.
Philo, *Nobility*, 1.

588.9 Nobility and honor always go together.
Ponte, *Don Juan*, 1787, 1.8.

588.10 The nobility to which you cannot raise yourself, cannot give you a patent of nobility.

Sanders, *366 Sprüche*, 1892, #288.

588.11 The fragrant, waving reed grows
tall
From feeble root and thin,
And uncouth worms that lowly
crawl
Most lustrous silk do spin. . . .
The goshawk, know, can soar on
high,
Yet low he nests his brood.
A Jew true precepts doth apply
Are they therefore less good?

Santob de Carrion, *Proverbios Morales*, 1350.

588.12 Who acts nobly, him will I account noble.

Süsskind of Trimberg. q *JE*, xi. 603.

589. NONSENSE

589.1 Nonsense is often the wisest form of allegory.

Leftwich. *Menorah Journal*, Spring 1952, x1. 59.

589.2 At times a little nonsense avails more than knowledge and honor.

Leon of Modena, *On Games of Chance*, 1596, tr Gollancz, 180.

590. NOSE

590.1 The proportion of so-called "Semitic" noses is very much greater among the non-Jewish population.

*Dixon, *Racial History of Man*, 1923, p. 172.

590.2 It is unbecoming for the waterspout to be at the entrance of a palace; yet the Supreme Architect created man with a spout over his mouth, and it constitutes his beauty and his pride!

Levi b. Haytha. *Gen. R.*, 12.1.

591. NOVELTY

591.1 There arose a new king over Egypt, who knew not Joseph.

Bible: Exod., 1.8.

591.2 There is nothing new under the sun.

Bible: Eccles., 1.9.

591.3 Novelty is an essential attribute of the beautiful.

Disraeli, *Vivian Grey*, 1827.

591.4 The sight of that to which one has long been accustomed does not produce such an ardent desire as of objects new in form and character.

Maimonides, *Guide for the Perplexed*, 1190, 3.49.

591.5 Praised be Thou . . . who hast kept us alive, preserved us, and brought us to this season.

Mishna: Berakot, 9.2. Benediction for anything new.

591.6 Bach is just as new today as he ever was—a continual revelation. Truly good things are new.

Schoenberg. Armitage, *Schoenberg*, p. 256.

592. NOVICE

592.1 It is said that a bird never makes so much noise as when she lays her first egg.

Disraeli, speech, House of Commons, June 28, 1858. Ref. to a maiden speech.

592.2 When the infant begins to walk, it thinks it lives in strange times.

Disraeli, *Sybil*, 1845.

592.3 Then there was a maiden speech, so inaudible that it was doubted whether, after all, the young orator really did lose his virginity.

Disraeli, *The Young Duke*, 1831.

593. NUDE

593.1 They were both naked, the man and his wife, and were not ashamed.

Bible: Gen., 2.25.

593.2 Naked came I out of my mother's womb, and naked shall I return thither.

Bible: Job, 1.21.

593.3 There is nothing more abominable than for a man to appear nude in public.

Talmud: Yebamot, 63b.

594. NUMBER

594.1 Two are better than one.

Bible: Eccles., 4.9.

594.2 The sand of the sea, the drops of rain, and the days of eternity—who can number?

Apocrypha: Ben Sira, 1.2.

594.3 Too many sailors will wreck the ship.

Bonsenyor, *Dichos y Sentencias*, 14C, #618.

594.4 When the trouble strikes many, there is some consolation.

Gentili, *Mleket Mahshebet, Ki Tabo*, 1710.

594.5 The cause of truth counts not the number of its adherents.

S. R. Hirsch, *Nineteen Letters*, (1836), #18, p. 208.

594.6 Better two than three [Better two feet without need of a cane].

José b. Kisma. *Talmud: Sabbath*, 152a.

594.7 When I find the road narrow, and can see no other way of teaching a well-established truth except by pleasing one intelligent man and displeasing ten thousand fools, I prefer to address myself to the one man, and to take no notice whatever of the contemplation of the multitude.

Maimonides, letter to Joseph Ibn Aknin, c.1189. *Guide for the Perplexed*, 1190, Introduction.

594.8 The folly of many is worldly wisdom.

Mendelé, Introd. to *Sefer HaBehemot*, 1913.

594.9 A pot with two cooks is neither hot nor cold.

Proverb. q Raba of Parazika. *Talmud: Erubin*, 3a. q Kahana. *Baba Bathra*, 24b. Cf Petronius, *Cena Trimalchionis. JQRo*, v. 168ff.

594.10 Precious is the seventh.

Proverb. q Schechter, *Seminary Addresses*, 195.

595. OATH

595.1 He who admits a portion of the claim, must take an oath.

Admon. *Mishna: Shebuot*, 6.3.

595.2 "No" is an oath, and "Yes" is an oath.

Eleazar. *Talmud: Shebuot*, 36a.

595.3 One who is not believed without an appeal to God stands condemned already.

Josephus, *Wars*, 2.8.6. Essene principle.

595.4 All swearing to, as well as all swearing away, of principles and dogmas is inadmissible; and when done, binds to nothing but to repentance of blamable levity thus shown.

M. Mendelssohn, *Jerusalem*, (1783), ii. 62f.

595.5 Think not that you may swear by My name, even in truth.

Tanhuma, Matot, 1, ed Buber, 79a. See *NT: Matt.*, 5.34. Bahya, *Hobot HaLebabot*, 8.3.17.

595.6 The oath of a Jew in the name of God is binding without further ceremony.

Versammlung deutscher Rabbiner, 1844. PRM, 153.

595.7 Throughout the Scriptures we find that a judicial oath is mandatory only in fiscal claims, as in *Exodus* 22.10, but nowhere do we find that the court may demand an oath in spiritual disputes.

Yehiel b. Joseph, 1240. q Official, *Disputation*. EOV, 83a.

596. OBEDIENCE

596.1 All that the Lord has spoken we will do and obey.

Bible: Exod., 24.7.

596.2 To obey is better than sacrifice.

Bible: I Sam., 15.22.

596.3 The best way to insure implicit obedience is to commence tyranny in the nursery.

Disraeli, speech, House of Commons, June 15, 1874.

596.4 Human history begins with man's act of disobedience which is at the same time the beginning of his freedom and development of his reason.

Fromm, *Psychoanalysis and Religion*, 1950, p. 84.

596.5 All who know well how to obey will know also how to rule.

Josephus, *Antiquities*, 4.8.2.

596.6 Involuntary obedience corrupts the soul.

Lewisohn, *Creative Life*, 1924, p. 71.

596.7 Who wishes to obey will be given the opportunity to obey.

Mekilta, to *Exod.*, 15.26.

596.8 A slave is bound to obey his master's orders, given solely in the master's interest. A son obeys his father's orders, given in his own interest. A subject obeys the order of the sovereign power, given for the common interest, wherein he is included.

Spinoza, *Theologico-Political Treatise*, 1670, ch 16.

596.9 Obedience is the primary and irremissible motive and the foundation of all morality.

Stahl, *Philosophie des Rechts*, (1837) 1854, ii. 106. q MRR, 372.

597. OBSCURITY

597.1 The obscure is the principal ingredient of the sublime.

Disraeli, *Contarini Fleming*, 1832.

597.2 When a thing is obscure, you can accomplish more.
Nahman Bratzlav. q ZRN, 225.

598. OBSTINACY

598.1 Stubbornness is as idolatry.
Bible: I Sam., 15.23.

598.2 A stubborn heart shall fare ill.
Apocrypha: Ben Sira, 3.26.

598.3 Dispute not with the obstinate, not even on matters of Torah.
Ibn Tibbon, *Tzavaah*, c.1190.

598.4 Stubbornness was the dominant trait, the distinguishing quality of the ancient Hebrew. He possessed a strength of will, a doggedness, rarely found in the Occidentals.
*Leroy-Beaulieu, *Israel Among the Nations*, 1895, p. 192.

599. OCCIDENT and ORIENT

599.1 Hopeless is your state in the West; the star of your future gleams in the East.
Bilu, *Manifesto*, Constantinople, 1882.

599.2 The Occidental would rebuild *society;* the Oriental strives to rebuild *man.* The Occidental politician is an organizer on business lines; the Oriental is a priestly educator of men.
Ehrenpreis, *Soul of the East*, 1927, 189.

599.3 Where the Orient and the Occident meet, there lies the land of Canaan. . . . From the Occident there beats a wild continuous wave . . . a thirst for life and personality, a will for action, for happiness, for power. . . . But from the east there comes a message of gentle wisdom. . . . Non-resistance, . . . passivity, renunciation. . . .
In that tiny land dwelt the folk of Israel, keen of eye and of ear. . . . And the little nation writes the two books which have most of all changed the face of the world, the great Book of Deeds, the Old Testament, and the great Book of Renunciation, the New Testament. But the stubborn desire for immortality remains the dominant note in all its living and writing.
Feuchtwanger, *Power*, 1925, p. 349f.

599.4 Wherever Israel went, God went with him, and while our face is ever turned in reverential awe at the rising sun, whence we started on our world mission, we have learned from history that westward wends the course of civilization's empire.
Kohler, address, Jan. 22, 1913.

599.5 Perhaps it is the great world-historical task of the Jewish settlement in Palestine to effect a synthesis of Europeanism and Orientalism.
F. Oppenheimer. *Reflex*, July, 1927, p. 68.

599.6 His soul was of the Orient, but his brain was of the Occident. His intellect had been nourished at the breast of Science, that classified everything and explained nothing. . . . Oh, it was a cruel tragedy, this Western culture grafted on an Eastern stock, untuning the chords of life, setting heart and brain asunder. But then Nature *was* cruel.
Zangwill, *Dreamers of the Ghetto*, 1898, p. 499f, 503f.

600. OCCUPATION

600.1 Artisans maintain the fabric of the world, and in the handiwork of their craft is their prayer.
Apocrypha: Ben Sira, 38.34. See E. J. Goodspeed, *Apocrypha*, 1938, p. 298.

600.2 A man who goes driving about from one trade to another is sure to drive himself into ruin eventually.
B. Auerbach, *Little Barefoot*, 1856, ch 9.

600.3 The concentration of Jewish labor in any occupation varies directly with the remoteness of that occupation from nature.
Borochov. *Yidisher Kempfer*, 1916. BNC, 68.

600.4 I don't believe in this superstitious prejudice that only the man who works with his hands is socially useful.
M. R. Cohen, *Reflections of a Wondering Jew*, 1950.

600.5 Out with you, lazy people. Stop idling away your time! Enter on some useful work. You, become a carpenter, you a mason, you a tailor, and you a fisherman!
Elisha b. Abuya, to Torah students. *Talmud J: Hagiga*, 2.1.

600.6 Medicine, the noblest of all human occupations.
Falaquera, *Sefer HaMaalot*, (13C) 1894, p. 63.

600.7 A trade is a fence: it protects against trespassers.
Gamaliel II. *Tosefta: Kiddushin*, 1.11.

600.8 Torah is excellent when combined with a worldly occupation.
Gamaliel III. *Mishna: Abot*, 2.2.
Ishmael b. Elisha. *Talmud: Berakot*, 35b.

600.9 All Torah and no work ends in futility and sin.
Ibid.

600.10 Both perfumers and tanners are needed; yet happy he whose craft is perfume, and woe to him whose trade is tanning!

Judah HaNasi. *Talmud: Pesahim,* 65a. Bar Kappara. *Talmud: Baba Bathra,* 16b.

600.11 It is a romantic myth that the country is pure and the city foul, that a merchant is essentially and necessarily more ignoble than he who cultivates the soil, that the work of the hand has a moral value which the work of the mind lacks. In a complicated modern civilization, whatever its specific economic forms, every function is as necessary as every other.

Lewisohn, *Israel,* 1925, p. 105.

600.12 Teach your son a clean and easy trade, and pray to the Giver of all wealth and prosperity.

Meir. *Mishna: Kiddushin,* 4.14. See *Eccles. R.,* 6.8.

600.13 Who teaches not his son a trade teaches him robbery.

Judah b. Ilai. *Tosefta: Kiddushin,* 1.11.

600.14 Boys and girls should be taught trades: idleness and want are the beginning of sin.

I. B. Levinsohn, *Teuda BeYisrael,* 1823.

600.15 A salesman . . . is a man way out there in the blue, riding on a smile and a shoestring. . . . A salesman is got to dream, boy. It comes with the territory.

Miller, (Charley in) *Death of a Salesman,* 1949.

600.16 Unlike other trades, Torah gives sustenance in youth and security in old age.

Nehorai. *Mishna: Kiddushin,* 4.14.

600.17 Let us change the merchant's yardstick and the Canaanitish scales for spade and plow!

Pinsker, speech, Katowice, 1886. q BRD, 45f.

600.18 He alone succeeds who has *one* occupation.

Proverb. q S. Levin, *The Arena,* 84.

600.19 Everyone's trade seems fine in his own eyes.

Rab. *Talmud: Berakot,* 43b.

600.20 A famine may last seven years, yet it does not pass through the artisan's gate.

Raba. *Talmud: Sanhedrin,* 29a.

600.21 Engage not in an occupation which will not permit you to fix times for study.

Sefer Hasidim, 13C, #830, p. 210.

600.22 Be whatever you want to be, but be it with all your heart.

Wolffsohn, letter to Hans Herzl. q Cohn, *David Wolffsohn,* 154.

601. OFFERING

601.1 Nadab and Abihu . . . offered strange fire before the Lord.

Bible: Lev., 10.1.

601.2 When people offer themselves willingly, bless ye the Lord.

Bible: Judg., 5.2.

601.3 Of Thine own have we given Thee.

Bible: I Chron., 29.14.

601.4 What is an offering to God? Charity to His children.

Akiba. *Midrash Zuta* to *Cant.* 1.15, ed Buber, 19.

601.5 Only the best should be brought to the sanctuary.

Akiba. *Sifré,* #68, to *Deut.* 12.11, ed Friedmann, 88b.

601.6 If you build a synagog, let it be more beautiful than your house. When you feed the hungry, clothe the naked, or devote anything to a holy purpose, it must be from your finest.

Maimonides, *Yad: Issuré HaMizbeah,* 1180, 7.11.

601.7 One must not devote all one's property to the Most High.

Eleazar b. Azariah. *Sifra,* to *Lev.* 25.25.

601.8 Render unto God what is His, and bear in mind that you and yours are His.

Eleazar b. Judah of Bartota. *Mishna: Abot,* 3.7.

601.9 You mustn't give money and not yourself.

Fels. q Zangwill. *Fortnightly Review,* June 1920.

601.10 A poor man's offering is esteemed doubly by God, for with the sacrifice he brings also his own flesh and blood.

Zohar, Lev., 9b.

601.11 The essence of the offering is that it be analogous to the sin, that a man offer to God his desires and passions.

Ibid.

602. OFFICE

602.1 Sometimes it is not the office that

makes the man, but the man that makes the office.

Agnon, *Shebuat Emunim*, 1943.

602.2 The civil servant will not discharge his duty fairly if he is only loyal to the State and does not greet the common man with sympathy and affection.

Ben Gurion, "Call of the Spirit." *IGY*, 5712.

602.3 All my life I have hoped to see an alleviation of the suffering of the world's disinherited. Should I then now, when the opportunity comes to me to assure those of France a larger measure of justice, abandon them? I accept the challenge which comes to me as a Jew and as a citizen of France.

Blum, 1936, to a delegation of Jews who urged him to decline the premiership in a Leftist coalition for fear of anti-Semitic repercussions.

602.4 Ministers fall like buttered bread: usually with the good side down.

Boerne, *Fragmente & Aphorismen*, 1840, #1. See 270.5; 657.1.

602.5 Remain obscure [out of office], and live.

Eleazar (b. Pedat). *Talmud: Sanhedrin*, 14a.

602.6 Do you think I offer you rulership? It is servitude that I offer you!

Gamaliel II, to disciples who declined office. *Talmud: Horayot*, 10a.

602.7 Beware of government officials. They permit only such contacts as will serve their selfish interests.

Gamaliel III. *Mishna: Abot*, 2.3.

602.8 Shame on the community whose physician is gouty, whose governor is one-eyed, and whose advocate acts as a prosecutor!

Levi. *Lev. R.*, 5.6.

602.9 To accept an office for personal profit is adultery.

Pesiḳta Rabbati, 111a.

602.10 When a man is chosen for public office, he becomes rich.

Samuel. *Talmud: Yoma*, 22b.

602.11 Woe to high office, which buries its occupants!

Seder Eliyahu Rabbah, ch 12, ed Friedmann, p. 55.

602.12 When Akiba was to be appointed to a communal office, his wife said: "Take it if you are ready to be cursed and despised."

Talmud J: Peah, 8.7

602.13 The office seeks him who would escape it.

Tanhuma, VaYiḳra, 4, ed Buber, 2b.

603. ONE

603.1 Nought beside Thee is really one, . . . for it is composite, . . . has a beginning and an end, . . . an opposite and a like

Bahya, *Hobot HaLebabot, Baḳasha*, 1040.

603.2 One grape will not make a bunch.

Disraeli, *Tancred*, 1847.

603.3 Where one is nothing, all are nothing.

Hoffenstein, *Pencil in the Air*, 1923, p. 148.

603.4 One defective verse can spoil a whole poem.

M. Ibn Ezra, *Shirat Yisrael*, (12C) 1924, p. 133.

603.5 There is but one sun in the sky, one song in the heart.

I. Najara, 1587. q Z. Shazar. *JS*, Oct. 1950.

603.6 All in one is nowhere found.

Proverb (Yiddish). *JE*, x. 228b.

603.7 One is none.

Proverb. q Syrkin. *Day*, March 1923. SGZ, ii. 214.

603.8 When man is at one, God is one.

Zohar. q Fleg, *Life of Moses*, 1928.

604. OPINION

604.1 How long halt ye between two opinions?

Bible: I Kings, 18.21.

604.2 Often are we but shadows of other lives. . . . We are good or bad, as public opinion bids us.

F. Adler, *Creed and Deed*, 1877, p. 84.

604.3 Let it not be said of me, he changed his opinion for the sake of power.

Akabia b. Mahalalel. *Mishna: Eduyot*, 5.6.

604.4 Public opinion is a people's invincible armor.

Boerne, *Die Freheit der Presse in Baiern*, 1818.

604.5 What we call public opinion is generally public sentiment.

Disraeli, speech, House of Commons, Aug. 3, 1880.

604.6 From your opinion of others we know their opinion of you.

M. Ibn Ezra, *Shirat Yisrael*, (12C) 1924, p. 123.

604.7 The weak-minded change their opinions because they are easily influenced by others, and the strong-minded change their opinions because they have complete mastery of their opinions.

Klatzkin, *In Praise of Wisdom,* 1943, p. 310.

604.8 Consideration of what people will say, what bigots will whisper, what crafty enemies will scheme—questions such as these can have but one effect—to darken the intellect and confuse the faculty of judgment.

Krochmal, letter to a student, q SSJ, i. 53f.

604.9 Follow your own bent, no matter what people say.

Marx, *Capital,* 1867, Preface.

604.10 Intelligent people ought to examine all different opinions.

Maimonides, *Guide to the Perplexed,* 1190, 3.13. See 3.4.

604.11 Every judge must voice his own opinion.

Maimonides, *Yad: Sanhedrin,* 10.6.

604.12 A judge must express his own carefully considered opinion.

Mekilta de Simeon b. Yohai, to *Exod.* 23.2.

604.13 The older I get the more clearly do I perceive how important it is, *first* to learn, and *then* to form opinions.

F. Mendelssohn.

604.14 Why are the unaccepted opinions of Shammai and Hillel recorded? To teach future generations not to persist in an opinion.

Mishna: Eduyot, 1.4. See Samuel. *Talmud: Erubin,* 13b.

604.15 It is evil pride to . . . regard one's own opinion as the best, since such an attitude bars progress.

Orhot Tzaddikim, 15C, ch 1.

605. OPPOSITION

605.1 When a downward-thrusting root encounters a stone . . . and cannot split it, it seeks ways of getting round it.

Asch, *What I Believe,* 1941, p. 23.

605.2 Judaism has always and everywhere stood . . . against any religion that controlled the land. . . . Stoutly the Jews were and are, as the famous Baptist preacher, Charles Haddon Spurgeon put it, "the great non-conformists in this world" —indeed, God's dissenters.

Baeck, *Judaism,* 1949.

605.3 Like the course of the heavenly bodies, harmony in national life is a resultant of the struggle between contending forces.

Brandeis, *Gilbert vs. Minn.,* 1920.

605.4 No government can long be secure without a formidable opposition.

Disraeli, *Coningsby,* 1844, 2.1.

605.5 Yes, I advocate the uttermost opposition to all injustice and untruth!

J. Jacoby, 1841. q LJG, 283.

605.6 It is wrong to suppress the views of an opponent; it is more fitting to ponder their meaning. . . . It would therefore be wrong to silence a person who expresses himself against religion.

Judah Löw, *Geburot HaShem,* 1582, ch 19. q BWC, 83. See *Beer HaGola,* 1598, ch 7. q Bokser, *Wisdom of Talmud,* 184.

605.7 From the true antagonist illimitable courage is transmitted to you.

Kafka, *Reflections,* #23. *Dearest Father,* 1954, p. 36.

605.8 God has spared us from hard feelings when someone contradicts or criticizes us. The Creator knows that we would rejoice even if the least scholar or colleague or opponent would answer us, provided the answer be true and reveal something that had been concealed from us. Nor would we hate or drive away or take to task the respondent who happens to be mistaken or hazy in his reply.

Maimonides, *Responsa,* ed Freimann, #69, p. 68.

605.9 The Jew . . . was the first and fiercest Nonconformist of the East.

Schechter, *Studies in Judaism,* 1896, i. p. xxi.

605.10 Good cannot come without opposition.

Shalom Shakna. See BTH, ii. 14.

605.11 Sometimes a man serves his party best by standing out, if need be, alone against his party.

S. S. Wise, *Sermons and Addresses,* 1905, p. 20.

606. OPPRESSION

606.1 Thou shalt not oppress thy neighbor, nor rob him.

Bible: Lev., 19.13.

606.2 What mean ye that ye crush My people, and grind the face of the poor?

Bible: Isa., 3.15.

606.3 He who oppresses the poor blasphemes his Maker, but he who is gracious to the needy honors Him.
Bible: Prov., 14.31.

606.4 Be of the persecuted, not of the persecutors.
Abbahu. *Talmud: Baba Kamma,* 93a.

606.5 Woe to you who devour the finest of the wheat . . . and tread under foot the lowly with your might.
Apocrypha: Enoch, 96.5.

606.6 Woe to you who build your palaces with the grievous toil of others! Each stone, each brick, of which it is built, is a sin!
Ibid., 99.13.

606.7 Nations are like olives. To gentle pressure they respond with sweet oil, to hard pressure with bitter oil.
Boerne, *Briefe aus Paris,* #77, Feb. 26, 1832.

606.8 Persecution made the Jews' law of brotherhood self-enforcing. It taught them the seriousness of life; it broadened their sympathies; it deepened their passion for righteousness; it trained them in patient endurance, in persistence, in self-control, and in self-sacrifice.
Brandeis. *Menorah Journal,* Jan. 1915.

606.9 French Jews, let us be the first to come to the aid of our Christian brothers. . . . A permanent committee in each country, with eyes open to all victims of fanaticism, regardless of religion, must be created and supported.
Crémieux, appeal in behalf of Lebanese Catholics, 1860.

606.10 To oppress the Jews has never brought prosperity to any government.
*Frederick the Great. q Farrar, *Social . . . Questions,* 356.

606.11 There is a love of oppression in human nature. . . . The small citizen of Frankfort worries over the privileges of the nobility, but he worries even more when anyone suggests the emancipation of the Jews.
Heine, *English Fragments,* 1828, ch 11.

606.12 Whom do you respect more, who is really the stronger, the down-trodden Jew, who in the dust of humility possesses sufficient strength of mind and character to pity his opponent and to accept the scorn heaped upon him as a trial sent by God . . . , or the ruffian, who in his overweening

pride . . . seems to consider himself privileged to revile the feeble and impotent and to find therein his claim to greatness?
S. R. Hirsch, *Nineteen Letters,* (1836), #15, p. 144f.

606.13 Why is Israel compared to an olive-tree? Because just as an olive yields its oil only when pounded, so Israel is at its best under oppression.
Johanan. *Talmud: Menahot,* 53b.

606.14 Among vigorous races . . . the scorn of the mob renders the individual greater in his own eyes. Against this rock, the darts of the adversary are broken. This is the casket in which the family is preserved, the mould in which character is cast.
D. Levi, *Vita di Pensiero,* 1875. q *JQRo,* xi. 369.

606.15 Blessed are they that are persecuted for righteousness sake, for theirs is the kingdom of heaven.
New Testament: Matt., 5.10.

606.16 God loves the persecuted and hates the persecutors.
Pesikta Rabbati, ed Friedmann, 193b.

606.17 God will do justice to the oppressed, be he Jew or Gentile.
Sefer Hasidim, 13C, #133, p. 62.

606.18 Persecution is often preservation.
Zangwill, *Speeches, Articles and Letters,* 26.

607. OPTIMISM

607.1 God saw everything He had made, and behold, it was very good.
Bible: Gen., 1.31.

607.2 Whatever the All Merciful does is for good.
Akiba. *Talmud: Berakot,* 60b.

607.3 God's works are all good, they supply every need in its season!
Apocrypha: Ben Sira, 39.33.

607.4 Through the darkest hours of its tragic history, Israel has kept burning the undying fire of its inextinguishable hope for the world.
*Baldwin. *B'nai Brith News,* Oct. 1923.

607.5 Like the ants, the Jews never lose faith in life. . . . Hamans and Hitlers everywhere; yet they live on, and enjoy life.
Berenson, Nov. 17, 1943. *Rumor and Reflection,* 156.

607.6 The vital impulse is optimistic. All the religious representations . . . are defensive reactions of nature against the representation, by the intelligence, of a depressing margin.

Bergson, *Two Sources of Morality and Religion*, 1935, p. 130.

607.7 Surely the measure of divine goodness is greater than that of evil dispensation.

Meir. *Talmud: Sanhedrin*, 100b.

607.8 This, too, is for good!

Nahum of Gimzo. *Talmud: Taanit*, 21b.

607.9 An optimist is the kind of person who believes a housefly is looking for a way to get out.

G. J. Nathan, *The Theater in the Fifties*, 1953, p. 105.

607.10 It is all for my good that my cow broke her leg.

Proverb. q Ishmael. *Sifré, Num.*, #119.

607.11 The Jewish race . . . is characterized by this somewhat contradictory combination: a strong optimism in material and social matters along with a deep philosophical pessimism. . . . Such a combination . . . in the same men makes an extraordinary type of human being, which, if properly adapted and used in a country, may bring a remarkable contribution of wealth, power and thought.

*Siegfried. *American Hebrew*, Nov. 22, 1929.

608. ORDER

608.1 In honoring, we begin with the most prominent, but in censuring, we begin with the least important.

Judah HaNasi. *Talmud: Berakot*, 61a.

608.2 Beauty is absent where order is lacking.

Philo, *Creation*, 7.

608.3 Answer the first point first and the last point last.

Talmud: Derek Eretz, 1.21.

609. ORIGINALITY

609.1 The originality of a subject is in its treatment.

Disraeli, *Lothair*, 1870.

609.2 Originality is the only thing that counts. But the originator uses material and ideas that occur round him and pass through him. And out of his experience comes the original creation or work of art.

Gershwin. q Sayler, *Revolt in the Arts*, 1930, p. 266.

609.3 When is the knowledge of literature bad? When it impairs a man's originality.

q M. Ibn Ezra, *Shirat Yisrael*, (12C) 1924, p. 78.

609.4 Better translate something useful from another language than compose some original nonsense.

K. Schulman. q MGU, 378.

610. ORPHAN

610.1 Ye shall not afflict . . . a fatherless child.

Bible: Exod., 22.21.

610.2 Who rears an orphan is deemed as though he had begotten him.

Joshua b. Karha. *Talmud: Sanhedrin*, 19b.

610.3 Hurray, I'm an orphan!

Sholom Aleichem. q SWS, 190.

611. OWN

611.1 Drink waters out of your own cistern, and running waters out of your own well.

Bible: Prov., 5.15.

611.2 First drink from your cistern, and then waters will be running out of your own well.

Ulla. *Talmud: Aboda Zara*, 19a.

611.3 They made me keeper of the vineyards, but my own vineyard have I not kept.

Bible: Cant., 1.6.

611.4 Who eats of his own field is like a baby nursed by its mother; who depends on the market is like a baby nursed by a stranger.

Ahai b. Josiah. *Abot de R. Nathan*, ch 30.

611.5 One measure of my own rather than nine of a neighbor's.

Kahana. *Talmud: Baba Metzia*, 38a.

611.6 Every fox praises his own tail.

I. B. Levinsohn, "Yehoshaphat."

611.7 Man has a portion only in his own toil.

Midrash Tehillim, on *Ps*. 146, #2, 267b.

611.8 Your own takes precedence.

Rab. *Talmud: Baba Metzia*, 30b.

611.9 I love what is fine,
Although 'tis not mine! . . .
The sun and the rose
And the loveliest child!

Rodenberg, "Ich liebe was fein ist," 1864.

611.10 Rather herbs and sacks among your own than cake and silks where you're unknown.
Samuel HaNagid, *Ben Mishlé,* 11C, #38.

611.11 Nothing I have is important to me, for this world is not mine.
Talmud: Derek Eretz, 1.1.

611.12 What is yours is not yours, then how can you regard what is not yours as yours?
Ibid., 1.24.

611.13 The only thing we, as free agents, really own in full inalienable right, is upright walking in the fear of God; hence we may glory in the knowledge of God.
Tosafot of the Pentateuch, 13C.

612. OX

612.1 When an ox falls, many are the slaughterers.
Proverb (Babylonian). *Lam. R.,* 1.34.

612.2 When an ox falls, men sharpen their knives.
Proverb (Palestinian). *Ibid.* Cf. Raba. *Talmud: Sabbath,* 32a.

612.3 When the oxen run and fall, he puts the horses in the stall.
Proverb. q Papa. *Talmud: Sanhedrin,* 98b.

612.4 An ox has a long tongue, yet cannot blow the shofar.
Proverb (Yiddish). BJS, #221. ATJF, p. 641.

612.5 An ox for a penny! But what if you don't have the penny!
Proverb (Yiddish). BJS, #223. See 940. 17.

612.6 You can't get two skins off one ox.
Proverb (Yiddish). BJS, #227. ATJF, p. 641.

613. PAIN

613.1 If you want life, expect pain.
Azariah. *Midrash Tehillim,* to *Ps.* 16.11, ed Buber, 62a.

613.2 Pain leads to reconciliation with our Father.
Eliezer b. Jacob. *Sifré,* #32, to *Deut.* 6.5.

613.3 The sublime poetry of pain.
Heine, *Harz Journey,* 1824.

613.4 Pain spiritualizes even beasts.
Heine, *Gedanken und Einfälle,* 1869.

613.5 Whom the Lord loves, He crushes with pain.
Huna. *Talmud: Berakot,* 5a.

613.6 Pain and suffering should lead to liberty.
Johanan b. Nappaha. *Talmud: Berakot,* 5a.

613.7 Those whom God chastises bear His name.
Jose b. Judah. *Midrash Tehillim,* ed Buber, 209.

613.8 Pain begets endurance.
Mendelé, *Shem VeYafet BaAgala,* 1890. q *Israel Argosy,* 1953, 29.

613.9 There are blows which do not hurt.
Molnar, *Liliom,* 1912.

613.10 The greatest pain is that which you can't tell others.
Proverb (Yiddish). BJS, #1368.

613.11 Not to have had pain is not to have been human.
Proverb (Yiddish). YFS, i. 418.

613.12 Any ache but heart ache; any pain but head pain.
Rab. *Talmud: Sabbath,* 11a.

613.13 If you are visited by pain, examine your conduct.
Raba. *Talmud: Berakot,* 5a.

613.14 Love will sprout out of the seed of pain.
Shimonovitz, "Milhama," 1921. *Shirim,* i. 327. q WHJ, iv. 315.

613.15 It is always only a question of a moment, for the pain which has passed is no longer present, and who would be so foolish as to concern himself with future pain!
Yitzhak Isaac of Kalev. q BTH, ii. 102.

614. PANTHEISM

614.1 All is one, and nothing is separated from Him.
Cordovero, *Shiur Koma,* (16C) 1883, ch 22.

614.2 He fills everything, and He *is* everything.
Gikatila. q SMT, 222.

614.3 Pantheism is the public secret in Germany. In fact, we have outgrown deism. We are free, and do not want a thundering tyrant; we are grown-up, and require no fatherly care. Nor are we the bungled work of a great mechanic. Deism is a religion for slaves, for children, for Genevese, for watch-makers.
Heine, *Germany from Luther to Kant,* 1834.

614.4 During the whole Middle Ages, till today, the predominant view of all things was not in direct contradiction with that idea with which Moses burdened the Jews. . . . But if Satan or sinful pantheism—from which may all the saints of the Old and New Testaments as well as the Koran protect us!—should conquer, there will fall on the heads of the poor Jews a tempest of persecution which will far surpass all their previous sufferings.
Heine, *Shakespeare's Maidens: Portia,* 1839.

614.5 Pantheists are only Atheists ashamed.
Heine, *Memoirs,* ed Karpeles, ii. 228.

615. PARABLE

615.1 By the ministry of the prophets have I used similitudes.
Bible: Hos., 12.11.

615.2 The legs hang limp from the lame; so is a parable in the mouth of fools.
Bible: Prov., 26.7.

615.3 Do not underestimate the parable, for it leads to the Torah's true meaning. A penny wick may help to find a lost pearl.
Cant. R., 1.1.8.

615.4 It was truth, it was a parable.
Judah b. Ilai. *Talmud: Sanhedrin,* 92b.

616. PARADISE
616.A. Conception

616.A.1 The reward of the souls in the world beyond is their ability to attain the true concept of God which is a source of the most wonderful felicity, an attainment impossible for man in this earthly life because of the disturbances on the part of matter.
Abravanel, *Commentary,* on *I Sam.* 25.29, (1511) 1686, p. 128c. q NDI, 296.

616.A.2 Eden is the Holy of Holies, the dwelling of the Lord.
Apocrypha: Jubilees, 8.19.

616.A.3 They who honor the true and everlasting God inherit life throughout the aeonian time, dwelling in the fertile garden of Paradise, feasting on sweet bread from the starry heaven.
Apocrypha: Sibyls, Fragment iii. 46–49.

616.A.4 If they will not admit me in the Garden of Eden, I shall get up on the roof of Gehenna and recite Torah; the righteous will gather about me, and the Garden of Eden will be there.
Baruch of Mezbizh. q *Siah Sarfé Kodesh,* 5688, p. 76.

616.A.5 A man's kind deeds are used as seed in the Garden of Eden; thus every man creates his own Paradise.
Ber. q Berger, *Eser Orot,* 1913, p. 32.

616.A.6 For the pious, Paradise exists everywhere.
Disraeli, *Venetia,* 1837.

616.A.7 Every righteous man has an Eden for himself.
Eleazar b. Menaham. *Lev. R.,* 27.1.

616.A.8 Every righteous man has a tree of his own in Eden.
Ragoler, *Maalot HaTorah,* (1828) 1946, p. 10.

616.A.9 In Paradise God will set a table for Israel. They will sit at ease and eat, while idolaters will watch and melt away.
Exod. R., 25.7. *Num. R.,* 21.21.

616.A.10 Not a day passes in which the Holy One does not teach a new law in the Heavenly Court.
Gen. R., 49.2.

616.A.11 In Heaven roast geese fly round with gravy-boats in their bills; tarts grow wild like sun-flowers; everywhere there are brooks of bouillon and champagne, everywhere trees on which napkins flutter, and you eat and wipe your lips and eat again without injury to your stomach; you sing psalms, or flirt with the dear, delicate little angels.
Heine, *Reisebilder,* ii. 1826.

616.A.12 Wherefore Paradise, where no
    beauty dwells,
    Only women dark as pitch,
    Old, afflicted with the itch,
    Whose somber company the
      heart with sadness swells?
Immanuel, *Mahberot,* c. 1300 (1491), ch 16.

616.A.13 The Prophets prophesied only concerning the messianic age, but as for the world-to-come, "men have not heard, neither has the eye seen" [*Isa.* 64.2].
Johanan b. Nappaha. *Talmud: Berakot,* 34b.

616.A.14 Where there is no toil, no burning heat, no piercing cold, nor any briars . . . that place we call the Bosom of Abraham.
Josephus, *Discourse to the Greeks Concerning Hades.*

616.A.15 When the rabbis speak of paradise and hell . . . these are only metaphors for the agony of sin and the happiness of virtue.
Kohler, *Jewish Theology,* 1918, p. 308.

616.A.16 In the hereafter, the Holy One will prepare a banquet for the righteous, and there will be no need of balsam or choice spices, for the North and South winds will waft all the perfumes of the Garden of Eden.

Num. R., 13.2. See Eleazar b. Pedat. *Talmud: Taanit, 31a.*

616.A.17 A wise man's soul has heaven for its country, and looks upon earth as a foreign land.

Philo, *Husbandry, 14.*

616.A.18 In the future world there is no eating, drinking, propagation, business, jealousy, hatred or competition, but the righteous sit, with their crowns on their heads, enjoying the brilliance of the Divine Presence.

Rab. *Talmud: Berakot, 17a.*

616.A.19 All Indo-European antiquity had placed paradise in the beginning; all its poets had swept a vanished golden age. Israel placed the age of gold in the future.

*Renan, Life of Jesus, 1863, p. 74.

616.A.20 The heathen nations have only a lost paradise behind them; the Jews have one also before them.

*Rosenkranz, Philosophy of Education, (1848) 1886, p. 249.

616.A.21 In this world, a dog may become a lion and a lion a dog; in the world-to-come, a lion remains a lion and a dog a dog.

Ruth Rabbah, 3.2.

616.A.22 In the world-to-come there is no death, sin, affliction, but everyone delights in wisdom and understanding.

Seder Eliyahu Rabbah, ch 2, ed Friedmann, p. 7.

616.A.23 In the world-to-come, the Holy One will hold sessions in His great academy for the righteous of the world.

Ibid., ch 3, ed Friedmann, p. 14.

616.A.24 Eden is without limit.

Talmud: Taanit, 10a.

616.A.25 It is not the saints that are in Paradise, but Paradise that is in the saints.

Teitelbaum. q B. Ehrman, *Peer Kabod,* 12a; BTH, ii. 190.

616.B. Candidates

616.B.1 Work righteousness on earth, that ye may have it as a treasure in heaven.

Apocrypha: Patriarchs, Levi, 13.5.

616.B.2 Alexander knocked at the gate of Paradise, and the guardian angel asked, "Who is there?" "Alexander," was the answer. "Who is Alexander?" came the further question. "Alexander, you know, *the* Alexander, Alexander the Great, Conqueror of the World." "We know him not," was the reply; "he cannot enter here. This is the gate of the Lord; only the righteous may enter" [*Ps.* 118.20].

Hertz, *DPB,* 1948, p. 770. See *Talmud: Tamid, 32b.*

616.B.3 These are among those who will enter the world-to-come: he who resides in Israel, he who teaches his children Torah, and he who recites the *habdala* at the conclusion of the Sabbath.

Johanan b. Nappaha. *Talmud: Berakot, 33a.*

616.B.4 Every man who ennobles his soul with excellent morals and wisdom based on faith in God, certainly belongs to the men of the world-to-come.

Maimonides, letter to Hasdai Halevi. KTJ, 197.

616.B.5 He who resides in Israel, recites *Shema* morning and evening, and speaks Hebrew will have a share in the world-to-come.

Meir. *Sifré,* #333, to *Deut.* 3.43.

616.B.6 All Jews have a portion in the world-to-come.

Mishna: Sanhedrin, 10.1.

616.B.7 These have no portion in it: he who maintains that resurrection is not a biblical doctrine, he who asserts that the Torah was not revealed divinely, and he who is an *epikoros.*

Ibid. See Jose b. Halafta. *Talmud: Tosefta Derek Eretz, 6.*

616.B.8 My father laid up treasures of Mammon, I treasures of souls. . . . They hoarded for this world, I for the world-to-come.

Monobaz, after being rebuked for squandering in alms the wealth of his fathers. *Talmud: Baba Bathra, 11a.*

616.B.9 I saw the sons of the future world, and they are but few!

Simeon b. Yohai. *Talmud: Sukka, 45b.*

616.B.10 A jailer who shields his prisoners against sin, and who informs the rabbis of the tyrant's projected decrees, and comedians who entertain and cheer the depressed and promote peace, are destined for the world-to-come.

Talmud: Taanit, 22a, abridged.

616.B.11 Those who suffer for their sins in this world, while maintaining their Jewish faith and cleaving to the Lord and His Law, have a portion in the world-to-come.

Usque, *Consolação às Tribulaçoes de Yisrael*, 1553, ed Remedios, iii. 49b. q NLG, 128.

617. PARENTS

617.1 Honor thy father and thy mother.
Bible: Exod. 20.12. Deut., 5.16.

617.2 Ye shall fear every man his mother and his father.
Bible: Lev., 19.3. See *Talmud: Kiddushin*, 30b–31a.

617.3 Hear, my son, the instruction of your father, and forsake not the teaching of your mother.
Bible: Prov., 1.8.

617.4 Remember your father and mother when you sit in council amidst the mighty.
Apocrypha: Ben Sira, 23.14.

617.5 There is one thing a man cannot change—his parents.
Ben Gurion, to Anglo-American Committee of Inquiry, March 19, 1946.

617.6 Both parents have an equal claim on the child.
Eliezer b. Hyrcanus. *Mekilta, to Exod.* 12.1, 20.12.

617.7 A son is compelled to support his parent.
Jonathan. *Talmud J: Nedarim*, 9.1.

617.8 The honor due to parents is like the honor due to God.
Judah HaNasi. *Mekilta, to Exod.* 20.12.

617.9 Man should revere his father and mother as he reveres God, for the three are partners in him.
Judah HaNasi. *Sifra*, 86d, to *Lev.* 19.3. *Talmud: Kiddushin*, 30b.

617.10 Parents who expect gratitude from their children (there are even some who insist on it) are like usurers who gladly risk their capital if only they receive interest.
Kafka, *Diaries*, Nov. 12, 1914, ii. 97.

617.11 Children are unruly where parents are untruthful.
Nahman Bratzlav. See BHH, 487.

617.12 What God is to the world, parents are to their children.
Philo, *Honor Due to Parents*, 1.

617.13 To honor parents is more important even than to honor God.
Simeon b. Yohai. *Talmud J: Peah*, 1.1.

617.14 Some provide luxury to their parents, yet are destined for Gehenna; others make their parents work, yet earn Paradise.
Talmud J: Peah, 1.1.

618. PARTY

618.1 Accursed, thrice accursed, is that fell spirit of party which desecrates the noblest sentiments of the human heart!
Benjamin, reply to Seward, U.S. Senate, March 1858.

618.2 Parties like only men who wear blinders and have committed a section of their conscience to their chief.
Darmsteter, *Ernest Renan*, 1893. *Selected Essays*, 235.

618.3 Party is organized opinion.
Disraeli, speech, Oxford, Nov. 25, 1864.

618.4 Without party, Parliamentary Government is impossible.
Disraeli, speech, Manchester, April 4, 1872.

618.5 It is a common enough phenomenon in party life: the men with the most similar ideas fight each other most bitterly.
S. Levin, *The Arena*, 1932, p. 282.

618.6 No shoulders can carry responsible burdens if they are already loaded with partisan chips.
Ribicoff. q *Look*, Sept. 20, 1955, p. 24.

618.7 The Party is always right.
Trotsky. q Souvarine, *Stalin*, 362.

619. PASS

619.1 Thou shalt not pass.
Bible: Num., 20.18.

620. PASSION

620.1 Be not a slave to your passions, lest they consume your strength like a bull.
Apocrypha: Ben Sira, 6.2.

620.2 Passions are cured not by reason, but by other passions.
Boerne, *Fragmente und Aphorismen*, 1840, #89.

620.3 Man is truly great only when he acts from the passions.
Disraeli, *Coningsby*, 1844, 4.13.

620.4 Only through some manifestation of passion can men earn fame.
Heine, *Lutetia*, #54, June 21, 1843.

620.5 Beware of a dog and a savior frothing.
Hoffenstein, *Pencil in the Air*, 1923, p. 148.

620.6 A publicist without a passion cannot make a place for himself.
S. Levin, *The Arena*, 1932, p. 271.

620.7 The quintessence of every passion is selfishness.
Saphir, *Papilloten*. SHW. iv. 56.

620.8 An emotion ceases to be a passion as soon as we form a clear and distinct idea of it.
Spinoza, *Ethics*, 1677, v. Pr. 3.

620.9 We can know phenomena, we can know human beings, only through the fire that is in them, only through their passions.
S. Zweig, *Conflicts*, 1927, p. 189.

621. PASSOVER

621.1 Ye shall observe the feast of unleavened bread.
Bible: Exod., 12.17.

621.2 The Seder nights . . . tie me with the centuries before me.
L. Frank, *Aufsätze, Reden und Briefe*, 1924.

621.3 Jews who long have drifted from the faith of their fathers, . . . are stirred in their inmost parts when the old, familiar Passover sounds chance to fall upon their ears.
Heine, *Rabbi von Bacharach*, 1840. q KJL, 345.

621.4 Passover affirms the great truth that liberty is the inalienable right of every human being.
M. Joseph, *Judaism as Creed and Life*, (1903) 1909, p. 168.

621.5 Even the poorest Jew, a recipient of charity, must, on the eve of Passover, eat only in a reclining position, as a mark of freedom, and drink no less than four cups of wine.
Mishna: Pesahim, 10.1.

621.6 On Passover eve the son asks his father, and if the son is unintelligent, his father instructs him to ask: Why is this night different from all other nights?
Ibid., 10.4.

622. PAST

622.1 Say not, "How was it that the former days were better than these?"
Bible: Eccles., 7.10.

622.2 Uneasy is the present when no past supports it.
M. Adler. *Opinion*, Jan. 1952, p. 11.

622.3 It is not I that belong to the past, but the past that belongs to me.
Antin, *Promised Land*, 1912, p. 364.

622.4 Our past is not only behind us, it is in our very being.
Ben Gurion, "Call of the Spirit," IGY, 5712.

622.5 The past only buries the present, and the old swallows the young.
Berdichevsky, *Al HaPerek, Tze'irim*, 1899, p. 79.

622.6 The legend of the past is Israel's bane.
Disraeli, *Alroy*, 1833, 7.1.

622.7 There is so much to lament in the world in which we live that I can spare no pang for the past.
Disraeli, (Stephen Morley in) *Sybil*, 1845.

622.8 To preserve the past is half of immortality.
D'Israeli, *Literary Characters*, 1795, ch 7.

622.9 That which we possess fully and in whole, obtains only in the past; and the poet, who desires to draw from the full and the whole, turns to the past, must turn to the past.
Eliashev, *Der Zeidé un der Enikel*, 1929.

622.10 Genuine talent cannot thrive without a ground under the feet; and when life does not provide a present, then we fuse ourselves with the past.
Ibid.

622.11 Whatever will be in the future already was in the past.
U. Z. Greenberg. q *Israel Argosy*, Autumn 1952, p. 113.

622.12 He has a great future, for he understands the past.
Heine, of Louis Blanc, *Lutetia*, April 30, 1840.

622.13 The man who seeks to wipe out his own past is thrown into a state of constant hatred of himself. . . . The old cannot be cut out clean. There ensues a sort of spiritual gangrene.
S. Levin, *Youth in Revolt*, 1930, p. 101.

622.14 The future of Judaism belongs to that school which can best understand the past.
Loew, written beneath a picture of his. q Schreiber, *Reformed Judaism*, 270.

622.15 Who cries over the past offers a vain prayer.
Mishna: Berakot, 9.3.

622.16 Oh, seek, my love, your newer way;
I'll not be left in sorrow.
So long as I have yesterday,
Go take your damned tomorrow!
Parker, "Godspeed," *Enough Rope,* 1926, p. 69.

622.17 Only the past is immortal.
D. Schwartz, "The Repetitive Heart," iii. *In Dreams Begin Responsibilities,* 1938, p. 93.

622.18 *Was* pretty, *had* money, *could* sing—all these things are damned useless.
Sholom Aleichem, *Maase fun Toiznt un ein Nacht,* 1915.

622.19 All the times run into the past, yet the past is not full.
J. Steinberg, *Mishlé Yehoshua,* 1885, 1.1, p. 1.

622.20 When mankind desires to create something big it must reach down deep into the reservoir of its past.
Stekel. q *American Zionist,* Nov. 5, 1953, p. 13.

622.21 The destruction of the past is perhaps the greatest of all crime.
S. Weil, *The Need for Roots,* 1952.

622.22 We cannot rid ourselves of our past without destroying our present and ruining our future.
Wolfson, "Escaping Judaism." *Menorah Journal,* 1921, vii. 72.

622.23 The past is our cradle, not our prison, and there is danger as well as appeal in its glamor. The past is for inspiration, not imitation, for continuation, not repetition.
Zangwill. *Fortnightly Review,* April 1919.

623. PATIENCE

623.1 The patient in spirit is better than the proud in spirit.
Bible: Eccles., 7.8.

623.2 Suffer patiently the wrath that comes upon you from God.
Apocrypha: I Baruch, 4.25.

623.3 Be patient in disease and poverty; for gold is proved in fire, and acceptable men in the furnace of affliction.
Apocrypha: Ben Sira, 2.4f.

623.4 In patience and meekness spend the number of your days, that you may inherit endless life.
Apocrypha: II Enoch, 50.2. See 51.3.

623.5 Patience yields many good things.
Apocrypha: Patriarchs, Joseph, 2.7.

623.6 Not through patience, but through impatience, are peoples liberated.
Boerne, *Menzel der Franzosenfresser,* 1836.

623.7 Patience is a necessary ingredient of genius.
Disraeli, *Contarini Fleming,* 1832, 4.5.

623.8 Through patience men can avert still greater trouble.
Ibn Gabirol, *Mibhar HaPeninim,* c. 1050, #104.

623.9 Misfortune may become fortune through patience.
Ibid., #146.

623.10 The powerless has nothing better than patience.
Ibid., #147.

623.11 Nothing reduces misfortune like patience.
Ibid., #153.

623.12 There are two main human sins from which all the others derive: impatience and indolence.
Kafka, *Reflections,* #3. *Dearest Father,* 1954, p. 34.

623.13 In your patience possess ye your souls.
New Testament: Luke, 21.19.

623.14 Be patient toward all men.
New Testament: I Thess., 5.14.

623.15 Ye have heard of the patience of Job.
New Testament: James, 5.11.

623.16 Here is the patience of the saints.
New Testament: Rev., 14.12.

623.17 It belongs to God to act . . . to creatures to suffer. He who accepts this . . . will bear with patience what befalls him.
Philo, *Cherubim,* 24.

624. PATRIARCHS

624.1 The Eighteen Benedictions open with "God of Abraham, God of Isaac, and God of Jacob"—not God of Abraham, Isaac and Jacob—because each patriarch sought and served God for himself, and did not accept blindly the God of his fathers.
Eisenstadt, *Panim Meirot,* 1715, i. #39. See HMI, 164.
Baal Shem. See BTH, i. 48.

624.2 The patriarchs' merit will aid Israel in the messianic era.
Gen. R., 70.8.

624.3 *Genesis* portrays Abraham as active, enterprising, trail-blazing, pioneering. . . . Great fathers seldom have great sons. . . . So Isaac is passive, without a strong will or character, distinguished only by patience. . . . Then came Jacob, full of life, energy, initiative.
Gordin, *Idishé Etik,* 1937, p. 193ff.

624.4 The first of the Eighteen Benedictions speaks of "the fathers," not "our fathers," because the patriarchs attained universal glory and were, in a sense, the fathers of all men.
Isserlein. q Joseph b. Moses, *Leket Yosher,* (1488) 1904, i. 21.

624.5 Jacob our father is not dead.
Johanan. *Talmud: Taanit,* 5b.

624.6 Neither we nor any generation that preceded us can claim credit for God's grace in choosing our nation, only the Patriarchs, as is explained in the Torah.
Krochmal, *Moré Nebuké HaZman,* (1851) 1924, ch 7, p. 38f.

624.7 All three patriarchs carry the Throne of Glory in their hearts.
Maimonides, *Iggeret Teman,* 1172, tr Cohen, p. xiii.

624.8 These ancient patriarchs of the Syrian deserts were in reality the cornerstones for humanity.
*Renan, *History of Israel,* 1888, i. 51.

624.9 The patriarchs are the Heavenly Chariot.
Simeon b. Lakish. *Gen. R., 47.6, 82.6.*

625. PATRIOTISM

625.1 It seems to be a patriotic duty to lie for the fatherland.
V. Adler. q London, speech, U.S. Congress, May 1, 1918.

625.2 Oh, dark is the spirit that loves
    not the land
    Whose breezes his brow have in
      infancy fanned;
    That feels not his bosom responsively thrill
    To the voice of her forest, the gush
      of her rill.
Aguilar, *Song of the Spanish Jews,* c. 1850.

625.3 Give us the fatherland to which we belong by birth, custom and love, and we will faithfully lay on its altar our means and our blood. Forget, and teach us to forget, the dark dividing wall that separated us . . . because you have so often coupled

your patriotism with demonic hatred of Jews.
Auerbach, *Judentum und . . . Literatur,* 1836, p. 67. q LGS, 88f.

625.4 Love of fatherland has no degrees: who does not all, does nothing; who gives not all, denies all.
Boerne, *Wage,* Pref. to 2d ed., 1819.

625.5 What misery has not love of one's fatherland already brought to mankind! . . . Is a country's selfishness less of a vice than an individual's? Does justice cease to be a virtue as soon as it is applied to a foreign people? A fine honor it is which forbids us to declare ourselves against our fatherland when justice is not on its side!
Boerne, *Introduction à la Balance,* 1836.

625.6 Patriotism springs from such noble roots and bears such bloody blossoms!
Goldberg. *Reflex,* July 1927, p. 28.

625.7 Living, just as much as dying
For one's fatherland, is sweet.
Heine, "Two Knights," 1851.

625.8 The Jewish religion is, above all, Jewish patriotism.
Hess, *Rome and Jerusalem,* (1862), #4, p. 64.

625.9 The Prophets were the conscious destroyers of their national state whenever that state became tyrannous. Of romantic patriotism . . . they were wholly innocent.
Lewisohn, *Israel,* 1925, p. 221.

625.10 Let us abandon this narrow conception of patriotism which consists of the doctrine "My country, right or wrong." There is a nobler doctrine, . . . "My country must always be right."
London, speech, U.S. Congress, Jan. 18, 1916. q RES, 73.

625.11 Praised be He who inspires inhabitants of a town with a love for it.
Simeon b. Lakish. *Gen. R. 34.15.*

625.12 Duties towards one's country are the highest that man can fulfil.
Spinoza, *Theologico-Political Treatise,* 1670, ch 19.

625.13 It is good to die for our country!
Trumpeldor, last words, March 1, 1920.

625.14 It is surprising that the Jew, treated as a stranger everywhere in Europe, still persists in ingratiating himself into the national bond.
Vambéry. q Zangwill. *JQRo,* xvii. 412.

625.15 We must make of our country not an idol, but a stepping-stone toward God.

S. Weil, *Gravity and Grace*, 1952, p. 202.

626. PAUL

626.1 The Jews . . . never have needed anything that Paul or any other Christian missionary had to offer them.

*Herford, *Judaism in NT Period*, 1928, p. 231.

626.2 With all Paul's faults, . . . we have more reason to be grateful to him than we have cause for censure. As Jews, we are indebted to him for spreading the ethics of Judaism in a Gentile world. . . . As members of civilized society, we owe him unstinted praise for . . . showing countless successors the way in which light, cheer and comfort, faith, hope and charity may be introduced in a benighted and a cruel world.

Krauskopf, *A Rabbi's Impressions*, 1901, end.

626.3 In spite of Paul's historic inaccuracies, in spite of his amazing forgetfulness of the Jewish doctrine of repentance and atonement, . . . we may still admire the profundity of his genius, and adopt many true and noble elements of his religious and ethical teaching.

Montefiore, *Liberal Judaism*, 1903, p. 174.

626.4 No one misunderstood Judaism more profoundly than Paul.

Montefiore, *A Rabbinic Anthology*, 1938, p. xiii.

626.5 What Paul says about Peter tells us more about Paul than about Peter.

Spinoza. q Fromm, *Psychoanalysis and Religion*, 56.

626.6 All Jews of all ages hoped and expected that the kingdom of heaven would encompass all nations and tongues; but Paul undertook to realize this hope, this is his title to greatness.

I. M. Wise, *Paul and the Mystics*, 1870. *Selected Writings*, 352.

627. PAUSE

627.1 The pause is an essential part of music.

S. Zweig, *Conflicts*, 1927, p. 194.

628. PEACE

628.1 Peace be to you.
Bible: Gen., 43.23.

628.2 Go in peace.
Bible: Exod., 4.18.

628.3 The work of righteousness shall be peace.
Bible: Isa., 32.17.

628.4 There is no peace, says the Lord, unto the wicked.
Ibid., 48.22.

628.5 How beautiful upon the mountains are the feet of the messenger of good tidings, that announces peace.
Ibid., 52.7.

628.6 Peace, peace to him that is far off and to him that is near.
Ibid., 57.19.

628.7 Peace, peace, when there is no peace.
Bible: Jer., 6.14, 8.11.

628.8 I will make a covenant of peace with them—it shall be an everlasting covenant with them.
Bible: Ezek., 37.26.

628.9 My covenant was with him of life and peace.
Bible: Mal., 2.5.

628.10 In peace will I both lay me down and sleep.
Bible: Ps., 4.9.

628.11 The Lord will bless His people with peace.
Ibid., 29.11.

628.12 Seek peace, and pursue it.
Ibid., 34.15.

628.13 There is a future for the man of peace.
Ibid., 37.37.

628.14 Great peace have they that love Thy Law.
Ibid., 119.165.

628.15 Peace be within thy walls, and prosperity within thy palaces.
Ibid., 122.7.

628.16 When the mountains bear grain, the people enjoy peace.
Aha. *Gen. R.,* 89.4.

628.17 Tranquil peace shall make its way to Asia, and Europe shall then be happy.
Apocrypha: Sibyls, 3.367f.

628.18 For the sake of domestic peace, Scripture misquotes [*Gen.* 18.12].
Bar Kappara. *Lev. R.,* 9.9.
Ishmael School. *Talmud: Yebamot,* 65b.

628.19 Peace, like charity, begins at home.
Ben Zevi, Inauguration Address, Knesset, Dec. 10, 1952.

628.20 Are immutable friendship and eternal peace among all nations dreams? No, hatred and war are dreams, from which we shall some day awake.

Boerne, *Introduction à la Balance*, 1836.

628.21 Peace cannot be kept by force. It can only be achieved by understanding.

Einstein, *Cosmic Religion*, 1931, p. 67.

628.22 Peace . . . is the essence of all the prophecies.

Eleazar b. Shammua. *Sifré*, #42, to *Num.* 6.26.

628.23 Peace . . . is the climax of all blessings.

Eleazar HaKappar. *Ibid.*

628.24 The disciples of the wise increase peace in the world.

Hanina b. Hama. *Talmud: Berakot*, 64a.

628.25 Other precepts are performed when the occasion arises . . . but of peace it is written, "Pursue it" [*Ps.* 34.15].

Hezekiah b. Hiyya. *Lev. R.*, 9.9. Cf *ARN*, ch 12.

628.26 Be of the disciples of Aaron, one who loves peace and pursues it, who loves all men and brings them near to the Torah.

Hillel. *Mishna: Abot*, 1.12.

628.27 Peace is indivisible.

Litvinov, at League of Nations, 1934.

628.28 Peace without truth is a false peace.

Mendel of Kotzk. q BTH, ii. 284.

628.29 Jerusalem will be rebuilt only through peace.

Nahman Bratzlav, *Sefer HaMiddot, Shalom*, 1821.

628.30 Where there is no peace, prayers are not accepted.

Ibid.

628.31 Blessed are the peacemakers, for they shall be called the children of God.

New Testament: Matt., 5.9.

628.32 Glory to God in the highest, and on earth peace, good will toward men.

New Testament: Luke, 2.14.

628.33 Would you end war?
Create great Peace . . .
The Peace that demands all of a man,
His love, his life, his veriest self.

Oppenheim, "1914—And After." *War and Laughter*, 1916, p. 148.

628.34 How could you . . . not grieve at war and delight in peace, being children of one and the same Father?

Philo, *Confusion of Languages*, 11.

628.35 You cannot find peace anywhere save in your own self.

Simha Bunam. q Buber, *Way of Man*, 31.

628.36 World peace is possible only through the application of the laws of morality, justice and righteousness in international relations.

Syrkin, "International." *Idisher Kempfer*, 1916. SGZ, ii. 223.

628.37 The blessing of the Holy One is peace.

Talmud: Megilla, 18a.

628.38 Grant us peace, Thy most precious gift, O Thou eternal source of peace, and enable Israel to be its messenger unto the peoples of the earth. Bless our country that it may ever be a stronghold of peace, and its advocate in the council of nations. . . . Strengthen the bonds of friendship and fellowship among the inhabitants of all lands.

Union Prayer Book, 1940, i. 22.

628.39 The world is established only in peace.

Zohar, Lev., 10b.

628.40 God is peace, His name is peace, and all is bound together in peace.

Ibid.

629. PEARL

629.1 Cast not your pearls before swine.

New Testament: Matt., 7.6.

629.2 Pearls round the neck, stones upon the heart.

Proverb (Yiddish). BJS, #2833.

629.3 Pearls are not sold in the vegetable market.

Tanhuma, Behukotai, 3.

629.4 Sometimes in a beggar's wallet one finds a pearl.

Zohar, Num., 157b.

630. PEN

630.1 My pen, though frail and slim of figure,
Has a serpent's tooth and a lion's vigor.

Al-Harizi, *Tahkemoni*, 13C, ch 9. q CHH, 67.

630.2 The pen is the interpreter of the heart.

J. Delmedigo, *Nobelot Hokma*, 1631.

630.3 Consider a pen. . . . It comes new and shining into your hand. It gets blackened working for you. You let it rust. And when it is worn out and can no longer serve you, you discard it with scorn. Remarkable, is it not? A pen has about the same fate as a good servant of the rich, or as a laborer in a factory.

Winchefsky, 1889. *Der Meshugener Filozof*, 17.

631. PEOPLE

631.1 Before all the people will I be glorified.
Bible: Lev., 10.3.

631.2 Hearken unto the voice of the people.
Bible: 1 Sam., 8.7.

631.3 Like people, like priest.
Bible: Hos., 4.9.

631.4 It was only for the sake of the people that God spoke to Moses their leader.
Akiba. *Mekilta*, to *Exod.* 12.1.

631.5 Sin not against the public.
Apocrypha: Ben Sira, 7.7.

631.6 The Tzaddik must descend to the level of the people, to make them understand the word of God.
Baal Shem. q Aaron Cohen, *Kether Shem Tob*, 29.

631.7 Thy will, O people, is the only righteous source of power.
Heine, *English Fragments*, Conclusion. Nov. 29, 1830.

631.8 Princes have long arms,
Parsons have long tongues,
And the people have long ears!
Heine, *Zeitgedichte*, #3, *Warning*.

631.9 Leave it to the people: if they are not prophets, they are the sons of prophets!
Hillel. *T: Pesahim*, 66a.

631.10 Always respect the public.
Isaac b. Phineas. *T: Sota*, 40a.

631.11 People are not as good as their friends describe them, nor as bad as their enemies portray them.
Lazerov, *Enciklopedie fun Idishe Vitzen*, 1928, #424.

631.12 Because Phineas was with the people even in wrath [*Num.* 25.11f], God gave him the priesthood.
Levi Yitzhok, *Kedushat Levi*, 1866, 58a.

631.13 An uneducated man said to Yannai: "I heard it said, 'The Torah is the inheritance of the congregation of Jacob'

[*Deut.* 33.4], not of the congregation of Yannai!"
Leviticus Rabbah, 9.3. Cf Finkelstein, *Pharisees*, 35f.

631.14 You must appear justified before men as well as before God.
Mishna: Shekalim, 3.2.

631.15 Nine *tzaddikim* do not make a *minyan*, but one common man, joining them, completes the *minyan*. Truly, "in the multitude of people is the king's glory" [*Prov.* 14.28].
Nahman Bratzlav, *Meshibat Nefesh*, 1842.

631.16 People are more fun than anybody.
Parker.

631.17 There are all sorts of people in the world: asses and mules, and dogs and hogs, and also worms.
Sholom Aleichem, *Kever Oves*, 1909.

631.18 The history of Israel, from Moses downwards, is not the history of an inspired book, or an inspired order, but of an inspired people.
*Stanley, *History of the Jewish Church*, (1862) 1896, i. 143.

631.19 The voice of the people is like the voice of the Almighty.
Uceda, *Midrash Samuel* (*1 Kings* 18.41 and *Ezek.* 1.24).

632. PERFECTION

632.1 Human perfection may be attained by fulfilling a single commandment of the Law of Moses.
Albo, *Ikkarim*, 1428, 1.23.5.

632.2 Neither in love nor in work, neither in society nor in solitude, neither in the arts nor in the sciences will the world of actuality permit us to attain perfection.
M. R. Cohen. *New Republic*, June 25, 1919.

632.3 The culminating sense of a form arriving at perfection excites us and we rise to the experience of beauty.
Guggenheimer, *Creative Vision*, 1950, p. 3.

632.4 The Bible addresses mankind with a flaming proclamation: The perfect world can be accomplished here!
Gutkind. *Freeland*, Jan. 1953, vii. 6.

632.5 Nothing is perfect in this world of ours.
Heine, *Romancero: Lazarus, Imperfection*, 1851.

632.6 The perfectibility of mankind on this earth is the characteristic work of Judaism.

S. Hirsch. q PRM, 176.

632.7 He who endeavors to perfect himself succeeds.

Hoshaia Rabbah. *Talmud: Nedarim, 32a.*

632.8 Perfection belongs only to God.

M. Ibn Ezra, *Shirat Yisrael,* (12C) 1924, p. 71.

632.9 How can you expect me to be perfect . . . when I am composed of contradictions?

q *Ibid.,* 157.

632.10 Man, being incomplete, is not at rest and is therefore always striving for his completion. . . . And this itself is his perfection.

Judah Löw, *Netibot Olam,* 1595. q BWC, 69f.

632.11 As a man must perfect himself as a man, so must a Jew strive to reach perfection as a Jew.

Z. Katzenellenbogen, letter to his son Gerson, Feb. 16, 1845.

632.12 The New Hasidim maintain that man can reach highest perfection only when he regards himself . . . as an organ of the Godhead.

S. Maimon, *Autobiography,* (1793) 1947, p. 50.

632.13 Ultimate perfection does not include any action or good conduct, but only knowledge.

Maimonides, *Guide for the Perplexed,* 1190, 3.27.

632.14 Be ye therefore perfect, even as your Father . . . is perfect.

New Testament: Matt., 5.48.

632.15 In intellectual perfection the highest good should consist.

Spinoza, *Theologico-Political Treatise,* 1670, ch 4.

632.16 Tinnius Rufus asked, "Why did not God make man exactly as He wants him to be?" Akiba replied, "For the very reason that man's duty is to perfect himself."

Tanhuma, Tazria, 7, ed Buber, 18a.

632.17 The desire to seek perfection, to overcome the physical, and find harmony of being, has been the affirmative note in Jewish history.

Weizmann. *N.Y. Herald Tribune* Annual Forum, Oct. 21, 1947.

633. PERFUME

633.1 Ointment and perfume rejoice the heart.

Bible: Prov., 27.9.

633.2 Perfumes are the feelings of flowers.

Heine, *Harz Journey,* 1824.

633.3 Sellers of spice cannot prevent one another from going to any town. Ezra granted them freedom of movement, to satisfy the daughters of Israel.

Huna b. Joshua. *Talmud: Baba Bathra,* 22a.

633.4 What would the world do without fragrance? We would pine away without it; and so we burn myrtle at the conclusion of the Sabbath.

Zohar, Exod., 20a.

634. PERSEVERANCE

634.1 Bricks are fallen, but we will build with hewn stones; sycamores are cut down, but cedars will we put in their place.

Bible: Isa., 9.9.

634.2 We are beaten down, but we will return and build the waste places.

Bible: Mal., 1.4.

634.3 A righteous man falls seven times and rises up again.

Bible: Prov., 24.16.

634.4 Waters wear the stones.

Bible: Job, 14.19.

634.5 Akiba, illiterate at the age of forty, saw one day a stone's perforation where water fell from a spring, and having heard people say, "Waters wear stones," he thought: If soft water can bore through a rock, surely iron-clad Torah should, by sheer persistence, penetrate a tender mind; and he turned to study.

Abot de R. Nathan, ch 6.

634.6 Talent made a poor Appearance
Until he married Perseverance.

Guiterman, *A Poet's Proverbs,* 1924, p. 69.

634.7 Who persists in knocking will succeed in entering.

M. Ibn Ezra, *Shirat Yisrael,* (12C) 1924, p. 113.

634.8 Perseverance prevails even against Heaven.

Nahman. *Talmud: Sanhedrin,* 105a.

634.9 Persistent dripping will bore through a rock.

Satanov, *Mishlé Asaf,* 1789. q CPP, #2058.

635. PERSONALITY

635.1 I would call the personality of man the gland of creativity.
Asch, *What I Believe,* 1941, p. 173.

635.2 Personality is in the very intention of the evolution of life, and the human personality is just one mode in which this intention is realized.
Bergson. q GIE, 128.

635.3 The humblest of human beings possesses the mystery of personality that infinitely transcends the material products of human skill.
Gompers, *Seventy Years of Life and Labor,* 1925, ii. 285.

635.4 The Old Testament presents *a rich and varied gallery of personalities.* ... This is the real greatness of the Hebrew religion. For this reason alone it is an insult to the historical spirit even to name Babylonians and Egyptians in one breath with Israel. ... Israel was never great in works of external civilization; but in the sphere of spiritual things it produced the highest that was achieved anywhere throughout the East—human personality living its own life in the presence of God. ... And because of that achievement, Israel is "the chosen people" and "salvation is of the Jews."
*Gunkel, *"What Remains of the OT,"* (1914) 1928, p. 52f.

635.5 It's not what you say, it's how you say it—because personality always wins the day.
A. Miller, *Death of a Salesman,* 1949, Act 1.

635.6 All that we cherish must rest on the dignity and inviolability of the person.
Proskauer, *Declaration of Human Rights,* 1945. *A Segment of My Times,* 217.

636. PERSPECTIVE

636.1 If forsooth we have failed to achieve happiness by conquering more lands, ... by traveling faster on the surface of things, why not try digging deeper in our own domain, ... making our life more significant by making it more profound?
Baron, *In Quest of Integrity,* 1936, p. 34.

636.2 How often do the events that determine our lives ... seem obscure when viewed from close up.
Brod, *The Master,* 1951, ch 1.

636.3 When you see yon mountain summits
From a distance, they are gleaming
As though decked with gold and purple.
Heine, *Atta Troll,* 1841, ch 16.

636.4 From the lofty mountain tops of science, the dawn of a new day is seen earlier than below in the turmoil of daily life.
Lassalle, *Workingmen's Programme,* 1862.

636.5 Our concepts of age . . . vary with our perspectives.
S. Levin, *Youth in Revolt,* 1930, p. 84.

637. PESSIMISM

637.1 Pessimism is not a philosophy, but a temperament. . . . It is evident that a period which suffers from general organic fatigue must necessarily be a pessimistic period.
Nordau, *Degeneration,* (1893), 3.4, p. 498.

637.2 Once again, we hear echoes of Indian pessimism, of life bound to a "melancholy wheel," and of human existence condemned to meaningless repetition. For mankind's break with this form of determinism, we have to look . . . to Jewry, who were the first to believe that history itself has meaning and that progress, not repetition, is the law of life.
*Ward, *Faith and Freedom,* 1954, p. 47.

638. PHARISEE

638.1 Pharisaism represents a great attempt to achieve the full domination of religion over life.
Baeck, *The Pharisees,* 1947, p. 50.

638.2 The Pharisees built up religious individualism and a purely spiritual worship; they deepened the belief in a future life; they championed the cause of the laity against an exclusive priesthood; they made the Scriptures the possession of the people, and in the weekly assemblages of the Synagog they preached to them the truths and hopes of religion out of the Sacred Books. . . . The Pharisees consistently strove to bring life more and more under the dominion of religious observance. . . . But the outward was subordinated to the inward.
*Box, 1911. q HBJ, 153.

638.3 Pharisaism was Prophecy in action; the difference is merely one between denunciation and renunciation.

Finkelstein, *The Pharisees,* 1940, p. xvi.

638.4 Pharisaism became the foundation for the foremost intellectual and spiritual structure the world has yet seen, Western civilization.

Ibid., 99.

638.5 The Pharisees survived because they had developed a type of Judaism which was not dependent on the Temple and its ritual, but had its roots in the Synagog and the School. . . . The Pharisees were able to do this because they were the only exponents of Judaism who discovered in it the principle of continuous revelation.

*Herford. *Menorah Journal,* 1919, v. 208f.

638.6 Of all the strange ironies of history, perhaps the strangest is that the word "Pharisee" is current as a term of reproach among the theological descendants of the sect of Nazarenes who, without the martyr spirit of those primitive Puritans, would never have come into existence. They, like their historical successors, our own Puritans, have shared the general fate of the poor wise men who save cities.

*Huxley. q Finkelstein, *Pharisees,* p. xvii.

638.7 The Pharisees are affectionate to each other, and cultivate harmonious relations with the community.

Josephus, *Wars,* 2.8.14.

638.8 Pharisaism shaped the character of Judaism and the life and thought of the Jew for all the future.

Kohler, "Pharisees." *JE,* ix. 666.

638.9 Too much credit cannot be given to the greatly maligned and misunderstood Pharisees. . . . The world owes the Bible with its Psalms, the Sabbath, the church, the school, the hospital, and the gospel of love to these modest and self-sacrificing servants of the Lord. They saved the Jew and Judaism from extinction.

F. A. Levy, *Crossroads in Judaism,* 1954, p. 13.

638.10 Judaism is the monument of the Pharisees.

*Moore, *Judaism,* 1927, ii. 193.

638.11 A Pharisee is one who separates himself from all uncleanness.

Nathan b. Yehiel, *Aruk,* 1101. q Moore, *Judaism,* i. 60.

638.12 The Pharisees permitted no discord between religion and life. . . . Jesus criticized not their doctrine, but its misapplication.

*Solovyov, "Talmud." *Ruskaya Mysl,* 1886.

639. PHILISTINE

639.1 The Philistines are upon you, Samson!

Bible: Judg., 16.9.

639.2 Be mulled wine or cool spring water, but not stale liquid that disgusts everybody; be no Philistines!

Boerne, *Der ewige Jude,* 1821.

640. PHILOSOPHY

640.1 What is philosophy? To deliberate well in reference to any question that emerges, never to be carried away by impulses, but to ponder over the injuries that result from the passions, and to act rightly as the circumstances demand, practicing moderation.

Apocrypha: Aristeas, 256.

640.2 Sarah, the mistress, is the Torah; her handmaiden, Hagar, is Philosophy . . . that sought to flee from her rule into the wilderness . . . but the angels taught her that it were better for her to be a servant in Sarah's house than a mistress in the desert.

Arama, *Hazut Kasha,* x. 1552. q *JE,* i. 410a.

640.3 God revealed philosophy first to His saints, to whom He also gave the Law . . . because philosophy was indispensable to the understanding, promulgation . . . and defense of the Law. Hence it was delivered, complete in all details, in the Hebrew language.

*R. Bacon, *Opus Tertium,* 13C, x. 32.

640.4 The most ancient of all forms of wisdom is incontrovertibly the philosophy of the Hebrews.

*Clement, *Stromateis,* c.200, i. 21. q John Patrick, *Clement of Alexandria,* 1914, p. 270.

640.5 The busines of the philosopher is well done if he succeeds in raising genuine doubts.

M. R. Cohen, *A Dreamer's Journey,* 1949, p. 165.

640.6 Great men absorb themselves in metaphysics only after they have acquired a thorough knowledge of other, more practical branches of learning.

Frances, *Zevi Muddah*, (17C) 1885. q Rhine, *JQR*, 1910, i. 277.

640.7 There is but one God, and this God is Being, that is the corner-stone of all Christian philosophy, and it was not Plato, it was not even Aristotle, it was Moses who put it in position.

*Gilson, *Spirit of Medieval Philosophy*, (1932) 1940, p. 51.

640.8 Philosophers and critics gain in importance as science makes life more complex—more rational in some ways, more irrational in others.

Flexner, *Universities*, 1930, p. 21.

640.9 In truth it is a puzzle to me
Why people study philosophy.
It is such tedious and profitless stuff,
And is moreover godless enough;
In hunger and doubt their votaries dwell,
Till Satan carries them off to hell.

Heine, *Latest Poems: Ascension*, 1853.

640.10 Philosophy will be of value so long . . . as it keeps itself independent of any special religion or other dogmatic doctrine.

Husik, *Philosophical Essays*, 1952, p. 69.

640.11 The aim of philosophic theory is the practical realization of all moral purposes, and this is the essence of religion.

Ibn Daud, *Emuna Rama*, 1168, Preface.

640.12 True philosophy seeks to subject the lower to the higher, i.e., reason should control the natural tendencies.

M. Ibn Ezra, *Shirat Yisrael*, (12C) 1924, p. 71.

640.13 Philosophy is to care and think and deal with death.

q *Ibid.*, 198.

640.14 The Aristotelian laws make men; Jewish laws make Jews.

Ibn Shem Tob, *Kebod Elohim*, 15C (1556). q *JE*, vi. 541b.

640.15 Greek philosophy, especially in this generation, not only does not render its students wiser and better, it does not even make them happier. On the contrary, it turns their natural joy into sadness. How many delightful youths were led by these studies to melancholy, misanthropy and self-hatred, and finally to suicide!

S. D. Luzzatto, *Peniné Shadal*, 1883, p. 417.

640.16 When you understand Physics, you have entered the hall; and when . . . you master Metaphysics, you have entered the innermost court and are with the King in the same palace.

Maimonides, *Guide for the Perplexed*, 1190, 3.51.

640.17 There exists not a Jewish Philosophy.

Munk, *La Philosophie chez les Juifs*, (1849) 1881, p. 14.

640.18 It is the way of philosophic works to ask questions which seem very difficult, and to offer answers which are very weak.

Nahman Bratzlav, *Maggid Sihot*, p. 22.

640.19 The influence of Jewish philosophy reaches deep into the development of modern philosophic thought, down to our time.

Neumark, *Essays*, 21.

640.20 Beware lest any man spoil you through philosophy.

New Testament: Col., 2.8.

640.21 To philosophize is but to desire to see things accurately.

Philo, *Confusion of Languages*, 20.

640.22 Philosophy is the handmaid of wisdom [i.e., Torah].

Philo, *Seeking Instruction*, 14.

640.23 It is Heaven which has showered philosophy upon us.

Philo, *Special Laws*, iii. 34.

640.24 Without Judaism no scholasticism, and without scholasticism no progress in philosophy.

*Schleiden, *Jews in Revival of Learning*, 1876.

640.25 All speculation, perhaps all philosophizing, is but thinking spirals: we go higher but get no farther.

Schnitzler, *Buch der Sprüche und Bedenken*, 1927, p. 47.

640.26 I do not know how to teach philosophy without becoming a disturber of established religion.

Spinoza, when offered a chair at Heidelberg, c.1670.

640.27 Philosophy has no end in view save truth; faith looks for nothing but obedience and piety.

Spinoza, *Theologico-Political Treatise*, 1670, ch 14.

640.28 It will not be long now before all philosophy will be scrapped, except for those who are incapable of being educated.
L. Stein, *Journey into the Self*, 1950, p. 108.

640.29 Philosophy is like the ocean: there are pearls in its depths, but many divers find nothing for all their exertion and perish in the attempt.
Zerahia, *Sefer HaYashar*, (c.1300) 1853, ch 6, p. 25.

640.30 A former theologian is always a philosopher!
Zunz, when young Hermann Cohen was first introduced to him as "a former theologian, now a philosopher." q AMP, 58.

641. PHYSICIAN

641.1 Is there no balm in Gilead? Is there no physician there?
Bible: Jer., 8.22.

641.2 Ye are plasterers of lies, ye are all physicians of no value.
Bible: Job, 3.4.

641.3 A protracted disease defies the physician.
Apocrypha: Ben Sira, 10.10.

641.4 Cultivate the physician as you need him, for him too has God ordained.
Ibid., 38.1.

641.5 Honor the physician even before you need him.
Ibid. q as Proverb, Eleazar b. Pedat. *Exod. R.*, 21.7.

641.6 A physician's skill lifts his head, and he may stand before nobles.
Ibid., 38.3.

641.7 A patient who lies to his physician cheats only himself.
Bahya, *Hobot HaLebabot*, 1040, 3.5.

641.8 Jewish doctors are good-natured and obliging, hasten to help the poor and needy, do not press for payment, and are highly experienced in their art.
*Boniface IX, c.1400. q Bloch, *My Reminiscences*, 291.

641.9 Anyone who goes to a psychiatrist ought to have his head examined.
Goldwyn, attributed to.

641.10 The best of doctors are destined for Gehenna.
Guria. *Mishna: Kiddushin*, 4.14.

641.11 If you charge the rich, heal the poor gratis.
Ibn Tibbon, *Tzavaah*, c.1190.

641.12 Comfort the sufferer by the promise of healing, even when you are not confident, for thus you may assist his natural powers.
Israeli, *Manhig HaRofeim*, c.930. q *Legacy of Islam*, 326.

641.13 It was difficult for the Angel of Death to kill everybody in the whole world, so he appointed doctors to assist him.
Nahman Bratzlav, *Likkuté Moharan Tanina*, 1809, 2.

641.14 If your time hasn't come, not even a doctor can kill you.
Perlstein. q Fabricant, *Amusing Quotations*, 27.

641.15 Pediatricians eat because children don't.
Ibid., 102.

641.16 Physician, heal your own limp!
Proverb. q *Gen. R.*, 23.4. See *Luke*, 4.23.

641.17 Ask the patient, not the doctor.
Proverb (Yiddish). See Yannai. *Talmud: Yoma*, 83a.

641.18 Three things need not be done: shoveling snow, for the snow will ultimately disappear of itself; seeking to marry off girls, for they will finally marry themselves off; and calling a doctor—for man will at last die without one.
Saphir, *Leichtfasslicher Unterricht.* SHW, ii. 123.

641.19 Who is a skilled physician? He who can prevent sickness.
Sefer Hasidim, 13C, #17, p. 22.

641.20 A physician who heals for nothing is worth nothing.
Talmud: Baba Kamma, 85a.

641.21 If the oculist is far, the eye may go blind.
Ibid.

641.22 When Prof. Frank, on leaving Vilna, was asked in whose charge he was leaving the public health, he answered, referring to Dr. Jacob Liboschütz, "In charge of *Deus et Judaeus.*"
Waldstein. JE, viii. 71a.

641.23 Both the doctor and the Angel of Death kill, but the former charges a fee.
Zabara, *Sefer Shaashuim*, 13C. q Falaquera, *HaMebakesh*, (1264) 1779, p. 15b. See *JQR*, i. 159.

642. PIETY

642.1 Be ever subtle in piety.
Abayé. *Talmud: Berakot,* 17a.

642.2 A pious man is worth a whole world.
Abba b. Kahana. *Talmud: Berakot,* 6b.

642.3 Piety is the preeminent form of beauty, and its power lies in love, which is the gift of God.
Apocrypha: Aristeas, 229.

642.4 From the sages let us learn,
From the holy men of old,
Let the fool for riches yearn,
Piety outshineth gold.
Asch, "Sanctification of the Name," tr Samuel. HGT, 256.

642.5 Without wisdom no piety, without piety no wisdom.
Eleazar b. Azariah. *Mishna: Abot,* 3.17.

642.6 Ah! happy is he whose heart trembles with the joy of the Lord, and is forever singing to his Maker! He bears patiently the divine yoke; he is humble and self-denying; he scorns the world's vain pleasures; he lives by his faith.
Eleazar b. Judah, *Rokeah,* 13C. q JJC, 253.

642.7 I do not know what a pious man is . . . but I fancy it must have to do with a kind of cloak: the material is made of arrogance, the lining of grudges, and it is sewed with the threads of dejection.
N. Friedman. q BTH, ii. 74.

642.8 The Holy One is particularly strict with the pious.
Hanina b. Hama. *Talmud: Yebamot,* 123b.

642.9 Beware of a pious fool, and of a wise sinner.
Ibn Gabirol, *Mibhar HaPeninim,* c.1050, #74.

642.10 A pious fool, a cunning rogue, a sanctimonious woman, and the plague of Pharisaism ruin the world.
Joshua b. Hanania. *Mishna: Sota,* 3.4.

642.11 Pernicious piety is when a man . . . will not touch a woman to save her from drowning.
Talmud: Sota, 21b.

642.12 A pious fool is he who sees a child struggling in water and says, "I'll take off my *tefillin* and then save the child."
Talmud J: Sota, 3.4.

642.13 An over-pious girl, a gadabout widow, and a half-baked scholar ruin the world.
Talmud: Sota, 22a.

642.14 True piety is determined by one's attitude to money.
Z. H. Kaidanover, *Kab HaYashar,* 1705, ch 52. q MJM, 462.

642.15 All our exercises in piety are only introductory to our union with God.
Katz, *Toldot Jacob Joseph,* (1780) 1903, p. 278.

642.16 Don't be extravagant in piety at the expense of others.
Lipkin. q KTH, i. 273.

642.17 If a man, out of his abundant wealth, builds a temple at a vast expense, and adorns it with costly offerings, let him not be classed with the pious, for he has gone astray, regarding ceremonious worship as holiness, and giving gifts to Him who cannot be bribed.
Philo, *The Worse Attacks the Better,* 7.

642.18 Piety, great God! and religion are become a tissue of ridiculous mysteries; men, who flatly despise reason, who reject . . . understanding are naturally corrupt; these, . . . of all men, are thought, O lie most horrible! to possess light from on high.
Spinoza, *Theologico-Political Treatise,* 1670, Preface.

642.19 With the Jews, . . . piety meant justice, impiety meant injustice and crime.
Ibid., ch 17.

642.20 Judah b. Ezekiel: To be pious, one must first be correct in civil matters.
Raba: One must be ethically meticulous.
Others: One must observe the ritual regulations.
Talmud: Baba Kamma, 30a.

643. PIONEER

643.1 We Jews have been taught by our history to appreciate the real value of laying foundations for future developments. Our share, as a people, in the building up of the general culture of Humanity has been nothing else than the laying of its foundations long before the superstructures were built by others.
Ahad HaAm, letter to Weizmann, Aug. 12, 1918. AEL, 294.

643.2 No man becomes a pioneer by order.
Ben Gurion, *Call of the Spirit.* IGY, 5712.

643.3 Thank Providence we have come to a wasteland, not a ready-made country, or we would have exchanged one exile for another. Only through the trials and tribulations of pioneering can a nation acquire true title to its country.
Bialik, in Kovno, 1930. See OMB, 23; *JS*, Dec. 1951, p. 10.

643.4 A pioneer has no specialty, no likes and dislikes, no "ego." He is but a nail, driven wherever the country demands. The *halutz* is a drop of the national will.
Jabotinsky, *Gan Zari*. q *HaDoar*, Sept. 22, 1950, p. 1063.

643.5 The difference between a refugee and a pioneer is a difference of prepositions. A pioneer goes *to*, and a refugee comes *from*.
M. Samuel, at National Assembly for Labor Israel, N.Y., Dec. 16–17, 1950.

644. PIT

644.1 A pit cannot be refilled with its own earth.
Johanan b. Nappaha. *Talmud: Berakot*, 3b.

644.2 Before the wise descends into a pit, he fixes the ladder to climb out of it.
Samuel HaNagid, *Ben Mishlé*, 11C, #61.

644.3 Seven pits lie open before the good, and he escapes; before the wicked there is only one, and he falls into it.
Talmud: Sanhedrin, 7a.

645. PITY

645.1 Pity is the deadliest feeling that can be offered to a woman.
Baum, *And Life Goes On*, 1931, p. 201. Cf Rabelais, *Works*, iv. ch 37.

645.2 Pity was invented by the weak.
Mendelé, *Dos Kleine Mentshelé*, 1864.

645.3 To be unhappy is only half the misfortune—to be pitied is misery complete.
Schnitzler, *Anatol: Questioning Fate*, 1893.

646. PLACE

646.1 The Lord did not choose the nation for the sake of the place; He chose the place for the sake of the nation.
Apocrypha: II Macc., 5.19.

646.2 There is not a thing that has not its place.
Ben Azzai. *Mishna: Abot*, 4.3.

646.3 And so man, too, has his own place. Then why do people sometimes feel so crowded? Because each wants the other's place.
Abraham Yaakov. q BTH, ii. 72.

646.4 It is the place which sanctifies the object.
Sifré, to *Num.*, 10.

647. PLAGIARISM

647.1 I am against the prophets, saith the Lord, that steal My words one from his neighbor.
Bible: Jer., 23.30.

648. PLANTS

648.1 Trees and plants and flowers have language, feeling and prayer of their own.
Baal Shem. q Kolitz, *The Tiger Beneath the Skin*, 61.

648.2 In plants, as in sleeping bodies, there is life.
Ibn Daud, *Emuna Rama*, 1168, 15.

648.3 Not a blade or herb but it manifests God's wisdom.
Zohar, Exodus, 80b.

649. PLAY

649.1 George (Gershwin) played good tennis almost by ear.
Levant, *A Smattering of Ignorance*, 1940, p. 186.

649.2 If your stomach be angry, appease it with play.
Pinski, *Abigail. King David and His Wives*, tr I. Goldberg, 1923, p. 48.

649.3 Man is the only adult creature who is concerned to amuse himself.
L. Stein, *Journey into the Self*, 1950, p. 167.

649.4 Every man has his hobby, every man has his folly.
Twerski. q CPP, #1135.

650. PLEASURE

650.1 Who loves pleasure shall be a poor man.
Bible: Prov., 21.17.

650.2 That every man should eat and drink, and enjoy pleasure for all his labor, is the gift of God.
Bible: Eccles., 3.12f. See 5.17, 8.15.

650.3 Man's like a bird all the days of
his breath,
And pleasures are nets that allure
him to death.
Al-Harizi, *Tankemoni*, 13C, ch 33.

650.4 My son, do as much good to yourself as you can, for there is no pleasure in the nether-world, and death will not be long in coming. Should you desire to leave an inheritance to your children,—who will tell you in the grave? The children of man are like the grass of the field: some blossom and some fade.

Apocrypha: Ben Sira, 14.11ff. q *Talmud: Erubin,* 54a.

650.5 Pleasures are manifestations of God's love.

Baal Shem. q SSJ, i. 28.

650.6 Pleasure, after all, is at best an intensely exquisite, convulsive pain!

Heine, *From Munich to Genoa,* 1828, ch 18.

650.7 A pretty maiden, a cup of wine, a beautiful garden, the song of a bird, and the murmur of a brook are the cure of the lover, the joy of the lonely, the wealth of the poor, and the medicine of the sick.

A. Ibn Ezra. q WHJ, i. 228.

650.8 For each pleasure accepted in this world, there is a deduction in the next; and for pleasures declined here, there are pleasures added to the account there.

Judah HaNasi. *Abot de R. Nathan,* ch 28.

650.9 Enjoy the honored vessel today: tomorrow it may be broken.

Proverb. q Eleazar b. Azariah. *Talmud: Berakot,* 28a.

650.10 Hurry and eat, hurry and drink, for the world is like a wedding feast, from which we must depart.

Samuel. *Talmud: Erubin,* 54a.

650.11 Nothing forbids man to enjoy himself save grim and gloomy superstition. . . . The greater the pleasure with which we are affected, the greater the perfection to which we pass.

Spinoza, *Ethics,* 1677, iv. Pr 45, Note.

650.12 A pleasure not shared is only half a pleasure.

Stekel, *Autobiography,* 1950, p. 64.

650.13 Pleasant sounds, sights and smells put one in good spirit.

Talmud: Berakot, 57b.

650.14 When pleasure-seekers multiplied, justice became perverted, and morals deteriorated.

Talmud: Sota, 47b.

650.15 Let us start a new religion with one commandment: "Enjoy thyself."

Zangwill, *Children of the Ghetto,* 1892, ii. ch 6.

651. PLEDGE

651.1 If you at all take your neighbor's garment to pledge, restore it to him by sunset, for that may be his only covering.

Bible: Exod., 22.25f.

651.2 No man shall take the mill or the upper millstone to pledge, for he takes a man's life to pledge.

Bible: Deut., 24.6.

651.3 When you lend your neighbor any loan, go not into his house to fetch his pledge. Stand outside, and the man to whom you lend shall bring out the pledge to you.

Ibid., 24.10f.

652. PLURALISM

652.1 Let all the peoples walk each one in the name of its God, but we will walk in the name of the Lord our God for ever.

Bible: Mic., 4.5.

652.2 We shall treasure and cultivate the variety of forms that human thought and activity has taken, and abhor, as leading to complete stagnation, all attempts to impress one pattern of thought upon whole nations or even upon the whole world.

Boas, *Mind of Primitive Man,* (1911) 1938, p. 272.

652.3 America has believed that in differentiation, not in uniformity, lies the path of progress.

Brandeis, address, Boston, April 6, 1915.

652.4 The great America for which we long is unattainable unless the individuality of communities becomes far more highly developed and becomes a common American phenomenon.

Brandeis. *The Survey,* Nov. 13, 1920.

652.5 A richer American culture can come only if the Jews, like other elements, are given a chance to develop under favorable conditions their peculiar genius.

M. R. Cohen, *A Dreamer's Journey,* 1949, p. 220.

652.6 Out of man's present spiritual chaos may emerge an ordered, pluralistic universe of thought. It will be a universe in which the principle of federalism is applied to the realm of the spirit, as it has been in the realm of political life. Unity will be achieved with no sacrifice of liberty; cooperation without imposing uniformity.

Finkelstein, *The Pharisees,* 1940, p. xxxiv.

652.7 There is nothing unnatural in running a track with two centers; several comets do it and all planets.

M. Heimann, *Aphorismen über Deutschtum und Judentum.*

652.8 Varieties of character and experience enrich civilization. States and institutions are barbarous in proportion as they insist on a dead unanimity.

Lewisohn. *Nation*, July 27, 1921, p. 102.

652.9 If it be genuine piety you aim at, let us not feign consonance, when manifoldness is the design and end of Providence.

Mendelssohn, *Jerusalem*, (1783), ii. 170.

652.10 Many pathways may all lead Godward, and the world is richer for that the paths are not a few.

Montefiore. *JQRo*, 1895, viii. 216.

652.11 We should get out of the ghetto, but we should get out as Jews, with our own spiritual treasures. We should interchange, give and take, but not beg. Ghetto is impotence. Cultural cross-fertilization is the only possibility for human development.

Peretz, *Vegn vos Firn op fun Yidishkeit*, 1911. LP, 378.

652.12 If they, as individuals or as a group, owe any debt to America, the payment can only be made by their remaining Jews, and the same holds true for all nationalities that have come here.

*Rolvaag, *Their Fathers' God*, 1931, p. 209.

652.13 I have learned from [Rabbi] Nobel that in the soul of a great Jew there is place for many things. False doctrines are dangerous only for the little ones.

F. Rosenzweig, *Briefe*, 1937, 420. q AMP, 140.

652.14 The Holy One revealed the Torah to Israel not in one language, but in four.

Sifré de Simeon b. Yohai, #343 (5708, p. 188).

652.15 What sort of God would that be who has only one way in which He can be served!

Yaakov Yitzhak. q Buber, *Way of Man*, 18. BTH, i. 313.

652.16 In a royal park one finds
Lovely flowers of all kinds,
In God's world in many ways
Through many faiths all the same
God praise.

Zweifel, *Here and There*. LGP, 860.

653. POCKET

653.1 The longest distance is to the pocket.

Proverb (Yiddish). BJS, #1366.

654. POETRY

654.A. General

654.A.1 Poetry has injured Religion in many ways. It has introduced indecision where certainty and precision are imperative. It has also done some harm by stereotyping and perpetuating false conceptions of Religion by the abiding tyranny of the beautiful phrase. Chiefly, it has wronged Religion by intruding its creative energy where it has no right of entry. There is no prophetical Hell. . . . The authors of apocalypses were poets, not prophets.

Abrahams, *Poetry and Religion*, 1920, p. 76.

654.A.2 As long as the soul animates man, and longs for light and thirsts for beauty, man needs the fountain of poetry.

Bialik. q OMB, 56.

654.A.3 Were it not for poetry, life would be a constant bleeding. Poetry grants us what nature denies us: a golden age which never rusts, a spring which never fades, unbeclouded happiness and eternal youth.

Boerne, *Memorial Address on Jean Paul*, Dec. 2, 1825.

654.A.4 He who discovered poetry, discovered God.

Esselin, "Fun Opgrunt." *Unter der Last*, 1936, p. 42.

654.A.5 Wisdom is fruit, and poetry is leaves.

Falaquera, *HaMebakesh*, (1264) 1779, p. 49.

654.A.6 Is perhaps poetry itself a disease of man, just as the pearl is only the material of a poor oyster's disease?

Heine, *Romantic School*, 1833, ii. ch 4.

654.A.7 The best of poets lie. . . . A poem stripped of deception ceases to be a poem.

q M. Ibn Ezra, *Shirat Yisrael*, (12C) 1924, p. 98.

654.A.8 The best in poetry is its fiction.

Immanuel, *Mahberot*, c. 1300 (1491), ch 8.

654.A.9 It is impossible to learn the art of poetry second-hand. Poetic inspiration comes only from the depths of the soul.

Ibn Ezra, *Shirat Yisrael*, 111.

654.A.10 The best of poems is that which . . . people understand.
Ibid., 120.

654.A.11 The lines must not drag, verbosity must be eschewed. The words must be harmonious to the ear and light on the tongue. Use no rare constructions or foreign idioms.
Ibn Tibbon, *Tzavaah*, c. 1190. AHE, 69.

654.A.12 Woe to him who wishes to rob life of the splendid poetry that inheres in it! He destroys the inwardness of life and its truth.
Kook, *HaMahshaba HaYisraelit*, 1920, p. 23. q ABJ, 165.

654.A.13 He who cherishes an intimate love of poetry must be pious, for poetry is a full sister of religion, of genuine, soulful piety.
J. Rapoport. *Davḳé*, 1952, xiii. 377.

654.A.14 Many people like a poet just as they like their cheese: they find him good only when moldered by maggots.
Saphir, *Humoristische Abende*, 1830.

654.A.15 Every poet re-expresses the universe in his own way, and every poem is a new and independent expression.
Spingarn, *New Criticism*, March 9, 1910.

654.A.16 My days I'll pass in quiet—
Those left to me on earth—
Nor sing for those who not yet
Have learned a poet's worth.
Süsskind von Trimberg, *Why Should I Wander?* c. 1300.

654.A.17 The new man cannot be formed without a new lyric poetry.
Trotsky, *Literature and Revolution*, 1925, p. 170.

654.A.18 God made the world with rhythm and rime. . . .
And thus the very soul of Song
Was woven in the scheme of things. . . .
I saw it in the town and field,
I heard it in the singing rain. . . .
And then I saw how closely knit
Were God and Poetry with man.
L. Untermeyer, "Poetry."

654.A.19 Poetry is the best way to arouse the feelings of the reader and to stimulate his understanding, for on account of the brevity of the form, its words are impressed

upon the soul and are retained in memory.
Wesseley, *Shiré Tiferet*, 1782, i., p. vii. q WHJ, iii. 88.

654.B. Jewish

654.B.1 The Hebrews had no Great Drama, but in their Great Lyric they were not only supreme, they were original and unique.
Abrahams, *Poetry and Religion*, 1920, p. 56.

654.B.2 It was for the prophet to find God, for the Psalmist to praise Him; in prophecy God speaks to man, in psalmody man sings to God. The prophet makes religion, the Psalmist experiences and acclaims it.
Ibid., 58.

654.B.3 Jewish poetry . . . has become the bearer of fulsome praise to the Occident which in Rome devoutly kisses the slipper of the Pope, and in Germany the tiara of philosophy. The cowherd's tune of its homeland no longer awakens in it that home-sickness which erstwhile, in the Exile, was an inexhaustible fount of tears and songs. Poetry struggles, like its singers, after emancipation; and the emancipation of national poetry is its self-destruction. Medieval Jewish poetry is the document of the freedom of the people in slavery; modern Jewish poetry that of the slavery of the people in freedom. May future Jewish poetry be the living portrayal of the people in freedom.
*Delitzsch, *Jüdische Poesie*, 1836, p. 95. q SHR 72.

654.B.4 Unhappy the man to whose portion it fell
A poet to be among Jews.
Frug, "A Leaflet of Confessions." *JQRo*, xiv. 551.

654.B.5 Am I the last of Zion's bards,
And you the last to read?
J. L. Gordon, "LeMi Ani Amel?" 1880. *Kol Shiré*, i. 104.

654.B.6 A people that was able to lament, to sing, to laugh in rhythmic measures, that possessed the faculty of pouring forth its feelings and thoughts in beautiful forms, was not spiritually dead. And these poets did not sing in solitude, but found a numerous audience.
Graetz, *Blumenlese neu-hebräischer Dichtungen*, 1862.

654.B.7 It is a characteristic of the poetry of the Hebrews, that, as a reflex of monotheism, it always embraces the universe in its unity. . . . The Hebrew poet does not depict nature as a self-dependent object, glorious in its individual beauty, but always as in relation and subjection to a higher spiritual power. Nature is to him a work of creation and order, the living expression of the omnipresence of the Divinity in the visible world.

*Humboldt, *Cosmos,* 1849, ii., 1.1.

654.B.8 The Arabs sing of love and
    passion,
The Romans of war and vengeance,
The Greeks of science and speculation,
The Hindus of proverbs and riddles,
The Jews offer psalms to the
    Lord of hosts.

A. Ibn Ezra. q Johanan Alemano, *Shaar HaHeshek,* (1790), 1860, 45b.

654.B.9 In the depths of the Ghetto the Jew preserved his Bible and his Agada, two wells of poetry at which he could ever refresh himself. . . . The sons of Jacob had, as it were, a latent, subterranean, poetic fire, ready to burst forth wherever Israel's soul had not become too parched by ritual and form, or too degraded by oppression and dishonoring trades.

*Leroy-Beaulieu, *Israel Among the Nations,* (1893), p. 238.

654.B.10 These same Jews, from time immemorial, have been the chief dreamers of the human race, and beyond all comparison its greatest poets. It was Jews who wrote the magnificent poems called the Psalms, the Song of Solomon, and the Books of Job and Ruth. . . . No heritage of modern man is richer and none has made a more brilliant mark upon human thought.

*Mencken, *Treatise of the Gods,* 1930.

654.B.11 Psychologically, all Jewish poetry is a translation from the Hebrew. There is far greater soul-relation between Untermeyer, Bialik and Yehoash, writing in three different languages, than between Untermeyer, Lindsay and Frost writing in the same language.

Raskin, *Anthology of Modern Jewish Poetry,* 1927, p. 8f.

654.B.12 Idea and pathos are the two most prominent characteristics of the Jewish Muse.

Ibid., 9.

654.B.13 In the whole compass of religious poetry, Milton's and Klopstock's not excepted, nothing can be found to surpass the elegy of Zion [of Judah Halevi].

*Schleiden, *Bedeutung d. Juden für d. Erhaltung d. Wissenschaften im Mittelalter,* 1879, p. 37. q KJL, 28.

654.B.14 The Hebrew, in those strains where he communes with God alone, other protectors having failed him, is at the climax of emotional song.

*Stedman, *Nature and Elements of Poetry,* 1892, p. 85.

654.B.15 I have heard that you wrote Hebrew poetry. Tell me in what century did you live?

Zunz, when he met J. L. Gordon. q D. Schwartz, *Wisconsin Jewish Chronicle,* Sept. 3, 1954.

655. POLAND

655.1 What else has it ever meant to love Poland but to love freedom, to have deep sympathy for misfortune, to admire the enthusiasm of the struggler? Poland is the symbol of all who have loved the loftiest ideals of humanity and have fought for them.

Brandes. q LGF, 507.

655.2 Long ago, when the single-headed white eagle was full-plumaged, when its eyes were clear and piercing, and its talons firm and relentless in their grip, it was a proud and noble bird that held its own against both West and North, and protected all who took refuge under its wing most generously. . . . But when the eagle grew old and weak, and the other birds of prey round about had deprived it of many of its feathers, it became cowardly, sly, and cruel; and because it did not dare to attack its enemies, it turned its wrath upon the defenseless Jews.

Franzos, *Two Saviors,* 1870. *Jews of Barnow,* 128.

655.3 The Pole will wield the pen as skillfully as the lance, and will show himself as brave in the fields of knowledge as on the tried fields of battle.

Heine, *Essay on Poland,* 1823. EPP, 805.

655.4 In their seclusion the character of the Polish Jews became a whole. . . . Their inner man is not stunted.
Ibid.

655.5 The honest Jew loves his country like a Pole!
*Mickiewicz, *Pan Tadeusz,* 1834, (tr Noyes, p. 326).

655.6 In the name of the Eternal God of Israel, and with the accord of all prominent members of our community, we turn to you, brothers of Israel, children of Poland, to fight bravely and courageously, . . . and to work whole-heartedly together with your fellow countrymen. . . . Their welfare is also yours.
Polish Rabbis, proclamation, 1863.

655.7 German city children are essentially proletarians, without tradition, without substance, and hence without imagination. Here the five-year-olds already live in a context of three thousand years.
Rosenzweig, letter from Warsaw, June 3, 1918. GFR, 77.

656. POLICE

656.1 If there be no policeman, there need be no judge.
Eleazar. *Tanhuma, Shoftim,* 3, ed Buber, 15a.

656.2 Every policeman knows that though governments change, the police remain.
Trotsky, *What Next?* 1932, i.

657. POLITICS

657.1 Ministers fall like buttered bread; usually on the good side.
Boerne, *Ges. Schr.,* 1829, iv. 48. Based on 270.5. See 602.4.

657.2 You cannot eradicate disease from the human body unless you eradicate it from the body politic.
Brandeis. *Boston Herald,* June 15, 1905.

657.3 I persist in avowing my conviction that the inspired poets, historians and sentenaries of the Jews are the clearest teachers of political economy; in short, that their writings are the statesman's best manual.
*Coleridge, *A Lay Sermon,* Introduction, 1816.

657.4 Real politics are the possession and distribution of power.
Disraeli, *Endymion,* 1880.

657.5 This career of plundering and blundering.
Disraeli, letter to Lord Grey de Wilton, Oct. 1873.

657.6 In politics experiments mean revolutions.
Disraeli, *Pompanilla,* 1828, ch 4, Note.

657.7 In politics nothing is contemptible.
Disraeli, *Vivian Grey,* 1827.

657.8 In politics there is no honor.
Ibid., 4.1.

657.9 Points of practical politics.
Ibid., ch 14 (earliest use of the phrase).

657.10 When the gigantic Roman Empire was endeavoring to wean its provinces from all independent political action, . . . the only message of the New Testament is subjection to the State. . . . There is a different message in the Old Testament . . . a magnificent combination of piety and patriotism. . . . Jahveh's faithful servants . . . felt most deeply the fate of their nation and took part with all their might in public affairs in the name of their God.
*Gunkel, *What Remains of the OT,* (1914) 1928, p. 42.

657.11 Just as a man of muscle may be attracted to pugilism, so a man without character is drawn into politics. It is a calling that turns his flaws into assets.
Hecht, *A Child of the Century,* 1954, p. 363.

657.12 Politics—where they pat you on the back so they'll know where to stick the knife.
Hershfield, *Now I'll Tell One,* 1938, p. 84.

657.13 Politics is the science of how who gets what, when and why.
Hillman, *Political Primer for All Americans,* 1944.

657.14 Ninety-nine percent of all activity is economic and practical, and only one percent is political; but the one percent is the beginning of the whole sequence.
Jabotinsky. q Heller, *Zionist Idea,* 149.

657.15 No political system has the privilege of immortality.
Laski. *New Republic,* May 3, 1939.

657.16 Politics . . . is one of the basic spiritual, intellectual and practical concerns of life. The prophets of Israel never dissociated politics from religion. On the contrary, they were passionately interested in politics. Zion must be redeemed through justice.

Magnes. *Foreign Affairs*, 1943.

657.17 The premises of politics lie in the conclusions of ethics.

H. Samuel, *A Book of Quotations*, 1947, p. 156.

657.18 If the world is not to perish in its blindness, it must revert to the leadership of thinkers and men of faith. Politics . . . must become religion instead of religion —at the first real call upon it—becoming politics.

Zangwill, *Voice of Jerusalem*, 1921, p. 128.

658. POPULARITY

658.1 Speak gently, control your temper, promote peace even with a stranger in the street, that you may be beloved above and below.

Abayé. *Talmud: Berakot*, 17a.

658.2 A scholar is beloved in his community, not because of his superior learning, but because he does not rebuke the people for neglecting their religious duties.

Abayé. *Talmud: Ketubot*, 105b.

658.3 Three are endearing: an open hand, a set table, and jollity.

Abot de R. Nathan, B, ch 31, ed Schechter, p. 68.

658.4 Greatness with the mob is deficiency and inferiority with those searching for the true rank.

Abulafia. *Shaaré Tzedek*, 1295. q SMMP, 29. SMT, 152. See 347.2.

658.5 To be popular with all men is the best of good gifts.

Apocrypha: Aristeas, 225.

658.6 Be absolutely indifferent to popular approval or disapproval. . . . To achieve this indifference, practice constant devotion to the Creator, which leaves little opportunity for petty thoughts.

Baal Shem. q Setzer, *Reb Yisroel*, 87.

658.7 What sin have I committed to be afflicted with such widespread popularity?

Ber. q MRH, 128; BTH, i. 99.

658.8 Write for the mob, not for posterity,

> Let blustering noise your poem's lever be,—
> You'll then be by the public deified.

Heine, *Sonnets*, #7, *In Fritz Steinmann's Album*.

658.9 To please all is an impossible aim, and to escape some criticism is an unattainable goal.

M. Ibn Ezra, *Shirat Yisrael*, (12C) 1924, p. 121.

658.10 It is easy to say "permitted" to all that the people desire.

Lerner, *Hayyé Olam*, 1905. q FRJ, 135.

658.11 I'm a controversial figure. My friends either dislike me or hate me.

Levant.

658.12 Woe unto you when all men shall speak well of you!

New Testament: Luke, 6.26.

658.13 The demagogue, mounting the platform, like a slave in the market, is a slave . . . and because of the honors which he seems to receive, is the captive of ten thousand masters.

Philo, *Joseph*, 7.

658.14 He whose honor is rooted in popular approval must day by day . . . scheme to retain his reputation. The populace is inconstant, so that if a reputation is not kept up, it quickly withers away.

Spinoza, *Ethics*, 1677, iv. Pr 58, Note.

658.15 Woe to the man who is hated by all, and woe to the man who is popular with all.

J. Steinberg, *Mishlé Yehoshua*, 1885, 17.21, p. 99.

658.16 I cannot give you the formula for success, but I can give you the formula for failure—which is: Try to please everybody.

Swope, address, Dec. 20, 1950.

659. POPULARIZATION

659.1 Of what use are locked granaries if the people have no key to them?

Heine, *Germany in the Time of Luther*, 1834.

659.2 Nearly all philosophers . . . addressed their philosophy to the few, . . . whereas our lawgiver, by making practice square with precept, not only convinced his own contemporaries, but so firmly implanted this belief concerning God in their descendants to all future generations that it cannot be moved.

Josephus, *Against Apion*, ii. 16.

659.3 The Judeans who believed in the popular dissemination of their studies retained their learning, while the Galileans, who did not believe in it, did not retain their learning.

Rabina. *Talmud: Erubin*, 53a.

660. POPULATION

660.1 I will multiply your seed as the stars of heaven, and as the sand which is upon the seashore.
Bible: Gen., 22.17.

660.2 Who has counted the dust of Jacob?
Bible: Num., 23.10.

660.3 The Lord increase you more and more!
Bible: Ps., 115.14.

660.4 Europe is over-populated, the world will soon be in the same condition, and if the self-reproduction of man is not "rationalized," as his labor is beginning to be, we shall have war. In no other matter is it so dangerous to rely upon instinct. Antique mythology realized this when it coupled the goddess of love with the god of war.
Bergson, *Two Sources of Morality and Religion,* 1935, p. 279.

660.5 May He make our numbers as the sand again, and as the stars of night!
Ibn Ghayat, "Habdala Hymn," tr Lucas, *Jewish Year,* 1898, 169.

660.6 "Men superfluous to the state, men of whom a country can make no use," seem to me terms which no statesman should employ. . . . No country can, without serious injury to itself, dispense with the humblest, the seemingly most useless of its inhabitants, and to a wise government, not even a pauper is one too many—not even a cripple altogether useless.
M. Mendelssohn, Preface to *Vindiciae Judaeorum,* 1782.

660.7 It is a truth . . . that the comforts and well-being of the poor cannot be permanently secured without some regard . . . to regulate the increase of their numbers, and to render less frequent among them early and improvident marriages.
Ricardo, *Principles of Political Economy,* 1817, p. 5.

661. POSSESSION

661.1 Better a drumstick in hand than a wing in the pot of others. Better a sheep at hand than a heifer far off. . . . Better one sparrow in hand than a thousand on the wing.
Apocrypha: Ahikar, 2.51.

661.2 Rather the possession of one than the expectation of two.
Berekia HaNakdan, *Mishlé Shualim,* c. 1260, 21.

661.3 I never possessed a thing which I would grieve to lose.
q Ibn Gabirol, *Mibhar HaPeninim,* c. 1050, #118.

661.4 You must sow the wheat you have, though it be inferior.
Isaac Nappaha. *Gen. R.,* 59.8.

661.5 Well do millers say, Everyone carries his worth in his tub.
Mana. *Talmud J: Peah,* 1.1.

661.6 Leave the property with him who has it.
Nahman. *Talmud: Ketubot,* 20a.

661.7 It is presumed that a thing belongs to its possessor.
Z. H. Chajes, *Mebo HaTalmud,* 1845, ch 15.

661.8 A man's life consists not in an abundance of possessions.
New Testament: Luke, 12.15.

661.9 Moses expressed it by the name of Cain, meaning "possession," a feeling foolish to the core or rather impious, for instead of regarding all possession as God's, Cain fancied that they were his own, though he could not possess securely even himself.
Philo, *Cherubim,* 20.

661.10 Neither glory, riches, honors, authority, nor anything else concerning our body or soul is really our own, not even life itself. If we recognize that we have but their use, we shall take care of them as God's possessions, being well aware beforehand that the master may, when he pleases, reclaim his own. By this we shall diminish our grief when deprived of them.
Philo, *Cherubim,* 33.

661.11 Rather a little pumpkin in hand than a big one in the field.
Proverb. q Abayé. *Talmud: Sukka,* 56b.

661.12 Rather one bird in the cage than a hundred in flight.
Proverb. q Isaac Nappaha. *Eccles. R.,* to 4.6.

661.13 Rather a pepper-corn today than a basket of pumpkins tomorrow.
Proverb. q *Talmud: Hagiga,* 10a.

661.14 Rather one cow in the stall than ten in the field.
Proverb (Yiddish). BJS, #495.

661.15 He who has the cash has the advantage.
Simeon. *Mishna: Baba Metzia,* 4.2.

661.16 Power and wealth take wings and fly away. These and cleverness are gifts of

God; therefore let none glory in their possession.

Tosafot of the Pentateuch, 13C.

661.17 Help us, O God, to banish from our hearts all vainglory, pride of worldly possessions, and self-sufficient leaning upon our own reason. . . . May we never forget that all we have and prize is but lent to us, a trust for which we must render account to Thee.

Union Prayer Book, 1940, 101f.

661.18 Like a child falling asleep over his toys, man loosens his grasp on earthly possessions only when death overtakes him.

Ibid., 1922, ii. 325.

661.19 Chained to his possessions, man is but a slave.

J. Wassermann, *Lebensdienst*, 1928, p. 188.

661.20 We only possess what we renounce; what we do not renounce escapes from us.

S. Weil, *Gravity and Grace*, 1952, p. 80.

662. POSTURE

662.1 I have broken the bars of your yoke and made you go upright.

Bible: Lev., 26.13.

662.2 A wise man should not . . . stoop like a hunchback.

Maimonides, *Yad: Deot*, 1180, 5.8.

662.3 Your eyes should look down, your heart up.

Nahmanides, letter to his son Nahman, 1268.

662.4 Men are like ears of corn: the emptier the head the more and the lower they stoop.

Saphir, *Badmantel-Gedanken*. SHW, i. 376.

662.5 God created man in a noble, upright stature.

Symmachus. q *JE*, vii. 361b.

663. POVERTY

663.1 If your brother become poor, . . . uphold him.

Bible: Lev., 25.35.

663.2 The poor shall never cease out of the land.

Bible: Deut., 15.11.

663.3 He raises the poor out of the dust.

Bible: I Sam., 2.8.

663.4 The needy shall not always be forgotten.

Bible: Ps., 9.19.

663.5 I know that the Lord will maintain the cause of the poor.

Ibid., 140.13.

663.6 All the days of the poor are evil.

Bible: Prov., 15.15. See *Ben Sira*, q *Talmud: Ketubot*, 110b; Charles, *Sirach*, 40.22, Note.

663.7 The poor man's wisdom is despised, his words are not heard.

Bible: Eccles., 9.16.

663.8 When a Jew must eat carobs, he repents.

Aha. *Lev. R.*, 35.6.

663.9 Poverty was created only to provide the well-to-do with an opportunity for charity.

Anav, *Sefer Maalot HaMiddot*, 13C, ch 23.

663.10 A scanty bread is the life of the poor; he who deprives him of it is a man of blood.

Apocrypha: Ben Sira, 34.21.

663.11 The life of the poor is a curse of the heart.

Ibid., 38.19.

663.12 Poverty is a sand-bank, riches a rock in the sea of life. The fortunate will sail through between them.

Boerne, *Der Narr im weissen Schwan*, ch 2.

663.13 Neglect not the children of the poor, for from them will go forth the Law.

Eleazar b. Pedat. *Talmud: Nedarim*, 81a.

663.14 Ever pray to be spared poverty, for if you are not reduced to it, your son or grandson may be.

Eleazar HaKappar. *Talmud: Sabbath*, 151b.

663.15 Who are God's people? The poor.

Exod. R., 31.5, on *Exod.* 22.24.

663.16 Poverty outweighs all other troubles.

Exod. R., 31.14. See 31.12.

663.17 The great concern of Moses was . . . to lay the foundation of a social state in which deep poverty and degrading want should be unknown.

*George, *Moses*, 1878.

663.18 Poverty is no disgrace.

Ginzberger, *Mareh Musar*, 1610.

663.19 It is no disgrace, but neither can you be proud of it.

Lazerov, *Enciklopedie fun Idishe Vitzen*, 1928, #489.

63.20 Poverty rocks the cradle of all our great men, and remains their faithful companion throughout life.

Heine. See CPQ, 320.

663.21 The worst conclusion is when people think that the poorer man is the less worthy.

M. Ibn Ezra, *Shirat Yisrael*, (12C) 1924, p. 147.

663.22 None is as poor as he who worries about poverty.

Ibn Gabirol, *Mibhar HaPeninim*, c. 1050, #563.

663.23 Rather the grave than poverty.

Ibid., #564.

663.24 Poverty is a wheel revolving in the world.

Ishmael School. *Talmud: Sabbath*, 151b.

663.25 Let the poor be members of your household.

Jose b. Johanan. *Mishna: Abbot*, 1.5.

663.26 Judaism has never seen anything specially meritorious in self-imposed poverty.

Max Joseph, *Sittenlehre d. Judentums*, 1902, p. 52.

663.27 Just when you are reduced materially, take care not to be impoverished also spiritually.

J. Kimhi, *Shekel HaKodesh*, 12C.

663.28 The poor are the King's true "Court."

Leon, *Sefer HaRimon*, 1287. See *SMT*, 234.

663.29 Poor is he who sees the world in the purse.

Sam Liptzin, *A Vort far a Vort*, 1955, p. 13.

663.30 Poverty at birth has never hampered great minds.

Magnin, *How to Live*, 1951, p. 141.

663.31 Poverty brings baseness along with it.

Manasseh b. Israel, *Vindiciae Judaeorum*, 1656, sect. 6.

663.32 Pauperism is the hospital of the labor army.

Marx, *Capital*, i. 1867.

663.33 Half a century on my back, and still a pauper!

Marx, May 4, 1868. q Mehring, *Karl Marx*, tr., 257.

663.34 A poor Jew must not be angry.

Mendelé, *Dos Vintshfingerl*, 1865.

663.35 Respect the children of the poor! From them come most poets.

Ibid.

663.36 Nothing is more poetical than poverty. Poverty makes wise. . . . Poverty refines the soul for noble emotions and good deeds.

Mendelé. See SHR, 250.

663.37 A Jew lives on the go. Want compels him to run, to hover, to act, to work; let want weaken in him the least bit, and he becomes passive and inert.

Mendelé, *Fishke der Krumer*, 1869. See *Poet-Lore*, 1922, xxxiii. 261.

663.38 All Israel is one pauper.

Mendelé, *ibid.*

663.39 The Jewish people as a whole is incomparably the poorest in the world.

Nordau, speech, V. Zionist Congress, Dec. 27, 1901.

663.40 Poverty in a house is more bitter than fifty plagues.

Phineas b. Hama. *Talmud: Baba Bathra*, 116a.

663.41 Poverty is becoming to a Jewess as a red ribbon on the nape of a white horse.

Proverb. q Akiba. *Lev. R.*, 35.6.

663.42 When the bread basket is empty, strife knocks at the door.

Proverb. q Papa. *Talmud: Baba Metzia*, 59a.

663.43 Poverty trails the poor.

Proverb. q Raba. *Talmud: Baba Kamma*, 92a.

663.44 When a Jew grows poor, he looks into his old accounts.

*Proverb (Arab). q C. Field, *Dictionary of Oriental Quotations*, 127.

663.45 Poverty is no disgrace, but neither is it an honor.

Proverb (Yiddish). BJS, #258.

663.46 Poverty and pride don't go well together.

Ibid., #1004.

663.47 The poor are always liberal.

Proverb (Yiddish). q *JE*, x. 229a.

663.48 If a poor man eats chicken, either he is sick or the chicken was sick.

Ibid.; BJS, #263.

663.49 When does a poor man rejoice? When he loses something and finds it again.

Proverb (Yiddish). q SWS, 186.

663.50 When is a poor man miserable? When he's invited to two weddings in one day.

Proverb (Yiddish). BJS, #299. ATJF, p. 641.

663.51 Who steals from the poor steals from God.

Proverb (Yiddish). BJS, #300.

663.52 God examined all good attributes, and found none as suitable to Israel as poverty, for in poverty they fear God.

Seder Eliyahu Zuta, ch 5, ed Friedmann, 18. *Hagiga*, 9b.

663.53 God must hate a poor man, else why did He make him poor?

Sholom Aleichem, *Tevyé: Hodel*, 1904. See HGT, 174.

663.54 The rich eat no ducats, and the poor eat no stones.

Sholom Aleichem, *Heintike Kinder*, 1899.

663.55 The rich are puffed up, and the poor burst.

Sholom Aleichem, *SAB*, 1926, p. 350.

663.56 Four may be regarded as dead: the poor, the blind, the leprous, and the childless.

Talmud: Aboda Zara, 5a.

664. POWER

664.1 With man, might is right; but the Almighty "loves justice."

Abbahu. *Exod. R., 30.1.* See *Isa.* 61.8, *Ps.* 99.4.

664.2 The secret of each power is in knowing that others are even more cowardly than we.

Boerne, *Der Narr im weissen Schwan*, ch 2.

664.3 Power must always feel the check of power.

Brandeis. q MBF, 578.

664.4 Power abdicates only under stress of counter-power.

Buber, *Paths in Utopia*, 1950, p. 104.

664.5 All power is a trust.

Disraeli, *Vivian Grey*, 1827, 6.7.

664.6 Power is the god of the one who accepts only himself.

W. Frank. *New Republic*, March 14, 1928, p. 118.

664.7 The lust for power is not rooted in strength but in weakness.

Fromm, *Escape from Freedom*, 1941, p. 162.

664.8 We have learned in a hard school that, while you can have power without freedom, you cannot have freedom without power.

Gelber, *Reprieve from War*, 1950, p. ix.

664.9 The love of power comes from a lack of the most important power, that of living a life of eternity with every creature.

A. D. Gordon, *On Power.* See *Avukah Annual*, 1925–30, p. 65.

664.10 The decline of a nation begins when it becomes power-conscious.

Gutkind, *Choose Life*, 1952, p. 13.

664.11 The heart declines when power mounts to the head.

H. Hurwitz. *Menorah Journal*, Spring 1954, xlii. 5.

664.12 Power covers many faults, . . . while exile exposes and exaggerates minor blemishes.

Ibn Verga, *Shebet Yehuda*, (1550) 1855, #8, p. 27.

664.13 Might is the greatest blessing under heaven
When it supports a great and righteous cause;
A miserable toy, when to sustain
Some tinsel state it cumbereth the hand
Wherein it rests!

Lassalle, *Franz von Sickingen*, 1859.

664.14 The powers that be are ordained of God.

New Testament: Rom., 13.1.

664.15 Everyone has as much right as he has might.

Spinoza, *Theologico-Political Treatise*, 1670.

664.16 Have we the moral fiber to keep alive our sense of justice as our physical prowess increases?

A. H. Sulzberger, speech, Sept. 12, 1951.

664.17 Power buries those who wield it.

Talmud: Yoma, 86b.

665. PRAISE

665.1 Praise is comely for the upright.

Bible: Ps., 33.1

665.2 Let another praise you, not your own mouth.

Bible: Prov., 27.2.

665.3 Let another praise you; and if not, your own mouth.

Zohar, Num., 193b.

665.4 Let her works praise her in the gates.
Bible: Prov., 31.31.

665.5 The work praises its master.
Apocrypha: Ben Sira, 9.17.

665.6 If you want to praise, praise God; if you want to blame, blame yourself.
Bahya. q Schechter, *Seminary Addresses,* 76.

665.7 Do not indulge in praising your friend; you may thus draw attention to his faults.
Dimi. *Talmud: Baba Bathra,* 164b.

665.8 Some of a man's praise may be sung in his presence, all of it in his absence.
Eleazar b. Azariah. *Sifré,* #102, to *Num.* 12.5.

665.9 If you are praised for parts not thine,
Strive hard to justify that line!
Samuel HaNagid, *Ben Mishlé,* 11C, #90.

665.10 I want neither your compliments nor your insults!
Talmud: Baba Kamma, 102b.

665.11 Pallor is a sign of anger, talk is a sign of folly, and self-praise is a sign of ignorance.
Zohar, Num., 193b.

666. PRAYER

666.A. Meaning

666.A.1 Let your prayer be a window to Heaven.
Baal Shem. q Simeon Zeeb, *Derash Tob,* 55, 97.

666.A.2 The purpose of prayer is to leave us alone with God.
Baeck, *Essence of Judaism,* 1936, p. 146.

666.A.3 All things pray, and all things exhale their souls. . . . Creation is itself but a sweetness and a longing, a sort of prayer to the Almighty, blessed be He.
Berdichevsky, *Meditations,* 1899, q FJA, 318.

666.A.4 Prayer is a bridle to desire.
Caspi, *Sefer HaMusar,* 14C, ch 11.

666.A.5 Brethren, give me a God, for I am full of prayer!
Frishman, "HaYadaata?" *Kol Kitbé,* 1951, ii. 25. q WHJ, iv. 218.

666.A.6 True worship is not a petition to God: it is a sermon to our own selves.
E. G. Hirsch. *Reform Advocate,* 1892, iii. 109.

666.A.7 The aim of our worship is the purification, enlightenment, and uplifting of our inner selves.
S. R. Hirsch, *Nineteen Letters,* (1836), #14, p. 129.

666.A.8 God longs for the prayer of the righteous.
Isaac. *T: Yebamot,* 64a.

666.A.9 Prayer is conversation with God.
Josippon, 9C or 10C, ch 1.

666.A.10 By prayer, we lift ourselves to a world of perfection.
Kook, *Olat R'iya,* 1923, Introduction, p. 13.

666.A.11 To pray is not the same as to pray for.
Montefiore, *Liberal Judaism,* 1903, p. 51.

666.A.12 Prayer sometimes dulls the hunger of the pauper, like a mother's finger thrust into the mouth of her starving baby.
Peretz. q SPG, 162.

666.A.13 Every thought of God is prayer. Holy, true and honest purposes are prayer. Earnest thought, search without vanity is prayer.
Varnhagen, letter to Count Custine, Jan. 1817. JRL, 186.

666.A.14 In prayer we open the gates . . . of our larger self. . . . God comes in to us and claims his own.
Weinstein, *Gentle Rain,* 1953, p. 22.

666.A.15 Let others rely on their hands; Israel's weapon is prayer!
Yalkut, to *Gen.,* 27.22.

666.B. Preparation

666.B.1 A man must purify his heart before he prays.
Exod. R., 22.3.

666.B.2 Not until a man has become absolute master of the warring forces within him . . . will his prayer prove acceptable.
Figo, *Bina Lalttim,* 1648, ii. 35b. Summ. BSJ, 255.

666.B.3 Before prayer, one must feel the need and joy of prayer.
Kook, *Olat R'iya,* 1923, 14. q ABJ, 218.

666.B.4 True worship is possible only when correct notions of God have previously been conceived.
Maimonides, *Guide for the Perplexed,* 1190, 3.51.

666.B.5 He who is about to pray should learn from a common laborer, who sometimes takes a whole day to prepare for a job. A wood-cutter, who spends most of the day sharpening the saw and only the last hour cutting the wood, has earned his day's wage.

Mendel of Kotzk. q Shemen, *Lublin*, 423.

666.B.6 The early Hasidim used to tarry an hour before prayer in order to attune their hearts to God.

Mishna: Berakot, 5.1.

666.B.7 First a Jew must wash . . . then he recites the benedictions.

Natronai b. Hilai, *Responsum* to Lucena, c. 850. q Amram Gaon, *Responsum* to Isaac b. Simeon. See KTJ, 76.

666.C. Mood

666.C.1 In my distress I called upon the Lord.

Bible: II Sam., 22.7.

666.C.2 Out of the depths have I called Thee, O Lord.

Bible: Ps., 130.1.

666.C.3 The soul that is greatly vexed, . . . the hungry soul, will give Thee glory and righteousness, O Lord.

Apocrypha: I Baruch, 2.18.

666.C.4 Prayer is acceptable only if the soul is offered with it.

Ammi b. Nathan. *T: Taanit*, 8a.

666.C.5 When is prayer heard? When the soul is subdued.

Al-Harizi, *Tahkemoni*, 13C, ch 24.

666.C.6 Blessed is the man who . . . praised the Lord with his heart.

Apocrypha: II Enoch, 52.1.

666.C.7 "Upon thy heart" [*Deut.* 6.6], i.e., with due attention.

Akiba. *T: Berakot*, 13b. See Abayé. *Ibid.*, 34a.

666.C.8 If a man can concentrate, let him pray; not otherwise.

Eleazar b. Pedat. *T: Berakot*, 30b.

666.C.9 When your mind is not at ease, do not pray.

Rab. *T: Erubin*, 65a.

666.C.10 Prayer is the service of the heart.

Talmud: Taanit, 2a.

666.C.11 Prayer needs attuning of the mind.

Talmud J: Berakot, 4.1.

666.C.12 Prayer without the heart is like a body without a spirit.

Bahya, *Hobot HaLebabot*, 1040, 8.3.9.

666.C.13 Is this a service of the heart, when the body is in the synagog and the mind in the market?

Lenczicz, *Amudé Shesh*, 1617, 23c.

666.C.14 The main thing in worship is the feeling of oneness with God, the ecstasy with which one serves Him and studies Torah, the attitude which is free of selfish motivation.

Baal Shem. q Aaron Cohen, *Keter Shem Tob*, (1795) 1864.

666.C.15 God hears not those who nurse unjust enmity.

Didascalia, ii. ch 55.

666.C.16 An angry man is unfit to pray.

Nahman Bratzlav, *Likkuté Etzot Ha-Shalem*, (1913), p. 48.

666.C.17 When you pray, know before whom you stand!

Eliezer b. Hyrcanus. *T: Berakot*, 28b.

666.C.18 At worship, cast down your eyes and lift up your heart.

Jose b. Halafta. *T: Yebamot*, 105b.

666.C.19 Whenever there rises in man's heart a joyous thought, a feeling of happiness, a sense of love for His law, that moment is auspicious for prayer.

Kaidanover, *Kab HaYashar*, 1705, 71, 8.

666.C.20 Rise to pray only in a humble, reverent frame of mind.

Mishna: Berakot, 5.1.

666.C.21 Rise not to recite the Benedictions in a mood of sorrow, indolence, laughter, chatter, frivolity, or idle talk, but only in a mood of joyous piety.

Talmud: Berakot, 31a. See 802.23.

666.C.22 Man must lose himself in prayer and forget his own existence.

Nahman Bratzlav. q HLH, 94.

666.C.23 When you pray, remove from your heart all worldly concerns.

Nahmanides, letter to his son Nahman, c. 1268.

666.C.24 A worshiper should visualize the Shekina: "I have set the Lord always before me" [*Ps.* 16.8].

Simeon HeHasid. *T: Sanhedrin*, 22a.

666.C.25 On Rosh Hashana and Yom Kippur, Jews should appear not depressed and in somber clothes, as suppliants before a human judge, but joyous, dressed in festive white, betokening a cheerful and confident spirit.

Talmud J: Rosh Hashana, 1.3.

666.D. Form

666.D.1 Repeat not your words in your prayer.

Apocrypha: Ben Sira, 7.14.

666.D.2 Avoid lengthy repetitions, and thus prevent the desecration of the Name, for the rumor has spread among Gentiles that Jews spit and cough and chatter during their prayers.

Maimonides, *Responsa,* ed Freimann, #36, p. 37.

666.D.3 Gentiles join their hands in prayer, signifying that their hands are bound. We express the same idea by putting our feet together when we rise for the Benedictions. This symbolizes greater humility; for with the hands bound, one can still run for pleasure, but not with the feet bound.

J. M. Epstein, *Kitzur Shné Luhot Ha-Berit,* 1683, 1689, 48b.

666.D.4 Who prays in Aramaic will receive no aid from the angels, for they do not understand Aramaic.

Johanan b. Nappaha. *T: Sabbath,* 12b.

666.D.5 Recite the *Shema* in any language you understand.

Talmud: Berakot, 13a.

666.D.6 Who prays without knowing what he prays, does not pray.

Maimon b. Joseph, *Letter of Consolation,* 1160.

666.D.7 Let those who do not know Hebrew learn the prayers in their own vernacular, for prayer must be understood. If the heart does not know what the lips utter, it is no prayer.

Sefer Hasidim, 13C, #11, p. 9.

666.D.8 The significance of the prayers consists not alone in their content but also in their traditional forms, in the verbiage in which they have been bequeathed to us, hence, also in the Hebrew language. This must remain, therefore, with few exceptions, the language of prayer.

Geiger, *Israelitisches Gebetbuch,* 1854, Introduction. q Philipson, *Centenary Papers,* 124.

666.D.9 Jewish prayer means praying in Hebrew.

Rosenzweig, letter to G. Scholem, March 10, 1921. GFR 102.

666.D.10 You may abbreviate your prayers.

Jose b. Halafta. *T: Berakot,* 3a.

666.D.11 When you address the Holy One, let your words be few.

Meir. *T: Berakot,* 61a.

666.D.12 The prayer of the righteous is short.

Mekilta, to *Exod.* 15.25.

666.D.13 When the children of Israel came to the Red Sea, and Moses prayed long, the Holy One said to him: "My children are in trouble, the sea before them and the enemy behind them, and you stand here indulging in long prayers!"

Eliezer b. Hyrcanus. *Mekilta,* to *Exod.* 14.15.

Judah b. Ilai. *T: Sota,* 37a.

666.D.14 In prayer, there is a time to be brief and a time to be profuse.

Eliezer b. Hyrcanus. *Mekilta,* to *Exod.* 14.15.

666.D.15 He who expects his prayer to be answered just because he drew it out, will be disappointed.

Johanan b. Nappaha. *T: Berakot,* 32b.

666.D.16 Rather a short prayer recited slowly and with devotion, than a long prayer recited hurriedly and without devotion.

Sefer Hasidim, 13C, #839, p. 212.

666.D.17 If you recite the Benedictions in a form other than the traditional, you do not fulfil your duty.

Jose b. Halafta. *Tosefta: Berakot,* 4.5.

666.D.18 Change not the form in which the sages cast the prayers.

Talmud J: Berakot, 5.2.

666.D.19 Haggai, Zechariah and Malachi, together with a hundred and twenty elders, arranged for us the Eighteen Benedictions, in which the learned and the unlearned may be equal, the former adding nothing to it, the latter omitting nothing from it.

Maimon b. Joseph, *Letter of Consolation,* 1160. See *Yoma* 69b.

666.D.20 Our prayer is acceptable if we recite it exactly as the Men of the Great Synod ordained it, even though we do not understand the words, which is not so when we pray in another language.

Sofer, *Elé Dibré HaBerit,* 1819.

666.D.21 The old prayers, . . . in which our fathers poured out their hearts to God, awaken our personal religious sentiments and blend them with the religious sentiments of the ages.

Steinthal. q *HaShiloah*, 1901, v. 423.

666.D.22 If a worshiper is unable to face toward Jerusalem, let him concentrate mentally on the Holy of Holies.

Mishna: Berakot, 4.5.

666.D.23 A worshiper should turn in his mind toward . . . the Holy of Holies. Thus will all Jews turn their hearts toward one place.

Talmud: Berakot, 30a.

666.D.24 When you pray to God, you need not specify your needs, or indicate the way of deliverance, as you would to a mortal. God knows better than you wherein your true welfare lies.

Norzi, *Marpé LaNefesh*, c. 1561, 20a. See JJC, 262.

666.D.25 Do not let your prayer become perfunctory.

Simeon b. Nathaniel. *Mishna: Abot*, 2.13.

666.D.26 Use a different form of words each day, lest by familiarity the prayers lose their spontaneity.

Landsofer, *Tzavaah*, 1710. AHE, 288.

666.D.27 Offer your prayers and meditations not as a commandment of men learned by rote, for only prayers that express your own heart and mind can bring you nigh to your Father in heaven.

Eybeshitz, *Yaarot Debash*, 1782, ii. 65.

666.D.28 It would be better for every man to pray when he feels inspired, to pray his own prayer and in a language familiar to him.

Nahman Bratzlav. q HLH, 94.

666.D.29 Prayer should be recited softly, so as not to put transgressors to shame.

Simeon b. Yohai. *T: Sota*, 32b.

666.D.30 He who recites his prayer aloud, in order that it may be heard, belongs to those of little faith.

Talmud: Berakot, 24b.

666.D.31 The prayers must be enunciated distinctly, but the voice should not be raised.

Hamnuna. *T: Berakot*, 31a.

666.D.32 Say your prayers softly, for thus is devotion aroused.

Judah b. Asher, *Tzavaah*, 14C. AHE, 175.

666.D.33 The voice is not prayer. . . . It behooves us to pray silently.

Zohar, Gen., 210a.

666.D.34 Pronounce your prayers clearly and precisely, so that each word may illumine the skies.

Zevi HaCohen. q Yekutiel Arieh, *Mebaser Tob*, 1900, p. 12.

666.D.35 Israel is the creator of true prayer.

*Wellhausen. q Hertz, *DPB*, p. xii.

666.D.36 Certainly the Jew has cause to thank God and the fathers before him, for the noblest Liturgy the annals of faith can show.

*Biddle. *JQRo*, Jan. 1907.

666.D.37 The Jew sings logic and prays metaphysics.

Zunz. q Schreiber, *Reformed Judaism*, 125.

666.E. Time

666.E.1 Call upon Me in the day of trouble.

Bible: Ps., 50.15.

666.E.2 Let my prayer be . . . in an acceptable time.

Bible: Psalms, 69.14.

666.E.3 There are times specially suitable for prayer.

Jose b. Halafta. *TJ: Makkot*, 2.6.

666.E.4 Would that man could pray all day; prayer never loses its value.

Johanan. *TJ: Berakot*, 1.1.

666.E.5 Every day I will bless Thee.

Bible: Ps., 145.2.

666.E.6 When Daniel knew that the writing was signed, he went into his house —his windows being open in his upper chamber toward Jerusalem—and he knelt upon his knees three times a day, and prayed and gave thanks before his God, as he did aforetime.

Bible: Dan., 6.11.

666.E.7 The gates of prayer are never closed.

Anan. *Deut. R.*, 2.12.

666.E.8 It is good to go morning, midday and evening into the Lord's dwelling, for the glory of your Creator.

Apocrypha: II Enoch, 51.4.

666.E.9 Happy shall those men be throughout the earth who shall truly love the Mighty God, blessing Him before eating and drinking.

Apocrypha: Sibyl, 4.24. See Assi. *T: Berakot*, 20b.

666.E.10 Pray and pray again, and you may light upon the hour when your prayer will be answered.

Hiyya Rabba. *Deut. R.*, 2.12.

666.E.11 It is meritorious to pray at twilight.

Johanan b. Nappaha. *T: Berakot*, 29b.

666.E.12 Saints . . . wake early every dawn to seek Thine house.

Judah Halevi, *Selected Poems*, 119.

666.E.13 Attend not to business before offering your devotions.

Zera. *T: Berakot*, 14a.

666.F. Place

666.F.1 Out of His temple He heard my voice.

Bible: II Sam., 22.7.

666.F.2 A man needs no fixed places to say his prayers, no synagogs; among the trees of the forest, everywhere one can pray.

Baal Shem. q HLH, 10.

666.F.3 It is better to pray at home, for in the synagog it is impossible to escape envy and hearing idle talk.

Elijah Gaon, *Alim LiTerufa*, 1836. AHE, 321.

666.F.4 Even from the mud, I will sing unto Thee, my God, even from the mud.

Glatstein, *Ven Yash Is Gekumen*, 1938.

666.F.5 Pray only in a room with windows.

Johanan b. Nappaha. *T: Berakot*, 34b.

666.F.6 Pray in a place set aside for prayer.

Johanan b. Nappaha. *TJ: Berakot*, 4.4.

666.F.7 Who prays at home is as if he had raised an iron wall.

Ibid., 5.1.

666.F.8 Rise and pray on a high place.

Johanan b. Nappaha. *TJ: Megilla*, 1.9.

666.F.9 Offer your devotions while on the road.

Jose b. Halafta. *T: Berakot*, 3a.

666.F.10 When Jews respond in synagog and school to the call for prayer with "May His great Name be praised!" the Holy One nods and says, "Happy the King who is thus praised in this house!"

Ibid.

666.F.11 With a pure mind and will, you can approach God anywhere.

Judah Halevi, *Cuzari*, c. 1135, 5.22.

666.F.12 Praying in Jerusalem is like praying before the Throne of Glory, for the gate of heaven is there.

Midrash Tehillim, 91.7, ed Buber, 400.

666.G. Public Prayer

666.G.1 In prayer, always associate yourself with the congregation, and say: *our* God, lead *us*, etc.

Abayé. *T: Berakot*, 30a.

666.G.2 The righteous pray for the world, . . . even for the wicked.

Aha, Simon. *Tanhuma, VaYera*, #9, ed Buber, p. 91.

666.G.3 Because David prayed alone, he said, "in an acceptable time" [*Ps.* 69.14]. A community's prayer is acceptable at all times.

Deut. R., 2.12.

666.G.4 Include in your prayer for your own sick all the sick.

Hanina b. Hama, Jose b. Halafta. *T: Sabbath*, 12b.

666.G.5 To be heard, a prayer must be for, or in, a congregation.

Judah Halevi, *Cuzari*, c. 1135, 3.17.

666.G.6 Praying only for oneself is like . . . refusing to assist fellow citizens in the repair of their walls. . . . In a congregation, one makes up for the defects of the other.

Ibid., 3.19.

666.G.7 An angel collects all the prayers offered in the synagogs, weaves them into garlands, and puts them on God's head.

Meir. *Exod. R.*, 21.4. *Zohar, Gen.*, 167b, names Sandalphon.

666.G.8 "*Ye* shall serve the Lord . . . and He will bless *thy* bread" [*Exod.* 23.25]. One eats by oneself, even in company, but should pray in communion with all Israel, even when alone.

Mendel of Kotzk. See SRT, ii. 38; BTH, ii. 282.

666.G.9 It is this merging with a congregation that makes prayer unselfish.

Moses Hasid, *Iggeret HaMusar*, 1717. AHE, 292.

666.G.10 Include friend and foe in your petitions, for how can one ask God for blessings which he does not want others to have?

Orhot Tzaddikim, 15C, ch 9.

666.G.11 He is a sinner who refuses to pray for his fellow.

Rab. *T: Berakot*, 12b.

666.G.12 A priest is not blameless who fails to pray for his generation.

Raba. *T: Makkot*, 11a.

666.G.13 We who are scattered to the four winds of heaven, should supplicate Almighty God for the peace of *all* the inhabitants of the world . . . for in their peace we, too, have peace.

Rossi. q Hertz, *DPB*, 507.

666.G.14 A prayer not spoken in the name of Israel is no prayer.

P. Shapiro. q BTH, i. 126.

666.G.15 He who prays for his fellow-man, while he himself is in the same need, will be answered first.

Talmud: Baba Kamma, 92a.

666.H. Praise

666.H.1 This is my God, and I will glorify Him.

Bible: Exod., 15.2.

666.H.2 I will speak of His excellencies.

Akiba. *T: Sefer Torah*, 3.10.

666.H.3 Ascribe greatness to our God.

Bible: Deut., 32.3.

666.H.4 They shall declare My glory among the nations.

Bible: Isa., 66.19. See *Ps.*, 96.3.

666.H.5 What is His glory? That His children declare His glory among the nations.

Eleazar b. Pedat. *Midrash Tehillim*, 44.1.

666.H.6 Exalt ye the Lord our God.

Bible: Ps., 99.9.

666.H.7 Praise the name of the Lord.

Ibid., 113.1.

666.H.8 Let them bless Thy glorious name that is exalted above all blessing and praise.

Bible: Neh., 9.5. See *Kaddish; Talmud: Berakot*, 33a.

666.H.9 Good is a psalm sung to God from a glad heart.

Apocrypha: Psalms of Solomon, 3.2.

666.H.10 We know that praise does not profit Thee, . . . yet the moral consciousness with which Thou hast endowed us dictates that we acknowledge Thy wondrous favors unto us by praise . . . according to our ability.

Bahya, *Hobot HaLebabot, Bakasha*, 1040.

666.H.11 God created man to admire the splendor of the world. Every author, be he

ever so great, desires the praise of his work.

Heine, *Harzreise*, 1826.

666.H.12 He is forgiven, even for a touch of idolatry, who responds with all his might, "Amen, the name of the Lord be praised!"

Johanan b. Nappaha. *T: Sabbath*, 119b.

666.H.13 Magnified and sanctified be His great name in the world which He created according to His will.

Kaddish. See *II Sam.* 7.26; *DPB*, ed Singer, 37.

666.H.14 The universe throbs with Thy pauseless praise.

Kalir, *The Lord Is King*, tr ZVJ, 158.

666.H.15 Thy praise, O our God, shall never depart from our mouth.

Kedusha. See *DPB*, ed Singer, 46; *UPB*, i. 126.

666.H.16 Praise God for misfortune as well as for good fortune.

Meir. *Mishna: Berakot*, 9.5. See *Lev. R.*, 36.2.

666.H.17 I know your Lord. . . . He permits Himself what He forbids others. Others must do good without thought of reward, . . . but He wants to be thanked and adored. . . . And you, who do His will, are not niggardly. You lay it on thick, you abject flatterers!

Mendelé, (Ashmedai in) *Di Kliatshé*, 1873, ch 20.

666.H.18 This was the purpose of the whole creation, that man should recognize and know Him and give praise to His name.

Nahmanides, *Commentary.* q SSJ, i. 121.

666.H.19 God is not dependent on being glorified by His creatures. . . . But all creatures justify their creation by honoring the Lord.

Judah Löw. See BWC, 90.

666.H.20 Though we on earth a thousand years shall dwell,
Too brief the space Thy marvels forth to tell!

I. Najara, "Yah Ribbon," 1587, tr Abrahams.

666.H.21 He who has God for his heritage should bless and praise Him, since this is the only return he can offer.

Philo, *Sobriety*, 11. See *Sacrifices of Abel and Cain*, 18. *Seder Eliyahu Rabbah*, ch 15 (14), ed Friedmann, 69.

666.H.22 Praise the Lord before you supplicate Him.
Simlai. *T: Berakot,* 32a.

666.H.23 All the world shall come to
serve Thee
And bless Thy glorious Name.
Yom Kippur Musaf Hymn, 7C, author unknown, tr ZVJ, 237.

666.I. Petition

666.I.1 Pour out your heart before Him.
Bible: Ps., 62.9.

666.I.2 Pray not for material prosperity: a partition rises when the material is introduced into the spiritual.
Baal Shem. See HLH, 10; SSJ, i. 24.

666.I.3 If I recite my wants, it is not to remind Thee of them, but only that I may be conscious of my dependence upon Thee.
Bahya, *Hobot HaLebabot,* 1040, 8.3.18.

666.I.4 Supplication is good both before and after the pronouncement of the doom.
Isaac b. Phineas. *T: Rosh Hashana,* 16a.

666.I.5 We should beseech God, not to give us blessings, . . . but for capacity to receive, and, having received, to keep them.
Josephus, *Against Apion,* ii. 23.

666.I.6 To pray that the expected baby be a boy is a vain prayer. . . . To pray, on hearing cries of distress, "that it be not in my house," is a vain prayer.
Mishna: Berakot, 9.3.

66.I.7 There is no prayer so blessed as the prayer which asks for nothing.
O. J. Simon, *Faith and Experience,* 1895, p. 13.

66.I.8 A poor man's prayer breaks through all barriers and storms its way into the presence of the Almighty.
Zohar, Gen., 168b.

666.J. Thanksgiving

666.J.1 It is good to give thanks unto the Lord.
Bible: Ps., 92.2.

666.J.2 Give thanks to the Lord, for He is good.
Ibid., 106.1. See *Isa.,* 12.4; *Jer.,* 31.11.

666.J.3 Be not like those who honor their gods in prosperity and curse them in adversity. In pleasure or pain, give thanks!
Akiba. *Mekilta,* to *Exod.* 20.20.

666.J.4 Give thanks unto Him before the Gentiles. . . . Extol Him before all the living.
Apocrypha: Tobit, 13.3f.

666.J.5 Lord, I thank Thee for the goodness of growth, I thank Thee for the slice of bread and the prayerful mood.
Ben Amittai. q HMH, 210.

666.J.6 Blessed be our God, in whose abode is joy, of whose bounty we have partaken, and through whose goodness we live.
Grace after a wedding feast. *DPB,* ed Singer, 300.

666.J.7 Who directed the first prayer of thanksgiving to God? A woman, Leah, when she cried out in the fullness of joy, "Now again will I praise the Lord!"
Johanan b. Nappaha. q KJL, 114.

666.J.8 Rock from whose store we have
eaten. . . .
His is the bread we have eaten,
His is the wine we have drunken,
Wherefore with lips let us laud
Him.
Medieval table hymn, tr ZCG, ch 21.

666.J.9 In the future, all sacrifices and prayers will be abolished, except that of thanksgiving.
Menahem of Gallia. *Lev. R.,* 9.7.

666.J.10 If a Jew breaks a leg, he thanks God he did not break both legs; if he breaks both, he thanks God he did not break his neck.
Proverb (Yiddish). q *JE,* x. 229a.

666.J.11 As long as the soul is within me, I will give thanks unto Thee, O Lord, my God and God of my fathers.
Talmud: Berakot, 60b. *UPB,* i. 101.

666.K. Meditation

666.K.1 Commune with your own heart upon your bed, and be still.
Bible: Ps., 4.5.

666.K.2 Words are the shell, meditation the kernel. Words are the body of the prayer, and meditation its spirit.
Bahya, *Hobot HaLebabot,* 1040, 8.3.9.

666.L. Efficacy

666.L.1 Before they call, I will answer.
Bible: Isa., 65.24.

666.L.2 If My people . . . pray . . . and turn from their evil ways, then will I hear from heaven, forgive their sin, and heal their land.
Bible: II Chron., 7.14.

666.L.3 Pious men . . . can change the laws of nature by prayer.
Albo, *Ikkarim,* 1428, 1.21.1.

666.L.4 Prayer, if offered from the heart and for the sake of heaven, even though the worshiper does not know its meaning, ascends on high and pierces the firmament.
Baal Shem. q Kleinman, *Or Yesharim*, 1924.

666.L.5 There was none greater in good deeds than Moses, yet he was answered only after prayer.
Eleazar b. Pedat. *T: Berakot*, 32a.

666.L.6 Who blesses God in adversity will have his prosperity doubled.
Eleazar HaKappar. *T: Berakot*, 63a.

666.L.7 If a man's prayers are not answered, let him pray more.
Hama b. Hanina. *T: Berakot*, 32b.

666.L.8 *Atar*, "entreaty," has the same root as the word for pitchfork, for as a pitchfork turns sheaves from one position to another, so does the prayer of the righteous move the dispensations of the Holy One from the attribute of anger to that of mercy.
Isaac. *T: Yebamot*, 64a.

666.L.9 The Holy One responds to the prayer of adults only after the little ones offered their supplication.
Seder Eliyahu Rabbah, ch 8, ed Friedmann, p. 44.

666.L.10 The Holy One delights in the prayer of the righteous, yet He does not always grant their requests.
Zohar, Exod., 15a.

666.M. Prayers

666.M.1 May the words of my mouth and the meditation of my heart be acceptable before Thee, O Lord, my Rock and my Redeemer.
Bible: Ps., 19.15.

666.M.2 We beseech Thee, O Lord, save now! We beseech Thee, O Lord, make us now to prosper!
Ibid., 118.25.

666.M.3 Lord, forgive me for that which cannot harm Thee, and give me that of which I cannot deprive Thee.
Al-Harizi, *Tahkemoni*, 13C, ch 48.

666.M.4 May it be Thy will . . . to give everyone his needs.
Eliezer b. Hyrcanus. *Tosefta: Berakot*, 3.11.

666.M.5 May it be Thy will to remove all barriers between Thee and us. . . . Endow us with the vision to see in everyone

his good qualities and to overlook his defects. Then will our prayers raise us to ever higher levels, and bring us ever nearer to Thee.
Elimelek, Introd. morning prayer (Azulai, *Likkute Zevi*, Vienna, 1869, end). See Hertz, *DPB*, 2.

666.M.6 My God, before I was formed, I was worthless, and now I am as if I had not been formed. Dust am I in life, and all the more so in death. Lo, I am before Thee like a vessel full of shame and confusion. May it be Thy will that I sin no more, and the sins which I have committed, purge away in Thine abounding mercies, but not through pain and sore diseases.
Hamnuna, Confession. *T: Berakot*, 17a.

666.M.7 Unite our hearts, O God, to fear Thy name. Keep us far from what Thou hatest, bring us near to what Thou lovest, and deal mercifully with us for Thy name's sake.
Hiyya b. Abba. *TJ: Berakot*, 4.2.

666.M.8 Lord of the universe, since both the besieged and the besiegers are Thy people, answer not, I pray Thee, the curses which they may pronounce against each other.
Honi HaMe'aggel. q Josephus, *Antiquities*, 14.2.1.

666.M.9 Help me, O Father, to break all bonds that imprison the soul. Help me to set my heart free from selfishness, hatred, jealousy, and enable me thus to reveal my better nature.
Mendes. q Hertz, *DPB*, 22f.

666.M.10 Our Father who art in Heaven, hallowed be Thy name. Thy kingdom come. Thy will be done in earth as it is in Heaven. Give us this day our daily bread. Forgive us our debts, as we forgive our debtors. Lead us not into temptation, but deliver us from evil. For Thine is the kingdom and the power and the glory for ever.
New Testament: Matt., 6.9–13.

666.M.11 "May all unite to do Thy will with a perfect heart!" . . . Thus prays the Jew. Have you more beautiful prayers to offer?
Peretz, *Advice to the Estranged*. LP, 348.

666.M.12 Since there are many good things in nature, grant me that which is best adapted to me, though it be the most trifling; looking to one thing only, that I shall be able to bear it with equanimity, and not, like a wretch, be overwhelmed by it.

Philo, *Change of Names*, 40.

666.M.13 May it be Thy will . . . to grant us long life, a life of peace, goodness, blessing, sustenance and vigor, a life marked by fear of sin and freedom from shame and confusion, a life of prosperity and honor, in which we may be imbued with love of Torah and fear of Heaven, a life in which all our heart's desires for good shall be fulfilled!

Rab. *T: Berakot*, 16b.

666.M.14 O God, keep my tongue from evil and my lips from speaking guile. Be my support when grief silences my voice, and my comfort when woe bends my spirit. Implant humility in my soul, and strengthen my heart with perfect faith in Thee. Help me to be strong in temptation and trial and to be patient and forgiving when others wrong me. Guide me by the light of Thy countenance that I may ever find strength in Thee, my Rock and my Redeemer.

Union Prayer Book, 1940, i. 140. See *T: Berakot*, 17a.

667. PREACHING

667.1 The supreme object of preaching must ever be to lead souls unto God; to wean men and women from the pursuit of low and earthly aims to all that is good, pure and true; to build up within them the grace of patience, the power of self-discipline, and the instinct of loving helpfulness, the spirit of sacrifice and of service.

H. Adler. q Hertz, *DPB*, 525.

667.2 Before delivering a lecture, review and revise it carefully. God revised the Torah four times before giving it to Israel.

Aha. *Exod. R.*, 40.1.

667.3 A preacher owes it to the congregation to be deliberate, not impetuous, and, above all, content with few words.

Bahya b. Asher, *Kad HaKemah*, 14C, 160.

667.4 Sermons, it has been said, though dealing with eternal subjects, are the most ephemeral form of literature.

Bentwich, *For Zion's Sake*, 1954, p. 44.

667.5 The sermon is the peculiar product of the Jewish mind. . . . It had its origin in . . . the ancient Synagog, and has

continued to this very day to form an integral part of Jewish worship.

Bettan, *Studies in Jewish Preaching*, 1939, p. 3.

667.6 Preachment is becoming to one who practices.

Eleazar b. Azariah. *Tosefta: Yebamot*, 8.4.

667.7 It is unfortunate that our preachers perpetually deal with themes relating to our duties to God. . . . Let the preacher . . . raise his voice in protest against the malpractices of men of prominence, and the people will soon learn to love him and to delight in his sermons.

Eybeshitz, *Yaarot Debash*, 1782, ii. 17b. q BSJ, 328f.

667.8 The best preacher is a man's upright life. That speaks to the heart, even though it utter not a sound. What the preacher does, and not what he says, makes a lasting impression. . . . My only justification for lifting my voice at all is that I am my own best audience. I preach mostly to myself.

Figo, *Bina Lalttim*, 1647, ii. 40. q BSJ, 235.

667.9 Let not our bad traits prevent you from listening to our good preachment.

q M. Ibn Ezra, *Shirat Yisrael*, (12C) 1924, p. 157.

667.10 If a lecture is not as delicious to the audience as honey from the comb, it were better had it not been delivered.

Jose b. Hanina. *Cant. R.*, 4.11.1.

667.11 If a lecture is not as alluring to the audience as a bride to her groom, you had better not deliver it at all.

Simeon b. Lakish. *Exod. R.*, 41.5.

667.12 A sermon is worthwhile if it inspires one person to pray fervently, even if that one person is myself.

Lipkin. q KTH, i. 277.

667.13 Preachment is but babbling.

Maimonides. q SSJ, iii. 63.

667.14 A preacher shall employ beauty of expression, cogent reasoning, logical construction, but, above all, exemplify in his conduct the truths he seeks to inculcate. A preacher deficient in any of these should refrain, or be restrained, from speaking in public.

Moscato, *Nefutzot Yehuda*, (1588) 1859, 34a. q BSJ, 203.

667.15 The foolishness of preaching. *New Testament: I Cor.,* 1.21.

667.16 A homily which cannot be turned into a prayer is a misfit.

q Schechter, June 2, 1912. SSA, 228.

667.17 Sensational preachers are comedians.

I. M. Wise, "The Rabbi," 1871. *Selected Writings,* 387.

667.18 Let the speaker be called what he will . . . so long as he expounds the word of God from Bible and Agada, extracts pure gold from old and new fields, teaches the present generation its true work and reaches all hearts by skillful speech. Then the divine spirit will return to thy temples, O daughter of Zion, and will become manifest in deeds flowing from words of enthusiasm.

Zunz, *Gottesdienstliche Vorträge,* 1832, p. 481.

668. PREJUDICE

668.1 In all . . . history there never lived but one man who could qualify as a one hundred per cent American; and men who deny or abridge the rights of others for religion or race should remember that that man was a Jew.

*Bok, *Americanization of Edward Bok,* 1920.

668.2 It is a common theological process to brighten the foreground by darkening the background. The tendency of the early Christian chroniclers was to enhance the virtues of the new faith and its founder at the expense of his correligionists and contemporaries.

Harrison, *Religion of a Modern Liberal,* 1931, p. 98.

668.3 A bias is not actionable.

Lassalle, *Science and the Workingmen,* 1863.

668.4 Reason and Humanity raise their voices in vain, for hoary Prejudice has completely lost its hearing.

M. Mendelssohn, Preface to *Vindiciae Judaeorum,* 1782.

668.5 Every corrupting prejudice begets, as carrion breeds maggots, a thousand accretions.

J. Wassermann. LCJ, 1929, p. 120.

669. PREPAREDNESS

669.1 Prepare to meet thy God, O Israel. *Bible: Amos,* 4.12.

669.2 Before you fight, seek an ally; before you are ill, seek a physician. *Apocrypha: Ben Sira,* 18.19.

669.3 Prepare the reply while you still have time.

Bahya, *Hobot HaLebabot,* 1040, 7.10, tr Hyamson, iv. 54.

669.4 I am prepared for the worst, but hope for the best.

Disraeli, *Alroy,* 1833, 10.3.

669.5 Preparing for the performance of a divine command is greater than the performance.

J. L. Eger. q Shemen, *Lublin,* 430.

669.6 Among the naked gods and goddesses who make merry there over nectar and ambrosia, you may see one goddess who, though surrounded by such festivity and gaiety, ever wears a coat of mail and bears helmet on head and spear in hand. It is the Goddess of Wisdom.

Heine, *Germany from Kant to Hegel,* 1834.

669.7 Who prepares before the Sabbath can eat on the Sabbath.

Jonathan b. Eleazer. *Pesikta Rabbati,* 198b. See *AZ,* 3a.

669.8 If you do not plow in summer, what will you eat in winter? *Midrash Mishlé,* 6.

669.9 Wise men do not wait till the calamity is upon them.

Philo, *Moses,* 59.

669.10 Prepare for the time when the possible will become the probable.

L. Stein, *Journey into the Self,* 1950, p. 256.

670. PRESENT

670.1 Your present is . . . elastic to embrace infinity.

Anspacher, *The Future Speaks.*

670.2 If not now, when? Hillel. *Mishna: Abot,* 1.14.

670.3 All our seeming contradictions arise from the equation between the today that is merely a bridge to tomorrow, and the today that is a springboard to eternity.

F. Rosenzweig, letter to G. Oppenheim, Feb. 5, 1917. GFR 47.

670.4 Unless it is a present which forms a link between two eternities, representing an answer of Amen to the past and an

Opening Prayer to the future, it will be a very petty present indeed.

Schechter, Apr. 26, 1903. *Seminary Addresses*, 45.

670.5 Detachment from the present gives the Jew the faculty of speculation: on the philosophic plane—and on the material.

*Thiebault.

670.6 For Judaism the center of gravity is here and now. Though we were immortal, yet eternity is only a succession of todays. The whole problem of life faces us today.

Zangwill. *North American Review*, April 1895.

671. PRESS

671.1 The function of the press is very high. It is almost holy. It ought to serve as a forum for the people, through which the people may know freely what is going on. To misstate or suppress the news is a breach of trust.

Brandeis. *Collier's Weekly*, March 23, 1912.

671.2 Newspaper jobs would be eagerly sought,
If all that was needed were printer's ink.
It is not enough that one cannot think:
One must also know how to express lack of thought.

Kraus, *Poems*, 1930, p. 57.

671.3 Give the news, all the news, in concise and attractive form, in language that is permissible in good society, and give it early, . . . impartially, without fear or favor, regardless of party, sect, or interest involved.

Ochs. *N.Y. Times*, Salutatory, Aug. 18, 1896.

671.4 Our Republic and its press will rise or fall together!

Pulitzer. q U.S. commemorative stamp, 1947. See his Salutatory, N. Y. *World*, May 10, 1883.

671.5 Always fight for progress and reform, never tolerate injustice or corruption, always fight demagogues of all parties, never belong to any party, always oppose privileged classes and public plunderers, never lack sympathy with the poor, always remain devoted to the public welfare, . . . never be afraid to attack wrong, whether by predatory plutocracy or predatory poverty.

Pulitzer, on retiring from editorship of St. Louis *Post Dispatch*, Oct. 16, 1890.

671.6 It is generally presumed that there are four great powers which govern society, viz., the sword, the pen, money, and woman. The fifth great power in this nineteenth century is Journalism.

I. M. Wise, 1893. *JWP*, 402.

671.7 When a man who could do better turns journalist, the angels in heaven weep for his lost soul.

I. M. Wise. *Deborah*, Nov. 5, 1896; *AJA*, June 1954, p. 124.

672. PRETENSE

672.1 Feign no interest in a purchase when you have no money.

Ishmael b. Jose. *T: Pesahim*, 112b.

673. PRIEST

673.1 The Lord spoke to Aaron saying: Drink no wine . . . when ye go into the tent of meeting . . . that ye may put difference between the holy and the common, between the unclean and the clean, and that ye may teach the children of Israel all the statutes.

Bible: Lev., 10.9ff.

673.2 The Lord said to Aaron: You shall have no inheritance in their land . . . I am your portion and inheritance among the children of Israel.

Bible: Num., 18.20.

673.3 The law of truth was in his mouth . . . he walked with Me in peace and uprightness, and turned many away from iniquity. For the priest's lips should keep knowledge, and they should seek the law at his mouth, for he is the messenger of the Lord of hosts.

Bible: Mal., 2.6f. See Huna b. Joshua. *T: Yoma*, 19a.

673.4 The priest is not superior to his fellow men, nor has he access to those transcendental regions which are closed to others. His power is in this, that he speaks what all feel. And he shall be counted an acceptable teacher then only, when the slumbering echoes within you waken to the music that moves and masters him.

F. Adler, *Creed and Deed*, 1877, p. 87.

673.5 Sometimes also the priests convey from their gods gold and silver, and bestow it upon themselves.

Apocrypha: Jeremy, 10.

673.6 Priesthood was merely tolerated in Judaism, and the whole history of Judaism contains a continual war against it.

Geiger, *Judaism and Its History*, ch 5, tr 1886, p. 99.

673.7 Like altar, like priests.

Jose of Maon. *TJ: Sanhedrin*, 2.6. See *T: Arakin*, 17a.

673.8 The High Priest may judge and be judged, testify and be testified against.

Mishna: Sanhedrin, 2.1.

673.9 The most indispensable virtue in a high priest is piety.

Philo, *Moses*, 3.1.

673.10 Most priests are affluent.

Proverb. q *Sifré*, #352, to *Deut.* 33.11, ed Friedmann, 145a.

673.11 Woe is me because of the house of Boethus! . . . They are high priests, their sons are financiers, their sons-in-law trustees, and their servants beat the people!

Saul of Batnit. *T: Pesahim*, 57a.

673.12 Priests do not bless Israel; it says, "*I* will bless them."

Sifré, #43, to *Num.* 6.27, ed Horvitz, p. 49.

673.13 For transgression, a high priest ranks as a commoner.

Talmud: Sanhedrin, 18a.

673.14 The laws of priesthood do not apply today.

Yannai. *TJ: Berakot*, 3.1.

673.15 A priest who loves not the people, or whom they love not, may not pronounce the blessing.

Zohar, Num., 147b.

674. PRINCE

674.1 Know ye not that there is a prince and a great man fallen this day in Israel?

Bible: II Sam., 3.38.

674.2 He brings princes to nothing.

Bible: Isa., 40.23.

674.3 Put not your trust in princes.

Bible: Ps., 146.3.

674.4 Happy are you, O land, when . . . your princes eat in due season, in strength, and not in drunkenness!

Bible: Eccles., 10.17.

674.5 To their entertainments princes invite only the nobility; but when they meet with misfortune, they invite also citizens.

Boerne.

675. PRINCIPLE

675.1 It is easier to fight for principles than to live up to them.

A. Adler.

675.2 We must have principles in order to have programs and to follow a given direction rather than get lost and wander aimlessly; but we must not follow a principle to destruction—that is the essence of fanaticism.

M. R. Cohen. *L. I. D. Monthly*, March 1932 (*Faith of a Liberal*, 66).

675.3 A precedent embalms a principle.

Disraeli, speech, House of Commons, Feb. 22, 1848.

675.4 No single principle can answer all of life's complexities.

Frankfurter, *Minersville School District vs. Gobitis*, 1940. 310 U.S. Reports, 586.

675.5 There is nothing more dangerous than a principle which appears in false and perverted form.

Lassalle, *The Workingmen's Programme* 1862.

676. PRINT

676.1 They do not know how they stumble, those pious fools, when they rely on everything found in print without knowing its nature, root and origin.

Emden, *Mitpahat Sefarim*, 1769, 78. q CJE, 259.

676.2 Not all that is thought should be spoken, not all that is spoken deserves to be written, and not all that is written is meant to be printed.

Lipkin. q KTH, i. 277.

676.3 The art which enables one man to write with many pens.

q Steinschneider, *Jüdische Typographie* (Ersch and Gruber, *Allgemeine Encyclopädie*, ii. 28).

677. PRIVACY

677.1 Enter not without permission your neighbor's premises, even to take something which belongs to you.

Ben Bag Bag. *T: Baba Kamma*, 27b.

677.2 What is improper in public, is forbidden in secret.

Rab. *T: Sabbath*, 64b.

677.3 Be chaste in private even as in the open market place, for your walls are witnesses against you.

Sefer Hasidim Zuta. q Güdemann, *Culturgeschichte*, iii. 214.

677.4 Privacy is a right. Damage by seeing is damage.
Talmud: Baba Bathra, 2b.

678. PRIVILEGE
678.1 A frying egg will not wait for the King of Cordova.
Disraeli, *Count Alarcos,* 1839.
678.2 Not everybody is privileged to enjoy two tables (wealth and wisdom).
Johanan b. Nappaha. *T: Berakot,* 5b.
678.3 Those who desire the good of all begin by the abolition of special privilege.
Laski, *A Grammar of Politics,* 1925.

679. PRODUCTION
679.1 The method of production of the material things of life generally determines the social, political and spiritual currents of life.
Marx, *Critique of Political Economy,* Preface, 1859.
679.2 An object of art creates a public capable of finding pleasure in its beauty. Production, therefore, not only produces an object for the subject, but also a subject for the object.
Ibid.
679.3 Not he alone who labors with his hands, but whoever does . . . or facilitates anything for the benefit or comfort of his fellow creatures, deserves to be called a producer.
M. Mendelssohn, Preface to *Vindiciae Judaeorum,* 1782.
679.4 The cheapest labor is that which is most productive.
O. S. Straus, address, May 22, 1907. *American Spirit,* 228.
679.5 Fifty productive are better than two hundred unproductive.
Talmud J: Peah, 8.8.

680. PROFIT
680.1 He errs who pursues profit.
Apocrypha: Ben Sira, 31.5.
680.2 Better a small profit at home than a large one from abroad.
Rab. *T: Pesahim,* 113a.
680.3 Nothing contributes so much to the prosperity and happiness of a country as high profits.
Ricardo, *On Protection to Agriculture,* 1820.
680.4 Big business is when the profit is big; small business is when the profit is small.
Talmud: Ketubot, 66b.

681. PROGRESS
681.1 There must be a daily advance in the knowledge and love of the Divine Master.
Baal Shem. q SSJ, i. 33.
681.2 Progress is nothing but the victory of laughter over dogma.
De Casseres, *Fantasia Impromptu,* 1933.
681.3 The European talks of progress because by the aid of a few scientific discoveries he has established a society which has mistaken comfort for civilization.
Disraeli. q Inge, *Outspoken Essays,* 179.
681.4 Belief in the progress of mankind, creating by its progress the Kingdom of God—this was and is the faith of Israel.
Dunner, *Republic of Israel,* 1950, p. 12.
681.5 The measure of progress is co-operation.
Filene. q Landman, *Christian & Jew,* 1929, p. 97.
681.6 Man shall climb ever upwards despite everything.
Herzl, letter to Baron de Hirsch, June 3, 1895.
681.7 In holy matters, we may promote, but not demote.
Hillel School. *T: Sabbath,* 21b.
681.8 The future has better things in store than had the past; upward runs the course of humanity, not downward.
E. G. Hirsch. *Reform Advocate,* 1893, v. 205.
681.9 Progress is slow, retrogression swift.
q M. Ibn Ezra, *Shirat Yisrael,* (12C) 1924, p. 83.
681.10 Progress is the fruit of devotion.
q *Ibid.,* 112.
681.11 Chief among the contrasts which differentiate the Bible from the other Sacred Books of the East is the notion of progress.
Jacobs, *Jewish Contributions to Civilization,* 1919, p. 84.
681.12 Israel must go forward!
Joshua b. Hanania. *Mekilta,* to *Exod.* 14.15.
681.13 To be a Jew means to favor progress without disregarding the old. The inner life-force of Judaism has always consisted in building further on existing foundations. We do not wish to be *Shulhan Aruk* mummies.
Karpeles, *Unsere Orthodoxie.* AZJ, 1898. q PRM, 487.

681.14 "If ye *walk* in My statutes" [*Lev.* 26.3]. The Torah must not be static.
Levi Yitzhok, *Kedushat Levi*, (1798) 1886, 50a.

681.15 The two essential factors of progress: morality and knowledge.
Luzzatti, *Evolution*, Aug. 15, 1876. LGF, 210.

681.16 Progress is the effect of an ever more rigorous subjugation of the beast in man, of an ever tenser self-restraint, an ever keener sense of duty and responsibility.
Nordau, *Degeneration*, 1893, 5.2, tr 1895, p. 560.

681.17 What good is there in life if my work today remains what it was yesterday?
Samuel HaNagid, *Ben Mishlé*, 11C. AHE, 74.

681.18 There is no cause for jitters as long as we hold fast to the certainty that material progress is not an end in itself but a means to a fuller, nobler, more satisfying life.
Sarnoff, *Youth in a Changing World*, June 12, 1954.

681.19 A human being must either climb up or climb down.
Talmud: Erubin, 21a.

681.20 It is difficult to realize what a startling break with universal thought the Jews made when they saw in history not conditioned recurrence but progressive manifestation of a divine plan for the human race.
*Ward, *Faith and Freedom*, 1954, p. 49. See Whitehead. *Atlantic Monthly*, March 1939, p. 315.

681.21 Progress never marches in a parade.
Winchell, Oct. 27, 1951.

681.22 All of human existence is a pilgrimage toward a better world.
Zuckerman. *Reconstructionist*, May 15, 1953, p. 15.

682. PROMISE

682.1 When a man vows a vow . . . he shall not break his word.
Bible: Num., 30.3.

682.2 When you vow a vow . . . be not slack to pay it.
Bible: Deut., 23.22. See *Ps.*, 50.14, *Eccles.* 5.3.

682.3 That which I have vowed I will pay.
Bible: Jon., 2.10.

682.4 Who shall sojourn in Thy tabernacle? . . . He who swears to his own hurt, and changes not.
Bible: Ps., 15.1, 4.

682.5 When in trouble, I vow; when relieved, I forget it.
Abba b. Kahana. *Gen. R.*, 81.2.

682.6 Vows are a fence for abstinence.
Akiba. *Mishna: Abot*, 3.13.

682.7 Beware of him who promises something for nothing.
Baruch, reply to Brooks Preparatory School, June, 1950.

682.8 The righteous promise little and perform much; the wicked promise much and perform not even a little.
Eleazar b. Pedat. *T: Baba Metzia*, 87a.

682.9 A pledge unpaid is like thunder without rain.
Hasdai, *Ben HaMelek VeHaNazir*, c. 1230, ch 5.

682.10 It is human nature to care much less for those who protect our goods than for those who promise us more.
Heine, *Lutetia*, Sept. 17, 1842.

682.11 The liberal's promise is a gift; the miser's gift is a promise.
Ibn Gabirol, *Mibhar HaPeninim*, c. 1050, #365.

682.12 Rain is withheld because of pledges unpaid.
Johanan b. Nappaha. *T: Taanit*, 8b.

682.13 Let not your legal contract or the presence of witnesses be more binding than your verbal promise made privately. Woe to him who builds on subterfuge and evasion.
Maimonides, *Shaaré HaMusar*. See *JQRo*, iii. 452.

682.14 Who alters or retracts a contract is at a disadvantage (in court).
Mishna: Baba Metzia, 6.1.

682.15 I promised him Holland and Brabant.
Proverb. q Lipperheide, *Spruchwörterbuch*, p. 936.

682.16 When a cock coaxes his mate, he tells her: "I'll buy you a cloak that will reach to your feet." After the event, he tells her: "May a cat tear off my crest if I do not buy you one when I have money."
Rab. *T: Erubin*, 100b.

682.17 Vows lead to folly.
Talmud: Derek Eretz, 2.5.

682.18 Never promise a child what you do not intend to give.
Zera: *T: Sukka*, 46b.

683. PROOF

683.1 The burden of proof is on the claimant.
Mishna: Baba Kamma, 3.11.

683.2 "We have not seen" is no proof.
Mishna: Eduyot, 2.2.

683.3 The proof of the pudding is in the digesting.
H. Samuel, *A Book of Quotations*, 1947, p. 192.

683.4 Proof is not obtained from fools.
Talmud: Sabbath, 104b.

684. PROPAGANDA

684.1 In propaganda the appeal of love is slow and lumbering in comparison with the appeal of hatred. Hatred is the piquant sauce which accelerates both the swallowing and the digestion of ideas and policies.
Jabotinsky, *The War and the Jew*, 1942, p. 45.

684.2 Education by means of pre-fabricated ideas is propaganda.
Kaplan. *Reconstructionist*, April 1950, p. 28.

684.3 Much of what had been achieved by the art of education in the nineteenth century has been frustrated by the art of propaganda in the twentieth.
Laski, *A Grammar of Politics*, 1925, p. 147.

684.4 While other sects are extending the means of Divine Worship to the remotest quarters of the habitable globe, . . . we are totally disregarding the fairest opportunities of increasing our own numbers, . . . enlarging our resources, and effectually perpetuating our national character.
Moise, *Memorial to Kehal Kodesh Beth Elohim*, 1824.

685. PROPERTY

685.1 The right of the inventor to his discovery, the right of the poet to his inspiration, depends upon those principles of eternal justice, which God has implanted in the heart of man.
Benjamin, speech, U.S. Senate, March 11, 1858.

685.2 When property is used to interfere with that fundamental freedom of life for which property is only a means, then property must be controlled.
Brandeis. q E. Poole. *American Magazine*, Feb. 1911.

685.3 Property has its duties as well as its rights.
Disraeli, *Sybil*, 1845, 2.11.

685.4 Private property was never
Made by Nature. . . .
With no pockets in our skins, we
Every one the world first entered.
Heine, *Atta Troll*, 1841, ch 10.

685.5 The time may come when society will rise to a better constitution, when what is created by all will revert to the uses of all.
E. G. Hirsch. *Reform Advocate*, 1894, viii. 202f.

685.6 Wherever the right of property clashes with a duty toward humanity, the former has no credentials that are entitled to consideration.
Ibid., 1897, xiii. 208.

685.7 A true Israelite . . . looks upon all his property as only a means of doing what is pleasing in the sight of God.
S. R. Hirsch, *Horeb*, 1838, ch 13.

685.8 Property is a form of power, and, like all power of man over man, must be responsible, and therefore limited.
Hook. *New York Times Magazine*, July 9, 1950.

685.9 Property is the source of affliction.
M. Iban Ezra, *Shirat Yisrael*, (12C) 1924.

685.10 Lo, strangers shall seize thy loved estate,
And empty thou shalt go away.
Ibn Gabirol, *Selected Religious Poems*, 62.

685.11 Property is theft.
Ibn Tibbon, *Tzavaah*, 1190. q KJL, 39.

685.12 The court has the power to expropriate.
Isaac Nappaha. *T: Gittin*, 36b.

685.13 Man is not the master of what he has, but only its guardian.
Jacob b. Asher, *Tur*, c. 1300, ii. 247.

685.14 Respect your neighbor's property like your own.
Jose HaCohen. *Mishna: Abot*, 2.12.

685.15 I, a wanderer through life on the way to eternity, believe in traveling light.

Why should I be burdened with possessions which I cannot take with me hence?
Kagan, to an American visitor. q *JS*, Sept. 1953, p. 20.

685.16 The only dependable foundation of personal liberty is the personal economic security of private property.
Lippmann, *The Method of Freedom*, 1934, p. 101.

685.17 Property remains in its status (in the absence of evidence to the contrary).
Mishna: Baba Bathra, 9.8.

685.18 There are four types of men: the neutral, who says, "Mine is mine and yours is yours"; the boor, who says, "Mine is yours and yours is mine"; the pious, who says, "Mine is yours and yours is yours"; and the wicked, who says, "Mine is mine and yours is mine."
Mishna: Abot, 5.10.

685.19 He who doesn't care to prevent wasting another's property is like a thief.
Nahman Bratzlav. q BHH. 487.

685.20 We brought nothing into this world, and it is certain we can carry nothing out.
New Testament: I Tim., 6.7.

685.21 A garment is precious to its wearer.
Rab. *T: Sabbath*, 10b.

685.22 Private property goes ultimately to the State if wages are withheld, employees deceived, the burden of taxes and public service shifted to others, and people are arrogant.
Rab. *T: Sukka*, 29b.

685.23 He who in his lifetime transfers his property to his children acquires a master, and can get no relief in court.
Talmud: Baba Metzia, 75b.

685.24 It is presumed that no man remains indifferent when his property is threatened.
Talmud: Sanhedrin, 72b.

686. PROPHETS

686.A. Prophecy

686.A.1 Hebrew prophecy was history and Hebrew history was prophecy.
*H. B. Adams, *Columbus*, Oct. 10, 1892. *Johns Hopkins Univ. Studies in Historical and Political Science*, x. 11.

686.A.2 Prophecy is characteristic of the lazy.
Gabishon, *Omer HaShikha*, c. 1600.

686.A.3 Since the destruction of the Temple, prophecy has been taken from prophets and given to fools and children.
Johanan. *T: Baba Bathra*, 12b.

686.A.4 Only prophecies of permanent value were published.
Johanan b. Nappaha. *Cant. R.*, 4.11.

686.A.5 Prophecy is certainly stronger than logical inference.
Judah Halevi, *Cuzari*. q FJR, 14.

686.A.6 Among the heathen, oracles were presented in an ambiguous form, . . . but among the Jews, prophecy is clear.
Levi. *Esther Rabbah*, 7.24.

686.A.7 Prophetism . . . founded the religion of humanity.
*Renan, *History of Israel*, 1889, ii. 414.

686.B. Prophets

686.B.1 Would that all the Lord's people were prophets.
Bible: Num., 11.29.

686.B.2 Is Saul also among the prophets?
Bible: I Sam., 10.11.

686.B.3 I hate him because he does not prophesy good concerning me.
Bible: I Kings, 22.8.

686.B.4 Speak to us smooth things, prophesy delusions.
Bible: Isa., 30.10.

686.B.5 The prophet is a fool, the man of the spirit is mad.
Bible: Hos., 9.7.

686.B.6 I am neither a prophet, nor the son of a prophet.
Bible: Amos, 7.14.

686.B.7 Touch not Mine anointed ones, do My prophets no harm.
Bible: Ps., 105.15. *I Chron.*, 16.22.

686.B.8 There shall be false prophets like tempests, and they shall persecute all righteous men.
Apocrypha: Patriarchs, Judah, 21.9.

686.B.9 No oracle-monger I of a false Phoebus, whom vain men have called a god and falsely termed a seer.
Apocrypha: Sibyl, 4.4f.

686.B.10 The Orientals are a shrewder race, they honor a maniac as a prophet, but we look upon prophets as maniacs.
Heine, *Baths of Lucca*, 1828, ch 1.

686.B.11 The prophet is an authentic, a true prophet because he dare oppose his own people on great moral and social and political issues.

Magnes. q Bentwich, *For Zion's Sake,* 286.

686.B.12 Whether one should yield credence to a prophet or not depends on the nature of his doctrines, not on his race.

Maimonides, *Iggeret Teman,* 1172, tr Cohen, p. x.

686.B.13 Beware of false prophets, who come to you in sheep's clothing, but inwardly they are ravening wolves.

New Testament: Matt., 7.15.

686.B.14 A prophet is not without honor, save in his own country and in his own house.

New Testament: Matt., 13.57.

686.B.15 None is a prophet in his own town.

Algazi, *Ahabat Olam,* 1642.

686.C. Prophets of Israel

686.C.1 See, I have this day set thee over the nations and over the kingdoms, to root out and to pull down, to destroy and to overthrow, to build and to plant.

Bible: Jer., 1.10.

686.C.2 If I say, "I will not . . . speak any more in His name," then there is in my heart, as it were, a burning fire shut up in my bones, and I weary myself to hold it in but cannot.

Ibid., 20.9.

686.C.3 The boldness of the ancient prophets . . . could have been possible only in a country where freedom of speech was a fact.

*Abbott, *Life and Literature of Ancient Hebrews,* 1901, 126.

686.C.4 The ancient prophets walk through the world of Judaism, like living geniuses reawaking from generation to generation.

Baeck, *Essence of Judaism,* 1936, p. 24.

686.C.5 The prophets of Israel discovered the non-egoistic element in man and founded upon it the ethical demand.

Baeck, *Judaism and Ethics,* 1949, p. 20.

686.C.6 Let us recall the tone and accents of the Prophets of Israel. It is their voice we hear when a great injustice has been done and condoned. From the depths of the centuries they raise their protest.

Bergson, *Two Sources of Morality and Religion,* 1935, p. 67.

686.C.7 The prophet is appointed to oppose the king and, even more, history.

Buber, *Israel and the World,* 1948, p. 130.

686.C.8 The letter of the prophets is in the church, and their spirit in science.

Darmsteter, *Selected Essays,* 1895, p. 11.

686.C.9 The prophets were the first to utter this cry [of justice and pity], and they did so for all time.

Ibid., 102.

686.C.10 The triumph of the prophets' religion . . . lay in their discovery of the idea of Humanity.

Enelow. *CCAR Yearbook,* 1924, p. 245, quoting H. Cohen.

686.C.11 The prophet was essentially a man of the future: he did not live in the past, the past lived in him.

Enelow, *Selected Works,* i. 187.

686.C.12 It was the noble series of Hebrew Prophets . . . who led the way . . . to the truly monotheistic conception of one sole God of the whole world, . . . disregarding all barriers of race and space and time.

*Hume, *World's Living Religions,* (1924) 1933, p. 184.

686.C.13 The greatest things that have been done to raise men's lot have been done always in the spirit, often in the name, of the Hebrew prophets.

Jacobs, *Jewish Contributions to Civilization,* 1919, p. 10.

686.C.14 The moral feelings of men have been deepened and strengthened, . . . and almost created, by the Jewish prophets. In modern times we hardly like to acknowledge the full force of their words, lest they should prove subversive to society. And so we explain them away or spiritualize them. . . . And still, . . . the force of the words remains, and a light of heavenly truth and love streams from them even now more than twenty-five hundred years after they were first uttered.

*Jowett. q HBJ, 145.

686.C.15 The Prophets started a revaluation of all accepted values. This new valuation has not been accepted—either by the Jews or by humanity—but it has acted as a powerful leaven and restraint in history.

H. Kohn, *Idea of Nationalism,* 1944, p. 40.

686.C.16 I believe with perfect faith that all the words of the Prophets are true.

Maimonides, *Commentary to Mishna: Sanhedrin,* 1168, 10.1. *Thirteen Principles,* #6.

686.C.17 There were three types of prophets: one insisted on the honor due the Father as well as the son [Israel]; one, on the honor due the Father; and one, on the honor due the son.

Mekilta, to *Exod.,* 12.1.

686.C.18 The prophets always strove to express their thoughts clearly.

M. Mendelssohn, *Biur to Exod.* 15.

686.C.19 Israel has supplied prophets without number. What is more, Israel is itself a prophet, is in itself the prophetic race. . . . Israel asks one thing only: to avoid giving the prophets grounds for prophecy. She knows the cost of this.

*Péguy. *Notre Jeunesse,* 1910, xi. 12. *Basic Verities,* 133.

686.C.20 The prophets are the interpreters of God.

Philo, *Special Laws,* i. 11.

686.C.21 The Prophets made religion moral and universal.

*Renan, *Le Judaisme comme Race et comme Réligion,* 1883.

686.C.22 The oldest advocates of the oppressed were the prophets of Israel, and that is why we accord them so eminent a place in the history of civilization.

*Renan, *History of Israel,* 1891, iii. 185.

686.C.23 The authority of the prophets has weight only in matters of morality; their speculative doctrines affect us little.

Spinoza, *Theologico-Political Treatise,* 1670, Preface.

686.C.24 Wherever the prophetic spirit rules, the walls between Christians and Jews are torn down.

*Tillich, address, Feb. 16, 1942. *Congress Weekly,* Feb. 27. 1942.

686.C.25 The socialistic monotheism of our prophets marks such a tremendous advance in the evolution of the human spirit that, placed beside their works, even such a book as Karl Marx's *Capital* seems like a small pile of sand gathered by children at the foot of a great mountain.

Zhitlovsky, *Gezamelté Shriften,* ii. 152.

686.D. Isaiah

686.D.1 The Lord has appointed me to bring good tidings to the humble. He has sent me to bind up the broken-hearted, to proclaim liberty to the captives, the opening of the eyes to them that are bound, . . . to comfort all that mourn.

Bible: Isa., 61.1f.

686.D.2 The Revolution with its hopes is in its issue nothing more than the actual testamentary execution of the will of Isaiah.

*Leroy-Beaulieu. q Peters, *Jew as a Patriot,* p. xvi.

686.D.3 Isaiah, seven hundred and fifty years before Jesus, made bold to say that sacrifices were of little consequence, and that the one thing which availed was clean hands and purity of heart.

*Renan, *Spinoza,* Feb. 21, 1877.

686.D.4 Isaiah, by the ardor of his convictions, by the example of his life, and by the beauty of his style, . . . is the true founder (I do not say inventor) of the messianic and apocalyptic doctrine.

*Renan, *History of Israel,* 1889, ii. 424.

687. PROSPERITY

687.1 My cup runneth over.

Bible: Ps., 23.5.

687.2 Prosperity comes not in anything weighed, measured or counted, but only in things hidden from view.

Isaac Nappaha. *T: Taanit,* 8b.

687.3 Our fathers said, "We have forgotten prosperity" [See *Lam.* 3.17]; but we have never seen it!

Judah HaNasi. *T: Nedarim,* 50b.

687.4 The prosperity of our people is not dependent upon civil emancipation, but upon the love of a man for his neighbor.

S. D. Luzzatto, letter to Jost, 1840. q SRH, 90. (*Igrot Shadal,* i. 660, #267).

687.5 Prosperity, obtained through truth and righteousness, is built on a sure rock. Happiness derived from falsehood, injustice and lust, is built on sand.

Maimonides, *Shaaré HaMusar.* See AHE, 108.

687.6 Prosperity and failure are twins: evil holds on the heel of each good, and good is joined to the heel of each evil.

Mandelstamm, *Mishlé Binyamin,* 1884, 2.15.

688. PROTEST

688.1 May we, like our fathers, still stand out against the multitude, protesting with all our might against its follies and its fears. May a divine discontent give color to our dreams, and a passion for holy heresy set the tone of our thoughts. May the soul of the rebel still throb in us as it throbbed in our forefathers, that today and forever we may still be a light unto those who stumble in darkness.

Browne, Prayer, 1924. *Wisdom of Israel,* 1945, p. 730.

688.2 Elders sin by not protesting the sins of princes.

Hanina b. Hama. *T: Sabbath,* 54a.

688.3 Ten thousand souls cry from within me!

Koreff, response to rebuke for being too loud in protest against Maria Theresa's decree of banishment against the Jews of Prague, Dec. 18, 1744. See *JE,* vii. 561b.

688.4 When men hold their peace, the stones will cry out.

Lassalle, speech, Assize Court, Aug. 11, 1848.

688.5 The real Israel is ever catholic, must be catholic, just as he must ever protest, must ever be protestant.

Lubin, letter to Enelow, June 1912. q ADL, 77.

686.6 In the second and third exiles we have served as a living protest against greed and hate, against physical force, against "might makes right"!

Peretz, Preface to *Idishé Bibliotek,* i. 1890.

688.7 The Jews were a living protest against superstition and religious materialism. An extraordinary movement of ideas, ending in the most opposite results, made of them, at this [Maccabean] epoch, the most striking and original people in the world.

*Renan, *Life of Jesus,* 1863, p. 75.

688.8 Judaism was always a protesting religion.

Schechter, *Studies in Judaism,* 1896, i. p. xxi.

688.9 Who can protest and does not, is an accomplice in the act.

Talmud: Sabbath, 54b.

688.10 The mere existence of the Jew today has been a triumph of idealism; it marks a dissent for the sake of an idea from the dominant forces of Asiatic or European civilization, a protestantism persisted in despite the ceaseless persecution of all the centuries of Pagan or Christian supremacy.

Zangwill, *Voice of Jerusalem,* 1921, p. 233.

689. PROTESTANTISM

689.1 The religion of the Scotch Protestants is simply pork-eating Judaism.

Heine, *Confessions,* 1854.

689.2 The Reformation was a return to primitive Christianity, and above all towards the democracy of the prophets of the Old Testament, which was alive with the breath of liberty and resistance to absolutism.

*Laveleye, Introduction to Straus, *Origin of Republican Form of Government,* (1885) 1926, p. xix. See Renan, *History of Israel,* ii. 421.

689.3 The Reformation was in large measure a reaffirmation of the Old Testament and of Judaism.

*Masaryk, *Grundlagen des Marxismus,* 1899, Sec. 120.

690. PROVERB

690.1 Despise not the discourse of the wise, but acquaint yourself with their proverbs.

Apocrypha: Ben Sira, 8.8.

690.2 A proverb without wisdom is like a body without a foot.

A. Ibn Ezra, *Commentary,* to *Prov.* 27.7.

690.3 A proverb has three characteristics: few words, right sense, fine image.

M. Ibn Ezra, *Shirat Yisrael,* (12C) 1924, p. 197. Arab Proverb, q Ayalti, *Yiddish Proverbs,* 1949, p. 10.

691. PROVINCIALISM

691.1 The only Czechoslovaks are the Jews: everyone else is either a Czech or a Slovak.

S. Levin, to Masaryk. q Namier, *Conflicts,* 166.

691.2 The sabra is in fact what few Jews outside of Israel have ever been able to be —a contented provincial.

*McDonald, *My Mission in Israel,* 1951, p. 294.

691.3 At the time of the last census I was staying in the house of a Scottish friend who, proudly but incorrectly, entered her nationality as "Scottish." A "depressed" Englishman in protest entered himself as "English." I alone put myself down as "British," and could not have done otherwise had I wished to.

Namier, *Conflicts,* 1943, p. 166.

692. PROVOCATION

692.1 Do not provoke a little heathen, a little snake, or a humble pupil.

Talmud: Pesahim, 113a.

693. PRUDENCE

693.1 Discretion shall preserve you.

Bible: Prov., 2.11.

693.2 As a ring of gold in a swine's snout, so is a fair woman that turns aside from discretion.

Ibid., 11.22.

693.3 The prudent man looks well to his going.

Ibid., 14.15.

693.4 A prudent man sees the evil and hides himself, but the thoughtless pass on, and are punished.

Ibid., 22.3.

693.5 Hearken with your ears that ye may know prudence.

Apocrypha: Baruch, 3.9.

693.6 Open not thy heart to every man.

Apocrypha: Ben Sira, 8.19.

694. PSALMS

694.1 Along every lyric of the Psalmist thrills a deep spirit of human enjoyment; he was alive as a child to the simple aspects of the world.

Bagehot, Macaulay. National Review, Jan. 1856.

694.2 I may truly name this book the anatomy of all parts of the soul; for no one can feel a movement of the spirit which is not reflected in this mirror. All the sorrows, troubles, fears, doubts, hopes, pains, perplexities, stormy outbreaks, by which the souls of men are tossed, are depicted here to the very life.

*Calvin. q BSL, 21f.

694.3 David, king of Judah, a soul inspired by divine music and much other heroism, was wont to pour himself in song; he, with seer's eye and heart, discerned the Godlike amid the human; struck tones that were an echo of the sphere-harmonies, and are still felt to be such. Reader, art thou one of a thousand, able still to *read* a Psalm of David, and catch some echo of it through the old dim centuries; feeling far off, in thy own heart, what it once was to other hearts made as thine? To sing it attempt not, for it is impossible in this late time; only know that it once was sung. Then go to the Opera, and hear, with unspeakable reflections, what things men now sing!

Carlyle, The Opera, 1852.

694.4 As Israel is preeminently the religious race, the Psalms are the prayer-book and the hymn-book of the whole world . . . they are religion itself put into speech.

Cornill, 1897. Culture of Ancient Israel, 1914, p. 162.

694.5 The 19th Psalm is the most magnificent of sacred songs. The 150th Psalm is the most glorious ascription of praise to God ever written.

C. W. Eliot. Menorah Journal, 1919, v. 151.

694.6 The religion of the Psalms lives amongst us still; in our hearts it is more effective than many of the Christian dogmas.

Gunkel, What Remains of the OT, (1914) 1928, p. 52.

694.7 In other portions of Scripture God speaks to us, but in the Psalms men speak to God and to their own hearts.

*M. Henry. q BSL, 22.

694.8 The triumphant strains resounding in this Hallelujah finale [*Ps.* 150] make a noble and fitting conclusion to the Psalms, the grandest symphony of praise to God ever composed on earth.

Oesterley, The Psalms in the Jewish Church, 1910; *The Psalms,* 1939, ii. 593.

694.9 The Book of Psalms contains the whole music of the heart of man, swept by the hand of his Maker. In it are gathered the lyrical burst of his tenderness, the moan of his penitence, the pathos of his sorrow, the triumph of his victory, the despair of his defeat, the firmness of his confidence, the rapture of his assured hope.

Prothero, The Psalms in Human Life, 1903.

694.10 In every country, the language of the Psalms has become part of the daily life of nations, passing into their proverbs, mingling with their conversation, and used at every critical stage of existence.

Ibid.

694.11 They are the songs of the human soul, timeless and universal; it is the sacred poets of Israel who, more than any others, have well and truly interpreted the spirit of man.

T. H. Robinson, A History of Israel, 1932, p. 447.

694.12 The veracity of the Hebrew Psalmists is nowhere more thorough than in such self-examination and faithful dealing with their souls. . . . No wonder that the Psalm-book of that little Hebrew people should have become the confessional of half mankind.

*G. A. Smith, *The Hebrew Genius*, 1927. BSL, 23.

695. PUBLICITY

695.1 Before all your people will I do marvels.
Bible: Exod., 34.10.

695.2 Tell it not in Gath, publish it not in the streets of Ashkelon.
Bible: II Sam., 1.20.

695.3 Hide not your wisdom.
Apocrypha: Ben Sira, 4.23.

695.4 Hidden wisdom and concealed treasure, what profit is there in either?
Ibid., 20.30.

695.5 Without publicity there can be no public spirit.
Disraeli, Aug. 8, 1871.

695.6 Advertising is necessary for business, and life is a business like any other.
Heine. q T. W. Evans, *Memoirs of Heinrich Heine*, 1884.

695.7 Why synagogs have no bells? Go to a fish market, and you will see that the high quality stalls are silent.
Kara, to a monk, 12C. q *Commentary*, May 1954, p. 447.

695.8 What does the splendor of the sun avail us unless it send forth its beams?
Lefin, letter to S. D. Luzzatto. *Kerem Hemed*, 1833, i. 74. q SHR, 103.

695.9 The Euphrates was asked, "Why are you inaudible?" It answered, "My deeds make me known; near me plants ripen in thirty days." The Tigris was asked, "Why are you so noisy?" It answered, "May my sound be heard, lest I be overlooked!"
The fruit trees were asked, "Why are you inaudible?" They replied, "We need no noise; our fruits testify for us." The other trees were asked, "Why are you so loud?" They replied, "That we may be noticed!"
Levi. *Gen. R.*, 16.3.

695.10 Only then is a man's service of God sincere when he wants no publicity for it.
Nahman Bratzlav, *Sefer HaMiddot, Teshuba*, 1821.

695.11 Publicity, *publicity*, PUBLICITY is the greatest moral factor and force in our public life.
Pulitzer, to editors of N.Y. *World*, Dec. 29, 1895.

695.12 Publicity is a very dangerous thing; great things can best be done in quiet.
E. de Rothschild, q Naiditsch, *Rothschild*, 28.

695.13 Judaism needs not to be advertised. Judaism needs to be taught.
Schechter, June 2, 1912 (*Seminary Addresses*, 227).

695.14 Publicity is immortality on a cash basis.
Shatzky, to J. L. Baron, 1951.

696. PUNISHMENT

696.1 Eye for eye, tooth for tooth.
Bible: Exod., 21.24. Cf *Lev.*, 24.20; *Jubilees*, 4.32.

696.2 This means monetary indemnity.
Ishmael. *Mekilta*, to *Exod.* 21.24.

696.3 Let it not enter your mind to take this law literally. As in the case of smiting a beast, compensation is to be paid.
Talmud: Baba Kamma, 83b. See Hananel b. Hushiel, *Commentary on Pentateuch.* q FJA, 173f.

696.4 Do unto him as he had proposed to do unto his brother.
Bible: Deut., 19.19.

696.5 Never act insolently or tyrannically in your treatment of offenders.
Apocrypha: Aristeas, 191.

696.6 I fear not punishment but to deserve punishment.
Boerne, *Eine Kleinigkeit*, 1821.

696.7 We are not punished *for* our sins, but *by* them.
Harrison, *Religion of a Modern Liberal*, 1931, p. 76.

696.8 Penalty is incurred only after warning.
Ishmael School. *T: Yoma*, 81a. *Sifré, Num.*, #113.

696.9 God does not punish a sinner under twenty.
Jonathan. *T: Sabbath*, 89b.

696.10 God does not punish without forewarning.
Jose b. Halafta. *T: Sanhedrin*, 56b.

696.11 When your sieve has become clogged, beat upon it.
Levi. *Gen. R.*, 81.2.

696.12 From the moment an offending scholar received his punishment, he is your brother. And it is proper the punishment be administered privately, not to diminish his dignity.

Maimonides, *Responsa,* ed Freimann, #18, p. 17.

696.13 Who holds the lash wields it.

Mendelé, *BaYamim HaHem,* 1912.

696.14 The judges are to be reminded that they . . . must esteem the tooth of the peasant as much as the tooth of the nobleman, especially since the peasant has to eat crusts while the nobleman is able to eat rolls.

*Michaelis, *Mosaisches Recht,* v. 242. q BEJ, 205f.

696.15 Fines are the same for all.

Mishna: Ketubot, 3.7.

696.16 To punish a pupil, use nothing harder than a shoe-lace.

Rab. *T: Baba Bathra,* 21a.

697. PUPIL

697.1 Respect your disciple as you respect your colleague.

Eleazar b. Shammua. *Mishna: Abot,* 4.12.

697.2 A teacher should cherish his pupil as much as himself.

Mekilta, to *Exod.* 18.9.

697.3 Raise many disciples.

Mishna: Abot, 1.1.

697.4 Teachers learn from their students' discussions.

Rashi, *Commentary, Prov.,* 13.23.

697.5 Without an army there is no king, and without pupils the sages gain no glory.

Saadia, letter to an Egyptian community, May 22, 928. KTJ, 84.

698. PURIM

698.1 Purim is the birthday of the first *Schutz-Jude,* the first Jewish toady to foreign royalty.

Peretz, *Purim,* 1896. *Alle Verk,* xii. 137. q SPG, 123.

698.2 Fever is no sickness, and Purim is no holiday.

Proverb (Yiddish). BJS, #2798.

698.3 On Purim one should drink till he cannot tell the difference between "Cursed be Haman" and "Blessed be Mordecai."

Raba. *T: Megilla,* 7b.

698.4 Should all the festivals be abolished, Purim will remain.

Yotzer to *Parashat Zakor* (D. W. Libshitz, *Tefilot MiKol HaShana,* 1878, p. 419), based on view that even if Hagiographa be abolished, the Scroll of Esther will be retained (Simeon b. Lakish. *TJ: Megilla,* 1.5). See *Sefer Hasidim,* 13C, #1055, p. 267.

699. PURPOSE

699.1 The purpose of man's life is not happiness, but worthiness.

F. Adler, *Creed and Deed,* 1877, p. 127.

699.2 Life in this world is an end in itself.

Baal Shem. q Setzer, *Reb Yisroel,* 90.

699.3 Philosophers may argue as to whether there is a purpose *to* the world; for religious people there is no question about having a purpose *in* the world.

Baron, *In Quest of Integrity,* 1936, p. 12.

699.4 If no vineyard, why a fence? If no sheep, why a shepherd?

Ben Azzai. *Mekilta,* to *Exodus* 12.1.

699.5 Criticism has few terrors for a man with a great purpose.

Disraeli, *Life of Lord George Bentinck,* 1852.

699.6 The secret of success is constancy to purpose.

Disraeli, speech, June 24, 1872.

699.7 To make clear fundamental ends and valuations, and to set them fast in the emotional life of the individual, seems to me precisely the most important function which religion has to perform in the social life of man. . . . They come into being not through demonstration but through revelation, through the medium of powerful personalities.

Einstein, *Out of My Later Years,* 1950, p. 22.

699.8 Even those things in the world which seem superfluous have a divine purpose.

Gen. R., 10.7.

699.9 Unless a life is activated by sustained purpose it can become a depressingly haphazard affair.

Guggenheimer, *Creative Vision,* 1950, p. 86f.

699.10 The Skillful Bowman and the Man of Action

Aim high, allowing for the Earth's Attraction.

Guiterman, *A Poet's Proverbs*, 1924, p. 68.

699.11 Our children should be fitted for bread-winning, but they should be taught that bread-winning is only a means, not the purpose of life, and that the value of life is to be judged . . . by the good and the service to God with which it is filled.

S. R. Hirsch, *Nineteen Letters*, (1836), #19, p. 200.

699.12 In the whole realm of nature there is nothing purposeless, trivial, or unnecessary.

Maimonides, *Guide for the Perplexed*, 1190, 3.25.

699.13 He who does not pursue ultimate goals is wasting his days.

Nahman Bratzlav. q Gutkind, *Choose Life*, 11.

699.14 If anyone should ask me what was the motive for the creation of the world, I will answer what Moses taught, that it was the goodness of the Existent.

Philo, *Unchangeableness of God*, 23.

699.15 Adopt, as far as you can, an unrestrained life purpose.

Ibid., 24.

699.16 The Holy One created not a thing without a purpose.

Rab. *T: Sabbath*, 77b.

699.17 Nature has no particular goal in view, and final causes are mere human figments.

Spinoza, *Ethics*, 1677, i. Appendix.

699.18 As a man thinks of ultimates, so he tends to deal with immediates.

M. Steinberg, *A Believing Jew*, 1951, p. 44.

699.19 Life consists also of something which is higher than physiology. Human labor, that very thing which distinguishes man from the animal, is thoroughly teleological. . . . Art, even the "purest," is thoroughly teleological, because if it breaks with great aims, no matter how unconsciously felt by the artist, it degenerates into a mere rattle.

Trotsky, *Literature and Revolution*, 1925, p. 106.

699.20 What is Revolution, if it is not a mad rebellion in the name of the conscious, rational, purposeful and dynamic principle of life, against the elemental, senseless,

biologic automatism of life, that is, against the peasant roots of our old Russian history, against its aimlessness, its non-teleological character?

Ibid., 109.

700. PUSH

700.1 A common person always pushes himself to the front.

Kahana. *T: Megilla*, 12b.

700.2 If a Jew does not push himself he will wait forever.

Mendelé, *Dos Vintshfingerl*, 1865.

701. PYRAMID

701.1 As for the pyramid, it has a suggestion of restful compactness, and benefits by the ease with which memory calls up Egypt and shapes that at Gizeh have overwhelmed us with pride in the audacity of mere men, like ourselves, who dared to build on the scale of the horizon, and to insert into the pell-mell of nature rational geometric shapes in harmonious contrast with it.

Berenson, *Aesthetics and History*, 1948.

701.2 From the foot of the pyramids I contemplate twenty centuries, buried in the sand. . . . I used to consider myself as great as a pyramid, and now I realize that I am only a shadow that passes, that has passed away. I came here to hold on to fleeting life, and I see all about me only death. . . . I write this, not quite knowing what I'm saying, but I dry the ink with the dust of Egyptian queens.

Rachel, letter to Arsène Houssaye, 1856.

702. QUANTITY

702.1 Better is little with the fear of the Lord, than great treasure and turmoil therewith.

Bible: Prov., 15.16.

702.2 His teaching is small but clear.

Abayé. *T: Erubin*, 62b, ref. to Eliezer b. Jacob.

702.3 Piety, especially Jewish piety, respects the little—the little man, the little matter, the little task, the little duty. Through the little, religion meets the greatness that lies behind.

Baeck, *Judaism*, 1949, p. 26.

702.4 The little and pure is much, the much and impure is little.

Bahya, *Hobot HaLebabot*, 1040, 5.6.

702.5 Were I asked to sum up the age-long trend of Jewish history, I should answer in three words: Quality versus Quantity. All down the years, from Joshua to the War of Independence, we have been the few withstanding the many.

Ben Gurion, "Call of the Spirit." *IGY*, 1951; BRD, 441.

702.6 In creative work, never consider quantity. Obadiah consists of one chapter, yet it found its place in the Book of Books.
Bialik. q OMB, 54.

702.7 Better a little near than much far away.
Rab. *T: Pesahim*, 113a.

702.8 There often comes a meaning home
Through simple verse and plain,
While in the heavy, bulky tome
We find of truth no grain.
Santob de Carrion, *Proverbios Morales*, 1350.

703. QUARREL

703.1 Let there be no strife, I pray you, between me and you.
Bible: Gen., 13.8.

703.2 Woe is me, mother, that you have borne me a man of strife and contention to the whole earth!
Bible: Jer., 15.10.

703.3 It is an honor for a man to keep aloof from strife.
Bible: Prov., 20.3.

703.4 Palestinians regard him of nobler birth who, in a quarrel, is the first to be silent.
Abbahu. *T: Kiddushin*, 71b.

703.5 Tarry not where there is contention; strife leads to murder.
Apocrypha: Ahikar, 2.55.

703.6 Quarrel not with a loud man, and put not wood on fire.
Apocrypha: Ben Sira, 8.3.

703.7 Keep far from strife, and sin will keep far from you.
Apocrypha: Ben Sira, 28.8.

703.8 Contention is the smoke of love.
Boerne, *Der Narr im weissen Schwan*, ch 5.

703.9 Strife is an opening which widens as the water presses on.
Huna. *T: Sanhedrin*, 7a, on *Prov* 17.14.

703.10 Hard-heartedness and a temper that will not resolve quarrels are a heavy burden of sin, unworthy of a Jew.
Moses of Coucy, *Semag*, 1245.

703.11 Every city or house divided against itself shall not stand.
New Testament: Matt., 12.25.

703.12 The Holy One obliterates all memory of one who foments strife.
Num. R., 18.4.

703.13 Refer not to a past quarrel, lest the dead embers be rekindled.
Orhot Tzaddikim, 15C, ch 21.

703.14 No good ever comes of strife.
Simeon. *Exod. R.*, 30.17.

703.15 Dissension in a house will lead to its destruction.
Talmud: Derek Eretz, 7.37. See *Matt.* 12.25.

703.16 Quarrelsome people soon come to grief.
Zohar, Gen., 76b.

704. QUESTION

704.1 Ask and learn.
Apocrypha: I Macc., 10.72.

704.2 He who asks too much goes astray.
Auerbach, *Little Barefoot*, 1856, ch 4.

704.3 As a rule, he who asks questions is ignorant.
Bacharach, *Havot Yair*, 1699, 209.

704.4 I have heard of the Yankee method of answering one question by asking another.
Benjamin, Debate with Sumner, U.S. Senate, June 1854.

704.5 It is an old saying: Ask a Jew a question, and he answers with a question.
Baeck, *Judaism and Philosophy*, 1949, p. 11.

704.6 The fool wonders, the wise man asks.
Disraeli, *Count Alarcos*, 1839.

704.7 The burning question of the day.
Disraeli, speech, House of Commons, March 1873.

704.8 Questions are always easy.
Disraeli, *Sybil*, 1845.

704.9 Never hesitate to ask where the acquisition of virtue is concerned.
Elijah b. Raphael, *Tzavaah*, 18C. AHE, 309.

704.10 One fool can ask what a thousand sages can't answer.
Emden, *Torat HaKanaut*, 1752, ch 9.

704.11 'Tis better Thrice to ask your way
Than even Once to go astray.
Guiterman, *A Poet's Proverbs*, 1924, p. 50.

704.12 Who is ashamed to ask will diminish in wisdom among men.
M. Ibn Ezra, *Shirat Yisrael*, (12C) 1924, p. 116.

704.13 A wise man's question is half the answer.
Ibn Gabirol, *Mibhar HaPeninim*, c. 1050, #3 (Lokman).

704.14 Inquiry is man's finest quality.
Ibid., #44.

704.15 There are lions before you, and you ask of foxes?!
Jeremiah. *TJ: Shebiit*, 9.4.

704.16 No questions concerning contradictions in the Agada.
Maimonides, *Guide to the Perplexed*, 1190, Introduction.

704.17 We ask no question on a story.
Proverb (Yiddish). BJS, #2366.

704.18 Not all questions may be asked, nor is there an answer for every question.
Mendelé, *Di Kliatshé*, 1873, ch 12.

704.19 Ask and it shall be given you; seek and ye shall find; knock, and it shall be opened to you.
New Testament: Matt., 7.7.

704.20 Each wherefore has its therefore.
Proverb (Yiddish). BJS, #1252.

704.21 Is there any greatness in propounding problems?
Raba. *T: Sanhedrin*, 106b.

704.22 Each question which we think through to its ultimate, leads to the supermundane.
Rathenau, *Mechanik des Geistes*, 1913, p. 1.

704.23 Who is not ashamed to ask will in the end be exalted.
Samuel b. Nahman. *T: Berakot*, 63b.

704.24 The wise man questions the wisdom of others because he questions his own, the foolish man because it is different from his own.
L. Stein, *Journey into the Self*, 1950, p. 257.

704.25 A scholar asks to the point and answers to the point.
Talmud: Derek Eretz, 1.1.

704.26 What is man after all but a question? To ask and only to ask, to ask honestly and boldly, and to wait humbly for an answer is he here.
Varnhagen, letter to Adam v. Müller, Dec. 15, 1820.

705. QUIETUDE

705.1 Keep calm, and be quiet.
Bible: Isa., 7.4.

705.2 The mind stayed on Thee Thou keepest in perfect peace.
Ibid., 26.3.

705.3 In quietness and confidence shall be your strength.
Ibid., 30.15.

705.4 Jacob shall again be quiet and at ease, and none shall make him afraid.
Bible: Jer., 30.10; 46.27.

705.5 I will walk at ease, for I have sought Thy precepts.
Bible: Ps., 119.45. See 131.2.

705.6 A tranquil heart is the life of the flesh.
Bible: Prov., 14.30.

705.7 Better is a dry morsel and quietness therewith, than a house full of feasting with strife.
Ibid., 17.1.

705.8 Better is one handful of quietness than both hands full of labor and striving after wind.
Bible: Eccles., 4.6.

705.9 As long as you have no equanimity and can still feel the sting of insult, you have not attained to the state where you can connect your thoughts with God.
Abner. q Isaac of Acre, *Me-irat Enayim* (Jellinek, *Beiträge zur Geschichte der Kabbala*, ii. 45). Bahya, *Hobot HaLebabot*, 5.5. See SMT, 97.

705.10 His [Jacob's] tranquil heart carried his feet.
Aha, on *Gen.* 29.1. *Gen. R.*, 70.8.

705.11 *Shivithi*, I have made all things *equal* in my eyes, because "I have set the Lord always before me" [*Ps.* 16.8]. It is immaterial to me whether I'm praised or abused. I've reached a state of absolute equanimity, because of my all-absorbing consciousness of God, which leaves no room for concern with anything else.
Baal Shem, *Tzavaat Ribash*, 1797, 1f. See AHE, 297.

705.12 The great victories of life are oftenest won in a quiet way, and not with alarms and trumpets.
Cardozo, speech, Free Synagog, 1915.

705.13 Not lightly vacated are the verdicts of quiescent years.
Cardozo.

705.14 Do Thy will, O God, in heaven above, and grant tranquility of spirit to those who fear Thee below.
Eliezer b. Hyrcanus. *T: Berakot,* 29b.

705.15 Real wealth is the soul in repose.
Hoffenstein, *Pencil in the Air,* 1923, p. 148.

705.16 The wise will remain serene in the face of trouble.
Ibn Gabirol, *Mibhar HaPeninim,* c. 1050, #10.

705.17 Wisdom leads to tranquility, gold and silver to anxiety.
Ibn Gabirol, *Mibhar HaPeninim,* c. 1050, #10.

705.18 Tranquility is the summit of felicity.
Ibid., #123.

705.19 The perfect man desires tranquility.
Philo, *Unchangeableness of God,* 6.

705.20 Inner riches without the capacity for inner composure is a buried treasure.
Schnitzler, *Buch der Sprüche & Bedenken,* 1927, p. 228.

705.21 Anyone desiring a quiet life has done badly to be born in the twentieth century.
Trotsky. q *N.Y. Times Magazine,* Sept. 14, 1952, p. 3.

705.22 Every artist harbors a mysterious duality: if life tosses him about stormily he yearns for peace; but no sooner is peace given him than he longs for the old agitation.
S. Zweig, *World of Yesterday,* 1943, p. 357.

706. QUORUM

706.1 Any ten men were competent to form themselves into a congregation, and to discharge all the duties of religion.
F. Adler, *Creed and Deed,* 1877, p. 209.

706.2 Rise early and go to synagog, so that you may have the merit of making up the quorum of ten.
Joshua b. Levi. *T: Berakot,* 47b.

706.3 A large town is one that has ten men of leisure who attend synagog. A settlement that has less is a village.
Mishna: Megilla, 1.3.

706.4 This does not mean that there are ten men that have no work, but ten men that can lay aside their work and come to the synagog when there is a sacred duty or a public matter to attend to.
Maimonides, *Responsa,* ed Freimann, #13, p. 14.

706.5 Ten bad Jews suffice to damn us, ten good Jews to save us. Which *minyan* will you join?
Montefiore, address, Cambridge, 1900.

706.6 Nine rabbis can't make a *minyan,* but ten cobblers can.
Proverb (Yiddish). BJS, #3479. ATJF, p. 644.

707. QUOTATION

707.1 When you have good news about your neighbor, mention the source of your information, but not when you have bad news.
Abbahu. *Midrash Samuel,* 7.5.

707.2 Those who never quote in return are seldom quoted.
D'Israeli, *Curiosities: Quotation,* 1823.

707.3 The wisdom of the wise and the experience of ages may be preserved by quotations.
Ibid.

707.4 As it is a virtue to quote something authentic, so is it a virtue not to quote anything inauthentic.
Eleazar b. Simeon. *T: Yebamot,* 65b.

707.5 Who doesn't mention the author of his quotation is a robber.
Johanan b. Nappaha. *Tanhuma, BaMidbar,* #27, ed Buber, 11a.

707.6 No proof from a word torn from its context.
Maimonides, *Iggeret Teman,* 1172.

707.7 Who quotes a thing in the name of him who said it brings redemption to the world.
Mishna: Abot, 6.6.

707.8 There are two kinds of marriages: where the husband quotes the wife, and where the wife quotes the husband.
Odets, *Rocket to the Moon,* Act 1. *Six Plays,* 1939, p. 347.

707.9 A quotation at the right moment is like bread in a famine (to the famished).
Raba. *T: Kalla Rabbati,* ch 1.

707.10 I understand I was put in a sermon yesterday and my book was referred to as "the sublime book of a new thinker who lives in our midst." But it won't be really good until they use me in sermons without quoting me, and best of all, without even knowing that it is me they are using.

Rosenzweig, letter to his mother, Oct. 5, 1921. GFR, 104.

707.11 The lips of a deceased scholar tingle pleasantly in the grave when a traditional statement is quoted in his name.

Simeon b. Yohai. *T: Yebamot,* 97a.

707.12 The poet paints the thought of the philosopher, the philosopher analyzes the picture of the poet, and hence arises the stereotyped form of quotation.

Steinschneider, *Jewish Literature,* 1857, p. 172.

708. RABBI

708.A. Rabbinic Authority

708.A.1 It is a precept to obey the rulings of the sages. . . . Who follows the rulings of the sages is called a holy man.

Abayé. *T: Yebamot,* 20a.

708.A.2 Who does not follow them is called a wicked man.

Raba. *Ibid.*

708.A.3 Who are the ministering angels? The rabbis.

Amemar. *T: Nedarim,* 20b.

708.A.4 When a rabbi commands, his commands are obeyed.

Anski, *Dybbuk,* 1918, Act 1.

708.A.5 We entertain no doubt that all the rabbis' teachings which have reference to the foundations of our faith and principles of the Torah were orally transmitted to them from Sinai.

Z. H. Chajes, *Mebo HaTalmud,* 1845, ch 17, (tr 1952, p. 141).

708.A.6 It is absolutely against the spirit of our holy religion to condemn or excommunicate a rabbi because of individual views or opinions concerning the temporary forms of our faith.

Chorin, *Rabbinische Gutachten,* 1842, i. 32.

708.A.7 Whatever the rabbi ordains must be.

Franzos, *Child of Atonement,* 1872. *Jews of Barnow,* 167.

708.A.8 You [rabbis] wish to convince, to lead to the truth, not to forge bonds and fetters; you know . . . that you have no sovereign power over the inalienable religious freedom of congregations and individuals; nay, you would repudiate such power were it offered you, for true religion can prosper only in an atmosphere of freedom of conviction.

Geiger, at Conference of German Rabbis, July 13, 1846.

708.A.9 The rabbis . . . stand . . . as the legitimate successors and continuators of the prophets.

*Herford, *Pharisaism,* 1912, p. 66.

708.A.10 No rabbi of one congregation shall interfere with the internal affairs of another congregation, nor shall any of his decisions be valid in a congregation which has its own rabbi.

Italian Congregations, *Takkanot,* Ferrara, June 21, 1554. See Samuel of Modena, *Responsa* (15C) 1582, iv. 14; *JE,* vi. 262a.

708.B. Rabbinic Profession

708.B.1 The Rabbis . . . were men distinguished for superior erudition and the blamelessness of their lives, and these qualities formed their only title to distinction.

F. Adler, *Creed and Deed,* 1877, p. 209.

708.B.2 I have chosen the way of modesty, and I hate the rabbinate.

Emden, *Megillat Sefer,* (18C) 1896, p. 59. q CJE, 57.

708.B.3 Blessed is He who has not made me a rabbi.

Emden, *Edut BeYaakob,* 1756, 46a. q CJE, 77.

708.B.4 There is no sharp distinction in religious status between the rabbi and the layman in Judaism.

Finkelstein, *Religions of Democracy,* 1941, p. 13.

708.B.5 The first and holiest duty of a rabbi is to disseminate the Torah.

Güdemann, *Geschichte des Erziehungswesens,* 1888, iii. ch 2.

708.B.6 We shall henceforth call them Protest Rabbis.

Herzl. *Die Welt,* July 10, 1897. Ref. to rabbis who opposed convening the Zionist Congress in Munich.

708.B.7 At first I did not want to be a rabbi, for a rabbi has to flatter his flock, and I thought of being a tailor. Then I saw that a tailor has to flatter his customers, and so has a shoemaker, and a bath-attendant; and I said to myself, "Where, then, is a rabbi worse off?" And so I became a rabbi.

N. Z. Horowitz. q Lipson, *MiDor Dor,* i. 109, #278.

708.B.8 When Levi Yitzhok was about to be born, Satan complained that if that soul were to descend on earth, it would reform the world, and his own power would come to an end. Then the Holy One comforted Satan, and said: "But he will be a rabbi, and he will be too occupied with communal affairs."

A. Kahana, *Sefer HaHasidut*, 1922, p. 250.

708.B.9 All the knowledge the future rabbi acquires must be subordinate to the higher task of practical communal service which he is expected to assume.

Kohler, *Inaugural Address*, Oct. 18, 1903.

708.B.10 Judaism in these days of skepticism, of religious apathy, of Mammon worship, of wholesale apostasy, requires men of power and undaunted courage, men of the spirit, men with the zeal of an Elijah and the tongue of an Isaiah . . . to be safe and trusted guides amidst all the perplexities of life, towers of strength when all things give way.

Kohler. *HUC Annual*, 1904, p. 18.

708.B.11 A rabbi whom they don't want to drive out of town isn't a rabbi, and a rabbi whom they actually drive out isn't a man.

Lipkin. q KTH, i. 276.

708.B.12 He who accepts a rabbinic position must be able to fulfil the command, "Ye shall not be afraid of any man" [*Deut.* 1.17].

Ibid., 277.

708.B.13 I regard the so-called pastoral ministry as the most sacred vocation. I revere it even above the offices of teaching and preaching. With admonition and serenity, religion should accompany man from the cradle to the grave.

I. N. Mannheimer, letter to A. Wolff, July 22, 1829.

708.B.14 "The law of the Lord is perfect" [*Ps.* 19.8] when it is taught by a righteous man who strives for perfection.

Midrash Tehillim, 19.14.

708.B.15 It was hard for Satan alone to mislead the whole world, so he appointed prominent rabbis in different localities.

Nahman Bratzlav, *Likkuté Moharan*, 1806. q HHH, iii. 27.

708.B.16 The rabbi is primarily a teacher; such is the tradition from all our past, such must be our aim and purpose now.

Philipson, at H.U.C., June 14, 1913. *Centen. Papers*, 255.

708.B.17 The rabbi's first concern is learning and scholarship.

Ibid., 259.

708.B.18 Unless you can play baseball, you'll never get to be a rabbi in America.

Schechter, to L. Finkelstein. q *Time*, Oct. 15, 1951, 54.

708.B.19 Rabbis must be God-fearing men.

Sefer Hasidim, 13C, #820, p. 208.

708.B.20 Love work, hate the rabbinate.

Shemaiah. *Mishna: Abot*, 1.10.

708.B.21 The rabbi is the teacher in Israel, no more and no less.

I. M. Wise, *The Rabbi*, 1871. *Selected Writings*, 387.

708.B.22 When in former days, a young man was ordained to the Rabbinate, the elders bade him remember, "We give you not dominion but services."

S. S. Wise, June 11, 1905. *Sermons and Addresses*, 76.

708.C. Hasidic Rabbi

708.C.1 The *tzaddik* is the foundation of the world. . . . No revelation is possible except through him.

Abraham Malak, *Hesed LeAbraham*, 1851.

708.C.2 The will of the *tzaddik* agrees with the will of God.

Ber, *Or Torah*, 1804, 13. q WHJ, iii. 38.

708.C.3 Elijah Gaon passed away, and left behind books. . . . Israel Baal Shem passed away, and left behind men.

Horodetzky. *HaShiloah*, 1907, xvii. 353, 356.

708.C.4 You deem it a miracle when God does the will of your *tzaddik*; we deem it a miracle if it can be truthfully asserted that the *tzaddik* does the will of God.

L. Kagan. q YSS, 175.

708.C.5 The *tzaddik* is the soul of the world; the rest of the generation is like the body. He is the channel through which the divine influence flows to the common people.

Katz, *Toldot Jacob Joseph*, 1780, Introduction.

708.C.6 To join with the common man, in order to lift him to a higher level, the *tzaddik* must himself have a particle of uncleanness.
Ibid., 40.

708.C.7 Lord, if ever Thou shouldst issue a hard decree against the Jews, we *Tzaddikim,* will not fulfill Thy commands!
Levi Yitzhok. q HLH, 43.

708.C.8 The Hasid will be held accountable for saying, "I have a rabbi, why do I need a book?" and the anti-Hasid for saying, "I have a book, why do I need a rabbi?"
Lipkin. q Mark, *Gdolim fun Undzer Tzeit,* 95.

708.C.9 The Hasidim think they have a rabbi; their opponents think they need no rabbi. Both are mistaken.
Lipkin. q KTH, i. 278.

708.C.10 It is the Hasidim who make the rabbi.
Mendel of Kotzk. q BTH, ii. 9.

708.C.11 The *tzaddik* is he who embraces in one harmonious synthesis the heavenly and the earthly, the spiritual and the material, and transforms it into an organic whole. He is like the neck which joins the head with the body.
Simha Bunam. q Shemen, *Lublin,* 161f.

709. RACE

709.1 The Jews are the only pure race in Europe, besides the gipsies.
*Andree, *Zur Volkskunde der Juden,* 1881.

709.2 An honorable race is what? The race of men! The race that fears God. A despicable race is what? The race of men! The race that transgresses the commandments.
Apocrypha: Ben Sira, 10.19.

709.3 No matter what learned scientists may say, race is, politically speaking, not the beginning of humanity but its end, not the origin of peoples but their decay, not the natural birth of man but his unnatural death.
Arendt, *Origins of Totalitarianism,* 1951, p. 157.

709.4 Society will be built even as the tabernacle in the wilderness, following a heavenly pattern in which red, yellow, black and white fires blended harmoniously. These are the colors of the races of men, and all of them together constituted the celestial design which the Holy One revealed to Moses as a model for His dwelling on earth.
J. L. Baron, Sermon, Feb. 9, 1934, based on *Pesikta Kahana,* ch 1, ed Buber, 1925, 4a.

709.5 Racial consciousness is absolutely necessary in music even though nationalism is not.
Bloch. q Ewen, *Book of Modern Composers,* 255.

709.6 There is no more a Semitic than there is an Aryan race, since both terms define linguistic groups, not human beings.
Boas, *Aryans and Non-Aryans,* 1934.

709.7 There is no evidence that the differences between . . . races . . . have any directive influence upon the . . . development of culture.
Boas, *Mind of Primitive Man,* (1911) 1938, p. 195f.

709.8 The Jews also have been proved by physical examination as well as by blood tests to be of highly mixed origin.
Ibid., 258, ref to J. Brutzkus' paper at Congrès de la Population, Paris, 1937.

709.9 Since a remote period there have been no pure races in Europe and it has never been proved that continued intermixture has brought about deterioration.
Ibid., 259.

709.10 The greatness of a nation does not depend on the character of its blood or race . . . [but] consists of the values it produces.
Brod, *Rassentheorie und Judentum,* 1934.

709.11 It is not race that has made the differences between the Jews and us; it is we and our ancestors that have made them.
*Brunetière. *Revue des Deux Mondes,* June 1, 1886.

709.12 Priggism . . . is as essentially a Teutonic vice as holiness is a Semitic characteristic.
*Butler, *Alps and Sanctuaries,* 1879, p. 142.

709.13 We contrast the Aryan with the "Semite," by whom we ordinarily mean "the Jew."
*Chamberlain, *Foundations,* (1899) 1911, i. 263.

709.14 Lack—or let us say poverty—of imagination is a fundamental trait of the Semite.
Ibid., 418.

709.15 A race manifests its proper genius, in all its brilliance and all its soundness, when there is mingled with it a spark of foreign genius.
Darmsteter, *Race and Tradition. Selected Essays,* 176f.

709.16 Race is everything; there is no other truth. And every race must fall which carelessly suffers its blood to become mixed.
Disraeli, *Coningsby,* 1844.

709.17 No one will treat with indifference the principle of race. It is the key of history.
Disraeli, *Endymion,* 1880, ch 2.

709.18 The Aryans have a sense of form and the Jews have not.
*Driesmans, *Cultural History of Race-Instincts,* 1899, i. 23.

709.19 Race is a controlling influence in the Jew, who, for two millenniums, under every climate, has preserved the same character and employments.
*Emerson, *English Traits: Race,* 1856.

709.20 It is impossible for the individual to be a Man as long as his people, the creator of his concrete life, is a Beast. . . . All ideals and ancient strivings of humanity disappear behind the crass egoism of the race. . . . Who can understand this as well as we Jews? We were the first to proclaim that man was created in the image of God, we must go further and say: the race must be created in the image of God.
A. D. Gordon. q *Avukah Annual,* 1925–1930, p. 63.

709.21 All nations, the most primitive that we meet with at the first dawn of historic times, will be for us the products of a process of amalgamation (already ended during the prehistoric times) among the heterogeneous ethnic elements.
Gumplowicz, *Rassenkampf,* 1883.

709.22 Race theory is as false in theory as it is foolish in practice. . . . I lay stress upon the ability and character of the citizens. . . , upon their loyalty and patriotism. When you think of these things, the so-called Jewish question becomes everywhere very easy to solve in accordance with the dictates of justice.
*Hainisch. *Pester Lloyd (American Hebrew,* April 18, 1924, 698).

709.23 All nations are composed of the most manifold racial elements, and we even

see that the most mixed stand in the foremost ranks of civilization.
F. Hertz, *Race and Civilization,* 1928, p. 321. See 135.

709.24 Racialism, if not vigorously kept in bounds, fosters the growth of injustice, inhumanity and fanaticism in general.
F. Hertz, *Nationality in History and Politics,* 1944, p. 54.

709.25 The Jewish race is one of the primary races of mankind that has retained its integrity, in spite of the continual change of its climatic environment.
Hess, *Rome and Jerusalem,* (1862), #4, p. 59.

709.26 In spite of the fact that they have hitherto remained an unmixed nation among the nations, present-day Jews are generally no longer real Semites.
*Hommel, *Semitische Völker & Sprachen,* 1883, i. Vorwort, (10 May 1881), p. viii.

709.27 There is no Ammonite and Moabbite today. King Senacherib of Assyria long ago mixed up all the nations.
Joshua b. Hanania. *T: Berakot,* 28a.

709.28 Do we know whence we are descended? Perhaps from those of whom it is written, "They ravished the women in Zion" [*Lam.* 5.11].
Judah b. Ezekiel. *T: Kiddushin,* 71b.

709.29 Not blue eyes, ergo, I am ill-bred;
My head is short, wherefore, I
   am too long
By a head!
A. M. Klein, *Hath Not a Jew,* 1940, p. 8.

709.30 Israel today is a race in transition.
Koestler, *Promise and Fulfilment,* 1949, p. 225.

709.31 Race is a fiction . . . human races are not pure, i.e., strictly speaking, there is no such thing as a race.
Lazare, *Antisemitism,* (1892) 1903, p. 227.

709.32 The idea of Semitic superiority is in no way more justifiable than the idea of Aryan superiority.
Ibid., 239.

709.33 With the mingling of races there is increasing life and vigor.
L. Levi, *International Law,* 1888, p. 80.

709.34 There will be strange ebbs and flows in the tide of race feelings.
Amy Levy, *Reuben Sachs,* 1888.

709.35 The declaration that blood prevails over ideals is the very antithesis of Judaism. It is the motto of the swastika.
Loewe, *Rabbinic Anthology*, 1938, p. lxxxi.

709.36 This same simple and sensuous quality shows itself in another way—in the inexpugnable racial tendency of the Hebrew mind to express not only emotions, but ideas, in apt and telling imagery.
*Lowes, *Essays in Appreciation*, 1936, p. 9.

709.37 The racial conception of society is essentially Jewish and non-Aryan.
*Macmurray, *Clue to History*, 1939, p. 232.

709.38 He made of one blood all nations of men to dwell on all the face of the earth.
New Testament: Acts, 17.26.

709.39 Those who have no true excellence of character should not pride themselves on the greatness of their race.
Philo, *Virtues*, 38.

709.40 It is the Semitic race which has the glory of having made the religion of humanity.
*Renan, *Life of Jesus*, 1863, p. 70.

709.41 One of the principal defects of the Jewish race is its harshness in controversy. . . . It is the faculty of nice discernment which makes the polished and moderate man. Now, the lack of this faculty is one of the most constant features of the Semitic mind.
Ibid., 297.

709.42 The boasted purity of descent of the Jews is a myth.
*Ripley, *Races of Europe*, 1899, p. 390.

709.43 The destruction of race prejudice is the beginning of the higher civilization.
Rosenwald, speech, 1911.

709.44 In the final analysis all the moral precepts, religious impulses and spiritual tendencies of an individual proceed out of deeply rooted racial memories.
J. Wassermann, *My Life as German and Jew*, 1933, p. 259.

709.45 Abraham had three wives: Sarah, a daughter of Shem; Keturah, a daughter of Japheth; and Hagar, a daughter of Ham.
Yalkut, Job, ch 8.

710. RAIN

710.1 Rain is greater than the resurrection, since that is only for the righteous, while rain is for all.
Abbahu. *T: Taanit*, 7a. Cf *Gen. R.*, 13.6.

710.2 Rain descends only on account of those who have faith.
Ammi b. Nathan. *T: Taanit*, 8a.

710.3 Praised be Thy name . . . for each drop which Thou bringest down and keepest apart from the others.
Ezekiel. *Gen. R.*, 13.15.

710.4 When do Jews and Gentiles rejoice together? When it rains.
Joshua b. Levi. *Gen. R.*, 13.6.

710.5 Earth, like a little child, was sucking

But yesterday the rains of winter, with a cloud for nurse.
Judah Halevi, *Selected Poems*, 71.

710.6 Rain is withheld only because of slanderers.
Simeon b. Pazzi. *T: Taanit*, 7b.

710.7 Rain is greater than the Revelation, for that brought joy to Jews, while rain brings joy to all men.
Tanhum b. Hiyya. *Midrash Tehillim*, 117.1.

711. RAINBOW

711.1 Behold the rainbow and bless its Maker.
Apocrypha: Ben Sira, 43.11.

712. RANK

712.1 The Holy One seized Jeroboam by his garment and urged him, "Repent, then I, you and Jesse's son will walk in the Garden of Eden." "And who will be first?" he inquired. "The son of Jesse." "Then I don't want it," he replied.
Abba. *T: Sanhedrin*, 102a.

712.2 Be servant to the noble rather than chief of the vulgar.
Berekia HaNakdan, *Mishlé Shualim*, c. 1260.

712.3 Be tail among lions rather than head among foxes.
Mathia b. Heresh. *Mishna: Abot*, 4.15. Cf *TJ: Sanhedrin* 4.8.

712.4 A churl should not ride the king's horse.
Proverb (Yiddish). *JE*, x. 229a.

713. READING

713.1 If we consider men and women generally, and apart from their professions or occupations, there is only one situation I can think of in which they almost pull themselves up by their bootstraps, making an effort to read better than they usually do. When they are in love and are reading a love letter, they read for all they are worth. They read every word three ways; they read between the lines and in the margins; they read the whole in terms of the parts, and each part in terms of the whole; they grow sensitive to context and ambiguity, to insinuation and implication; they perceive the color of words, the odor of phrases, and the weight of sentences. They may even take the punctuation into account. Then, if never before or after, they read.

M. J. Adler, *How to Read a Book,* 1940, p. 14.

713.2 Read ten books on one theme or personality rather than a hundred books concerning different subjects.

Brandes. q Niger, *Geklibene Shriften,* 1928, i. 66.

713.3 There is an art of reading, as well as an art of thinking and an art of writing.

D'Israeli, *Literary Character,* 1795, ch 11.

713.4 Reading is a dynamic act: the creative coming together of minds.

W. Frank. Schreiber, *Portraits and Self-Portraits,* 1936, 44.

713.5 I've given up reading books; I find it takes my mind off myself.

Levant.

713.6 There are two kinds of readers of serious books. The first is like unto a man who squeezes grapes with his finger tips, extracting mere watery juice. When the stuff fails to ferment, he blames the grapes. The second is like unto a man who crushes grapes thoroughly, extracting all their richness. Such a one is never moved to complain, for the stuff will readily ferment, and he is left with most excellent wine.

Midrash Ribesh Tov. q Browne, *Wisdom of Israel,* p. ix.

713.7 I prefer to pray the less so as to read the more.

Moses Hasid, *Iggeret HaMusar,* 1717. AHE, 290.

713.8 Everyone reads out of a work as much as he is capable of reading into it. Only in the material realm is "a receiver not a giver." Spiritually, you can't take unless you give. To apprehend God's or a man's creation, you must put in your share and become a partner in the creative work.

Niger, *Geklibene Shriften,* 1928, i. 19.

713.9 The Catholics have read only for two centuries, the Protestants only since Calvin, but the Jews for two thousand years.

*Péguy. q Siegfried. *American Hebrew,* Nov. 22, 1929.

713.10 There are readers who read only the dead letters, whose eyes touch the words and the words are for them nothing but lead. They do not penetrate beyond the eye.

J. Rosenfeld. q Niger, *Geklibene Shriften,* 1928, i. 73f.

713.11 It's a continuous conversion. . . . The real question is what changes will be made in you as a result of really reading a book.

L. Stein, *Journey into the Self,* 1950, p. 156.

714. REALITY

714.1 You cannot seek for the ideal outside the realm of reality.

Blum, *New Conversations,* 1901. q FNL, 128.

714.2 God is all reality, but not all reality is God.

Cordovero, *Elima Rabbati,* (16C) 1881, 24d. q SMT, 252f.

714.3 Reality will always remain unknowable.

Freud, *Outline of Psychoanalysis,* 1949, p. 106.

714.4 Little by little we subtract
Faith and Fallacy from Fact,
The Illusory from the True,
And starve upon the residue.

Hoffenstein, *Rag-Bag,* ii. *Year In, You're Out,* 1930. *Complete Poetry,* 1954, p. 212.

714.5 Nothing is real but what is felt or believed.

F. Mendelssohn, letter to Pastor Bauer, March 4, 1833.

714.6 What inexorably destroys neurasthenics is that they do not know how to come to terms with reality.

Nordau, *Degeneration,* (1893), 5.1, p. 540.

714.7 You cannot transfer what does not exist.

Rami b. Hama. *T: Baba Metzia,* 33b.

714.8 The praiseworthy wise man is he who makes reality his guiding principle and bases his belief thereon.

Saadia, *Emunot VeDeot,* 933, Introd., 3, tr Rosenblatt, 14f.

715. REASON

715.1 Come now, and let us reason together.
Bible: Isa., 1.18.

715.2 If men would follow the dictates of reason and live according to nature, they would all mutually love one another.
Acosta. q SMMP, 93.

715.3 There are men who are bound by the chains of reason, and for such men there is no aerial soaring.
Ahad HaAm. q Leftwich. *Menorah Journal,* Spring 1952, p. 60.

715.4 Never seek gratification at the expense of reason.
Apocrypha: Aristeas, 215.

715.5 By their contempt for pain, yea, even unto death, [martyrs] proved that Reason rises superior to the passions.
Apocrypha: IV Macc., 1.9.

715.6 Reason is a spark kindled by the beating of our heart.
Apocrypha: Wisdom of Solomon, 2.2.

715.7 *Homo sapiens,* the only creature endowed with reason, is also the only creature to pin its existence to things unreasonable.
Bergson, *Two Sources of Morality and Religion,* 1935, p. 92.

715.8 Man is not an angel that his reason should always work perfectly, nor is he a mule that it should never be active at all.
Caspi, *Yoré Deah,* 14C, ch 3. AHE, 134.

715.9 Reason cannot be forced into belief.
Crescas, *Or Adonai,* c. 1400.

715.10 Reason is the mediating angel between God and man.
A. Ibn Ezra, *Commentary to Pentateuch,* Introd., 12C.

715.11 Reason is God's emissary.
A. Ibn Ezra, *Commentary,* to *Prov.* 22.20.

715.12 Reason cannot injure true Religion, for true Religion is reason.
Joseph, *The Ideal in Judaism,* 1893, p. 13.

715.13 Mankind has lost its morality because it has lost its God. Perhaps it has lost both because of the irrational element in both of them.
Klausner, *Christian and Jewish Ethics. Judaism,* Jan. 1953, 29.

715.14 I cannot sate my soul
With love that comes from logic's bonds.
Kook, *Zikkaron,* 12. q ABJ, 169.

715.15 The law cannot prevent us from considering as true what our reason urges us to believe.
Levi b. Gerson, *Milhamot Adonai,* (1329) 1560, Introd.

715.16 Whatever light I may receive, I shall always illumine it with the light of reason. . . . My religion enjoins me to *believe* nothing, but to *think* the truth and to *practice* goodness.
S. Maimon, *Autobiography,* (1793) 1947, p. 91.

715.17 Reason is more to be trusted than the eye.
Maimonides, *Commentary to Mishna,* 1180, *Zeraim,* Preface.

715.18 Without reason there is no perfection of soul.
Norzi, *Seah Soleth,* 1561, 7a.

715.19 Wherein shall a man find complete repose, save in reason?
Philo, *Dreams,* i. 18.

715.20 Any interpretation that conforms to reason must be correct.
Saadia, *Emunot VeDeot,* 933, 9.3.

715.21 Reason knows itself and its limitations. It knows that it is but a modest light in the dusk of infinitude, yet the only one at our disposal.
Schnitzler, *Buch der Sprüche & Bedenken,* 1927, p. 43.

715.22 Virtue arising from Reason is higher than virtue which is not founded on Reason.
Shneor Zalman, *Tanya,* 1796. q HLH, 60.

715.23 True virtue is life under the direction of reason.
Spinoza, *Ethics,* 1677, iv. Pr 24, Proof; Pr 37, Note 1.

715.24 Reason can do much to restrain and moderate the passions, but . . . the road which reason herself points out is very steep, so that such as persuade themselves that the multitude of men distracted by politics can ever be induced to live according to the bare dictate of reason, must be dreaming of the poetic golden age, or of a stage-play.
Spinoza, *Political Treatise,* 1677, 1.5.

715.25 The Bible leaves reason absolutely free.
Spinoza, *Theologico-Political Treatise,* 1670, Preface.

715.26 Reasonable people are not commonly reasoners, and reasoners not usually reasonable.

L. Stein, *Journey into the Self*, 1950, p. 256.

715.27 Where reason speaks, malice cannot be.

I. M. Wise. *Deborah*, Jan. 21, 1897. See *AJA*, June 1954, p. 136.

715.28 Inclination, being tough and hard, is normally stronger than reason, which is gentle and delicate. But even when both forces are equal, man must assist the intellect in its battle with the will.

Zerahia, *Sefer HaYashar*, (c. 1300, 1526) 1853, ch 6, p. 28.

716. REBELLION

716.1 Rebellion is as the sin of witchcraft.

Bible: I Sam., 15.23.

716.2 We have no portion in David, . . . every man to his tents!

Bible: II Sam., 20.1. *I Kings*, 12.17.

716.3 If ye refuse and rebel, ye shall be devoured with the sword.

Bible: Isa., 1.20.

716.4 Fight not against the Lord . . . for ye shall not succeed.

Bible: II Chron., 13.12.

716.5 By sedition ye have settled, and by sedition will your children fall.

Apocrypha: Jubilees, 10.30.

716.6 Rebellion! the very word is a confession; an avowal of tyranny, outrage, and oppression. It is taken from the despot's code, and has no terror for others than slavish souls.

Benjamin, *Farewell to the Union*, U.S. Senate, 1861.

716.7 God adjured Israel not to rebel against the Governments.

Helbo. *Cant. R.*, 2.7.

Jose b. Hanina. *T: Ketubot*, 111a.

716.8 Having no hope of future reward the Jew could not resign to the misfortunes of life. . . . To the scourges befalling him he replied neither with the Mohammedan's fatalism, nor with the Christian's resignation, but with revolt.

Lazare, *Antisemitism*, (1892) 1903, p. 279.

716.9 Insurrection is an art.

Marx. q Souvarine, *Stalin*, 86.

716.10 Lord of the universe, . . . send us our Messiah, for we have no more strength to suffer. Show me a sign, O God. Give me the force to rend the chains of exile. Otherwise, . . . otherwise . . . I rebel against Thee. If Thou dost not keep Thy covenant, . . . then neither will I keep that agreement, and it is all over, we are through being Thy chosen people, Thy peculiar treasure!

Mendel of Kotzk. q Cahn, *Der Rebbe fun Kotzk*, Introd., 9.

716.11 An elder is liable for *acting* contrary to a Supreme Court decision, not for dissenting from it and for persisting in communicating his opinion. Scripture says, "the man that *does* presumptuously" [*Deut.* 17.12], not that *speaks* presumptuously.

Talmud: Sanhedrin, 88b. Maimonides, *Yad: Mamrim*, 3.6.

716.12 A rebellious elder . . . is a judge who gives a practical ruling contrary to the decision of the Supreme Court.

Maimonides, *Yad: Mamrim*, 1180, 3.4.

717. RECORD

717.1 Let giving and receiving all be in writing.

Apocrypha: Ben Sira, 42.7.

717.2 Why is the unaccepted opinion of a single person recorded? So that if someone say, "I learned the tradition thus," he may be told, "You learned the refuted opinion."

Judah HaNasi. *Mishna: Eduyot*, 1.6.

717.3 The unaccepted minority opinion of a single person is recorded, so that if a [future] court prefers that opinion, it may depend on his authority.

Mishna: Eduyot, 1.5.

718. REDEMPTION

718.1 Let my people go!

Bible: Exod., 5.1.

718.2 A redeemer will come to Zion.

Bible: Isa., 59.20.

718.3 Lord . . . enable us to . . . rebuild Thy city. . . . Then shall we chant unto Thee a new song on our redemption and salvation.

Akiba. *Mishna: Pesahim*, 10.6.

718.4 Had we not a biblical verse [*II Sam.* 7.23], we could not say it: Israel said to God, Thou hast redeemed Thyself!

Akiba. *Sifré, Num.*, #84.

718.5 Gather our dispersion, free those in bondage, look upon them that are despised, and let the nations know that Thou art God!

Apocrypha: II Macc., 1.27.

718.6 Israel's redemption is like a harvest [*Joel* 4.13],—if a field is reaped too early, even its straw is not good. It is like a vineyard [*Isa.* 27.2],—if the grapes are picked at the right time, even the vinegar is good. It is like a woman with child [*Mic.* 5.2],—if born prematurely, a baby is not viable.

Cant. R., 8.14.

718.7 God of Abraham, Thou knowest well
that Moses shall be born again,
and that in vain maternal pain
shall seek a bullrush clump beside
    a river's swell
to shield his cradle, in a fashion.
Thou, who didst all evil fell,
grant to me the reeded mat
for that soft cradle woven by my
    passion!

*De la Vega, The Cries of Jewry.

718.8 Redeem us speedily for the sake of Thy name!

Eighteen Benedictions, 2C B.C.E., #7.

718.9 Redemption, like a livelihood, must be earned each day.

Eleazar. *Gen. R.*, 20.9.

718.10 The Jews' redemption depends on their repentance.

Eliezer b. Hyrcanus. *T: Sanhedrin*, 97b.

718.11 Whoever lives a godly life may become, not alone his own redeemer, but also in some degree the redeemer of the world.

Enelow, *Selected Works*, 1935, i. 170.

718.12 Through himself alone can man be redeemed—through himself and in himself.

Franzos, *Shylock of Barnow*, 1873. *Jews of Barnow*, 47.

718.13 We must . . . redeem our minds before we redeem our bodies.

J. L. Gordon, letter to S. Bernfeld, Jan. 31, 1888. *Igrot*, ii. 248. q Rhine, *Leon Gordon*, 82.

718.14 No redemption without faith and Torah!

Hazaz. q *JF*, Dec. 1950, p. 28.

718.15 Man's good deeds are single acts in the long drama of redemption.

Heschel, *The Earth Is the Lord's*, 1950, p. 72.

718.16 Like the dawn, Israel's redemption will come gradually.

Hiyya Rabba. *TJ: Berakot*, 1.1. Cf *Cant. R.*, 6.10.1.

718.17 The Jews will be redeemed by divine grace, not by merit.

Joshua b. Hanania. *T: Sanhedrin*, 97b.

718.18 The redemption requires preparation, its prerequisite is practical work in the Land of Israel.

Kalischer. q *HaDoar*, June 4, 1954, p. 578.

718.19 We shall not be redeemed until our exile is brought to an end.

Katznelson, *The Unfailing Source. Israel Argosy*, 1952, 161.

718.20 The redemption depends only on faith.

Nahman Bratzlav, *Likkuté Moharan*, 1806.

718.21 When lions roar, Oh, deign Thy flock to free!

I. Najara, "Yah Ribbon," 1587, tr Abrahams.

718.22 You are the weakest and the least, and the last to be redeemed. . . . You will be freed, when man will rise above the earthly, when human worms will turn into human eagles.

Peretz, *The Day*, 1906. *Alle Verk*, xii. 319.

718.23 Jerusalem's redemption will come only through righteousness.

Ulla b. Ishmael. *T: Sabbath*, 139a.

718.24 When the Jewish people will have redeemed the Land of Israel, the Land of Israel will redeem the Jewish people.

Ussishkin. *Eretz Israel*, 1932, p. 4.

718.25 Believe not thy foes when they say thou art forsaken like a useless slave, an old outworn servant who is summarily driven out of the house. Do not believe it, Israel! Between thy God and thee there is an unsettled reckoning that will one day be settled in thy favor, when grace will have struck the balance.

Werfel, *Between Heaven and Earth*, 1944, p. 211f.

719. REFINEMENT

719.1 Many refined people will not kill a fly, but eat an ox.

Peretz, *Taanis Gedanken*, 1896. *Alle Verk*, xii. 77.

720. REFORM

720.1 Mostly, reform in religion is rational. But if the religion be already too rational, reform must be emotional.

Abrahams, *Poetry and Religion*, 1920, p. 39.

720.2 The formulation of the highest truth needs constant revision, and even more surely do the forms in which that truth is clothed. . . . A liturgy that cannot expand, that cannot absorb the best religious teaching of the age, that cannot dare to sing unto the Lord new songs, . . . is a printed page, not a prayer-book for the supplicant's heart.

Abrahams. q PRM, 421.

720.3 Religion must change her dress according to the times and the climate . . . according to the dictates of advanced science, enlightened insight, more cultured taste, broadening conditions of life—in short, according to the needs of the world today.

S. Adler, sermon, 1860, at Anshe Hesed, N.Y.

720.4 As little as the ripe fruit can be forced back into the bud or the butterfly into the chrysalis, so little can the religious idea in its long process from generation to maturity be bound to one and the same form.

Einhorn, sermon, Sept. 27, 1855.

720.5 Not emancipation but reform is the leading issue of the day for the Jews.

Geiger, letter to M. A. Stern, 1836. q PCP, 100.

720.6 Every reform is a transition from the past into a regenerated future. Such reform does not break with the past but rather preserves carefully the bond which connects the present with the past. . . . It follows the law of historical development.

Geiger, "Unser Gottesdienst." *JZWL,* 1868, vi. 4. q PCP 102.

720.7 There are no drag-chains in Judaism, from which we must forcibly release ourselves; it does not come forward with orders that mock reason or violate conscience, that we should discard it; it needs inner reform, and itself offers the handle for it.

Geiger, letter to Bischoffsheim, Oct. 8, 1872.

720.8 Shall I shrink from initiating religious changes that the age demands, merely because my fathers remained passive? No; I claim the very changes as my merit, as a token of my zeal for the true welfare of the faith.

Joseph, *The Ideal in Judaism,* 1893, p. 48.

720.9 Hezekiah "broke in pieces the brazen serpent that Moses had made" [*II Kings* 18.4], and that Hezekiah's predecessors had spared when they suppressed every form of idolatry. Hezekiah's ancestors left something undone whereby he might distinguish himself, and my ancestors left room for me to distinguish myself!

Judah HaNasi. *T: Hullin,* 6b–7a.

720.10 True honoring of the old consists in our nursing it, not in our permitting it to decay. A wine dresser knows that if his vine is to bring forth . . . much and good fruit, he must cut away the rank sprigs of the vine lest it shoot into wood. But he knows also that if he cuts away all twigs the stem withers.

M. Lazarus, address, Leipzig Synod, 1869, q PRM, 295.

720.11 Every petrified religion is like a blasphemy.

Werfel, *Between Heaven and Earth,* 1944, p. 144.

721. REGIMENTATION

721.1 I fear you. As victors, you may become the bureaucracy: doling out to each his bit as in a poorhouse, assigning to each his task as in a prison. And you will exterminate the creator of new worlds,—the free human will, and stop up the purest well of human happiness—the power of the one to face thousands, to stand up to peoples and generations.

Peretz, *Hofnung un Shrek,* 1906. LP, 279.

722. REGRET

722.1 Regret is the most stupid feeling one can possibly cherish.

Auerbach, *Little Barefoot,* 1856, ch 17.

722.2 To regret nothing is the beginning of all wisdom.

Boerne, *Fragmente und Aphorismen,* 1840, #202.

722.3 A series of congratulatory regrets.

Disraeli, speech, July 30, 1878.

722.4 Regret is of no avail to a maiden who has lost her maidenhood, to a shooter who has flung the stone from the sling, and to a speaker who has uttered the word, which cannot be recalled.

Foundations of Religious Fear, 12C. See tr Gollancz, 1915.

722.5 Could we reach into the concealed rumination of the elderly, we could find as many regretful saints as repentant sinners.
Myerson, *Speaking of Man*, 1950, p. 110.

722.6 Regret is a woman's natural food—she thrives upon it.
Pinero, *Sweet Lavender*, 1893, Act 3.

722.7 Sense and regret come too late.
Sholom Aleichem, *A Boidem*, 1899.

723. REGULAR

723.1 The regular takes precedence over the irregular.
Mishna: Zebahim, 10.1.

724. RELATIVITY

724.1 No midgets, no giants.
Agnon, *Sippur Pashut*, 1935.

724.2 If a flame among the cedars fall,
What chance has hyssop on the wall?
If Leviathan be hauled by hooks,
What hope have fish in shallow brooks?
Bar Kipok. *T: Moed Katan*, 25b.

724.3 If my theory of relativity is proven successful, Germany will claim me as a German and France will declare that I am a citizen of the world. Should my theory prove untrue, France will say that I am a German and Germany will declare that I am a Jew.
Einstein, address at Sorbonne.

724.4 A giant in your eyes, a dwarf in ours.
Eleazar b. Simeon. *Gen. R.*, 65.11.

724.5 The big you have seems small, the small you haven't seems big.
Hanina. *T: Berakot*, 33b.

724.6 God alone is eternal and absolute; all else is relative.
Herberg, *Judaism and Modern Man*, 1951, p. 142.

724.7 A little sin is a big sin when committed by a big man.
A. Ibn Ezra, *Commentary*, to Gen. 32.9.

724.8 What to a fool is a thorn, to a wise man is corn.
Proverb (Yiddish). YFS, i. 420.

725. RELIGION

725.1 Though religion . . . always envelops conduct, the sentiment of religion and the sense of moral value are distinct.
S. Alexander, *Space, Time and Deity*, (1920) 1927, ii. 404.

725.2 The old conceptions of religion can be overcome only through more religion, not through irreligion.
B. Auerbach. q L. Geiger, *Deutsche Lit. & Juden*, 243.

725.3 This has been the lesson of religion through the ages . . . that time . . . may be swallowed up in the splendor of eternity, that experience . . . may be elevated into unconquerable immortality, that little men and women, born of earth, may rise to the heavenly throne of glory by losing themselves in an overbounding love of humanity.
Baron, *In Quest of Integrity*, 1936, p. 35f.

725.4 The spectacle of what religions have been in the past, of what certain religions still are today, is indeed humiliating for human intelligence. What a farrago of error and folly!
Bergson, *Two Sources of Morality and Religion*, 1935, p. 92.

725.5 Religion is love and reconciliation; the very word connotes it: it rebinds what was separated. . . . But what have men made of it! A stream of blood flows through eighteen centuries, and on its banks dwells Christendom. How they have desecrated the holiest! Religion was a weapon in rapacious, murderous hands.
Boerne, *O närrische Leute*, 1819.

725.6 The submergence of self in the pursuit of an ideal, the readiness to spend oneself without measure, prodigally, almost ecstatically, for something intuitively apprehended as great and noble, spend oneself one knows not why—some of us like to believe that this is what religion means.
Cardozo, *Values*, 1931.

725.7 We recognize in every religion an attempt to grasp the Infinite.
CCAR, *Pittsburgh Platform*, 1885.

725.8 For the ancient Roman his State was his Religion, and for the Jew his Religion was his State.
*Chamberlain, *Foundations*, (1899) 1911, ii. 12.

725.9 Religion is the link between soul and body, the point where heaven and earth meet in friendly encounter.
I. Deutsch, sermon, July 2, 1839.

725.10 Religion should be the rule of life, not a casual incident in it.
Disraeli, *Lothair*, 1870, ch 17.

725.11 The cosmic religious experience is the strongest and noblest driving force behind scientific research.

Einstein, *Cosmic Religion*, 1931, p. 52.

725.12 Religion is comparable to a childhood neurosis.

Freud, *Future of an Illusion*, tr 1949, p. 92.

725.13 Longing after the Highest and Noblest, attachment to the Whole, soaring up to the Infinite, despite our finiteness and limitedness—this is religion.

Geiger, *Judaism and Its History*, 1866, p. 18.

725.14 There is something odd about the weakness which irreligious men feel for religion. Almost invariably it becomes their favorite topic.

Guedalla, *A Gallery*, 1924, p. 42f.

725.15 Genuine religion is a call to revolt.

Gutkind, *Choose Life*, 1952, Preface.

725.16 Beautiful women without religion are like flowers without perfume.

Heine, *City of Lucca*, 1828, ch 11.

725.17 Monopoly is as injurious to religions as to trades; they are only strong and energetic by free competition.

Ibid., ch 14.

725.18 Human misery is too great for men to do without faith.

Heine. q L. Kalisch, *Pariser Skizzen*, 334. q KJL, 365.

725.19 You must not break friendship on account of different religious opinions, for it is universally agreed that all religions are matters of imagination.

Ibn Verga, *Shebet Yehuda*, (1550) 1855, #7, p. 16. q NLG 95.

725.20 Religion is a perception of the Divine existence, issuing in duty.

Joseph, *Judaism as Creed and Life*, (1903) 1909, p. 5.

725.21 Our lawgiver . . . did not make religion a part of virtue, but had the insight to make the virtues parts of religion. . . . For all our actions and studies and words have a connection with piety towards God.

Josephus, *Against Apion*, ii. 17.

725.22 The essence of religion is the human quest for salvation.

Kaplan, *Future of the American Jew*, 1948, p. 72.

725.23 When a man is on a low cultural level, he can satisfy his spiritual needs with outward religious observances; but as he becomes more highly developed, he wants to grasp the spirit of religion.

Krochmal, *Moré Nebuké HaZeman*, 1851, ch 7.

725.24 Some philosophers hold that all religions have a common aim, toward which they tend in different ways. Each employs parables and images according to the style of its generation and country and suitable to the intelligence of its followers, but all aim to lead people to justice, truth and bliss.

Levi b. Abraham, *Livyat Hen*, 1315, ed 1872, p. 140.

725.25 The plainest historical evidence for the effectiveness of religion as a positive social form lies in the history of the Jews.

*Macmurray, *Creative Society*, 1935.

725.26 Religion is the sigh of the oppressed creature, the feeling of a heartless world, just as it is the spirit of unspiritual conditions. It is the opium of the people.

Marx, *Critique of Hegelian Philosophy of Right*, 1844.

725.27 The first requisite for the people's happiness is the abolition of religion.

Ibid.

725.28 Religion should have not only the sacrament of prayer but also the sacrament of social service.

Mattuck, sermon, April 12, 1918.

725.29 True divine religion needs neither arms nor fingers for its use; it is all spirit and heart.

M. Mendelssohn, Preface to *Vindiciae Judaeorum*, 1782.

725.30 True religion . . . must be basically universalistic, must proclaim and strive for ultimate world-unity.

J. Morgenstern. Weller, *World Fellowship*, 1935, p. 64.

725.31 Pure religion . . . is this, To visit the fatherless and widows in their affliction, and to keep unspotted from the world.

New Testament: James, 1.27.

725.32 Religion is a functional weakness.

Nordau, *Conventional Lies*, 1884.

725.33 Religion is a sum of scruples which impede the free exercise of our faculties.

S. Reinach, *Cultes, Mythes et Religions*, i. 1904.

725.34 The pure religion which we dream of as the bond that shall in days to come hold together the whole of mankind in one communion, will be the realization of the religion of Isaiah, the ideal Jewish religion, freed from all admixture of impurity.
*Renan. q KJJ, 81.

725.35 In religion, which with me pervaded all the hours of life, I had been moved by the Jewish ideal, and as the perfect color and sound gradually asserted their power on me they seemed finally to agree in the old article of Jewish faith that things done delightfully and rightfully were always done by the help and spirit of God.
*Ruskin. q Sokolow, *History of Zionism*, 1919, i. 3.

725.36 The Bible is not the sole basis of our religion, for in addition to it we have two other bases. One is anterior to it, namely, the fountain of reason. The second is posterior to it, namely, the source of tradition.
Saadia, *Emunot VeDeot*, 933, 3.10, tr Rosenblatt, 174.

725.37 It rests with us to elect between archaeology and religion.
O. J. Simon, *Faith and Experience*, 1895, p. 105.

725.38 Religion is the everlasting dialogue between humanity and God. Art is its soliloquy.
Werfel, *Between Heaven and Earth*, 1944, p. 216.

725.39 Religion and morality, the way to God and the way to man, coincide.
M. Wiener, *Die Religion der Propheten*, 11f. q BKF, 38.

725.40 I would think of my religion as a gamble rather than think of it as an insurance premium.
S. S. Wise, *Religion*.

725.41 A Prusso-Jewish conscript replied in bewilderment when asked to state his religion: *Die Christen haben Religion: wir sind doch Juden"* (Christians have a religion; but we are Jews).
Zangwill. *JQRo*, xvii. 408.

725.42 Only charlatans make new religions.
Zunz. q SSJ, iii. 115.

726. REMNANT

726.1 A remnant shall return, even the remnant of Jacob.
Bible: Isa., 10.21.

726.2 I will rejoice over the few that shall be saved, inasmuch as they it is that make the glory prevail.
Apocrypha: II Esdras, 7.60.

727. REPENTANCE

727.1 Let the wicked forsake his way and . . . return unto the Lord.
Bible: Isa., 55.6. See 44.22.

727.2 Amend your ways and your doings.
Bible: Jer., 7.3, 26.13.

727.3 Make you a new heart and a new spirit; for why will ye die, O house of Israel?
Bible: Ezek., 18.31. See 18.23.

727.4 Return, O Israel, unto the Lord your God.
Bible: Hos., 14.2.

727.5 Rend your heart, not your garments, and turn to the Lord.
Bible: Joel, 2.13.

727.6 Return to Me . . . and I will return to you.
Bible: Zech., 1.3.

727.7 Turn us to Thee, O Lord, and we shall be turned.
Bible: Lam., 5.21.

727.8 If trouble cross your path, repent and void the wrath.
Abba b. Kahana. *Eccles. R.*, 7.13.1.

727.9 Where penitents stand, the wholly righteous cannot stand.
Abbahu. *T: Berakot*, 34b.

727.10 He who confesses his sin and does not turn away from it is like one bathing and holding on to a defiling reptile.
Adda b. Ahaba. *T: Taanit*, 16a.

727.11 Great is repentance! It cancels heavenly decrees and vows.
Aha b. Papa. *Cant. R.*, to 8.6.

727.12 Great is the art of writing music or literature. . . . But greater still is the art of bringing about one's regeneration.
Almi, *Our Unfinished World*, 1947.

727.13 Bad men are full of repentance.
*Aristotle, *Nicomachean Ethics*, 9.4, tr Meir Alguadez, *Sefer HaMiddot*, 15C, 9.5. See Wolfson, *Philo*, ii. 253.

727.14 Israel can be restored on the Day of Atonement, even as a nut may be picked up from the dirt, washed and made fit again.

Azariah. *Cant. R.,* 6.11.1.

727.15 Each penitent thought is a voice of God.

Baal Shem. q SSJ, i. 31.

727.16 Abandon transgression out of shame before the Creator, not out of fear of men or hope of their reward.

Bahya, *Hobot HaLebabot,* 1040, 7.5.

727.17 Humble yourself here, and you won't be humbled hereafter.

Ben Zoma. *Exod. R.,* 30.19.

727.18 Who does not accept the penitent is a fratricide.

Didascalia, ii. ch 21.

727.19 Though blasphemed in public, God demands penitence in private.

Eleazar b. Pedat. *Pesiḳta Kahana,* ch 25, ed Buber, 147a.

727.20 Repent one day before your death.

Eliezer b. Hyrcanus. *Mishna: Abot,* 2.10.

727.21 "How does one know which is the day before death?" . . . "Therefore repent today."

Abot de R. Nathan, ch 15. Cf Browning, *Ben Karshook's Wisdom.*

727.22 Like an architect, the Holy One modelled the world, and it would not stand, until He created repentance.

Eliezer b. Hyrcanus. *PRE,* ch 3.

727.23 Penitence and good deeds shield against retribution.

Eliezer b. Jacob. *Mishna: Abot,* 4.11.

727.24 Great is repentance: it brings healing to the world.

Hama b. Hanina. *T: Yoma,* 86a.

727.25 God's hand is spread out to shield penitents from Justice.

Ishmael b. Jose. *T: Pesahim,* 119a.

727.26 One hour of repentance and good deeds in this world is more beautiful than all the life in the world to come.

Jacob b. Kurshai. *Mishna: Abot,* 4.17.

727.27 Great is repentance: it prolongs life.

Jonathan b. Eleazar. *T: Yoma,* 86b.

727.28 Prayer does half, repentance does all.

Joshua b. Levi. *Lev. R.,* 10.5.

727.29 The test of repentance is refraining from sin on two occasions when the same temptation returned.

Judah (b. Ezekiel). *T: Yoma,* 86b.

727.30 If Jews would repent thoroughly even one day, they would be redeemed at once.

Levi. *Cant. R.,* 5.2.2.

727.31 As long as the candle burns, I can still do some mending.

Lipkin. q *HaMelitz,* 1897, #88. S. Rosenfeld, *Israel Salanter,* 38.

727.32 Repentance means that the sinner forsake his sins, cast them out of his mind, and resolve in his heart to sin no more.

Maimonides, *Yad: Teshuba,* 1180, 2.2.

727.33 Awake, sleepers, from your sleep, and ye who are sunk in slumber rouse yourselves and examine your actions. Repent and remember your Creator, ye who forget the truth because of transient vanities, who go astray all year after idle and useless things which cannot deliver. Look to your souls, amend your ways and deeds, and let everyone of you forsake his impure thoughts.

Ibid., 3.4.

727.34 For the sake of one true penitent, the whole world is pardoned.

Meir. *T: Yoma,* 86b.

727.35 My hands are stretched out toward the penitent. I reject no creature that gives me his heart. Whoever comes toward Me, I go toward him, and heal him.

Midrash Tehillim, 120.7.

727.36 If one says, I'll sin again and repent again, he'll have no opportunity to repent.

Mishna: Yoma, 8.9.

727.37 Whenever night falls, whenever day breaks, search well into your dealings, so will your whole life be one Day of Atonement.

Moses of Evreux, 1240.

727.38 Repentance should be attained through joy.

Nahman Bratzlav. q BHH, 487.

727.39 Refer not to a penitent's evil deed, not even in jest.

Orhot Tzaddiḳim, 15C, ch 21.

727.40 Repentance: a fierce battle with the heart.

Ibid., ch 26.

727.41 Happy he who repents while still a man [in full vigor].

Rab, on *Ps.* 112.1. *T: Aboda Zara,* 19a.

727.42 Be not a fool who brings a sin offering without repenting.

Raba. *T: Berakot,* 23a.

727.43 All sins are atoned for by repentance, except such as entail irretrievable harm, e.g., corrupting, misleading and misinforming a multitude, ruining the reputation of an innocent person, and keeping misappropriated articles.

Saadia, *Emunot VeDeot,* 933, 5.6.

727.44 The gates of penitence are always open.

Samuel b. Nahman. *Lam. R.,* 3.44.9.

727.45 Great is repentance: it turns sins into incentives for right conduct.

Simeon b. Lakish. *T: Yoma,* 86b.

727.46 Repentance is pain, accompanied by the idea of oneself as cause.

Spinoza, *Ethics,* iii. Pr 51, Note.

727.47 Repentance, like the sea, is always open to the venturers.

Yalkut, Psalms, #789.

727.48 Happy are the penitent who, in one day, one hour, aye, one second, can draw as near to the Holy One as the righteous do in many years.

Zohar, Gen., 129a. See Simeon b. Yohai. *Tosefta: Kiddushin,* 1.14.

728. REPROOF

728.1 Rebuke your neighbor, and bear no sin because of him.

Bible: Lev., 19.17.

728.2 Reproofs of instruction are the way of life.

Bible: Prov., 6.23.

728.3 Reprove not a scorner, lest he hate you; reprove a wise man, and he will love you.

Ibid., 9.8.

728.4 A rebuke enters deeper into a man of understanding than a hundred stripes into a fool.

Ibid., 17.10.

728.5 Better open rebuke than hidden love.

Ibid., 27.5.

728.6 It is better to hear the rebuke of the wise than the song of fools.

Bible: Eccles., 7.5.

728.7 First investigate, then rebuke.

Apocrypha: Ben Sira, 11.7.

728.8 Censuring past omissions may but help one to evade a present task.

Baeck, Founder's Day Address, HUC, 1953.

728.9 I wonder whether there is anyone in our generation competent to rebuke another.

Eleazar b. Azariah. *T: Arakin,* 16b.

728.10 As one is commanded to speak when he is likely to be obeyed, so is one commanded not to speak when not likely to be obeyed.

Eleazar b. Simeon. *T: Yebamot,* 65b.

728.11 It is a duty to reprove, regardless whether the reproof is likely to be heeded or to be ignored.

Abba. *Ibid.*

728.12 Let a Jew sustain material loss, let him find himself the victim of political persecution, and all his fellow-Jews will rush to his rescue. . . . Yes, . . . we do love one another. But that love is purely physical. Of spiritual love, that is, love for the soul of our neighbor, there is but little in our midst. One may fritter away one's life in unseemly practices, and none will venture to remonstrate with him.

Eybeshitz, *Yaarot Debash,* 1779, i. 67a. q BSJ, 330f.

728.13 Jerusalem was destroyed because its people did not reprove one another.

Hanina b. Hama. *T: Sabbath,* 119b.

728.14 Reproof is the flash of friendship between faithful brothers.

q M. Ibn Ezra, *Shirat Yisrael,* (12C) 1924, p. 95.

728.15 If only the sinless would reprove, none would ever reprove.

q *Ibid.,* 157.

728.16 My friend is he who will tell me my fault in private.

Ibn Gabirol, *Mibhar HaPeninim,* c.1050, #277.

728.17 If you see a scholar commit an offense at night, do not cavil the next day; he may have already done penance.

Ishmael School. *T: Berakot,* 19a.

728.18 By what merit did Jeroboam become king? By reproving Solomon. And why was he punished? Because he reproved him in public.

Johanan b. Nappaha. *T: Sanhedrin,* 101b.

728.19 It is meritorious to rebuke a colleague for the sake of heaven.

Jonathan b. Eleazar. *T: Tamid,* 28a.

728.20 Love your admonisher, hate your flatterer.

Meir. *Abot de R. Nathan,* ch 29.

728.21 Reproach not a neighbor for a fault which is also yours.

Nathan. *Mekilta,* to *Exod.* 22.20. *Talmud: Baba Metzia,* 59b.

728.22 If he doesn't heed your warning, throw a wall at him.

Proverb. q Raba. *T: Baba Kamma,* 92b.

728.23 He who can reprove the masses and does it, pleases God.

Seder Eliyahu Rabbah, ch 3, ed Friedmann, p. 17.

728.24 Peace without reproof is no peace.

Simeon b. Lakish. *Gen. R.,* 54.3.

728.25 Those who carp at mankind, and are more skilled in railing at vice than in instilling virtue, and who break rather than strengthen man's dispositions, are hurtful both to themselves and to others.

Spinoza, *Ethics,* 1677, iv. Appendix 13.

728.26 Leave Israel alone: let them sin unwittingly rather than willfully.

Talmud: Sabbath, 148b.

729. REPUTATION

729.1 Ye shall be clear before God and before Israel.

Bible: Num., 32.22.

729.2 I'd rather be called a fool all my life than commit wrong in the sight of God for one moment.

Akabia b. Mahalalel. *Mishna: Eduyot,* 5.6.

729.3 The dough must be bad, indeed, if the baker himself declared it so.

Proverb. q Hiyya Rabba. *Gen. R.,* 34.10.

729.4 Thus did my father counsel me in bygone days: "Samuel, destroy not what I have built up!"

Samuel b. Adiya. q GHJ, iii. 70.

729.5 If you can be good, do not call yourself bad.

Sheshet. *T: Berakot,* 30a.

730. RESEARCH

730.1 Investigate everything in the universe, from the smallest creature to the largest.

Bahya, *Hobot HaLebabot,* 1040, 8.3.23. See 1.3.

730.2 Inquiry is a duty, and error in research is not a sin.

Benjamin b. Moses, *Sefer Dinim,* c.800. q GHJ, iii. 152.

730.3 Happy are we whose goodly portion is the Word of God and the Law of Truth, that need not fear research and testing from any side and in any manner.

Krochmal. q SHR, 106.

730.4 The essential thing is not to find truth but to investigate and search after it.

Nordau, *Paradoxes,* 1885, Preface.

730.5 It is inconceivable that honest investigation should have been forbidden us.

Saadia, *Emunot VeDeot,* 933, Introduction.

730.6 The beginning of research is curiosity, its essence is discernment, and its goal truth and justice.

Satanov, *Mishlé Asaf,* 1789, 1792, 7.5f. q SRH, 43.

731. RESIDENCE

731.1 I dwell among my own people.

Bible: II Kings, 4.13.

731.2 Live not in a city whose heads are scholars.

Akiba. *T: Pesahim,* 112a.

731.3 Dwell not too long by the river. Move to the hill on account of rain.

Hai Gaon, *Musar Haskel,* c.1000. HPB, 75.

731.4 Don't build on the summit your
cottage,
But down in the valley.

Heine, *Hebrew Melodies, Motto,* 1851.

731.5 If you gave me all the silver and gold and jewels in the world, I would not dwell anywhere but in the home of Torah.

Jose b. Kisma. *Mishna: Abot,* 6.9.

731.6 Try to live in a new town: it has less corruption.

Rab. *T: Sabbath,* 10b.

731.7 Reside not in a town where no horses neigh or no dogs bark. Reside not in a town where the head is a physician.

Rab. *T: Pesahim,* 113a. See *T: Sanhedrin,* 17b.

732. RESIGNATION

732.1 Resign yourself to the Lord, and wait patiently for Him.

Bible: Ps., 37.7.

732.2 Let come on me what will.

Bible: Job, 13.13.

732.3 Gnaw the bone that falls to your lot, be it good or bad.

Alphabet of Ben Sira, 3.

732.4 Lord, whate'er Thy will imposes
on me
I'll bear like a crown, not like a
yoke.
Beer-Hofmann, *Jacob's Dream*, 1919.

732.5 Accept your affliction with love
and joy.
Eleazar b. Judah, *Rokeah*, 13C.

732.6 If you are abused by a wicked
man, accept the ordeal with love, and say,
"He is God's agent on account of my sin."
J. M. Epstein, *Kitzur Shné Luhot Ha-
Berit*, (1683), 8a.

732.7 Delight in what comes from God,
and say, "This, too, is for the best."
Hai Gaon, *Musar Haskel*, c.1000.

732.8 Rejoice in what you have; sigh not
for what you lost.
Hasdai, *Ben HaMelek VeHaNazir*,
c.1230, ch 21.

732.9 Pain must be borne willingly and
lovingly.
Huna. *T: Berakot*, 5a.

732.10 Who refuses to accept God's decrees is incurably stupid.
Ibn Gabirol, *Mibhar HaPeninim*, c.1050,
#125.

732.11 Resignation makes free.
Ibid., #173.

732.12 Who accepts affliction cheerfully
brings salvation to the world.
Joshua b. Levi. *T: Taanit*, 8a.

732.13 Well, we bear what we cannot
change.
Mosenthal, *Das goldene Kreuz*, 1875.

732.14 Resignation is the surrender of
the human freedom to choose, to judge, to
decide, in the face of a paramount loyalty.
It is the greatest manifestation of human
freedom, the relinquishment of all the
petty forms of freedom for the exercise of
the greatest of its forms, the assertion of
one's inner self as the master of all external conduct.
Wolfson, "Escaping Judaism." *Menorah
Journal*, 1921, vii. 71.

733. RESISTANCE

733.1 Stand not against the stream.
Apocrypha: Ben Sira, 4.26.

733.2 Evil cannot be persuaded to good.
It must be extirpated.
Brod, *The Master*, 1951, ch 7, p. 423.

733.3 If you had lived in the dread days
of martyrdom, . . . you would surely, as

did so many, have given your life in defense of your faith. Well, then, fight now
the fight laid on you in better days, the
fight with evil desire; fight and conquer!
Eleazar b. Judah, *Rokeah*, 13C. ZEH, 17.

733.4 If I were a Jew and were born in
Germany and earned my livelihood there,
I would claim Germany as my home even
as the tallest Gentile German may, and
challenge him to shoot me or cast me in the
dungeon; I would refuse to be expelled or
to submit to discriminating treatment.
*Gandhi. *Christian World*, Jan. 18, 1939.

733.5 Resist not evil.
New Testament: Matt., 5.39.

733.6 Whoever resists the power, resists
the ordinance of God.
New Testament: Romans, 13.2.

733.7 Blessed are they to whom it is
given to resist with superior strength the
weight that would pull them down, taught
by the guiding lines of right instruction to
leap upward from earth and earth-bound
things.
Philo, *Special Laws*, iv. 21.

733.8 Beneath the yoke of barbarism one
must not keep silence; one must fight.
Whoever is silent at such a time is a traitor
to humanity.
S. Zweig, on the day the Nazis burned
his books. *World of Yesterday*, 1943.

734. RESOLUTION

734.1 I will go in unto the king, which
is not according to the law; and if I perish,
I perish.
Bible: Esther, 4.16.

734.2 A shipload of Jewish refugees
from Spain, swept by the plague, was compelled to land on a desolate coast. Among
them was a man, his wife and two children. As they struggled on through the
waste, the wife died. The man carried his
two sick children, but at last he fainted
from fatigue and hunger. When he awoke,
he found his two children dead by his side.
He rose to his feet and said in his grief:
"Lord of the universe, much hast Thou
done to make me forsake my faith. But
know for a certainty that nothing which
Thou hast brought, or may still bring, over
me will make me change. In spite of all, a
Jew I am and a Jew I shall remain!"
Ibn Verga, *Shebet Yehuda*, (1550) 1855,
p. 90. See SSA, 201; Silver, *World Crisis*,
51f.

735. RESPECT

735.1 In the academy, follow wisdom; at a banquet, age.

Ammi b. Nathan. *T: Baba Bathra,* 120a.

735.2 Respect is accorded only to a personality which respects itself, to character, and not to a servile creature which surrenders its all and permits the effacement of its own individuality.

Dubnow, *Pisma,* 1907. q *JP,* 1948, ii. 315.

735.3 Respect one another.

Eleazar b. Azariah. *T: Pirke Ben Azzai,* 1.4.

735.4 Despise no man: many pearls are found in a poor man's tunic.

Eliezer b. Isaac, *Orhot Hayyim,* c.1050. AHE, 40.

735.5 Respect is not the root from which love grows, but the elm on which it creeps up and brings forth its precious blossoms.

M. Jacobs. q TL, p. 80.

735.6 Suspect all and respect all.

Joshua b. Levi. *T: Pirke Ben Azzai,* 3.3.

735.7 I must respect the opinions of others even if I disagree with them.

Lehman. E. R. Murrow, *This I Believe,* 1952, p. 99.

735.8 Respect your fellow as you respect your teacher.

Mekilta, to *Exod.* 17.9.

735.9 How foolish are those who rise before a Scroll and not before a great man!

Raba. *T: Makkot,* 22b.

736. RESPECTABILITY

736.1 To secure respect for law, we must make the law respectable.

Brandeis, speech, Oct. 15, 1912.

736.2 Their only ability was respectability.

Zangwill.

737. RESPONSE

737.1 The song that from the heart would spring
Is dead for want of echoing.

Peretz, *In Alien Lands,* tr Leah W. Leonard.

738. RESPONSIBILITY

738.1 Your destroyers and wasters shall go forth from you.

Bible: Isa., 49.17. q in the sense: your destroyers are your own people.

738.2 A Jew used often to say to me: "You don't have to answer for Lenin being a Russian, while I shall have to answer for Trotsky being a Jew. Isn't that a flagrant injustice?"

*Berdyaev, *Christianity and Anti-Semitism,* tr 1952, p. 32.

738.3 The great developer is responsibility.

Brandeis, letter to R. W. Bruere, Feb. 25, 1922.

738.4 It was as Beaconsfield that he acted in [the Congress of] Berlin, but the Jews of Russia paid for Disraeli.

S. Levin, *Childhood in Exile,* 1929, p. 253.

738.5 If one man sins, the whole generation suffers. . . . If there is one righteous man, the whole world stands for his sake.

Marmorstein, *Old Rabbinic Doctrine of God,* 1927, p. 48.

738.6 The Trotskys make the revolutions and the Braunsteins pay the bills.

Mazé, comment in Moscow, 1921. q *Reflex,* Nov. 1927, p. 8.

738.7 I am responsible for any damage caused by my charge.

Mishna: Baba Kamma, 1.2.

738.8 Man is always responsible, whether his act is intentional or inadvertent, whether he is awake or asleep.

Ibid., 2.6.

738.9 An encounter with a deaf-mute, an idiot, or a minor is bad, for you are liable and they are not.

Ibid., 8.4

738.10 One is not responsible when in distress (under torture).

Raba. *T: Baba Bathra,* 16b.

738.11 There are all sorts of flight from responsibility: There is flight into death, flight into sickness, and finally flight into folly. The last is the least dangerous and most convenient, and even to the wise, the way to it is usually not as far as they like to imagine.

Schnitzler, *Buch der Sprüche & Bedenken,* 1927, p. 78.

738.12 All Jews are sureties for one another.

Sifra, 112a, to *Lev.* 26.37. *Talmud: Shebuot,* 39a.

738.13 A man on a boat began to bore a hole under his own seat. His fellow passengers protested: "Unfortunately, when the water enters, the whole boat sinks."

Simeon b. Yohai. *Lev. R.,* 4.6.

411

738.14 All men are responsible for one another.

Talmud: Sanhedrin, 27b.

738.15 Wherever a Jew lives, Judaism is on trial. . . . Every Jew, Atlas-like, bears upon his shoulders the burden of the whole world's Jewry.

S. S. Wise, *Sermons and Addresses,* 1905, p. 124.

739. REST

739.1 The spirit of the Lord caused them to rest.

Bible: Isa., 63.14.

739.2 Find rest for your souls.

Bible: Jer., 6.16.

739.3 Repose is good when it is rest, when we have chosen it . . . it is not good when it is our sole occupation.

Boerne, *From My Diary,* #12, May 22, 1830.

739.4 Rest is a state of peace between man and nature. . . . Work is a symbol of conflict and discord; rest is an expression of dignity, peace and freedom.

Fromm, *Forgotten Language,* 1951, p. 244, 247.

739.5 Moses does not give the name of rest to mere inactivity.

Philo, *Cherubim,* 26.

740. RESURRECTION

740.1 The dead live not, the shades rise not.

Bible: Isa., 26.14.

740.2 Thy dead shall live, my dead bodies shall arise.

Ibid., 26.19.

740.3 I will open your graves, and cause you to come up.

Bible: Ezek., 37.12.

740.4 If a man die, may he live again?

Bible: Job, 14.14.

740.5 Many of them that sleep in the dust of the earth shall awake, some to everlasting life, and some to reproaches and everlasting abhorrence.

Bible: Dan., 12.2.

740.6 All who have fallen asleep in hope of Him shall rise again.

Apocrypha: II Baruch, 30.2.

740.7 They who died in grief shall arise in joy, . . . and they who are put to death for the Lord's sake shall awake to life.

Apocrypha: Patriarchs, Judah, 25.3f.

740.8 We reject as ideas not rooted in Judaism, the beliefs both in bodily resurrection and in Gehenna and Eden.

CCAR, *Pittsburgh Platform,* 1885.

740.9 Almighty God will Himself raise us up . . . with all that have slept from the beginning of the world, whether we die at sea, are scattered on earth, or torn to pieces by beasts or birds.

Didascalia, v. ch 6. q *JE,* iv. 592b.

740.10 First to be resurrected . . . will be those buried in Eretz Israel.

Gen. R., 74.1.

740.11 The righteous buried in other lands will roll through subterranean channels to the Land of Israel, where the Holy One will breathe into them a spirit of life, and they will arise.

Simon. *Ibid.,* 96.5. See *T: Ketubot,* 111a; *Zohar, Gen.* 69a.

740.12 The grave, like the womb, receives and gives forth.

Josiah. *T: Berakot,* 15b, on *Prov.* 30.16.

740.13 I believe with perfect faith that there will be a revival of the dead at the time when it shall please the Creator.

Maimonides, *Commentary to Mishna: Sanhedrin,* 1168, 10.1. *Thirteen Principles,* #13.

740.14 If a grain of wheat, buried naked, sprouts forth in many robes, how much more so the righteous!

Meir. *T: Sanhedrin,* 90b.

740.15 He who maintains that the resurrection is not a biblical doctrine has no share in the world to come.

Mishna: Sanhedrin, 10.1.

740.16 Our life consists of resurrections.

Pacifici, *Fragments on Unity of Israel,* 1912. LR, 112.

740.17 The kernel which is sown in earth must fall to pieces so that the ear of grain may sprout from it.

P. Shapiro. q BTH, i. 123.

740.18 A rabbi was asked: At the resurrection, will the dead need to be sprinkled with the water of purification? He replied: We shall go into this matter at the time of the resurrection, for inasmuch as Moses will be there, we shall know what to do.

Talmud: Nidda, 70b. See Saadia, *Emunot VeDeot,* 7.7.

741. RETRIBUTION

741.1 If ye walk in My statutes . . . I will give your rains in their season, . . . and ye shall . . . dwell in your land safely.

Bible: Lev., 26.3–5.

741.2 As I have done, so God has requited me.
Bible: Judg., 1.7.

741.3 Them that honor Me I will honor.
Bible: I Sam., 2.30.

741.4 They that forsake the Lord shall be consumed.
Bible: Isa., 1.28.

741.5 They shall eat the fruit of their doings.
Ibid., 3.10.

741.6 They sow the wind, and they shall reap the whirlwind.
Bible: Hos., 8.7. See 10.13.

741.7 As you have done shall be done to you.
Bible: Obad., 1.15.

741.8 Nations sink in the pit they made.
Bible: Ps., 9.16.

741.9 The wicked is snared in the work of his own hands.
Ibid., 9.17.

741.10 In keeping of them is great reward.
Ibid., 19.12.

741.11 Thou renderest to every man according to his work.
Ibid., 62.13.

741.12 Who digs a pit shall fall therein.
Bible: Prov., 26.27.

741.13 Your work shall be rewarded.
Bible: II Chron., 15.7.

741.14 He is paid wtih the clue his own hands had wound.
Abayé *T: Pesahim*, 28a.

741.15 God revealed the reward of only two precepts, the weightiest and the lightest—honoring parents and letting the mother bird go—and the reward for both is the same: length of days.
Abba b. Kahana. *Deut. R.*, 6.2. Ref. to *Exod.* 20.12, and *Deut.* 22.7.

741.16 For the elect a covenant, for sinners an inquisition.
Apocrypha: Enoch, 60.6.

741.17 ..He is unworthy of reward unless . . . he recognize that it is accorded as a mark of God's grace.
Bahya, *Hobot HaLebabot*, 1040, 4.4.

741.18 The recompense of virtue is virtue, and of sin, sin.
Ben Azzai. *Mishna: Abot*, 4.2.

741.19 The reward of the Law is only in the world to come.
Exod. R., 52.3. See Jacob. *T: Kiddushin*, 39b.

741.20 God is long-suffering, but He collects His due.
Hanina. *TJ: Taanit*, 2.1.

741.21 Because you drowned others, others drowned you; and those who drowned you will in turn be drowned.
Hillel, to a floating head. *Mishna: Abot*, 2.6.

741.22 Sin must prosper, or it's bored,
While virtue is its own reward.
Hoffenstein, "As the Crow Flies," viii. *Year In, You're Out*, 1930. *Complete Poetry*, 1954, p. 256.

741.23 God does not withhold reward even for a decorous speech.
Johanan b. Nappaha. *T: Nazir*, 23b.

741.24 Unhappy Israel! . . . You would not serve God in love, now you serve your enemy in hate. You would not serve God in plenty, now you serve the enemy in hunger. You would not serve God when you were well-clothed, now you serve your enemy naked!
Johanan b. Zakkai. *Mekilta*, to *Exod.* 19.1.

741.25 The reward of such as live exactly according to the laws is not silver or gold, not a garland of olive-branches or of smallage, nor any such public sign of commendation; but every good man is content with the witness that his own conscience bears him.
Josephus, *Against Apion*, ii. 31.

741.26 Villainy escapes not the wrath of God.
Josephus, *Wars*, 7.2.2.

741.27 I believe with perfect faith that the Creator . . . rewards those who keep His commandments and punishes those who transgress them.
Maimonides, *Commentary to Mishna: Sanhedrin*, 1168, 10.1. *Thirteen Principles*, #11.

741.28 The reward of the righteous in the world to come is spiritual bliss; the punishment of the wicked is exclusion from it: light everlasting for the one, death for the other.
Maimonides, *Yad: Teshuba*, 1180, 8.1.

741.29 If a man sought the best course in life, reward awaits him beyond the grave; there he finds the table set for a joyous feast that will last through eternity.

Meir. *Eccles. R.,* 5.14.

741.30 Where the sin was committed the judgment takes place.

Nahmanides, *Commentary.* q SSJ, i. 126.

741.31 There is not a precept in the Torah, however light, for which there is not reward in this world; but as to reward in the world to come, I know not.

Nathan. *T: Menahot,* 44a.

741.32 Then came a dog and bit the cat that ate the kid.

Passover Hagada, Had Gadya.

741.33 Each virtue is its own reward.

Philo, *Honor Due to Parents,* 10.

741.34 A novel punishment: that he should live continually dying, that he should endure an undying and never ending death.

Philo, *Rewards and Punishments,* 12.

741.35 Snarer, how you have been snared! Gate breaker, how your gates have been broken!

Proverb. q Eleazar b. Simeon. *Gen. R.,* 67.2.

741.36 With the ladle which the artisan hallowed out, his own tongue shall be burned.

Proverb. q Joseph. *T: Pesahim,* 28a.

741.37 None ever took a stone out of the Temple, but the dust did fly into his eyes.

Proverb. q D'Israeli, *Curiosities: Philosophy of Proverbs.*

741.38 God waits long, but pays with interest.

Proverb (Yiddish). *JE,* x. 228b.

741.39 God gives nothing for nothing.
Ibid.

741.40 The arrow maker is shot with the arrow he made.

Raba. *T: Pesahim,* 28a.

741.41 The same . . . fire will illumine the righteous and burn the sinners.

Saadia, *Emunot VeDeot,* 933, 9.5.

741.42 For the good they do, the righteous are rewarded in the world to come, and the wicked in this world.

Samuel HaKatan. *Midrash Tehillim,* 94.4, to *Ps.* 94.15.

741.43 Father in Heaven, the Torah I observed was yours, the loving-kindness I did was of yours, yet Thou hast rewarded me with this world, the messianic age, and the world to come!

Seder Eliyahu Rabbah, ch 18, ed Friedmann, 89.

741.44 The reward of the righteous is endless.

Sefer Hasidim, 13C, #633, p. 170.

741.45 The loaf and the rod came from heaven wrapped together, and God said: "If ye will and obey, ye shall eat; if ye refuse and rebel, ye shall be devoured" [*Isa.* 1.19f].

Simeon b. Yohai. *Lev. R.,* 35.6. *Sifré,* #40, to *Deut.* 11.12, ed Friedmann, 79a.

741.46 Refraining from sin is rewarded like observing the precepts.

Simeon. *Seder Eliyahu Rabbah,* ch 15, ed Friedmann, 69.

741.47 Wickedness flies, retribution crawls.

J. Steinberg, *Mishlé Yehoshua,* 1885, 5.22, p. 30.

741.48 When Akiba was being tortured to death, the angels cried out: "Is this the Torah, and this its reward?!" Then a heavenly voice proclaimed: "Happy Akiba, destined for life eternal!"

Talmud: Berakot, 61b.

741.49 Your Employer is trustworthy: He will pay your wage.

Tarfon. *Mishna: Abot,* 2.16.

741.50 The reward of the righteous is in the world to come.
Ibid.

742. REVELATION

742.1 The Lord spoke unto Moses face to face.
Bible: Exod., 33.11.

742.2 We have seen this day that God does speak with man.
Bible: Deut., 5.21.

742.3 The glory of the Lord shall be revealed, and all flesh shall see it together.
Bible: Isa., 40.5.

742.4 Verily Thou art a God that hidest Thyself.
Ibid., 45.15.

742.5 In the whirlwind and in the storm is His way, and the clouds are the dust of His feet.
Bible: Nahum, 1.3.

742.6 Reason must surrender some rights to the divine revelations.

Arama, *Akedat Yitzhak,* 15C, ch 25.

742.7 He conceals Himself in His manifestations, and reveals Himself in His concealments.

Baal Shem. q Setzer, *Reb Yisroel*, 69.

742.8 In each movement of man there is the Creator, . . . even in evil.

Ber. q *Tzavaat Ribash*, 1797.

742.9 God can be manifest in His absence as well as in His presence.

Gutkind, *Choose Life*, 1952, p. 75.

742.10   I see Thee in the starry field,
I see Thee in the harvest's yield,
In every breath, in every sound,
An echo of Thy name is found.
The blade of grass, the simple flower,
Bear witness to Thy matchless power.

A. Ibn Ezra, tr E. de L.

742.11   In the mirror of thought,
By the light of his mind,
The wise man perceives all about him
His Creator's glory.
In his own body—
In the four elements of its substance,
In the design of its structure,
In the concord and symmetry of its parts—
He beholds God.

M. Ibn Ezra, *Selected Poems*, 94.

742.12 Each word uttered by God split itself into the seventy languages of the world.

Johanan b. Nappaha. *Exod. R., 5.9. T: Sabbath*, 88b.

742.13 His revelation is continuous. New aspects of the Torah unfold constantly. The more we study it, the more it expands.

Judah Arieh, *Sefat Emet*, 1926, p. 278, on *Ps.* 146.19.

742.14   The Creator . . . is revealed to the heart, not to the eye. . . .
Thou wilt find thy God within thy bosom,
Walking gently in thine heart.

Judah Halevi, *Selected Poems*, 94.

742.15 The grandeur of natural order, man's pursuit of truth, his appreciation of beauty, his drive toward justice and holiness—it is all one. . . . One God, one Mind, one Will, one Beauty, one Love.

Lazaron, *Common Ground*, 1938, p. 298f.

742.16 Revelation is the silent, imperceptible manifestation of God in history. It is the still, small voice: it is the inevitableness, the regularity of nature.

Loewe, *Rabbinic Anthology*, 1938, p. lxxiii.

742.17 The great principle of Judaism is nothing but the belief in revelation and acceptance of the burden of the Mitzvot.

S. D. Luzzatto, *Mehkeré HaYahadut*, ii. 19. q WHJ iii. 395.

742.18 The Israelites have a divine code . . . but no dogmas, no saving truths, no general self-evident propositions. Those the Lord always reveals to us as to the rest of mankind, by *nature and by events,* but never in *words* or *written characters*.

M. Mendelssohn, *Jerusalem*, 1783, tr Samuels, ii. 89.

742.19 Our belief in a revealed religion is not founded on miracles but on a public legislation.

M. Mendelssohn, *Supplementary Remarks*, 1770. SMM, 93.

742.20 The "hidden God" [*Isa.* 45.15; Pascal, *Pensées*, iv. 242] of the physical universe is revealed in the moral life.

Roth, *Jewish Thought*, 1927. BSL, 435.

742.21 All that man sees—sky, earth, and its fullness—are God's outer garments, manifesting an inner spirit, the divine vital elan which permeates them.

Shneor Zalman, *Tanya*, 1796, ch 42.

743. REVOLUTION

743.1 The revolutionist has no personal right to anything. Everything he has or earns belongs to the Cause. Everything, even his affections.

Berkman, *Prison Memoirs of an Anarchist*, 1912, p. 73.

743.2 We are right in doubting whether that is a crime which, if consummated is requited with a crown of laurel, and if merely attempted is rewarded with a crown of thorns.

Boerne, *Kritiken, De la peine de mort, par Guizot*, 1822.

743.3 No revolution can ever succeed as a factor of liberation unless the Means used to further it be identical in spirit and tendency with the Purposes to be achieved. . . . The ultimate end of all revolutionary social change is to establish the sanctity of human life, the dignity of man, the right of every human being to liberty and well-being.

E. Goldman, *My Further Disillusionment*, 1924, p. 175.

743.4 Revolution is war, a zoological rather than a human method.

H. Greenberg, *To a Communist Friend*, 1936. GIE, 260.

743.5 Whether a revolution succeeds or miscarries, men of great hearts will always be its victims.

Heine, *Salon*, 1834.

743.6 To accept the workers' Revolution in the name of a high ideal means not only to reject it, but to slander it. All the social illusions which mankind has raved about in religion, poetry, morals or philosophy, served only the purpose of deceiving and blinding the oppressed. . . . The Revolution is strong to the extent to which it is realistic, rational, strategic and mathematical.

Trotsky, *Literature and Revolution*, 1925, p. 88.

743.7 Woe to the revolutionary who does not know that the fighting fronts of necessary revolt are constantly changing, and with them, the targets for his weapons.

Werfel, *Between Heaven and Earth*, 1944, p. 223.

743.8 Woe to the times when sheep kill lions!

Zabara, *Sefer Shaashuim*, 13C, ch 8, ed Davidson, 98.

744. RICHES

744.1 As a partridge that broods over young which she has not brought forth is he who gets riches and not by right.

Bible: Jer., 17.11.

744.2 Woe to him who increases what is not his!

Bible: Hab., 2.6.

744.3 He reaps riches, and knows not who shall gather them.

Bible: Ps., 39.7.

744.4 When he dies he shall carry nothing away; his wealth shall not descend after him.

Ibid., 49.18.

744.5 Who trusts in his riches shall fall.

Bible: Prov., 11.28.

744.6 A rich man has many friends.

Ibid., 14.20. See 19.4.

744.7 Weary not yourself to be rich.

Ibid. 23.4.

744.8 Riches certainly make themselves wings.

Ibid., 23.5. See 27.24.

744.9 He that makes haste to be rich shall not be unpunished.

Ibid., 28.20.

744.10 Give me neither poverty nor riches.

Ibid., 30.8.

744.11 Who loves silver shall not be satisfied with silver.

Bible: Eccles., 5.9.

744.12 All the prophets complained of the silver and gold which went forth with the children of Israel from Egypt.

Akiba. *Gen. R.*, 28.7.

744.13 Our rich cast off everything that reminds them of Judaism; they seek to dazzle by luxury.

Alami, *Iggeret Musar*, 1415. q *JE*, i. 317a.

744.14 Strive to acquire wealth honestly, that you may benefit in this world and in the world to come. . . . Wealth is a gift from God.

Anav, *Maalot HaMiddot*, 13C, ch 23. See *Ben Sira*, 40.13.

744.15 There is glass in the window and in the mirror, but in the mirror the glass is covered with a little silver; now, lo and behold, no sooner is a little silver added than you cease to see others and see only yourself.

Anski, *Dybbuk*, 1918.

744.16 Wealth has led astray the hearts of princes.

Apocrypha: Ben Sira, 8.2.

744.17 Wealth is affliction disguised as a good.

Bahya, *Hobot HaLebabot*, 1040, 6.4.

744.18 Too much riches is as bad for the soul as too much blood is for the body.

Bahya b. Asher, *Perush al HaTorah: Tzav*, 14C.

Norzi, *Orah Hayyim*, 1579, p. 16b.

744.19 Riches hardens the heart faster than boiling water an egg.

Boerne, *Fragmente und Aphorismen*, 1840, #12.

744.20 From poverty our own power can save us, from riches only divine grace.

Boerne, *Der Narr im weissen Schwan*, ch 2.

744.21 Wealth has great nobility.

Bonsenyor, *Dichos y Sentencias*, 14C, #471.

744.22 He is rich who can forget his lot.
Braude. q Glenn, *Israel Salanter*, 73.

744.23 We call our rich relatives the kin we love to touch.
Cantor.

744.24 No riches can equal the vast store accumulated by the mountain in our l'Argentière, yet it is but a soulless heap!
Caspi, *Yoré Deah*, 14C, ch 10. See AHE, 145.

744.25 Great wealth is a great blessing to a man who knows what to do with it.
Disraeli, *Edymion*, 1880.

744.26. The salvation of the Jews was never wrought by the rich.
Ginzberg, *Students, Scholars and Saints*, 1928, p. 13.

744.27 Excessive wealth is perhaps harder to endure than poverty.
Heine, *Lutetia*, May 5, 1843.

744.28 The more wealth the more worry.
Hillel. *Mishna: Abot*, 2.7.

744.29 Lodge in the lair of lions; roam the hills
With the leopard; couch thee with the meadow-snake;
But from the rich man's dwelling keep afar,
And of his hand, nor gift nor honor take.
M. Ibn Ezra, *Selected Poems*, p. 89.

744.30 Told that a certain man had acquired great wealth, a sage asked: "Has he also acquired the days in which to spend it?"
Ibn Gabirol, *Mibhar HaPeninim*, c. 1050, #537.

744.31 Many men hoard for the future husbands of their wives.
Ibid., #547.

744.32 Wealth—an illusion,
Power—a lie.
Over all dissolution
Creeps silent and sly.
Unto others remain
The goods thou didst gain
With infinite pain.
Ibn Gabirol, *Meditation*, tr E. Lazarus. AJ, 1883, p. 225f.

744.33 Wealth found, peace lost.
Jeiteles. *Bikkuré Halttim*, 5587.

744.34 Too often, art emerging from garrets, in the plenitude of strength and promise, has been undone in palaces.
O. H. Kahn, *Of Many Things*, 1926, p. 85.

744.35 The richer Jew was ne'er in my esteem the better Jew.
*Lessing, (Templar in) *Nathan der Weise*, 1779, 2.5.

744.36 Who is rich? He who enjoys his wealth.
Meir. *T: Sabbath*, 25b.

744.37 It is easier for a camel to go through the eye of a needle than for a rich man to enter into the kingdom of God.
New Testament: Matt., 19.24.

744.38 Why snatch at wealth, and hoard and stock it?
Your shroud, you know, will have no pocket!
Paoli, *Neueste Gedichte*, 1870.

744.39 If you rub elbows with a rich man, you get a hole in your sleeve.
Proverb (Yiddish). q Zhitlovsky. 1921, p. 234.

744.40 Do not be fooled into believing that because a man is rich he is necessarily smart. There is ample proof to the contrary.
J. Rosenwald.

744.41 None is poorer than the rich who knows not how to spend.
Schnitzler, *Buch der Sprüche & Bedenken*, 1927, p. 230.

744.42 Men are like weasels: weasels drag and lay up and know not for whom, and men save and hoard and know not for whom.
Talmud J: Sabbath, 14.1.

744.43 The safest wealth is lack of needs.
Werfel, *Between Heaven and Earth*, 1944, p. 217.

744.44 Wisdom and wealth usually don't go together in one person.
Zabara, *Sefer Shaashuim*, 13C, ch 7.

745. RIDDLE

745.1 If ye had not plowed with my heifer, ye had not found out my riddle.
Bible: Judg., 14.18.

745.2 An Athenian in Jerusalem gave a child a penny and asked him to bring something of which he could eat his fill and have plenty left over to take on his journey. The child brought him salt.
Lam. R., 1.7.

745.3 An Athenian in Jerusalem took a broken mortar to a tailor for repair. The tailor picked up a handful of sand and said: "Twist this into thread, and I'll sew the mortar."
Ibid., 1.8.

745.4 An Athenian in Jerusalem had a child bring him eggs and cheeese, and asked him to tell which cheese came from a white goat and which from a black goat. The child replied: "You are a grown man. You tell me which egg is from a white hen and which from a black hen!"
Ibid., 1.9.

746. RIGHTEOUS

746.1 Noah was . . . righteous and whole-hearted: Noah walked with God.
Bible: Gen., 6.9.

746.2 Glory to the righteous.
Bible: Isa., 24.16.

746.3 Open the gates, that the righteous . . . may enter.
Ibid., 26.2.

746.4 Who walks righteously . . . shall dwell on high.
Ibid., 33.15f.

746.5 They sold the righteous for silver, and the poor for a pair of shoes.
Bible: Amos, 2.6.

746.6 The righteous deals graciously, and gives.
Bible: Ps., 37.21. See *Ezek.*, 18.5–9.

745.7 I have not seen the righteous forsaken.
Ibid., 37.25.

746.8 The righteous shall flourish like the palm tree.
Ibid., 92.13.

746.9 The path of the righteous is as the light of dawn, that shines more and more to the perfect day.
Bible: Prov., 4.18.

746.10 Is it any advantage to the Almighty that you are righteous?
Bible: Job, 22.3.

746.11 There is the righteous who perishes in his righteousness, and there is the wicked who prolongs life in his evil-doing.
Bible: Eccles., 7.15.

746.12 God said: I rule man; who rules Me? The righteous: for I issue a decree, and he may annul it.
Abbahu. *T: Moed Katan*, 16b. Cf Assi. *Sabbath*, 63a.

746.13 The tzaddik orders and the Holy One does.
Proverb. q YSS, 175. See *T: Taanit*, 23a. *Zohar, Gen.*, 245b. Kahana, *Sefer Ha-Hasidut*, 258.

746.14 No flesh is righteous in the sight of the Lord.
Apocrypha: Enoch, 81.5.

746.15 The righteous must be a lover of men.
Apocrypha: Wisdom of Solomon, 12.19.

746.16 This world would have been created even for one righteous man.
Eleazar b. Pedat. *T: Yoma*, 38b.

746.17 The world abides even for the sake of one righteous man.
Johanan b. Nappaha. *Ibid.*

746.18 When the righteous depart, the blessing departs.
Eleazar b. Simeon. *Sifré*, #38, to *Deut.* 11.10.

746.19 Only he is righteous before God who is also good to man.
Iddi. *T: Kiddushin*, 40a.

746.20 Even in His wrath, the Holy One remembers the righteous.
Johanan b. Nappaha. *T: Berakot*, 54b.

746.21 One righteous man does not die till another, equally righteous, is born.
Johanan b. Nappaha. *T: Yoma*, 38b.

746.22 The Holy One saw that the righteous were but few, so He planted them throughout all generations.
Ibid.

746.23 The righteous are superior to angels.
Johanan b. Nappaha. *T: Sanhedrin*, 93a.

746.24 Disaster comes because of the wicked, but usually its first victims are the righteous.
Jonathan b. Eleazar. *T: Baba Kamma*, 60a.

746.25 There are always thirty righteous men among the nations, by whose virtue those nations abide.
Judah b. Ilai. *T: Hullin*, 92a. See Simeon b. Yohai. *Gen. R.*, 35.2.

746.26 The righteous is a town's luster, majesty and glory. When he departs, the luster and glory depart.
Judah b. Simeon, Samuel b. Isaac. *Gen. R.*, 68.6.

746.27 Let us pray that the mind be in the soul like a pillar in a house, and that

the righteous be likewise firmly established in the human race for the relief of all diseases.
Philo, *Migration of Abraham*, 22.

746.28 The world is sustained by Divine Grace, and the righteous by their own force.
Rab. *T: Berakot*, 17b.

746.29 Righteous men do not take what is not theirs.
Rab. *T: Sanhedrin*, 99b.

746.30 The righteous . . . are called God's brothers and friends.
Seder Eliyahu Rabbah, ch 18, ed Friedmann, 109. *Ps.* 122.8.

746.31 The righteous men of all nations are priests of the Holy One.
Seder Eliyahu Zuta, ch 20.

746.32 The righteous gives a little more than the scale indicates.
Sefer Hasidim, 13C, #1217, p. 303.

746.33 The righteous protect a city more than sand the sea.
Simeon b. Lakish. *T: Baba Bathra*, 7b.

746.34 Wherever the righteous go, the Shekina goes with them.
Simeon b. Yohai. *Gen. R.*, 86.6.

746.35 The world must have no less than thirty-six righteous men in each generation who are privileged to view the Shekina.
Abayé. *T: Sanhedrin*, 97b. Cf Berekia. *Gen. R.*, 49.3. See above, 746.25.

746.36 The righteous is an everlasting foundation [*Prov.* 10.25],— the *Tzaddik* supports the world.
Targum, to *Prov.*, 10.25.

746.37 All human beings, endowed with the spirit of holiness, are of the category of *Tzaddik*.
Zohar, Gen., 33a.

747. RIGHTEOUSNESS

747.1 So shall my righteousness witness against me hereafter.
Bible: Gen., 30.33.

747.2 The work of righteousness shall be peace; and the effect of righteousness quietness and confidence for ever.
Bible: Isa., 32.17.

747.3 Offer the sacrifices of righteousness.
Bible: Ps., 4.6. See *Deut.* 33.19.

747.4 In righteousness shall I behold Thy face!
Ibid., 17.15.

747.5 Righteousness and peace have kissed each other.
Ibid., 85.11.

747.6 Righteousness looks down from heaven.
Bible: Ps., 85.12.

747.7 Righteousness shall go before him.
Ibid., 85.14.

747.8 Righteousness and justice are the foundation of Thy throne.
Ibid., 98.15.

747.9 Open to me the gates of righteousness, I will enter them.
Ibid., 118.19.

747.10 Righteousness exalts a nation.
Bible: Prov., 14.34.

747.11 To do righteousness and justice is more acceptable to the Lord than sacrifice.
Ibid., 21.3.

747.12 They that turn many to righteousness are like the stars for ever.
Bible: Dan., 12.3.

747.13 Blessed the man who dies in righteousness and goodness.
Apocrypha: Enoch. 81.4.

747.14 Who sows righteeousness shall reap sevenfold.
Apocrypha: II Enoch, 42.11.

747.15 When righteousness is at stake, the strength of youth returns to my Reason.
Apocrypha: IV Macc., 5.31.

747.16 Righteousness casts out hatred.
Apocrypha: Patriarchs, Gad, 5.3.

747.17 Righteousness is immortal.
Apocrypha: Wisdom of Solomon, 1.15.

747.18 The intense and convinced energy with which the Hebrew . . . threw himself upon his ideal of righteousness . . . has belonged to Hebraism alone.
Arnold, Culture and Anarchy, 1869, Preface.

747.19 As long as the world lasts, all who want to make progress in righteousness will come to Israel for inspiration.
Arnold, Literature and Dogma, 1873, p. 56.

747.20 Thou hast made this world a battlefield for righteousness.
Didascalia, v. ch 6. See *JE*, iv. 593b.

747.21 The world rests on a single pillar, Righteousness.
Eleazar b. Shammua. *T: Hagiga*, 12b, on *Prov.* 10.25.

747.22 I declare righteousness . . . the true and pure Judaism.
S. Holdheim, Letter to Jews in Arad, 1848.

747.23 Righteousness is not an inheritance, but one's own.
Midrash Tehillim, 146.7. *Numbers Rabbah,* 8.2.

747.24 Blessed are they who hunger and thirst after righteousness.
New Testament: Matthew, 5.6.

748. RIGHTS

748.1 Woe to them that . . . take away the right of the poor.
Bible: Isa., 10.1f.

748.2 One may have a right to speak, but that does not mean that he is right when he speaks.
Aarons, *The Lawyer Out of Court,* Oct. 23, 1950.

748.3 The first right of our fellow creatures is to get the truth from us.
Benamozegh, *Storia degli Esseni,* 1865. q PUS, 133.

748.4 What you call human rights—to seek and consume food, to sleep, to reproduce—belong also to the brute in the field, until you kill it, and these you would grant also to Jews. But civic rights alone are human rights: for man becomes man only in civic society.
Boerne, *Der ewige Jude,* 1821.

748.5 The makers of our Constitution . . . sought to protect Americans. . . . They conferred, as against the government, the right to be left alone—the most comprehensive of rights and the right most valued by civilized men. To protect that right, every unjustifiable intrusion by the government upon the privacy of the individual, whatever the means employed, must be deemed a violation of the Fourth Amendment. And the use, as evidence in a criminal proceeding, of facts ascertained by such intrusion must be deemed a violation of the Fifth.
Brandeis, dissent, *Olmstead vs. U.S.,* 1928.

748.6 Not toleration, but the unrestricted exercise of all their rights shall we demand for our coreligionists.
*Bülow, to Alliance Israélite Universelle representatives who had asked, at Berlin Congress, 1878, toleration for Balkan Jews.

748.7 To enforce one's rights when they are violated is never a legal wrong, and may often be a moral duty.
Cardozo. *N.Y. Reports,* vol. 211, p. 468.

748.8 Only by declaring equal rights for all will you make good citizens.
Crémieux. q Peters, *Jew as a Patriot,* 95.

748.9 We demand our rights. We do not beg for a favor.
Einhorn, letter to L. Löw, Dec. 27, 1844.

748.10 Can it be denied that the mere doctrine of the rights of man has played into the hands of the selfish? . . . The bald theory of rights has prospered the capitalist and none other.   ..
E. G. Hirsch. *Reform Advocate,* 1897, xiii. 188.

748.11 The idea of legally establishing inalienable, inherent and sacred rights of the individual is not of political but religious origin.
G. Jellinek, *Declaration of Rights of Man,* 1895, ch 7, tr Farrand, 1901, p. 77.

748.12 Every State is known by the rights it maintains.
Laski, *A Grammar of Politics,* 1925, p. 89.

748.13 Neither Pagan nor Mahometan nor Jew ought to be excluded from the civil rights of the Commonwealth because of his religion. . . . If we allow the Jews to have . . . dwellings amongst us, why should we not allow them to have synagogs?
*Locke, *Letter Concerning Toleration,* 1689.

748.14 On every principle of moral obligation I hold that the Jew has a right to political power.
*Macaulay, speech, House of Commons, April 5, 1830.

748.15 I seat myself [in Austrian Parliament] on the left, because we Jews have no right.
Meisels, to representative of autocracy. See M. Jastrow. *Activities of the Rabbi,* 1892, p. 72.

748.16 From equal rights to brotherhood is still quite far.
Mendelé, *A Sgule tzu di Idishe Tzores,* 1899.

748.17 It would be painful to me to beg for that permission to exist which is the natural right of every human being who lives as a peaceful citizen. If, however, the State has weighty reasons for tolerating my nation only to a certain number, what privilege ought I to claim over my fellow countrymen that I should ask for an exception in my favor?

M. Mendelssohn, to Marquis d'Argens, who asked Mendelssohn to petition for the right of residence in Berlin.

748.18 To be despoiled as a Jew, or to need protection as a Jew, is equally disgraceful.

Pinsker, *Auto-Emancipation,* 1882.

748.19 No plea of sovereignty shall ever again . . . permit any nation to deprive those within its borders of these fundamental rights on the claim that these are matters of internal concern.

Proskauer, *Declaration of Human Rights,* 1945. *Segment,* 217.

748.20 The greatest right in the world is the right to be wrong.

H. Weinberger. N.Y. *Evening Post,* April 10, 1917.

748.21 In the whole of modern Jewish history before the Zionist movement, there is only one statesmanlike episode—the refusal of civil rights by the Jewish community of Amsterdam.

Zangwill. *JQRo,* xvii. 411.

749. RISE

749.1 In descent, there is ascent.

Anski, *Dybbuk,* 1918.

749.2 Descent is only a means of ascent.

Judah Arieh, *Sefat Emet,* 1926, p. 66.

749.3 Rise is not as a sluggard, but with eagerness to serve your Maker.

Asher b. Yehiel, *Hanhaga,* c. 1320. AHE, 120.

749.4 Let man strengthen himself like a lion and rise in the early morning to render service to his Creator, as David said, "I will awake the dawn" [*Ps.* 57.9].

Caro, *Shulhan Aruk: Orah Hayyim,* 1564, 1.1.

749.5 If man does not rise, he falls.

J. Y. Hurwitz. q *JP,* 1948, ii. 116.

750. RIVER

750.1 Are not Amanah and Pharpar, the rivers of Damascus, better than all the waters of Israel?

Bible: II Kings, 5.12.

750.2 The river appears less grandiose when it has no stones over which to wend its way.

Herzl, *Das Palais Bourbon,* 1895.

750.3 Each river has its own course.

Joseph. *T: Hullin,* 18b.

751. ROME

751.1 I said to deceitful Uz: Shall you forever walk in your wantonness? Gehenna is prepared for you as your appointed lot!

Abitur, hymn based on *Ps.* 120, 10C.

751.2 Esau [used symbolically for Rome] said to Jacob: . . . When wolves make peace with lambs, . . . then shall there be peace in my heart towards you.

Apocrypha: Jubilees, 37.20f.

751.3 Woe to you, unclean city of Latin land, frenzied and poison-loving, in widowhood shall you sit beside your banks, and Tiber shall mourn for you.

Apocrypha: Sibyl, 5.168–170.

751.4 The Holy Roman Empire—neither holy, nor Roman, nor an empire.

Boerne.

751.5 Titus destroyed the Temple. The religion of Judea has in turn subverted the fanes which were raised to his father and to himself in their imperial capital; and the God of Abraham, of Isaac and of Jacob is now worshipped before every altar in Rome.

Disraeli, *Tancred,* 1847.

751.6 Rome would always rule, and when her legions fell, she sent dogmas into the provinces. Like a giant spider, she sat in the center of the Latin world, and spun over it her endless web.

Heine, *North Sea: Norderney,* 1826.

751.7 Wicked Rome looks with greedy eyes [*Dan.* 7.8] at other people's property: This one is rich, let us make him a magistrate; that one is rich, let us make him a senator.

Johanan b. Nappaha. *Gen. R.,* 76.6. See *Pesahim* 118b.

751.8 Great are their possessions, the people that won them are greater still!

Josephus, *Wars,* 3.5.7.

751.9 God was on the Roman side.

Ibid., 5.9.3.

751.10 On the day Solomon married Pharaoh-Necho's daughter, archangel Michael descended from heaven and stuck a great pole in the sea, which gathered mud about it, so that the place became like a thicket of reeds and formed the site of Rome. On the day Jeroboam made the golden calf, two huts were built in Rome, and Abba Kolon taught the people there to make their buildings firm. On the day Elijah departed, a king was established in Rome.

Levi. *Cant. R.*, 1.6.4.
Samuel. *T: Sabbath*, 56b.

751.11 Like arrows that strike suddenly are the imperial edicts, unnoticed till one finds oneself on the way to execution.
Midrash Tehillim, 120.4. See 104.21.

751.12 Merciful God, either under Thy protection, or under Rome's!
Rabba b. Hana. *T: Gittin*, 17a.

751.13 When a swine lies down, it spreads out its paws, as if to say, "I am clean!" So wicked Rome robs and oppresses, yet pretends to be executing justice.
Simeon. *Gen. R.*, 65.1.

751.14 Roman civilization was all selfish: they built marketplaces to harbor harlotry, baths for their own refreshment, bridges to exact tolls.
Simeon b. Yohai. *T: Sabbath*, 33b.

752. ROOT

752.1 From the false what can be true?
Apocrypha: Ben Sira, 34.4. See 40.15.

752.2 The same root bears the same figs.
Brod, *The Master*, 1951, ch 4, p. 201.

752.3 If you take hold of the root, love also the fruit.
Hasdai, *Sefer HaTapuah*, c. 1230.

752.4 Fruits take after their roots.
A. Ibn Ezra, *Commentary*, to *Ruth* 2, end.

752.5 The fruit and the root resemble each other.
Isaac Halevi, *Paaneah Raza*, (13C), 1607, 12a.

752.6 Plants bear witness to the reality of roots.
Maimonides, *Iggeret Teman*, 1172.

752.7 The branch does not belie the root.
Trabotti, *Farewell Address*, 1653. AHE, 277.

752.8 To be rooted is perhaps the most important and least recognized need of the human soul.
S. Weil, *The Need for Roots*, 1952.

752.9 One has to have an anchorage from which one can set out and to which one can always return.
S. Zweig, *World of Yesterday*, 1943, p. 160.

753. ROSE

753.1 Let us crown ourselves with rosebuds before they wither.
Apocrypha: Wisdom of Solomon, 2.8.

753.2 All the world glows with roses, roses, roses.
Chernihovsky. q SHR, 318.

753.3 The finest rose is the Persian, which is said never to open.
Dunash Ibn Tamim. q Ibn Baitar. *JE* v. 13b.

753.4 Paper roses perish in the rain, while a live rose blossoms in the rain.
Hazaz, *End of Days*. q *JF*, Dec. 1950, p. 26.

753.5 Who reaches with a clumsy hand for a rose must not complain if the thorns scratch.
Heine, *Rabbi of Bacharach*, (1840), 1947, ch 3, p. 60.

753.6 A rose, bent by the wind and pricked by thorns, yet has its heart turned upwards. So Israel, though taxed and tortured, has its heart fixed upon the Father in heaven.
Huna. *Cant. R.*, 2.2.5.

753.7 A rose is a rose is a rose.
G. Stein, *Geography & Plays: Sacred Emily*, 1922.

754. RUINS

754.1 Men moralize among ruins.
Disraeli, *Tancred*, 1847, 5.5.

754.2 We do not understand ruins, until we ourselves have become ruins.
Heine, *Thoughts and Fancies*, 1869. EPP, 653.

754.3 Ruins are our monuments. Ruins —except for the immortal spirit that broods here despite a hundred conquests.
Lewisohn, *Israel*, 1925, p. 132.

755. RULE

755.1 No rule without an exception.
Johanan b. Nappaha. *T: Erubin*, 27a.

755.2 An exception throws light on the rule.
Num. R., 3.7.

756. RULER

756.1 Who made you a ruler and a judge over us?
Bible: Exod., 2.14.

756.2 Provide out of all the people able men, such as fear God, men of truth, who

hate unjust gain, and place such . . . to be rulers.
Ibid., 18.21.

756.3 I will not rule over you, neither shall my son rule over you; the Lord shall rule over you!
Bible: Judg., 8.23 (Gideon).

756.4 A ruler over men shall be the righteous.
Bible: II Sam., 23.3.

756.5 To rule is an art, not a science.
Boerne, *Fragmente und Aphorismen*, 1840, #7.

756.6 A smile for a friend and a sneer for the world, is the way to govern mankind.
Disraeli, *Vivian Grey*, 1827.

756.7 To rule men we must be men.
Ibid.

756.8 Who is fit to rule? A sage invested with power, or a king who seeks wisdom.
Ibn Gabirol, *Mibhar HaPeninim*, c. 1050, #4.

756.9 All who know well how to obey will know also how to rule.
Josephus, *Antiquities*, 4.8.2.

756.10 In our holy language, the words for ruler (*Moshel*) and for peace (*sholem*) consist of the same letters, suggesting that a ruler's duty is to maintain peace.
Kook, to Storrs. q Tzoref, *Hayye Ha-Rav Kook*, 1947, p. 192.

756.11 One reign may not overlap another even by a hair's breadth.
Rab. *T: Sabbath*, 30a.

756.12 Seek no intimacy with the ruling power.
Shemaiah. *Mishna: Abot*, 1.10.

756.13 "Nor curse the ruler" [*Exod.* 22.27], as long as he acts in the spirit, and obeys the laws, "of thy people."
Talmud: Baba Kamma, 94b.

757. RUN

757.1 Come what may, I will run.
Bible: II Sam., 18.23.

757.2 To the synagog, it is meritorious to run.
Abayé. *T: Berakot*, 6b.

757.3 Run less, and you'll have less to return.
Hiyya Rabba. *Eccles. R.*, 11.9.

757.4 The merit of attending a lecture is in the running to it.
Zera. *T: Berakot*, 6b. See Joshua b. Levi.
Ibid.

758. RUSSIA

758.1 All my soul belongs to my native land. . . . There, in the North, my heart beats more sturdily, I breathe more deeply, and am more sensitive to all that occurs.
Antokolski, letter to Stasov, Dec. 29, 1882.

758.2 Here all are convinced that I am a Russian, and in Russia all are convinced that I am an alien. . . . O Russia, how cruelly you requite my loyalty!
Ibid., letter received Jan. 8, 1883.

758.3 Let our last farewell be lit by the hope of a better future for our poor, poor motherland which lies so close to our heart.
Cohan-Bernstein, letter from his death chamber in Yakutsk, Aug. 6, 1889. q Olgin, *Soul of the Russian Revolution*, 1917, p. 338.

758.4 Scientists tell us that coal is nothing but concentrated sunlight. . . . The story of the Russian Jew is the story of coal. Under a surface marred by oppression and persecution he has accumulated immense stores of energy, in which we may find an unlimited supply of light and heat for our minds and hearts. All we need is to discover the process, long known in the case of coal, of transforming latent strength into living power.
I. Friedlander, *Jews of Russia and Poland*, 1915, p. 209.

758.5 Come, all who do not want to be lackeys of the lackeys, . . . come, and help the Jews.
*Gorky. q Singer, *Russia at the Bar*, 1904, p. 214.

758.6 Comrades, if before the Revolution the Russian state was an immense prison, . . . the most horrible cell it contained, the torture-chamber, was reserved for us, the Jewish people. . . . Nevertheless, we have always loved . . . our great fatherland. Why? Because of the restless soul of the Russian people, . . . because of its eternal hungering after truth, because of the imperishable spirit of love in its masses.
Grusenberg, to Council of Workers and Soldiers Delegates, 1917. q FJA, 262f.

758.7 It is difficult to be a Jew, . . . but to be simultaneously a Russian proletarian and a Jew—that means suffering beyond endurance. . . . If such an oppressed class as the Jewish proletarians in Russia is able to rise and to overcome stupendous obstacles with a superhuman energy, then we may boldly . . . look at the future.

*Kautsky, *Justice*, Feb. 22, 1902. q *HJ*, Apr. 1953, p. 39.

758.8 The final collapse of the Russian Czarist government began with the pogrom of Kishinef.

S. Levin, *The Arena*, 1932, p. 252.

758.9 The pogroms are oil for the wheels of revolution.

Medem. See 768.8.

758.10 The only habeas corpus of the Russian citizen was the institution of bribery. . . . It gave relief. It slackened the grip of petty and stupid regulations. It was perhaps the most human institution among the barbed-wire entanglements of the Russian order.

Olgin, *Soul of the Russian Revolution*, 1917, p. 77. See Pares, *Russia*, (1943) 1953, p. 31.

758.11 A Russian to hate a Jew! Out of the wall of his vast cathedrals he carves the figures of his twelve holy apostles—and every one a Jew. He enters and prostrates himself before the picture of a Hebrew child in the arms of a Hebrew mother. He mutters a creed that declares a Jew to be the Son of God, the Savior of the world—then he goes out and kills the first Jew he meets because he is a Jew. It is irony to move the laughter of devils and the tears of the just.

*Stafford, speech, Jan. 21, 1906.

758.12 In Vilna there was a young Jewish sculptor of great promise who was expected to become one of the historic exponents of the Jewish culture. The young man's promise was fulfilled, but Jewry's hope was disappointed; for the *chef d' oeuvre* in which this Jewish artist eventually gave expression to his genius was a statue of the Russian Orthodox Christian Czar Ivan the Terrible! Under the duress of the "Pale," Jewish genius had been perverted to the glorification of Jewry's oppressors.

Weizmann, as told by Toynbee, *Study of History*, 1934, ii. 242f.

759. SABBATH

759.A. Institution

759.A.1 God blessed the seventh day and hallowed it.

Bible: Gen. 2.3.

759.A.2 Remember the sabbath day, to keep it holy.

Bible: Exod., 20.8. Cf *Deut.*, 5.12.

759.A.3 The Sabbath institution permeates all of Mosaism, hence the sanctification of the seventh week, seventh month, seventh year, and finally the jubilee year.

J. Auerbach. III Versammlung deutscher Rabbiner, 1846.

759.A.4 An entire cessation of all the affairs of life on each seventh day is a Jewish institution, and is not prescribed by the laws of any other people.

D'Israeli, *The Genius of Judaism*, 1833.

759.A.5 The Sabbath will never be abolished in Israel.

Mekilta, to *Exod.* 20.13.

759.A.6 When the Sabbath complained, "All the days of the week are paired, I alone am an odd number, without a mate," the Holy One replied, "The congregation of Israel is your mate!"

Pesikta Rabbati, ch 23, ed Friedmann, 117b.

759.A.7 Thou hast given us in love this great and holy day.

Zadok. q by his son Eleazar. *Tosefta: Berakot*, 3.7.

759.B. Meaning

759.B.1 It is a sign between Me and the children of Israel forever.

Bible: Exod., 31.17.

759.B.2 Call the Sabbath a delight.

Bible: Isa., 58.13.

759.B.3 The Sabbath was given only for pleasure.

Hiyya b. Abba. *Pesikta Rabbati*, ch 23, ed Friedmann, 121a.

759.B.4 This is the meaning of the Jewish Sabbath, to give to man peaceful hours, hours completely diverted from everyday life, seclusion from the world in the midst of the world.

Baeck, *Essence of Judaism*, 1936, p. 147.

759.B.5 The law of the Sabbath is the quintessence of the doctrine of ethical monotheism. . . . It is the epitome of the love of God.

H. Cohen, *Die Religion der Vernunft*, 1919, pp. 181, 183.

759.B.6 The Sabbath is the day of peace between man and nature. . . . By not working—by not participating in the process of natural and social change—man is free from the chains of nature and from the chains of time, although only for one day a week.

Fromm, *Forgotten Language,* 1951, p. 244f.

759.B.7 A king built a bridal chamber, plastered, painted and adorned it. Now what was needed to complete it? Why, a bride! So with the world, after the six days of creation, what was needed to finish it? The Sabbath!

Geniba, on *Gen.* 2.2. *Gen. R.,* 10.9.

759.B.8 The Sabbath is the incomplete form of the world to come.

Hanina b. Isaac. *Gen. R.,* 17.5. See *Mekilta,* to *Exod.* 31.13.

759.B.9 The Sabbath is a mirror of the world to come.

Zohar, Gen., 48a.

759.B.10 The Sabbath is the anticipation of the Messianic time, just as the Messianic period is called the time of "continuous Sabbath."

Fromm, *Forgotten Language,* 1951, p. 244.

759.B.11 The Sabbath has been instituted as an opportunity for fellowship with God, and for glad, not austere, service of Him.

Judah Halevi, *Cuzari,* c.1135, 3.5.

759.B.12 The Sabbath is the heart of Judaism.

Kagan. q YSS, 148.

759.B.13 The Sabbath signifies an abdication on that day of the right to be master of certain things enjoyed during the six other days. It means not only resting oneself, but letting all other things rest; creating nothing—neither fire nor sound, excepting when it be for the sake of the Creator Himself. A Sabbath so observed . . . is an essential affirmation of faith.

Ibid., 150.

759.B.14 An artist cannot be continually wielding his brush. He must stop at times in his painting to freshen his vision of the object, the meaning of which he wishes to express on his canvas. Living is also an art. . . . The Sabbath represents those moments when we pause in our brushwork to renew our vision of the object.

Kaplan, *The Meaning of God,* 1937, p. 59.

759.B.15 In love and favor Thou hast given us Thy Holy Sabbath as an inheritance, a memorial of the Creation, . . . in remembrance of the departure from Egypt.

Kiddush. See *DPB,* ed Singer, 124; *UPB,* 1940, i. 93.

759.B.16 All the moral doctrines of Judaism may be grouped around the idea of the Sabbath.

Magnes, 1911, *Gleanings,* 1948, p. 58.

759.B.17 The perfect Sabbath rest is the attuning of the heart to the comprehension of God.

Maimonides, *Tzavaah.* AHE, 101.

759.B.18 To observe the Sabbath is to bear witness to the Creator.

Mekilta, to *Exod.* 20.13.

759.B.19 The Jew's struggles of the week are but preparation for the finer things of the Sabbath. This is the all-pervading aim of his life.

Mendelé, *Feast of Weeks.* LEJS, 33.

759.B.20 The Sabbath *is* a world revolution.

F. Rosenzweig, letter to E. Rosenstock, Aug. 25, 1924. GFR, 135.

759.B.21 The Sabbath is the visible sign of the insufficiency of the material and the need for its re-integration with the spiritual It is a standing protest against the doctrine of wage-slavery.

L. Roth, *Jewish Thought,* 1954, p. 47.

759.B.22 Ours it is to bear the Sabbath in our souls.

Salaman, "Saturday." *Songs of Many Days,* 1923, p. 18.

759.B.23 The Sabbath and festivals were given for devotion to Torah.

Samuel b. Nahman. *Pesikta Rabbati,* ch 23, ed Friedmann, 121a.

759.B.24 One does not nap on the Sabbath in order to work better the next day, even on Torah, for Sabbath rest is for Sabbath enjoyment, not for the sake of a weekday's work.

Sefer Hasidim, 13C, #608, p. 164.

759.B.25 The Holy One lends man an extra soul on the eve of the Sabbath, and withdraws it at the close of the Sabbath.

Simeon b. Lakish. *T: Betza,* 16a.

759.B.26 The Sabbath is the hub of the Jew's Universe; to protract it is a virtue; to love it is a liberal education.

Zangwill. q Berkowitz, *Sabbath Sentiment,* (1898) 1921, p. 3.

759.B.27 As the Sabbath commences, all harmful fires are suppressed, including that

of Gehenna, so that sinners obtain a respite.
Zohar, Exod., 203b.

759.C. Observance

Laws

759.C.1 In it thou shalt not do any manner of work.
Bible: Exod., 20.10.

759.C.2 Kindle no fire throughout your habitations on the Sabbath day.
Ibid., 35.3.

759.C.3 Blessed art Thou . . . who hast sanctified us by Thy commandments, and bidden us kindle the Sabbath light.
Amram Gaon, *Siddur*, 9C, 24b.

759.C.4 Every man who does any work, or goes on a journey, or tills his farm, . . . or lights a fire, or rides on a beast, . . . or catches an animal or bird or fish, or fasts, or makes war on the Sabbath . . . shall die.
Apocrypha: Jubilees, 50.11ff.

759.C.5 Whoever attacks us on the Sabbath, let us fight against him, that we may not die.
Apocrypha: 1 Macc., 2.41.

759.C.6 Religious accounts may be calculated and discussed on Sabbath.
Hamnuna, Hisda. *T: Sabbath*, 150a.

759.C.7 Matters of life and death, and communal affairs in general, may be attended to on the Sabbath.
Johanan b. Nappaha. *Ibid.: Ketubot*, 5a.

759.C.8 To save a life, disregard a Sabbath, that the endangered may observe many Sabbaths.
Jonathan. *Mekilta*, to *Exod.* 31.1.
Simeon b. Menasya. *T: Yoma*, 85b.

759.C.9 The Sabbath has been given to you, not you to the Sabbath.
Jonathan. *T: Yoma*, 85b.
Simeon b. Menasya. *Mekilta*, to *Exod.* 31.14.

759.C.10 Since woman extinguished the "light of the world," she atones for it by lighting the Sabbath candles.
José b. Katzarta. *Gen. R.*, 17.8. *TJ: Sabbath*, 2.6.

759.C.11 The desecration of the Sabbath in an emergency is not delegated to strangers, minors, servants or women . . . but is done by prominent Jews and sages.
Maimonides, *Yad: Sabbath*, 1180, 2.3.

759.C.12 A girl's betrothal and a child's education or vocational training may be arranged for on the Sabbath.
Manasseh School. *T: Sabbath*, 150a.

759.C.13 "Nor pursuing your business, nor speaking thereof" [*Isa.* 58.13]—*your* business is forbidden, not the business of Heaven.
Ibid.

759.C.14 No Sabbath laws apply where life is in danger.
Mathia b. Heresh. *Mishna: Yoma*, 8.6.

759.C.15 You may violate the Sabbath to relieve pain.
Mathia b. Heresh. *T: Yoma*, 84a.

759.C.16 Who puts out a light for fear of robbers . . . or to enable a patient to sleep is not guilty; to save oil or wick, is guilty.
Mishna: Sabbath, 2.5.

759.C.17 Desecrate the Sabbath and extinguish a man-made candle, rather than let a soul, the God-made candle, be extinguished.
Rab. *T: Sabbath*, 30b.

759.C.18 Tell nothing on the Sabbath which will draw tears.
Sefer Hasidim, 13C, #625, p. 167.

759.C.19 Let melancholy and passion, born of spleen and bile, be banished from all hearts on the Sabbath day.
Moses Hasid, *Iggeret HaMusar*, 1717. AHE, 291.

759.C.20 The Sabbath may be desecrated for a living infant of a day, but not for dead King David.
Simeon b. Eleazar. *Tosefta: Sabbath*, 17.19.
Simeon b. Gamaliel II. *T: Sabbath*, 151b.

759.C.21 In this world, a man picks figs on the Sabbath and the figs say nothing; in the next world, they will shout: Today is Sabbath!
Simeon HeHasid. *Midrash Tehillim*, 73.4, ed Buber, 168a.

Customs

759.C.22 Desist from speech on the Sabbath day.
Abbahu. *TJ: Sabbath*, 15.3.

759.C.23 "Remember the Sabbath"—keep it in mind from Sunday on, and hold for it anything good that may come your way.
Eleazar b. Hanania. *Mekilta*, to *Exod.* 20.8.

759.C.24 It is a great merit to prepare personally for the Sabbath. Such chores are not undignified. It is an honor to honor the Sabbath.

> Epstein, *Kitzur Shné Luhot HaBerit*, (1683), 61a.

759.C.25 Have another cloak for the Sabbath.

> Hanina b. Hama. *Pesikta R.*, ch 23, 115b. *TJ: Peah*, 8.7.

759.C.26 Sanctify the Sabbath with food, drink, clean garments and pleasure, and God will reward you for it!

> Hiyya b. Abba. *Deut. R.*, 3.1. See Johanan b. Nappaha. *Cant. R.*, 5.16. *Tanhuma, VaYetzé*, 22, ed Buber, 80b.

759.C.27 Gather congregations each Sabbath and assemble in houses of study to instruct Jews in the laws of the Torah.

> *Midrash Abkir. Yalkut Shimoni*, #408, to *Exod.* 35.1.

759.C.28 Jews occupy themselves every seventh day with the philosophy of their fathers, dedicating that time to the acquisition of knowledge and the study of the truths of nature.

> Philo, *Moses*, ii. 39.

759.C.29 To the Jews the Sabbath is a day of happiness. The synagog liturgy of the Sabbath is full of the joyous note. It is marked by gay dress, sumptuous meals, and a general sense of exhilaration. The Puritans knew little or nothing of synagog worship or of Jewish homes. They had no experience of "the joy of the commandment"—a phrase often on Jewish lips and in Jewish hearts.

> *Selbie, *Influence of OT on Puritanism*, 1927. BSL 423.

759.C.30 Devote part of the Sabbath to Torah and part to feasting.

> *Talmud J: Sabbath*, 15.3.

759.C.31 Sleep on the Sabbath is a pleasure.

> *Yalkut Reubeni, VaEthhanan*, 1660.

759.C.32 Eat three meals on the Sabbath.

> Zerika. *Mekilta*, to *Exod.* 16.25. *T: Sabbath*, 117a.

Reception

759.C.33 Beloved, come, the Bride to meet,
> The Princess Sabbath let us greet.

> Alkabetz, "Leka Dodi," c. 1540. *UPB*, 1940, i. 26.

759.C.34 Come, let us welcome Queen Sabbath!

> Hanina b. Hama. *T: Sabbath*, 119a.

759.C.35 Welcome the Sabbath as one welcomes a great and renowned king, with reverence and joy. From synagog return home to find lamps lit, chairs set, table laid, and a tranquil happiness in the heart of wife and family.

> Joel b. Abraham Shemaria, *Tzavaah*, 1800. AHE, 347.

759.C.36 On Sabbath eve, a good angel and an evil angel accompany a man from the synagog to his home. If the man finds the candles lit, the table set, and the bed made, the good angel says, "May next Sabbath be like this!" and the evil angel answers perforce, Amen. Otherwise, the evil angel says, "May next Sabbath be like this!" and the good angel is compelled to respond, Amen.

> José b. Judah. *T: Sabbath*, 119b.

759.C.37 Bring fruits and wine and sing a gladsome lay,
> Cry, "Come in peace, O restful Seventh Day!"

> Judah Halevi, tr S. Solis-Cohen.

759.C.38 Yannai would don his robes on Sabbath eve, and call: "Come, O bride! Come, O bride!"

> *Talmud: Sabbath*, 119a.

759.C.39 Two angels accompany the worshiper on Sabbath eve, place their hands over his head, and say: "Thine iniquity is taken away, and thy sin purged" [*Isa.* 6.7].

> Ukba. *T: Sabbath*, 119b.

759.D. Value

759.D.1 Jerusalem was destroyed because it had desecrated the Sabbath.

> Abayé. *T: Sabbath*, 119b.

759.D.2 More than Israel kept the Sabbath, the Sabbath has kept Israel.

> Ahad HaAm. *HaShiloah*, 1898, iii. 6. *Al Parashat Derakim*, iii. 79.

759.D.3 There is no Judaism without the Sabbath.

> Baeck, address, Jan. 20, 1935.

759.D.4 The Sabbath became the most effective patron-saint of the Jewish people. . . . The ghetto Jew discarded all the toil and trouble of his daily life when the Sabbath lamp was lit. All insult and outrage was shaken off. The love of God, which returned to him the Sabbath each seventh day, restored to him also his honor and human dignity even in his lowly hut.

> H. Cohen, *Die Religion der Vernunft*, 1919, p. 184.

759.D.5 Had Judaism brought into the world only the Sabbath, it would thereby have proved itself to be a producer of joy and a promoter of peace for mankind. The Sabbath was the first step on the road which led to the abrogation of slavery.

Ibid., p. 540.

759.D.6 Sabbath's holiness extends over the week days, which draw inspiration from it as from a central source.

Danzig, *Hayyé Adam*, 1810.

759.D.7 Sabbath observance balances all the commandments of Torah.

Eleazar b. Abina. *TJ: Nedarim*, 3.9.

759.D.8 That there is one day in the week that the working man may call his own, one day in the week on which hammer is silent and loom stands idle, is due, through Christianity, to Judaism—to the code promulgated in the Sinaitic wilderness.

*George, *Moses*, 1878.

759.D.9 Who worships on Sabbath eve is as God's partner in creation.

Hamnuna. *T: Sabbath*, 119b.

759.D.10 Of a prince by fate thus treated
    Is my song. His name is Israel,
    And a witch's spell has changed him
    To the likeness of a dog. . . .
    But on every Friday evening,
    On a sudden, in the twilight,
    The enchantment weakens, ceases,
    And the dog once more is human.

Heine, "Princess Sabbath," 1851, tr M. Armour. See J. H. Hertz, *Affirmations of Judaism*.

759.D.11 The Falashas . . . were some generations ago sorely harassed by hired missionaries to name the Savior and Mediator of the Jews. They spoke wiser than they knew when they answered, "The Savior of the Jews is the Sabbath.

J. H. Hertz, *Daily Prayer Book*, 1948, p. 341.

759.D.12 Jews will be redeemed by virtue of their Sabbath observance.

Hiyya b. Abba. *Lev. R.*, 3.1.

759.D.13 If we the Sabbath keep with faithful heart,
    The Lord will Israel keep with love divine.

A. Ibn Ezra, Sabbath Table Hymn, c. 1158. *DPB*, ed Hertz, 569.

759.D.14 The Sabbath is . . . the greatest wonder of religion. Nothing can appear more simple than this institution. . . . Yet no legislator in the world hit upon this idea! To the Greeks and Romans it was an object of derision, a superstitious usage. But it removed with one stroke a contrast between slaves who must labor incessantly and their masters who may celebrate continuously.

B. Jacob, "The Decalogue." *JQR*, 1923, xiv. 165.

759.D.15 Anyone who observes the Sabbath properly, even if he be an idolater, is forgiven his sins [against God].

Johanan. *T: Sabbath*, 118b.

759.D.16 We have a certain seasoning, called Sabbath, which lends an unusual flavor to our dishes; but it works only for him who observes the Sabbath.

Joshua b. Hanania. *T: Sabbath*, 119a.

759.D.17 The Sabbath is the choicest fruit and flower of the week, the Queen whose coming changes the humblest home into a palace.

Judah Halevi, *Cuzari*, c. 1135, 3.5.

759.D.18 The tumult of my heart is stilled,
    For thou art come, Sabbath my love!

Judah Halevi, tr Solis-Cohen.

759.D.19 He who keeps one Sabbath properly is accounted as if he had observed all the Sabbaths from Creation to the Resurrection.

Judah HaNasi. *Mekilta*, to *Exod.* 31.13.

759.D.20 I am black on week days, but comely on the Sabbath.

Levi b. Haytha. *Cant. R.*, 1.5.2.

759.D.21 Treasure of heart for the broken people,
    Gift of new soul for the souls distrest,
    Soother of sighs for the prisoned spirit—
    The Sabbath of rest

I. Luria, Sabbath Table Hymn, 1560, tr Nina Salaman.

759.D.22 If a man keeps the Sabbath properly, the Lord also keeps him.

Maaseh Book, (1602) 1934, #8, p. 13.

759.D.23 The Jew sings to his bride, Sabbath, . . . and the depression of his spirit vanishes, his will is submerged in God's will.

Mendelé, *Feast of Weeks*. LEJS, 33.

759.D.24 The Sabbath . . . prevents us reducing our life to the level of a machine. . . . If to labor is noble, of our own free will to pause in that labor which may lead to success, . . . may be nobler still.

Montefiore, *Bible for Home Reading,* 1896, i. 86.

759.D.25 The Sabbath is . . . an efficacious level for the religious education of children. Parents will neglect it at the peril of their spiritual life.

Montefiore, *Liberal Judaism,* 1903, p. 142.

759.D.26 The Sabbath was like a field of reunion whither, at the beginning of each week, all Hebrews had to repair in spirit. It was the monument which declared their political existence, the bond which clasped the bundle of their institutions.

*Proudhon, *De la Célébration du Dimanche,* 1850, Pref. viii.

759.D.27 Our modern spirit, with all its barren theories of civic and political rights, and its strivings towards freedom and equality, has not thought out and called into existence a single institution that, in its beneficent effects upon the laboring classes, can in the slightest degree be compared to the Weekly Day of Rest promulgated in the Sinaitic wilderness.

Ibid., p. 12. q Hertz, *DPB,* 338f.

759.D.28 The lamp is lit, and sorrows flit.

Proverb. q AJL, 154.

759.D.29 The Jewish tradition, with its love of home life and its devotion to study, has shown how the Sabbath can be made not only a day of respite from work but a positive factor in human development and well-being.

L. Roth, *Jewish Thought,* 1954, p. 47.

759.D.30 If Israel observed properly two Sabbaths, they would be redeemed immediately.

Simeon b. Yohai. *T: Sabbath,* 118b.

759.D.31 If Israel kept properly one Sabbath, the Son of David would come, for Sabbath is equivalent to all commandments.

Levi. *Exod. R.,* 25.12. *TJ: Taanit,* 1.1.

759.D.32 Man's [annual] budget is fixed for him between Rosh Hashana and Yom Kippur, except his expenses for Sabbaths and festivals and his children's tuition: if he spends less [for these], he is given less, and if he spends more, he is given more.

Tahlifa. *T: Betza,* 16a.

759.D.33 Who spends for the Sabbath is repaid by the Sabbath.

Talmud: Sabbath, 119a.

759.E. Problem

759.E.1 Every Jew who has it within his power should aid in the effort to restore the Sabbath.

C. Adler. q Hertz, *DPB,* 383.

759.E.2 The Sabbath is a human want. . . . The old Jewish Sabbath is dead. To successfully revive it, seclusion on the part of the Jews from the outer world in a new Ghetto would be the price.

E. G. Hirsch, 1885. q Schreiber, *Reformed Judaism,* 237.

759.E.3 No community steps out of Judaism which celebrates the Sabbath on a day other than that observed up to this time.

S. Hirsch. III Versammlung deutscher Rabbiner, 1846.

759.E.4 If we transfer the Sabbath to Sunday, we will bury Judaism on Friday evening to permit it to be resurrected on Sunday morning as another religion.

L. Stein, *ibid., Protokolle,* 119. q PRM, 210.

759.E.5 The great majority of Jews . . . have really no holidays. The children attend school on the Sabbath, the apprentice must work on this day, . . . and when the young man has finally become his own master, he will scarcely be inclined to observe a day to which he has not been accustomed from childhood.

Versammlung deutscher Rabbiner, Memorial Address, 1845. q PRM, 189.

759.E.6 The old Sabbath is gone. Saturday, for the Jew as for the rest of our citizens, is a workday.

Voorsanger. CCAR, 1903, xiii. 166.

760. SACRIFICE

760.1 There shall not be found among you anyone who makes his son or his daughter to pass through the fire.

Bible: Deut., 18.10.

760.2 To what purpose is the multitude of your sacrifices to Me?

Bible: Isa., 1.11. See *Ps.,* 50.12f.

760.3 I spoke not unto your fathers, nor commanded them . . . concerning burnt-offerings or sacrifices.

Bible: Jer., 7.22.

760.4 The sacrifices of God are a broken spirit.
Bible: Ps., 51.19.

760.5 He who offers a sacrifice offers also of his soul in all its moods.
Apocrypha: Aristeas, 170.

760.6 Disown all temples and altars, vain erections of senseless stones, befouled with constant blood of living things!
Apocrypha: Sibyl, 4.24–31.

760.7 A handful of flour brought by a poor man voluntarily is more precious than two handfuls of incense brought by the High Priest.
Isaac Nappaha. *Eccles. R.,* to 4.6.

760.8 See how the Holy One tried to spare the people expense: if one became liable to sacrifice, he was commanded to bring from the herd [*Lev.* 1.3]; if he could not afford it, he was told to bring a lamb [4.32]; and if he could not afford that, he could bring a goat [3.12], or a fowl [1.14], or just a measure of fine flour [6.12].
Levi. *Lev. R.,* 8.4.

760.9 We strike from all bequeathed prayer-books any line that reminds us of the temple and sacrifices.
M. Lilienthal, address, 1876.

760.10 I believe in the national meaning of the Messianic dogma and hope for a national restoration, yet I am free to confess that the reinstitution of the bloody sacrificial ritual does not form part and parcel of these hopes and promises.
I. N. Mannheimer, *Theologische Gutachten über das Gebetbuch,* 1842, p. 94f. q PRM, 87. See Maimonides, *Guide for the Perplexed,* 3.32.

761. SALT

761.1 With all your offerings, offer salt.
Bible: Lev., 2.13. See *Num.,* 18.19.

761.2 The world can get along without pepper, not without salt.
Johanan. *TJ: Horayot,* 3.5.

761.3 Ye are the salt of the earth.
New Testament: Matt., 5.13. See ZVJ, 59.

761.4 All dishes require salt.
Talmud: Betza, 14a.

761.5 I do not consider it a compliment to be called "the salt of the earth." Salt is used for some one else's food. It dissolves in that food. And salt is good only in small quantities.
Weizmann, *Trial and Error,* 1949, p. 274. See ZVJ, 59.

762. SALVATION

762.1 I wait for Thy salvation, O Lord.
Bible: Gen., 49.18. Cf *I Sam.,* 2.1, *Ps.,* 119.81.

762.2 My salvation shall be for ever.
Bible: Isa., 51.6.

762.3 Salvation is of the Lord.
Bible: Jon., 2.10. Cf *Jer.,* 3.23, *Ps.,* 3.9.

762.4 The salvation of Israel is the salvation of the Holy One.
Abbahu. *Lev. R., 9.3.*

762.5 Many have been created, but few shall be saved.
Apocrypha: II Esdras, 8.3.

762.6 Salvation is attained not by subscription to metaphysical dogmas, but solely by love of God expressed in action.
Crescas, *Or Adonai,* c. 1400, ii. 6.1.

762.7 My salvation depends upon me alone!
Eleazar b. Dordia. *T: Aboda Zara,* 17a.

762.8 Woe to the nations that have no salvation!
Johanan b. Nappaha. *T: Rosh Hashana,* 23a.

762.9 For the sake of Torah and Israel, let the world be saved!
Judah b. Simon. *Lev. R.,* 23.3.

762.10 Judaism combines the idea of salvation of the individual with that of the salvation of the social unit.
Mattuck, sermon, May 12, 1918.

762.11 When he who walks in the dark of night gets a lantern [commandment], he is safe from thorns and pits. When dawn breaks [Torah], he is safe also from beasts and robbers. When he reaches the cross-roads [Death], he is saved from all.
Menahem b. José. *T: Sota,* 21a.

762.12 Salvation is of the Jews.
New Testament: John, 4.22.

762.13 Through their fall, salvation is come to the Gentiles.
New Testament: Rom., 11.11.

762.14 He who has Torah, good deeds, humility and the fear of Heaven will be saved.
Pesikta Rabbati, ed Friedmann, 198a.

762.15 Only then does the soul begin to be saved when . . . reason is the charioteer, and toil creates not self-satisfaction but a readiness to yield honor to God, the bestower of the boon.
Philo, *Allegorical Interpretation,* 3.46.

763. SAMARITANS

763.1 The blood-groups of the Samaritans show no affinity to those of the Hebrews.

*Huxley & Haddon, We Europeans, 1936, p. 151.

763.2 When the Jews are in difficulties, the Samaritans deny that they have kinship with them, thereby indeed admitting the truth, but whenever they see some splendid bit of good fortune come to them, they suddenly grasp at the connection with them, . . . tracing their line back to Ephraim and Manasseh.

Josephus, *Antiquities*, 11.8.6. See also 9.14.3. See above 16.2.

763.3 The Samaritans are an eloquent illustration of what happens in Israel to any group which surrenders to the letter of the Torah.

F. A. Levy, *Crossroads in Judaism*, 1954, p. 8.

763.4 The precepts which the Cutheans adopted, they observe meticulously, even more so than the Israelites.

Simeon b. Gamaliel. *T: Kiddushin*, 76a.

763.5 The Samaritan poor and the Jewish poor are to be treated alike.

Tosefta: Peah, 4.1.

764. SAND

764.1 As dust is found from one end of the earth to the other, so will the children of Israel be everywhere on earth.

Gen. R., 41.9.

764.2 Like dust, the children of Israel will be trodden; but as dust wears out even metal, so will Israel outlast the Powers.

Ibid.

764.3 Jews are likened to sand: tiny grains, dry and scattered, each separate from the other.

Peretz, *Reb Nohemkes Myses*, 1904, 200.

764.4 Wisdom's race is likened to sand, both because it is innumerable and because sand-banks force back the inroads of the sea as trained wisdom keeps back sinful and unjust deeds.

Philo, *Dreams*, i. 28.

764.5 Israel is likened to sand [*Hos.* 2.1], for as sand remains immutable when put in hot or cold, so Jews swerve not from their religion even when they pass through fire or water.

Tanhuma, ed Buber, Introduction, #35, p. 134.

764.6 As the waves of the raging sea hurl themselves against the earth, but their force is broken by the sand on the shore, . . . so do the nations roar and fume and seek to overwhelm the world, but recede, broken and powerless, when Israel cleaves to God.

Zohar, Exod., 225b.

765. SATAN

765.1 Satan stood up against Israel.

Bible: I Chron., 21.1.

765.2 God may use Satan to His own purposes. Elements emerge from the chaos of evil and are built up into good.

S. Alexander, *Space, Time and Deity*, (1920) 1927, ii. 411.

765.3 The devil came, wearing the form and brightness of an angel.

Apocrypha: Adam and Eve (Slavonic), 38.1.

765.4 Save me from the foe who pursues me as a lion, from Satan.

Apocrypha: Asenath, 1.

765.5 When the fool curses Satan, he curses his own soul.

Apocrypha: Ben Sira, 21.27.

765.6 There is no fellowship between God and Satan.

Didascalia, ii. ch 62.

765.7 Satan enters through a needle's eye.

Hagiz, *Leket HaKemah*, (1697) 1897, p. 103a.

765.8 He is . . . really a handsome and and charming man. . . .
    A diplomat too, well skilled in debate,
    He talks quite glibly of church and state.

Heine, *Return Home*, 1826, #37.

765.9 Satan's torment was worse than Job's: he was like a servant told to break the cask without spilling the wine.

Isaac. *T: Baba Bathra*, 16a.

765.10 Never give Satan an opening.

Jose b. Halafta. *T: Berakot*, 60a.

765.11 Get thee behind me, Satan: thou art an offense unto me.

New Testament: Matt, 16.23. See 4.10.

765.12 Resist the devil, and he will flee from you.

New Testament: James, 4.7.

765.13 Be sober, be vigilant, because your adversary, the devil, walks about as a roaring lion, seeking whom he can devour.

New Testament: I Peter, 5.8.

765.14 We are like fish
In this vast sea.
And Satan fishes
For you and me.
Peretz, "Monish" (tr LGP, 56), 1888.

765.15 Satan, the Evil Inclination, and the Angel of Death, are all one and the same.
Simeon b. Lakish. *T: Baba Bathra*, 16a.

765.16 It is necessary to put a pacifier in Satan's mouth.
Yalkut, Lev., #521.

766. SATIETY

766.1 Ye have sown much and brought in little, ye eat but have not enough, ye drink but are not filled, ye clothe you but there is none warm, and he who earns wages earns for a bag with holes.
Bible: Hag., 1.6.

766.2 There are three things that are never satisfied, yea, four: . . . the grave, the barren womb, the earth that is not satisfied with water, and the fire that says not, Enough.
Bible: Prov., 30.15f.

766.3 All the rivers run into the sea, yet the sea is not full.
Bible: Eccles., 1.7.

766.4 The eye is not satisfied with seeing, nor the ear with hearing.
Ibid., 1.8.

766.5 The sated is disgusted with honey.
Immanuel, *Mahberot*, c. 1300 (1491), 11.

766.6 The sated believes not the hungry.
Proverb (Yiddish). See S. Levin, *Youth in Revolt*, 234.

767. SCALDING

767.1 Scalded by the hot, he blows on the cold.
Proverb (Yiddish). BJS, #2.

767.2 Who burned his fingers, mistaking a glowing coal for a gem, will not touch a gem, lest it be a coal.
Simon. *Deut. R.*, 1.8.

768. SCAPEGOAT

768.1 Aaron shall lay both his hands upon the head of the live goat, confess over him all the iniquities of the children of Israel, . . . and shall send him away . . . into the wilderness.
Bible: Lev., 16.21.

768.2 He was wounded because of our transgressions, . . . and with his stripes we were healed.
Bible: Isa., 53.5.

768.3 Scapegoats for economic sins called Jews.
Berenson, March 4, 1944. *Rumor and Reflection*, 257.

768.4 All the leaden-cheeked Christian onion-eaters of Upper and Lower Egypt understood admirably that a war against the Jews could, in the end, be an excellent dodge for healing up many a bankruptcy or reviving many a decrepit business.
*Bloy, *Le Salut par les Juifs*, (1892) 1947, p. 246f.

768.5 The Jews are more stupid than cattle when they persuade themselves that the governments will protect them when revolution breaks out. No, they will be offered as a sacrifice to popular hatred. The governments will seek to ransom themselves with this price. In India, when they want to kill the frightful boa, they drive an ox toward it; when it devours the ox and can no longer move, they kill it. The Jews will be the oxen, driven into the jaws of the revolution.
Boerne, *Briefe aus Paris*, #51, Oct. 8, 1831.

768.6 So long as gentiles are ill at ease with themselves they want Jews to be there, to bear the blame for all conceivable ills.
q *H. Ellis, *Questions of Our Day*, 1936, p. 40.

768.7 The Pestilence like fury broke
And took its thousands of our folk;
The Earth against us fiercely turned,
And many Jews were therefore burned.
*Henricus of Erfurt, 1348. q LJG, 125.

768.8 Jewish blood is the best for oiling the wheels of progress.
q Jabotinsky, *The War and the Jew*, 1942, p. 48. See 758.9.

768.9 If the Jew did not exist as an outlet for the wrath of those who are despoiled, . . . he would be invented.
Lazare, *Nationalism and Jewish Emancipation*, 1889. LJD 85.

768.10 He being rich and a Jew, that is enough for me.
*Lessing, (Sittah in) *Nathan der Weise*, 1779, 2.3.

768.11 A sinful world needs a scapegoat.
T. Lessing, *Der jüdische Selbsthass*, 1930, Introd. LR 188.

768.12 Psychologically speaking, . . . each individual Christian has to deal in some way with the problem of his share in Christ's death. One way of atonement is through Holy Communion. . . . Another way to lessen the burden of guilt is to throw it all on the Jews. . . . The next step is to project onto them also the secret sin of every Christian, of unconsciously rejoicing in Christ's crucifixion.

Loewenstein, *Christians and Jews,* 1951, p. 190f.

768.13 All reactions begin by creating a case against the Jews.

Luzzati, letter to E. Rothschild, Oct. 31, 1913. LGF 474.

768.14 So long as the world is a place in which life to the ordinary man means insecurity, frustration and unemployment, so long will he need some scapegoat for his feelings; and the position of the Jews, and their powerlessness, make them the perfect scapegoat.

*Parkes, *An Enemy of the People: Antisemitism,* 1946, 132.

768.15 Nothing gratifies the mob more than to get a simple name to account for a complex phenomenon, and the word "Jew" is always at hand to explain the never-absent maladies of the body politic.

Zangwill, *Voice of Jerusalem,* 1921, p. 199.

769. SCHLEMIHL

769.1 Phineas, blind with fury,
In the sinner's place, by ill-luck
Chanced to kill a guiltless person,
Named Schlemihl ben Zuri Shaddai.
He, then, this Schlemihl the First,
Was the ancestor of all the
Race Schlemihls.

Heine, *Jehuda Ben Halevy,* 1851, 4. See *Num.,* 1.6.

769.2 To say that a schlemihl is a luckless person . . . is to touch only the negative side. It is the schlemihl's avocation and profession to miss out on things, to muff opportunities, to be persistently, organically, preposterously, and ingeniously out of place. A hungry schlemihl dreams of a plate of hot soup, and hasn't a spoon.

M. Samuel, *World of Sholom Aleichem,* 1944, p. 187.

769.3 Even when he falls on straw, Schlemihl stumbles on a stone.

Sholom Aleichem, *Mottel Pesses,* 1907.

770. SCHOLAR

770.1 To dine with a scholar is to feast also on the Shekina.

Abin Halevi. *T: Berakot,* 64a.

770.2 A scholar who is not as unyielding as iron is no scholar.

Ashi. *T: Taanit,* 4a.

770.3 As a shell shields the fruit, so do common Jews shield scholars.

Azariah. *Cant. R.,* 6.11.1.

770.4 Treating scholars to wine is like offering libations to God.

Berekia. *T: Yoma,* 71a. See *Ketubot,* 105b.

770.5 Nor rock nor flint can e'er in hardness vie
With a Hebrew boy whose Torah is his fare.

Bialik, "HaMathmid," 1895. FTH, 32.

770.6 Many a scholar is like a cashier: he has the key to much money, but the money is not his.

Boerne, *Der Narr im weissen Schwan,* ch 2.

770.7 How does the uneducated regard a scholar? At first like a gold ladle; if he converses with him, like a silver ladle; and if the scholar is his beneficiary, like an earthen ladle.

Eleazar b. Pedat. *T: Sanhedrin,* 52b.

770.8 Who will not support a scholar will see no blessing.

Ibid., 92a.

770.9 A table is not blessed, if it has fed no scholars.

Seder Eliyahu Rabbah, ch 13, ed Friedmann, p. 91.

770.10 A scholar is not a robber, and a robber is not a scholar.

Eleazar b. Perata. *T: Aboda Zara,* 17b.

770.11 Two scholars, traveling together, who do not discuss Torah, deserve to be burned.

Elia b. Berekia. *T: Taanit,* 10b. See *Sota,* 49a.

770.12 Great is the reward for hospitality to a scholar!

Eliezer b. Jose. *T: Berakot,* 63b.

770.13 A Jewish scholar must master all the seven branches of knowledge.

Elijah Gaon. q GSS, 223.

770.14 A scholar who busies himself with communal affairs forgets his learning.

Exod. R., 6.2.

770.15 Scholars promote peace in the world.

Hanina. *T: Yebamot,* 122b.

770.16 It is a disgrace for a scholar to walk out with patched shoes.

Hiyya b. Abba. *T: Berakot,* 43b. See *Sabbath,* 114a.

770.17 Scholars have no rest even in the world to come.

Hiyya b. Ashi. *T: Moed Katan,* 29a. See Rab. *Berakot* 64a.

770.18 For what scholar must the people do his work? For him who ignores his own wants and busies himself with Heaven's wants.

Johanan b. Nappaha. *T: Sabbath,* 114a.

770.19 What scholar may be appointed community head? He who can answer a legal question in any area of the law.

Ibid.

770.20 A scholar commits a capital offense if he appears with a stain of grease on his garment.

Ibid.

770.21 Scholars are builders, builders of the world.

Ibid.

770.22 If three consecutive generations are scholars, the Torah will not depart from that line.

Johanan b. Nappaha. *T: Baba Metzia,* 85a.

770.23 Woe to scholars of Torah who lack fear of God.

Jonathan b. Eleazar. *T: Yoma,* 72b.

770.24 Jerusalem was destroyed for not respecting scholars.

Judah b. Ezekiel. *T: Sabbath,* 119b.

770.25 Rather a corpse than a scholar without sense.

Lev. R., 1.15.

770.26 A student who permits everybody to tread over him will retain his learning.

Mathna. *T: Erubin,* 54a. See *Derek Eretz,* 1.2.

770.27 A scholar who willfully forgets and rejects one item of his study is guilty of a mortal sin.

Meir. *Mishna: Abot,* 3.8.

770.28 There are four types of students: the sponge, who absorbs all; the funnel, who lets it in at one end and out at the other; the strainer, who lets out the wine and retains the dregs; and the sieve, who lets out the coarse and keeps the fine flour.

Mishna: Abot, 5.15.

770.29 A young scholar can kindle the mind of an older one.

Nahman b. Isaac. *T: Taanit,* 7a.

770.30 A disciple of the sages should have a measure of pride.

Rab. *T: Sota,* 5a.

770.31 You will find no Torah in one who, because of some knowledge, exalts himself to the sky.

Raba. *T: Erubin,* 55a.

770.32 Two scholars in one town who are intolerant of one another in matters of law, invite wrath upon themselves.

Raba. *T: Taanit,* 8a.

770.33 Though the shell is soiled, the nut is not spoiled; so a scholar may have sinned, yet his Torah is not contemned.

Raba. *T: Hagiga,* 15b.

770.34 "Bring the precious out of the vile" [*Jer.* 15.19]. Even a vile person may be a source of knowledge.

Meir. *Midrash Mishlé,* 2.6.

770.35 A student who did not wait on scholars remains a boor.

Samuel b. Nahman. *T: Sota,* 22a.

770.36 A tent cannot be kept up without pegs and cords, and Israel cannot stand without scholars.

Seder Eliyahu Rabbah, ch 28 (30), ed Friedmann, 148.

770.37 Scholars are an atonement for Israel in foreign lands.

Seder Eliyahu Zuta, ch 2, ed Friedmann, p. 173.

770.38 You can tell scholars on the street by their walk, speech and dress.

Sifré, #343, to *Deut.* 33.2, ed Friedmann, 143b.

770.39 A scholar, like a bride, should be retiring and discreet, without blemish and above reproach.

Simeon b. Lakish. *Cant. R.,* 4.11.

770.40 A scholar who is not vindictive like a snake, is not a scholar.

Simeon b. Yehozadak. *T: Yoma,* 22b–23a. See Bloch, *Hekal leDibré Hazal,* pp. 72–75; Solomon Pucher. *HaAsif,* 1887, IV, 120–124.

770.41 The Holy One avenges the offended dignity of a rabbinical scholar.

Talmud: Berakot, 19a.

770.42 The ignorant hate scholars more than heathens hate Jews, and their wives hate them even more.
Talmud: Pesahim, 49b.

770.43 Who marries his daughter to a scholar, or who supports scholars, is as if he cleaved to the Shekina [*Deut.* 30.20].
Talmud: Ketubot, 111b.

770.44 A scholar should be like a leather bottle, which admits no wind; like a deep garden bed, which retains its moisture; like a pitch-coated vessel, which preserves its wine, and like a sponge, which absorbs everything.
Talmud: Derek Eretz, 1.2. Cf 1.20.

770.45 Hama said, pointing to Lydda's synagogs, "O how much money my fathers sank in these buildings!" Said Hoshaia: "Think of how many lives they sank here, for they might have spent their money far better in supporting poor scholars!"
Talmud J: Peah, 8.8.

770.46 As a spice-box contains all sorts of spices, so should a scholar be full of all branches of learning.
Tanhuma b. Abba. *Cant. R.,* 5.13.

770.47 A scholar unafraid
To follow thought to any sea,
Or back to any fount.
Zangwill, Pref. to Jacobs, *Barlaam and Josaphat.*

771. SCHOOL

771.1 The heart of the Jewish people has always been in the Bet HaMidrash; there was the source from which they drew the strength and the inspiration that enabled them to overcome all difficulties and withstand all persecutions. If we want to go on living, we must restore the center to the Bet HaMidrash, and make that once more the living source of Judaism.
Ahad HaAm, letter to B. Benas & I. Raffalowich, Oct. 26, 1915. AEL, 272.

771.2 The people of Neshwies . . . wore rags on their feet and ate white bread only on the Sabbath, but no child went without schooling.
M. R. Cohen, *A Dreamer's Journey,* 1949, p. 224.

771.3 The Common School is the Greatest Discovery Ever Made by Man.
Flexner, inscription in Hall of Fame.

771.4 The school is the most original

institution created by post-biblical Judaism.
L. Ginzberg, *Students, Scholars and Saints,* 1928, p. 5.

771.5 Jerusalem was destroyed because its children were in the streets [*Jer.* 6.11], not in schools.
Hamnuna. *T: Sabbath,* 119b.

771.6 A synagog may be turned into a school.
Joshua b. Levi. *T: Megilla,* 27a.

771.7 A school may not be turned into a synagog.
Papi. *Ibid.*

771.8 The world abides only for the sake of school children.
Judah HaNasi. *T: Sabbath,* 119b.

771.9 The studies of school children may not be interrupted even for the building of the Temple.
Ibid.

771.10 Accept no pupil under six; from that age on, stuff them with Torah.
Rab. *T: Baba Bathra,* 21a. See Kattina. *Ketubot,* 50a.

771.11 A teacher is assigned twenty-five pupils.
Raba. *Ibid.*

771.12 No teacher should teach more than ten children in a class.
Huké HaTorah, 12C or 13C. q S. Asaf, *Mekorot LeToldot HaHinuk,* 1925, i. 11.

771.13 Better expel one annoying pupil than ruin a whole class.
Sefer Hasidim, 13C, #184, p. 72.

771.14 A town without schools is doomed to destruction.
Simeon b. Lakish. *T: Sabbath,* 119b.

771.15 Synagogs and houses of study are Israel's towers [*Cant.* 8.10].
Simeon b. Lakish. *T: Baba Bathra,* 8a.

771.16 You don't tell tales out of school.
Zunser, refrain of a popular song. q LEZ, 25.

771.17 Our advance and salvation, our retreat and destruction, are linked with the prosperity or failure of school and synagog.
Zunz.

772. SCIENCE

772.1 The Greeks stole their wisdom from Israel.
*Al-Ghazali. q NDI, 100.

772.2 All sciences originated among the sons of Israel, the reason being the existence of prophecy among them.

*Averroes. q *ibid.*

772.3 From the beginning the Hebrews have been very skillful in the knowledge of astronomy; and all nations have obtained this science as well as other sciences from them.

*R. Bacon, *Opus Majus,* 4.4.16. tr Burke, i. 301.

772.4 The roots and principles of all sciences were handed down from the Hebrews first to the Chaldeans, then to the Persians and Medians, then to the Greeks and finally to the Romans.

Judah Halevi, *Cuzari,* i. 63; ii. 66. q NDI, 100.

772.5 Every answer given arouses new questions. The progress of science is matched by an increase in the hidden and mysterious.

Baeck, *Judaism and Science,* 1949, p. 6.

772.6 We cannot abandon science, the breath of our nostrils. . . . We will set our goods, our children, our lives at stake for it.

Bedersi, *Iggeret HaHitnatzlut,* 1305.

772.7 Not logic alone, but logic supplemented by the social sciences becomes the instrument of advance.

Cardozo, *Growth of the Law,* 1924, p. 73.

772.8 None really knows the true meaning of loving and fearing God, unless he is acquainted with natural science and metaphysics.

Caspi, *Sefer HaMusar,* 14C (Ashkenazi, *Taam Zeḳenim,* 1854). q AJL, 370. See Immanuel, *Commentary* to *Prov.* 1.7.

772.9 Without science, no Judaism.

Brann. *MGWJ,* li. 1893.

772.10 The study of science . . . leads to a knowledge of . . . the Creator.

E. Delmedigo, *Behinat HaDat,* 1519. q FJR, 16.

772.11 Torah and science are intertwined.

Elijah Gaon, to Baruch b. Jacob, 1778. q Baruch b. Jacob, *Euclid,* 1780, Introduction.

772.12 A knowledge of all the sciences is necessary to understand the Torah. These are all comprehended in it,—algebra, geometry, music, etc.

Elijah Gaon. q Israel b. Samuel Ashkenazi of Shklov, *Peat HaShulhan,* 1836, Preface.

772.13 There are many who have dabbled a little in science, and . . . since in such men the light of investigation has extinguished the light of belief, the multitude think it dangerous, and shrink from it. In Judaism, however, knowledge is a duty, and it is wrong to reject it.

Ibn Daud, *Emuna Rama,* 1168, 2.83, 4.103. q GHJ, iii. 364.

772.14 The only reason why the love of physical science has been implanted in man is that it might support the science of religion and its law, both together making an excellent combination.

Saadia, *Emunot VeDeot,* 933, 10.14, tr Rosenblatt, 394.

772.15 Science does not derogate from worship. It may exalt it immeasurably.

H. Samuel, *Belief and Action,* 1937, p. 88.

772.16 The sciences are pearls strung on a cord of faith.

J. Steinberg, *Mishlé Yehoshua,* 1885, 14.37, p. 80.

772.17 Science equips man, but does not guide him. It illumines the world for him to the region of the most distant stars, but it leaves night in his heart. It is invincible, but indifferent, neutral, unmoral.

Darmsteter, *Selected Essays,* 1895, p. 6.

772.18 Judaism is the only religion that has never entered into conflict, and never can, with either science or social progress. . . . They are old friendly voices, which it . . . salutes with joy, for it has heard them resound for centuries already, in the axioms of free thought and in the cry of the suffering heart.

Ibid., 274.

772.19 Let us . . . be more humble, more reasonable, in the evaluation of the competence of our science. Let us not continue to mistake the constructs of our scientifically disciplined imaginations for reality. Perhaps then we may regain insight and even faith.

Efroymson. *Reconstructionist,* June 12, 1953, p. 20.

772.20 It was the scientists who first made true democracy possible, for not only did they lighten our daily tasks but they made the finest works of art and thought, whose enjoyment was until recently the privilege of the favored classes, accessible to all.

Einstein, *Cosmic Religion,* 1931, p. 95.

772.21 Science without religion is lame, religion without science is blind.

Einstein, *Out of My Later Years*, 1950, p. 26.

772.22 Science belongs in common to all nations, and is not the special domain of any specific nation.

Falaquera, *Sefer HaMaalot*, (13C) 1894, p. 75.

772.23 Science, in the very act of solving problems, creates more of them.

Flexner, *Universities*, 1930, p. 19.

772.24 Science itself would not have existed were it not that Jewish piety, learning, and unrivaled penetration and clarity of thought have freed the mind of man of the condition in which the phenomena of nature appeared to him actuated—and thus explained—by the free-will of separate independent deities.

Haffkine. *Menorah Journal*, 1916, ii. 77.

772.25 The science that spares is the science that smites.

Harrison, *Religion of a Modern Liberal*, 1931, p. 46.

772.26 If physicians more learned than I wish to counsel me, inspire me, O God, with confidence in and obedience toward the recognition of them, for the study of science is great. It is not given to one alone to see all that others see. May I be moderate in everything, except in the knowledge of this science. . . . Grant me the strength and opportunity always to correct what I have acquired, always to extend its domain; for knowledge is boundless, and the spirit of man can also extend infinitely and enrich itself daily with new acquisitions.

M. Herz. "Physicians' Prayer." *Deutsches Museum*, 1783. Attributed to Maimonides.

772.27 As for secular sciences, blessed be the Merciful One who saved me from them.

Judah b. Asher. q LJG, 103.

772.28 Science too springs from God, and differs from Torah only in subject matter.

Judah Löw. q NDI, 104.

772.29 The pursuit of science in itself is never materialistic. It is a search for the principles of law and order in the universe, and as such an essentially religious endeavor.

Koestler, *Arrow in the Blue*, 1952, p. 52.

772.30 Whoever obstructs scientific inquiry clamps down the safety valve of public opinion, and puts the State in train for an explosion.

Lassalle, *Science and the Workingmen*, 1863.

772.31 What is false in science cannot be true in religion. Truth is one and indivisible. God is bound by His own laws.

Loewe, *A Rabbinic Anthology*, 1938, p. lxix.

772.32 Not one of the theoretical doctrines of Judaism was ever refuted by scientific arguments, nor will ever be subject to such refutation.

Neumark, *Philosophy of Judaism*, Jan. 29, 1908. *Essays*, 6.

772.33 What the world needs is a fusion of the sciences and the humanities. The humanities express the symbolic, poetic, and prophetic qualities of the human spirit. Without them we would not be conscious of our history; we would lose our aspirations and the graces of expression that move men's hearts. The sciences express the creative urge in man to construct a universe which is comprehensible in terms of the human intellect. Without them, mankind would find itself bewildered in a world of natural forces beyond comprehension, victims of ignorance, superstition and fear.

Rabi, *Engineering and Science*, Calif. Inst. of Technology, Commencement Address, June 1954.

772.34 The thesis that there is an inherent conflict between science and our immortal souls is simply untrue. . . . Virtue does not of necessity go hand in hand with primitive plumbing, and nobility can be found in a skyscraper no less than in a log-cabin.

Sarnoff, *Youth in a Changing World*, June 12, 1954.

772.35 Man is an inquisitive, an observing, a classifying animal.

C. Singer, *Religion and Science*. NSR, 1925, p. 118.

772.36 Each science is political, for science is coherent knowledge of the formation and progress of a creative thought and of that which this thought produces in the human race.

Zunz, *Politisch & Unpolitisch*, 1862, (*Gesam. Schr.* 1875, i. 338).

773. SCIENCE OF JUDAISM

773.1 That is the science of Judaism, a vivid realization of its great history and its peculiar doctrines . . . an irresistible impulse of self-examination.
Graetz, *History of the Jews*, 1895, v. 590.

773.2 Jews still have money for their cripples. . . . Only that poor cripple, the science of Judaism, which helped to tear down the fences of intolerance, still has no sheltering home.
D. Kaufmann, letter to Zunz, May 10, 1878.

773.3 . . . and I expect no improvement in this regard.
Zunz, letter to D. Kaufmann, June 24, 1878.

773.4 Zunz knows all the details of Rashi's life, what he did and where he lived and travelled; but I know what Rashi said and wrote.
Oettinger.

773.5 Equality for Jews in practice and life will result from the equality achieved by the Science of Judaism.
Zunz, *Zur Geschichte und Literatur*, 1845, i. 21.

774. SCORN

774.1 Fear not the taunt of men.
Bible: Isa., 51.7. See 28.22; *T: Aboda Zara*, 18b.

774.2 How long will scorners delight in scorning?
Bible: Prov., 1.22.

774.3 Cast out the scorner, and contention will go out.
Ibid., 22.10.

774.4 God created all things, great and small, and he who disdains the face of man disdains the face of the Lord.
Apocrypha: II Enoch, 44.1f. Cf 52.2.

775. SCRIBES

775.1 A ready scribe in the Law of Moses.
Bible: Ezra, 7.6.

775.2 (That) Jerusalem became the Holy City of the world was due not to the Temple and priests, but to the Levites and scribes.
Finkelstein, *The Pharisees*, 1940, p. 23.

775.3 The Scribes succeeded where the Prophets had failed. Through them the teachings proclaimed in the schools of the Prophets became the common property of the whole people.
L. Ginzberg, *Students, Scholars and Saints*, 1928, p. 2.

775.4 There is more stringency in respect to the teachings of the Scribes than of the Torah.
Mishna: Sanhedrin, 11.3. See Johanan. *TJ: Berakot*, 1.4. Raba. *T: Erubin*, 21b.

775.5 Except your righteousness exceed that of the scribes and Pharisees, ye shall in no wise enter the kingdom of heaven.
New Testament: Matt., 5.20.

775.6 The prophet and the elder [scribe] are messengers of God; the prophet needs His seal, the sign and the miracle, the elder does not need it, for he proves himself by the Torah.
Tanhum b. Hiyya. *TJ: Berakot*, 1.4.

776. SCROLL

776.1 Skins of sacred scrolls, pure white swaddlings of your soul.
Bialik, *In the Slaughter Town*, 1904. LGP, 31.

776.2 I see the Scroll aflame, and its letters soaring upward!
Hanina b. Teradion. *T: Aboda Zara*, 17b.

776.3 Even he who inherited a Scroll should write one himself.
Rabba b. Nahmani. *T: Sanhedrin*, 21b.

776.4 Sell not a Torah Scroll, even though you may not need it.
Talmud: Megilla, 27a.

776.5 The letters of the Torah Scroll must not be gilded.
Talmud: Sefer Torah, 1.7.

777. SEA

777.1 The sea is His, and He made it.
Bible: Ps., 95.5. See 107.23f.

777.2 Thus far shall you come, but no further; and here shall your proud waves be stayed.
Bible: Job, 38.11.

777.3 A people whose sons sail the seas cannot die, for its way is ever through water and burning.
U. Z. Greenberg, *Maasé BiYerushalmi. Israel Argosy*, 1952, p. 138.

777.4 I often feel as if the sea were really my own soul, and . . . from time to time there rise wondrous flower forms from the depths of my soul, and breathe forth perfume, and gleam, and vanish.

Heine, *Norderney*, 1826.

777.5 The face of the waters and the face of the heavens. . . .
And between them is my heart, a third sea,
Lifting up ever anew my waves of praise.

Judah Halevi, *Selected Poems*, 13.

777.6 They wander, they wander,
The waves of the sea.
In haste they are flowing;
Their faces are glowing
And sparkling with glee.
And while they're rejoicing
And making us gay,
They're mixing and mingling
And gone are for aye.
Yea, scattered and tossed;
Forever are lost!

Letteris, "Waves of the Sea," (*Tofes Kinor VeUgav*, 1860). tr FHH, 19.

777.7 The ocean is the world's great heart,
Beating eternally,
And bearing on its gloomy tide
The sky diurnally. . . .
O may my heart find rest with thee
In peace, fraternally.

Rodenberg, "Hymn," 1864, *Poems*, tr. Wm. Vocke, 1869, p. 46f.

777.8 It is not the seas that divide the peoples, but the peoples that divide the seas.

Sholom Aleichem, *Yidishé Folks Tzeitung*, 1902.

777.9 By the seashore, thorn-bushes are fir trees.

Talmud: Pesahim, 4a.

778. SEASON

778.1 Lo, the winter is past, the rain is over and gone; the flowers appear in the earth; the time of singing is come, and the voice of the turtle is heard in our land.

Bible: Cant., 2.11f.

778.2 Dawn crawls around naked on all four.
The threshold sleeps mist-covered at the door.
Tree stripped, house heavy like wet clay,
And Father Summer has gone away.
Dawn stretches out his gnarled hand tremblingly,

Pulls off a last leaf, to cover his nudity.

Bialostotzky, "Autumn." (*Lider un Essayn*, 1932, ii. 57). LGP, 348.

778.3 One swallow is no harbinger of spring.

Bonafos, *Sefer HaGedarim*, c. 1500.

778.4 The spring and two fair eyes together
Against my heart an oath have taken.

Heine, *New Spring: Lyrics*, 1844, #11.

778.5 Earth was a bride prisoned by the winter,
Whose soul was yearning for the times of love.

Judah Halevi, *Selected Poems*, 71.

778.6 In the winter the earth is pregnant. It bears within itself a great secret. In the summer, the secret is disclosed.

Nahman Bratzlav. q ZRN, 60.

778.7 If you sing through the summer, you weep in the winter.

Proverb (Yiddish). BJS, #1464.

778.8 The sweetest melody
Your heart can sing,
Keep for your autumn hour,
Not for the spring.
Glad is the blossom-time
With its own tune and chime;
Ah, but the sunset-day
Sing it away.

A. Raisen, tr M. Syrkin. *Reflex*, Sept. 1927, p. 109.

778.9 The end of the summer is more trying than the summer itself.

Talmud: Yoma, 29a.

779. SECRET

779.1 Bread eaten in secret is pleasant.
Bible: Prov., 9.17.

779.2 A bird of the air shall carry the voice.
Bible: Eccles., 10.20.

779.3 Your secret confide to but one in a thousand.
Apocrypha: Ben Sira, 6.6.

779.4 Secrecy necessarily breeds suspicion.

Brandeis, letter to C. Adler, Aug. 10, 1915. q LBG, 203.

779.5 If I cannot keep my secret, why expect another to keep it?

M. Dari, *Diwan*, 12C. S. Pinsker, *Likuté Kadmoniyot*, 94.

779.6 What you'd hide from an enemy, disclose not to a friend.

Ibn Gabirol, *Mibhar HaPeninim*, c. 1050, #315 (Lokman).

779.7 If you keep a secret, it's your prisoner; if you let it out, you're its prisoner.

Ibid., #321.

779.8 We know that the wages of secrecy are corruption. We know that in secrecy, error undetected will flourish and subvert.

J. Robert Oppenheimer, Feb. 1950.

779.9 Where people pass, tell no secrets.

Proverb. q *Gen. R.*, 74.2.

779.10 Confide a secret to a woman, but cut off her tongue.

Proverb. q Lipperheide, *Spruchwörterbuch.*

779.11 What three know is no secret.

Proverb (Yiddish). BJS, #1357.

779.12 What is told may not be spread without the teller's permission.

Rabba b. Nahmani. *T: Yoma*, 4b.

780. SECTARIANISM

780.1 Jews were not exiled till they separated into sects.

Johanan b. Nappaha. *TJ: Sanhedrin*, 10.5.

780.2 On Judgment Day, God will not ask to what sect you belonged, but what manner of life you led.

Kagan, *Hafetz Hayyim*, 1873.

780.3 Schismatics of one faith hate each other more cordially than they hate outsiders.

S. Levin, *The Arena*, 1932, p. 83.

780.4 "Ye shall not dissect yourselves" [*Deut.* 14.1],—ye shall not cut yourselves into separate sects.

Simeon b. Lakish. *T: Yebamot*, 13b.

781. SECURITY

781.1 The beloved of the Lord shall dwell in safety by Him.

Bible: Deut., 33.12.

781.2 They shall sit every man under his vine and under his fig tree, and none shall make them afraid.

Bible: Mic., 4.4.

781.3 The righteous are secure as a young lion.

Bible: Prov., 28.1.

781.4 You could best establish security if you imitate God's unceasing benignity.

Apocrypha: Aristeas, 188.

781.5 To attain the stability we yearn for in this world, we must first find stability within ourselves.

Baruch. q Sarnoff, *Youth in a Changing World*, June 12, 1954.

781.6 No passenger on board the most seaworthy vessel may rejoice in his sense of security as long as there be one compartment not properly safeguarded.

Eybeshitz, *Yaarot Debash*, 1779, ii. 55b. q BSJ, 356.

781.7 Culture cannot flourish amid privation and want; men must have physical security.

M. Ezekiel, *$2500 a Year*, 1936.

781.8 Your greatest security lies in your friendships.

Fink, *Release from Nervous Tension*, 1943, p. 228.

781.9 It is the emancipation from the security of Paradise which is the basis for man's truly human development.

Fromm, *Psychoanalysis and Religion*, 1950, p. 84.

781.10 Security and equality cannot bring man happiness . . . but they can bring him something no less important—dignity—a sense of social value and individual worth.

H. Greenberg, "To a Communist Friend," 1936. GIE, 254.

781.11 Dine on onions in security rather than on geese while your heart is restless.

Judah b. Ilai. *T: Pesahim*, 114a.

781.12 Rather herbs in safety than meat in danger.

Samuel HaNagid, *Ben Mishlé*, 11C, #39.

781.13 Is there anywhere, east or west, a place where we are safe?

Judah Halevi. See GHJ, iii. 346.

781.14 The virtue of a state is its security.

Spinoza, *Political Treatise*, 1677, 1.6.

782. SEED

782.1 Seed for posterity; bread for the present.

Boerne, *Ankündigung der Zeitschwingen*, July 1819.

782.2 If you have a seedling in your hand, and they say to you: "Look, here comes the Messiah!" go on and plant the seedling first, and then come out to meet Messiah.

Johanan b. Zakkai. *ARN* B, ch 31, ed Schechter, p. 34. q Klausner, *Messianic Ideal in Israel*, 1955, p. 396.

782.3 God has a hidden and wise design . . . in the seed which . . . transforms earth and water into its own substance.
Judah Halevi, *Cuzari*, c. 1135, 4.23.

782.4 Before the seed in the ground begins to sprout, it must first be decomposed.
Kagan, *Hafetz Hayyim*, 1873. q YSS, 168. See Nahman Bratzlav, letter to his brother, q MRH, 151.

783. SEEKING GOD

783.1 You shall find Him, if you search after Him with all your heart and with all your soul.
Bible: Deut., 4.29. Cf *Jer.*, 29.13.

783.2 Seek ye the Lord while He may be found.
Bible: Isa., 55.6.

783.3 It is time to seek the Lord.
Bible: Hos., 10.12.

783.4 Seek Me, and live.
Bible: Amos, 5.4. Cf *Ps.*, 9.11.

783.5 Seek ye the Lord, all ye humble of the earth.
Bible: Zeph., 2.3.

783.6 In the day of my trouble I seek the Lord.
Bible: Ps., 77.3.

783.7 Happy are they that . . . seek Him with the whole heart.
Ibid., 119.2.

783.8 Can you by searching find out God?
Bible: Job, 11.7.

783.9 Oh that I knew where I might find Him!
Ibid., 23.3.

783.10 Ye cannot find the depth of man's heart, . . . then how can ye search out God?
Apocrypha: Judith, 8.14.

783.11 Before you can find God, you must lose yourself.
Baal Shem. q SSJ, i. 30.

783.12 In their hearts will all that seek Thee comprehend Thee, and in their thoughts will they find Thee.
Bahya, *Hobot HaLebabot, Bakasha*, 1040.

783.13 I seek my God: dost thou know where He may be?
Chernihovsky, *In the Thick Cloud*, 1902, tr Snowman.

783.14 Dark are Thy ways! O who can find them?
O Lord of distance, and yet we see

the dayspring a wisp of Thy glory behind them,
the nightfall a step on the path to Thee.
Fleg, *Wall of Weeping*, 1919, tr H. Wolfe, 101.

783.15 Judaism makes man find God where he finds himself.
S. R. Hirsch, "Mila." *Gesam. Schr.*, 1921, iii. 293.

783.16 Judaism makes man find God in the act of seeking Him.
Ibid. q BKF, 204.

783.17 At the dawn I seek Thee, Rock and Refuge tried.
Ibn Gabirol, *Selected Religious Poems*, #1, tr Zangwill.

783.18 Longing I've sought Thy nearness,
With all my heart have I called Thee,
And going out to meet Thee,
I found Thee coming toward me.
Judah Halevi, *Selected Poems*, 134f; 168.

783.19 Whatever the creed of his father, . . . a religious man must seek and discover God for himself.
L. H. Montagu. *JQRo*, xi. 231.

783.20 If you are seeking God, O mind, go out of yourself and seek diligently; but if you remain amid the heavy encumbrances of the body or the self-conceits with which the understanding is familiar, . . . not yours is the quest for the things of God.
Philo, *Allegorical Interpretation*, 3.15.

783.21 Nothing is better than to search for the true God, even if the discovery of Him eludes human capacity, since the very wish to learn, if earnestly entertained, produces untold joys and pleasures.
Philo, *Special Laws*, i. 7.

783.22 He is ever to be sought, though mysterious and unrevealable.
Zohar, Gen., 1b.

784. SEGREGATION

784.1 Separate yourself from the nations, and eat not with them, . . . for their works are unclean. . . . They offer sacrifices to the dead, worship evil spirits, . . . and have no heart.
Apocrypha: Jubilees, 22.16ff.

784.2 Away from the hive, the bee pines away and dies; isolated from society or sharing insufficiently in its activities, man suffers from a similar malady very little studied up to now, called listlessness; when isolation is prolonged, as in solitary confinement, characteristic mental troubles appear.

Bergson, *Two Sources of Morality and Religion*, 1935, p. 95.

784.3 We decree and order that from now on, and for all time, Christians shall not eat or drink with Jews, nor admit them to feasts, nor cohabit with them, nor bathe with them.

*Eugenius IV, *Decree*, 1442.

784.4 How could the holy flame have been kept burning in our breasts had there been no distinctive laws . . . to remind us that we are consecrated to . . . a divine mission? But whosoever honestly thinks that our isolation is the result of pride or hostility to our fellow beings is the victim of a deplorable delusion.

S. R. Hirsch, *Nineteen Letters*, (1836), #15, p. 141f. See #7, p. 69.

784.5 They say we Jews are clannish. It is true, and I hope it will remain true until conditions change. We are not clannish from choice. We are not willing to be received on sufferance or with reservations. Until the time comes when social barriers are so completely destroyed that we mingle among men and women of all creeds and races without thought of distinction we must needs remain clannish and cling to our own if we would preserve our self-respect.

S. Untermeyer, speech, April 27, 1923.

785. SELF

785.1 "That your brother may live *with* you" [*Lev.* 25.36],—your own life comes first.

Akiba. *T: Baba Metzia*, 62a.

785.2 There is one who is wise for many, but for himself is a fool.

Apocrypha: Ben Sira, 37.19.

785.3 No relation like oneself.

Arama, *Akedat Yitzhak, Ruth*, 15C.

785.4 Life with others is good, but to live with oneself is better.

Auerbach, *Landhaus am Rhein*, 1869.

785.5 Sociability is the art of unlearning to be preoccupied with yourself.

O. Blumenthal. q TL, p. 271.

785.6 The phrase "self-made man" is most misleading. We have power to mar, but we alone cannot make.

Brandeis, *A Call to the Educated Jew*, 1916.

785.7 Without being and remaining oneself, there is no love.

Buber, *Between Man and Man*, 1947, p. 43.

785.8 Who tends to himself as to his cattle will never be sick.

Caspi, *Commentary*, to *Prov.*, 12.

785.9 The eye which sees all things cannot view itself.

D'Israeli, *Literary Character*, 1795, ch 8.

785.10 The true value of a human being is determined primarily by the measure and sense in which he has attained to liberation from the self.

Einstein, *The World As I See It*, 1934, p. 245.

785.11 In Hebrew, the word for "I" consists of the same letters as the word for "nothing."

J. Falk, *Binyan Yehoshua*, 5548, 12.9.

785.12 That which cannot maintain itself by its own power, has no right to exist.

Heine, *Norderney*, 1826.

785.13 No bird can fly over itself.

Ibid. (Fichte, *Transcendental Idealism*).

785.14 If a people cannot help itself, it cannot be helped at all.

Herzl, address, I Zionist Congress, Aug. 29, 1897.

785.15 If I am not for myself, who is for me? And if I am [only] for myself, what am I?

Hillel. *Mishna: Abot*, 2.4.

785.16 First become a blessing to yourself that you may be a blessing to others.

S. R. Hirsch, *Nineteen Letters*, (1836), #12, p. 113.

785.17 He who does not love himself, does not love well; and he who does not hate himself, does not hate well.

Koestler, *Arrow in the Blue*, 1952, p. 26.

785.18 It is my profound belief that man has the power to pull himself by his own hair out of the mire.

Ibid., 38.

785.19 Every human being must know how . . . to be himself.

Lazare, *Nationalism and Jewish Emancipation*, 1889.

785.20 Only few men are found that do not sin against themselves.

Maimonides, *Guide for the Perplexed*, 1190, 3.12.

785.21 A man can see all plague-spots, except his own. . . . A man may annul all vows, except his own.

Mishna: Nega'im, 2.5.

785.22 We are never more modern, never more progressive, than when we are ourselves.

Nordau, speech, Aug. 14, 1907.

785.23 I am formed of soul and body, I seem to have mind, reason, sense, yet I find that none of them is really mine. Where was my body before birth, and whither will it go when I have departed? What has become of the changes produced by life's various stages in the seemingly permanent self? Where is the babe that once I was . . .? Whence came the soul, whither will it go?

Philo, *Cherubim*, 32.

785.24 When the kettle boils over, it pours on its own side.

Proverb. q Judan. *Eccles. R., 7.9.*

785.25 If a man spits in the air, it will fall on his own face.

Proverb, *ibid.*

785.26 Ten enemies can't harm a man as much as he harms himself.

Proverb (Yiddish).

785.27 Everyone is related to oneself; none can incriminate himself.

Raba. *T: Sanhedrin, 9b.*

785.28 He who promotes Heaven's glory promotes his own too.

Seder Eliyahu Rabbah, ch 14, ed Friedmann, 65.

785.29 No tongue speaks as much ill of us as our own.

Sholom Aleichem, *Olom Habo*, 1904.

785.30 The first and only foundation of virtue, or the rule of right living, is seeking one's own true interest.

Spinoza, *Ethics*, 1677, v. Pr 41, Proof. See iv. Append. 8.

785.31 To continue to be whatever we happen to be is in the long run for the greatest human happiness.

Wolfson, "Escaping Judaism." *Menorah Journal*, 1921, vii. 72.

785.32 The strength whereby God saves is the strength that is our own.

Zangwill, "Our Own." ZVJ, 307.

786. SELF-CONFIDENCE

786.1 Self consciousness, extending to pride, if properly directed, can become a safe moral principle.

Auerbach, *Das Landhaus am Rhein*, 1869.

786.2 In matters of holiness, man has a moral right to lift his heart to God.

Baal Shem. q Petahia Azriel, *Or HaGanuz*, 42.

786.3 He who places implicit confidence in his genius will find himself some day utterly defeated and deserted.

Disraeli, *Alroy*, 1833, 10.17.

786.4 The worst of poisons: to mistrust one's power.

Heine, *Sonnets*, #1, 1821.

786.5 Trust not in yourself till the day of your death.

Hillel. *Mishna: Abot*, 2.4.

786.6 Who has confidence in himself will gain the confidence of others.

Lazerov, *Enciklopedie fun Idishe Vitzen*, 1928, #469.

786.7 Everyone is wise in one's own eyes.

Proverb. q Spinoza, *Ethics*, i. Appendix.

786.8 Rely not on what your predecessors composed, for none but you can know the trouble of your heart, and none but you can heal your wound.

Zerahia, *Sefer HaYashar*, (c. 1300) 1853, Preface, p. 2.

787. SELF-CONTEMPT

787.1 Our greatest need is emancipation from self-contempt.

Ahad HaAm, *Some Consolation*, 1892. *Selected Essays*, 202.

787.2 Of all afflictions, the worst is self-contempt.

Auerbach, *Lucifer*, 1847.

787.3 My grandmother, the beautiful daughter of a family which had suffered much from persecution, had imbibed that dislike for her race which the vain are too apt to adopt when they find that they are born to public contempt.

Disraeli, *Life and Writings of Isaac D'Israeli*, 1848.

787.4 He who cannot at times hate himself or despise himself must needs be lacking in conscience.

Klatzkin, *In Praise of Wisdom*, 1943, p. 310.

787.5 Self-hatred is the Jew's patriotism.
Koestler, *Thieves in the Night,* 1946, p. 278.

787.6 A strong feeling of being part and parcel of the group and having a positive attitude toward it is . . . the sufficient condition for the avoidance of attitudes based on self-hatred.
Lewin, "Self-Hatred Among Jews." CJR, 1941; LRS, 199.

787.7 Christians feel nothing but contempt for the Jew ashamed of his faith.
*Saniford, 1932. q BSS, 47.

787.8 The ancient Temple was treated irreverently by non-Jews only after Jews had done so first [*Jer.* 7.11, *Ps.* 80.13]. . . . Scholars are not held in contempt unless they first hold one another in contempt.
Sefer Hasidim, 13C, #224, p. 78f.

787.9 Three hate their own kind: dogs, cocks, and prostitutes.
Talmud: Pesahim, 113b.

788. SELF-CONTROL

788.1 He that is slow to anger is better than the mighty, and he that rules his spirit than he that takes a city.
Bible: Prov., 16.32.

788.2 What is the highest form of rulership? To rule oneself and not to be carried away by impulses.
Apocrypha: Aristeas, 222.

788.3 If ye rule over your inclinations and discipline your heart, ye shall be preserved in life, and after death obtain mercy.
Apocrypha: IV Ezra, 14.34.

788.4 The greatest of virtues, self-control.
Apocrypha: IV Macc., 1.2.

788.5 Blessed Israel! When they are busy with Torah and good deeds, they master their inclination, not their inclination them.
Banaah. *T: Aboda Zara,* 5b.

788.6 Who is a hero? He who conquers his will.
Ben Zoma. *Mishna: Abot,* 4.1.

788.7 One is master of oneself only to decline the first cup, not the second.
Boerne.

788.8 Self-control is not worth a farthing unless we build up a great self worth controlling.
M. R. Cohen. *New Republic,* Aug. 31, 1918, p. 143. *Faith of a Liberal,* 76.

788.9 The world exists only because of self-restraint in strife.
Eleazar b. Pedat. *T: Hullin,* 89a.

788.10 Be kings, not slaves, of your passions.
Elijah b. Raphael, *Tzavaah,* 18C. AHE, 308.

788.11 Trust not in your wisdom, unless you can master your desire.
Ibn Gabirol, *Mibhar HaPeninim,* c. 1050, #184.

788.12 Happy is he who controls his inclination.
Joshua b. Levi. *T: Aboda Zara,* 19a.

788.13 Liberty is not fool-proof. For its beneficent working it demands self-restraint.
O. H. Kahn, speech, University of Wisconsin, Jan. 14, 1918.

788.14 Who cannot command oneself shall not command others.
Leon of Modena, *Tzemah Tzaddik,* 1600.

788.15 Man has six organs to serve him, and he is master only of three. He cannot control his eye, ear or nose, but he can his mouth, hand and foot.
Levi. *Genesis Rabbah,* 67.3.

788.16 Rule your spirit, lest others rule your body.
Satanov, *Mishlé Asaf,* 1789, 1792, 24.2 (q SRH, 44).

788.17 Man who makes a harness for his beast should certainly fashion one for his appetites.
Talmud J: Sanhedrin, 10.1.

789. SELF-EMANCIPATION

789.1 The emancipation of the Jewish people can be gained only by our own efforts.
Borochov, *National Self Help,* Aug. 6, 1915. BNC, 87.

789.2 No savior from without can come
To those that live and are enslaved.
Their own Messiah they must be.
Frug, "Resurrection." FJA, 388.

789.3 There is no hero anywhere in this wide world who can free the man that forgets his own chains.
Mendel of Kotzk. q Cahn, *Der Rebbe fun Kotzk,* p. 132.

789.4 They can only set free men free. . . .
And there is no need of that!
Free men set themselves free.
Oppenheim, "The Slave," *Songs for the New Age,* 1914, p. 24.

789.5 A prisoner cannot free himself.
Talmud: Berakot, 5b.

790. SELF-RESPECT

790.1 Ancestors who wandered from land to land, ragged and disgraced, the dust of all the highways in their hair and beards, every man's hand against them, despised by the lowest yet never despising themselves, honoring God but not as a beggar honors an almsgiver, calling out in their suffering not to the Lord of Mercy but to the God of Justice.
Beer-Hofmann, *Der Tod Georgs*, 1900. q LRB, 19.

790.2 All must respect those who respect themselves.
Disraeli, *Coningsby*, 1844.

790.3 As a man thinks of himself, so will he be.
Gentili, *Mleket Mahshebet, VaYehi*, 7.

790.4 I have been wont to bear my head right high.
Heine, *Sonnets: To my Mother*, #1, 1821.

790.5 Scholars die prematurely for lack of self-respect.
Jose b. Judan of Kfar Babli. *ARN*, ch 29.

790.6 We cannot do without being needed, and without something of which we are proud.
Kaplan, *Future of the American Jew*, 1948, p. 82.

790.7 Despite all his humiliations, the Jew has never been degraded in his own eyes.
Lehmann. *L'Universe Israélite*, Nov. 1, 1891.

790.8 Raising the self-esteem of the minority groups is one of the most strategic means for the improvement of inter-group relations.
Lewin. *Journal of Issues*, 1946. LRS, 215.

790.9 You feel oppressed by your Judaism only as long as you do not take pride in it.
Pappenheim, *Blätter d. jüd. Frauenbundes*, July 1936, p. 33.

790.10 A quiet, dignified pride in the creative achievements of Jewish history is no ugly chauvinism. It is the only effective answer to the filth of the agitator.
Sachar.

790.11 The greatest evil urge is to forget that you are the child of a king.
Solomon of Karlin. q YHS, ii. 178.

790.12 The chief merit of your leadership is that it seeks to restore or create the self-respect of the Jewish people. . . . In Palestine the Jew is on horseback, head up, free from the care what others think of him.
*Wedgewood, to Zionist Agency. Parliamentary Debate, June 9, 1942.

790.13 Help and respect can come to a people only through self-help and self-respect.
S. S. Wise, *Sermons and Addresses*, 1905, p. 5.

791. SELF-RIGHTEOUSNESS

791.1 Say not in your heart: "For my righteousness the Lord has brought me in to possess this land," whereas for the wickedness of these nations the Lord drives them out from before you.
Bible: Deut., 9.4.

791.2 We do not present our supplications before Thee because of our righteousness, but because of Thy great compassions.
Bible: Dan., 9.18.

791.3 Justify not yourself in the sight of God.
Apocrypha: Ben Sira, 7.5.

791.4 As you lie down at night, you add up everything you did that day. And when a man calculates his hours and sees that he did not waste a moment, when his heart beats high with pride, then—up in Heaven —they take all his good works, crush them into a ball, and hurl it down into the abyss.
Ber. q BTH, i. 106.

791.5 The merit one attributes to oneself Scripture attributes to others.
Jose b. Zimra. *T: Berakot*, 10b.

791.6 The soul should not attribute to itself, but to God, its toil for virtue.
Philo, *Allegories*, 3.46.

791.7 Even if all the world tells you, "You are righteous," consider yourself a sinner.
Simlai. *T: Nidda*, 30b.

791.8 I prefer the wicked, who knows that he is wicked, to the righteous, who regards himself as righteous. . . . He who feels that he is a *tzaddik*, is thereby no longer a *tzaddik*.
Yaakov Yitzhak of Lublin. q Shemen, *Lublin*, 161.

792. SELF-SACRIFICE

792.1 Not alms but self-sacrifice leads man to perfection.
Aaron of Karlin. q YHS, ii. 167.

792.2 Let us die manfully for our brethren, and not leave a cause of reproach against our glory!
Apocrypha: 1 Macc., 9.10.

792.3 In critical times men can save their lives only by risking them.
Blum, *For All Mankind,* (1941) 1946, p. 128.

792.4 They will let you live only when you learn to die.
Herzl, *Das neue Ghetto,* 1896.

792.5 It is the duty of the individual to bear hardships, even to suffer martyrdom, for the common welfare.
Judah Halevi, *Cuzari,* c. 1135, 3.19.

792.6 The patriarchs and prophets offered their lives for Israel.
Nathan. *Mekilta,* to *Exod.* 12.1. See *Gen.* 44.33; *Exod.* 32.32; *Apocalypse of Sedrach,* 5.

792.7 Greater love has no man than this, that a man lay down his life for his friends.
New Testament: John, 15.13.

792.8 Who sacrifices himself for Israel is worthy of greatness and of the Holy Spirit.
Num. R., 15.20.

792.9 Not by worshipping themselves but by sacrificing themselves to something conceived as larger than themselves, have nations or institutions become saturated with the spirit of greatness.
Zangwill, *War for the World,* 1915, 1921, p. 130.

793. SELF-SUFFICIENCY

793.1 There is no barber that cuts his own hair.
Abin. *Lev. R.,* 14.9.

793.2 Lord, be Thou neither against us nor for us!
Bar Kochba, attrib. to. *TJ: Taanit,* 4.6.

794. SELFISHNESS

794.1 It is the individual who is not interested in his fellow men who has the greatest difficulties in life.
A. Adler, *Social Interest,* 1939.

794.2 The man who is always watching for his own gain is a traitor at heart.
Apocrypha: Aristeas, 270.

794.3 There is no room for God in him who is full of himself.
Baal Shem. q MRH, 371.

794.4 Work and trouble are redoubled because everyone wants his portion for himself alone.
Bahya, *Hobot HaLebabot,* 1040, 8.3.22.

794.5 The strongest barrier to faith is selfishness.
Baron, *In Quest of Integrity,* 1936, p. 14.

794.6 It does not pay even a people to live only for itself.
Beer-Hofmann, *Young David,* 1933.

794.7 The most hardened egotism is but frozen compassion, and the most tender sympathy is but dissolved selfishness.
Boerne, *Fragmente und Aphorismen,* 1840, #268.

794.8 Self-centeredness is a form of infantilism.
J. Gordon, "Growing Up Jewishly." CCAR, 1952.

794.9 Torah abides only in him who ignores himself.
Johanan b. Nappaha. *T: Sota,* 21a.

794.10 Men in general, but more particularly the insane, love to speak of themselves, and on this theme, they even become eloquent.
Lombroso, *The Man of Genius,* 1889, iv. ch 1.

794.11 An ignorant man believes that the whole universe exists only for him. . . . If, therefore, anything happens to him contrary to his expectations, he at once concludes that the whole universe is evil.
Maimonides, *Guide for the Perplexed,* 1190, 3.12.

794.12 It is not only individuals—peoples too cannot live merely for themselves. The whole world must be redeemed.
Peretz, *Der Dichter,* 1910. LP, 325.

794.13 Many a one prays and is not heard, because he remains heedless of the plight and needs of others.
Sefer Hasidim, 13C, #1023, p. 257.

794.14 He who thinks himself more blessed because he enjoys benefits which others do not, . . . is ignorant of true blessedness.
Spinoza, *Theologico-Political Treatise,* 1670, ch 3.

794.15 Heaven's gate is shut to him who comes alone,
Save thou a soul, and it shall save thine own.
*Whittier, "The Two Rabbis," 1868.

794.16 "I stood between the Lord and you" [*Deut.* 5.5]. The "I" always stands between God and us.

Yehiel Michal. q Moshe Eliakim, *Kehilat Moshé*, 1906, p. 30. Attrib. to Ber. See J. L. Maimon, *Saré HaMeah*, i. 218.

794.17 Selfishness is the only real atheism; aspiration, unselfishness, the only real religion.

Zangwill, *Children of the Ghetto*, 1892, ch 16.

795. SENSE

795.A. Sense Perception

795.A.1 If you wish to be pure in mind, guard your senses.

Apocrypha: Patriarchs, Reuben, 6.1.

795.A.2 We only see what we desire, only hear what we long for.

M. H. Luzzatto, *LaYesharim Tehilla,* 1743, 2.1.

795.A.3 He who is held in bondage by his senses can never enjoy even a dream of freedom. It is only by complete escape from them that we arrive at a state of freedom from fear.

Philo, *Cherubim,* 23.

795.A.4 Describe a tune to the deaf and a rainbow to the blind.

Proverb (Yiddish). BJS, #74.

795.B. Common Sense

795.B.1 In America we have not decreed that common sense and erudition are incompatible.

A. Jacobi. q Truax, *The Doctors Jacobi,* p. 149.

795.B.2 I speak to you common sense, and you say "Heaven will have mercy!"

Jose b. Kisma. *T: Aboda Zara,* 18a.

795.B.3 Solid good sense is often nonsense solidified.

L. Stein, *Journey into the Self,* 1950, p. 256.

796. SERVANT

796.1 A servant of servants shall he be unto his brethren.

Bible: Gen., 9.25.

796.2 Oppress not a hired servant, . . . whether he be of thy brethren or of thy strangers in the land.

Bible: Deut., 24.14.

796.3 Also upon the servants and handmaids in those days will I pour out My spirit.

Bible: Joel, 3.2.

796.4 Did I despise the cause of my manservant or maid-servant when they contended with me? . . . Did not he who made me in the womb make him?

Bible: Job, 31.13, 15.

796.5 The great happiness in life is not to donate but to serve.

Brandeis, address, Boston, March 20, 1913.

796.6 The more maids the more lewdness, the more servants the more exploitation.

Hillel. *Mishna: Abot,* 2.7.

796.7 Make not heavy your Gentile servant's burden; oppress him not; give him of all you eat and drink; offend him not with words.

Maimonides, *Yad: Abadim,* 1180, 9.8. Caro, *Yoré Deah,* 1564, #267.

796.8 Servants, be obedient to your masters.

New Testament: Eph., 6.5. See *I Peter,* 2.18.

796.9 Behave to your servants as you desire God to behave to you.

Philo. q Antonius, *Sermons,* 57. See *Eph.,* 6.9; *Col.* 4.1.

796.10 It is enough for a servant that he be like his master.

Proverb. q Ulla. *T: Berakot,* 58b. *NT: Matt.,* 10.25.

796.11 If you have hired yourself to someone, pull his wool!

Rab. *T: Yoma,* 20b.

796.12 None has a worse servant than he who is his own master.

Saphir, *Badenmantel-Gedanken.* SHW, i. 375.

796.13 Sell not your servant to a cruel master.

Sefer Hasidim, 13C, #141, p. 64.

797. SERVICE OF GOD

797.1 Thou Israel . . . art My servant.
Bible: Isa., 41.8f.

797.2 My servant . . . shall make the right to go forth to the nations.
Ibid., 42.1.

797.3 My servant . . . shall not lift his voice . . . A bruised reed shall he not break, and a dimly burning wick shall he not quench.
Ibid., 42.2f.

797.4 Serve Him with a whole heart and with a willing mind.
Bible: 1 Chron., 28.9.

797.5 Serve the Lord in all things, even in trifles.

Baal Shem. q Dubnow, *History of Jews in Russia,* i. 226.

797.6 Service of God consists in what we do to our neighbor.

Baeck, *Essence of Judaism,* 1936, p. 197.

797.7 Proclaim yourself solemnly and joyfully, "Servant of God."

S. R. Hirsch, *Nineteen Letters,* 1836, #4.

797.8 Him will I serve. . . . I ask not to be free.

A. Ibn Ezra, tr Lucas. *Jewish Year,* 1898.

797.9 God's service spells freedom.

Judah Halevi, *Cuzari,* c.1135, 5.25. See *Selected Poems,* 121.

797.10 If you weary in the service of God, it means you are carrying other burdens, not that of the yoke of Heaven.

Kranz. q Mendel, *Emeth VeEmuna,* 1940, p. 27.

797.11 The purpose of man's creation is the service of God.

Landsofer, *Tzavaah,* c.1710 (1717). AHE, 286.

797.12 Every tzaddik has his own way of serving God.

Leib of Spola. q HLH, 74.

797.13 One Yom Kippur, when the service was completed, Joseph Duber said to a rich man who remained in the synagog to join in the reading of Psalms: "A soldier who of his own will deserts from one branch of the service to another is court-martialed and disciplined. You have joined the poor, whose piety demands the recital of Psalms; but your post is among the rich, whose service is to lift not their voice but their hand, to do charity!"

Michelson, *Shemen HaTob,* 1905, p. 140.

797.14 The purpose of serving God . . . is to promote man's perfection.

Norzi, *Orah Hayyim,* 1579, p. 2b.

797.15 To be the servant of God is man's greatest boast.

Philo, *Cherubim,* 31.

797.16 Uninterrupted service under Thee is better not only than freedom, but even than the most extensive dominion.

Philo, *Noah's Planting,* 12.

797.17 You wish to serve the Most High —serve your self.

Solomon of Karlin. q YHS, ii. 178.

797.18 For the Jew, nature and men are nothing of themselves; they are for the service of God.

*Taine, *History of English Literature,* 1864, ii. 169f.

797.19 To serve Him is perfect freedom and to worship Him the soul's purest happiness.

Union Prayer Book, 1940, i. 34.

797.20 Just as our fathers, Abraham, Isaac and Jacob, founded . . . each a new service according to his character: one the service of love, the other that of stern justice, the third that of beauty, so each one of us in his own way shall devise something new in the light of teaching and of service, and do what has not yet been done.

Yehiel Michael. q Buber, *Way of Man,* 16.

797.21 All service of God must be performed with gladness and zest, otherwise it is not perfect.

Zohar, Lev., 8a.

798. SEX

798.1 Male and female created He them.
Bible: Gen., 1.27.

798.2 Am I to lose because I am a male?
Admon. *Mishna: Ketubot,* 13.3.

798.3 Sex-appeal is the keynote of our whole civilization.

Bergson, *Two Sources of Morality and Religion,* 1935, p. 291.

798.4 Much of our most highly valued cultural heritage has been acquired at the cost of sexuality.

Freud, *Outline,* 114.

798.5 Amoebas at the start
Were not complex;
They tore themselves apart
And started sex.
Guiterman, "Sex."

798.6 Breathes there a man with hide so tough
Who says two sexes aren't enough?
Hoffenstein, *Love Songs,* #3 (*Poems,* 1928, p. 206).

798.7 Sensual desire has merely pleasure for its object; amorous desire . . . aims at more, at procreation. . . . To counteract willfully this aim of nature, when it may be obtained, is downright sinning.

M. Mendelssohn, letter, Apr. 24, 1773. *Jerusalem,* ii. 248.

798.8 The act of sexual union is holy and pure. . . . The Lord created all things in accordance with His wisdom and whatever He created cannot possibly be shameful or ugly. . . . When a man is in union with his wife in a spirit of holiness and purity, the Divine Presence is with them.
Nahmanides, *Iggeret HaKodesh*, 13C. q BWC, 75.

798.9 Men would not vie with women, nor women with men, in those matters which concern only the opposite sex.
Philo, *Sacrifices of Abel and Cain*, 30.

798.10 All that the Holy One created, He created male and female.
Rab. *T: Baba Bathra*, 74b.

798.11 Jews were too busy having children to bother with sex.
M. Samuel, *World of Sholom Aleichem*, 1944, p. 283.

798.12 Wherever you find sexual license you may expect disease.
Simlai. *Gen. R.*, 36.5. *TJ: Sota*, 1.5.

798.13 The bond between male and female is the secret of true faith.
Zohar, Gen., 101b.

799. SHADE

799.1 Shadows tell that light is near.
I. Friedmann, *Imré Bina*, 1912, p. 29. q CPP, #1963.

799.2 Light and shade go together in the world.
Mendelé, *BeSether Raam*, 1886.

799.3 The shadows show off the light.
Montefiore, *Rabbinic Anthology*, 1938, p. xv.

800. SHAME

800.1 There is shame that brings sin and shame that brings honor.
Apocrypha: Ben Sira, 4.21.

800.2 Many precepts are fulfilled only out of shame.
Bahya, *Hobot HaLebabot*, 1040, 2.5.

800.3 Be ashamed before God as you are before His creatures.
Hasdai, *Ben HaMelek VeHaNazir*, c.1230, ch 26.

800.4 The chief of all the ten virtues is a sense of shame.
Ibn Gabirol, *Mibhar HaPeninim*, c.1050, #48.

800.5 Shyness is a good trait. It leads to fear of sin.
Mekilta, to *Exod.*, 20.17. *T: Nedarim*, 20a.

800.6 Shame is an iron fence against sin.
Orhot Tzaddikim, 15C, ch 3.

800.7 Where there's no shame before men, there's no fear of God.
Proverb (Yiddish). BJS, #368.

800.8 If one is ashamed of a sin, all his sins are forgiven.
Rab. *T: Berakot*, 12b.

800.9 Humiliation is worse than physical pain.
Talmud: Sota, 8b.

800.10 Jerusalem was destroyed because its people had no shame.
Ulla b. Ishmael. *T: Sabbath*, 119b.

801. SHECHEM

801.1 Henceforth Shechem shall be called a city of imbeciles.
Apocrypha: Patriarchs, Levi, 7.2.

802. SHEKINA

802.1 The Lord thy God walketh in the midst of thy camp . . . therefore shall thy camp be holy.
Bible: Deut., 23.15.

802.2 In Thy presence is fullness of joy.
Bible: Ps., 16.11.

802.3 Cast me not away from Thy presence.
Ibid., 51.13.

802.4 God stands in the congregation of God; in the midst of the judges He judges.
Ibid., 82.1.

802.5 Where men gather for worship, where judges sit as a court and where even one man engages in Torah, the Shekina is there.
Abin b. Adda. *T: Berakot*, 6a. Cf *Matt.*, 18.20.

802.6 The Shekina accompanied Israel wherever they were exiled, and will return with them at the restoration.
Akiba. *Mekilta*, to *Exod.* 12.41.
Nathan. *Num. R.*, 7.10.

802.7 The Shekina will one day fill the world from end to end.
Cohen b. Abba. *Esther Rabbah*, 1.4.

802.8 Little children, too, receive the Divine Presence.
Eleazar b. Shammua. *Midrash Tehillim*, #32, to *Ps.* 22.27.

802.9 When you sit at your table to eat, remember you are in the presence of the King.
Eliezer b. Isaac, *Orhot Hayyim*, c.1050. AHE, 43.

802.10 There is no place on earth devoid of the Shekina.

Gamaliel. *Pesikta Kahana,* ch 1, ed Buber (1898) 1925, 2b.

802.11 Even when Jews are unclean, the Shekina is with them.

Hanina b. Hama. *T: Gittin,* 57a. *Sifré, Num.,* #1.

802.12 If I am here, all is here; if I am not here, what is here?

Hillel. *T: Sukka,* 53a. Ref. to God.

802.13 The Divine Presence is everywhere.

Hoshaia Rabba. *T: Baba Bathra,* 25a. See *Kiddushin,* 31a.

802.14 As long as the Shekina is in exile, the Name is incomplete.

Jose. *Zohar, Num.,* 147b.

802.15 The beauty and magnificence of the Shekina can be revealed only in a people that lives a fully rounded life on its own land.

Kook, *Azkara,* 1937, i. q ABJ, 82.

802.16 When the tide rises and a cave on shore is filled with water, the sea is not diminished. So when the Tent of Meeting was filled with Shekina's radiance, the world was no less full of the Glory of God.

Levi. *Num. R.,* 12.4.

802.17 If we desire to . . . be truly men of God, we must wake from our sleep and bear in mind that the great King is over us.

Maimonides, *Guide for the Perplexed,* 1190, 3.52.

802.18 God gave the Jewish soul a special grace, by which it is enabled to feel His sensible presence.

Manasseh b. Israel, *Nishmat Hayyim,* 1652. q SHZ, i. 30.

802.19 Guard your mouth from all evil, purify and sanctify yourself from all sin, and I shall be with you everywhere.

Meir. *T: Berakot,* 17a.

802.20 In all your doings, in all your resolves, forget not that you stand before Him, whose glory fills the whole earth.

Moses of Evreux, 1240. Nahmanides, letter to his son Nahman, c. 1268.

802.21 The Shekina did not rest on the Second Temple. The Holy One said: When all Israel immigrate here, the Shekina will

rest here; now they shall be served only by the Heavenly Voice.

Pesikta Rabbati, ch 35, ed Friedmann, 160a. Cf Isaac. *Ibid.*

802.22 I am willing to be condemned to all tortures in hell, if only the Shekina will cease to suffer.

Samuel Shinaver, *Ramathaim Tzofim,* 1881, 33b. q SSJ i. 230.

802.23 The Shekina does not rest amidst gloom, sloth, frivolity, levity, or idle talk, but only in the joy of a precept.

Talmud: Sabbath, 30b. *Midrash Tehillim,* 102b, on *Ps.* 24.3. See 666.C.21.

802.24 The Shekina rests only on the wise, strong, rich and tall.

Ibid. 92a. Cf Johanan. *T: Nedarim,* 38a.

802.25 The Holy Spirit rests on him only who has a joyous heart.

Talmud J: Sukka, 5.1.

802.26 The Shekina rests on Israel only when they do some work.

Tarfon. *Abot de R. Nathan,* ch 11.

803. SHEMA

803.1 He who has not seen a Jew say *Shema Yisrael* at the Ne'ila service or at the confession before death, has never seen religious ecstasy.

H. Cohen.

803.2 Happy are we! How goodly is our portion, how pleasant our lot, how beautiful our heritage! Happy are we who, early and late, morning and evening, twice each day, declare: "Hear, O Israel, the Lord our God, the Lord is One!"

Daily Prayer Book, ed Singer, 8.

803.3 *Shema Yisrael* was on the lips of those who suffered and were tortured for the sake of the Law. . . . It is the password by which one Jew recognizes another in every part of the world.

Eisenstein, "Shema," 1905. *JE,* xi. 267b.

803.4 The *Shema,* wherein we briefly confess the divine Unity, . . . made our religion the fundamental religion for the whole world; for the divine Unity embraced as its consequence the ultimate unity of mankind.

*G. Eliot, *Daniel Deronda,* 1876, ch 60.

803.5 Nowhere else in Scripture are the elements of universalism and particularism in the Jewish conception of God expressed so completely or so forcefully.

Finkelstein, *The Pharisees,* 1940, p. 63f.

450

803.6 The *Shema* is the basis of all higher, ethical, spiritual religion; an imperishable pronouncement, reverberating to this day in every idealistic conception of the universe.

*Gunkel. q Hertz, *DPB*, 269.

803.7 The last letter of the first word, *Shema*, and . . . of the [last] word, *Ehad*, are written large in the Hebrew Bible. These two large letters form the word *ed*, "witness"; i.e., every Israelite by pronouncing the *Shema* becomes one of "God's witnesses," testifying to His Unity before the world.

Hertz, *Daily Prayer Book*, 1948, p. 438.

803.8 There is a chapter in Holy Writ . . . which we inscribe on our doorposts and bear on our forehead during prayer, which is not a prayer but which we consider as the most important of prayers, . . . a chapter which every mother teaches to her child as soon as it begins to lisp its first words, a chapter which for centuries has consoled the suffering and sweetened the last hours of the dying; a chapter . . . so rich in its simplicity, so expressive in its conciseness, that it sums up our principal duties and awakens in us a crowd of memories and thoughts, . . . all the glories of our past and all the hopes of our future.

Z. Kahn, *Sermons et Allocutions*, 1896, p. 55.

803.9 It was undeniably a stroke of true religious genius . . . to select . . . this one verse [*Deut.* 6.4] as the inscription for Israel's banner of victory. Throughout the entire realm of literature, . . . there is probably no utterance to be found that can be compared in its intellectual and spiritual force, or in the influence it exerted upon the whole thinking and feeling of civilized mankind, with the six words which have become the battle-cry of the Jewish people for more than twenty-five centuries.

Kohler. q Hertz, *DPB*, 269.

803.10 Read the *Shema* on retiring to rest. . . . 'Tis a ladder set up on earth for thy soul's ascent on high, especially if the words are accompanied with copious tears.

Moses Hasid, *Iggeret HaMusar*, 1717. AHE, 289f.

803.11 Everyone who says the *Shema* is our brother.

Nordau. q *Maccabean*, April 1903, p. 221.

803.12 When Jews proclaim constantly, each day, the *Shema*, He responds, "I am the Lord your God, who delivers you from trouble!"

Pirké de Rabbi Eliezer, ch 4.

803.13 If you only recite the *Shema* morning and evening, you will not be conquered!

Simeon b. Yohai. *T: Sota*, 42a. See *Menahot*, 99b.

803.14 How many tyrants are bound hand and foot before them when they open their mouths on their beds with *Shema*, and seek compassion from the Holy King with many appropriate verses!

Zohar, Num., 211a.

804. SHEPHERD

804.1 I shall give you shepherds according to My heart.

Bible: Jer., 3.15.

804.2 Woe to the shepherds of Israel that have fed themselves!

Bible: Ezek., 34.2.

804.3 Woe to the worthless shepherd that leaves the flock!

Bible: Zech., 11.17.

804.4 When shepherds are in debt, goats are taken in pledge.

Isaac b. Zeira. *T: Sabbath*, 33b.

804.5 The Holy One tests the righteous in the pasture. There Moses, David and Amos proved themselves.

Isaac Nappaha. *Tanhuma, Shemot*, 10, ed Buber, 3b.

804.6 No occupation is more degraded than that of a shepherd, who walks about in beggarly fashion with staff and bag, yet Jacob applied this epithet to God [*Gen.* 48.15], and David said, "The Lord is my shepherd" [*Ps.* 23.1].

Jose b. Hanina. *Midrash Tehillim*, 23.2.

804.7 How beautiful, how sweet, is the lot of the young shepherd of flocks! . . . Poor though he be, he is happy.

M. H. Luzzatto, *Migdal Oz*, (1727) 1837, Act 3, Sc. 1. q SRH, 22.

804.8 The good shepherd gives his life for the sheep.

New Testament: John, 10.11.

804.9 There shall be one fold and one shepherd.

Ibid., 10.16.

804.10 When the shepherd is lame and the goats are fleet, there will be an accounting at the gate of the fold.

Proverb. q Mar Ukba. *T: Sabbath*, 32a.

804.11 When the shepherd is on the right path, the sheep too are on the right path.

Reuben. *Pirké de R. Eliezer,* ch 42.

804.12 To rove with herds demurely,
In olden days was surely
A royal usage, full of fame:
Saul was a herdsman only,
Who strayed in deserts lonely,
And great King David was the
same.
O shepherds' fortune,
Thou fairest fortune!
Free words thy praise proclaim.

Rodenberg, "Shepherds' Song," 1855, *Poems,* 1869, p. 73.

805. SHIP

805.1 Ships are usually wrecked near the shore.

Boerne, *Fragmente und Aphorismen,* 1840, #156.

805.2 At night there is something uncanny and mysterious in meeting strange ships at sea, and we imagine that our best friends . . . sail silently by, and that we are losing them forever.

Heine, *Norderney,* 1826.

805.3 The waters roar and far the shore,
My ship, my ship goes down.

M. Rosenfeld, "O Long the Way," *Songs of Labor,* tr 1914, p. 40.

806. SHOE

806.1 Put off your shoes . . . for the place whereon you stand is holy ground.

Bible: Exod., 3.5.

806.2 No path can give Delight
To him whose Shoes are tight.

Guiterman, *A Poet's Proverbs,* 1924, p. 22.

806.3 The shoe is a venerable symbol, first of wandering; second, of rest and possession.

Harrison, *Religion of a Modern Liberal,* 1931, p. 113.

806.4 Sell the beams of your house and buy shoes for your feet.

Judah b. Ezekiel. *T: Sabbath,* 129a.

806.5 A husband must provide his wife with new shoes for each of the three annual festivals.

Mishna: Ketubot, 5.8.

806.6 Stripped naked, yet wearing shoes!

Proverb. q *Talmud: Sota,* 8b.

806.7 Before going to synagog or school, inspect your shoes.

Sefer Hasidim, 13C, #432, p. 127.

806.8 Who has no shoes is worse than dead and buried.

q *Talmud: Sabbath,* 152a.

806.9 When the Aaronites rise to bless the congregation, they remove their shoes out of respect for the people.

Talmud: Sota, 40a.

806.10 Always think of your shoes. A man is judged by his shoes.

Wolffsohn's mother. q Cohn, *David Wolffsohn,* p. 8.

807. SHOPPING

807.1 What gathering flowers in a wood is to children, shopping in large towns is to women.

Auerbach, *On the Heights,* 1865.

808. SHROUD

808.1 Give shrouds for the dead,
For the living give bread.

Frug, "Have Pity."

808.2 Place not many shrouds on me.

Judah HaNasi. *TJ: Ketubot,* 12.3.

808.3 The shroud should be always kept clean and ready.

Maasé Book, (1602) 1934, #9, p. 14.

808.4 Even a Nasi may not be buried in silk shroud or embroidered garments, which is arrogance, extravagance, and heathenish.

Maimonides, *Yad: Ebel,* 4.2.

808.5 Shrouds are made without pockets.

Proverb (Yiddish). BJS, #3974.

808.6 Women don't reprove the tailor when he sews their shrouds.

Proverb (Yiddish). *JE,* x. 228b.

808.7 A daughter complained: You taught me such a lugubrious trade, sewing shrouds, and the men keep away from me! Said her father: My daughter, in due time, they will all come to you!

Sefer Hasidim, 13C, #1, p. 2; #588, p. 161.

808.8 Bury me neither in white nor in black, for I know not whither I go, and I don't wish to appear as a groom among mourners or as a mourner among grooms.

Yannai Rabba. *T: Sabbath,* 114a.

809. SHYLOCK

809.1 I believe there are few
But have heard of a Jew
Named Shylock of Venice,

As errant a "Screw"
In money transactions,
As ever you knew.
*Barham, "Merchant of Venice," 1842.

809.2 The great wrong that Shakespeare did the Jewish people was . . . that by emphasizing at every evil point Shylock's race and religion, he made him as a type of his people. . . . Shakespeare painted many other villains . . . yet never did he associate their religious creed with them. . . . The villainies they executed were individual, the villainy of Shylock was made to be Jewish.
Calisch, *The Jew in English Literature,* 1909, p. 75f.

809.3 Mean as Shylock was, you cannot but feel that the Christians were meaner—that they returned evil for evil, . . . encouraged swindling trickery and domestic abduction, . . . and even when Doctor Portia's quibble triumphs, . . . the most excited playgoer cannot but be aware . . . that a certain amount of injustice has been done to the miserable old man, cheated at once out of "his ducats and his daughter," nay, of the very ring that "he had from Leah when he was a bachelor."
*Craig. *Macmillan's Magazine,* April 1863.

809.4 This is the Jew that Shakespeare drew.
*Pope, attrib. to, when Macklin played Shylock, Feb. 14, 1741. Attrib. also to Johnson. See *Biographia Dramatica,* 1:2, p. 469.

809.5 In terming Shylock "the Jew that Shakespeare drew," there is a perfect logic, for Shylock is, of all Shakespeare's characters, the only one untrue to nature. He is not a Jew.
*Bryant. q BSS, 59.

810. SIGH

810.1 One sigh uttered in prayer is of more avail than all the choirs and singers.
Agnon, *Hemdat. Israel Argosy,* 1952, p. 101.

810.2 Don't sigh over what's lost.
Hasdai, *Ben HaMelek VeHaNazir,* c. 1230, ch 21.

810.3 A sigh can break a body.
Johanan b. Nappaha. *T: Berakot,* 58b.

810.4 Sighing always through my laughter crept.
M. Rosenfeld, *Songs of Labor,* tr 1914, p. 45.

811. SILENCE

811.1 The prudent keeps silence in such a time.
Bible: Amos, 5.13.

811.2 Let all the earth keep silence before Him.
Bible: Hab., 2.20. See *Zech.,* 2.17.

811.3 To Thee silence is praise.
Bible: Ps., 65.2.

811.4 Silence is often the highest form of praise. To praise a flawless pearl is to deprecate it.
Judah of Kfar Neburya. *TJ: Berakot,* 9.1.

811.5 Even a fool, when he holds his peace, is counted wise.
Bible: Prov., 17.28.

811.6 Silence is a fence for wisdom.
Akiba. *Mishna: Abot,* 3.13.

811.7 Silence often expresses more powerfully than speech the verdict and judgment of society.
Disraeli, speech, House of Commons, Aug. 1, 1862.

811.8 If speech is silver, silence is gold.
q M. Ibn Ezra, *Shirat Yisrael,* (12C) 1924, p. 132.

811.9 A man's faults may be concealed by his intelligence, money and wife. If he have no wife, then silence is important; and if he cannot keep silence, the best thing for him is the grave.
Ibn Gabirol, *Mibhar HaPeninim,* c. 1050, #310.

811.10 The best of all medicines is Silence.
Judah of Kfar Gibboraya. *T: Megilla,* 18a.

811.11 For each second of silence, of no evil talk, man will enjoy supernal light in the hereafter.
Kagan, *Shemirat HaLashon,* 1879, i. 11.

811.12 The merit of a condolence call is in the silence observed.
Papa. *T: Berakot,* 6b.

811.13 A silence that spoke more clearly than speech.
Philo, *Moses,* 12.

811.14 A word for a dollar, silence for two.
Proverb. q Joshua b. Levi. *Lev. R.,* 16.5.

811.15 In Babylon, silence is a mark of nobility.
Rab. *T: Kiddushin,* 71b.

811.16 Silence and meditation are the rungs on which one climbs to the Higher Worlds.

Sackler, *The Tzaddik's Journey. Reflex,* Nov. 1927, 76.

811.17 Silence is the only successful substitute for brains.

M. Samuel. q Leon Gutterman, JTA, 1952.

811.18 There was a vast oppressive silence. . . . Only man speaks, said I to myself. Graves and stars are still. For a short while I sat, awake and not awake, then thought to myself again: Only man is silent; graves and stars speak.

Shenberg, *Like a Lengthening Shadow. Under the Fig Tree,* 94f.

811.19 Haply greater strength is required to listen than to sing?
To be silent as a stone than to think in loud voice?

Shneor, "Song of the Prophet," 1903, tr FTH, 170.

811.20 There is nothing better than silence.

Simeon b. Gamaliel I. *Mishna: Abot,* 1.17.

811.21 The world would be much happier if men were as fully able to keep silence as they are able to speak.

Spinoza, *Ethics,* 1677, iii. Pr 2, Note.

811.22 Silence is becoming to the wise a..d even more so to the fool.

Talmud: Pesahim, 99a.

811.23 Be clever, and keep silence.

Talmud: Yoma, 7a.

811.24 Your silence is better than your speech.

Talmud: Yebamot, 65a.

811.25 Silence is admission.

Ibid., 87b.

811.26 Silence is good everywhere, except in connection with Torah.

Zohar, Gen., 245a.

811.27 Give bread to a dog, oil to a door, blows to a squabbler, and board to a scoffer, and you'll silence all the four.

q Zunz, *Nachlese zur Spruchkunde,* 1869. *Gesam. Schr.* iii. 265.

812. SILVER LINING

812.1 If you have no linen, you save on laundry.

Proverb (Yiddish). BJS, #1392.

813. SIMPLICITY

813.1 The Lord preserves the simple.
Bible: Ps., 116.6.

813.2 The essential tenet of Judaism is that a man should walk in a spirit of wholesome simplicity, without any subtleties.

H. Bloch, *Kobetz Miktabim Mekoriyim,* 1920, p. 66.

813.3 The sweet simplicity of the three percenters.

Disraeli, *Endymion,* 1880, ch 96. Speech, Feb. 19, 1850.

813.4 He knows the Truest Way to Teach
Who puts Great Thoughts in Simple Speech.

Guiterman, *A Poet's Proverbs,* 1924, p. 45.

813.5 Simplicity is a fundamental feature of Hebrew religion.

*Gunkel, *What Remains of the OT,* (1914) 1928, p. 37.

813.6 The really great of the earth are always simple. Pomp and ceremonial, popes and kings, are toys for children.

Heine. q Zangwill, *Dreamers of the Ghetto,* 360.

813.7 Art has no excellence higher than true simplicity. Art has no abomination baser than artificial simplicity.

Klatzkin, *In Praise of Wisdom,* 1943.

813.8 The higher the truth the simpler it is.

Kook, *Orot HaKodesh,* 1938, 4. q ABJ, 154.

813.9 The simple wealth of nature is food and shelter.

Philo, *Rewards,* 17.

813.10 Simplicity is the peak of civilization.

Sampter, *The Emek,* 1927, p. 60.

813.11 Simplicity, above all, characterizes alike the noblest and the loveliest poems,—simplicity of art and of feeling. There are no better examples of this, as to motive and construction, than those two episodes of Ruth and Esther. . . . There is not a phrase, an image, an incident, too much or too little in either; not a false note of atmosphere or feeling. These works, so naively exquisite, are deathless.

*Stedman, *Nature and Elements of Poetry,* 1892, p. 174.

813.12 Oh, for the simple life,
For tents and starry skies!

Zangwill, "Aspiration."

814. SIN

814.A. Definition

814.A.1 Sin is not offense against God, but against our humanity.
E. G. Hirsch. *Reform Advocate*, 1894, vii. 135.

814.A.2 Sin is not sinful because God forbade it, but God forbade it because it is sinful.
Saadia, *Emunot VeDeot*, 933.

814.A.3 All crimes against men are sins against God.
Sifré, to *Num.*, #2.

814.A.4 The basic formula of all sin is: frustrated or neglected love.
Werfel, *Between Heaven and Earth*, 1944, p. 189.

814.B. Original Sin

814.B.1 Behold, I was brought forth in iniquity, and in sin did my mother conceive me.
Bible: Ps., 51.7.

814.B.2 Adam says: You die on your own account, not on mine.
Ammi b. Nathan. *Tanhuma, Hukkat*, 16.

814.B.3 Say not from God is my transgression, for He made not what He hates.
Apocrypha: Ben Sira, 15.11.

814.B.4 Sin was not sent on earth. Man himself created it.
Apocrypha: Enoch, 98.4.

814.B.5 No more abhorrent doctrine than original depravity has ever been conceived. It is completely alien to Jewish thought and to the Bible, even though Christians use the Garden parable to give it divine sanction.
*V. Fisher. *American Zionist*, Nov. 5, 1953, p. 14.

814.B.6 Judaism has not allowed the doctrine of original sin to be grafted on to it.
Geiger, *Das Judentum u.s. Geschichte*, 1865, i. 145.

814.B.7 You die because of the sin of the first man.
Levi. *Deut. R.*, 9.8. Cf Simeon b. Eleazar. *Sabbath*, 55b.

814.B.8 The Evil Desire grows strong in man by dint of the pollution thrust into him by the serpent of old.
Moscato, *Nefutzot Yehuda*, 1588, p. 70a.

814.B.9 There is no hereditary wickedness in Israel.
Pesikta Kahana, ch 26, ed Buber, 150a.

814.B.10 God created you upright, and it is you who soil your souls with wickedness.
Saadia, letter to an Egyptian community, 928. See KTJ, 89.

814.B.11 Why was only a single man created first? That virtue and vice may not be claimed as hereditary.
Tosefta: Sanhedrin, 8.4.

814.C. Universality

814.C.1 There is no man that sins not.
Bible: I Kings, 8.46. See *Eccles.*, 7.20.

814.C.2 He that is without sin among you, let him first cast a stone at her.
New Testament: John, 8.7.

814.C.3 Jews and Gentiles are all under sin.
New Testament: Rom., 3.9.

814.C.4 All of us share in the sin of others. The High Priest and Ezra [9.6] include themselves among the sinners of Israel.
Sefer Hasidim, 13C, #74, p. 52.

814.D. Causes

814.D.1 We are sinful not merely because we have eaten of the Tree of Knowledge, but also because we have not yet eaten of the Tree of Life.
Kafka, *Paradise. Parables*, 25.

814.D.2 Jews sin out of depression, Gentiles out of prosperity.
Kaminer, *Baraitot de R. Yitzhak*, 1885.

814.D.3 The heart and the eyes are the panderers of sin.
Levi. *TJ: Berakot*, 1.5.

814.D.4 Three sins none can escape on any day: sinful thoughts, the presumption that God must answer our prayers, and dust of slander.
Rab. *T: Baba Bathra*, 164b.

814.D.5 None sins unless struck by folly.
Simeon b. Lakish. *T: Sota*, 3a.

814.D.6 We presume none sins unless he stand to profit by it.
Talmud: Baba Metzia, 5b. *Shebuot*, 42b.

814.E. Forms

814.E.1 Remember not the sins of my youth.
Bible: Ps., 25.7.

814.E.2 Transgression, in small things or in great, is equally heinous, for in either case the Law is despised.
Apocrypha: IV Macc., 5.20f.

814.E.3 Under coercion a man may sin, except with respect to idolatry, incest and murder.
Council of Lydda, 132. *T: Sanhedrin,* 74a. See *Yoma,* 9b.

814.E.4 A sin against man is far more reprehensible than a sin against God.
A. Danzig. q *JE,* iv. 439a.

814.E.5 No sin is so light that it may be overlooked; no sin is so heavy that it may not be repented of.
M. Ibn Ezra, *Shirat Yisrael,* (12C) 1924, p. 92.

814.E.6 We must distinguish between sin by word and sin by deed.
Maimonides, *Iggeret HaShemad,* 1160. q GHJ, iii. 455.

814.E.7 Who doesn't attempt to prevent sin is answerable for the sin.
Talmud: Sabbath, 54b.

814.E.8 A big sin is forgotten, a little sin is not.
Talmud: Pesahim, 7b.

814.F. Effect

814.F.1 Your iniquities have separated you from your God.
Bible: Isa., 59.2.

814.F.2 Sin is a reproach to any people.
Bible: Prov., 14.34.

814.F.3 One sinner destroys much good.
Bible: Eccles., 9.17.

814.F.4 Each sin is recorded the same day in heaven.
Apocrypha: Enoch, 98.7.

814.F.5 After sin, what is there but death?
Apocrypha: II Enoch, 30.16.

814.F.6 Think not of the smallness of your sin, but of the greatness of Him against whom you have sinned!
Bahya, *Hobot HaLebabot,* 1040, 7.7.

814.F.7 A sin in this world dogs the sinner in the world to come.
Eleazar. *T: Sota,* 3b.

814.F.8 It is not the lizard but the sin that kills.
Hanina b. Dosa. *T: Berakot,* 33a.

814.F.9 Sin dulls the heart.
Ishmael School. *T: Yoma,* 39a.

814.F.10 One day's sin spoils the record of a year.
Johanan b. Nappaha. *T: Hagiga,* 5b.

814.F.11 A sin's beginning is sweet, but its end is bitter.
Simeon b. Halafta. *Eccles. R.,* 3.2.3.

814.F.12 Sins considered trifling beset man on Judgment Day.
Simeon b. Lakish. *T: Aboda Zara,* 18a.

814.F.13 Unintentional sin taints the higher man.
Vidas, *Reshit Hokma,* 1578, 1.5.

814.G. Growth

814.G.1 Sin begins as a spider's web and becomes as a ship's rope.
Akiba. *Gen. R.,* 22.6.

814.G.2 No sin is too big for God to pardon, and none is too small for habit to magnify.
Bahya, *Hobot HaLebabot,* 1040, 7.7.

814.G.3 Commit a little sin, and you'll commit a big sin.
Sifré, Shoftim, #187, to *Deut.* 19.11, ed Friedmann, 108b.

814.G.4 A sin leaves a mark; repeated, it deepens the mark; when committed a third time, the mark becomes a stain.
Zohar, Gen., 73b.

814.H. Fear of Sin

814.H.1 A man may have studied Midrash, Halaka, Agada,—but if he have no fear of sin, he has nothing.
Exod. R., 30.14.

814.H.2 Where fear of sin precedes wisdom, wisdom is retained; where wisdom precedes fear of sin, wisdom is not retained.
Hanina b. Dosa. *Mishna: Abot,* 3.9.

814.H.3 The wages of sin are high.
Hoffenstein, *Pencil in the Air,* 1923, p. 149.

814.H.4 The key which unlocks the Torah is the fear of sin.
Hoshaia. *Exod. R.,* 40.1.

814.H.5 Who has knowledge without fear of sin is like a carpenter without tools.
Johanan b. Zakkai. *Abot de R. Nathan,* ch 22.

814.H.6 To worry over sin is itself a sin. It leads to melancholy, which makes true penitence impossible.
I. Landa, *Toldot Yitzhak,* 1929, p. 89.

814.H.7 Tremble before a minor sin, lest it lead you to a major one.
Talmud: Derek Eretz, 1.26.

814.H.8 He who is afraid of his sins has cause to fear.

Zohar, Gen., 178a.

814.I. Conquest of Sin

814.I.1 Sin couches at the door . . . but you may rule over it.

Bible: Gen., 4.7.

814.I.2 Though your sins be as scarlet, they shall be white as snow.

Bible: Isa., 1.18.

814.I.3 Thou wilt cast all their sins into the depths of the sea.

Bible: Mic., 7.19.

814.I.4 Contemplate three things, and you will avoid sin: whence you came, whither you go, and to whom you must account.

Akabia b. Mahalalel. *Mishna: Abot,* 3.1.

814.I.5 As the goldsmith refines gold in his powerful flame, as the farmer winnows the grain from the chaff, so must sin be refined of its uncleanness, until only its holiness remains.

Anski, *Dybbuk,* 1918, Act 1.

814.I.6 Moral instruction is a barrier to sin; it leads us to despise this transient world and to love the eternal.

Ibn Gabirol, *Mibhar HaPeninim,* c. 1050, #8.

814.I.7 Contemplate three things, and avoid sin: Over you is a seeing eye, a hearing ear, and a record of all your deeds.

Judah HaNasi. *Mishna: Abot,* 2.1.

814.I.8 To forsake one transgression means more than all [rituals].

Saadia, letter to an Egyptian community, 928.

814.I.9 If one guards himself against sin three times, the Holy One guards him from then on.

Samuel b. Isaac. *TJ: Kiddushin,* 1.9.

814.I.10 The very fire of sin must be sublimated into a sacred flame.

Shneor Zalman, *Likkuté Torah, Deut.,* (1848) 1928, p. 160.

814.I.11 He who deliberately and forcibly restrains himself from sinning has already entered the Kingdom of Heaven.

Sifra, to *Lev.* 20.26.

814.I.12 Elijah told Judah, brother of Sala the Pious: Fall not into a passion, drink not to excess, and before setting out on a journey seek counsel of your Maker, and you will not sin.

Talmud: Berakot, 29b.

814.I.13 He who talks about and reflects on the evil he did, is thinking evil, and what one thinks, therein is one caught. . . . Stir filth this way or that, and it is still filth. . . . In the time I brood, I could be stringing pearls for the joy of heaven. This is what is written: "Depart from evil, and do good" [*Ps.* 34.15]—turn wholly from evil, do not brood over it, but do good. You have done wrong? Then balance it by doing right.

Yitzhak Meir, sermon. See GIT, 111.

814.J. Sinner

814.J.1 Sinners are enemies to their own life.

Apocrypha: Tobit, 12.10.

814.J.2 Sinners are mirrors. When we see in them faults, we must realize that they but reflect the evil in us.

Baal Shem. See AKS, 1793.

814.J.3 "Let *sins* cease" [*Ps.* 104.35]. Pray not that sinners die, but that they repent, and thus "the wicked will be no more."

Beruria. *T: Berakot,* 10a. See *Midrash HaNe'elam,* i. 105a.

814.J.4 The Hebrew myth of the deluge embodied the truth that destruction of sinners can never cure the world of sin.

Abbott, Life and Literature of Ancient Hebrews, 1901, p. 80.

814.J.5 Lovers of God who commune with sinners are . . . imitators of their Father in heaven, who makes His sun rise on the righteous and the wicked, and sends His rain alike upon the evil and good.

Didascalia, ii. ch 14. q *JE,* iv. 589b. Cf *Agadat Shir,* ed Schechter, 4; *Matt.* 5.45; *II Tim.* 2.5.

814.J.6 Sinners should be offered comfort and hope.

Ibid.

814.J.7 We hate the criminal, and deal severely with him, because we view in his deed, as in a distorting mirror, our own criminal instincts.

Freud. q F. Wittels, *Freud and His Time,* 368.

814.J.8 As malodorous galbanum was included in the Temple incense [*Exod.* 30.34], so must sinners be included among worshippers.

Hisda. *T: Keritot,* 6b.

814.J.9 Great is he whose sins are counted.

Judah Halevi, *Cuzari,* c. 1135, 1.93.

814.J.10 Despise not those who are obliged to violate the Sabbath, but admonish them gently not to forsake the Law.

Maimonides, *Iggeret HaShemad*, 1160. q GHJ, iii. 456.

814.J.11 Wisdom said "Evil pursues sinners" [*Prov.* 13.2]. Prophecy said, "The soul that sins shall die" [*Ezek.* 18.4]. But the Holy One said, let them repent and be forgiven! "Therefore doth he instruct sinners in the way" of repentence [*Ps.* 25.8].

Pesikta de R. Kahana, #25, 158b.

815. SINAI

815.1 The territory is unique in that it has only one page in all human history—it was Israel's wander-land for forty years.

Haas, *Theodor Herzl*, 1927, ii. 110.

815.2 At Sinai, God was the groom, Israel the bride, Torah the marriage certificate, and Moses the best man.

Hakinai. *PRE*, ch 41.

815.3 The souls that were yet to be created were there. . . . So did the sages of all generations receive their wisdom from Sinai.

Isaac. *Exod. R.*, 28.6.

815.4 When God proclaimed the Torah at Sinai, no bird twittered, no fowl flew, no ox lowed, no angel stirred a wing, the sea did not roar, the creatures did not speak, the whole world was hushed into breathless silence, and the Voice went forth, "I am the Lord thy God!"

Johanan b. Nappaha. *Exod. R.*, 29.9.

815.5 The Torah was given publicly in the wilderness, in no man's land, so that Jews may not say to others, You have no share in it! Anyone wishing to accept it is welcome to it.

Mekilta, to *Exod.*, 19.2.

815.6 All the commandments were spoken at Sinai.

Sifra, to *Lev.*, 27.34, ed Weiss, 115b.

815.7 The voice that sounded at Sinai was never silenced.

M. Steinberg, *Partisan Guide*, 1945, p. 188.

815.8 What is the meaning of *Sinai*? The mountain on which *sinah* ("hostility") toward idolatry descended.

Talmud: Sabbath, 89a.

816. SINCERITY

816.1 Speak not one thing with the mouth and another with the heart.

Abayé. *T: Baba Metzia*, 49a.

816.2 If you are a Jew, be a Jew; if a heathen, be a heathen!

Abba b. Zabina. *TJ: Shebiit*, 4.2.

816.3 "A just hin" [*Lev.* 19.36]. Let your "yes" [*hin*] be just, and let your "no" be just.

Jose b. Judah. *T: Baba Metzia*, 49a.

816.4 Sincerity makes an untruth seem like a truth, while insincerity makes a truth seem like an untruth.

Lipkin. q GSS, 190.

816.5 Overwhelm not your neighbor with invitations and offers which you expect him to decline.

Meir. *Tosefta: Baba Bathra*, 6.14.

816.6 Anything done in sincerity and fear of God, though it have nothing to do with Torah, will ensure us eternal life.

Norzi, *Marpé LeNefesh*, c. 1561, 6a.

816.7 With us deeds accord with words and words with deeds.

Philo, (Calanus to Alexander) *Every Good Man Is Free*, 14.

816.8 As my mouth, so my heart.

Talmud: Megilla, 16b.

817. SIZE

817.1 The fact that the heavenly bodies are large, while man is small, is no proof of their greater importance.

Abravanel, *Commentary*, Gen. 1.16, (1579) 1862, 12d; *I Sam.* 25.29, (1511) 1686, 128a. q NDI, 114f.

817.2 None foregoes a large entrance and comes through a small one.

Adda b. Mattena. *T: Erubin*, 10b.

817.3 A little fire will burn many sheaves of grain.

Alphabet of Ben Sira, 14.

817.4 From a little spark comes a large conflagration.

Apocrypha: Ben Sira, 11.32. Cf *NT: James*, 3.5.

817.5 The curse of bigness has prevented proper thinking.

Brandeis, 1935.

817.6 Learn the great art of being small.

Brenner. q *UJE*, ii. 519a.

817.7 Some of the greatest military feats have been performed by small armies.

Disraeli, speech, House of Commons, March 30, 1874.

817.8 All the great things have been done by little nations.

Disraeli, *Tancred*, 1847.

817.9 A circle may be small, yet it may be mathematically as beautiful and perfect as a large one.

D'Israeli, *Literary Miscellanies,* 1796.

817.10 A little hole will sink a large ship.

Domoratzki, *Mishlé Agur,* 1910, 67.16, p. 85.

817.11 Big doesn't necessarily mean better. Sunflowers aren't better than violets.

Ferber, *Giant,* 1952, p. 94.

817.12 Who scorns the little was not born for the great.

I. Friedmann, *Imré Bina,* 1912, p. 50. q CPP, #1737.

817.13 Who watches pennies will accumulate dollars.

Ibid., p. 90.

817.14 The great and terrible is much easier to set forth in art than the little and neat.

Heine, *Romantic School,* 1833.

817.15 A tiny fly has sometimes choked the big man.

Ibn Gabirol, *Mibhar HaPeninim,* c. 1050, #618.

817.16 The giant feels the stinging fly.

Immanuel, *Mahberot,* c. 1300. q CHS, 22.

817.17 Your heart, a span in size, will a universe comprise.

Lipkin. q KTH, i. 270.

817.18 Prosperity may be found in small as in big business.

Peretz, *Fir Dores Fir Tzavoes,* 1901. *Alle Verk,* iv. 237.

817.19 Napoleon was a little fellow; so is the uranium atom.

L. Stein, *Journey into the Self,* 1950, p. 256.

817.20 A gnat frightens a lion; a mosquito can hurt an elephant.

Talmud: Sabbath, 77b.

817.21 God has always chosen small countries through which to convey His messages to humanity.

Weizmann, *Trial and Error,* 1949, p. 386.

817.22 Bulky books and tight shoes have always been most uncomfortable for me.

I. M. Wise. *Deborah,* Sept. 17, 1896, p. 5.

818. SKILL

818.1 They that are deft with their hands and skilled in their work are indispensable in a city; wherever they dwell, they hunger not.

Apocrypha: Ben Sira, 38.31.

818.2 Skill is a superb and necessary instrument but it functions at its highest level only when it is guided by a mature mind and an exalted spirit.

Guggenheimer, *Creative Vision,* 1950, p. 107.

818.3 It is not labor by itself, but labor with skill, that is good.

Philo, *The Worse Attacks the Better,* 7.

819. SLANDER

819.1 Who shall sojourn in Thy tabernacle? . . . He that has no slander upon his tongue.

Bible: Ps., 15.1, 3. See 101.5.

819.2 Who utters slander is a fool.

Bible: Prov., 10.18.

819.3 Slander not a servant to his master.

Ibid., 30.10.

819.4 Scholars passed by a dead dog. The disciples said: "How awful its smell!" Their master said, "How white its teeth!"

Bahya, *Hobot HaLebabot,* 1040, 6.6.

819.5 Guard yourself from slander, at least one hour each day.

Braude. See Glenn, *Israel Salanter,* 73.

819.6 When Abbahu called Caesarea "a city of cursing and blaspheming," Resh Lakish offered him a little sand for his mouth, saying, "God is not pleased with one who calumniates Israel!"

Cant. R., 1.6.1.

819.7 If you slander, you'll commit other sins too.

Eleazar HaKappar. *T: Derek Eretz,* ch 7.

819.8 Cast no aspersion on whom the Torah shielded.

Judah b. Bathyra. *T: Sabbath,* 96b.

819.9 When Moses said of Israel, "they will not believe me" [*Exod.* 4.1], God rebuked him and said, "How do you know?"

Judah Halevi b. Shalom. *Num. R.,* 7.5.

819.10 The soul of a slanderer transmigrates into a silent stone.

Naphtali Hertz, *Emek HaMelek,* 1648, 153b.

819.11 Isaiah suffered martyrdom for having said, "I dwell in the midst of a people of unclean lips" [*Isa.* 6.5].

Raba. *T: Yebamot,* 49b.

819.12 For saying it, a seraph flew to him with a glowing stone.

Simon. *Cant. R.,* 1.6.1.

819.13 No individual should ever pronounce a sentence of condemnation against a whole ethnic group.

Rathenau, *Staat & Judentum*, 1911. *Gesam. Schr.*, i. 193.

819.14 Because Moses called the people "rebels" [*Num.* 20.10], he was not permitted to enter the Promised Land.

Simon. *Cant. R.*, 1.6.1.

819.15 There is no cure for a slanderer.

Talmud: Derek Eretz, 1.13.

819.16 The penalty for slander equals that of all the cardinal sins.

Tosefta: Peah, 1.2.

819.17 A slanderer deserves to be stoned.

Ukba. *T: Arakin*, 15b.

819.18 The Holy One said: There is no room in the world for the slanderer and Me.

Ibid.

820. SLAVERY

820.1 If you buy a Hebrew servant, six years he shall serve, and in the seventh he shall go out free for nothing.

Bible: Exod., 21.2.

820.2 If the servant shall plainly say . . . I will not go out free, then his master . . . shall bore his ear through with an awl.

Ibid., 21.5f.

820.3 They are My servants . . . they shall not be sold as bondmen.

Bible: Lev., 25.42.

820.4 Thou shalt not rule over him with rigor.

Ibid., 25.43.

820.5 When you let him go free, you shall not let him go empty; you shall furnish him liberally.

Bible: Deut., 15.13.

820.6 The Merciful demands that your servant be your equal. You should not eat white bread, and he black bread; you should not drink old wine, and he new wine; you should not sleep on a feather-bed and he on straw. Hence it was said, Whoever acquires a Hebrew slave acquires a master.

Abayé. *T: Kiddushin*, 20a.

820.7 Praised be Thou . . . who hast not made me a slave.

Aha b. Jacob. *T: Menahot*, 43b. *DPB*, ed Singer, p. 5.

820.8 A wise slave love as yourself, and withhold not his freedom.

Apocrypha: Ben Sira, 7.21.

820.9 What is a slave? He is a human being. He has feelings and passions and intellect. His heart, like the white man's, swells with love, burns with jealousy, aches with sorrow, pines under restraint and discomfort, boils with revenge and ever cherishes the desire for liberty.

Benjamin, *Lockett vs. Merchants Insurance Co.*, 1845.

820.10 A slave who fled for refuge to the Land of Israel shall not be deported to slavery. His master shall be asked to release him and specify the price, and as soon as the slave can afford it, he shall pay it. If the master is unwilling to free him, the Sanhedrin shall proclaim his emancipation.

Caro, *Shulhan Aruk: Yoré Deah*, 1564, #268.

820.11 I cannot recall an instance in Hebrew literature where the master of slaves is designated as *baal* ["owner"]. . . . He is always referred to as *adon* ["possessor"], and thus the Hebrew language, as an involuntary vehicle of the Hebrew spirit, asserts that slavery is a relationship not founded in natural law, . . . but merely an empirical condition, something that came into being and may properly go out of existence.

*Cornill, *Israel and Humanity*, Jan. 8, 1895.

820.12 The Essenes first declared slavery to be a crime.

Crémieux, address, International Anti-Slavery Congress, 1840.

820.13 We prefer death to slavery.

Eleazar b. Yair. q Josephus, *Wars*, 7.8.6.

820.14 The slavish gesture breeds the slavish soul.

Fleg, *Vision of Isaac. Jewish Anthology*, 385.

820.15 Though the law permits us to impose hard labor on a Canaanite slave, piety and wisdom command us to be kind and just.

Maimonides, *Yad: Abadim*, 1180, 9.8.

820.16 A son or pupil may, but a Hebrew slave may not, wash his master's feet, or put his shoes on him, . . . as slaves do.

Mekilta, to *Exod.* 21.2.

820.17 Like a hired man, a Hebrew slave cannot be forced to do anything other than his trade.

Ibid.

820.18 "I will bring you out from under the bearings of Egypt" [*Exod.* 6.6]. Why "bearings"? Because there was something worse than bondage, namely, . . . that they were willing to bear the Egyptian yoke, and it was from these "bearings" that they had first to be delivered.

Mendel of Kotzk. q Cahn, *Der Rebbe fun Kotzk*, 3.1, p. 110. BTH, ii. 260f., attrib. it to Simha Bunam of Pzhysha.

820.19 It was with the Jews that the revolt of the slaves begins in the sphere of morals.

*Nietzsche, *Genealogy of Morals*, 1887, 1.7. See *Beyond Good and Evil*, 1885, #195.

820.20 Servants rank lower in fortune, but in nature can claim equality with their masters, and in the law of God the standard of justice follows nature, not fortune.

Philo, *Special Laws*, iii. 25.

820.21 Our bondage is that we choose to be bondmen.

Ragoler, *Maalot HaTorah*, (1828), 114.

820.22 You were permitted to have slaves for labor, not for humiliation.

Samuel. *T: Nidda*, 47a.

820.23 The true slave is he who is led away by his pleasures and can neither see what is good for him nor act accordingly.

Spinoza, *Theologico-Political Treatise*, 1670, 16.

820.24 A master may not deduct for his Hebrew bondman's idleness due to trouble or illness.

Talmud: Abadim, 2.2.

821. SLEEP

821.1 He giveth His beloved sleep.
Bible: Ps., 127.2.

821.2 Drowsiness shall clothe a man with rags.
Bible: Prov., 23.21.

821.3 I sleep, but my heart wakes.
Bible: Cant., 5.2.

821.4 Sweet is the sleep of the laboring man.
Bible: Eccles., 5.11.

821.5 Sleep is the incomplete experience of death.
Hanina b. Isaac. *Gen. R.*, 17.5.

821.6 Sleep, the most precious invention!
Heine, *William Ratcliff*, 1822, Scene 10.

821.7 When God created Adam, the angels mistook him for a deity. . . . But when God put him to sleep, they knew he was a mortal.
Hoshaia Rabba. *Gen. R.*, 8.10.

821.8 Good sleep is a skill in relaxation and self-control.
E. Jacobson.

821.9 "Sleep to fall" [*Gen.* 2.21]. The beginning of a man's downfall is sleep.
Levi. *Gen. R.*, 17.5.

821.10 Fear God by day, and you'll sleep soundly at night.
Zabara, *Sefer Shaashuim*, 13C, 7.26. ed Davidson, 69.

821.11 A healthy man may live seven days without food, five without drink, but only three without sleep.
Ibid., ch 8, ed Davidson, 86f; ed Hadas, 115.

822. SLOWNESS

822.1 When you can't speed, you crawl.
Brenner, *HaYerushalmi*, ch 1.

822.2 Deities are formed slowly.
Levi, *Demeter*, tr Mary A. Craig. q *JQRo*, ix. 387.

822.3 What we conquer inch by inch will be a lasting gain.
Schreiber, *Reformed Judaism*, 1892, p. 84.

823. SMILE

823.1 Pack up your troubles in your old
      kit-bag,
And smile, smile, smile.
G. Asaf, song, 1915.

823.2 To smile at your neighbor is more important than to treat him to a drink.
Johanan b. Nappaha. *T: Ketubot*, 111b.

823.3 The Americans are very sensitive people because they are new, but your people, being so old, can afford to smile.
*Kipling, to Zangwill. q Zangwill, *New Jew*, Oct. 24, 1898.

824. SMOKE

824.1 Before the fire is the smoke of the furnace.
Apocrypha: Ben Sira, 22.24.

824.2 More smoke than roast.
Rabbinic maxim.

824.3 There is no smoke without fire, and no fire without smoke.
Zohar, Num., 137b. See *Zohar, Gen.*, 70a.

825. SMUGNESS

825.1 They were filled . . . therefore they have forgotten Me.
Bible: Hos., 13.6.

825.2 Woe to them that are at ease in Zion.
Bible: Amos, 6.1.

825.3 Hebraism—and here is the source of its wonderful strength—has always been severely preoccupied with an awful sense of the impossibility of being at ease in Zion.
*Arnold, *Culture and Anarchy,* 1869, p. 116.

825.4 If a man after prayer be conscious of the least pride or self-satisfaction . . . then let him know that he has prayed not to God but to himself. And what is this but disguised idolatry?
Baal Shem. q SSJ, i. 30.

825.5 If you were completely free of sin, I would be apprehensive of something in you worse than sin,—haughtiness and pride.
Bahya, *Hobot HaLebabot,* 1040, 3.4, 7.8.

825.6 Self-complacency is the companion of ignorance.
Schechter, March 20, 1904. *Seminary Addresses,* 60.

825.7 When prosperous, men find it easy to dispense with God.
Silver, *World Crisis,* 1941, p. 56.

826. SNAKE

826.1 The serpent has no feet or hands,
Yet makes his way in many lands;
But who would on his belly crawl
In order to avoid a fall?
Hoffenstein, "Songs About Life," #9. *Poems in Praise of Practically Nothing,* 1928, p. 93.

826.2 Bitten by a snake, afraid of a rope.
Proverb. q Levi. *Cant. R.,* 1.2.3.

826.3 The best of snakes, crush its head.
Simeon b. Yohai. *TJ: Kiddushin,* 4.11. *Mekilta,* to *Exod.* 14.7.

827. SNOB

827.1 Snobbery is but a point in time. Let us have patience with our inferiors. They are ourselves of yesterday.
I. Goldberg, *Tin Pan Alley,* 1930.

827.2 He lies below, correct in cypress wood,
And entertains the most exclusive worms.
Parker, "The Very Rich Man," *Death and Taxes,* 1932, p. 28.

827.3 Snobbery is pride in status without pride in function.
Trilling, "Manners, Morals and the Novel," 1947. *The Liberal Imagination,* 1950, p. 209.

828. SOCIALISM

828.1 The Israel Kibbutz is altogether differentiated from the Russian collective. . . . It is socialism by consent.
Bentwich, *Israel,* 1952, p. 118.

828.2 Socialism at its best is the fruit of the Jewish spirit.
Bialik. q Livneh, *BeShaar HaTekufa. JS,* Dec. 1952, p. 13.

828.3 The aim of Socialism is to set up a universal society founded on equal justice for all men and on equal peace for all nations.
Blum, *For All Mankind,* (1941) 1946, p. 177.

828.4 Socialism has several aspects. Economically, it means the socialization of the means of production; politically, the establishment of the dictatorship of the toiling masses; emotionally, the abolition of the reign of egotism and anarchy which characterizes the capitalistic system.
Borochov, at Poalé Zion Conference, Kiev, 1917. BNC 125.

828.5 The Russian Revolution has demonstrated beyond doubt that the State idea, State Socialism, in all its manifestations . . . is entirely and hopelessly bankrupt.
E. Goldman, *My Further Disillusionment,* 1924, p. 160.

828.6 Socialism holds nothing but unhappiness for the human race. It destroys personal initiative, wipes out national pride . . . and plays into the hands of the autocrats. . . . Socialism is the end of fanatics, the sophistry of so-called intelligentsia, and it has no place in the hearts of those who would secure and fight for freedom and preserve democracy.
Gompers, *Seventy Years of Life and Labor,* 1925, ii. 431.

828.7 Socialism . . . aims at a saner, higher and nobler social order. . . . The spirit of Socialism, which places the welfare of society above the selfish interests of the individual, clearly characterizes the whole modern trend of American governmental policy.
Hillquit, *Loose Leaves from a Busy Life,* 1934, p. 328.

828.8 He who has eyes to see understands that the individualistic age is at an end, and that soon . . . the socialistic period will begin, for the individualistic time is but a stepping-stone to that form of society where the individual knows that beyond his rights, and before his rights, come certain duties and certain obligations.

E. G. Hirsch, "Stepping Stones." *Reform Advocate*, 1891, i. 266.

828.9 Socialism is really the most consistent scheme of militarism. It puts us all into battalions and into regiments. . . . We are all under discipline, and our individuality is chilled and killed.

E. G. Hirsch, *My Religion*, 1925, p. 136.

828.10 After World War II, when socialism had a sweeping victory in England, it proved . . . that it can be as fanatically nationalist, and as indifferent to the fate of the oppressed of other people, as the most greedy capitalist society.

Kaplan, *Future of the American Jew*, 1948, p. 7.

828.11 That industries like coal and electric power, transport and banking, the supply of meat and the provision of houses, should be left to the hazards of private enterprise will appear as unthinkable to a future generation as it is unthinkable to our own that the army of the State should be left to private hands. . . .That does not mean direct operation by government. . . . It means the planning of constitutions for essential industries.

Laski, *A Grammar of Politics*, 1925.

828.12 Their [socialists'] destructive criticism, wherein they show the material evils of society, is just and pitiful. But their remedies are ridiculous, powerless, false.

Luzzatti, letter to Elia Lattes, 1861. LGF, p. xvii.

828.13 Socialism is not Jewish. Theoretical and practical Socialism existed before Marx and Lassalle. The philosophical foundations of Marxism are to be found in Protestant Hegelianism and in Feuerbach. In the formation of Marxism, the Protestant Engels exerted as determining an influence as Marx. . . . Socialism appeals to Jews because it embraces the interests of all the oppressed.

*Masaryk, *Grundlagen des Marxismus*, 1899, #126, p. 477.

828.14 The socialist revolution begins on national grounds, but it cannot be completed on these grounds. Its maintenance within a national framework can only be a provisional state of affairs.

Trotsky, *The Permanent Revolution*, 1932, Introduction.

829. SOCIAL JUSTICE

829.1 Service to mankind must not be seen in the throwing of crumbs to the poor. . . . We must work out a world order which shall rest upon equal distribution of labor and rewards.

Asch, *What I Believe*, 1941, p. 198f.

829.2 In Judaism social action is religiousness, and religiousness implies social action.

Baeck, *Essence of Judaism*, 1936, p. 197.

829.3 From the time of the Prophets, Judaism has welcomed all aspiration for a just order. It has meant a passion to defend the weak against the strong and to strive for a society built on justice and mercy.

Bentwich. LJC, Dec. 18, 1953, p. 15.

829.4 The suppression of poverty, of the scourges of cold, hunger, and disease, are not "purely material ends."

Blum, *For All Mankind*, (1941) 1946, p. 177.

829.5 We deem it our duty to participate in the great task of modern times, to solve, on the basis of justice and righteousness, the problems presented by the contrasts and evils of the present organization of society.

CCAR, *Pittsburgh Platform*, 1885.

829.6 A sage who heeds not the appeal of widows and orphans and declines to act as a judge on the ground that he is too busy with his studies, is a "man of separation" . . . and he appears as one who overthrows the land! [*Prov.* 29.4].

Exod. R., 30.13.

829.7 With trenchant power they [Prophets] hammered into the hearts of their people, and, through their writings, into the heart of all mankind, the truth that the essence of sin among men is oppression of the lowly, and that righteousness consists in worthy treatment of the poor and the oppressed.

*Gunkel, *What Remains of the OT*, (1914) 1928, p. 39f.

829.8 All modern social legislation is an outcome of the prophetic spirit, and the spirit of these Hebrew teachers will continue to urge the nations to ever fresh reforms.

Ibid., p. 40.

829.9 Away with all this charity. Justice we need. Social justice everywhere.

E. G. Hirsch. *Reform Advocate*, 1893, v. 205.

829.10 Never forget that you have been the people . . . which brought justice into the world and earn yourself forgiveness for having given a god to men by being forever the soldiers of justice and of human brotherhood.

Lazare, *Jewish Nationalism*, 1897. LJD, 79.

829.11 Dedicate all your strength to the unification of all in the perfection of humanity, and to the establishment of the kingdom of Labor, Brotherhood, and Justice.

A. Lieberman, letter to his brother Abraham Isaac, 1875. q Marmor, *Letters of Aaron Lieberman*, 41.

829.12 Whilst the organization of Israel could not withstand the world pressure of its time, its spiritual and moral characteristics have always remained as enticing ideals in the minds of men, and thereby provide not only a proof that they are to find another opportunity of expression in society, but an earnest that the world pressure will change so as to aid rather than stultify that opportunity.

*J. R. Macdonald, *The Socialist Movement*, 1911, p. 21f.

829.13 Burn the sun on the altar of infinite love, offer the whole world as a holocaust on the battlefield of right! Break the rainbow in two, make of one half a bow for Amor, and of the other half a fiery sword for Justice!

Moyshé Oyved. q ZVJ, 236.

829.14 According to Israel's law no man has a right to more than bread, water and wood, as long as the poor are not provided with the necessaries of life.

Schechter. *American Hebrew*, Jan. 1916.

829.15 When asked by his father, Joshua b. Levi, what he had seen in a trance, Joseph replied: "I saw a world upside down, the upper below and the lower above." Whereupon Joshua said: "You saw a well-ordered world!"

Talmud: Pesahim, 50a.

830. SOCIETY

830.1 Their [Essenes'] example testifies to how great a height religious men were able to raise their conception of society even without the succor of the New Testament.

*Acton, *Freedom in Antiquity*, 1877 (*Essays on Freedom & Power*, 1948, p. 55).

830.2 Blessed be He who created all these people to attend to my needs! How much Adam had to toil! He had to plow and plant, cut and bind sheaves, thresh and winnow grain, grind and sift flour, and knead and bake before he could eat a piece of bread. He had to shear and wash wool, hatchel and dye and spin and weave and sew before he had a shirt to put on. But I rise in the morning, and find everything ready for me!

Ben Zoma. *Tosefta: Berakot, 7.2.*

830.3 There are many things men can do without, except men.

Boerne, *Umgang mit Menschen*, 1824.

830.4 It is a community of purpose that constitutes society.

Disraeli, *Sybil*, 1845.

830.5 The structure of modern society affects man in two ways simultaneously: he becomes more independent, self-reliant, and critical, and he becomes more isolated, alone and afraid.

Fromm, *Escape from Freedom*, 1941, p. 104.

830.6 Hebraic religion cannot and will not admit that society is the whole of life or that any social institution whatever is above judgment and criticism in terms of the "higher law" revealed in the divine imperative. It says *no* to society or the state or the church when any of these dares to exalt itself and call for the worship of total allegiance.

Herberg, *Judaism and Modern Man*, 1951, p. 143.

830.7 Judaism is rooted in the love of family; patriotism and nationalism are the flower of its spirit, and the coming regenerated state of human society will be its ripe fruit.

Hess, *Rome and Jerusalem*, (1862), #2, p. 48.

830.8 The group to which an individual belongs is the ground on which he stands, which gives or denies him social status, gives or denies him security and help.

Lewin. *Menorah Journal*, 1940. LRS, 174.

830.9 True salvation can come only to a person who renders service to the community.

Lipkin. q Glenn, *Israel Salanter*, 20. See *Tebuna*, 1862. p. 39; GIS, 172.

830.10 Human society should be something more than a mere aggregation of

bipeds each seeking to devour the other.
London, speech, U.S. Congress, 1916. q
RES, 88.

830.11 Man is naturally a social being.
Maimonides, *Guide for the Perplexed*,
1190, 2.40.

830.12 Man . . . can develop into an individual only in society.
Marx, *Criticism of Political Economy*,
1859.

830.13 The course of our individual lives
often depends more on the fate of the
group to which we belong—family, union,
class or race—than on our own individual
merits.
Pekelis. *New Republic*, Oct. 29, 1945, p.
570.

830.14 God made nought complete in
itself. . . . Through reciprocity and combination, even as a lyre is formed of unlike
notes, God meant that they should come to
fellowship and concord and form a single
harmony, that a universal give and take
should govern them. . . . Thus each wants
and needs each; all need all, so that this
whole of which each is a part, might be
that perfect work worthy of its architect.
Philo, *Cherubim*, 31. See 332.7.

830.15 None of us has solid ground under his feet; each of us is only held up by
the neighborly hands grasping him by the
scruff, with the result that we are each
held up by the next man, and often, indeed
most of the time, hold each other up mutually.
F. Rosenzweig, letter to Ilse Hahn,
March 11, 1920. GFR 92.

830.16 Man is a social animal. . . .
Men can provide for their wants much
more easily by mutual help, and only by
uniting their forces can they escape from
the dangers that beset them.
Spinoza, *Ethics*, 1677, iv. Pr 35, Note.

830.17 How much we owe to the labors
of our brothers! Day by day they dig far
from the sun that we may be warm, enlist
in outposts of peril that we may be secure,
and brave the terrors of the unknown for
truths that shed light on our way. Numberless gifts and blessings have been laid in
our cradles as our birthright.
Union Prayer Book, 1940, i. 45.

831. SOFTNESS

831.1 This people has refused the waters
of Shiloah that go softly.
Bible: Isa., 8.6.

831.2 I shall go softly all my years.
Ibid., 38.15.

831.3 A soft answer turns away wrath.
Bible: Prov., 15.1.

831.4 A wise man must be . . . soft-spoken with all.
Maimonides, *Yad: Deot*, 1180, 5.7.

831.5 A worthy scholar lets his learning
"distil as the dew"; an unworthy one lets
it "drop as the rain" [*Deut.* 32.2].
Raba. *Yalkut Shimoni*, #942.

831.6 Be not sweet lest they swallow you;
Be not soft lest they trample you.
Uceda, *Midrash Samuel*, to *Abot*, 1579.

832. SOLITUDE

832.1 Woe to him who is alone when he
falls.
Bible: Eccles., 4.10.

832.2 "Alone" is the best conveyance, for
then the horses are always harnessed.
Auerbach, *Little Barefoot*, 1856, ch 56.

832.3 The chief support for purity of
heart is love of solitude.
Bahya, *Hobot HaLebabot*, 1040, 8.17.

832.4 The right to be alone—the most
comprehensive of rights, and the right most
valued by civilized men.
Brandeis, *Olmstead vs. U.S.*, 1928.

832.5 There is a society in the deepest
solitude.
D'Israeli, *Literary Character*, 1795, ch 6.

832.6 Solitude is the nurse of enthusiasm, and enthusiasm is the parent of genius.
Ibid.

832.7 Quiet intercourse with ourselves
is all-important, but for that we never
have time.
Ehrenpreis, *Soul of the East*, 1928, p.
166.

832.8 I live in that solitude which is
painful in youth, but delicious in the
years of maturity.
Einstein, *Out of My Later Years*, 1950.

832.9 Lone as the blessed Jew.
*Emerson, *Quatrains: Shakespeare.*
(*May-Day*, 1867, p. 190).

832.10 At bottom, we live spiritually
alone.
Heine, *Norderney*, 1826.

832.11 A life of seclusion, devoted only
to meditation and prayer, is not Judaism.
S. R. Hirsch, *Nineteen Letters*, (1836),
#15, p. 150.

832.12 Against the love of pleasure, effective beyond all else, is solitude. For he who puts out of sight the things that are worldly loses the desire for them.

M. H. Luzzatto, *Mesillat Yesharim,* (1740), ch 15, p. 134.

832.13 Every pious man should seek retirement and seclusion, and should only in case of necessity associate with others.

Maimonides, *Guide for the Perpexed,* 1190, 3.51.

832.14 Moses received the Torah when he was alone with the mountain, because he was in retreat and solitude. Hence the expressions, "A law unto Moses from Sinai," and "Moses received the Torah from Sinai" [*Mishna: Abot,* 1.1].

Morawczyk, *Minha Hadasha* (1576) 1722, ch 1, p. 6b.

832.15 Solitude is the highest stage. Only in solitude can man attain . . . union with the eternal God. Therefore a man must seek to be alone, at least for an hour each day, especially at night, when everyone is asleep and all things are quiet. Solitude in the open air, in the forest or in the desert, is of the utmost importance.

Nahman Bratzlav. q HLH, 95f.

832.16 It is well to be alone. It fertilizes the creative impulse.

Nordau. q A. & M. Nordau, *Max Nordau,* 87.

832.17 Rather a stone, but to be alone!

Peretz, *Oich a Feleton,* 1894. *Alle Verk,* xii. 64.

832.18 Even in paradise, it's not good to be alone.

Proverb (Yiddish). BJS, #166.

832.19 One can eat alone, but not work alone.

Ibid., #167.

832.20 For solitude doth cause a dearth
Of fruitful, blessed thought,
The wise would pray to leave this earth,
If none their friendship sought.

Santob de Carrion, *Proverbios Morales,* 1350.

832.21 How strange we grow when we're alone,
And how unlike the selves that meet and talk.

Sassoon, *Heart's Journey,* 1928, p. 18.

833. SOLOMON

833.1 You covered the earth with your soul, and gathered parables like the sea.

Apocrypha: Ben Sira, 47.15.

834. SON

834.1 A wise son makes a glad father, but a foolish son is the grief of his mother.

Bible: Prov., 10.1.

834.2 There are four types of sons: the wise, the simple, the wicked, and the one who does not know enough to ask.

Mekilta, to *Exod.* 13.14.

834.3 A son is his father's foot.

Raba. *T: Erubin,* 70b.

834.4 He who is survived by a son devoted to Torah is as though he had not died.

Simeon b. Yohai. *Gen. R.,* 49.4.

834.5 The Holy One is angry at him who does not leave a son to be his heir.

Simeon b. Yohai. *T: Baba Bathra,* 116a.

834.6 He who has not a son is called childless.

Zohar, Gen., 90b. See 48a.

835. SONG OF SONGS

835.1 The most noteworthy day in history is that on which the Song of Songs was composed. All the other Hagiographa books are holy, but this one is the Holy of Holies.

Akiba. *Mishna: Yadayim,* 3.5.

836. SORROW

836.1 Sorrow has killed many, and there is no profit therein.

Apocrypha: Ben Sira, 30.23.

836.2 When your friend is bereaved, bear with him in sorrow; when your friend dies, throw off sorrow.

Proverb. q *Gen. R.,* 96.5.

836.3 The deeper the sorrow, the less tongue it has.

Proverb. ATJF, p. 640.

836.4 Who broods excessively over his sorrow will weep for yet another death.

Rab. *T: Moed Katan,* 27b.

837. SOUL

837.1 He who injures the soul of man, injures his own soul.

Apocrypha: II Enoch, 60.1.

837.2 Apply torment to my body; my soul ye cannot reach.

Apocrypha: IV Macc., 10.4.

837.3 No deed is perfect without the impulse of the soul.

Bahya, *Hobot HaLebabot*, 1040, Introduction.

837.4 The soul is a stranger in this world.
Ibid., 4.4.

837.5 O give me a soul, for my heart is full of love.

Frishman, "HaYadaata?" *Kol Kitbé*, 1951, ii. 25. q WHJ, iv. 218.

837.6 A soul, because of its heavenly origin, will no more be satisfied with worldly luxuries than a princess can be with a peasant for a husband, though he bring her everything on earth.

Hanina b. Isaac. *Eccles. R.*, 6.6.

837.7 Happy the soul which has not been sullied by evil deeds, which has discerned its Creator and understood its Origin, and returns to its habitation cheerfully and joyously after a strenuous life spent in noble deeds.

Hasdai, *Sefer HaTapuah*, c. 1320, tr Gollancz, 116.

837.8 I never praise the deed, but the human soul whose garment it is, and history is nothing but the soul's old wardrobe.

Heine, *Journey from Munich to Genoa*, 1828, ch 29.

837.9 The hand obeys the soul.

Heine, *Lutetia*, Oct. 3, 1840.

837.10 If there is a transmigration of souls then I am not yet on the bottom rung. My life is a hesitation before birth.

Kafka, *Diaries*, Jan. 24, 1922, ed Brod, ii. 210.

837.11 The soul sings all the time; joy and sweetness are her garments; high-minded tenderness envelops her.

Kook, *Orot HaKodesh*, 1938, p. 174. q ABJ, 189.

837.12 The human soul is one, though it has many diverse activities.

Maimonides, *Eight Chapters*, 1168, ch 1.

837.13 Man's supreme and final battles are to be fought out in his own soul.

Neuman, address, May 24, 1942. NLG, 302.

837.14 What is a man profited if he gain the whole world and lose his own soul?

New Testament: Matt., 16.26.

837.15 He created no soul barren of virtue.

Philo, *Allegorical Interpretation*, 1.13.

837.16 Man's soul will not find rest in this world, even if it obtains the kingdoms of the whole earth, for it knows that it has a world to come. There, and there alone, will it find rest.

Saadia, letter to an Egyptian community, 928. See KTJ, 87.

837.17 Even though man's body is of small dimension, his soul is more extensive than heaven and earth, because his knowledge embraces all that they contain.

Saadia, *Emunot VeDeot*, 933, 4.2, tr Rosenblatt, p. 183.

837.18 As the Holy One fills and sustains the universe, sees and is not seen, abides in the innermost precincts and is pure, so the soul fills and sustains the body, sees and is not seen, abides in the innermost recesses, and is pure.

Shimi b. Ukba. *T¡ Berakot*, 10a. Cf *Lev. R.*, 4.8.

837.19 He who reaches the depth of his own soul is at the core of the world.

Simmel. summ. Lewisohn, *Expression in America*, 337.

838. SOUL AND BODY

838.1 The soul must not boast that it is more holy than the body, for only in that it has climbed down into the body and works through its limbs can the soul attain to its perfection. The body on the other hand, may not brag of supporting the soul, for when the soul leaves, the flesh falls into decay.

Buber, *Tales of the Hasidim*, 1947, i. 7.

838.2 Forego not the sublimely spiritual for the lowly physical.

Falaquera, *Sefer HaMaalot*, (13C) 1894, p. 51.

838.3 I was the lamp's wick; I must now
Consume away; the spirit, thou,
Wilt be selected by-and-by
To sparkle as a star on high
Of purest radiance.

Heine, *Latest Poems: Body and Soul*, 1853.

838.4 Is not the soul a guest in our body, deserving of our kind hospitality? Today it is here, tomorrow it is gone.

Hillel. *Lev. R.*, 34.3.

838.5 The body of man is light when the soul is therein.
But when the soul is gone, it sinks heavily to the ground.

M. Ibn Ezra, *Selected Poems*, 18.

838.6 All of us have mortal bodies, composed of perishable matter, but the soul lives forever: it is a portion of the Deity housed in our bodies.

Josephus, *Wars*, 3.8.5.

838.7 Longeth not the soul to separate
　　from the body
　　And return to the majesty of her
　　trappings?

Judah Halevi, *Selected Poems*, 108.

838.8 For yourself, give precedence to the soul; but for others, forego not the demands of the body. Your neighbor's physical needs are your spiritual affairs.

Lipkin. q KTH, i. 273.

838.9 It may happen that in one human body more than one soul may suffer a new incarnation. . . . It may be that the one soul is balsam, the other poison. . . .Now they are confined in one place, . . . they interpenetrate, they bite into each other. . . . But though ever bruising each other, recreating each other, always this union is the means by which one soul aids another.

I. Luria. q Feuchtwanger, *Power*, 248f.

838.10 The properties of the soul depend on the condition of the body.

Maimonides, *Guide for the Perplexed*, 1190, 3.12.

838.11 Jewish spirituality combines heaven and earth, as it were. It does not separate soul from body or mind from nature, but understands man and history in the unity of man's physical and spiritual life.

*R. Niebuhr, Introd. to Frank, *Jew in Our Day*, 1944, p. 3.

838.12 We are corpse-bearers, the soul raising and carrying without toil the body. . . . And note, how strong the soul is.

Philo, *Allegorical Interpretation*, 3.22.

838.13 When we are alive, we are as though our soul is dead and entombed in our body; but when we die, our soul lives its proper life, released from the evil, dead body, to which it was bound.

Philo, *Allegories*, 1.33, interpreting Heraclitus.

838.14 As from the fire of the soul was, according to Ibn Gabirol, the body created, so from the sparks struck out by two souls is the body of Truth created.

Zangwill, *Voice of Jerusalem*, 1921, p. 4.

839. SOUND

839.1 A donkey likes its snort as a canary its song.

Caspi, *Commentary*, to *Prov.* 23.15.

839.2 We can seldom see a flaw in a bell; we must hear its ring to know if it exists.

Heine, *Baths of Lucca*, 1828, ch 1.

839.3 Who shouts of his labor covets another's yield.

Hoffenstein, *Pencil in the Air*, 1923, p. 148.

839.4 Burning thorns crackle, as if to say, "We too are wood!"

Levi b. Zeira. *Eccles. R.*, 7.6.

839.5 Neighbors cannot protest the noise of an artisan's hammer, or of mill-stones, or of children.

Mishna: Baba Bathra, 2.3.

839.6 One coin in a bottle rattles (Little learning boasts).

Proverb. q Hezekiah b. Hiyya. *Midrash Tehillim*, 1.21.

839.7 Noisy as in a synagog.

*Proverb. q Zoozman, *Zitatenschatz der Weltliteratur*.

839.8 It is not for the shouter to complain of the echo.

H. Samuel, *A Book of Quotations*, 1947, p. 192.

839.9 Nothing is done in this world without producing a sound.

Zohar: Gen., 92a.

840. SOUR GRAPES

840.1 Who cannot afford meat say, it is foul.

Meiri, *Commentary*, to *Prov.*, c. 1300.

841. SOVEREIGNTY

841.1 Sovereignty is transferred from nation to nation on account of the violence of pride.

Apocrypha: Ben Sira, 10.8.

841.2 It is a dangerous mistake to think that an international institution can obtain permanent peace without having the authority to intervene in the legislation of the various countries, and even perhaps in their government.

Bergson, *Two Sources of Morality and Religion*, 1935, p. 279.

841.3 As long as there are sovereign nations possessing great power, war is inevitable.

Einstein. *Atlantic Monthly*, Nov. 1945.

841.4 The nations, in their assumption of the right of absolute sovereignty, are still under the sway of paganism. . . . In the Jewish prayer-book we read: "Our

Father, our King, we have no sovereign but Thee."
Lubin, letter to Brandeis, March 20, 1918. q ADL, 343.

842. SPACE

842.1 A needle's eye is not too narrow to hold two friends who agree.
Kimhi, *Shekel HaKodesh*, 12C.

842.2 There is always room for sweet things.
Proverb. q Abayé. *T: Megilla*, 7b.

842.3 Let us love each other more, and we shall have a feeling of spaciousness.
Raphael of Bershad. q BTH, i. 130.

843. SPAIN

843.1 How can you call Ferdinand of Aragon a wise king, the same Ferdinand who impoverished his own land and enriched ours?
*Sultan Bajazet, on Spain's expulsion of Jews, 1492. Frishman (*Alle Verk*, iv. 196) attrib. it to Manuel of Portugal, 1497.

843.2 Ever since the time of the Maranos, all Spaniards of superior rank have Jewish blood.
Hermann. q Julius Bab. *Aufbau*, July 30, 1954, p. 16.

843.3 The Spanish noon is a blaze of azure fire, and the dusty pilgrims crawl like an endless serpent along treeless plains . . . O bird of the air, whisper to the despairing exiles, that today, today, from the many-masted, gayly-bannered port of Palos, sails the world-unveiling Genoese, to unlock the golden gates of sunset and bequeath a Continent to freedom!
E. Lazarus, *Little Poems in Prose.*

843.4 Where, we are tempted to ask, when we behold the persecution of an innocent, industrious people for the crime of adhesion to the faith of their ancestors, where was the charity, which led the old Castilian to reverence valor and virtue in an infidel, though an enemy?
*Prescott, *Ferdinand and Isabella*, (1837) 1868, i. 263.

843.5 We turn to our exiled sons for inspiration in the work of carrying on the great traditions of our land. In them, who throughout the far-flung parts of the earth demonstrate the lasting vigor and undying spiritual worth of our culture, we find nourishment for our spirits.
*Pulido. *American Israelite*, Feb. 5, 1925.

844. SPECIALIZATION

844.1 Each gifted people, like every gifted individual, has a specialty.
Hess, *Rome and Jerusalem*, 1862.

844.2 You cannot be everything if you want to be anything.
Schechter, *Studies in Judaism*, 1896. i. 150.

845. SPEECH

845.A. Value

845.A.1 Wisdom is known through utterance.
Apocrypha: Ben Sira, 4.24.

845.A.2 Regard the speech, not the speaker.
Caspi, *Yoré Deah*, 14C, ch 16. AHE, 155.

845.A.3 The need for speech and work is greater than the need for silence and rest.
M. Ibn Ezra, *Shirat Yisrael*, (12C) 1924, p. 132.

845.A.4 When a man refrains from speech, his ideas die, his soul stops, and his senses deteriorate.
Ibid., 133.

845.A.5 We own no master to our lips.
Ibn Gabirol, *Selected Religious Poems*, 31.

845.A.6 Speech is often more effectual than arms.
Josephus, *Wars*, 5.9.2.

845.A.7 Speech has no value unless it can be translated into action, and action has no value unless it cannot be retranslated in speech.
Klatzkin, *In Praise of Wisdom*, 1943, p. 310.

845.A.8 Speech, the mother of thought.
K. Kraus. q Armitage, *Schoenberg*, p. 253.

845.A.9 Talk is valuable only when talk is action.
London, speech, U.S. Congress, Jan. 18, 1916. q RES, 71.

845.A.10 He who masters his speech will not be overcome.
Nahman Bratzlav, *Sefer HaMiddot, Meriba*, 1821.

845.A.11 Speech is light and winged by nature.
Philo, *Change of Names*, 43.

845.A.12 Wherein will a man find tranquility . . . except in speech?
Philo, *Dreams*, 1.18.

845.A.13 Before speaking, weigh your words.
Talmud: Derek Eretz, 1.30.

845.B. Danger

845.B.1 Talk . . . tends to penury.
Bible: Prov., 14.23.

845.B.2 As it is a duty to say what will be heard, so is it a duty not to say what will not be heard.
Eleazar b. Simeon. *T: Yebamot*, 65b.

845.B.3 Do what you say, but say not what you do.
Elijah b. Raphael, *Tzavaah*, 18C. AHE, 309.

845.B.4 Before I speak I am master of the word; after I speak, the word is master of me.
Ibn Gabirol, *Mibhar HaPeninim*, c. 1050, #338.

845.B.5 The less you speak, the less you err.
Ibid., #354.

845.B.6 Speech is well calculated to conceal and obscure faults.
Philo, *Dreams*, 1.17.

845.B.7 A fool says what he knows, a sage knows what he says.
Simha Bunam. q BTH, ii. 256.

845.B.8 Do not speak what is superfluous.
Zalman of St. Goar, *Tzavaah*. q SSJ, i. 146.

845.C. Loquacity

845.C.1 There is nothing in the world better for the purification of the soul than the curbing of idle talk.
Agnon, *Days of Awe*, 1948, p. 20.

845.C.2 The fault with charity—too little; with speech—too much.
Al-Harizi, *Tahkemoni*, 1218, ch 44.

845.C.3 The speaking ceased and they proceeded to enjoy themselves.
Apocrypha: Aristeas, 202.

845.C.4 Prate not in the assembly of elders.
Apocrypha: Ben Sira, 7.14.

845.C.5 Let your speech be short, comprehending much in few words.
Ibid., 32.8.

845.C.6 Be liberal with your wealth, not with your words.
Bahya, *Hobot HaLebabot*, 1040, 8.3.17.

845.C.7 Beware of idle talk.
Ben Azzai. *ARN*, ch 1. See Nahman b. Isaac. *T: Yoma*, 77a.

845.C.8 Tell not all you know.
Mendelé, *Di Kliatshé*, 1873, ch 12.

845.C.9 There is overreaching in trade, and in—talk.
Mishna: Baba Metzia, 4.10.

845.C.10 Use not vain repetitions.
New Testament: Matt., 6.7.

845.C.11 Much talk leads to sin.
Simeon b. Gamaliel I. *Mishna: Abot*, 1.17.

845.D. Fair Speech

845.D.1 Be fair in speech to all alike.
Apocrypha: Aristeas, 191.

845.D.2 Gentle speech multiplies friends.
Apocrypha: Ben Sira, 6.5.

845.D.3 Like cooling dew on parched soil is gentle speech on a gift.
Ibid., 18.15.

845.D.4 Speech finely framed delights the ears.
Apocrypha: II Macc., 15.39.

845.D.5 I grew intoxicated with my own eloquence.
Disraeli, *Contarini Fleming*, 1832, 1.7.

845.D.6 Eloquence is the child of knowledge.
Disraeli, *Young Duke*, 1831, 5.6. See *Endymion*, 1880.

845.D.7 Can fine words feed the hungry?
Hasdai, *Ben HaMelek VeHaNazir*, c. 1230, Introduction.

845.D.8 The branches' length depends on the tree's roots, and right speech on the man's sense.
Ibn Gabirol, *Poems*.

845.D.9 Always use refined speech.
Ishmael School. *T: Pesahim*, 3a.

845.D.10 Well-chosen phrases are a great help in the smuggling of offensive ideas.
Jabotinsky, *The War and the Jew*, 1942, p. 120.

845.D.11 God withholds not reward even for an elegant phrase.
Johanan. *T: Baba Kamma*, 38b.

845.D.12 Let your utterance be clear, tranquil, and apt to the point.
Maimonides, *Shaaré HaMusar*. AHE, 106. See Nahmanides, letter to his son Nahman, c. 1168. *NT: Col.* 4.6.

845.D.13 Stronger than giant still
Are tongues that gently speak,
Nothing will malice kill
Like tender words and meek.

Santob de Carrion, *Proverbios Morales*, 1350, 583.

845.D.14 When you speak of someone, tell the good you know of him.

Sefer Hasidim, 13C. ZEH, 20.

845.E. Evil Speech

845.E.1 A man accustomed to disgraceful speech will never learn wisdom.

Apocrypha: Ben Sira, 23.15.

845.E.2 A worthy man who utters a reprehensible word is like a parlor through which runs a tanner's pipe.

Eliezer b. Jacob. *T: Pirké Ben Azzai*, 1.3.

845.E.3 All know why a bride enters the bridal chamber; yet if one befouls his mouth with a word of folly, he forfeits the prosperity of a lifetime.

Hanan b. Rabbah. *T: Sabbath*, 33a.

845.E.4 Gehenna is made deep for a lewd speaker.

Hisda. *T: Sabbath*, 33a.

845.E.5 A famous man once asked God to remove the evil tongue and perverse lips against him, and God said: "How shall I do for you what I do not for Myself?"

M. Ibn Ezra, *Shirat Yisrael*, (12C) 1924, p. 96.

845.E.6 Ignorant people sin mortally when they call the Holy Ark a chest, or the Synagog a public house.

Ishmael b. Eleazar. *T: Sabbath*, 32a.

845.E.7 Never utter an ugly word.

Joshua b. Levi. *T: Pesahim*, 3a.

845.E.8 Who defiles his mouth with profanity has no share in the bliss of the world to come.

Leon of Modena, *On Games of Chance*, tr Gollancz, 188.

845.E.9 Speech is a God-given boon peculiar to man, and must not be employed for that which is degrading.

Maimonides, *Guide for the Perplexed*, 1190, 3.8.

846. SPINOZA

846.1 This little man with the gigantic spirit emerged out of the Middle Age as a rock towering from the water.

Antokolski, letter to S. I. Mamontoff, Dec. 1877.

846.2 Spinoza was drunk with eternity.

Benda, *Belphégor*, (1919) 1929, p. 52.

846.3 It is true that Spinoza rejects the idea of an anthropomorphic God who will respond to our flattering prayers. . . . If, however, religion consists in humility (as a sense of infinite power beyond our scope), charity and love (as a sense of the mystic potency in our fellow human beings), and spirituality (as a sense of the limitations of all that is merely material, actual or even attainable), then no one was more deeply religious than Spinoza.

M. R. Cohen, *A Dreamer's Journey*, 1949, 217.

846.4 Through a thousand veins and arteries, through the mysterious sluiceways and channels of the philosophic, economic and literary mind, the doctrines of Benedict de Spinoza are flowing into the universal consciousness of the world.

De Casseres. *Reflex*, Aug. 1927, p. 36.

846.5 The theoretical portion of our scientific teaching is really—systematic Spinozism.

*Fichte, *Works*, i. 102. q *JQRo*, viii. 65.

846.6 Spinoza is one of the great heroes of humanity. He has delivered men from the vain fear and the vain hope of being immortal, in making them know and feel that they are eternal.

*France. *Chronicon Spinozanum*, iii. (*Menorah Journal*, 1924, x. 199).

846.7 Spinoza is the chief point of modern philosophy; either Spinozism or no philosophy.

*Hegel, *Works*, xv. 374. q *JQRo*, viii. 65.

846.8 If one begins to philosophize, one must first be a Spinozist. The soul must bathe in this ether of one Substance, in which everything that men have looked upon as true has sunk!

Ibid.

846.9 In reading Spinoza, we are seized by a feeling as when contemplating Nature in her grandest aspects of life-inspired repose, a forest of thoughts, high as heaven, whose blooming summits are in wavy motion, while their immovable trunks are deep-rooted in earth. There is a certain air in the writings of Spinoza which is inexplicable; we are breathed on as by the breezes of the future. The spirit of the Hebrew prophets, it may be, rested on their remote descendant.

Heine, *Germany from Luther to Kant*, 1834.

846.10 All of our modern philosophers, perhaps unconsciously, see through the glasses which Baruch Spinoza ground.

Heine, *Romantic School,* 1835, ii. ch 3.

846.11 Love is the highest reason, as well as the purest, most divinely willing; if we will not believe this from St. John, we may do so from the undoubtedly *still more godly Spinoza,* whose philosophy and morality move entirely round this axis.

*Herder, *On Perception and Feeling,* 1778.

846.12 Spinoza's doctrine is Jewish to the core: Nature and God ... are different modes of one ... energy that spans the All. Nature is God. God is nature. But mind in man is also in nature. Mind in man being personal, ... we have the right to urge that in nature is personality.

E. G. Hirsch. *Reform Advocate,* 1897, xiii. 73.

846.13 When we combine the de-anthropomorphized Deity of Maimonides with the eternity of matter of Gersonides, the determinism of Crescas and the immanence of Divinity in all things taught by the Cabala, and cast them into the mould of Cartesian method, we have the materials for the so-called Pantheism of Spinoza.

Jacobs, *Jewish Ideals,* 1896, p. 53f.

846.14 There is but one philosphy, the philosophy of Spinoza.

*Lessing. q Jacobi (q *JE,* xi. 519b).

846.15 A man may adopt a Spinozistic attitude towards the conception of God, and yet claim to be a Jew.

Montefiore, *Liberal Judaism,* 1903, p. 5.

846.16 Spinoza is a God-intoxicated man (*Gott-trunkener Mensch*).

*Novalis, *Glauben und Liebe, Paralipomena,* #355. *Schriften,* 1923, ii., 292.

846.17 Judaism gave the world the greatest herald of the new era in Spinoza.

Oko. *Menorah Journal,* 1919, v. 129.

846.18 Spinozism ... is not a system but a habit of mind.

*Pollock, *Spinoza,* (1880) 1899, p. 381.

846.19 This powerful tradition of idealism and of hoping against all hope, this religion which demanded of its adherents the most heroic sacrifices without (and which was of its very essence) promising anything certain in return beyond this life, was the healthy and bracing atmosphere in which Spinoza was reared. ... At bottom he was at one with the true fathers of Judaism, especially with that great Maimonides, who had been instrumental in introducing into Judaism the boldest philosophy.

*Renan, *Spinoza,* Feb. 21, 1877.

846.20 This man from his granite pedestal will point out to all men the way of blessedness which he found; and ages hence the cultivated traveler passing by this spot will say in his heart: "The truest vision ever had of God came, perhaps, here."

*Renan, at Spinoza's statue in The Hague, 1882. q Sachar, *History of the Jews,* 1940, p. 248.

846.21 Spinoza is the noblest and most lovable of the great philosophers. Intellectually, some others have surpassed him, but ethically, he is supreme.

*Russell, *History of Western Philosophy,* 1945, p. 569.

846.22 O thou most vilely misjudged sage, modest and virtuous Spinoza, forgive me for having shared the error of all concerning thy books before I had read them, and receive today the tribute of gratitude due to thee. If in an age of corruption and madness, and in the capital famed for its talents and its pleasures, I have remained true to the faith of my fathers, it is thou whom I have to thank.

*Abbé Sabatier de Castres, *Apologie de Spinoza,* 1766. q *JQRo,* viii. 59.

846.23 No one can really hope to reach what is true and perfect in philosophy, who has not at least once in his life plunged into the abyss of Spinozism.

*Schelling, *Works,* 1.5.10, p. 33.

846.24 Offer respectfully with me a fillet to the manes of the sainted, outcast Spinoza! He was penetrated by the high world-spirit, the Eternal was his beginning and end, the Universe his one and everlasting love; in sacred innocence and deep humility he reflected himself in the eternal world, and say, too, how he was its most lovable reflecting-glass. Full of religion was he, and full of the Holy Spirit; and thus here also he stands alone and unapproached, master in his art, but exalted above the profane vulgar, without flowers and without rights of citizenship.

*Schleiermacher, *Works on Theology,* i. 190.

846.25 I see how much Benedict owes to Baruch.

q Zangwill, *Dreamers of the Ghetto,* 211.

847. SPINSTER

847.1 Being an old maid is like death by drowning, a really delightful sensation after you cease to struggle.
Ferber.

847.2 Rather a young widow than an old maid.
Proverb (Yiddish). BJS, #492.

848. SPIRIT

848.1 I will put a new spirit within you.
Bible: Ezek., 11.19.

848.2 Renew a steadfast spirit within me.
Bible: Ps., 51.12.

848.3 The spirit of man will sustain his infirmity; but a broken spirit who can bear?
Bible: Prov., 18.14.

848.4 The spirit of man is the lamp of the Lord, searching all the inward parts.
Ibid., 20.27.

848.5 So act as to elicit the latent spiritual possibilities in others, and therefore in thyself.
F. Adler, *Life and Destiny*, 1903, p. 82.

848.6 The capacity of a man to withstand fire and death, to fight and be victorious, depends not only on his technical capacity and professional knowledge but on the spirit within him.
Ben Gurion, *How Secure Is Israel? JS*, July 1951, p. 18.

848.7 A people profoundly religious, a people whose very history has been the history of an idea, are to be made to feel again the truth, that the life of the spirit is not a thing apart, that it is in every thought and every word and every act.
Cardozo, speech, Free Synagog, 1915.

848.8 Judaism is fundamentally opposed to paganism . . . [in that] the former subjected nature to the spirit.
Graetz, *Construction of Jewish History.* summ. WHJ, iii. 536.

848.9 While among the Phoenician people the Spiritual was still limited by Nature, in the case of the Jews we find it entirely purified. . . . Nature—which in the East is the primary fundamental existence—is now depressed to the condition of a mere creature; and Spirit now occupies the first place.
*Hegel, *Philosophy of History*, 1830, 1.3.4. tr Sibree, 195.

848.10 To be sure, the very essence of Judaism is the struggle of the spirit with the flesh. Nevertheless, neither the prophets, . . . nor the authors of the Talmud put undue emphasis on this antithesis, nor did they seek to mortify the flesh and make man entirely spiritual.
Klausner, *From Jesus to Paul*, 1944, p. 487f.

848.11 The spiritual is automatic, that is, its functioning is its essence.
Krochmal, *More Nebuke HaZeman*, (1851) 1924, ch 7, p. 36.

848.12 If there is one thing fundamental to the life of the spirit it is the absence of force.
Laski, *A Political Grammar*, 1925, p. 33.

848.13 Spirituality is like a bird: if you hold on to it tightly, it chokes, and if you hold it loosely, it escapes.
Lipkin. q KTH, i. 275.

848.14 The Jewish spirit, the Jewish soul, is the most important thing we have. In some sense it is all we have, all that is worth having and living and struggling for.
Magnes, 1916. q BFZ, 283.

848.15 We are not here for the sake of possession, or of power, or of happiness, but we are here to transfigure the divine out of the human spirit.
Rathenau, *Von kommenden Dingen*, 1917, Conclusion.

848.16 In the spiritual realm too no atom is lost; what was remains indestructible. In our spirits there survive all the spirits of all the ages.
H. Steinthal, *Mythos und Religion*, 1870, p. 1.

848.17 Faith in Isreal means faith in the spiritual strength of the world.
N. Syrkin, 1924.

849. SPIRIT OF GOD

849.1 Who has meted out the spirit of the Lord?
Bible: Isa., 40.13.

849.2 The spirit of the Lord caused them to rest.
Ibid., 63.14.

849.3 I will put My spirit in you, and ye shall live.
Bible: Ezek., 37.14.

849.4 I will pour out My spirit upon all flesh.
Bible: Joel, 3.1. See *Ezek.*, 39.29.

849.5 I am full of power by the spirit of the Lord.
Bible: Mic., 3.8.

849.6 My spirit abides among you; fear not.
Bible: Hag., 2.5.

849.7 Not by might, nor by power, but by My spirit.
Bible: Zech., 4.6.

849.8 Take not Thy holy spirit from me.
Bible: Ps., 41.13.

849.9 Let Thy good spirit lead me in an even land.
Ibid., 143.10.

849.10 The Creator planted His sweet spirit in all, and made it a guide to all mortals.
Apocrypha: Sibyl, 1.5f.

849.11 The spirit of God cannot lie.
Ibid., 3.701.

849.12 "The spirit of God hovered" [*Gen.* 1.2]—like a dove brooding over her young, barely touching them.
Ben Zoma. *T: Hagiga,* 15a. See *Gen. R.,* 2.4.

849.13 Glorious edifices and the drama of a magnificent liturgy do not enhance the power of church and synagog when the spirit of God has fled!
Lazaron, *Common Ground,* 1938, p. 317.

849.14 Where the spirit of the Lord is, there is liberty.
New Testament: II Cor., 3.17. See *Gal.,* 5.22f.

849.15 I call heaven and earth to witness that, whether Jew or Gentile, man or woman, servant or maid, according to one's deeds does the Holy Spirit rest upon him.
Seder Eliyahu Rabbah, ch 10 (9), ed Friedmann, 48.

849.16 All that the righteous have accomplished, they have accomplished through the Holy Spirit.
Tanhuma, VaYehi, #14, 78a.

850. STARS

850.1 There shall step forth a star out of Jacob.
Bible: Num., 24.17.

850.2 The stars in their courses fought against Sisera.
Bible: Judg., 5.20.

850.3 The beauty and glory of heaven are the stars, gleaming ornaments in the heights of God. At the word of the Holy One they take their prescribed places, and sleep not at their watches.
Apocrypha: Ben Sira, 43.9f.

850.4 Stars in which one no longer believes grow pale.
Heine, *Lutetia,* March 31, 1841.

850.5 Are ye God's meditations, thoughts indeed,
Engraved upon the annals of the skies?
M. J. Lebensohn, "To the Stars," #5 (*Kinor Bat Tziyon,* 7) tr FHH, 26.

850.6 The large stars—like an evening reception, the milky way—like a great society.
Pasternak, *Safe Conduct,* 2.8. *Prose Works,* 1945, p. 82.

850.7 Don't look up to heaven, for what will you see in the sky, except stars, luminous but cold, wholly insensitive to pity?
Peretz, *Drei Matones,* 1904-15. LP, 187.

850.8 When one star is visible, it is day; when two stars appear, it is twilight; and when three stars are seen, it is night.
Samuel. *T: Sabbath,* 35b.

850.9 God, if You wish for our love,
Fling us a handful of stars!
L. Untermeyer, "Caliban." *Challenge,* 1915, p. 104.

851. STATE

851.1 The struggle for God and His commandments was often a struggle against the commandments of the State.
Baeck, *The Pharisees,* 1947, p. 48.

851.2 The state, cradle of humaneness, has become its coffin.
Boerne, *Kritiken,* 1825, #5.

851.3 If the moral and physical fiber of its manhood and its womanhood is not a state concern, the question is, what is?
Cardozo, *Adler vs. Deegan,* 1929, 251 N.Y. Reports, 467.

851.4 The state is made for man, not man for the state.
Einstein, *The World As I See It,* 1924, p. 204.

851.5 The state must perish if man becomes tied to it in such a way that the welfare of the state, its power and its glory become the criteria of good and evil.
Fromm, *Psychoanalysis and Religion,* 1950, p. 84f.

851.6 The redemption toward which Jews have striven for thousands of years, is not identical with State, government, military power, war and diplomacy, but is as different from all this as day is from night.

Hofshi, 1950. *Selected Essays,* i. 1952, p. 57.

851.7 When the human being has attained true maturity, the state will become obsolete. It will finally be done away with as an unnatural infringement upon human liberty, and as a perversion of life's inherent simplicities.

Judah Löw. summ. BWC, 85f.

851.8 The State, according to Jewish interpretation, rests on two mutually complimentary foundations: the need for duly constituted authority, and the necessity to delimit its powers.

Livneh, *BeShaar HaTekufa,* 1952, *JS,* Dec. 1952, p. 9.

851.9 A State, not guarded against those to whom a State means the highest ideal, always devours its own children.

Maybaum. *Judaism,* 1954, iii. 105.

851.10 The majesty and sanctity of the State consists above all in the firm administration of justice.

Stahl, *Staatslehre,* 1847.

851.11 The State is the folk constituted as a personality.

Stahl. q BRN, 96.

851.12 The state system of Europe is akin to the system of cages in an impoverished provincial zoo.

Trotsky, *What Next?* 1932.

851.13 Judaism imposes upon its adherents the duty of serving the state to which they belong with devotion, and promoting its national interests with all their heart and might.

Verein duetscher Rabbiner, *Declaration,* July 6, 1897.

852. STATESMAN

852.1 An elder statesman is somebody old enough to know his own mind and keep quiet about it.

Baruch.

852.2 The extreme scarcity of political leaders of any caliber is owing to the fact that they are called upon to decide at any moment, and in detail, problems which the increased size of societies may well have rendered insoluble.

Bergson, *Two Sources of Morality and Religion,* 1935, p. 264.

852.3 The world is weary of statesmen whom democracy has degraded into politicians.

Disraeli, *Lothair,* 1870.

852.4 The politician says: "I will give you what you want." The statesman says: "What you think you want is this. What it is possible for you get is that. What you really want, therefore, is the following."

Lippmann, *A Preface to Morals,* 1929, p. 281f.

852.5 Statesmen . . . are suspected of plotting against mankind, rather than consulting their interests, and are esteemed more crafty than learned.

Spinoza, *Tractatus Politicus,* 1677, 1.2.

853. STATION

853.1 Great duties could alone confer great station.

Disraeli, speech, House of Commons, July 12, 1839.

853.2 The man most fit for high station is not he who demands it.

M. Ibn Ezra, *Shirat Yisrael,* (12C) 1924, p. 83.

853.3 It is of great advantage that man should know his station, and not erroneously imagine that the whole universe exists only for him.

Maimonides, *Guide for the Perplexed,* 1190, 3.12.

854. STATISTICS

854.1 There are three kinds of lies: lies, damned lies, and statistics.

Disraeli, attributed to.

854.2 Statistics in Israel today are like potatoes: they lie in the mud, but they're growing!

q S. J. Kahn. *Menorah Journal,* 1954, xlii. 125.

854.3 Statistics are the heart of democracy.

Strunsky, *Topics of the Times,* Nov. 30, 1944.

855. STATURE

855.1 The Holy One takes pride in the stature of tall men.

Abbahu. *T: Bekorot,* 45b.

856. STIMULATION

856.1 A sluggish soul needs stimulation just as much as a sluggish liver.

O. H. Kahn, *Of Many Things,* 1926, p. 73.

857. STONE

857.1 The stone which the builders rejected has become the chief corner-stone.
Bible: Ps., 118.22.

857.2 Throw no stones into the well from which you have drunk.
Proverb. q Raba. *T: Baba Kamma,* 92b.

857.3 Men spend their days in cages of stone,
And in their death slabs of stone close the graves:
Stone, stone, stone.
Shneor, *Shira SheBeHed,* 1908 (Shirim, 1952, ii. 49). q WHJ, iv. 290.

857.4 Whether the stone falls on the pot, or the pot on the stone, woe to the pot!
Simeon b. Jose b. Lakunia. *Esther Rabbah,* 7.10.

858. STRANGER

858.1 One law for the native and the stranger among you.
Bible: Exod., 12.49.

858.2 The stranger . . . you shall love as yourself.
Bible: Lev., 19.34. See 24.22, *Exod.* 22.20, *Num.* 15.16, *Deut.* 10.18f.

858.3 Also the aliens . . . will I make joyful in My house of prayer.
Bible: Isa., 56.6f. See *1 Kings,* 8.41ff.

858.4 Divide this land . . . to you and the strangers . . . among you.
Bible: Ezek., 47.21f.

858.5 He that is surety for a stranger shall smart for it.
Bible: Prov., 11.15.

858.6 Strangers will one day be ministering priests in the Temple.
Berekia. *Exod. R.,* 19.4.

858.7 No ancient constitution accorded to strangers such a position as they enjoyed under the Mosaic code.
Butcher. q JQRo, xvii. 415.

858.8 With the law of shielding the alien, true religion begins. . . . In the alien, man discovered the idea of humanity.
H. Cohen. q *DPB,* ed Hertz, 90f. See BEJ, 202.

858.9 The Jewish codes were more favorable to strangers than those of any other people.
Döllinger, Heidentum und Judentum, 1857, p. 788.

858.10 Scripture warns us, there is a bad streak in the stranger.
Eliezer b. Hyrcanus. *Mekilta,* to *Exod.* 22.20.

858.11 Build your home in such a way that a stranger may feel happy in your midst.
Herzl, *Diary,* Aug. 6, 1896.

858.12 The Lacedaemonians made a practice of expelling foreigners and would not allow their own citizens to travel abroad, in both cases apprehensive of their laws being corrupted. . . . We, on the contrary, while having no desire to emulate the customs of others, yet gladly welcome any who wish to share our own.
Josephus, *Against Apion,* ii. 36.

858.13 In our law it is a greater sin to rob or defraud a stranger than a fellow Jew. A Jew must show his charity to all men.
Manasseh b. Israel, *Vindiciae Judaeorum,* 1656.

858.14 Wherever a religious act is prescribed in Israel, strangers must be especially included.
Mekilta, to *Exod.* 12.19.

858.15 A stranger's rose is but a thorn.
Peretz, *In Alien Lands,* tr Leah W. Leonard.

858.16 In a strange place, a dog does not bark for seven years.
Proverb. q Lipperheide, *Spruchwörterbuch: Fremde.*

858.17 The native below, and the stranger on top?!
Proverb. q Raba. *T: Erubin,* 9a.

858.18 On strangers' graves, we don't weep our eyes out.
Proverb (Yiddish). BJS, #1334.

858.19 Wresting the judgment of a stranger is like wresting the judgment of God.
Simeon b. Lakish. *T: Hagiga,* 5a.

858.20 Are you, Jew, ever a stranger? God is with you everywhere.
Tanhuma. *Deut. R.,* 2.16.

858.21 To be a stranger is a prodigious occupation requiring diligence and skill.
Werfel, *Between Heaven and Earth,* 1944, p. 215.

859. STRENGTH

859.1 As thy days, so shall thy strength be.
Bible: Deut., 33.25.

859.2 Not by strength shall man prevail.
Bible: I Sam., 2.9.

859.3 Be strong, and quit yourselves like men.
Ibid., 4.9.

859.4 The Lord will give strength to His people.
Bible: Ps., 29.11.

859.5 A mighty man is not delivered by great strength.
Bible: Ps., 33.16.

859.6 Happy is the man whose strength is in Thee.
Ibid., 84.6.

859.7 They go from strength to strength.
Ibid., 84.8.

859.8 Strength and dignity are her clothing.
Bible: Prov., 31.25.

859.9 When you see a man stronger than you, rise before him.
Apocrypha: Ahikar, 2.61.

859.10 For what God demands, He provides us with strength.
S. R. Hirsch, *Horeb*, 1838, #519.

859.11 Only the strong are to be strengthened, and the quick to be quickened.
Judah b. Bathyra. *Sifré*, to *Num.*, #1.

859.12 There are ten strong things in the world: Rock, but iron cleaves it. Iron, but fire softens it. Fire, but water quenches it. Water but clouds bear it. Clouds, but wind scatters them. Wind, but the body withstands it. The body, but fright crushes it. Fright, but wine banishes it. Wine, but sleep works it off. Death is stronger than all, and charity saves from it [*Prov.* 10.2].
Judah b. Ilai. *T: Baba Bathra*, 10a.

859.13 The strong ought to bear the infirmities of the weak.
New Testament: Rom., 15.1.

859.14 Our strength is rooted not in our being a world power, but in our being the people of the Lord.
Opatoshu, *Last Revolt*, 1952, ch 41, p. 263.

859.15 Is not bodily strength a shadow which any chance disease can destroy?
Philo, *Posterity of Cain*, 33.

859.16 I'll be the strongest amid you,
Not lightning, stream or mountain blue,
But dew that, falling to the earth,
Gives strength....

I'll be the strongest in the land.
I'll be the word that heals, the hand
That unseen, still, as from above,
Gives love.
Yehoash, "The Strongest," tr M. Syrkin. *Reflex*, July 1927, 62.

859.17 In Jewish blood and muscle, not in Jewish weeping and wailing, lies the hope of our people.
Zangwill, speech, VI Zionist Congress, Sept. 1903.

860. STUDY
860.A. Evaluation

860.A.1 Much study is weariness of the flesh.
Bible: Eccles., 12.12.

860.A.2 Study must precede practice.
Abbahu et alia. *TJ: Pesahim*, 3.7. See *T: Kiddushin*, 40b.

860.A.3 Neglect not the discourse of the wise.
Apocrypha: Ben Sira, 8.9.

860.A.4 Study from love, and honor will follow.
Bahya, *Hobot HaLebabot*, 1040, Introduction.

860.A.5 Were an angel to reveal to me all the mysteries of the Torah, it would please me little, for study is more important than knowledge. Only what man achieves through effort is dear to him.
Elijah Gaon. See *Reflex*, Dec. 1927, p. 57.

860.A.6 It was the Holy Book, and the study of it, that kept the scattered people together.
Freud, *Moses and Monotheism*, 1939.

860.A.7. What *virtus*, taken as fortitude, and philosophy meant to the Roman, the Bible and study are to the Jew. Abravanel wrote his commentary after his diplomatic activities had proved futile and the splendor of life a mere vanity. He fled to the realm of eternity, in order to find there his anchorage and to create values which no storm can dissipate.
I. Heinemann. *MGWJ*, Nov. 1938.

860.A.8 They [Jews in Russia] study the Talmud because it is the spirit and aim of their life, not in order to know and use this knowledge for ulterior purposes. . . . They study with their hearts.
M. Lilienthal, *My Travels in Russia*, 288.

860.A.9 I thank Thee . . . that Thou hast set my lot with those who attend the house of study, not with those who frequent circuses. Both they and I rise early, they for frivolity, I for Torah. They and I labor, and are on the march: they toward the pit of destruction, I toward the world of eternity.

Nehunia b. HaKana. *T: Berakot,* 28b.

860.A.10 God to David: I prefer one day you spend in study to a thousand offerings Solomon will bring on the altar.

Rab. *T: Sabbath,* 30a. Cf *Erubin,* 63b.

860.A.11 Study, though you may forget, though you do not fully understand.

Raba. *T: Aboda Zara,* 19a.

860.A.12 I will not shut myself up in the house of study, while there is no bread in my home [*Isa.* 3.7].

Talmud: Sabbath, 120a.

860.B. Subjects

860.B.1 I hope the time will come when the laws and literature of the ancient Hebrews will be studied in all of our schools as now are studied the laws and literature of the ancient Greeks and Romans, and when it will be universally recognized that no man ignorant of the laws and literature of the ancient Hebrews is a well-educated man.

Abbott, The 250th Anniversary of . . . Jews in U.S., 1905, 232.

860.B.2 Study . . . man, and . . . when we arrive at an understanding of man, much of the mystery of the universe will be clear to us.

Bahya, *Hobot HaLebabot,* 1040, 2.5.

860.B.3 Delve deep into the study of Mishna.

Banaah. *Pesikta Kahana,* ch 27, ed Buber, 158a.

860.B.4 His admirable elasticity of mind the Jew owes, first and foremost, to the study of the Talmud.

Cassel, *Lehrbuch d. jüd. Gesch. & Lit.,* 1879, p. 198.

860.B.5 It is within man's province to explore all things, above and below, created by God, but he must not pass beyond these boundaries to investigate the essence of God.

Dunash Ibn Tamim, *Commentary to Sefer Yetzira,* 955. q FJR, 12.

860.B.6 Askest thou in what to set thy lore?

In Grammar much, but in the Talmud more.

Ezobi, *Kaarat Kesef,* 1270 (tr *JQRo,* viii. 537).

860.B.7 Let the study of Torah be the foundation, and the study of other things secondary.

Falaquera, *Iggeret HaVikuah,* 13C.

860.B.8 I regretted my years at college. . . . I should have studied Hebrew, learned to know my race, its origins, its beliefs, its role in history, its place among the human groups of today; to attach myself through it to something that should be I, and something more than I, to continue through it something that others had begun and that others after me would carry on.

Fleg, *Why I Am a Jew,* 1929, p. 41.

860.B.9 A scholar of the traditional text, who learns nothing else, is like a camel carrying a load of silk: silk and camel are of no use to each other.

A. Ibn Ezra, *Yesod Mora,* 1158, ch 1, 1840, p. 4.

860.B.10 I will make the wisdom of the ancients my portion. . . .
When I dive into the sea of their knowledge,
I bring forth pearls to adorn my neck.

M. Ibn Ezra, tr Solis-Cohen, 7f.

860.B.11 To talk of the inconceivable is foolishness, and to argue about the incomprehensible is a sin.

q M. Ibn Ezra, *Shirat Yisrael,* (12C) 1924, p. 84.

Ibn Gabirol, *Mibhar HaPeninim,* c. 1050, #76.

860.B.12 Nothing sharpens the intellect like moral instruction.

Ibn Gabirol, *Mibhar HaPeninim,* #2.

860.B.13 Who wishes to become wise should study civil law.

Ishmael. *T: Berakot,* 63b.

860.B.14 A father is obliged to teach his son civics.

Judah HaNasi. *Mekilta,* to *Exod.* 13.13.

860.B.15 Above all, study astronomy, for through it we can learn the greatness and power of the Lord.

Judah Löw. q LJG, 104.

860.B.16 Why should we nibble at the bones of later authors when we can feast on meat upon the golden tables of the Talmud, Alfasi, Maimonides, Asher, the pegs on which everything hangs?

A. S. Kaidanover, letter to Samuel Ha-levi, *Nahalat Shiva,* 1667, #50.

860.B.17 How shall man obtain a conception of the majesty of the Divine . . . ? Through the expansion of his scientific faculties; through the liberation of his imagination. . . ; through the disciplined study of the world and of life; through the cultivation of a rich, multifarious sensitivity to every phase of being. All these desiderata require obviously the study of all the branches of wisdom, all the philosophies of life, all the ways of the diverse civilizations and doctrines of ethics and religion in every nation and tongue.

Kook, *HaMahshaba HaYisraelit,* 1920, 15. q ABJ, 167f.

860.B.18 Before studying ethics, I blamed the whole world and justified myself; after I started the study, I blamed myself and also the world; but finally I blamed only myself.

Lipkin. q KTH, i. 274.

860.B.19 He who wishes to attain perfection must first study logic, next the various branches of mathematics in their proper order, then physics, and lastly metaphysics.

Maimonides, *Guide for the Perplexed,* 1190, 1.34.

860.B.20 It is ignorance or a kind of madness to weary our minds with subjects which are beyond our reach.

Ibid., 2.24.

860.B.21 Forbidden sexual relations may not be expounded in the presence of three, esoteric cosmogony in the presence of two, and the mysteries of the "Chariot" not even in the presence of one who is not a sage with an understanding of the subject by himself.

Mishna: Hagiga, 2.1.

860.B.22 Only he who dips into the wisdom of the "ancient ones" will drink the pure wine.

Nahmanides. q SSJ, i. 111.

860.B.23 Why venture to determine the indeterminate? . . . Rather make yourself the object of your impartial scrutiny. . . . Before you have investigated thoroughly your tenement, is it not an excess of madness to examine that of the universe?

Philo, *Dreams,* i. 10.

860.B.24 Wisdom's task is to investigate all that nature has to show.

Philo, *Providence,* 1.

860.B.25 It is mournful to observe how entirely we have turned our backs on the Hebrew sources. In the obscure, insolvable riddles of the Egyptian hieroglyphics the learned have been hoping to find the key of ancient doctrine, and now we hear of nothing but the language and wisdom of India, while the writings and traditions of the Rabbins are consigned to neglect without examination.

*Schelling. q Coleridge, *The Friend, Second Landing Place,* iv. 1818. See Moulton, *Literary Study of the Bible,* 1899, 2d ed, Preface, p. xii–xiii.

860.B.26 One cannot understand the Christian religion if one is not instructed in that of the Jews, whose faith was its pattern.

*R. Simon, French tr of Leon of Modena's *Historia dei Riti Ebraici,* (1674) 1684, Dedication. q PUS, 31.

860.B.27 Huna asked his son why he absented himself from Hisda's lectures. "Because," said the youth, "he treats of secular subjects, of the anatomy of glands, the function of elimination, even of the dangers in forcing oneself in a privy, and of ruptures and dislocations." "He treats of health," exclaimed the father, "and you call these secular subjects? All the more reason for attending!"

Talmud: Sabbath, 82a.

860.B.28 The Bible has been compared to water, the Mishna to wine, and the Gemara to liqueur. All three are necessary, and a rich man enjoys them all.

Talmud: Soferim, 15.7. See 15.8.

860.C. Time

860.C.1 When I lived in royal courts, I . . . had no time to delve into books. . . . It was only after I became a wanderer on the earth, going penniless from kingdom to kingdom, that I became a student of the Book of God.

Abravanel, response to Saul Cohen Ashkenazi, *Sheelot,* 1547. q I. Blumenfeld, *Otzar Nehmad,* 5617.

860.C.2 Say not, when I have leisure I will study; you may not have leisure.

Hillel. *Mishna: Abot,* 2.4.

860.C.3 Constant study is not study all day, but each day.

Lipkin, on *Exod.* 29.42. q KTH, i. 270.

860.C.4 The Torah says: If you forsake

me one day, I forsake you two days, like two going in opposite directions.

Megillat Hasidim. q Simeon b. Lakish. *TJ: Berakot, 9.5.*

860.C.5 Designate fixed times for the study of Torah.

Raba. *T: Erubin,* 54b.

860.C.6 Make your study of Torah a fixed engagement.

Shammai. *Mishna: Abot,* 1.15.

860.D. Companionship

860.D.1 Take care to study in company.

Eleazar b. Pedat. *T: Nedarim,* 81a. See *Sabbath,* 63a.

860.D.2 As "iron sharpens iron" [*Prov.* 27.17], so do two scholars sharpen one another's mind in law.

Hama b. Hanina. *T: Taanit,* 7a.

860.D.3 Who studies in a synagog will not easily forget.

Johanan b. Nappaha. *TJ: Berakot,* 5.1.

860.D.4 Provide yourself a teacher, acquire a comrade.

Joshua b. Perahia. *Mishna: Abot,* 1.6.

860.D.5 Move to a center of Torah, and expect not the Torah to follow you. Only colleagues will sustain your learning.

Nehorai. *Mishna: Abot,* 4.14.

860.D.6 *Jeremiah* 23.29 likened Torah to fire: as fire does not ignite of itself, so Torah lacks spark and endurance if one studies alone.

Rabbah b. Hana. *T: Taanit,* 7a.

860.D.7 God loves two students who arrange to study together.

Simeon b. Lakish. *T: Sabbath,* 63a.

860.D.8 When two merchants exchange goods, each one surrenders part of his stock; but when two students exchange instruction, each one retains his own learning and acquires also the other's. Is there a bigger bargain than this?

Simeon b. Lakish. *Tanhuma, Teruma,* 1.

860.D.9 Organize yourselves into classes for the study of Torah, since it can best be acquired in association with others.

Talmud: Berakot, 63b.

860.E. Miscellaneous

860.E.1 At times you should study one page of Gemara ten hours, and at times ten pages of Gemara one hour.

Hayyim b. Isaac. q Niger, *Geklibene Shriftn,* i. 36.

860.E.2 Who studies with a view to teach will have opportunity to learn and to teach; who studies with a view to practice, will have opportunity to learn, teach and practice.

Ishmael b. Johanan. *Mishna: Abot.* 4.5.

860.E.3 Study in joy and good cheer, in accordance with your intelligence and heart's dictates.

Rashi, *Commentary, Sabbath,* 63b.

861. STYLE

861.1 The moorish style is least expressive of the spirit of Judaism. It is too light, too coquettish; it has an enchanting splendor which surrounds kings in fairy-tales, but is by no means conducive to devotion and awe. . . . The Jews could sooner lay claim to the Egyptian style, for did they not occupy themselves, during their four hundred years of bondage, with building, and there is no doubt that they created something grandiose.

Antokolski, letter to Stassov, Nov. 6, 1879.

861.2 Style, folk say, was given at Sinai.

Bialik, "On Mendelé." *HaShiloah,* 1912, xxvi. 182.

861.3 In creative work, style and content are one.

Bialik. q OMB, 53.

861.4 It is the interaction of his personality and period that results in the formation of a composer's style.

Copland, *What to Listen for in Music,* 1939.

861.5 An author can have nothing truly his own but his style.

D'Israeli, *Literary Miscellanies: Style.*

861.6 The style is the man himself.

Ezobi. q *Buffon, Discourse,* 1753. See KJL, 89.

861.7 To write a consummate prose, a great mastery in metric form is requisite, among other things.

Heine, *Ludwig Boerne,* 1840, i.

861.8 Endeavor to cultivate conciseness and elegance. . . . Avoid heaviness, which spoils a composition.

Ibn Tibbon, *Tzavaah,* c. 1190. AHE, 69.

861.9 The same message is revealed to many prophets, yet no two of them prophesy in the same style.

Isaac Nappaha. *T: Sanhedrin,* 89a.

861.10 Who tells the truth needs no fancy phrases.

Peretz, *Yohanan Melameds Maaselach*, 1904. *Alle Verk*, vi. 181.

862. SUBLIMITY

862.1 The feeling of the sublime is the root of the religious sentiment.

F. Adler, *Creed and Deed*, 1877, p. 38.

862.2 Sublimity is Hebrew by birth.

*Coleridge, *Table Talk*, July 25, 1832.

862.3 We have long been induced to suspect that the seeds of true sublimity lurk in a life which, like this book, is half fashion and half passion.

Disraeli, *Young Duke*, 1831.

863. SUBMISSION

863.1 There is nothing to check blows like submission, and the resignation of the wronged victim puts the wrongdoer to confusion.

Agrippa II. q Josephus, *Wars*, 2.16.4.

863.2 To each wave that approached me, I bent my head.

Akiba, on how he was saved in a shipwreck. *T: Yebamot*, 121a.

863.3 The human race loves those who are willing to be in subjection to them.

Apocrypha: Aristeas, 257.

863.4 Every Jew in exile illustrates "He was oppressed . . . and opened not his mouth." He opens not his mouth to protest that he is more righteous than his tormentor, but only keeps his look directed toward God.

A. Ibn Ezra, *Commentary*, to *Isa.* 53.7.

863.5 The height of intellect is distinguishing between the real and the impossible, and submission to what is beyond one's power.

Ibn Gabirol, *Mibhar HaPeninim*, c. 1050, #209.

863.6 Whoever shall smite you on your right cheek, turn to him the other also.

New Testament: Matt., 5.39.

863.7 Men are especially intolerant of serving, and being ruled by, their equals.

Spinoza, *Theologico-Political Treatise*, 1670, ch 5.

864. SUCCESS

864.1 Success depends on faith and good deeds, . . . not upon the knowledge of the proofs which lead to them.

Abravanel, *Ateret Zekenim*, (1557) 1894, 42. q NDI, 291.

864.2 Whom God prospers, you too honor.

Apocrypha: Ahikar, 2.64.

864.3 Success is as ice cold and lonely as the North Pole.

V. Baum, *Grand Hotel*, (1929) 1931, p. 134.

864.4 The recognized professions definitely reject the size of the financial return as the measure of success.

Brandeis, address, Brown University, 1912.

864.5 We Jews, we of the blood of Amos and Jeremiah, of Jesus and Spinoza and all the earth-shatterers who died unsuccessful, we know a different world-history from this one which subscribes to success.

Buber, *Zion and Youth*, 1918. *Avukah Annual*, 1925–30, 52.

864.6 Success is the child of Audacity.

Disraeli, *Rise of Iskander*, 1834, ch 4.

864.7 Most successes come to harm the successful.

Gentili, *Mleket Mahshebet, VaYera*, 11. 1710.

864.8 Success is little more than a chemical compound of men and moment.

Guedalla.

864.9 Asked to explain his success, an official replied: "I kept my mind awake and my desire asleep."

M. Ibn Ezra, *Shirat Yisrael*, (12C) 1924, p. 144.

864.10 Accidental success is a temptation to improvidence.

Josephus, *Wars*, 3.5.6.

864.11 Great successes never come without risks.

Ibid., 3.10.4.

864.12 Nothing succeeds like success, except the failure that reverses it.

L. Stein, *Journey into the Self*, 1950, p. 256.

864.13 Success has the character of a cat. It won't come when coaxed.

Werfel, *Between Heaven and Earth*, 1944, p. 219.

864.14 Success in life depends on two things: luck and pluck, luck in finding someone to pluck.

Wynn. q Leon Gutterman, JTA, 1952.

865. SUFFERING

865.1 God has made me fruitful in the land of my affliction.

Bible: Gen., 41.52.

865.2 Only those who have suffered and endured greatly have achieved greatly. . . . Man has ever risen nearer to God by the altar-stairs of pain and sorrow.

S. A. Adler, *The Discipline of Sorrow*, 1906.

865.3 All the instruction which wicked King Manasseh had received from his father proved futile. The only teacher that finally proved effective was affliction. Precious affliction!

Akiba. *Sifré to Deut.*, #32.

865.4 It was only through suffering that Israel obtained three priceless and coveted gifts: the Torah [*Ps.* 94.12], the Land of Israel [*Deut.* 8.5, 7], and the world to come [*Prov.* 6.3].

Akiba. *T: Sanhedrin*, 101a.

865.5 There is no man without suffering. Happy is he whose suffering is for the Torah.

Alexandri. *Gen. R.*, 92.1.

865.6 He lives most who suffers most.

Boerne.

865.7 Suffering should lead man to self-inspection, . . . to the admission of errors, . . . and to prayer and forgiveness.

Büchler, *Studies in Sin and Atonement*, 1928, p. 345.

865.8 What makes a son a delight to his father? Suffering.

Eliezer b. Jacob. *Mekilta, to Exod.* 20.20.

865.9 It is only the strong who are strengthened by suffering; the weak are made weaker.

Feuchtwanger. *Paris Gazette*, 1940.

865.10 Sick people are invariably more refined than the robust, for only the sick man is really a man; his limbs have a history of suffering, they are spiritualized.

Heine, *Journey from Munich to Genoa*, 1828, ch 27.

865.11 Suffering is good, for through it men attain the world to come.

Huna. *Gen. R.*, 9.8.

865.12 Suffering is precious: it is a divine covenant.

Jonathan. *Mekilta, to Exod.* 20.20.

865.13 Precious are afflictions: they are accompanied by God's glory.

Jose b. Judah. *Sifré, to Deut.* 6.5.

865.14 It is not why I suffer, that I wish to know, but only whether I suffer for Thy sake!

Levi Yitzhok. q BTH, i. 213.

865.15 How dear and agreeable to me are all these tortures and blows! Through them the name of God is sanctified and celebrated.

Levi Yitzhok. q HLH, 45.

865.16 Suffering excels sacrifice for atonement: sacrifice involves property, suffering affects the person.

Nehemiah. *Mekilta, to Exod.* 20.20. *Sifré*, #2, to *Deut.* 6.5.

865.17 On the road of affliction
Marches redemption.

Shimonowitz, "Al Sfod," 1921, (*Shirim*, i. 343).

865.18 God said to David: If life is what you seek, meditate on suffering, for "the reproofs of instruction are the ways of life."

Zera. *Yalkut, Ps.*, 67, quoting *Prov.* 6.23.

865.19 Suffering befalls a righteous man on account of God's love for him. He crushes his body to strengthen his soul.

Zohar, Gen., 180b.

865.20 If there are ranks in suffering, Israel takes precedence of all nations; if the duration of sorrows and the patience with which they are borne ennoble, the Jews can challenge the aristocracy of every land; if a literature is called rich in the possession of a few classic tragedies—what shall we say to a national tragedy lasting for fifteen hundred years, in which the poets and the actors were also the heroes?

Zunz, *Synagogale Poesie*, 1855, p. 9. q Eliot, *Daniel Deronda*, 6.42.

865.21 Perhaps this may be the meaning of the eternal persecution driving us across the face of the whole earth: that holy things may become still holier if far away, and our hearts even more humble through overweight of sorrow.

S. Zweig, *The Buried Candelabrum*, 1936.

866. SUICIDE

866.1 The nearer the relation to the murdered person, the more heinous the crime . . . and man is closest to himself. A suicide is a sentinel who deserted his post.

Bahya, *Hobot HaLebabot*, 1040, 4.4.

866.2 One is considered a suicide only when there is absolute certainty that he premeditated and committed the act with a clear mind, not troubled by some great fear or worry which might have . . . caused him temporarily to lose his mind.

CCAR, xxxiii. 63.

Sofer, *Responsa (Yoré Deah)*, #326.

866.3 "Surely your blood of your lives will I require" [*Gen.* 9.5]. This includes suicide, except in a case like that of Saul. *Gen. R.*, 34.13.

866.4 Razors pain you;
Rivers are damp;
Acids stain you;
And drugs cause cramp.
Guns aren't lawful;
Nooses give;
Gas smells awful;
You might as well live.
Parker, "Résumé," *Enough Rope*, 1926, p. 61.

866.5 Suicide is extraordinarily rare among Jews.
*Ripley, *Races of Europe*, 1899, p. 385.

866.6 Suicides are weak-minded, and are overcome by external causes repugnant to their nature.
Spinoza, *Ethics*, 1677, iv. Pr 18, Note.

867. SUN

867.1 Sun, stand thou still upon Gibeon; and thou, Moon, in the valley of Ajalon!
Bible: Josh., 10.12.

867.2 Her sun has gone down while it was yet day.
Bible: Jer., 15.9.

867.3 The sun shall not smite you by day, nor the moon by night.
Bible: Ps., 121.6.

867.4 The sun changes oft for a blessing or a curse.
Apocrypha: Enoch, 41.8.

867.5 The sun bleaches the linen, but tans the laundress.
Bahya b. Asher, *Kad HaKemah*, 14C, p. 174. q BSJ, 115.

867.6 Behold the heavens! A devouring flame
Has taken hold of them.
The sun with fiery kiss has touched
And set afire their hem.
J. Cahan, "Shekiat Hama," 1901. q WHJ, iv. 302.

867.7 The sight of the sun is life, and life is love.
Chernihovsky, "Agadot HaAviv," c. 1900. *Kitbé*, i. 112.

867.8 Sunshine on the Sabbath is benevolence to the poor.
Isaac Nappaha. *T: Taanit*, 8b.

867.9 When the sun rises, the patient improves.
Proverb. q Abayé. *T: Baba Bathra*, 16b.

867.10 A sunbeam took human shape when he was born.
Zangwill, *Melting Pot*, 1908, Act 1.

868. SUPERNATURAL

868.1 Speak not of matters superhuman, over which we have no control.
Akiba. *Tanhuma*, to *Lev.* 12.3, ed Buber, iii. 18a.

868.2 Neither Moses nor Elijah ever went up to heaven, nor did the Glory ever come down to earth.
Jose b. Halafta. *Mekilta*, to *Exod.* 19.20. *T: Sukka*, 5a.

868.3 Among us, supernaturalism is bound up with national pride, with the conviction that Judaism has a divine origin and a sublime superiority to all culture and civilization. . . . It is blended with a primitive simplicity, with a mistrust of all that appears modern, with sorrow over the degradation of those Jews who, chosen to be teachers and models to mankind, think only of aping their neighbors.
S. D. Luzzatto, letter to Reggio, Nov. 26, 1838.

868.4 The account of the Witch of Endor is unacceptable literally, in spite of what is implied by the rabbis, because it is contrary to reason.
Samuel b. Hofni, c.1025. q D. Kimhi, *Commentary* to *I Sam.* 28.24.

869. SUPERSTITION

869.1 Turn not to ghosts, nor to familiar spirits.
Bible: Lev., 19.31.

869.2 Strict adherence to the teachings of our holy religion is the best check to superstitious beliefs.
M. Friedlander, *The Jewish Religion*, (1891) 1922, p. 7.

869.3 Do not let the convulsions of inanimate nature disturb you. . . . These accidents . . . have physical causes.
Herod I. q Josephus, *Wars*, 1.19.4.

869.4 Give your whole heart to God. Trust not in dreams or omens, inquire not of fortune-tellers. Such things show a lack of faith.
Jacob b. Asher, *Tokaha*, 14C. See AHE, 205.

869.5 All beliefs in eclipses as ill omens belong to non-Jews.
Johanan. *Mekilta*, to *Exod.*, 12.2.

869.6 All these are false and fraudulent notions with which old idolators used to mislead the ignorant masses in order to exploit them. It is unfit for Jews, intelligent people, to succumb to such superstitions.

Maimonides, *Yad: Akum*, 11.16.

869.7 Superstition, sister of impiety.
Philo, *Sacrifices of Abel and Cain*, 4.

869.8 I deny the existence of demons and Lilith, and the efficacy of witchcraft and amulets. I repudiate all deviations from law.
Philosophy's Challenge, 16C. See *JQRo*, xii. 142.

869.9 Even at this remote [nomadic] epoch, the Semite shepherd bore upon his forehead the seal of the absolute God, upon which was written, "This race will rid the earth of superstition."
*Renan, *History of Israel*, 1888, i. 42f. See ii. 421f.

869.10 Since the necromancer cannot cause light to shine for himself, how can he cause it to shine for others?
Simeon b. Lakish. *Lev. R.*, 6.6.

869.11 How blest would our age be if it could witness a religion freed from all the trammels of superstition!
Spinoza, *Theologico-Political Treatise*, 1670, ch 11.

869.12 Fervently we pray that the day may come . . . when superstition shall no longer enslave the mind.
Union Prayer Book, 1940, i. 71.

870. SUSPENSE

870.1 Decision destroys suspense, and suspense is the charm of existence.
Disraeli, (Mrs. Coningsby in) *Tancred*, 1847.

871. SUSPICION

871.1 Who wrongly suspects a neighbor must beg his pardon and bless him.
Eleazar. *T: Berakot*, 31b. See Jose. *T: Moed Katan*, 18b.

871.2 Do not try to identify the Tree of Knowledge. Heaven forfend that we cast suspicion on any tree!
Joshua b. Levi. *Gen. R.*, 15.7.

871.3 He who suspects innocent people will be punished.
Joshua b. Levi. *T: Yoma*, 19b.
Simeon b. Lakish. *T: Sabbath*, 97a.

871.4 Innocent suspects will have good children.
Proverb (Yiddish), based on *Num*. 5.28.

871.5 One is not suspected unless he has done it, at least in part, or had a mind to do it, or enjoyed seeing others do it.
Reuben b. Estrobile. *T: Moed Katan*, 18b.

871.6 A suspect in regard to one law is not necessarily suspect in regard to the whole Law, unless he is an apostate.
Talmud: Erubin, 69a. See *Hullin* 4b, *Bekorot*, 30ab.

872. SWAN

872.1 When the swans begin singing,
They presently must die.
Heine, *Early Poems: Evening Songs*, #2.

872.2 In a thousand little streams
I want to flow with the swan,
Who is without speech or sound
And without thought.
A beast that is dumb,
A beast that is beautiful,
No spirit and no symbol.
Kolmar, *Parting*. q *Commentary*, Nov. 1950, p. 463.

873. SWEAT

873.1 In the sweat of your face shall you eat bread.
Bible: Gen, 3.19.

873.2 Sweating is something Jewish.
Mendelé, *Fishke der Krumer*, 1869.

873.3 There is a difference between voluntary perspiration and enforced sweating.
Mendelé, *Shem VeYefet BaAgala*, 1890.

874. SWEETNESS

874.1 Out of the strong came forth sweetness.
Bible: Judg., 14.14.

874.2 Beware of sweets.
Ibn Tibbon, *Tzavaah*, c. 1190. AHE, 76.

874.3 Little girl, don't be so sweet, lest you be consumed.
Proverb (Yemenite), recorded by Moses Levi Nahum.

874.4 Don't be too sweet, lest you be eaten up; don't be too bitter, lest you be spewed out.
Proverb (Yiddish). BJS, #1470.

875. SWIMMING

875.1 A father must teach his child to swim.
Akiba. *Mekilta*, to *Exod*. 13.13. *T: Kiddushin*, 29a.

875.2 Fame is not to the wise, nor favor to the men of skill,

Save only to them that have skill
to swim.

Judah Halevi, *Selected Poems*, 31.

876. SWINE

876.1 The swine . . . is unclean to you.
Of their flesh ye shall not eat, and their
carcasses ye shall not touch.

Bible: Lev., 11.7f. Cf *Deut.* 14.8.

876.2 When the swine that had been
to the baths saw a muddy ditch, he went
down and washed in it, and cried to his
companions, "Come and wash."

Apocrypha: Ahikar, 8.8.

876.3 A pig is a pig, even when it plays
a trick.

Mendelé, *In a Sturem Tzeit*, 1913.

876.4 Hang a palm on a pig, and it
will do the usual thing.

Proverb. q Papa. *T: Berakot*, 43b.

877. SWITZERLAND

877.1 Neuchatel wants to expel the
Jews. Strange. That town manufactures
annually 130,000 watches, and yet does
not know what time it is!

Boerne, *Fragmente & Aphorismen*,
1840, #301.

877.2 Switzerland, to the uninformed
observer, must always seem to be one of
those fortunate countries . . . which have
a great deal of geography and very little
history.

Guedalla, *Master of Men*, 1923, p. 17.

878. SWORD

878.1 By the sword shall you live.

Bible: Gen., 27.40.

878.2 The Lord saves not with the
sword and spear.

Bible: I Sam., 17.47.

878.3 His sword is drunk with their
blood.

Apocrypha: Enoch, 62.12.

878.4 O worthy sir! Think better of
the sword!

A sword when swung in freedom's sacred cause,
Becomes the Holy Word. . . .
All great things, which e'er will
come to pass
Will owe their final being to the
sword.

Lassalle, *Franz von Sickingen*, 1859.

878.5 The sword comes into the world
because justice is delayed or perverted,
and Torah is misinterpreted.

Mishna: Abot, 5.8.

878.6 I came not to send peace, but a
sword.

New Testament: Matt., 10.34.

878.7 All they that take the sword shall
perish by the sword.

Ibid., 26.52.

878.8 He that has no sword, let him
sell his garment and buy one.

New Testament: Luke 22.36.

879. SYMBOL

879.1 In Judaism there was always a
tendency to recognize the peculiar con-
catenation and permeation of the two
worlds. . . . I visualize in the Shield of
David the symbolical presentation of that
permeation: two triangles, one pointing
upward, the other downward, are interwoven to such an extent that they appear
to be a new phenomenon which cannot
be split into its parts again. Our God is
one.

Brod, *Das Diesseitswunder*, 1939. q *Reconstructionist*, Nov. 30, 1951, p. 11.

879.2 Out of the expression and ex-
uberance, the failures and triumphs of
human experience, religious geniuses of
the world have imagined symbols. They
have made banners for the spirit to follow, patterns by which men might passionately and completely live.

Edman, *Adam, the Baby and the Man
from Mars*, 1929, p. 118.

879.3 Most mistakes in philosophy and
logic occur because the human mind is
apt to take the symbol for the reality.

Einstein, *Cosmic Religion*, 1931, p. 101.

879.4 The symbol—the outward expression of the inward signification—
should above all charm the senses by and
for itself.

Heine, *The Salon*, 1831.

879.5 We lean on such crutches as the
poor symbolism of human speech to represent what is finally unrepresentable.

E. G. Hirsch. *Reform Advocate*, 1897,
xiv. 519.

879.6 In relation to God, Israel is sym-
bolized by a dove [*Hos.* 11.11]; in relation to Gentiles, by untamed animals
[*Gen.* 49].

Johanan b. Nappaha. *Exod. R.*, 21.5.

879.7 The seven loaves represented the
planets; the loaves on the table, twelve in
number, the circle of the zodiac and the
year.

Josephus, *Wars*, 5.5.5.

879.8 The seven-branched candelabrum is a symbol of the five senses and the powers of the soul, all functioning in the service of Him who is blessed.

Maimonides, *Perakim BeHatzlaha. Responsa,* ii. 32b.

879.9 Other kings carry rods in their hands as scepters, but my scepter is the book of the Sequel of the Law.

Philo, *Special Laws,* iv. 32.

880. SYMPATHY

880.1 God with a heart afflicted me
That feels another's misery,
When it hears of sufferings tell,
It burns in everybody's hell.

Bialik, *The Last Word.* LGP, 26.

880.2 Mere knowledge alone will not enable us to solve the profound problems of life. . . . Sympathy is an essential part of a right attitude to the riddles of the universe. You must tune up your heart to catch the music of the spheres.

M. R. Cohen, *A Dreamer's Journey,* 1949, p. 118.

880.3 I am a Jew because in all places where there are tears and suffering, the Jew weeps.

Fleg, *Why I Am a Jew,* 1929, p. 94.

880.4 We do not rejoice at the punishment meted out to an enemy; we have been taught by the holy laws to have human sympathy.

Philo, *Flaccus,* 14.

881. SYNAGOG

881.1 "He may be found" [*Isa.* 55.6], —in school and synagog.

Abbahu. *TJ: Berakot,* 5.1. See *Deut. R.,* 7.2.

881.2 Any ten men were competent to form themselves into a congregation, and to discharge all the duties of religion.

F. Adler, *Creed and Deed,* 1877, p. 209. See p. 228.

881.3 Mystery upon mystery! This is indeed a puzzle. I came to a city and it was empty. I entered the synagog and it was full.

Agnon, "HaMeshulah", 1925. tr *Avukah Annual,* 1932, p. 714.

881.4 Jews may not enlarge, elevate or beautify their synagogs.

*Alfonso X, 1261. q Lindo, *Jews of Spain and Portugal,* 99.

881.5 If Jewish life survived the destruction of the Temple, that was because the synagog had been prepared to take over the whole burden and carry it onward for generations to come.

Finkelstein, *The Pharisees,* 1940, p. 569.

881.6 The religion of Torah learned to do without the Temple, but it never dreamed of doing without the synagog.

*Herford, *Pharisaism,* 1912, p. 30f.

881.7 The essence of the Synagog is congregational worship and edification, conducted by the congregation through their own members, not by priests on their behalf. . . . To have created the Synagog is perhaps the greatest practical achievement of the Jews in all their history.

*Herford, *Judaism in NT Period,* 1928, pp. 23, 26.

881.8 *Shools* . . . we call our houses of worship, and that is what they should be, schools for the grown-up.

S. R. Hirsch, *Nineteen Letters,* (1836), #14, p. 131.

881.9 Don't wreck the old synagog before you build the new.

Hisda. *T: Baba Bathra,* 3b.

881.10 On the way from synagog, don't take long strides.

Huna. *T: Berakot,* 6b.

881.11 When the Holy One enters a synagog and does not find there ten men, his wrath is kindled.

Johanan b. Nappaha. *T: Berakot,* 6b.

881.12 The more I do for my congregation, the more I am insulted.

J. Jonas, letter to Isaac Leeser, May 5, 1852 (unpublished, in possession of J. R. Marcus).

881.13 The synagog is the one unfailing wellspring of Jewish feeling. There we pray together with our brethren, and in the act become participators in the common sentiment, the collective conscience, of Israel. There we pray with a mightier company still, with the whole house of Israel.

M. Joseph, *Judaism as Creed and Life,* 1903, p. 219.

881.14 Woe unto American Israel when the day comes and we are found an unorganized bundle of atoms; and woe to us if we organize on any but ecclesiastical, that is, religious lines! We must unify our societies and place them under the roof of the synagog. Whatever is inimical or even indifferent to the synagog must be wiped out of existence.

Margolis, *Theological Aspect of Reform Judaism,* 1903.

881.15 There [Russian church], the large mass of people stood quiet, grave and silent, and only the priest and the choir spoke and sang . . . in lovely, carefully harmonic and measured tones. But here [Minsk synagog, 1899], it was as though I had fallen among torrential waves. Hundreds and hundreds of worshipers—each one taking his own case to God, each one in a loud voice with passionate eagerness. Hundreds of voices ascended to the heavens, each for himself, without concord, without harmony, yet all joining together in one tremendous, clamorous sound. No matter how strange to the Western ear, it makes a deep impression and has a great beauty derived from the passion of the mass feeling.

Medem, *Fun Mein Leben,* 1923. q *Commentary,* Nov. 1950, 481.

881.16 The Shekina is in the synagog . . . even when one man is there.

Mekilta, to *Exod.* 20.21.

881.17 What are our places of prayer . . . but schools of prudence, courage, temperance and justice, of piety, holiness and virtue?

Philo, *Moses,* ii. 39 (iii. 37).

881.18 A city where the roofs of private houses are higher than the roof of the synagog, is doomed to destruction.

Rab. *T: Sabbath,* 11a.

881.19 The synagog has been the most original and fruitful creation of the Jewish people.

*Renan, *History of Israel,* 1895, iv. 192.

881.20 Even now in our own day synagogs are the strength of Judaism,—a strength that others envy, the ground of many a jealous calumny, to which there is but one answer to be made: Go, and do thou likewise.

Ibid., 194. See *Life of Jesus,* 1863, p. 165.

881.21 He who knows . . . what potentialities lie dormant even . . . in a mere Yom Kippur Judaism . . . will guard against speaking disdainfully of the synagog.

F. Rosenzweig, *Bildung und kein Ende,* 1920. GFR, 220.

881.22 It is one of the most interesting of religious phenomena to observe the essential unity that the Synagog maintained. . . . Dispersed among the nations, without a national center, without a synod to formulate its principles, or any secular power to enforce its decrees, the Synagog found its home and harmony in the heart of a loyal and consecrated Israel.

Schechter, *Some Aspects of Rabbinic Theology,* 1910, p. xvi.

881.23 He who does not worship in the synagog of his own town is called a bad neighbor.

Simeon b. Lakish (Bacher: Levi). *T: Berakot,* 8a.

881.24 Israel lives in its congregations!

I. M. Wise. *American Israelite,* July 29, 1887.

881.25 If only two Jews remained in the world, one would summon to the synagog, and the other would go there.

Yiddish Saying. q *JE,* x. 229a.

881.26 Woe to him who carries on conversation in the synagog!

Zohar, Gen., 256a. See NTA, 455.

881.27 The Synagog service was a rallying point to the Jews, and proved the safeguard of Israel's faith.

Zunz, *Gottesdienstliche Vorträge,* 1832, Preface.

882. SYSTEM

882.1 Men like to have things neatly explained and ticketed and systematized. It takes spiritual grandeur to admit that we cannot synthesize the deepest realities of our experience, and yet cling to all of them.

B. Bamberger, *Fallen Angels,* 1952, p. 250.

882.2 The Jew has—whether to his advantage or not—a certain aversion towards systems and the solemnity of robes of state: he takes things easily.

Mauthner, "Skepticism and the Jews." *Menorah Journal,* 1924, x. 14.

882.3 The more genuinely and characteristically Jewish an idea or doctrine is, the more deliberately unsystematic is it. Its principle of construction is not that of a logical system.

Scholem, *Major Trends in Jewish Mysticism,* 1941, p. 158.

883. TACT

883.1 Difficulties melt away under tact.

Disraeli, *Tancred,* 1847.

883.2 A want of tact is worse than a want of virtue.

Disraeli, *Young Duke,* 1831.

884. TAILOR

884.1 There is always a thread on a tailor.

Tanhuma, ed Buber, Introduction, 79a.

885. TALE

885.1 The world says that tales put people to sleep. I say that with tales you can rouse people from their sleep.

Nahman Bratzlav, *Hayyé Moharan.* q ZRN, 225.

886. TALENT

886.1 The more gifted we are, the more we owe to God.

Baron, sermon, 1928, based on M. H. Luzzatto, *Mesillat Yesharim,* 1740, ch 22.

886.2 There he sits with all his talent
Turning it to no account!

D. Kalisch, *Berlin bei Nacht,* 1850.

886.3 There can be no doubt that the Jews . . . have given proportionately more men of talent to our Aryan civilization than the so-called Aryans themselves.

*Leroy-Beaulieu, *Israel Among the Nations,* 1895, p. 230.

886.4 One should be born with the talent to enjoy, and not only to create, art.

J. Rosenfeld. q Niger, *Geklibene Shriften,* 1928, i. 74.

886.5 A great talent fares like a paper kite: the higher it rises, the more street-arabs gather to pull it down.

Saphir, *Warum giebt es kein Narrenhaus.* SHW, i. 367.

886.6 To have talent, one must have character: abilities and natural disposition by themselves make no talent.

Varnhagen. q KRV, 278.

887. TALMUD

887.1 It is possible to stand firmly on the basis of positive Judaism without swearing unswerving allegiance to Talmudism.

Aub. *Rabbinische Gutachten,* Breslau, 1842, ii. 10.

887.2 If I were to know that I had neglected even one of the commandments of the Talmud, I should not want to live.

Baruch of Tultshin. q *JE,* ii. 562b.

887.3 The pregnant thought of this book, devoted as it is almost exclusively to the preservation of the cult, is that the cult is transitory, and that, when Jewish truths shall be universally recognized, Jewish rites will cease.

Darmsteter, *Selected Essays,* 1895, p. 260.

887.4 The vast ocean of Talmud—that strange, wild, weird ocean, with its leviathans, and its wrecks of golden argosies, and with its forlorn bells that send up their dreamy sounds ever and anon, while the fisherman bends upon his oar, and starts and listens, and perchance the tears may come into his eyes.

E. Deutsch, *The Talmud,* 1867.

887.5 The Talmud is a literary monument of the national hegemony established and maintained by the autonomous communities of Roman Palestine and Persian Babylonia—a monument embodying the efforts of the leaders to build a strong shell of the Law around the shattered kernel of the nation.

Dubnow, *Weltgeschichte des jüdischen Volkes,* 1927, Introd.

887.6 The Talmud preserved and promoted the religious and moral life of Judaism; it held out a banner to the communities scattered in all corners of the earth, and protected them from schism and sectarian divisions; it acquainted subsequent generations with the history of their nation; finally it produced a deep intellectual life which preserved the enslaved and proscribed from stagnation and lit for them the torch of science.

Graetz, *History of the Jews,* 1893, ii. 635.

887.7 The Talmud is the Catholicism of the Jews. It is a Gothic cathedral, overloaded with child-like grotesqueness, yet amazing with its heaven-soaring grandeur. It is a hierarchy of religious laws, which often treat of the drollest, most ridiculous subtleties, yet are so intelligently arranged . . . and coincide with such tremendous logical force, that they constitute a formidable and colossal whole.

Heine, *Germany from Luther to Kant,* 1834.

887.8 The inner meaning of Talmudism is unshakable trust in God and unreserved obedience to His declared will.

*Herford, *Menorah Journal,* 1919, v. 204, 206.

887.9 Were it not for the men of the Great Assembly and the men who produced the Mishna and the Talmud, the Torah of our God would have long since been lost and forgotten. It was they who confirmed the commandments and elucidated them thoroughly.

A. Ibn Ezra, *Yesod Mora,* 1158.

887.10 Why does each tract of the Talmud begin with page 2, and not with page 1? To remind us that no matter how much we study and learn, we have not yet come to the first page!

Levi Yitzhok. q Kahana, *Sefer HaHasidut*, 1922, p. 243.

887.11 That book of gems, that book of gold,
Of wonders many and manifold.

*Longfellow, *Wayside Inn*, 1863, 2d Interlude.

887.12 All matters in the Babylonian Talmud are mandatory on all Jews.

Maimonides, *Yad*, 1180, Introduction.

887.13 The Talmud is not there for any scurvy fellow to run over it with unwashed feet and say he knows it all.

*Reuchlin. q VA, 277.

887.14 The "sea of the Talmud" has also its gulf stream of mysticism.

Schechter, *Studies in Judaism*, 1896, i. p. xxiii.

887.15 So says Rabbi Talmud (*Ut narrat Rabbinus Talmud*).

*Henricus Seymensis. See *JQRo*, xiii. 615.

887.16 To oppose a single word of the teachings of the Talmud is to oppose God and His Law.

Sherira Gaon. q *Shaaré Tzedek*, Introd.

887.17 The Talmud has been a fortress which has helped the Jews to maintain their distinctiveness amidst the peoples, a fortress which the Christian world has, for fifteen centuries, vainly sought to batter with all the material and spiritual weapons at its disposal.

*Solovyov, "Talmud." *Ruskaya Mysl*, 1886.

887.18 We are prepared to die for the Talmud. . . . Our bodies are in your power, but not our souls!

Yehiel of Paris, to Queen Blanche, 1240.

887.19 The very incoherence of the Talmud, its confusion of voices, is an index of free thinking.

Zangwill, *Chosen Peoples*, 24.

888. TASTE

888.1 If a serpent were to eat the most luscious delicacies, he would still feel only the taste of dust.

Ammi b. Nathan. *T: Yoma*, 75a. See Assi. *ibid.*

888.2 Taste everything, "and see that the Lord is good" [*Ps.* 34.9].

Baal Shem. q Simeon Zeeb, *Derash Tob*, 23; HHH, 51.

888.3 To know the taste of the wine, it is not necessary to drink the whole barrel.

Bialik. OMB, 58.

888.4 Only dancing in the market
For a Jew shall not be lawful. . . .
For a sense of style, of rigid
Plastic art in motion's wanting
To that race, who really ruin
What there is of public taste.

Heine, *Atta Troll*, 1841, ch 6.

888.5 All food in the mouth of the healthy is like honey,
But honey in the mouth of the sick is like juniper.

Judah Halevi, *Selected Poems*, 79. Cf Marcus Aurelius, 6.52.

888.6 Taste teaches morality and power teaches taste.

Pasternak, *Safe Conduct*, 2.3. *Collected Prose Works*, 74.

888.7 The flute admired by nobles is rejected by weavers.

Rab. *T: Yoma*, 20b.

888.8 Some prefer vinegar and some prefer wine.

Talmud: Kiddushin, 48b.

889. TATTOO

889.1 Ye shall not make any cuttings in your flesh for the dead, nor imprint any marks upon you.

Bible: Lev., 19.28.

890. TAXES

890.1 Governments last as long as the undertaxed can defend them against the overtaxed.

Berenson, Feb. 25, 1944, *Rumor and Reflexion*, 1952, p. 248.

890.2 No taxation without misrepresentation.

Hoffenstein, *Pencil in the Air*, 1923, p. 149.

890.3 All must contribute to the building of town gates, even orphans, but not rabbis, since they need no protection. All must contribute to the digging of a well, including rabbis.

Judah b. Ezekiel. *T: Baba Bathra*, 8a.

890.4 Edom [used symbolically for Rome, Imperial Government] is never satisfied; what flows thither never returns.

Midrash. q Zunz, "Leiden." *Synagogale Poesie*, 1855.

890.5 Our taxes today . . . are simple robbery. The Mishna lists tax collectors with murderers and pillagers [*Nedarim*, 3.4].

Mordecai, *Nezikin*, 13C, 190. q HSJ, 79.

890.6 Taxation under every form presents but a choice of evils.

Ricardo, *Principles of Political Economy*, 1817, 9.

890.7 Income tax returns are the most imaginative fiction being written today.

Wouk. q Leon Gutterman, JTA, 1952.

891. TEACHER

891.1 Each community must engage teachers for the children.

Alnaqua, *Menorat HaMaor*, (14C), 1932, iv. 138.

891.2 Teachers and school-children are society's most beautiful ornaments.

Cant. R., 1.10.2. See Feldman, *Jewish Child*, 275.

891.3 It is the supreme art of the teacher to awaken joy in creative expression and knowledge.

Einstein. Motto for Astronomy Building, Pasadena Junior College.

891.4 Academic chairs are many, but wise and noble teachers are few.

Einstein, *The World As I See It*, 1934, p. 243.

891.5 Revere your teacher as you revere Heaven.

Eleazar b. Shammua. *Mishna: Abot*, 4.12.

891.6 He who gives a legal decision in the presence of his teacher commits a capital offense.

Eliezer b. Hyrcanus. *T: Erubin*, 63a.

891.7 Let your children's tutor be constantly in your house, and pay him liberally.

Elijah Gaon, *Alim LiTerufa*, 1836.

891.8 No printed word nor spoken plea
　　Can teach young hearts what men
　　　　should be,
　　Not all the books on all the shelves,
　　But what the teachers are themselves.

Guiterman, *The Light Guitar*, 1923, p. 20.

891.9 Who pleases his teachers is destined for the world to come.

Hanina b. Hama. *T: Sabbath*, 153a.

891.10 An impatient man cannot be a teacher.

Hillel. *Mishna: Abot*, 2.5.

891.11 To oppose a teacher is to oppose the Shekina.

Hisda. *T: Sanhedrin*, 110a. See Zera. *TJ: Sanhedrin*, 11.4.

891.12 Turn to books only when you have no teacher.

M. Ibn Ezra, *Shirat Yisrael*, (12C) 1924, p. 116.

891.13 Banned by a teacher, banned by his disciple.

Johanan b. Nappaha. *T: Moed Katan*, 17a.

891.14 Teachers may not accept remuneration for teaching Torah, but may for teaching punctuation marks and accents.

Johanan b. Nappaha. *T: Nedarim*, 37a.

891.15 He is your teacher if he enlightened you in but one *Mishna*.

Jose b. Halafta. *T: Baba Metzia*, 33a. See *Mishna:Abot*, 6.3.

891.16 A disciple, who is present when his master sits in judgment, and sees a point in favor of a poor man, should not be silent.

Joshua b. Karha. *T: Sanhedrin*, 6b.

891.17 Ammi and his colleagues, on an educational inspection tour, came to a town and asked for its guardians. The councilmen appeared, but the rabbis said, "These are not guardians, but wreckers of a town! The guardians are the teachers of the young and instructors of the old, as is written [*Ps.* 127.1], 'Except the Lord keep the city, the watchman wakes but in vain.'"

Lam. R., Proem 2. *TJ: Hagiga*, 1.7.

891.18 One teacher is not sufficient. Study with another too.

Meir. *Abot de R. Nathan*, ch 3, ed Schechter, p. 16.

891.19 An unmarried man may not be an elementary teacher.

Mishna: Kiddushin, 4.13.

891.20 Conscientious teachers of small children are destined to sit on the right hand of God.

Pesikta Kahana, ch 28, ed Buber, 1925, 161b.

891.21 If you are to conquer the land you are about to enter, it will be largely through the arts and achievements of the teacher.

Philipson, at HUC, June 14, 1913. *Centen. Papers,* 225.

891.22 A pupil eats by the merit of his master.

Proverb. q *T: Yoma,* 75b.

891.23 Who withholds a law from his pupil robs him of his inheritance.

Rab. *T: Sanhedrin,* 91b.

891.24 If a student finds his studies hard, blame his teacher.

Raba. *T: Taanit,* 8a.

891.25 Let not your master's table be empty, while yours is ample.

Abba Saul. *T: Betza,* 20b.

891.26 There are three teachers: parents, instructors, and comrades.

Sefer Hasidim, 13C, #820, p. 208.

891.27 The robe of the professor must be as stainless as the ermine of the judge.

Seligman. q Flexner, *Universities,* 1930, p. 207.

891.28 To serve a teacher is greater than to study Torah.

Simeon b. Yohai. *T: Berakot,* 7b.

891.29 If you see cities uprooted, know that it came about because they did not maintain teachers' salaries.

Simeon b. Yohai. *Lam. R.,* Proem 2. *TJ: Hagiga,* 1.7.

891.30 God said: You must teach, as I taught, gratuitously.

Talmud: Nedarim, 37a.

891.31 The business of the American teacher is to liberate American citizens to think apart and to act together.

S. S. Wise. q *N.Y. Times Magazine,* March 22, 1953, p. 46.

892. TEACHING

892.1 My doctrine shall drop as the rain, my speech shall distill as the dew.

Bible: Deut., 32.2.

892.2 The Lord was pleased for His righteousness' sake to make the teaching great and glorious.

Bible: Isa., 42.21.

892.3 Only if a scholar is like a bed of spices, the perfume reaching others, will his learning be preserved.

Eleazar b. Pedat. *T: Erubin,* 54a.

892.4 To transmit wisdom to the un-worthy is like throwing pearls before swine.

q M. Ibn Ezra, *Shirat Yisrael,* (12C) 1924, p. 198.

892.5 Who learns and does not teach is like a myrtle in the desert.

Johanan. *T: Rosh Hashana,* 23a.

892.6 Who teaches a neighbor's son Torah earns a seat in the Academy on High. Who teaches the son of a common man, the Holy One annuls evil decrees for his sake.

Jonathan b. Eleazar. *T: Baba Metzia,* 85a. See *Sanhedrin* 19b.

892.7 An error in teaching amounts to presumption.

Judah b. Ilai. *Mishna: Abot,* 4.13.

892.8 Always teach the shortest way.

Meir. *T: Pesahim,* 3b.

892.9 A teacher should cheerfully explain again and again, in accordance with the pupils' intelligence, the difficult parts till they understand them fully.

Orhot Tzaddikim, 15C, ch 2.

892.10 Teach not Torah in public unless you studied all its branches.

Seder Eliyahu Rabbah, ch 14, ed Friedmann, 67.

892.11 Who teaches Torah in this world will do so also in the next.

Sheshet. *T: Sanhedrin,* 92a.

892.12 Teaching an unworthy student is like worshiping idols.

Simeon b. Eleazar. *Tosefta: Aboda Zara,* 6.18.

892.13 In Rab's days, there was a teacher whose prayer for rain was answered promptly. Asked to tell of his special merit, he said: I teach children of the poor as well as of the rich; I accept no fee from any who cannot afford it; and I have a fishpond to delight the children and to encourage them to do their lessons.

Talmud: Taanit, 24a.

892.14 Let not your mouth drop any word of Torah of which you are uncertain, which you have not learned from an authority.

Zohar, Gen., Prologue, 5a.

893. TEARS

893.1 The Lord God will wipe away tears from all faces.

Bible: Isa., 25.8.

893.2 Oh that my head were waters, mine eyes a fountain of tears!
Bible: Jer., 8.23.

893.3 I melt away my couch with my tears.
Bible: Ps., 6.7.

893.4 My tears have been my food day and night.
Bible: Ps., 42.4.

893.5 O Thou who hearest weeping, healest woe,
Our tears within Thy vase of crystal store!
Amittai b. Shefatia, "Adonoy, Adonoy," tr N. Davis. *JQRo*, ix. 722.

893.6 Tears shed at the demise of a good man are counted by the Holy One and deposited in His treasury.
Bar Kappara. *T: Sabbath*, 105b.

893.7 Jewish tears are the heaviest. They have the weight of many centuries.
*Bloy, *Le Sang du Pauvre*, 1909. BPA, 264.

893.8 Since the Temple was destroyed, the gates of prayer have been closed, but not the gates of tears.
Eleazar b. Pedat. *T: Berakot*, 32b.

893.9 The deepest grief is tearless.
Franzos, *Child of Atonement*, 1872. *Jews of Barnow*, 165.

893.10 What poetry there is in human tears!
Heine, *Memoirs of Herr von Schnabelewopski*, 1834. EPP 646.

893.11 If my tears would flow according to my woes, there'd be no dry spot on which to set my toes.
A. Ibn Ezra, *Shirim*, ed Kahana, 19.

893.12 A tear is deeper than the sea.
S. J. Imber, *When Harvests Fail*. LGP, 250.

893.13 Lips that taste of tears, they say, Are the best for kissing.
Parker, *Enough Rope*, 1926, p. 11.

893.14 Tears are no payment on debts.
Proverb (Yiddish). BJS, #1335.

893.15 There is a palace that opens only to tears.
Tikkuné Zohar, 13C, ch 11, p. 26b.

893.16 There is no gate which tears cannot break through.
Zohar, Exod., 12b.

894. TEFILLIN

894.1 Thou shalt bind them for a sign upon thy hand, and they shall be for frontlets between thine eyes.
Bible: Deut., 6.8.

894.2 The God of might, who conquered Canaan with storm,
How they have bound Him with tefillin straps!
Chernihovsky, "LeNokah Pesel Apollo," 1911. *Kol Shire*, i. 205.

894.3 Tefillin demand a pure body.
Yannai. *T: Sabbath*, 49a.

895. TEL AVIV

895.1 I love Tel Aviv . . . because all of it, from the foundation to the coping, was established by our own hands . . . because we need not feel obligated to anyone for its good points or apologetic for its bad points. Is not this the whole aim of our redemption, . . . to be owners of our body and soul, masters of our spirit and creation?
Bialik. OMB, 24.

895.2 Something perfectly new and peculiar has come forth here from a desert: a Jewish city that is not a ghetto.
Ehrenpreis, *Soul of the East*, 1927, p. 84f.

896. TEMPLE

896.A. Sanctuary

896.A.1 [In the building of Solomon's Temple,] the stones carried themselves and placed themselves on the row.
Berekia. *Cant. R.*, 1.1.5.

896.A.2 The Temple windows were . . . narrow within and widening outward, in order to send forth light into the world.
Bezalel. *Pesikta Kahana*, ch 21, ed Buber, 130a. See *1 Kings*, 6.4.

896.A.3 The Temple gave light to the whole world.
Exod. R., 36.1.

896.A.4 The Temple court was a hundred cubits long, yet all Israel stood there!
Jose b. Halafta. *Gen. R.*, 5.7.

896.A.5 The people stood there pressed together, yet when they prostrated themselves, they had ample room.
Mishna Abot, 5.5.

896.B. Cult

896.B.1 Who has required this at your hand, to trample My courts?
Bible: Isa., 1.12.

896.B.2 The most complete silence reigns. . . . Everything is carried out with reverence and in a way worthy of the great God.

Apocrypha: Aristeas, 95.

896.B.3 Wolf! Wolf! You have consumed the substance of Israel, and failed us in our hour of need!

Miriam bath Bilga, at Syrian invasion, 165 B.C.E. q *Tosefta: Sukka,* 4.28.

896.C. Destruction

896.C.1 Since the Destruction, the Holy One has not laughed.

Aha. *T: Aboda Zara,* 3b.

896.C.2 Ye priests, take the keys of the sanctuary, cast them into the height of heaven, and give them to the Lord, saying: "Guard Thy house Thyself, for lo! we are found false stewards!"

Apocrypha: II Baruch, 10.18. See *Zohar, Gen.,* 202b.

896.C.3 When our fathers were to be led to Persia, the godly priests of that time took some of the fire of the altar, and hid it secretly in the hollow of a sort of empty cistern.

Apocrypha: II Macc., 1.19.

896.C.4 When the Temple was destroyed, an iron wall was removed from between Israel and their Father in heaven.

Eleazar b. Pedat. *T: Berakot,* 32b.

896.C.5 On the lordly heights of Zion, . . .
Once in every year, on every
Ninth of Ab, the stones are
mourning.

Heine, *Jehuda Ben Halevy,* 1850, 2.

896.C.6 Since the destruction, there has never been a perfectly clear sky.

Hisda. *T: Berakot,* 59a.

896.C.7 There were more righteous people at the time of the destruction than at its construction [*Isa.* 54.1].

Johanan b. Nappaha. *Pesikta Kahana,* ch 20, ed Buber, 127b.

896.C.8 The Destruction is no less precious to me than the Holy Temple itself. The Destruction yielded our most treasured poetry, created an entire culture.

Mendelé. q Anski, *Gezamelté Shriften,* x. 186.

896.C.9 Since the Destruction there has been no joy above or below.

Zohar, Gen., 61b.

897. TEMPTATION

897.1 Who is the strange god *in* man [*Ps.* 81.10]? Temptation.

Abin. *T: Sabbath,* 105b. Cf *TJ: Nedarim,* 9.1.

897.2 When you come to serve God, prepare your soul for temptation.

Apocrypha: Ben Sira, 2.1.

897.3 The most effective antidote to temptation: shut the eyes.

Ibn Gabirol, *Mibhar HaPeninim,* c. 1050, #181.

897.4 To withstand temptation is a deed of great merit.

Isaac Nappaha. *Cant. R.,* 4.4.3.

897.5 If the Ugly One meet you, drag him to the house of study: if he be stone, he'll be washed away there, and if iron, he'll be shattered.

Ishmael School. *T: Sukka,* 52b.

897.6 I never wasted energy resisting temptation.

M. J. Lewi, on 94th birthday. q *N.Y. Times,* Dec. 19, 1951.

897.7 The greater the day the greater its temptations.

Lipkin. q KTH, i. 272.

897.8 Invite not temptation.

Rab. *T: Sanhedrin,* 107a.

897.9 If the Tempter attacks you, think of how you would act in time of martyrdom, how you would defy torture and death!

Sefer Hasidim, 13C, #2, p. 4f.

897.10 They caught and imprisoned the Tempter for three days, and then could not find a fresh egg in the whole Land of Israel. Said they, "If we kill him, the world will go under." So they put out his eyes, and let him go.

Talmud: Yoma, 69b.

897.11 Put no temptation before an honest man, let alone a thief, as the sages' proverb goes: Put no fire next to tow.

Tanhuma, Matzora, 13, ed Buber, 26b.

897.12 Only he is worthy of reward who withstood temptation.

Zera. *TJ: Kiddushin,* 1.9.

897.13 In the Messianic age, the Holy One will kill the Tempter before the eyes of the righteous, and he will cease forever.

Zohar, Gen., 190b.

898. TESTIMONY

898.1 One witness shall not rise up against a man. . . . At the mouth of two

or three witnesses shall a matter be established.
Bible: Deut., 19.15.

898.2 The stone shall cry out of the wall, and the beam out of the timber shall answer it.
Bible: Hab., 2.11.

898.3 The man who has seen and not declared it, be he accursed.
Apocrypha: Jubilees, 4.5.

898.4 Witnesses were created only against liars.
Ashi. T: Kiddushin, 65b.

898.5 A man's own soul, his own limbs, testify against him.
Hidka. T: Taanit, 11a.

898.6 It is the plaintiff who has to submit evidence.
Immi. TJ: Baba Metzia, 7.1.

898.7 When you are in court and have evidence in favor of the poor and against the rich, you are not permitted to be silent.
Joshua b. Karha. Tosefta: Sanhedrin, 1.8.

898.8 These are ineligible as witnesses: gamblers, usurers, betters, traders in illegal wares, and slaves.
Mishna: Rosh Hashana, 1.8.

898.9 No one may testify concerning himself.
Mishna: Ketubot, 2.9.

898.10 Before submitting testimony, witnesses are told that false witnesses are despised even by those who hire them.
Nathan b. Mar Zutra. T: Sanhedrin, 29a.

898.11 Who intends to lie seeks witnesses from a distance.
Proverb. q Asher b. Yehiel, Halakot: Shebuot, ch 6, #13.

898.12 Four eyes see more than two.
Proverb (Yiddish).

898.13 Who lends money without witnesses transgresses the law, "Put not a stumbling block before the blind" [Lev. 19.14].
Rab. T: Baba Metzia, 75b.

898.14 A borrower may not be a witness in a case involving the lender.
Raba. T: Sanhedrin, 25a.

898.15 Two angels accompany everyone and testify against him.
Shila School. T: Taanit, 11a.

898.16 "Ye are My witnesses . . . I am

the Lord" [Isa. 43.10f]: Only when you are My witnesses am I God.
Simeon b. Yohai. Pesikta Kahana, ch 12, ed Buber, 91b.

898.17 Evidence voided in part is voided altogether.
Talmud: Baba Kamma, 73a.

898.18 The Holy One detests him who has evidence and witholds it.
Talmud: Pesahim, 113b.

898.19 Relatives are disqualified to serve as witnesses.
Talmud: Sanhedrin, 28a.

898.20 "God came down to see" [Gen. 11.5]. Here Scripture stresses an important lesson: Not to judge, not to talk, till we have seen.
Tanhuma, Noah, 28, ed Buber, 28b.

898.21 The evidence of one is not valid against that of two.
Ulla. T: Yebamot, 88b.

898.22 The soul testifies at night to what the man does by day.
Zohar, Gen., 92a.

899. THEATRE

899.1 There is that smaller world which is the stage, and that larger stage which is the world.
Goldberg, Theatre of G. J. Nathan, 1926, p. 3.

899.2 The theatre is not a game. It is a spiritual compulsion. Once it celebrated the gods. Now it broods over the fate of man.
Lewisohn, Creative Life, 1924, p. 131f.

899.3 The theatre is an escape from reality.
G. J. Nathan, The Theatre, 1921, p. 168.

900. THEOLOGY

900.1 Theology is flourishing at the expense of religion.
F. Adler, Creed and Deed, 1877, p. 1.

900.2 The very absence of formal theology in Judaism is a virtue.
Bentwich. LJC, Dec. 18, 1953, p. 15.

900.3 Theology: that madness gone systematic which tries to crowd God's fulness into a formula and a system!
Blau, "My Uncertain God." Menorah Journal, 1924, x. 470.

900.4 The theology of original sin is not as monstrous as the original sin of theology.
Ibid., 470f.

900.5 The scholastic tree is covered with prodigal foliage, but is barren of fruit.
D'Israeli, *Curiosities: Quodlibets*, 1791.

900.6 The most significant feature of the rabbinical system of theology is its lack of system.
Ginzberg, *Students, Scholars and Saints*, 1928, p. 92.

900.7 The moment a religion seeks support from philosophy, its ruin is inevitable. ... Religion, like every other form of absolutism, should be above justification.
Heine, *Germany from Luther to Kant*, 1834.

900.8 Moral experience is autonomous of any theological truth.
Hook, letter to *N.Y. Times*, June 22, 1952.

900.9 The divine test of a man's worth is not his theology but his life.
Joseph, *Judaism as Creed and Life*, 1903, p. 116.

900.10 The greater the jurist, the smaller the theologian.
S. Levin, *Youth in Revolt*, 1930, p. 55.

900.11 It was said by a great writer that the best theology is that which is not consistent, and this advantage the theology of the Synagog possesses to its utmost extent.
Schechter, *Studies in Judaism*, 1896, i. 231.

900.12 Reason, however sound, has little weight with ordinary theologians.
Spinoza, *Theologico-Political Treatise*, 1670, ch 5.

900.13 All theology is to the religious life of prayer, of mystical experience and of good works, as the theory of harmony is to music.
Werfel, *Between Heaven and Earth*, 1944, p. 144.

900.14 Fortunately, religion depends as little upon theology as love upon phrenology.
Zangwill, *Send-Off to Dr. Schechter*, April 1902.

900.15 In the crude working world religion depends less on the belief than on the believer.
Zangwill, *Italian Fantasies*, 1910, p. 13.

901. THEORY

901.1 Purely theoretic studies seem to me to be of those fine flowers which relieve the drabness of our existence and help to make the human scene worth while.
M. R. Cohen. *New Republic*, Dec. 3, 1919, p. 19. *Faith of a Liberal*, 86.

901.2 In the whole realm of the Divine Law, not one single truth is revealed to us which is only of theoretical interest.
S. R. Hirsch, "Die Stiftshütte." *Gesam. Schr.*, 1921, p. 371. q BKF, 62.

901.3 The history of our modern technic shows that nothing is as practical as theory.
Oppenheimer. *Reflex*, July 1927, p. 72.

901.4 People prefer theory to practice because it involves them in no more real responsibility than a game of checkers, while it permits them to feel they're doing something serious and important.
L. Stein, *Journey into the Self*, 1950, p. 107.

902. THIEF

902.1 Thou shalt not steal.
Bible: Exod., 20.13.

902.2 Men do not despise a thief, if he steal to satisfy his soul when he is hungry.
Bible: Prov., 6.30.

902.3 Stolen waters are sweet.
Ibid., 9.17.

902.4 A thief is a thief, whether he steal much or little, from Jew or Gentile.
Caro, *Hoshen Mishpat*, 1564, #369.

902.5 The last of the robbers is the first to be hanged.
Eccles. R., 7.26.1.

902.6 A benediction over stolen things is blasphemy.
Eliezer b. Jacob. *T: Baba Kamma*, 94a.

902.7 Before a thief steals, he has learned to lie.
I. Friedmann, *Imré Bina*, 1912, p. 15.

902.8 Men in fact are but pickpockets!
Heine, *Atta Troll*, 1841, ch 10.

902.9 While forcing the lock, the burglar calls on divine aid.
Immanuel, *Mahberot*, (c. 1300), ch 11.

902.10 When thieves fall out, the theft is revealed.
Ibid.

902.11 To rob a friend even of a penny is like taking his life.
Johanan b. Nappaha. *T: Baba Kamma*, 119a. See *Lev. R.*, 33.3.

902.12 A thief is punished harder than a robber, for a thief, who works stealthily, seems to fear man more than God.
Johanan b. Zakkai. *Mekilta, to Exod.* 22.6.

902.13 Not the mouse but the hole is the thief.
Joseph b. Hiyya. *T: Gittin,* 45a.

902.14 If there were no receivers of stolen goods, there would be no thieves.
Lev. R., 6.2.

902.15 Stealing time is also robbery.
M. H. Luzzatto, *Mesillat Yesharim,* 1740, ch 11.

902.16 The breach invites the thief.
Proverb. q Raba. *T: Sukka,* 26a.

902.17 If you steal from a thief, you taste of thieving.
Proverb. q *T: Berakot,* 5b.

902.18 When the thief is needed, he's taken off the gallows.
Proverb (Yiddish). BJS, #828.

902.19 Every thief has his alibi.
Proverb (Yiddish). BJS, #829.

902.20 You can keep one from stealing, but not from being a thief.
Schnitzler, *Buch der Sprüche & Bedenken,* 1927, p. 225.

902.21 A thief may go unhanged for two or three thefts; eventually he will be caught.
Talmud: Sanhedrin, 7a.

902.22 When courage fails him, the thief becomes virtuous.
Ibid., 22a.

902.23 First among thieves is a deceiver.
Tosefta: Baba Kamma, 7.8.

903. THIRST

903.1 Ho, every one that thirsts, come ye for water.
Bible: Isa., 55.1.

903.2 In my thirst, they gave me vinegar to drink.
Bible: Ps., 69.22.

903.3 Who blows off the foam from his glass is not thirsty.
Alphabet of Ben Sira. q *T: Sanhedrin,* 100b.

904. THORN

904.1 Thorns do not impede the rose.
Hoffenstein, *Pencil in the Air,* 1923, p. 148.

904.2 From the thorn-bush comes forth the rose.
Proverb. q *Cant. R.,* 1.1.6.

904.3 No thorn but seeks to prick.
Twerski, *Rashi,* 1946.

905. THOUGHT

905.1 As he thinks in his heart, so is he.
Bible: Prov., 23.7.

905.2 Thought encompasses the earth, and its seat is in a tiny attic the size of a man's palm.
Bedersi, *Behinat Olam,* c. 1305, ch 1.

905.3 Thinking is a strenuous art—few practice it: and then only at rare times.
Ben Gurion, speech, April 18, 1940. BRD, 105.

905.4 In the heyday of prosperity Americans never think. In suffering, they sometimes do.
Brandeis, letter to Paul U. Kellogg, June 9, 1924.

905.5 Thinking is not a heaven-born thing. . . . It is a gift men and women make for themselves. It is earned, and it is earned by effort. There is no effort, to my mind, that is comparable in its qualities, that is taxing to the individual, as to think, to analyze fundamentally.
Brandeis. q CGP, 322f.

905.6 It is depth of understanding, nobility of thought, that constitutes the crown of the righteous.
Figo, *Bina Lalttim,* 1648, ii. 16a, on Rab's dictum, *T: Berakot,* 17a.

905.7 The thought precedes the deed as the lightning the thunder.
Heine, *Religion and Philosophy in Germany,* 1834.

905.8 Ye fools, so closely to search my trunk! . . . My contraband goods I carry about in my head, not hid in my clothing.
Heine, *Germany: A Winter Tale,* 1844, ch 2.

905.9 Thought is invisible nature; nature, visible thought.
Heine, *Gedanken und Einfälle,* 1869.

905.10 Wise men think out their thoughts; fools proclaim them.
Ibid.

905.11 Thoughts, beautifully combed and curled.
Ibid.

905.12 Dive into the sea of thought, and draw precious pearls.
M. Ibn Ezra, *Shirat Yisrael,* (12C) 1924, p. 102.

905.13 Thought serves man as a mirror: it shows him the ugliness and the beauty within him.
Ibid., 111.

905.14 Alone, without a brother, I have no friends but my thoughts.
Ibn Gabirol, "On Leaving Saragossa." HPB, 83.

905.15 My thoughts form an Eden in my heart.
Judah Halevi. q Jacobs, *Jewish Ideals,* 119.

905.16 The Hebrew form of thought rebels against the very idea of a distinction between the secular and the religious aspects of life. It demands the synthesis of action and reflection.
*Macmurray, *Clue to History,* 1939, p. 29.

905.17 To stop thinking means for me to stop living.
Mendelé, letter to Binstok, 1877. q Z. Raisen, *Lexicon,* i. 21.

905.18 Art can rise above mere handicraft only by being devoted to the expression of a lofty thought.
F. Mendelssohn, *Memorandum on a Music Academy,* May 1841.

905.19 Think and thank.
M. Montefiore family escutcheon, 1846.

905.20 If you can't help it, don't think about it.
C. Myers, *Don't Think About It,* 1952.

905.21 Think before you speak.
Nahmanides, letter to his son, 1267. q SSJ, i. 110.

905.22 Rather talk to a woman and think of God than talk to God and think of a woman.
Proverb (Yiddish). YFS, i. 414.

905.23 Let your thought belong to the world, but your love to your people. Yet let your thought be ever filled with love, and your love be ever led by thought.
Rülf, inscription in a young admirer's album. q *JGL,* 1912, xv. 200.

905.24 A humble man walks on earth, yet his thoughts reach the sky.
Samuel HaNagid, *Diwan,* ed Harkavy, #15, ed Brody, #36.

905.25 Don't attempt to drive folly out of your mind by force. Rather ignore evil thoughts, and concentrate on God.
Shneor Zalman, *Likkuté Amarim,* (1796) 1912, p. 70.

905.26 No man can bid a fool or sage
from thought abstain,
A thought can glide through
stone and steel and iron chain.
Süsskind of Trimberg. q GHJ, iii. 420. See KJL, 182.

905.27 To think is to dig and to measure with a plummet. Many have no strength to dig; others have not the courage to let the plummet sink into the depths.
Varnhagen, *Diary,* April 10, 1806.

906. THREE

906.1 A threefold cord is not quickly broken.
Bible: Eccles., 4.12.

907. THRIFT

907.1 Teach craft to Scots and thrift to Jews.
*Cowley, *The Prophet,* 1647.

907.2 Rare are seven things:
A nun who never sings,
A maid without a lover,
A fair without a robber,
A goat of beard bereft,
A Jew that knows no thrift,
A granary without mice,
And a Cossack without lice.
*Ditty (German). q Sombart, *Jews and Modern Capitalism,* 319.

907.3 Expenses properly managed make half an income.
Ibn Gabirol. q Ibn Tibbon, *Tzavaah.* AHE, 79.

907.4 To dissipate your inheritance, wear linen, use glass, and be an absentee employer.
Johanan b. Nappaha. *T: Hullin,* 84b.

907.5 Small pennies add up to a large sum.
Meir. *Tosefta: Sota,* 3.1.

908. TIME

908.A. Concept

908.A.1 Wherever anything lives, there is open somewhere a register in which time is being inscribed.
Bergson, *Creative Evolution,* 1908, ch 1.

908.A.2 To express all spatial concepts in terms of time is perhaps one of the most important tasks of the humanity of the future.

G. Landauer, *Scepticism and Mysticism*. q LR, 121.

908.A.3 Time is a part of eternity, and of the same piece with it.

M. Mendelssohn, *National Instruction. Jerusalem*, tr Samuels, ii. 179, Note 4.

908.A.4 Time is change, transformation, evolution. Time is eternal sprouting, blossoming, the eternal tomorrow.

Peretz, *Hofnung un Shrek*, 1906. *Alle Verk*, xiii. 9.

908.A.5 It would be correct to say that the world was not made in time, but that time was formed by means of the world, for it was heaven's movement that was the index of the nature of time.

Philo, *Allegorical Interpretation*, 1.2.

908.B. Tenses

908.B.1 Draw from the past, live in the present, work for the future.

Geiger, motto. q *Menorah Journal*, 1917, iii. 6. Cf CCAR, liv. 225.

908.B.2 The present is the spinning wheel, the past the thread that is spun, the future the wool for men to weave their years.

Mandelstamm, *Mishlé Binyamin*, 1884, 9.16.

908.C. Power

908.C.1 Time will show.

Apocrypha: II Macc., 4.17.

908.C.2 Time will accomplish what ingenuity will not.

Bacharach, *Hoot HaShani*, 1679, 102.

908.C.3 The stream of time sweeps away the errors, and leaves the truth for the inheritance of humanity.

Brandes, *Ferdinand Lassalle*, 1881, p. 6.

908.C.4 Time wounds all heels.

Cerf, attributed to. q FAT, 1009.

908.C.5 Nothing can withstand time.

J. S. Delmedigo, *Nobelot Hokma*, 1631, Introduction.

908.C.6 Time will teach more than all our thoughts.

Disraeli, *Alroy*, 1833, 9.6.

908.C.7 Time, the great destroyer of other men's happiness, only enlarges the patrimony of literature to its possessor.

D'Israeli, *Literary Character*, 1795, ch 22.

908.C.8 Time will free the fly and cage the eagle.

Hasdai, *Ben HaMelek VeHaNazir*, c. 1230, ch 5.

908.C.9 No man can give comfort, only Time. Time, sly Saturn, heals all our wounds, only to deal our hearts fresh ones with his scythe.

Heine, letter to Varnhagen, March 28, 1833. EPP, 407.

908.C.10 Man decides to join, and Time parts.

M. Ibn Ezra, *Shirat Yisrael*, (12C) 1924, p. 83.

908.C.11 Time is the teacher most sublime.

Ibid., 84.

908.C.12 Time was but created to destroy.

M. Ibn Ezra, *Selected Poems*, 31.

908.C.13 Time is blind.

Immanuel, *Mahberot*, c. 1300, ch 1.

908.C.14 Time, the deceiver of all men.

Judah Halevi, *Selected Poems*, 80.

908.C.15 He that puts Time to proof, a traitor finds.

M. Ibn Ezra, *Selected Poems*, 54.

908.C.16 This people has established its home not in space but in time and in eternity, and therefore time has no power over it.

H. Kohn, *Die politische Idee des Judentums*, 1924. LR, 125.

908.C.17 People do not consume time, time consumes people.

Lazerov, *Enciklopedie fun Idishe Vitzen*, 1928, #513.

908.C.18 Time and patience will remedy every evil.

M. Lilienthal, *My Travels in Russia*, 350.

908.C.19 Time is a physician.

Philo, *Joseph*, 2.

908.C.20 Who forces time is pushed back by time; who yields to time finds time on his side.

Samuel. *T: Erubin*, 13b.

908.C.21 Time is the school in which we
learn,
Time is the fire in which we
burn.

D. Schwartz, "For Rhoda." *In Dreams Begin Responsibilities*, 1938, p. 95.

908.C.22 Time's violence rends the soul: by the rent eternity enters.

S. Weil, *Gravity and Grace*, 1952, p. 134.

908.C.23 Time the body sickens, and the passions quickens.
Zabara, *Sefer Shaashuim*, 13C, ch 7.

908.C.24 A youth asked an old man, who walked with difficulty, "Who put chains on your feet?" The old man replied, "Time, and it forges daily your chains too."
Zabara, *Sefer Shaashuim*, 13C, ed Davidson, p. 74.

908.C.25 Fear time, even when it smiles at you.
Ibid., 7.81, ed Davidson, p. 76.

908.D. Value

908.D.1 Is a land born in one day? Is a nation brought forth at once?
Bible: Isa., 66.8.

908.D.2 So teach us to number our days that we get us a heart of wisdom.
Bible: Ps., 90.12.

908.D.3 Days should speak and . . . years should teach wisdom.
Bible: Prov., 32.7.

908.D.4 With the Most High account is not taken of much time or of a few years. What did it profit Adam that he lived nine hundred and thirty years, and transgressed. . . ? Or wherein did Moses lose by living only one hundred and twenty years, and . . . lit a lamp for the nation of Israel?
Apocrypha: II Baruch, 1f, 4.

908.D.5 We mustn't waste time for that's the stuff life's made of.
Belasco, *Return of Peter Grimm*, 1911, Act 1.

908.D.6 Who gains time gains everything.
Disraeli, *Tancred*, 1847, 4.3.

908.D.7 If time is money, then everybody lives beyond his means.
Fulda, *Sprüchen in Prosa*.

908.D.8 An honest man keeps a strict account of his time, . . . lest he be morally bankrupt.
Hildesheimer. q MGU, 175.

908.D.9 The Hebrews affirmed the reality and importance of time. To them it was not an illusion, something from which man must escape, but something which must be redeemed.
*Hyatt, *Prophetic Religion*, 1947, p. 76.

908.D.10 A Jew never has time, he is always on the run.
Mendelé, *In a Sturem Tzeit*, 1886.

908.D.11 The welfare of a day ranks as far above an eternity of years, as the briefer daylight above an eternity of darkness.
Philo, *Who Is Heir*, 58.

908.D.12 It is well to economize time.
Philo. q John of Damascus, *Parallels*, p. 563c.

908.D.13 Rely on time for discipline.
Samuel HaNagid, *Ben Mishlé*, 11C. AHE, 71.

908.D.14 No loss like the loss of time.
Uceda, *Midrash Samuel*, 1579, to *Abot* 5.23.

908.D.15 "To kill time," what a profound and terrifying expression! Vaguely uneasy in the presence of what is really worth while, we amuse ourselves, we "kill" the brief time of our lives by playing cards, going to tedious . . . plays, or plunging into the meaningless whirl of society.
Werfel, *Of Man's True Happiness*, 1937. *Between Heaven and Earth*, 13.

908.E. Transience

908.E.1 A thousand years in Thy sight are but as yesterday when it is past, and as a watch in the night.
Bible: Ps., 90.4.

908.E.2 Our time is a very shadow that passes away.
Apocrypha: Wisdom of Solomon, 2.5.

908.E.3 Remember the companionship of time is but of short duration. It flies faster than the shades of evening. We are like a child that grasps a sunbeam. When he opens his hand, he is surprised to find it empty and the brightness gone.
Bedersi, *Behinot HaOlam*, c. 1310.

908.E.4 A day passes creeping,
A year, as on wings.
Frug, "Hot and Cold," tr Frank. *JQRo*, xiv. 560.

908.E.5 The hours are only a slothful race!
Heine, *Songs*, #2, 1827.

908.E.6 There is pathos in the things that pass, but in things that never pass there would be despair.
H. Samuel, *Belief and Action*, 1937, p. 96.

908.F. Times

908.F.1 My times are in Thy hand.
Bible: Ps., 31.16.

908.F.2 Observe times and seasons.
Apocrypha: Ben Sira, 4.20.

908.F.3 Let not your spirit be troubled on account of the times.
Apocrypha: Enoch, 90.2.

908.F.4 Woe to the princes and people that obey the times, instead of commanding the times! The times will devour them. It was not the times that made France, it was France that made the times!
Boerne, *Menzel der Franzosenfresser,* 1836.

908.F.5 The man who anticipates his century is always persecuted when living, and is always pilfered when dead.
Disraeli, (Sievers in) *Vivian Grey,* 1827.

908.F.6 Who ignores the time walks in darkness, and who explores it is illumined by a great light.
q M. Ibn Ezra, *Shirat Yisrael,* (12C) 1924, p. 84.

908.F.7 Time is the same for pauper and priest.
Talmud: Berakot, 2b.

908.F.8 Man is the child of his times.
Zabara, *Sefer Shaashuim,* 13C, ch 7.

908.G. Timeliness

908.G.1 Is it a time to receive money?
Bible: II Kings, 5.26.

908.G.2 I will hasten it in its time.
Bible: Isa., 60.22.

908.G.3 A word in due season, how good it is!
Bible: Prov., 15.23. See *Ben Sira,* 4.23.

908.G.4 To everything there is a season, and a time to every purpose under the heaven.
Bible: Eccles., 3.1.

908.G.5 If a fig is plucked at the proper time, it is good for the fig and good for the tree, but not when gathered prematurely.
Abbahu. *Gen. R.,* 62.2.

908.G.6 Strike while the iron is hot.
Abulafia, *Yosef Lekah,* 1730.

908.G.7 Observe the opportunity.
Apocrypha: Ben Sira, 4.20.

908.G.8 A parable from the mouth of a fool is worthless, for he utters it out of season.
Ibid., 20.20.

908.G.9 At an unseasonable time display not your wisdom.
Ibid., 32.4.

908.G.10 Everything avails in its season.
Ibid., 39.34.

908.G.11 While the rope is in your grip, pull your cow.
Arama, *Akedat Yitzhak: Eccles.,* 15C.

908.G.12 How precious is a good deed done in due time!
Eleazar b. Shammua. *Sifra,* 25a, to *Lev.* 5.11. See Simeon. *T: Pesahim,* 68b.

908.G.13 A coal that does not burn in time does not burn.
Isaac b. Eleazar. *TJ: Maaser Sheni,* 5.3.

908.G.14 Attack not the wicked when fortune smiles on him.
Isaac b. Phineas. *T: Berakot,* 7b.

908.G.15 While your fire is burning, roast your pumpkin.
Johanan. *T: Sanhedrin,* 33b.

908.G.16 Rejoice at a time of joy, and mourn at a time of mourning.
Joshua b. Karha. *Gen. R.,* 27.4.

908.G.17 When an opportunity presents itself to do a good deed, do it at once.
Josiah. *Mekilta,* to *Exod.* 12.17.

908.G.18 If you have a rendezvous with destiny, be sure to come on time.
Kaplan. *Reconstructionist,* April 7, 1950, p. 27.

908.G.19 A Jew is never on time. . . He marries, begets children, ages and dies before his time.
Mendelé, *In a Sturem Tzeit,* 1886.

908.G.20 All depends on the time.
Mishna: Baba Metzia, 3.7.

908.G.21 Eat at eating-time, and you'll sleep at sleeping-time.
Nahmanides. q H. Kaidanover, *Kab Ha-Yashar,* 1705, ch 8.

908.G.22 When the festival is past, its duties have passed.
Proverb. q Beth Hillel. *T: Betza,* 20b.

908.G.23 While you have the sandal on, tread the thorn down.
Proverb. q Levi (Bacher: Isaac Nappaha). *Gen. R.,* 44.12.

908.G.24 Driver, when you open the door and see rain, put down your sack and go to sleep again.
Proverb. q Papa. *T: Berakot,* 59a.

908.G.25 Defer not till tomorrow what you can do today.
Proverb (Yiddish).

908.G.26 Two things it's never too late to do: to die and to become a teacher in a *heder.*
Proverb (Yiddish). q S. Levin, *Childhood in Exile,* 45.

908.G.27 The zealous perform their duty as soon as possible.

Raba. *T: Yoma*, 28b.

908.G.28 To be ready is much, to have the capacity for waiting is more, but to be able to utilize the right moment is everything.

Schnitzler, *Buch der Sprüche & Bedenken*, 1927, p. 227.

908.G.29 No time is ever out of time.

Toller. *Machine-Wreckers*, (1922) 1926.

908.G.30 Only the best people are punctual.

Varnhagen. q KRV, 170.

909. TITHE

909.1 At the end of every three years . . . bring forth all the tithe of your increase . . . And the Levite, . . . the stranger, the fatherless, and the widow . . . shall be satisfied.

Bible: Deut., 14.28f.

909.2 Tithes are a fence for wealth.

Akiba. *Mishna: Abot*, 3.13.

909.3 Tithe, and you'll be rich.

Johanan b. Nappaha. *T: Taanit*, 9a.

910. TOLERANCE

910.1 We ought to show the same keen spirit of generosity to our opponents so that we may win them over to the right.

Apocrypha: Aristeas, 227.

910.2 Good will is mightier than the strongest weapons and guarantees the greatest security.

Ibid., 230.

910.3 The good man shows mercy to all, even to sinners.

Apocrypha: Patriarchs, Benjamin, 4.2.

910.4 Provoke not one of another belief.

Asher b. Yehiel, *Hanhaga*, c.1320.

910.5 The supreme rule of the road is the rule of mutual forbearance.

Cardozo, *Ward vs. Clark*, 1921. 232 N.Y. Reports, 195.

910.6 You can never make your own religion look so well as when you show mercy to the religion of others.

*Dibdin, (Abednego in) *The Jew and the Doctor*, 1800.

910.7 A brotherly forbearance
Has united us for ages:
You, you tolerate my breathing
And I tolerate your rages!

Heine, *To Edom*. Letter to Moses Moser, Oct. 25, 1824. q *Rabbi of Bacherach* (Schocken ed), 72.

910.8 The proud monuments of liberty knew that . . . the Ruler of the universe would receive with equal benignity the various offerings of man's adoration if they proceed from an humble spirit and sincere mind; that intolerance in matters of faith had been from the earliest ages of the world the severest torment by which mankind could be afflicted; and that governments were only concerned about the actions and conduct of man, and not his speculative notions.

Henry, speech, North Carolina House of Commons, Dec. 6, 1809.

910.9 The tone of the great Jewish writers in reference to Christianity was as different from that of their opponents as light from darkness. Criticism and dissent were of course to be found in Jewish writings, but not the execration which filled so many Christian pages.

*Herford. *Menorah Journal*, 1919, v. 147. See *Pharisaism*, 333; BSL, 124.

910.10 In the midst of all triumphs of Christianity, it is well that the stately synagog should lift its walls by the side of the aspiring cathedral, a perpetual reminder that there are many mansions in the Father's earthly house as well as in the heavenly one; that civilized humanity, longer in time and broader in space than any historical form of belief, is mightier than any one institution or organization it includes.

*Holmes. *American Hebrew*, April 4, 1890; *Over Teacups*, 1892, 197.

910.11 Which is the greatest virtue? Patience with others' vices.

Ibn Gabirol, *Mibhar HaPeninim*, c.1050, #84.

910.12 Thy glory is not diminished by those who worship aught beside Thee,
For the yearning of them all is to draw nigh to Thee.

Ibn Gabirol, *Royal Crown*, 11C. *Selected Religious Poetry*, 86.

910.13 A wise man's duty is to be scrupulously faithful to the religious laws of his country, and not to abuse those of others.

Josephus, *Against Apion*, 2.13.

910.14 Our legislator expressly forbade us to deride or blaspheme the gods recognized by others [*Exod.* 22.28].

Ibid., 2.33.

910.15 I will not speak of tolerance. The freedom of conscience is a right so sacred that even the name of tolerance involves a species of tyranny.

*Mirabeau, at National Convention, 1791. q *Moniteur.*

910.16 What business has a drunken peasant in God's world? But if God gets along with him, can I reject him?

Moshe Leib of Sasov. q BTH, ii. 85.

910.17 Good will and amity among faiths and peoples . . . like the bluebird of happiness, are rarely attainable through frantic pursuit.

Neuman, address, March 12, 1948. NLG, 331.

910.18 A freer intercourse wtih Jews and Christians would have a good effect on both.

*Priestley, *Address to the Jews.* May 20, 1791. *Evidence of Revealed Religion,* 1794, i. 398, Note.

910.19 The soul of a *great* Jew can accommodate many things. There is danger only for the little souls.

F. Rosenzweig, letter to J. Prager, Jan. 1922. GFR, 107.

910.20 Who fears God neither gets angry nor insists on his ways.

Saadia, *Maggen uMehayé,* 10C.

910.21 The world is big enough for two such grand faiths as the Hebrew and the Christian.

Schechter. q J. G. Huneker, *Variations,* 101.

910.22 While the most atrocious persecution of the Jews was the order of the day . . . a French Jew, Judah HeHasid, wrote: "Treat the Christian as your brother in faith. If he errs to his loss, call his attention to it. Do not discriminate against him in the collection of taxes. . . . Never rob a Christian. God helps all who are oppressed." Contrast this with the pronouncement of the Christian Church, that "one need not keep faith in dealing with heretics."

*Schleiden, *Jews in Revival of Learning,* 1876.

910.23 Once a heavenly voice was heard saying: Akiba's prayer was answered not because he is greater . . . but because he is forbearing.

Talmud: Taanit, 25b.

910.24 Even the word Tolerance is intolerable. No person has a right to tolerate another.

Taubels, letter to S. Holdheim, c.1839.

911. TOMORROW

911.1 Boast not of tomorrow, for you know not what a day may bring.

Bible: Prov., 27.1.

911.2 Say not, Tomorrow I will do, for the day of death is hidden from every living being.

Bahya, *Hobot HaLebabot,* 1040, 7.7.

911.3 Know your Tomorrow while your Today lasts.

Judah Halevi, *Selected Poems,* 110.

911.4 Take no thought for the morrow; for the morrow will take thought for things of itself.

New Testament: Matt., 6.34.

911.5 Have your task of tomorrow done since the day before yesterday.

Spector. q CPP, #1822.

911.6 Learn the difference between to-day and tomorrow.

Talmud: Derek Eretz, 1.24.

912. TONGUE

912.1 Their tongue is a sharpened arrow, it speaks deceit.

Bible: Jer., 9.7.

921.2 Keep thy tongue from evil, and thy lips from speaking guile.

Bible: Ps., 34.14.

912.3 My tongue is the pen of a ready writer.

Ibid., 45.2.

912.4 A soothing tongue is a tree of life.
Bible: Prov., 15.4.

912.5 Death and life are in the power of the tongue.

Bible: Prov., 18.21.

912.6 A soft tongue will break a bone.
Ibid., 25.15. See Ben Sira, 28.17; Alnaqua, *Menorat HaMaor,* 14C, ed Enelow, iv. 139.

912.7 Many have fallen by the edge of the sword, but not as many as have fallen by the tongue.

Apocrypha: Ben Sira, 28.18.

912.8 The tongue is the heart's pen and the mind's messenger.

Bahya, *Hobot HaLebabot,* 1040, 2.5, tr Hyamson, ii. 20.

912.9 The tongue's sin weighs as much as all other sins together.
Elijah Gaon, *Alim LiTerufa,* 1836.

912.10 Let your tongue be imprisoned in your mouth!
Hai Gaon, *Musar Haskel,* c.1000.

912.11 Some sin against man, some against God; but an evil tongue sins against both.
Hanina b. Hama. *Eccles. R.,* 9.12.

912.12 The worst of men is he whose tongue is mightier than his mind.
q M. Ibn Ezra, *Shirat Yisrael,* (12C) 1924, p. 78.

912.13 Man's shame is between his legs, and a fool's between his cheeks.
q *Ibid.,* 80.

912.14 Thoughts rooted in the heart are branched forth by the tongue.
Ibid., 93. See 140.

912.15 The tongue is set between two cheeks, and a water channel passes beneath it, arranged in numerous folds; yet see how many conflagrations it has caused!
Jose b. Zimra. *Lev. R.,* 16.4.

912.16 The Holy One said to the tongue: All human limbs are standing, you are lying; all are outside, you are inside; not only that, but I surrounded you with two walls, one of bone and one of flesh, "what more could be given or added to you, deceitful tongue!" [*Ps.* 120.3].
Jose b. Zimra. *T: Arakin,* 15b.

912.17 A pedlar once came to Sepphoris and called out, "Who wants the elixir of life?" R. Yannai wanted to buy, but the pedlar said, "You don't need it." Showing him his article, a Psalter, he pointed to [*Ps.* 34.13] "Who is the man that desires life? Keep your tongue from evil."
Lev. R., 16.2.

912.18 Both the day Simeon b. Gamaliel wanted something good to eat and the day he wanted something cheap, his servant Tabbai brought him tongue. Asked to explain, Tabbai said: "Both good and evil are in the tongue. If it is good, there is nothing better; and if it is bad, there is nothing worse."
Ibid., 33.1.

912.19 The tongue and the heart may be far apart, yet rain from the skies makes plants to rise.
Lipkin. q KTH, i. 272.

912.20 The tongue rules over all the bodily organs.
Midrash Tehillim, 39.2, ed Buber, 128a.

912.21 If a horse with four legs can sometimes stumble, how much more a man with only one tongue.
Sholom Aleichem. q SWS, 47.

912.22 In the future, all the beasts of prey will say to the serpent: a lion claws and eats, a wolf tears and eats, but why do you bite? The serpent will reply: "Why does an evil tongue talk?"
Simeon b. Lakish. *T: Arakin,* 15b.

912.23 Men can govern anything more easily than their tongues.
Spinoza, *Ethics.* 1677, iii. Pr 2, Note.

912.24 An ass is known by his long ears, a fool by his big tongue.
Steinberg, *Mishlé Yehoshua,* 1886.
Weissmann-Chajes, *Hokma uMusar,* 1875.

912.25 He who desires a portion in the higher life . . . should above all guard his mouth and tongue.
Zohar, Lev., 41a.

913. TOOL

913.1 When the maker of stocks is put in the stocks, he is paid with his own handiwork.
Abayé. *T: Pesahim,* 28a.

913.2 When a maker of arrows is shot by an arrow, he is paid with his own handiwork.
Raba. *Ibid.*

913.3 The tiger's claws are meant to bring him food.
Alharizi, *Tahkemoni,* 13C. q CHS, 16.

913.4 Said the tree to the woodcutters, "If you had not something from me, you would not have fallen on me."
Apocrypha: Ahikar, 3.24.

913.5 The workman's tool is the continuation of his arm. . . . Nature, in endowing us with an essentially tool-making intelligence, prepared for us in this way a certain expansion.
Bergson, *Two Sources of Morality and Religion,* 1935, 298.

913.6 The fetters which bind the people are forged from the people's own gold.
Brandeis, *Other People's Money,* 1914.

913.7 When iron was created, the trees trembled. Said the Holy One: If you won't supply the handle, the ax will not hurt you.

Gen. R., 5.9. Cf Simeon b. Yohai. Sanhedrin, 39b.

913.8 A carpenter without tools is no carpenter.

Hoshaia. Exod. R., 40.1.

913.9 How many spun the rope that became their noose! How many quarried the rock by which they were stoned!

Immanuel, Mahberot, c.1300, ch 10.

913.10 A robber knows his weapons.

Johanan b. Nappaha. T: Baba Metzia, 84a.

913.11 A plain lead pencil can record the most precious thoughts.

Sam Liptzin. A Vort far a Vort, 1955, p. 16.

913.12 The spoon he fashioned will carry the mustard to burn his tongue.

Proverb. q Joseph b. Hiyya. T: Pesahim, 28a.

913.13 A good tool is half an artisan.

Proverb (Yiddish). YFS, i. 412.

913.14 Pincers are made with pincers; work is promoted by work, and science by science.

Satanov, Mishlé Asaf, 1789, 34.23.

914. TOOTH

914.1 I am escaped with the skin of my teeth.

Bible: Job, 19.20.

914.2 Thy teeth are like a flock of ewes, come from the washing.

Bible: Cant., 6.6.

914.3 A toothache in the heart.

Heine, Buch Le Grand, 1827, ch 20.

914.4 You can't chew with somebody else's teeth.

Proverb. ATJF, p. 639.

914.5 If a man of Naresh kissed you, count your teeth.

Rab. T: Hullin, 127a.

915. TORAH

915.A. Definition

915.A.1 Torah represents the accumulated literary and spiritual heritage of the Jewish people through the centuries.

Chipkin. Religious Education, Sept. 1953, p. 338.

915.A.2 Torah is not law. It is an expression for the aggregate of Jewish teachings.

Ginzberg, Students, Scholars and Saints, 1928, p. 65.

915.A.3 Torah meant divine teaching upon all and everything that concerned religion.

*Herford, Pharisaism, 1912, p. 74.

915.A.4 The real Torah is not merely the written text of the Five Books of Moses; the real Torah is the meaning enshrined in that text, as expounded . . . and unfolded . . . by successive generations of Sages and Teachers in Israel.

Hertz, Daily Prayer Book, 1948, p. 35f.

915.A.5 The real Torah is the unwritten moral law which underlies the precepts of both the written law and its oral interpretation.

Kohler, Jewish Theology, 1918, p. 46.

915.A.6 Torah in one aspect is the vehicle, in another and deeper view it is the whole content, of revelation.

*Moore, Judaism, 1927, i. 263.

915.A.7 Every living soul is a letter of the Torah, wherefore all souls taken together make up the Torah.

Nathan of Nemirov. q Peretz, SPG, 180.

915.A.8 Torah is the distillation of the soul of Israel into the written words of its classic literature, in the institutions in which it has taken shelter. But the Torah in the ideal cannot be chained to the written word nor contained wholly in the institutions designed for human beings. It is the indwelling of the divine spirit in living souls as expressed in the genius of Israel.

Neuman, address, March 12, 1948. NLG, 322f.

915.A.9 The Torah is the map of the world.

Z. Rabinowitz, Tzidkat HaTzaddik, 1902, #4.

915.B. Contents

915.B.1 The Law of Moses does not include philosophical theories, or logical investigations, or proofs involving high inquiries. For man's success is above Reason and beyond Nature.

Abravanel, Ateret Zekenim, (1557) 1894, 42. See NDI, 291.

915.B.2 Our law forbids us to injure anyone by word or deed.

Apocrypha: Aristeas, 168.

915.B.3 What brief verse contains the whole substance of the Torah? *Proverbs,* 3.6, "In all thy ways acknowledge God, and He will direct thy paths."

Bar Kappara. *T: Berakot,* 63a.

915.B.4 Every glory and wonder, every deep mystery and all beautiful wisdom are hidden in the Torah, sealed up in her treasures.

Nahmanides, *Commentary on Pentateuch,* Introd. q SSJ, i. 127.

915.B.5 There is no branch of wisdom, natural or divine, but is contained in the profound depths of our perfect Torah.

Norzi, *Orah Hayyim,* 1579, 15a.

915.B.6 Is there aught in the vain events of everyday life not already contained in the Law of Moses?

Rossi, *Meor Enayim,* 1573 (ed Cassel) 264.

915.B.7 What does the Torah say? Submit to the yoke of the kingdom of heaven, excel in the fear of God, and love one another.

Sifré, #323, to *Deut.* 32.29, 138b.

915.C. Character

915.C.1 What great nation . . . has statutes . . . so righteous as all this law?

Bible: Deut., 4.8.

915.C.2 The law of the Lord is perfect, restoring the soul; the testimony of the Lord is sure, making wise the simple.

Bible: Ps., 19.8.

915.C.3 Thy testimonies are my delight.

Ibid., 119.24.

915.C.4 Thy law is truth.

Ibid., 119.142.

915.C.5 All thy righteous ordinance endures for ever.

Ibid., 119.160.

915.C.6 It would be impossible to mention any people of even a much later age . . . whose law and constitution embodied an ideal so noble as that embodied in the Hebrew civil laws, or any people whose history shows the existence of political institutions so essentially just, free, and humane.

*Abbott, *Life and Literature of Ancient Hebrews.* 1901, p. 127.

915.C.7 Though we depart, the Law abides.

Apocrypha: II Baruch, 77.15.

915.C.8 The first man knew her not perfectly, neither will the last trace her

out, for her understanding is fuller than the sea, and her counsel is greater that the deep.

Apocrypha: Ben Sira, 24.28f.

915.C.9 The sun gives light by day, the Torah by day and night.

Asher b. Saul. q *Kol Bo,* 8.

915.C.10 God has concentrated Himself in the Torah.

Ber, *Or HaEmet,* 1899, 15.

915.C.11 Like rain, the Torah nourishes useful plants and poisonous weeds.

Elijah Gaon, *Commentary,* to *Prov.* 24.31 and 25.4.

915.C.12 Down to modern times, no State has had a constitution in which the interests of the people are so largely taken into account, in which the duties, so much more than the privileges, of rulers are insisted upon, as that drawn up for Israel in *Deuteronomy* and in *Leviticus;* nowhere is the fundamental truth that the welfare of the State, in the long run, depends on the uprightness of the citizen so strongly laid down.

*T. H. Huxley, *Controverted Questions,* 1892.

915.C.13 The Torah is intrinsically perfect; it requires no external evidence for the truths it teaches.

A. Ibn Ezra, *Commentary,* to *Ps.,* 19.8.

915.C.14 The Torah and all its commandments . . . form a great and mighty Divine poem, a poem of confident trust and love.

Kook, *Eder HaYekor,* 1906, p. 44. q ABJ, 199.

915.C.15 We have in the Mosaic code and its amplifications the most careful safeguards against slavery and a deadening poverty.

*J. R. Macdonald, *Socialist Movement,* 1911, p. 20.

915.C.16 The Torah . . . was not written in ink, nor was it engraved on stone. It was white fire carved on black fire.

Opatoshu, *Last Revolt,* 1952, ch 10, p. 71.

915.C.17 I think it strange that the first law of the world happens to be the most perfect, so that the greatest legislators have borrowed their laws from it.

*Pascal, *Pensées,* 1670, #619.

915.C.18 If Torah is here, wisdom is here.

Proverb (Yiddish). Mendele, *BaYamim HaHem,* 1912.

915.C.19 Let not the Torah seem to you antiquated, which nobody minds, but new, to which all run.

Sifré, #33, to *Deut.* 6.6, ed Friedmann, 74a. See Rashi, *Commentary,* on *Exod.* 19.1.

915.C.20 Like water, the Torah cleanses, and is priceless and free.

Sifré, #48, to *Deut.* 11.22, ed Friedmann, 84a.

915.C.21 Like wine, the Torah rejoices the heart and improves with age.

Ibid.

915.C.22 A sin may extinguish a commandment, but not the Torah.

Talmud: Sota, 21a.

915.C.23 The Torah has been likened to a sword [*Gen.* 3.24], to fire [*Deut.* 33.2] and to water [*Isa.* 55.1]. As a sword may shield or slay, as water may satisfy or drown, and as fire may sustain or destroy, so Torah may spell life or retribution.

Yalkut Shimoni, #951.

915.C.24 The Torah is a vestment to the Shekina.

Zohar, Gen., 23ab.

915.D. Purpose

915.D.1 The purpose of the divine law is to guide men to obtain . . . spiritual happiness and immortality.

Albo, *Ikkarim,* 1428, 1.7, tr Husik, i. 79.

915.D.2 What can it profit a man to study Torah all his life, if he never attempts to fathom the real purpose of such study?

Anatoli, *Malmad HaTalmidim,* 1149, 148b. q BSJ, 82.

915.D.3 The object of the whole Torah is that man should become a Torah himself.

Baal Shem. q SSJ, i. 29.

915.D.4 Thou hast favored us with a law of loving-kindness and made known to us precepts of truth . . . to guide us in the paths of equity, . . . to purify our souls from the dross of daily desires, to redeem our spirits from the temporal shackles of this world.

Bahya, *Hobot HaLebabot, Bakasha,* 1040, tr Hyamson, v. 55.

915.D.5 It is not the protection of property, but the protection of humanity, that is the aim of the Mosaic code. Its sanctions are not directed to securing the strong in heaping up wealth so much as to prevent-ing the weak from being crowded to the wall.

*George, *Moses,* 1878.

915.D.6 The dietary laws are not incumbent upon us because they conduce to moderation, nor the family laws because they further chastity. . . . The law as a whole is not the means to an end, but the end in itself; the Law is active religiousness, and in active religion lies what is specifically Jewish.

Ginzberg, *Students, Scholars and Saints,* 1928, p. 208.

915.D.7 Israel accepted the Torah only that the Angel of Death should have no dominion over them.

Jose. *T: Aboda Zara,* 5a.

915.D.8 The whole Torah exists only for the sake of peace.

Joseph. *T: Gittin,* 59b.

915.D.9 We possess a code excellently designed to promote piety, friendly relations . . . and humanity toward the world, besides justice, hardihood and contempt of death.

Josephus, *Against Apion,* ii. 14.

915.D.10 The essence and aim of the whole Torah is love for God and devotion to Him.

Katz, *Toldot Jacob Joseph,* 1780. q HLH, 32.

915.D.11 The corner-stone of the Torah . . . is to strengthen in the human heart the quality of mercy and love, to remove confidence in our own power and in the might of our hands, and to put our trust in divine Providence which follows not intelligence but justice and loving-kindness and sincerity.

S. D. Luzzatto, *Yesodé HaTorah,* 1880, p. 9.

915.D.12 All the commandments and exhortations in the Pentateuch aim at conquering the desires of the body.

Maimonides, *Guide for the Perplexed,* 1190, 3.8.

915.D.13 The general object of the Law is the well-being of the soul and of the body.

Ibid., 3.27.

915.D.14 It is the object . . . of the whole Law to abolish idolatry . . . and to overthrow the opinion that stars can interfere for good or evil in human affairs.

Ibid., 3.37.

915.D.15 The Torah was given to sanctify His great name.
Seder Eliyahu Rabbah, ch 26, (28), ed Friedmann, 140.

915.E. Value

915.E.1 Happy are they . . . who walk in the law of the Lord.
Bible: Ps., 119.1.

915.E.2 Great peace have they that love Thy law.
Ibid., 119.165.

915.E.3 Believe with perfect faith in the Torah of Moses, . . . the basis of all wisdom and mysteries. . . . Upon its ladder will your soul ascend and turn into its place.
Alami, *Iggeret Musar*, 1415. q GIS. 124.

915.E.4 If ye prepare your hearts to sow in them the Law, it shall protect you when the Almighty will shake the whole creation.
Apocrypha: II Baruch, 32.1.

915.E.5 If you respect the Law . . . a lamp will not be wanting, a shepherd will not fail, a fountain will not dry up.
Ibid., 77.16.

915.E.6 We have nothing now save the Almighty and His law.
Ibid., 85.3.

915.E.7 The world was created only for the sake of the Torah.
Banaah. *Gen. R.*, 1.4.

915.9.8 For me the Torah reflects the universe.
Benamozegh, letter to Luzzatto. q PUS, 170.

915.E.9 Our teachers . . . knew that the bonds of the Torah would be able to keep them [Jews] together.
Z. H. Chajes, *Mebo HaTalmud*, 1845, ch 8. tr 1952, p. 47.

915.E.10 It was life under the yoke of the Law which implanted freedom and peace in the heart of the Jew, so that hatred and vengeance could not lodge there.
H. Cohen, *Die Religion der Vernunft*, 1919, p. 542.

915.E.11 Torah and loving-kindness will spare you the tribulations which are to attend the advent of Messiah.
Eleazar b. Shammua. *T: Sanhedrin*, 98b.

915.E.12 Without Torah, man stumbles against sin and dies; with Torah . . . he walks like a man in the dark with a lantern. . . . God said: Hold My lamp [Torah], and I'll hold yours [soul].
Exod. R., 36.3.

915.E.13 From the free spirit of the Mosaic Law sprang the intensity of family life that amid all dispersions and persecution has preserved the individuality of the Hebrew race; that love of independence that under the most adverse circumstances has characterized the Jew; that burning patriotism that flamed up in the Maccabees and bared the breasts of Jewish peasants to the serried steel of Grecian phalanx and the resistless onset of Roman legion; that stubborn courage that in exile and in torture held the Jew to his faith. It kindled that fire that has made the strains of Hebrew seers and poets phrase for us the highest exaltations of thought; that intellectual vigor that has over and over again made the dry staff bud and blossom. And passing outward from one narrow race it has exerted its power wherever the influence of the Hebrew Scriptures has been felt. It has toppled thrones and cast down hierarchies. It strengthened the Scottish Covenanter in the hour of trial, and the Puritan amid the snows of a strange land. It charged with the Ironsides at Nasby; it stood behind the low redoubt on Bunker Hill.
*George, *Moses*, 1878.

915.E.14 Who fills his mind with Torah clears it of fear and folly.
Hanania Sgan Kohanim. *ARN*, ch 20.

915.E.15 The Torah is a crown for the head [*Prov.* 1.9], a string of pearls for the neck [*ibid.*], a balm for the heart [*Ps.* 19.9], a salve for the eyes [*ibid.*], and a drug for the bowels [*Prov.* 3.8].
Hezekiah b. Hiyya. *Lev. R.*, 12.3.

915.E.16 The more Torah, the more life.
Hillel. *Mishna: Abot*, 2.7.

915.E.17 With the Torah, freedom came into the world.
Isaac. *Gen. R.*, 53.7.

915.E.18 Torah is a city's rampart, and students are its towers.
Johanan b. Nappaha. *T: Baba Bathra*, 7b–8a.

915.E.19 A drug may be beneficial to one and not to another, but the Torah is a life-giving medicine for all Israel!
Judah b. Hiyya. *T. Erubin*, 54a, on *Prov.* 4.22.

915.E.20 Israel could dispense with its State and its Temple, but not with its storehouse of divine truth, from which it constantly derives new life and new youth.

Kohler, *Jewish Theology*, 1918, p. 361.

915.E.21 It is in and through the Torah that we are teachers of the nations, that we exist today, and are saved for an eternal salvation.

Krochmal, *Moré Nebuké HaZeman*, 1851.

915.E.22 A little of Torah's light will push back much of exile's night.

Lipkin. q KTH, i. 270.

915.E.23 The cord of God's ordinances and Law are suspended from heaven to earth, and whoever lays hold of it has hope.

Maimon b. Joseph, *Letter of Consolation*, 1160.

915.E.24 The Torah clothes its devotee with meekness and piety. . . . It magnifies and exalts him above all creatures.

Meir. *Mishna: Abot*, 6.1.

915.E.25 Man's end is death. . . . Happy he who was brought up in Torah, labored in Torah, and gave pleasure to his Creator.

Meir. *T: Berakot*, 17a.

915.E.26 A commandment, like a lamp, is a momentary aid; the Torah, like light, is a permanent protection.

Menahem b. Jose. *T: Sota*, 21a.

915.E.27 To have Torah is greater than to have priesthood or royalty.

Mishna: Abot, 6.5.

915.E.28 A man of Torah is one who knows his place, rejoices in his lot, makes a fence to his words, claims no credit to himself, . . . loves the Omnipresent, loves all creatures, . . . welcomes criticism of himself, . . . keeps away from honors, is not puffed up because of his learning, delights not in giving legal decisions, shares the burden of a colleague, . . . listens to others, adds to his knowledge, learns in order to teach and to practice, . . . notes with precision what he hears, and quotes in the name of him who said it.

Ibid., 6.6.

915.E.29 As soon as they received the Torah, they [Jews] became a whole nation.

Pesikta Kahana, ch 1, ed Buber (1898) 1925, 2a.

915.E.30 Through Torah . . . man becomes God's partner in creation.

Ragoler, *Maalot HaTorah*, (1828) 1946, p. 44.

915.E.31 You cannot buy Torah with money!

Samuel b. Nahman. *Num. R.*, 2.16.

915.E.32 A scholar, constantly occupied with Torah for the glory of Heaven, needs no weapon for protection. The Holy One is his protector, and the ministering angels are his body guard.

Seder Eliyahu Rabbah, ch 4, ed Friedmann, p. 19.

915.E.33 The Torah is God's most precious treasure, . . . because it tips the scale of Israel toward merit, trains them in the commandments, and leads them to the life of the world to come.

Ibid., ch 15, ed Friedmann, p. 71.

915.E.34 Though exiled, when Jews engage in Torah, they are at home.

Ibid., ch 28 (30), p. 148.

915.E.35 The soul's delights come only after the comprehension of the Torah's mysteries.

Shneor Zalman, *Torah Or: Shemot*, 1837.

915.E.36 If not for Torah, Israel would not at all differ from the nations of the world.

Sifra, 112c.

915.E.37 If Israel heeded the Torah, none would prevail over them.

Sifré, to *Deuteronomy*, 32.29, #323, ed Friedmann, 138b.

915.E.38 It took six days to make the world, forty to give the Torah.

Simlai. *Pesikta Rabbati*, ch 21, ed Friedmann, 110a.

915.E.39 Israel accepted Torah so that no nation or tongue should prevail over them.

Talmud: Aboda Zara, 5a.

915.E.40 Why is Israel called God's people? Because of the Torah.

Tanhuma, VaEra, ed Buber, 9a.

915.E.41 The altar will abide as long as the Temple, but the light of the Torah will abide for ever.

Tanhuma, BeHaAloteka, 6, ed Buber, 24b.

915.E.42 Woe is me that I made use of the crown of the Torah!

Tarfon. *T: Nedarim*, 62a.

915.E.43 Make not of the Torah a crown to magnify yourself, or a spade with which to dig.

Zadok. *Mishna: Abot*, 4.5.

915.E.44 The terrestrial world was not freed from the defilement of the serpent until Israel stood at Mount Sinai.

Zohar, Gen., 36b.

915.F. Acceptance

915.F.1 The Holy One suspended Mount Sinai over Israel like a vault, and said: "If you accept the Torah, well and good; if not, you will find your grave here!"

Abdimi b. Hama. T: Sabbath, 88a. See Aboda Zara, 2b.

915.F.2 All souls stood at Sinai, each accepting its share in Torah.

Alshek. q Ragoler, Maalot HaTorah, 111.

915.F.3 The Holy One offered the Torah to all nations, and none but Israel accepted it.

Johanan b. Nappaha. T: Aboda Zara, 2b. See Pesikta Rabbati, ch 21, ed Friedmann, 99b. Mekilta, to Exod. 20.2.

915.F.4 As God permeates the universe, so the Law has found its way among all mankind.

Josephus, Against Apion, ii. 39.

915.F.5 Scripture likens the Torah to the desert, to fire, and to water, for like these three, it is free to all.

Mekilta, to Exod. 20.2.

915.F.6 The Torah was given in the third month, the zodiac symbol of which is Gemini, to indicate that it was for both, Jacob and Esau.

Pesikta de R. Kahana, ch 12, p. 95b.

915.F.7 Our laws . . . attract and win the attention of all, of barbarians, of Greeks, of dwellers on the mainland and islands, of nations of the east and west, of Europe and Asia, of the whole inhabited world from end to end.

Philo, Moses, ii. 4.

915.F.8 When God created the world, He stipulated: If Israel accept My law, well and good; if not, let chaos return.

Simeon b. Lakish. T: Aboda Zara, 3a.

915.G. Application

915.G.1 The Law must be revealed to all human beings, since the world was created for all of them, and in the hearts of all of them God planted faith and good understanding.

Apocrypha: Sibyl, 3.261f. q Klausner, From Jesus to Paul, 149, omitted in Charles ed.

915.G.2 The written and oral laws, which jointly form our revealed religion, are binding on our nation only. "Moses commanded us a law" [Deut. 33.4]. All the other nations of the earth, we believe, have been bidden by God to be guided by the laws of Nature and the religion of the patriarchs. Those who regulate their lives according to the laws of this natural and rational religion are called "the virtuous of other creeds," and are "children of eternal salvation."

M. Mendelssohn, Letter to Lavater, 1770.

915.G.3 The Torah was not given to angels!

Raba. T: Berakot, 25b. See Joshua b. Levi. Sabbath, 88b.

915.G.4 In Morals, Jew and non-Jew stand under the same law.

Sifra, to Lev. 18.6, ed Weiss, 85b.

915.G.5 Positive laws which depend on a specific time are to be observed by men, not women, by the ritually fit, not the unfit.

Simeon. Sifré, Num., #115.

915.G.6 The whole Torah was inscribed on the altar in seventy tongues.

Talmud: Sota, 36a.

915.G.7 Seven precepts were imposed on the children of Noah [i.e., all men]: civil justice, and the prohibition of blasphemy, idolatry, incest, bloodshed, robbery, and meat cut from a live animal.

Talmud: Sanhedrin, 56a.

915.G.8 God gave Israel the Law that all nations may be made happy.

Tanhuma, Debarim, ed Buber, p. 2.

915.H. Origin

915.H.1 Moses commanded us a law, an inheritance of the congregation of Jacob.

Bible: Deut., 33.4.

915.H.2 I doubted whether Moses' law was really God's law, and decided that it was of human origin, as many others have been.

U. Acosta, Exemplar Humanae Vitae, 1647, 1687.

915.H.3 The Torah was given in rolls [sections, later joined].

Banaah. T: Gittin, 60a.

915.H.4 A ruling derived from common sense is also designated by the Rabbis as "Words of Torah."

Z. H. Chajes, Mebo HaTalmud, (1845) 1952, ch 4, p. 31.

509

915.H.5 Wisdom and Torah flow from one source.

Elijah Gaon. q J. B. Agus. *Commentary*, Apr. 1951, p. 387.

915.H.6 Whatever the Prophets were to prophesy, whatever the sages of future generations were to teach, they received from Sinai.

Isaac Nappaha. *Exod. R.*, 28.6. See *Berakot*, 5a.

915.H.7 The Holy One showed Moses all the minutiae of the Torah, and all the innovations which would be introduced by the Scribes.

Johanan. *T: Megilla*, 19b.

915.H.8 I believe with perfect faith that the whole Torah, now in our possession, is the same that was given to Moses our teacher.

Maimonides, *Commentary to Mishna: Sanhedrin*, 1168, 10.1. *Thirteen Principles*, #8.

915.I. Development

915.I.1 Ye shall not add to the word which I command you, neither shall ye diminish from it.

Bible: Deut., 4.2.

915.I.2 The Torah will never change, for truth is unchangeable.

Albo, *Ikkarim*, 1428, 1.17.8.

915.I.3 The Torah is eternal, but its explanation is to be made by the spiritual leaders of Judaism . . . in accordance with the age.

Baal Shem. q SSJ, i. 29.

915.I.4 We have enlarged the sphere of our duty and made many things, which are in themselves indifferent, a part of our religion, that we may have more occasions of showing our love to God, and in all the circumstances of life be doing something to please Him.

Castro. q Limborch, *Amica Collatio de Veritate Religionis Christianae cum Erudito Judaeo*, 1687. q Addison, *Spectator*, #213, Nov. 3, 1711.

915.I.5 Development is of the essence of Judaism. Jewish history proves the richness of its power of adaptability . . . To the Jew it has been a veritable "tree of life." A living, growing tree.

F. A. Levy, *Crossroads in Judaism*, 1954, p. 31.

915.I.6 As times change, so the laws change.

Medina, 16C. q *American Zionist*, Feb. 5, 1953, p. 17.

915.I.7 When Moses was on high, he found the Holy One decorating the Torah's letters with coronets. He asked the meaning of this, and the Holy One said, "After many generations, a man by the name of Akiba will expound heaps and heaps of laws on each of these tittles." Moses went and sat down behind eight rows of disciples listening to Akiba's discourse, but he was unable to follow the discussion. At one point, the disciples asked, "Whence do you know it?" and Akiba replied, "It is a law given to Moses on Sinai." Said Moses, "Lord, Thou hast such a man, and Thou givest the Torah by me?" God replied, "Such is My decree!"

Rab. *T: Menahot*, 29b.

915.I.8 Forty-eight prophets and seven prophetesses prophesied to Israel, and none subtracted aught from, or added aught to, what is written in the Torah, save the reading of the Esther scroll.

Talmud: Megilla, 14a.

915.J. Oral Law

915.J.1 The oral law is as truly the word of God as the written law.

Godscheaux and Lambert, Manifesto, March 31, 1846. *AZJ*, 1846, p. 290f. q PRM, 460.

915.J.2 It is to this oral development of the law that Judaism owes its existence during the two thousand years of exile.

Hess, *Rome and Jerusalem*, (1862), p. 104.

915.J.3 God made His covenant with Israel only for the sake of the Oral Law.

Johanan. *T: Gittin*, 60b.

915.J.4 All the precepts were given to Moses at Sinai with their interpretations.

Maimonides, *Yad*, 1180, Introduction.

915.J.5 Words were given orally and words were given in writing, and the former are more precious.

Samuel b. Nahman. *TJ: Peah*, 2.4.

915.J.6 The Oral Law is but the interpretation of the Written Law.

Talmud: Sabbath, 31a.

915.K. Halaka

915.K.1 Halaka is the ultimate essence of Agada. The rumble of our heart's desire on its stormy way to the goal is Agada; the gratification of the desire, and the repose which follows, that is Halaka. Halaka does not deny emotion, it conquers it.

Bialik, "Halaka VeAgada." *Knesset*, 1917, p. 12 (tr *Law and Legend*, 1923).

915.K.2 It is only in the Halaka that we find the mind and character of the Jewish people exactly and adequately expressed.

Ginzberg, *Students, Scholars and Saints*, 1928, p. 117.

915.K.3 The Halaka would not be a true mirror of Jewish life, if it were free from all logical inconsistencies.

Ibid., 124.

915.K.4 Make a fence for the Torah.

Mishna: Abot, 1.1.

915.K.5 Make not the fence higher than the Law itself.

Hiyya Rabba. *Gen. R.*, 19.3.

915.K.6 "Watch My watch" [*Lev.* 18.30]—provide a protection to My protection.

Kahana. *T. Yebamot*, 21a.

915.K.7 Each halaka is the wisdom and will of God.

Shneor Zalman, *Tanya*, 1796. q HLH, 60.

915.K.8 Since the Temple was destroyed, the Holy One has in this world only the four cubits of Halaka.

Ulla b. Ishmael. *T: Berakot*, 8a.

915.K.9 There is even something to be said for the "legal fictions" which, corrosive of conscience as they were, were probably meant to show that the unavoidable breach of law in a difficult world did not mean repudiation of the Law.

Zangwill, *Voice of Jerusalem*, 1921, p. 63.

915.L. Suspension and Abrogation

915.L.1 Like man himself, the child of God, the divine law has a perishable body and an imperishable spirit. The body is intended to be the servant of the spirit, and must disappear as soon as bereft of the latter.

Einhorn, sermon, Sept. 27, 1855.

915.L.2 What human being can claim a right to abolish laws given by the Almighty?

Friedlander, *Jewish Religion*, (1891) 1922, p. 417.

915.L.3 We are sure that, in case of such abrogation taking place, it will be done by a revelation as convincing as that of Sinai.

Ibid.

915.L.4 The divine law is immutable and eternal like its Author; neither time nor conditions can change, much less abrogate, it.

Godscheaux and Lambert, Manifesto, March 31, 1846. *AZJ*, 1846, p. 290f. q PRM, 460.

915.L.5 A rabbinic court may lay down a condition which abrogates a biblical law.

Hisda. *T: Yebamot*, 89b.

915.L.6 The divinity of . . . the Torah has been admitted by both Jesus and Mohammed; we need not prove it. But the divine authority asserted by them for its abrogation or change . . . must be proved. And since no proof has been given, it must be rejected.

Ibn Daud, *Emuna Rama*, 1168, ch 2. q FJR, 220.

915.L.7 If anything arise that the former teachers knew not or were not called upon to decide, then surely a change is as necessary as any alteration mentioned in the Talmud.

Isserles, *Teshubot Rema*, 21. q PRM, 69.

915.L.8 The commandments will be abolished at the Resurrection.

Joseph b. Hiyya. *T: Nidda*, 61b.

915.L.9 I believe . . . that this Torah will not be exchanged, and that there will never be any other Law from the Creator.

Maimonides, *Commentary to Mishna: Sanhedrin*, 1168, 10.1. *Thirteen Principles*, #9.

915.L.10 As a surgeon must sometimes amputate a limb to save a life, so may the authorities decree the temporary suspension of some laws to sustain the Law.

Maimonides, *Yad: Mamrim*, 1180, 2.4.

915.L.11 What God has bound, man cannot dissolve.

Mendelssohn, *Jerusalem*, 1783, tr Samuels, ii. 164.

915.L.12 No court may abrogate the decision of another court unless it is its superior in wisdom and numbers.

Mishna: Eduyot, 1.5.

915.L.13 There are times which call for the voidance of a law in order to work for the Lord.

Nathan, on *Ps.* 119.126. *Mishna: Berakot*, 9.5.

915.L.14 Moses is alone in this, that his laws . . . remain secure from the day they were first enacted to now, and we may hope that they will remain for all future ages.

Philo, *Moses*, ii. 3.

915.L.15 A time will come when the Torah will be forgotten in Israel.

Rab. *T: Sabbath*, 138b.

915.L.16 Anyone in discomfort is exempt from the Sukka ritual.

Raba. *T: Sukka*, 26a.

915.L.17 A [Roman] decree is likely to be repealed. Hence, we do not set aside a rabbinic ordinance on account of it.

Rabbah. *T: Ketubot*, 3b.

915.L.18 Sometimes to suppress a law is to confirm the Law.

Simeon b. Lakish. *T: Menahot*, 99ab.

915.M. Authority

915.M.1 Any Jew who resorts to a civil court, thus evidencing greater esteem for secular than for divine legislation, is guilty of profaning God's name.

Bahya b. Asher, *Kad HaKemah*, 14C. q BSJ, 99.

915.M.2 Allegiance to the authority of the rabbinic tradition is binding upon all sons of Israel.

Z. H. Chajes, *Mebo HaTalmud*, (1845) 1954, ch 1, p. 4.

915.M.3 A decision according to the rabbis is law.

Eliezer b. Isaac, *Orhot Hayyim*, c. 1050. AHE, 34.

915.M.4 Mishna and Talmud . . . have no eternal obligatory authority.

J. A. Friedlander. *Rabbinische Gutachten*, 1842. q PRM, 62.

915.M.5 The Torah you heard from the mouth of a sage, esteem it as though you had heard it from Mount Sinai.

Helbo. *Eccles. R.*, 1.10.

915.M.6 No one has a right to contradict the rabbinical works that have been accepted by the majority of Israel.

Isserlein, *Terumat HaDeshen*, 1519, #241. q *JE*, i. 283b.

915.M.7 We believe all that is written in the Torah.

Judah Halevi, *Cuzari*, c. 1135, 1.8.

915.M.8 A court has the right to follow its own reasoning and legislate contrary to the decision of an earlier court.

Maimonides, *Yad: Mamrin*, 1180, 2.1.

915.M.9 Any practice introduced by the Gaonim is inviolable.

Nahmanides. q I. H. Weiss. *JQRo*, i. 295.

915.M.10 In an hour of peril the spoken word is as holy as God's Torah.

Opatoshu, *Last Revolt*, 1952, ch 10, p. 71.

915.N. Observance

915.N.1 He that keeps the law, happy is he.

Bible: Prov., 29.18.

915.N.2 God is strict, even to a hair's breadth, with . . . His saints.

Abba. *T: Yebamot*, 121b.

Aha. *T: Baba Kamma*, 50a.

915.N.3 If you can bear the whole yoke of the Lord, you will be perfect; if not, do what you can.

Didache, 6.2.

915.N.4 Greater is he who does when commanded than he who does without having been commanded.

Hanina b. Hama. *T: Kiddushin*, 31a.

915.N.5 God said: If ye keep the Torah, I shall consider you as though you had made yourselves [*Lev.* 26.3].

Hanina b. Pappi. *Lev. R.*, 35.7. Cf Johanan. *Tanhuma, Tabo*, 3, ed Buber, 23b.

915.N.6 As a moral agent, man is his own creator.

M. Lazarus, *Ethics*, (1898) 1900, i. 163, #122.

915.N.7 Would they had forsaken Me but kept My law, for the light of the law would have led them back to the right path!

Hiyya b. Abba, on *Jer.* 16.11. *TJ: Hagiga*, 1.7.

915.N.8 Who is lenient with himself and strict with others is a cunning rogue.

Huna. *T: Sota*, 21b.

915.N.9 Who observes the Law in poverty will yet observe it in prosperity. Who neglects the Law in prosperity will yet be compelled to neglect it through poverty.

Jonathan. *Mishna: Abot*, 4.9.

915.N.10 Above all we pride ourselves on the education of our children, and regard as the most essential task in life the observance of our laws.

Josephus, *Against Apion*, i. 12.

915.N.11 Anyone who has had the opportunity of knowing the inner life of present-day Jewish families that observe the Law of the fathers with sincere piety and in all strictness, will have been astonished at the wealth of joyfulness, gratitude and sunshine, undreamt of by the outsider, which the Law animates in the Jewish home.

*Kittel, *Religion of the People of Israel*, 1925, p. 192.

915.N.12 In observing Torah, be not extravagant at someone else's expense.

Lipkin, q S. Rosenfeld, *Israel Salanter*, 37.

915.N.13 Think not that I came to destroy the Law. . . . I came not to destroy, but to fulfil. Verily, till heaven and earth pass, one jot or tittle shall in no wise pass from the law till all be fulfilled.

New Testament: Matthew, 5.17f.

915.N.14 One sees that this nation that clings to this Law is in a state of humiliation and contempt. Our answer is that if the adherents of the Law had been granted perpetual sovereignty, the non-believers might have said about them that the only reason they served their Lord was in order to preserve their favorable situation.

Saadia, *Emunot VeDeot*, 933, 3.10, tr Rosenblatt, 179.

915.N.15 Who studies Torah and does not practice it is punished more severely than if he had not studied.

Simeon b. Halafta. *Canticles Rabbah*, 1.1.

915.N.16 Pure reason was given to angels, but human beings must observe Torah and commandments.

Yaabetz, *Or HaHayyim*, 1555, ch 2.

915.O. Study

915.O.1 This book of the law shall not depart out of thy mouth, but thou shalt meditate therein day and night.

Bible: Josh., 1.8. Cf *Isa.* 59.21; *Ps.* 1.2, 119.92.

915.O.2 Remember the law of Moses My servant.

Bible: Mal., 3.22.

915.O.3 Open mine eyes that I may behold wondrous things out of Thy law.

Bible: Ps., 119.18.

915.O.4 Turn it again and again, for everything is in it; contemplate it, grow gray and old over it, and swerve not from it, for there is no greater good.

Ben Bag Bag. *Mishna:Abot*, 5.22.

915.O.5 Study Torah diligently. Learn how to refute an unbeliever.

Eleazar b. Arak. *Mishna: Abot*, 2.14.

915.O.6 Even if compelled to solicit for tuition, let not the young of either sex go without instruction in Torah.

Eliezer Halevi, *Tzavaah*, c. 1350.

915.O.7 If you study the laws of sacrifices, I account it as though you had offered the sacrifices.

Hanina b. Papa. *Lev. R.*, 7.3.

915.O.8 . . . as though the Temple were rebuilt.

Johanan b. Nappaha. *T: Menahot*, 110a.

915.O.9 Where two meet in Torah, the Shekina is present.

Hanina b. Teradion. *Mishna: Abot*, 3.2.

915.O.10 The Shekina attends even one who is engaged in Torah.

Halafta (b. Dosa) of Kfar Hanania. *Mishna: Abot*, 3.6.

915.O.11 The Holy One studies with him who studies alone.

Seder Eliyahu Rabbah, ch 18, ed Friedmann, 89.

915.O.12 Study of Torah is superior to honoring parents.

Isaac b. Samuel b. Martha. *T: Megilla*, 16b.

915.O.13 Let us review the laws again and again, that no rust gather on them.

Jacob b. Hanina. *Sifré, Debarim*, #306.

915.O.14 It is more important to study Torah than to fast.

Jacob b. Hayyim Tzemah, *Nagid uMetzavé*, 1712.

915.O.15 A house where Torah is studied at night will not be ruined.

Jeremiah b. Eleazar. *T: Erubin*, 18b.

915.O.16 As there is always a fruit when the tree is searched, so is there always a pleasant surprise when Torah is searched.

Johanan b. Nappaha, on *Prov.* 27.18. *T: Erubin*, 54a.

915.O.17 If you have learned much Torah, do not arrogate to yourself much credit, because you were created for that purpose.

Johanan b. Zakkai. *Mishna: Abot*, 2.8.

915.O.18 Wherever scholars engage in Torah, they are, as it were, offering incense to My Name.

Jonathan b. Eleazar. *T: Menahot*, 110a.

915.O.19 Fit yourself to learn Torah; it does not come by inheritance.

Jose HaCohen. *Mishna: Abot*, 2.12.

915.O.20 He [Moses] appointed the Law to be the most excellent . . . form of instruction, ordaining . . . that each week men should . . . assemble to listen to the Law and to obtain a thorough and accurate knowledge of it, a practice which all other legislators seem to have neglected.

Josephus, *Against Apion*, ii. 17. See ii. 18.

915.0.21 "The writing was . . . graven [*harut*] upon the tables" [*Exod.* 32.16]. Read not *harut* but *herut* ["freedom"], for none is free who does not study Torah.

Joshua b. Levi. *Mishna: Abot*, 6.2. Cf Tanhuma, *Ki Tissa*, #12, ed Buber, 112; *NT: John*, 8.32.

915.0.22 Former generations made study of Torah their main concern, and other work secondary, and both prospered. Later generations have made secular work their main concern and study of Torah subsidiary, and neither has prospered.

Judah b. Ilai. *T: Berakot*, 35b.

915.0.23 Each congregation of thirty members is bound to provide for six talmudic students and six apprentices.

Judah Löw, *Takkanot*, c. 1600.

915.0.24 The study of Torah is more essential than Eretz Israel, yea, even more than the building of the Temple.

Kagan. q YSS, 92.

915.0.25 Every Jew, rich or poor, or even a beggar, healthy or not, young or old, is obliged to study Torah.

Maimonides, *Yad: Talmud Torah*, 1180, 1.8.

915.0.26 Who engages in Torah to escape physical labor and to qualify for charity, desecrates the Name . . . and forfeits life eternal, for it is forbidden to benefit from Torah in this world.

Ibid., 3.10.

915.0.27 Take time off from your business and engage in Torah.

Meir. *Mishna: Abot*, 4.10.

915.0.28 Who occupies himself with Torah for its own sake makes the world worth while. . . . He is called a lover of God and man.

Meir. *Mishna: Abot*, 6.1.

915.0.29 . . . promotes peace in heaven and on earth.

Alexandri. *T: Sanhedrin*, 99b.

915.0.30 . . . will find in it his elixir of life.

Banaah. *T: Taanit*, 7a.

915.0.31 . . . shields the whole world.

Johanan b. Nappaha. *T: Sanhedrin*, 99b.

915.0.32 . . . is as though he built the heavenly and earthly Temples.

Rab. *T: Sanhedrin*, 99b. Cf *Megilla*, 16b.

915.0.33 Study My ways with all your heart and soul. Keep watch at the gates of My law. Enshrine My law in your heart!

Meir. *T: Berakot*, 17a.

915.0.34 "If a man do" [*Lev.* 18.5]. It does not say Priests, Levites, Israelites, but "a man," teaching us that even a Gentile who studies Torah is equal to a High Priest.

Meir. *T: Baba Kamma*, 38a. See 325.15.

915.0.35 On the day of his martyrdom, Eleazar b. Shammua told his disciples: "I see the two martyrs, Judah b. Baba and Akiba, carried on their biers, discussing a halaka."

Midrash Elé Ezkera, tr Gollancz, *The Targum*, 143.

915.0.36 This is the way of Torah: eat a morsel of bread with salt, drink water by measure, sleep on the ground, live a life of privation, and toil in the Torah.

Mishna: Abot, 6.4.

915.0.37 To study Torah, you must cultivate the habit of an ox for bearing a yoke, and that of an ass for carrying burdens.

Seder Eliyahu. q *T: Aboda Zara*, 5b.

915.0.38 The Torah was given in the desert, teaching us that to merit Torah, a man must renounce himself like the desert.

Pesikta de R. Kahana, ch 12, ed Buber, 95b.

915.0.39 Study of Torah leads to precision, precision to zeal, zeal to cleanliness, cleanliness to restraint, restraint to purity, purity to holiness, holiness to meekness, meekness to fear of sin, fear of sin to saintliness, saintliness to the holy spirit, the holy spirit to life eternal.

Phineas b. Yair. *T: Aboda Zara*, 20b. Cf *Mishna: Sota*, 9.15; *TJ: Sabbath*, 1.3. See A. Büchler, *Types of Jewish Palestinian Piety*, pp. 42–67.

915.0.40 Who studies Torah needs no burnt-offering . . . or sin-offering.

Raba. *T: Menahot*, 110a. See *Zohar, Lev.*, 35a.

915.0.41 Children of Israel, support those who study Torah!

Saadia, letter to an Egyptian community, 928. See KTJ 88.

915.0.42 May it be Thy will, O Lord our God, to establish peace among the disciples who engage in Thy Torah.

Safra. *T: Berakot*, 16b–17a.

915.O.43 The study of Torah, which means the revelation of God to man, and the cultivation of prayer, which means the revelation of man to God, were the grand passions of old Judaism.

Schechter. London *Jewish Chronicle,* Oct. 15, 1897. SSJ, ii. 9.

915.O.44 Everyone who studies halakot is assured of the world to come.

Seder Eliyahu Zuta, ch 2, p. 173. q *T: Megilla,* 28b.

915.O.45 You must not interrupt your study of halaka for prayer.

Shneor Zalman, *Tanya,* 1796. q HLH, 60.

915.O.46 To study Torah, just as to worship at the altar, is to "serve Him with all your heart and soul" [*Deut.* 11.13].

Sifré, #31, to *Deut.* 11.13, ed Friedmann, 80a.

915.O.47 When three people eat at one table and converse Torah, it is as if they were eating at God's board.

Simeon b. Yohai. *Mishna: Abot,* 3.3.

915.O.48 Let the words of Torah be clear on the tip of your tongue [play on words of *Deut.* 6.7], so that if you are asked something, you do not hesitate, but answer readily.

Talmud: Kiddushin, 30a.

915.O.49 If Israel occupy themselves with Torah, it is as though they were not in exile.

Tanna debe Eliyahu, ed Friedmann, 148.

915.O.50 Each fresh discovery by a Torah student creates a new heaven.

Zohar, Gen., Prologue, 4b.

915.O.51 Torah study endows one with an extra soul.

Ibid., 12b.

915.O.52 Torah is the very fulness of life, life of bliss without gloom. It is freedom, complete freedom.

Ibid., 131b.

915.O.53 Words of Torah uttered at night ascend and are woven into a garland before the Almighty.

Ibid., 178b.

915.O.54 Students of Torah are superior to Prophets.

Zohar, Lev., 35a.

915.P. Attitude to Torah

915.P.1 My soul breaks with longing for Thine ordinances at all times.

Bible: Ps., 119.20.

915.P.2 Divine Glory will satisfy him who devotes himself to Torah in poverty.

Abbahu. *T: Sota,* 49a.

915.P.3 As the fish said to the fox, We prefer to live in the river, infested as it is with nets, rather than on dry land, outside of our vital atmosphere, so we would rather face Roman threats than forsake the Torah, our "life and length of days" [*Deut.* 30.20].

Akiba. *T: Berakot,* 61b.

915.P.4 Heaven forbid that we should forsake the Law!

Apocrypha: I Macc., 2.21.

915.P.5 Be zealous for the Law and give your lives for the covenant of your fathers.

Ibid., 2.50.

915.P.6 Be strong, and show yourselves men on behalf of the Law, for therein shall ye obtain glory.

Ibid., 2.64.

915.P.7 Deliver yourselves whole-heartedly to Torah, and you will not be delivered to the tyrant.

Ilai b. Berekia. *T: Sanhedrin,* 94b.

915.P.8 Where is there another people on earth, among whom studies which aimed only at truth and the development of the spiritual life were cultivated with such pure, devoted and selfless love as in Israel?

Jellinek, 1882. q HBJ, 95.

915.P.9 Who honors Torah is honored; who dishonors it is dishonored.

Jose b. Halafta. *Mishna: Abot,* 4.6.

915.P.10 Torah abides with him who sacrifices all for it.

Jose b. Hanina. *T: Sota,* 21b. Cf *Tanhuma, Noah,* #3, 15b. See Simeon b. Lakish. *T: Berakot,* 63b.

915.P.11 *Simhat Torah* means "the Torah's joy," and implies that it is not enough for a Jew to find joy in the Torah, but the Torah should also find joy in him.

Jose-Ber of Brisk.

915.P.12 Time and again the sight has been witnessed of prisoners enduring tortures and death in every form in the theatres, rather than utter a word against the laws and the allied documents.

Josephus, *Against Apion,* i. 18.

915.P.13 We, not withstanding the countless calamities . . . never even in the direst extremity proved traitors to our laws.

Ibid., ii. 30. See ii. 37.

915.P.14 Israel cannot exist without devotion to Torah.

Joshua b. Hanania, or Eleazar Hisma. *Mekilta*, to *Exod.* 17.8.

915.P.15 A heavenly voice proclaims daily from Mt. Horeb: Woe to men who scorn the Torah!

Joshua b. Levi. *Mishna: Abot*, 6.2. See *T: Hagiga*, 5b.

915.P.16 Obedience to His law is the noblest form of devotion to God.

M. Lazarus, *Ethics*, 1901, ii. 46, #203.

915.P.17 We honor not the commandments but the Commander, who saved us from groping in the dark and provided us with a lamp to make clear what is obscure.

Maimonides, *Yad: Shehita*, 1180, 14.16.

915.P.18 Open my heart in Thy law, and may my soul pursue Thy precepts.

Mar b. Abina. *T: Berakot*, 17a.

915.P.19 If civil union cannot be obtained on any other term than that of departing from the Law, . . . we are heartily sorry for what we deem necessary to declare—that we will rather renounce civil union.

M. Mendelssohn, *Jerusalem*, 1783, tr Samuels, ii. 165.

915.P.20 Approach the Torah with joy, and also with trembling.

Rab. *T: Yoma*, 4b.

915.P.21 When the Jew is attacked, he is not to keep the Torah in front of him as a shield, but he is to keep himself as a shield in front of the Torah.

F. Rosenzweig, letter to his Freiburg students. *Briefe*, 1935.

915.P.22 A traveler through the countryside is guilty of a mortal sin if he interrupts his thoughts of Torah to admire a beautiful tree or field.

Simeon b. Yohai. *Mishna: Abot*, 3.7.

915.P.23 Even if there were no hope for our redemption, we would still owe allegiance to the Torah.

Sofer. See SSJ, iii. 61.

915.P.24 Love the Torah, and honor it.

Talmud: Derek Eretz, 1.9.

915.P.25 Who starves for Torah here will be satisfied hereafter.

Tanhum b. Hanilai. *T: Sanhedrin*, 100a.

915.P.26 Enlighten our eyes in Thy Torah that we may cling to Thy commandments.

Union Prayer Book, i. 118. DPB, ed Singer, 40.

915.P.27 The Hebrew Torah, which cried anathema on idols, became itself an idol, swathed in purple, adorned with golden bells, and borne round like a Madonna for reverent kisses.

Zangwill, *Italian Fantasies*, 1910, p. 14.

915.P.28 Far from Torah, far from God.

Zohar, Lev., 21a, 89b.

915.P.29 He who is not occupied with Torah and its precepts is a subject of an earthly power; he who is so occupied is a citizen of the Kingdom of Heaven.

Ibid., 29a.

916. TORTURE

916.1 Clean shall my fathers receive me, unafraid of your torments even unto death!

Apocrypha: IV Macc., 5.37.

916.2 Under every form of torture, . . . devised to make them acknowledge Caesar as Lord, not one submitted. . . . But most of all were the spectators struck by the children of tender age, not one of whom could be prevailed upon to call Caesar lord.

Josephus, *Wars*, 7.10.1.

916.3 The Spanish Inquisition, with all their torments and cruelties, could make any Jew become a Christian. For unreasonable beasts are taught by blows, but men are taught by reason.

Manasseh b. Israel, *Vindiciae Judaeorum*, 1656, #5.

916.4 After a man has determined to surrender his life in martyrdom, he is absolutely insensible to torture.

Meir of Rothenburg, *Responsa*, (13C) 1891, #517.

917. TRADITION

917.1 Remove not the ancient landmark which the fathers have set.

Bible: Prov., 22.28, 23.10.

917.2 Haven't the words of the wise been compared to nails? The nails are fixed, while the generations suspend from them . . . their thoughts and aspirations. . . . Thus, the burden of the heritage grows in extent and profundity. But while the generations come and go, the nails remain.

J. B. Agus. *Jewish Frontier*, July 1952, p. 6f.

917.3 Tradition is a fence for Torah.

Akiba. *Mishna: Abot*, 3.13.

917.4 Blessed is he who keeps the foundations of his fathers.

Apocrypha: II Enoch, 52.9.

917.5 Without the aid of tradition, neither the rational nor the scriptural laws can be completely fulfilled.

Bahya, *Hobot HaLebabot*, 1040, 5.5.

917.6 We are our fathers' sons, not their coffins.

Berdichevsky, *Arakin*, 1900, p. 23.

917.7 Tradition does not imply standing still; it expresses the continuity of nature and history.

Blum, *New Conversations*, 1901. q FNL, 114.

917.8 Liberalism and traditionalism are contrasts; liberty and tradition are not. Tradition is true and living only if it renews itself constantly in liberty, and the will to preserve brings forth inner transformations. And as to liberty—from where shall it take the substance for its work, if not from the depths of tradition?

M. Buber, *For M. M. Kaplan*, 1951, p. 4.

917.9 The enactments which came down by tradition have the same authority as the commands of Scripture.

Z. H. Chajes, *Mebo HaTalmud*, (1845) 1952, ch 3, p. 24.

917.10 Tradition is the life-giving soul in Judaism, it is the daughter of Revelation, . . . it is the fountain that will ever fertilize the times and, whenever it will come in contact with the outer world, create new formations, according to the ever-changing wants and necessities of life.

Geiger, *Judaism and Its History*, 1865, p. 135f. See *Nachgelassene Schriften*, i. 205.

917.11 When a man turns his back on tradition, he really severs himself from Judaism itself and from its national essence.

Hess, *Rome and Jerusalem*, (1862), p. 111.

917.12 The tradition of all past generations weighs like an Alp upon the brain of the living.

Marx, *18th Brumaire*, 1852.

917.13 Reform Judaism differentiates between *tradition* and *the traditions;* it considers itself, too, a link in the chain of Jewish tradition, the product of this age as Talmudism was of its age.

Philipson, *Reform Movement in Judaism*, (1907) 1931, p. 5.

917.14 Feed no more on effete fables, which the long course of the ages has handed down for the deception of mortals, but rather receive in full and generous measure new, fresh, blessed thoughts from the ever ageless God.

Philo, *Sacrifices of Abel and Cain*, 21.

918. TRAFFIC

918.1 Like the driving of Jehu . . . for he drives furiously.

Bible: II Kings, 9.20.

918.2 The chariots rush madly in the streets, they jostle one against another in the broad places; the appearance of them is like torches, they run to and fro like lightnings.

Bible: Nah., 2.5.

919. TRANSLATION

919.1 A translator must know three things: the genius of the language from which he translates, the genius of the language into which he translates, and the subject matter.

Al-Harizi, Pref. to his tr of Maimonides, *Commentary to Zeraim*.

919.2 All translation is commentary.

Baeck, *The Pharisees*, 1947, p. 35.

919.3 If one translates a verse literally, he is a liar; and if he adds thereto he is a blasphemer and a libeller.

Judah b. Ilai. *T: Kiddushin*, 49a.

919.4 The best translation cannot fully convey the exact meaning.

M. Mendelssohn, *Or LiNethiba*, 1783, p. 11.

919.5 Seventy elders wrote the whole Torah in Greek for King Ptolemy, and that day was as ominous for Israel as the day on which Israel made the golden calf, for the Torah cannot be translated adequately.

Talmud: Sefer Torah, 1.6.

920. TRAVEL

920.1 Travel teaches toleration.

Disraeli, *Contarini Fleming*, 1832, 5.7.

920.2 Travel is hard on clothes, person, and purse.

Eleazar. *Midrash Tehillim*, 23.3.

920.3 Traveling may be . . . an experience we shall always remember, or an experience which, alas, we shall never forget.

J. Gordon, *Your Sense of Humor*, 1930.

921. TREE

921.1 Where the tree falls, there shall it be.

Bible: Eccles., 11.3.

921.2 He who spares a tree is apt to spare a man.

Blau, *The Wonder of Life*, 1925, p. 98.

921.3 Trees grow upward: so should men. Trees, with their green leaves and tenderly tinted blossoms, seek the light: so should men.
Ibid., 99.

921.4 The little birch-woods on the wide and endless spaces,
The only luminous dreams in a waste of black woe.
Einhorn, "Lithuania," 1907 (*Gez. Lider,* 1952, p. 75). LGP, 514.

921.5 Trees were created for man's companionship.
Gen. R., 13.2.

921.6 So came the trees at the call of God,
And all the trees are holy.
Guiterman, *Song and Laughter,* 1929, p. 199.

921.7 A nut tree will not grow apples.
Jacob Tam, *Sefer HaYashar,* 12C. q CPP, #479.

921.8 Who sees trees in blossom shall pronounce a benediction.
Judah b. Ezekiel. *T: Berakot,* 43b.

921.9 If a man kills a tree before its time, it is as though he had murdered a soul.
Nahman Bratzlav. q *Menorah Journal,* 1924, x. 88.

921.10 An acacia's no good before it's chopped wood.
Proverb. q *Exod. R.,* 6.5.

921.11 Each of Job's friends had a tree identified with him, and when it drooped, they knew he was in trouble.
Talmud: Baba Bathra, 16b.

922. TRIAL

922.1 Ye shall not try the Lord . . . as ye tried Him in Massah.
Bible: Deut., 6.16.

922.2 I have tried thee in the furnace of affliction.
Bible: Isa., 48.10.

922.3 The righteous God tries the hearts and reins.
Bible: Ps., 7.10.

922.4 All men are tried by fire and the balance.
Apocrypha: Testament of Abraham, 13.

922.5 A farmer puts the yoke on his strong cow, not on his weak cow.
Eleazar b. Pedat. *Gen. R.,* 32.3.

922.6 No limit to trials, but the wise learns thereby.
Ibn Gabirol, *Mibhar HaPeninim,* c. 1050, #223.

922.7 As a potter does not test defective vessels, which would break with one blow, so the Holy One tests only the righteous.
Jonathan b. Eleazar. *Gen. R.,* 32.3.

922.8 The better the flax the more it is beaten, and the more it improves and glistens.
Jose b. Hanina. *Gen. R.,* 32.3.

922.9 Rejoice in your trials here; they save you hereafter.
Talmud: Derek Eretz, 7.23.

922.10 Trials challenge, persecution strengthens, and isolation exalts, provided they do not break one.
S. Zweig, *World of Yesterday,* 1943, p. 343.

923. TRIFLE

923.1 The smallest shall become a thousand, and the least a mighty nation.
Bible: Isa., 60.22.

923.2 Who has despised the day of small things?
Bible: Zech., 4.10.

923.3 Sometimes small things lead to great joy.
Agnon, *Shebuat Emmunim,* 1943.

923.4 Some desirable lesson is often taught by the most insignificant affairs of life.
Apocrypha: Aristeas, 285.

923.5 Who despises small things shall become poor.
Apocrypha: Ben Sira, 19.1.

923.6 The true artist . . . is not afraid of banality, and is therefore never banal.
Bialik. q OMB, 61.

923.7 History wends its way through a road littered with the seemingly insignificant.
Borochov, *Nationalism and Class Struggle,* (1907) 1937, p. 102.

923.8 The Holy One confers distinction on a person only after examining him in some small matter.
Cant. R., 2.

923.9 Blessed are the unimportant, as much as the important.
Chernihovsky. q WHJ, iv. 267.

923.10 Little things affect little minds.
Disraeli, *Sybil,* 1845, 3.2.

923.11 The faithful in little is faithful in much.
New Testament: Luke, 16.10.

923.12 Nobody ever stubs his toe against a mountain. It's the little temptations that bring a man down.
Peretz, *All for a Pinch of Snuff,* c.1910. q SPG, 64.

923.13 The tiniest smoldering spark, when blown up, lights a great pile; so the least particle of virtue, when warmed into life by great hopes.
Philo, *Migration of Abraham,* 21.

923.14 Drop by drop, the measure is filled.
Proverb. q *Num. R.,* 17.3.

923.15 A mere extra two measures of silk, which Jacob gave Joseph, started a chain of events which led our forebears down to Egypt.
Rab. *T: Megilla,* 16b.

923.16 Very minor sins have led to great catastrophes, and for very minor good deeds, some met with enormous rewards.
Seder Eliyahu Rabbah, ch 14, ed Friedmann, 65.

923.17 The tiny needle will support a house.
J. Steinberg, *Mishlé Yehoshua,* 1885, 26.29, p. 146.

923.18 A minor transaction yields a minor profit.
Talmud: Ketubot, 66b.

923.19 No great issues are possible without small achievements.
Trotsky, *Problems of Life,* 1923, p. 5.

924. TROUBLE

924.1 Is it you, you troubler of Israel?
Bible: I Kings, 18.17, ref. to Elijah.

924.2 Man is born unto trouble, as the sparks fly upward.
Bible: Job, 5.7. Cf 14.1.

924.3 An individual's trouble is real trouble, not a community's.
Akiba. *Deut. R.,* 2.22.

924.4 Shared trouble is half consolation.
Gentili, *Mleket Mahshebet, Tabo,* 1710.

924.5 The trouble of many is half consolation.
S. Levi, *Lehem Shelomo,* 1597, p. 171a.

924.6 The art of living lies less in eliminating our troubles than in growing with them.
Baruch.

924.7 Troubles are quick to come and slow to leave.
I. Friedmann, *Imré Bina,* 1912, p. 119. q CPP, #1497.

924.8 Trouble is universal, and so must be help.
Guttmacher. q Brod, *Heidentum* etc., 1921. q LR, 198.

924.9 One thing obtained with trouble is treasured more than a hundred acquired with ease.
Ishmael. *Abot de R. Nathan,* ch 3.

924.10 Who passed forty days without trouble has received his paradise on earth.
Ishmael School. *T: Arakin,* 16b.

924.11 Trouble shared by all is real trouble, not trouble confined to Jews only.
Johanan b. Nappaha. *Deut. R.,* 2.22.

924.12 There's no trouble for one without profit for another.
Levi. *Gen. R.,* 38.10.

924.13 Ease destroys bravery, trouble . . . creates strength.
Maimonides, *Guide for the Perplexed,* 1190, 3.24.

924.14 The transition from trouble to ease gives more pleasure than continual ease.
Ibid.

924.15 One does not meet trouble half way.
Raba. *T: Gittin,* 18a.

924.16 Troubles in this world are meant to wash away sins.
Seder Eliyahu Rabbak, ch 15 (14), ed Friedmann, 69.

924.17 The more trouble, the more faith.
Sholom Aleichem, *A Boidem,* 1899.

924.18 Little troubles are really a good thing—for someone else.
Sholom Aleichem, *Yidishé Folks Tzeitung,* 1902.

924.19 Later troubles make us forget the earlier troubles.
Simeon b. Yohai. *Mekilta,* to *Exod.* 13.2. Cf *Berakot,* 13a.

924.20 Today's troubles make us forget yesterday's.
Ahad HaAm, letter to L. Simon, May 23, 1924. AEL, 296.

924.21 One trouble makes you forget another; therefore they always come in teams.
Steinberg, *Mishlé Yehoshua,* 1885.

925. TRUST

925.1 What is trust? Tranquility of soul in the one who trusts.

Bahya, *Hobot HaLebabot*, 1040, 4.1, tr Hyamson, iii. 8.

925.2 A trustee is held to something stricter than the morals of the market place. Not honesty alone, but the punctilio of an honor the most sensitive, is then the standard of behavior.

Cardozo, *Meinhard vs. Salmon*, 1928, 294 N.Y. Reports 458.

925.3 Excessive confidence throws men off their guard, whereas fear teaches precaution.

Herod I. q Josephus, *Wars*, 1.19.4.

925.4 One can positively never be deceived if one mistrusts everything in the world, even one's own scepticism.

Schnitzler, *The Road to the Open*, (1908) 1923.

926. TRUST IN GOD

926.1 Cursed is the man who trusts in man, who makes flesh his arm, and whose heart departs from the Lord.

Bible: Jer., 17.5. See *Isa.*, 3.1.

926.2 Blessed is the man that trusts in the Lord.

Bible: Jer., 17.7.

926.3 Though the fig-tree shall not blossom, neither shall fruit be in the vines, the labor of the olive shall fail, and the fields shall yield no food, the flock shall be cut off from the fold, and there shall be no herd in the stalls, yet will I rejoice in the Lord, I will exult in the God of my salvation.

Bible: Hab., 3.17f.

926.4 Put your trust in the Lord.

Bible: Ps., 4.6. See 37.3, 5, 40.5, 62.9, 112.7.

926.5 It is better to take refuge in the Lord than to trust in man. It is better to take refuge in the Lord than to trust in princes.

Ibid., 118.8f.

926.6 Trust in the Lord with all your heart, and lean not upon your own understanding.

Bible: Prov., 3.5.

926.7 Though He slay me, yet will I trust in Him; but I will maintain mine own ways before Him.

Bible: Job, 13.15.

926.8 Then in His hand myself I lay
And trusting, sleep; and wake with cheer;
My soul and body are His care;
The Lord doth guard, I have no fear.

Adon Olam, tr F. de Sola Mendes.

926.9 Who trusts God fears no man.

Bahya, *Hobot HaLebabot*, 1040, 4, Preface, tr Hyamson, iii. 3.

926.10 This is just the heroic feature in the faith of the Old Testament that, in the midst of the riddle of this life, and face to face with the impenetrable darkness resting on the life beyond, it throws itself without reserve into the arms of God!

*Delitzsch. q *JQRo*, 1888, i. 161.

926.11 They trust in the multitude of their troops . . . but we trust in the Lord, who can save by many or by few.

Josippon, iv. ch 20.

926.12 We trust a star to guide our way
Upon the open sea.
Why trust we not the Lord of stars
On earth our Guide to be?

M. E. Kuh, *Hinterlassene Gedichte*, 1792.

926.13 "When Moses held up his hand, Israel prevailed" [*Exod.* 17.11]. . . . When Moses raised his hand, Israel turned their thoughts and hearts toward their Father on high, and that led them to prevail. The same in regard to the brass serpent [*Num.* 21.8], which in itself cannot kill or heal, and the blood token on the lintel [*Exod.* 12.7].

Mekilta, to *Exod.* 17.11. *Mishna: Rosh Hashana*, 3.8.

926.14 It is not the iron, but the force which moves the iron, that fells the tree. Think not that without your present employment you must needs starve. Put your entire trust in God, who will support you in some other manner, for He has many messengers ever ready for His service.

Orhot Tzaddikim, 15C.

926.15 It is best to trust in God, not in our dim reasonings and uncertain conjectures.

Philo, *Allegories*, iii. 81.

927. TRUTH

927.1 Speak every man the truth with his neighbor.

Bible: Zech., 8.16.

927.2 Thou desirest truth in the inward parts.
Bible: Ps., 51.8.

927.3 Truth springs out of the earth.
Ibid., 85.12.

927.4 The truth of the Lord endures for ever.
Ibid., 118.2.

927.5 They that deal truly are His delight.
Bible: Prov., 12.22.

927.6 All His works are truth, and all His ways justice.
Bible: Dan., 4.34.

927.7 God is a lover of truth.
Apocrypha: Aristeas, 206.

927.8 Truth and peace shall be associated together.
Apocrypha: Enoch, 11.2.

927.9 Blessed is he in whom is truth.
Apocrypha: II Enoch, 42.12.

927.10 Above all things truth bears away the victory.
Apocrypha: I Esdras, 3.12.

927.11 Great is truth, and mightier than all.
Ibid., 4.35, 41.

927.12 Truth abides, and is strong for ever.
Ibid., 4.38.

927.13 Love truth, and it will preserve you.
Apocrypha: Patriarchs, Reuben, 3.9. See *Dan.*, 2.1.

927.14 A little truth overcomes much falsehood, as a little light dispels much darkness.
Bahya, *Hobot HaLebabot*, 1040, 5.5.

927.15 Blessed be He who knoweth the truth.
Bertinoro, letter to his father, 1488. KTJ 309.

927.16 Truth often serves only as a ladder to falsehood.
Boerne, *Fragmente und Aphorismen*, 1840, #115.

927.17 When Pythagoras discovered his well-known doctrine, he offered a hecatomb to the gods. Since then oxen tremble whenever a new truth comes to light.
Ibid., #258.

927.18 The truth is neither shy nor timid.
Caspi, *Yoré Deah*, 14C, ch 15. Duran, *Tashbetz*.

927.19 God Himself cannot alter the laws of *a priori* truth.
Crescas, *Or Adonai*, c. 1400, 1556.

927.20 Truth and nature can never be obsolete.
D'Israeli, *Curiosities: Philosophy of Proverbs*, 1823.

927.21 No personal regard where truth is involved.
Elijah Gaon. q Hayyim b. Isaac, *Hoot HaMeshulash*, #9, p. 39. q GSS, 136.

927.22 Know the truth, and you will know its Master.
Falaquera, *Iggeret HaVikuah*, 13C.

927.23 Learn from any source and seek truth wherever you may obtain it, even from apostates, just as honey is taken from bees.
Ibid., 1875, p. 3.

927.24 Truth is to be accepted from any man. Its touch-stone is not the rank or position of its professor, but its intrinsic worth.
Falaquera, *Sefer HaMaalot*, (13C) 1894, p. 11.

927.25 The seal of the Holy One is truth.
Hanina b. Hama. *T: Sabbath*, 55a.

927.26 The deepest truth blooms only from the deepest love.
Heine, *English Fragments*, 1828, ch 13.

927.27 Truth is the center of the circle.
A. Ibn Ezra, *Commentary*, Introduction.

927.28 Endure the truth, though it be bitter.
Ibn Gabirol, *Mibhar HaPeninim*, c. 1050, #135.

927.29 Seek where the truth is found—
    if in the Lord
    Or in another—be the truth
    adored.
J. Ibn Ghayat, "Elijah's Prayer," tr Lucas. *JQRo*, viii. 609.

927.30 Accept truth from whatever quarter it may come. . . . Whoever calls logic a "foreign" science, or speaks contemptuously of Plato and Aristotle because they did not belong to the Jewish nation, is like the sluggard who cries, "A lion is in the way."
Immanuel, *Commentary*, to *Prov.* 26.13.

927.31 The homely woman hates the mirror.
Immanuel, *Mahberot*, c. 1300, ch 5.

927.32 Accept the truth, whatever its source. . . . Take the pearls from the sea,

the gold from the dust, and the roses from amidst the thorns.
Ibid., ch 19.

927.33   Truth is Thy primal word.
Judah HeHasid, *Hymn of Glory*, c. 1200, tr Zangwill.

927.34   Truth will teach its way.
J. Kimhi, *Sefer Hukka*, (12C) 1868.

927.35   The ultimate truth is penultimately always a falsehood.
Koestler, *Darkness at Noon*, 1941.

927.36   There can be no negotiation with truth.
Lassalle, *Franz von Sickingen*, 1859.

927.37   Truth and justice even toward an adversary—this is the first duty of man.
Lassalle, *Open Letter to the Central Committee*, 1863.

927.38   Nowadays Jews tell lies in the street and the truth in the synagog. Alas for the good old days when they used to tell the truth in the street and lies in the synagog!
Levi Yitzhok, ref. to the Confessions. q SWS, 213.

927.39   The truth is often too plain to find credence.
Lewald, *Deutsche Lebensbilder*, 1856, 1, 17.

927.40   Accept the truth from whomsoever speaks it.
Maimonides, *Commentary to Mishna*, Introduction, 1168.

927.41   A truth established by proof neither gains force or certainty by the consent of all scholars, nor loses by general dissent.
Maimonides, *Guide for the Perplexed*, 1190, 2.15.

927.42   Wish to learn the truth, not just to win a wordy victory.
Maimonides, *Shaaré HaMusar*.

927.43   A truth does not become greater by frequent repetition.
Maimonides, *Tehiyat HaMethim. Responsa*, ii. 9d.

927.44   Imprisonment is sweetened to man if the truth is in prison with him.
Meir of Rothenburg. q Kolitz, *Tiger Beneath the Skin*, p. 135.

927.45   Truth is not compatible with dogma.
Melamed, *Spinoza and Buddha*, 1933, Preface, p. viii.

927.46   Truth is a word which each one understands in his own way, according to his own needs, as it suits him.
Mendelé, *Dos Kleine Mentshelé*, 1864.

927.47   I acknowledge no immutable truths, but such as not only may be made conceivable to the human understanding, but as also admit of being demonstrated and warranted by human faculties.
M. Mendelssohn, *Jerusalem*, 1783, tr Samuels, ii. 89.

927.48   Nothing is beautiful but the truth.
Minkowski, 1882.

927.49   The truth is its own witness.
Moses b. Joshua, *Commentary to Moré Nebukim*, (14C) 1852, p. 22.

927.50   Ye shall know the truth, and the truth shall make you free.
New Testament: John, 8.32.

927.51   There are not many in the world who recognize the truth.
Orhot Tzaddikim, 15C, Introduction.

927.52   He who comprehends that his soul is extracted from the very source of truth, will never permit a lie to enter truth's sanctuary.
Ibid., ch 23.

927.53   What honor can there be where there is not also truth?
Philo, *Decalogue*, 2.

927.54   Truth . . . is its own reward.
Philo, *Honor Due to Parents*, 10.

927.55   A half truth is a whole lie.
Proverb (Yiddish). BJS, #178. (Yemenite), recorded by Moses Levi Nahum.

927.56   Words of truth are recognizable.
Rab. T: *Sota*, 9b.

927.57   A sophism is seldom a black untruth; mostly it's a strong concoction of lies, infected by a drop of truth.
Schnitzler, *Buch der Sprüche & Bedenken*, 1927, p. 232.

927.58   Truth is its own excuse for being.
L. Stein, letter, Sept. 19, 1902. *Journey into the Self*, 1950, p. 12.

927.59   Truth is not always the best basis for happiness. . . . There are people who perish when their eyes are opened.
Stekel, *Autobiography*, 1950, p. 260f.

927.60   Truth can stand, falsehood cannot.
Talmud: Sabbath, 104a.

927.61 The truth is heavy, therefore its bearers are few.

Uceda, *Midrash Samuel*, 1579.

927.62 O Lord, open our eyes that we may see and welcome all truth, whether shining from the annals of ancient revelations or reaching us through the seers of our own time.

Union Prayer Book, 1940, i. 34.

927.63 Truth, the redeemer, the savior, and the messiah.

I. M. Wise, *Outlines of Judaism,* 1869. *Selected Writings,* 220.

927.64 Truth does not contradict truth.

L. Zweifel. *HaAsif,* 1885.

928. TURKEY

928.1 Great Turkey, . . . where the gates of freedom and equal opportunity for the unhindered practice of Jewish worship are ever open! There, Israel, you can renew your inner life.

Usque, *Consolação às Tribulaçoes de Yisrael,* 1553, Dialogue 3, 53b. q GHJ, iv. 400.

929. TWILIGHT

929.1 The nightingale of poetry, like that bird of wisdom, the owl, is heard only after the sun is set. The day is a time for action, but at twilight feeling and reason come to take account of what has been accomplished.

Trotsky, *Literature and Revolution,* 1925, p. 19.

930. TYRANNY

930.1 How has the oppressor ceased . . . that smote the peoples in wrath . . . with a persecution that none restrained! . . . Your pomp is brought down to the netherworld, . . . and the worms cover you. How you have fallen from heaven, O Lucifer, son of the morning!

Bible: Isa., 14.4, 6, 11f.

930.2 Is this the man that made the earth to tremble, that shook the kingdoms?

Ibid., 14.16.

930.3 The removal of a tyrant is not merely justifiable; it is the highest duty of every true revolutionist.

Berkman, *Prison Memoirs of an Anarchist,* 1912, p. 7.

930.4 Tyrants in our days are the most dangerous preachers of liberty.

Boerne, *Aus meinem Tagebuch,* May 3, 1830.

930.5 I believe it to be an invariable rule that tyrants of genius are succeeded by scoundrels.

Einstein, *World As I See It,* 1934, p. 240.

930.6 God spoke to Moses respectfully, not like a tyrant.

Eleazar b. Arak. *Mekilta de Simeon b. Yohai.*

930.7 All dictatorships originated as temporary military necessities.

Harrison, *Religion of a Modern Liberal,* 1931, p. 51.

930.8 Tyranny is but the act of a mortal, here today and in the grave tomorrow, . . . and the righteous shall inherit the earth.

Ibn Pulgar, *Ezer HaDat,* 14C, 53a. q *JQRo,* xvii. 45.

930.9 Ever since the time of Revelation, every despot or slave that attained to power has made it his first aim and final purpose to destroy our law and to vitiate our religion by the sword, by violence, and by brute force . . . Tyranny oppresses us and kings are hard on us, but they cannot destroy us.

Maimonides, *Iggeret Teman,* 1172.

930.10 Despotism has one advantage, it is cogent. . . . It has definite answers to every question. Never mind limits; for with him who has got all, "more or less" is of no farther consideration.

M. Mendelssohn, *Jerusalem,* 1783, tr Samuels, ii. 4.

930.11 Despotism annihilated multiplicity under the pretense of the most perfect unity. But under pretense only, for inasmuch as it totally annuls the free will of the members, the state ceases to be a union of moral beings, and we obtain a physical aggregate instead of a moral system.

M. Mendelssohn, *On National Instruction (ibid.,* ii. 183).

930.12 Then shall iniquity be dumb and all wickedness end like smoke, when Thou removest tyranny from the earth, and Thou alone reignest.

Rab, Kingdom Prayer for Rosh Hashana. See UPB, 1945, ii. 56, 140, 206.

930.13 It is to the eternal glory of the Jews that, in the midst of this ignoble idolatry [Caligula self-deification], they uttered the cry of outraged conscience. . . . Alone affirming their religion to be the absolute religion, they would not bend to the odious caprice of the tyrant.

*Renan, *The Apostles,* 1866, ch 11 (tr, p. 180).

930.14 It is better to grow wings and fly away than to submit to a godless king.

Simeon b. Lakish. *Esther Rabbah,* Proem 9.

930.15 The Holy One does not deal despotically with His creatures.

Simlai. *T: Aboda Zara,* 3a.

930.16 The most tyrannical governments are those which make crimes of opinions, for everyone has an inalienable right to his thoughts.

Spinoza, *Theologico-Political Treatise,* 1670, ch 18.

930.17 It is a consoling fact that, in the end, the moral independence of mankind remains undestructible. Never has it been possible for a dictatorship to enforce one religion or one philosophy upon the whole world. Nor will it ever be possible, for the spirit always escapes from servitude; refuses to think in accordance with prescribed forms, to become shallow and supine at the word of command, to allow uniformity to be permanently imposed upon it.

S. Zweig, *The Right to Heresy,* 1936, p. 10.

931. UNDERSTANDING

931.1 With all your getting, get understanding.

Bible: Prov., 4.7.

931.2 Good understanding gives grace.

Ibid., 13.15.

931.3 The thunder of His mighty deeds who can understand?

Bible: Job, 26.14.

931.4 You are unable to understand what belongs to you, . . . how then should your vessel comprehend the way of the Most High?

Apocrypha: II Esdras, 4.10f.

931.5 Dwellers on earth can understand only what is on earth.

Ibid., 4.12.

931.6 I shall light a candle of understanding in your heart, which shall not be put out.

Ibid., 14.25.

931.7 Where mutual understanding ends, vexation begins.

Auerbach, *Little Barefoot,* 1856, ch 5.

931.8 Nine-tenths of the serious controversies which arise in life result from misunderstanding.

Brandeis, address, Boston Typothetae, Apr. 22, 1904.

931.9 All but the crudest scientific work is based on a firm belief . . . in the rationality and comprehensibility of the world.

Einstein, *Cosmic Religion,* 1931, p. 98.

931.10 The most inexplicable thing about the world is that the world is inexplicable.

Einstein q Baeck, *Judaism & Philosophy,* 1949, p. 12.

931.11 Without understanding no knowledge; without knowledge no understanding.

Eleazar b. Azariah. *Mishna: Abot,* 3.17.

931.12 Men hate what they cannot understand.

M. Ibn Ezra, *Shirat Yisrael,* (12C) 1924, p. 96.

931.13 Man, who does not understand why it is the dark part of the eye that sees, shall he presume to explain the ways of God?

Johanan b. Nappaha. *Tanhuma, Tetzavé,* 4, ed Buber, p. 97.

931.14 The prayer for Understanding is first [in the Eighteen Benedictions], for it is intellect that brings man near to God, and the prayer of Repentance follows immediately, to teach us that our Understanding should be applied to His Law and service.

Judah Halevi, *Cuzari,* c. 1135, 3.19.

931.15 If a great man makes a seemingly illogical statement, do not laugh; try to understand it.

Kahana. *T: Berakot,* 19b.

931.16 The ignorant always adores what he cannot understand.

Lombroso, *The Man of Genius,* 1889, iii. ch 3.

931.17 Repeating a tradition is rewarded by understanding it.

Raba. *T: Berakot,* 6b.

931.18 A student of laws who doesn't understand their meaning or can't explain their contradictions, is but a basket full of books.

Rashi, *Commentary,* to Nahman's statement. *T: Megilla,* 28b.

931.19 The more we understand particular things, the more do we understand God.

Spinoza, *Ethics,* 1677, v. Pr 24.

931.20 I have learned not to mock, lament or execrate, but to understand human actions.

Spinoza, *Political Treatise,* 1677, 1.4.

931.21 When you do not understand, be not ashamed to admit it.

Talmud: Derek Eretz, 1.22.

932. UNEMPLOYMENT

932.1 The reserve to ensure regularity of employment is as imperative as the reserve for depreciation.

Brandeis. q *Survey Graphic,* April 1929.

932.2 The periods of unemployment accompanying depression in the business cycle . . . present a challenge to all our claims to progress, humanity, and civilization.

Gompers, *Seventy Years of Life and Labor,* 1925, ii. 3f.

932.3 Society produces the causes of unemployment, and society must meet the problem.

Rogoff, *An East Side Epic,* 1930, p. 86.

933. UNITED NATIONS

933.1 The continuation of the existence of human beings is in serious doubt if no supra-national solution can be achieved.

Einstein, letter, February 1952.

933.2 The world state is inherent in the United Nations as an oak tree is in an acorn.

Lippmann, *One World or None,* 1946.

934. UNITY

934.1 Let us be one band, for we are all children of one man.

Adret, *Second Epistle,* c. 1300. q HPB, 181.

934.2 Observe the waters: when they flow together, they sweep along stones, trees, earth, and other things; but if they are divided into many streams, the earth swallows them up, and they vanish. So shall ye also be if ye be divided.

Apocrypha: Patriarchs, Zebulun, 9.1–3.

934.3 In a religion, which alone among all religions had a clear conception of the descent of all men from one single father and which set the value of the human being so exceedingly high, there could be no room for a generic differentiation between nation and nation, for a division into higher and lower races.

*Chrysanth, *Religyi Drevnyago Mira,* 1878, iii. 326. q BKF, 173.

934.4 Unity of form is of little import for the future. This unity exists only in the vision of imbecile advocates of outward conformity, the Torquemadas or the Pobiedonostshefs.

J. Darmsteter, *Selected Essays,* 1895, p. 10.

934.5 The unity of man is to the Jew an article of faith.

Fleg, *Why I Am a Jew,* 1929, p. 68. See p. 83, 95.

934.6 All human beings descend from one father.

Fränkel, *Korban HaEda,* 1757, to *TJ: Nedarim,* 9.4.

934.7 Our sacred Scriptures presuppose the unity of God, in spite of the apparent variety which the world presents, and the unity of the human genus, notwithstanding the differences of races; because the total plan of the history of the world seems to have been always present to the spirit of the Jewish people.

Hess, *Rome and Jerusalem,* (1862), p. 182.

934.8 A man is like a letter of the alphabet: to produce a word, it must combine with another.

Mandelstamm, *Mishlé Binyamin,* 1885.

934.9 This little people, speaking through its prophets, dared to answer the principle of world-unity through world-conquest, world-empire and world-exploitation, reformulated . . . by Assyria and its successors, with the counter-principle of world-unity through a world-God, world-brotherhood, world-purpose, world-justice, world-peace, universal in extent and eternal in application.

J. Morgenstern. q Weller, *World-Fellowship,* 1935, p. 61.

934.10 There is neither Jew nor Greek, there is neither bond nor free, there is neither male nor female, for ye are all one.

New Testament: Gal., 3.28.

934.11 The chain which . . . makes us one, is to honor the one God.

Philo, *Special Laws,* i. 9.

934.12 May all become a single band to do Thy will with a perfect heart.

Rab, Kingdom Prayer for Rosh Hashana. See *UPB,* 1945, ii. 54.

934.13 The League of Nations is first of all the vision of a great Jew about 3,000 years ago—the Prophet Isaiah.

*Smuts.

934.14 A bundle of reeds cannot be broken by a man; but taken singly, even a child can break them.

Tanhuma, Nitzabim, 4, ed Buber, 25a.

934.15 O may all, created in Thine image, recognize that they are brethren, so that, one in spirit and one in fellowship, they may be forever united before Thee. Then shall Thy kingdom be established on earth.
Union Prayer Book, 1940, i. 71f.

934.16 One humanity on earth as there is but one God in heaven.
Ibid., 1945, ii. 345. See Einhorn, *Olat Tamid.*

934.17 The Jewish mind runs to Unity by an instinct as harmonious as the Greek's sense of Art. It is always impelled to a synthetic perception of the whole.
Zangwill, *Voice of Jerusalem,* 1921, p. 148.

934.18 All souls in the world, the Almighty's handiwork, are mystically one; but when they descend on earth, they are separated.
Zohar, Gen. 85b.

934.19 When man is at one, God is at one.
Zohar. q Fleg, *Life of Moses,* 128.

934.20 All hardships become lighter if borne in common, and all goodness becomes better before the Lord if practiced in unison.
S. Zweig, *Buried Candelabrum,* 1936.

935. UNIVERSE

935.1 Everything above and below is one unity.
Baal Shem. q Aaron Cohen, *Keter Shem Tob,* 7.

935.2 The heavens and the heavens of heavens together with the depths of the earth constitute one unit, one world, one being.
Kook, *Orot HaKodesh,* 1938, p. 144. q ABJ, 136.

935.3 All forms of existence are linked and connected with each other, but derived from His existence and essence.
Leon, *Sefer HaRimon,* 1287. q SMT, 223.

935.4 Whether the universe was created or is eternal cannot be answered with mathematical certainty.
Maimonides. *Commentary to Mishna,* 1168, Introduction.

935.5 The universe in its entirety is nothing but one individual being . . . there is no vacuum whatever therein.
Maimonides, *Guide for the Perplexed,* 1190, i. 72.

935.6 The microscope, no less than the telescope, has revealed unknown galaxies moving in tune to the same music of the spheres—a clue to the most awesome mystery of all, which is the Divine unity in Nature.
Sarnoff, *Youth in a Changing World,* June 12, 1954.

935.7 The slightest movement records the motion of higher worlds. Not only the commandments and customs, but all that man does, sees, hears, touches and feels, points to divinity. Everything everywhere in existence is a challenge, prompting and stirring man to forsake what is external, carnal, earthy, and to immerse himself in the eternal life of the Deity.
Zeitlin. *HaTekufa,* 1920, vi. 315.

936. UNIVERSITY

936.1 Character-building—morality in its larger sense—must be the cornerstone of the edifice and the keystone of the arch.
Brandeis, letter to J. W. Mack, June 3, 1925. q LBG, 74.

936.2 A university should be a place of light, of liberty, and of learning.
Disraeli, speech, House of Commons, March 8, 1873.

936.3 If it is not prepared for the free competition of ideas, it is not, in the true sense, a university.
Laski, *I Believe,* 1939.

936.4 The business of a university is . . . teaching the student how facts are converted into the truth.
Laski.

936.5 I hope our University will . . . send forth a new gospel to the World, blend all cultures into a new and unique harmony, a truly human harmony.
Shimoni, *Orot,* May 1950.

937. USE

937.1 The brain is like the hand. It grows with using.
Brandeis. *Filene Cooperative Ass'n Echo,* May 1905. q LBG, 97.

937.2 A civilization which is devoted exclusively to the utilitarian is at bottom not different from barbarism. The world is sustained by unworldliness.
Heschel, *The Earth Is the Lord's,* 1950, p. 55.

937.3 Utility is represented as the purpose of all conduct regulated by moral law. . . . . This notion is alien to the spirit of Judaism.

Lazarus, *Ethics of Judaism*, 1900, i. 163, #122.

937.4 If you're a cow, give milk! if an ox, plow! if a sheep, let yourself be sheared! if a horse, let yourself be ridden!

Mendelé, *Sefer HaBehemot*, 1913.

938. USURY

938.1 To a foreigner you may lend on interest.

Bible: Deut., 13.21.

938.2 Lord, who shall sojourn in Thy tabernacle? . . . He that puts not out his money on interest.

Bible: Ps., 15.1, 5.

938.3 This means; no interest even from a heathen.

Simlai. *T: Makkot*, 24a.

938.4 The Torah did not forbid taking interest from non-Jews, for commerce entails such; but that cannot be construed as favoring usury, since the Talmud forbids what excites disgust.

S. Abel, *Beth Shelomo*, 1893. See *JE*, i. 50b.

938.5 Who lends on interest . . . is as though he denied . . . God.

Caro, *Yoré Deah*, 1564, 159.5.

938.6 A usurer is ineligible to act as witness or judge.

Mishna: Sanhedrin, 3.3.

938.7 Who breaks the law against usury breaks the yoke of heaven.

Sifra, to *Lev.* 25.37, ed Weiss, 109b.

938.8 Go where you will through Christendom and you shall have of the Jews under ten in the hundred, yea, sometimes for five, whereas our Englsh usurers exceed all God's mercy.

*Thomas Wilson, *Discourses on Usury*, 1572. See Péguy, *Notre Jeunesse*, 1910, xi. 12. *Basic Verities*, 147.

939. VACILLATION

939.1 Are you for us, or for our adversaries?

Bible: Josh., 5.13.

939.2 It is good that you should take hold of the one; yea, also from the other withdraw not your hand.

Bible: Eccles., 7.18.

939.3 Push him with the left hand, pull him with the right.

Eleazar of Modin, or Eliezer b. Hyrcanus. *Mekilta*, to *Exod.* 18.6. Ref to would-be proselyte.

939.4 Be This or That when Things are said or done.
Both Rain and Snow have Friends, but Slush has None.

Guiterman, *A Poet's Proverbs*, 1924, p. 77.

939.5 Lot's wife hesitated, though angels led the way. Naturally, she was petrified where she stood, a monument of vacillation.

Harrison, *Religion of a Modern Liberal*, 1931, p. 72.

939.6 Legend tells that Abraham, who broke the idols of his father courageously, braved the fire of Nimrod's furnace and was saved by the power of his faith in God, whereas Haran, who wavered, not knowing whether to bow to the idol of Nimrod or to worship Abraham's Only One, went into the fire and was consumed.

Kohler, *Inaugural Address*, Oct. 18, 1903.

939.7 You would hold the rope by both ends.

Proverb. q Azariah. *Lev. R.*, 10.1.

939.8 In dealing with temptation, children and women, let your left hand repel and your right hand attract.

Simeon b. Eleazar. *T: Sota*, 47a.

940. VALUE

940.1 Better is a little that the righteous has than the abundance of many wicked.

Bible: Ps., 37.16. See *Ben Sira*, 29.11.

940.2 What the hand did not acquire, the eye did not spare.

Apocrypha: Ahikar, 3.3.

940.3 Better the life of the poor under a shelter of logs, than sumptuous fare in the house of strangers.

Apocrypha: Ben Sira, 29.22.

940.4 Rather death with renown than life with pollution.

Apocrypha: II Macc., 6.19.

940.5 Not more things but higher values —this has been the historic challenge of religion.

Baron, *In Quest of Integrity*, 1936, p. 34.

940.6 The setting enhances the gem's charm, not its worth.

Boerne, *Denkrede auf Jean Paul*, Dec. 2, 1825.

940.7 A man's inner significance manifests itself in the kind of forces released vigorously within him by misfortune.

Brodnitz. q PZL, 120.

940.8 It is the appreciation of beauty and truth, the striving for knowledge, which makes life worth living.

M. R. Cohen, *A Dreamer's Journey*, 1949, p. 166.

940.9 Teach us that wealth is not elegance, that profusion is not magnificence, that splendor is not beauty.

Disraeli, *Young Duke*, 1831.

940.10 A successful man is he who receives a great deal from his fellowmen. . . . The value of a man, however, should be seen in what he gives and not in what he is able to receive.

Einstein, *Out of My Later Years*, 1950, p. 34f.

940.11 Only things acquired by hard labor and great struggle are of any value.

Elijah Gaon. q SSJ, i. 87.

940.12 We Jews have always known how to respect spiritual values.

Freud, letter to Jacob Meitlis, Nov. 30, 1938.

940.13 Friendship, love, philosopher's
    stone—
    These three things men value
    alone.

Heine, *Lyrical Interlude*, 1823, #44.

940.14 The gem held firmly in the bosom of the earth, the pearl concealed in the bottom of the sea, man holds as the greatest treasure; he would regard it as of little worth had nature laid it at his feet like pebbles and shells.

Heine, *Buch der Lieder*, Preface to 2nd ed., 1837.

940.15 He that regards the precious
    things of earth
    With wisdom's eyes, holds them
    of little worth.

M. Ibn Ezra, *Selected Poems*, p. 55.

940.16 Nothing can have value without being an object of utility.

Marx, *Capital*, 1867.

940.17 In hell an ox is worth a groschen, but nobody has that groschen.

Proverb (Yiddish). q *JE*, x. 229a. See 612.5.

940.18 The terms *good* and *bad* indicate no positive quality in things regarded in themselves. . . . Thus one and the same thing can be at the same time good for the melancholy, bad for the mourner, and neither good nor bad for the deaf.

Spinoza, *Ethics*, 1677, iv. Preface.

941. VANITY

941.1 The daughters of Zion are haughty, walk with stretched-forth necks and wanton eyes, walking and mincing as they go, and making a tinkling with their feet.

Bible: Isa., 3.16.

941.2 When the Evil Will sees a man walking mincingly, preening his garments and curling his hair, he says, "This is my man!"

Ammi. *Gen. R.*, 22.6.

941.3 Feminine vanity, that divine gift which makes women charming.

Disraeli, *Tancred*, 1847, 2.8.

941.4 The ugliest vanity is the vanity of one who boasts of his humility.

Klatzkin, *In Praise of Wisdom*, 1943, p. 306.

941.5 When we see people . . . poise over their head golden wreaths, . . . what else can we think than that they are slaves of vainglory, though they assert that they are . . . rulers of many others?

Philo, *Dreams*, ii. 9.

941.6 Vanity is the cause of a great deal of virtue in men; the vainest are those who like to be thought respectable.

Pinero, *Notorious Mrs. Ebbsmith*, 1895, Act 4.

942. VARIETY

942.1 The heart of man seeks variety.

Agnon, *Sippur Pashut*, 1935.

942.2 Man is all the higher in the scale of civilization the oftener he changes his clothes in material, cut and color.

Auerbach, *On the Heights*, 1865.

942.3 Variety is the mother of enjoyment.

Disraeli, *Vivian Grey*, 1827, 5.4.

942.4 The pleasure increases when the objects placed before the senses vary.

M. Ibn Ezra, *Shirat Yisrael*, (12C) 1924, p. 35.

942.5 See how many different kinds of living beings there are in the world, and the voice, appearance, intelligence and taste of one is different from those of the others!

Seder Eliyahu Rabbah, ch 2, ed Friedmann, p. 10.

943. VEHEMENCE

943.1 Three are especially vehement: among beasts, the dog; among fowl, the cock; and among nations, Israel.

Simeon b. Lakish. *T: Betza,* 25b. Yakim. *Exod. R.,* 42.9.

944. VENGEANCE

944.1 Thou shalt not take venegeance, nor bear a grudge.

Bible: Lev., 19.18.

944.2 Vengeance is Mine, and recompense.

Bible: Deut., 32.35.

944.3 Say not, "I will do to him as he has done to me."

Bible: Prov., 24.29.

944.4 Revenge becomes great souls!

Abravanel, *Commentary* on *Gen.* 15.1, (1579) 1862, p. 39d.

944.5 Requite not evil to your neighbor for any wrong.

Apocrypha: Ben Sira, 10.6.

944.6 Leave to God the avenging.

Apocrypha: Patriarchs, Gad, 6.7.

944.7 Say not, Since I have been humiliated, let my neighbor be humiliated. Know it is the image of God you would thus humiliate.

Ben Azzai, Tanhuma. *Gen. R.,* 24.7.

944.8 No root of hatred, not a blade of vengeance....

> What will they? Why stretch out
> their hands to Me?
> Has none a fist? And where's a
> thunderbolt
> To take revenge for all the gen-
> erations,
> To blast the world and tear the
> heavens asunder
> And wreck the universe, My
> throne of glory.

Bialik, "In the Slaughter Town," 1904. q ZVJ, 178.

944.9 Repay not shame with shame, deception with deception.

J. M. Epstein, *Kitzur Shné Luhot HaBrit,* (1683) 1698, 8a.

944.10 Who takes vengeance destroys his own house.

Proverb. q Papa. *T: Sanhedrin,* 102b.

944.11 If a Jew wrong a Christian, what is his humility? Revenge. If a Christian wrong a Jew, what should his sufferance be by Christian example? Why revenge. The villainy you teach me, I will execute, and it shall go hard but I will better the instruction.

Shakespeare, Merchant of Venice, 1597, 3.1.

944.12 If you refuse assistance to a neighbor because he had been unkind to you, you are guilty of revenge; if you grant him his request for aid and remind him of his unkindness, you are guilty of bearing a grudge.

Sifra, to *Lev.* 19.18, ed Weiss, 89a.

944.13 This shall be our revenge: we shall quicken what they will kill, and raise what they will fell. . . . This is the banner of vengeance which we shall set up, and its name is—Jerusalem!

Smolenskin, *Nekam Brith,* 1882.

944.14 Who takes vengeance or bears a grudge acts like one who, having cut one hand while handling a knife, avenges himself by stabbing the other hand.

Talmud J: Nedarim, 9.4.

945. VICARIOUS

945.1 I will not destroy it [Sodom] for the sake of the ten.

Bible: Gen., 18.32.

945.2 Visiting the iniquity of the fathers upon the children unto the third and fourth generation of them that hate Me, and showing mercy unto the thousandth generation of them that love Me.

Bible: Exod., 20.5f.

945.3 Shall one man sin, and wilt Thou be wroth with all . . . ?

Bible: Num., 16.22.

945.4 The fathers shall not be put to death for the children, neither shall the children be put to death for the fathers.

Bible: Deut., 24.16.

945.5 The fathers have eaten sour grapes, and the children's teeth are set on edge.

Bible: Jer., 31.29. *Ezek.,* 18.2.

945.6 Happy the man who has a peg to hang on!

Akiba *TJ: Berakot,* 4.1.

945.7 Everyone shall bear his own righteousness or unrighteousness.

Apocrypha: IV Ezra, 7.105.

945.8 Be merciful to Thy people, and let our punishment be a satisfaction in their behalf. Make my blood their purification, and take my soul as ransom for theirs.

Apocrypha: IV Macc., 6.27–29.

945.9 Shila sins and Johanan is punished!
Gen. R., 25.3.

945.10 May I be an expiation sacrifice for the house of Israel.
Ishmael b. Elisha. *Mishna: Negaim*, 2.1.

945.11 Toby did a bad jobbing, and Ziggad got a drubbing.
Proverb (Babylonian). *T: Makkot*, 11a.

945.12 In Judaism there is no vicarious atonement.
Remy. q Hertz, *DPB*, 906.

945.13 Judaism . . . has no doctrine of vicarious salvation.
M. Steinberg. *Reconstructionist*, 1947.

945.14 That's the penalty we have to pay for our acts of foolishness,—someone else always suffers for them.
Sutro, *The Perfect Lover*, 1905, Act 2.

945.15 If heathens say, "Give us one of you to kill, or we shall kill all of you," let them all be killed rather than deliver one soul, unless they specified a particular man they wanted.
Tosefta: Terumot, 7.20. See *Mishna: Terumot*, 8.12.

946. VICE

946.1 What is crime amongst the multitude is only vice among the few.
Disraeli, *Tancred*, 1847.

946.2 Parsimony, soft-heartedness, and naïveté are vices in a man but virtues in a woman.
Hasdai, *Ben HaMelek VeHaNazir*, c. 1230, ch 30.

946.3 I have seen women on whose cheeks red vice was painted, and in whose hearts dwelt heavenly purity.
Heine, *English Fragments*, 1828, ch 2.

946.4 Vices will exist while men do.
Spinoza. *Political Treatise*, 1677, 1.2.

947. VICTORY

947.1 Victory is of the Lord.
Bible: Prov., 21.31. Cf *II Chron.* 20.15.

947.2 The race is not to the swift, nor the battle to the strong.
Bible: Eccles., 9.11.

947.3 Victory in battle stands not in the multitude of a host.
Apocrypha: I Macc., 3.19.

947.4 In defeat we are victorious; in death we are reborn.
Asch, *Tales of My People*, 1948, Motto, v.

947.5 As a coach I have always tried to emphasize that winning is not enough. The game must be played right. . . . I would rather see my teams lose a game in which they played well than win with a sloppy performance that reflected no credit.
Holman. E. R. Murrow, *This I Believe*, 1952, p. 74.

947.6 The stronger wins.
Huna b. Tahlifa. *T: Gittin.* 60a.

947.7 Who wins through evil loses.
Ibn Gabirol, *Mibhar HaPeninim*, c.1050. #643.

947.8 If Victory makes the hero, raw Success
The stamp of virtue, unremembered
Be then the desperate strife, the storm and stress
Of the last Warrior Jew. But if the man
Who dies for freedom, loving all things less, . . .
Nobler the conquered than the conqueror's end!
E. Lazarus, "Bar Kochba." *Poems*, 1888, ii. 22.

947.9 "Not for victory will He contend" [*Ps.* 103.9]. Did I not contend with the generations of the flood, of the dispersion, and of Sodom, and won the dispute and lost the people? And when Moses won over Me [*Exod.* 32], did I not gain in My world?
Midrash Tehillim, 103.12, ed Buber, 218b. See *Pesikta Rabbati*, ch 9, ed Friedmann, 32b.

947.10 Short-range defeats are often long-range victories.
Pekelis. *New Republic*, Oct. 29, 1945, p. 571.

947.11 Faith in victory has helped us to attain victory.
Veit. q L. Geiger. *JGL*, 1910, xiii. 157.

947.12 Now, in the atomic age, victory has become almost indistinguishable from defeat.
J. P. Warburg, *Last Call for Common Sense*, 1949, p. 3.

948. VILLAGE

948.1 In the working village, in God's open country, there is the best soil for the creation and development of sacred, lasting values, just as in the past it was the village that produced the prophets, sages and teachers of our people.

Hofshi, "Man & Agriculture." *Freeland,* Sept. 1952, p. 8.

948.2 It is in the village that the real soul of a people—its language, its poetry, its literature, its traditions—springs up from the intimate contact between man and soil. The towns do no more than "process" the fruits of the villages.

Weizmann, *Trial and Error,* 1949, p. 278.

949. VILNA

949.1 The great Pentecost of my life was Vilna.

S. Levin, *The Arena,* 1932, p. 268.

949.2 All men of all races who love liberty and peace have a special relation to the Jews of Vilna.

Lewisohn, *Israel,* 1925, p. 105.

949.3 Vilna, the Jerusalem of Lithuania. *Napoleon. See J. Raisin, *Haskalah,* 197.

949.4 Vilna, . . . city and mother in Israel, . . .
　　Even thy drawers of water were drawn from the source of the great in Torah.

Shneor, *Hezyonot,* 1923, p. 268. q SHR, 162.

949.5 Is Jerusalem ready . . . to become the Vilna of Israel as Vilna had been the Jerusalem of Lithuania? For what was in essence the colorful folklore and creative folk spirit of East European Jewry? It was its deeply earnest attitude toward things spiritual, its anti-militarist and anti-chauvinist character.

I. N. Steinberg. *Reconstructionist,* Dec. 15, 1950, p. 18.

950. VINE

950.1 As the vine among trees, short yet pre-eminent, is Israel among the nations: inferior in appearance, yet mighty in spirit.

Lev. R., 36.2.

950.2 As on a vine, the leaves cover the clusters, so in Israel: the uneducated shield the scholars. . . . As on a vine, the larger clusters weigh down lower than the smaller ones, so in Israel: those who bear a larger burden of Torah are lowlier and humbler than others.

Ibid.

950.3 The tree of which Adam ate was the vine, since its fruit has caused the most wailing in the world.

Meir. *T: Berakot,* 40a.

950.4 Like the fruit of the vine, first trodden, then placed on the royal table, is Israel: first oppressed, but ultimately destined for greatness.

Talmud: Nedarim, 49b.

950.5 As the vine will receive no graft from another tree, so the Community of Israel accepts no master but God.

Zohar, Genesis, 239b.

951. VIOLENCE

951.1 He looked for justice, but behold violence.

Bible: Isa., 5.7.

951.2 The violence of the wicked shall drag them away.

Bible: Prov., 21.7.

951.3 A branch [sprung] of violence has no tender twig.

Apocrypha: Ben Sira, 40.15.

951.4 Nothing established by violence and maintained by force . . . can endure.

Blum, *For All Mankind,* (1941) 1946, p. 30.

951.5 My throat is parched from crying, Violence!

Gershom b. Judah. q WHJ, i. 247.

951.6 Violence breeds violent succession.

Ibn Gabirol, *Selected Religious Poetry,* 26.

951.7 As among fish, so among men: the larger swallow the smaller.

Talmud: Aboda Zara, 4a.

952. VIOLET

952.1 The blue eyes of spring-time.

Heine, *New Spring,* 1844, #13.

953. VIRTUE

953.1 Reverence for superiors, respect for equals, regard for inferiors—these form the supreme trinity of the virtues.

F. Adler, *Creed and Deed,* 1877, p. 204.

953.2 In virtue are immortality and remembrance.

Apocrypha: Wisdom of Solomon, 4.1.

953.3 Self-control and understanding, righteousness and courage, there is nothing in life more profitable than these.

Ibid., 8.7.

953.4 Virtues and girls are prettiest before they know that they are pretty.

Boerne, *Kritiken: Hist. de la Révol. française.*

953.5 Goodness shall endure for ever,
Virtue nevermore shall perish.
Frug, "Two Pictures," tr Frank. *JQRo*, xiv. 557.

953.6 Virtue will last when beauty has passed.
Heine, *Rabbi of Bacharach*, (1840), ch 3, 1947, p. 65.

953.7 It is not a virtue to refrain from hurting others, but it is a virtue to bear a hurt patiently.
Ibn Gabirol, *Mibhar HaPeninim*, c. 1050, #83.

953.8 The Holy One proclaims daily the virtue of these three: a bachelor in a big city who remains chaste, a poor man who restores a find, and a rich man who tithes in secret.
Johanan b. Nappaha. T: *Pesahim*, 113a.

953.9 Follow and worship God in the exercise of virtue, for this way of worshipping God is the most holy.
Josephus, *Against Apion*, ii. 23.

953.10 These are the things of which a man eats the fruit in this world and the principal remains in the future world: honoring parents, practicing charity, promoting peace, but the study of Torah is equal to all of them.
Mishna: Peah, 1.1. Cf Johanan. T: *Sabbath*, 127a.

953.11 The wise turns vices into virtues; the fool, virtues into vices.
Orhot Tzaddikim, 15C, Introduction.

953.12 Virtue is the art of the whole life.
Philo, *Allegorical Interpretation*, 1.17.

953.13 Each of the four main virtues—wisdom, courage, temperance, justice—is a sovereign wielding authority.
Philo, *Prosperity & Exile of Cain*, 37.

953.14 Virtue has no room in her home for a grudging spirit.
Philo, *Special Laws*, i. 59.

953.15 Virtue and goodness are judged not by quantity but by quality; hence one day spent with perfect correctness is of equal value with the entire good life of a wise man.
Philo, *Rewards and Punishments*, 19.

953.16 Four virtues refresh the world: charity, justice, truth and peace.
Seder Eliyahu Rabbah, ch 16, ed Friedmann, 74.

953.17 The virtuous among the wicked is superior to the virtuous among the righteous; a sinner among the righteous is worse than a sinner among the wicked.
Sefer Hasidim, 13C, #16, p. 22.

953.18 The source of all virtue is wisdom, reason, knowledge.
Shneor Zalman, *Tanya*, 1796. q HLH, 59.

953.19 Virtue is action in accord with the laws of one's own nature.
Spinoza, *Ethics*, 1677, iv. Pr. 18, Note.

953.20 Virtue's foundation is the endeavor at self-preservation.
Ibid. See Pr 22, corollary.

953.21 Virtue is to be desired for its own sake.
Ibid.

953.22 Virtue, not blessedness, is the reward of virtue.
Ibid., v. Pr 42.

953.23 In every age, virtue has been exceedingly rare.
Spinoza, *Theologico-Political Treatise*, 1670, ch 12.

953.24 The Holy One loves him who does not display temper, does not become intoxicated, and does not insist on his full rights.
Talmud: Pesahim, 113b.

953.25 To him who loves his neighbor, befriends a relative, marries his sister's daughter, and lends to a man in need, Scripture refers: "Thou shalt call and the Lord will answer" [*Isa*. 58.9].
Talmud: Yebamot, 62b–63a.

953.26 Justice for others, courage for ourselves. These are the two virtues in which all the others consist.
Varnhagen, *Briefe*, 1877. q JRL, 233.

953.27 If you conceal your vices, conceal your virtues.
Zabara, *Sefer Shaashuim*, 13C, 7.42.

953.28 Certain virtues are always fashionable, but not virtue.
Zunz, *Predigten*, 1822, Preface.

954. VISION

954.1 I will set no base thing before mine eyes.
Bible: Ps., 101.3.

954.2 Where there is no vision, the people perish (JPS ed: cast off restraint).
Bible: Prov., 29.18.

954.3 Our movement will be tested by its fealty to the vision.
Ben Gurion, *Hazon VeDerek*, 1951, i.

954.4 Sometimes it is best not to try to see too far into the unknowable future.
Brandeis. q *Survey Graphic,* Nov. 1936.

954.5 O lift your eyes to where the dawn appears,
   stripped of the blinding bandage of your tears.
Fleg, *Wall of Weeping,* (1919) 1929, tr Wolfe, 16.

954.6 How short-sighted is man! He cannot even fully comprehend his own short-sightedness.
M. Friedlander, *Jewish Religion,* 1891, p. 32.

954.7 True vision requires far more than the eye. It takes the whole man. For what we see is no more and no less than what we are.
Guggenheimer, *Creative Vision,* 1950, p. 4.

954.8 Be not like a bird that sees the grain but not the trap.
Ibn Tibbon, *Tzavaah,* c. 1190. KTJ, 159.

954.9 Only the inward vision can reach that heavenly goal.
Judah Halevi, tr Lucas, *Jewish Year,* 1926, p. 62.

954.10 Our deeds cannot be measured except by the yardstick of the vision which brought us hither.
Katznelson, *Ktabim,* ix. 301.

954.11 Stoop to get a view of the inside, . . . and never either willingly or unwillingly close your eyes.
Philo, *Migration of Abraham,* 39.

954.12 A guest for a while sees a mile.
Proverb (Yiddish). BJS, #733.

954.13 In sooth, there must be lives of
   dreams, lives of visions!
   If not here—in a land unexplored and uncharted;
   If not now—in an age not yet started!
J. Steinberg, "My Yearning." tr FTH, 116.

954.14 Without inspection drink no wine nor dare a document to sign.
Twerski, *Rashi,* 1946.

954.15 Open my eyes to visions girt
   With beauty, and with wonder lit—
   But let me always see the dirt,
   And all that spawn and die in it.
L. Untermeyer, "Prayer." *Challenge,* 1915, p. 7.

954.16 A man sees first of all what he fears to see.
Wallenrod. *HaDoar,* Feb. 25, 1955, p. 324.

954.17 The true artist and poet exalts what he sees in reality into a vision.
Werfel, *Between Heaven and Earth,* 1944, p. 39f.

954.18 Vision looks inward and becomes duty. Vision looks outward and becomes aspiration. Vision looks upward and becomes faith.
S. S. Wise, June 11, 1905. *Sermons & Addresses,* 72.

955. VISIT

955.1 Let your foot be seldom in your neighbor's house.
Bible: Prov., 25.17.

955.2 Who does not visit the sick is like a murderer.
Akiba. *T: Nedarim,* 40a.

955.3 Forget not to visit the sick; you will be loved for it.
Apocrypha: Ben Sira, 7.35. See Eleazar. *T: Nedarim,* 41a.

955.4 Visit the sick, for sympathy lightens pain. . . . Fatigue him not by staying too long. . . . Enter cheerfully, for his heart and eyes are on those who come in.
Eliezer b. Isaac, *Orhot Hayyim,* c. 1050. AHE, 40.

955.5 When you visit an indigent patient, go not with empty hands.
Ibid. AHE, 44.

955.6 Visiting is like rain: prayed for when withheld, loathsome when overdone.
Ibn Gabirol, *Mibhar HaPeninim,* c. 1050, #405.

955.7 Neglect not to visit and treat the poor; there is no nobler work.
Israeli, *Manhig HaRofeim,* c. 930. q *Legacy of Islam,* 326.

955.8 Visit not your neighbor in the hour of his disgrace.
Simeon b. Eleazar. *Mishna: Abot,* 4.18.

955.9 When you visit a patient, sit not on his bed.
Talmud: Sabbath, 12b.

956. VOICE

956.1 The voice is the voice of Jacob.
Bible: Gen., 27.22.

956.2 After the fire a still small voice.
Bible: I Kings, 19.12.

956.3 A voice crying in the wilderness.
Bible: Isa., 40.3 (as read in *Matt.* 3.3).

956.4 She raised her voice against Me, therefore I hated her.
Bible: Jer., 12.8.

956.5 If a house could be built by a loud voice, the ass would build two in a day.
Apocrypha: Aḥiḳar, 2.8.

956.6 A hidden voice, a mighty voice,
    From early times is borne,
    A voice of men who fought with gods,
    And mocked foes' sword with scorn.
Chernihovsky, "A Melody," 1916. *Kitbé,* ii. 10. tr FTH, 64.

956.7 Sweet is the voice of a sister in the season of sorrow.
Disraeli, *Alroy,* 1833.

956.8 There is no index of character so sure as the voice.
Disraeli, *Tancred,* 1847, 2.1.

956.9 A hard voice in a woman is a physical defect.
Hisda. *T: Ketubot,* 75a.

956.10 God personified Himself to the Jews not in the image, but in the call. In Jewish prayers and in Jewish literature the "Hear" sounds again and again. When Elijah perceived God, he heard only a still, small voice. . . . The word, logos, was for the Jew the intermediary between infinity and the individual being. . . . The name and the sound . . . conjured and created.
H. Kohn, *Idea of Nationalism,* 1944, p. 32.

956.11 One voice can enter ten ears, but ten voices cannot enter one ear.
Levi. *Pesiḳta Rabbati,* ch 21, ed Friedmann, 100b.

956.12 The voice is on the borderline between the physical and the spiritual.
Peretz, *Meḳubolim,* 1906. *Alle Verk,* vi. 53. See LP, 227.

956.13 Man has been likened to an earthen pot. . . . You have but to tap the pot with your finger. If it rings back full and true, all is well; there is your perfect pot. And if not—man, alas, has been likened to a broken potsherd.
Peretz, *Mesiras Nefesh,* c.1910. *Alle Verk,* vii. 142. SPG, 22.

956.14 "Honor the Lord with thy substance" [*Prov.* 3.9]. If you have a beautiful voice and are in the synagog, honor the Lord with it.
Pesiḳta Rabbati, ch 25, ed Friedmann, 127a.

956.15 Sweet of voice, short of brains.
Proverb. q Immanuel, *Mahberot,* (c. 1300) 1870, ch 20, p. 159.

956.16 A woman's voice is an excitement.
Samuel. *T: Beraḳot,* 24a.

956.17 Whenever the voice of Jacob is interrupted, the hands of Esau are reinforced.
Zohar, Gen., 171a.

957. VOTE

957.1 Votes should be weighed, not counted.
M. Mendelssohn, *An Niḳolai. Gesam. Werke,* 1838, iii.

958. VULGARITY

958.1 If it were not for the leaven and manure in the spirit of man, the ripe fruit, delighting God and man, would not have grown.
Kook, *Orot HaKodesh,* 1938, p. 432. q ABJ, 186.

958.2 In the soil of every fetching man, there is a streak of ingratiating commonness; in the heart of every alluring woman, there is a touch of calico.
G. J. Nathan, *Autobiography of an Attitude,* 1925, p. 64.

958.3 By vulgarity I mean that vice of civilization which makes man ashamed of himself and his next of kin, and pretend to be somebody else.
Schechter, *Abraham Lincoln,* Feb. 11, 1909.

959. WAGE

959.1 The wages of a hired servant shall not abide with you all night until the morning.
Bible: Lev., 19.13. See *Deut.* 24.15.

959.2 As is the share of him who goes down to battle shall be the share of him who tarries by the baggage; they shall share alike.
Bible: I Sam., 30.24.

959.3 The wage is according to the labor.
Ben He He. *Mishna: Abot,* 5.23.

959.4 Low wages are not cheap wages.
Brandeis, *Stettler vs. O'Hara,* 243 U.S. Reports 629, Dec. 17, 1914.

959.5 Nature has her laws, and this is one—a fair day's wage for a fair day's work.

Disraeli, (Nixon in) *Sybil*, 1845.

959.6 No man can claim to be free unless he has a wage that permits him and his family to live in comfort.

Hillman, speech, Aug. 2, 1918. q JSH, 175.

959.7 Be content with your wages.

New Testament: Luke, 3.14.

959.8 Wages are payable at the conclusion of the work.

Raba. *T: Baba Metzia*, 73a.

959.9 Wages should be left to the fair and free competition of the market, and should never be controlled by the interference of the legislature.

Ricardo, *Principles of Political Economy*, 1817, 5.

959.10 There is no way of keeping profits up by keeping wages down.

Ricardo, *On Protection to Agriculture*, 1820.

960. WAITING

960.1 Though it tarry, wait for it.
Bible: Hab., 2.3.

960.2 Happy is he that waits.
Bible: Dan., 12.12.

960.3 Everything comes if a man will only wait.
Disraeli, (Fakredeen in) *Tancred*, 1847, 4.8.

960.4 Waiting demoralizes.
Herzl, *Das Palais Bourbon*, 1895.

960.5 We wait for Messiah, to be rewarded [for waiting].
Jonathan. *T: Sanhedrin*, 97b.

960.6 Anxious waiting is affliction, but no disgrace.
Nordau, speech, IX Zionist Congress, Dec. 26, 1909.

960.7 Wise men do not wait till the calamity is upon them.
Philo, *Moses*, 59.

960.8 Wait and see what happens.
Pinero, *Preserving Mr. Panmure*, 1911, Act 3.

961. WAITING FOR GOD

961.1 Happy are all they that wait for Him.
Bible: Isa., 30.18.

961.2 They that wait for the Lord shall renew their strength.
Ibid., 40.31.

961.3 Wait for your God continually.
Bible: Hos., 12.7.

961.4 Only for God does my soul wait in stillness.
Bible: Ps., 62.2.

961.5 My soul waits for the Lord more than watchmen for the morning.
Ibid., 130.6. See 69.4.

961.6 It is good that a man should wait quietly for the salvation of the Lord.
Bible: Lam., 3.26.

961.7 In all time we look to Thee and wait.
Amittai b. Shefatia, *Adonoy, Adonoy*, c. 900. *JQRo*, ix. 722.

962. WAKE

962.1 Awake, my people! How long will you sleep?
J. L. Gordon, "Hakitza Ammi," 1863. q HMH, 40.

962.2 Wake, Israel, wake! Recall today
The glorious Maccabean rage!
E. Lazarus, "Banner of the Jew," 1882. *Poems*, 1889, ii. 11.

963. WALK

963.1 No one can walk backward into the future.
Hergesheimer, *The Three Black Pennys*, 1917.

963.2 Long strides reduce the eyesight by a five hundredth part.
Ishmael b. Jose. *T: Sabbath*, 113b. See *Berakot*, 43b.

963.3 It is forbidden to take long strides on the Sabbath.
Judah HaNasi. *T: Sabbath*, 113b.

963.4 You can tell by a man's walk whether he is wise and intelligent or foolish and ignorant.
Maimonides, *Yad: Deot*, 1180, 5.8.

963.5 If you don't walk four cubits after a meal you won't digest your food.
Samuel. T: Sabbath, 41a.

964. WALL

964.1 We are not defenders of the wall, but the wall itself, and each and every one of us is a living brick of this wall.
Arlosoroff, *Leben und Werk*, 1936, p. 184.

964.2 Verily, a mere *walking wall* is this

people, always firm, upstanding, never falling, never to be consumed.

Frishman, "Western Wall." *Avukah Annual*, 1932, p. 694.

964.3 The walls of Jericho fell to the sound of shouts and trumpets. I never heard of walls being raised by that means.

Weizmann, at Zionist Congress, 1931. *Trial & Error*, 338.

965. WANDERING JEW

965.1 Yet still they come across the sand
Following a bright and holy star,
Seeking peace for every land
And Liberty both near and far;
They come with their unfaltering will,
And their flag is bright and blue,
And the dream is glittering still
Promising Zion to the Jew.

*Dimitrov, "Jews." *Subrani Suchineniya*, 1931, ii. 120. tr Joy Davidman.

965.2 The Wandering Jew wanders no more. He has arrived.

*Dumas fils, (Daniel in) *La Femme de Claude*, 1873, 2:1.

965.3 Our people wandered before they were driven.

*G. Eliot, (Joseph Kalonymos in) *Daniel Deronda*, 1876.

965.4 The ungainly figure of the Wandering Jew . . . acquires a heroic dignity when one realizes that he could have thrown off his rags, and clad himself in scarlet, and enjoyed peace and quiet and affluence, by pronouncing one single word —a word which he did not pronounce.

Golding, *The Jewish Problem*, 1938, p. 70. See Judah Halevi, *Cuzari*, 1.115, 4.23.

965.5 That mummy of a race which wanders over the world wrapped in most ancient swathing-bands of letters, a petrified fragment of the History of the World, a specter which gets its living by trading in bills of exchange and old pantaloons.

Heine, *City of Lucca*, 1828, ch 13.

965.6 Oh, the weary march, . . . oh the blankness of the receding goal! . . . for the West hath cast them out, and the East refuseth to receive.

E. Lazarus, *The Exodus. Poems*, ii. 60. Ref to Spanish expulsion, Aug. 3, 1492.

965.7 As soon as father Abraham conceives of Judaism, the process of "Go forth" begins.

Mendelé, *Di Alte Maasé*, 1865.

965.8 For this people, so proud and yet so humble, there is no home upon this earth. Wanderers they have been. Wanderers they are destined ever to remain.

*O'Connor, *Vision of Morocco*, 1924, p. 6.

965.9 To be elsewhere—the great vice of this race, its great, secret virtue. . . . The most comfortable houses . . . will never mean any more to them than a tent in the desert. . . . This people is always on camel back.

*Péguy, *Notre Jeunesse*, 1910. *Basic Verities*, 1943, 141.

965.10 To the millenial wanderer, no road, however far, need be too long.

Pinsker, *Auto-Emancipation*, 1882.

965.11 With a wanderer's staff in hand,
Without a home, without a land,
No friend, no helper on the way,
No tomorrow and no today.

M. Rosenfeld, "Exile Song." LGP, 143.

965.12 The Jew of whom I spake is old, so old
He seems to have outlived a world's decay;
The hoary mountains and the wrinkled ocean
Seem younger still than he; his hair and beard
Are whiter than the tempest-sifted snow. . . .
. . . but from his eye looks forth
A life of unconsumèd thought which pierces
The present, and the past, and the to-come.

*Shelley, *Hellas*, 1821.

965.13 The hour of night, and in the night
A memory drifts. An endless road
Walked by a homeless tribe . . .
The load
Of the world's pain weighs down their flight.

The hour of night, and in the night
A hoarse and supplicating cry;
But rusty are the keys of the sky
And a deaf God sits in that height.

*Yavorov, "Hebrews." *Suchineniya*, 1920, i. 94. tr Joy Davidman.

965.14 I figure the Jew as the eldest-born of Time, touching the Creation and reaching forward into the future, the true *blasé* of the Universe; the Wandering Jew who has been everywhere, seen everything, done everything, led everything, thought everything, and suffered everything.

Zangwill, *Children of the Ghetto*, 1892, ii. ch 6, p. 408.

966. WAR

966.1 Shall your brethren go to war, and ye sit here?

Bible: Num., 32.6.

966.2 You shed blood abundantly and made great wars: you shall not build a house to My name.

Bible: I Chron., 22.8, 28.3.

966.3 War once set on foot cannot be lightly either broken off or carried through without risk of disaster.

Agrippa II. q Josephus, *Wars,* 2.16.4.

966.4 We fight for our lives and our laws.

Apocrypha: I Macc., 3.21.

966.5 Then at last war's piteous ruin shall stop, and none shall fight any more with sword and steel and spear, for this shall be unlawful henceforth.

Apocrypha: Sibyls, 5.381-3.

966.6 The appalling thing about war is that it kills all love of truth.

Brandes, letter to Clemenceau, March 1915.

966.7 Disputes about war, . . . like the showy magnificence of military parades, may be of interest to government officials, but what, besides the wasting of time, can such things mean to us?

Eybeshitz, *Yaarot Debash,* 1779, p. 29a. q BSJ, 340.

966.8 It simply is not true that war never settles anything.

F. Frankfurter.

966.9 That battle-madness which we find among the ancient Teutonic races who fought neither to kill nor to conquer, but for the very love of fighting itself.

Heine, *Germany from Kant to Hegel,* 1834.

966.10 Each new year carries on the old
year's shame
And crowns the butchers of mankind with fame
And drinks a health to the defilers of creation.

Kraus, "New Year 1917." *Poems,* 1930, p. 72.

966.11 Who can reflect on the sacredness of human life, in view of its eternal destinies, without coming to the conclusion that war, with its attendants, hatred, destruction and slaughter, is incompatible with the high dictates of religion?

L. Levi, *International Law,* 1888, p. 4.

966.12 Let us concentrate on the one great job of civilization—the complete elimination of war.

Levinson. Weller, *World Fellowship,* 1935, p. 35.

966.13 War is no more inevitable than the plague is inevitable. War is no more a part of human nature than the burning of witches is a human act.

London, speech, U.S. Congress, March 17, 1916. q RES, 79.

966.14 It is not Carnegie's millions, nor millions added to those millions, that can kill war and bring peace. It is the "just weight" and the "just measure" which . . . shall kill war.

Lubin, letter to *American Agriculturist,* 1910. q ADL, 6.

966.15 Call the War what you will, but call it not Just. At best, we may say that it appears necessary, because due to our weakness and wickedness we see no other way to remove the evil from the earth.

Magnes, 1940. *Gleanings,* 1948, p. 62.

966.16 The self-restraint which Scripture imposed on the children of Israel in regard to Ammon, Moab and Seir [*Deut.* 2.5, 9, 19] carries a prohibition against all aggressive war.

Nahmanides, *Sefer HaMitzvot,* #47.

966.17 The wars of the Greeks and the barbarians . . . have all flowed from one source, greed, the desire of money, glory, or pleasure, for it is on these that the human race goes mad.

Philo, *Decalogue,* 28.

966.18 So far as war has any biological effect, it is rather to kill off the fittest than to preserve them.

H. Samuel, *Belief and Action,* 1937, p. 206.

966.19 Moloch comes riding,
With uplifted sword,
And all men acclaim him,
Their chosen lord.
So join in the shouting,
Like fools and slaves,
And let him thrust you
Into your graves.

Shneor, "War Comes." LGP, 114.

966.20 War never ends war.

S. S. Wise, *Rededication*, 1932.

966.21 War does not permit itself to be coordinated with reason and righteousness.

S. Zweig, *World of Yesterday*, 1943, p. 234.

967. WARNING

967.1 A person is not punishable unless he had been forewarned.

Simeon. *Sifré, #173*, to *Deut.* 18.12. Jose. *T: Sanhedrin*, 56b.

968. WATCH

968.1 A watched pot never boils.

Perelman, *Crazy Like a Fox*, (1928) 1947, p. 14.

969. WATER

969.1 Water spilt on the ground . . . cannot be gathered up again.

Bible: II Sam., 14.14.

969.2 The waters are come in even unto the soul.

Bible: Ps., 69.2.

969.3 Pour not out the water which others may need.

Judah HaNasi, Joseph. *T: Yebamot*, 11b.

969.4 None shall cut off a stream of water.

Philo. q Eusebius, *Preparation of the Gospel*, 8.7.

969.5 Don't pour out dirty water before you have clean water.

Weissmann-Chajes, *Hokma uMusar*, 1875, p. 3.

970. WAY

970.1 God led them not by way of the land of the Philistines, because it was near.

Bible: Exod., 13.17.

970.2 Ask for the old paths, where is the good way.

Bible: Jer., 6.16.

970.3 The ways of the Lord are right: the just walk in them, but transgressors stumble in them.

Bible: Hos., 14.10.

970.4 Thou makest me to know the path of life.

Bible: Ps., 16.11.

970.5 All the paths of the Lord are mercy and truth.

Ibid., 25.10.

970.6 Blessed is he who . . . walks along the straight path.

Apocrypha: II Enoch, 42.10.

970.7 Who desires his Creator's favor will enter by the narrow door, through which the pious and patient come.

Bahya, *Hobot HaLebabot*, 1040, 7.10. See *Matt.* 7.13f.

970.8 Enjoy the Road. The Best is lost
    to those
Who hurry blindly toward the
    Journey's Close.

Guiterman, *A Poet's Proverbs*, 1924, p. 27.

970.9 God's road is all uphill,
    And man climbs slowly.

Guiterman, *Brave Laughter*, 1943, p. 103.

970.10 All roads are dangerous.

Hanina. *TJ: Berakot*, 4.1.

970.11 He who warns us against the useless road, serves us as well as he who points out to us the right way.

Heine, *Germany from Kant to Hegel*, 1834.

970.12 Where there is no road, a new road must be trodden.

J. Y. Hurwitz, q *JP*, 1948, ii. 116.

970.13 Ride the public highway and leave the winding paths.

q M. Ibn Ezra, *Shirat Yisrael*, (12C) 1924, p. 148.

970.14 Show us not the aim without the
    way.
For ends and means on earth are
    so entangled.

Lassalle, *Franz von Sickingen*, 1859.

970.15 Carve your own way!

Mosen, "Zuruf." *Gedichte*, 1836.

970.16 The road through life is like the edge of a blade, with the netherworld on either side.

Moshe Leib of Sasov. See BTH, ii. 92.

970.17 The road to pleasure is downhill and very easy, so that one does not walk but is dragged along; the way to self-control is uphill, toilsome no doubt, but profitable exceedingly.

Philo, *Special Laws*, iv. 20.

970.18 There is no highway without ambushes, and there is no highway without cross-roads.

Sifré, #20, to *Deut.* 1.22, ed Friedmann, 69b.

970.19 I like roads that don't care much where they are going.

Stampfer, *Jerusalem Has Many Faces*, 1950, p. 18.

971. WEAKNESS

971.1 Everything that is weak is found to be useless.

Apocrypha: Wisdom of Solomon, 2.11.

971.2 We are weak—and that is our crime!

Ben Gurion, speech, Palestine Labor Party, 1931.

971.3 Few people are bad but many are weak.

Brandeis, to Alfred Lief, May 19, 1934. LBG, 93.

971.4 Man's biological weakness is the condition of human culture.

Fromm, *Escape from Freedom,* 1941, p. 33.

971.5 The authoritarian character feels the more aroused the more helpless his object has become.

Ibid., 168.

971.6 The virtue of powerlessness, the power of helplessness, the company of the dispossessed, the sanctity of the insulted and the injured—these are the great themes of Yiddish literature.

Howe & Greenberg, *A Treasury of Yiddish Stories,* 1954, 38.

971.7 In this world it is very dangerous to be weak.

Peretz, *Shreib a Feleton,* 1895. *Alle Verk,* xii. 77.

971.8 To the tune of the strong, the weak must dance.

Syrkin, "Natzionale Freiheit," 1917. SGZ, ii. 280.

972. WEATHER

972.1 Everything is in Heaven's hands, except cold and heat.

Hanina. *T: Ketubot,* 30a.

972.2 One day it will become a science, and we shall then be able to compound weather as we now do medicine.

Varnhagen. q JRL, 234.

973. WEEPING

973.1 Weep not for the dead . . . but weep sore for him who goes away, for he shall return no more, nor see his native country.

Bible: Jer., 22.10.

973.2 Rachel weeping for her children.

Ibid., 31.15.

973.3 Weeping is an exceeding great evil . . . unless it come through joy.

Baal Shem. See AHE, 299.

973.4 I saw a bride weep because she was happy. Niggardly life grants us nothing, we must pay for everything with tears. Who bought much, wept much.

Boerne, *Die Sylvesternacht eines alten Herzens,* Jan. 1. 1827.

973.5 Jews ought to weep when they are born and when they die, and in the days in between.

Ibn Verga, *Shebet Yehuda,* 1550.

973.6 Israel's only treasure amid its evils, the power of bewailing its present distresses.

Philo, *Confusion of Tongues,* 20.

973.7 If every woman in the world was weeping her heart out, men would be found dining, feeding, feasting.

Pinero, *The Benefit of the Doubt,* 1895, 1.

974. WEIGHT

974.1 The lighter rises higher.

Gentili, *Mleket Mahshebet,* 1710.

975. WET

975.1 One can't get wetter than wet.

B. Auerbach, *Waldfried,* 1875, p. 11.

976. WHIP

976.1 They use the Whip, the horse complains,
  Who have no Sense to use the Reins.

Guiterman, *A Poet's Proverbs,* 1924, p. 30.

977. WICKED

977.1 He said to the wicked, "Why do you smite your fellow?" (Usually quoted, "Wicked one, why do you smite your fellow?")

Bible: Exod., 2.13.

977.2 The wicked are like the troubled sea: it cannot rest, and its waters cast up mire and dirt.

Bible: Isa., 57.20.

977.3 Six things the Lord hates, yea, seven are an abomination to Him: haughty eyes, a lying tongue, and hands that shed innocent blood; a heart that devises wicked thought, feet that are swift in running to evil, a false witness that breathes out lies, and he that sows discord among brethren.

Bible: Prov., 6.16–19.

977.4 The wicked flee when no man pursues.

Ibid., 28.1.

977.5 The triumph of the wicked is short, the joy of the godless but for a moment.
Bible: Job, 20.5. See 8.13; *Ps.*, 37.35f, 94.3.

977.6 Though wickedness be sweet in his mouth . . . it is the gall of asps within him.
Bible: Job, 20.12, 14.

977.7 Wherefore do the wicked live, . . . yea, wax mighty in power?
Ibid., 21.7.

977.8 Plunder comes to a sudden end.
Apocrypha: Ben Sira, 40.14.

977.9 Wickedness is a coward, and witnesses its own condemnation.
Apocrypha: Wisdom of Solomon, 17.11.

977.10 If you yield not to wickedness, it will not follow you.
Johanan. *Tanhuma, Tazria*, #11, ed Buber, 20a.

977.11 Even a criminal has his good side.
Nahman Bratzlav. q HLH, 98.

977.12 The wicked do not repent even at the gates of Gehenna.
Simeon b. Lakish. *T: Erubin*, 19a.

977.13 There is grief above when the wicked suffer destruction.
Zohar, Gen., 57b.

977.14 God is glorified by a good deed the wicked happens to do.
Zohar, Exod., 11a.

978. WIDOWHOOD

978.1 Ye shall not afflict any widow.
Bible: Exod., 22.21.

978.2 I caused the widow's heart to sing for joy.
Bible: Job, 29.13.

978.3 The world is darkened for him who is widowed.
Alexandri. *T: Sanhedrin*, 22a.

978.4 Losing one's first wife is like witnessing the Destruction of the Temple.
Johanan b. Nappaha. *Ibid.*

978.5 Everything can be replaced, except the wife of one's youth.
Samuel b. Nahman. *Ibid.*

978.6 Rather than widowed remain, 'tis better to marry again.
Simeon b. Lakish. *T: Ketubot*, 75a. *Yebamot* 118b.

979. WIFE

979.A. A Blessing

979.A.1 A virtuous woman is a crown to her husband.
Bible: Prov., 12.4.

979.A.2 Who finds a wife finds a great good.
Ibid., 18.22.

979.A.3 A prudent wife is from the Lord.
Ibid., 19.14.

979.A.4 Who is rich? He who has a wife beautiful in deeds.
Akiba. *T: Sabbath*, 25b.

979.A.5 A beautiful wife is a joy to her husband; she shall double the days of his life.
Apocrypha: Ben Sira, 26.1. q *T: Yebamot*, 63b. Original text: A good wife.

979.A.6 Each day with her is as good as two.
Rashi, *Commentary*, to *Yebamot* 63b.

979.A.7 A good wife is a good gift. . . . Rich or poor, his heart is merry, and his face cheerful at all times.
Apocrypha: Ben Sira, 26.3f.

979.A.8 Who gets a wife gets the choicest possession, a help meet for him and a pillar of support.
Ibid., 36.24.

979.A.9 A man without a wife is not a man.
Eleazar b. Pedat. *T: Yebamot*, 63a.

979.A.10 As soon as a man takes a wife, his sins are arrested.
Hama b. Hanina. *T: Yebamot*, 63b.

979.A.11 A home is blessed only on the wife's account.
Helbo. *T: Baba Metzia*, 59a.

979.A.12 Without a wife, no help, joy, blessing or atonement.
Jacob. *Gen. R.*, 17.2.
Tanhum b. Hanilai. *T: Yebamot*, 63b.

979.A.13 The joy of the heart is a wife.
Joshua b. Karha. *T: Sabbath*, 152a.

979.A.14 Who has no wife lives without peace.
Joshua b. Levi. *Gen. R.*, 17.2.

979.A.15 Home means wife.
Judah HaNasi. *Mishna: Yoma*, 1.1.

979.A.16 No life without a wife.
Levi. *Gen. R.*, 17.2.

979.A.17 A pious wife, remaining modestly within her domestic circle, is like the altar, an atoning power for her household.
Tanhuma, VaYishlah, 6.

979.B. Shrew

979.B.1 The contentions of a wife are a continual dropping.
Bible: Prov., 19.13. Cf 27.15.

979.B.2 Better to dwell in an attic nook than in a house together with a contentious woman.
Ibid., 21.9, 25.24.

979.B.3 I would rather dwell with a lion and dragon than keep house with a wicked woman.
Apocrypha: Ben Sira, 25.16.

979.B.4 May God preserve you from an evil worse than death—a contentious woman.
Hiyya Rabba. *T: Yebamot,* 63a.

979.B.5 All are carried off by the devil, except a shrew.
Proverb. q Lipperheide, *Spruchwörterbuch,* 976.

979.B.6 Any ill and cruel fate rather than a cruel mate.
Rab. *T: Sabbath,* 11a; Myers, *Gems from the Talmud,* 47.

979.B.7 How baneful is a bad wife, with whom Scripture compares Gehenna!
Raba. *T: Yebamot,* 63b. Cf *Erubin,* 41b.

979.C. Treatment

979.C.1 A man is forbidden to compel his wife to her duty.
Assi. *T: Erubin,* 100b.

979.C.2 As a man should provide for the dignity of his widow, so should he provide for the honor of his divorcee.
Eleazar b. Pedat. *TJ: Ketubot,* 11.3. Jose HaGelili. *Ibid.*

979.C.3 Husbands must honor their wives more than themselves, and treat them with tender consideration.
Eliezer Halevi, *Tzavaah,* c. 1350. AHE, 210. See Maimonides, *Shaaré HaMusar.* AHE, 116.

979.C.4 A man does not proceed against his wife unless he becomes possessed.
Ishmael School. *T: Sota,* 3a.

979.C.5 Wife-beating is a thing not done in Israel.
Jacob Tam, c. 1150. q AJL, 89. See Meir of Rothenburg, *Responsa,* (1557), p. 291.

979.C.6 Who neglects his marital duty to his pious wife is a sinner.
Joshua b. Levi. *T: Yebamot,* 62b.

979.C.7 When a wife is ill-treated, she recalls her honeymoon.
Lam. R., 1.34.

979.C.8 If your wife is short, bend down and listen to her whisper.
Proverb. q Papa. *T: Baba Metzia,* 59a.

979.C.9 Beware of wronging your wife: she is easily hurt and her tears are ready.
Rab. *Ibid.*

979.C.10 A man should not quarrel with his wife to satisfy his parents.
Sefer Hasidim, #953, p. 234.

979.C.11 When asked why he constantly brought his wife presents, though she was continually tormenting him, Hiyya Rabba replied: They do enough for us, rearing our children and delivering us from sin!
Talmud: Yebamot, 63a.

979.C.12 Never be angry with your wife; if you put her off with your left hand, hurry and draw her back with your right hand.
Talmud: Sota, 47a.

979.C.13 Marital companionship must be loving and unconstrained.
Zohar, Gen., 49ab.

979.C.14 A man may not take his wife to another land without her consent.
Ibid., 79a.

979.D. Miscellaneous

979.D.1 Enjoy life with the wife you love.
Bible: Eccles., 9.9.

979.D.2 All wives will give honor to their husbands, great and small.
Bible: Esther, 1.20.

979.D.3 It is slavery and a disgrace if a wife support her husband.
Apocrypha: Ben Sira, 25.22.

979.D.4 No poet has yet sung the beautiful eyes of his own wife.
Boerne, *Kritiken,* 1824, #24.

979.D.5 An obedient wife commands her husband.
Disraeli, *Count Alarcos,* 1839.

979.D.6 It destroys one's nerves to be amiable every day to the same human being.
Disraeli, *Young Duke,* 1831.

979.D.7 Wives, honor your husbands; be their garland of roses!
Elijah b. Raphael, *Tzavaah*, 18C. AHE, 305.

979.D.8 A wife is mainly for beauty, and for having children.
Hiyya. *T: Ketubot*, 59b.

979.D.9 I have never called my wife "wife," but "home."
Jose b. Halafta. *T: Sabbath*, 118b.

979.D.10 One's wife is like oneself.
Joseph b. Nehunya. *T: Berakot*, 24a.

979.D.11 Manoah was an ignoramus: he followed his wife in everything.
Nahman b. Jacob. *T: Berakot*, 61a. Ref. to *Judg.* 13.1.

979.D.12 A man's wife is his compromise with the illusion of his first sweetheart.
G. J. Nathan, *Autobiography of an Attitude*, 1925, p. 271.

979.D.13 If the husband sits on a chair in the Garden of Eden, his wife is his footstool.
Peretz, *Sholom Bayis*, 1889. LP, 153.

979.D.14 Give your ear to all, your hand to friends, but your lips only to your wife.
Proverb (Yiddish).

979.D.15 A wife exalts her husband, and a wife casts him down.
Proverb (Yiddish).

979.D.16 Honor your wives that you may be enriched.
Raba. *T: Baba Metzia*, 59a.

979.D.17 A proper wife is she that does her husband's will.
Seder Eliyahu Rabbah, ch 10, ed Friedmann, 51.

979.D.18 Every man gets the wife he deserves.
Simeon b. Lakish. *T: Sota*, 2a.

979.D.19 Scholars should not be constantly in their wives' company, like cocks and hens.
Talmud: Berakot, 22a.

979.D.20 At the time of the Golden Calf, the women refused their golden ornaments for idolatry, therefore they rule over their husbands and all men are now hen-pecked.
Yalkut Reubeni. See *JQRo*, ii. 175.

980. WILL

980.1 God created man . . . and put him in the power of his will.
Apocrypha: Ben Sira, 15.14.

980.2 When Jews engage in Torah and good deeds, they control their will.
Banaah. *T: Aboda Zara*, 5b.

980.3 Man's will is the God of the universe.
Berdichevsky, *BaDerek*, 1922, i. 17. q HMH, 92.

980.4 It is the will that is the father to the deed.
Disraeli, *Alroy*, 1833, 1.1.

980.5 If you will, 'tis not a myth.
Herzl, Motto in *Altneuland*, 1902.

980.6 Skill is nil without a will.
Ibn Tibbon, *Tzavaah*, c. 1190.

980.7 The righteous are judged by the Good Will, the wicked by their Evil Will.
Jose HaGelili. *T: Berakot*, 61b.

980.8 Happy is he who conquers his will like a man [*Ps.* 112.1].
Joshua b. Levi. *T: Aboda Zara*, 19a.

980.9 All is possible to him who wills.
Morawczyk, *Minha Hadasha*, 1576.

980.10 Nothing can withstand the will.
Proverb.

980.11 Dare to investigate the sources of your will.
Rathenau. *Kunst und Leben*, Jan. 26, 1917.

980.12 The hand to break my will is not created yet!
Shneor, "Song of the Prophet," 1903. tr M. Samuel. *Reflex*, Aug. 1927, p. 111.

980.13 Will and understanding are one and the same.
Spinoza, *Ethics*, 1677, ii. Pr. 49, Corollary.

980.14 Bend our will that we may submit unto Thee.
Talmud: Berakot, 60b. DPB, ed Singer, 7.

980.15 I'll deny my will temporarily, that I may not lose my eternity.
Yalkut Shimoni, Proverbs, #947.

981. WILL OF GOD

981.1 Now, Israel, what doth the Lord thy God require of thee, but . . . to keep for thy good the commandments of the Lord.
Bible: Deut., 10.12f.

981.2 It hath been told thee, O man, what . . . the Lord requireth of thee: only to do justly, to love mercy, and to walk humbly with thy God.
Bible: Mic., 6.8.

981.3 Teach me to do Thy will.
Bible: Ps., 143.10.

981.4 Lord, . . . Thou knowest full well that our will is to do Thy will, and what prevents us? The yeast in the dough [the evil that works in us like ferment] and subjection to foreign powers. May it be Thy will to deliver us from their hand, that we may do Thy will with a perfect heart.
Alexandri. *T: Berakot,* 17a.

981.5 What He wills is done.
Apocrypha: Ben Sira, 43.26.

981.6 In all you propose, add the proviso, "if the Lord will."
Eliezer Halevi, *Tzavaah,* c. 1350. AHE, 213.

981.7 Make His will yours, so that He make your will His.
Gamaliel III. *Mishna: Abot,* 2.4.

981.8 When Jews do God's will, no nation has power over them. When they do not, He delivers them to the beasts among the low.
Johanan b. Zakkai. *T: Berakot,* 66b.

981.9 Be bold as a leopard, swift as an eagle, fleet as a deer, and strong as a lion to do the will of your Father in Heaven.
Judah b. Tema. *Mishna: Abot,* 5.20.

981.10 When God wills it, even a broom can shoot.
Mendelé, *BiYeme HaRaash,* 1895.

981.11 If Israel do God's will, they are as stars; if they do not, they are as dust.
Sifré, #47, Deut., ed Horovits, 105.

981.12 Men will pursue their questions from cause to cause, till at last they take refuge in the will of God—in other words, the sanctuary of ignorance.
Spinoza, *Ethics,* 1677, i. Appendix.

982. WILL AND TESTAMENT

982.1 The will of the dying must be carried out.
Meir. *T: Taanit,* 21a.

982.2 A father should arrange his estate and write a will.
Sefer Hasidim, 13C, #959, p. 236.

983. WINE

983.1 Wine cheers God and man.
Bible: Judg., 9.13. See *Ps.,* 10.15.

983.2 Wine is a mocker, strong drink is riotous.
Bible: Prov., 20.1

983.3 Wine . . . at last bites like a serpent and stings like a basilisk.
Ibid., 23.32.

983.4 Wine is an unreliable emissary: I sent it down to my stomach, and it went up to my head!
Al-Harizi, *Tahkemoni,* 13C, ch 3.

983.5 Show not your valor in wine: it has been the ruin of many.
Apocrypha: Ben Sira, 31.25.

983.6 Wine is as good as life to a man, if he drink in moderation.
Ibid., 31.27.

983.7 Wine turns the mind . . . to lust, and leads the eyes into error.
Apocrypha: Patriarchs, Judah, 14.1. See *I Esdras,* 3.18.

983.8 Wine is the cause of war and confusion.
Apocrypha: Patriarchs, Judah, 16.5.

983.9 Old wine is a comfort to old men.
Eleazar b. Pedat. *T: Megilla,* 16b.

983.10 Wine is a bad thing.
It makes you quarrel with your neighbor,
It makes you shoot at your landlord,
It makes you—*miss* him.
Gabrilowitsch. q CMH, 140.

983.11 Wine was created only to comfort mourners and requite sinners.
Hanan. *T: Sanhedrin,* 70a.

983.12 When wine enters, counsel leaves.
Hiyya Rabba. *T: Erubin,* 65a.

983.13 When wine goes in, the secret will out.
Hiyya Rabba. *T: Sanhedrin,* 38a.

983.14 Bitter is wine, but it sweetens all bitterness.
M. Ibn Ezra, *Selected Poems,* 17.

983.15 My wine is a stripling without sword or spear,
But he shall put to flight the host of my sorrows.
Ibid., 44.

983.16 Wine cooleth man in summer's heat,
And warmeth him in winter's sleet.
M. Ibn Ezra. q KJL, 204.

983.17 How can we waken a song or a laugh
When we find that we simply have nothing to quaff?
Ibn Gabirol, "Water Song." q CHH, 60.

983.18 Wine is the beginning of all sin.
Meiri. *Bet HaBehira*, to *Abot*, c. 1300.

983.19 Praised be Thou . . . who hast created the fruit of the vine.
Mishna: Berakot, 6.1.

983.20 Where there's wine, there's immorality.
Num. R., 10.3.

983.21 The wise becomes genial after a drink of wine.
Philo, *Noah's Work as a Planter*, 40.

983.22 Vinegar brings down the price of wine.
Proverb. q *Gen. R.*, 39.11.

983.23 Wine whets the appetite.
Raba. *T: Pesahim*, 107b.

983.24 Old wine is good for the stomach.
Talmud: Berakot, 51a. See *I Tim.*, 5.23.

983.25 One cup of wine is becoming to a woman; two are degrading.
Talmud: Ketubot, 65a.

983.26 Wine is at the head of all medicines.
Talmud: Baba Bathra, 58b.

984. WINGS

984.1 Hide me in the shadow of Thy wings.
Bible: Ps., 17.8.

984.2 On the wings of song.
Heine, *Lyric Interlude*, 1823, #9.

984.3 O that I might fly on eagles' wings!
Judah Halevi, *Selected Poems*, 19.

984.4 When the Holy One will renew His world, He will make wings like eagles' for the righteous.
Seder Eliyahu. q *T: Sanhedrin*, 92b.

985. WISDOM

985.1 Happy is the man who finds wisdom. . . . Her ways are ways of pleasantness, and all her paths are peace. She is a tree of life to them that lay hold on her.
Bible: Prov., 3.13, 17f.

985.2 The beginning of wisdom is: Get wisdom.
Ibid., 4.7.

985.3 Who finds me finds life.
Ibid., 8.35.

985.4 The fear of the Lord, that is wisdom.
Bible: Job, 28.28.

985.5 In much wisdom is much vexation.
Bible: Eccles., 1.18.

985.6 Wisdom is better than strength.
Ibid., 9.16. See 9.18.

985.7 He gives wisdom to the wise, and knowledge to them that know.
Bible: Dan., 2.21.

985.8 There is no wisdom more comprehensive, more ancient, and more exalted than that embodied in our Law.
Abravanel, *Rosh Amana*, (1505) 1861, p. 29a. See NDI 100.

985.9 Wisdom is the soul's natural food.
Anatoli, *Malmad HaTalmidim*, 1149.

985.10 Wisdom lifts the poor man's head, and sets him among princes.
Apocrypha: Ben Sira, 11.1.

985.11 Wisdom went forth to reside among men, and found no dwelling. Wisdom returned to her place, and took her seat among the angels.
Apocrypha: Enoch, 42.2.

985.12 The wisdom of the wise nought can take away. . . . Even among enemies it is a glory, and in a strange country a fatherland.
Apocrypha: Patriarchs, Levi, 13.7f.

985.13 Wisdom will not . . . dwell in a body enslaved by sin.
Apocrypha: Wisdom of Solomon, 1.4.

985.14 Wisdom is the spirit of human love.
Ibid., 1.6.

985.15 Wisdom's true beginning is desire of instruction, . . . and that brings near to God. So desire of wisdom promotes to a kingdom.
Apocrypha: Wisdom of Solomon, 6.17, 20.

985.16 Wisdom, properly used, is a remedy for every ill; but when misdirected, becomes an incurable disease.
Bahya, *Hobot HaLebabot*, 1040, 5.5.

985.17 Pain is the father, and love the mother, of wisdom.
Boerne, *Fragmente und Aphorismen*, 1840, #203.

985.18 Wisdom is the ability to do good and to abandon sin.
Gerondi, *Shaaré Teshuba*, 13C, 3.3.

985.19 Wisdom begets humility.
A. Ibn Ezra, *Commentary to Eccles.*, 8.1, 1167.

985.20 I will make the wisdom of the ancients my portion. . . .

When I dive into the sea of their
   knowledge,
I bring forth pearls to adorn my
   neck. . . .
They are light to mine eyes, they
   are music to mine ears,
They are honey to my palate,
   they are savor to my nostril.
M. Ibn Ezra, *Selected Poems,* 8f.

985.21 Wisdom is like fire: a little enlightens, much burns.
M. Ibn Ezra, *Shirat Yisrael,* (12C) 1924,
p. 37.

985.22 A short life with much wisdom is better than a long life with little wisdom.
Ibid., 113.

985.23 Wisdom is like gold ore, mixed with stones and dust.
Ibid., 119.

985.24 Seek wisdom from sceptics.
Ibn Gabirol, *Mibhar HaPeninim,* c. 1050,
#49.

985.25 There is no intellectual wisdom which in itself, without a belief in Providence, is able to save man and assure him bliss.
S. D. Luzzatto, *Yesodé HaTorah,* 1880,
p. 12.

985.26 The wisdom of this world is foolishness with God.
New Testament: I Cor., 3.19.

985.27 Wisdom has no kinship with a sophist's culture.
Philo, *Cherubim,* 3.

985.28 The mind is cleansed by wisdom.
Philo, *Special Laws,* i. 50.

985.29 The Chaldeans and Hebrews alone got wisdom as their destiny.
*Porphyry. q *JE,* iv. 108b.

985.30 With wisdom only, you don't go to market.
Proverb (Yiddish). BJS, #1572.

985.31 The aim of wisdom is penitence and good deeds.
Raba. *T: Berakot,* 17a.

985.32 Because God loved Wisdom, He adopted her as His daughter, and lovingly brought her up. Before He made heaven and earth, she was His delight . . . and He took counsel with her. . . . Then, because God loved man, He sent Wisdom to walk upon the earth, that her delightful employ be with man, who would choose her in order to survive unto great salvation.
Satanov, *Mishlé Asaf,* 1789. q HMH, 38.

985.33 Worldly wisdom means: take all things as much as possible seriously, but nothing too gravely.
Schnitzler, *Buch der Sprüche & Bedenken,* 1927, p. 228.

985.34 A king said to his favorite councilor, "Ask what you will and I shall grant it." The councilor asked for his daughter in marriage, knowing that thus all else will be his. Similarly, God asked Solomon [*I Kings* 3.5] what he would have, and Solomon asked for—Wisdom.
Simeon b. Halafta. *Eccles. R.,* 1.1.1.

985.35 Wisdom without fear of God is despicable.
Talmud: Tosefta Derek Eretz, 1.9.

985.36 Love is the best relationship, wisdom the best pedigree.
Zabara, *Sefer Shaashuim,* 13C, ch 7, ed Davidson, p. 75.

986. WISE

986.1 A wise man is strong.
Bible: Prov., 24.5.

986.2 They that are wise shall shine as the bright firmament.
Bible: Dan., 12.3.

986.3 A wise man is superior to a prophet.
Amemar. *T: Baba Bathra,* 12a.

986.4 Who is wise? He who learns from everybody.
Ben Zoma. *Mishna: Abot,* 4.1.

986.5 A tenacious memory, a quick perception, and other mental equipments enable men to acquire information; but to be a . . . "sage" . . . one must be in possession of a great soul.
Ginzberg, *Students, Scholars and Saints,* 1928, p. 242.

986.6 Who never acted foolishly,
He also ne'er was wise.
Heine, *Zum "Lazarus,"* 1854, 6.

986.7 Kings are the judges of the earth, and sages the judges of kings.
Ibn Gabirol, *Mibhar HaPeninim,* c. 1050,
#25.

986.8 Man is wise only while in search of wisdom; when he imagines he has attained it, he is a fool.
Ibid., #21.

986.9 A sage who was asked, "Why are you wiser than your friends," said, "Because I spent more on oil than they on wine."
Ibn Gabirol, *Mibhar HaPeninim,* c. 1050,
#16.

986.10 The wise knows what he tells, the fool tells what he knows.

Lazerov, *Enciklopedie fun Idishe Vitzen,* 1928, #416.

986.11 Just as the ideal type of the Christian, the sum of evangelical virtue, is the saint . . . so it might be said that the ideal type of Israel, he who climbed to the topmost rounds of Jacob's ladder, is the sage.

*Leroy-Beaulieu, *Israel Among the Nations,* 1895, p. 222.

986.12 Give us wisdom in place of a prophet, and endow us with a wise heart that we may understand Thy law and be at rest in it.

Maimon b. Joseph, *Letter of Consolation,* 1160.

986.13 A sage is more of an asset to a nation than its king.

Maimonides, *Commentary to Mishna: Horayot,* 3, end. 1168.

986.14 Anyone who follows a middle course is called a sage.

Maimonides, *Yad: Deot,* 1180, 1.4.

986.15 Let your house be a meeting place for the wise. Powder yourself in the dust of their feet, and avidly drink in their words.

Mishna: Abot, 1.4.

986.16 Seven characteristics distinguish the wise: he does not speak before his superior, does not interrupt, is not hasty to answer, asks and answers to the point, talks about first things first and about last things last, admits when he does not know, and acknowledges the truth.

Ibid., 5.7.

986.17 A sage has no house or kin or country, save virtue.

Philo, *Abraham,* 6.

986.18 Only the wise is free and a ruler, though he have ten thousand masters over his body.

Philo, *Prosperity and Exile of Cain,* 41.

986.19 Better a slap from the wise than a kiss from a fool.

Proverb (Yiddish). BJS, #506.

986.20 Rather with the wise in Gehenna than with a fool in Eden.

Ibid., #522.

986.21 Rather lose with the wise than win with a fool.

Ibid., #523.

986.22 Only those are called wise who do the will of the Holy One.

Sefer Hasidim, 13C, #13, p. 11.

986.23 When a sage dies, all are his kin, obliged to mourn.

Talmud: Sabbath, 105b.

986.24 Who is wise? He who foresees results.

Talmud: Tamid, 32a.

986.25 Better a hostile sage than a friendly fool.

Zabara, *Sefer Shaashuim,* 13C, ch 7.

986.26 A pupil who suggests new ideas to his master is a sage.

Zohar, Exod., 201a.

986.27 A man of discernment . . . knows both his own view and that of others.

Ibid.

987. WIT

987.1 There is a laughing anger, and we call it wit. There is a laughing wisdom, and we call it humor. And there is, blended of the two, a laughing banter, which we call satire.

O. Blumenthal, *Das zeite Gesicht,* 2d ed, 1898, Pref., 4f.

987.2 Understanding is bread, which satisfies; wit is spice, that makes it appetizing.

Boerne, *Der Narr im weissen Schwan,* ch 3.

987.3 Wit is the best safety valve modern man has evolved; the more civilization, the more repression, the more need there is for wit.

Brill, *Basic Writings of Sigmund Freud,* 1938, p. 21.

987.4 Wit . . . like champagne, not only sparkles, but is sweet.

Disraeli, *Young Duke,* 1831.

987.5 For wit and borrowers it is wholesome when they surprise us unannounced.

Heine, *English Fragments,* 1828, ch 10.

987.6 What preachers' admonitions and whole dissertations, composed with much seriousness and logical proof, cannot accomplish, is often accomplished by a little wit and satire.

Levinsky. *HaMelitz,* 1893, #156.

987.7 Jewish wit is the foundation and pinnacle of all wit.

Moszkowski. q *UJE,* x. 545b.

987.8 The Jews seized the weapon of wit, since they were interdicted the use of every other sort of weapon.

Saphir, *Literatur-Briefe.* SHW, iv. 81.

988. WOMAN
988.A. Enigma

988.A.1 The mystery of women is largely the product of the romantic imagination of men.

Angoff. *American Mercury*, Sept. 1950.

988.A.2 Would you know a woman? Her soul has seven seals.

S. J. Imber, "Woman." LGP, 251.

988.B. Character

988.B.1 A woman of valor who can find? Her price is far above rubies.

Bible: Prov., 31.10.

988.B.2 One man among a thousand have I found; but a woman among all those have I not found.

Bible: Eccles., 7.28.

988.B.3 Women are . . . not so well able to comprehend a thing which is appreciable only by the intellect.

Agrippa I, letter to Caligula, 40. KTJ, 58.

988.B.4 Any wickedness, only not the wickedness of a woman!

Apocrypha: Ben Sira, 25.13.

988.B.5 No wrath above that of a woman.

Ibid., 25.15.

988.B.6 A silent woman is a gift from the Lord.

Ibid., 26.14.

988.B.7 Woman is as intelligent as man, but less capable of emotion.

Bergson, *Two Sources of Morality and Religion*, 1935, p. 36.

988.B.8 Woman constitutes the horizon of men, where heaven and earth meet. Angel and devil get along there as nowhere else. The gentlest, noblest woman possesses at least one full coal-pan from hell, and there is none so wicked as not to bear in her one little nook of Paradise.

Boerne, *Fastenpredigt über die Eifersucht*.

988.B.9 A storm, however sudden, is yet preceded by a warning breeze; but how can one guard against a woman's temper?

Boerne, *Der Narr im weissen Schwan*, ch 2.

988.B.10 Why is a man more easily pacified than a woman? Because man was made out of soft earth, and woman out of a hard rib.

Dosetai b. Yannai. *T: Nidda*, 31b. See *Gen. R.*, 17.7

988.B.11 A woman craves for jewelry.

Eleazar. *T: Ketubot*, 65a.

988.B.12 A woman will uncover a pot to see what her neighbor's cooking.

Eliezer b. Philo. *Mishna: Tohorot*, 7.9.

988.B.13 No woman ever faithful hold Unless she ugly be and old.

Immanuel, *Mahberot*. q KJL, 220.

988.B.14 Women are inquisitive.

Isaac. *Yalkut, Esther*, #1049.

988.B.15 Women are a distinct race.

Joseph. *T: Sabbath*, 62a.

988.B.16 Woman was endowed with more intelligence than man.

Judah HaNasi. *T: Nidda*, 45b. See *Gen. R.*, 18.1.

988.B.17 When God was about to create Eve, He considered well from what part of Adam to create her. Said He: "I will not use the head, lest she be swell-headed; not the eye, lest she be a coquette; not the ear, lest she be an eavesdropper; not the mouth, lest she be a gossip; not the heart, lest she be prone to jealousy; not the hand, lest she be light-fingered; not the foot, lest she be a gadabout; I shall make her from a hidden part of man, that she be modest." Yet in spite of all the precautions, she is subject to all these faults.

Levi. *Gen. R.*, 18.2. Cf Chaucer, *The Parsones Tale*, 79; A. Lincoln, *Adam and Eve's Wedding Song*.

988.B.18 Women are fond of talking.

Nathan. *T: Berakot*, 48b.

988.B.19 Women are more firm than men.

Nathan, *Sifré*, #133, to *Num.*, 27.4.

988.B.20 Woman has a thousand souls.

Proverb. q Lipperheide, *Spruchwörterbuch*, 986.

988.B.21 Woman prefers a little with levity to much with gravity.

Proverb (Yiddish). q Dukes, *Rabbin. Blumenlese*, 1844, 235.

988.B.22 Women's styles may change, but their designs remain the same.

Rolnick. q *Look*, Aug. 9, 1955, p. 13.

988.B.23 Women are tender-hearted.

Shila. *T: Megilla*, 14b.

988.B.24 Women are fickle.

Simeon b. Yohai. *T: Sabbath*, 33b.

988.B.25 Every woman has a mind of her own.

Talmud: Berakot, 45b.

988.C. Virtue

988.C.1 A virtuous woman is a crown to her husband.
Bible: Prov., 12.4.

988.C.2 Israel's deliverance was in reward for righteous women.
Avira, or Akiba. *T: Sota,* 11b.

988.C.3 In the generation of the wilderness, the women built up the fences which the men broke down.
Num. R., 21.10. See *PRE,* ch 45.

988.C.4 Women are more prompt than men in fulfilling the commands.
Exod. R., 28.2.

988.C.5 Man's virtues are chiefly those of power, woman's of patience.
Harrison, *Religion of a Modern Liberal,* 1931, p. 114.

988.C.6 Ugliness in a woman is already half way to virtue.
Heine, *Gedanken und Einfälle,* 1869, #6.

988.C.7 When you find an all-white raven, you'll find also a virtuous woman.
Huppat Eliyahu Rabbah. EOM, 171a.

988.C.8 The best protection of a woman's virtue is a homely face.
Immanuel, *Mahberot,* c. 1300, ch 4.

988.C.9 Virtue dwells rarely in the bright-eyed and fair, but in wrinkled old crones with silvery hair.
Ibid. q CHH, 93. Cf *JQRo,* iv. 78.

988.C.10 The glory of woman is in the home.
Maimonides, *Tzavaah.* q CPP, #1430.

988.C.11 Nowadays, all Jewesses are women of surpassing merit.
Mordecai, 13C; Maharil, 14C. q AJL, 155.

988.C.12 Women lie even when they are silent.
Proverb. q Lipperheide, *Spruchwörterbuch,* 986.

988.C.13 A woman is easy to persuade.
Proverb. *Ibid.*

988.D. Form

988.D.1 Daughters are corner-pillars carved after the fashion of a palace.
Bible: Ps. 144.12.

988.D.2 Alas, all women are as frail as any porcelain.
Heine, *Atta Troll,* 1841, ch 26.

988.D.3 God built Eve in the shape of a store-house, wide below and narrow above, that she may hold comfortably her produce.
Hisda. *T: Erubin,* 18b.

988.E. Beauty

988.E.1 She will be known by her eyelids.
Apocrypha: Ben Sira, 26.9.

988.E.2 Israel's daughters are all beautiful, only poverty disfigures them.
Ishmael b. Elisha. *Mishna: Nedarim,* 9.10.

988.E.3 The Lord . . . took the finest of materials in His possession: the white of lilies for cheeks, the red of coral for lips, the blue of heaven for eyes, the black of ravens for hair; added the grace of loveliness, kindness and tenderness, mixed all these ingredients together, and out of it came forth beautiful Adelle!
Mendelé, *Dos Vintshfinger,* 1865.

988.E.4 A woman is permitted to make her toilet during the festival week, to plait and part her hair, treat her eyes with kohl, manicure her nails, and apply rouge to her face. Said Huna b. Hinena: Only the young do that. Said Hisda: Even your mother does it, even your grandmother, even a woman on the brink of the grave.
Talmud: Moed Katan, 9b.

988.E.5 At times a woman of pleasant homeliness is more attractive than a woman of unpleasant beauty.
Twerski, "Hegyonot." *HaPoel HaTzair,* 1951, #38.

988.F. Lure

988.F.1 I find more bitter than death the woman, whose heart is snares and nets, and her hands are as bands.
Bible: Eccles., 7.26.

988.F.2 Many have perished through the beauty of woman, and her love has been as a fire that burns.
Apocrypha: Ahikar, 2.72.

988.F.3 A woman's beauty brightens the countenance, and excels every delight of the eye. When she possesses also a soothing tongue, her husband is not like other sons of men.
Apocrypha: Ben Sira, 36.22f.

988.F.4 Better a man's wickedness than a woman's blandishments.
Apocrypha: Ben Sira, 42.14.

988.F.5 Her sandal ravished his eye, her beauty took his soul captive.
Apocrypha: Judith, 16.9.

988.F.6 Beauty has beguiled you, base passion!
Apocrypha: Susanna, 56.

988.F.7 A wise man saw a hunter conversing with a woman, and he remarked: Take care that you don't become the game.
Hasdai, *Ben HaMelek VeHaNazir,* c. 1230, ch 30.

988.F.8 Youthful one! Foolish one!
Poor little simpleton!
In the flame rushes he,
Little bee! Little bee!
Now the flame flickers high,
In the flame he must die:
'Ware of the maidens, then,
Sons of men! Sons of men!
Heine, *Early Poems: The Lesson.*

988.F.9 Yes, woman is a dangerous being.
Heine, *Letters on Germany,* 1846, #1.

988.F.10 A wife solicits in silence, a husband by speech; and this is a fine trait in woman.
Isaac b. Abdimi. *T: Erubin,* 100b.

988.F.11 Follow a lion rather than a woman.
Johanan b. Nappaha. *T: Erubin,* 18b.

988.F.12 Beautiful gazelle, with golden hair,
How like a lion thou thy prey dost tear!
Judah Halevi, *Shirim,* 131.

988.F.13 Cursed be the woman who has a husband and strives not to be attractive.
Meir of Rothenburg, *Responsa,* #199.

988.F.14 A glance at a woman's soul is like
A glance at heaven's realm.
Rodenberg, "Die reinen Frauen," 1864.

988.F.15 How miserable women are in their perpetual, unconscious bluff, with their useless primming and resort to every outer fluff.
Varnhagen, *Briefe,* 1877.

988.G. Love

988.G.1 A woman that is loved always has success.
Baum, *Grand Hotel,* (1929) 1931, p. 132.

988.G.2 One heavenly bliss alone does woman know:

The bliss to love and be loved here below.
M. Beer, *Der Paria,* (1823) 1829, Act 1.

988.G.3 A woman lives only when she loves; she finds herself only when she loses herself in a man.
Boerne, *Fastenpredigt über die Eifersucht.*

988.G.4 A woman prefers poverty with love to luxury without it.
Joshua. *Mishna: Sota,* 3.4.

988.G.5 They say there are sixty-seven different ways in which a woman can like a man.
Sutro, *Walls of Jericho,* 1904, Act. 1.

988.G.6 Is it proper for a good Jewish mother to concern herself about love? Love is revolting idolatry. A Jewess may love only God, her husband, and her children.
A. Weill. q KJL, 123.

988.H. Power

988.H.1 Every wise woman builds her house, but the foolish plucks it down with her own hands.
Bible: Prov., 14.1.

988.H.2 Women have dominion over you: do ye not labor and toil, and give and bring all to women?
Apocrypha: I Esdras, 4.22. See 4.26.

988.H.3 Women bear rule over king and beggar alike.
Apocrypha: Patriarchs, Judah, 15.5.

988.H.4 Today, since men of the world are killing themselves with work and have neither time nor taste for leisured activities, the leadership in things mental and spiritual is in good society monopolized entirely by women.
Benda, *Belphégor,* (1919) 1929, p. 123.

988.H.5 A woman's wisdom is only at her spindle.
Eliezer b. Hyrcanus. *T: Yoma,* 66b.

988.H.6 It all depends on the woman.
Gen. R., 17.7.

988.H.7 O woman! woman! what a benefactor to his race is that man who frees us from your chains!
Heine, *Baths of Lucca,* 1828, ch 10.

988.H.8 Every woman has her weapons on her.
Iddi. *T: Yebamot,* 115a.

988.H.9 It is the way of men to follow the opinion of women.
Phineas. *Pirké de R. Eliezer,* ch 41.

988.H.10 A woman who marries assumes her husband's name, even as a victor assumes that of the battle he won.

Saphir, *Warum giebt es kein Narrenhaus.* SHW, i. 366.

988.H.11 God told Moses to speak first to the women and then to the men [*Exod.* 19.3], "because at Creation, when I commanded Adam, Eve upset the world."

Tahlifa of Caesarea. *Exod. R.,* 28.2.

988.I. Attitude to Woman

988.I.1 From a woman did sin originate, and because of her we all must die.

Apocrypha: Ben Sira, 25.24.

988.I.2 Who shall despise this people, that have such women!

Apocrypha: Judith, 10.19.

988.I.3 Meddle not with affairs of womankind.

Apocrypha: Patriarchs, Reuben, 3.10.

988.I.4 A female friend, amiable, clever, and devoted, is a possession more valuable than parks and palaces; and without such a muse, few men can succeed in life, none can be content.

Disraeli, *Henrietta Temple,* 1837.

988.I.5 Talk to women as much as you can. This is the best school.

Disraeli, *Vivian Grey,* 1827.

988.I.6 Nothing is of so much . . . use to a young man . . . as to be well criticized by women. It is impossible to get rid of those thousand bad habits which we pick up in boyhood, without this.

Ibid.

988.I.7 Let the Law be burned rather than entrusted to a woman.

Eliezer b. Hyrcanus. *Mishna: Sota,* 3.4.

988.I.8 Let there be from now on no distinction between duties for men and women unless flowing from the natural laws governing the sexes; no assumption of the spiritual minority of woman.

A. Geiger. *WZJT,* 1837. q PRM, 473.

988.I.9 The Bible is the only literature in the world up to our own century which looks at women as human beings, no better and no worse than men. . . . After a long acquaintance with the remarkable ladies of the romancers and poets of other lands, it is refreshing to stand on firm ground with the author of the last chapter of *Proverbs,* . . . who had never an idea that woman was the lesser man or some bright angelic visitant.

Hamilton, Spokesmen for God, 1936, 1949, p. 99f.

988.I.10 As long as woman regards the Bible as the charter of her rights, she will be the slave of man. The Bible was not written by a woman. Within its lids there is nothing but humiliation and shame for her.

Ingersoll, Liberty of Man, Woman and Child, 1877.

988.I.11 If our wives are not prophetesses, they are daughters of prophetesses and of great men, and one may rely on their customs.

Isaac b. Samuel HaZaken, 12C. q GGE, i. 232.

988.I.12 A lady asked why God acted like a thief, stealing a rib from Adam while he was asleep. Jose replied: If someone gave you secretly an ounce of silver and you returned publicly twelve ounces, would you call that stealing?

Jose b. Halafta. *Gen. R.,* 17.7. Cf *T: Sanhedrin,* 39a. Attr. also to Imma Shalom, sister of Gamaliel II.

988.I.13 Engage not in too much conversation with women.

Jose b. Johanan. *Mishna: Abot,* 1.5. See *Erubin,* 53b.

988.I.14 Woman, says the Law, is in all things inferior to man. Let her accordingly be submissive, not for humiliation, but that she may be directed; for authority has been given by God to man.

Josephus, *Against Apion,* ii. 24.

988.I.15 Praised be Thou . . . who hast not made me a woman. This is said daily, for a woman is exempt from many of the commandments.

Judah b. Ilai. *Tosefta: Berakot,* 7.18.

988.I.16 . . . who hast made me according to Thy will.

Corresponding benediction for women. *DPB,* ed Singer, 6. Abudraham, *Hibbur Perush HaBerakot,* 1340.

988.I.17 Man, waging the battle for existence, fighting to provide for his family, and his wife, remaining at home to fulfill her household duties, together must share alike.

Kagan, on *I Sam.* 30.24. See YSS. 227.

988.I.18 Man was not created for the woman, but woman for the man.

New Testament: I Cor., 11.9.

550

988.I.19 Moses calls sense Woman, suggesting Mind as her husband.
Philo, *Fugitives,* 34.

988.I.20 Scripture made woman equal to man in respect to penalties.
Rab. Ishmael School. *T: Pesahim,* 43a.

988.I.21 A man killed by a woman was no man.
Raba. *T: Baba Metzia,* 97a. See *Judg.,* 9.54.

988.I.22 Man prefers men to women [in distributing property], but the Creator shows equal consideration to all.
Sifré, Num., #133. See *Num.,* 27.7.

988.I.23 Adam was created from the dust and Eve from Adam; but henceforth, it shall be "in our image" [*Gen.* 1.26]: not man without woman, nor woman without man, and neither without the Holy Spirit.
Simlai. *Gen. R.,* 8.9. See *I Cor.* 11.11f.

989. WONDER

989.1 What hath God wrought!
Bible: Num., 23.23. First telegram, sent from Washington to Baltimore, May 24, 1844.

989.2 One who has never been bewildered, who has never looked upon life and his own existence as phenomena which require answers and yet, paradoxically, for which the only answers are new questions, can hardly understand what religious experience is.
Fromm, *Psychoanalysis and Religion,* 1950, p. 94.

989.3 Wonder, rather than doubt, is the root of knowledge.
Heschel, *Man Is Not Alone,* 1951, p. 11.

989.4 The greatest wonder is that true wonders are so common.
Karpeles, *Jewish Literature,* 1895, p. 140.

989.5 Where all walk on stilts nobody will stop to wonder.
Koestler, *Thieves in the Night,* 1946, p. 153.

989.6 Be open-eyed to the great wonders of nature, familiar though they be. But men are more wont to be astonished at the sun's eclipse than at its unfailing rise.
Orhot Tzaddikim, 15C, see Hertz, *DPB,* 993.

990. WORD

990.1 I am not a man of words.
Bible: Exod., 4.10.

990.2 Pleasant words are as a honeycomb, sweet to the soul, and health to the bones.
Bible: Prov., 16.24.

990.3 Who spares his words has knowledge.
Ibid., 17.27.

990.4 A word fitly spoken is like apples of gold in settings of silver.
Bible: Prov., 25.11.

990.5 How forcible are right words!
Bible: Job, 6.25.

990.6 Do you hold words to be an argument, but speeches of a desperate one to be wind?
Ibid., 6.26.

990.7 Let thy words be few.
Bible: Eccles., 5.1.

990.8 A fool multiplies words.
Ibid., 10.14. See *Job.* 35.16, 38.2.

990.9 The words of the wise are as goads, and as nails well fastened are those that are composed in collections.
Bible: Eccles., 12.11.

990.10 Ye wise, be heedful of your words.
Abtalion. *Mishna: Abot,* 1.11.

990.11 He who puts devices in the heart, puts words in the mouth.
Agnon, *Shebuat Emunim,* 1943.

990.12 A plurality of words does not necessarily represent a plurality of things.
Albo, *Ikkarim,* 1428, 2.9. tr Husik, ii. 51.

990.13 There is a good word which is better than a gift.
Apocrypha: Ben Sira, 18.17.

990.14 The words of the wise are weighed in the balance.
Ibid., 21.25.

990.15 You make a bolt for your silver and gold; make a balance and weight for your words.
Ibid., 28.25.

990.16 Issue no base coin from your lips, weigh your words in the balance of your judgment.
Asher b. Yehiel, *Hanhaga,* c.1320. AHE, 120.

990.17 With words we govern men.
Disraeli, *Contarini Fleming,* 1832, 1.

990.18 Let your words be pleasant with the children of men.
Epstein, *Kitzur Shné Luhot HaBrit,* (1683) 1698, 8a.

990.19 Spinning words, we are much like the spider spinning its web out of its own body. We, however, unlike the spider, may be enmeshed in our own web.

Goldberg, *The Wonder of Words,* 1938, p. 298.

990.20 Pleasant words—can they satisfy the hungry?

Hasdai, *Ben HaMelek VeHaNazir,* c. 1230, Introduction.

990.21 If the word lives, dwarfs may carry it; if it is dead, no giant can uphold it.

Heine, *Germany from Luther to Kant,* 1834.

990.22 When the arrow has left the bow-string it no longer belongs to the archer, and when the word has left the lips it is no longer controlled by the speaker.

Heine, *Germany,* Pref. to 2d ed, 1852.

990.23 Respect yourself in your purest emanation, your word.

S. R. Hirsch, *Nineteen Letters,* (1836), #11, p. 112.

990.24 Words are like bodies, and meanings like souls.

A. Ibn Ezra, *Commentary,* to *Exod.* 20.1.

990.25 A word without thought is like a foot without sinew.

M. Ibn Ezra, *Selected Poems,* 92.

990.26 Wounds heal, but not words.

J. Kimhi, *Commetary* to *Prov.* 28.

990.27 Keep firmly to your word.

Maimonides, *Shaaré HaMusar.* See *JQRo,* iii. 452.

990.28 Where the rabbi's word is, there he himself is.

Mendel of Kotzk. q BTH, ii. 271.

990.29 He who punished the generations of the flood and of the dispersion will punish him who does not stand by his word.

Mishna: Baba Metzia, 4.2.

990.30 The more words the more foolishness.

Mordecai b. Judah Lev, *Maamar Mordecai,* 1719, to *Prov.*

990.31 All words are in a sense tombs of a forgotten past.

Morrison, *Wonderful Words,* 1954.

990.32 By your words will ye be justified, and by your words will ye be condemned.

New Testament: Matt., 12.37.

990.33 The word once spoken cannot return.

Philo, *Change of Names,* 43.

990.34 Words should be weighed, not counted.

Proverb (Yiddish). BJS, #1263.

990.35 A wise word is no substitute for a piece of herring or a bag of oats.

Sholom Aleichem, *Tevyé the Milkman.* q SWS, 10.

990.36 Verbal wrong is worse than monetary wrong.

Simeon b. Yohai. *T: Baba Metzia,* 58b.

990.37 Words should be clean and tough
    as cobble-stones,
    That simple people, in the market-place,
    Should grip them with their feet and never stumble.

Stampfer, *Jerusalem Has Many Faces,* 1950, p. 89.

990.38 One word comes and cancels another.

Talmud: Gittin, 32b.

990.39 Judge your words before you utter them.

Talmud: Derek Eretz, 2.

990.40 Words neither kill nor quicken.

Talmud: Semahot Zutarti. q Caspi, *Yoré Deah,* ch 13. q AHE, 151; *JQRo,* iii. 320.

990.41 Words . . . conceal one's thought as much as they reveal it; and the uttered words of philosophers, at their best and fullest, are nothing but floating buoys which signal the presence of submerged unuttered thoughts.

Wolfson, *Philo,* 1948, i. 107.

991. WORD OF GOD

991.1 Thy words are truth.

Bible: II Sam., 7.28. Cf *Ps.* 119.160.

991.2 The word of our God shall stand for ever.

Bible: Isa., 40.8.

991.3 I will send a famine in the land, not a famine of bread . . . but of hearing the words of the Lord.

Bible: Amos, 8.11.

991.4 Thy word is a lamp unto my feet, and a light unto my path.

Bible: Ps., 119.105.

991.5 They bound it with phylacteries round heart and head; they fastened it to their doors; they opened and closed the day with it; as sucklings they learned the

Word, and they died with the Word on their lips. From the Word they drew the strength to endure the piled-up afflictions of their way. Pale and secretive they smiled over the might of Edom, over its fury and the madness of its past works and its future plans. All that would pass; what remained was the Word.

Feuchtwanger, *Power*, 1925, p. 165f.

991.6 "Is not My word like a hammer that breaks the rock?" [*Jer.* 23.29]. As the hammer's blow yields many sparks, so each word from the Holy One split into seventy different tongues.

Ishmael School. *T: Sabbath.* 88b.

991.7 "By the word of the Lord were the heavens made" [*Ps.* 33.6]: not by labor or toil, but only by a word!

Judah b. Simeon. *Gen. R.*, 3.2.

991.8 The words of God are pure; they are more precious than rubies. They are wrapped up in hearts, they are bound up in souls.

Judah Halevi, tr N. Salaman, 144.

991.9 Some believe that God commands an action in words consisting, like ours, of letters and sounds. . . . All this is the work of the imagination, in fact, identical with evil inclination.

Maimonides, *Guide to the Perplexed*, 1190, 2.12.

991.10 In the beginning was the word of God.

New Testament: John, 1.1.

991.11 "All the people saw the voice" [*Exod.* 20.15]. The voice of God is visible, because it speaks not in words but in deeds.

Philo, *Decalogue*, 11.

991.12 Praised be Thou . . . by whose word the twilight comes.

Talmud: Berakot, 12a. *DPB*, ed Singer, 96.

992. WORLD

992.1 I am a sojourner in the earth.

Bible: Ps., 119.19. See *I Chron.*, 29.15.

992.2 Who speaks of worldly matters and religious matters as though they were distinct, is a heretic.

Baal Shem. q SSJ, i. 28.
P. Shapiro. q BTH, i. 134.

992.3 The world is like a house, with the sky as a ceiling, the earth spread out like a carpet, the stars arrayed like lamps, . . . and man its master.

Bahya, *Hobot HaLebabot*, 1040, 1.6.

992.4 In this world, man is a prisoner.

Ibid., 6.5.

992.5 The world is like a fair: people gather for a while, then part; some profit and rejoice, others lose and grieve.

Ibid., 8.3.13.

992.6 Renounce not [this] world; it gives provisions for the eternal world.

Ibid.

992.7 A heart occupied by love of the world has no room for the love of God.

Ibid., 10, Introduction.

992.8 The world is a stormy sea . . . and Time forms a frail bridge over it. . . . Intoxicated with the wine of your vanity, you sway hither and thither, and fall into the terrifying abyss.

Bedersi. *Behinat HaOlam*, c.1310, ch 8.

992.9 To me the whole world is one gallows.

Bialik, "O Heaven, You Must Pray for Me," 1904.

992.10 The world is a mirror: what looks in looks out. It returns only what you lend it.

Boerne, *Aus meinem Tagebuch*, April 29, 1830.

992.11 What a man does now and here with holy intent is no less important, no less true—being a . . . link with divine being—than the life in the world to come.

Buber, *The Way of Man*, 1950, p. 44.

992.12 The grandeur of the world is always in accordance with the grandeur of the mind that contemplates it. The good finds here his paradise, the bad partakes here already of his hell.

Heine, *Gedanken und Einfälle*, 1869, #2.

992.13 We live in a divine world.

S. R. Hirsch, *Nineteen Letters*, (1836), #3, p. 26.

992.14 A hero is he who despises this world, and a weakling is he who honors it.

M. Ibn Ezra, *Shirat Yisrael*, (12C) 1924, p. 88.

992.15 The world is like a woman of
      folly. . . .
   She speaks sweet words, but
      verily
   Under her tongue is a snare.

M. Ibn Ezra, *Selected Poems*, p. 47.

992.16 Reject the world, that enriches to
      impoverish,

And exalts the station of men to
cast them down,
That multiplies their children to
diminish them, . . .
Leaving not one to remain or
escape.
Ibid., 57.

992.17 Man is like one who flees from
his enemies and is surrounded by wild
beasts. He who understands the world will
not rejoice in good fortune, nor grieve
at ill fortune.
Ibn Gabirol, *Mibhar HaPeninim,* c.1050,
#510. See HMP, #43.

992.18 The world is an enemy cloaked
as a friend. . . . Divorce from this world is
betrothal to the next world.
Immanuel, *Mahberot,* c.1330, ch 19.

992.19 This world is like an antecham-
ber to the next. Prepare yourself here that
you may be admitted to the banquet hall
there.
Jacob. *Mishna: Abot,* 4.16.

992.20 Judaism claims for the ideal the
whole domain of the actual; it has an-
nexed the world, and established there the
kingdom of heaven.
Joseph, *The Ideal in Judaism,* 1893, p. 7.

992.21 A servant of God . . . loves the
world and long life, because it affords him
opportunities to earn the world to come.
Judah Halevi, *Cuzari,* c.1135, 3.1.

992.22 We are Nihilistic thoughts,
thoughts of suicide, that have arisen in
the mind of God. . . . Our world is only
a practical joke of God, like a bad day.
Kafka.

992.23 The world is an expensive hotel:
you pay dearly for each pleasure.
Lipkin. q KTH, i. 270.

992.24 The world gnaws away your life,
day and night.
Maimon b. Joseph, *Letter of Consolation,*
1160.

992.25 There is nothing in this entire
world for the sake of which it is worth
becoming obligated to a fellow-man.
Mendel of Kotzk. q CRK, 3.2, p. 132.

992.26 We are today more exercised
about our life with God on earth than on
what will happen to us after . . . death.
Montefiore, *Liberal Judaism,* 1903, p. 56.

992.27 My kingdom is not of this world.
New Testament: John, 18.36. See *James,*
4.4.

992.28 There are some who admire the
world rather than the world's maker, and
pronounce it to be without beginning.
Philo, *Creation,* 2.

992.29 The whole world is one town.
Proverb. ATJF, p. 640.

992.30 The righteous servant of God
loves the life of this world merely because
it serves as a step-ladder to the next world.
Saadia, *Emunot VeDeot,* 933, 10.11, tr
Rosenblatt, 387.

992.31 Take in all you can of food and
drink, since the world from which we must
depart is like a wedding-feast.
Samuel. *T: Erubin,* 54a.

992.32 If in our world there are vales
of tears, there are hillsides also of joy and
laughter and peaks of splendor shining in
the sun.
H. Samuel, *Belief and Action,* 1937, p.
107.

992.33 Life is good and a gracious gift
of God. To love God one need not hate the
world. Life should not be feared or contemned or renounced, but sanctified and
enjoyed through wholesome living in
which the whole of man—body, mind and
soul—are fulfilled.
Silver, address, H.U.C., June 7, 1952.

992.34 The world rests on three things:
justice, truth and peace.
Simeon b. Gamaliel II. *Mishna: Abot,*
1.18. See *Zech.* 8.16.

992.35 The three are really one, for
when justice is done, truth prevails and
peace is established.
Talmud J: Taanit, 4.2.

992.36 The world is based on three
things: on Torah, worship, and loving-
kindness.
Simeon the Just. *Mishna: Abot,* 1.2.

992.37 When Simeon b. Yohai and his
son Eleazar emerged from their twelve-
year confinement in a cave, they saw men
plowing and sowing, and they exclaimed:
"These people forsake life eternal and give
themselves to things temporal!" Whatever
they cast their eyes upon was immediately
burnt up. Then a heavenly voice called
out: "Did you come forth to destroy My
world? Return to your cave!"
Talmud: Sabbath, 33b.

992.38 Let all the world be one Jerusalem!
I. M. Wise. *American Israelite,* Aug. 31,
1866.

992.39 Ah, I wish I could get you to see with the eyes of the great rabbis and sages in Israel. . . . Nothing on God's earth common or purposeless. Everything chanting the great song of God's praise!
Zangwill, *Children of the Ghetto*, 1892, ii. ch 2, p. 343.

992.40 This world is like the night.
Zera, or Joseph. *T: Baba Metzia*, 83b. See M. H. Luzzatto, *Mesillat Yesharim*, ch 3, p. 25.

993. WORM

993.1 Wherever the worm turns, he is still a worm.
Hoffenstein, *Pencil in the Air*, 1923, p. 147.

993.2 At night a glowing coal, in the morning but a worm.
Judah b. Simeon. *Pesikta Rabbati*, ch 33, 151b.

993.3 I am a rainworm, buried deep
Among the oozing, slimy things,
Yet of an eagle's nest I dream,
And eagle's wings.
Peretz, "I Am a Rainworm," 1900 tr J. Robbins, (LGP, 83).

993.4 The worm regards its cauliflower as the world.
Sanders, *366 Sprüche*, 1892, #314.

993.5 The worm in the radish thinks there's nothing sweeter.
Sholom Aleichem, *Menahem Mendel: London*, 1892, #8.

994. WORRY

994.1 Fret not thyself, it tends only to evil-doing.
Bible: Ps., 37.8.

994.2 Care in the heart of a man bows it down, but a good word makes it glad.
Bible: Prov., 12.25.

994.3 Remove vexation from your heart.
Bible: Eccles., 11.10. See 7.3.

994.4 You may not be here tomorrow, and you will have worried about a world which is not yours.
Apocrypha: Ben Sira. q *T: Yebamot*, 63b.

994.5 Let not anxiety enter your heart, for it has killed many strong men.
Apocrypha: Ben Sira, 30.23, as q Abayé. *T: Sanhedrin* 100b.

994.6 Anxiety brings on old age prematurely.
Ibid., 30.24.

994.7 From the day man comes forth from his mother's womb, to the day he returns to the mother of all living: preoccupation and anxiety and watchfulness for the future—from him who sits in exultation on a throne to him who is clothed with dust and ashes.
Apocrypha: Ben Sira, 40.1-3.

994.8 Anxiety is the worst demon in life.
B. Auerbach, *Waldfried*, 1874.

994.9 You don't get ulcers from what you eat. You get them from what's eating you.
V. Baum. q Leon Gutterman. JTA, 1952.

994.10 Care is a god, invisible but omnipotent. It steals the bloom from the cheek and lightness from the pulse; it takes away the appetite, and turns the hair grey.
Disraeli, *Alroy*, 1833, 5.5.

994.11 Anxiety destroys our figure.
Disraeli, *Young Duke*, 1831.

994.12 Oh man, why worry and pry?—
The Past is gone,
The Future yet to come,
The Present as a twinkle of the eye—
Then, worry, why?
Hahn, *Yosif Ometz*, (1723) 1928, p. 294f. q GIS, 179.

994.13 He who worries about this world is like him who pushes his finger against the compartment wall of his train to make it go faster.
J. Y. Hurwitz. q GIS, 87.

994.14 Worry over what has not occurred is a serious malady.
Ibn Gabirol, *Mibhar HaPeninim*, c. 1050, #140.

994.15 Drink poison rather than worry.
Ibid., #141.

994.16 All worries are forbidden, except worry about worrying.
M. Jaffe. q Kleinman, *Or Yesharim*, 8. q BTH, ii. 154.
Lipkin. q KTH, i. 272.

994.17 When you are annoyed by something you could not avoid, don't aggravate it by useless worry.
Lefin, *Heshbon HaNefesh*, 1809.

994.18 Have you ever seen an undomesticated beast or bird with a craft? Yet they are sustained without anxiety. Now, if they who were created to serve me, get along thus, surely I, who was created to serve my Master, should make a living without anxiety!

Mishna: Kiddushin, 4.14. Cf *Matt.*, 6.26. See Simeon b. Eleazar. *T: Kiddushin,* 82b.

994.19 These are worries about unlaid eggs.

Proverb. q Lipperheide, *Spruchwörterbuch*, 810.

994.20 All worry: some because their pearls are too sparse, others because the beans in their soup are too sparse.

Proverb (Yiddish). BJS, #1421.

995. WORSHIP

995.1 Bring no more vain oblations.

Bible: Isa., 1.13.

995.2 I cannot endure iniquity along with solemn assembly.

Ibid. See *Amos*, 5.21.

995.3 We shall render for bullocks the offering of our lips.

Bible: Hos., 14.3.

995.4 It is good to declare Thy lovingkindness in the morning and Thy faithfulness in the night seasons.

Bible: Ps., 92.3.

995.5 Worship the Lord in the beauty of holiness; tremble before Him, all the earth.

Ibid., 96.9.

995.6 One moment of worship, motivated by joy and love, is better than a hundred fasts.

Baal Shem. q Gutman, *Derek HaEmuna uMaasé Rab*, 96.

995.7 Thou wilt not be appeased by a multitude of words, . . . but only by a broken spirit, trembling soul and softened heart.

Bahya, *Hobot HaLebabot, Bakasha,* 1040, tr Hyamson, v. 63.

995.8 Man is made to adore and obey; but . . . if you give him nothing to worship, he will fashion his own divinities and find a chieftain in his own passions.

Disraeli, *Coningsby*, 1844.

995.9 The practice of virtue, that is the most saintly manner of worshipping God.

Josephus, *Against Apion*, ii. 22.

995.10 The true worship of God is possible only when correct notions of Him have previously been conceived.

Maimonides, *Guide for the Perplexed*, 1190, 3.51.

995.11 It were better if he, who is careless with the honor due to his Maker, had not come into the world.

Mishna: Hagiga, 2.1. *T: Kiddushin,* 40a.

995.12 God delights in altars beset by a choir of Virtues, albeit no fire burn on them.

Philo, *Noah's Work as a Planter,* 25.

995.13 In bringing themselves, worshipers offer the best of sacrifices, the full and truly perfect oblation of noble living.

Philo, *Special Laws,* i. 50.

995.14 Genuine worship is that of the soul offering plain truth, the only sacrifice, and rejecting displays of external riches and extravagance, which are spurious ministrations.

Philo, *The Worse Attacks the Better,* 7.

995.15 How shall I be silent when I see many of my people . . . pilgrimage to shrines of pious dead, light candles and burn incense there!

Sahal b. Matzliah, *Iggeret Tohakat,* 10C. q GHJ, iii. 205.

995.16 On his return from work, a man should stop at the synagog, review a section of Bible or Mishna, recite his prayers, and then go home. If he first go home for his meal and a nap, he may forget about his spiritual duties.

Talmud: Berakot, 4b.

995.17 While the breath of life is within me, I will worship Thee, Sovereign of the world and Lord of all souls.

Ibid., 60b. *Union Prayer Book,* 1940, i. 101.

995.18 We can worship Thee in holiness only as we serve our brothers in love.

Union Prayer Book, 1940, i. 45.

996. WRITING

996.1 In the same hour came forth fingers of a man's hand, and wrote over . . . the wall . . . *Mene, Mene, Tekel Upharsin.*

Bible: Dan., 5.5,25.

996.2 He [fallen angel] instructed mankind in writing with ink and paper, and thereby many have sinned . . . to this day.

Apocrypha: Enoch, 9.

996.3 In his penmanship man stands revealed—

Purest intent by chastest style is sealed.

Ezobi, *Kaarat Kesef*, 1270. *JQRo.* viii. 537.

556

996.4 To give me your refusal,
You need not write so long!
Heine, *New Spring,* 1844, #34.

996.5 With pen of scribe the great man
shall attain
Ends that the warrior's sword can
never gain.
M. Ibn Ezra, *Selected Poems,* p. 92.

996.6 From the scribes rather than from
their scripts.
q M. Ibn Ezra, *Shirat Yisrael,* (12C)
1924, p. 117.

996.7 If you write aught, read it through
a second time, for no man can avoid slips.
Let not any consideration of hurry prevent
you from revising a short epistle. . . . A
man's mistakes in writing bring him into
disrepute; they are remembered against
him all his days. As our sages say: "Who
is it that uncovers his nakedness here and
it is exposed everywhere? It is he who
writes a document and makes mistakes
therein."
Ibn Tibbon, *Tzavaah,* c. 1190. AHE, 68.

996.8 Be careful in your work, which is
a divine art, for by omitting or adding a
letter, you may cause the world's ruin.
Ishmael b. Elisha, to Meir, a scribe. *T:
Sota,* 20a.

996.9 The Men of the Great Synagog
undertook twenty-four fasts, praying that
scribes, who write holy books and ritual
objects, should not become rich, lest they
stop writing.
Joshua b. Levi. *T: Pesahim,* 50b.

996.10 Writing is one of the easiest
things; erasing one of the hardest.
Lipkin. q KTH, i. 277.

996.11 The diffusion of writings and
books . . . has entirely transformed man.
. . . We teach one another by writings; we
learn to know nature and man out of
writings; we toil and repose over, edify
and amuse ourselves with writings. . . .
Dead letter all; spirit of living conversation
none!
M. Mendelssohn, *Jerusalem,* 1783, tr
Samuels, ii. 111.

996.12 Writers in Israel are as holy as
the Land of Israel.
Pesikta Kahana, ch 5, ed Buber, 1925,
41a.

996.13 Moses wrote [the last eight verses
of *Deut.*] with tears.
Simeon. *T: Baba Bathra,* 15a.

996.14 How many pens were broken,
how many ink bottles were consumed, to
write about things that have never happened!
Tanhuma, Shoftim, 18. q Browne, *Wisdom of Israel,* 295.

997. YELLOW MARK

997.1 King Joseph I once indicated to
his Prime Minister Pombal that, to distinguish the Jews and to free the Spaniards
from Jewish infection, he would have the
Jews wear yellow caps. The following day
the minister appeared before the state council with three yellow caps, and said to the
king: "One for myself, one for the Grand
Inquisitor, and one for your Majesty!"
C. Brunner. *Reflex,* Aug. 1927, p. 68.

997.2 If the Germans want to put the
yellow Jewish star in Denmark, I and my
whole family will wear it as a sign of the
highest distinction.
*King Christian, to leaders of Danish
Lutheran Church. q AP, Oct. 11, 1943.

997.3 Noble sir! Would you be my
knight, then you . . . must sew yellow
wheels upon your mantle, or bind a blue-
striped scarf about your breast. For these
are my colors, the colors of my house,
named Israel, the unhappy house mocked
at on the highways and byways by the
children of fortune.
Heine. *Rabbi von Bacherach.* q KJL, 348.

997.4 The stain of our shame shall become the sheen of our glory!
Herzl. *Die Welt,* June 3, 1897, ref. to
color of cover.

997.5 Wear it with pride, the yellow
badge!
R. Weltsch. *Jüdische Rundschau,* April
1, 1933.

998. YESTERDAY

998.1 Yesterday will never return.
Weigh, count, consider what you did then.
Bahya, *Hobot HaLebabot,* 1040, 7.7.

998.2 Yesterday, by virtue of being yesterday, undermines the foundations of today. . . . Let us walk our own way; let
us breathe with our own lungs.
Berdichevsky, *Al HaPerek, Tze'irim,*
1899, p. 79. q *Reconstructionist,* Dec. 15,
1950, p. 10.

998.3 Yesterday did not vanish, but
lives.
Elisheba. q WHJ, iv. 333.

999. YIDDISH

999.1 Our hope for the future would be much stronger, if we did not rob our sons and daughters of our tongue. . . . One word, one expression, taken from the speech of the people, is more effective than ten abstract ideas.
Ahad HaAm. *HaShiloah,* 1900, ii. 574.

999.2 With this cosmopolitan jargon, made of the rags of every language, he [Morris Rosenfeld] created a music like that of a lamenting harp.
*Bloy, *Le Sang du Pauvre,* 1909. *Pilgrim,* 1947, p. 262.

999.3 There is no room in the sphere of civilization for this jargon. It is a barbarian and a pan-Judaic circle.
W. Feldmann. *Ojczyzna,* Dec. 15, 1890. q *YAJ,* v. 67.

999.4 If Hebrew was nobler and more dignified—the exterior of the coat—Yiddish was warmer and more comfortable—the lining of the coat.
S. Levin, *Childhood in Exile,* 1929, p. 105.

999.5 Come what may! I will fight above all for this Jargon and serve my people!
Mendelé, letter. q KJG, 325.

999.6 To feel ashamed of the Yiddish language is to be guilty of anti-Semitism.
Nordau. q R. Brainin. *The Day,* Feb. 4, 1923.

999.7 Yiddish, the language which will ever bear witness to the violence and murder inflicted on us, bear the marks of our expulsions from land to land, the language which absorbed the wails of the fathers, the laments of the generations, the poison and bitterness of history, the language whose precious jewels are the undried, uncongealed Jewish tears.
Peretz, "*Manginot HaZman.*" *HaAsif,* 1886, p. 729f.

999.8 In all the attics and cellars from Warsaw to New York you lay your head,
You come like an old mother, wearing an old apron, into the home of your daughters,
And they are ashamed of you, and your grandchildren greet you with scoffing laughter,
And often enough one of your sons has lost his temper at the sight of you,

And kicked you out of his rich home at the point of his elegant shoe.
Ravitch, "Song on the Seas to My Mother-Tongue." LGP, 238.

999.9 Classic Yiddish writing derives its stylistic strength and charm from the deliberate emphasis on Hebrew phraseology. Yiddish had a policy which gave it its folk-character—and that was to keep Hebrew alive.
M. Samuel, *Prince of the Ghetto,* 1938, p. 280.

999.10 Six million speakers are sufficient to give historic dignity to any language! One great writer alone is enough to make it holy and immortal. . . . The main point is that Yiddish incorporates the essence of a life which is distinctive and unlike any other.
Zangwill, 1906.

999.11 The only superiority of Yiddish over German is that there is only one gender.
Zangwill, *Speeches, Article and Letters,* 8.

999.12 Yiddish far more than Hebrew or neo-Hebrew was the living Jewish tongue. It was the language of the Jewish masses; it vibrates with their history, follows the mould of their life and thought, and colors itself with their moods. It is to Yiddish that we must look for the truest repository of specifically Jewish sociology. From Yiddish we can build up a picture of the life of the Judengasse.
Zangwill. q Leftwich. *JS,* May 1952, p. 19.

1000. YOUTH

1000.1 It is good for a man that he bear the yoke in his youth.
Bible: Lam., 3.27.

1000.2 Rejoice, O young man, in your youth.
Bible: Eccles., 11.9.

1000.3 There is youth, so men told me—
Where is mine?
Bialik, *Be a Refuge,* 1908. LGP, 40.

1000.4 No man the battling heart of youth can pry.
Bialik, *HaMathmid,* 1895. FTH, 37.

1000.5 Almost everything that is great has been done by youth.
Disraeli, *Coningsby,* 1844, 3.1.

1000.6 The Youth of a Nation are the trustees of Posterity.

Disraeli, *Sybil*, 1845.

1000.7 The two greatest stimulants in the world are youth and debt.

Disraeli, *Tancred*, 1847.

1000.8 Years of youth, years of folly.

Figure of Speech (Yiddish). BJS, #1762.

1000.9 Youth must fade and charms will vanish,

    Passing like the summer roses.

Frug, *Two Pictures*, tr Frank. *JQRo*, xiv. 557.

1000.10 The younger the tree, the more greenly bitter the fruit.

Heine, *Lutetia*, Aug. 25, 1840 (ref. to *parvenu*).

1000.11 Woe to that which passes, never to return!

Jose b. Kisma. *T: Sabbath*, 152a.

1000.12 Youth has ever been, and will ever be, the age of disinterestedness, enthusiasm, and ready sacrifice.

Lassalle, speech, Assize Court, Aug. 11, 1848.

1000.13 To be young is to hope; to be young is to love simply and naturally; to be young is to rejoice in one's own health and strength, and in that of all human beings, and of the birds of the air and the beetles in the grass.

Nordau, *Degeneration*, (1893), 5.2, p. 554.

1000.14 With youth all things are possible. It is the spirit of youth that declares, "I can prevail." It is the spirit of youth that keeps the man on the firing line, ready always to do his part even when the hair begins to whiten.

Philipson, at H. U. C., June 14, 1913. *Centen. Papers*, 260.

1000.15 Youth is not a time of life—it is a state of mind. It is not a matter of ripe cheeks, red lips and supple knees. It is a temper of the will, a quality of the imagination, a vigor of the emotions. It is a freshness of the deep spring of life.

S. Ullman, *From the Summit of Four Score Years*, [1920?], p. 13.

1000.16 I pity all your youth, and all your charm;

    And even as I stroke your cheek aglow,

    My fingers feel the mighty frost of death

    And non-existence creeping through us go.

Yehoash, "Evanescence." LGP, 122.

1001. ZEAL

1001.1 My zeal has undone me.

Bible: Ps., 119.139.

1001.2 Let us renounce our parents, kinsmen and friends, wife and children, all possessions and enjoyments of life, if they become an impediment to piety.

Didascalia. v. ch 6. q *JE*, iv. 592b.

1001.3 In my youth, when I was fired with the love of God, I thought I would convert the whole world to God. But soon I discovered that it would be quite enough to convert the people who lived in my town, and I tried for a long time, but did not succeed. Then I realized that my program was still too ambitious, and I concentrated on the persons in my household. But I could not convert them either. Finally it dawned on me: I must work upon myself, so that I may give true service to God. But I did not accomplish even this.

H. Halberstam. q BTH, ii. 214.

1001.4 Like a swift moving fire which ceases not nor rests, until it has accomplished its purpose, so must man's energy be in the service of God.

M. H. Luzzatto, *Mesillat Yesharim*, 1740, ch 7.

1001.5 For our children's sake how can we . . . be lax and indifferent? Should we not give them a force and a sword with which they may battle against temptation, with which they may keep themselves clean and pure, filled with high aims and holy thoughts?

Montefiore, *Liberal Judaism*, 1903, p. 216.

1002. ZION

1002.1 Out of Zion shall go forth the law, and the word of the Lord from Jerusalem.

Bible: Isa., 2.3.

1002.2 The Lord has founded Zion, and in her shall the afflicted of His people take refuge.

Ibid., 14.32.

1002.3 For Zion's sake I will not . . . rest, until her triumph go forth as brightness, and her salvation as a torch that burns.

Ibid., 62.1.

1002.4 The Lord dwells in Zion.

Bible: Joel, 4.21.

1002.5 The Lord shall yet comfort Zion!
Bible: Zech., 1.17.

1002.6 Out of Zion, the perfection of beauty, God has shone forth.
Bible: Ps., 50.1.

1002.7 Morning and evening omit not to remember Zion . . . with a broken heart and bitter tears.
Asher b. Yehiel, *Hanhaga,* c. 1320. AHE, 125.

1002.8 Zion is greater than a piece of land in the Near East. Zion is greater than a Jewish commonwealth in this land. Zion is memory, admonition, promise. Zion is . . . the foundation stone of the messianic upbuilding of humanity. It is the unending task of the Jewish people.
M. Buber, *Zion and Youth,* 1918. *Avukah Annual,* 1925, p. 49.

1002.9 We come to Zion only by way of Zion.
M. Buber, *Zion als Ziel und Aufgabe,* 1936.

1002.10 O lift Zion's banner, ye Fighters of Judah,
Our God is Almighty to shield and to aid;
If we have no bulwarks—let us be the fortress,
Our bodies the rampart, our hearts the stockade!
Chernihovsky, "O Lift Zion's Banner," 1897, tr I. Abrahams.

1002.11 Let our eyes behold Thy return to Zion in mercy!
Daily Prayer Book, ed Singer, 51.

1002.12 To keep our Judaism, we need not go back to Zion, but must bring Zion hither, live after its spirit, and incarnate it in our deeds and thoughts.
Enelow, *Selected Works,* 1935, i. 135.

1002.13 In the heart of the Jew is the true Zion, not in success nor in some faraway land.
*Huneker, *Variations,* 1922, p. 110.

1002.14 Oh, who will give me wings
That I may fly away,
And there, at rest from all my wanderings,
The ruins of my heart among thy ruins lay?
Judah Halevi, *Zionides,* tr Lucas. *Jewish Year,* 1898, 129.

1002.15 Perfect in beauty, Zion, how in thee

Do love and grace unite!
Ibid., p. 132.

1002.16 My heart is in the East, though in the West I live,
The sweet of human life no happiness can give. . . .
No joy in sunny Spain mine eyes can ever see,
For Zion, desolate, alone hath charms for me!
Judah Halevi, *Zionides,* tr H. Pereira Mendes.

1002.17 Zion, old and suffering
Victim of long oppression,
Sublime in woe and patience,
Witness to truth immortal!
D. Levi, "The Bible," 1846. tr M. A. Craig. *JQRo,* ix. 380.

1002.18 Turn to Thy city, Zion's sacred shrine!
On yon fair mount again let beauty shine!
I. Najara, "Yah Ribbon," 1587, tr Abrahams.

1002.19 Itoism says, "Zion is where the Jew lives as a Jew."
Zangwill, *Territorialism as Practical Politics,* 1913.

1002.20 God started the earth from Zion, from the spot where faith culminates in its full perfection. Zion is thus the citadel and central point of the universe, from which it began to be fashioned and from which the whole world is nourished.
Zohar, Gen., 186a.

1003. ZIONISM

1003.A. General

1003.A.1 There is a country without a nation; and God now, in His wisdom and mercy, directs us to a nation without a country.
*Ashley, May 17, 1854. q BSS, 426.

1003.A.2 For hundreds of years the Jewish masses have blindly searched for a way that will return them to nature, to the soil. At last we have found it. Zionism is the way.
Borochov, *Nationalism & Class Struggle,* (1907) 1937. p. 74.

1003.A.3 In our age, the choice for the Jew is between Zionism or ceasing to be a Jew.
*Crossman, *Palestine Mission,* 1947, p. 66.

1003.A.4 We are in an era in which each race has resolved to reclaim and repossess its soil, its homeland, its language and its temple. We Jews . . . no longer wish to be a group; we want to be a people, yea, more than a people, a nation. . . . We need once again a fixed, territorial fatherland. . . . Every one has his ideal or folly. That which led us and which for centuries we have recited on our feast days is: Next year in Jerusalem!

*Dumas fils, (Daniel in) *La Femme de Claude*, 1873, 2:1.

1003.A.5 Palestine is not primarily a place of refuge for the Jews of Eastern Europe, but the embodiment of the reawakening corporate spirit of the whole Jewish nation.

Einstein, *The World As I See It*, 1934, p. 154.

1003.A.6 Looking toward a land and a polity, our dispersed people . . . may share the dignity of a national life which has a voice among the peoples of the East and the West. . . . Let us . . . claim the brotherhood of our nation, and carry it into a new brotherhood with the nations of the world.

*Eliot, *Daniel Deronda*, 1876, ch 42.

1003.A.7 A people without a center or a government of its own can never attain to honor among the nations of the world. We must therefore demonstrate that the desire for rebirth still lives within us.

Z. Frankel, 1845. q *CCAR*, 1951, p. 268. See GSS, 210.

1003.A.8 The wealthy . . . have for the most part been indifferent to the appeal of Zionism. The power of the magnet is not felt by gold!

Friedenwald. q P. Goodman & A. D. Lewis, *Zionism*, 1916, p. 136.

1003.A.9 I am told Zionism is a Utopia. I do not know; perhaps. But inasmuch as I see in this Utopia an unconquerable thirst for freedom, one for which the people will suffer, it is for me a reality. With all my heart I pray that the Jewish people, like the rest of humanity, may be given spiritual strength to labor for its dream and to establish it in flesh and blood.

*Gorky. q *Maccabean*, April 1902, ii. 213.

1003.A.10 In the last resort, if the highest argument for Zionism is to be found in the prophet Isaiah, the case for it on the narrowest grounds is—Kishineff.

Guedalla, *Supers and Supermen*, 1920, p. 69.

1003.A.11 The Jews have but one way of saving themselves—a return to their own people and an emigration to their own land.

Herzl, *The Jewish State*, 1896.

1003.A.12 The world will be freer by our liberty, richer by our wealth, greater by our greatness.

Ibid., ch 6.

1003.A.13 Zionism was the Sabbath of my life.

Herzl, *Diary*, Jan. 24, 1902.

1003.A.14 March forward, Jews of all lands! The ancient fatherland of yours is calling you. . . . March forward, ye noble hearts! The day on which the Jewish tribes return to their fatherland will be epoch-making in the history of humanity. Oh, how will the East tremble at your coming! How quickly, under the influence of labor and industry, will the enervation of the people vanish, in the land where voluptuousness, idleness and robbery have held sway for thousands of years.

Hess, *Rome and Jerusalem*, (1862), p. 158f.

1003.A.15 As long as in our heart of hearts
There throbs a Jewish soul,
And in the Orient, in Zion,
We envision our goal,
Our cherished hope is not yet lost,
The ancient hope not damped—
To regain our fatherland,
Where David once encamped.

Imber, *HaTikva*, 1876, tr Baron.

1003.A.16 Zionism means one man persuading another man to give money to a third man to go to Palestine.

q Koestler. *Arrow in the Blue*, 1952, p. 114.

1003.A.17 To be a Zionist is to be a Jew. . . . Jews who are not Zionists at heart, are not Jews.

M. Mandelstamm, *Open Letter*, 1899. q *HaDoar*, July 1, 1955, p. 626c.

1003.A.18 We only have not the right to live for ourselves. We only are the natural domestic servants of all nations, whom the master can dismiss when he believes he no longer needs them, but who cannot give notice to their employers. . . . We Zionists are the first who endeavor to introduce the system of being able to give notice in this painful condition of service.

Nordau, speech, V Zionist Congress, Dec. 27, 1901.

1003.A.19 In order that we may not be compelled to wander from one exile to another, we must have a place of refuge, a rallying point, of our own.

Pinsker, *Auto-Emancipation,* 1882.

1003.A.20 Zionism, ingenious diagnostician but very mediocre practitioner, has recognized the disease but applied the wrong therapy.

F. Rosenzweig, *Zweistromland,* 1926, p. 40.

1003.A.21 I do not think I have ever heard the arguments of the Jews as to why they should not have a free State, schools and universities, where they can speak and argue without danger. Then alone can we know what they have to say.

*Rousseau, *Emile,* 1762.

1003.A.22 Zionism is not a mere national or chauvinistic caprice, but the last desperate stand of the Jews against annihilation.

Ruppin, *The Jews of Today,* (1904) 1913, p. 300.

1003.A.23 What should we want with Zion now, we Jews ...
In whom a fresh and fiery energy
Has blossomed into psalms and saviors, turned
A savage tribe to kings and priests that burned
To set a whole world free?

L. Untermeyer, *Lost Jerusalem. Roast Leviathan,* 1923.

1003.A.24 If before I die there are half a million Jews in Palestine, I shall be content because I shall know that this "saving remnant" will survive. They, not the millions in the Diaspora, are what really matter.

Weizmann, to McDonald, 1933, q McDonald, *My Mission,* 251.

1003.B. Political

1003.B.1 His Majesty's Government view with favor the establishment in Palestine of a national home for the Jewish people, and will use their best endeavor to facilitate the achievement of this object, it being clearly understood that nothing shall be done which may prejudice the civil and religious rights of existing non-Jewish communities in Palestine or the rights and political status enjoyed by the Jews in any other country.

*Balfour, letter to Lord Rothschild, Nov. 2, 1917.

1003.B.2 The State is not in itself an aim: it is a means to an end, the end of Zionism.

Ben Gurion, speech, Aug. 13, 1948. BRD, 276.

1003.B.3 Zionism aims to create for the Jewish people a publicly recognized and legally secured home in Palestine.

Herzl, *Basle Program,* 1897.

1003.B.4 If the Jew entertains as a religious tenet and as a matter of conscientious conviction the belief that the Jewish state will again arise, then he cannot possibly be in earnest in the matter of the separation of the religious and political elements and its implied corollary of true loyalty to the fatherland.

Holdheim, *Autonomie der Rabbinen,* 1843, p. 54.

1003.B.5 Loyalty to America demands that each American Jew become a Zionist.

Brandeis, *The Jewish Problem,* 1915.

1003.B.6 I would not even shrink from the scaffold if I could restore them to a position of respect among the nations. Whenever I indulge in childish dreams, I prefer to picture myself sword in hand, at the head of the Jews, leading them to recover their independence.

Lassalle. q Brandes, *Ferdinand Lassalle,* 9.

1003.B.7 Palestine must belong to the Jews, and Jerusalem is destined to become the seat of a Jewish Commonwealth.

M. Montefiore, 1885. q SHZ, i. 120.

1003.B.8 National independence and unity within the vast Arab territories, and extensive help in developing them, must surely count as sufficient compensation for a strip of country the size of Wales which even now is bi-national, and is to the Jews the one and only place in the entire world which they can claim as their national heritage.

Namier, *Conflicts,* 1943, p. 162.

1003.B.9 The national rebirth of the Jews must be launched through a congress of prominent Jews.

Pinsker, *Auto-Emancipation,* 1882.

1003.B.10 Audacity created the Zionist Congress. It was Theodor Herzl's only weapon. . . . The Zionist Congress enabled us to regain corporate responsibility of our national destiny. It gave a Galuth people status and an address. It is the forerunner of the Jewish State.

Lipsky, Nov. 1921. *Selected Works*, 1927, i. 161.

1003.B.11 Either the Jews remain by their faith, and await the coming of the Messiah . . . there you deny the divinity of Jesus, and we cannot help you; or you enter without any religion. Then we surely cannot be for you.

*Pius X, to Herzl, 1903. q HTH, ii. 200.

1003.B.12 Leave the country to its own rightful people; let them come in in peace and take possession of that land!

*Shaftesbury, address, June 1860. London *Hebrew Review*, June 1860.

1003.B.13 It (is) more than ever necessary to define Zionism clearly as a modern political movement, having for its aim the re-establishment of Israel as a political entity, and incidentally the salvation of the masses of Russia and Roumania.

Zangwill. q Philipson, *Centenary Papers*, 76.

1003.C. Cultural and Spiritual

1003.C.1 All over the world Jews are resolved that our common Judaism shall not be crushed out by short-sighted fanatics for local patriotism; and, in so far as Zionism strengthens this sense of the solidarity of our common Judaism, we are all Zionists.

Abrahams, 1905. q HBJ, 120.

1003.C.2 The heart of the people—that is the foundation on which the land will be regenerated.

Ahad HaAm, "The Wrong Way," 1889. *Ten Essays*, 14.

1003.C.3 In Palestine we can and should found for ourselves a spiritual center of our nationality.

Ahad HaAm, "Dr. Pinsker & His Pamphlet," 1892. *Ten Essays*, 121.

1003.C.4 Palestine will become our spiritual centre only when the Jews are a majority of the population and own most of the land.

Ahad HaAm, letter, July 27, 1903. AEL, 282.

1003.C.5 Zionism cannot put an end to the material Jewish problem, because not all the Jews can migrate to Palestine. Therefore the object of the movement is only to create for our people a national center, the influence of which *on the diaspora* will be spiritual only.

Ahad HaAm, letter to M. Ehrenpreis, Jan. 7, 1904. AEL 287.

1003.C.6 It is not the Mandate which is our Bible; it is the Bible which is our Mandate.

Ben Gurion.

1003.C.7 If we wish that the name Israel be not extinguished, then we are in duty bound to create something which may serve as a center for our entire people, like the heart in an organism, from which the blood will stream into all the arteries of the national body and fill it with life.

Ben Yehuda, "Sheela Nikbada." *HaShahar*, 1879.

1003.C.8 One people, one land, one language!

Ben Yehuda. q Hemda Ben Yehuda. *New Palestine*, Dec. 1950.

1003.C.9 The aim [of Zionism] is the creation of a new type of Jew. In place of the Jew who is a victim of the merely material and who worships lifeless things a Jew is to appear whose life is rooted in the spirit, who is animated by love and sacrifice.

Bergmann, *Jawne und Jerusalem*, 1919. LR, 133.

1003.C.10 The purpose of establishing Jewish settlements [in Palestine] is not to provide a living for a number of people, but to revive the spirit of our Holy Land; not to upbuild Palestine, but to bring into being the holiness of the Land of Israel.

N. Z. J. Berlin. q ABJ, 21.

1003.C.11 Shall we, with our inheritance, do less than the Irish, the Serbians, or the Bulgars? And must we not, like them, have a land where the Jewish life may be naturally led, the Jewish language spoken, and the Jewish spirit prevail?

Brandeis, *A Call to the Educated Jew*, 1916.

1003.C.12 The attempt of Zionism to lead Israel, nation and land, into the "normalcy" of the other nations, has no future. It is only God's kingly will, God's revealed Torah, that can shelter Israel, the people and the land, in Jerusalem's two-fold peace.

Breuer, *The Challenge to Israel*. JJCW, 190.

1003.C.13 It is not a commonwealth of Jews that should be established, but a truly Jewish commonwealth. A truly Jewish commonwealth can be none other than one in which the precepts of Moses with regard to the equalization of property, the appeals of the Prophets for social justice, are translated into reality.

M. Buber, *Zion and Youth*, 1918. *Avukah Annual*, 1930, 50.

1003.C.14 Upon you, upon the youth, will it depend whether Palestine is to become the center of mankind or a Jewish Albania, the salvation of nations or the toy of the Powers. Zion will not arise in the physical world if you do not prepare for it in your souls.

Ibid. (p. 53).

1003.C.15 The cause of Zionism has great claims upon those who are interested in the future organization of the peaceful intercourse of nations. . . . Moreover the Zionistic state would stand forth to the world as an inspiring symbol of victory against great odds, against seemingly insuperable odds, of the rights of nationality to be itself.

*Dewey. *Menorah Journal*, 1917, iii. 207f.

1003.C.16 The force of a historic factor will remain . . . with that form of Zionism which posits, along with the objectives of a Jewish national revival throughout the world, also the aim of creating another accumulator of spiritual energy to sustain the diaspora.

Dubnow, *Pisma o Starom i Novom Yevreistvie*, 1907, p. 320.

1003.C.17 It is a nationalism whose aim is not power but dignity and health. If we did not have to live among intolerant, narrow-minded and violent people, I should be the first to throw over all nationalism in favor of universal humanity.

Einstein, *The World As I See It*, 1934, p. 167.

1003.C.18 Revive the organic center: let the unity of Israel which has made the growth and form of its religion be an outward reality.

*Eliot, *Daniel Deronda*, 1876, ch 42.

1003.C.19 Our national life was a growing light. Let the central fire be kindled again, and the light will reach afar.

Ibid.

1003.C.20 From a centralized nation, honestly trying to become a model nation,

. . . will go forth a mightier and more wholesome influence upon the other nations, than can be expected from the efforts of thousands of a disorganized and widely diffused multitude of disjointed and unassociated individuals.

Flesenthal. *Maccabean*, March 1903, p. 135.

1003.C.21 Unless the religious spirit is allowed to take a new flight, and unless Jews feel themselves to be the messengers of God's truth, no gathering, no talking of Jewish nationality has any meaning, or will have any beneficial result either for the Jews or for the rest of the world.

M. Gaster. *Zionism and the Jewish Future*, 1916.

1003.C.22 He has fought his God; he has fought his environment; now he is fighting for his ancient homeland. If this . . . is only to become a nation like other nations, it is a sad struggle. If, on the other hand, it is a species of *reculer, pour mieux sauter*—a digging in for reinforcement of a new spurt—the spectacle assumes a dignity and a grandeur that are absent from the incorporated selfishness that we call nationality.

Goldberg. *Reflex*, July 1927, p. 30.

1003.C.23 Do we really want to be only that which the best people of the other living races no longer want to be? . . . In my naïveté I believed that we were striving to create a race of men upon whose banner of rebirth is inscribed, not "By Fire and Sword Will Judah Arise," but: "Nation shall not lift up sword against nation, neither shall they learn war any more."

A. D. Gordon. See *Avukah Annual*. 1925–30, p. 65.

1003.C.24 Before, or at least along with, the redemption of the soil there must be also the redemption of the soul.

J. L. Gordon, letter to S. Bernfeld, Jan. 31, 1888. *Igrot*, ii. 248.

1003.C.25 Zionism and Judaism are not the same. They are utterly different, perhaps contradictory, certainly not interchangeable, terms. When one cannot be a Jew, he turns Zionist.

Hazaz, *Boiling Stones*, 1946, p. 240. See *Judaism*, Jan. 1953, p. 12.

1003.C.26 As the Ghetto melts away under the disintegrating forces of modernity, a new cement must be created to hold together whatever is individual in the Jew.

Nationality is the rationale and Zionism the saving policy of modern Judaism.

M. Heller. *Maccabean,* July 1903, p. 34.

1003.C.27 Out of the old dreams of a monumental temple, smoking with bloody sacrifice, of a miraculous scion of David, ruling mankind in justice and peace, we extract the spiritual kernel when we strive for a state that shall be humanity's one sanctuary, for a nation that shall be the world's heaven-sent redeemer. Reform Judaism teaches us how to be Zionists in the full light of modern culture.

M. Heller. Baltimore *Jewish Comment.* q *Maccabean,* March 1903, p. 176.

1003.C.28 Zionism is the return of the Jews to Judaism, before their return to the Jewish land.

Herzl, address, I Zionist Congress, Aug. 29, 1897.

1003.C.29 With the sure instinct of its historic and cultural vocation to unite man and his world and to create human brotherhood, this people [Jews] has preserved its nationality *within* its religion and has connected both inseparably with the inalienable land of its fathers.

Hess, *Rome and Jerusalem,* 1862. LR, 3.

1003.C.30 Zionism is the affirmation of our personality. We have faith in ourselves, our spirit, our destiny to be worthy of our past.

Lazare, *Le National Juif,* 1898. q SHZ, i. 293.

1003.C.31 A Zionist is a Jew who, though not persecuted by Gentiles, wishes to revive Israel, because of his inner need and voluntary choice.

Liebenstein. *Jewish Frontier,* Sept. 1950, p. 27.

1003.C.32 The promulgation of the Mission of Israel demands a world center, a world authority whence the forces actuating it could radiate in every direction.

Lubin, letter to Brandeis, March 20, 1918. q ADL, 343.

1003.C.33 Zionism is an idea, a necessity, a moving force in the lives of all Jews, not merely of the oppressed. A race cannot give full expression to its genius except in its own home on indigenous soil.

Magnes, 1904. q BFZ, 53.

1003.C.34 The generation of Jews we wish to raise in the Land of Israel will be not of the twelfth or of the twentieth century, but, on the one hand, of the thirtieth,

and, on the other hand, of a much earlier age, earlier than your entire era, of the period of the Prophets and the Hasmoneans.

Mohilever, letter to S. Reinach. 1896. q MGU, 245.

1003.C.35 We will return to Zion as we went forth, bringing back the faith we carried away with us.

M. M. Noah, 1824. q HBJ, 123.

1003.C.36 Judaism is Zionism, and Zionism is Judaism.

Nordau, address, II Zionist Congress, Aug. 28, 1898.

1003.C.37 Judaism will be Zionist, or Judaism will not be.

Nordau, address, Amsterdam, April 1899.

1003.C.38 The rebirth of Israel's national consciousness and the revival of Judaism are inseparable. When Israel found itself, it found its God. When Israel lost itself, or began to work at its self-effacement, it was sure to deny its God.

Schechter, 1906. q HBJ, 116f.

1003.C.39 The ultimate aim of the Zionists is to liberate the Jewish people from the peculiar psychological complex induced by the penalization to which they have been subject for centuries in the Gentile world.

*Toynbee, *A Study of History,* 1934, ii. 252.

1003.C.40 I sympathize from the bottom of my heart with the Zionist propaganda as a protest against the universal opinion in which the Jew is held not only in Russia but in West Europe.

*Tugan-Baranowsky. q *Maccabean,* April 1902, ii. 213.

1003.C.41 The association of Jews with the Mahometan world is one of the great facts of history from which modern civilization is derived. . . . Palestine is placed exactly at the sensitive point where the Western world touches Mahometan life. . . . There is a new world waiting to be born, stretched along the eastern shores of the Mediterranean and western shores of the Indian Ocean. The condition of its life is the fusion of Mahometan and Jewish populations, each with their own skills and their own memories, and their own ideals.

*Whitehead. *Atlantic Monthly,* March 1939, p. 319f.

1003.C.42 Zionism, as conceived and in part executed by Theodor Herzl, was the half-conscious instinct of a people integrating past and future together into the totality of the will to live and to be itself and only itself.

S. S. Wise, *A Century of Jewish Progress,* 1933.

1003.C.43 Palestine needs a people; Israel needs a country. If, in regenerating the Holy Land, Israel could regenerate itself, how should the world be other than the gainer?

Zangwill, *Zion, Whence Cometh My Help,* July 1903.

1003.D. Practical

1003.D.1 The great miracle, the unique miracle in Eretz Israel, is the Jewish worker who does everything—in the field and garden, in the vineyard and orange-grove, in trade and industry, on the roads and railways, in electricity and water-works, in the quarry and the port.

Ben Gurion, March 1932. *Ben Gurion Selections,* 1948, p. 11.

1003.D.2 Building a State means for us a return to the soil. We found hundreds of Arab villages. We didn't take them away. . . . We established hundreds of new Jewish villages on new soil. . . . We didn't merely buy the land, we recreated the land. We did that in rocky hills like Motza. . . . In the swamps of Hedera hundreds of Jews died of malaria, and they refused to leave that place until it was made healthy. . . . We did it on the sand dunes of Rishon le-Zion. With our toil, our sweat, and with our love and devotion, we are remaking the soil to enable us to settle there, not at the expense of anybody else.

Ben Gurion, to Anglo-American Committee of Inquiry, March 19, 1946.

1003.D.3 Almighty God, help me to get there, . . . that I may till the sacred soil, aye, that I may labor there, work there!

M. Eliasberg. q MGU, 161f.

1003.D.4 It is the task of Zionism in the Diaspora to transform the Jews domiciled there into workers and producers. There, too, the chief thing is creation, not wealth.

A. D. Gordon. q SHR, 416.

1003.D.5 There is no greater service for the pious Jew to perform than to rebuild the ruins of the Holy Land.

Kalischer, *Derishat Zion,* 1862. q Hess, *Rome & Jerusalem,* 264.

1003.D.6 This is what our philosophy and propaganda aims at. To return to the Land, and within the Land to the soil; to cure that nervous over-strungness of exile and dispersion; to liquidate the racial inferiority complex and breed a healthy, normal earth-bound race of peasants.

Koestler, *Thieves in the Night,* 1946, p. 153.

1003.D.7 I dreamed of gathering a group of like-minded comrades who . . . would create a kind of nucleus for the mankind of the future. . . . Science would be their sacred hope, and labor their source of wisdom. Not slavery to machine and brute labor in the factory, but devotion as a conscious free being to work which, in proportion to the effort and imagination poured into its creation, would bring joy and happiness to the creator.

Schatz, *Memoir.* SMMP, 429.

1003.D.8 To bring water to the thirsty earth, shade to the sun-parched sands, the laughter of children to a countryside where only jackals howl; to unearth the good soil under the rocks, to push back the desert, and remove the last swamps—these are among the tasks of the Jewish National Fund in its second fifty years.

Weizmann, message, Jan. 19, 1951. *N.Y. Times,* Jan. 20, 1951.

1003.D.9 The task of Zionism is the strengthening of the State of Israel, the ingathering of exiles in the Land of Israel, and the fostering of the unity of the Jewish people.

World Zionist Congress, Aug. 29, 1951, Resolution.

1004. ZOHAR

1004.1 When I open the *Zohar,* I see the whole world.

Baal Shem. q Setzer, *Reb Yisroel,* 139.

1004.2 The contents of the Zohar were given at Sinai.

Isserles, *Torat HaOla,* (1570) 1659, ii. ch 1.

1004.3 What is the *Zohar?* . . . The Holy One took a gem from His crown and dropped it on the earth. The gem split and scattered into millions of brilliant gleams, . . . which came from eternity to brighten all the somber nooks, to satisfy all the famished who thirst for light, and to quicken and warm all that had been killed by the cold of science and the darkness of ignorance, by the blindness of nature and the cruelty of men.

Zeitlin. *HaTekufa,* 1920, vi. 314.

Glossary

Ab Fifth Hebrew month, corresponding to July or August.

Abba "Father." Title of some of the sages in the Talmud.

Agada Non-legal portions of rabbinic literature and lore.

Amora (pl., *Amoraim*) Term applied to the sages, from c. 200 to c. 500, whose teachings constitute the *Gemara*.

Baal Shem (*Tob*) "Master of the (Good) Name." Term applied to presumed healers and miracle-workers; specifically to Israel ben Eliezer (c. 1700–1760), founder of Hasidism.

Ben "Son," "son of."

Beth HaMidrash "House of Study." Term applied also to synagog.

Brith "Covenant." Specifically, the covenant of circumcision.

Cabala Jewish mystical lore.

Cohen "Priest." Name indicating descent from Aaron.

Eighteen Benedictions A collection of prayers occupying a central place in the daily Jewish services.

Edoth "Testimonies." Certain biblical precepts.

Epikoros "Heretic."

Eretz Israel "Land of Israel."

Ethrog A fruit of the citrus family, one of the four symbolic plants used in the ritual on the Feast of Tabernacles.

Galuth or **Galut** "Diaspora," "exile."

Gaon "Excellency." Title of the heads of the Babylonian academies from 589 to 1038; in modern times, applied to Elijah of Vilna (1720–1797).

Gemara "Learning." The part of the Talmud which is the Amoraim's exposition of, and supplement to, the *Mishna*.

Habdala "Separation." The ceremony, after sunset, which ushers out the Sabbath or festival.

Hagada The manual for the Seder service on Passover eve.

Halaka The legal part of rabbinic tradition and literature.

Halla The priest's share of the dough (*Num.* 15.21; *Ezek.* 44.30) which, in the diaspora, is symbolically cast into the fire. Ceremonial loaf eaten on Sabbath eve.

Halutz "Vanguard." Specifically, pioneer in modern Israel.

Hanukka (Hanucca) Festival of Dedication, of Lights, of the Maccabees.

Haroseth Mixture of apples, nuts and wine, symbolizing mortar, eaten at the Seder feast on Passover eve.

Hasid (pl., **Hasidim**) "Pious." Follower of the pietistic movement (*Hasidism*) inspired by Israel Baal Shem.

Haskala Enlightenment movement.

Heder Elementary classroom or school.

Hillul HaShem "Defamation of the Name" of God, or of Israel.

Jabneh Judean port city, where Johanan b. Zakkai, at the time of the Roman destruction of Jerusalem, established an academy and preserved the Torah.

Kaddish Doxology in Aramaic, recited at the conclusion of each service, and by the bereaved at time of mourning.

Karaite Follower of an anti-rabbinic sect, which arose within Judaism in the eighth century.

Kasher (Kashrut, Kosher) "Fit," "permitted." Term applied particularly to food prepared according to dietary regulations.

Ketuba "Document." Specifically, marriage-contract.

Kiddush "Sanctification." Benediction over wine and ceremony ushering in the Sabbath or festival.

Kiddush HaShem "Sanctification of the Name" of God. Martyrdom.

Kneseth or **Knesset** "Assembly." Israeli Parliament.

Levite Member of the tribe of Levi.

Lulab Palm branch, to which myrtle and willows are attached. It is used, with the ethrog, in Succoth ritual.

Matza Cake of unleavened bread, eaten on Passover.

Mazal "Constellation." Luck.

Megilla "Scroll." Specifically, Scroll of Esther.

Mezuza "Doorpost." A small case, containing verses from *Deuteronomy*, attached to the doorpost. See *Deut.* 6.9.

Midrash (pl., **Midrashim**) "Study," "research," "homily." There are a number of midrashic works of *halaka*, but most midrashim contain *agada*, or non-legal homilies.

Minyan "Number," "count," or "quorum" of ten requisite for congregational worship.

Mishna The code of the Tannaim, edited by Judah HaNasi, c. 200.

Mitzva "Commandment," "precept."

Nasi "Prince," "chief." Head of the Sanhedrin.

Nazir One who vows to abstain from wine and hair-cutting.

Ne'ila Concluding service on the Day of Atonement.

Pe-ah Corner of field, left for the poor. See *Lev.* 19.9ff.

Purim Festival of Lots, ordained in the Book of Esther.

Rosh Hashana New Year Day.

Rosh Hodesh First day of the month, New Moon.

Sanhedrin Court of law and justice, before the year 70.

Schlemihl (Schlemiel) Yiddish term for clumsy, unlucky man.

Seder "Order" of service. Passover eve ceremony.

Sefer Torah "Book of the Law." Scroll of the Pentateuch.

Sgan Kohen (Sgan Kohanim) Deputy High Priest.

Shabuot Festival of Weeks, of Revelation, of Early Harvest.

Shehita Ritual form of slaughtering animals for food.

Shekina Divine Presence, often used as a synonym for God.

Shema " 'Hear,' O Israel" (*Deut.* 6.4), recited in daily service and in confession of faith.

Shofar "Ram's horn," used on solemn ritual occasions.

Shool "School." Popular Yiddish term for synagog.

Succa "Booth."

Succoth Festival of Tabernacles.

Talith "Cloak," "garment." Prayer shawl.

Talmud "Learning," "teaching." Rabbinic compendium, including the *Mishna* and the *Gemara*. There are two distinct *Talmudim*, the Palestinian (*Jerushalmi*), edited 4th century, and the Babylonian, (*Babli*, or just *Talmud*), edited c. 500.

Tanna (pl., **Tannaim**) Term for the sages whose work and teachings constitute the *Mishna*.

Tefillin "Phylacteries." Small cases, containing biblical verses, worn by men on forehead and left arm during the morning prayers on week-days.

Torah Term variously applied to Pentateuch, Bible, Law, and Jewish learning.

Tosafists Medieval French and German authors of critical glosses on Rashi and the Talmud.

Tzaddik "Righteous," "pious" man. Hasidic rabbi.

Tzedaka "Righteousness," "charity."

Tzitzith "Fringes," prescribed in *Num.* 15.38.

Yom Kippur "Day of Atonement."

Zecut (Yiddish: **Zchoos**) "Merit."

Zohar "Radiance," "splendor." Title of the most important mystical work, the Bible of the Cabala, introduced into Spain by Moses de Leon at the end of the thirteenth century.

Bibliography

While the standard English translations of the classics constitute the basic sources of the entries in this volume, these have not been followed in all instances. Many of the quotations were drawn from different versions for reasons of greater brevity, superior epigrammatic effect, or popular familiarity, and thousands appear here in direct new renditions. In each case meticulous care has been taken to convey faithfully the spirit and intent of the original text and context.

The standard translations include *The Holy Scriptures* (Jewish Publication Society, 1917), R. H. Charles' *Apocrypha and Pseudepigrapha of the Old Testament* (Oxford University Press, 1913), both the C. D. Yonge and the Loeb Classical Library editions of Philo, the Authorized Version of the *New Testament*, the Whiston and Loeb renditions of Josephus, and the Soncino Press editions of *Midrash Rabbah* (1939) and *The Babylonian Talmud* (1935–1952).

Unless otherwise noted in the individual items, excerpts from other classical works refer to the following specific editions:

Aaron Halevi. *Sefer HaHinuk,* (13C). Warsaw, 5640.

Abba Mari Astruc. *Minhat Kenaot,* (1303). Pressburg, 1838.

Abot de Rabbi Nathan. S. Schechter, ed. London, 1887.

Abraham bar Hiyya HaNasi. *Hegyon HaNefesh,* (12C). Freimann, ed. Leipzig, 1860.

Agadat Bereshith. S. Buber, ed. Vilna (1902), 2nd ed., 1925.

Agadat Samuel (Midrash Samuel). S. Buber, ed. (1892), 1925.

Ahad HaAm. *Al Parashat Derakim,* (1895). Berlin, 1920.
Selected Essays. L. Simon, tr. Jewish Publication Society, 1912.
Ten Essays on Zionism and Judaism. L. Simon, tr. George Routledge & Sons, London, 1922.

Albo, Joseph. *Sefer Halkkarim,* (1428). I. Husik, tr. Jewish Publication Society, 1929f.

Al-Harizi, Judah. *Tahkemoni,* (1218). Vienna, 1845.

Anatoli, Jacob. *Malmad HaTalmidim,* (c. 1250). Lyck, 1866.

Apocalypse of Sedrach. A. Rutherfurd, tr., in *Ante-Nicene Fathers,* 2nd ed., 1897.

Asher b. Yehiel. *Orhot Hayyim,* (c. 1320). Piotrkow, 1907.

Bahya b. Asher. *Kad HaKemah,* (14C). Breit, ed. Lemberg, 1880.

Bahya Ibn Pakuda. *Hobot HaLebabot,* (1040). M. Hyamson, tr. New York, 1925–1947.

Baraita di Samuel, (8C?). A. L. Lipkin, ed. Vilna, 1925.

Berekia HaNakdan. *Mishlé Shualim,* (1260?). Warsaw, 1874.

Chajes, Zevi Hirsch. *Mebo HaTalmud,* (1845). J. Schachter, tr. East & West Library, London, 1952.

Donnolo, Shabbethai. *Hakemani,* (982). D. Castelli, ed. Florence, 1880.

Franzos, Karl Emil. *Die Juden von Barnow,* (1877). M. W. Macdowall, tr. New York, 1883.

Friedländer, Michael. *Jewish Religion,* (1891). Shapiro, Valentin, London, 1922.

Gabishon, Abraham. *Omer HaShikha,* (16C). Leghorn, 1748.

Gunkel, Hermann. *What Remains of the Old Testament,* (*Deutsche Rundschau,* 1914). A. K. Dallas, tr. Macmillan, 1928.

Hasdai, Abraham. *Ben HaMelek VeHaNazir,* (c. 1230). Zhitomir, 1850.

Herzl, Theodor. *Excerpts from his Diaries.* Scopus, New York, 1941.
The Jewish State, (1896). S. D'Avigdor, tr. 3rd ed., New York, 1917.

Hess, Moses. *Rome and Jerusalem,* (1862). M. Waxman, tr. Bloch, New York, 1918.

Hirsch, Samson Raphael. *The Nineteen Letters of Ben Uziel,* (1836). B. Drachman, tr. Funk & Wagnalls, New York, 1899.

Ibn Ezra, Abraham. *Yesod Mora,* (1158). J. Baer, ed. Frankfurt, 1840.

Ibn Ezra, Moses. *Shirat Yisrael,* (12C). B. Halper, ed. Leipzig, 1924.

Ibn Gabirol, Solomon. *Ethics (Improvement of the Moral Qualities,* 1045). S. S. Wise, tr. New York, 1901.
Mibhar HaPeninim, (c. 1050). B. H. Ascher, tr. London, 1859.
Selected Religious Poems. I. Zangwill, tr. Jewish Publication Society, 1923.

Ibn Verga, Solomon. *Shebet Yehuda,* (1550). M. Wiener, ed. Hannover, 1855f.

Immanuel (of Rome). *Mahberot,* (c. 1330). Lemberg, 1870.
Tophet and Eden (c. 1330). H. Gollancz, tr. London, 1921.

Judah Halevi. *Cuzari,* (c. 1135). H. Hirschfeld, ed. Leipzig, 1887. Hirschfeld, tr. London, 1931.
Diwan. H. Brody, ed. Berlin, 1896–1901.
Selected Poems. Nina Salaman, tr. Jewish Publication Society, 1924.

Kimhi, Joseph. *Shekel HaKodesh,* (12C). H. Gollancz, ed. London, 1919.

Legacy of Islam, The. T. Arnold & A. Guillaume, eds. Oxford, 1931.

Levi b. Abraham. *Livyat Hen,* (1315). Kabak, ed. Bomberg, 5632.

Luzzatto, Moses Hayyim. *Mesillat Yesharim,* (1740). M. M. Kaplan, tr. Jewish Publication Society, 1936.

Maimon, Solomon. *Autobiography.* J. C. Murray, tr. (London, 1888) Schocken Books edn., 1947.

Maimonides, Moses. *Eight Chapters,* (1168). J. I. Gorfinkle, tr. Columbia University Press, 1912.
    Guide for the Perplexed, (1190). M. Friedländer, tr. George Routledge & Sons, 2nd ed., London, 1904.
    Iggeret HaShemad (Maamar Kiddush Ha-Shem). A. Geiger, ed. Breslau, 1850.
    Iggeret Teman, (1172). A. S. Halkin, ed. B. Cohen, tr. New York, 1952.
    Responsa: Kobetz Teshubot HaRambam. Lichtenberg, ed. Leipzig, 1859. *Teshubot,* Freimann, ed. Jerusalem, 1934.
    Yad HaHazaka (Mishne Torah). Vilna, 1924.

Marx, Karl. *On the Jewish Question,* (1844). In his *Selected Essays,* H. J. Stenning, tr. International Publishers, New York, 1926.

Mekilta (de R. Ishmael), (3C). J. Z. Lauterbach, ed. Jewish Publication Society, 1949.

Mekilta de R. Simeon. D. Hoffmann, ed. Frankfurt, 1905.

Mendelssohn, Moses. *Jerusalem,* (1783). M. Samuels, tr. London, 1838.

Midrash Agada. S. Buber, ed. Vienna, 1894.

Midrash Mishlé. S. Buber, ed. 1893.

Midrash Mishlé Rabbati. D. Z. Ashkenazi, ed. Stettin, 1861.

Midrash Rabbah. Romm, ed. Vilna, 1878.

Midrash Ruth HeHadash (Midrash HaNe'-elam). Warsaw, 5625.

Midrash Samuel (Agadat Samuel). S. Buber, ed. (1892), 1925.

Midrash Tanaim. D. Hoffmann, ed. Berlin, 1908f.

Midrash Tehillim (Shoher Tob). S. Buber, ed. Vilna, 1891.

Midrash Zuta. S. Buber, ed. Berlin, 1894; Vilna, 1925.

Mishna, (c. 200). Horeb, ed. 1924.

Morawczyk, Jehiel Michael. *Minha Hadasha,* (1576). Frankfurt, 1722.

Moscato, Judah Arieh. *Nefutzot Yehuda,* (1588). Lemberg, 1859.

Nahman Bratzlav. *Sefer HaMiddot,* (1821). Warsaw, 5687.

Najara, Israel. *Zemirot Israel,* (1587). J. Fries, ed. Horeb, 1946.

Pesikta (de R.) Kahana. S. Buber, ed. Lyck, 1868; Vilna, 1925.

Pesikta Rabbati. M. Friedmann, ed. Vienna, 1880.

Pesikta Zutarti (Tobia. Lekah Tob). S. Buber, ed. Vilna, 1879.

Pirke de Rabbi Eliezer (8C). Lemberg, 1874.

Ragoler, Abraham. *Maalot HaTorah,* (1828). M. Feinstein & N. Waxman, eds. New York, 1946.

Saadia. *Emunot VeDeot,* (933). S. Rosenblatt, tr. Yale University Press, 1948.

Samuel HaNaggid. *Ben Mishlé,* (11C). A. E. Harkavi, ed. Petersburg, 1879.

Seder Eliyahu Rabbah and *Zuta.* M. Friedmann, ed. Vienna, 1902.

Sefer Hasidim, (13C). J. Wistinetzki, ed. 2nd edn, Frankfurt, 1924.

Sifra. Weiss, ed. Vienna, 1862.

Sifré, Numbers and *Sifré Zuta.* H. S. Horovitz, ed. Leipzig, 1917.

Sifré, Numbers and *Deuteronomy.* Friedmann, ed. Vienna, 1917.

Talmud: Talmud Babli. Romm, ed. Vilna, 1884.
    Talmud Jerushalmi. Romm, ed. Vilna, 1922.
    Treatises Derek Eretz (Derek Eretz, Pirké Ben Azzi, Tosefta Derek Eretz). M. Higger, ed. New York, 1925.
    Seven Minor Treatises (Sefer Torah, Mezuza, Tefillin, Zizith, Abadim, Kutim, Gerim, and *Soferim II).* M. Higger, ed. Bloch, New York, 1930.

Testament of Abraham. W. A. Craigie, tr., in *The Ante-Nicene Fathers.* 2nd edn, New York, 1897.

Testament of Job. K. Kohler, tr., in *Kohut Memorial Volume,* 1897.

Theodosian Code. C. Pharr, tr. Princeton University Press, 1952.

Tosefta. S. Zuckermandel, ed. Pasewalk, 1880.

Yalkut HaMakiri. S. Buber, ed. Berditchev, 1899.

Zabara, Joseph. *Sefer Shaashuim,* (13C). I. Davidson, ed. New York, 1914. M. Hadas, tr. Columbia University Press, 1932.

Zohar, (13C). Amsterdam, 1728. H. Sperling & M. Simon, trs. Soncino Press, 1949.

Long titles are not always given in full. Where the source is clear and easily ascertainable, these are occasionally curtailed. Thus, (the omitted portions given here in parentheses):

Apocrypha: (*The Testaments of the Twelve*) *Patriarchs.*

*Bloy, *Pilgrim (of the Absolute).*

Blum, *New Conversations (of Goethe with Eckermann).*

Brandes, *Main Currents (of the Nineteenth Century).*

*Chamberlain, *Foundations (of the Nineteenth Century).*

Dubnow, *Pisma (o Starom i Novom Yevreistvie).*

Edman, *Adam, (the Baby, and the Man from Mars).*

Freud, *Outline (of Psychoanalysis),* (1940) 1949.

Krauskopf, *A Rabbi's Impressions (of the Oberammergau Passion Play).*

Lewin, *Resolving (Social Conflicts).*

Magnin, *How to Live (a Richer and Fuller Life).*

Maimonides, *Yad (HaHazaka, Mishné Torah).*

Weiss, *Dor (Dor VeDorshov).*

Recurrent titles are designated, especially in cross references, by initials. the key to which is given in the List of Abbreviations.

Subject Index
and
Index of Authors

Subject Index

The numbers following each entry denote topics. Sub-topics are entered without repetition of main entries, as 155B4, 12, 15. The reference is to items 4, 12 and 15 under 155B.

Large and small capitals are used for topic headings found in the text. The symbol *s* ("see") indicates cross-references.

Infant *s* Baby, 592.3
Infanticide *s* Abortion, 2.2
Inferior 953.1
INFERIORITY 161.1, 284B1, 327B2, 421.1, 450L15, 953.1
Infinite 372.14, 373.28, 670.1, 725.7, 13
INFLUENCE 415.2, 422.1–12
Informer 374.11
Ingathering *s* Israel: Restoration, 269.25, 718.5, 1003D9
INGENUITY 146.4, 423.1f, 908C2
Ingratitude 5.12, 345.1f, 4f, 395.4, 450J22–34
INHERITANCE 424.1f, 915H1
Iniquity 419.1, 930.12
Initiation 425.2
INITIATIVE 425.1–3
Injustice 687.5
Inn 299B14
INNER & OUTER *s* Appearance, Dress, Form, 35.9, 306.2, 372.4, 403.17, 426.1–16, 450-E76, 638.2, 946.3
INNOCENCE 427.1–4
Innocent 324.5
Inquiry 704.14, 730.2, 772.29
INQUISITION 386.2, 428.1–4, 741.16, 916.3
Inquisitive 772.35, 988B14
Insane 794.10
Insight 434.5, 466D13
Insolence 244.16, 540C6, 696.5
Inspection 440.2, 954.14
INSPIRATION 423.2, 429.1–3
INSTABILITY 430.1–3
INSTINCT 431.1f
INSTITUTION 432.1–4, 560.11, 575-B3, 915A8
Instruction *s* Teaching, 617.3, 814I6, 860B12
INSULT 327A2, 335Z20, 433A1–9, 665.10
Insults 433B1–3
Insurgent 151.13
Insurrection *s* Rebellion, 716.9
INTEGRITY *s* Character, 360.3, 387.3, 434.1–7
Intellect *s* Mind, 369C6, 546.13–15, 24, 559.14, 632.15, 863.5, 931.14
INTELLIGENCE 203.4, 232C5, 398.27, 435.1–13, 450E20–30, 88, 510.4, 811.9, 988B3, 7, 16
Intensity 40.25, 450E31–36
INTENTION 436.1–12, 866.2
Intercessor *s* Mediator
Interest 83.1, 5, 8, 938.1–5
Intermarriage *s* Marriage: Intermarriage, 522E1–7, 709.9, 15f, 21, 33
Internationalism 455B10, 576-A2
INTERPRETATION 65C, 437.1–7, 715.20, 915J4
Interpreter 219.14
Interruption 521.4, 16, 986.16
Intolerance *s* Bigotry, 450J41, 770.32
Intoxication 953.24
Introduction 86.1
INTUITION 438.1–7, 572.1
Invective 524.4
INVENTION 439.1–5, 477C3, 546.15
INVENTORY 440.1f
Investigation 728.7, 730.1, 4f, 772.13
Investment 554.18
Invisible 40.16, 63.23
INVITATION 441.1f, 816.5
Inwardness 426.16
Iraq 202.10
IRELAND 442.1

IRON 300.11, 443.1–3, 859.12, 926.14
Wall 896C4
IRONY 444.1–3
Isaac *s* Patriarchs, 393.3, 488-A7, 624.3
ISAIAH 65A5, 117.13, 133A4, 236.15, 450E11, 574.13, 686-D1–4, 708B10, 725.34, 819.11f, 934.13, 1003A10
Ishmael 238.6, 8, 257.34
Ishmaelite 449.9
Islam 117.9, 523.3, 716.8, 1003-C41
Isolation *s* Segregation, 467B18, 784.2, 4
ISRAEL *s* Jews, 202.31, 36, 304.1, 335X17, 385.17, 455B3, F2, 556.5, 560.6, 14, 21, 569F2, 607.4, 709.30, 753.6, 797.1, 950.1f, 973.6
Baal Shem 708.C3
Eternal 445B9, 450M2, 9
Fall 445E1–5
Land 115F3, 163.2, 202.26, 385.22, 445D1–44, 450F1–4, 467B2, 540E3, 718.25, 740.10f, 820.10, 828.1, 865.4
Residence in 616B5
Mission of 202.6, 27, 35, 236.9, 445C1–27, G6, 450H24, 628.38
Name 445A1–4, 1003C7
People p. xiv; 159.9, 445B1–65, 450J8, 455B2f, 536.4, 631.18
Beloved of God 234.4, 335-Y2, 445B19–41, 802.18
Bride of God 815.2
Character 445B1–18
Vehemence 943.1
Chosen 445B42–65, 635.4
Congregation 507B7
Holy 385.17
Indestructible 450M20
Influence 450E8
Marriage to God 540E2, 815.2
a Prophet 686C19
Servant of God 797.1
Restoration 445F1–49, 718.25
State 36.4, 159.4, 445C19, G1–11, 1003B2, D9
Israelite 450A2
Italy 202.34, 236.2, 450E45
Itoism 1002.19
Ivan the Terrible 758.12

JABNEH 446.1
Jacob *s* Patriarchs, 70.1, 269.26, 419.4, 624.3, 5, 751.2, 923.15, 956.1
(Jews) 281.21, 419.4, 450F10, 705.4, 751.2, 956.17
Jahrzeit 185J22
Jailer 616B10
James I 450I1
Japheth 348.5, 709.45
Jargon 999.2f, 5
JEALOUSY 234.7, 335Z28, 447.1–7, 540E26, 666M9
Jehu 918.1
Jephtha 321.9
Jeremiah 335U7
Jericho 964.3
Jeroboam 712.1, 728.18, 751.10
JERUSALEM 123.8, 159.3, 193.10, 244.8, 384.12, 445D36, F36, 39, 448.1–26, 450F8, M15, 455B4, 483.3, 563.7, 628.29, 666D22, F12, 718.23, 728.13, 745.3f, 759D1, 770.24, 771.5, 775.2, 800.10, 944.13, 949.5, 992.38, 1002.1, 1003B7

Children 745.2, 4
Destruction 244.8, 335P16, 483.3, 728.13, 759D1, 770.24, 771.5, 800.10
the Golden 448.9
Heavenly 448.16
Symbolic 455B4, 944.13, 992.38
Jeshurun 278.1
Jesse 540B1
Jest 255.5
JESUS *s* Christianity, 32A3, 8, 170.3, 6, 449.1–14, 638.12
Jewelry 988B11
Jewess 450F20, 22–24, 27
Jewish Blood *s* Blood, Jewish
Consciousness 445B51, 450-E116, F14, O8, P1–6
Contributions to Civilization, 24B7, 159.6, 193.1, 18, 240.13, 15, 450E51, 53, I1–20, 657.3, 762.12, 771.4, 886.3
Dignity 450E107, L10
Education 450P3
Life 450E76
Nation 236.5, 8
National Fund 1003D8
People 202.19, 23f
Problem, Question, 275.8, 450-N1–4, 709.22, 1003C5
Soul 471.2
JEWS 450A–Q, 228.13, 236.5, 814-D2
Alienation 450C1–4
Antiquity 450G8, J15, M17
Aristocracy 450G8, 10
Attitude to 450J1–66
Apathy & Tolerance 450J18–21
Appreciation 450J8–17
Barometer 450J1–7
Hostility 32A6, 16, 202.7, 450J35–66, L7, 625.3
Ingratitude 450J22–34
Challenge & Role 445C7–9, 11, 450H1–35, P6
Conscience 146.10, 450H32, J45
Creative Minority 450H4, 13
Critic 450H13, 688.1, 5–8
Ferment 450H6, 15, 18, 20, 31, 478.5
God-Bearing 170.4, 7
Lightning-Rod 450J1
Revolutionary Factor 65-B11, 450H4, 688.1, 820.19
Scapegoat 768.3–10, 12f, 14f
Touchstone of Nations 450-J5
Witness 445C3, 23, 450H16, 803.7
Character 445B16, 450E1–119, 915K2
Adaptability 450E107
Artists 450E25
Characteristics 63.12
Civility 450E103
Cleverness 129.4, 450E104
Cosmopolitanism 159.11
Conservatism 148.2, 4, 450-E93
Courage 450E1–6, 98
Dreamers 450E25, 55, 654-B10
Fear 450L15
Freedom-Loving 258.4, 450-E56f
Generosity 450E107
Heroism 236.15, 450L10
Humaneness 450E7–15
Idealism 450E64, 66
Imitativeness 412.1
Impetuosity 450E16–19
Intelligence 450E20–30, 39, 88, K21, 860B4

Soothsaying 213.1f
Sophism 927.57, 985.27
Sophisticate 176.3
Sorcery 456C7
SORROW s Grief, 335Y11, 351.8, 397.3, 450K36, 466A1, 666-C21, 836.1-4, 956.7
SOUL 77.2, 4, 16, 265.11, 335F6, 396.15, 23, 488D27, 503.2, 515.1, 654A2, 666M9, 837.1-19, 856.1, 898.22, 934.18
AND BODY 257.7, 360.2, 367.5, 456A10, 725.9, 785.23, 838.1-14, 865.19
Extra 759B25, 915O51
Jewish 503.7, 802.18, 848.14
SOUND 227.9, 529.4, 695.9, 839.1-9
SOUR GRAPES 840.1, 945.5
South Africa 46.5
SOVEREIGNTY 748.19, 841.1-4
Sow 361.3
SPACE 24A11, 455A36, 569A7, 842.1-3
SPAIN 36.3, 202.34, 450K30, 843.1-5, 997.1, 1002.16
Expulsion from 232E9, 509.29, 734.2
Refugee 734.2
Spark 817.4
Spartans 348.1
SPECIALIZATION 142.3, 844.1f
Speculation 670.5
Speculator 467A31
SPEECH 206.4, 471.14, 24, 770.38, 811.8
Danger 845B1-8
Evil 845E1-9
Fair 741.23, 845D1-14
Limitation 492.6, 759C22
Loquacity 845C1-11
Value 845A1-13
Speed 124.2
Spending 487.8, 554.7, 744.41, 759D33
Speyer 123.7
Spice 633.3, 770.46
SPINOZA 328.10, 450E22, H23, 30, 846.1-25
SPINSTER 847.1f
SPIRIT 77.7, 133D2, 185A5, 246.4, 295.3, 5f, 306.6, 372.21, 569-A7, 576B15, 848.1-17, 930.17, 950.1
and Matter 569A7
Jewish 848.14
of Age 18A1f
OF GOD 739.1, 742.21, 796.3, 849.1-16
of Law 483.1, 7
of Prophecy 233.10
Spiritual 838.2
Spirituality 307.7, 372.10, 450-E67-78, 524.3, 575B5, 576-B15, 19, 838.11, 848.13, 16f
Spitting 785.25
Splendor 940.9
Spring 778.1, 3f, 8
Sprinkling 398.44
Spurgeon 605.2
Stability s Security
Stage 899.1
Standing 367.9
STAR s Astrology, 244.7, 307.12, 445B7, 450E33, 569B2, 577.3, 811.18, 850.1-9, 915D14, 926.12, 981.11
of David 879.1
Starling 16.3
STATE s Church & State, Israel: State of, 341.8, 391.13, 445-G1-11, 450I7, 473.7, 725.8, 781.14, 828.5, 851.1-13, 1003-B2, D2
Stateless 122.3

STATESMAN 341.15, 381.4, 852.1-5
STATION 853.1-3
STATISTICS 854.1-3
STATURE 456C7, 662.5, 802.24, 855.1
Status 827.3
Stealing s Thief, 325.26
Stepmother 561.11
STIMULATION 856.1
Stomach 265.12, 649.2
STONE 291.2, 339C6, 445D11, 557.1, 605.1, 634.5, 741.37, 814C2, 857.1-4, 896A1
Stoop 355.3
Storm 742.5, 988B9
Straight Line 559.20
Strange Fire 601.1
STRANGER 112G2, 275.2, 369C4, 395.1f, 13, 418.3, 531.5, 796.2, 858.1-21, 909.1, 940.3
Straw 525.1
Street 229.13
STRENGTH 18C3, 68.1, 169.1, 367.10, 372.4, 396.13, 450E79-84, H7, 466C8, 705.3, 785.32, 811.19, 859.1-17, 985.6
Strictness 487.10, 642.8
Strife s Quarrel, 299B8, 11, 335-Z1, 540E26, 663.42, 703.1-3, 5, 7, 9, 12, 14, 705.7
Strike (Labor) 467B9
Strong 225.8, 802.24, 865.9, 874.1, 947.2, 6, 971.8, 986.1
Struggle s Controversy, Fight, 153.5, 311.45, 529.4
Stubbornness s Obstinacy 598.1, 2, 4
Student s Pupil, Scholar, 495.8, 628.24, 770.26, 28, 30, 35
STUDY 7.9, 189.34, 272.6, 456A18, 558.2, 600.21, 860E1-3
Companions 860D1-9
Evaluation 860A1-12
Love of 450E88, 477B11, C10, 759D29
Motive 232D11, 272.6
Subjects 770.13, 46, 772.12, 860B1-28
Agada 17.3
Alfasi 860B16
Anatomy 860B27
Ancients 860B10, 16, 22, 985.20
Asher 860B16
Astronomy 860B15
Bible 860B28
Cabala 94.2
Civics 860B14
Esoterics 860B5, 20f
Ethics 860B12, 18
Forbidden 860B21
Gemara 860B28
God 860B5
Grammar 860B6
Greek 348.6
Hebrew 860B1, 8
Law 860B13
Logic 860B19
Maimonides 860B16
Man 860B2, 23
Mathematics 860B19
Metaphysics 860B19
Mishna 860B3, 28
Nature 860B24
Physics 860B19
Physiology 860B27
Rabbinics 860B25
Science 772.12
Social Science 474.3
Talmud 860B4, 6
Torah 860B7, 915O1-54
World 860B17
Time 860C1-6
Stumbling 265.15
Stupidity 244.4

STYLE s Fashion, 65B18, 125.5, 253.1, 496.10, 861.1-10, 888.4, 988B22
Subject 596.8
Subjection 657.10
Sublime 373.29, 597.1, 613.3, 862.1
SUBLIMITY 373.22, 29, 862.1-4
SUBMISSION 43.15, 445C26, 863.1-7
Subordinate 15.4, 244.12, 398.42
Subtlety 129.2, 5, 282.7, 546.11, 642.1
SUCCESS 14, 7, 142.1, 146.7, 205.4, 268.3, 335P12, 347.8, 372.6, 600.18, 699.6, 864.1-14, 940.10
Succoth 81.1f, 325.8, 455B18, 915L16
SUFFERING s Adversity, Pain, 14.3, 257.16, 304.6, 335V11, 450E27, 613.6, 616B11, 623.17, 865.1-21
Sugar 71.5
Suggestion 306.1
SUICIDE 43.2, 229.5, 450E3, 455-E18, 866.1-6, 992.22
Sukka s Booths, Succoth, 915-L16
Summer 778.2, 6, 9
SUN 422.5, 548.6, 558.1, 577.3, 695.8, 867.1-10
Superfluous 513.4f
Superior 327B2, 463.32, 487.9, 953.1
Superiority 8.5, 244.13, 307.7, 709.32
Supermundane 704.22
SUPERNATURAL 868.1-4
SUPERSTITION 105.4, 167.4, 575-B5, 650.11, 869.1-12
Suppression 104.2, 153.2
Surprise 347.22, 987.5
Survival 271.10
Suspect 456B16, 735.6
SUSPENSE 870.1
SUSPICION 735.6, 779.4, 871.1-6
Swabian 450F18
Swallow 403.6, 778.3
SWAN 507D17, 872.1f
Swear 595.4f, 682.4
SWEAT 873.1-3
Sweatshop 467B11
Sweet 152.12, 255.9, 426.3, 569-F1, 831.6, 842.2
SWEETNESS 494.3, 561.14, 874.1-4, 983.14
SWIMMING 875.1f
SWINE 876.1-4
SWITZERLAND 877.1f
SWORD 21.1, 79.8, 197.6, 448.3, 671.6, 878.1-8
SYMBOL 879.1-9
Symmetry 58.19
SYMPATHY 507C14, 794.7, 880.1-4, 955.4
SYNAGOG 24B9, 93.9, 112B6, 241.3, 562.37, 569E6, 601.6, 638.5, 695.7, 706.2-4, 757.2, 759C29, 770.45, 771.6f, 15, 17, 839.7, 845E6, 860D3, 881.1-27, 910.10, 927.38
of Satan 450B22
Syria 509.7
SYSTEM 477B19, 882.1-3, 900.6

Tabbai 912.18
Tabernacle 709.4
Table 21.2, 112C18, 770.9, 802.9
Manners 521.1, 6
of Law 18D16, 187.1f, 7f
Tabor 467A44
TACT 883.1f
Tail 72A8, 309.2, 365.1, 476.13, 712.3

Index of Authors

This index includes the name of every author directly quoted in the *Treasury,* together with a brief characterization and the years of his birth and death or the century in which he lived. It includes also an entry for each work generally quoted by title rather than author.

The numbers following each entry refer to the pages. A *b* following the number is used only when the author is quoted in the second column of the page.

Composition or Redaction Dates of Classical Works

Apocrypha:
Adam and Eve. 30 B.C.E.
Additions to Esther. 125 B.C.E.–90 C.E.
Ahiḳar. 5C B.C.E.
Aristeas. 130 B.C.E.–64 C.E. or 100 B.C.E.
Asenath. 1C C.E.
Assumption of Moses. 1C.
I Baruch. c.150 B.C.E.–78 C.E.
II Baruch. c. 70–90 C.E.
III Baruch. 2C.
Ben Sira. c. 300–190 B.C.E.
Enoch. 1C B.C.E.
II Enoch. c. 30 B.C.E.
I Esdras. 3–1C B.C.E.
II Esdras (IV Ezra). c. 100.
Jeremy. c. 300 B.C.E. or 1C B.C.E.
Jubilees. 2C B.C.E.
Judith. c. 150 B.C.E.
I Maccabees. c. 120 B.C.E.
II Maccabees. 1C B.C.E.
III Maccabees. c. 1C B.C.E.
IV Maccabees. Between 63 B.C.E. & 38 C.E.
Martyrdom of Isaiah. 1C.

Patriarchs (Testaments of Twelve). c. 200 B.C.E. or c. 107 B.C.E.
Psalms of Solomon. c. 50 B.C.E.
Sibyls. 160 B.C.E. to 5C C.E.
Susanna. c. 95–c. 60 B.C.E.
Testament of Abraham. 2C.
Testament of Moses. 7–29. C.E.
Tobit. c. 300 B.C.E., or 190–20 B.C.E.
Wisdom of Solomon. 125–100 B.C.E., or 50 B.C.E.
Didache. 2C.
Didascalia. 1C.
Mekilta. Palestine, 2–3C.
Mishna. Palestine, c. 200.
New Testament. c. 50–150.
Sifré. c. 100.
Tanna de be Eliyahu. 10C.
Targum to *Canticles.* 3C.
Tosefta. Palestine, c. 300.
Zohar. c. 1300.
Talmud (Babylonian). c. 500.
Talmud Jerushalmi. 4C.